D0622840

I WANT YOU!

The Evolution of the All-Volunteer Force

BERNARD ROSTKER

The research described in this report results from the RAND Corporation's continuing program of self-initiated independent reserach. Support for such reserach is provided, in part, by donors and by the independent reserach and development provisions of RAND's contracts for the operation of its US Department of Defense federally funded research and development centers. This research was conducted within the RAND National Security Research Division(NSRD) of the RAND Corporation. NSRD conducts research and analysis for the Office of the Secretary of Defense, the Joint Staff, the Unified Commands, the defense agencies, the Department of the Navy, the U.S. Intelligence Community, allied foreign governments, and foundations.

Library of Congress Cataloging-in-Publication Data

Rostker, Bernard
 I want you! : the evolution of the All-Volunteer Force / Bernard Rostker.
  p. cm.
 "MG-265."
 Includes bibliographical references.
 ISBN 0-8330-3895-8 (hardcopy with dvd : alk. paper)—ISBN 0-8330-3896-6 (hardcopy without dvd)
  1. Military service, Voluntary—United States—History—20th century. 2. United States—Armed Forces—Recruiting, enlistment, etc.—History—20th century. I. Title.

 UB323.R67 2006
 355.2'23620973—dc22

                   2006009100

The RAND Corporation is a nonprofit research organization providing objective analysis and effective solutions that address the challenges facing the public and private sectors around the world. RAND's publications do not necessarily reflect the opinions of its research clients and sponsors.

RAND® is a registered trademark.

Cover image courtesy of www.archives.gov from original art by James Montgomery Flagg. The artist used himself as a model for this illustration which was used on World War I recruitment posters and revived during World War II.

© Copyright 2006 RAND Corporation

Published 2006 by the RAND Corporation
1776 Main Street, P.O. Box 2138, Santa Monica, CA 90407-2138
1200 South Hayes Street, Arlington, VA 22202-5050
4570 Fifth Avenue, Suite 600, Pittsburgh, PA 15213
RAND URL: http://www.rand.org/
To order RAND documents or to obtain additional information, contact
Distribution Services: Telephone: (310) 451-7002;
Fax: (310) 451-6915; Email: order@rand.org

Author Preface

This is a story that needs to be told, one about how the American military has transformed itself over the past 30 years from a force of mostly conscripts and draft-motivated "volunteers" held in low esteem by the American public to a force of professionals sustained in peacetime, tested in battle, and respected throughout the world. It is a story of how a determined group of public servants used analysis to bring about one of the most fundamental changes in American society. Many have spoken about the all-volunteer force as a classic marriage between political decisionmaking and policy analysis. Over the last 30 years, a rich body of analysis has developed that is largely unavailable to the general public or even to the general analytical community. The purpose of this book is to create a comprehensive record of the more than 30 years of policy and economic analysis that was responsible for today's all-volunteer force. Using the historic context, the book traces the critical policy questions of the day, how these questions changed over time, and the analysis that provided decisionmakers with the insights to manage the all-volunteer force effectively.

Not Without Its Critics

From its inception, the all-volunteer force has not been without its critics. Military sociologists in particular were dismayed by the very thought that the nation would give up conscription, which for them epitomized the social contract between the citizen and the state. They worried that what they saw as a shift to a "market paradigm" would compromise the legitimacy of the military and reduce its effectiveness as a fighting force. Their concerns were presented in journal articles, papers at academic conferences, op-ed pieces in magazines and newspapers, and congressional testimony. From time to time, these views influenced decisionmakers and their decisions. Sometimes, they were in direct opposition to the work of the analysts trying to foster the all-volunteer force. Their arguments are also considered here, when and where appropriate.

How to Read This Book

This is at once a history of the evolution of America's all-volunteer force and a review of the major policy questions and the research undertaken to support Department of Defense (DoD) decisionmakers over the past 30 years. Each period has at least two chapters: one that covers the history of the period and another that reviews the major analytic studies used to inform the debate.

Scholars are often frustrated when they try to find the material referenced in footnotes or in a bibliography. At best, this takes time and much effort. At worst, while you might have a reference, the material may not be easily available. I have tried something different here. An accompanying DVD—available in the expanded DVD edition—contains the full text of the book and provides an archive of much of the related policy and analytic literature of the past 30 years, allowing the reader to see original source materials firsthand. The documents in this archive are linked from citations in the electronic version of the book. It is my hope that scholars and students of military affairs and public administration will use this book as an extended annotated bibliography and that access to these sources will enable better understanding and interpretation of the events reported here.

My 40-Year Odyssey

This book is also something of a memoir. I have had the honor and pleasure to participate in many of the events covered here as an analyst, a supervisor of research, a government official, and a decisionmaker. Throughout the book, I have included Author's Notes as footnotes to provide a personal context.

In addition, many of the people mentioned in the book have also played many roles over the years of this story. In fact, this is an important part of the story. For example, during the late 1990s, the Deputy Secretary of Defense was Dr. John White. In our story Dr. White first appears as a researcher at the RAND Corporation and a member of the Gates Commission staff.[1] He was later to lead the Air Force's Manpower, Personnel, and Training Program at RAND and the team that convinced the DoD to put the Defense Manpower Analysis Center at RAND. Several years later, he became Assistant Secretary of Defense for Manpower, Reserve Affairs, and Logistics and then became Deputy Director of the Office of Management and Budget. He played a central role in the creation of a viable standby draft and the revitalization of the Selective Service System and draft registration in 1980.

In my case, I was a captain in the Army assigned to the Office of the Assistant Secretary of Defense for Systems Analysis during the period of the Gates Commission

---

[1] More formally known as the President's Commission on an All-Volunteer Armed Force, the Gates Commission was set up by President Richard Nixon.

(1968–1970). Although I was in the Pentagon during these critical years, I observed the events recounted here from a distance and through the filter of a junior staff officer. After my Pentagon service, I went to RAND (1970) and led a number of studies concerning the all-volunteer force and the Air Reserve Forces. The research and policy analysis done for the Air Reserve Forces is presented here. I eventually followed Dr. White as Director of the Air Force's Manpower, Personnel, and Training Program at RAND. In 1977, both Dr. White and I left RAND to join the Carter administration, he as Assistant Secretary of Defense for Manpower, Reserve Affairs, and Logistics and I as Principal Deputy Assistant Secretary of the Navy for Manpower and Reserve Affairs. In that job, I sponsored the Navy recruiting experiments that are also discussed here. In 1979, Dr. White was instrumental in my appointment by President Jimmy Carter to the position of Director of Selective Service. The lack of a creditable standby draft had become a significant charge against the all-volunteer force, and I was asked to build a new, postmobilization, standby system. Before the end of my tenure at Selective Service, my name would be associated with a landmark Supreme Court case concerning the power of Congress to legislate on the basis of gender. The case of *Rostker v. Goldberg* is also discussed in this book.

In later years, I was never far from the all-volunteer force. In 1985, I helped establish the Arroyo Center at RAND, the Army's federally funded research and development center for studies and analysis. I initially supervised the manpower studies the Arroyo Center did for the Army. In 1990, I took over the leadership of the Defense Manpower Research Center at RAND. The center was established in 1971 at the start of the all-volunteer force. I left that position in 1994 to join the Clinton administration and spent the next four years as Assistant Secretary of the Navy for Manpower and Reserve Affairs. I did additional service as Special Assistant to the Deputy Secretary of Defense for Gulf War Illnesses. The Deputy Secretary at the time was Dr. John White. I must have done something right in those jobs because, in 1998, Secretary of Defense William Cohen asked me to move from the Navy and become the 25th Under Secretary of the Army (1998–2000). Finally, in 2000, I was reassigned to the position of Under Secretary of Defense for Personnel and Readiness (2000–2001). This is effectively the same position that Dr. White had held 23 years earlier as Assistant Secretary of Defense and that Dr. David S. C. Chu, another alumnus of RAND's manpower programs, holds today.

Finally, this study was conducted by RAND as part of its continuing program of self-sponsored research. We acknowledge the support for such research provided by the independent research and development provisions of RAND's contracts for the operation of its DoD federally funded research and development centers: Project AIR FORCE (sponsored by the U.S. Air Force), the Arroyo Center (sponsored by the U.S. Army), and the National Defense Research Institute (sponsored by the Office of the Secretary of Defense, the Joint Staff, the unified commands, and the defense agencies). The Office of the Under Secretary of Defense for Personnel and Readiness provided additional funds.

Contents

CHAPTER SEVEN
Analytic Studies During the Initial Transition Period (1969–1972)

CHAPTER TEN

The Second Inning: Analytic Studies (1973–1976)

CHAPTER THIRTEEN
The Carter Years: Analytic Studies (1977–1980)

CHAPTER FOURTEEN
Sustaining the All-Volunteer Force: The Reagan-Bush Years (1981–1992)

CHAPTER FIFTEEN

The Role of Women in the All-Volunteer Force

CHAPTER EIGHTEEN
Reaping What You Sow: Analytic Studies of the Clinton and Bush Years (1992–2004)

CHAPTER NINETEEN
Why Has the All-Volunteer Force Been a Success?

Figures

Tables

Foreword

In September 2003, it was my privilege to participate in a two-day conference at the National Defense University. The occasion was the 30th anniversary of the all-volunteer force. Those assembled included some who were present at the start of the all-volunteer force and others who shared responsibility for the future all-volunteer force and for national security policy. I noted then the importance of such an event. We would remind ourselves of where and how the all-volunteer force started, of the successes and difficulties of the all-volunteer force through the ensuing three decades, and of what needs to be done to ensure positive future chemistry between the all-volunteer force and national security strategy.

The conference was a success. Yet two days of presentations and discussions are scarcely sufficient to identify, explore, and analyze in depth the myriad issues the all-volunteer force involves. Justice to the all-volunteer force and its seminal role in national policy requires an in-depth pioneering study—wide in scope, accurate in detail, rich in analysis, penetrating in insight, and most importantly, accessible to a vast audience.

Bernard Rostker is delivering that justice. The research and analysis presented in this volume are at once comprehensive in both scope and depth. Indeed, the work constitutes a virtual archive of the many events, issues, facets, and fundamentals constituting the all-volunteer force. The research and documentation exceed by far, in my judgment, any prior attempts to explore this subject.

Few people have the motivation, the capacity, or the endurance to undertake quality research into such a complex array of political, economic, social, and technical issues. The shift from conscription to an all-volunteer force involved a rich recipe of all those aspects and more. Bernard Rostker deserves our gratitude for this ambitious and major contribution.

As an aside, it may be noted that the personalities involved in molding such a complex ingredient mix into effective public policy necessarily reflected a wide array of motivations, insights, biases, and emotions. Trying to capture these personality insights is among the most difficult of research tasks. In reading this volume, one could infer that, while Secretary of Defense, I hesitated on occasion in my support for the Gates Commission or was not aggressive in implementing changes in personnel acquisition practices. Such is not the case. The times were complex; the changes were significant; and our efforts had to be orchestrated carefully. We were prosecuting two wars (the Cold War and Southeast Asia); I had to manage the impact of a declining defense budget; and, politically, we faced major opposition in the Services, the Congress, and even from some in the White House as we moved away from the draft. It was mandatory, in my judgment, that we proceed deliberately and thoughtfully toward an all-volunteer force.

Time was needed. Congressional support was, of course, essential. It took months and substantial effort to garner that support. Likewise, it was desirable for other reasons to convince the Services and the military leadership of the all-volunteer force's value. Again, that took some cultivation. Most importantly, the strategy of Total Force in which the all-volunteer force would be embedded required explanation. Total Force involved not only revising the integration, use, and cultures of the active and reserve components but also incorporating other nations more effectively into a cohesive defense effort. Altering the active and reserve structure was by itself a major task. Attempting to increase the defense value of our many bilateral and multilateral security relationships would likewise take time. Accelerating the pace of change toward the all-volunteer force would have risked failure. It was crucial, in my judgment, that the all-volunteer force succeed.

It is important to note that Rostker does not attempt to render a final verdict in the concept or future of the all-volunteer force. The all-volunteer force is dynamic, requiring study and understanding. Those who are interested in or, especially, engaged in national security, economic, political, or social policy would do well to use Bernard Rostker's work to the fullest extent possible, especially as they deal with the all-volunteer force issues in the future.

Melvin R. Laird
Secretary of Defense (1969–1973)
Counselor to the President (1973–1974)
Nine-Term Member of the United States House of Representatives (1952–1968)

Acknowledgments

The *evolution* described in this book is not only about the all-volunteer force, it is also about my own evolution over the almost 40 years of my professional career. As the all-volunteer force advanced from a concept to a proposal, to a faltering reality, to a mature and resilient institution, I grew from a young Army captain, to an economist at the RAND Corporation, to a senior executive at the Department of Defense. The all-volunteer force was the result of the hard work of a large number of dedicated people—many highlighted in this book. My personal evolution was also the result of the support I received from a great many people. You never do it alone. This book is about them as much as it is about me and the all-volunteer force.

First and foremost is the support and encouragement I received from my wife, Louise, and our sons, David and Michael. Louise was there from the very beginning of both stories and even before. Through graduate school at Syracuse University, to my Army service at the Pentagon, out to California, and back and forth across the country four times, she raised a family, had a career, and was able to even put up with me with good humor. My late parents, Madeline and Leon Rostker, provided the intellectual stimulation and opportunities for me to discover my calling and then follow it. After my military tour in the Pentagon's Systems Analysis office, it was my father who was most enthusiastic about me taking up RAND's offer of employment. He said he was sure that it would be the best of all my offers to launch a career, and he was right.

RAND as an institution has had many lives and has changed and adapted over the nearly 40 years I have been associated with it. I am sure that each generation of RANDites thinks that it arrived during RAND's golden years, but I am sure that when I came in 1970, it *was* RAND's golden years. We had a privileged relationship with the Air Force and the Office of the Secretary of Defense. We had a small, dedicated, and outstanding young staff that lived and worked together in the sunshine of Santa Monica. Military manpower was a new area for economists, and there was a whole world to discover. The person who recruited me to RAND and would be my mentor for the rest of my life was John White. John and I were both graduate students at Syracuse University's Maxwell School of Citizenship and Public Affairs at the same time. While John was several years ahead of me, we shared many of the same professors and the same dissertation advisor, Jerry Miner. When I went off to the Pentagon to do my Army service, John went to RAND, and after my tour was over, he was instrumental in recruiting me to RAND.

At RAND, I was fortunate to meet and work with Rick Cooper, David S. C. Chu, Bob Roll, Glenn Gotz, John McCall, David Greenberg, Frank Camm, Dave Armor, Mike Polich, Bruce Orvis, Steve Drezner, and Jim and Susan Hosek and, in later years, Beth Asch, Jim Dertouzos, Dick Buddin, Mike Hix, and Larry Hanser—all soldiers in the cause of the all-volunteer force. I learned more from them than from any other group of people, and that continues to this day. In 1973, when John White moved up to become a vice president at RAND, I was fortunate enough to take over as Director of the Air Force Manpower, Personnel and Training Program. With his support and that of RAND President Don Rice, I honed my skills and learned my craft; then, in 1977, Don was instrumental in me getting a position as Principal Deputy Assistant Secretary of the Navy in the Carter administration.

In my new job at the Pentagon, I was exposed to people and issues that I had never known about as a simple action officer just eight years earlier. I met people who were struggling to make the all-volunteer force work and who would be my colleagues for the rest of my professional life. In the pages of this book, you will meet them, but a number require special recognition. In the Navy, I worked directly for two Washington legends, Graham Claytor and Jim Woolsey, then the Secretary and Under Secretary of the Navy, respectively. I learned about the Navy and military life from my executive assistant, Commander Mike Boorda. In later years, Mike would say that he learned from me, and that was high praise from someone who would become Chief of Naval Operations.

I also worked closely with my counterparts in the Office of the Secretary of Defense. John White had left RAND and was the Assistant Secretary for Manpower and Reserve Affairs. Former RAND colleague Gary Nelson worked for White, as did Richard Danzig and Robin Pirie. Both Richard and Robin would be colleagues again in the 1990s when we all returned to work in the Navy Secretariat. The irrepressible Johnny Johnston made things happen then and for years to come.

In the early years of the all-volunteer force, and in my early years at the Pentagon, there was a dedicated group of people who would sustain the all-volunteer force (and me) in good times and bad. You will also meet them in these pages: Irv Greenberg, Jeanne Fites, Eli Flyer, Al Martin, Steve Sellman, Paul Hogan, Bill Carr, Saul Pleeter, Marty Binkin, Joyce Shields, and Curt Gilroy in "The Building," as the Pentagon is often called, and, Anita Lancaster, Ken Scheflin, and Robbie Brandewie from the Defense Manpower Data Center. Steve Herbits, Martin Anderson, Bill Brehm, and Don Srull provided leadership at critical times, and each shared with me his experiences. Tom Stanners and Gene Devine were legends at the Office of Management and Budget, as were Arnold Punaro, Frank Sullivan, P. T. Henry, and Charlie Abell from the Senate Armed Services Committee and Kim Winkup, Karen Heath, and John Chapla from the House Armed Services Committee. The other federally funded research and development centers joined RAND in helping decisionmakers grapple with a seemingly never-ending list of management issues, their representatives including Stan Horowits, Chris Jehn, Aline Quester, Martha Koopman, Bill Simms, Bob Lockman, John Tilson, Larry Goldberg, Dave Kassing, and John Bringerhoff. They, as well as Bob Goldich and Lawrence Kapp of the Congressional Research Service, who provided sage advise to Congress over the years, were most helpful to me in the preparation of this book.

Ultimately, however, it was the military that had to make the all-volunteer force work. I was fortunate to work directly with a number of outstanding officers who steered their respective services' personnel programs during the most trying years of the all-volunteer force and who were patient with me when the positions I held were more senior than my age or the experience I brought to the job normally demanded. Without their support, my service would have been much more difficult and certainly less enjoyable. In the Air Force, then–Major General John Roberts held the critical positions of Director of Personnel Plans and later Deputy Chief of Staff for Personnel of the Air Force when I headed the Air Force's Manpower, Personnel, and Training Program at RAND; in the Navy, then–Vice Admiral James Watkins was the Chief of Naval Personnel during my time as the Principal Deputy Assistant Secretary of the Navy for Manpower and Reserve Affairs; and in the Army, Major General Maxwell Thurman headed the Army Recruiting Command when I was Director of Selective Service. He later served as the Deputy Chief of Staff for Personnel of the Army. All three eventually achieved four-star rank, General Roberts as Commander of the Air Training Command, Admiral Watkins as Chief of Naval Operations—after retirement, he served as Secretary of Energy under President George H. W. Bush—and General Thurman as Vice Chief of Staff of the Army and commander U.S. Southern Command during the invasion of Panama.

John White, Richard Danzig, and Robin Pirie gave me the opportunity to guide the Selective Service System, and when President Carter decided to change course, we had a workable plan that could be put in place to register over 2 million young men during the summer of 1980 and the winter of 1981. Without their confidence, encouragement and—when things got hot—direct support, the 1980–1981 registration would not have been as effective as it was. Almost 15 years later, Richard Danzig smoothed the way for my return to government, when I worked for him and John Dalton, as the Assistant Secretary of the Navy for Manpower and Reserve Affairs. And it was John White, then Deputy Secretary of Defense, who reached down into the Navy Department and gave me the "tarbaby" that was the Gulf War Illness problem, which resulted in probably the most significant single thing I did for DoD and our service men and women during my entire career. John gave me the opportunity to serve and help explain to those suffering from unexplained illness after their service in the Gulf War what may have happened and what did not happen during the war and, it was hoped, provide some measure of comfort, if not always relief.

Secretary of Defense William Cohen was one of my strongest supporters when I was the Director of Selective Service and he was the junior senator from Maine. After moving to DoD in 1997, he promoted me to be Under Secretary of the Army and then Under Secretary of Defense for Personnel and Readiness. Much of the later chapters of the book covers this period.

I am indebted to the RAND Corporation for the opportunity to work on this book, and when the scope of the book took off, its continued support went far beyond the point that any of us had originally thought would be needed. Jim Thomson, President of RAND; Michael Rich, Executive Vice President; and Brent Bradley, Assistant to the President for Corporate Strategy, gave me the resources to do the job. Their task was helped when Jeanne Fites and Curt Gilroy of the Office of the Under Secretary of Defense for Personnel and Readiness took up sponsorship. They provided additional funds that covered some of the costs of preparing the final manuscript. David S. C. Chu, the current Under Secretary, read every word of the final draft and not only provided insightful comments from the prospective only he could have, having served as the Assistant Secretary of Defense for Program Analysis and Evaluation from 1980 to 1993, but also opened his papers at the Library of Congress, allowing me to review the inner workings of the Defense Resources Board during those important years.

Two of the giants of the all-volunteer force, Walter Oi and John Warner, both were available to me as I wrote this book. Walter's engagement with this issue goes back to the early 1960s as the Director of Research on the original 1964 Pentagon Draft Study. In 2006, Walter is still engaged as a member of the Defense Military Compensation Commission, as is John White. John Warner has also been engaged at every critical point since he first provided insightful analysis to the Gates Commission. He continues to provide support for the current Defense Military Compensation Commission.

The original plan for this book envisioned a short history to set the stage for a discussion of the economic analysis used by decisionmakers. After I was exposed, however, to the primary source materials contained in the 60 archive boxes of the Steve Herbits collection at the Hoover Institution at Stanford University, I was hooked. For me, the words contained in the reports and memorandums archived at Hoover jumped off the pages and brought alive the critical discussions that took place so many years ago. I felt I was in the room and that I could hear people talking. Elena Danielson, the archivist at Hoover, was kind enough to allow me to copy 400 pages of these critical documents. But, alas, Herbits' papers covered only a small portion of the all-volunteer force period I wanted to cover. I was delighted to find, in the "Bibliographic Note" at the end of Robert Griffith's book, *The U.S. Army's Transition to the All-Volunteer Force 1968–1974,* a reference to papers in Record Group 330 at the National Archives' Washington National Records Center at Suitland Maryland. David O. (Doc) Cook, the Pentagon's Director for Administration and Management, told me that Record Group 330 was all DoD papers; since I held the needed security clearances, he approved my access to these papers, subject to final security review and declassification. He asked Harold Neeley at Washington Headquarters Services to facilitate access to the stored files. Sandy Meagher and her supervisor, Robert Storer, provided direct support. As the size and importance of this collection became apparent and as my requests for documents grew to the many hundreds and consisted of thousands of pages, their support was critical. The timely and professional way they did their jobs made this book possible.

At the Records Center, Elizabeth Sears and Mike Waesche provided workspace and access to the 332 boxes of materials that DoD indicated contained materials on the all-volunteer force. Unlike the boxes at the Hoover Institution, which were neatly arranged and catalogued archive boxes, the boxes at the National Records Center were moving boxes, and the materials they contained had been dumped into them when file cabinets had been emptied 25 years before. When I was finished going through all the moving boxes, it was clear that, like the Herbits collection, these materials also stopped in the mid-1970s, when the formal all-volunteer force transition programs ended.

When I explained my problem to Elizabeth and Mike, they told me that there was a better way to get to related papers in the later years. They gave me a copy of the DoD record coding system, and I was able to identify specific codes for the all-volunteer force, Selective Service, recruiting and retention, and enlisted and officer personnel management. They then led me to a mass of filing cabinets that contained all the "accessions" received by the Records Center, including those from DoD. Eventually, I was able to locate folders for all four codes for each year from 1960 through 2002. These folders came from accessions marked "Official Records 1960," "Official Records 1961," and so on. I learned that these were accessions from the immediate office of the Secretary and Deputy Secretary of Defense, and that each year their staffs went through their files and sent anything that was two years old or older to the Records Center. After another round of requests and approvals, an additional 67 boxes were made available, together with 50 folders that were removed from their boxes. All in all, I copied and Sandy Meagher and her staff reviewed and declassified over 5,600 pages from 960 documents. Joanne Palmer at RAND did an outstanding job of scanning all these and more into Portable Document Format (PDF) files that are contained on the DVD.

Further documents were obtained from the Presidential libraries of President Gerald Ford at the University of Michigan in Ann Arbor, President Jimmy Carter at the Carter Center in Atlanta, and President Ronald Reagan in Simi Valley, California, as well as from the Nixon Presidential Materials that are being held by the National Archives in College Park, Maryland. Melvin Laird recommended that I review his papers that were at the Ford Presidential Library. Martin Anderson's White House papers, which cover the Military Manpower Task Force established in 1980, required special clearance from the Office of the White House General Counsel, and I am indebted to David Chu and to Paul Koffsky and Stewart Aly of the DoD General Counsel's office for their help in getting the White House to approve the release of these documents. Many former government officials retained copies of important documents from their time in service. They literally scoured attics and garages and sent me folders and boxes of documents. Invariably, each new package of documents shed new light on some incident I thought I understood. For these invaluable sources of materials, I am indebted to Martin Anderson, Al Martin, Steve Sellman, Jeanne Fites, Joyce Shields, Gene Devine, Bill Brehm, Don Srull, Stu Rakoff, Eli Flyer, John Johnston, Irv Greenberg, Bill Carr, Jeff Goldstein, Bob Goldich, and Anita Lancaster. All these documents and more are available on the accompanying DVD, and since the text is linked to these documents, this book is a guide to over 1,700 primary source documents.

The Internet was also an important source of material, including the audio files of John Ford and my seminars at the U.S. Military Academy at West Point. My wife, Louise, edited President Carter's 1980 State of the Union address to highlight the parts where he called for a return to active draft registration. Photographs were provided courtesy of the Jimmy Carter Library and the National Archives.

One advantage of modern information technology is the ability to hyperlink materials. Stand-alone encyclopedias have used linking, and legal reference services link over the internet. When I ran the DoD Gulf War Illness Office, we produced online Case Narratives with footnotes that were linked to source material. When I discovered the vast number of government documents, the number of links for this book took off. I estimate that there may be as many as 6,000 links in this book. Managing such a large number of supporting documents was a major undertaking made manageable by a bibliographic program, EndNote, which is integrated into Microsoft Word. Word and Adobe Acrobat allow me to enter links one at a time, clearly a daunting task that would have taken time but would have been prone to human error. My son Michael suggested that a computer program could be written that would read the information inserted in Word by EndNote and automatically write the link without further intervention. In fact, Michael S. Tseng at RAND wrote just such a program for me, and we were able to automate the linking process. I am indebted to both Michaels for saving me the time and the tedium. The resourceful people at EEI Communications were able to take the Word document with the automated links and transfer the whole document into Adobe's InDesign program for final layout of both the book and the DVD.

Throughout this project, I benefited from the superb support I received from RAND staff. My long-serving administrative assistant, Nancy Rizor, read and reread countless drafts and made valuable suggestions. Gail Kouril and the rest of the RAND Library staff were able to locate the most obscure references. The Publications and Creative Services group at RAND maintains an archive of every RAND document published since the founding of the corporation in 1948. Michael Rich, RAND's Executive Vice President, facilitated the use of historically important RAND documents that helped tell the story of the evolution of the all-volunteer force. The Pentagon Library, damaged in the attack of September 11, 2001, was a valued source of one-of-a-kind documents. They are an important resource for the whole defense community.

I am indebted to Jim Hosek and Robin Pirie for taking on the task of formally reviewing the manuscript for this book. Both excel in their firsthand knowledge of the events and technical studies described in this book. The book is all the better for their efforts. Phyllis M. Gilmore edited the book with a light but firm hand and, for good or bad, let my voice come through. Finally, halfway through my Army tour at the Pentagon, Congressman Melvin Laird took over as Secretary of Defense. To an Army captain, but one of the 50,000 people working in the building at that time, Secretary Laird was a storied figure. I could never have imagined that, 35 years later, I would write a book about the all-volunteer force or that Secretary Laird would honor me by writing a foreword to that book. If someone at the time had told me that would happen, I would have said, "fiction," but this only goes to show that life is often stranger than fiction.

Bernard Rostker
Arlington, Virginia
January 2006

CHAPTER ONE

What Have We Done?
A Summary of Then and Now (1960–2006)

> Lapses in discipline within elements of the Army have caused me serious concern. Some instances have been obvious, grave in nature, and well publicized. These, along with other[s] . . . dictate the need to give special attention to the subject throughout the chain of command.
>
> —General William C. Westmoreland
> Chief of Staff, U.S. Army[1]—1971

> We have the finest military on Earth because we have the finest people on Earth, because we recruit and we retain the best that America has to offer.
>
> —William S. Cohen
> Secretary of Defense[2]—2001

Introduction[3]

As this was being written, in spring 2006, 157,000 American service members were at war: 137,000 in Iraq and 20,000 in Afghanistan. All were volunteers. While some worry about the resiliency of the all-volunteer force during periods of prolonged stress and long-term commitment, and others decry the perceived lack of social representativeness of the all-volunteer force, no one can deny that it is the finest fighting force the United States has ever fielded.

---

[1] Letter of September 15, 1971, to Major Field Commanders (Westmoreland, 1971).

[2] Farewell to U.S. Armed Forces, January 17, 2001 (Cohen, 2001).

[3] An earlier version of this chapter was presented at a conference at the American Center of Sciences Po in Paris in June 2002. The conference was cosponsored by the Strategic Studies Institute of the U.S. Army War College, the Royal United Services Institute, the French Ministry of Defense Center for Social Studies in Defense, the Association of the U.S. Army, the Förderkreis Deutches Heer, and the U.S. Embassy in Paris.

Janice Laurence (2004a) provides an excellent short review of the history of the all-volunteer force.

Looking back, there are at least five reasons that the United States moved to an all-volunteer force in 1973. First, the norm throughout American history has been a volunteer military. Second, the size of the eligible population of young men reaching draft age each year in the 1960s was so large and the needs of the military so small in comparison that, in practice, the draft was no longer universal. By the late 1960s, the American system of conscription had lost legitimacy and support among the vast majority of the American people. It was viewed as unfair, the universality of the World War II draft having been replaced by a system encapsulated in the title of a landmark blue ribbon commission report, *Who Serves When Not All Serve* (Marshall, 1967). The large population of military age also meant that obtaining enough volunteers was possible at budget levels that were seen as acceptable. Third, the Vietnam War was unpopular. As the war went on, draft calls increased and deferments were cancelled; more and more young Americans became subject to an institution they had been able, up to that point, to largely ignore. It was an institution that tied them to an unpopular war. Fourth, as one historian has written, there was a "rational, intellectual basis for the volunteer force" that told young men that they did not have a moral obligation to serve. Finally, the Army itself had lost confidence in the draft as discipline problems among draftees mounted in Vietnam. The Army was ready for a change. Moreover, there was a group of inspired leaders that pressed forward and would not be deterred. Notwithstanding all this, some argued against the end of conscription. Most students of military sociology argued in favor of reforming, not ending, the draft. Some liberals and some conservatives in Congress were fearful of an all-volunteer force, albeit for very different reasons.

The Move to End Conscription

Conscription is not the norm for America. Americans have historically distrusted standing militaries. A citizen militia—the National Guard of today—is provided for in the Constitution as a counter to a strong standing federal army. While there was an implied obligation for all to "provide for the common defense," the first national draft did not come until the Civil War. After the war, the Adjutant General of the State of Illinois set down a design for a future draft system that would be the model for the future conscription system in the United States. The model was based on federalism, as it existed in the 1860s. It apportioned the requirement for future conscripts to the states and through the states to individual counties. This plan, together with the concept of "channeling" draft-eligible men into whatever military or civilian occupation best supported the war effort—a concept that led to the term *Selective Service*—was implemented during World War I and again in 1940, on the eve of World War II. President Harry Truman ended conscription for a time in 1947 but, following the same model, reinstated the draft as a Cold War measure in 1948. It remained in place until 1973.

If America has no tradition of a draft absent an ongoing war, hot or cold, we have a tradition of the intellectual elite longing for some form of national service. The issue is not so much the need of the country for the labor of these conscripted citizens, but the benefits that would be wrought on a young person having served the country for some period of time.[4] Voluntary programs, such as the Peace Corps, were fine for those who already had a calling for service. What was needed, they argued, was compulsory service to transform the unredeemed and to make them better citizens. The attraction was not so much for military service as for any service. If other forms of national service were constitutionally prohibited, military service would do.[5]

In reality, the Cold War draft of the pre-Vietnam period was a poor substitute for universal service. As the size of the draft age group expanded and the needs of the military fell, draft calls fell, and the universality of the system became a sham.[6] While other countries, France for example, facing a similar situation tried to maintain universal conscription by reducing terms of service to fit their demographics and their budgets, this was not really an alternative for America, given the worldwide military commitments it had accepted after World War II. By the early 1960s, the Selective Service had became "a draft agency that did more deferring than drafting" (Flynn, 1985, p. 218). In 1962, only 76,000 were drafted. By comparison, more than 430,000 draft eligible men were given educational or occupational deferments that year, and over 1,300,000 were deferred because of paternity. In fall 1962, President John Kennedy extended deferments to married men, even if they were not fathers. For all practical purposes, this meant that anyone who wanted to could avoid military service. What was left of the draft became politically sensitive because of the perception that the system of deferments had gotten out of control. The need for a draft was openly questioned. Pressure mounted in Congress to reform Selective Service and, at least, study the feasibility of an all-volunteer force. In 1963, President Lyndon Johnson announced that the Pentagon would undertake a comprehensive study of the draft system.

While there was a movement in favor of some form of compulsory national service as a responsibility of citizenship, there was also a movement that believed that the

---

[4] The renowned anthropologist Margaret Mead argued that "Universal national service, in addition to solving the problem of fairness for those who are asked to serve in the military, in contrast to those who are not, is above all a new institution for creating responsible citizens alert to the problems and responsibilities of nationhood in a rapidly changing world" (Mead, 1967, p. 109).

[5] The 13th Amendment to the Constitution prohibits involuntary servitude. The only exception is the authority the Constitution grants Congress to raise an Army and support a Navy. A more complete treatment of the constitutional questions associated with a number of national service schemes can be found in Danzig and Szanton (1986).

[6] In 1948, when President Truman asked Congress to reinstate the draft to deal with the threat of communism in Europe, he also called for universal service. On March 17, 1948, he told Congress, "There is no conflict between the requirements of selective service for the regular forces and universal training for the reserve components" (O'Sullivan and Meckler, 1974, p. 206). Universal military training failed, but the draft was passed, and Truman signed a new Selective Service Act into law on June 24, 1948. On September 21, 1950, within weeks of the start of the Korean War, Truman again called for universal military service. Congress went as far as to create the National Security Training Commission to study the issue, but nothing more ever came of it.

draft was "inconsistent with a free society" (Friedman, 1967). The leading proponent was University of Chicago Professor Milton Friedman. Economists and those who accepted Professor Friedman's argument dominated the Pentagon study of the draft. The task of the study, as they saw it, was to estimate the cost of shifting from the draft to a voluntary system of manpower procurement. The study group drew the distinction between the cost to society of having a draft and the budget costs of moving to an all-volunteer force. Their argument was that the cost to society is very high when the cost of the military is not paid for by the general public but by a small group of draftees forced to serve at below-market wages. They argued that, by comparison, the budget cost of the all-volunteer force was "affordable." The analysis was set aside, however, as the country moved to increasing draft calls for the Vietnam War.

By fall 1968, the unpopularity of the draft and the Vietnam War motivated the Republican candidate for President, Richard Nixon, to publicly announce that if elected he would move the country to an all-volunteer force. In a campaign speech, Nixon said that a draft that "arbitrarily selects some and not others simply cannot be squared with our whole concept of liberty, justice and equality under the law. . . . in the long run, the only way to stop the inequities is to stop using the system" (Nixon, 1968).

The Army itself was also ready for a change. As the official Army history of the period put it, "well before the Gates Commission rendered its report, the Army's leadership had concluded that an end to conscription was in the service's best interest. . . ." (Griffith, 1997, p. 17).

On February 20, 1970, the Gates Commission, set up by President Nixon to advise him on establishing an all-volunteer force reported that "We unanimously believe that the nation's interest will be better served by an all-volunteer force, supported by an effective standby draft, than by a mixed force of volunteers and conscripts" (Gates, 1970).

The recommendation by the Gates Commission must be seen against the backdrop of the Vietnam War. By the late 1960s, the widespread opposition to the Vietnam War had moved from the burning of draft cards to riots in the streets of Chicago during the Democratic National Convention of 1968. Finally, with an unpopular war in a stalemate and at the request of President Nixon, the House of Representatives moved to an all-volunteer force by approving Public Law 92-129 by a vote of 297 to 108 on August 4, 1971. The Senate followed on September 21, 1971, by a vote of 55 to 30. On September 28, 1971, President Nixon signed the bill that extended the draft for only two years and committed the country to transition to an all-volunteer force (Lee and Parker, 1977, pp. 138–147).

A Model for Other Countries

While the Gates Commission accepted Friedman's arguments, European countries that have moved to an all-volunteer force more recently were not very moved by the argument that conscription is "inconsistent with a free society."[7] In fact, the historical view on the European continent is that every citizen has an obligation to perform some service at the call of the state. The end of the Cold War, however, led to cost-motivated downsizing that sharply cut the number of conscripts, thereby sowing "the seeds of an upcoming public debate about who serves and who . . . [does] not" (Haltiner and Klein, 2005, p. 10). Echoing the debate that had occurred in the United States in the 1960s, "the problem of burden-sharing in defense matters grew acute and there was strong political pressure in favor of a complete suspension of the draft, [in such countries as] France, Italy, Slovenia and Spain" (Haltiner and Klein, 2005, p. 11). These new converts to an all-volunteer force found universal military service both unaffordable and inconsistent with maintaining a competent, modern military. Most recently, Anthony Cordesman, in his review of NATO military operations in Kosovo, found that

> Kosovo seems to have reinforced the lessons that many military experts drew about the value of conscripts versus professionals after the Gulf War. . . . The level of technology and the tactical demands of Kosovo clearly required highly trained and proficient soldiers. . . . This experience helps validate the decision to phase out conscription to many French officers. It also raised growing concerns among German officers over their government's insistence that conscription was necessary to ensure a democratic force. Some senior German officers feel that the net result is to alienate German conscripts while wasting scarce resources on useless low-grade manpower. (Cordesman, 2000, p. 260)

Effects on the Military: From 1973 to the Present

The all-volunteer force has changed the American military in remarkable ways. The "quality" of the force, measured by scores on standardized IQ tests, has improved. The percentage of new recruits who are high school diploma graduates was increased. The all-volunteer force has dramatically increased the number of career personnel and increased the proficiency and professionalism of the force. Despite fears that an all-volunteer force would separate the Army from the American people, the all-volunteer force is broadly representative of the American people. Some have argued that this has come at the expense of widening the political gap between the military and society and

---

[7] Jehn and Selden, in their review of the more-recent experience in Europe, argue that

> Countries that have chosen to adopt voluntarism have cited only its expected positive effect on military effectiveness and, less often, the inequity of selective conscription. Absent from the justification for adopting an AVF [All-Volunteer Force] have been the economic inefficiency of conscription and the involuntary servitude which conscription represents. (Jehn and Selden, 2001, p. 13)

> The effects on the state in terms of budgetary expenditures and military capability are what appears to drive the debate in Europe; the effects of conscription on the individual citizen and his basic rights do not often enter into the discussion. By contrast, these issues were an undercurrent of the debate about conscription in the United States. (Jehn and Selden, 2002, p. 99)

have blamed this on the lack of a draft. This is a new kind of representationalism, based not on race, gender, socioeconomic status, educational achievement, or geography but on political values.

Quality

The quality of personnel that the services access under the all-volunteer force has remarkably improved since the days of the draft. Under the Vietnam War–era draft, the services used a quota system to ensure the "equitable" distribution of manpower on the basis of mental ability. Each service was required to take a specified percentage of Mental Category IV personnel.[8] Mental Category IV personnel are between the 10th and 30th percentile of the population. On a standard intelligence test—the Stanford-Binet IQ test—this represents a test score range between about 72 and 91. Mental Category V, the lowest 10 percent of the population, is never taken.[9] Those opposed to the all-volunteer force in Congress, who were unsuccessful in their attempts to block President Nixon's initiative, turned their attention to the issue of quality. If there was going to be an all-volunteer force, it would have to have a 55-percent floor on high school graduates, as opposed to the 45-percent floor the services had had, and a ceiling of 18 percent on Mental Category IV personnel. Many at the time, particularly opponents of the all-volunteer force in Congress, thought these levels could not be achieved. To make a very long story short—discussed in the rest of this book—about 93 percent of accessions today are high school graduates, and the services take very few—in effect, no—Mental Category IV personnel.

Representativeness

The issue of representativeness had surfaced during the early debates about the all-volunteer force, during the deliberations of the Gates Commission; as the Army transitioned to the all-volunteer force; and, most recently, during the current war in Iraq and the War on Terrorism. In 1973, the recently retired Army Chief of Staff, General William Westmoreland, told the *New York Times* that "The social composition . . . (of the all-volunteer Army) bothers me. I deplore the prospect of our military forces not representing a cross-section of our society" (Franklin, 1973, p. 1).

For the last 26 years, the Department of Defense has annually reported on social representation in the U.S. Military. The most recent report noted the following (Chu, 2004):

---

[8] The Department of Defense has a conversion table of "Mental Category Scores from AFQT to IQ Scores" as noted in Martin (1980).

[9] The "categories" used here are aggregations of scores from the Armed Force Quality Test. In *Performance of the All-Volunteer Force,* Janice Laurence provides an excellent summary of this test in the overall context of measuring the performance of soldiers, tracing the history of aptitude and performance measurement to the current policy of recruiting that a minimum of 60 percent of new accessions must come from Category I–IIIA and 90 percent be high school graduates. See Laurence (2004b).

- **Age.** The active-duty population is younger than the overall civilian sector. Military personnel between the ages of 17 and 24 make up 49 percent of the active-duty force, compared to about 15 percent of the civilian workforce. Officers, while older than enlisted personnel—mean ages of 34 and 27, respectively—are younger than their civilian counterparts. The mean age of civilian college graduates in the 21–49 cohort is 36.

- **Gender.** While the number of females has risen sharply—17 percent of active component accession and 24 percent of reserve component accession—they are still underrepresented. However, today 15 percent of the active-duty enlisted force is female, compared with less than two percent when the draft ended. The representations of women among active-duty officer accessions and in the officer corps in FY 2002 were 19 and 16 percent, respectively.

- **Marital status.** In addition to the increase in the number of women, the larger career force has meant that the number of service members who are married has also increased. At the start of the all-volunteer force, approximately 40 percent of enlisted members were married. At a high in 1994, 57 percent were married. Today, the number is 49 percent. Sixty-eight percent of all active-duty officers are married. Today's military is family friendly. As a result, newcomers to the military are less likely than their civilian age counterparts to be married, but as time goes on, military members are more likely to be married than those in the civilian sector.

- **Educational level.** The most recent statistics show that 92 percent of the new accessions to the active component are regular high school graduates. The figure for the reserve components was 87 percent. Compare this with the 1973 goal of 45 percent and with the 79 percent for all 18- to 24-year-olds today. Ninety-five percent of active-duty officers have baccalaureate degrees, and 38 percent have advanced degrees.

- **Mental aptitude.** Today's American military scores well above the general civilian population on standard tests of intelligence.[10] The services currently accept almost no one from the two lowest mental categories, IV and V (scoring roughly 72 to 91), with one percent from Category IV and none from Category V. In contrast, 30 percent of civilians fall into these categories. For the top two categories, I and II (above 108), the military takes more than its fair share, with 41 percent of military personnel but only 36 percent of civilians falling into these two categories. Finally, more than twice as many military personnel as civilians fall into the middle category, III (92 to 107), with 58 percent for the military and 34 percent for civilians. Moreover, the reading level of new recruits is one year higher than their civilian counterparts.

- **Socioeconomic status.** The Survey of Recruit Socioeconomic Backgrounds—parents' education, employment status, occupation, and home ownership—shows that

---

[10] As noted earlier, the scores used to describe these mental categories are the AFQT score converted to a Stanford-Binet IQ score, as noted in Martin (1980).

recruits come primarily from families in the middle or lower middle class. The high end of the distribution was not well represented.

- **Race and ethnicity.** In FY 2002, African Americans were slightly overrepresented among new enlisted accessions relative to the civilian population, 16 percent compared with 14 percent. This is considerably below the 1973 level of 28 percent. African Americans make up 22 percent of the total enlisted force but only 13 percent of the 18- to 44-year-old civilian workforce.

  Hispanics are underrepresented, making up 16 percent of all civilians but only 11 percent of new accessions.

  The situation for officers is reversed; eight percent of newly commissioned officers were African Americans, and four percent were Hispanic. Interestingly, the prevalence of African American and Hispanic officers in the active-duty officer corps closely reflects the proportion of these groups in the relevant civilian, college-graduate population.

- **Geographic representation.** The geographic distribution of enlisted accessions for FY 2002 shows that the South continues to be overrepresented, with more than 40 percent of accessions. Compared with the civilian population, the representation ratio for 18- to 24-year-olds was 1.2 for the South and 0.8 for the Northeast. The ratio for the North Central and West was 0.9.

Professionalization of the Military

Probably the most important change in the all-volunteer force has been the professionalization of the military as retention increased and as the services were able to devote fewer resources to training new personnel. In 1969, when President Nixon established the Gates Commission, only 18 percent of the Army had more than four years of service. The corresponding numbers for the Navy, Marine Corps, and Air Force were 31, 16, and 46 percent, respectively. By 1977, the percentages had grown to 37 percent for the Army and 42, 26, and 54 percent for the other services, respectively. Today, having fully achieved an all-volunteer force, the numbers stand at 51 percent for the Army, 49 percent for the Navy, 35 percent for the Marine Corps, and 66 percent for the Air Force. In the early 1970s, before the all-volunteer force, the services routinely retained about 15 percent of the cohort of true volunteers, draft-motivated volunteers, and draftees who were eligible to reenlist. Today, the corresponding number is about 53 percent. The exception is the Marine Corps, which restricts reenlistments to about 25 percent of those eligible to reenlist to maintain the desired force profile.

The Political Gap Between the Military and Society

It has become popular to argue that the all-volunteer force is responsible for, as the title of one book puts it, *Widening the Gap Between the Military and Society* (Ricks, 1997). Those who hold this view argue that, because we do not have a draft, the ignorance of American elites about the military has deepened. But when, short of mobilization, have "American elites" had a firsthand knowledge of the military? While it cannot be denied that fewer current members of Congress have served in the military than those serving in Congress when conscription was ended in 1973, the large number of veterans serving in the past was the result of the mass mobilizations of World War II and Korea. Unlike the World War II and Korea generations, many from the draft-era Vietnam generation serving today in Congress did not serve in the military. The basic point is that there are no clear linkages, from the past or with respect to the current situation, that demonstrate how differences between the military leadership's political orientation and that of the political elite, especially elected members of Congress, have translated to a less-capable military, a weakened nation, a disaffected youth, or disproportionate burdens on certain segments of society. To claim that differences have changed in an adverse way since the advent of the all-volunteer force is to assume knowledge of adverse consequences even though actual evidence is lacking.

The Final Chapter Has Not Been Written

In January 2002, William Cohen spoke to the men and women of the armed forces about his four years as Secretary of Defense. He ended his remarks by saying:

> On countless occasions I've been asked by foreign leaders, "How can our military be more like America's?" I'll repeat here today what I've said time and time again. It's not our training, although our training is the most rigorous in the world. It's not our technology, although ours is the most advanced in the world. And it's not our tactics, although ours is [sic] the most revolutionary in the world. We have the finest military on Earth because we have the finest people on Earth, because we recruit and we retain the best that America has to offer. (Cohen, 2001)

In the final account, when the draft ceased to be a means of universal service, it lost its legitimacy and was doomed. The alternative to the draft, the all-volunteer force, has been a resounding success for the American military and the American people. It has resulted in a professional, career-oriented military that has proven itself on battlefields throughout the world. It is a force that is generally representative of American society and has provided outstanding employment opportunities for groups that have long been excluded from the mainstream of society. It is a leading employer of women, with equal pay for equal work. It is the most racially integrated institution in America.[11] It is a resilient and flexible force that has integrated the

---

[11] Aline Quester and Curtis Gilroy, in their review of the changing status of women and minorities (Quester and Gilroy, 2002, p. 120), found that

> In the years since the advent of the volunteer force, the U.S. military has become more racially and ethnically diverse. It also appears to have successfully integrated women. Moreover, even though the process from entry-level to top leadership positions has taken a long time, both the current top enlisted and officer ranks have richer minority and female representation than the accession cohorts from which they were drawn.

full-time, active-duty soldier with his part-time, civilian reserve counterpart to form a truly total force. Moreover, this has been done with an affordable budget and with a competitive wage. Today, people join because they want to join, not because someone is forcing them to serve. Today the all-volunteer force is one that values the individual, and through increased levels of retention, individuals signal back that they value the all-volunteer force.

The last chapter of the evolution of the all-volunteer force has not yet been written. As demonstrated countless times over the past 30 years, the all-volunteer force is a fragile institution. In the past, insensitivity to the needs of service members and their families resulted in low enlistments and poor-quality recruits. Today, the fragility of the all-volunteer force comes from extended operations in Afghanistan and Iraq. To date, the increase in operational tempo for active and reserve forces has not resulted in significant recruitment shortages, although the active Army, the Army National Guard and the Army Reserve are having increasing difficulty recruiting new personnel. For the total force, the picture is not as bleak as it might be because of good retention. The professionalism of the all-volunteer force is paying off. As the Army struggles, those charged with managing the force are vigilant and, with the knowledge gained over 30 years, certainly will certainly do their utmost to ensure the continued success of the all-volunteer force. However, only time will tell.

Then, Now, and the In-Between: The Plan for This Book

Having discussed the conditions of the late 1960s leading to an all-volunteer force—the *Then*—and the force that resulted—the *Now*—the remainder of the book tells the story of how the all-volunteer force evolved—the *In-Between*. The remaining 18 chapters follow roughly the chronology of events, with each period covered in two chapters. Three chapters depart from this format, however. The period of the Carter administration is covered in three chapters, including a stand-alone chapter called the "Selective Service Side Show." The Reagan and Bush years of the 1980s are also covered in three chapters, with one devoted to the role women have played in the success of the all-volunteer force. A final chapter explores why the all-volunteer force has been a success.

The chronology of events can sometimes become confusing. An event will carry the normal calendar notation of date of month, day year, e.g., July 1, 1973, the first official day of the all-volunteer force, but that day is also the first day of fiscal year (FY) 1974. On any given day, such as July 1, 1973, the Department of Defense will be spending money from one fiscal year, e.g., FY 1973, defending its budget request for the next fiscal year before Congress, e.g., FY 1974, and preparing the details of its budget to be submitted to the President for his consideration that covers a third fiscal year, e.g., FY 1975. An appendix to this book contains a timeline that should help the reader make sense of what often can become a confusing set of dates.

The first chapter for each period is the history of the period. It is largely based on government documents, particularly those from the original Project Volunteer Office in the Pentagon and those that were in the files of the immediate office of the Secretary of Defense before they were sent to the National Records Center.[12] They have been supplemented with archived papers from the Executive Office of the President for the Nixon, Ford, Carter, and Reagan administrations. Papers from the Bush and Clinton administrations have been embargoed by a recent Executive Order and were not available. In addition, a large number of documents were obtained from former government officials who had taken copies with them when they left office.

The second chapter for each period focuses on the research used to inform the decisionmakers as they were managing the all-volunteer force. While this is also largely chronological, adding this material to the history chapter would have hopelessly diverted the story. As a result, and since each chapter is meant to stand alone, there is some unavoidable repetition between each and its associated history chapter. The second chapters present material that some readers will find very technical. These chapters can be easily scanned or skipped entirely without loosing much of the story of the evolution of the all-volunteer force. For those interested, however, they do present a more in-depth understanding of how decisionmakers used analysis, an important theme in the story.

The remaining chapters of this book roughly correspond to the administrations of the eight Presidents since Lyndon Johnson ordered the Pentagon study of the draft in 1964. Key to the story are the ten men who have served as Secretary of Defense and the Under Secretaries and Assistant Secretaries that supported them over the last 35 years. Most noteworthy are Secretary of Defense Melvin Laird; Assistant Secretary for Manpower and Reserve Affairs Roger Kelley; Kelley's replacement, William K. Brehm; and the secretaries he served, James Schlesinger and Donald Rumsfeld. They had the very hard job of initiating and nurturing the all-volunteer force during its most formative years. The Carter administration's Secretary of Defense was Harold Brown; his assistant secretaries in the manpower "shop" were John White and Robin Pirie.

---

[12] *Author's Note:* There is a requirement to preserve government records, but in practice, most offices in the Pentagon, with the exception of the immediate Office of the Secretary and Deputy Secretary of Defense, do not systematically preserve their records. For example, at one point, the Accessions Policy Office sent their "old" records to a contractor for "safekeeping." When the contractor moved to a smaller location, the records were destroyed. Documents are often retained as souvenirs by departing officials, myself included. Some of these will eventually find their way back into the Presidential archives, or to private archives. Unfortunately, most will eventually be thrown out during some episode of spring cleaning.

The staff of the Secretary of Defense, however, is dutiful in maintaining its files and uses a formal classification system. Every year, staff members remove items that have been in the file for two years and send them to the National Records Center. My extensive use of documents that were in the files of the Secretary of Defense not only screened the documents for relative importance but introduces a bias into the research. It was a screen because it is presumed only "important" issues are brought to the attention of the Secretary of Defense. This will, however, introduce a bias into the research because the available record is hardly a random sample of documents covering all aspects of the all-volunteer force. For example, the chapter that deals with women and the all-volunteer force focuses largely on the Army. The Air Force is hardly covered, which was a reflection of the documents obtained from the Secretary of Defense's office.

They had to deal with the all-volunteer force at its lowest. Assistant Secretaries Larry Korb and Chris Jehn served Secretaries of Defense Caspar Weinberger, Frank Carlucci, and Richard Cheney as the Cold War came to an end. Edwin Dorn, Rudy Deleon, and Bernard Rostker were under secretaries—the position of assistant secretary was elevated one level in the hierarchy—serving secretaries Les Aspin, William Perry, and William Cohen during the 1990s, as the force transitioned to a new world order after the fall of the Soviet Union. Since 2001, David S. C. Chu has been Under Secretary of Defense for Personnel and Readiness, the new name for the old position; he works for Secretary of Defense Donald Rumsfeld, returning for the second time. The events of September 11, 2001, and the wars in Afghanistan and Iraq mark their administration.

The success of the all-volunteer force can be clearly linked to the expertise these men brought to the job. A number of the Secretaries of Defense served as members of Congress—Laird, Rumsfeld, Cheney, Aspin, and Cohen. Several had also held senior positions at the White House—Rumsfeld and Cheney had been chiefs of staff to the President. Carlucci had been national security advisor to the President and Schlesinger had been the Director of Central Intelligence and Associate Director of the Office of Management and Budget. The under and assistant secretaries who served during these 35 years were also very well qualified. Many were trained analysts. Brehm, White, Pirie, Korb, Jehn, Dorn, Rostker, and Chu all contributed to the development of the all-volunteer force before they took their posts at the Pentagon. The reader will meet these men and many more as this story unfolds.

Besides the qualifications of the people who managed the all-volunteer force throughout the years, there are number of themes that mark the evolution of the all-volunteer force which come up time and again. The reader will find many examples of how resistant the institution was to change; the importance of analysis in asking the right questions and providing decisionmakers with the costs and benefits of alternative courses of action; the importance that pay has in recruiting the right force; how hard it has been to determining what was the right force to recruit and than how to actually recruit it. Finally, repeatedly, when the "wrong" decisions were made prospective recruits and those in service told those in charge when things were not right. They told them not in words, but by actions—by not enlisting and not reenlisting. In one way, this is the story of how those in charge reacted to the messages they were sent.

References

Chu, David S. C., *Population Representation in the Military Services—Fiscal Year 2002,* final report, Washington, D.C.: Office of the Under Secretary of Defense (Personnel and Readiness), 2004. G1209.pdf.

Cohen, William S., *Farewell to Armed Forces,* Washington, D.C.: U.S. Department of Defense, 2001. S0178.pdf.

Cordesman, Anthony H., *The Lessons and Non-Lessons of the Air and Missile Campaign in Kosovo,* Washington, D.C.: Center for Strategic and International Studies, 2000.

Danzig, Richard, and Peter Szanton, *National Service: What Would It Mean?* Lexington, Mass.: Lexington Books, 1986.

Flynn, George Q., *Lewis B. Hershey, Mr. Selective Service,* Chapel Hill, N.C.: University of North Carolina Press, 1985.

Franklin, Ben A., "Lag in a Volunteer Force Spurs Talk of New Draft," *New York Times,* July 1, 1973, pp. 1–3.

Friedman, Milton, Statement by Professor Milton Friedman, hearing before the 90th Cong., 1st Sess., Washington, D.C., U.S. Government Printing Office, Vol. 113, March 9, 1967.

Gates, Thomas S., Jr., *The Report of the President's Commission on an All-Volunteer Armed Force,* Washington, D.C., 1970. S0243.pdf.

Griffith, Robert K., Jr., *The U.S. Army's Transition to the All-Volunteer Force 1968–1974,* Washington, D.C.: U.S. Army Center of Military History, 1997. S0186.pdf.

Haltiner, Karl W., and Paul Klein, "The European Post-Cold War Military Reforms and Their Impact on Civil-Military Relations," in Franz Kernic, Paul Klien and Karl Haltiner, eds., *The European Armed Forces in Transition,* New York: Peter Lang, 2005.

Jehn, Christopher, and Zachary Selden, "The End of Conscription in Europe?" Western Economic Association International Annual Meeting, San Francisco, July 5–8, 2001. S0228.pdf.

———, "The End of Conscription in Europe?" *Contemporary Economic Policy,* Vol. 20, No. 2, April 2002, pp. 93–100.

Laurence, Janice H., *The All-Volunteer Force: A Historical Perspective,* Washington, D.C.: Office of Under Secretary of Defense (Force Management Policy), 2004a. S0840.pdf.

———, *Performance of the All-Volunteer Force,* Washington, D.C.: Office of the Under Secretary of Defense (Force Management Policy), 2004b. S0838.pdf.

Lee, Gus C., and Geoffrey Y. Parker, *Ending the Draft: The Story of the All-Volunteer Force,* Washington, D.C.: Human Resources Research Organization, FR-PO-771, 1977. S0242.pdf.

Marshall, Burke, *In Pursuit of Equity? Who Serves When Not All Serve? Report of the National Advisory Commission on Selective Service,* Washington, D.C.: National Advisory Commission on Selective Service, 1967. G1428.pdf.

Martin, Albert J., "Relationship Between AFQT and IQ Inclusion for ASVAB Back-Up Book," memorandum to Richard Danzig, Washington, D.C., September 4, 1980. G1471.pdf.

Mead, Margaret, "A National Service System as a Solution to a Variety of National Problems," in Sol Tax, ed., *The Draft: A Handbook of Facts and Alternatives,* Chicago: The University of Chicago Press, 1967, pp. 99–109.

Nixon, Richard M., *The All-Volunteer Armed Force: A Radio Address by the Republican Presidential Nominee,* Washington, D.C.: Republican National Committee, 1968. G0251.pdf.

O'Sullivan, John, and Allen M. Meckler, eds., *The Draft and Its Enemies: A Documentary History,* Champaign, Ill.: University of Illinois Press, 1974.

Quester, Aline O., and Curtis L. Gilroy, "Women and Minorities in America's Volunteer Military," *Contemporary Economic Policy,* Vol. 20, No. 2, April 2002, pp. 111–121.

Ricks, Thomas E., "The Widening Gap Between the Military and Society," *The Atlantic Monthly,* July 1997. S0817.pdf.

Westmoreland, William C., "Discipline in the Army," letter to Major Field Commanders, Washington, D.C., September 15, 1971. S0119.pdf.

CHAPTER TWO

The Coming of the All-Volunteer Force (1960–1968)

> The Vietnam War bruised American Society like nothing else in this century. The nation split over the war, as did the generation that has now come of age.
>
> —Robert Timberg
> Reporter and Author[1]

> Today all across our country we face a crisis of confidence. Nowhere is it more acute than among our young people. They recognize the draft as an infringement on their liberty, which it is. To them, it represents a government insensitive to their rights, a government callous to their status as free men. They ask for justice, and they deserve it.
>
> —Richard M. Nixon
> President of the United States[2]

Introduction

In their comprehensive history, *Ending of the Draft*, Gus Lee and Geoffrey Parker attributed the early success of the all-volunteer force to nine "conditions" (1977, pp. 524–526). The first was the "establishment of the rational, intellectual basis for the volunteer force." If this is so, the father of that "rational, intellectual basis" was economist Professor Milton Friedman of the University of Chicago. But, if he was the father, who was the mother? Senator Sam Nunn of Georgia (D-Georgia) would suggest that the mother of the all-volunteer force was the Vietnam War.[3] "The All-Volunteer Force is

---

[1] *The Nightingale's Song* (Timberg, 1995).

[2] Radio Address, October 17, 1968 (Nixon, 1968).

[3] In 1973, shortly after becoming a U.S. senator, Nunn told the Georgia State Assembly that "this concept [of the all-volunteer force] is a clear result of the Vietnam war which, because of its unpopularity, it caused the President and Congress to yield to the tremendous pressure to end the draft at almost any price" (Nunn, 1973).

to a large extent a political child of the draft card burning, campus riots, and violent protest demonstrations of the late 1960s and early 1970s," Nunn told Congress (1978, p. 50). Moreover, as with any offspring, one can argue about whether the child owes more to its father or its mother. So it is with the all-volunteer force.

The Rational, Intellectual Basis for the All-Volunteer Force

In December 1966, at a conference at the University of Chicago,[4] Professor Friedman pronounced the draft "inconsistent with a free society" (Friedman, 1967, p. 53). He argued that "The disadvantages of our present system of compulsion and the advantage of a voluntary army are so widely recognized that we can deal with them very briefly." To Professor Friedman, the "more puzzling question [was] why we have continued to use compulsion."[5] His answer was "the tyranny of the status quo." Not so fast. While there is a clear case that, in a free society, the state should not use its power to compel without careful consideration, many have argued that each citizen owes service for the defense of his country.[6]

A Little History

Professor William H. McNeill, at the same conference, argued in support of Friedman's proposition that "from the Iron Age to the present, the prevailing form of military establishment among civilized states has been the tax-supported professional army" (McNeill, 1967, p. 118). His argument notwithstanding, the compulsory provision of labor to serve the state in fact has a long history. Conscription is implied in the Bible (Deuteronomy 20:5), which lists specific exemptions from military service—who "may leave and return home." Moreover, the effectiveness of conscripts is questioned, as it is written, "Whoever is afraid and faint-hearted must leave and return home, so that his fellows may not become faint-hearted like him." McNeill would have been more correct if he had said that countries have used *both* professional and conscript soldiers since the dawn of history and that the use of one over another continues to be a very controversial issue.

---

[4] The proceedings of the conference were published as Tax (1967).

[5] Friedman not only argued against compulsory service, but also argued that society's best interest could be served by allowing free choice. This meant both allowing young people the freedom to choose their occupations and providing equal opportunity in education. Friedman would argue that, if each citizen owes service for the betterment of society, this service can best be provided by a system of free individual choice—including the choice to work in the private market and not be constrained to engage in activities politicians deem to be true social service.

[6] For example, Eliot Cohen quotes Jefferson on "the necessity of obligating every citizen to be a soldier; this was the case of Greeks and Romans and must be that in every free state" (as quoted in Cohen, 1985, p. 148). This also follows the teachings of the French philosopher Jean-Jacques Rousseau. In 1772, he wrote that "It was the duty of every citizen to serve as a soldier" (as quoted in Flynn, 2002, p. 3).

The history of Britain is most instructive on this point. It is also very relevant, since it has shaped the American experience and the military system we observe today.

The British Tradition

W. E. Lunt, in his history of England, recalled the system of militia that existed in Anglo-Saxon England and the mixed force of professionals and militia that fought for King Harold at the battle of Hastings (1066).[7] He characterized the militia as "poorly armed, badly disciplined," especially when compared with the professional knights who carried the battle, and Harold therefore used the militia "on the rear and flanks" (Lunt, 1956, p. 59). Then as now, consideration of military effectiveness is a timeless issue in the debates over the choice between a professional and a conscript force.

After Hastings, the feudal system the Normans brought to England was based on the granting of estates to William's followers in exchange for a specific obligation to serve the king. John Green noted in his (not so) *Short History of the English People* that

> Great or small . . . each estate . . . was granted on condition of its holder's service at the king's call; and when the larger holdings were divided by their owners into smaller sub-tenancies, the under-tenants were bound by the same conditions of service to their lord. . . . A whole army was by this means encamped upon the soil, and William's summons could at any moment gather an overwhelming force around his standard. (Green, 1908, p. 107)

Under Henry II, the feudal organization was replaced by the *Assize of Arms of 1181*. Henry's aim was to create an efficient fighting force where every freeman was required to supply himself with arms "and to bear these arms (in the King's) service" (Lunt, 1956, p. 115). In addition, the compulsory service of "jurors" was also instituted under Henry II, a further example of the use of state power to compel service (Lunt, 1956, p. 120). Henry's regulations were extended in 1285 under Edward I's Statute of Winchester to "specify the military obligations of a subject according to income" (Schwoerer, 1974, p. 14). They were extended again in 1558, under Elizabeth I so that "the armies of the Tudors and early Stuarts . . . were composed of men who were conscripted to defend the state, to man an expedition, or to fight a war and who were then disbanded" (Schwoerer, 1974, p. 2). While reporting that "the gentry . . . regularly evaded their military responsibilities," Schwoerer also noted that "the notion that men of substance should compose the trained bands [of militia] and should be prepared to defend the country persisted" (Schwoerer, 1974, p. 15). The writings of the period reinforce such ideas, as in Sir Thomas More's *Utopia* (1518) and Niccolo Machiavelli's *The Prince* (1513), which expounded on the dangers of a professional army and argued that, in a free state, "the defense of the land should be entrusted to its own citizens . . . a good citizen should serve his government in both a political and

---

[7] Ralph Witherspoon provides a very readable history on this subject in his doctoral dissertation (Witherspoon, 1993, pp. 76–153).

military capacity" (Schwoerer, 1974, pp. 16–17). This was countered by critics who thought it unwise to believe "that untrained subject[s] could defend a country better than a paid professional soldier[s]" (Schwoerer, 1974, p. 16), and the issue of a standing and professional army was hotly debated.

During the following century—the 17th—the issue of the maintenance of a "standing army" and military policies was "part of every major political and constitutional confrontation" between crown and Parliament, but the right to compel service was never seriously questioned. It is true that, during the Cromwellian period of the New Model Army (1645), the more-radical groups proposed to strip Parliament of "the power of impressment" because (as quoted in Schwoerer, 1974, p. 54) "every man's conscience . . . should be satisfied in the justness of that cause wherein he hazards his life," but such rules never passed. With the restoration of Charles II (1630), Parliament not only agreed to leave command of the citizen militia in the hands of the king, it gave him authority to raise as many soldiers as he wished, presumably professional soldiers, *as long as he paid them.*[8] This was reversed when James II (1685) replaced Charles II. By the time of the Glorious Revolution and the ascendancy of William of Orange to the English throne, the Bill of Rights of 1689 had expressly prohibited the King from "raising and keeping a standing army within this kingdom in time of peace unless with consent of Parliament" (Lords Spiritual and Temporal and Commons Assembled at Westminster, 1689). Thereafter, and through the zenith of an expanding British Empire, British power rested largely on a professional army of volunteers.[9]

---

[8] Schwoerer maintains that it was "inevitable" that a standing, professional army be established "given the technological and political changes on the continent" (Schwoerer, 1974, p. 5). As it is today, it was the romantic and utopian who longed for the conscript force of citizens. Rather than arguments concerning "the rational, intellectual basis for the volunteer force," it was the practical consideration that a conscript force could no longer produce a viable military institution that moved England toward a professional military.

[9] There was still the responsibility to serve in the local militia, and thanks to "the Ballot Act of 1757, the crown could force men into the militia, then call up this force." For most of its modern history, however, Britain's small standing professional army was made up of volunteers and "functioned mainly in the pacification and policing of the empire" (Flynn, 2002, p. 12–13).

It was not just in England that the use of conscripts was coming into question. Conscripts largely manned the Swedish navy when Admiral Klas Fleming complained to King Gustavus Adolphus that his better seamen defected to foreign fleets, where the wages were better. The king thought that "the Swedes are no worse seamen than the Dutch, as long as they get proper wages and are treated well" (Museum, 2004, p. 33). When the fleet arrived in Stockholm in the autumn of 1627, the crews were force to stay in the capital because of "the fear that the ships would lack crews when they went out to sea again in the spring" (Museum, 2004, p. 33). The burghers of Stockholm were required to provide board and lodging for the crews and complained bitterly about the additional tax.

The first conscription law in Sweden was written in 1618. It was changed several times before King Karl XI developed "the new allotment system." Between 1682 and 1901, Sweden had its own version of a professional army. Local communities were responsible for recruiting soldiers. The local community provided each recruit with a small wage, housing, food, and clothing. The government provided each soldier with a weapon and a uniform to wear when he was called to serve. "The idea was that the soldier should support himself and his family by working on his own land at the cottage. . . . If the soldier had to go to the wars, his wife had the right to stay on at the cottage" (Blent et al., 2004). This system was "attractive," and there were "no problems with recruits" (Hoglund, 2004). In 1901, compulsory national service was introduced.

The American Tradition—Conscription and Voluntarism

During most of our history the United States has, like Britain, relied on volunteers to provide the personnel to sustain its armed forces. Federal drafts have been employed only four times, with mixed results.

From the Revolution to the Civil War. The events of the 17th century in England were all familiar to the American colonists of that and the following century, as were the writings of such Renaissance authors as More and Machiavelli. Ideas concerning service, the role of the militia, and the hostility toward a "standing army" "were carried to the English colonies in America where they had a profound impact on the thinking of American leaders" (Schwoerer, 1974, p. 5) and on the *Declaration of Independence* and the *Constitution.* The Army's official history of military mobilization notes that, in the colonies "every able-bodied man, within prescribed age limits, . . . [was] required by *compulsion* to possess arms, to be carried on muster rolls, to train periodically, and to be mustered into service for military operations whenever necessary" (Kreidberg and Henry, 1955, p. 3, emphasis added). During the Revolution, several of the newly formed states used compulsion, and from 1777 on, the "annual pattern of recruiting" included a congressional allocation of quotas to the states and through the states to the towns; when voluntarism failed, citizens were drafted. Charles Royster explained the process:

> The local militia commanders held a muster and called for volunteers. A few men enlisted. Then weeks of dickering started. The state or the town or private individuals or all three sweetened the bounty. Meanwhile, citizens who did not want to turn out with the militia were looking for militia substitutes to hire. . . . By the spring or summer, all of the men who were going to enlist that year on any terms had done so, whereupon the state found that it had not filled its quota. . . . Drafting began in 1777 and sent men for terms ending in December, which ensured that the whole process would begin again next January.
>
> Those who enlisted wanted to be paid. After army pay became low, rare and depreciated, these men sought their main compensation in the bounty given at the time of recruitment. . . . When drafting began, it often did not mean selecting an unwilling man to go, but selecting from among the unwilling one man who had to pay one of the willing to go as a substitute. Even then the draftee got a bounty. . . . Apart from the handling of army supplies, recruiting introduced more corruption into American society than any other activity associated with a standing army. . . . Bounties inspired some soldiers to enlist several times with several units within a few days. (Royster, 1979, pp. 65–71)

George Washington saw the draft as a "disagreeable," but necessary, "alternative." On January 28, 1778, reacting to the "numerous defects in our present military establishment" and the need for "many reformations and many new arrangements" he wrote to the "Committee of Congress with the Army":

> Voluntary inlistments [sic] seem to be totally out of the question; all the allurements of the most exorbitant bounties and every other inducement, that could be thought of, have been tried in vain, . . . some other mode must be concerted, and

no other presents itself, than that of filling the Regiments by drafts from the Militia. This is a disagreeable alternative, but it is an unavoidable one.

As drafting for the war, or for a term of years, would probably be disgusting and dangerous, perhaps impracticable, I would propose an annual draft of men, without officers, to serve 'till the first day of January, in each year; . . . .This method, though not so good as that of obtaining Men for the war, is perhaps the best our circumstances will allow; and as we shall always have an established corps of experienced officers, may answer tolerably well. (Washington, 1931–1944, vol. 10, p. 366)[10]

On February 26, 1778, Congress acted on the report of the "Committee of Congress at camp" that had been appointed to work with General Washington in developing recommendations "as shall appear eligible" (Washington, 1931–1944, p. 362) by passing a resolution extolling the states to revert to coercion if necessary to meet their quotes for the militia to serve with the army. The resolution said, in part,

that the several states hereafter named be required forthwith to fill up by drafts from their militia, [or in any other way that shall be effectual,] . . . .That all persons drafted, shall serve in the continental battalions [sic] of their respective states for the space of nine months. (Ford, 1904–37, p. 200)

While the details of the drafting varied among the states, there was a common goal of "obtaining recruits with a minimum of governmental coercion" (Royster, 1979, p. 66). By 1781, however, the majority of those who took the field at Yorktown were militiamen, many of whom had been drafted.[11]

After the war, in 1783, Washington wrote Alexander Hamilton to endorse the concept of a citizen's obligation to the state: "Every Citizen who enjoys the protection of a free Government, owes not only a proportion of his property, but even of his personal services to the defense of it" (Washington, 1974). The preamble to the U.S. Constitution starts with the words "We the People" and includes the words "provide for the common defense." The Knox Plan of 1790 envisioned universal military service. Suspicion of a professional army was one reason for the militia clause of the

---

[10] There is some disagreement as to whether this was a national or state draft; Kestnbaum referred to this as "federal conscription" (Kestnbaum, 2000, p. 28), while Kreiberg, in the Army's *History of Military Mobilization,* noted that

The quotas still could not be filled until the states, on advice of Washington and on recommendation of the Continental Congress, resorted to coercion—a draft. This draft was a state Militia draft and varied from state to state as to details. Most of the states reluctantly resorted to a draft after exhausting all other possible methods of raising the men requested by the Continental Congress. The draft was never all-embracing because of the means of evading it, such as the payment of a fee in lieu of service or the furnishing of a substitute. (Kreidberg and Henry, 1955, p. 15)

[11] See Table 1, *Troops Furnished in the Revolutionary War, by Year* (in Kreidberg and Henry, 1955, p. 28). See also Kestnbaum (2000), p. 28.

Constitution (Art. I, Sec. 8).[12] The second amendment to the Constitution—the right to bear arms—also reflects the basic suspicion 18th century Americans had of a professional Army and the confidence they had in the militia as the protector of their freedoms. The militia, by the Act of 1792, was to be made up of "each and every free able-bodied white male . . . [above] the age of eighteen years and under the age of forty-five years" (O'Sullivan and Meckler, 1974, pp. 36–37). Nevertheless, when Alexis de Tocqueville traveled through the United States in the 1830s, he concluded that

> In America conscription is unknown and men are induced to enlist by bounties. The notions and habits of the people of the United States are so opposed to compulsory recruiting that I do not think it can ever be sanctioned by the laws. (de Tocqueville, 1835, Bk. 1, Ch. 13)

By the time of the Mexican War (1846–1848), compulsory service in the militia had been replaced by voluntary membership in local military companies, which Congress allowed to be organized under the militia clause of the Constitution.[13] The small professional army of the federal government was never designed to do more than maintain the military infrastructure of the nation and to provide a core on which the militia and those who voluntarily answered "the call to the colors" could build.[14] The tremendous manpower demands of the Civil War changed that and resulted in America's first federal and national draft.

---

[12] Article 1, Section 8 provides for both the militia and a national army and navy:

> The Congress shall have Power . . .
>
> To raise and support Armies . . . ;
>
> To provide and maintain a Navy . . . ;
>
> To provide for calling forth the Militia to execute the Laws of the Union, suppress Insurrections and repel Invasions;
>
> To provide for organizing, arming, and disciplining, the Militia, and for governing such Part of them as may be employed in the Service of the United States, reserving to the States respectively, the Appointment of the Officers, and the Authority of training the Militia according to the discipline prescribed by Congress; . . .

The clauses on the armies and navy are also the basis for Congress's power to order a national conscription. See the Selective Draft law cases in O'Sullivan and Meckler (1974, pp. 140–149).

[13] Cutler reported that

> Between 1815 and 1846, the years of Jacksonian democracy, militia service was everywhere allowed to become voluntary; the law of the United States was tacitly annulled by the states. Volunteer companies . . . sprang up in large numbers as substitutes for the older force. . . . Congress decreed that they should be regarded as militia and organized under the militia clause of the Constitution. (Cutler, 1923, p. 171)

[14] The Army was disbanded after the Revolution, on July 2, 1784, with the exception of one company of soldiers retained to protect the military stores of the nation at West Point and Fort Pitt (Cutler, 1922, p. 47). By 1798, the Army totaled 2,100. At the start of the War of 1812, about 80,000 volunteers and militia augmented the regular Army of 6,744. At the start of the Mexican War, the regular Army numbered 8,349; at the start of the Civil War, it was 16,367 (Cutler, 1922, p. 49).

The term "call to the colors" is technically a bugle call to render honors to the nation. It is used when no band is available to render honors or in ceremonies requiring honors to the nation more than once. "To the Color" commands all the same courtesies as the National Anthem.

The Civil War. Ironically, the first American legislature to pass a *national* conscription law without going through the states was the Congress of the Confederate States of America.[15] On April 16, 1862, the Confederate Congress provided that every able-bodied white male between the ages of 18 and 35 would serve in the Army for three years (Cutler, 1922, p. 83). It also extended the enlistments of those who had already volunteered for the duration of the war.

The draft was extremely unpopular in the South. While 21 percent of Confederate soldiers were conscripts, it "engendered much discontent and considerable resistance" (Chambers, 1991). By one account, "the Rebel soldiers hated the Conscript Law. It was unfair, and they knew it. It took the glory out of the war, and the war was never the same for them."[16] A Confederate general summed up the situation: "It would require the whole army to enforce conscription law, if the same thing exists through the Confederacy which I know to be the case in Georgia and Alabama, and Tennessee" (as quoted in Cutler, 1922, p. 86). But was this not to be expected? Albert Moore, in his definitive account, *Conscription and Conflict in the Confederacy,* saw the difficulties the South faced as inhering

> in a system of compulsory service among a proud and free people. Conscription was not only contrary to the spirit of the people but to the genius of the Confederate political system. It seemed unnatural that the new government, just set up as the agent of the sovereign States, should exercise such compelling and far-reaching authority over the people, independent of the States. . . . Conflict with State authorities in the enforcement of it—conscription—seriously impaired its efficiency. (Moore, 1924, p. 354)

Nevertheless, conscription in the South fared far better than in the North, and, throughout the war, it provided the manpower the South needed to carry on the fight.

In the North, at the start of the Civil War, President Abraham Lincoln called for 75,000 militia and volunteers, the former to serve for a matter of months and the latter for one or two years (Chambers, 1987, p. 87). By 1863, it was clear that something more than the militia was required. On March 3, 1863, Lincoln signed the first federal draft law, the Enrollment Act (O'Sullivan and Meckler, 1974, pp. 63–66). Unlike the resolution Congress had made during the Revolutionary War, the Enrollment Act made no mention of the militia and asserted, for the first time, the federal government's authority to directly draft people into the national army.[17]

---

[15] It was ironic because, in 1814, those who now made up the Confederacy had argued that it was the right of the states to raise the militia and had blocked President Madison's proposal for a national—federal—draft. Now, in 1862, it was the "Confederate Congress [that] threw the theory of states' rights to the winds and enacted the first 'Conscription Law'" (Cutler, 1923, p. 172).

[16] As discussed in Harper (2001).

[17] The act provided that those drafted would "remain in service for three years or the war, whichever ended first" (Kreidberg and Henry, 1955, p. 105).

The Civil War draft was a despised institution because, as de Tocqueville (1835, Bk. 1, Ch. 23) had argued, there was little sense of equal sacrifice.[18] As had been the practice during the Revolution and was the practice in France, wealthy men were able to buy their way out of service—commutation—or hire a substitute to serve in their stead.[19] The riots in Boston, New York, and other northern cities attested to the unpopularity of the draft.[20] In the most perverse way, however, the draft was effective in the North not because it brought in large numbers of people, but because it persuaded "elected officials to raise much higher bounties to entice men to enlist and thus avert the need for governmental coercion" (Chambers, 1987, p. 64). Local bounties soared to as high as $1,500 (Kreidberg and Henry, 1955, p. 110).

By the end of the Civil War, states and localities had paid almost a quarter of a billion dollars in bounties to encourage young men to volunteer, with the federal government spending an amount only slightly greater. By one estimate, "Bounties cost about as much as the pay for the Army during the entire war . . . and five times the ordnance costs" (Kreidberg and Henry, 1955, p. 110). In fact, the bounty program became so popular that many men volunteered again and again. One "bounty-jumper"—as such men were known—was reported to have enlisted 32 times (Cutler, 1922, p. 64). By the end of the war, 2.1 million men saw service in the blue uniform of the Union. Of this number, the draft produced 46,000 conscripts and 116,000 substitutes, and 87,000 paid the commutation fee to buy their way out of service. The rest were volunteers.

From the Civil War to World War I. One lasting legacy of the Civil War was the *Report on the Draft in Illinois* (see Oakes' report in O'Sullivan and Meckler, 1974, pp. 93–101), prepared in 1865 by the Acting Assistant Provost Marshal General of the State of Illinois, Brevet Brigadier General James Oakes. This report became the blueprint for the next draft—but not until World War I. Between the Civil War and World War I, including the Indian Wars and the Spanish-American War, America relied on volunteers, many of them newly arrived immigrants, and the *new* volunteer militia of the states, the National Guard, to provide the manpower needed to defend the country.

---

[18] Alexis de Tocqueville saw the importance of equal sacrifice when, in 1835, he wrote of the condition required for conscription to work:

> Military service being compulsory, the burden is shared indiscriminately and equally by all citizens. That again necessarily springs from the condition of these people and from their ideas. Government can do nearly what it wants, provided that it addresses itself to everyone at once; it is the inequality of its weight, and not its weight, that ordinarily makes one resist it. (de Tocqueville, 1835, Bk. 1, Ch. 23)

[19] John O'Sullivan and Allen Meckler noted that "At the heart of the antagonism to the draft law lay the realization that the commutation fee of $300, not to mention the possibilities of hiring a substitute, was far beyond the means of most workmen" (O'Sullivan and Meckler, 1974, p. 66).

[20] On July 2, 1863, the second day of the battle of Gettysburg, Lincoln called for 300,000 men to be drafted—20 percent of those enrolled. In New York City, names were drawn on July 11. The papers the next day contained both the names of those drafted and the lists of those killed at Gettysburg. The next morning, riots broke out that lasted three days.

In 1915, with war raging in Europe, and a growing preparedness movement at home, the idea of universal military training and service, already popular in Europe, was being widely discussed. President Woodrow Wilson, reflecting the traditional American view, did not want to increase the size of the regular army. In his State of the Union address that year, he told Congress that "our military peace establishment [should be] no larger than is actually and continuously needed for the use of days in which no enemies move against us" (Wilson, 1915). He did, however, reluctantly call on Congress to approve an increase in the standing Army of some 31 percent, to 141,848. The major increase in the Army, however, was to come from a new force of "disciplined citizens, raised in increments of one hundred thirty-three thousand a year through a period of three years [for] training for short periods throughout three years . . . [not to] exceed two months in the year" to supplement the army. Even though he wanted this force to make "the country ready to assert some part of its real power promptly and upon a larger scale, should occasion arise," he did not want a draft. While he saw "preparation for defense as. . . absolutely imperative," he wanted to "depend upon the patriotic feeling of the younger men of the country whether they responded to such a call to service or not" (Wilson, 1915).[21]

Wilson's views about a draft changed as it became increasingly clear that America would enter the war. On April 2, 1917, he asked Congress for a declaration of war. Four days later, the day Congress actually declared war on Germany, he asked for a draft; on May 18, 1917, he signed the *Selective Service Act of 1917* into law. Unlike the Civil War, the new draft was widely accepted. Cutler describes the "marvelously complete response; . . . the popular support and approval accorded the selective service" and how, on the day young men reported for registration, "a feeling of solemnity possessed all hearts; a holiday was declared; at the stated hour, church bells rang as though summoning men to worship" (Cutler, 1923, p. 174).[22]

The new Selective Service law provided that both draftees and enlistees should serve for the duration of the war and that compulsory military service should cease four months after a proclamation of peace by the President. While the law did not offer bounties or permit personal substitution, it did provide for deferments based on essential work. The term *Selective Service* was used to capture the idea that, while all men of a specific age group—eventually 18 to 45—might be required to register, only some would be selected for military service, in line with the total needs of the nation. Of the approximately 23.9 million men who were registered and classified during World

---

[21] The National Defense Act of June 3, 1916, actually raised the standing Army to 175,000 and provided for a reserve of 450,000 (O'Sullivan and Meckler, 1974, p. 104).

[22] *Author's Note:* September 16, 1918, was the appointed day for the nation to register. Both of my grandfathers registered for the draft; one in New York City and the other in Kenosha, Wisconsin. They were 40 and 45 years of age, and conscription had already shaped their lives. They both had fled Europe to avoid being drafted. My mother's father emigrated in 1897 at the age of 25 to avoid service in the Austrian army, and my father's father in 1911 at the age of 33 to avoid being drafted a second time into the Russian Army. I doubt that, when they registered that day in 1918, either of them could imagine that sixty-one years later their grandson would become head of the Selective Service System and would be responsible for the mass registration of 1980. Only in America.

War I, only a fraction, 2.8 million men, were actually drafted. Draftees, however, made up 72 percent of the armed forces. This made a better case for equality of sacrifice than the draft had made during the Civil War (Chambers, 1991).

When the war was over and the need for a mass army had ended, so did the legitimacy of the draft.[23] While there was some interest in retaining some form of involuntary military training after World War I,[24] limited budgets and a relatively small standing army could not lay claim to the compelling argument of "equal sacrifice" that had been so successfully used at the beginning of World War I. It was not until 1940, months after the start of World War II in Europe, that the conditions were again right for Congress to vote for a draft.

World War II. In 1920, through the efforts of a number of people who had participated in the wartime Selective Service System, Congress passed the National Defense Act of 1920, which authorized the War Department General Staff to plan for the "mobilization of the manhood of the Nation . . . in an emergency" (as quoted in Hershey, 1942). It took six years, however, before the secretaries of War and the Navy created the Joint Army-Navy Selective Service Committee (JANSSC). In 1936, when Army Major Lewis B. Hershey was assigned to head the office, the "entire operation consisted of two officers and two clerks" (Flynn, 1985, p. 63). Hershey was selected for this job because of his reputation of being a good staff officer, because of his "talents at management and personnel" and the fact that he "had originally come from the National Guard, an outfit which had to play a big role in the conscription plan" (Friedman, 1967, p. 63). Under Hershey's leadership, the JANSSC annual budget was increased to $10,000. He brought in National Guard officers and started to promote training through conferences held throughout the United States. After Congress authorized the draft in 1940, the Joint Committee became the national headquarters of the newly authorized Selective Service System.

An important principal of the World War II draft was the concept of equal sacrifice. While President Franklin Roosevelt did not mention de Tocqueville's admonition that "it is the inequality of its weight, and not its weight, that ordinarily makes one resist it [conscription]" when he signed the bill on September 16 1940, he talked about the "duties, obligations and responsibilities of equal service" (as quoted in Flynn, 1993, p. 2). In the preamble of the act, Congress "declares" the following:

> In a free Society the obligation and privileges of military training and service should be shared generally in accordance with a fair and just system of selective compulsory military training and service. (As quoted in Hershey, 1942, p. 33)

---

[23] Chambers noted that

> What was most significant about the draft in the immediate post–World War I period is how quickly America abandoned it. . . . By the spring of 1920 Congress had rejected any kind of compulsory military training in peacetime and reduced the wartime army of nearly 4,000,000 citizen-soldiers to [a volunteer] force that numbered only 200,000 regulars. (Chambers, 1987, p. 252)

[24] See General Leonard Wood's call for universal military training (O'Sullivan and Meckler, 1974, pp. 117–120).

One month later, October 16, 1940, all men between the ages of 21 and 36 registered. A national lottery was held on October 1, 1940, to establish the order of call, and, with President Roosevelt looking on, Secretary of War Henry Stimson drew the first number, 158 (Flynn, 1993, p. 22). On November 8, 1940, President Roosevelt ordered the selection and induction of a number of men "not to exceed" 800,000 by July 1, 1941 (Hershey, 1942, p. 27). The prescribed period of active service was one year, to be followed by 10 years in the reserves. On June 28, 1941, the President ordered that an additional 900,000 be "selected and inducted" during FY 1942. On August 19, 1941, by one vote in the House of Representatives (and, some say, only by the employment of a quick gavel by Speaker of the House Sam Rayburn), Congress extended the period of service to 18 months by passing the Service Extension Act of 1941.[25] Congress also reduced the maximum age at which a person might be inducted to 28 years of age, allowing some 193,000 to leave service before their training period had been completed.

The 1940 draft used the Selective Service model first introduced in America during World War I. Deferments were provided for government officials and for those "employed in industry, agriculture or other occupations or employments" who were "necessary to the maintenance of the public health, interest and safety" (Hershey, 1942, p. 35). The law prohibited deferments for "individuals by occupational groups or of groups of individuals in any plant or institutions" (Hershey, 1942, p. 37). Given, as one historian noted, that "the draft had been sold as a democratic mechanism" (Flynn, 1993, p. 41), students were only allowed to complete the academic year. The "importance of universality of service as befitting a democracy" and "social and economic realities" of the nation was also tested when it came to married men and fathers. While not specifically identifying these two classes, the law allowed the President to defer "those men in a status with respect to persons dependent upon them for support which renders their deferment advisable" (Hershey, 1942, p. 35).

The Cold War Draft: 1947–1973. Even before the end of World War II, but with victory clearly in sight, Congress, under considerable pressure from the public, pressed the new Truman administration to end the draft. It made little difference that America faced a sizable need for military manpower to meet the new occupation requirements in Germany and Japan. Flynn notes that "The public's position on the draft seemed clear: bring the troops home and immediately and stop taking boys through the draft" (Flynn, 1993, p. 89). For President Harry Truman, reviving the notion of universal military training, which had not taken hold after World War I, was the best way to have sufficient manpower to meet the needs of the occupation and to forestall the call to end the wartime draft. Unable to move either the public or Congress to accept universal military training, Truman agreed to end the draft on March 31, 1947. In less than a year, however, the world situation had so deteriorated and the Army's experience

---

[25] George Flynn has described the summer 1941 debate (1993, pp. 51–52).

with this version of an all-volunteer force had been so poor—30,000 recruits a month were required, but only 12,000 volunteers enlisted—that Truman asked for a resumption of the draft.

In spring 1948, reinstatement of the draft seemed imperative. The communist coup in Czechoslovakia in February 1948 and General Lucius Clay's warning on March 5 about the possibility of imminent conflict with the Soviet Union led President Truman to called for the "temporary reenactment of selective service" (as quoted in Friedberg, 2000, pp. 174–175).[26] The "danger," however, passed, and the call-up lasted only three months. By February 1949, inductions were suspended, and by summer 1949, the Associated Press reported that "unless an unforeseen emergency develops, the peacetime draft of manpower for the armed forces is expected to expire June 25, 1950" (The Associated Press, 1949). On June 24, 1950, with Congress considering an extension of the Military Selective Service Act and with the Selective Service System being placed on standby, North Korean forces invaded South Korea. Three days later, Congress voted the full extension of military conscription. Nearly 600,000 men were inducted in FY 1951, with 87,000 in a single month; by the end of the war 1.5 million men had been induced, with about 750,000 Reservists involuntarily called to active duty (Magruder, 1967, p. II-3).

After the Korean War, the draft remained in place in what Aaron Friedberg called "a state of equilibrium." It was an "equilibrium," he argued, that was "less sturdy and less stable than it appeared," noting that

> Limited conscription—from Korea to Vietnam—aroused little opposition so long as the number of those drafted remained relatively small, the use to which they were put retained broad public approval, those who preferred to avoid service could do so with relative ease, and the inevitable inquiry of the selection process did not receive undue attention. If one of these parameters changed, support for the draft would weaken; if all of them changed at once, it would disappear altogether. (Friedberg, 2000, p. 179)

Conscription in the Early 1960s, the Call for Reform, and the Vietnam War

When John Kennedy took the oath of office on the steps of the Capitol on January 20, 1961, peacetime conscription had "become the new American tradition" (O'Sullivan and Meckler, 1974, p. 220).[27] It was a tradition, however, that did not affect most Americans.

---

[26] General Clay was the U.S. military Governor in occupied Germany at the time.

[27] In the words of one author,

> John Kennedy primed the pump, [which would eventually lead to Vietnam and the end of conscription]. He proclaimed the United States willing to "pay any price, bear any burden, meet any hardship" to advance the cause of freedom around the world. (Timberg, 1995, p. 85)

Monthly draft calls were low.[28] Lieutenant General Lewis B. Hershey, the Director of Selective Service—the same person who had been assigned to the JANSSC in 1936[29]—put it this way: "We deferred practically everybody. If they had a reason, we preferred it. But if they didn't, we made them hunt one" (as quoted in Flynn, 1985, p. 218).

In 1961, draft calls dropped to 113,000. In 1962, only 76,000 were called, and in 1963, 119,000 were drafted. In comparison, by January 1962, more than 430,000 draft-eligible men had educational or occupational deferments. An additional 1,300,000 had been deferred because of paternity. On September 10, 1962, with DoD requirements at historically low levels and the pool of draft age males increasing, President Kennedy extended deferments to "married, non-fathers" (Flynn, 1985, p. 219). The zenith of support for Selective Service came the next spring. On March 5, 1963, the House of Representatives voted 387 to 3 to extend induction authority. The Senate approved the extension by voice vote on March 15th. President Kennedy signed the extension of the draft into law on March 28, 1963 (Flynn, 1985, p. 222).

Despite the strong support Congress showed in extending the draft authority, questions were being increasingly asked concerning the equity of conscription and the policies Selective Service[30] was following because of the perception that the system of deferments was unfair.[31] In November, only eight months after the favorable vote by Congress, Hershey was before the Senate Committee on Labor and Public Welfare to answer questions about the feasibility of abolishing the draft and moving to an all-volunteer force (U.S. Congress, 1963). He maintained that an all-volunteer system would never work as long as the armed forces needed more than one million men.[32] Nevertheless, pressure mounted in Congress both to reform Selective Service and to at least study the feasibility of an all-volunteer force. When Senator Barry Goldwater (R-Arizona), then a prospective presidential nominee of the Republican Party, announced his intention to end the draft, President Johnson moved to "defuse" the issue. On April 18, 1964, he announced his plan for a "comprehensive study of the draft system" (Flynn, 1985, p. 226). The *New York Times,* for one, questioned whether

---

[28] O'Sullivan and Meckler argued that, because of deferments in the early 1960s, the burden of service fell on the "least vocal and least powerful group in society" (O'Sullivan and Meckler, 1974, p. 220). Janowitz, however, found that "those whose education ranged from having completed nine years of school to those who had completed college, roughly the same proportion [about 70 percent] had had military" service (Janowitz, 1967, p. 76).

[29] *Author's Note:* General Hershey was the second Director of Selective Service (National Headquarters, 1968). I became the fourth director in 1979 and established the draft registration and revitalization programs of 1980 and 1981.

[30] The operations of the Selective Service System are described in Chapter 2 of Watson (1967).

[31] The noted military sociologist James Burk found that

> the perception of inequities eroded public confidence in the draft. In 1966, for the first time since the question was asked, less than a majority (only 43 percent) believed that the draft was handled fairly in their community. . . . Although the public still supported the draft, the problems protesters exposed raised serious questions about its operation during the Vietnam War. (Burk, 2001)

[32] The following summer, General Hershey told the Senate that "equity was unattainable" and that "we defer people . . . because we can't use them all" (as quoted in Flynn, 1985, p. 225).

he really wanted an "independent study," since he asked DoD to undertake the study. The *Times* observed in an editorial that, "if Congress and the nation are to have a really thoroughgoing study ... a Presidential commission, or a committee ... should be established" (*New York Times* Editorial Board, 1964, p. 42).[33] The resulting Pentagon Draft Study (1964–1965) nevertheless proved to be a turning point in the development of the all-volunteer force and the training ground for those, mainly economists, who worked on the study and who would see an all-volunteer force a decade later.

The 1964 Pentagon Draft Study

Secretary of Defense Robert McNamara named William Gorham, a Deputy Assistant Secretary of Defense, to lead the study team. Dr. Walter Oi, then a professor of economics at the University of Washington and a central figure in the all-volunteer force story for decades to come, was recruited to head the Economic Analysis Division.[34] The task of the study was to "estimate the budgetary cost of shifting from the draft to a voluntary system of manpower procurement" (Oi, 1996, p. 42). Dr. Oi, remembers it as a "massive study" with serious research that commenced in June 1964 and was to be completed by June 1965.[35]

The timing is significant because this was the period of the initial manpower buildup for Vietnam and the rapid increase in draft calls.[36] When the study was finally finished, Assistant Secretary of Defense for Manpower and Reserve Affairs, Thomas D. Morris, withheld the study group's report from the public for a year. He feared that, if the study group's conclusion in favor of an all-volunteer force were acted upon, it would become difficult, if not impossible, to meet the increasing manpower demands of an enlarging Vietnam War (Greenberg, 2001). It was finally released to Congress as part of Secretary Morris's testimony (Morris, 1966) before the House Armed Services Committee on June 30, 1966.[37]

---

[33] Witherspoon noted that, in fact, "the White House had effectively deflected ... [congressional] efforts to launch an investigation of wider dimensions of the draft" (Witherspoon, 1993, p. 176).

[34] Oi recalls that William Gorham called the labor economist Professor Greg Lewis at the University of Chicago to check on a number of candidates. Lewis recommended his former student, Walter Oi (as told to the author by Oi, 2001). Also see Professor Friedman's comment in Friedman (1998).

[35] Oi signed on as a consultant to the Department of Defense on June 18, 1964. He headed the Economic Analysis Section, which included six economists. He initially requested a "part-time leave of absence for the fall quarter" of 1964, expecting most of the research to be completed by December, with a study deadline of March 1, 1965. (See Oi, 1964.) The study director, Bill Gorham, provided an "expanded version of the outline of the final report" to the study group on December 15, 1964 (Gorham, 1964). Oi's initial projection of how long the study would take proved optimistic. Late into February 1965, he and his team were still "attempt[ing] to state succinctly the assumptions underlying nine basic sets of projections" (Oi, 1965).

[36] For a more complete presentation of the events of this period, see Witherspoon (1993, pp. 154–222).

[37] In 1967, Congressman Donald Rumsfeld (R-Illinois) complained to the Senate Armed Services Committee that

> An extensive manpower study by the Department of Defense, requested by the President in response to growing criticism of the draft, was withheld upon its completion, then revised in light of the escalation in Vietnam, and finally reported to the Congress, in 1966, by Assistant Secretary of Defense Thomas D. Morris in brief summary form only. (Rumsfeld, 1967, p. 425)

While Morris faithfully presented the numerical analysis—analysis that would later find its way into the leading economic journals and conference papers—the policy recommendations he drew from the research and the views of members of the study team were sharply different.[38] Morris concluded that

> we cannot look forward to discontinuing the draft . . . unless [we can] . . . reduce the force levels substantially below those needed since Korea. [And] increases in military compensation sufficient to attract an all-volunteer force cannot be justified. (Morris, 1966, p. 9,942)

Oi saw it another way:

> The report was not released to the public for a year. In his testimony before the House Armed Services Committee, Assistant Secretary of Defense Thomas D. Morris stated that an all-volunteer force would entail an incremental cost of 4 to 17 billion dollars per year, depending on the supply response to envisioned pay increases. The estimate from the 1965 Department of Defense study was $5.5 billion, close to the low end of the range. More important, the DoD report pointed out that this was an incremental budget cost that concealed the real social cost of allocating manpower to the nation's defense. (Oi, 1996, p. 42)

Failure to Reform the Draft

By summer 1966, with opposition to the Vietnam War increasing and congressional reauthorization of induction authority pending, both the President and Congress saw the need to act—and act they did, but *separately.* On July 2, 1966, just two days after Morris's difficult testimony before the House Armed Services Committee, President Johnson issued an Executive Order that created the Presidential Advisory Commission on Selective Service. Burke Marshall, at the time General Counsel of the International Business Machines (IBM) Corporation, agreed to head this commission.[39] Many in Congress and the press saw this as another Johnson ploy to "subvert" Congress (Witherspoon, 1993, pp. 222–223). On December 7, 1966, the House Armed Services Committee chartered their own group based on a civilian advisory panel that had been formed the month before and was headed by retired Army General Mark Clark.[40]

The Marshall commission summed up the prevailing problem with conscription in the title of its report, *In Pursuit of Equity: Who Serves When Not All Serve?* (Marshall,

---

[38] See the discussion between Congressman Rumsfeld and Dr. Harold Wool at the 1966 University of Chicago Conference on the Draft in Tax (1967, p. 387).

[39] Marshall was well known to President Johnson, having served as Assistant Attorney General for Civil Rights during the Kennedy administration (Barnes, 2003).

[40] Witherspoon notes that "The Clark Panel report was not a very impressive document; the substantive portion of the report consisted of only about 18 pages, . . . Reportedly, the Panel members only met about six times to consider substantive issues" (Witherspoon, 1993, p. 240).

1967). The commission rejected the idea of a volunteer force as too expensive and argued for a number of fundamental changes to the Selective Service System to include:

- eliminating most educational and occupational deferments because of their unfairness
- changing the order of call to youngest rather than oldest first, to be less disruptive to career planning
- adopting a national lottery
- consolidating the local boards

The Clark Panel also dismissed the notion of an all-volunteer force as being too expensive but disagreed with the Marshall Panel over the issue of deferments and the lottery.

It appears, however, that the only thing that the administration, Marshall commission and Clark Panel could agree on in the spring of 1967 was that the country should not move to an all-volunteer force. On March 6, 1967, President Johnson told Congress he was

> Instructing the Secretary of Defense, the Director of the Selective Service System and the Director of the Bureau of the Budget jointly to establish a Task Force to review the recommendations for a restructured Selective Service System made by the National Advisory Commission. . . . (Watson, 1967, p. I-1)

The Task Force reported in the fall that, "The Selective Service System with its present structure is thoroughly competent to carry out appropriate policy given to it" (Watson, 1967 p. I-14). The members of the Task Force rejected all recommendations for change. They concluded that the states should be retained, automation was "undesirable . . . special panels to hear conscientious objector cases should not be provided . . . a new plan of organization . . . [was] unnecessary . . ." and the "present structure of the Selective Service be retained" (Watson, 1967, p. I-14). It would take four more years of war and a new administration before the recommendations of the Marshall commission would be even partially implemented.

When the issue of extending the draft law came up in spring 1967, some in Congress were willing to press the case for an all-volunteer force. A young Republican congressman from the 13th Congressional District of Illinois, Donald Rumsfeld, was one who challenged the prevailing view. He asked the Senate Armed Services Committee[41] to vote to extend the Selective Service Act for two years and "declare its intention

---

[41] *Author's Note:* Thirty-four years later, as the outgoing Under Secretary of Defense for Personnel and Readiness, I met with now–Secretary of Defense Donald Rumsfeld. I told him I was planning to write a book on the all-volunteer force. He mentioned he was one of the earliest supporters of the all-volunteer force and had vivid memories of the 1966 conference at the University of Chicago. He also remembered his feelings of angst about pressing the issue of an all-volunteer force when he testified before the Senate Armed Services Committee and its chairman, "the great" Senator Richard Russell (D-Georgia).

to establish a volunteer military force and conduct the necessary investigation and study to determine the best means to establish such a force" (Rumsfeld, 1967, p. 427).[42] Congress voted the full four-year extension of the Selective Service Act. Lee and Parker summed up the significance of that vote:

> Congress . . . (rejected the idea of an all-volunteer force and) all the substantive proposals for reform and, in June, passed the Military Selective Service Act of 1967. The Act prevented the President from implementing a lottery or provisions to draft younger men first without congressional approval. Congress also reaffirmed the "1951 proviso" and protected undergraduate deferments from presidential tampering except in national emergencies. . . .
>
> The failure of Congress and the Johnson Administration to reform the draft in 1967 was important to the evolution of the All-Volunteer Force. That failure, continued high draft calls, and increased opposition to the war and the draft assured that the draft would be a major issue during the 1968 presidential campaign. In October of that year, the Republican candidate for president, Richard Nixon, declared his intention to move toward ending the draft when the war in Vietnam was over. (Lee and Parker, 1977, p. 29)

Arguments Against an All-Volunteer Force

While in 1967 Professor Friedman argued that the case for an all-volunteer force was "widely recognized," there was, in fact, substantial opposition to an all-volunteer force. In June 1966, DoD told Congress "a volunteer force was unfeasible and the costs were prohibitive" (Lee and Parker, 1977, p. 26). In addition, both the Marshall and Clark commissions concluded that the nation could not "afford" the risk of moving to an all-volunteer force. Other voices were also to be heard. These most often took the form of arguments in favor of universal national service as the appropriate alternative to the then-current draft service. The noted anthropologist Margaret Mead saw a national service system as a solution to a variety of national problems. She wrote:

> Universal national service would provide an opportunity for young adults to establish an identity and a sense of self-respect and responsibility as individuals before making career choices or establishing homes. At present a very large number go from dependency on their parents into careers that have been chosen for them, or use early marriage as a device to reach pseudo-adult status. (Mead, 1967, p. 105)

---

[42] Rumsfeld had attended the conference at the University of Chicago the previous December. In his prepared statement, he quoted from Milton Friedman's presentation at the conference. He had Friedman's remarks and a statement and article by Walter Oi added to the *Congressional Record* (Rumsfeld, 1967, p. 430). Friedman also authored an extensive article for the *New York Times Magazine,* which appeared on May 14, 1967. Rumsfeld added that to the *Congressional Record* as well (Rumsfeld, 1967).

The leading military sociologist in the country, Morris Janowitz, thought an all-volunteer force would create "a predominantly or even all Negro enlisted force in the Army, an 'internal foreign legion' which would be disastrous for American political democracy" (Janowitz, 1967, p. 75). Dr. Harry A. Marmion, President of Saint Xavier College in Chicago, wondered whether arguments against compulsory service were nothing more than "pragmatic self-interest" for those who "did not want to serve." He put it this way:

> In point of fact, an all-volunteer army would liberate the middle class from the legal necessity of serving but commit others to compulsory service by economic circumstance. Is this not, in effect, forcing the poor and the less fortunate into the armed forces? Is this truly democratic? (Marmion, 1971, p. 46)[43]

Candidate Nixon Speaks Out

In 1967, Richard Nixon, then a candidate for the Republican nomination for President, named Martin Anderson, an associate professor of business at Columbia University, his "research director."[44] Anderson was a conservative thinker who had taken on a number of liberal programs, most notably the federal urban renewal program (Anderson, 1964). He now focused on conscription and would be a central figure in the draft debate for years to come. In April, Anderson sent Nixon a memorandum he had written arguing for an all-volunteer force (Anderson, 1967a). He prepared a more-extensive memorandum in July[45], *An Analysis of the Factors Involved in Moving to an All-Volunteer Armed Force* (Anderson, 1967c).

---

[43] Professor Friedman countered these arguments when he wrote that

> Clearly, it is a good thing not a bad thing to offer better alternatives to the currently disadvantaged. The argument to the contrary rests on a political judgment: that a high ratio of Negroes in the armed services would exacerbate racial tensions at home and provide in the form of ex-soldiers a militarily trained group to foment violence. (Friedman, 1967, p. 260)

Friedman's point apparently rang true for those very individuals being discussed at the conference at the University of Chicago. Professor Charles Moskos, Jr., one of the severest critics of the all-volunteer force for decades to come, showed in 1969 that

> Negroes . . . are still much more likely than whites to have positive views towards the draft and military life. . . . Negro youths by seeking to enter the armed forces are saying that it is even worth the risk of being killed in order to have a chance to learn a trade, to make it in a small way, to get away from a dead-end existence, and to join the only institution in this society that seems really to be racially integrated. (Moskos, 1969, p. 161)

[44] Anderson has recounted how, in December 1966, Nixon's law partner Leonard Garment recruited him to become a "brain truster" for Nixon (Anderson, 1991). This essay is also contained in Anderson (1993).

[45] On July 5, 1967, Anderson called Nixon's office and was told by Pat Buchanan that Nixon was out of town and "will be back next week and we will present him with your effort" and that they would call "if he wants [the] draft file" (Anderson, 2005, p. 3).

Anderson's July paper was a tightly reasoned summary of the recent draft debate.[46] He echoed Friedman's arguments that "no one has any duty to serve the state" (Anderson, 1967b, p. 2) and asserted that "virtually all men would agree that" an all-volunteer force is right. He argued that the effect on national security would be positive because the draft system produced "a high number of trainees and inexperienced men who must constantly be replaced" (Anderson, 1967b, p. 3). He told Nixon that the "basic reason why the draft is necessary today is simply that we have not been willing to pay even reasonably fair wages to our men in the military" (Anderson, 1967b, p. 5). He challenged the Pentagon's pessimistic estimate of the cost of an all-volunteer force, choosing to side with Walter Oi's assessment that "even in times of hostilities . . . the additional cost is feasible within the context of the federal budget" (Anderson, 1967b, p. 17). He concluded as follows:

> Therefore, because it is moral and fair, because it increases our national security, and because it is economically feasible, we should establish a volunteer armed force that will offer the young people of our country the opportunity to participate in her defense with dignity, with honor, and as free men. (Anderson, 1967b, p. 39)

Nixon sent Anderson's paper to a number of his informal advisors. On August 16th, Thomas Evans called from Nixon's office to ask a number of questions and to see if Anderson might be available for "consultations." Anderson followed up the next day with a letter to Evans explaining the effect of a phase-out of the draft on the officer corps and the reenlistment of specialists. He sent him a number of papers that Oi and Stuart Altman had prepared as part of the ill-fated Pentagon study. He also told Evans that a group of congressman known as the "Wednesday Group" were "planning to publish a book under their auspices proposing an all-volunteer professional army" (Anderson, 1967d). On the evening of August 23, 1967, Anderson received a phone call from Alan Greenspan, who told him that Leonard Garment had "put a 30-man task force to work on [his] paper, [and said it was to be treated] "as a major question" (Anderson, 2005, p. 7). A few weeks later, the issue of the draft was raised again in a free-ranging review of "tentative thoughts regarding the research area" (Anderson, 1967f).

Anderson's paper also found its way to Kent Crane of the Republican National Committee's Research Division, who read it "with great interest . . . [and took] the liberty of reproducing the paper and sending one copy to Ambassador Robert Hill and another to Doug Bailey on Capitol Hill" (Crane, 1967). At his law firm, Nixon asked his colleagues for their opinion and to call around and try out the idea. They reported that several congressmen indicated they were "opposed to abolition of the draft at this

---

[46] In this paper, Anderson recounted "a 17-page policy memorandum for Nixon that spelled out the essential arguments, pro and con, for ending the draft and setting up an all-volunteer force" (Anderson, 1991, p. 3). In Anderson's "White House papers" at the National Archives, however, there is only a seven-page undated memorandum for Nixon, titled "An Outline of the Factors Involved in Establishing an All-Volunteer Armed Force" (Anderson, 1967a). This is most likely the paper sent to Nixon because it is clearly the outline for the longer papers, dated July 4, 1967 (Anderson, 1967b) and the final paper dated July 10, 1967 (Anderson, 1967c).

time and suggested that they should be contacted prior to any announcement" (Evans, 1967). After reading Anderson's paper, Frank Lincoln, who headed Nixon's military advisory group, was "tentatively in favor of gradual transition to the concept of a voluntary army" (Evans, 1967) but indicated that Adm. (Ret.) Arleigh Burke, the former Chief of Naval Operations, was opposed.

Comments came from other quarters. In October, Tom Huston told Pat Buchanan that Anderson's paper was "a first-rate job"—dispassionate, logical, and convincing— and suggested that he and Buchanan "discuss how to gain the maximum exposure for its conclusions." Nixon even received encouragement from those who did not know he was considering taking a public position in favor of ending the draft. In October, William H. Peterson wrote to ask whether he had "considered coming out for a voluntary army after Vietnam" (Peterson, 1967). Pointing out that Representatives Donald Rumsfeld and Thomas B. Curtis (R-Missouri)[47] had already "introduced a billing calling for a study of the feasibility of terminating the draft," Peterson reminded Nixon that "absolution of the draft has won over quite an usual conglomerate of individuals and organizations" (Peterson, 1967), including the Republican Ripon Society.[48] He ended by asking Nixon, "What do you think?"

Nixon was inching closer to taking a public position. In October 1967, Anderson provided Nixon with "a recently revised draft of the original paper . . . recent articles by Senator Mark Hatfield [D-Oregon] and Professor Milton Friedman, as well as some miscellaneous clippings," and suggested that on an upcoming trip he might take a "quick look at them."[49]

Nixon did more than take a "quick look." During his visit to the University of Wisconsin the following month, on November 16, 1967, he told the Student Bar Association that "What is needed is not a broad based draft, but a professional military corps. The nation must move toward a volunteer army by compensating those who go into the military on a basis comparable to those in civilian careers" (Semple, 1967). The next day, a headline, albeit not a front-page headline, in the *New York Times* announced Nixon's coming out: "Nixon Backs Eventual End of Draft." By August 1968, these views were a plank in the Republican Party platform: "When military manpower needs can be appreciably reduced, we will place the Selective Service System

---

[47] Congressmen Curtis and Rumsfeld kept pushing the issue of draft reform and the all-volunteer force. On July 2, 1967, they publicly demanded that President Johnson provide Congress with the staff papers of the Marshall Commission.

[48] The previous November 29, 1966, the Ripon Society publicly called for a "gradual phasing out of the draft" (Parsons, 1966).

[49] Anderson also told Nixon about a new book, *How to End the Draft,* by five Republican congressmen, and that they intended

> to press for legislation to raise military pay and improve other conditions so the draft could be abandoned in favor of a volunteer armed force. They have a specific 31 point plan and estimate the additional annual cost at $4.38 billion. (Anderson, 1967e)

The book (Stafford et al., 1967) received some publicity (Neff, 1967).

on standby and substitute a voluntary force obtained through adequate pay and career incentives."[50]

Almost a year later, on October 17, 1968, when he was the official candidate of the Republican Party for President, Nixon spoke to the subject of conscription in a radio address over the CBS Radio Network.[51] He put himself squarely on the side of an all-volunteer force:

> I feel this way: a system of compulsory service that arbitrarily selects some and not others simply cannot be squared with our whole concept of liberty, justice and equality under the law. Its only justification is compelling necessity. . . . Some say we should tinker with the present system, patching up an inequity here and there. I favor this too, but only for the short term. But in the long run, the only way to stop the inequities is to stop using the system. (Nixon, 1971, p. 77)

Nixon hedged when he recognized the economists' argument about the hidden tax of conscription but put "practical" constraints on budget affordability. He noted that, "Our servicemen are singled out for a huge hidden tax—the difference between their military pay and what they could otherwise earn" (Nixon, 1971, p. 79). He then added that

> the draft can be phased out of American life, . . . if we find we can reasonably meet our peacetime manpower needs by other means. . . . It will cost a great deal to move to a voluntary system, but unless that cost is proved to be prohibitive, it will be more than worth it. (Nixon, 1971, p. 80)[52]

---

[50] As quoted in Witherspoon (1993, p. 325). Witherspoon also notes that this was in "stark contrast" to the Democratic platform, which maintained "support (for a) random system of selection which will reduce the time period of eligibility for the draft and ensure equality in selection procedures."

[51] From the "News Release from the Nixon-Agnew Campaign Committee" (Klein, 1968).

[52] Professor Milton Friedman took exception to this line of argument. At the 1966 conference on the draft at the University of Chicago, he said

> I would like to emphasize that we are now paying larger costs than that [$4 billion to 8 billion—Oi's estimate of the cost of an all-volunteer force]. The costs he estimates are the budgetary costs. They are not the real cost because the situation is now that we have two kinds of taxes. We have taxes that you and I pay in money, and we have taxes that the young men who are forced to serve pay in compulsory service. . . . This is no less a tax because you exact it in the form of service than if you exact it in the form of money. (Friedman, 1967, p. 365)

References

Anderson, Martin C., *The Federal Bulldozer,* New York: McGraw Hill Book Company, 1964.

———, "An Outline of the Factors Involved in Establishing an All-Volunteer Armed Force," memorandum to Richard M. Nixon, New York, April 1, 1967a. G1122.pdf.

———, "An Analysis of the Factors Involved in Moving to an All-Volunteer Armed Force," unpublished paper, July 4, 1967b. S0032.pdf.

———, "An Analysis of the Factors Involved in Moving to an All-Volunteer Armed Force," unpublished paper, New York, July 10, 1967c. A0013.pdf.

———, "I have looked into those questions we discussed," memorandum to Thomas Evans, New York, August 18, 1967d. A0014.pdf.

———, "In regard to your trip next week," memorandum to Richard M. Nixon, New York, October 14, 1967e. A0020.pdf.

———, "Tentative Thoughts Regarding the Research Area," letter to Leonard Garment, New York, September 8, 1967f. S0033.pdf.

———, *The Making of the All-Volunteer Armed Force,* Palo Alto, Calif.: Hoover Institution Press, 1991.

———, "The Making of the All Volunteer Armed Force," in Leon Friedman and William F. Levantrosser, eds., *Cold War Patriot and Statesman: Richard M. Nixon,* Westport, Conn.: Greenwood Press, 1993.

———, "Notes From the Summer of 1967," letter to Bernard Rostker, Stanford, Calif., November 9, 2005. S0906.pdf.

Associated Press, "Army Manpower Draft Expected to End in June," *New York Times,* August 5, 1949, p. 3.

Barnes, Bart, "Burke Marshall, 80, Dies; JFK's Civil Rights Enforcer," *Washington Post,* June 3, 2003, p. B6.

Blent, Karin, Anna Dahlen, Mora Larsson, and Marita Wikander, *Skansen,* Stockholm, Sweden: Skansen, 2004.

Burk, James, "The Military Obligation of Citizens Since Vietnam," *Parameters,* Summer 2001, pp. 48–60.

Chambers, John Whiteclay II, *To Raise and Army: The Draft Comes to Modern America,* New York: The Free Press, 1987.

———, "Conscription," in Eric Foner and John A. Garraty, eds., *The Reader's Companion to American History,* New York: Houghton Mifflin Company, 1991.

Cohen, Eliot A., *Citizens and Soldiers: The Dilemmas of Military Service,* Ithaca, N.Y.: Cornell University Press, 1985.

Crane, Kent, "I Have Read Your Paper," memorandum to Martin C. Anderson, Washington, D.C., August 14, 1967. A0015.pdf.

Cutler, Frederick Morse, *The History of Military Conscription with Special Reference to the United States,* dissertation, Worcester, Mass: Clark University, 1922.

———, "Military Conscription, especially in the United States," *The Historical Outlook,* Vol. XIV, No. 5, May 1923, pp. 170–175.

Evans, Thomas, "Proposal for Volunteer Army," memorandum to Richard M. Nixon, New York, August 8, 1967. A0016.pdf.

Flynn, George Q., *Lewis B. Hershey, Mr. Selective Service,* Chapel Hill, N.C.: University of North Carolina Press, 1985.

———, *The Draft, 1940–1973,* Lawrence, Kan.: University Press of Kansas, 1993.

———, *Conscription and Democracy: The Draft in France, Great Britain, and the United States,* Westport, Conn.: Greenwood Press, 2002.

Ford, Worthington C., ed., *Journals of the Continental Congress: 1774–1789,* Washington, D.C.: 1904–1937. G1400.pdf.

Friedberg, Aaron L., *In the Shadow of the Garrison State: America's Anti-Statism and Its Cold War Strategy,* Princeton, N.J.: Princeton University Press, 2000.

Friedman, Milton, "Discussion: Recruitment of Manpower Solely by Voluntary Means," in Sol Tax, ed., *The Draft: A Handbook of Facts and Alternatives,* Chicago: University of Chicago Press, 1967.

———, "Why Not a Volunteer Army?" in Sol Tax, ed., *The Draft: A Handbook of Facts and Alternatives,* Chicago: University of Chicago Press, 1967, pp. 200–207. S0240.pdf.

———, *Two Lucky People,* Chicago: University of Chicago Press, 1998.

Gorham, William, "Expanded Version of the Outline of the Final Report," memorandum to Military Manpower Study Group, Washington, D.C., December 15, 1964. G0245.pdf.

Green, John Richard, *A Short History of the English People,* New York: London George Newnes Limited, 1908.

Greenberg, I. M., "Interview with Bernard Rostker," September 1, 2001.

Harper, Douglas, "The American Civil War: Conscription," 2001. Online at http://www.etymonline.com/cw/conscript.htm (as of May, 18, 2005).

Hershey, Lewis B., *Selective Service in Peacetime: A Report to the President,* Washington, D.C.: Selective Service System.

Hoglund, Patrik, "Recruiting in Sweden in the 17th Century," letter to Bernard Rostker, Stockholm, August 25, 2004.

Janowitz, Morris, "The Logic of National Service," in Sol Tax, ed., *The Draft: A Handbook of Facts and Alternative,* Chicago: University of Chicago Press, 1967, pp. 73–90.

Kestnbaum, Meyer, "Citizenship and Compulsory Military Service: The Revolutionary Origins of Conscription in the United States," *Armed Forces & Society,* Vol. 27, No. 1, pp. 7–36.

Klein, Herbert G., "Program for Abolishing the Draft," News Release New York, October 17, 1968. G1124.pdf.

Kreidberg, Marvin R., and Merton G. Henry, *History of Military Mobilization in the United States Army 1775–1945,* Washington, D.C.: U.S. Government Printing Office, No. 20-212, 1955.

Lee, Gus C., and Geoffrey Y. Parker, *Ending the Draft: The Story of the All Volunteer Force*, Washington, D.C.: Human Resources Research Organization, FR-PO-771, April 1977. S0242.pdf.

Lords Spiritual and Temporal and Commons Assembled at Westminster, *English Bill of Rights*, Westminster, England: Parliment, 1689.

Lunt, W. E., *History of England*, New York: Harper & Brothers, 1956.

Magruder, Carter B., *Report of the Task Force on the Structure of the Selective Service System*, Washington, D.C.: Task Force on the Structure of the Selective Service System, October 1967. G1475.pdf.

Marmion, Harry A., *The Case Against a Volunteer Army: Should America's Wars be Fought Only by the Poor and the Black?* Chicago: Quadrangle Books, 1971.

Marshall, Burke, *In Pursuit of Equity? Who Serves When Not All Serve? Report of the National Advisory Commission on Selective Service*, Washington, D.C.: National Advisory Commission on Selective Service, February 1967. G1428.pdf.

McNeill, William H., "The Draft in the Light of History," in Sol Tax, ed., *The Draft: A Handbook of Facts and Alternatives*, Chicago: University of Chicago Press, 1967, pp. 117–121.

Mead, Margaret, "A National Service System as a Solution to a Variety of National Problems," in Sol Tax, ed., *The Draft: A Handbook of Facts and Alternatives*, Chicago: The University of Chicago Press, 1967, pp. 99–109.

Moore, Albert Burton, *Conscription and Conflict on the Confederacy*, New York: Macmillan Co., 1924.

Morris, Thomas D., Assistant Secretary of Defense (Manpower), Statement, hearing before the House Committee on Armed Services, Washington, D.C., U.S. Government Printing Office, June 30, 1966. S0273.pdf.

Moskos, Charles C., Jr., "The Negro and the Draft," in Roger W. Little, ed., *Selective Service and American Society*, New York: Russell Sage Foundation, 1969, pp. 139–162.

Museum, The Vasa, *VASA*, Stockholm, Sweden: The Vasa Museum, 2004.

National Headquarters, Selective Service System, Office of Public Information, "Biographical Outline: Lt. General Lewis Blaine Hershey—Director, Selective Service System," April 1, 1968. G1027.pdf.

Neff, Edwin D., "Republican Legislators Propose End of the Draft in Just-Published Book." A0021.pdf.

New York Times Editorial Board, "The Draft Studies," New York Times, April 20, 1964, p. 42.

Nixon, Richard M., *The All-Volunteer Armed Force: A Radio Address by the Republican Presidential Nominee*, Washington, D.C.: Republican National Committee, October 17, 1968. G0251.pdf.

Nunn, Sam, "Remarks by US Senator Sam Nunn before the George General Assembly," news release, Washington, D.C., March 5, 1973. S0118.pdf.

U.S. Congress, Costs of the All-Volunteer Force, hearing before the Senate Armed Services Subcommittee on Manpower and Personnel, 95th Cong., 2nd Sess., Washington, D.C., U.S. Government Printing Office, February 6, 1978. S0443.pdf.

O'Sullivan, John, and Allen M. Meckler, eds., The Draft and Its Enemies: A Documentary History, Champaign, Ill.: University of Illinois Press, 1974.

Oi, Walter Y., "Request for Leave to Participate in the Department of Defense Draft Study," memorandum to Department of Economics Chairman, University of Washington, Seattle, Wash., July 29, 1964. G0244.pdf.

———, "Assumptions Underlying Projections," memorandum to William Gorham and Harold Wool, Washington, D.C., February 25, 1965. G0246.pdf.

———, "Historical Perspectives on the All-Volunteer Force: The Rochester Connection," in Curtis L. Gilroy J. Eric Fredland, Roger D. Little, and W. S. Sellman, ed., Professionals on the Front Line: Two Decades of the All-Volunteer Force, Washington, D.C.: Brassey's, 1996.

———, "Interview with Bernard Rostker," July 6, 2001.

Parsons, W. Stuart, Ripon Society Blasts Democrats' Lottery, National Service Corps: Insists Draft Can Be Phased Out, Cambridge, Mass.: The Ripon Society, November 29, 1966. A0023.pdf.

Peterson, William H., Have You Considered Coming Out for a Volunteer Army, Princeton, N.J., October 5, 1967. A0017.pdf.

Royster, Charles, A Revolutionary People at War: The Continental Army and American Character, 1775–1783, Chapel Hill, N.C.: The University of North Carolina Press, 1979.

Rumsfeld, Donald, A U.S. Representative in Congress from the 13th Congressional District of the State of Illinois on Amending and Extending the Draft Law and Related Authorities, Statement, hearing before the Senate Committee on Armed Services, Washington, D.C.: April 18, 1967. G1168.pdf.

Schwoerer, Lois G., 'No Standing Army': The Antiarmy Ideology in the Seventeenth-Century England, Baltimore, Md.: The Johns Hopkins University Press, 1974.

Semple, Robert B., Jr., "Nixon Backs Eventual End of Draft," New York Times, November 18, 1967, p. 21.

Stafford, Robert T., Frank J. Horton, Richard S. Schweiker, Garner E. Shriver, and Charles W. Whalen, Jr., How to End the Draft: The Case for an All-Volunteer Army, Washington, D.C.: National Press, Inc., 1967.

Tax, Sol, ed., The Draft: A Handbook of Facts and Alternatives, Chicago: University of Chicago Press, 1967.

Timberg, Robert, The Nightingale's Song, New York: Simon and Schuster, 1995.

Tocqueville, Alexis de, "Democracy in America," 1835. Online at http://xroads.virginia.edu/~HYPER/DETOC/1_ch13.htm (as of March 15, 2005).

U.S. Congress, Nation's Manpower Revolution, Statement, hearing before the Senate Committee on Labor and Public Welfare, 88th Cong., 1st Sess., Washington, D.C.: November 22, 1963.

Washington, George, "To the Committee of Congress with the Army: Head Quarters, January 29, 1778," in John C. Fitzpatrick, ed., *The Writing of George Washington for the Original Manuscript Sources,* Washington, D.C.: U.S. Government Printing Office, 1931–1944, pp. 364–367. G1401.pdf.

———, "Sentiments on a Peace Establishment," in John O'Sullivan and Alan M. Meckler, eds., *The Draft and Its Enemies: A Documentary History,* Champaign, Ill.: University of Illinois Press, 1974.

Wilson, Woodrow, *1915 State of the Union Address,* December 7, 1915.

Witherspoon, Ralph Pomeroy, *The Military Draft and the All-Volunteer Force: A Case Study of a Shift in Public Policy,* dissertation, Blacksburg, Va.: Virginia Polytechnic Institute and State University, 1993.

CHAPTER THREE

The Coming of the All-Volunteer Force: Analytic Studies (1960–1968)

[W]e cannot look forward to discontinuing the draft . . . unless [we can] . . . reduce the force levels substantially below those needed since Korea. . . . Increases in military compensation sufficient to attract an all-volunteer force cannot be justified.

—Thomas D. Morris
Assistant Secretary of Defense
(Manpower)[1]

The estimate from the 1965 Department of Defense study was $5.5 billion, close to the low end of the range. More important, the DoD report pointed out that this was an incremental budget cost that concealed the real social cost of allocating manpower to the nation's defense.

—Walter Oi
Head, DoD Economic Analysis Section
for the 1964 Pentagon Draft Study[2]

The Inequities of the Draft

The debate concerning the draft and the feasibility of an all-volunteer force resulted in a number of studies, both inside the government and at universities. The common view was that the system of conscription had to be changed. Even after the increased draft calls associated with the escalation of the conflict in Vietnam, the system of delays, exemptions, and deferments was no longer creditable in the eyes of most Americans.

---

[1] Statement to the House Committee on Armed Services, June 30, 1966 (Morris, 1966, p. 9,942).

[2] From his retrospective essay prepared for the 20th anniversary of the all-volunteer force in 1993 (Oi, 1996, p. 42).

Lawrence M. Baskir and William A. Strauss, *Chance and Circumstance: The Draft, the War, and the Vietnam Generation,* New York: Alfred A. Knopf, 1978

Excerpt from the Preface:

Chance and Circumstance focuses on that part of the American people who were confronted most immediately with the reality of Vietnam—the 27 million draft-age men we call the Vietnam generation. Yet this book is not about those who actually fought the war. Their first hand accounts are eloquent, tortured, and tragic, and are perhaps the most important single chronicle of the Vietnam experience. We have written about the 25 million men who did not fight. Our purpose is to show who they were and how they escaped the war—and yet, in truth did not escape it. Vietnam was, as a *Washington Post* editorial once observed, "a generation-wide catastrophe." In its wreckage lay an astonishing variety of victims.

Lawrence M. Baskir and William A. Strauss wrote the most definitive empirical study of inequities during the Vietnam period. Although published five years after the last person was drafted, it illustrates why the issue of "equity" was so important in shaping public opinion.

In 1974, President Gerald Ford established the Presidential Clemency Board. Baskir was its General Counsel and Chief Executive Officer. Strauss was the Director of Planning and Management. In their book *Chance and Circumstance: The Draft, the War, and the Vietnam Generation,* they produced what Rev. Theodore M. Hesburgh, a member of the board, characterized as the "first comprehensive study of the Vietnam generation" (Hesburgh, 1978). Table 3.1 shows the results of their calculations of the likelihood of service by income status and education. Figure 3.1 shows that the majority of young men who were draft age during the Vietnam War (August 4, 1964, to March 28, 1973) did not serve.

Table 3.1
Likelihood of Vietnam-Era Service (%)

	Military Service	Vietnam Service	Combat Service
Income			
Low	40	19	15
Middle	30	12	7
High	24	9	7
Education			
High school dropout	42	18	14
High school graduate	45	21	17
College graduate	23	12	9

SOURCE: Baskir and Strauss (1978, p. 9).

Figure 3.1
Vietnam Generation

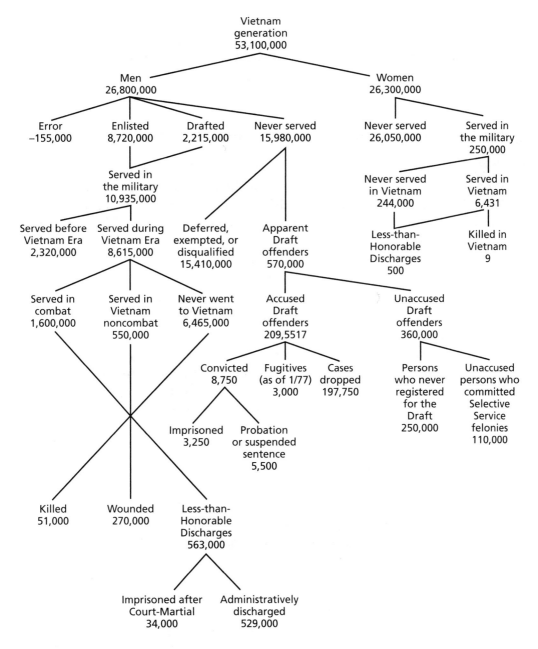

In fact, the dislocation caused by the war and the large number of "apparent draft offenders" shows how unpopular the draft had become. According to Baskir and Strauss, the number of young men who were apparent draft offenders was equal to one-quarter of those who actually served in Vietnam. The one thing that those who favored national service and those who favored an all-volunteer force could agree on was that the Selective Service System was not working.

A New Paradigm for the Study of Military Manpower

In 1963, when President Johnson asked Secretary of Defense Robert McNamara to study options for reforming the Selective Service System, including the feasibility of an all-volunteer force, he could not have anticipated the revolution in military manpower that would follow. From World War I to that time, military personnel issues were generally the purview of psychologists, psychometricians, and sociologists.

For the psychologists and psychometricians, the basic issue was "selection and classification," i.e., who would be selected from the pool of potentially available draft age males and, once selected, what jobs should they be assigned to do.[3] Starting with World War I, their efforts brought mental testing into the American mainstream and established psychological testing and the intelligence quotient—the IQ score—in the public consciousness. Psychological screening was important in World War II. Such programs as the one to select and classify Navy and Army aircrews were considered one of the triumphs of applied psychology. The issue of an all-volunteer force was, however, seen by the Pentagon as largely outside the realm of psychologists.

Sociologists and anthropologists researched the issues of group dynamics, relations between society and the military, and social relations within the military.[4] Sociologists, such as Morris Janowitz of the University of Chicago and Charles Moskos, Jr., of Northwestern University, emphasized their concern about the relationship between the military and society, as well as the internal social organization and the effectiveness of alternative military organizations.[5] At the conference in 1966 at the University of Chicago, they argued against an all-volunteer force in favor of national service. In con-

---

[3] A whole section of the American Psychological Association is devoted to military psychology.

[4] The premier sociological journal that covers this subject is appropriately titled *Armed Forces and Society.*

[5] Moskos saw this as a competition between "economics" and "sociology." In 1985, he lamented how things had developed and charged that the sociologist's views had "conflicted with the econometric mindset that had become dominant in the Office of the Secretary of Defense and in sponsored research in military manpower." He favored "a sociological construct in contrast to the econometrics of the policy analyst," with its "explicit recognition of the trade-offs involved in military manpower." He argued that "the econometric approach tends to define issues that are amenable to existing methodologies and thus concentrates on narrowly conceived comparisons of variables to the neglect of the more difficult issues of institutional change and civilian-military relations." He argued that his approach reinforced the "contextual factors" and that "in place of the individual atomism of the econometric mold, it presented military life in a dynamic organizational framework" (Moskos and Wood, 1988, p. 4).

trast, the involvement of economists in issues of military manpower was new in 1966 and was even commented on by George Hildebrand at the annual meeting of the American Economic Association.[6]

> There can hardly be a better subject for economic analysis than comparative methods for the recruitment of military manpower. The problem has both micro- and macroeconomic aspects. It involves both allocative and distributive effects. It raises questions of wage structure and of labor mobility. It combines the tasks of formal analysis and of statistical estimation. Above all, given the highly controversial ambient of issues surrounding military recruitment in the United States today, the economist who ventures into the field has both the challenge and the opportunity to separate clearly his scientific findings from the normative aspects of the question. (Hildebrand et al., 1967, p. 63)[7]

Given Secretary McNamara's penchant for quantitative analysis and with the assignment of an economist, Deputy Assistant Secretary William Gorham, to head the 1964 Pentagon Draft Study, action on the all-volunteer force shifted to labor economists. Until the early 1960s, labor economists had generally focused on studying the issues of wage determination and labor unions. However, within the economic profession, things were changing. In 1964, future Nobel Prize winner Garry Becker published his landmark book, *Human Capital* (Becker, 1964). Using the tools of human capital theory, economists would address a wide range of social problems from military manpower to marriage and the formation of families.[8] In addition, development of new programs as part of President Johnson's Great Society, the establishment of the Manpower Administration in the Department of Labor and the Office of Economic Opportunity, provided resources for a new generation of economists that revolutionized

---

[6] A landmark book, *The Economics of Defense in the Nuclear Age* (Hitch and McKean, 1960), did not even mention the subject of military manpower.

[7] Two other reviewers of the papers presented at the 1966 meeting of the American Economic Association also commented on the new involvement of economists in this area of policy analysis. Paul Weinstein noted that

> These research papers mark a significant genesis in the economic analysis of military manpower which is long overdue. It is hoped that we have unlatched the gate that separates the academic from the military establishment. (Weinstein, 1967, p. 66)

Harold Wool, the Pentagon's Director of Procurement Policy, mentioned that

> Those concerned with formulating our long-range manpower policies turned to the economists for answers to the following questions: Will it be economically feasible to recruit and maintain peacetime military forces of the size required in recent years on a completely voluntary basis? And, if so, how much would it cost? (Wool, 1967, p. 69)

[8] Later, the pendulum would swing backward, with a new focus on jobs-based analysis as *personnel economics* addressed more traditional management questions. Edward Lazear summed up the changes this way:

> Human-capital theory is primarily a supply-side approach that focuses on the characteristics and skills of the individual worker. It pays far less attention to the environments in which workers work. The entire notion of a "job," which seems central to the thinking of businesspersons and administrators, is virtually absent from most labor-market analyses. . . . The institutional literature, and especially the work on internal labor markets, asks questions that differ from those asked by human-capital theory. (Lazear, 1995)

the field of labor economics.[9] New journals, such as the *Journal of Human Resources,* appeared. It was against that background that a team of economists took on the issue of the "feasibility" of an all-volunteer force.

Budget Versus Economic Costs

The distinction between *budget costs* and *economic costs* was critical to the debate over the all-volunteer force. The bureaucracy wanted *budget costs* to be the basis for any decision on an all-volunteer force. These were the costs they had to deal with when working with Congress. The economists they hired, despite their charter to look at budget costs, followed the lead of Professor Milton Friedman of the University of Chicago, and insisted that *economic costs* be considered in any decision. Friedman saw it this way:

> The question [of] how much more we would have to pay to attract sufficient volunteers has been studied intensively in the Department of Defense study of military recruitment. . . . On a more mundane budgetary level, the argument that a voluntary army would cost more simply involves a confusion of apparent with real cost. . . . When he is forced to serve, we are in effect imposing on him a tax in kind equal in value to the difference between what it would take to attract him and the military pay he actually receives. This implicit tax in kind should be added to the explicit taxes imposed on the rest of us to get the real cost of our armed forces. If this is done, it will be seen at once that abandoning the draft would almost surely reduce the real cost—because the armed forces would then be manned by men for whom soldiering was the best available career, and hence who would require the lowest sums of money to induce them to serve. Abandoning the draft might raise the apparent money cost to the government but only because it would substitute taxes in money for taxes in kind. (Friedman, 1967, pp. 203–204)

First Estimates of the Military Supply Curve Without a Draft

The initial work on estimating a supply curve for volunteers in the absence of a draft was done for the 1964 Pentagon Draft Study by Stuart Altman of Brown University and Alan Fechter of the Institute for Defense Analyses. Results of their work were first released to Congress by DoD on June 30, 1966, and, the following December, were

---

[9] *Author's Note:* I was fortunate to be one who benefited from support from the Manpower Administration. In the summer of 1967, as a student at Syracuse University's Maxwell School of Citizenship and Public Affairs I received a grant to write my doctoral dissertation. My topic was the theoretical underpinning of manpower retraining and the elasticity of substitution between various categories of labor and other factors of production employing the newly developed constant elasticity of substitution production function. Empirically, if a category of labor was inelastic, retraining might be necessary to prevent a shortage of labor and a curtailment of production. If labor was very elastic, wage-inducted factor substitution would ensure that shortages did not result in production bottlenecks, and the case for retraining would be less compelling.

presented at the annual meeting of the American Economic Association and published in the American Economic Review (Altman and Fechter, 1967). They were also presented in a later article in the Journal of Human Resources (Altman, 1969).

In their presentation, Altman and Fechter first noted that "legal and administrative constraints on recruiting practices . . . made it difficult to separate variations in the number of new enlistees and officers recruited caused by supply factors from those caused by demand factors" (Altman and Fechter, 1967, p. 19). This is the classic "identification problem," which was significant when economists were trying to estimate a military supply curve without a draft from data from years with a draft. Clearly, during these years, the total number of men enlisted in the armed forces consisted of both true volunteers and those induced to join because they feared that they would be drafted (the so-called "draft-motivated volunteers"). Someone motivated by the draft to "volunteer" could either ask Selective Service to move up his draft date to a time of his choosing or enlist in a service of his choice and for a program of his choice, rather than to serve in the Army. Those who took the draft option were inducted for two years; those who selected the enlistment option were sometimes enlisted for longer periods to qualify for specific programs.

Altman and Fechter worked around this "identification problem" by searching out a group that was "relatively free from these constraints." They chose "Army enlistees in Mental Group I–III and officers commissioned through ROTC programs in 'Voluntary' schools" (Altman and Fechter, 1967, p. 19). They estimated a supply equation using quarterly data for 1956 through 1965. The dependant variable in their enlisted supply equation was the ratio of total Army Mental Group I–III divided by the 18- to 19-year-old male population. Their independent variables were the unemployment rate for males 18 to 19 years of age, "dummy variables" reference for periods of high and low draft calls, and seasonal variables. They noted the importance of military earnings but concluded, "its effects could not be estimated directly from time series data because of insufficient statistical variability over the period studied"(Altman and Fechter, 1967, p. 20).

Using this equation, they estimated future enlistments *with a draft* based on the projected 18- to 19-year-old male population for 1970 through 1975, with two levels of assumed unemployment.

To estimate future enlistments *without a draft,* they used estimates of "draft motivation" from survey data to

> determine the extent to which the existence of the draft has influenced the level of voluntary enlistments. . . . [They] reduc[ed] the enlisted and officer continued draft projections by the appropriate draft-motivation factor from the Department of Defense Survey. (Altman and Fechter, 1967, p. 23)

Using this equation, they estimated future enlistments *with a draft* based on the projected 18- to 19-year-old male population for 1970 through 1975, with two levels of assumed unemployment. They estimated two equations: one for the Army and one

Stuart H. Altman and Alan E. Fechter, "The Supply of Military Personnel in the Absence of a Draft," *American Economic Review,* **Vol. 57, No. 2, May 1967, p. 20**

It was found that the following variables were important determinants of the level of enlistments, given the existence of military conscription: (1) the size of the 18- to 19-year-old male population; (2) the male 18- to 19-year-old unemployment rate: (3) major changes in draft pressure; and (4) seasonal factors. These variables were incorporated into the following equation, estimated from quarterly data for the period July 1956, to June 1963.

(1)
$$\frac{E}{P} = .03018 + .35670\ U* + .02007 D_H†$$
$$\phantom{\frac{E}{P} = .03018 +}(.07696)\quad\ (.00865)$$

$$- .01341\ D_L - .01024\ S_p$$
$$(.00703)\quad\ (.00522)$$

$$+ .02107\ S_M^* - .00517\ F$$
$$(.00620)\quad\ (.00588)$$

$$R^2 = .67$$

NOTE: Figures in parenthesis denote standard errors.
  * Significant at the .01 level.
  † Significant at the .05 level.

where,

E/P = quarterly Army Mental Group I–III enlistments divided by the 18- to 19-year-old male population.

U = the 18- to 19-year-old male unemployment rate.

D_H = a dummy variable for periods of high draft pressure (the four quarters during the Berlin buildup crisis).

D_L = a dummy variable for periods of low draft pressure (the four quarters of FY 1965 during which time draft calls were low and there was extensive publicity about the long-run possibility of eliminating the draft).

S_p = a spring seasonal dummy variable.

S_M = a summer seasonal dummy variable.

F = a fall seasonal dummy variable.

Stuart H. Altman and Alan E. Fechter, "The Supply of Military Personnel in the Absence of a Draft," *American Economic Review,* **Vol. 57, No. 2, May 1967, p. 28**

For enlisted men, the following equation was estimated from 1963 data for nine Census regions [4]:

(2)
$$\log c_i = b_1 + b_2 \log Y_i + b_3 \log U_i$$

$$\text{where } c_i = \left[(1) - \left(\frac{D_i \cdot E_i}{p_i}\right)\right]$$

and,

E_i = 1963 enlistments in the ith region in Mental Groups I–III.

D_i = the proportion of draft-motivated volunteers within Mental Groups I–III in the ith region as measured by the Department of Defense Survey.

P_i = the estimated number of 17- to 20-year-old physically and mentally qualified males (Mental Groups I–III) in the civilian labor force?

Y_i = relative earnings in the ith region-the ratio of (a) average annual military pay over the first term to (b) full-time civilian earnings of 16- to 21-year-old males not enrolled in school in the ith region.

U_i = unemployment rate of 16- to 21-year-old civilian males not enrolled in school in the ith region.

for "all services." They noted that higher budgetary costs were associated with the all-volunteer force but argued that the economic costs would be lower (Altman and Fechter, 1967, p. 31). It would be left to Walter Oi to estimate the economic costs.

An extensive treatment of the above model is presented in Altman's 1967 article in the *Journal of Human Resources* (Altman, 1969). Altman estimated an equation "with a draft" adding the "percentage of military men in a region who are white" as an explanatory variable. The effect of the draft was again accounted for by creating a "nondraft enlistment rate" using the results of the 1964 DoD survey. However, his regression results, as he said, "present a somewhat confusing picture. How are we to interpret the findings that the no-draft pay elasticity estimates are uniformly higher than the elasticities estimated with a draft?" (Altman, 1969, p. 52) He overcame this problem, as well as the problem that his original estimates provided a constant pay elasticity over the entire range of projected enlistments, by reestimating his supply equation using the "complement of the no-draft enlistment rate" as the new dependant variable. His new results showed an Army pay elasticity of 1.18, which decreased as Army enlistments rose. He noted that these results were similar to those that Anthony Fisher had obtained—as discussed below—"using a different theoretical model and time-series data," and it is this formulation that Walter Oi used when costing the all-volunteer force (Altman, 1969, pp. 55–57).

Harold Wool of DoD, another member of the 1964 Pentagon Draft Study team, reviewed Altman and Fechter's paper at the 1966 annual meeting of the American Economic Association. He pointed out that the "statistical foundation" of the study consisted of only nine observations from 1963 "adjusted" for voluntary enlistment rates. He argued that the "implicit assumption . . . is a nearly instantaneous adjustment of military manpower supply to adjustments in first-term pay" was questionable (Wool, 1967, p. 69). At the time, with the war in Vietnam raging, the official position of the Pentagon was not to favor a move to an all-volunteer force. Wool's critique summed up the Pentagon's view of the work of Altman and Fechter:

> These estimates and assumptions are inevitably fraught with great uncertainties. There is much which we still have to learn about the mechanism of occupational choice—about the influences which condition young men to choose a military career as against other alternatives in civilian life. We do, however, know from a variety of sources that attitudes towards military service as well as to other occupational careers are often formed early in adolescence and are influenced by many cultural sociological factors other than pay. In fact, some of our surveys have shown widespread ignorance of the true level of military compensation on the part of civilian youth. It is most unlikely, therefore, that short-range supply elasticities would approach those suggested by the cross-sectional analysis.
>
> Our uncertainties concerning the responsiveness of recruitment to pay incentives are compounded by uncertainties concerning the effects of changes in the civilian labor market on recruitment. . . .

For these and many related reasons, I believe that any single unqualified estimate of the "cost of an all-volunteer force," tempting though it may be, exceeds our capability at the present time. At best, these cost estimates must be stated in a broad range to suggest the limits of our knowledge and the inherent error of estimate in such projections. (Wool, 1967, p. 69–70)

The Economic Cost of the Draft

Walter Oi and other economists argued that the military payroll "is not the economic cost of labor resources allocated to the uniformed services" (1967b, p. 40). He presented three ways to measure the "cost" of the draft. Budget cost is one. A second is the value of the output that those in service could have produced if they were employed in the civilian economy.[10] A third measure, Oi suggests, is the full economic cost. He argued that, following the classic approach developed by Alfred Marshall, economic costs should account for the occupational preferences of those forced to serve because of the draft, or the value of the compensating payment necessary to induce individuals to volunteer (Marshall, 1920, pp. 547–570). This payment would, of course, have to increase to encourage more men to join voluntarily as requirements increased and thus leads to the familiar upward-sloping supply curve with respect to military pay and number of total enlistments. More simply, if the military had to compete freely in the national labor market for recruits, the market-clearing wage rate would rise or fall depending on the number of recruits required.

With this framework, Oi suggests,

> The draft imposes costs on men . . . in at least three ways. First, more men . . . are demanded [and drafted] . . . because of the high turnover of draftees and reluctant [draft-motivated] volunteers. Second, some men are coerced . . . without being compensated for their aversion to service life. . . . Finally, true volunteers who enlist at a low level of pay . . . are denied the higher pay that would have prevailed in an all-volunteer force. (Oi, 1967a, pp. 242–243)

In other words, they would forego some amount of what economists refer to as economic rent, because of the imposition of a draft.

Oi tried to estimate the various costs of the draft. Using the results of the 1964 DoD survey, he projected that the "effects of the draft on voluntary enlistments" for the FY 1970–1975 period at an assumed military end strength of 2.65 million men (Table 3.2). From Altman and Fechter, Oi obtained an estimated pay elasticity of 1.36, with an increase of 68 percent in basic first-term pay being necessary to sustain an all-volunteer force (Oi, 1967b, p.48). These costs would be, he argued, somewhat offset

---

[10] Oi calls this "a measure of technical efficiency," but it is classically thought of as the value of the marginal product of those drafted if they were free to work in the civilian economy, or the opportunity cost of the draft.

because the lower personnel turnover associated with the increased propensity of a force of all "true volunteers" to reenlist would result in a "career ratio of regular Army enlisted men [moving] from .431 to .537" (Oi, 1967b, p. 49).

Table 3.2
Effects of the Draft on Voluntary Enlistment-Survey Responses (by age and education)

Age at Entry and Education	True Volunteers[a] (%)	Number of DoD Sample[b]		With Draft[c]	Voluntary Enlistments in FY 1970–75 No Draft		
		No.	%		No.[d]	%	
17–19							
Less than high school	79.3	167.8	27.7	122.2	96.2	36.6	
High school graduate	63.7	247.1	40.8	188.0	119.7	45.5	
Some college	55.9	44.0	7.3	18.3	10.2	3.9	
Total	68.7	438.9	75.8	328.5	226.1	86.0	
20 and over							
Less than high school	60.2	20.2	3.3	14.3	8.6	3.3	
High school graduate	42.3	61.7	10.2	42.8	18.1	6.9	
Some college	32.7	64.4	10.6	31.1	10.2	3.9	
Total	40.5	146.4	24.2	88.2	36.9	14.0	
All ages							
Less than high school	77.4	31.1	31.1	136.3	104.8	39.8	
High school graduate	59.5	51.0	51.0	230.8	137.8	52.4	
Some college	42.1	17.9	17.9	49.4	20.4	7.8	
Total	61.9	100.0	100.0	416.7	263.0	100.0	

SOURCE: Adapted from Oi (1967b, p. 46).

[a] Based on responses of regular enlisted men in their first term of service to the question, "If there had been no draft and if you had no military obligation, do you think you would have volunteered for active military service?" Entries denote the percentage who responded, "Yes, definitely," or, "Yes, probably."

[b] Figures may differ from force strength statistics due to elimination of nonrespondents and sampling variability.

[c] Estimates of voluntary enlistments in FY 1970–75 if the draft is continued.

[d] Obtained by multiplying columns one and four. Assumes that the draft is eliminated but pay and recruitment incentives are unchanged.

Walter Oi, "The Economic Cost of the Draft," *American Economic Review,* **Vol. 57, No. 2, May 1967, pp. 55–58**

If the draft is eliminated with no pay changes, the annual supply of voluntary enlistments is projected to be around 263 thousand men at a first-term pay $M_0 =$ $2,500 If pay is increased by a factor of 1.88 to $M_1 = $4,700$, the annual supply of recruits climbs to 416.7 thousand men; i.e., from OA to OB accessions.

The reluctant volunteers (the line segment AB) enlist at the lower pay M0 in order to avoid being drafted. The difference between their minimum supply prices and the current first-term pay M0 represents an implicit tax, which is borne by these men. The aggregate annual cost fro the 153.7 thousand reluctant volunteers is thus given by the area of the triangle, DB'E, or $141 million. This estimate tacitly assumes that each reluctant volunteer is compensated in a discriminatory fashion without compensating the true volunteers. If, however, pay were raised to $4,700 for all recruits including true volunteers, the annual cost of the draft is increased by the additional amount M0DEM1 or $917 million. The lower annual cost of $141 million, which excludes rents, represents an implicit tax levied against reluctant volunteers who were coerced to enlist by the draft liability. In a sense, each reluctant volunteer pays, on average, an implicit tax of $915 in each of the 3.5 years

of his first term of service. If the point estimate of β had been used in these calculations, the aggregate annual cost, DB'E, is estimated to be $192 million. Since each regular enlistee serves for 3.5 years, the total tax (excluding rents) borne by the reluctant volunteers in an age class is conservatively estimated to be $493 million; the best estimate is $672 million.

The economic cost of conscripting men into military service is harder to assess. The Selective Service System does not attempt to draft men with the least aversion for military life. The supposition that draftees were next in line above the point E in the Figure is less plausible than in the case of reluctant volunteers. However, a lower bound estimate is again obtained by assuming that draftees had the smallest equalizing income differentials and hence the lowest minimum supply prices. In Figure 1, first term pay must be raised from M1 = $4,700 to M2 = $5,900 to attract the 55.3 thousand (the line segment BC) on a voluntary basis. If each draftee is compensated in a discriminatory fashion, the implicit annual tax which is borne by involuntary draftees Is given by the area EB'C'F or $175 million. Since the average active duty tour for a draftee is about 1.9 years, the total implicit tax for draftees in an age class is $333 million.

Each reluctant volunteer and draftee could, in principle, have been induced to enter active military service on a voluntary basis. The draft, however, compels some to serve while others are coerced to enlist at military pay scales, which are below their minimum supply prices. The difference between minimum supply price and current first-term pay is simply an implicit tax—the economic cost of active military service for reluctant service participants. A lower bound estimate of this cost (for those who serve in enlisted ranks) is derived from the area DC'F and is approximately equal to $826 million for reluctant participants in an age class.

The economic cost or implicit tax placed on men who were coerced to serve by the draft provides a lower bound estimate of the opportunity cost of acquiring enlisted men.

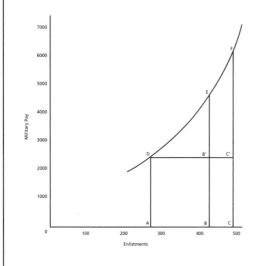

Walter Oi, "The Economic Cost of the Draft," *American Economic Review,* **Vol. 57, No. 2, May 1967, pp. 55–58—continued**

The estimates . . . are biased downward because the men who bear the cost are assumed to be those with the lowest supply prices in the absence of a draft. These estimates also neglect the rents that would have been paid to true volunteers in a competitive labor market. Under a draft, we not only tax the reluctant service participants but we also prevent true volunteers from collecting these rents. The full economic cost which includes these rents is estimated to be $5,364 million. . . .

Estimating a Supply Curve from the Underlying Economic Theory

The work of the 1964 Pentagon Draft Study was critical to the political debate during the late 1960s. It provided a counter to the Pentagon and the several commissions that studied the Selective Service System and its alternatives and their conclusions that an all-volunteer force was "unaffordable." The study's analysis, however, was far from robust when compared with estimates made only a few years later because, unlike later studies, Altman and Fechter's estimates did not include a wage variable, and their measures of draft pressure were taken from an independent survey rather than from a direct analysis of the effect of draft calls on enlistment.

Anthony Fisher provided a much-improved estimate in 1970, the basic form of which has become the "gold standard" for estimating military supply. As Benjamin Klotz noted in his review of Fisher's study, this was the "first attempt to derive a supply curve of military volunteers from an underlying economic theory" (Klotz, 1970, p. 970). In a 1970 article in the *American Economic Review,*[11] Fisher presented a model of an "individual decision to enlist" that can be estimated statistically. In Fisher's formulation, an individual decides to enlist in the absence of a draft by comparing two income streams, the "present value of volunteering" and the "present value of not volunteering" (Fisher, 1969, p. 240), where earnings include "nonpecuniary, or psychic, as well as pecuniary components" (Fisher, 1969, p. 241). For the first time anywhere, Fisher derived a true supply from a theoretically correct structural model rather than a "reduced form" statistical model. In the model, the dependant variable was the enlistment rate, and the independent variable was the log of the ratio of military wage to civilian alternative wages, corrected for the probability of being unemployed (Fisher, 1969, p. 244).

Fisher estimated the supply curve using quarterly time-series data from the third quarter of 1957 through the fourth quarter of 1965. He used enlistments in mental categories I to III for 17- to 20-year-olds to get around the identification problem and used population number as reported in the Current Population Survey. Quarterly data were generated by linear interpolation. His civilian earnings were "the median income

---

[11] Based on his 1968 doctoral dissertation from Columbia University under Gary Becker and Jacob Mincer.

of year round, full time male workers, age 14–19 and 20–24," weighted for the two years spent in the military. The unemployment rate was the rate for males aged 18 to 19 reported by the Bureau of Labor Statistics. He constructed a "draft pressure" variable based on draft calls rather than on the results of a survey. His results suggested that the "earnings elasticity at the mean enlistment rate (without a draft) is . . . 1.44" (Fisher, 1970, p. 981).

Anthony C. Fisher, "The Cost of the Draft and the Cost of Ending the Draft." *American Economic Review,* **Vol. 59, No. 3 (1970): 239–54**

I. A Model for the Supply of Enlisted Volunteers

Enlistment in the Absence of a Draft

The Individual Decision to Enlist. In deciding whether or not to enlist in the absence of a draft, an individual is deciding between the returns to enlistment and the returns to some (best) civilian alternative. If he enlists, he may expect to receive a stream of earnings in the military $W_{M1}, W_{M2} \ldots W_{Mn}$ over periods $1, 2, \ldots n$ respectively. If he does not enlist, his (best) alternative is a stream of earnings in the civilian economy $W_{C1}, W_{C2} \ldots W_{Cn}$. The returns to enlistment would be the present value of the sum over periods one to n of earnings in M (the military), and the returns to nonenlistment would be the present value of the sum of earnings in C (the civilian sector). In deciding whether or not to enlist, then, the individual compares the present value of volunteering

$$(1) \qquad V_M = \sum_{j=1}^{n} \frac{W_{Mj}}{(1+i)^j}$$

to the present value of not volunteering

$$(2) \qquad V_C = \sum_{j=1}^{n} \frac{W_{Cj}}{(1+i)^j}$$

Earnings in the discussion in principle include nonpecuniary, or psychic, as well as pecuniary components. The influence of the nonpecuniary on the supply of volunteers will be made explicit in the next section. At this point it is sufficient to think of it as included in the W_{Mj} and W_{Cj}.

Some modification of the present value stream V_M seems to be indicated by empirical considerations. Few servicemen reenlist, and fewer still remain in service for 20 years, the minimum necessary to qualify for a pension. V_M then becomes approximately . . .

$$\sum_{j=4}^{n} \frac{W_{MCj}}{(1+i)^j} \simeq \sum_{j=4}^{n} \frac{W_{Cj}}{(1+i)^j}$$

(T)he enlistment decision would be based on a comparison of

$$\sum_{j=1}^{3} \frac{W_{Mj}}{(1+i)^j} \text{ with } \sum_{j=1}^{3} \frac{W_{Cj}}{(1+i)^j} .$$

In comparing

$$\sum_{j} \frac{W_{Mj}}{(1+i)^j} \text{ and } \sum_{j} \frac{W_{Cj}}{(1+i)^j} ,$$

note that discounting is important only if the time patterns of returns in M and C differ significantly. In fact, earnings increased monotonically over the first three years in both sectors, providing some justification for neglecting discounting over the three-year enlistment period. If discounting can be neglected over the relatively short period, it is possible to simplify still further. The decision to enlist would then be based on a comparison of

$$W_M = \sum_{j=1}^{3} W_{Mj} \text{ and } W_C = \sum_{j=1}^{3} W_{Cj} ,$$

with enlistment taking place if $W_M > W_C$.

Anthony C. Fisher, "The Cost of the Draft and the Cost of Ending the Draft." *American Economic Review,* **Vol. 59, No. 3 (1970): 239–54—continued**

The Aggregate Enlistment Rate. The number of volunteers depends, therefore, on the distribution of civilian alternatives W_c.

Since W_c has been defined to include both money and psychic income, an individual can be said to enlist if $W_M > W_c + dW_c$, where W_M is redefined as money earnings in M, W_c as money earning in C, and d is a coefficient measuring the taste or relative preference for military service.

(30)

Enlistment with a Draft

In the preceding sections we have specified a model of the individual decision to enlist and the aggregate enlistment rate in a free labor market, i.e., in a market with no compulsory military service or draft system. In this section the draft in introduced as an additional determinant of the supply of volunteers for military service.

It is introduced explicitly through it's effect on expected earnings in the civilian economy, or more correctly, expected earnings associated with a decision not to enlist. It will be recalled that $\widetilde{W}_c{}^* = p_c \widetilde{W}_c$ has been defined as expected earnings in the civilian economy in the absence of a draft. But if some proportion of those who elect to remain in the civilian economy will be taken into the military, then expected earnings in the civilian economy are a weighted average of civilian and military earnings. The expected wage associated with a decision not to enlist may be represented as:

(18) $$\widetilde{W}_c{}' = p_c \widetilde{W}_c{}^* + p_d W_{M'},$$

a weighted average of expected civilian earnings $\widetilde{W}_c{}^*$ and military earnings W_M, the respective weights being p_c, the probability of remaining a civilian, and p_d, the probability of being taken into the military.

Time Series: Results

Results of the estimation of the parameters of equation (25) are presented, with some explanation, in equation (30) below.

$$\frac{E}{P} + .00751 - \underset{(.00324)}{.00709} \ln\left(\frac{\widetilde{W}_c}{W_M}\right)$$

$$- \underset{(.01018)}{.00891} \ln(1 - U)$$

$$- \underset{(.041)}{.312} \ln\left(1 - \frac{A}{P}\right)$$

$$- \underset{(.00069)}{.00133} SP + \underset{(.00065)}{.00254} SU$$

$$- \underset{(.00056)}{.00196} A \qquad R^2 = .90$$

(a) $\ln(\widetilde{W}_c/W_M)$ and $\ln(1 - U)$ are lagged one period.

(b) SP, SU, and A are seasonal dummy variables for spring, summer and autumn respectively.

(c) The figures in parentheses are standard errors.

. . .

A property of equation (25) noted earlier is that elasticity would be relatively large with a relatively small proportion of the population already enlisted, and relatively small with a relatively large proportion of the population already enlisted. Thus, elasticity of enlistments without a draft is (absolutely) larger $(-.74)$ than elasticity of enlistments with a draft $(-.46)$, since the proportion of the population enlisted is smaller.

. . .

Suppose the induction rate I/P is set equal to zero, its value if inductions were eliminated. The enlistment rate E/P in equation (38) is reduced by the amount of the term $[(-b_3/1 + b_3)(I/P)]$, which drops out of the equation. The average enlistment rate is 0.153 and the enlistment rate calculated from equation (38) (with $[(-b_3/1 + b_3)(I/P)] = 0$) is .0117, a reduction of about 24 percent.

This is less than perfectly consistent with the 38 percent reduction implied by the attitude survey. . . .

Anthony C. Fisher, "The Cost of the Draft and the Cost of Ending the Draft." *American Economic Review,* **Vol. 59, No. 3 (1970): 239–54—continued**

Attitude survey response is in general unreliable and may here lead to an overestimate of the effect of the draft on enlistments. Error typically accompanies the reporting even of items, such as consumer income, capable of exact evaluation and representation. It might be expected, then, that response to a subtle question of motivation, and for an action (the decision to enlist) taken perhaps several years prior to the time of the question, is likely to be still more subject to error, still less reliable. It is conceivable, for example, that the draft (as motivation for enlistment) represents a convenient catch-all or excuse. This would be especially true for those unable to realize original hopes or objectives in enlisting, a failure perhaps difficult to admit. (2) Prediction from a regression line is associated with increasing error as the difference between the projected value of the independent variable and its mean increases. Thus, the coefficient $-b_3/1 + b_3$ may reliably predict the effect on the enlistment rate of small movements around the mean induction, but not of a change of 100 percent (drop to zero) in the rate. Nothing is implied about the direction of error, but caution is suggested in interpreting the predicted enlistment rate. (3) While a drop to zero in the induction rate could be and has been interpreted as elimination of the service obligation, legal elimination might have a stronger effect on the enlistment rate. An induction rate equal to zero could leave some potential enlistees uninfluenced (at least for some time) by the draft, but others might prefer to persistence of the obligation.

References

Altman, Stuart H., "Earnings, Unemployment and the Supply of Enlisted Volunteers," *The Journal of Human Resources,* Vol. 4, No. 1, Winter 1969. S0801.pdf.

Altman, Stuart H., and Alan E. Fechter, "The Supply of Military Personnel in the Absence of a Draft," *The American Economic Review,* Vol. 57, No. 2, May 1967, pp. 19–31. S0232.pdf.

Baskir, Lawrence M., and William A. Strauss, *Chance and Circumstance: The Draft, the War, and the Vietnam Generation,* New York: Alfred A. Knopf, 1978.

Becker, G. S., *Human Capital: A Theoretical and Empirical Analyses, with Special Reference to Education,* New York: Columbia University Press, 1964.

Fisher, Anthony C., "The Cost of the Draft and the Cost of Ending the Draft," *The American Economic Review,* Vol. 59, No. 3, June 1969, pp. 239–254. S0192.pdf.

———, "The Cost of Ending the Draft: Reply," *The American Economic Review,* Vol. 60, No. 5, December 1970, pp. 979–983. S0234.pdf.

Friedman, Milton, "Discussion: Recruitment of Manpower Solely by Voluntary Means," in Sol Tax, ed., *The Draft: A Handbook of Facts and Alternatives,* Chicago: University of Chicago Press, 1967.

Hesburgh, Theodore M., "Foreword," in Lawrence M. Baskir and William A. Strauss, eds., *Chance and Circumstance: The Draft, the War, and the Vietnam Generation,* New York: Alfred A. Knopf, 1978.

Hildebrand, George H., Paul A. Weinstein, and Harold Wool, "Discussion," *The American Economic Review,* Vol. 57, No. 2, May 1967, pp. 63–70. S0229.pdf.

Hitch, Charles J., and Roland McKean, *The Economics of Defense in the Nuclear Age,* Cambridge, Mass.: Harvard University Press, 1960.

Klotz, Benjamin P., "The Cost of Ending the Draft: Comment," *The American Economic Review,* Vol. 60, No. 5, December 1970, pp. 970–978. S0230.pdf.

Lazear, Edward P., "A Jobs-Based Analysis of Labor Markets," *The American Economic Review,* Vol. 85, No. 2, May 1995, pp. 260–265.

Marshall, Alfred, *Principles of Economics,* 8th ed., New York: Macmillan and Co., 1920.

U.S. Congress, Statement of the Honorable Thomas D. Morris, Assistant Secretary of Defense (Manpower), hearing before the House Committee on Armed Services, Washington, D.C., U.S. Government Printing Office, June 30, 1966. S0273.pdf.

Moskos, Charles C., Jr., and Frank R. Wood, "Introduction," in Charles C. Moskos and Frank R. Wood, eds., *The Military: More Than Just a Job?* New York: Pergamon-Brassey's International Defense Publishers, Inc., 1988, pp. 3–14.

Oi, Walter Y., "The Cost and Implications of an All-Volunteer Force," in Sol Tax, ed., *The Draft: A Handbook of Facts and Alternatives,* Chicago: University of Chicago Press, 1967a, pp. 221–251.

———, "The Economic Cost of the Draft," *The American Economic Review,* Vol. 57, No. 2, May 1967b, pp. 39–62. S0236.pdf.

————, "Historical Perspectives on the All-Volunteer Force: The Rochester Connection," in Curtis L. Gilroy, J. Eric Fredland, Roger D. Little, and W. S. Sellman, ed., *Professionals on the Front Line: Two Decades of the All-Volunteer Force,* Washington, D.C.: Brassey's, 1996.

Weinstein, Paul A., "Discussion," *The American Economic Review,* Vol. 57, No. 2, May 1967, p. 66. S0229.pdf.

Wool, Harold, "Discussion," *The American Economic Review,* Vol. 57, No. 2, May 1967, pp. 63–70. S0229.pdf.

CHAPTER FOUR

The President's Commission on an All-Volunteer Armed Force—the Gates Commission—and Selective Service Reform (1969–1970)

> We unanimously believe that the nation's interest will be better served by an all-volunteer force, supported by an effective stand-by draft, than by a mixed force of volunteers and conscripts.
>
> —The Gates Commission[1]

Acting on a Campaign Promise

Richard Nixon was elected President on November 5, 1968. He immediately set up a transition team that included distinguished economist Arthur Burns, assisted by Martin Anderson.[2] Burns and Anderson were both from Columbia University and both had been part of Nixon's campaign organization. By one account, W. Allen Wallis,[3] President of the University of Rochester, approached Burns in December and reminded him of the President-elect's pledge to end the draft. According to Walter Oi, who had moved to the University of Rochester by then, this is what happened:

> Burns said that if Wallis could show how the draft could be abolished at an extra cost of no more than $1 billion in the first year, he would bring the matter before President-elect Nixon. When Wallis returned to Rochester on December 19, 1968, he called William H. Meckling, dean of the Graduate School of Management. Meckling quickly assembled a research team consisting of Martin J. Bailey, Harry J. Gilman, and Walter Oi. In the next ten days, this team prepared a short position paper that developed a plan to end conscription and outlined the steps needed to

---

[1] February 20, 1970 (Gates, 1970, p. iii).

[2] Friedman notes that "Nixon appointed Arthur [Burns] counselor to the president as a temporary post until he could appoint him chairman [of the Federal Reserve] the next year. Martin Anderson served as an assistant to [Burns]" (Friedman, 1998, p. 377).

[3] For Wallis's views on the draft and an all-volunteer force see his speech before the Rochester, New York, chapter of the American Legion, November 11, 1968, see Wallis (1976).

implement the plan. This paper, accompanied by a cover letter to Arthur Burns, was carried by a messenger to New York City on December 31, 1968. . . . When this plan was forwarded to Mr. Nixon's transition team on December 31, 1968, a decision was made to establish a presidential commission. It is Wallis's impression that the idea for a presidential commission came from Arthur Burns. (Oi, 1996, p. 44)[4]

Anderson's recollections are somewhat different. He recalls that he and Burns were charged to develop an action plan for the initial days of the new administration. Such efforts always start with a list of campaign promises (Anderson, 2001), and there was no more prominent a campaign promise for Nixon than to end conscription. On January 6, 1969, Burns sent their paper, *Suggestions for Early Action, Consideration or Pronouncements,* to the President-elect. The section of this report that deals with conscription started by noting that "one of your strongest pledges during the campaign was the eventual abolition of the draft" (Burns, 1969).[5]

Even before that, on December 24, 1968, Anderson wrote secretary-designate Melvin Laird to remind him of "President-Elect Nixon's . . . policy statements on an All Volunteer Armed Force [and asked for] any early reactions, however, tentative" (Anderson, 1968). Laird recalls "it was suggested in Key Biscayne, in the third week of December 1968, that a commission be set up to study the idea of an all volunteer force" (Laird, 2003a, p. 4).[6]

Five days after the inauguration (January 25, 1969), at a meeting of the National Security Council, President Nixon raised the issue of the Selective Service and the all-volunteer force. From this beginning, the two issues—moving to an all-volunteer force and reforming Selective Service—were tied together in a White House strategy that saw progress on both fronts as necessary and complementary, even though the all-volunteer force would negate the need for the draft. At this point in the new administration, it was not possible to see which military personnel procurement alternative, conscription or an all-volunteer force, would prevail. Reflecting this dual strategy, Nixon asked Laird for

---

[4] The Rochester group prepared four "working papers." A copy of the "Policy Options and Discussion" sent to Arthur Burns on December 31, 1968, was among the papers of former Secretary of Defense Melvin Laird archived at the Ford Presidential Library (Wallis et al., 1968). The cover letter and two other working papers—"Military Manpower Requirements: FY 1969–71" and "Force Reductions"—are in the archives of the University of Rochester. The working paper, "Military Pay Proposal for FY 1970," is apparently missing.

[5] While Burns's paper makes no reference to a paper from the University of Rochester, Wallis would be one of the members of the soon-to-be-established Presidential commission, and people from Rochester filled many key positions on the staff.

[6] Laird recalls that several alternatives were discussed at Key Biscayne, but

> those present . . . decided that this approach—an independent commission—was the best, particularly given the considerable opposition to the concept of all-volunteer service in the military, especially from the Joint Chiefs and the service secretaries. (Laird, 2003a, p. 5)

two papers relating to Selective Service. The first paper was to concern itself with the possibility of a transition to an all-volunteer Army, or Armed Forces. . . . The second paper was to provide . . . [Laird's] views on the draft. (Laird, 1969b)[7]

A Special Commission

Four days after the meeting of the National Security Council, Nixon directed Laird to "begin immediately to plan a special Commission to develop a detailed plan of action for ending the draft" (Nixon, 1969a). The commission was to report to Nixon by May 1, 1969. Laird was, however, not enthusiastic about a special commission. While he favored an all-volunteer force, he did not want to start with a special commission so early in the new administration. He was wary of the new White House and National Security Council teams and wanted time to get prepared before undertaking such a major effort, especially one that was as politically charged as ending the draft. In a memorandum back to Nixon, Laird suggested he had both good and bad news. The good news was that "the initial steps for moving towards this goal [of an all-volunteer force] are already underway." The bad news was that

> these initial steps, of themselves, make inappropriate at this time the establishment of a special Commission to develop a plan of action for ending the draft. In my judgment, such a Commission should begin its work later, after the Department of Defense has had the opportunity to work out and promulgate the absolutely vital measures now under review. . . . We call the plan I am proposing "Project Volunteer." (Laird, 1969a)

Laird concluded his reply to Nixon with a the final thought: "If you still feel that an outside commission should be announced prior to completion . . . [of the Pentagon study], please advise me and I will be pleased to submit a list [of] suggested members for the Commission" (Laird, 1969a).

Project Volunteer: Laird's Alternative to a Special Commission

When Laird got to the Pentagon, his inclination was to try to slow the rush to an all-volunteer force. It was not that he disagreed with Nixon on the goal of moving away from conscription; rather, he wanted to better position himself for the coming debate, and he thought that it would take a little time, given the more-pressing issues of the war in Vietnam. Fortunately, DoD was already gearing up for a new study of the

---

[7] The fact that there was a dual strategy at work was not lost on Congress, as noted by John Ford in his lecture to the cadets at West Point on November 25, 1980. See Ford (1980). After the 30th Anniversary Conference, Ford provided his personal recollection in a short paper, *Looking Back on the Termination of the Draft.* See Ford (2003). In the early 1970s, Ford was on the staff of the House Armed Services Committee, which took the lead on issues of selective service and the all-volunteer force. Ford would later become the committee's staff director.

feasibility of the all-volunteer force, and if Nixon agreed to wait for the results of that study, it would give him the time he needed to sort things out at the Pentagon.

The idea for the new study had taken hold the previous fall, before the election, when the chairman of the House Armed Services Committee, Congressman L. Mendel Rivers (D-North Carolina), asked the Pentagon if

> any current studies [were] being made by the Department of Defense on this [the all-volunteer force] subject [and any recent efforts by the Department] to provide new incentives to attract more volunteers for military service. (Rivers, 1968)[8]

Assistant Secretary of Defense (Manpower and Reserve Affairs) Alfred Fitt sent an extensive list of relevant projects to Rivers on October 2, 1968. These included economic studies of manpower supply, surveys of enlisted motivation, and Project 100,000 (Fitt, 1968a).[9] Two weeks later, Fitt wrote the chairman that he had decided to "initiate a more comprehensive planning study to systematically re-examine all possible ways to maximize the number of volunteers" (Fitt, 1968b). The fact there was to be a new study was reported in *The New York Times* within days, under the heading, "Pentagon is Re-examining Feasibility of an All-Volunteer Force to End Draft" (Beecher, 1968).

On October 4, 1968, Fitt told his colleagues at the Pentagon, the assistant secretaries of the military departments, of his intent to undertake a new, comprehensive study and that he had selected Harold Wool to head the "ad hoc planning group" (Fitt, 1968a).[10] Before the end of October, Wool provided a study plan and selected the title *Project Volunteer,* as he said, "in the absence of any convenient rubric" (Wool, 1968a). Given the outcome of the election, however, Wool suggested they make no "major commitments . . . pending discussions with representatives of the incoming Administration" (Wool, 1968b).[11]

After the change of administration, Fitt—still on the job until his replacement was confirmed—told Laird, the new Secretary of Defense, about the study.[12] Laird asked to

---

[8] Chairman Rivers noted that his committee had given "careful consideration" to the all-volunteer force during the hearings in 1966 and 1967 on reauthorizing the Selective Service Act, and found that

> the all-volunteer force concept . . . impracticable and, therefore, rejected by the Committee . . . and ultimately endorsed by the entire Congress. . . . there nonetheless continues to be substantial public interest . . . and interest manifested by many Members of Congress. (Rivers, 1968)

[9] Project 100,00 was a test program to see whether the military could use "men who were being disqualified for military service under previous mental standards and some men with physical defects which were correctable within a short period of time" (Greenberg, 1972).

[10] Wool was the Director of Procurement and General Research Policy and had helped Fitt prepare for the new study. He also worked on 1964 Pentagon Draft Study.

[11] Wool, however, was eager to get on with the long-lead-time research, particularly "one or more intensive motivational surveys among civilian youth, designed to elicit their military service plans and their responsiveness to various types of recruitment incentives" (Wool, 1968c).

[12] On January 11, 1969 Wool submitted to Fitt a revised plan, noting that "[n]one of the Services, however, have taken exception to the very comprehensive scope of the study plan . . . in fact, [they] provided mainly for inclusion of additional areas of study" (Wool, 1969).

see the study plan. Several days later, the same day Nixon signed his directive to Laird to "begin immediately to plan a special Commission to develop a detailed plan of action for ending the draft" (Nixon, 1969a), Fitt provided Laird a copy of the "Project Volunteer" study plan. In the accompanying memorandum (Fitt, 1969b), he took the position that "it would be far better for the President to direct you [Laird] to perform the study than to give the task to a Presidential Commission." He assured Laird that

> [i]nstitutionally we [DoD] prefer volunteers, for many reasons, and there is no bias here against (a) thorough, objective analysis, or (b) change. . . .
>
> If there must be a Presidential Commission . . . then I hope . . . [it will occur] after DOD has had a year or so to develop all the facts and its own recommendations. (Fitt, 1969b)[13]

President Nixon's memorandum of January 29, 1969, was sent to Fitt's office for "appropriate action." His staff prepared a draft of a memorandum to Laird that Fitt was "very much alarmed at the course of action directed by the President . . . on the subject of the all-volunteer force." It laid out in detail the current state of affairs and pressed the argument to slow "the President down a little bit on this incredibly important and complicated issue" (Fitt, 1969d). In the file, however, the draft memorandum is marked "NOT SENT." What was sent to Laird is not known, but the memorandum Laird signed and sent to Nixon followed the arguments Fitt had made when he sent him the study plan.

Nixon Acts

Laird's response to Nixon did not go over well with Nixon's senior staff. In a memorandum on "Secretary's Laird's answer to President's directive in regard to the All-Volunteer Armed Force," Anderson told Burns, "Secretary Laird has declined to comply with the President's request . . . " (Anderson, 1969b). He characterized Laird's plan as "unwise" and, while admitting that DoD's arguments had "merits," he told Burns he thought they were "not convincing." He prepared for Burns's consideration a draft of a response for the President to sign and suggested it be forward to Nixon (Anderson, 1969a)—the letter Nixon actually signed was slightly different from Anderson's draft but conveyed the same sentiments.

On February 6, 1969, Nixon "advised" Laird he wanted to go ahead with the outside commission. He congratulated him on the fact the department "has already taken the initial steps for moving toward an all-volunteer armed force . . . [and should] continue, at full speed, with the efforts you currently have underway" (Nixon, 1969b).

---

[13] The same day, in a separate note, Fitt warned Laird against

> economists at the Council of Economic Advisors who were fanatic opponents of the draft. . . .
>
> many economists have closed minds on the subject. . . .
>
> My concern is that the economists (whom I respect greatly as a general rule) with the President's ear do not stack the deck against a thoughtful, careful objective study of the problem. (Fitt, 1969a)

But, he said, these efforts made him "feel all the more strongly that the time has come to develop a detailed plan . . . [and that] . . . [such] a plan should be developed by an outside Commission." He also told Laird that the commission should "draw heavily on the experts in your department [and] [w]hen the special Commission reports to *me,* I will want you to review their work and give me your recommendations" (Nixon, 1969b, emphasis added). He again asked Laird for a list of names of people who might serve on the special commission. The next day, Laird provided his list. The first name on it was Thomas S. Gates, Jr.[14]

On March 27, the President announced the formation of a commission, under the leadership of former Secretary of Defense Thomas Gates, Jr. The commission was charged to "develop a comprehensive plan for eliminating conscription and moving toward an all-volunteer armed force" (Nixon, 1969c).

Setting Up the Commission

Great care was taken in choosing the commissioners. Anderson recalls that the White House decided not to "stack the deck" with commissioners all committed to an all-volunteer force. The reasoning was that a commission that contained a mix of people, including some who did not support the all-volunteer force, would be more creditable in the final analysis. In fact, the chairman of the commission that would forever bear his name, the Gates Commission, told Nixon that he was "opposed to the whole idea of a volunteer force." Nixon then told him that "that's exactly why I want you as the Chairman. . . . If you change your mind and think we should end the draft, then I'll know it is a good idea" (Anderson, 1991, p. 5).

If the commission was not "stacked" in numbers, it was, in Anderson's mind, stacked intellectually. As an advocate of the all-volunteer force, Anderson counted on the substantial powers of persuasion of economists Milton Friedman and Alan Greenspan to drive the commission to recommend the end of conscription (Anderson, 2001).[15] It was a calculated decision that proved correct. In fact, Friedman was able to deliver a unanimous recommendation in favor of an all-volunteer force.

The commission included a number of people who had already made their mark on the debate over the draft during the previous decade. Besides Milton Friedman, the commission included two other outspoken proponents of the all-volunteer force, H. Allen Wallis and Stephen Herbits. Herbits was the token "student" on the commis-

---

[14] Other names on the list, which can be found in Laird (1969c), included Allen Wallis, President of the University of Rochester, and William Meckling, also of Rochester. By the end of February, a tentative list of commissioners was available (Mack, 1969). The final list of commissioners was agreed to "at a meeting at the White House" on March 26, 1969 (Feulner, 1969).

[15] By 1969, Friedman had become a very public critic of the draft, testifying before Congress and pressing his views in his *Newsweek* column. In 1968, he wrote that the draft adds "to the strains on our society by using a method of manning our armed forces that is inequitable, wasteful and basically inconsistent with a free society" (Friedman, 1968b). In his *Newsweek* column on March 16, 1970, he noted that he "was much impressed by the emergence of unanimity out of initial disagreement" (Friedman, 1970b).

sion.[16] While he was a law student, he was also one of the principal architects of the influential 1967 congressional monograph, *How to End the Draft: The Case for an All-Volunteer Army.* In later years, as a staffer on the Hill, he shepherded the all-volunteer force legislation through Congress and eventually became the Pentagon's "special assistant" in charge of the all-volunteer force. The commission also included such notables as Father Theodore Hesburgh and Generals Alfred Gruenther and Lauris Norstad.

The research staff was drawn largely from the group that prepared the Rochester memorandum for Arthur Burns and from those who had worked on the 1964 Pentagon Draft Study. Notably, this included Walter Oi and Stuart Altman. The federally funded research and development centers that supported the Pentagon also provided staff: the Center for Naval Analyses, then a subsidiary of the University of Rochester; the Institute for Defense Analysis; and RAND. The Assistant Secretary of Defense for Systems Analysis (SA) and the Assistant Secretary of Defense for Manpower and Reserve Affairs (M&RA) were also told to cooperate.[17]

Selective Service Reform

The second subject Nixon raised at the National Security Council meeting of January 25, 1969, was reform of Selective Service. The new administration faced two issues: what reforms to initiate, given the long history of past commissions and failed efforts, and what to do about the controversial, 75-year-old, Director of Selective Service, Lieutenant General Lewis B. Hershey.

Laird Favors a Lottery

On February 3, 1969, as requested by the President, Laird laid out his views on reforming the draft. He saw the long-range answer to the problem as being the all-volunteer force. Since he had submitted his memorandum to the President concerning the best path to follow to get to at all-volunteer force and had not yet received Nixon's response, he reiterated that his study program constituted "an effective approach to the longer-term issues. In the meantime," he acknowledged that "we do have the short-term problem of resolving draft inequities and improving draft procedures" (Laird, 1969b).

Reflecting Fitt's assessment, Laird told Nixon that the basic problem was "we need to draft only about a quarter of the . . . fully qualified men in the draft-liable

---

[16] A number of Congressmen (Stafford, 1969) pressed to make Stephen Herbits a member of the commission. They told the President that

> [t]he exhaustive research effort which went into our analysis of the draft and potential avenues for change was undertaken by Stephen E. Herbits, whose expertise on current manpower systems and alternatives is extraordinary. (Stafford et al., 1969)

and sought to gain Secretary Laird's support for his appointment.

[17] *Author's Note:* At the time, I was a staff officer in the Manpower Requirements Directorate of the Office of the Assistant Secretary of Defense (SA). I was a member of the SA team that supported the Gates Commission.

manpower pool—and the figure will become only one in seven if and when we revert to pre-Vietnam strengths" (Laird, 1969b, p. 1).[18] He noted that both the Marshall and Clark commissions

> agreed on the general proposition that men should be exposed to the draft for 12 months at about their 20th year. If a man was not inducted, his draft liability should then end . . . except in emergency situations. . . .
>
> I believe that a reform of the draft selection system along these lines makes good sense and that you should support it. . . . In addition to this needed reform . . . I hope that when the time comes to select a new Selective Service Director, it will be possible for him to be a civilian. (Laird, 1969b, pp. 1, 3)

Even though key members of the White House staff considered reforming Selective Service as merely applying cosmetics to a system many "viewed as inequitable and capricious" (Rose, 1969), the legislative proposal Laird sent the Bureau of the Budget on March 4, 1969, which included the use of a lottery, drove the agenda.[19] It also set up a direct conflict between the Secretary of Defense and the Director of Selective Service. Laird told the President that

> General Hershey concur[red] in the draft reform bill, as restoring the broad authority of the President to determine the manner of selection for induction, and he suggested a technical addition with which we agree. However, his suggested revision . . . eliminates all references to lottery. It is not advisable to submit a bill to the Congress to reassert the President's broad authority without explaining that he intends to institute lottery selection. (Laird, 1969d)

The lottery issue, as proposed by Laird, was discussed at a Cabinet meeting on April 30, 1969 (Rose, 1969).[20] After the Cabinet meeting, the administration adopted Laird's position and the procedures recommended by the Burke Marshall commission in 1967 (Marshall, 1967). Nixon asked Congress on May 13, 1969, "to amend the

---

[18] Several days after the initial National Security Council meeting on January 25, 1969, Laird received a comprehensive review of the Selective Service problem from Fitt. Fitt told Laird that "the short term problem . . . [is] that the armed forces need only about half the fully qualified young men who turn 19 each year. . . . the figure will become only 1 in 7 . . . when we revert to pre-Vietnam strengths" (Fitt, 1969c).

[19] Anderson was one of the White House staffers who thought the move to a lottery was "cosmetic." He told Arthur Burns on March 3, "A move to a lottery draft system . . . may lull enough people into thinking that meaningful reform has been achieved, thus delaying effective action" (Anderson, 1969c).

[20] Anderson tried again to persuade Arthur Burns just days before the upcoming Cabinet meeting of scheduled for April 30, 1969. On April 24th, Anderson told Burns that the

> institution of a lottery would increase draft calls. . . . A lottery would tend to focus dissatisfaction with the draft on the White House, rather than diffusing it on many thousands of local draft boards. . . . A lottery is a cosmetic type of form that would not focus on fundamental problems. (Anderson, 1969e)

His concern that this was in conflict with the ongoing efforts of the Gates Commission, and that, "[we] should wait until they have finished their report before taking any action on this issue" (Anderson, 1969e) suggests that either he was not attuned to the dual strategy of working both the all-volunteer force and selective service reform issues simultaneously, or that following such a path had not been a conscious decision on the part of the administration.

Military Service Act of 1967, returning to the President the power, which he had prior to June 30, 1967, to modify call-up procedures" (Nixon, 1969d). In late June, John Ehrlichman, one of Nixon's most senior aides, asked Laird to report on "the status of the draft reform proposal" (Laird, 1969e). Laird responded that, "[s]ince General Hershey is responsible for administering the draft law, the draft reform legislation was actually forwarded to the Congress by Selective Service concurrent with the President's Message" (Laird, 1969e). Having said that, Laird told Ehrlichman he had already approached the two Armed Services Committee Chairmen, John Stennis (D-Mississippi) and L. Mendel Rivers, but they were noncommittal on when they might hold hearings.

At the end of August, Laird reported to Nixon that "Congress will not act on your draft reform legislation in this year without an all out campaign by the Administration" (Laird, 1969f). He pressed the President to consider moving forward by Executive Order.[21] The White House was desperate and considered launching "a new program to give the widest publicity to the President's program on the 19-year-old [lottery] draft" (Klein, 1969).

What to Do About General Hershey?

Just as Martin Anderson was the point man on the all-volunteer force, Peter Flanigan was the point man on Selective Service and dealing with General Hershey. By 1969, Hershey, who had held the job since 1940, had become a very controversial figure. Even before the administration took office, Congressman Donald Rumsfeld (R-Illinois) lobbied the transition team to replace Hershey: "it would be a terrible, terrible mistake if he were not replaced" (Rumsfeld, 1968). Laird felt the same way. He told the President that

> We have no control over, and no responsibility for, the policies and operations of Selective Service. Yet because it is run by a man who is technically on active duty as a Lieutenant General, most people think Selective Service is an arm of the Department of Defense. The Armed Forces have enough of an image problem as it is without being blamed for the wrongs or apparent wrongs of Selective Service. (Laird, 1969b)

On February 17, 1969, H. R. Haldeman conveyed Nixon's decision to replace Hershey to Peter Flanigan but was concerned about the political fallout and the need to "lay the ground work first by using our veterans groups to give us recommendations on a replacement" (Haldeman, 1969a). As Haldeman saw it, "The problems . . . will come . . . from the organized veterans groups, the draft boards, and the Congress; so it

---

[21] The "Executive Order" option had been developed by Assistant Secretary of Defense Roger Kelley (1969a). In September 1969, Laird reported to Nixon,

> General Hershey is initiating a pilot test in collaboration with Defense to define these procedures, to determine whether the system is fully workable and whether it can be made readily understandable to the public. . . . I believe these efforts will put us in a sound position to choose the most effective alternative in case we cannot obtain early congressional action. (Laird, 1969g)

is important to have it properly prepared before any action is taken" (Haldeman, 1969a).[22] In fact, it would take a year before Hershey was replaced.

The issue of what to do about Hershey dragged on through the spring and summer,[23] but by September, with the debate on Selective Service reform finally moving ahead and with Hershey's opposition to key features of the reform package,[24] it was becoming critical. Herb Klein, the White House Director of Communications, raised with Flanigan and Ehrlichman his concerns about replacing "Lewis Hershey so this doesn't come in the middle of . . . [the draft reform] campaign" (Klein, 1969). By early October, arrangements had been made for Hershey to step aside. As part of the arrangements, Hershey wanted the dignity of a meeting with the President.[25] At the meeting on October 10, 1969, Nixon thanked Hershey for his service and told the General how much he looked forward to his guidance in the future regarding matters of manpower mobilization (Flanigan, 1969c). After the meeting, the White House announced that, effective February 16, 1970—one day short of a year since Nixon made the decision to replace Hershey—Lieutenant General Lewis Hershey would be promoted to General and moved to a new position, "Advisor to the President on Manpower Mobilization, . . . [to] advise the President on a broad range of manpower mobilization problems" (White House Press Secretary, 1969a).

Push for Selective Service Reform

The renewed push for Selective Service reform started on September 19, 1969 with a statement from the Secretary of Defense on the draft. Laird started by noting the President's "decision to move forward through executive action to put into effect major portions of his draft proposals" (Laird, 1969h). The campaign had immediate results; a subcommittee of the House Armed Services Committee held hearings on September 30, 1969. With the movement in Congress, Flanigan was concerned that

> Secretary Laird's public statements may undermine the efforts to get lottery and "moving age" legislation through Congress by pledging the Administration to act

---

[22] Haldeman also reported that Nixon wanted the post "filled by a civilian rather than a military officer" (Haldeman, 1969a).

[23] During the spring, Haldeman, citing "the significance this will have in the youth community" (Haldeman, 1969b), was pressing Flanigan to "find out who can talk to Hershey and persuade him to submit his resignation now" (Haldeman, 1969b).

[24] Hershey wrote the President on September 3, 1969,

> Implementation of the so-called Mark Clark conveyor belt is far more complicated than would appear on its face and is extremely difficult of explanation to the point of acceptance by the public. While on its face it would appear a simple compression of the present method of calling people from age 19 to age 26 to age 19 to age 20, this very compression would multiply the present administrative difficulties and opportunities for legal action to the point they could seriously endanger the successful operation of the System. (Hershey, 1969a)

[25] In the preparation for the meeting, Flanigan told the President, "General Hershey requested the opportunity to meet with you prior to the announcement of his transfer from the post of Director of Selective Service" (Flanigan, 1969b).

by executive action . . . [a]nd commit the Administration to adoption of a "moving age" system that is, at best, untested and difficult to administer. (Lynn, 1969)

He recommended to the President that he direct Laird to curtail "additional public speculation concerning the adoption of an Executive Order . . . until Congress has been given a chance to act" (Lynn, 1969). In fact, Congress did act and passed H.R. 14001, An Act to Amend the Military Selective Service Act of 1967. President Nixon signed it into law on November 26, 1969, in a ceremony in the Roosevelt Room. At the signing the President said,

> As far as this draft reform bill is concerned, it does not remove all of the inequity of the draft, because there will be inequity as long as any of our young men have to serve when others do not have to serve. But the agony and suspense and uncertainty which has hung over our young generation for seven years can now be reduced to one year, and other very needed reforms in the draft can be made by Executive Order. (Nixon, 1969g)

Nixon singled out the DoD initiative and the bipartisan support in Congress and said he would not be "satisfied until we finally can have the system, which I advocated during the campaign of a completely volunteer system" (Nixon, 1969g). By proclamation, he directed

> [t]hat a random selection sequence will be established by a drawing to be conducted in Washington, D.C., on December 1, 1969 and will be applied nationwide. . . . The random selection sequence . . . shall determine the order of selection. . . . (Nixon, 1969f)[26]

The details were specified in an accompanying Executive Order (Nixon, 1969e).[27]

When the lottery was finally implemented on December 1, 1969, it was done the old-fashioned way, by drawing balls out of two bowls. Ignoring suggestions that the random selection be done by computer, Hershey insisted on using the same fishbowls that had been used in 1940 during the mobilization for World War II. The drawings were made from one bowl that contained letters of the alphabet and another that contained numbers from one to 366.[28] To the dismay of many in the White House, statisticians quickly determined that the results were not statistically random. The old method of hand drawing, rather than a more modern method employing computers, became a cliché for everything that was wrong with the Selective Service System;

---

[26] The results of the lottery were widely reported in the media. For example, one issue of *U.S. News & World Report* (1969) contained a "Clip Out and Save" display of the lottery results.

[27] A fact sheet was also prepared and distributed by the White House Press Office (White House Press Secretary, 1969b).

[28] The scene is described in Flynn (1985, p. 283).

Hershey could not even run a lottery without fouling things up. On December 26, 1969, Kissinger told Nixon that "the Selective Service's mismanagement of the lottery and the procedures by which it is applied have created serious problems in its implementation" (Kissinger, 1969b). Apparently, "the balls were placed in the jar in calendar order, . . . not random order [and] the stirring did not randomize the balls in the jar" (Kissinger, 1969b). In the eyes of the White House staff, a change in leadership at Selective Service could not come too quickly.

NSSM 78

By the fall of 1969, with the broad outline and procedures for Selective Service reform finally moving through Congress, the more-technical issue of specific deferment and exemption standards needed to be addressed. In October 1969, with the backing of Flanigan, National Security Advisor Henry Kissinger recommended that the National Security Council staff "undertake a 'low profile' review of Selective Service standard guidelines and procedures for deferments and exemptions" (Flanigan, 1969a). On October 8, 1969, National Security Study Memorandum (NSSM) 78 directed that a review of U.S. deferment and exemption policy take place (Kissinger, 1970a). The directive called for the study to be completed by December 1, 1969. Stephen Enke, a consultant from the General Electric Company's Center for Advanced Studies (also referred to as GE Tempo) was selected as the study director. Harold Wool from DoD and Professor Walter Oi from the Gates Commission and a number of other people from around the government assisted him. While two colonels from Selective Service were also asked to assist, General Hershey did not feel he had been adequately consulted, particularly not "informed of the nature of Dr. Enke's report" (Hershey, 1969b).

On December 18, 1969, Enke's *Draft Review of Deferments and Exemptions from Selective Service (NSSM 78)* was circulated among government agencies to solicit comments so that a final revision might be prepared for submission to the President on January 16, 1970 (Enke, 1969).[29] During the comment period, Kissinger told Nixon that "this review has pointed out several serious shortcomings in the operation of the new draft lottery system." Besides the fact that "the random process developed by the Selective Service for use in the lottery was not random" (Kissinger, 1969b), Enke found that the

> certainty granted by having an assigned order of call has been reduced greatly by the wide disparities among the procedures of local boards . . . [and] treatment of deferred persons under the new lottery system, because all eligible registrants were assigned a permanent rank of call in the first lottery. (Kissinger, 1969b)

---

[29] DoD's comments on the draft report were sent to Kissinger on January 19, 1970 (Laird, 1970a). Laird's recommendations were incorporated in the final version except for two points dealing with student deferments (Kelley, 1970a). Enke prepared summary comments and forwarded them to Selective Service and the White House staff (Enke, 1970a). Enke also prepared a draft of a memorandum for the President and sent it to John Court of the National Security Council and Jonathan Rose and Martin Anderson of the White House (Enke, 1970b).

Nixon was particularly concerned that

registrants with relatively late lottery sequence numbers may be drafted by some boards ahead of registrants with earlier sequence numbers, because physical examinations have not been completed for some with early sequence numbers. (Flanigan, 1970a)

He directed Flanigan to get General Hershey to adjust procedures. The President wanted "to prevent the development of dramatic and unnecessary disparities in the sequence numbers of those called throughout the country in a particular month," Flanigan told Hershey (Flanigan, 1970a). Hershey was less than cooperative. As Flanigan's staff saw it, Hershey was

out of sympathy . . . with our efforts to implement the lottery program in a rational manner. . . . Hershey has been most reluctant to give us the information required to figure out where the problem is, and what size of call the System could meet without reaching some ridiculously high sequence number this early in the year. Apparently the good General prefers a filibuster to hard facts. (Rose, 1970)[30]

Hershey might be able to stonewall the White House, but he could not delay his departure from Selective Service. On February 16, 1970, as scheduled, Hershey left Selective Service, and Colonel Dee Ingold was designated Acting Director of Selective Service (Flanigan, 1970b) and (Nixon, 1970a).[31] Several weeks later, Flanigan, still distressed by the random sequence number problem, told Ingold "to place strong emphasis on the timely preinduction physical examination of registrants with low sequence numbers" (Flanigan, 1970e).

What Flanigan had not appreciated was the depth of Hershey's rejection of the underlying concept of random selection and a direct national order of call. As far as Hershey was concerned, the new procedures went against everything he knew was responsible for Selective Service's success since 1940. In his new capacity as the Manpower Mobilization Advisor to the President, Hershey tried once more to change the direction of the administration. In a paper prepared for the National Security Council meeting of March 25, 1970 Hershey told Nixon:

---

[30] *Author's Note:* On March 2, 1970, the new Acting Director, Colonel Dee Ingold, explained to Flanigan that "[r]evival of support for the frequently reviewed proposal to compute fixed calls at a central point for all 4,100 local boards suggests the advisability of reassessing some of the arguments in opposition" (Ingold, 1970). He still concluded it would not be advisable to have a single national call. In 1980, when I was Director of Selective Service, the procedures I put into place provided for a single national order of call. If Selective Service were activated today, it would operate with a single national order of call.

[31] In the Washington fashion, Hershey's move out of Selective Service became irreversible the next night—Tuesday, February 17, 1970—when President Nixon hosted a dinner at the White House in honor of the General and Mrs. Hershey. Those attending included the civilian and military leadership of the federal government and members of the Gates Commission (White House Staff, 1970). The Army Chief of Staff, General William Westmoreland, told the President how he and the other military leaders appreciated the dinner for Hershey, a man they all admired for "his dedication, integrity and steadfastness over the years" (Westmoreland, 1970).

I recommend that the staff of the White House refrain from attempting a day to day supervision which inevitably results in interference with the operation of the Selective Service System. . . .

I recommend strongly against any adoption of centralization, ignoring of states, and centralizing power here that have been heretofore delegated to the states and to the communities.

The strength of the Selective Service System has been in the individual's acceptance of responsibilities by Governors and by local board members with local board areas. This must not be tampered with in the name of equity, in the name of machine operation, or some other thing except understanding and ability to devise some other system which can replace one which has heretofore been able under all circumstances, difficult and otherwise, to carry out its function. (Hershey, 1970a, pp. 2, 3)

He argued that the White House had "completely misunderstood the purpose that Congress intended in restoring to the President his former powers." The present system was a "perversion," he told the President, that ignored "the clear letter and intent of Congress to use the sequence only in determining priority within the local boards and not nationally" (Hershey, 1970a, pp. 2–3). Finally, to the heart of the NSSM 78 issue, he recommended that the President take no actions until Congress abolished or restricted student deferments.

On March 30, 1970, he again wrote Nixon to press his case:

I repeat my recommendation that unless and until the Congress legislates on the student deferment, the President refrain from issuing an Executive Order removing deferment from registrants in the field of education, occupation, or dependency. (Hershey, 1970b)

A decade later, everything that Hershey had rejected was included in the Selective Service Revitalization Plan of 1981.[32]

Selecting a New Director of Selective Service

With Hershey gone, Flanigan focused on finalizing the nomination of his replacement and getting him confirmed. The leading candidate—Charles DiBona, President of the Center for Naval Analyses (CNA)—was, however, running into trouble in the Senate. The Chairman of the Committee, Senator Stennis, told Ken BeLieu of the White House:

I like him personally but if he doesn't tone down his remarks about the all-volunteer army he can torpedo the Draft, the Committee and the President. It's probably just a lack of experience, but all he needed to say is I follow the President on the all-

---

[32] *Author's Note:* I developed that plan when I was President Carter's Director of Selective Service. It was not until I reviewed the material for this book that I realized that the system I put in place was so antithetical to the one Hershey had built. This help explains the hostility I received from several of the "old guard." The design I implemented, however, stands today.

volunteer army. He brought up the all-volunteer army when he should have confined his remarks to Draft problems and need for its extension. (BeLieu, 1970a)[33]

The center of the opposition came from Senator Margaret Chase Smith (R-Maine). She told BeLieu, "I doubt very much if I could agree to him at this time because I think he opposes the draft. I'm disturbed because of his outright championing of the volunteer army before facts are in" (BeLieu, 1970a). She had made the connection between CNA, the University of Rochester, the Gates Commission, and the All-Volunteer Force.[34] The final blow came when Senator Barry Goldwater (R-Arizona) told BeLieu six senators would "[join] Senator Smith against DiBona" (BeLieu, 1970b). The President withdrew DiBona's nomination.

With DiBona out of the way, a new search started for Hershey's replacement. Laird weighed in, initially suggesting that the Assistant Secretary of the Army for Manpower and Reserve Affairs, William K. Brehm, should be considered. He quickly withdrew the recommendation when the Secretary of the Army, Stan Resor, objected, saying he needed Brehm at the Pentagon (Wallace, 1970). Next up was Curtis Tarr, the Assistant Secretary of the Air Force for Manpower and Reserve Affairs. Tarr had been considered early in the search but said that he preferred to stay with the Air Force. Now, with DiBona's withdrawal, he became the leading candidate. Nixon approved his nomination on March 2, 1970, when Flanigan told Nixon that Tarr's "experience as a university president, a vice president of a manufacturing company and a Republican candidate for Congress make him uniquely qualified both to meet the congressional objections and to handle the job." Tarr's only request was a "few minutes with you [the President] so that you can express the importance of, and your interest in, his taking over the Selective Service System at this difficult moment" (Flanigan, 1970c). On March 4, 1970, the President met with Tarr.[35] On March 10, 1970, the President was advised that "All necessary checks have been completed," and on March 12, 1970, the Press Office released the "intent to nominate" press notice (White House Press Secretary, 1970b). His nomination "sailed through" the Senate Armed Services Committee on March 18, 1970, with no dissenting votes (Bullen, 1970).

---

[33] *Author's Note:* I had the same experience with Senator Stennis in 1979, except the issue came up before my confirmation hearing. At the actual hearing, I ducked all questions on the volunteer force and answered only questions about the draft. The *Army Times* headline after my confirmation hearing was "Draft System Nominee Ducks All-Vol Question."

[34] On January 30, 1969, David J. Callard and Chairman Gates visited Senator Stennis and Ed Brasswell, Stennis' senior aide, to "inform the Senator of the Commission's progress." After the meeting, he visited with Senator Smith for about 30 minutes. Callard noted that Senator Smith

> had no particular questions to ask about the Commission's work. She was extremely interested in the Center for Naval Analyses, of which Charles DiBona is President. She seems to know that CNA has done a considerable amount of work for the Commission, and she showed keen interest in exactly what CNA had done. (Callard, 1970a)

[35] Flanigan's "talking points" for President Nixon provide some insight on how the Nixon White House was managed (Flanigan, 1970d).

Whether by design or, more likely, by happenstance and with Tarr in place and NSSM 78 completed, the issues of draft reform and the all-volunteer force merged again as they had at the first National Security Council meeting on January 25, 1969.[36] Tarr played a prominent role at the National Security Council meeting on March 25, 1970, leading that portion of the discussions that dealt with Selective Service reform. The outcome of that meeting was incorporated in Nixon's address to Congress on April 23, 1970, which covered both the issues of the all-volunteer force and draft reform (Nixon, 1969a). In the meantime, with the "credibility of the President's lottery program in large part rest[ing] upon a successful solution to the problems of quotas and calls," Tarr was told to "correct any existing difficulties with as little public fanfare as possible" (Flanigan, 1970f).[37] He reorganized Selective Service National Headquarters (White House Press Secretary, 1970b) and, the following October, sent Nixon "a short report on our progress and some of our problems" (Tarr, 1970b, p. 1). He acknowledged that

> the random selection system . . .was not operating as well as its proponents hoped that it would . . . . One of my first decisions was to hold each State Director responsible for providing not only those inductees requested in the ensuing months, but also to make up for his early shortages. . . .
>
> By the end of August we had eliminated completely our shortages. (Tarr, 1970b, p. 2)

Addressing one of the critical problems, the unevenness in sequence numbers called, he told the President that

> [t]his year we do not expect to exceed random selection number 195 anywhere in the United States. . . .
>
> Thus your Administration has fulfilled the desiderata set forth when random selection was adopted last fall. (Tarr, 1970b, p. 2)

The Gates Commission

Parallel to the workings of Selective Service reform, the Gates Commission was formed, did its work and reported to the President. At the outset, as an indication of the importance of the commission to the administration, Anderson suggested to the President

---

[36] On February 10, 1970, Stephen Enke, working for the National Security Council, prepared and circulated an outline "of some alternative 'scenarios,' integrating interim draft reform into the larger goal of the AVAF" (Enke, 1970c).

[37] There were even suggestions from Congress that "the President or the Selective Service Director appoint a three-man board of high level 'mathematicians' to recommend a fair and equitable selection procedure" (Baroody, 1970). Tarr was concerned because, as he told the Assistant Chief Counsel of the House Armed Services Committee,

> we have assurances from statisticians that it is not possible to get a truly random selection . . . from some kind of mechanical drawing [and] . . . the reservation[s] the average American has . . . [if] we might substitute a computer or a table of random numbers. (Tarr, 1970a)

that the first meeting of the commission be held in the White House. Nixon agreed, and the first meeting was scheduled for the Roosevelt Room on Thursday, May 15, 1969. The meeting was to start at 9:30 a.m., with the President to "drop-by at approximately 10:15 a.m." (Anderson, 1969d).

The tone for the Gates Commission was set at the first meeting, when Crawford Greenewalt asked the chairman "whether the Commission was obligated to recommend an all-volunteer force plan." He was told "it was not necessary for the Commission members to assume at the outset that an all-volunteer solution was either feasible or desirable." Greenewalt replied that "his only concern was that he be free to reject the all-volunteer solution" (President's Commission on an All-Volunteer Armed Force [Gates Commission], 1969).

While there was initial skepticism on the part of the noneconomists on the commission about the arguments that had been honed during the previous years of debate, the views expounded on by the economists who had taken part in the earlier debate prevailed.[38] Lee, citing the transcripts of the commission's public sessions, noted that Chairman Gates questioned the "hidden tax" argument

> on the grounds that it was difficult to understand and involved "fairly esoteric reasoning." Some members thought it was politically unrealistic to advocate an All-Volunteer Force on the grounds that it would involve no increase in true economic costs, since both Congress and the public would think in terms of the increase in budgetary expense and taxes that might be required if the draft were eliminated.[39]
>
> Mr. Greenewalt thought that the burden of combat in a volunteer force would fall upon "the poor and the black" and that there was something immoral about seducing them to die for their country with offers of higher pay.
>
> General Norstad . . . felt that elimination of the draft could mean that people with better education and backgrounds would not enlist and the Military Services would be less effective as a result. (Lee and Parker, 1977, p. 43)

By December 1969, after the commissioners reviewed the staff papers that had been prepared for them, they came together in the unanimous recommendation that the nation's interests would be better served by an all-volunteer force.[40] The commission argued in their February 1970 report that

---

[38] A more-complete discussion of the deliberations of the commission can be found in Witherspoon (1993, pp. 343–365).

[39] Oi recalled that the "conscription tax" argument was "drummed into the heads of the commission members" (Oi, 1996, p. 45) by the economists.

[40] It is noteworthy that this Presidential commission did its work without holding public hearings. The prevailing view seemed to be that "hearings would only impede the staff and Commission's work, and delay the submission of a report to the President" (Callard, 1969a). David Callard, the commission's administrator, expressed his concern to Martin Anderson that "The Commission's failure to solicit public opinion vigorously on a very important and sensitive issue is all the more glaring in view of the President's sincere interest in generating more public participation in the governmental process" (Callard, 1969a). Nevertheless, this was one commission that did its work behind closed doors.

The United States has relied throughout its history on a voluntary armed force except during major wars and since 1948. A return to an all-volunteer force will strengthen our freedoms . . . . It is the system for maintaining standing forces that minimizes government interference with the freedom of the individual to determine his own life in accord with his values.

The often-ignored fact . . . is that our present armed forces are made up predominantly of volunteers. . . .

Reasonable improvements in pay and benefits in the early years of service should increase the number of volunteers by these amounts. . . .

In any event, such improvements are called for on the ground of equity alone. Because conscription has been used to provide raw recruits, the pay of men entering the services has been kept at a very low level. It has not risen nearly as rapidly as the pay of experienced military personnel, and it is now about 60 percent of comparable civilian pay. Similarly, the pay of first-term officers has not been kept in line with the pay of more experienced officers, or with comparable civilians. . . .

If the Commission's recommendations are put into effect for fiscal 1971, they will entail a budget increase of an estimated $3.3 billion. . . . (Gates, 1970, pp. 6–7)

Commission's Review and Rejection of Arguments Against an All-Volunteer Force

In reaching their recommendation, the commissioners reviewed and dismissed the major arguments that had been put forward by opponents of an all-volunteer force. Table 4.1 shows the arguments and the counterarguments cited in the commission's February 1970 report.

The commission's recommendation to move to an all-volunteer force echoed the arguments that had been heard at the University of Chicago Conference on the Draft in 1966. First, as the commission put it, "conscription is a tax." They found the tax to be inequitable and regressive. They argued that a full accounting for the true cost of the draft meant that, even given the higher budget costs of an all-volunteer force, a mixed system of volunteers and conscripts was more costly to society than an all-volunteer force. Second, by not accounting for the true cost of the labor the DoD employed, the armed forces were "inefficient" and were wasting society's resources.

Conscription is a Tax. The role of the conscription tax in arguing for an all-volunteer force was so central to the commission's conclusion that they devoted a whole chapter— Chapter 3—to presenting their argument. They invoked Benjamin Franklin's writings on the impressing of American sailors to ask if it was "just . . . that the richer . . . should compel the poorer to fight for them and their properties for such wages as they think fit to allow, and punish them if they refuse?" The importance of this argument was highlighted, as the final report notes:

> This shift in tax burden lies at the heart of resistance on "cost" grounds to an all-volunteer armed force. Indeed, this shift in tax burden explains how conscription gets enacted in the first place. In a political democracy conscription offers the general public an opportunity to impose a disproportionate share of defense costs on a minority of the population. (Gates, 1970, p. 25)

Table 4.1
Resolution by the Gates Commission of Arguments Against an All-Volunteer Force

Arguments Against an All-Volunteer Force	Findings by the Gates Commission
An all-volunteer force would be very costly— so costly the nation cannot afford it.	Although the budget for a volunteer armed force will be higher than that for a mixed force (volunteers and conscripts), the actual cost will be lower. This is not really a paradox because many of the costs of manning our armed forces are not reflected in the budget. Men who are forced to serve at artificially low pay are actually paying a form of tax, which subsidizes those who do not serve. Furthermore, the output of the civilian economy is lower because more men serve in the military than necessary for an all-volunteer force of the same strength.
An all-volunteer force would not be flexible enough to expand rapidly for a sudden crisis.	A standby draft could be put into effect promptly if circumstances required mobilization of large numbers of men.
An all-volunteer force would undermine patriotism by weakening the tradition that each citizen has a moral responsibility to serve his country.	Compelling service through a draft undermines respect for government by forcing an individual to serve when and how the government decides, regardless of his own values and talents.
Draftees guard against the growth of a separate military ethos.	The existing loyalties and political influence of the force cannot be materially changed by eliminating conscription in the lowest ranks.
The higher pay for a voluntary force will appeal especially to blacks, who have fewer civilian opportunities.	Ending conscription will not fundamentally change the composition of the armed force; further, denying such opportunities would be seen as either bias or a paternalism, as though blacks are not capable of making the "right" decisions about their lives.
An all-volunteer force would consist of mercenaries.	Mercenaries are men who enlist for pay and nothing else, usually in the service of a foreign power. Those who volunteer for the armed forces do so many reasons, including a sense of duty. Moreover, we do not consider career commissioned and noncommissioned officers to be mercenaries.
It will stimulate foreign military adventures.	The President can always increase enlistments, through a standby draft and calling up reserves under an all-volunteer force, or by increasing draft calls under conscription.
The all-volunteer force will be less effective because highly qualified youths will be unlikely to enlist or to make the military a career.	A force of men who have freely chosen to serve should enhance the dignity and prestige of the military. Every man in uniform would be serving as a matter of choice rather than coercion.

NOTE: The table paraphrases points made in the commission report.

The report followed Oi's argument, originally presented in the 1966 papers given at the University of Chicago Conference (Oi, 1967b) and the annual meeting of the American Economic Association (Oi, 1967a). The commission accepted the estimate of the lost wages that draftees could have earned in their best civilian alternatives—estimated to be $2 billion—as their measure of the conscription tax. They added to that the income forgone by volunteers who did not get the benefit of the wage rate that would be required to attract the marginal volunteer. This was estimated at an additional $1.5 billion.[41]

Specifically, the commissioners noted,

> This concept of the tax does not include the income loss suffered by true volunteers whose military compensation is held below the level which would be required to maintain an all-volunteer force, nor does it include the amount by which all-volunteer pay rates would exceed the pay levels at which some of the current draftees and draft-induced enlistees would enter on a voluntary basis. (Gates, 1970, p. 26)

To these costs, a new category was added to reflect the experience of the Vietnam War draft. These were the costs that prospective inductees incurred to escape conscription, which manifested themselves in a variety of ways, such as additional college attendance, movement into occupations that carry deferments, immigration, etc. The commission recognized that

> The fact that conscription imposes a tax is not in itself immoral and undesirable. Taxes are required to enable government to exist. What is of questionable morality is the discriminatory form that this implicit tax takes, and even more, the abridgement of individual freedom that is involved in collecting it.
>   The tax is discriminatory because the first-term servicemen who pay it constitute a small proportion of the total population. . . . The extent of the discrimination resulting from conscription depends on the proportion of the population forced to serve, and on the level of compensation provided to those who serve. . . . In addition to being discriminatory, conscription as a tax is also generally regressive, falling on individuals whose income is low. (Gates, 1970, pp. 27–28)

The argument concerning the discriminatory nature of the "conscription tax" not only swayed the commission, it also proved critical when Congress debated the commission's recommendations. Lee noted that

> It was also important that the Administration spokesmen separated the issue of military compensation from the more controversial issues of the draft extension, the war in Vietnam, and the [all-]volunteer force. Though increased compensation was the main tool for achieving the volunteer force, the Administration supported the pay raise primarily on the grounds of equity and fairness, and was thus able to draw nearly universal support for increased compensation from both sides of the AVF [All-Volunteer Force] draft issue and the war issue. Administration witnesses

---

[41] Economists refer to this category of lost income as "economic rent."

frequently argued that competitive pay was a sound policy because it was intrinsically fair, rather than because it would obtain more voluntary enlistments. (Lee and Parker, 1977, p. 98)

The Draft Misallocates the Nation's Resources. Besides the issue of the "conscription tax," the commission argued that an all-volunteer force would be a more effective force than a mix of volunteers and conscripts. As the commission saw it,

[c]onscription induces the military services to use manpower inefficiently. They make manpower decisions on the basis of the costs as they perceive them, namely, those that are reflected in their budget. (Gates, 1970, p. 29)

The commissioners projected that

[w]hen military compensation is raised to a level consistent with an all-volunteer armed force, the services will find it desirable to economize on manpower. In particular, they will discover ways to substitute non-human resources for manpower in a wide variety of activities. (Gates, 1970, p. 30)

They also projected that

[p]ersonnel turnover in an all-volunteer force will be reduced for several reasons. If the draft is continued, it is projected that about 42 percent of accessions into the Army (for a force of 2.5 million men) will be draftees who serve for only two years, compared with three and four-year tours for voluntary enlistments. Moreover, the re-enlistment rates of draftees and draft-motivated volunteers are considerably lower than those of men who voluntarily choose military service. . . . Our projections indicate that, by 1980, 45 percent of Army enlisted men will have four years or more of service experience, as compared with 31 percent for a mixed force of the same size. (Gates, 1970, pp. 40–41)

The Standby Draft

The commission saw a standby draft as an integral part of an all-volunteer force. In their report, the members explicitly cited "[t]he rationale for providing a standby draft is the possible urgent need for the nation to act quickly" (Gates, 1970, p. 120). The commission understood, however, that "a standby draft will not supply effective military forces in [the beginning] . . . [but would] provide manpower resources for the second stage of expansion" (Gates, 1970, p. 120). They believed a standby system that authorized the President to invoke the draft at his discretion could lead to adventurism on the part of the President. Because of the issue of personal freedom and inequities inherent in conscription, invocation of a draft should require congressional approval.

The commission did not have specific recommendations concerning how a standby system might be organized or managed, except that the authority to conscript should be held by Congress. The organization of the Selective Service System and its ability to implement a standby draft would, however, become a significant issue later in the decade. The failure of the administration to develop a feasible standby draft would be one argument that the opponents of the all-volunteer force would use to return to conscription.

Means of Achieving an All-Volunteer Force

Although the commissioners argued that "[p]ay is not the only, and perhaps not even the primary motivating force for joining or remaining in the military services" and recommended "a number of changes in military manpower procurement and management practices to improve the non-monetary conditions of military life and thereby help increase the attractiveness of military careers" (Gates, 1970, p. 49), their clear emphasis was on increasing first-term pay.

Views on Compensation. As the commission saw it,

> [m]ilitary compensation in the early years of service is now so low that it will not sustain an all-volunteer force of the quality desired. Until that condition is corrected, an all-volunteer force cannot be realized. (Gates, 1970, p. 49)

At the heart of their recommendations was the research done by their staff. In the final report, the commission noted that it had

> used several methods to estimate directly the effect of increases in first and second term pay on voluntary enlistments and re-enlistments. Based on these studies, and on the observed impact on retention of proficiency pay and the variable re-enlistment bonus, we estimate that a 10 percent increase in the current value of first-term regular military compensation will result in an increase of about 12.5 percent in the voluntary enlistment rate from the 17 to 21 year old civilian population. In the case of the Army, a 40 percent pay raise would increase the voluntary enlistment rate from about 1.388 to about 2.079 per 100 men in the 17 to 21 age cohort. The same percentage increase in officer compensation will induce a roughly comparable rise in the voluntary enlistment rate from the college population. (Gates, 1970, p. 56)

Besides an across-the-board increase in first-term pay, the commission called for skill differentials and hostile-fire pay. The skill differentials were to "attract some persons with special skills or unusual aptitudes" (Gates, 1970, p. 60). The hostile-duty pay was "a matter of equity . . . [and would] provide compensation flexibility in conflict situations" (Gates, 1970, p. 61).

Views on "Compensation in Kind" and "Fringe Benefits." One of the most important decisions made by the commission was to endorse the

> development of a military salary system comparable to that in the civilian sector, including the substitution of cash for some benefits that are now provided in-kind, and the modification of the present retirement system, including the introduction of vesting. (Gates, 1970, p. 56)

As far as it went, this was consistent with the recommendations for structural reform that came out of the First Quadrennial Review of Military Compensation, a study lead by Navy Rear Admiral Lester Hubbell (Hubbell, 1967). This was predictable, given the underlying bias of the economists on the commission and their staff. The commission accepted the argument that

[p]roviding compensation in cash has an inherent advantage in that . . . it allows each individual to decide how he or she will use whatever he earns. He can thus get the full value of whatever costs are incurred by the government in paying him. When he is compensated in non-cash form, however, the value of what he receives is often less to him than its cost to the government. (Gates, 1970, p. 63)

The problem, however, was that the Hubbell recommendations were for a salary system for the career force only, with first-term personnel continuing to be covered by a pay and allowance system. The low pay for first-term personnel that the Hubbell system also recommended had assumed the continuation of the draft and was out of step with the transition to an all-volunteer force. As a result, the administration withdrew support for the Hubbell salary system, and a unique opportunity to transform military compensation was lost. While a number of commissions have proposed over the past 30 years converting the military to a salary system, the military has never implemented such a system. Steadfast opposition to a salary system from the enlisted leadership of the services has replaced the support the concept enjoyed in the late 1960s.[42] The military continues to use a "pay and allowances" system where "compensation-in-kind" is a significant part of total remuneration.

In practice, military leaders charged with managing the transition to an all-volunteer force had to work within the existing system of pay and allowances. They tried to develop a balanced program. Unlike the commission, the services recommended that funds be provided to improve benefits and income-in-kind. In fact, over time, billions of dollars would be spent to improve the quality of life of service members and their families as an inducement to enlist or reenlist in the military. It can be debated whether or nor this was the most efficient use of resources. What cannot be debated, however, was the commission's decision "against recommending general increases in . . . benefits or in income-in-kind items of pay" (Gates, 1970, p. 63). This placed it at odds with those charged with implementing the commission's recommendations. For example, the program "to improve the conditions of military service" that the commission recommended was much smaller than the program the services had recommended. The commission's notion of "improving the conditions of military service and the quality of military life" to attract and retain "higher quality personnel" (Gates, 1970, p. 64) was limited to the following:

---

[42] For example see the statements of support from the Army (Resor, 1969), Navy (Chafee, 1969), Air Force (Brown, 1969) and Joint Chiefs of Staff (McConnell, 1969).

- "elimination of the present system of obligated terms of service so that enlisted personnel would be recruited and retained on the same basis as commissioned officers" (Gates, 1970, p. 64)
- "expansion of the current program whereby enlistees are permitted to specify their choice of occupation as a condition of enlistment" (Gates, 1970, p. 65)
- expansion of the "entitlement to reimbursement of family travel expense and dislocation allowance . . . to all enlisted personnel" (Gates, 1970, p. 67)

Views on Recruiting. Anticipating what would become a sustained theme over the next thirty years, the commission recognized the importance of recruiters.[43] In their report they noted that

> [s]tudies indicate that a relatively small increase in recruiting expenditures would produce as much as a 10 to 20 percent rise in enlistment rates. . . . Clearly, elimination of the draft will increase the need for effective recruiting and the budget required. (Gates, 1970, pp. 83–84)

The commission understood that managing recruiters would demand new concepts; for example, "successful recruiters should be allowed to extend their tours of duty, while the unsuccessful are assigned elsewhere" (Gates, 1970, p. 85). The commission also anticipated the need for an "improved incentive system for recruiters" and the

> elimination of the present system under which each district, city and individual recruiter receives an enlistment quota. Substantial evidence indicates that this system eliminates the incentive to seek enlistees in excess of one's quota. (Gates, 1970, p. 85)

In what would prove to be an understatement, the commission felt "[m]ore advertising in mass media will be both required and rewarding" (Gates, 1970, p. 85). Over time, advertising became the most-flexible tool that personnel managers had in supporting the all-volunteer force.

Areas of Concern

The commission recognized that in two areas of concern, they were not sanguine that they knew how they would meet the manpower needs of the armed forces without conscription. But, as the commission saw it, "there is time not only for further study, but for experimentation" (Gates, 1970, p. 87). The areas of concern were physicians and reserves.

Physicians. The critical need for physicians and the central role the draft played in making sure that the military services had the physicians they required was illustrated by data presented in the final report. According to the commission, "[e]ighty percent of

---

[43] The commission staff prepared a review of recruiter productivity based on commissioned studies done for the Assistant Secretary of Defense (Manpower) by Marcom Economics, Inc. (See Kemp, 1970).

all male physicians in the United States under 35 have served in the armed forces or have held reserve commissions" (Gates, 1970, p. 87). Even more impressive, "[o]nly four percent of male physicians under 35 who are eligible for service have not yet served" (Gates, 1970, p. 87). The commissioners understood that, "[i]f the draft is eliminated, dramatic action will be required to insure the continuation of health care now provided by the military medical system" (Gates, 1970, p. 90). They recommended both reducing the demand for military physicians through civilianization, e.g., using civilian doctors to treat military personnel and their dependants on military bases, and increasing the remuneration of military physicians. Anticipating a program that would be very effective over the coming years, the commission focused on "[a] variety of forms of subsidies to medical students." This would eventually include the scholarship programs at civilian medical schools (Gates, 1970, p. 93) and the creation of DoD's own medical school, the Uniformed Services University of the Health Sciences.

Reserve Forces. Citing survey results that showed that "perhaps 75 percent of the enlisted personnel fulfilling their initial six-year military service obligation in the reserves are there only because of the draft" (Gates, 1970, p. 97), the commission identified the reserves as a "special . . . problem." The commission thought the problem could be significantly reduced by eliminating

> approximately 113,000 men in paid drill status ("spaces") without significantly affecting reserve effectiveness. . . .
> [S]hortfalls from present levels in the reserves are *not* a serious threat to national security. (Gates, 1970, p. 100, emphasis in the original)

Again, anticipating research that would come later in the 1970s (Shishko and Rostker, 1976), the commission argued that the reserves had the potential to be a significant "part-time" job. Without the formal analysis of the economics of moonlighting, the commission noted that

> [t]he prospect of securing volunteers for reserve service is surely related to pay levels. All too often it is said that drill pay is nearly irrelevant to a young man deciding whether to devote free time to unit activity. Yet almost one-third of men with less than six years of service describe drill pay as one of the most significant factors in their decision. . . .
> [While drill pay] is not a large amount compared to total family earnings . . . the more meaningful economic comparison is with part-time employment alternatives. . . . The typical E4 . . . closely resembles the Department of Labor's portrait of the typical multiple jobholder—"a comparatively young married man with children who feels a financial squeeze." . . .
> [A] necessary if not sufficient condition for voluntary reserve participation is a level of drill pay attractive enough to make military instruction preferable to other part-time activities. (Gates, 1970, p. 102)

The commission also understood that, because of the Vietnam War (and the related ease the reserves had had in attracting draft-induced, non–prior service volunteers), the personnel profiles of the reserve components was skewed in favor of new recruits. The reserve components did not try to attract personnel who were leaving active service,[44] and their own reenlistment rates were pitifully low. The commission noted that, between 1962 and 1969, over 4.8 million men left active service, while reserve components recruited "fewer than 900,000 of them into paid drill status" (Gates, 1970, p. 110). The reserve components reported a reenlistment rate during these years of 7.2 percent. The commission suggested that, by focusing on prior service personnel and reenlistments and with a pay elasticity of 1.25, "the projected enlistments appear to be adequate for the reserve forces associated with the 2.25 million force and 2.5 million man active forces" (Gates, 1970, p. 116).

The Gates Commission Finishes Its Work

Within the Gates Commission, not only had there been unanimity that the nation should move toward an all-volunteer force, but they all agreed on how it should be done. However, DoD had formed its own options on the best way to achieve an all-volunteer force. As the Gates Commission proceeded to "prebrief" the services on their emerging recommendation, it became clear that the commissioners' views were different from those prevailing in the Pentagon. The Gates Commission, while saying that "[p]ay is not the only, and perhaps not even the primary motivating force for joining or remaining in the military services" (Gates, 1970, p. 49), emphasized programs to "increase . . . military compensation . . . required to sustain an all-volunteer force" (Gates, 1970, p. 50). Assistant Secretary of Defense Roger Kelley's staff thought that changes in personnel management practices were the way to implement the all-volunteer force.

In August 1969, in response to a request for comments on proposals being considered by the commission staff, Kelley told Harry Gilman, the commission's Director of Military Manpower, Supply, and Compensation, that DoD objected to the use of pay differential and bonuses (Kelley, 1969b). After the commission's vote in December, Gates tried to persuade senior members of DoD to go along with the commission. On the evening of January 9, 1970, over dinner, he privately discussed the commission's recommendations with Secretary of the Army Stanley Resor and his Assistant Secretary for Manpower, Bill Brehm. Resor had been well prepared by his staff and told Gates of the Army's concerns, both "the more technical aspects of the staff analysis upon which cost estimates and hence feasibility ultimately will be based . . . [and some] qualitative points" (Resor, 1970). Clearly, the Army had the details of the commission's recommendations and methodologies before the meeting because, the next day, Resor sent Gates a substantial paper detailing the Army's concerns and raising questions about the commission's methodologies. Resor ended the paper by telling Gates "I hope you will

---

[44] In FY 1970, of the 105,172 first-term airmen who separated from the regular Air Force, only 289 joined the Air Reserves Forces—the Air National Guard and the Air Force Reserve (Rostker, 1973, p. 36).

give serious thought to these questions in your deliberation. We have at stake both the security of the nation, and how we shape its future" (Resor, 1970). Resor and the Army, however, were not the only opposition the commission would face.

The Gates Commission Reports to the President

On February 21, 1970, the Gates Commission forwarded its recommendation to end conscription to President Nixon. The commission unanimously found the cost of an all-volunteer force was "a necessary price of defending our peace and security [and that conscription was] . . . intolerable when there is an alternative consistent with our basic national values" (Gates, 1970, p. 10). The commission made three recommendations to the President for implementing an all-volunteer force: (1) raise military pay, (2) improve the conditions of military service and recruiting, and (3) establish a standby draft system by June 30, 1971.

With Kissinger's backing, Anderson suggested the President meet with the commission to formally receive the final report in person, since "members of the Commission, most of them of great distinction, can be extremely helpful—if they are properly motivated" (Anderson, 1970c).[45] On February 21, 1970, the President met with the commissioners in the Cabinet Room (Figure 4.1).[46] Anderson recalled that the President spent 90 minutes with the commissioners rather than the planned 30 minutes:

> While . . . [he] did not commit himself to my specific recommendations . . . he did express enthusiasm and sympathy for an all-volunteer force, making the point that even a reformed draft is unfair, i.e. some go, some do not go. (Anderson, 1970h)

Following the meeting with the President, the White House Press Office released a summary of the Presidential commission's report on an all-volunteer armed force (White House Press Secretary, 1970c).[47] The commission had designed, and the White House had agreed to, a public-relations campaign that included a private printing of

---

[45] Anderson had provided Kissinger with a summary of the commission's findings, noting that they had "concluded that the armed forces including reserve forces, can and should be raised by voluntary means" (Anderson, 1970e). Kissinger's only concern was to "ensure that this meeting is not over-publicized and that the President's remarks are not interpreted as a public endorsement of the Commission's findings" (Kissinger, 1970a). Anderson provided an attendance list (Anderson, 1970f).

Several options for the meeting were presented to Nixon, who personally decided on 30 minutes with a "photo opportunity" (Chapin, 1970a).

[46] At Laird's request, the meeting was moved from Friday, February 20, to Saturday, February 21, 1970, to avoid congressional questions on Friday (Chapin, 1970b). Anderson prepared a set of talking points for the President (Anderson, 1970g).

[47] The White House Press Office also prepared the transcript of a press conference involving Thomas S. Gates, Chairman, Presidential Commission on All-Volunteer Armed Forces; members of the commission; Dr. Martin Anderson, Special Assistant to the President; and Ronald L. Ziegler, Press Secretary to the President (Gates et al., 1970).

Figure 4.1
The President's Commission on an All-Volunteer Force meeting with President Nixon in the Cabinet Room on Saturday, February 21, 1970, together with Martin Anderson's "Memorandum for the President's Files" describing the meeting (Anderson, 1970h).

SOURCE: National Archives.

THE WHITE HOUSE
WASHINGTON
February 21, 1970

MEMORANDUM FOR THE PRESIDENT'S FILE

FROM: Martin Anderson

SUBJECT: Meeting with the President's Commission on
               An All-Volunteer Armed Force

On Saturday, February 21, 1970 at 11:00 A.M. the President met
with his Commission on An All-Volunteer Armed Force in the
Cabinet Room. Those present at the meeting were:

Commission Members	Commission Staff	White House Staff
Thomas Gates	William Meckling	Martin Anderson
Thomas Curtis	Stuart Altman	Ron Ziegler
Frederick Dent	David Callard	
Alan Greenspan	Harry J. Gilman	
Gen. Alfred Gruenther	David Kassing	
Stephen Herbits	Walter Y. Oi	
Fr. Theodore Hesburgh		
Jerome Holland		
John Kemper		
Jeanne L. Noble		
W. Allen Wallis		

At the beginning of the meeting there was a brief "photo opportunity."
Thomas S. Gates, the Chairman of the Commission, then made a
short statement and presented the President with a bound copy of the
report.

Instead of the planned 30 minutes the President spent 90 minutes
discussing the implications of moving, and not moving, toward an
all-volunteer armed force with the members of the Commission.

While the President did not commit himself to any specific recommendations of the Commission he did express enthusiasm and sympathy for an
all-volunteer force, making the point that even a reformed draft is
unfair, ie. some go, some do not go.

-2-

The President made the point that if the members of the Commission,
most of whom were opposed or neutral to the idea of a volunteer force
when they began their deliberations, could unanimously recommend
such a course and change their views, then the country can change
its views.

At the end of the meeting he requested that a massive educational
campaign be started. A copy of the Commission's report, accompanied
by a letter from Thomas Gates, the Chairman of the Commission, is
to be sent to the top "movers and shakers" -- educators, media people,
heads of voluntary organizations, etc. -- in the country. He wants
thoughtful people to "read the report and become convinced."

the report by the Macmillan Company, with an initial press run of 100,000 in paperback and 5,000 to 7,000 in hardback, with distribution of the paperback copies starting on March 6, 1970 (Callard, 1970b).[48]

Laird's Turn

Now, as promised, it was Laird's turn to opine on the subject.[49] While he would not oppose the basic contention and recommendations of the commission, he took exception to a move to an all-volunteer force by June 30, 1971, and made no attempt to hide his position from the public.[50] On March 11, 1970, he wrote the President to formally "endorse" the basic conclusion of the report.[51] In a subtle but meaningful turn of phrase, he suggested that "the main emphasis should be on reducing draft calls to zero rather than achieving an All-Volunteer Force, even though the objective of each is identical" (Laird, 1970d). Anticipating the strategy that would work in Congress, he explained that it would "be easier to reach your objective by focusing public attention on eliminating the draft rather than stirring those who object to the concept of an All-Volunteer Force" (Laird, 1970d). Accordingly, the following October, he established

---

[48] The commission had considered a number of publishing alternatives but had wanted to "contract a paperback book distribution" in addition to the standard press run from the Government Printing Office (Callard, 1969b). Even before the report had been presented to the President, the White House agreed to have it published as a paperback (Anderson, 1969f).

[49] Kelley had provided DoD's informal comments to Martin Anderson on February 27, 1970 (Kelley, 1970b).

[50] On January 29, 1970, Laird met with the 1970 Senate Youth Program Group. In answering a question on the volunteer force, he expresses some concern about whether "we have the kind of support presently in the Congress for the additional funding that would be necessary" to move to an all-volunteer force (Laird, 1970b, p. 5). The following day, the *Washington Post* carried a headline: "Laird Dim on Prospects for All-Volunteer Army" (Wilson, 1970). Anderson was concerned that "statements like Laird's undercut the President in an important policy area." In a memorandum to John Ehrlichman, Anderson recommended that Laird "be reminded of the President's policy and instructed to support that policy until it is changed" (Anderson, 1970b). The record does not show who, if anyone, was so bold as to "instruct" Secretary Laird on this point. Moreover, on March 2, 1970, Laird received from the Systems Analysis office an assessment that supported his judgment that the demands the war in Vietnam made on the Pentagon would have to come down before the country could move to an all-volunteer force:

> With a 20% first term pay increase, we expect modest enlistment surpluses in all Services by FY 73. . . . In summary, all-volunteer Service is a viable goal. . . . It is not practical during FY 71, would be difficult in FY 72, but will be feasible . . . in FY 73. (OASD[SA], 1970a)

Making his position on when to move to an all-volunteer force public resulted in a sharp exchange of letters with commissioner Milton Friedman (see Friedman, 1970a). Laird replied, assuring Friedman that he supported the objectives of the all-volunteer force but that it could not be achieved by mid-1971 because of the "well known budget strictures for FY 1971" (see Laird, 1970c). Laird also wrote Senator Stennis expressing his "deep concerns and strong opposition" to ending conscription on July 1, 1971. He told the Chairman: "I am convinced that military manpower needs will require the continuation of the draft beyond this date. . . . To fix the date of July 1, 1971 . . . needlessly endanger[s] our national security" (Laird, 1970e).

[51] Two weeks earlier (February 27, 1970), Kelley had sent Anderson a memorandum that summarized "major DoD observations about the All-Volunteer Armed Force which result from our discussions and the report of the President's Commission" (Kelley, 1970c).

"the goal of zero draft calls by the end of FY 1973" (Laird, 1970f). His final words, however, were cautionary:

> The Administration cannot be placed in the position of having to reduce forces below National Security Council recommendations because it has acted too soon in taking irreversible steps to eliminate the draft. (Laird, 1970d, p. 6)

The President Has Decided . . .

Martin Anderson was given the job of preparing an issue paper for the President incorporating the views of the Gates Commission and DoD, the National Security Council, the Bureau of the Budget, and other interested administration parties.[52] He had very little time to do it, especially since the paper needed to be a joint project, combining the results of the working group on draft reform, which Peter Flanigan chaired, and the results of the working group on the all-volunteer force, which Anderson chaired (Anderson, 1970m).[53] While the original plan had "a decision memorandum . . . ready for the President by February 23, 1970 to anticipate a possible message [to Congress] in the third week of March 1970" (Anderson, 1970), the issue was not taken up by the President until March 25, 1970, at a special meeting of the National Security Council.

In preparation for the March 25, 1970, meeting, Kissinger's staff prepared a "red book" (with backup materials) for the President. It contained "a brief summary of the issues and alternatives prepared by Peter Flanigan and Martin Anderson, [and] Secretary Laird's views on the all-volunteer army and draft reform," e.g., Laird's March 11, 1970 Memorandum (Kissinger, 1970b). At the meeting, Nixon made several critical decisions. He rejected the recommendation of the Gates Commission to end the draft June 30, 1971, noting that it "can't be done," and changed the target date for ending the draft to January 1973 (Kissinger, 1970b).[54] After the March 25, 1970, meeting, Anderson prepared a decision memorandum on an all-volunteer force and draft reform

---

[52] This issue paper went through a number of drafts: March 2, 1970 (Anderson, 1970i); March 17, 1970 (Anderson, 1970j) and (Anderson, 1970k); March 20, 1970 (OASD[M&RA], 1970a); March 22, 1970 (OASD[SA], 1970b); March 23, 1979 (Davis, 1970); and March 25, 1970 (OASD[M&RA], 1970b).

Kelley laid out the "tight timetable" in his memorandum of March 3, 1970 (1970d).

[53] The first meeting of Anderson's Task Force on All-Volunteer Armed Force was held on February 7, 1970, well before the commission briefed the President (Anderson, 1970d). On March 2, 1970, Bill Meckling, the Staff Director of the Gates Commission, shared with Anderson that they were confronting "three types of uncertainty . . . in planning the transition to an All-Volunteer Force" (Meckling, 1970).

[54] The following day, March 26, 1970, the Budget Director, Robert Mayo, was still pressing for the lowest-budget option. He told Nixon, "this approach affords a reasonable possibility of ending draft calls early in FY 1973 without the major budgetary problems created by all the other options with their emphasis on FY 1972 or earlier expenditures" (Mayo, 1970).

Figure 4.2
President Nixon's Decisions About the All-Volunteer Force

THE WHITE HOUSE
WASHINGTON

April 9, 1970

MEMORANDUM FOR

HENRY KISSINGER
MARTIN ANDERSON
JOHN EHRLICHMAN
BILL TIMMONS
PETER FLANIGAN

The President has decided the following regarding the All-Volunteer Army and Draft Reform:

1. We should move toward reducing draft calls and achieving an all-volunteer force with the following provisos:

   (a) We cannot spend the additional $3.4 billion in FY 1971 recommended by the Gates Commission.

   (b) We should emphasize to Congress and the public that our goal is to reduce draft calls to zero.

   (c) We must not commit ourselves to a timetable for ending the draft that we cannot achieve.

   (d) We must get the draft renewed on July 1, 1971, if we expect our foreign policy to be credible.

   Within this framework, he agrees that the following steps should be taken to reduce draft calls over the next few years:

   --- During FY 1971, a $300 million (20 percent) increase in first term military pay should be made to demonstrate our tangible commitment to the zero draft objective.

   --- During FY 1972, a large commitment of funds ($2 billion) should be made toward substantially reducing draft calls.

   --- During FY 1973, a larger expenditure ($3.5 billion) should be made in the expectation that draft calls could be ended between July 1972 and July 1973.

- 2 -

2. He has approved the following on draft reform:

   (a) Request Congress to amend the law to permit Selective Service to induct men according to their random sequence number. In effect this would provide what the public has expected from the draft lottery system - that those with lottery number one will be drafted before those with lottery number two, etc.

   (b) Request Congress to amend the Military Service Act to restore discretionary authority over undergraduate student deferments to the President. Then issue an Executive Order providing that those college students, who do not now hold II-S deferments, would not be granted such deferments in the future.

   (c) Continue to bar graduate student deferments except for students in medical and allied fields, for which DOD foresees a special draft call.

   (d) Issue an Executive Order phasing out occupational, agricultural, and paternity deferments -- except in case of "hardship." A man not now holding one of these deferments would not be granted that deferment in the future.

3. The President has decided he will take action independent of the Congress in issuing an executive order to phase out occupational, agricultural and paternity deferments. He will request Congress to permit student deferments to be phased out at the same time.

4. The President wants to hold action on the following until next year:

   (a) Extension of the draft.

   (b) Request for a stand-by draft.

   (c) Doctor's Draft.

KEN COLE

cc: Jim Keogh
     Jeb Magruder
     Bryce Harlow
     H. R. Haldeman
     Ron Ziegler

SOURCE: Cole (1970).

that incorporated the results of the meeting and sent it to John Ehrlichman on March 31, 1970 (Anderson, 1970m).[55] On April 9, 1969, Ken Cole reported to the White House senior staff the President's decision.[56] Figure 4.2 shows Cole's memorandum reporting Nixon's decision.

It fell to Kelley to tell Laird of the President's decisions. His memorandum to Laird did not, however, stress the "provisos" which started Cole's memorandum to the White House staff. Kelly summed it up by saying that

---

[55] Anderson's decision memorandum records that the meeting took place on March 24, 1970, although the documents prepared for the meeting state that it was to take place on March 25, 1970. Subsequently, on April 14, 1970, the National Security Advisor, Dr. Henry Kissinger, published National Security Decision Memorandum (NSDM) number 53, which recorded Nixon's decisions. "Pertinent extracts" were provided the senior staff at the Pentagon on April 17, 1970 (ASD[ISA], 1970).

[56] In 1968, Cole was director of scheduling for Richard Nixon's successful presidential campaign. Immediately after the election, Cole worked in the presidential transition office at the Pierre Hotel in New York City. On President Nixon's Inauguration in 1969, Cole became staff secretary, reporting to H. R. Haldeman, Chief of Staff. In 1970, Cole became Deputy Assistant to the President and coordinated the activities of the Domestic Council for the Presidential Domestic Assistant John Ehrlichman and for Melvin Laird, Ehrlichman's successor. On Laird's departure from the White House, Cole was appointed Assistant to the President and Head of the Domestic Council. Cole continued leading the Domestic Council when President Ford assumed the presidency. During his time of service, he headed the Governors' Council and the White House Fellows Program among other duties.

The President has decided as follows:

1. He accepted the DoD plan for eliminating draft calls.
2. He defers extension of induction authority, doctor draft and related matters until next year.
3. He will go ahead now with an Executive Order to phase out occupational and paternity deferments.
4. He will recommend to Congress legislation to institute a direct national call and authority to phase out student deferments.

The President's message to Congress on the above will probably be next week. (Kelley, 1970e)

The President Addresses Congress

Even before the President had settled on a course of action, work went forward to craft the speech he would deliver to Congress. On January 10, 1970, Martin Anderson got the process started with a memorandum to the Deputy Assistant to the President, Ken Cole (Anderson, 1970a). On March 5, 1970, presidential speechwriter Pat Buchanan checked in with Anderson, telling him he had "been detailed to handle the Volunteer Army Message" (Buchanan, 1970). When the message was circulated for comment in early April, there was still one remaining pocket of opposition at the White House, President's Nixon's "new" Advisor to the President on Manpower Mobilization, General Hershey. With the President's decision before him, Hershey tried one last time to get Nixon to change his mind. He told the President that the "presumption that the national security can be maintained by armed forces provided by added pay incentives is based on hopes that have not been sustained by the history of the United States." He was particularly concerned, "The message gives encouragement to those who desire to be relieved from obligations of military service" (Hershey, 1970c, p. 1). Notwithstanding General Hershey's misgivings, Nixon sent the message to Congress on April 23, 1970.

The special address outlined the phased implementation of the Gates Commission's recommendations. On top of an already-approved 6-percent pay raise for all federal employees, Nixon asked Congress to approve a 20-percent pay increase for enlisted men with less than two years of service, as Laird had suggested. He promised an additional $2.0 billion the next fiscal year (FY 1972) "to help attract and retain the personnel we need for our Armed Forces" (Nixon, 1970b). Nixon also directed Laird to expand programs designed to increase enlistments and retention. Following Laird's recommendation, he did not endorse the move to an all-volunteer force by June 30, 1971.[57] Citing our "responsibilities in Vietnam and our overall foreign policy," Nixon

---

[57] Tarr favored a four-year extension, as noted in OASD[M&RA] (1971).

said that "no one can predict with precision whether or not, or precisely when, we can end conscription . . ." but also said that he was "confident that, barring any unforeseen development this proposed program will achieve our objective [of ending the draft]" (Nixon, 1970b).

He noted that the current authority to induct draftees into the armed services expired on July 1, 1971, and called on Congress to extend this authority. Nixon also called on Congress to implement a number of reforms to "deal with the draft as it now exists." He moved to phase out—not immediately eliminate—the system of deferments. He told Congress that, by executive order, he would direct that "no future deferments . . . be granted on the basis of employment . . . [or] paternity" (Nixon, 1970b). He asked Congress to restore his authority to control student deferments. Nixon also radically changed the system by which young men were called into service. He asked Congress to suspend the quota system in favor of a national random-selection system. He also committed himself, once these measures were approved, to "authorize the Selective Service System to establish a plan under which the draft call each month will be on a national basis, with the same lottery sequence number called throughout the country" (Nixon, 1970b).[58]

As had occurred the year before with Selective Service reform, there was a delay before Congress agreed to start hearings on the President's proposals. In fact, nothing happened during the remainder of 1970. In an end-of-year memorandum, eight months after the President's speech, Laird told Kissinger that he believed the Senate Armed Services Committee would hold hearings "as early as February 1 [1971], on the extension of Selective Service induction authority and other amendments to the Selective Service Act" (Laird, 1970h) and pressed his view on that and other related issues. In fact, in early January 1971, the White House got the same message from Chairman Stennis, who expressed his "desire for a prompt and firm Administration position on all items related to draft legislation" (Rose, 1971). By late January, Laird could report to Kissinger that

> Senator Stennis . . . has scheduled early hearings on extension of induction authority under the Selective Service Act and on other matters related to the Administration's plan to move toward an All-Volunteer Armed Force. I will be the first witness on Tuesday, February 2, 1971. (Laird, 1971a)

Laird also actively engaged with the chairman of the House Armed Services Committee. In what he would later describe as a "private agreement," Laird agreed with committee chairman F. Edward Hebert (D-Louisiana) that DoD would withdraw its

---

[58] The President also asked Laird "to give high priority to the expansion of programs to increase enlistments and retention in the Services and to report every quarter on the progress . . ." (Laird, 1971b).

opposition to the Military Medical School he had been trying to get through Congress in exchange for the his promise to move the draft legislation (Laird, 2003b).[59]

On January 28, 1971, President Nixon sent a second message to Congress "to move toward an all-volunteer force" (Nixon, 1971b) and to fund the transition program as part of the FY 1972 budget.[60] He proposed

> an additional $1.5 billion in making military service more attractive to present and potential members, with most of this to be used to provide a pay raise for enlisted men with less than two years of service, effective May 1, 1971. . . .
>
> [O]ne-fifth of the additional 1.5 billion [would] be devoted to expanding our efforts in the areas of recruiting, medical scholarships, ROTC, improvement of housing, and other programs to enhance the quality of military life. (Nixon, 1971b, p. 2)

He also told Congress that he had directed the Secretary of Defense to "recommend . . . such further additions to military compensation as may be necessary to make the financial rewards of military life fully competitive with those in the civilian sector" (Lee and Parker, 1977, p. 89). Again noting that "[n]o one knows precisely when we can end conscription," Nixon asked Congress to extend induction authority until July 1, 1973, and promised that "[w]e shall make every endeavor to reduce draft calls to zero by this time."

Congress Moves to End Conscription and Reform Selective Service

Reactions to President Nixon's messages were mixed both across the country and in Congress.[61] John Ford, member of the House Armed Services Committee's professional

---

[59] Laird not only withdrew is opposition but actively lobbied Elliot Richardson (Laird, 1970g), Secretary of Health, Education, and Welfare, to support the idea of a "National University of the Health Sciences." Richardson did not agree and told Laird that "HEW's earlier position should not be modified at this time" (Richardson, 1970). Louis M. Rousselot, Deputy Assistant Secretary of Defense for Health and Environment and a major proponent of the idea within the Pentagon, provided his boss, Roger Kelley, and, later, Martin Anderson at the White House with an assessment that could be used to rebut Richardson's opposition (Rousselot, 1971a) (Rousselot, 1971b). By early February, Anderson had drafted an "options paper" for the President (Anderson, 1971). Laird remembers that, in the end,

> the President told me to do what I thought best, and I testified for the medical university before Congress. The medical university was built in Bethesda, and the all-volunteer force sailed through the House Armed Services Committee—an example of how the consensus-building process sometimes worked. (Laird, 2003b)

[60] The day after the President's address, Deputy Secretary of Defense David Packard submitted proposed legislation "to make military pay more equitable" in a letter to the Speaker of the House of Representatives (Packard, 1971).

[61] To get a sense of the nation's take, DoD had assessed the reactions of 55 major news commentators.

> Forty-seven percent (26) favored the administration's plan. Thirty-three percent (18) were strongly opposed to establishing an all-volunteer force. Twenty percent (11) were strongly opposed to any further extension of the draft and wished to establish an all-volunteer force immediately. (Annunziata, 1971)

staff at the time and later its staff director, reflected years later on the mood of the committee in 1971. In 1980, he told cadets at West Point that some committee members had opposed the all-volunteer force, remembering the failure of the all-volunteer force in 1948, and that "some of the older ones . . . [had a] bias in favor of the draft . . . [and] great skepticism . . . that an all-volunteer force would work" (Ford, 1980).

This issue cut across traditional lines and made strange bedfellows.[62] Some in Congress who favored the all-volunteer force wanted to move forward on the timetable suggested by the Gates Commission and end conscription by July 1, 1971. Others favored the two-year extension requested by the President. Some liberals, like Senator Ted Kennedy (D-Massachusetts), thought that "a volunteer force during wartime would be mercenary, composed of the poor, black, and uneducated" (Lee and Parker, 1977, p. 96). Some conservatives, like Senator John Stennis, thought that a volunteer force was "a flight from reality." On the other side of the issue, liberals like Senator Mike Mansfield (D-Montana) and conservatives like Senator Barry Goldwater found common ground in supporting the abolition of the draft. The immediate issue was the extension of induction authority to accompany a pay increase for new recruits as the administration moved toward a "zero draft."[63]

While Congress eventually supported the President in his request for a two-year extension of induction authority, its members could not resist changing his compensation package. The House passed a pay increase in excess of what the administration had asked for and increased the allowances for subsistence, quarters, and dependents that the Gates Commission had argued against.[64] The Senate rejected the administration's pay proposal and eventually voted to support the original pay proposals of the Gates Commission.[65] The conference committee, however, rewrote the compensation package at the $2.4 billion level.[66] At the last minute, a glitch developed when Senator Gordon

---

[62] The White House communication group was concerned about who would get credit. After quoting a presidential news summary as referring to the efforts of a "unique Congressional coalition of Democrats and Republicans, blacks and whites, liberals and conservatives," Alexander Butterfield went on to stress "the importance of our getting credit for this, and making certain that we don't let this group steal our ideas" (Butterfield, 1969).

[63] John Ford saw the term "zero draft" as Nixon "hedging his bet by reducing draft calls to zero but keeping the authority on the books if needed" (Ford, 1980).

[64] Lee notes that

[t]he Administration had requested $79 million in quarters allowances, with all of it going to junior personnel, thereby allowing the repeal of the Dependents Assistance Act of 1950. The committeemen raised this amount to $824.2 million, with most of it going to the career force but still providing even greater allowances for first-termers than the Administration had requested. Finally, the committee allocated $37.8 million in subsistence allowances, with over 60 percent of it going to the career force. The Administration bill had provided no additional subsistence allowances. (Lee and Parker, 1977, p. 117)

[65] Kissinger reported to the President that the Senate was "considering a number of significant modifications . . . that will adversely affect our military capabilities and the foreign policies dependent upon them" (Kissinger, 1971). Nixon instructed Laird "[to] actively lead an Administration-wide effort aimed at preventing any substantial reduction by the Congress in the levels of our ground forces capabilities" (Nixon, 1971c).

[66] The administration had wanted $1.0 billion for FY 1971.

Allott (R-Colorado) objected to the conference report and tried to go around it by amending the upcoming military procurement bill (Allott, 1971). Nixon personally telephoned Senator Allott and committed to a later supplemental pay raise.[67]

After a decade of debate and an unpopular war, it was finally settled. Responding to what some saw as the "national will," on August 4, 1971, the House accepted the conference report by a vote of 250 to 150.[68] On September 21, 1971, the Senate accepted the conference report by a vote of 55 to 30. On September 28, 1971, President Nixon signed Public Law 92-129, and with that he kept his campaign promise to "stop the draft and put the selective service structure on stand-by" (Nixon, 1971a, p. 2).[69]

---

[67] This commitment to Allott played an important role in the future management of the all-volunteer force by limiting options available to the Pentagon.

[68] John Ford told the West Point cadets,

> More than any other bill I can think of, the Congress was responding to what they thought was the national will. They were doing what they thought the people want done, hoping that it would work, although a lot of them had reservations about it. One truism over time about the House of Representatives is they will eventually come around to do what they think the majority [of the people] wants. (Ford, 1980)

[69] H.R. 6531 authorized an extension of the draft for two years, until July 1, 1973. It increased military pay a total of $1.8 billion over nine months:

> The largest increase was in basic pay primarily for those with short service ($1.4 billion). Other increases included basic allowances for quarters ($305 million) and dependents assistance allowance ($120 million). . . .

> Enlistment bonuses are authorized . . . up to $6,000 for men enlisting in the combat elements . . . initial use of the authority would be to pay $3,000 bonuses . . . . (White House Press Secretary, 1971)

The bill "restores to the President discretionary authority which he had before the 1967 Selective Service amendments, over student deferments and establishing a uniform national call" (White House Press Secretary, 1971).

References

Allott, Gordon, "Military Pay Amendments of June 8, 1971," Dear Colleague letter to Members of the U.S. Senate, Washington, D.C., September 29, 1971. S0057.pdf.

Anderson, Martin C., "Information from President-Elect Nixon to Secretary-Designate Laird," memorandum to Secretary-Designate Melvin R. Laird, New York, December 24, 1968. G1130.pdf.

———, "Draft of 'Secretary's Laird's Answer to President's Directive in Regard to the All-Volunteer Armed Force'," Washington, D.C., February 2, 1969a. A0003.pdf.

———, "Secretary's Laird's Answer to President's Directive in Regard to the All-Volunteer Armed Force," memorandum to Arthur Burns, Washington, D.C., February 3, 1969b. A0002.pdf.

———, "A Move to a Lottery," memorandum to Arthur Burns, Washington, D.C., March 3, 1969c. A0004.pdf.

———, "First Meeting of the President's Commission on a All-Volunteer Armed Force," memorandum to Dwight Chapin, Washington, D.C., April 23, 1969d. G1077.pdf.

———, "Lottery Legislation Recently Submitted by Defense Department," memorandum to Arthur Burns, Washington, D.C., April 24, 1969e. G1462.pdf.

———, "Publication of the Report of the President's Commission on an All-Volunteer Armed Force as a Paperback Book," memorandum to Ken Cole, Washington, D.C., December 4, 1969f. G1080.pdf.

———, "Development of Presidential Message on All-Volunteer Armed Force," memorandum to Ken Cole, Washington, D.C., January 10, 1970a. A0012.pdf.

———, "Remarks by Secretary Laird on the Feasibility of an All-Volunteer Armed Force," memorandum to John Ehrlichman, Washington, D.C., January 30b, 1970. G1464.pdf.

———, "President's Commission on an All-Volunteer Armed Force," memorandum to Dwight Chapin, Washington, D.C., February 2, 1970c. G1082.pdf.

———, "1st Meeting of Task Force on All-Volunteer Armed Force," memorandum for file Washington, D.C., February 7, 1970d. A0008.pdf.

———, "Summary of Report of the President's Commission on an All-Volunteer Armed Force," memorandum to Henry Kissinger, Washington, D.C., February 17, 1970e. G1085.pdf.

———, "Attendance at presentation of the report of the Commission on an All-Volunteer Armed Force," memorandum to Steve Bull, Washington, D.C., February 18, 1970f. G1088.pdf.

———, "Meeting with Commission on an All-Volunteer Armed Force," memorandum to the President, Washington, D.C., February 21, 1970g. G1089.pdf.

———, "Meeting with the President's Commission on an All-Volunteer Armed Force," memorandum for the President's file Washington, D.C., February 21, 1970h. G1156.pdf.

————, "Alternative Option for All-Volunteer Armed Force discussed at meeting on March 2, 1970," memorandum to Ken BeLieu, William Brehm, David Callard, Chuck Colson, John Court, Steve Enke, Peter Flanigan, General Haig, Roger Kelley, William Meckling, Jon Rose, Jim Schlesinger, Tom Stanners and Paul Wollstadt, Washington, D.C., March 2, 1970i. A0009.pdf.

————, "All-Volunteer Armed Force," memorandum (draft) to Kenneth BeLieu, John Ehrlichman, Peter Flanigan, General Haig, Roger Kelley, Henry Kissinger, Secretary Laird, Robert Mayo and Jim Schlesinger, Washington, D.C., March 17, 1970j. L0018.pdf.

————, Martin Anderson's Personal Notes from AVAF/Draft Reform Meeting held in John Ehrlichman's Office on March 17, 1970, Washington, D.C., March 17, 1970k. A0010.pdf.

————, "All-Volunteer Force and Draft Reform," decision memorandum to John Ehrlichman, Washington, D.C., March 31, 1970m. G1142.pdf.

————, "Staff Action Concerning a Armed Forces Medical School," file notes, Washington, D.C., 1971. G1470.pdf.

————, The Making of the All-Volunteer Armed Force, Palo Alto, Calif.: Hoover Institution Press, 1991.

————, "Interview with Bernard Rostker," October 1, 2001.

Annunziata, Joseph, Press Reaction to the Administration's Plan for an All-Volunteer Force by July 1, 1973 (August 1970–August 1971), Washington, D.C.: Office of the Assistant Secretary of Defense (Public Affairs), August 27, 1971. G0229.pdf.

ASD[ISA]—See Assistant Secretary of Defense for International Security Affairs.

Assistant Secretary of Defense for International Security Affairs, "Draft Reform and the Elimination of Draft Calls (NSDM 53)," memorandum to Deputy Secretary of Defense, Secretaries of the Military Departments, Chairman Joint Chiefs of Staff, Assistant Secretaries of Defense, General Counsel and Assistant to the Secretary (Legislative Affairs), Washington, D.C., April 17, 1970. L0023.pdf.

Baroody, William J., Jr., "Random Selection System," memorandum to Curtis W. Tarr, Washington, D.C., April 27, 1970. L0035.pdf.

Beecher, William, "Pentagon Orders a Study of All-Volunteer Force," New York Times, October 20, 1968.

BeLieu, Ken, "Director of Selective Service Charles DiBona," memorandum to Bryce Harlow, Washington, D.C., January 27, 1970a. G1039.pdf.

————, "Director of Selective Service," memorandum to Bryce Harlow, Washington, D.C., January 28, 1970b. G1040.pdf.

Brown, Harold, "Proposed Military Pay Reform," memorandum to Deputy Secretary of Defense, Washington, D.C., February 10, 1969. G1446.pdf.

Buchanan, Patrick, "I Have Been Detailed," memorandum to Martin C. Anderson, Washington, D.C., March 5, 1970. A0006.pdf.

Bullen, Dana, "Tarr Backs Draft Reforms, Wins Senate Panel Approval," Washington Star, March 19, 1970. G1137.pdf.

Burns, Arthur F., Suggestions for Early Action and Considerations, or Pronouncement: A Report to the President-Elect, New York: Program Coordination Group, January 6, 1969. S0034.pdf.

Butterfield, Alexander P., "Credit for the Creation of the All-Volunteer Force," memorandum to John Ehrlichman, Washington, D.C., August 8, 1969. G1078.pdf.

Callard, David J., "Generating More Interest in the Commission's Work," memorandum to Martin C. Anderson, Washington, D.C., September 18, 1969a. G1465.pdf.

———, "Printing of Commission's Final Report," memorandum to Martin C. Anderson, Washington, D.C., November 26, 1969b. G1079.pdf.

———, "Meeting with Senators Stennis and Smith, January 30, 1970," memorandum Washington, D.C., January 30, 1970a. G1136.pdf.

———, "Public Relations Regarding an All-Volunteer Force," memorandum to Robert Odel, Washington, D.C., March 11, 1970b. G1133.pdf.

Chafee, John H., "Proposed Military Pay Reform," memorandum to Deputy Secretary of Defense, Washington, D.C., February 10, 1969. G1445.pdf.

Chapin, Dwight L., "Meeting to Receive the Report of the President's Commission on an All-Volunteer Armed Force," memorandum to the President, Washington, D.C., February 11, 1970a. G1081.pdf.

———, "The All-Volunteer Army Task Force Meeting," memorandum to H. R. Haldeman, Washington, D.C., February 18, 1970b. G1090.pdf.

Cole, Ken, "The President Has Decided," memorandum to Henry Kissinger, Martin C. Anderson, John Ehrlichman, Bill Timmons and Peter Flanigan, Washington, D.C., April 9, 1970. A0005.pdf.

Davis, Jeanne W., "Draft Reform and the All-Volunteer Forces: Paper," memorandum to Office of the Vice President, Office of the Secretary of State, Office of the Secretary of Defense, Office of the Director Emergency Preparedness, Office of the Director Selective Service System, Office of the Attorney General, Office of the Chairman Joint Chiefs of Staff, Peter Flanigan, Martin C. Anderson, John Ehrlichman and Office of the Under Secretary of State, Washington, D.C., March 23, 1970. L0019.pdf.

Enke, Stephen, *Draft Deferments and Exemptions from Selective Service,* Washington, D.C.: National Security Council, NSSM-78, December 18, 1969. G1143.pdf.

———, "Agency Comments on NSSM-78," memorandum to Dee Ingold, Jonathan Rose and Martin C. Anderson, Washington, D.C., January 15, 1970a. G1151.pdf.

———, "Presidential Memo on Draft Reform," memorandum to John Court, Jonathan Rose and Martin C. Anderson, Santa Barbara, Calif., January 22, 1970b. G1149.pdf.

———, "Scenarios for Integrating Interim Draft Reform Into the AVF," memorandum to Paul Wollstadt, Washington, D.C., February 10, 1970c. L0015.pdf.

Feulner, Edwin J., Jr., *For the Volunteer Army File,* Washington, D.C.: Office of the Special Assistant to the Secretary and Deputy Secretary of Defense, March 26, 1969. L0041.pdf.

Fitt, Alfred B., "Manpower Procurement Planning Study," memorandum to Assistant Secretaries of the Military Departments (M&RA), Washington, D.C., October 4, 1968a. G0247.pdf.

———, "Initiate a New Study on All Possible Ways to Maximize the Number of Volunteers," memorandum to L. Mendel Rivers, Washington, D.C., October 17, 1968b. G0248.pdf.

———, "Study Plan for 'Project Volunteer'," memorandum to Assistant Secretaries of the Military Departments (M&RA), November 15, 1968c. G0256.pdf.

———, "Arguments Against a Special Commission," memorandum to Melvin R. Laird, Washington, D.C., January 29, 1969a. G0260.pdf.

———, "'Project Volunteer' Instead of Nixon's Special Commission," memorandum to Melvin R. Laird, Washington, D.C., January 29, 1969b. G0261.pdf.

———, "Selective Service Matters," memorandum to Secretary Laird, Washington, D.C., January 29, 1969c. G0672.pdf.

———, "'Alarmed at the course of action …'—NOT SENT," memorandum to Melvin R. Laird, Washington, D.C., January 30, 1969d. G0262.pdf.

Flanigan, Peter M., "NSC Study of Selective Service Standards," memorandum to the President, Washington, D.C., October 6, 1969a. G1033.pdf.

———, "Meeting with Lieutenant General Lewis B. Hershey, Director of Selective Service," memorandum to the President, Washington, D.C., October 9, 1969b. G1024.pdf.

———, "Meeting with Lieutenant General Lewis B. Hershey, Director of Selective Service," memorandum for the record to President's File, Washington, D.C., October 14, 1969c. G1025.pdf.

———, "Increased Concern About Statements Concerning the Lottery," memorandum to Lewis B. Hershey, Washington, D.C., January 13, 1970a. G1038.pdf.

———, "Personnel Actions: General Hershey's Last Day," memorandum to the President, Washington, D.C., February 16, 1970b. G1068.pdf.

———, "Meeting with Curtis W. Tarr Assistant Secretary of the Air Force," memorandum to the President, Washington, D.C., March 2, 1970c. G1048.pdf.

———, "Meeting with Curtis W. Tarr Assistant Secretary of the Air Force," memorandum to the President, Washington, D.C., March 3, 1970d. G1047.pdf.

———, "Experience Using Random Sequence Numbers," memorandum to Colonel Dee Ingold Acting Director of Selective Service, Washington, D.C., March 4, 1970e. G1049.pdf.

———, "Draft Reform," memorandum to Curtis W. Tarr Director of Selective Service, Washington, D.C., October 23, 1970f. G1054.pdf.

Flynn, George Q., Lewis B. Hershey, Mr. Selective Service, Chapel Hill, N.C.: University of North Carolina Press, 1985.

Ford, John J., 1971 Draft Bill, West Point, New York: U.S. Military Academy at West Point, November 25, 1980. G1389.mov.

———, Looking Back on the Termination of the Draft, unpublished report, September 27, 2003. S0881.pdf.

Friedman, Milton, "The Draft," *Newsweek,* March 11, 1968, p. 82.

———, "Secretary of Defense Melvin R. Laird," letter to Melvin Laird, February 23, 1970a. G0537.pdf.

———, "The End of the Draft?" *Newsweek,* March 16, 1970b, p. 90.

———, *Two Lucky People,* Chicago: University of Chicago Press, 1998.

Gates, Thomas S. Jr., *The Report of the President's Commission on an All-Volunteer Armed Force,* Washington, D.C., February 1970. S0243.pdf.

Gates, Thomas S. Jr., Martin C. Anderson, and Ronald L. Ziegler, "On the Report of the Gates Commission," press conference Washington, D.C., February 21, 1970. G0541.pdf.

Greenberg, I. M., *Project 100,000: New Standards Program,* Washington, D.C.: U.S. Department of Defense. G1318.pdf.

Haldeman, H. R., "President's Decision to Replace General Hershey," memorandum to Peter Flanigan, Washington, D.C., February 17, 1969a. G1029.pdf.

———, "President is Anxious to Move Quickly on General Hershey," memorandum to Peter Flanigan, Washington, D.C., April 28, 1969b. G1030.pdf.

Hershey, Lewis B., "Action to Modify the Draft," memorandum to the President, Washington, D.C., September 2, 1969a. G1065.pdf.

———, "Review of Selective Service Guidelines," memorandum to Henry A. Kissinger, Washington, D.C., November 24, 1969b. G1036.pdf.

———, "For the NSC Meeting on All-Volunteer Army and Draft Reform," memorandum to the President, Washington, D.C., March 25, 1970a. G1154.pdf.

———, "Policies for Congressional Hearing on Manpower Legislation," memorandum to the President, Washington, D.C., March 30, 1970b. A0022.pdf.

———, "Proposed Message to the Congress on an All-Volunteer Armed Force and Draft Reform," memorandum to the President, Washington, D.C., April 10, 1970c. A0007.pdf.

Hubbell, Lester, *1967 Quadrennial Review of Military Compensation,* Vol. 1: *Active Duty Compensation,* Washington, D.C.: Office of the Assistant Secretary of Defense (M&RA), 1967. S0022.pdf.

Ingold, Dee, "National Calls Prorated Directly to Local Boards," memorandum to Assistant to the President Peter M. Flanigan, Washington, D.C., March 2, 1970. G1046.pdf.

Kelley, Roger T., "Reform of Draft System Through Executive Action in Lieu of Legislation," memorandum to Kenneth E. BeLieu Deputy Assistant to the President for Congressional Relations, Washington, D.C., August 13, 1969a. G1066.pdf.

———, "Department of Defense Views on Proposals Being Considered by the Commission Staff," memorandum to Harry J. Gilman, Director of Military Manpower Supply and Compensation Studies, President's Commission on an All-Volunteer Armed Force, Washington, D.C., August 29, 1969b. G1152.pdf.

———, "Final Version of Dr. Enke's Report, 'The President's Review of Deferments and Exemptions from Selective Service,'" memorandum to Secretary of Defense, Washington, D.C., February 16, 1970a. G0507.pdf.

———, "Department of Defense Observations of the All-Volunteer Force," memorandum to Special Consultant to the President Martin C. Anderson, Washington, D.C., February 27, 1970b. G0534.pdf.

———, "Major Department of Defense Concerns About Gates Commission Report," memorandum to Special Consultant to the President Martin C. Anderson, Washington, D.C., February 27, 1970c. G0289.pdf.

———, "Timetable," memorandum to Secretary Laird, Washington, D.C., March 3, 1970d. G0540.pdf.

———, "The President Has Decided," memorandum to Secretary Laird, Washington, D.C., April 9, 1970e. L0022.pdf.

Kemp, Stewart W., "Productivity of U.S. Military Recruiting Systems," in Gates Commission, ed., *Studies Prepared for the President's Commission on an All-Volunteer Armed Force,* Washington, D.C.: U.S. Government Printing Office, 1970, pp. IV-4-1 through IV-4-19. G1296.pdf.

Kissinger, Henry A., "National Security Study Memorandum 78: Review of U.S. Deferment and Exemption Policy," memorandum to Commerce Director of Selective Service Secretaries of Defense, Labor Health Education and Welfare, Director of the Bureau of the Budget, Director of the Office of Emergency Planning, Washington, D.C., October 8, 1969a. G1155.pdf.

———, "Draft Lottery Problems," memorandum to the President, Washington, D.C., December 26, 1969b. G1117.pdf.

———, "Presidential Meeting with Gates Commission," memorandum to Hugh Sloan, Washington, D.C., February 16, 1970a. G1084.pdf.

———, "NSC Meeting on All-Volunteer Army and Draft Reform," memorandum to the President, Washington, D.C., March 2, 1970b. G1153.pdf.

———, "Military Manpower and Congress," memorandum to the President, Washington, D.C., May 14, 1971. G1102.pdf.

Klein, Herbert G., "The Nixon Selective Service Plan," memorandum to Peter M. Flanigan and John Ehrlichman, Washington, D.C., September 15, 1969. G1032.pdf.

Laird, Melvin R., "Response to President's Memorandum on the All-Volunteer Force," memorandum to the President, Washington, D.C., January 31, 1969a. G0259.pdf.

———, "Selective Service Reforms," memorandum to the President, Washington, D.C., February 3, 1969b. G0263.pdf.

———, "Response to Nixon's February 6th Letter," letter to the President of the United States, Washington, D.C., February 7, 1969c. G0265.pdf.

———, "Status on Progress on Selective Service Reform Legislation," memorandum to the President, Washington, D.C., April 30, 1969d. G0684.pdf.

———, "Status of the Draft Reform Proposal," memorandum to John D. Ehrlichman, Counsel to the President, Washington, D.C., July 30, 1969e. G0682.pdf.

———, "Draft Reform," memorandum to the President, Washington, D.C., August 29, 1969f. G1121.pdf.

———, "Draft Reform," memorandum to the President, Washington, D.C., September 18, 1969g. G1118.pdf.

———, *Secretary of Defense Statement on the Draft,* Washington, D.C.: U.S. Department of Defense, September 19, 1969h. G1120.pdf.

———, "Draft Review of Deferments and Exemptions from Selective Service (NSSM-78)," memorandum to Henry A. Kissinger, Washington, D.C., January 10, 1970a. G1150.pdf.

———, *Remarks before 1970 Senate Youth Program Group,* Washington, D.C.: U.S. Department of Defense, January 19, 1970b. G1463.pdf.

———, "In response to your letter concerning my statement on Meet the Press," letter to Milton Friedman, Washington, D.C., March 4, 1970c. G0539.pdf.

———, "Future of the Draft," memorandum to the President of the United States, Washington, D.C., March 11, 1970d. G0268.pdf.

———, "Opposition to Terminating the Draft on July 1, 1971," memorandum to Senator John C. Stennis, Washington, D.C., August 14, 1970e. G1146.pdf.

———, "Zero Draft Calls by July 1, 1973," memorandum to Secretaries of the Military Department and Chairman Joint Chiefs of Staff, Washington, D.C., October 12, 1970f. G0511.pdf.

———, "Support for a National University of the Health Sciences," letter to Elliot Richardson, Washington, D.C., November 12, 1970g. G1466.pdf.

———, "Selective Service Act," memorandum to Assistant to the President for National Security Affairs, Washington, D.C., December 28, 1970h. G0187.pdf.

———, "Program for Moving to Zero Draft Calls," memorandum to the Assistant to the President for National Security Affairs, Washington, D.C., January 26, 1971a. L0029.pdf.

———, "Third Quarterly Report," memorandum to the President, Washington, D.C., February 27, 1971b. L0030.pdf.

———, "Introduction," in Barbara A. Bicksler, Curtis L. Gilroy and John T. Warner, eds., *The All-Volunteer Force: Thirty Years of Service,* Washington, D.C.: Brassey's, Inc., 2003a.

———, "Statement by Former Secretary of Defense Melvin Laird," Conference Celebrating the 30th Anniversary of the All-Volunteer Force, Washington, D.C., September 16, 2003b.

Lee, Gus C., and Geoffrey Y. Parker, *Ending the Draft: The Story of the All Volunteer Force,* Washington, D.C.: Human Resources Research Organization, FR-PO-771, April 1977. S0242.pdf.

Lynn, Laurence E., Jr., "Peter M. Flanigan Memo on Draft Reform," memorandum to Henry A. Kissinger, Washington, D.C., September 29, 1969. G1119.pdf.

Mack, W. P., *Draft Presidential Announcement of the Commission on an All-Volunteer Armed Force with List of Commissioners as of February 22, 1969,* Washington, D.C.: Office of the Assistant Secretary of Defense (M&RA), February 22, 1969. L0002.pdf.

Marshall, Burke, *In Pursuit of Equity? Who Serves When Not All Serve?: Report of the National Advisory Commission on Selective Service,* Washington, D.C.: National Advisory Commission on Selective Service, February 1967. G1428.pdf.

Mayo, Robert P., "Draft Reform and the All-Volunteer Armed Force," memorandum to the President, Washington, D.C., March 26, 1970. G1145.pdf.

McConnell, John P., "Proposed Military Pay Reform," memorandum to Secretary of Defense, Washington, D.C., February 10, 1969. G1447.pdf.

Meckling, William H., "All-Volunteer Force," memorandum to Martin C. Anderson, Washington, D.C., March 2, 1970. A0011.pdf.

Nixon, Richard M., "Plan for a Special Commission to Develop Plans to End the Draft," memorandum to Melvin R. Laird, Washington, D.C., January 29, 1969a. G0258.pdf.

———, "Names for the Commission on an All-Volunteer Force," memorandum to Secretary of Defense, Washington, D.C., February 6, 1969b. G0264.pdf.

———, *Statement by the President Announcing a Commission on an All-Volunteer Armed Forces,* Washington, D.C.: Office of the White House Press Secretary, March 27, 1969c. G0266.pdf.

———, *Message from the President of the United States Relative to Reform of the Selective Service System to the House of Representatives,* Washington, D.C.: The White House, May 13, 1969d. G0671.pdf.

———, *Executive Order: Amending the Selective Service Regulations to Prescribe Random Selection,* Washington, D.C.: The White House, November 26, 1969e. G1158.pdf.

———, *Proclamation by the President: Random Selection for Military Service,* Washington, D.C.: The White House, November 26, 1969f. G1200.pdf.

———, *Remarks of the President at Signing H.R. 14001, An Act to Amend the Military Selective Service Act of 1967,* Washington, D.C.: The White House, November 26, 1969g. G1159.pdf.

———, *Designation of Colonel Dee Ingold as Acting Director of Selective Service,* Washington, D.C.: The White House, February 16, 1970a. G1067.pdf.

———, *Message to Congress on Ending the Draft, April 23, 1970,* Washington, D.C.: The White House, April 23, 1970b. G1160.pdf.

———, "The All-Volunteer Armed Force: A Radio Address, October 17, 1968," in Harry A. Marmion, ed., *The Case Against a Volunteer Army,* Chicago: Quadrangle Books, 1971a, pp. 75–82. G0251.pdf.

———, *Message to the Congress: Ending the Draft,* Washington, D.C.: The White House, January 28, 1971b. G0646.pdf.

———, "Military Manpower Reductions," memorandum to Secretary of Defense, Washington, D.C., May 24, 1971c. G1103.pdf.

OASD[M&RA]—*See* Office of the Assistant Secretary of Defense for Manpower and Reserve Affairs.

OASD[SA]—*See* Office of the Assistant Secretary of Defense for Systems Analysis.

Office of the Assistant Secretary of Defense for Manpower and Reserve Affairs, Draft Reform and the All-Volunteer Armed Force, issue paper, Washington, D.C.: U.S. Department of Defense, March 20, 1970a. G0533.pdf.

———, *Draft Reform and the All-Volunteer Armed Force,* issue paper, Washington, D.C.: U.S. Department of Defense, March 23, 1970b. G0535.pdf.

———, *to be Discussed in DPRC Meeting on January 18, 1971,* Washington, D.C.: U.S. Department of Defense, January 1, 1971. L0028.pdf.

Office of the Assistant Secretary of Defense for Systems Analysis, *Active Force Manpower Needs and Supply in a Volunteer Service,* Washington, D.C.: U.S. Department of Defense, March 2, 1970a. G0545.pdf.

———, *Draft Reform and All-Volunteer Armed Forces,* Washington, D.C.: U.S. Department of Defense, March 22, 1970b. G0543.pdf.

Oi, Walter Y., "The Cost and Implications of an All-Volunteer Force," in Sol Tax, ed., *The Draft: A Handbook of Facts and Alternatives,* Chicago: University of Chicago Press, 1967a, pp. 221–251.

———, "The Economic Cost of the Draft," *The American Economic Review,* Vol. 57, No. 2, May 1967b, pp. 39–62. S0236.pdf.

———, "Historical Perspectives on the All-Volunteer Force: The Rochester Connection," in Curtis L. Gilroy J. Eric Fredland, Roger D. Little, and W. S. Sellman, ed., *Professionals on the Front Line: Two Decades of the All-Volunteer Force,* Washington, D.C.: Brassey's, 1996.

Packard, David, "Legislative Proposal to Make Military Pay More Equitable," memorandum to Speaker of the House of Representatives, Washington, D.C., January 29, 1971. G0192.pdf.

President's Commission on an All-Volunteer Armed Force [Gates Commission], *Minutes of the (First) Meeting of the President's Commission on an All-Volunteer Armed Force,* Washington, D.C. S0035.pdf.

Resor, Stanley R., "Proposed Military Pay Reform," memorandum to Deputy Secretary of Defense, Washington, D.C., February 8, 1969. G1444.pdf.

———, "Comments on the Gates Commission Report," memorandum to Thomas Gates, Washington, D.C., January 10, 1970. G0285.pdf.

Richardson, Elliott L., "HEW's Support for a National University of the Health Sciences," letter to Melvin Laird, Washington, D.C., January 4, 1971. G1467.pdf.

Rivers, L. Mendel, "Continued Public Interest In the 'All-Volunteer Force' Concept," letter to Assistant Secretary of Defense for Manpower Alfred B. Fitt, Washington, D.C., September 17, 1968. G0249.pdf.

Rose, Jonathan, "Interim Reform of Selective Service System During Approach to an All-Volunteer Force," memorandum to Peter M. Flanigan, Washington, D.C., April 26, 1969. G1127.pdf.

———, "Charles DiBona," memorandum to Bryce Harlow, Washington, D.C., February 9, 1970. G1043.pdf.

———, "Draft Meeting," memorandum to Peter M. Flanigan, Assistant to the President, Washington, D.C., January 7, 1971. G1101.pdf.

Rostker, Bernard D., *The Personnel Structure and Posture of the Air National Guard and the Air Force Reserve,* Santa Monica, Calif.: RAND Corporation, R-1049-PR, April 1973. S0794.pdf.

Rousselot, Louis M., "Comments on HEW's Rationale for Opposing the Uniformed Services University of the Health Sciences Concept," memorandum to Roger T. Kelley, Washington, D.C., February 3, 1971a. G1468.pdf.

———, "HEW's Position on H.R. 2," memorandum to Martin C. Anderson, Washington, D.C., February 19, 1971b. G1469.pdf.

Rumsfeld, Donald H., "General Hershey: Selective Service System," memorandum to Peter M. Flanigan, Washington, D.C., November 25, 1968. G1028.pdf.

Shishko, Robert, and Bernard D. Rostker, "The Economics of Multiple Job Holding," *The American Economic Review,* Vol. 66, No. 3, June 1976, pp. 298–308. S0159.pdf.

Stafford, Robert T., "Recommendation for Stephen Herbits," memorandum to Melvin R. Laird, Washington, D.C., March 11, 1969. L0039.pdf.

Stafford, Robert T., Richard S. Schweiker, Charles W. Whalen, Jr., Frank Horton, and Garner E. Shriver, "Recommendation for Stephen Herbits," memorandum to the President, Washington, D.C., March 11, 1969. L0040.pdf.

Tarr, Curtis W., "Random Selection System," memorandum to Assistant Chief Counsel House Armed Services Committee Frank Slatinshek, Washington, D.C., May 4, 1970a. L0037.pdf.

———, "Short Report," memorandum to the President, Washington, D.C., October 23, 1970b. G1054.pdf.

U.S. News & World Report Staff, "ABC's of Draft by Lottery," *U.S. News & World Report,* December 15, 1969.

Wallace, Carl S., "Consideration of William K. Brehm for Director of Selective Service," memorandum to Peter M. Flanigan Assistant to the President, Washington, D.C., February 17, 1970. G1050.pdf.

Wallis, W. Allen, *An Over Governed Society,* New York: The Free Press, 1976.

Wallis, W. Allen, William H. Meckling, Martin J. Bailey, Harry J. Gilman, and Walter Y. Oi, *Immediate Steps Towards Ending the Draft,* Rochester, New York: University of Rochester, December 31, 1968. L0001.pdf.

Westmoreland, William C., "Dinner Honoring General Hershey," memorandum to the President of the United States, Washington, D.C., February 18, 1970. G1045.pdf.

White House Press Secretary, *Appointment of General Hershey to New Job,* Washington, D.C.: The White House, October 10, 1969a. G1034.pdf.

———, *New Draft Selection System Fact Sheet,* Washington, D.C.: The White House, November 26, 1969b. G1157.pdf.

———, *Summary of the Report of the Presidential Commission on an All-Volunteer Armed Force,* Washington, D.C.: The White House, February 21, 1970a. G0542.pdf.

————, "Intention to Nominate Curtis W. Tarr to be Director of Selective Service," press release Washington, D.C., March 12, 1970b. G1070.pdf.

————, *Extension of the Draft and Increase in Military Pay,* Washington, D.C.: The White House, September 28, 1971. G0576.pdf.

White House Staff, *Scenario of Action on All-Volunteer Force,* Washington, D.C.: The White House, March 2, 1970. L0017.pdf.

Wilson, George C., "Laird Dim on Prospects for All-Volunteer Army," *Washington Post,* January 30, 1970, pp. A1-2.

Witherspoon, Ralph Pomeroy, *The Military Draft and the All-Volunteer Force: A Case Study of a Shift in Public Policy,* dissertation, Blacksburg, Va.: Virginia Polytechnic Institute and State University, 1993.

Wool, Harold, *The Military Specialist,* Baltimore, Md.: The Johns Hopkins University Press, 1968a.

————, "Study Plan for 'Project Volunteer,'" memorandum to Assistant Secretary of Defense (M&RA) Alfred B. Fitt, Washington, D.C., November 13, 1968b. G0254.pdf.

————, "Tentative Organization Plan for 'Project Volunteer,'" memorandum to Assistant Secretary of Defense (M&RA) Alfred B. Fitt, Washington, D.C., November 13, 1968c. G0255.pdf.

————, "Study Plan for 'Project Volunteer,'" memorandum to Assistant Secretary of Defense (M&RA) Alfred B. Fitt, Washington, D.C., January 11, 1969. G0257.pdf.

CHAPTER FIVE

The Studies of the All-Volunteer Armed Force (1969–1970)

> We unanimously believe that the nation's interest will be best served by an all-volunteer force, supported by an effective stand-by draft, than by a mixed force of volunteers and conscripts.
>
> —The Gates Commission[1]

Complementary Studies

The studies by the Gates Commission staff were done against the background of a number of other study efforts that were under way or had already been completed. Most noteworthy were the National Security Council's force sizing study, known as National Security Study Memorandum 3 (NSSM-3), and the Hubbell pay study.

NSSM-3

Early in the Nixon administration, the National Security Council undertook a study of alternative force structures and strategies that would provide the goal, e.g., the "required" number of military personnel, the Gates Commission worked toward. NSSM-3,[2] *Alternative Military Strategies and Budgets,* reviewed a number of post-Vietnam alternatives ranging from a high of 3.3 million men to a low of 1.9 million men in the active armed forces. The commission focused its projections and recommendations on sustaining an active military force that would number 2.25 million. In fact, the 2.2 million force level was reached in FY 1974; by FY 1975, the force level was 2.1 million men.

---

[1] From the report published February 20, 1970 (Gates, 1970, p. iii).

[2] NSSM-3 was based on a pilot study in 1968 done by the Pentagon's system analysis staff at the end of the Johnson administration. A senior member of the systems analysis staff had joined Dr. Henry Kissinger on the National Security Council and, during the transition period, brought the pilot study to Dr. Kissinger's attention. (See Bovey and Thomason, 1998.)

The Systems Analysis office briefed the Gates Commission on the results of NSSM-3 and privately told the Secretary of Defense that, while

> there is considerable uncertainty . . . the "shortage" of enlistments needed to maintain the force at the expected level (i.e., 2.0 to 2.5 million) would be small or even non-existent. Thus, the added cost, for increased pay or bonuses, would be modest, perhaps under $1 billion. (Rossotti, 1969)

The Hubbell Study

The Gates Commission was also briefed on the compensation reform initiatives pending at the end of the Johnson administration. The economists on the commission particularly liked the move to a salary system, and all assumed that first-term personnel would be included and that the new salary system would complement the all-volunteer force they were endorsing. Unfortunately, things did not work out quit as expected. Here is how it played out.

In 1966 Congress directed that, by January 1, 1967, and thereafter every four years, the President present to Congress "a complete review of the principles and concepts of the compensation system for members of the uniformed services" (ASD[M&RA], 1967, p. 151). The first Quadrennial Review of Military Compensation (QRMC) (Hubbell, 1967) was commonly referred to as the Hubbell Study, after the head of the interservice task force, Rear Admiral Lester E. Hubbell. As the Hubbell Study saw it, "the military is no longer so different from the rest of society that meaningful comparisons cannot be made between the two" (Hubbell, 1967, p. 6). The study team believed its

> most important conclusion [was] that a basic overhaul of career force compensation is needed. The existing system is not attaining its objective to the extent desired. Moreover, it is inefficient in accomplishing as much as it does. . . . The hard facts are that we are not now attracting, retaining and motivating to career military service the kind and numbers of people our uniformed services need. (Hubbell, 1967, p. 26)

In a series of findings and recommendations covering regular compensation (Hubbell, 1967, p. 6), special pays (ASD[M&RA], 1967), and retirement (U.S. Department of Defense, 1969), the Hubbell Study laid out the design of a fundamentally different compensation system that, while fully consistent with the market model the Gates Commission was developing, focused on career personnel.[3]

---

[3] A summary of the Hubbell reform proposals was published (described as an "in-depth report") in the *Commanders Digest* of May 11, 1968 (Staff of the *Commanders Digest,* 1968). The proposals enjoyed wide support and the endorsement of the Bureau of the Budget (Zwick, 1968). The new Secretary of Defense initially endorsed it as "a critical first step in moving to a volunteer force" (Packard, 1969), but with two major changes. He recommended an increase of 12.6 percent for noncareer personnel, rather than the 9.1 percent in the original proposal, and recommended an increase in the retirement floor by 9.1 percent. Tom Stanners, the long-serving senior-staff expert on military personnel at the Bureau of the Budget, reported that, "[a]ssuming favorable action by the Administration, Secretary Laird plans to personally discuss the proposal with Chairmen Stennis and Rivers" (Stanners, 1969b). That approval never came. The pay reform proposals were ultimately viewed as being inconsistent with the Nixon administration's move to an all-volunteer force.

With regard to first-term personnel, the Hubbell Study was out of step with the Nixon administration's notions about the all-volunteer force, for instance, that "[p]ay philosophy applied in the past has included the ideal of the citizen's obligation to serve a minimum period in uniform" (ASD[M&RA], 1967, p. 2). The Hubbell Study summed up their "compensation concepts" for the first term, noncareer force this way:

> Food, clothing, shelter, medical care, and other basic necessities are provided by the Government in kind to most noncareer members most of the time. This is appropriate and necessary because of the nature of the military activities—mostly training and operations—in which noncareer personnel are predominately engaged. The residual of basic pay after taxes is available to the single noncareer member to spend on other basic necessities. In those few cases where necessities are not furnished in kind, nontaxable cash allowances are furnished in lieu thereof.
>
> This concept of compensation assures that young, single soldiers, sailors, airmen, and marines who are members of largely self-contained military communities are properly cared for. . . . 84% of noncareer members have no dependents; therefore, measures designed to support most effectively the individual member himself under his particular conditions of service are appropriate in this part of the force. (Hubbell, 1967, p. 11)[4]

The details of the Hubbell pay proposals are less important here, and the issues would be revisited again and again through a series of quadrennial reviews and presidential commissions over the next three decades. What is important is that nothing directly came of these recommendations because of the Hubbell Study's focus on the career force and its design of a salary system that was not extended to first-term personnel, which was the focus of the administration's efforts to end the draft. Tom Stanners, the longtime military personnel expert at the Office of Management and Budget, prepared a summary of the Hubbell recommendations that was sent to Martin Anderson at the end of January 1969 (Stanners, 1969a). Stanners remembers how he, Admiral Hubbell and Hubbell's deputy, Army Colonel Gorman Smith tried to persuade Burns and Anderson to go along with a salary system for career personnel (Stanners, 2002).[5] Burns and Anderson opposed the reform because it did not include

---

[4] The issue of pay for first-term personnel was raided shortly after the Hubbell Study was released for review inside the Johnson administration in 1967. Gardner Ackley, Chairman of the Council of Economic Advisors, questioned Secretary of Defense Robert McNamara on the "plight of the drafted soldier" (Ackley, 1967). McNamara defended the pay and allowance system for first-term personnel and the "residual income standard" as appropriate (McNamara, 1967).

The issue was joined in correspondence between Merton J. Peck of the Council of Economic Advisors (Peck, 1967); Alfred B. Fitt, the Assistant Secretary of Defense for Manpower and Reserve Affairs and Reserve Affairs (Fitt, 1968); and Lt. Col. Gorman Smith (Smith, 1968), Admiral Hubbell's deputy on the pay study. Also joining the debate was Professor Walter Oi, a staff member of the DoD Compensation Policy Board. His critique of the Volume 1 of the Hubbell proposals was published in the Congressional Record on August 2, 1968 (Oi, 1968).

On March 14, 2005, Oi was appointed to the Defense Advisory Committee on Military Compensation and charged to "identify approaches to balance military pay and benefits in sustaining recruitment and retention of high-quality people, as well as a cost-effective and ready military force" (Secretary of Defense, 2005).

[5] Smith was a student of Burns at Columbia University, where his doctoral dissertation was on *Occupational Pay Differentials for Military Technicians* (Smith, 1964).

first-term personnel, the focus of the all-volunteer force effort, and the White House rejected the proposal.

The failure of the Johnson administration to send the Hubbell proposal forward in 1967 as originally directed by Congress led the chairman of the House Armed Services Committee, Congressman Mendel Rivers, to introduce an amendment into the 1967 Military Pay Act. The so-called "Rivers Amendment" provided that the military receive the same pay raises at the same time as civil service workers. It also provided that the civilian salary adjustments be concentrated in the basic pay segment of Regular Military Compensation (RMC). RMC was defined in the law as "basic pay, tax exempt quarters and subsistence allowances or their in-kind equivalents, and the Federal tax advantage from the allowances" (Rumsfeld, 1976, p. 3). While this did not address the issue of what an appropriate level for military compensation would be, it did ensure that military compensation would not lag further behind that of the civil service. The particular mechanism chosen was a problem. Concentrating the raises that had been figured on total RMC in only the basic-pay portion of RMC meant that basic pay rose much more rapidly than did average civil service salaries, and since retirement pay was calculated only on basic pay at retirement, the eventual cost growth in the retirement bill forced a change in 1974.[6]

Analytic Studies Undertaken for the Gates Commission (1970)

The research staff of the Gates Commission was drawn largely from economists who had worked on the 1964 Pentagon Draft Study or on the Rochester memorandum prepared for Arthur Burns in December 1968. William H. Meckling, Dean of Rochester's Graduate School of Management, was named staff director.[7] Four "research directors" supported him. Walter Oi, research director for the 1964 study, was given the responsibility to estimate manpower requirements and the lower turnover expected from a volunteer force. This included consideration of the influence that the greater use of civilians would have on requirements. Another veteran of the 1964 study, Stuart Altman, was asked to continue his work on the supply of officers. Harry Gilman from the University of Rochester supervised work on the supply of enlisted personnel, including the effects of pay and other variables that might induce enlistments and reenlistments. David Kassing from the Rochester's affiliate, the Center for Naval Analyses, was responsible for historical, political, and social research. They had working for them a number of economists from academia and the Pentagon's federally contracted research centers (FCRCs).

---

[6] The 1974 changes provided that

> military basic pay and the allowances for quarters and subsistence each be adjusted by the same average percentage and at the same time as Civil Service salary adjustments. A major consequence of this action was to reduce significantly the growth of retirement liabilities of future years. (Rumsfeld, 1976, p. 5)

[7] Henderson recounts Meckling's contribution to the Gates Commission in Henderson (1999).

The next several sections review the various staff studies. They are grouped into studies that considered the draft as a conscription tax, studies of the supply of first-term personnel, studies of the reenlistment of first-term personnel, and studies that address the efficient composition of an all-volunteer force.

The Economic Analysis of Conscription as a Hidden Tax

Larry A. Sjaastad and Ronald H. Hansen did the analysis of conscription as a tax, a central argument of the Gates Commission.[8] They started, as Walter Oi did in the original 1964 Pentagon Draft Study, by defining the components of the *conscription tax* as

> the difference between the earnings the draftee or draft motivated (reluctant) volunteer receives from the military (including income in kind) and the earnings that would cause that individual to be willing to enter the military. (Sjaastad and Hansen, 1970, p. IV-1-2)[9]

To this they added, as Oi had, "economic rents foregone." They argued that, while "it is true that rents are not necessary to attract the affected individuals to military service, . . . similar rents are . . . collected by [other] sellers of goods and services to the government," and, therefore, it is only proper that they be treated as part of the conscription tax (Sjaastad and Hansen, 1970, p. IV-1-2). In a later review, Richard V. L. Cooper noted that this also has the effect of increasing the number of people affected by the tax of conscription to include even those who volunteer for the military (Cooper, 1977, p. 83). The number of people paying the conscription tax also increased when Sjaastad and Hansen argued that the cost of "draft avoidance" should be included in the calculus of the conscription tax. In the final analysis, the Gates Commission argued that the conscription tax was being paid, not only by those who were drafted, but also by those who modified their behavior to avoid the draft and even by those who volunteered for military service.

A General Model of the Economic Cost of Conscription. The inclusion of the cost of draft avoidance enabled Sjaastad and Hansen to construct a general model of the economic cost of conscription. They showed how seemingly different schemes were simply variations of the selection process, which determines who would serve, when not all had to serve. They started by modeling the Civil War system, which permitted a draftee to hire a substitute. Given the free working of the market for substitutes, John

---

[8] Larry Sjaastad was Professor of Economics at the University of Chicago. Both Ronald Hansen and Richard Cooper were graduate students in the Economics Department at Chicago at the same time.

[9] This is the same definition Oi used during the 1964 Pentagon Draft Study. A number of alternative definitions, however, have also been used. Hansen and Weisbrod defined the tax as the "difference between their civilian opportunity cost and the military remuneration" (Hansen and Weisbrod, 1967). Cooper made the distinction between the two by noting that "the economic cost of military labor has tended to be interpreted as the alternative civilian wage, while the social cost has the straightforward interpretation of the individual's reservation wage" (Cooper, 1975).

Warner and Beth Asch would later argue that, theoretically, such a system would generate "the same force as a volunteer system. Allowing substitutes shifts [some of] the burden of paying for the military force from taxpayers to those who hire substitutes" (Warner and Asch, 2001). Going further, Sjaastad and Hansen argued that another variation on the Civil War theme was a system in which "every member of the eligible group receives a draft notice but, as the government wishes to recruit" a limited number of men, "it offers to sell exemptions" (Sjaastad and Hansen, 1970, p. IV-1-4).[10] Even the draft system used during most of the post–World War II period, until the lottery system was introduced in 1970, was shown to be a variation on the same model. For example, in the pre-lottery system, the cost to a potential draftee of avoiding military service, rather than being the dollars spent to buy an exemption or pay for a substitute took the "form of going to school, entering sheltered occupations, bearing legal and court fees as one fought induction, going to jail, emigrating to Canada, incurring disabilities, etc." (Sjaastad and Hansen, 1970, p. IV-1-6).[11]

The Economic Cost of a Random Lottery. The analysis of the economic cost of a random lottery draft system led to some very interesting and counterintuitive findings. Cooper showed that a random lottery actually has a larger economic cost than do alternative systems—hiring substitutes, purchasing exemptions, or "channeling" through exemptions and deferments—because some with a great aversion to serving in the military—such as a person with a high reservation wage—will be compelled to serve. Cooper noted that the

> irony is that the more random the draft policy, the larger the economic cost associated with those actually serving in the military. . . . For example, the excess economic cost of the pre-lottery draft is estimated to have been $850 million in the pre-Vietnam benchmark year of 1964; had the more random lottery draft been in effect, the excess economic cost would have been $1,350 million. . . .
>
> Therefore, the policymaker has the unenviable task of trading off economic cost against equity or "fairness." When the number of eligible men exceeds requirements, *there is no conscription policy that minimizes both economic cost and inequity.* (Cooper, 1977, pp. 73–74, emphasis in the original)

The Military as a Monopsonist. Those in favor of an all-volunteer force argued that, because conscription imposes a below-market wage and uses the power of the state to

---

[10] The French used this type of system from 1818 until 1870. After the fall of Napoleon, one of the first things the new king did in 1814 was end the draft. Conscription returned in 1818 in the form of a national lottery. Service fell, however, only on the unfortunates who both had a low lottery number and did not have the means to pay the Fr 2,000 "blood tax" for an "exemption." The resulting French Army was so ineffective that the Prussian Army of "conscripts" humiliated the French Army on the battlefield in 1870. In the United States, the Civil War Enrollment Act (March 3, 1863) followed the French example.

[11] It should be noted that joining the reserves during the Vietnam War period was also a "cost." The cost was serving in a reserve unit, which one would not have done in the absence of a draft. The benefit of joining the reserves was having very good chances of not serving on active duty and of not serving in Vietnam. See Rostker (1974) for a model of reserve-force participation that shows how the probability of being drafted and the probability of reserve mobilization affected the decision to join the military reserves.

compel people to serve at that wage, the military overemploys people, resulting in the waste of society's resources.[12] Thomas Borcherding was the first to note, however, that since the military faced an upward-sloping supply curve, it should be classified as a *monopsonist*.[13] Moreover, as a monopsonist it is possible that, with an all-volunteer force, the military would actually underemploy manpower. This also results in a misuse of society's resources. Moreover, he argues, "it is impossible to specify which inefficiency is more damaging," the overemployment of resources under a draft or "a possible deadweight burden associated with monopsonistic purchase of volunteers" (Borcherding, 1971, p. 196).[14]

The fact that the military faced an upward-sloping supply curve had other implications. Oi argued in the 1964 Pentagon Draft Study, to be followed later by the Gates Commission and by Sjaastad and Hansen, that a very large component of the cost of conscription was the economic rent foregone by volunteers.[15] They argued that this was a cost of conscription even though it was a transfer payment from the taxpayers, through the government, to the volunteers.[16] Borcherding's analysis implied, however, that while the rents may have been transfer payments, they were not *neutral* and had an impact on the optimal allocation of resources. His analysis showed that the payment of these *rents* was the source of the underutilization of manpower by a monopsonistic military.

The Military as a Discriminating Monopsonist. In his analysis of the military as a monopsonist, Borcherding noted that, from the point of view of society, the negative aspects of being a monopsonist would be ameliorated to the extent that the military can engage in wage discrimination. By *wage discrimination,* he meant that the military would not pay the first person it enlists the same wage it pays the last person it enlists. He assumed, however, that the military could not discriminate because equal wages for identically defined jobs are now the law of the land (Borcherding, 1971, p. 196).

The advantage of wage discrimination is clear. If the military *cannot* discriminate, the marginal cost of the last enlistee is not only the wage the military must pay but also the economic rent it paid previous enlistees. If the military *can* discriminate, however,

---

[12] One contributor to the *American Economic Review* suggested that, "It would appear without exception that economists believe that a voluntary military is preferable to conscription" (Borcherding, 1971, p. 195).

[13] Michael Brennan noted that

> Unlike a competitive resource buyer, a monopsonist . . . faces an upward sloping supply curve because he exercises control over the market price. . . . Control over demand depresses the price below competitive levels in favor of the buyer. (Brennan, 1965, pp. 309–315)

[14] Cooper argued that, while "the social welfare losses from underemployment of military labor remain a distinct possibility with the volunteer system, . . . these costs are considerably less than the social welfare losses incurred under the draft" (Cooper, 1975, p. 2).

[15] The estimate was that it was three quarters as large as the cost of wages foregone by draftees.

[16] Note that those who volunteered under the mixed draft-and-volunteer system received economic rent. But they received less rent than they would have if the system had been entirely volunteer. From the perspective of the volunteer in the mixed system, this was an actual cost—a loss of economic rent. From the perspective of the volunteer in an all-volunteer system, the rent that had been foregone would now be paid to the volunteer and would in effect be a transfer payment from the taxpayers to the volunteers.

Excerpted from Thomas E. Borcherding, "A Neglected Social Cost of a Voluntary Military," *American Economic Review* **Vol. 61, No. 1, March 1971, pp. 195–196**

It would appear without exception that economists believe that a voluntary military is preferable to conscription. It is my purpose to demonstrate that this institutional preference is questionable on purely a priori grounds. A *potentially* important welfare cost may arise under voluntarism from the monopsonistic behavior of the defense establishment as a purchaser of enlisted personnel. To analyze this possibility it will be necessary to develop a terse and simple model of choice in the "market" for enlisted personnel and to apply it to the institutions of conscription and voluntarism. . . .

Since the voluntarists hold that the draft leads to an excessive purchase of enlisted men, they implicitly assume that the military treats the budgetary cost of that input under conscription as the actual cost. Does not consistency require that this assumption hold under voluntarism as well? Fur-

ther, since the empirical evidence indicates that the supply function is upward sloping (see Stuart Altman and Alan Fechter, and Walter Oi), monopsonistic purchase is a distinct possibility unless wage discrimination is possible.

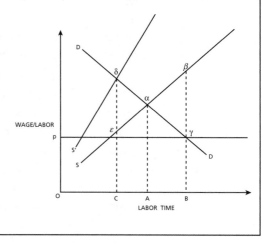

by paying each person just the wage necessary to entice him to join the military, the marginal value of the last person to join would be just equal the wage it took to get him to join. The military would use the *socially optimal* amount of manpower—it would not underemploy manpower.

The Military Tries to Minimize the Economic Rent Paid. What has become clear over the past 30 years is how important it is for the military to minimize economic rent and how expensive across-the-board pay increases are when given to all first-term personnel. This is true not only for minimizing budget outlays but also, as we have seen, for minimizing the negative effects of being a monopsonist, e.g., the underutilization of manpower. In fact, a more carefully crafted set of recruitment incentives built around bonuses and even payments in kind that are attractive to segments of the market has proven to be very important to the success of the all-volunteer force.

The military has been able to discriminate in the employment of first-term personnel by offering different segments of the market different money payments, conditions of service, and even payments in kind. For example, bonuses for the combat arms are occupationally specific, e.g., the military does not have to pay the economic rent that would result if the bonus wage level had been given as an across-the-board pay rate. By further limiting bonuses to high school graduates or to those who score highest on aptitude tests—presumably those with the highest *reservation wages*—the military can avoid paying economic rent to the less qualified—presumably those with the lowest *reservation wages*—who already have opted for combat arms. Negotiating with recruits over tour length, unit assignment, and duty location is a form of "wage discrimination" that has proven to be very effective. In addition, payments in kind are sometimes justified because of market imperfection, when the cost of the government providing a service is less than it would be for an individual to obtain that service on the open market.

In summary, the Gates Commission's argument that there was a "hidden tax of conscription" was supported by the economic analysis its staff had developed. Moreover, the argument clearly resonated with both those who supported and those who opposed an all-volunteer force. Regardless of their final views, both sides came together to vote for increases in first-term compensation. Also regardless of the sides' final views, increasing military compensation increased volunteers and moved the country toward zero draft calls and an all-volunteer force.

The arguments concerning foregone economic rents were more problematic. To the extent that these existed because the military faced an upward-sloping supply curve, the Gates Commission did not include the social costs of the possible underemployment of personnel associated with the all-volunteer force. To the extent a successful program of "wage discrimination" would be part of the management of an all-volunteer force, the Gates Commission overestimated the amount of economic rent foregone and thus also the final estimate of the conscription tax.

Subsequent Consideration of the Economics of Conscription. A consistent theme for both the 1964 Pentagon Draft Study and the Gates Commission was that economic, rather than budget, costs should be considered and that the difference was simply an appropriate "transfer of the burden of payment for national defense from draftees and reluctant volunteers to taxpayers in general" (Pauly and Willett, 1968). D. Lee and R. McKenzie (Lee and McKenzie, 1992), building on the work of Edgar Browning (1987), demonstrated that transfer payments were not neutral and showed that a volunteer force, with its greater budgetary cost, could impose higher deadweight losses from taxation than would a draft force of equal size.[17] John Warner and Beth Asch (Warner and Asch, 1996) extended Lee and McKenzie's one-period model to distinguish between first-term and career members of the military. They acknowledged that the social costs of a draft force could actually become less than the social costs of a volunteer force, considering the deadweight loss from taxation at some force levels, presumably when a large proportion of the eligible cohort of potential volunteers is needed when the marginal cost of an additional volunteer is extremely high. At this point, the social cost advantages of a volunteer force cannot overcome the added deadweight loss from raising large amounts of taxes to cover the extremely high marginal personnel cost and the

---

[17] In economics, a *deadweight loss* is a permanent loss of well-being to society that can occur when equilibrium for a good or service is not Pareto optimal (that is, that at least one individual could be made better off without others being made worse off). The draft thus causes a distortion in relative prices, which has an "income effect," making people feel poorer, and this income effect is a deadweight loss.

economic rent paid to the submarginal recruit. Parenthetically, Milton Friedman also acknowledged this point at the 1966 draft conference when he noted that

> [when] a very large fraction of the young men of the relevant age group are required . . . in the military . . . it might turn out that the implicit tax of forced service is less bad than the alterative taxes that would have to be used to finance a voluntary army. Hence for a major war, a strong case can be made for compulsory service. (Friedman, 1967, pp. 202–203)

Excerpted from John T. Warner and Beth J. Asch, "The Economics of Military Manpower," in Keith Hartley and Todd Sandler, eds., *Handbook of Defense Economics,* Vol. I, New York: Elsevier, 1995, pp. 375–379

Lee and McKenzie recognized that the military wage bill is not a pure transfer, but itself involves a cost. The reason is simple: when the government raises taxes (or prints money) in order to pay the military wage bill, the higher tax rates will, in general, cause distortions in economic behavior that impose deadweight losses on the economy. Browning (1987), for instance, finds the deadweight loss from income tax distortions to labor supply to be about 30–40 cents per dollar of tax revenue. Thus, a volunteer force, with its higher wage bill, will impose a larger deadweight loss from taxation than a draft force. It is therefore ambiguous whether a draft force has lower cost once the deadweight loss from taxation is considered. . . .

If the draft force is less than $2V$, it will be comprised only of volunteers: there is no distinction between the draft and the volunteer force. Therefore, below $2V$, $c_1 = 1$ and $TC_A = TC_D$. There is a discontinuity to TC_D at $F = 2V$. . . .

Which system to choose?[*] The answer depends on the desired force level and how it is determined. If all that matters is force size, then obviously choose the volunteer force if $F < F^*$ and the draft force if $F > F^*$. But the military is not concerned with forces of equal size so much as forces of equal readiness. There are three reasons to believe that a volunteer force will not need to be as large as a draft force to be equally ready. First, readiness is based on the number of ready personnel (denoted M above), not the total number F. Since the draft force has more personnel in training at any given time, and since some of the training must be provided by more experienced personnel, a draft force will not be as ready as a volunteer force of equal size. Second, to the extent that productivity rises with experience, a volunteer force will not need as many personnel to provide the same readiness. (Indeed, productivity studies reviewed in Section 3.2 above indicate big returns to experience in many military occupations.) Third, volunteers are likely to be more motivated than draftees, also making the volunteer force more productive than a draft force of equal size. (A theory of effort if developed in Section 5.) Importantly, as both forces increase in size, the difference in the average experience level and in personnel turnover also widens. Thus, a proportionate increase in the size of both

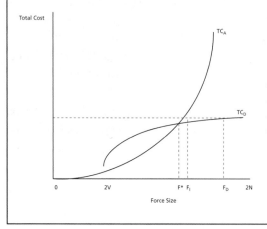

Excerpted from John T. Warner and Beth J. Asch, "The Economics of Military Manpower," in Keith Hartley and Todd Sandler, eds., *Handbook of Defense Economics,* Vol. I, New York: Elsevier, 1995, pp. 375–379—continued

forces will raise the effectiveness of the volunteer force relative to that of the draft force (i.e., $\partial R/\partial F_A$ increases relative to $\partial R/\partial F_D$ as F increases).

A second approach to the question of procurement method is to suppose that the military has an exogenous demand for a force with readiness level R^*. If F_A is the volunteer force and F_D is the draft force that will deliver the readiness level R^* (where $F_A < F_D$ for the reasons just stated), then the appropriate procurement method depends on a comparison of TC_A and TC_D for these two forces. As long as $F_A < F^*$, the volunteer force is unambiguously cheaper. Even above F^*, the volunteer force may be cheaper if the disparity in forces required to deliver readiness R^* is wide enough. Thus, in Figure 3 one would still choose the volunteer force F_A over the draft force F_D if $F_A < F_I$.

A third approach is to suppose that military planners, politicians, and the electorate somehow collectively determine the deterrent value of forces of different sizes and arrive at an optimal size force and procurement method by comparing the marginal cost of force size with the marginal benefit of force size or "value of marginal contribution of readiness" *(VMCR)*. VMCR is the social value placed on $\partial R/\partial F$ and probably rises as

the threat of war increases. Thus in Figure 4, the curves $VMCR_A$ and $VMCR_D$ represent the VMCR of a volunteer force and a draft force, respectively. For any force above $2V$, $VMCR_A > VMCR_D$ for the three reasons cited above, and the difference between them widens as F increases for the same reasons.

For either procurement method, the optimal force size is the one that equates *VMCR* with the marginal cost of force size. Thus, in Figure 4, F_A is the optimal volunteer force and F_D is the optimal draft force. Once these optimal size forces are determined, then the optimal procurement method is the one that maximizes the "surplus" from defense, i.e. the difference between the total value of the readiness provided *(VR)* and the total cost *(TC)*: $S = VR - TC$. (*VR* is the area under the relevant *VMCR* curve.) Thus, if S_A is the surplus from force F_A and S_D is the surplus from force F_D, choose the volunteer force if $S_A > S_D$. Figure 4 can be used to illustrate this approach. Suppose F_A is the optimal volunteer force and F_D is the optimal draft force. Then suppose that the volunteer force is expanded from F_A to F_D. The change in SA (∂S_A) is the area A, which is the excess of increase in cost over the value of readiness. Compare this to area D (∂S_D) which is the reduction in S_D brought about from reducing the draft force from F_D to F_A. The volunteer system is the optimal one if $S_A > S_D$. The additional insight that follows from this approach over previous ones is that S_D will rise relative to S_A the more elastic are the *VMCR* curves. That is, the less rapidly the value that the electorate places on additional units of defense readiness declines, the more likely the draft is to be the preferred procurement method. Outward shifts in the *VMCR* curves brought about by the threat of war mean larger optimal force levels and an higher likelihood that the defense surplus will be maximized through conscription.

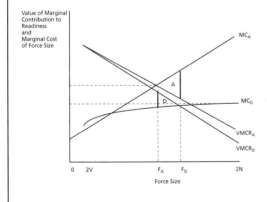

Warner and Asch acknowledged that, while the issue is ultimately empirical and hinges on questions about the deadweight loss from taxation, the elasticity of supply, and the productivity differences between volunteer and conscripted forces, they found the case for an all-volunteer force more compelling than Lee and McKenzie had suggested. Their analysis is particularly insightful when it examines why several European countries with strong historic ties to the draft as a legitimate form of national service decided to abandon conscription. Warner and Asch pointed out that the larger career forces associated with the all-volunteer policy yield a more-productive force than an equal-size force of conscripts and, thus, "conscription need not be the more efficient procurement method even if the draft force costs less." They further concluded that "the case for conscription has probably weakened over time due to improvements to military technology, which have served to increase the relative productivity of volunteer forces" (Warner and Asch, 1996, p. 311).

Supply of Personnel Available to the Military: Theory and Analysis

Theory

The economists on the Gates Commission staff developed a "theoretical model" of the choices each potential enlistee faced, e.g., to enlist or not to enlist, to derive a set of hypotheses and mathematical equations that could be estimated statistically. Alan Fechter provided a cogent presentation of this theoretical model in a way that has become the standard discussion about why the military faces an upward-sloping supply curve and why that supply curve has the familiar "S" shape. In his paper "Impact of Pay and Draft Policy on Army Enlistment Behavior" (Fechter, 1970), he developed the argument along these lines:

> Each potential enlistee is faced with a choice between enlisting and not enlisting. We shall classify the activities associated with the former choice as enlistment activity and activities associated with the latter choice as non-enlistment activity. In principle, each set of activities can be described in terms of pecuniary and non-pecuniary costs and benefits. Our model first assumes that the individual chooses the set of activities that provides him with the highest net pecuniary and non-pecuniary benefits. We further assume that, in principle, the individual can evaluate non-pecuniary costs and benefits in pecuniary terms. This implies, for example, that the individual is able to stipulate the number of dollars of additional pay, or pecuniary benefits, that he would require to offset the non-pecuniary cost associated with what he thinks are distasteful conditions of service life. . . .
>
> Given these assumptions, we can postulate that the potential enlistee can determine a reservation military wage . . . that would make the sum of the pecuniary and non-pecuniary benefits from choosing enlistment activity just equal to the sum of pecuniary and non-pecuniary benefits of choosing non-enlistment activity. At this wage, the potential enlistee would be indifferent between enlistment and non-

enlistment activity. If the military wage actually offered the potential enlistee . . . exceeded his reservation wage, he would enlist. If it did not, he would not.

One expects differences in reservation wages among potential enlistees. . . . Reservation wages may vary [because of] . . . differences in "tastes" for military activity. Individuals who find . . . military activity unpleasant will, other things equal, have a high reservation wage.

In principle, potential enlistees may be arrayed according to their reservation military wages, creating a frequency distribution like the one in Figure [5.1]. . . . [t]he shaded area under the frequency distribution . . . [Figure 5.2] can be transformed into a point on the enlistment supply schedule . . . . The entire enlistment supply schedule displays the number of enlistments that would be forthcoming at alternative military wages, other things held constant. . . . (Fechter, 1970, pp. II-3-2 to II-3-3)

If a normal curve best approximates the basic distribution of tastes, the cumulative distribution function of that curve is an inverted S-shaped function. This is the familiar S-shaped supply curve.

Analysis

The analysis of the supply of personnel available to the military reflects a fundamental conundrum of economic research. Some members of the Gates Commission staff thought the analysis would produce "precise estimates" (Fechter, 1970, p. II-3-1).

Figure 5.1
Frequency Distribution of Potential Enlistees Classified by Their Reservation Military Wage

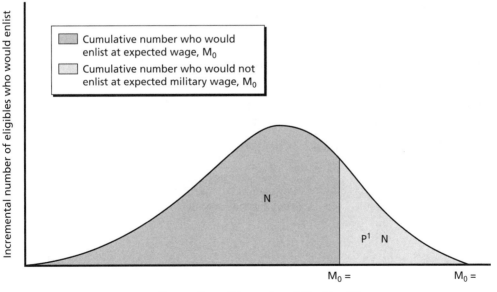

SOURCE: Fechter (1970, p. II-3-4).

Figure 5.2
Aggregate Enlistment Supply Curve

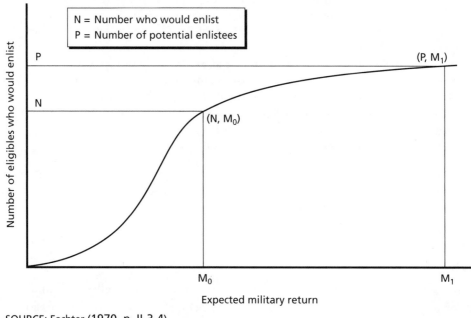

SOURCE: Fechter (1970, p. II-3-4).
RAND *MG265-5.2*

Others thought the analysis would provide "insights into the importance of possible changes in the environment" (Cook and White, 1970a, p. II-5-1). In fact, while the Gates Commission staff broke new ground by raising a number of methodological issues not previously considered in the published literature,[18] the commission's recommendations were not based on estimates of the elasticity of supply of new recruits from a single, definitive study.[19] In a supporting report that presented papers written by members of the commission's staff, Harry J. Gilman, who supervised those who worked on volunteer supply, went to great lengths to explain how they developed their statistical estimations of the supply elasticity for non–prior service personnel. He described the studies as collectively forming the underlying basis of the staff's estimates and the commission's recommendation:

> The terms "collectively" and "underlying bases" were used . . . to emphasize the fact that the recommended pay increases for military personnel, particularly for those in their first term of service, were based more on the collective conclusions of these studies than on specific estimates derived in them. In general, the studies were too diverse in methods and results and their data base too imperfect to enable the

---

[18] Gilman describes the two most significant previous studies of the draft as being those by Anthony Fisher and by Stuart Altman and Alan Fechter (Gilman, 1970 p. II-1-4).

[19] *Elasticity of supply* measures the change in the amount a firm supplies in response to a change in price.

Commission's staff to directly use the individual estimates derived. (Gilman, 1970, pp. II-1-1 to II-1-2)

Even Alan Fechter, who had worked on the original 1964 Pentagon Draft Study and who had seen his task as "obtaining precise estimates of the effects of pay and draft policy on enlistment behavior," concluded that "[t]he results reported should be viewed as tentative rather than final. Our results raised many questions that could not be adequately answered" (Fechter, 1970, p. II-3-1).

Notwithstanding the above, and with full consideration for the "collective, and underlying bases" of the staff studies, the commission staff settled on an elasticity of supply of 1.25 to be used when making projections of the influence of pay changes on the number of true volunteers.[20] That estimate has proven remarkably resilient, and, as one researcher remarked,

> The Gates Commission results on the effects of pay have stood the test of time. . . . If the Gates Commission work were being redone today (1983), it is quite possible its pay elasticity assumption would remain unchanged. (Nelson, 1986, p. 43)

Diverse Methods and Imperfect Databases

A significant reason for deciding not to use a single study or single estimate was that, as Gilman noted, the diverse "methods and results" and a database that was "too imperfect to enable the Commission's staff to directly use the individual estimates derived" (Gilman, 1970, p. II-1-2). The following are a number of examples of the diversity in methods and results.

Estimates of the Number of True Volunteers. Estimates of the number of true volunteers were critical to the analytic design because they determined the "manpower deficit" that an all-volunteer force pay raise had to overcome. The smaller the deficit, the smaller the pay raise; the smaller the deficit, the smaller the supply response required from a given pay raise; the smaller the deficit, the smaller the estimated supply elasticity required to overcome the deficit. Gilman highlights, as discussed in Chapter Two of this book, the two methods used to account for the effect of the draft and to estimate the manpower deficit: "the observed relationship between changes in the rate of inductions" that Fisher and others used in time series analysis and "the responses of first-termers to survey questionnaires" that Altman and Fechter and others used in cross-sectional analysis (Gilman, 1970, p. II-1-5). Gilman characterized the problem of estimating the then-current number of true volunteers as "no less serious in this [the Gates Commission] study than were those faced in the earlier studies." The draft pressure estimates produced for time series studies were characterized by the commission's staff itself in their various staff papers as "not too reliable" and "highly unstable."

---

[20] The Army suggested an elasticity between 0.5 and 1.0. The System Analysis staff told Secretary Laird's military assistant that there had "been little evidence to support an elasticity of less than 1.0. . . . The Gates Commission believed the best estimate was 1.25 and this appears to us to be on the conservative side" (Odeen, 1971).

However, Gilman considered the survey estimates used in cross-sectional analysis to be "at best highly subjective" (Gilman, 1970, p. II-1-6).

While Gilman and the Gates team expressed misgivings about their *specific* estimates of the effects of the draft and the true volunteer rate the military faced in 1970, they believed they had some reasonable insights into the size of the manpower deficit expected from the elimination of the draft. Gilman thought the draft pressure method produced estimates that implied a higher estimate of the number of true volunteers than did the survey method, and if the estimates were anywhere near correct, "the manpower deficits will be fairly small for the forces up to 2.5 million men" (Gilman, 1970, pp. II-1-7, II-1-10).

Supply-and-Demand Identification Problem. The Gates staff also noted the identification problem that had plagued earlier attempts to estimate military supply curves, a central theme of advances in supply modeling a decade later. Burton Gray summarizes the issues this way:

> If there are any queues, and if any of the services are turning away potential enlistees, then we are not observing points on the supply curve. This possibility appears to be greatest for the Air Force, followed by the Navy, and less for the Marines. It is unlikely that the Army and the Marines have been in a position to turn away enlistees in mental group I–III. The existence of unobserved queuing would cause us to underestimate the supply elasticities. (Gray, 1970, p. II-2-6)

Aside from measuring enlistments only for a subpopulation that was thought never to be in "excess supply"—white, male first-term enlistees in mental group I–III—only the studies by Alvin Cook and John White studies tried to explicitly deal with the *identification problem* (Cook, 1970) (Cook and White, 1970b).[21] Cook explains that

> The supply curve of Air Force volunteers . . . is not directly observable because data are not available on the number of individuals who volunteer but only on the number who actually enlist . . . so attempts to estimate supply curve parameters in traditional ways yield erroneous results. To circumvent this difficulty, we developed a supply curve adjusted by the quality of the recruits and demonstrate that this quality adjustment is an implicit equilibrating mechanism between demand for recruits and supply of volunteers. . . . [T]he parameters of the unobservable supply curve can then be inferred from the adjusted supply curve. (Cook, 1971, p. 4)

Cook includes a *quality variable* that equals "the average quality level of the recruits accepted" (Cook, 1970, p. II-4-10) for each quarter from the first quarter of 1958 through the second quarter of 1967. He also calculated and used as explanatory variables in his regression analysis the *net advantage* of being in the Air Force based on the ratio of military and civilian wages, *draft pressure* based on the Selective Service I-A pool

---

[21] *Author's Note:* Within the decade, John White would become the Assistant Secretary of Defense for Manpower and Reserve Affairs (1977–1978), then the Deputy Director of the Office of Management and Budget (1978–1981). He would also serve as Deputy Secretary of Defense during the Clinton administration.

and that part of the pool which called for preinduction physical examination, unemployment from seasonally adjusted youth unemployment rates from the Bureau of Labor Statistics, and dummy variables for exogenous influences—the Berlin crisis, the Vietnam War and the period when President Kennedy expanded marriage deferments.

He also calculated and used the following as explanatory variables in his regression analysis

- the *net advantage* of being in the Air Force, based on the ratio of military to civilian wages
- the *draft pressure,* based on the Selective Service I-A pool and the part of the pool that was called up for preinduction physical examination
- unemployment from seasonally adjusted youth unemployment rates from the Bureau of Labor Statistics
- dummy variables for exogenous influences, such as the Berlin crisis, the Vietnam War, and the effects of President Kennedy's expansion of marriage deferments.

His estimate of the elasticity of volunteers with respect to relative pay, given the average quality level of the recruit force, is 2.19. Cook also raises an important question concerning the role that quality will play in achieving an all-volunteer force, a question he partially answered in his second study with John White. In commenting on his projections of the cost of the all-volunteer force for the Air Force, Cook noted that

> This assumes that the average quality level of the recruit force remains constant. If the quality level is allowed to decrease, the amount of money required to fulfill the manpower requirements will also decrease. This raises questions about the decrease in quality that may be entertained without harming the Air Force's mission and about the preferred and feasible mix of various qualities of individuals under a binding budget constraint. We have not attempted to address these problems within the scope of this study, but they should not be idly dismissed, especially in a world fraught with budget constraints. (Cook, 1970, p. II-4-21)

In fact, in another study, Cook and White tried to address the issue by turning their regression equation on its end and by using quality of recruits as the dependent variable. They noted that "[t]he earnings ratio is the most significant variable for quality changes and has the largest elasticity" (Cook and White, 1970a, p. II-5-16). This is particularly significant, given the work Fechter did on the appropriateness of relative pay, e.g., the ratio of military to civilian wages, instead of including each pay variable separately.

Specification of Military and Civilian Pay. Most studies of enlisted supply incorporate *relative pay* as a key explanatory variable. The use of this ratio implies that equal and offsetting changes in civilian and military wages that leave the ratio unchanged have no effect on enlistments. Alternatively, the two pay measures—civilian pay and military pay—could enter the analysis as separate variables, each free to take on its own estimated value. In such a case, the *expected* positive sign on the coefficient for military pay would reflect the substitution effect of joining the military. An *expected* negative sign on the coefficient for civilian pay would reflect the substitution effect of increased opportunity costs of joining the military. In this case, however, the expected negative sign could, if "enlisting in the Army is considered a relatively discommodious activity" (Fechter, 1970, p. II-3-8), reflect an *income effect* as potential recruits turn away from the military. Thus, it is possible that service in the military is what economists call an *inferior good.* Empirically, Fechter notes from his analysis that

> Decomposition of relative pay into its components, military and civilian pay, produced the finding that civilian pay changes were causing most of the enlistment response. This finding could be attributed to possible multicollinearity or large measurement error in our estimate of military pay. It also could have arisen because of a shift on the part of potential enlistees away from military careers as their family incomes, . . . which correlated with our estimates of civilian pay, rose. (Fechter, 1970, p. II-3-22)

The policy implications of using each of these two specifications of the pay variables are striking. When using the relative military pay variable, economists implicitly assume symmetry between military and civilian pay. This precludes the possibility of a negative *income effect* that shows a decrease in the number of people joining the military as civilian incomes rise. Use of the absolute pay model is less restrictive. It allows for asymmetrical responses in pay and for the possibility that military service is an *inferior good.* Over time, as standards of living increase, this would suggest that it would be increasingly more difficult to attract people to join the military.

The Functional Form. Unlike earlier estimates of non–prior service supply, the Gates Commission staff considered how the mathematical formulation—the "functional form"—of the regression equation might affect the estimated coefficients. Concern for the specific form of the supply function starts with the underlying labor theory of *occupational preferences* and *compensating payments* that was discussed earlier in this Chapter. It is generally assumed that there is a distribution of *reservation wages* that has the general shape of a normal curve. Reservation wages reflect the population's taste for and attitudes toward the military. It follows then that the cumulative distribution function of this normal curve is an inverted S-shaped function, which economists refer to as a supply curve, with wages on the y-axis and quantity on the x-axis.

If the military wants to recruit at least cost, that is, to behave as a discriminating monopsonist, its wage offer will take into account the distribution of taste for military service in the population. Those with the highest taste (or preference) for military service will be willing to accept the lowest wage, other things being equal. By implication, the first individuals to enlist at the lowest wage will be those with the highest taste, and increases in the wage will be needed to bring in individuals with incrementally lower tastes. This process of self-selection into the military implies that recruits tend to be drawn from a particular portion of the taste distribution—the upper end. This remains true even over the rest of the upper range of the taste distribution because the value of the supply elasticity depends on the specific point of evaluation; it is not, however, true that the supply elasticity is in general constant, although it might be approximately constant over the range of recruiting observed empirically.

Early estimates that used functional forms that had uniformly declining elasticities of supply are clearly inconsistent with an S-shaped supply curve, which has different regions reflecting extreme tastes and attitudes—preferences—for and against military service. Gilman noted, however, that this may be more of a theoretical than a practical problem, since

> We may expect to observe a significantly declining elasticity only when the deficit is large because only then do the military services have to call on individuals whose tastes may be significantly different from those that preceded them into the military on a voluntary basis. . . . In our case . . . [a]lmost independent of the shape of the [supply] function, the elasticity of supply should be fairly constant over time. (Gilman, 1970, p. II-1-12)

Gray agreed and noted that

> For the purpose of extrapolation, we must specify the form of the supply function above the observed mean enlistment rates. Economic theory suggests that the supply elasticity probably decreases as we move up the supply function. (Gray, 1970, p. II-2-32)

He goes on to say that

> the range and variation of the data did not permit us to distinguish on statistical grounds alone which functional form gave the best fit. The elasticities computed at the mean values . . . were all very similar. (Gray, 1970, p. II-2-12)

Specification Errors, Measurement Errors, and Statistical Bias. The data the Gates Commission staff used generally go under the heading of nonexperimental data. As such, they are often proxies for more-specific data that would have been available if the studies were being done under controlled conditions, e.g., experiments. Such data, because they are collected from many generic sources, are often subject to all kinds of specification and measurement errors. Gilman notes, for example, "in the [cross-sectional] enlistment accession studies, the dependent variable . . . the enlistment rate . . . require[s] too many adjustments based on imperfect information" (Gilman, 1970, pp. II-1-13 to II-1-14) to provide reliable estimates. He characterizes the pay variables used in *time series* regression analysis as "imprecise," then admits that "even if they had been more precise, it would still be difficult to interpret their meaning and their impact on enlistments. We simply do not know enough about how individuals respond to expected pay raises" (Gilman, 1970, p. II-1-14). Finally, in terms that are reminiscent of Harold Wool's earlier critique of the results of the 1964 Pentagon Draft Study, he "confesses" that

> Unfortunately, complete isolation of the pay effects is almost impossible to achieve. Mostly, of course, this is a failure of the data rather than the method, for neither the civilian pay and population figures nor the military pay and enlistment or re-enlistment data nor any of the other data are available in sufficient detail or have been generated under sufficiently stable conditions to permit such isolation. (Gilman, 1970, p. II-1-13)

The individual authors of the component studies that supported the Gates Commission seem to concur with Gilman's rather gloomy assessment. Burton Gray worried about inconsistency between the data and the underlying theory. Specifically, he noted that "if reservations wages and civilian incomes are positively related we will overestimate the effects of military pay on enlistments" (Gray, 1970, p. II-2-2).[22]

Gray also notes that in his data "[f]ailure to account for military wage variation will produce a downward bias in our regression coefficients for relative income, and hence, the elasticity" (Gray, 1970, p. II-2-8). He explains, however, that "[a] more important and potent source of bias is random, nonsystematic errors of measurement of civilian incomes" (Gray, 1970, p. II-2-31). He concludes by saying,

> The evidence from our regressions and data is not sufficient to indicate the net effect of these sources of bias. We suspect that the net effect is to cause an underestimate of the elasticity, but we are not sufficiently confident to attempt to create a "fudge factor" to add to our actual estimates. (Gray, 1970, p. II-2-31)

He concluded, however, in the spirit of Gilman, *"collectively, underlying base"* argument, that, for first-term enlistments,

> [t]he results of this study imply higher elasticities than the results of the previous cross section work. The enlistment rates used were not significantly different, but the income measure and disaggregated data base were. We conclude that "the elasticity" of first term military supply with respect to the military wage is very probably above unity, that it may be as high as 1.5, but that it is very probably less than 2.0. (Gray, 1970, p. II-2-22)

Gilman told us that, "[b]ecause of some of the data and measurement problems . . . , [the Gates Commission] used an elasticity of supply for initial entrants of 1.25 rather than those reported in the respective studies" (Gilman, 1970, p. II-1-14).[23]

---

[22] Gray was a little ahead of the times. His point that reservation wage possibly correlated with "income" was addressed in later empirical work on recruiting that included family income, or parent education levels, among the explanatory variables.

[23] Gilman went on to note that they believed "that this elasticity is on the low side both because it is lower than the vast majority of the statistically significant estimates reported in the respective studies and because most of the identifiable biases are on the negative side" (Gilman, 1970, p. II-1-14).

Excerpted from Burton C. Gray, "Supply of First-Term Military Enlistees: A Cross-Section Analysis," in Gates Commission, eds., *Studies Prepared for the President's Commission on an All-Volunteer Armed Force*, Washington, D.C.: U.S. Government Printing Office, 1970, pp. II-2-24 and II-2-25

As we mentioned in section I above, we make the critical assumption that the distribution of reservation relative wages, r, is independent of the distribution of w_c. However, it is possible and even likely that reservation wages are not distributed independently of other variables such as regional attitudes toward the military, differences across socio-economic groups, ethnic differences, etc. In the context of cross section estimation, the socio-economic variables are likely to be the most troublesome. Groups whose education or family income is high may require larger relatively military to civilian wages in order to enlist, implying that r and w_c may be positively related. In figure II.2.3 we show two possible F functions for which r and w_c are positively related. If potential enlistees from each group receive the same military wage, w_m, then the points we actually observe will trace out an F function which has a higher slope than the group specific functions. Thus the effect of assuming only one taste function for the entire population will be to overestimate the elasticity of supply.

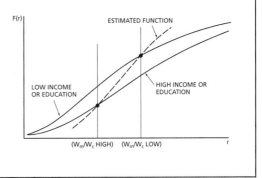

The Reenlistment of First-Term Personnel

The staff's analysis of the first-term reenlistment rate provided the commission with an estimate of the sensitivity of first-term reenlistment to economic variables and an estimate of the effect of the presence of draftees and draft-motivated enlistments on depressing the first-term reenlistment rate. The commission's staff used the measure of the depressed reenlistment rate to look at military turnover and the longer-term demand for enlistments; as Gary Nelson noted, "[a] critical source of supply of military personnel is the group of men completing the first term of military service" (Nelson, 1970, p. II-6-1).[24]

The staff's studies of reenlistment were a "special case of the more general decisions between any two employment alternatives" (Wilburn, 1970, p. II-7-1). The elasticity estimates were made using statistical techniques similar to those used in the analysis of first-term personnel. There was, however, some recognition that the decision a person considering reenlistment and potentially a career in the military makes might

---

[24] *Author's Note:* Gary Nelson was one of the Institute for Defense Analyses economists assigned to work on the staff of the Gates Commission. He would later move to RAND and then to the Congressional Budget Office. During the Carter Administration, he was a Deputy Assistant Secretary of Defense working for John White in the Manpower and Reserve Affairs office. He played an important role in the development of better econometric techniques for measuring retention. Gary would end his service in government as the Director of Compensation at the Office of Personnel Management. After government service, he had a long and distinguished career at the Systems Research and Analysis Corporation.

be different from one a person considering initial employment by one of the services would make. Specifically, while Nelson incorporated in his analysis estimates of expected future military and civilian income for the next three years after the decision to reenlist, he noted that, "[s]ince subsequent reenlistment rates are quite high (in excess of 75 percent), a more distant time horizon may be considered appropriate" (Nelson, 1970, p. II-6-6). Subsequent studies in the late 1970s would explicitly model the decision process that service members are assumed to go through when they make the decision to reenlist. These more-sophisticated models of the decision process would become one of the most productive lines of economic research that continue to the present.

The Supply of Officers

One of the most significant methodological departures from the work of the 1964 Pentagon Draft Study was in the estimation of the supply of officers. In the earlier study, Stuart Altman and Alan Fechter (1967) used substantially the same model that they had for the supply of enlisted personnel to model the supply of officers. They derived

---

Excerpted from Stuart H. Altman and Robert J. Barro, "Officer Supply: The Impact of Pay, the Draft, and the Vietnam War," *American Economic Review,* **Vol. 61, No. 4, September 1971, pp. 652-654**

II. The Effect of a Draft

With the introduction of a draft it is necessary to consider three occupations: civilian, officer, and draftee. As discussed below, there must be some distinction between being an officer and being a draftee if the introduction of a draft is to have any effect on the officer enlistment rate. In addition to the returns from the civilian and officer occupations, one must also calculate the return from the draftee occupation. For the following analysis we make the important simplifying assumption that the difference between the officer and draftee occupations can be captured solely as a pecuniary differential. Hence, the total monetized return from the draftee occupation is (see equations (1) and (3)):

(8) $\qquad M_d^i = w_d + p_d^i N_o = w_d(1 + \tau_o^i N_o)$

Where w_d is draftee pay and is assumed to be equal for all individuals. The inclusion of the officer nonpecuniary term, $\tau_o^i N_o$, reflects the assumption that the officer and draftee occupations can be distinguished solely on pecuniary grounds.

With the existence of a draft, an individual's choice is still between enlisting as an officer or remaining a civilian. The new element here is that there is some probability, p_i, of being drafted if one chooses to remain a civilian. Therefore, the civilian option amounts to the choice of a lottery where one obtains M_c^i with probability $(1 - p_i)$ and M_d^i with probability p_i. Assuming that (von Neumann-Morgenstern) utility is linearly related to the monetized returns in each occupation—that is, that individuals are (at least approximately) risk-neutral in the choice among these occupations, the officer enlistment condition is:

$$(1 - p_i)M_c^i + p_i M_d^i < M_o^i$$

Using equations (1), (3), (4), and (8), the condition for volunteering as an officer may be expressed as (assuming $w_o > w_d$):

(9) $\quad w_c^i(1 + \tau_i) < w_o + \dfrac{p_i}{1 - p_i}(w_o - w_d)$

Where $(1 + \tau_i)$ is the civilian/military taste factor, defined in equation (4).

Excerpted from Stuart H. Altman and Robert J. Barro, "Officer Supply: The Impact of Pay, the Draft, and the Vietnam War," *American Economic Review,* **Vol. 61, No. 4, September 1971, pp. 652-654—continued**

The enlistment condition in equation (9) indicates that the introduction of a draft ($p_i \neq 0$ for some i) has an impact on enlistment only if ($w_o \neq w_d$). If officer and draftee pay are equivalent (in a generalized sense), all individuals who would opt for civilian life in the absence of a draft would still desire civilian life when a draft was introduced? The essence of draft-induced enlistment is some distinction between the treatment of officers (enlistees) and draftees.

Again viewing w_c^i and $(1 + \tau_i)$ as subject to probability distributions, the fraction of individuals who enlist in the presence of a draft is given by:

(10)

$$\Phi^d = P_\tau \left[w_c^i (1 + \tau_i) < w_o + \frac{p_i}{1 - p_i} (w_o - w_d) \right]$$

In equation (10) individuals are viewed as comparing taste-adjusted civilian pay, $w_c^i(1 + \tau_i)$, with officer pay, w_o, augmented by a term to account for the effect of the draft: $[p_i/(1 - p_i)](w_o - w_d)$. Among a group of individuals with a single value of $p_i > p$, and a fixed distribution of $w_c^i(1 + \tau_i)$, the enlistment percentage increases with p if $w_o > w_d$, and increases with $(w_o - w_d)$ if $p > O$. In other words, with the presence of a draft, the military has two vehicles in addition to increases in pecuniary and nonpecuniary pay which can increase the number of officer accessions. First, the probability of being drafted may be raised, and, second, the conditions of draftees, w_d, may be worsened.

The fraction of officer entrants in the presence of a draft (equation (10)) may be compared with those in the nondraft model equation (6)). Since the left-hand variable in the probability statement, $w_c^i(1 + \tau_i)$ is the same for both models, it is possible, without knowledge of the explicit distributions of w_c^i and $(1 + \tau_i)$; to answer the following question. If there is currently a draft situation characterized by military wages w_o and w_d and draft probability p (which applies to all members of some group of individuals), and if Φ^d is the percentage of the eligible population which is voluntarily entering the military as officers, what increment in officer pay would be required to maintain the officer entrance rate if the draft were abolished? Since $\Phi = \Phi^d$ is required, the necessary increment in pay follows from equations (6) and (10):

$$\Delta w_o = \frac{p}{1 - p} (w_o - w_d)$$

As a numerical illustration, the data for 1964 are; $p = .358$, $(w_o - w_d) = \$2444/\text{year}$. Therefore, the pay increment which just maintains the enlistment percentage when p is set equal to zero is $\Delta w_o = \$1363/\text{year}$ which amounts to a 28 percent increase over 1964 first-term officer pay. Comparable figures for 1969 are: $p = .536$, $(w_o - w_d) = \$3619$, $\Delta w_o = \$4180$, or a 63 percent increment in pay. The greater percentage in the later year is accounted for by the higher percentage of officer enlistees who would otherwise be drafted.

In order to determine the entire officer supply curve, it is necessary to specify the joint distribution of w_c^i, $(1 + \tau_i)$ and p_i in equation (10). The analysis is facilitated if it is possible to segregate the total population into a few groups of equal draft probability. If a group with a single draft probability p is involved, and if w_c^i and $(1 + \tau_i)$ are, as in Section I, independently lognormally distributed, then:

(11)
$$\Phi^d = N \left[\frac{\log \dfrac{w_o^*}{\widetilde{w}_c(1 \mp \tau)}}{\sigma} \right]$$

where w_o^* is "effective" officer pay (explicit pay augmented by the effect of the draft), and is given from equation (10) by:

(12)
$$w_o^* = w_o + \frac{p}{1 - p} (w_o - w_d)$$

"estimates of the extent to which new officers could be attracted to military service through pay increases, . . . [based] on variations in ROTC enrollment rates in voluntary institutions in 1963" (Altman and Fechter, 1967, p. 27). Altman, in his work for the Gates Commission, this time with Robert J. Barro,[25] developed a much more sophisticated model of officer accession. The model Altman and Barro used was based on Fisher's (Fisher, 1969) occupational choice model; however, they explicitly considered the influence that the draft had on the earnings of those who were considering taking officer commissions.

Altman and Barro noted that the traditional economic model considered the choice between a civilian and a military occupation over the "short period corresponding to the length of initial duty obligation of an officer" (Altman and Barro, 1970, p. II-10-2). Unlike previous studies that added independent variables reflecting the differential pressure of the draft, constructed from either survey results or draft calls, a "reduced form" specification, they modeled explicitly the influence that the draft would have on alternative income streams. Seen this way, the draft created a third occupation that could be chosen. They argued that

> With the introduction of a draft [as was true during the period their data was collected] it is necessary to distinguish between three occupations: civilian, officer, and draftee. . . . [Moreover], there must be some distinction between being an officer and being a draftee if the introduction of a draft is to have any effect on the officer enlistment rate. . . .
>
> With the existence of a draft, an individual's choice is still between enlisting as an officer or remaining a civilian. The new element here is that there is some probability . . . of being drafted if one chooses to remain a civilian. . . .
>
> [W]ith the presence of a draft, the military has two vehicles in addition to increases in pecuniary and nonpecuniary pay which can increase the number of officer accessions. First, the probability of being drafted may be raised, and second, the conditions of draftees may be worsened. (Altman and Barro, 1971, pp. 652–653)

This notion that the probability of being drafted would influence the "effective" pay of the occupational alternatives is similar to the analysis of joining the reserve forces. During the Vietnam War, given that the likelihood a reserve unit would be called up was very small, joining a reserve unit was a hedge against being drafted and the loss of civilian earnings.

---

[25] Altman and Barro's work was among the Gates Commission's staff papers (Altman and Barro, 1970). It was also published in the *American Economic Review* (Altman and Barro, 1971).

Expanding the Supply of, and Reducing the Demand for, Military Manpower

To the Gates Commission, the feasibility of an all-volunteer force lay not only in increasing the supply of traditional volunteers to the military but also in expanding the pool of available young men and reducing the demand for new personnel. The analysis of the economics of conscription suggested that the military had little incentive to economize on its use of people by eliminating unnecessary jobs or substituting different types of personnel, such as women and civilians, for the white males who made up the vast majority of those being inducted. Moreover, the draft had allowed the services to set mental aptitude, physical, and moral standards at levels that might minimize budget costs but that were not necessarily economically efficient or even cost effective.

Quality of an All-Volunteer Force

The quality of personnel needed to man an all-volunteer force was a point of contention between those favoring the end of conscription and those wanting to retain the draft. Those arguing to end the draft saw the demands for a "high-quality" force as inflated and charged that the military was using this issue to sabotage the all-volunteer force.[26] Those favoring a draft feared the Gates Commission would trade "military effectiveness" for the unproven and risky scheme of an all-volunteer force.

David M. Reaume and Walter Y. Oi (1970) and John A. Sullivan (1970) examined the issue of mental standards for the Gates Commission. Reaume and Oi considered the civilian education distribution weighted by the actual 1969 enlisted force strengths assigned to the military occupational specialty corresponding to the civilian occupation against data on the educational attainment of enlisted men classified by major DoD occupations. They concluded that "the Air Force and Navy employ more talent than the civilian economy when talent is measured either by educational attainment or mental test scores" (Reaume and OI, 1970, p. I-3-18). They argued that their results were confirmed for the Army by a study by Worth Bateman (Bateman, 1965). Sullivan started his study by examining the proposition that "an all-volunteer force would have to be manned with lower-quality [mental quality] personnel" (Sullivan, 1970, p. I-2-1). He considered the proposition that the services needed high-quality recruits because of the demands of "modern military technology" by looking at changes in the mix of military occupations over time. Based on his assessment of the services' occupational structures, he concluded that the

> secular rise in the average mental ability of recruits . . . *cannot* . . . be explained by the *need* for high quality personnel, but must instead reflect other Service policies

---

[26] A *high-quality* service member is generally defined as one who scores in the upper half of the Armed Forces Qualifications Test (AFQT), i.e., groups I, II, and IIIA, and a high school graduate.

such as the use of mental standards to limit the supplies of potential volunteers. (Sullivan, 1970, p. I-2-16, emphasis in the original)

Sullivan argued, based on the experience with the so-called "New Standards" recruits of Project 100,000,[27] that higher-quality recruits were not needed. He cited the studies by I. M. (Irv) Greenberg (1969), who would later become a key DoD manager for the all-volunteer force implementation program,[28] that the marginal cost of training a New Standards man was approximately $200. Understanding the cost implications of trying to achieve an all-volunteer force by focusing on raising pay, Sullivan argued that

> the Services could obtain larger flows of volunteers by lowering mental standards or by raising pay. The former involves higher training costs, while the latter adds to the military pay budget. The comparatively small magnitude of the higher training costs suggests that if the draft were ended, it would be more economical to retain and possibly expand the New Standards program. (Sullivan, 1970, p. I-2-25)

Sullivan also questioned the use of written tests, citing Eli Flyer's work for the Air Force (Flyer), that "the possession of a high school diploma is a more significant predictor of future adjustment to the military than is measured mental ability" (Sullivan, 1970, p. I-2-27). Finally, Sullivan concluded that:

> The performance of NS [New Standards] men in relation to control groups that met the higher qualification standards that prevailed in FY1965 is clearly lower, especially when performance was measured by written tests. Attrition rates in formal training courses and incidence of disciplinary problems were also higher for NS men. All of these results were predictable from earlier studies. The magnitude of the differentials between NS men and Control groups is, however, an important finding of the Project 100,000 experience. The higher attrition rates in training NS men were found, for example, to add only 3 to 5 percent to the full training costs. When performance is measured by supervisory ratings, the difference between NS men and control groups

---

[27] Sullivan has observed that, in

October 1966, the Department of Defense launched Project 100,000 (also called the New Standards program) under which the Services were forced to accept some men in lower mental group IV . . . Project 100,000 was, to a considerable degree, a rehabilitation program for men with marginal mental and physical qualifications and does not reflect the Services' judgment of the effectiveness of these marginal men. (Sullivan, 1970, p. I-2-10)

[28] Mental Category IV and the New Standards Men were "related" in a very specific way. Greenberg noted that,

for the period October 1966 to December 1971, the Secretary of Defense established quotas for the percentage of non–prior service accessions who scored in mental group IV on the Armed Forces Qualification Test. These quotas varied by service to take into account the job mix differences by service. At least 50 percent of the CAT IV quota were required to be men who would have been rejected for military service immediately before Project 100,000. These newly eligible men were called New Standards Men. Furthermore, 50 percent of the New Standards quota was to be met with men scoring in AFQT band 10–15—the lower half of CATIV. Although test score standards were lowered, they still were somewhat higher than those in the Korean War and much higher than World War II standards. (Greenberg, 2004)

is negligible. One cannot help but conclude that the Project 100,000 experiment has been a success and should be continued. The Armed Services freely admit that the NS men have proven themselves to be effective soldiers in combat and logistical support units. Yet when the NS men reach the re-enlistment point, a majority of them are classified as "ineligible to re-enlist" mainly because they fail to pass the written mental and aptitude tests. . . . So long as a draft will assure the Services of adequate supplies of new recruits, there is little incentive to retain an enlisted man who is unlikely to be promoted to the top NCO rank. (Sullivan, 1970, pp. I-2-44 to I-2-46)

Using the 1964 and 1968 DoD personnel surveys, Sullivan found that "if the draft is ended with no pay changes about 50.6 to 53.6 percent of true volunteers to the Army are likely to have high school degrees." He argued that

[t]he evidence assembled in this study leads us to the conclusion that the relaxed mental standards . . . can provide the requisite quality to effectively man the enlisted billets in an all-volunteer force. . . . [Moreover], acceptable percentage[s] of mental group IV inputs (recruits) can be as high as 25 to 30 percent in the Army and Marine Corps, and 20 to 25 percent in the Navy and Air Force. (Sullivan, 1970, p. I-2-47)[29]

A Further Word About Project 100,000

The fact that Project 100,000 was often cited by those who thought the services overstated their need for high-quality personnel infuriated the generals and admirals in the Pentagon. From its very inception, they spoke about Project 100,000 in the most derogatory terms, often referring to it as another of President Johnson's Great Society "social experiments." If this was to be the cost of an all-volunteer force, it was a cost that they were not willing to pay, and they resisted every effort to force them to lower their recruiting standards. While the focus of a great deal of research during the 1980s was on entry standards—research that would eventually validate the benefits of keeping them high—the relevance of Project 100,000 was still a matter of great debate in the early 1970s.

Project 100,000 was Secretary of Defense Robert McNamara's response to the 1964 report of the President's Task Force on Manpower Conservation, *One-Third of a Nation: A Report on Young Men Found Unqualified for Military Service.*[30] With President Johnson's Great Society programs being implemented across the federal government, one of the purposes of Project 100,000 was to upgrade the qualification of disadvantaged youth to prepare them for more productive civilian lives. "DoD was

---

[29] Greenberg noted that

These percentages are somewhat higher than the Mental Group IV quota for Project 100,000 in effect from October 1966 to December 1971. The Army's quota ranged from 24.0 percent to 25.0 percent; Marine Corps from 18.0 percent to 24.0 percent; Navy from 15.0 percent to 18.0 percent; and Air Force from 15.0 percent to 18.0 percent. The CAT IV percentages were based on the job-mix of the Vietnam era force structure. (Greenberg, 2004)

[30] Greenberg discusses the early Project 100,000 in a 1969 article (1969).

convinced," Greenberg noted in a report on Project 100,000, "that the training and experience these men would receive would not only make then satisfactory servicemen, but would also prepare them for more productive lives when they returned to civilian lives" (Greenberg, 1972, p. 1).

In 1966, in an address before the Veterans of Foreign Wars, Secretary of Defense McNamara announced DoD would start a program to accept a limited number of young men who had previously been rejected for military service. Some of the men who would now be accepted had previously been disqualified for not meeting mental standards. Some had physical defects that appeared to be readily correctable. Project 100,000 qualified 100,000 men per year by lowering the minimum test scores and reducing educational standards to a level that was still slightly higher than what had been in effect during the Korean War. About 55 percent of those who joined were volunteers; the rest were drafted.

Men brought into the military under Project 100,000 were known as *New Standards Men*. To ensure that each service participated, the Secretary of Defense used a quota system. When the project started in October 1966, 25.9 percent of Army non–prior service enlisted accessions had to be from Mental Group IV on the Armed Forces Qualification Test. Greenberg, Project 100,000's Executive Director, noted that "[a]t least 50% of the Mental Group IV quota was to be met with New Standards Men. At least 50% of the New Standards Quota was to be met with men scoring in AFQT range 10–15" (Greenberg, 1972, p. 4).[31] Each service had its own quota. When the program began in October 1966, 25.9 percent of the Army's new non–prior service accessions had to be from Mental Group IV. The Army has a medically remedial quota of one percent. The other services had lesser quotas: Navy, 15 percent; Marine Corps, 18 percent; and Air Force, 15 percent. Quotas were adjusted slightly every year. Greenberg summed up the program in 1972:

> Between October 1966 and December 1971 [when the program was terminated], 354,000 men entered service under Project 100,000; 91% were accepted on the basis of lowered mental standards; the remaining 9% were Medically Remedial Men. Approximately 54% of the Project 100,000 men were volunteers; 46% were draftees. All services met their quotas for New Standards accessions. Approximately 67% of the new standards men entered the Army.

---

[31] Greenberg was hired in January 1965 by Gus Lee with the approval of Bill Gorham to work on civilian ceilings issues and to improve the efficiency of the support structure. He had had extensive manpower experience during World War II on General MacArthur's staff and on the Headquarters, Department of the Army staff. After graduating from the Industrial College of the Armed Forces (ICAF), he reported to the Office of the Assistant Secretary of Defense for Manpower and Reserve Affairs. Secretary of Defense McNamara was concerned about General Hershey's testimony before Congress that the Selective Service System was having difficulty filling draft calls because the Army-run examining stations were backlogged with 150,000 cases. He asked the newly appoint Assistant Secretary for Manpower and Reserve Affairs to clean up the backlog. The task fell to Greenberg. This was the beginning of a long association between Greenberg and Morris. From April to October 1966 Greenberg did the preparatory work to get Project 100,000 started. For example, he visited Job Corps centers to gain ideas on how to run the program. When Project 100,000 got started, he was appointed Executive Director. He was joined by Eli Flyer for about 18 months to develop reporting instruments for New Standards Men and a Control Group (Greenberg, 2004).

The peak year was 103,000 in FY 1969. Input of New Standards Men was curtailed as overall service accessions decreased in subsequent years. (Greenberg, 1972, p. 5)[32]

To monitor the progress of the New Standards Men, a control group was established. Compared to the control group, New Standards Men were more likely to be black (38 percent, compared to 10 percent for the control group) and less likely to have graduated from High School (47 percent, compared to 76 percent for the control group); they were also more likely have poorer reading skills and to score lower on the Armed Force Qualification Test. New Standards Men had a median percentile score of 13.6, compared to 56.8 percent for the control group. Despite these disadvantages, New Standards Men were almost as likely as the control group to complete basic training, at 94.6 percent compared to 97.5 percent, and only slightly less likely to complete their skill training courses, at 90 percent compared to 96 percent. Greenberg notes that they "made satisfactory promotion progress," although "they attained the higher pay grades later than the control group" (Greenberg, 1972, p. 7).

Project 100,000 was never a popular program among the services, and with the Nixon administration proposing to move to an all-volunteer force, the Defense Appropriation Act of 1972 prohibited the use of quotas based on mental category, effectively killing the program in December 1971. Congress did, however, reinstate quotas later in the decade—not to enforce a minimum on the services but to enforce a maximum. The services were prohibited from recruiting more than 45 percent of their new non–prior service accession from Mental Group IV.

The Legacy

A series of fateful decisions in 1964—Present Johnson's decisions to undertake a study of the viability of an all-volunteer force and to let Secretary of Defense McNamara organize the study and McNamara's decision to turn the effort over to an economist, Deputy Secretary of Defense William Gorham—were responsible for an intellectual revolution in the management of military personnel. Without these events, the groundwork would not have been set for the eventual successful work of the Gates Commission. The analysis that supported the Gates Commission's 1970 decision to recommend to President Nixon that the nation move to an all-volunteer force was firmly based on the decisions taken in 1964.

The commission's work was truly *remarkable*. The economic arguments developed in 1964 and later honed by the commission staff represented a "totally new paradigm for evaluating military" personnel issues (White, 2003, p. 2). It expanded the domain of military policy studies to the "macro operational issues of manning the

---

[32] For a more complete presentation, see ASD[M&RA] (1969) and Heisey et al. (1985)

force" (White, 2003, p. 2). The work of the Gates Commission was quantitative, allowing alternatives to be assessed in terms of both cost and benefits. It was academically rigorous, applying state-of-the-art econometric applications to new and challenging areas. It was robust, proving tools that future generations would use to manage the all-volunteer force, through easy and hard times and through periods of war and peace. At the 30th Anniversary Conference, Frederick D. Dent, one of the original commissioners said that

> A key to the successful execution of President Nixon' charge was the splendid commission staff. . . . The large staff, consisting of scholars, military personnel, and consultants, produced important and pertinent studies that became the basis of the commission's report to the President. These studies . . . [discussed here in his chapter] were nothing short of brilliant. (Dent, 2004, p. 8)

References

Ackley, Gardner, "The Salary Plight of the Drafted Soldier," memorandum to Secretary McNamara, Washington, D.C., July 27, 1967. G1449.pdf.

Altman, Stuart H., and Robert J. Barro, "A Model of Officer Supply Under Draft and No Draft Conditions," in Gates Commission, ed., *Studies Prepared for the President's Commission on an All-Volunteer Armed Force*, Washington, D.C.: U.S. Government Printing Office, 1970, pp. II-10-11 to II-10-31. S0716.pdf.

———, "Officer Supply: The Impact of Pay, the Draft, and the Vietnam War," *The American Economic Review*, Vol. 61, No. 4, September 1971, pp. 649–664. S0193.pdf.

Altman, Stuart H., and Alan E. Fechter, "The Supply of Military Personnel in the Absence of a Draft," *The American Economic Review*, Vol. 57, No. 2, May 1967, pp. 19–31. S0232.pdf.

ASD[M&RA]—*See* Assistant Secretary of Defense for Manpower and Reserve Affairs.

Assistant Secretary of Defense for Manpower and Reserve Affairs, *Report of the First Quadrennial Review of Military Compensation*, Washington, D.C.: U.S. Department of Defense, November 1, 1967. S0021.pdf.

———, *Project One Hundred Thousand: Characteristics and Performance of 'New Standards' Men*, Washington, D.C.: U.S. Department of Defense, December 1969. G1319.pdf.

Bateman, C. Worth, *Qualitative Requirements Study*, Washington, D.C.: Office of the Assistant Secretary of Defense/Manpower, March 1965.

Borcherding, Thomas E., "A Neglected Social Cost of a Voluntary Military," *The American Economic Review*, Vol. 61, No. 1, March 1971, pp. 195–196. S0233.pdf.

Bovey, Robert L., and James S. Thomason, *National Security Study Memorandum 3 (NSSM-3): A Pivotal Initiative in U.S. Defense Policy Development*, Washington, D.C.: Institute for Defense Analysis, D-2147, September 1998. S0302.pdf.

Brennan, Michael J., *Theory of Economic Statics*, Englewood Cliffs, N.J.: PrenticeHall, Inc., 1965.

Browning, Edgar K., "On the Marginal Welfare Cost of Taxation," *The American Economic Review*, Vol. 77, No. 1, March 1987, pp. 11–23. S0636.pdf.

Cook, Alvin A., Jr., "Supply of Air Force Volunteers," in *Staff Papers for the President's Commission on an All-Volunteer Force*, Washington, D.C.: U.S. Government Printing Office, 1970, pp. II-4-1 to II-4-34. S0476.pdf.

———, "Occupational Choice, the Draft, and the Excess Supply of Air Force Volunteers," Santa Monica, Calif.: RAND Corporation, P-46061, 1971. S0303.pdf.

Cook, Alvin A., Jr., and John P. White, "Estimating the Quality of Airman Recruits," in Gates Commission, ed., *Studies Prepared for the President's Commission on an All-Volunteer Armed Force*, Washington, D.C.: U.S. Government Printing Office, 1970a, pp. II-5-1 through II-5-23. S0714.pdf.

———, *Estimating the Quality of Air Force Volunteers*, Santa Monica, Calif.: RAND Corporation, RM-630-PR, September 1970b. S0301.pdf.

Cooper, Richard V. L., *The Social Cost of Maintaining A Military Labor Force*, Santa Monica, Calif.: RAND Corporation, R-17581-ARPA, August 1975. S0795.pdf.

———, *Military Manpower and the All-Volunteer Force*, Santa Monica, Calif.: RAND Corporation, R-1450-ARPA, September 1977. S0177.pdf.

Dent, Frederick D., "Reflections from the Gates Commission," in Barbara A. Bicksler, Curtis L. Gilroy and John T. Warner, eds., *The All-Volunteer Force: Thirty Years of Service*, Washington, D.C.: Brassey's, Inc., 2004.

Fechter, Alan E., "Impact of Pay and Draft Policy on Army Enlistment Behavior," in Gates Commission, ed., *Studies Prepared for the President's Commission on an All-Volunteer Armed Force*, Washington, D.C.: U.S. Government Printing Office, 1970, pp. II-3-1 to II-3-59. S0713.pdf.

Fisher, Anthony C., "The Cost of the Draft and the Cost of Ending the Draft," *The American Economic Review*, Vol. 59, No. 3, June 1969, pp. 239–254. S0192.pdf.

Fitt, Alfred B., "Analysis of First Term Military Pay," memorandum to Merton J. Peck, Washington, D.C., October 2, 1968. G1450.pdf.

Flyer, Eli S., *Factors Relating to Discharge for Unsuitability Among 1956 Accessions to the Air Force*, Lackland Air Force Base, San Antonio, Tex.: U.S. Air Force Personnel Research Laboratory, WADC TN 59201, December 1959.

Friedman, Milton, "Why Not a Volunteer Army?" in Sol Tax, ed., *The Draft: A Handbook of Facts and Alternatives*, Chicago: University of Chicago Press, 1967, pp. 200–207. S0240.pdf.

Gates, Thomas S. Jr., *The Report of the President's Commission on an All-Volunteer Armed Force*, Washington, D.C., February 1970. S0243.pdf.

Gilman, Harry J., "The Supply of Volunteers to the Military Services," in Gates Commission, ed., *Studies Prepared for the President's Commission on an All-Volunteer Armed Force*, Washington, D.C., 1970, pp. II-1-1 to II-1-26. S0711.pdf.

Gray, Burton C., "Supply of First-Term Military Enlistees: A Cross-Section Analysis," in Gates Commission, ed., *Studies Prepared for the President's Commission on an All-Volunteer Armed Force*, Washington, D.C.: U.S. Government Printing Office, 1970, pp. II-2-1 to II-2-40. S0712.pdf.

Greenberg, I. M., "Project 100,000: The Training of Former Rejectees," *Phi Delta Kappan*, June 1969, pp. 570–574. S0818.pdf.

———, *Project 100,000: New Standards Program*, Washington, D.C.: U.S. Department of Defense, 1972. G1318.pdf.

———, "Technical Comments," memorandum to Bernard Rostker, Washington, D.C., July 2004.

Hansen, W. Lee, and Burton A. Weisbrod, "Economics of the Military Draft," *The Quarterly Journal of Economics*, Vol. 81, No. 3, August 1967, pp. 395–421.

Heisey, Jane Gillette, Barbara Means, and Janice H. Laurence, *Military Performance of Low Aptitude Recruits: Project 100,000 and the ASVAB Misnorming*, Alexandria, Va.: Human Resources Research Organization, FR-PRD-85-2, February 1985. S0819.pdf.

Henderson, David R., "Thank You. William H. Meckling: We Owe a Debt to the Man Who Killed the Draft," *Red Herring Magazine*, January 1999.

Hubbell, Lester, *1967 Quadrennial Review of Military Compensation*, Vol. 1: *Active Duty Compensation*, Washington, D.C.: Office of the Assistant Secretary of Defense (M&RA), 1967. S0022.pdf.

Lee, D., and R. McKenzie, "Reexamination of the Relative Efficiency of the Draft and the All-Volunteer Army," *Southern Economic Journal*, Vol. 59, 1992.

McNamara, Robert, "Your Memorandum on the Salary Plight of the Drafted Soldier," memorandum to Chairman of the Council of Economic Advisors, Washington, D.C., August 8, 1967. G1452.pdf.

Nelson, Gary R., "Economic Analysis of First-Term Reenlistments in the Army," in Gates Commission, ed., *Studies Prepared for the President's Commission on All-Volunteer Armed Force*, Washington, D.C.: U.S. Government Printing Office, 1970, pp. II-6-II to II-6-31. S0715.pdf.

———, "The Supply and Quality of First-Term Enlistees Under the All-Volunteer Force," in William Bowman, Roger Little and G. Thomas Sicilia, eds., *The All-Volunteer Force After a Decade: Retrospect and Project*, New York: Pergamon-Brassey's, 1986.

Odeen, Philip A., "Zero Draft," memorandum to General Pursley, Washington, D.C., April 14, 1971. G0657.pdf.

Oi, Walter Y., "Modernizing Military Pay: A Critique," *Congressional Record*, Vol. 114, No. 137, August 2, 1968, pp. S10078–10084. G1454.pdf.

Packard, David, "Proposed Military Pay Reforms," memorandum to Secretaries of the Military Departments and Chairman of the Joint Chiefs of Staff, Washington, D.C., February 4, 1969. G1455.pdf.

Pauly, M., and T. Willett, "Efficiency in Military Procurement," in J. Miller, ed., *Why the Draft? The Case for a Volunteer Army*, Baltimore, Md.: Penguin Books, 1968, pp. 71–82.

Peck, Merton J., "Military Pay," memorandum to Assistant Secretary of Defense (Manpower and Reserve Affairs), Washington, D.C., September 16, 1968. G1453.pdf.

Reaume, David M., and Walter Y. OI, "The Educational Attainment of Military and Civilian Labor Forces," in Gates Commission, ed., *Studies Prepared for the President's Commission on an All-Volunteer Armed Force*, Washington, D.C.: U.S. Government Printing Office, 1970, pp. I-3-1 to I-3-23. G1461.pdf.

Rossotti, Charles O., "Reducing Reliance on the Draft," memorandum to Secretary of Defense, Washington, D.C., September 22, 1969. G0281.pdf.

Rostker, Bernard D., *Total Force Planning, Personnel Costs and the Supply of New Reservists*, Santa Monica, Calif.: RAND Corporation, R-1430-PR, October 1974. S0796.pdf.

Rumsfeld, Donald H., *Report of the Third Quadrennial Review of Military Compensation: Military Compensation—A Modernized System*, Washington, D.C.: U.S. Department of Defense. S0168.pdf.

Secretary of Defense, *Charter of the Defense Advisory Committee on Military Compensation*, Washington, D.C.: U.S. Department of Defense, March 14, 2005. G1433.pdf.

Sjaastad, Larry A., and Ronald W. Hansen, "The Conscription Tax: An Empirical Analysis," in President's Commission on an All-Volunteer Armed Force, ed., *Studies Prepared for the President's Commission on an All-Volunteer Armed Force*, Washington, D.C.: U.S. Government Printing Office, 1970. S0901.pdf.

Smith, Gorman C., *Occupational Pay Differentials for Military Technicians*, dissertation, New York: Columbia University, 1964. S0111.pdf.

———, *Council of Economic Advisor's Evaluation of Modernizing Military Pay*, Vol. I: *Active Duty Compensation*, Washington, D.C.: Deputy Director, Compensation and Career Development, 1968. G1451.pdf.

Staff of the *Commanders Digest*, "Hubbell Pay Review Finds Released by Defense Department: Special In-Depth Report," *Commanders Digest*, Vol. 4, No. 32, May 11, 1968. G1448.pdf.

Stanners, Thomas, "Military Compensation Reform (The Hubbell Plan)," memorandum to Martin C. Anderson, Washington, D.C., January 31, 1969a. G1123.pdf.

———, "Military Pay Modernization Proposal," memorandum to Director of the Bureau of the Budget, Washington, D.C., February 18, 1969b. G1457.pdf.

———, "Interview with Bernard Rostker," February 18, 2002.

Sullivan, John A., "Qualitative Requirements of the Armed Forces," in Gates Commission, ed., *Studies Prepared for the President's Commission on an All-Volunteer Armed Force*, Washington, D.C.: U.S. Government Printing Office, 1970, pp. I-2-1 to I-2-56. G1460.pdf.

U.S. Department of Defense, Modernizing Military Pay: Report of the First Quadrennial Review of Military Compensation, Vol. V: The Military Estate Program (Appendices), Washington, D.C.: U.S. Department of Defense, 1969. S0171.pdf.

Warner, John T., and Beth J. Asch, "The Economic Theory of a Military Draft Reconsidered," Defence and Peace Economics, Vol. 7, 1996, pp. 297–312.

———, "The Record and Prospects of the All-Volunteer Military in the United States," Journal of Economic Perspectives, Vol. 15, No. 2, Spring 2001. S0357.pdf.

White, John P., "Comments," 30th Anniversary Conference, Washington, D.C., September 2003. S0717.pdf.

Wilburn, Robert C., "Impact of Income, the Draft and Other Factors on the Retention of Air Force Enlisted Men: A Cross Section analysis," in Gates Commission, ed., Studies Prepared for the President's Commission on All-Volunteer Armed Force, Washington, D.C.: U.S. Government Printing Office, 1970.

Zwick, Charles J., "Military Compensation Reform," memorandum to the President, Washington, D.C., March 26, 1968. G1456.pdf.

CHAPTER SIX

The Pentagon's Response:
The Laird and Kelley Years (1969–1972)

> With the signing of the peace agreement in Paris today, and after receiving a report from the Secretary of the Army that he foresees no need for further inductions, I wish to inform you [the American people] that the Armed Forces henceforth will depend exclusively on volunteer soldiers, sailors, airmen and Marines. *Use of the draft has ended.*
>
> —Melvin Laird
> Secretary of Defense[1]

DoD's Project Volunteer Committee

Concurrent with the activities of the Gates Commission, DoD undertook its own planning studies. On April 10, 1969, Secretary of Defense Melvin Laird established the Project Volunteer Committee to develop "a comprehensive action program for moving toward a volunteer force" (Laird, 1969a). Roger Kelley, the new Assistant Secretary of Defense for Manpower and Reserve Affairs,[2] was appointed chairman. Other members of the committee were the Assistant Secretary of Defense for Systems Analysis, the Assistant Secretaries of the Military Departments for Manpower and Reserve Affairs, the Deputy Chiefs of Staff for Personnel from the Military Services, and the Joint Staff Director of Manpower and Personnel. The committee's secretary and staff

---

[1] News release of January 27, 1973 (Laird, 1973b, emphasis added).

[2] The responsibilities of the Assistant Secretary of Defense for Manpower and Reserve Affairs include "providing . . . [a] system of compensation and other benefit forms to attract and retain personnel" (OASD[M&RA], 1969).

director was Harold Wool, Director of Procurement Policy and General Research. Wool had held a similar position in the 1964 Pentagon Draft Study.[3]

From the very beginning, Kelley saw the move to an all-volunteer force as an effort that required "a redirecting of our thought processes and work rather than a new project separate and apart from on-going activities." On April 10, 1979, he told Ivan Selin and Charles Rossetti,[4] the new leadership team in Systems Analysis, that

> [v]irtually every manpower activity in Systems Analysis and Manpower and Reserve Affairs must be approached in terms of whether it will contribute toward the ultimate realization of this goal. So while some additional people may be needed along the way, we see 'Project Volunteer' as a major redirection of our total efforts rather than a separate and new layer of work activity. (Kelley, 1969a)[5]

At the first meeting of the committee on April 21, 1969,[6] Kelley explained his philosophy to the other members of the committee. He told the services he wanted them to be the prime agents for implementing the all-volunteer force. He asked them to develop their "own proposed program and recommendations" (Wool, 1969a), which he would approve.[7]

The role of the services was stressed again at the second meeting of the full Project Volunteer Committee several days later (April 23, 1969), when Kelley told the services they would brief the Gates Commission late in June (Wool, 1969c). The research program he developed "in support of Project Volunteer" stressed "projecting [the] future supply of volunteers for military service" (Kelley, 1969d), with the services providing an "evaluation of the relative effectiveness of [Project Volunteer] options" (Kelley, 1969d). While the full Project Volunteer Committee did not meet again until January 1970—one month before the Gates Commission released its report—a Steering Com-

---

[3] Kelley set up a "small 'shirt sleeves' group to meet regularly with Harold Wool to review work and critique results." Members of that group included his senior staff and the senior staff from Systems Analysis (see Kelley, 1969a). A week before the April 21, 1969, meeting, Wool met with Bill Meckling, Walter Oi, and Harry Gilman for lunch to "discuss arrangement for collaboration and support . . . and to discuss the public information guidelines." He had worked with both Oi and Gilman on the DoD draft study in 1964 and 1965. In a memorandum for the record, he noted that, "Dr. Oi has written a number of papers on the volunteer force issue and also testified with me on the subject in 1967 before the Joint Economic Committee." Meckling, he noted, "expressed an interest in the detailed statistical data banks being prepared by the Institute of Defense Analyses under contract with this office on Army and Navy recruitment and retention experience" (Wool, 1969b).

[4] *Author's Note:* Selin and Rossetti had been senior members of the former Systems Analysis Office. Selin had come from RAND and Rossetti from the Harvard Business School. They would see Systems Analysis through the transition and acceptance by the new Nixon administration. After leaving the Pentagon, they would found American Management Systems.

[5] This decision would become a point of contention between himself and Selin and later Gardiner Tucker as the implementation proceeded.

[6] The invitations for the meeting went out on April 15, 1969, with an agenda that included discussion of "(1) [the] role of DoD Project Volunteer in relation to the President's Advisory Committee on an All-Volunteer Force, (2) [r]eview of the Project Volunteer Study Plan, [and] (3) Organizational and Liaison Arrangements" (Kelley, 1969b).

[7] Wool asked the services to provide "liaison officers" to work on two ad hoc working groups (Wool, 1969d).

mittee was formed over the next several months. In July, Kelley chartered the Program Evaluation Group under the direction of the new Deputy Assistant Secretary of Defense for Manpower Research and Utilization, Paul Wollstadt, to work with the services and "develop a comprehensive master plan" (Kelley, 1969f).[8] In addition, he asked his staff to assess and evaluate "each Service recommendation in terms of . . . potential effectiveness, costs, and feasibility . . . [and develop] any additional or alternative recommendations" (Kelley, 1969e).[9]

Wool's assessment of the program the services submitted in July is noteworthy. While there were over 300 separate recommendations, the major proposals were increased pay and pay reform, authority to grant enlistment bonuses, increased Reserve Officer Training Corps (ROTC) scholarships, in-service and post-service educational benefits, better housing, expanded entitlements, and increased funding for advertising and survey research. He noted that there were

> few specific recommendations in the area of improved utilization, qualitative standards or civilian substitution. The special problems of the reserves and of physician-dentist recruitment and utilization are also not adequately treated by some Services. (Wool, 1969f)

The Program Evaluation Group reported to Kelley on January 14, 1970, just before the Gates Commission's report was made public, recommending a course of action that would become the services' preferred way to achieve an all-volunteer force—"provide sufficient incentives including, but not limited to, better pay" (Wollstadt, 1970a).[10]

The Services Prepare

Under Kelley's concept, each service was responsible for its own efforts, and each service responded differently, as measured by focus, intensity, and dedication. By early May, Wool reported to the Steering Committee that "all Services now had special Project Volunteer working groups in operation, or were setting up such groups, with the exception of the Navy" (Wool, 1969e).

---

[8] Wollstadt had taken over this post on July 1. From then on, Wool's office, the Directorate for Procurement Policy and General Research, and the Directorate for Manpower Utilization and Management Techniques reported to Wollstadt (Kelley, 1969c).

[9] Kelley separately asked the assistant secretaries for Installations and Logistics and for Pubic Affairs to "submit their recommendations . . . for policy review and evaluation prior to [his] preparation of a coordinated Project Volunteer program" (Kelley, 1969g).

[10] Kelley provided a copy of the Program Evaluation Group's report to the services on January 22, 1970, suggesting that the Project Volunteer Committee meet weekly each Saturday morning "to develop our specific recommendations and time-table for action to implement the All-Volunteer Force, . . . [through] a careful analysis of the [Program Evaluation Group] report, but a . . . careful evaluation of the Gates Commission recommendations" (Kelley, 1970a).

The Navy and Marine Corps

The Navy and Marine Corps gave responsibility for the all-volunteer force to their respective military personnel offices. In the case of the Navy, the Assistant Chief of Plans of the Bureau of Naval Personnel was responsible for Project Volunteer Committee activities. As far as the Navy was concerned, this was just another "personnel drill" to be managed using normal staff processes. It would employ its "current working staff to handle Project Volunteer matters" (OASD[M&RA], 1970d). When facing a suggestion that he examine the prospects of an all-volunteer military and how it might affect the Navy, the Chief of Naval Personnel decided not to engage the Navy's federal contract research center (FCRC), the Center for Naval Analyses. David Kassing, who then headed CNA's personnel research program and was a member of the Gates Commission staff, remembers having his proposal to help the Navy rejected because, in the view of the Navy leadership, "It—the all-volunteer force—will never happen."

The Marine Corps established Task Force Project Volunteer in May 1969 with "representation from all Staff Divisions and Departments within Headquarters, Marine Corps . . . and routed through the Deputy Chief of Staff/Manpower . . . to the Commandant, Marine Corps" (OASD[M&RA], 1970d).

The Air Force

Like the Navy and Marine Corps, the Air Force initially treated the all-volunteer force as business as usual. The Air Force established a "Project Volunteer Task Group" in the Directorate of Personnel Planning in the Office of the Deputy Chief of Staff (Personnel). It established "permanent working group[s] composed of members of [the] Air Staff under [the] control of [the] Project Volunteer Section" (OASD[M&RA], 1970d). In December 1968, the Air Force, unlike the Navy, asked its FCRC, the RAND Corporation, to research the likely quantity and quality of new personnel in a post–southeast Asia environment. The Project Volunteer Task Group had a first draft of RAND's plan by the end of June 1969, and in September, RAND made its first report to the Air Staff on the work it was doing for them and for the Gates Commission (Cook and White, 1969). The Air Force would later mount a sizeable internal study in the Office of the Assistant Chief of Staff for Studies and Analysis, called Saber Volunteer.

The Army

The Army was even faster out of the blocks than the Air Force. Not only was it the service that most directly benefited from the draft and thus had the most at stake, the new Army Chief of Staff, General William C. Westmoreland, had already commissioned a study of the feasibility of an all-volunteer force. When he took over this post in summer 1968—several months before Nixon's "all-volunteer force" speech of October 17, 1968—Westmoreland asked the Army to start a "close-hold" staff study to research the effects that ending the draft and shifting to an all-volunteer force would have on the

Army.[11] The so-called Career Force Study "was directed toward identifying the relationships between various factors which influence volunteering and assessed the Army's capability to support an all-volunteer force" (Butler, 1969, p. 1-1). The study's main conclusion, based largely on the work of the 1964 Pentagon Draft Study, was that the Army take a positive position on any future proposals for an all-volunteer force and "support a post [Vietnam] reduction in draft calls contingent upon the Army's ability to attract by voluntary means the number and quality of personnel needed" (Griffith, 1997, p. 19). They were concerned, however, that an all-volunteer force would be costly and possibly not representative of the American people, i.e., that it would be predominantly black (Griffith, 1997, p. 18).[12]

In early February, with a bootleg copy of Nixon's January 29, 1968, memorandum to Laird in hand, Westmoreland chartered a new study group—Project PROVIDE—to continue the work of the Career Force Study and to be the Army's staff contact with the Office of the Secretary of Defense.[13] Griffith, in his extensive history of this period, attributes the Army leadership's rather positive attitude to the "perceived . . . link between manpower procurement and the Army's social problems."[14] Sensing the mood on the Army staff, Griffith wrote that

> Conventional wisdom holds that the Army opposed ending conscription. . . . In fact, well before the Gates Commission rendered its report, the Army leadership had concluded that an end to conscription was in the service's best interest. (Griffith, 1997, p. 17)
>
> If the dissent, undisciplined, and drug and alcohol abuse were indeed imports from society, they reasoned, reduced reliance on the draft and unwilling draft-motivated volunteers might offer a way for the Army to solve some of its own social problems. In a smaller post-Vietnam Army of true volunteers, professional standards could be established and dissidents, malcontents, and misfits weeded out. (Griffith, 1997, p. 25)

---

[11] See Bill Brehm's account in Brehm (2002). Also, for a more complete discussion of actions being taken by the Army Staff, see Griffith (1997).

[12] Should the black content of the military have made a difference? In the racially charged atmosphere of the day, Janowitz and Moskos, the leading military sociologists, expressed their opposition to the all-volunteer force with the following rhetorical questions:

> Can a political democracy expect to have a legitimate form of government if its military is not broadly representative of the larger society? Can a military force whose combat units are overweighed with a racial minority have credibility in the world arena? (Janowitz and Moskos, 1974, p. 110)

[13] Project Provide made 33 specific recommendations, starting with "[s]upport a peacetime all-volunteer force in principle" (Directorate of Personnel Studies and Research, 1969).

[14] The Army Historical Summary recalled that

> In the summer of 1968 there were increasing indications that deliberate attempts were being made to undermine discipline and resist established authority. . . . Actions have taken the form of refusal to obey orders, publication of so-called underground newspapers, soldiers' participation in anti-war meetings and demonstrations, and petitions in civil courts to establish the rights of soldiers. (Bell, 1973a, pp. 44–45)

The work of the PROVIDE study group—after November 1969 designated as Task Group PROVIDE—together with what Griffith describes as an "early unity of effort" among Army's Deputy Chief of Staff for Personnel, Lieutenant General Walter T. "Dutch" Kerwin, and the Assistant Secretary of the Army for Manpower and Reserve Affairs, William K. Brehm, enabled the Army to take the lead on the Project Volunteer Committee.[15] The Army also established the Special Assistant for the Modern Volunteer Army as the single staff officer responsible to the Secretary of the Army and the Chief of Staff of the Army, giving him the authority to "[d]irect coordination with and tasking of (the) Army Staff and major commands" (OASD[M&RA], 1970d).

Project Volunteer, the Gates Commission's Recommendations and the FY 1972 Program

The efforts at the Pentagon were of some concern to members of the Gates Commission, both substantively and procedurally. In July, Gates told Laird that "several members of the Commission expressed great concern that a parallel formal report might be materially harmful" (Gates, 1969). Laird responded that the Pentagon's

> Project Volunteer . . . is designed to complement and support the Commission's studies. . . . [However,] to avoid any possible misunderstanding . . . all key personnel engaged in Project Volunteer . . . [were] instructed to avoid using the terms "report" or "study" in documents related to this Project. (Laird, 1969b)

The Army even classified the final report of the PROVIDE study group as SECRET.

The developing position at the Pentagon was also of some concern to the commission. The Pentagon's emerging position reflected the concerns of those in uniform that pressing too hard or being too optimistic about the ability to achieve an all-volunteer force could jeopardize "national security." While the members of the Program Evaluation Group thought that moving to an all-volunteer force might be possible, given the recommended pay increases, their approach was very different from the one the Gates Commission was developing. The services not only supported the pay increases the commission favored, they also favored a full-scale program of family and bachelor housing, as well as new programs for education and training.[16] They placed

---

[15] *Author's Note:* General Dutch Kerwin would later become the Army's Vice Chief of Staff. Assistant Secretary Brehm would, in 1973, succeed Roger Kelley as Assistant Secretary of Defense for Manpower and Reserve Affairs and would complete the transition to an all-volunteer force. In the mid-1980s, Brehm and I would be colleagues at the Systems Research and Analysis Corporation (SRA). SRA would be one of the few private consulting firms to develop a sustained capability to work on military manpower issues.

[16] Wollstadt told Anderson on February 9, 1970, that the "need for improved housing will be given even greater emphasis" (Wollstadt, 1970b).

the highest priority on building an effective recruiting force. In contrast, the Gates Commission recommended a small increase in recruiting resources, of $8 million annually. Finally, as previously noted, the Pentagon favored a longer transition period, with a two-year extension of the existing draft authority and an effective date for terminating conscription of July 1, 1973.

By late December 1969, Kelley knew enough about where both Project Volunteer and the Gates Commission were heading to know that, besides the overall agreement that a volunteer force was feasible, there was likely to be little agreement between the two groups.[17] Just before Christmas, Kelley forwarded to Laird a memorandum he had received from Wollstadt. He characterized the memorandum as "a succinct and an accurate summary of some key points to be considered in moving toward an All-Volunteer Force" (Kelley, 1969h). In the memorandum, Wollstadt expressed his concern that

> the staff of the Gates Commission has had a tendency to rely too heavily on increasing under-2 [years of service] pay as the solution to the All-Volunteer force problem. . . .
> Pay for all military people must be externally competitive and internally equitable if an All-Volunteer Force is to be sustained over the long term. (Kelley, 1969h)

In addition, "Better housing than exists or is now being planned will be necessary . . . [and] [b]etter [p]ersonnel [m]anagement" (Kelley, 1969h). Wollstadt believed that an all-volunteer force was feasible, but was

> concerned . . . that some of the ardent proponents of the All-Volunteer concept, particularly key members of the Gates Commission staff, may underestimate what it will take in terms of money and effort to sustain an All-Volunteer Force beyond the rapid draw-down period. (Kelley, 1969h)[18]

Formal consideration of a Pentagon position on the Gates Commission's recommendations started with a reconvening of the full Project Volunteer Committee on

---

[17] On October 16, 1969, months before the commission submitted its report, Nixon received a letter from the commission asking him to "correct the severe financial disadvantage imposed on draftees and on volunteers in their first two years of service" (Gates et al., 1969). This went directly to the recommendations of the Hubbell pay proposals for reforming the military compensation system. Nixon told Laird that he was "impressed" by the commission's suggestion that the "military pay increase now scheduled for Fiscal Year 1971 be concentrated in the initial years of service. . . ." He asked Laird to "evaluate the major military pay alternatives that are practically available to us for Fiscal Year 1971, given special consideration of their effect on moving towards an all-volunteer force" (Nixon, 1969). Laird thought the best course of action was

> to grant substantially larger general increases to the lower enlisted grades than to high enlisted grades and officers, and also to convert the present pay system to a salary system effective January 1, 1971, [and make] major changes in the military retirement system. (Laird, 1969c)

[18] Shortly after the Gates Commission reported, Kelley's staff prepared a "Comparison of Gates Commission and Department of Defense (Project Volunteer) Recommendation on an All-Volunteer Force (OASD[M&RA], 1970a), and a chapter-by-chapter review (OASD[M&RA], 1970a). Several months later they also sent Kelley a more formal "evaluation of the military compensation aspects of the Gates Commission Report" (Benade, 1970).

January 31, 1970.[19] While the committee agreed with the Gates Commission that an all-volunteer force was feasible with a large-enough pay raise and support for noncompensation programs, they sharply disagreed over the timetable for achieving an all-volunteer force.[20]

Laird was not entirely pleased with all the recommendations of the Gates Commission, particularly its recommendation to end conscription by June 1971. He made no attempt to hide his position from the public, resulting in a sharp rebuke from Gates Commissioner Milton Friedman.[21] On March 11, 1970, two weeks after the formal release of the Gates Commission's report to the public, Laird presented his own position and DoD's recommendations to the President.[22] He told Nixon that

> The Department of Defense endorses the basic conclusion of the Report of the President's Commission on an All-Volunteer Armed Force that the draft should be phased out. This should occur when assured of the capability to attract and retain an Armed Force of the required size and quality through voluntary means. (Laird, 1970)

Laird asked for a 20-percent increase in first-term enlisted pay starting on January 1, 1971; wanted additional funds for recruiting, housing, and quality-of-life programs; and wanted expansion of ROTC scholarships. Moreover, he thought the commission's report was "in serious error in suggesting that little or no problem exists with respect to compensation of career military personnel" (Laird, 1970b). The total costs added $2 billion in FY 1972 and $3.5 billion in FY 1973 to the Pentagon's budget—then at a wartime level of $75 billion. He also favored a two-year extension of the draft, compared to the one-year extension the Gates Commission had recommended. *A Comparison of Gates Commission and Department of Defense (Project Volunteer) Recommendations on an All-Volunteer Force,* prepared by Kelley's staff, showed how far DoD deviated from the recommendations of the Gates Commission (OASD[M&RA], 1970b).

---

[19] Lee suggested a strategy for DoD in a memorandum for Deputy Assistant Secretary Wollstadt (see Lee, 1970).

[20] At the same time, the press was reporting widespread opposition to the basic concept of an all-volunteer force among military officers. *U.S. News & World Report* quoted an Army general in the Pentagon as saying that, "[a]s of now, I do not know of a single Army officer who favors returning to an all-volunteer force, even if it could be done at this stage" (*U.S. News & World Report* Staff, 1970).

[21] This resulted in a sharp exchange of letters with Commissioner Friedman (Friedman, 1970). Laird assured Friedman that he supported the objectives of the all-volunteer force but that it could not be achieved by mid-1971 because of the "well known budget strictures for FY 1971" (Laird, 1970a). Laird also wrote Senator Stennis expressing his "deep concerns and strong opposition" to ending conscription on July 1, 1971. He told the chairman that he was "convinced that military manpower needs will require the continuation of the draft beyond this date. . . . To fix the date of July 1, 1971 . . . needlessly endangers our national security" (Laird, 1970e).

[22] Secretary of the Army Stanley Resor provided the Army's comments on March 8, 1970 (see Resor, 1970a). The Army Deputy Chief of Staff for Personnel also provided comments (Army ODCSPER Staff, 1970), as did the Air Force Personnel office (Air Force DCSP Staff, 1970), Kelley's staff (OASD[M&RA], 1970c), and the Navy (Crutchfield, 1970).

The next step was a meeting of the National Security Council, scheduled for March 25, 1970, after which, in an April 23, 1970, address to Congress, Nixon announced his determination to move to a volunteer force. The program he submitted to Congress, however, while consistent with the conclusions of the Gates Commission, largely reflected the program and schedule Secretary Laird had recommended (Nixon, 1970). On May 4, 1970 Laird asked the secretaries of the military departments for their comments on the report of the Project Volunteer Committee as the "initial Department of Defense plan for carrying out the President's program announced in his April 23, 1970 message on the draft to Congress" (Laird, 1970c). The Project Volunteer Committee finally reported to Laird on August 14, 1970, on their plans and actions for moving toward an all-volunteer force (Project Volunteer Committee, 1970).[23] Through the summer and fall, Laird kept Nixon informed on "progress on this program . . . to increase voluntary enlistment and retention and to move toward zero draft calls" (Laird, 1970d and Laird, 1970g). With no action in Congress, Laird and Kelley also tried to put their best foot forward and to keep their efforts in public view. In October, with members of the Project Volunteer Committee present, Kelley briefed the Pentagon press corps on "some of the things we are doing about . . . zero draft calls" (Kelley, 1970c).

Preparing the FY 1972 Budget

The main effort to develop an all-volunteer force program had to go through the congressional authorization and appropriations process as part of DoD's FY 1972 budget. DoD's comptroller agreed to give Assistant Secretary Kelley extraordinary authority to allocate the funds that were set aside for the transition to the all-volunteer force. Gus Lee, by then the Director of Procurement Policy and Director of the Project Volunteer Committee, noted that, by this action, "Kelley's influence over allocations of resources became his chief 'carrot' for obtaining cooperation from the Services in the early stages of Project Volunteer" (Lee and Parker, 1977, p. 78).

The Army, having relied on the draft as a significant source of its personnel, submitted a "robust" FY 1972 program that included improved benefits, as well as additional money for proficiency pay, a premium pay to enlistees in the ground combat arms, and paid radio and television advertising. While the Army's initial recommendation was that the "heavy investment in pay programs should be postponed until after FY 72, when the best results can be obtained with the fewest dollars" (Kester, 1970a), its request for nearly two-thirds of the "pie" was not well received by the other services.

---

[23] Also see the slides that Kelley used in briefing the House Armed Service Committee (Kelley, 1970b).

In the final FY 1972 budget, the Army, backed by the Assistant Secretary of Defense for Systems Analysis, got the largest share of the volunteer resources.[24] The Army had 52 percent of the projected accession requirement for FY 1972 but received 64 percent of the resources.[25] As finally allocated, the Project Volunteer program was overwhelmingly oriented toward the active force (98 percent of the resources), enlisted personnel (96 percent of the resources), and non–prior service accessions (85 percent of the resources).

The Army Moves Out

Even as the Army pressed for the majority of the FY 1972 budget, it did not want to wait for the new fiscal year. Instead, it moved ahead during the remainder of FY 1971 with an ambitious program to start to move toward an all-volunteer force. On October 13, 1970, at the annual meeting of the Association of the United States Army (AUSA)— a traditional forum for major Army policy announcements—General Westmoreland announced his intent to appoint a senior general officer to oversee the Army's program for an all-volunteer force (Westmoreland, 1970a).[26] One week later, Lieutenant General George Forsythe was appointed Special Assistant to the Secretary of the Army and the Chief of Staff of the Army for the Modern Volunteer Army, and Brigadier General Robert Montague was selected as his deputy (Westmoreland, 1970a).[27] By the end of the month, they had a charter signed by the Secretary of the Army, Stanley Resor (Resor, 1970a).[28] Forsythe was formally—"by Direction of the Chief of Staff"—

---

[24] Lee notes that,

> The Assistant Secretary of Defense (Systems Analysis) had presented a staff analysis to Secretary Laird and Deputy Secretary Packard which concluded that, given the pay raise, the Navy, Marine Corps, and Air Force would be able to meet their accession requirement on a volunteer basis without additional incentives. Therefore, Systems Analysis did not, in general, recommend additional funding for the Navy, Marine Corps, and Air Force in FY1972. This recommendation marked the beginning of bureaucratic differences between the ASD (M&RA) and the ASD (Systems Analysis)—particularly between their staffs—which persisted throughout the time Kelley remained in office. (Lee and Parker, 1977, p. 80)

[25] The ratios of requirements to resources were 1.23 for the Army, 0.60 for the Navy, 1.26 for the Marine Corps , and 0.75 for the Air Force.

[26] Westmoreland followed up the AUSA speech with an Army Commanders Conference in early December to direct "Army actions to improve Service attractiveness" (Westmoreland, 1970b).

[27] Griffith notes that Brehm and Kerwin,

> the two men in the Army leadership charged with the day-to-day development of the all-volunteer Army [were concerned about] . . . insufficient time and inadequate organization . . . They decided the Army needed a full-time advocate for the AVF supported by a special staff charged with coordinating plans, budget, and implementation. . . . Secretary Resor and General Westmoreland . . . agreed. (Griffith, 1997, p. 51)

[28] General Forsythe briefed the Chairman of the House Armed Service Committee on December 11, 1970, who expressed concern that "the HASC was being informed after the fact" (Burke, 1970).

"authorized direct access to the SA [Secretary of the Army] and CofSA [Chief of Staff of the Army] . . . [to] periodically report . . . on progress toward reducing to zero the Army's reliance on Selective Service inductions" (Bennett, 1970).

Pressing forward, on November 3, 1970, Resor informed Laird that the Army would make an "all-out effort to reach zero draft calls by the end of FY 73 [and of the Army's plan for a] publicity campaign to attract volunteers beginning in calendar 1971" (Resor, 1970b). On November 6, 1970, Under Secretary of the Army Beal provided revised and reduced advertising budget estimates and pressed Laird to

> approve the concept and the revised funding levels . . . [because] [w]ithout adequate funding support and an early go-ahead the momentum we have generated throughout the Army during the past month will be lost. (Beal, 1970)

On November 19, 1970, in a bold but ultimately unsuccessful bureaucratic move, Resor wrote Laird again

> to stress the urgency of our request, [to] emphasize the need to get underway with an integrated broad-scope program, and [to] urge that we may have your decision without delay. (Resor, 1970c)

The Army was asking the Secretary of Defense for $131 million for FY 1971 to strengthen the recruiting command—536 new personnel and 105 new recruiting stations—and to fund paid television advertising, improve the living conditions of soldiers, and provide proficiency pay for the combat arms. When the Army finally got the Secretary of Defense's decision, it was less than thrilled. Laird told the Army to reprogram—reallocate—funds from its own existing FY 1971 accounts. A total of $39.8 million was finally identified for reprogramming; $10.6 million went for a paid radio and television advertising campaign, $14 million to the Recruiting Command, and $25 million to fund Project VOLAR.[29]

Project VOLAR

Within a month of being set up the Special Assistant for the Modern Volunteer Army prepared an extensive "master program" to "improve service attractiveness, expand recruiting, increase reenlistments, and upgrade people and units" (Office of the Special Assistant for the Modern Volunteer Army, 1970). The centerpiece of the program was Project VOLAR, three field experiments at Fort Ord, Fort Carson, and Fort Benning to improve soldiers' living conditions. According to General Forsythe, it was "aimed at determining the effectiveness of certain resources applications in moving toward zero draft by 30 June 1973" (Forsythe, 1970). Its goals were laudatory:

---

[29] In FY 1971 the U.S. Army Recruiting Command recruiting force was more than doubled, from 2,969 to 6,080. In addition, the college graduation utilization program was tried to make sure the 25,296 college graduates who entered the Army in FY 1971 were given "challenging and demanding assignments" (Bell, 1973b, p. 49).

to apply the DoD "fly before you buy" principle in determining those "resource supported" actions that will have the greatest "pay off" in attracting new enlistments, raising reenlistments, and improving retention of high quality officers and enlisted men. (Forsythe, 1970)

It was based on a successful program that Major General Bernard Rogers, the Commander of the 5th Infantry Division (Mechanized) at Fort Carson, had developed. Rogers had recognized the futility of traditional Army attempts to "compel and intimidate" personnel into "acceptable behavior" and had developed a program to "co-opt" the mostly draftees and Vietnam returnees in his command. The command's retention rate had increased 45 percent within ten months.[30] The new program, building on the Fort Carson experience, would include more-comfortable barracks and increased privacy and would hire civilians to replace soldiers performing kitchen police and other menial duties. Besides Forts Carson, Benning, and Ord, Fort Bragg was added in the United States, and selected troop centers were added in Europe. Sixteen additional installations were to be added when funds became available.[31] Several snappy slogans were written to "publicize and sell the Modern Volunteer Army" (Office of the Special Assistant for the Modern Volunteer Army, 1970): "The Army is Changing— For the Better" and "Today's Army Wants to Join You," are most remembered. General Forsythe asked the Human Resources Research Office (HumRRO) to evaluate the program. When the FY 1972 program budget was finalized, the Army was given $72 million for Project VOLAR; $66 million was given to the other services to share.

Paid Radio and Television Advertising

While disappointed not to get additional funds for paid radio and television advertising, the Army nevertheless decided to move ahead and reprogram FY 1971 funds,[32] so advising Kelley's staff in early December (Wollstadt, 1970c).[33] Kelley agreed that the Army could test the value of paid advertising and told his staff that

> [a]s long as the evaluation is made by an outside organization (other than the advertising agency employed by the Army), I see no objection to confining the test to the Army. It must be monitored closely by your office, however, including the ad copy to insure basic fairness as far as the other Services are concerned. (Wollstadt, 1970c)[34]

---

[30] General Montague came from Fort Carson and was "convinced . . . that changes in life-style could make the Army more attractive to volunteers" (Griffith, 1997, p. 65).

[31] The new installations, 13 in CONUS and thee overseas, were added on July 1, 1971 (Bell, 1974, p. 57).

[32] The Army reprogrammed $39.8 million of its FY 1971 funds "for an FY 71 zero-draft effort . . . for increased advertising, recruiting and a three-post experiment in raising standards of living" (Resor, 1971a).

[33] See the timeline for discussions about paid radio and television advertising in OASD[M&RA] (1971d).

[34] See Kelley's handwritten note on Wollstadt's memorandum (Wollstadt, 1970c).

To the leadership in OSD and the other services, the issue of evaluation was critical for their acquiescence to the Army's proposal. The Deputy Secretary of Defense told the Secretary of the Army in early January "that the experiments in the use of paid TV/radio recruitment advertising during FY 71 are to be conducted under the supervision of ASD(M&RA)" (Packard, 1971a). The details of the oversight were clearly spelled out in meetings with the Army and in written instructions:

> [W]e must know and approve in advance messages to be used and the location of the proposed test broadcasts . . . [and] either (a) to examine and approve the Army's plan for evaluating the results or (b) to arrange for an outside evaluation by an independent organization obtained by OSD. (Wollstadt, 1971b)

While the Army agreed that, if OSD "desired it, we (the Army) will be happy to have an evaluation of an independent organization obtained by OSD" (Kester, 1971), they certainly did not wait for OSD to "supervise" their program.

The Army's program began on March 1, 1971, and was to run for only 13 weeks. The Navy, however, was still concerned that the Army's "advertising campaign will undermine the philosophy of free, public service advertising and will jeopardize the recruiting efforts of all Services" (Hittle, 1971).[35] The Navy also complained that "the Army's advertising plan exceeds the scope and density of coverage required for 'test' purposes" (Hittle, 1971). Matters were made worse by the fact that the "test" was not designed, as Kelley had stipulated, by an "outside organization—other than the advertising agency employed by the Army," but by N. W. Ayer & Sons, Inc., the Army's advertising agency.[36] Moreover, the test was poorly designed, with very little variation in the way advertising funds would be spent. Ayer & Sons had bought time in all the top 100 radio markets and saturated each market with spots. Their apparent goal was not to test the value of paid advertising, but to produce the maximum response possible. Two-thirds of the television funds were spent on network sales for national coverage. Only one-third of the television funds were allocated to the eight specially selected markets to test the effectiveness of television advertising.[37] The OSD staff believed that sometime after the advertising agency initiated the program, the Army decided to "forget about the test and go for accessions" (Lee and Parker, 1977, p. 159). By the time OSD realized what had happened, it was to late to do anything about it, and Kelley had no choice but to let the Army continue.

---

[35] A complete account of this program is in Foreman (1972). Kelley set out the terms and assurances of the test for the other services. He promised that, "When our evaluation of the Army test is completed, it will be fully discussed with all the Services" (Kelley, 1971d). The same concerns came up at the February 25, 1971, hearings of the House Armed Services Committee: "Two members reported that they knew of instances where broadcast stations have said to the other Services, 'If the Army can pay for its advertising, so can you'" (Lee, 1971b).

[36] See Lee's memorandum to Wollstadt (Lee, 1971a).

[37] A more complete discussion of the test design and the selection of the Army's theme, "Today's Army Wants to Join You" is in Foreman (1972).

At the end of the initial three-month "test" the Army was ready to move out again with another round of advertising. The Army asked for permission at a Project Volunteer Committee meeting to run a six-week paid radio and television advertising program later in the summer.[38] This second round of paid advertising would start on July 26, 1971; would run until September 3, 1971; and would cost $3.1 million. For Kelley, a July start was problematic because the Army's evaluation studies of the first 13-week test were due in August or September 1971 and "preliminary results of the OSD sponsored evaluation" would not be available until early August, with additional data in September, final results in December (OASD[M&RA], 1971f). Kelley's rejection of the proposal was emphatic, if not effective. He told the Army that

> Your request is denied. There is a lack of convincing evidence that enlistment gains realized in the past three months are due substantially to paid advertising. Lacking such evidence, there is no basis upon which we could justifiably authorize the additional paid advertising at this time. (Kelley, 1971i)

The Army immediately went over his head to the Secretary of Defense. "I request your immediate favorable decision on this request," Resor wrote Laird (Resor, 1971c). In what can only be described as a bizarre set of bureaucratic maneuvers, the Deputy Secretary of Defense finally overturned both Kelley's decision to wait for the evaluation to be completed and Laird's decision to side with the Army. The final decision was to approve a limited program in "selected markets only, rather than nation-wide as proposed by the Army" (Kelley, 1971h).[39]

What proved to be more problematic was the attitude of Congress. Some in Congress felt the new Army slogan, "Today's Army Wants to Join You," reflected a "weakening of discipline" and a "selling of the Pentagon." The Chairman of the House Armed Services Committee, Congressman F. Edward Hebert (D-Louisiana), told a senior delegation from the Army that, with regard to the public airways, "not one cent of appropriated money would be used to buy something that the Government already owned" (Forsythe, 1971). Hebert believed that in exchange for the licensing privileges the Federal Communications Commission grants, the electronic media should furnish the military services with free prime-time advertising spots.[40] Unfortunately, the Army was caught in the middle. The broadcast industry rejected

---

[38] Kelley's staff proposed to him an alternative. Rather than an extension of the Army's program they wanted "to discuss with the Services the feasibility of a joint DoD-sponsored advertising effort to publicize the new pay rates" (OASD[M&RA], 1971f).

[39] See Kelley's memorandum to the Army (Kelley, 1971i), Resor's to Laird (Resor, 1971), Chafee's memorandum to Laird (Chafee, 1971) and Kelley's memorandum to Laird (Kelley, 1971h). The endorsements on the latter show Laird's approval of the Army's plan on June 30, 1971, and Deputy Secretary of Defense David Packard's final decision on July 2, 1971. Chafee's memorandum to Laird also overturns not only the Navy's long-term position in regard to Army paid advertising, but also the specific position taken by his Assistant Secretary less than a month earlier (Johnson, James E., 1971a).

[40] Roy Burch covered this subject well in his "study essay" for the U.S. Army War College (Burch, 1972).

any suggestion that in allocating time to public service announcements the fact of a government license obligates a licensee to give a preferred position to announcements of any particular government agency or indeed to government agencies generally . . . [and] respectfully decline[d] to make any commitment of public service time of the scope suggested.[41]

On July 27, 1971, the new Secretary of the Army, Robert F. Froehlke, sought Laird's advice on "whether it is more important to the achievement of your goals for us to proceed with paid radio and TV advertising this summer or to accede to Chairman Hebert's views" (Froehlke, 1971). The Department of Defense was clear that, without Chairman Hebert's support, the summer paid-advertising program was cancelled. In early August, Laird told Nixon of Hebert's "strong determination to prevent further use of paid TV/radio advertising for recruiting" (Laird, 1971d). Congress went on to formally prohibit the use of FY 1972 funds for paid radio and television advertising.[42]

Recruiting

One of the most encouraging experiences the Army had during this early period was the effectiveness of its program of recruiting options for the combat arms. During 1970, with an active draft at hand, the Army had recruited an average of only 250 new personnel a month for the combat arms. The Unit-of-Choice option[43] and the Location-of-Choice option,[44] together with the emphasis recruiters placed on ground-combat enlistments, contributed to a rapid and significant increase in the number of ground-combat enlistments. The Army also aggressively moved to beef up the Recruiting Command by assigning it three new general officers. They initiated a number of new programs that proved to be very effective.[45] The Recruiter Assistants Program, initiated April 9, 1971, sent recent Advanced Individual Training (AIT) graduates back to their

---

[41] Letter from the president of the CBS Broadcast Group to the Secretary of the Army, October 8, 1971, cited in Foreman (1972).

[42] In subsequent years, in deference to Chairman Hebert's strong views, DoD did not use paid radio and television advertisements, relying on public-service advertising. The Army, however, conducted a modest radio campaign in 1975, and ASD(M&RA) conducted a modest joint test of radio time in 1976. When Congressman Hebert lost power and his chairmanship in 1976, the situation changed.

[43] The Unit-of-Choice Program, which began February 1, 1971, with seven combat units participating, was "designed to promote high morale among recruits by reducing or eliminating uncertainty and anxiety through early identification and association with a parent military organization" (Grissmer et al., 1973, p. 2).

[44] The CONUS Station of Choice Enlistment Option started in October 1972, offering qualified men assignment to one of 40 installations in the continental United States and training in one of over 250 entry-level occupations (Bell and Cocke, 1977, p. 65).

[45] The Army asked the General Research Corporation (GRC), successor to the Research Analysis Corporation (RAC), their former federal contract research center (FCRC), to undertake an evaluation of "the effectiveness of the . . . unit canvasser and recruiter assistant programs in terms of their contributions to the Army recruiting effort, and their cost effectiveness compared to other programs designed to attract volunteers" (Grissmer et al., 1973, p. 1). The GRC study found that "the marginal productivity of a unit canvasser or recruiter assistant appears to be significantly higher than that of an additional US Army Recruiting Command USAREC recruiter" (Grissmer et al., 1973, p. x).

home towns temporarily, to help recruiters locate new prospects. The Unit Canvasser Program, initiated in February 1972, had soldiers from the unit of choice help recruiters enlist prospects for the canvasser's own unit. As a result of these initiatives, Army enlistments in the combat arms increased to an average of over 3,000 per month. In one month, June 1971, the number of ground-combat enlistments exceeded 4,000 (Lee and Parker, 1977, p. 167). By February 1972, and ahead of schedule, over 2,300 new recruiters were in place, and 556 new recruiting stations had opened.

Enlistment Bonus

Besides a new emphasis on recruiting, the Army believed that "a new and dramatic pay incentive" was central to its volunteer Army program and wanted "something new and concrete for our recruiters to sell, and to concentrate our efforts where they will have the greatest payoff in lessening reliance on draftees, particularly in combat jobs" (Kester, 1970b).[46] The Army's support for special pay drew immediate opposition from the Navy. The Assistant Secretary of the Navy told Kelley that

> [a] specific bonus program for the Army's Combat Arms . . . is not compatible with the concept that our Marines are recruited, trained and motivated for . . . .
> [B]oth the Navy and the Marine Corps are opposed to a plan which may tend to overemphasize the monetary aspects of military service at the time of initial recruitment. (Hittle, 1970)

The Army not only supported legislation required for enacting an enlistment bonus but also favored expanding proficiency pay ("pro pay") for those already in service and wanted to reprogram funds to implement the pro pay program in FY 1971 (Kelley, 1971a). When the Secretary of the Army told Kelley that the Army had "allocated the additional $30 million for special pay (pro pay) of up to $150 per month for men on long tours of service (30 months or more after training) in the combat skills" (Resor, 1971c), Kelley and the new Assistant Secretary of Defense (Systems Analysis) Gardiner Tucker objected. The Systems Analysis office thought pro pay was "less 'efficient' than bonuses in attracting new enlistees, since you must pay it to a large number of men already in the Service who qualify" (Tucker, 1971a).

The Army's request was denied because, as the Secretary of Defense wrote the Secretary of the Army, "we have strongly favored the enlisted bonus over pro pay for combat personnel, believing that it would be very difficult to stop pro pay once it had been started" (Packard, 1971a).[47] After months of delay, with positive action in

---

[46] Also see Kester's memorandum of December 10, 1970, to Kelley (Kester, 1970c).

[47] In winter 1971, Packard and Resor agreed to use pro pay "as an interim tool to attract new entries, to be discontinued for first termers as soon as Congress authorized the use of the enlisted bonus" (Kelley, 1971c). Unfortunately, Jim Schlesinger at the Office of Management and Budget (OMB), later to be the Secretary of Defense, "strongly opposed . . . our recommendation." Kelley told Packard that, "[b]ased on Schlesinger's reaction, I doubt that this can be done" (Kelley, 1971c).

Congress (White House Press Secretary, 1971), and over continued objections from the Navy (Johnson, James E., 1971b), the Secretary of Defense authorized a $1,500 enlistment bonus in May 1972, to start in July 1, 1972, for the Army and Marine Corps in return for a four-year enlistment in the combat arms.[48] Initially, the program was to run for 90 days as a test, with "[b]onus payment [not] . . .to be paid to individuals who have already enlisted in the delay pool of another Service" (Kelley, 1972d). A test plan was built around a questionnaire administered to all volunteers who chose the bonus, interviews with recruiters, and a survey of 17- to 21-year-old males in the target population to study attitudes toward the bonus option. The plan also called for a cost-benefit analysis (OASD[M&RA], 1972b). A report by Kelley's staff found that the "test has been successful . . . Army and Marine Corps were authorized 7,500 and 3,300 bonus enlistments, respectively. Subsequently the test was extended to October 31, 1972 and quotas removed" (OASD[M&RA], 1972a). In April 1973, the bonus was raised to $2,500 and restricted to high school graduates, and the Army was asked to submit a new evaluation plan.

Kelley's own Special Assistant to ASD(M&RA) for All-Volunteer Force Action, General Montague, however, raised questions about both the original and new evaluation plans. Looking at the original research, among the things he questioned was

> the representativeness of the sample can only be assumed, [and] the questionnaires were developed hurriedly; they contained ambiguities, omitted important questions, included irrelevant questions, and are improperly organized. (Montague, 1973)

In the future, he recommended, "we should work more closely with PA&E [Program Analysis and Evaluation—the new name for Systems Analysis] before the fact when we decide to test various AVF initiatives."[49]

General Montague's concerns notwithstanding, David Grissmer et al. in a study for the Army found that "the presence of the combat arms bonus decreased the possible percentage decline in combat arms enlistments that would have occurred as additional options and emphasis were placed on other skills" (Grissmer et al., 1974). The effects of the $2,500 bonus were clearer and more dramatic. While the

> increases due to the $1,500 bonus were primarily in the IIIA, IIIB non–high school graduate group . . . the increases from the $2,500 bonus [were] among high school graduates in Mental Categories I–III. . . . [Moreover], [t]he additional volunteers who entered the Army as a result of the bonus appear to be primarily people who

---

[48] See the M&RA "Plan For Army Ground Combat Enlistment Bonus" (Lee, 1972b), Kelley's recommendation to the Secretary of Defense (Kelley, 1972b), and his recommendation to include the Marine Corps (Kelley, 1972c).

[49] Montague also recommended that the "plans for test and later evaluating the test of shorter reserve enlistments should be fully reviewed before the test begins. The RAND plan covering the Air Force is good. An Army plan, worthy of the name, doesn't exist to my knowledge" (Montague, 1973).

would not have entered the Service at all as opposed to people who would have entered another Service. (Grissmer et al., 1974, p. 281)[50]

The Other Services

While the other services announced programs to improve military life, they did not move as aggressively as the Army to reallocate funds to these new programs. In FY 1971, the Army reprogrammed just under $40 million. The other services reprogrammed fewer funds: the Navy, $1.2 million; Marine Corps, $15,000; and the Air Force, $4 million. Moreover, in the face of an aggressive Army effort, the other services lacking new programs of their own, and with draft calls decreasing, the number of "draft induced volunteers" entering the other services decreased.[51]

Navy

Admiral Elmo Zumwalt, Chief of Naval Operations (CNO), was outspoken in his support of the all-volunteer force and took the lead in the Navy's zero-draft program, but his initial attention was on reenlistments, not accessions. In his memoir, Zumwalt noted that, for years, the Navy's reenlistment rate had been 35 percent. In 1970, when he became the CNO, the reenlistment rate had fallen to 9.5 percent (Zumwalt, 1976, p. 167). He identified four things he felt "the Navy could do to make the service more attractive and more satisfying." They were: (1) reexamine regulations and practices dealing with personal behavior, (2) develop operational schedules to "lighten . . .the burden . . . (of) long separation from family," (3) increase job satisfaction "through more responsibility and greater opportunity for advancement," and (4) "throw overboard once and for all the Navy's silent but real and persistent discrimination against minorities" (Zumwalt, 1976, p. 168). Even before he formally took over the responsibilities of the CNO, Zumwalt established a series of retention study groups, a grassroots effort to form recommendations for improving retention. When Zumwalt became CNO, he met weekly with whatever retention working group was in Washington. He would later describe it as a "more than welcome opportunity to insert into the routine of paperwork and VIP meetings an encounter with sailors from the fleet" (Zumwalt, 1976, p. 172). Famous for his "Z-grams," messages to the whole Navy,[52] it was not

---

[50] For example, according to the FY 1972 Historical Summary,

> Enlistments in infantry, armor, and field artillery were averaging 300 a month. After extensive printed advertising, substantial increases in the recruiting force and in recruiting stations, and initiation of new and attractive enlistment options, combat arms enlistments jumped to almost 39,000 in fiscal year 1972 compared with less than 10,000 the previous year. Overall enlistments and the "number of true volunteers" jumped as well. Yet these successes were still short of requirements. (Bell, 1974, p. 58)

[51] Draft calls for the last six months of calendar year 1971, when compared with the same period in 1970, declined from 70,000 to 11,000.

[52] For a complete list of Z-grams, see Appendix D in Zumwalt (1976, pp. 530–532).

until Z-gram 109, issued on April 26, 1972, that he focused on recruiting and "declared recruiting is my top priority" (Zumwalt, 1972b).

"I paid little attention to recruitment, which seemed to me to be going reasonably well"—until late 1971, Zumwalt would later admit, and then only because between October and December 1971 the Navy missed accession goals by about 8,000.[53] It attributed this, in part, to the relatively slow expansion of its recruiting force. By February 1972, the Navy had placed only 68 percent of 500 recruiters it had programmed. The Navy had opened only 87 percent of the 175 stations that had been planned. Moreover, it was falling behind the other services. The 30-percent increase in recruiters the Navy achieved in FY 1972 was more than matched by the Army's increase of 71 percent and the Air Force's increase of 36 percent. The Navy exceeded only the Marine Corps, which increased its recruiter force by 18 percent in FY 1972. As one observer noted,

> [I]n all cases the increases in the other Services occurred earlier than the Navy's [and] . . . were more aggressive in their recruiting. . . . [The draw down in Vietnam,] made the Army much more attractive, relative to the Navy, then had previously been the case. (Jehn and Carroll, 1974, p. 5)

To make things worse, the Navy initiated new quality standards that made recruiting just that much harder. A research team at the Center for Naval Analyses estimated that the Navy's tightening "its screening of 'low quality' individuals . . . resulted in a probable loss of about 7,000 recruits during FY 1972. This figure represents over 93 percent of the true shortfall of 7,525 for FY 1972" (Jehn and Carroll, 1974, p. 5).[54]

To address these problems Admiral Zumwalt recommended the promotion of Rear Admiral David Bagley to Vice Admiral and assigned him to the job of Chief of Naval Personnel with oversight of the Naval Recruiting Command.[55] In March 1972,

---

[53] For an account of Zumwalt's new concerns about recruiting see Zumwalt (1976, p. 210).

[54] When the CNA team could not find any statistically significant relationship between the number of recruiters assigned and the number of recruits, they did not conclude that "recruiters don't matter," but pointed to the fact that they "were unable to measure such [things] as recruiter selection, training, motivation, and management" (Jehn and Carroll, 1974, p. 10); all problems during the period. The CNA team noted,

> Prior to 1972, when recruiting was a lower priority, recruiter billets were often used to alleviate the shore rotation problem. . . . Recruiters were not carefully screened for motivation or ability. . . . [Moreover, it was their impression] career counselors are often as poorly trained for their jobs as recruiters have been in the past. (Jehn and Carroll, 1974, p. 14)

[55] In April 1971, the recruiting function had been removed from the Bureau of Naval Personnel and "made a separate field command . . . to give recruiting greater visibility" (Jehn and Carroll, 1974, p. 5). The separation had only reduced the standing of recruiting.

On January 31, 1972, the Assistant Chief of Naval Personnel for Plans and Programs wrote the head of the Program Evaluation Group to apprise him of the actions the Navy had taken "in an attempt to provide the most responsive personnel and management techniques possible. . . . These actions will satisfy our immediate needs" (Finneran, 1972). On March 1, the Navy initiated new recruiting programs and asked that OSD consider the "special Navy problem[s] when apportioning the Project VOLUNTEER Funds for FY 74" (Bagley, 1972). On March 11, 1972, in response to a personal request from Laird, Secretary of the Navy John Chafee reported on the problems facing the Navy and actions underway to improve the situation (Chafee, 1972).

Zumwalt told his Flag Officers that he had "now placed recruiting as my TOP PRIOR-ITY!" He asked them that,

> while traveling about in your local areas take a few minutes of your time and visit the local recruiting stations. . . . Let them know you *are* interested. . . .
>
> We must all pull together in this endeavor and make our All Volunteer Navy a reality (Zumwalt, 1972a, emphasis in the original).

He also initiated a three-year enlistment option, "the shortest active obligation open to regular Navy enlistees, guaranteed duty with one of the Navy's seagoing units or an aviation unit, based on the coast of the enlistee's choice" (Greene, 1972). The Navy traditionally programmed fewer resources than any of the other services to attract new accessions. Its FY 1973 budget provided enough resources for the Navy to spend $540 per new recruit, based on a goal of 125,000 new recruits. The Army expected to spend $840 to attract a new recruit, while the Air Force and the Marine Corps planned on spending $660 and $770, respectively (Kelley, 1972e). When the Navy asked for more money, Laird, recognizing "the urgent and critical need to increase the number of vol-unteers for the Navy," agreed. Even though "there is no contingency fund for the All-Volunteer Force," he increased the Navy's recruiting budget by $29.2 million, noting this was still "$14 million less than the total stated Navy requirement" (Laird, 1972c).[56] After the Navy reassigned Rear Admiral Emmett Tidd to head the Recruiting Com-mand, things began to change, as Zumwalt would later note that, by FY 1994, Tidd

> achieved 103 percent of his numerical goal. . . . Fewer than 4 percent of all recruits in FY 74 were in Mental Group IV. Furthermore, as the result of the emphasis Emmett [Tidd] placed on minority recruiting, minority personnel in the Navy rose from less than 5 percent to almost 10, and in FY 74 as high a percentage of minor-ity recruits as of the total, some 80 percent, were school eligible. That was quite a job for anyone to do in less than two years, and he richly earned his promotion to vice admiral that I saw to it he got by upgrading his command to a three-star billet. (Zumwalt, 1976, p. 213)

Air Force

In the Air Force, Lieutenant General Robert J. Dixon, Deputy Chief of Staff (Person-nel) was also concerned about the all-volunteer force and not only for the regular Air Force. In summer 1970, he asked RAND for help in understanding the implications of a zero draft for the Air National Guard and the Air Force Reserve.[57] In December

---

[56] In September 1972, the Navy provided a fact sheet on the implications of the newly received FY 1973 funds on the recruiting budget for FY 1974 (Zech, 1972). The service asked Congress to approval reprogramming $14.2 mil-lion for recruiting (OASD[M&RA], 1972c).

[57] See Chapter Seven for a discussion of RAND's involvement with the Air Force and the Air Reserve Personnel Study.

1970, he commissioned the Saber Volunteer study.[58] Major General Glenn Kent, the Assistant Chief of Staff for Studies and Analysis, took General Dixon's tasking and assigned Major John Johnston as study director. Major Johnston was concerned that he already had a full plate. General Kent remembers telling him to take all the time he needed to finish up what he was doing, as long as he was ready for the new assignment after lunch. Major Johnston would not only complete the Saber Volunteer assignment, producing what one observer called "the most comprehensive collection of the data in a single study" (Lee and Parker, 1977, p. 461), but went on to the Brookings Institution to coauthor an important assessment of the all-volunteer force for the Senate Armed Services Committee,[59] and then on to serve on the Air Staff and the Office of the Secretary of Defense. The data from the two-year Saber Volunteer study were published in 24 volumes and helped shape the debate on the all-volunteer force in the White House and Congress. Johnston's arguments concerning the percentage of the high school graduating class the military needed to recruit was often quoted by those skeptical that the all-volunteer force was feasible.[60]

In summer 1971, the Air Force failed to meet its total non–prior service recruiting objectives for the first time in five years. The quality levels for these recruits also decreased slightly in comparison with those for FY 1970. The Air Force moved into action. In August, it asked Kelley for 31 percent of the uncommitted FY73 funds and asked that in the future OSD should allocate funds using a "formula [that] weights numbers of people and the length of time they may be utilized. This places proportional emphasis on both accessions and retention areas" (Borda, 1971). Under the Air Force proposal, the Army's share would drop to 36 percent of the total available funds, and the Air Force's share would increase to 31 percent.

In addition to asking for new money, in October 1971, the Air Force offered new recruits the job assignments of their choice in return for a six-year enlistment. This was an important early initiative that worked well for the Air Force; eventually, almost half of Air Force enlistments would take the six years option. In November, the Air Force submitted an aggressive new budget proposal for FY 1973 that included

> a $1,000 bonus . . . paid to those enlisting in high quality guaranteed assignment, Air Force Specialty Codes . . . for a six year enlistment. The Air Force can document enough cost savings of the six year enlistment to obviate the entire cost of the program. (Roberts, 1971, p. 2)

---

[58] The Saber Volunteer study is summarized in Johnson (1971).

[59] The Senate Armed Services Committee published the report that Johnson and Binkin prepared for its chairman, Senator Stennis, as Binkin and Johnson (1973).

[60] The argument was flawed. It assumed a high school graduate had only one chance to join the military. In fact, a graduate had many chances to join. The relevant pool was not one year's graduating class, but all those between the minimum and maximum ages for recruits, which was something on the order of ten times the size of a single graduating class. In fact, most recruits entered the military well after they graduated from high school, with more than half being older than 20.

In February 1972, the service revised the goal system for recruiters and put the emphasis on quality. From then on, the Air Force would no longer award points to a recruiter simply for meeting quotas.

The Air Force also reached out to industry for help. In May 1972, it held the Air Force-Industry Conference on the All-Volunteer (Zero Draft) Force "to seek the counsel and to profit from the experience of those already in the market place" (U.S. Air Force, 1972a, p. 1). At the conference, General Dixon laid out the Air Force's approach to meeting its all-volunteer force goals. He highlighted the $64 million to be spent to increase the number of recruiting personnel, opening additional recruiting stations, and adding new recruiting incentives and the $13 million for such educational programs as tuition assistance, educational counselors, and off-duty education. He identified "programs waiting in the wings" that included more ROTC scholarships and increased entitlements for junior-grade airmen. He stressed the commitment to a "codified" Air Force Personnel Plan that, as he saw it, provided a "management discipline, something to be lived up to and used in procurement, in training, and every other facet of personnel management" (Dixon, 1972, p. 18). Finally, he announced that volunteer accessions in the Air Force had grown from 50 to 86 percent (March 1972) and reenlistments were up from a 1971 level of 20 percent to 35 percent—a level he identified as needed to maintain a balanced force.

The "consensus" of the conference was that "representatives from the private sector . . . noted that they were surprised at the distance the Department of Defense had already traveled in making the transition to an all-volunteer force." They agreed that "both the business communities and the military paid insufficient attention to the question of the 'demand' for people" (U.S. Air Force, 1972a, p. 141).

Building the FY 1972 All-Volunteer Force Program

November and December is budget season at the Pentagon. In fall 1970, DoD, working with the volunteer-force spending limits Nixon had given them the previous spring, was putting the final touches on the FY 1972 budget. By at least one account, this one by Deputy Secretary Packard's military assistant, there were problems with Kelley's presentation of the Project Volunteer recommendations. In a memorandum for the record, he noted that his "overall impression of the presentation of Project Volunteer . . . [was that] there was no basis for acting on any of the items recommended . . . " (Furlong, 1970, p. 1). He concluded that "no data was presented which would permit a reasoned selection of proposed courses of action nor any basis for confidence that they would have the desired effect" (Furlong, 1970, p. 4).

Working the back channels through the military assistants of the Secretary and Deputy Secretary of Defense, System Analysis's point man on the all-volunteer force, Phil Odeen, characterized Kelley's program as providing "a conceptual framework and overview of the zero draft program" (Odeen, 1970). Setting the stage, he noted that, in FY 1972, there are $1.3 billion which can be allocated to the zero-draft concept. A number of alternative ways of spending this money have been proposed . . . [that] fall into three categories: (1) recruiting and advertising alternatives; (2) pay options; and (3) special problems. (Odeen, 1970, p. 1)[61]

He presented a number of options that included the proposals from the services, three options from Kelley's shop, and three options from his own shop. He argued that the services and Kelley's options did "not reduce the draft below what it would be if Volunteer Funds were not spent at all." System Analysis's options were more responsive. They "involve[d] a significant reduction in the draft call, [but] they require[d] large increases in pay and recruiting/advertising expenditures in order to attract a sufficient number of volunteers" (Odeen, 1970). Odeen's paper was the basis for the discussions and decisions made at the meeting on December 15, 1970, discussed below.

Systems Analysis Versus Manpower and Reserve Affairs

The conflict between the Systems Analysis and the Manpower offices over how to proceed with the "zero draft" program had started the previous summer, when the Project Volunteer Committee submitted its report (Project Volunteer Committee, 1970). The report did not contain a single budget number or budget alternative and was fiscally unconstrained. From the perspective of Systems Analysis, the Project Volunteer report was long on generalizations and short on specifics. During the fall, the new Assistant Secretary for Systems Analysis, Gardiner Tucker, undertook his own study. At the end of November, after trying to accommodate several comments from Kelley and Wollstadt, *The Volunteer Service: Prospects, Alternatives and Decision Criteria* (Tucker, 1970) was released.[62] The study tried to answer "three basic questions":

(1) [H]ow large is the potential manpower gap between the Services' demand for annual new accessions and the supply of true volunteers; (2) how much will it cost

---

[61] The Manpower and Systems Analysis shops had been battling from the very start. At the first meeting of the Project Volunteer Steering Committee, on May 14, 1969, they had "discussions of [the] respective roles of Manpower and Reserve Affairs and Systems Analysis" (Wool, 1969e). Wool noted that

[a]fter lengthy discussion in which Systems Analysis representatives repeatedly expressed concern over the availability of data bearing upon questions of requirements and annual gains/losses, Assistant Secretary Kelley instructed the Staff Director and Systems Analysis to work out any problems in this respect, and further instructed them to proceed on a close cooperative working relationship on a day-by-day basis. (Wool, 1969e)

In October 1969, Kelley and the acting head of Systems Analysis, Ivan Selin, got Packard's approval of a charter "to define the complementary responsibilities of our offices as they relate to manpower" (Selin and Kelley, 1969a); on October 29, 1969, they jointly signed a memorandum to "clarify the roles of Systems Analysis and Manpower & Reserve Affairs in matters related to manpower requirements and manpower utilization" (Selin and Kelley, 1969b). It was a compact that would not last.

[62] *Author's Note:* The Manpower Requirements Directorate worked for the Deputy Assistant Secretary for Resource Analysis and prepared the study. The head of the office was Frank Sullivan. I worked in that office from August 1, 1968, to July 31, 1970, and worked on early drafts of the report (OASD[SA], 1970). Frank Sullivan would later play a critical role in the development of the all-volunteer force as Staff Director of the Senate Armed Services Committee and one of Senator Stennis's top aides.

to eliminate the gap; and, (3) what schedules can be set to achieve a Volunteer Service. . . .

The costs of achieving a Volunteer Service depend directly on the size of the manpower gap and the methods used to close it. . . . It is doubtful that current Volunteer Service spending proposals could close that gap, assuming only $1.3 billion is available in FY 72. (Tucker, 1970, p. 1)

Systems Analysis was critical of many of the Project Volunteer Committee proposals, particularly those

aimed at improving the standard of living (e.g., housing) or lessening the aggravation of Service (e.g., reducing KP). While many of these may have merit, they may not have direct and immediate results in moving toward a zero draft. Furthermore, they tend to be high risk investments because we have no good ways to measure the elasticity of enlistments or reenlistments to changes in the standard of living. Thus we could spend volunteer service money to make small improvements in living conditions and not know whether or how they reduced reliance on the draft. Spending on these items should be small and experimental, designed to measure which of the proposals have the highest potential. (Tucker, 1970, p. 11)

Systems Analysis concluded that, "[w]ith the planned 20% pay raise for first term enlisted men and end strengths below FY 72 budget submissions, the Air Force, Navy, and Marine Corps should not have any manpower gaps under a Volunteer Service" (Tucker, 1970, p. 11).[63]

Working from this study, Systems Analysis proposed seven budget alternatives in an options paper circulated on December 14, 1970 (Odeen, 1970). The options were discussed at a meeting that Laird and Packard had with the services on December 15, 1970. Laird's military aid, Brigadier General Robert Pursley, recorded what happened at the meeting:

The principal objective of the zero draft program is to reduce reliance on the draft during FY 72 leading to a zero draft by the end of CY 72. . . . the costs of the program [is to] be within the funds currently available ($1.3 billion for FY 72 and $3.5 billion for FY 73). . . . (Pursley, 1971, p. 1)

Laird and Packard initially favored Option 6 [the midrange offer put forward by Tucker and Systems Analysis] because of its low planned draft call . . . [and] the other Services' acceptance of the program and possible Congressional difficulties

---

[63] The Navy provided Kelly its own assessment of the System Analysis study. The Navy thought the study had

fatal flaws in the basic assumptions and methodology which completely negate all the conclusions but two. The Navy supports the conclusion that more analysis of the labor market and recruiting potential is needed [and agrees with] . . . the fundamental criteria for evaluation of alternatives. (Navy paper, attachment to Tucker, 1970, p. A-1)

The service felt that the assumptions underlying the Systems Analysis study "grossly exaggerate[d] the magnitude of the problem[s] by minimizing the Navy's problem[s] and maximizing the Army's" (Tucker, 1970, p. A-2). This assessment concluded that "the concentration of all remaining Volunteer funds on the Army will in fact worsen our [the Navy's] position" (Tucker, 1970, p. A-3).

with the large contingency fund and only limited funds for the Services other than the Army. Consequently, the agreed upon strategy was to start with Option 2 but move toward Option 6 draft levels in FY 72. . . . . Mr. Kelley argued this option would be more acceptable to the other Services. The problem of the contingency funds was overcome by asking Congress for bonus authorizations for all Services, but initially allocating only the $3000 combat arms enlisted bonus to the Army. The remaining $446 million would be unallocated DOD funds available for other Service or additional Army enlistment bonus needs in FY 1972. (Pursley, 1971, p. 2)

The FY 1972 program that was finally approved contained $463 million for the 20-percent first-term pay raise, $105.2 million for recruiting and advertising, $66.5 million for such special problems as ROTC and medical, $209 million for quality-of-life "experiments," $10 million for an Army-only combat arms enlisted bonus, and $446 million of "unallocated" funds.

The difference between the option Systems Analysis favored and the one Kelley and all the services favored was indicative of the schism that had been growing for years between the "analytic" arm of the Office of the Secretary of Defense and the rest of the Pentagon. It was so deep that a plank in the Republican Party platform in 1968 called for elimination of the Systems Analysis Office. At an offsite weekend meeting with the senior leadership of the department shortly after he became Secretary of Defense, Laird managed to preserve Systems Analysis by agreeing to changes in its top leadership, downgrading the leadership of the office from an assistant secretary to an independent directorate, and changing its name. By fall 1970, the leadership had changed, but the name and organization restructuring had not yet taken place.

The option Systems Analysis favored reduced draft calls in FY 1972 from 100,000 to 36,000; recruiting and advertising budgets were large, as were Army bonuses. The contingency fund was quite large to cover unexpected shortfalls in both the Army and the other services. Only a small amount was provided for quality-of-life and special programs. By comparison, all the services favored the option that provided more money for quality-of-life programs. The Navy and Marine Corps wanted the bulk of the contingency fund for an additional 15-percent pay increase for all enlisted and officers with less than two years of service. They did not want to use enlistment bonuses, but agreed the Army might use them as long as they were "experimental." The Army preferred proficiency pay to enlistment bonuses. The Air Force thought that a combat bonus was all the Army needed "to make it competitive with the other Services," and complained that the program "favors the Army too strongly in the nonpay area" (Pursley, 1971).

The Manpower and Reserve Affairs (M&RA) staff prepared a succinct comparison of approaches between the two offices (OASD[M&RA], 1971b):

- Systems Analysis has concluded after a 20 percent pay raise only (the) Army would have supply problems.
- ASD(M&RA) believes that all Services would have supply problems after the end of the draft.

- ASD(SA) emphasizes the enlistment bonus because of its cost-effectiveness, particularly in a situation where problems are expected to be the exception rather than the rule.
- ASD(M&RA) would limit the bonus primarily to known manning problems which remain in a zero draft environment, rather than to solve FY 1972 problems while the draft authority exists.

With the final deadlines for submitting the FY 1972 budget almost on them and with an important meeting of the Defense Program Review Committee (DPRC), to be chaired by National Security Advisor Henry Kissinger, scheduled for early January, Kelley told Laird and Packard that he did

> not believe that we can reconcile [the] remaining differences at this time through further discussion with the Services. The practical next step is to discuss our tentative plans with the leadership of both Armed Services Committees as a means of getting their reactions and determining what is "do-able." (Kelley, 1970d, pp. 1–2)

Laird and Packard did meet with the leadership of the House Armed Services Committee (Packard, 1971c), and on January 18, 1971, Packard signed the Program Budget Decision (PBD) authorizing $1.4 billion in outlays and $1.52 billion in total obligation authority for "programs under Project Volunteer" (Deputy Secretary of Defense, 1971).[64] President Nixon confirmed this in his statement to Congress on January 29, 1971, asking for "an additional $1.5 billion [in total obligation authority] in making military service more attractive to present and potential members" (Nixon, 1971).[65]

What was also clear was that Systems Analysis, not the Manpower office, had taken the lead. Systems Analysis prepared the "point paper" on a zero draft for the DPRC meeting that Packard sent to Kissinger on January 15, 1971 (OASD[SA], 1971).[66] It addressed "ways to solve these problems, and considerations of timing and spending" (Packard, 1971b).[67]

Kelley was not at all happy and soon let Packard know it. On January 18, he spoke to Packard before their morning staff meeting and followed that discussion with a

---

[64] Further details of the $1.4 billion outlay program were provided in OASD[M&RA] (1971c).

[65] Army Secretary Resor was concerned that Kissinger had misled the President to thinking that FY 72 draft calls would be limited to 80,000. He told Packard, "these objectives [should] be described as a range of draft calls rather than as a single estimate. . . . A range of 80,000 to 110,000 for the FY 72 draft level at this time" (Resor, 1971b).

[66] Wollstadt provided Kelley an assessment of the point paper the Systems Analysis office had prepared: "Like several other recent Systems Analysis papers, this is primarily a sales pitch for extensive use of enlistment bonuses in FY 72, FY 73 and perhaps later. It contains no arguments that we haven't seen before" (Wollstadt, 1971a). He was particularly incensed that the letter Packard sent to Kissinger did not mention "that the only Service which favors enlistment bonuses at this time is the Air Force" (Wollstadt, 1971a).

[67] The budget issues were not the only things on the agenda for the meeting of the DPRC. The issue of "extend[ing] the induction authority, which expires July 1, 1971, for two years or for a longer period" was also to be taken up (OASD[M&RA], 1971a). On December 28, 1970, Laird told Kissinger he favored a two-year extension. The Director of Selective Service, Curtis Tarr, favored a four-year extension.

memorandum because, he said, "I believe I failed to convey my real concern." While he admitted that his office had "limited capability" in the "analysis of manpower force figures," he felt he should be consulted on "personnel policy questions," such as "pay forms and the definition of the overall problem." He reminded Packard that previously there had been a "complementary relationship" between Systems Analysis and Manpower and Reserve Affairs, reminding him of the memorandum he and former acting Assistant Secretary Ivan Selin had signed the previous year. Kelley also reminded Packard that this "relationship" had been "confirmed with Gardiner Tucker shortly after he took over Systems Analysis." Unfortunately, according to Kelley, things did not work out as planned, "of which the DPRC paper is the most recent example" (Kelley, 1971b).

In April 1971, Kelley's staff laid out the problem with Systems Analysis and the Project Volunteer Committee. As they saw it, the then-current "[e]valuation of the effects of the Zero Draft Program represents primarily an extension of the current analysis being made within the Services and by OASD(M&RA). . . ." As a result, they concluded that they would have to "plan the FY 1973 program without much to evaluate" (Lee, 1971b, attachment and p. 3).

Tucker, on the other hand, wanted a multiyear plan, not "just a one year FY 72 program" (Tucker, 1971b). In April, with some prodding from Laird, agreement between the two assistant secretaries seemed near on a formal evaluation system for Project Volunteer. Kelley, however, was clearly concerned about the bureaucratic status of his office. He told his staff that, as far as he was concerned,

> implementation [of the Evaluation System for Project Volunteer] will be the responsibility of M&RA but we should draw upon Systems Analysis in the process. There should be a clear understanding between our shops as to this relationship and the anticipated need for their services. Under no circumstances should there be two Evaluation Systems rivaling each other—one in M&RA measuring the effectiveness of action programs within the Services, and the other in Systems Analysis measuring the effectiveness of our measurement. (Kelley, 1971e)

It was clear that he and Tucker really were far apart in their concepts of how to evaluate the all-volunteer force initiatives. Central to Kelley's evaluation scheme was a belief that

> [e]ach of the Services is responsible, not only for cooperating with the OSD studies and analyses, but also for developing its own evaluation plans. Each service must subject the Project Volunteer programs to close-to-the-action scrutiny as an important part of the total evaluation process. (OASD[M&RA], 1971e, p. 1)

In late May, he indicated to Wollstadt that the center of his own evaluation system was still the Project Volunteer Committee. His increased commitment was obvious when he now stated "the Project Volunteer Committee should meet monthly rather than quarterly to review progress," as had been their schedule since 1970, and "the PEG—Program Evaluation Group—will require the full-time effort of a good action officer. There are many 'loose pieces' to be collected from the Services, and then to be put in usable form" (Kelley, 1971f). In early June, Kelley finally acted along a very familiar line. Two years earlier, on July 16, 1969, he established the Program Evaluation Group under the Project Volunteer Committee to facilitate the "development of a consolidated set of proposed actions . . . [to provide for] the optimum allocation of resources" (Kelley, 1969f). Now, in almost identical language, he rechartered the Program Evaluation Group, again under the Project Volunteer Committee, to "continuously review and evaluate overall program experience, interpret . . . significance in terms of program objectives, and report these interpretations to the Project Volunteer Committee" (Kelley, 1971g).[68]

Clearly, Tucker had more in mind. The list of studies and analyses that were already under way or planned that Kelley provided when he rechartered the Program Evaluation Group was long on tracking and short on analysis. It was dominated by surveys of "attitudes toward and perceptions of military life held by young American males" (Kelley, 1971g) and short on the type of analysis the White House would demand at the end of the year, such as assessments of how the military pay raise had been affecting enlistments and identification of which programs were most productive in terms of additional recruits. Systems Analysis had long held that "the next fundamental improvement in our ability to tune-up our initial program will be the collection of data from modest, but well designed field experiments" and for years had argued that "we need to start measuring these effects, not just re-study them" (Srull, 1970).

It was not only those in Systems Analysis who had understood the shortcomings, John Kester, the Deputy Assistant Secretary of the Army (Manpower and Reserve Affairs) told Kelley in 1970:

> We already have numerous studies which attempt to draw conclusions from the almost total lack of data. More studies manipulating the same sparse data (even with different statistical gymnastics) are unlikely to contribute anything significant. The next fundamental improvement in our ability to fashion our program will be the collection of data derived from testing of incentives now. (Kester, 1970b, p. 4)

Although Kelley and his staff felt there was a long list of "Project Volunteer accomplishments" (Lee, 1971c), Tucker continued active opposition to the initiatives Kelley and the services had agreed upon. He opposed the construction of new, improved barracks; the extension of travel entitlements; and improvement in educational benefits.[69] Tucker wanted to focus on the Army and saw military compensation as the prime policy instrument for achieving an all-volunteer force. He wanted to determine as soon as possible, but in any event no later than the following September (1972), whether the

---

[68] According to Lee, the evaluation of PROJECT VOLAR by HumRRO was "part of the old PEG evaluation plans. . . . The studies are primarily of attitudes towards reenlistment at VOLAR posts. . . . But the studies do not enable us to say that VOLAR is relatively cost-effective" (Lee, 1972a).

[69] He did support the need for enlistment bonuses, ROTC scholarships, improvement in subsistence payments, and additional funds for recruiting.

draft could actually be ended by July 1973 (Kelley, 1971k). With the cuts in the budget, the coming fiscal year would more closely resemble the program that Tucker had been proposing for some time. It was a program Kelley did not feel was adequate. Moreover, it would require zero-cost innovations that he was not prepared to implement.

Tucker's position was bolstered by a critical report he had received from a RAND evaluation of Kelley's program for the transition to the volunteer force and from a private report Dr. Stephen Enke had prepared for the Secretary of Defense. The RAND report criticized the Project Volunteer Committee, and by implication Kelley, for not undertaking formal evaluation of the initiatives they had previously funded (Hoffman and Fiorello, 1971).[70] Enke, who chided the department for its lack of adequate planning, echoed these concerns.[71] He predicted severe recruiting shortfalls and recommended the creation of a temporary planning staff.

In fact, all these efforts had ties back to Systems Analysis. The RAND study was commissioned by Systems Analysis and was authored by a former member of the Systems Analysis staff, Fred Hoffman. Steve Enke had also been on the Systems Analysis staff, as well as at RAND. Secretary Laird's Special Assistant, Brigadier General Robert Pursley, was Systems Analysis alum.

By the end of 1971, Tucker was in open revolt. Going around Kelley, he circulated a separate memorandum to "set up a separate Systems Analysis review with [the] Army on Project Volunteer and the need for renewal of the draft" (Lee, 1971e). Kelley's staff viewed this as "illegitimate." In their view, the "ASD(M&RA) [was] the responsible Assistant Secretary. If they want to make a study we could not oppose it," they told Kelley, and added that, "so far their studies have not been useful but there is always hope" (Lee, 1971e).

A Different Way of Looking at Things

The locus of the differences between the Manpower and Systems Analysis offices was not only bureaucratic; it was also intellectual.[72] The prevailing view of the Systems Analysis office[73]—a view developed and honed at RAND over the previous 20 years—

---

[70] Gus Lee's assessment of the RAND report was that it was "not as bad as most such efforts. It contains a number of suggestions to refine and sophisticate our Project Volunteer planning and evaluation. Not all of them are practical but some we would do anyway at the proper time, whether or not the report suggested them" (Lee, 1971d).

[71] Kelley's staff described the Enke Report "as a 'Little Gates Report'—pessimistic rather than optimistic and done with less competence than the Gates Report" (Lee, 1971e).

[72] Kelley insisted that "ASD (M&RA) is responsible for implementation of the OSD evaluation plan with the assistance of Systems Analysis" (OASD[M&RA], 1971e).

[73] The founder of the Systems Analysis Office was Alain Enthoven. He left RAND and moved to DoD in 1959 and founded the office under the Comptroller. After the 1960 election of John Kennedy and the appointment of Robert MacNamara as Secretary of Defense, Charles Hitch, the head of RAND's Economics Department, became the Comptroller of DoD. When Hitch left DoD in 1965 to become Chancellor of the University of California System, Enthoven was made an Assistant Secretary of Defense for Systems Analysis, and his office was elevated in status and greatly expanded. Hitch wrote many of the new defense management classics while at RAND, most notably Hitch and McKean (1960). Enthoven contributed to this classic by preparing the mathematic appendix on optimization. Other classics on "systems analysis" written by RAND staff of the period include McKean (1958), Fisher (1971), and Novick (1965).

was that programs like Project Volunteer were suited to assessment and analysis.[74] They fundamentally disagreed with the lack of formal evaluation and experimentation. On the other side of the argument, the Manpower staff thought such ideas "ignored the real world" (Lee and Parker, 1977, p. 473). Years later, Gus Lee, Kelley's Staff Director for the Project Volunteer Committee and the Director of Procurement Policy, explained that

> [f]rom the viewpoint of the Project Volunteer Committee there was not enough time. . . . The committee wished to use these funds as efficiently as possible but . . . [was] not persuaded that efficiency meant waiting for the research and analytical community to give them answers. . . . Over a year of study and analysis had preceded the formulation of the programs. The committee decided to go ahead and try the programs, and then modify or drop them if they were not effective. (Lee and Parker, 1977, p. 474)

Lee, however, later admitted that, even after a year trying to respond to Tucker's criticism, "empirical data on which to base new programs or terminate old ones were still not definitive" (Lee and Parker, 1977, p. 201).

Laird Reports to the President

All through the transition period, Laird reported on progress on "programs to increase enlistments and retention in the Services" (Laird, 1971a). In early 1971, he told the President that enlistment trends were up and that "there was an improvement in reenlistment rates during the first quarter of FY 1971 compared with FY 1970" (Laird, 1971a). He made a similar report in May (Laird, 1971b). In August, he reported to Nixon "an obstacle to continued progress in Army enlistments. The Chairman of the House Armed Services Committee has indicated a strong determination to prevent further use of paid TV/radio advertising for recruiting" (Laird, 1971c).

Fiscal Reality Sets in: The Development of the FY 1973 Program

The all-volunteer force program met the new realities of the federal budget in late winter 1971, just as the Pentagon was finalizing the FY 1973 budget. While it had been clear since March that congressional actions would "substantially reduce the funds

---

[74] *Author's Note:* The RAND connection is also shown by the proposal that John White, RAND's Program Director for the Manpower, Personnel, and Training Research Program sent to Frank Sullivan of the Systems Analysis Office (see White, 1971). The year before, I had left Systems Analysis for RAND. In 1971, I was working for John White, and that September, I took over the Air Force's Manpower, Personnel, and Training Program, which White had established in 1969. More important, in spring 1977, White became the Assistant Secretary for Manpower, the position Kelley held in 1971.

available for new initiatives in FY 73 given the $3.5 billion outlay ceiling" (Ryder, 1971), DoD thought that it would "still have about $400 million in FY 73 funds" (Odeen, 1971). The pay program that Congress approved, together with the commitments made to Senator Gordon Allott (R-Colorado) during debate to further increase entry pay, meant that the all-volunteer force program exceeded OMB's FY 1973 targets and that "planning funds" were no longer available for new nonpay initiatives.[75]

On December 8, 1971, Laird complained to the White House that the OMB target levels would "disallow any new initiatives to meet Volunteer force objectives above the first year program level. Such . . . limitation[s] would seriously constrain our efforts to attain an All-Volunteer force" (Laird, 1971e). The initial budget decision from the White House on December 22, 1971, included a "reduction . . . of about $350 million of additional All Volunteer Force funds pending assessment of the effects of the recent military pay raise on enlistments and identification of . . . most productive programs to attract added recruits" (Laird, 1971e). Accordingly, on December 23, 1971, Laird approved the deferral of all "uncommitted spending until FY 1974" (OASD, 1971).[76] The challenge now, Laird told Kelley, was for "us to put together a comprehensive, logical, and convincing manpower program. Any call on added manpower funds will rest on our ability to do the requisite homework" (Laird, 1971e). This was made all the more vital when Kissinger told Laird two weeks later that

> The President has directed that the Department of Defense review the military manpower situation including a detailed evaluation of past progress and future prospects for attaining the objectives of a zero draft by July 1973. . . . The study should be completed by April 9, 1972 for subsequent review by the Defense Program Review Committee (DPRC). (Kissinger, 1972a)

On January 3, 1972, as directed by Laird, Kelley proposed a new focus and structure to manage the transition to an All-Volunteer Force (Kelley, 1972a). The most important change, along the lines suggested by Enke in his report to Laird, was the establishment of the Central All-Volunteer Force Task Force to augment the Project Volunteer Committee. In a move that showed he still had confidence in Kelley, Laird

---

[75] In November, Kelley proposed that, in developing the budget, we "follow the same procedures as last year. After obtaining the views of the Project Volunteer Committee, I would make recommendations to Mr. Laird and Mr. Packard" (Kelley, 1971j). The services presented their proposed FY 1973 budgets. See the Navy budget (Department of the Navy, 1971) and the Army budget (Department of the Army, 1971). The Comptroller, however, believed that "nearly half of the service estimates for ongoing activities represent new starts in FY 1973. For this reason, we believe that these amounts should be placed in competition with the $3.5 billion outlay target" (Moot, 1971).

[76] Herbits also noted that the "absence of Martin Anderson in the White House has strengthened the arm of Kissinger's forces in this matter," and "the decision to deny the $400 million to the Pentagon may . . . have been made by the President himself on Kissinger's . . . recommendation" (Herbits, 1972, p. 5). The Pentagon staff believed the recommendation came from OMB (OASD[M&RA], 1971g). Herbits also noted the "increased participation by Kissinger's staff," and thought that Kissinger's "memo was prepared with the help of Systems Analysis" (Herbits, 1972, p.4). In fact, Phil Odeen had left Systems Analysis to join Kissinger's staff in November 1971. Griffith provides a cogent discussion of Odeen's role in Griffith (1997, pp. 57–58).

placed the new task force under his direction (Laird, 1972a).[77] Kelley selected Brigadier General Robert Montague to manage the new office.[78] He also made Kelley the point of contact between the Pentagon and the National Security Council (NSC) to answer Kissinger's inquiries.[79] To address the bickering within the Office of the Secretary of Defense, Kelley suggested, and Laird agreed to, a steering committee that would include Systems Analysis.[80] For the one year it was in existence, the task force employed ten military personnel detailed from the services, four civilians from OSD, and four contractors.[81]

In commissioning the new office, Laird asked the task force to determine what supplemental funds would be needed in FY 1973—that is, what needed to be done to fix the FY 1973 budget—and then to develop a "combination of manpower programs, policies and practices necessary to implement our national security policy in FY 1974 and beyond without reliance on the draft" (Laird, 1972a). According to Kelley (1972a, pp. 1–2), the task force was also to

(1) Develop and implement a system for monitoring and reporting manpower developments within the Services, to determine how particular components of current policies and programs are working in terms of their costs and their contributions to a viable AVF . . .
(2) Improve our projections of the demand for and supply of volunteers by Service, option, education and scores on mental and physical tests for FY 1974 and beyond . . .
(3) Identify likely shortfalls.
(4) Determine the sensitivity of these shortfalls to the personnel policies, requirements and manpower programs.
(5) Probe the validity of the rationale for the policies, requirements and programs.

---

[77] Herbits notes that the White House's decision to cut back $400 million had a "serious psychological impact . . . . those Pentagon proponents of the volunteer army had been given a sharp set-back: their credibility slightly reduced; their spirits severely dampened" (Herbits, 1972, p. 6). Doing anything other than appoint Kelley as the point of contact would have openly undercut him, most likely resulting in his resignation.

[78] Montague had been the deputy to the Special Assistant for the Modern Volunteer Army and became available as that office was being phased out. In the long run, Greenberg noted, "Montague's assignment as Special Assistant for AVF Matters adversely affect his career. Before his assignment to OSD some of his superiors felt he could become Chief of Staff of the Army" (Greenberg, 2004). Montague retired form the Army after his tour as the Deputy Commander of the Army Recruiting Command.

[79] The Army had decided that it could manage the Modern Volunteer Army through its normal staff entities. As the Chief of Staff of the Army saw it,

> Considerable and noteworthy progress has been made in developing a Master Program for the Modern Volunteer Army effort. . . . as has been our practice, your office should continue to phase out of activities whenever we are confident that desirable new initiatives are fully set as lasting Army practices. (Chief of Staff, 1972; as quoted in Lee and Parker, 1977, p. 192)

[80] Lee notes that the steering committee did not include representatives from the services, met only three times, and was "unable to accommodate the differences between ASD(M&RA) and ASD (Systems Analysis) staff" (Lee and Parker, 1977, p. 190, n. 2).

[81] General Montague would stay on the ASD(M&RA) staff for an additional year as the Special Assistant on Volunteer Force Matters, then return to the Army to serve as the Deputy Commander of the Army Recruiting Command (Lee and Parker, 1977, p. 199).

(6) Determine the correlation between present pre-induction selection techniques and satisfactory job performance . . . to determine whether more efficient selection amongst potential enlistees is possible.

The Task Force produced a number of studies

for the purpose of exploring options and alternatives to compensate for or to mitigate possible shortfalls in accessions in a zero draft environment and to provide a data base for the evaluation of optimum force mixes in future years. (Central All-Volunteer Force Task Force, 1972a, p. 21)

Each study was designed either to decrease the demand for new personnel or to increase the eligible pool of potential recruits. These efforts, recommended by the Gates Commission but not previously addressed by the services or the Project Volunteer Committee, were as follows:

- a study of the positions for which civilian personnel, direct hire or contract, could be substituted for male military personnel in the last half of FY 1973 and in FY 1974
- a study of the utilization of military women and alternative utilization plans for FYs 1973 through 1977
- a study of the qualitative accession needs of each service in terms of mental ability, as measured by scores on aptitude tests and the Armed Forces Qualification Test for FYs 1973 and 1974 and beyond
- a study of the reserves
- an independent investigation and analysis of possible measures for broadening the recruiting market, to be conducted by a group of officers, one from each service, with experience in recruiting.

The Civilian Substitution Study

One way the Gates Commission thought the Pentagon could reduce its requirements for military personnel and accessions was to replace them with civilians. The Central Task Force, based on inputs from the military services, accepted 103,000 as the lower bound of the number of military spaces that could be civilianized. The task force's report, however, noted that the services opposed "further civilianization" (Central All-Volunteer Force Task Force, 1972a, p. 17). By FY 1974, about 36,000 military positions had been eliminated. About 30,000 civilian positions had been added.

The Utilization-of-Women Study

The Gates Commission was conspicuous in its lack of attention to the role that women might play in reducing the demand for male recruits. In fact, years later, when Martin Binkin and Mark Eitelberg pointed this out in a paper (Binkin and Eitelberg, 1986) prepared for the ten-year anniversary conference commemorating the end of the draft, which was held at the U.S. Naval Academy in 1983, William Meckling, the Staff Director of the Gates Commission was "shocked" at Binkin and Eitelberg's "allegation." In a comment on their paper he noted, "My shock led me to canvass my files in search of contradictory evidence. I could find no record anywhere that we seriously considered the question of expanding the number of women in uniform" (Meckling, 1986, p. 112).

By 1972, the situation concerning the role of women had changed. On March 22, 1972, Congress passed the Equal Rights Amendment (ERA) and authorized women to enter the service academies starting in FY 1976. This raised expectations among service planners that final passage was inevitable; seeing what they believed was the hand-writing on the wall, they decided that it was in their own self-interest to act (Central All-Volunteer Force Task Force, 1972c).[82] All but the Marine Corps agreed to meeting or exceeding the goals Secretary Kelley had laid down and incorporated into the task force's study plan. The Army and Navy decided to double the number of women in uniform, and the Air Force chose to triple the number of women serving. Only the Marine Corps balked, rejecting a 40-percent increase in the number of women Marines. The Marine Corps did agree to half that goal, a 20-percent increase (Lee and Parker, 1977, p. 197). In 1972 only 1.9 percent of all active-duty military personnel were women. By September 1976, over 5 percent of the active force were women.

The Accession Quality Requirements Study

Validating the "qualitative needs for each Service" was one of the jobs of the Central All-Volunteer Force Task Force (Central All-Volunteer Force Task Force, 1972b). The Gates Commission's controversial finding that all the services overstated their requirements by demanding that new recruits have above-average mental test scores did not sit well with the services. Eventually, the work of the task force reinforced the conclusions of the Gates Commission. However, the task force's recommendations on quality standards were not implemented. The issue of mental quality requirements and standards remained a point of contention. Proponents of the all-volunteer force believed that the demand for excess quality would sabotage the all-volunteer force.[83]

Negotiations with Congress over Special Pay

In late January 1971, Gus Lee briefed Stephen Herbits, probably the most knowledge-able congressional staffer on the issue of an All-Volunteer Force, about the budget situation. Herbits had been a member of the Gates Commission and was now in a

---

[82] Binkin notes that while the ERA "left unclear its specific impact on the military, it did reinforce the impetus for change" (Binkin, 1993, p. 6). Also see the legal analysis prepared for the fall 1972 meeting of the Defense Advisory Committee on Women in the Services (DACOWITS) and its conclusions about the effects of the ERA on women in the military, which were deemed "tenuous and speculative" (Frings, 1972).

[83] Discussion with Steve Herbits (Herbits, 2001).

position to provide support and possibly to facilitate help from friendly members of Congress. Herbits agreed with what Kelly wanted to do.[84] Rather than an across-the-board pay raise, Kelly wanted to use the money to increase special pays and bonuses, as the Second Quadrennial Review of Military Compensation had recently recommended.[85] This also had the support of the Army leadership. The Army Chief of Staff, General Westmoreland, thought the money reserved for "the Allott Amendment could be better allocated to essential incentives and critical programs and experiments designed to meet Modern Volunteer Army objectives" (Westmoreland, 1972).

On February 9, 1972, Herbits laid out a strategy for Senators Stafford and Allott to shift them from an across-the-board pay raise to a more-focused approach.[86] Herbits told Stafford and Allott that it was "imperative that an item is selected which will both accomplish our limited goals [keep shortfalls to a minimum] *and* be politically feasible" (Herbits, 1972, p. A-21, emphasis in the original). He recommended that

> an increase in basic pay in the form of the "Allott" amendment not be one of those items on which we focus our priority attention. . . .
>
>   To obtain our limited objectives we must attract sufficient high-aptitude enlistees. If a general pay raise is used, the costs will be higher in the long run, and may not have sufficient flexibility to attract certain select groups. (Herbits, 1972, p. A-21)

This was part of an agreed-to plan worked out by Herbits and Kelley's deputy, Major General Leo Benade.[87] On March 22, 1972, Laird wrote Senator Allott that he "consider[ed] the [new] bill to be a sound approach for addressing the personnel supply needs of the Department of Defense as we move to an all-volunteer Armed Force" (Laird, 1972b). The next day, OMB Director George Shultz wrote Allott that he "consider[ed] it to be a desirable approach" (Shultz, 1972). Senator Allott filed the bill on March 23, 1972, as the Uniformed Services Special Pay Act of 1972 (Allott, 1972). Although the special-pay program did not pass Congress until 1974, the Pentagon was able, with Herbit's help, to get Senator Allott to agree to a more-productive approach to the All-Volunteer Force than an across-the-board pay raise. In addition, the support from OMB showed those within DoD that the administration was still committed to the All-Volunteer Force even after the budget setback the previous (1971) winter.

---

[84] Lee has noted that "Kelley gave Herbits full credit for accomplishing initial Congressional acceptance" (Lee and Parker, 1977, p. 200).

[85] In August 1972, Laird reported to Congress that "[t]hese special pay proposals are not flash ideas conceived in the pressure of ending the draft. They are carefully considered, and based on time-tested concepts which draw upon years of experience with special pays in the military services" (Laird, 1972f, p. 35).

[86] This was the same Senator Allott who held a $387 million IOU from the administration from the previous summer's all-volunteer force debate in the Senate.

[87] See Lee's discussion in Lee and Parker (1977, 200), and Herbits's account in "memorandum II" of Herbits (1972).

Responding to the President's Request for Detailed Evaluation of Past Progress and Future Prospects

On January 15, 1972, Kissinger told Laird that the "President has directed that the Department of Defense review the military manpower situation including a detailed evaluation of past progress and future prospects for attaining the objectives of a zero draft by July 1973" (Kissinger, 1972a). The required study dragged on for months. Finally, at the end of July, just a month before a report was due to the Congress, two memoranda were submitted to Kissinger that looked at the same facts, had entirely different tones, and came to very different conclusions.

The First—"Bad News"—Memorandum, by Odeen

The first memorandum, dated July 27, 1972, was written for Kissinger by his new deputy, Phil Odeen (Odeen, 1972a). Odeen had recently moved from the Pentagon to the National Security Council, but retained his interest in the all-volunteer force. He told Kissinger the required report had been substantively completed by April but "was mired in a mass of bureaucratic disagreement. As a result, the President does not have an analysis of the likelihood of attaining the FY 73 zero draft objective" (Odeen, 1972a, p. 1).[88] However, a "draft of the DoD study [was] given to me informally by the OSD staff." Its major conclusions were as follows (Odeen, 1972a, p. 1):

- In FY 1974, the Army might have a shortfall of between 15,000 and 85,000, resulting in an "overall reduction in Army force levels of one-third to almost two full divisions and associated support."
- If the Uniformed Services Special Pay Act that Senator Allott had submitted passed Congress, it would "reduce the Army shortfalls somewhat [but] not alleviate the Army's problem completely."
- More initiatives require management innovation, i.e., having more women and civilians, assigning more recruiters, and inducting lower-quality people, rather than increasing funding.

Odeen noted that "response to the November pay raise has been spotty" with increased enlistment in February and March. "In April and May, however, enlistments dropped off severely and only partially recovered in June. The Vietnam offensive may have been a major factor causing disappointing April and May results" (Odeen, 1972a, p. 3).

Odeen wanted Kissinger to sign a stern memorandum reminding Laird of his failure to provide the study for review by the DPRC and to provide a full review by September that could be submitted to Congress.

---

[88] As noted, Kelley had told Tucker that, with regard to the paper Systems Analysis had prepared, "I can agree with very little" (Lee, 1972c).

The Second—"Good News"—Memorandum, by Laird

The second memorandum was by Laird and arrived one day later, July 28, 1972. This memorandum was much more optimistic and included a lengthy report Laird was planning to send both the President and Congress at the end of the August, as required by Section 2111 of Public Law 92-129. The memorandum reviewed the "major administration initiatives and substantial progress toward final attainment of that goal" and noted "the remaining problems in ending reliance on the draft and the actions needed to solve these problems" (Laird, 1972e).

The Final Move to End the Draft

Laird's report, however, caused Kissinger some concern. When Nixon asked Kissinger's deputy, General Alexander Haig, if it were possible for a "near-term end of the draft" later in August, Kissinger responded that, since Laird was planning on providing Congress "considerable information on the current manpower shortages, planned draft calls, etc.," opposition from some senators and congressmen could be expected, citing "the Secretary's testimony and data in charging that the early end to the draft is a political act" (Kissinger, 1972b, p. 2). He suggested, and Nixon approved, several steps the President could take to "achieve maximum recognition of your progress in ending the draft" (Kissinger, 1972a).

The plan was to invite Laird to the Western White House to make the report (Laird, 1972f) public and brief the press.[89] Kissinger told Nixon that this would "commit you to ending the draft by July 1, 1973, if the legislation we have requested is passed with enough lead time to carry out the policy" (Kissinger, 1972b, p. 3).

At a meeting with the President set for Monday, August 28, 1972 (Kissinger, 1972c), Kissinger reviewed the plan for the final move to end conscription. Kissinger told Nixon that

> Laird's delivery of this optimistic report will give you an occasion to reaffirm your commitment to the All-Volunteer concept, recount your record of making the Selective Service System more equitable through introduction of the lottery while lowering annual draft calls from approximately 299,000 (1968) to below 50,000 (1972). (Kissinger, 1972c, p. 1)

One person who was unhappy about all this was Phil Odeen. For over a year, since the budget debacle in December 1971, he had been pressing for a "detailed analysis" that would push the Systems Analysis agenda. He told Kissinger that, while

---

[89] Laird told the press that we

will be able to reach the goal of no peace-time draftees by June 30, 1973. . . . There are only two reservations that do exist and those reservations I am confident will be handled by the Congress very shortly in legislation which is currently pending before the House and the Senate. (Laird, 1972d)

[t]he Laird report is a good statement of the problems which must be overcome to attain the AVF . . . it does not provide the detailed analysis of our overall manpower situation. (Odeen, 1972b, p. 2)

He wanted Kissinger to tell Laird that

the President asked me to reiterate his request of last January for a detailed analysis of the projected manpower situation in FY 74 [and to submit the study] by September 15, 1972, for presentation at a DPRC meeting in late September. (Odeen, 1972c, Enclosure: Odeen's draft of a letter to the Secretary of Defense)

Kissinger thought such action was unwise and had General Haig tell Odeen that "HAK [Henry A. Kissinger] says lay low on this for time being, we must focus on FY 74 budget" (Odeen, 1972c).

Laird and Kelley's Last Budget: FY 1974

The FY 1974 budget was a replay of the previous year, with one exception. By the winter, recruiting was high, and the 68-percent entry-level pay increase of November 14, 1971, was having the designed effect.[90] From the originally programmed volunteer force funds of $3.5 billion, $3.1 billion had previously been committed to ongoing programs that were to be continued during FY 1974, leaving "about $0.4B of the original fund[s]" for special programs of new starts, which Odeen told Kissinger "may be needed if we are to satisfy manpower needs in FY 74 without the draft" (Odeen, 1972d, p. 1). OMB, however, wanted to cut the $400 million from the Pentagon's budget.

The Manpower and Systems Analysis Offices: The Last Round

Kelley developed budget proposals for the $400 million (Kelley, 1972g). He presented the program in three priority bands. The first priority totaled $205 million and was accession-oriented, to improve that program. The second priority group of $80 million and a third priority of $103.6 million were oriented toward "quality of life" and retention, respectively. Systems Analysis, armed with the reports of the Central All-Volunteer Force Task Force, presented "alternative[s] to the Service proposals that [come] closer

---

[90] The Secretary of the Army congratulated his staff:

The recruiting and reenlistment results during the summer have been outstanding. Based on these results, we all should taste the fruits of success and make all necessary preparations to see this favorable trend continue. (Froehlke, 1972)

Tucker did not share the sense of success, however. In August 1972, he circulated an issue paper that drew an immediate response from Kelley. In a memorandum to the Deputy Secretary, Kelley wrote that,

[b]ecause the Draft Manpower Issue Paper circulated by Gardiner Tucker's memorandum of August 2, 1972 is critical of the All-Volunteer Force effort and reflects no recognition of the substantial successes to date, I am compelled to bring several points to your attention. (Kelley, 1972f)

to solving the problems and [cost] less" (Chapel, 1972). As they had the previous year, Systems Analysis wanted to increase enlisted bonuses and the employment of women, civilians, and Category IV personnel.[91] They placed the highest priority on recruiting, reserve force recruiting and advertising, and "civilianization of the K.P. [kitchen police] in Marine Corps" (Lee, 1972f). Systems Analysis considered that $330 million of the uncommitted $400 million "may have merit for other than AVF reasons, but . . . it would be difficult to justify on the basis of specific AVF problems" (Srull, 1972b). Odeen sided with Systems Analysis and recommended to Kissinger that only $170 million be "provided to fill out the Army's needs" (Odeen, 1972d).

Kelley's staff characterized the Systems Analysis proposal as "similar to last year's OASD(SA) alternatives in that it is 'bare bones' and excludes the Air Force" (Lee, 1972e). Lee told Kelley, "No action is necessary on your part except to encourage the OSD(SA) leaders to attend Project Volunteer meetings and to keep action in the volunteer channels" (Lee, 1972e). In a response to his Systems Analysis contact, Lee provided insight into the continuing tensions between the Manpower and Systems Analysis offices. He summarized the difference between the M&RA and SA approaches to the management of the volunteer force:

> While both SA and M&RA strive for cost-effectiveness, SA appears to adopt a higher risk level in gaining success of a volunteer force. SA puts priority on "bare bones" spending whereas M&RA puts priority on insured force effectiveness. Oversimplifying, SA stresses cost over effectiveness and M&RA stresses effectiveness over cost. In the face of sizable unknowns, this leads to quite different programs.
>
> SA would focus on imminent shortfalls in quantity of accessions, whereas M&RA gives greater weight than does SA to "follow through." . . . [and] a special obligation . . . to give balanced attention to the full system of conditions of service. (Lee, 1972e, p. 3)

Packard settled the budget dispute in a Program Budget Decision on December 5, 1972. He approved "items in priority groups one and two of the ASD (M&RA) program at a cost of $285.0 million" (OASD, 1972).[92] This, however, was still a reduction of over $100 million.[93] The budget decision also noted that,

---

[91] *Author's Note:* Over time, one of the problems with offices like Systems Analysis is that they become advocates and proponents for particular viewpoints. It may well have been that their original positions were based on sound analysis. But the effectiveness of the office was very much reduced when the positions presented to and rejected by decisionmakers returned year after year.

[92] The final budget decision accepted Kelley's recommendation of $205.6 million and rejected Tucker's recommendation of $103.6 million. Tucker was also unhappy that the Deputy Secretary's decision "approved a distribution of that money which bears little resemblance to the problem of closing potential gaps in FY 1974 accessions" (Tucker, 1972). He asked the Comptroller to "resubmit PBD 281 to the Deputy Secretary and I recommend two alternatives be presented to him" (Tucker, 1972).

[93] The Army did ask that the decision be reconsidered in a formal "Program/Budget Decision Reclama" (Department of the Army, 1972). The Air Force also filed a reclama (U.S. Air Force, 1972b).

During the early planning stages of the all-volunteer force, it was clear that a separate identification of funds for project volunteer was needed. . . . However, there is an increasing difficulty in distinguishing between those items that should be assigned to the basic budget and those that should be assigned to the special All-Volunteer Force project. Accordingly, starting in FY 75, . . . requirements for the All-Volunteer Force [shall] be contained within the basic budget. (OASD, 1972, p. 3)

Thus, the FY 1974 budget would be the last time that the Manpower and Systems Analysis offices would do battle over the all-volunteer force. It would also be the last time because, by the next year, Roger Kelley would be gone, replaced by Bill Brehm, formerly of the Systems Analysis office.

Recruiting for the All-Volunteer Force at the End of 1972

Laird's report to the President and Congress in August may have sounded optimistic at the time, but it turned out to be prophetic. In September, Laird updated the August report with the news that

[r]ecruiting during the traditionally favorable summer months exceeded our expectations. . . . [T]he 'true volunteer' component of total enlistments continued to climb beyond the 75 percent proportion noted among enlistees in FY 1972. (Laird, 1972g)

In a report to Kelley, Irv Greenberg noted,

Despite the sharp drop in draft calls [from a 1969 level of 289,900 to 1972 level of 50,000] [enlistments] and the proportion of true volunteers—that is, those who are not draft motivated—has grown significantly from about 40% in 1968 to over 75%. . . . Prospects of achieving the objectives of ending reliance on the draft by July 1, 1973 are excellent. (Greenberg, 1972)[94]

In fact, on January 27, 1973, as the new FY 1974 budget was sent to Congress, Laird made the announcement quoted at the beginning of this chapter: *"Use of the draft has ended."* But this was just the calm before the storm.

---

[94] In October, the staff reported the following to Kelley:

[We] apparently are now getting enough "true volunteers" to meet FY 1974 male accession requirements, except for the Army. . . . Even without continued improvement in recruiting the "gap" would be only 14,000. (Lee, 1972d)

Srull provided a comparison of the ASD(M&RA) and ASD (SA) estimates (Srull, 1972a).

Final Decision to End Conscription

On October 12, 1970, Secretary of Defense Melvin Laird "established the goal of zero draft calls by the end of FY 1973" (Laird, 1970f). With the passage of the two-year extension of conscription with the Selective Service Act of 1971, the final act in implementing the all-volunteer force was the decision to let induction authority lapse, rather than ask for another extension. On January 3, 1973, General Hershey, the President's Advisor on Manpower Mobilization, wrote Nixon to "recommend that Congress be requested to extend to June 30th, 1977, the authority of the President to induct under the Military Selective Service Act of 1971" (Hershey, 1973). Laird, of course, disagreed with General Hershey's recommendation and felt the matter well covered by NSSM 165 (Laird, 1973a). His successor as Secretary, Elliot Richardson, also advised the President, despite problems during winter 1973 in meeting Army accession requirements, that it would "not be necessary to extend induction authority" (Richardson, 1973a). On March 16, 1973, President Nixon thanked General Hershey for his 62 years of government service. He told him "[E]very American is profoundly grateful, and we join as one in wishing you the fullest measure of happiness in the years ahead" (Nixon, 1973). Five days later Secretary Richardson announced,

> on behalf of the Nixon Administration . . . [the Department of Defense] informed the Chairmen of the Armed Service Committee of the Senate and the House of Representatives that it will not be necessary to extend the draft induction authority beyond its expiration date of July 1[, 1973]. (Richardson, 1973b)[95]

---

[95] On April 12, 1973, Kelley wrote to Thomas Gates: "We in the Administration continue to be deeply appreciative of the clear course set for us in the report of the Gates Commission" (Kelley, 1973).

References

Air Force DCSP Staff, "Written Comments on Gates Report," memorandum to Gus C. Lee, Washington, D.C., April 3, 1970. G0295.pdf.

Allott, Gordon, *Allott Introduces the Uniformed Services Special Pay Act of 1972,* Washington, D.C.: U.S. Senate, March 23, 1972. S0071.pdf.

Army ODCSPER Staff, *Analysis of the Gates Commission Report,* Washington, D.C.: Deputy Chief of Staff for Personnel, Headquarters U.S. Army, April 1, 1970. G0294.pdf.

Bagley, David H., "Apportioning of AVF Resources," memorandum to Assistant Secretary of Defense (M&RA), Washington, D.C., March 7, 1972. G0142.pdf.

Beal, Thaddeus R., "Volunteer Army Actions," memorandum to Secretary of Defense, Washington, D.C., November 6, 1970. G0504.pdf.

Bell, William G., ed., *Department of the Army Historical Summary: Fiscal Year 1969,* Washington, D.C. : U.S. Army Center of Military History 1973a.

———, ed., *Department of the Army Historical Summary: Fiscal Year 1971,* Washington, D.C.: U.S. Army Center of Military History, 1973b.

———, ed., *Department of the Army Historical Summary: Fiscal Year 1972,* Washington, D.C.: U.S. Army Center of Military History, 1974.

Bell, William G., and Karl E. Cocke, eds., *Department of the Army Historical Summary: Fiscal Year 1973,* Washington, D.C. : U.S. Army Center of Military History, 1977.

Benade, Leo E., "Evaluation of the Gates Commission Report," memorandum to Roger T. Kelley, Washington, D.C., March 27, 1970. G0293.pdf.

Bennett, Warren K., "Special Assistant for the Modern Volunteer Army (SAMVA)," memorandum to Heads of Army Staff Agencies, Washington, D.C., October 31, 1970.

Binkin, Martin, *Who Will Fight the Next War? The Changing Face of the American Military,* Washington, D.C.: The Brookings Institution, 1993.

Binkin, Martin, and Mark Jan Eitelberg, "Women and Minorities in the All-Volunteer Force," in William Bowman, Rodger Little and G. Thomas Sicilia, eds., *The All-Volunteer Force After A Decade: Retrospect and Prospect,* New York: Pergamon-Brassey's, 1986.

Binkin, Martin, and John D. Johnson, *All Volunteer Armed Forces: Progress, Problems, and Prospects,* Washington, D.C.: Senate Armed Service Committee, June 1, 1973. S0148.pdf.

Borda, Richard J., "Fiscal Year 1973 Project Volunteer Funding," memorandum to Assistant Secretary of Defense (M&RA), Washington, D.C., August 24, 1971. G0226.pdf.

Brehm, William K., Interview with Bernard Rostker, January 31, 2002.

Burch, Roy D., *Madison Avenue and the U.S. Army: An Analysis of the Use of Broadcast Announcements, Paid or Free, to Recruit U.S. Army Personnel,* Carlisle Barracks, Pa.: Army War College, AD760473, December 29, 1972. S0112.pdf.

Burke, Lloyd L., "Volunteer Army Meeting (with Congressman Hebert)," memorandum for the record, Washington, D.C., December 11, 1970. G0313.pdf.

Butler, Jack Sibley, *Provide (U) Project Volunteer in Defense of the Nation,* Vol. II, Washington, D.C.: Directorate of Personnel Studies and Research, Department of the Army, 1969. G0335.pdf.

Central All-Volunteer Force Task Force, *Civilian Substitution: A Report on Substitution of Civilians for Military Personnel in the Armed Forces,* Washington, D.C.: Office of the Assistant Secretary of Defense (M&RA), AD 764523, October 1972a. G1227.pdf.

———, *Qualitative Accession Requirements: A Report on the Qualitative Accession Needs of the Military Services,* Washington, D.C.: Office of the Assistant Secretary of Defense (M&RA), AD764511, November 1972b. G1226.pdf.

———, *Utilization of Military Women: A Report of Increased Utilization of Military Women, FYs 1973–1977,* Washington, D.C.: Office of the Assistant Secretary of Defense (M&RA), AD764510, December 1972c. S0026.pdf.

Chafee, John H., "Army's Advertising," memorandum to Secretary of Defense, Washington, D.C., July 23, 1971. S0053.pdf.

———, "Navy Recruiting," memorandum to Secretary of Defense, Washington, D.C., March 11, 1972. G0563.pdf.

Chapel, Steve, "Systems Analysis AVF FY 1972 Funding Alternatives," memorandum to Gus Lee, Washington, D.C., November 10, 1972. G0088.pdf.

Chief of Staff, U.S. Army, "Guidance for the Special Assistant for the Modern Volunteer Army," memorandum to Lieutenant General Forsythe, Washington, D.C., January 15, 1972.

Cook, Alvin A., Jr., and John P. White, *A Briefing to the Air Staff (AFPDP): The Supply of Air Force Recruits in a Post-Southeast Asia Environment,* Santa Monica, Calif.: RAND Corporation, D-19610-PR, November 5, 1969. S0283.pdf.

Crutchfield, R. R., "(Navy) Comments on Gates Report," memorandum to Gus C. Lee, Washington, D.C., April 9, 1970. G0297.pdf.

Department of the Army, *Army Requests for FY 73 Project Volunteer Funds,* Washington, D.C., November 30, 1971. G0125.pdf.

———, *Program/Budget Decision Reclama—FY 1974 Budget,* Washington, D.C., December 15, 1972. G0149.pdf.

Department of the Navy, *FY 1973 Cost Estimates,* Washington, D.C., November 24, 1971. G0123.pdf.

Deputy Secretary of Defense, *Project Volunteer—FY 1972 Increment—Program/Budget Decision,* Washington, D.C.: Office of the Secretary of Defense, January 18, 1971. G0508.pdf.

Directorate of Personnel Studies and Research, *Provide: Project Volunteer in Defense of the Nation,* Vol. I, Washington, D.C.: Office of the Deputy Chief of Staff for Personnel, 1969. G0334.pdf.

Dixon, Robert J., "Keynote Address," Proceedings of the Air Force Industry Conference on the All-Volunteer (Zero-Draft) Force, Washington, D.C., May 4, 1972. G1307.pdf.

Finneran, John G., "All Volunteer Force Recruiting Problems," memorandum to Deputy Assistant Secretary of Defense (Manpower Research and Utilization), Washington, D.C., January 31, 1972. G0137.pdf.

Fisher, Gene H., *Cost Considerations in System Analysis,* New York: American Elsevier Publishing Company, Inc., 1971.

Foreman, Robert C., *Paid Radio and TV Advertising in Support of a Volunteer Army: A Historical View of the Essential Actions,* Washington, D.C.: Industrial College of the Armed Forces, M-7211, 1972. S0110.pdf.

Forsythe, George I., *Fact Sheet: Project VOLAR Experiment,* Washington, D.C.: Special Assistant for the Modern Volunteer Army, December 7, 1970. G0311.pdf.

———, "Discussion with Congressmen Hebert on Army Plans for Recruiting Advertising, August–September 1971," memorandum for the record, Washington, D.C., July 27, 1971. G0653.pdf.

Friedman, Milton, "Secretary of Defense Melvin R. Laird," letter to Melvin Laird, February 23, 1970. G0537.pdf.

Frings, Carole L., "The Effect of the Equal Rights Amendment on Women in the Military," in Central All-Volunteer Force Task Force, ed., *Utilization of Military Women: A Report on Increased Utilization of Military Women, FY 1973–1977,* Washington, D.C.: Office of the Assistant Secretary of Defense (M&RA), 1972. G1297.pdf.

Froehlke, Robert F., "Recruiting Advertising—Discussions with Congressman Hebert on Army Plans for Recruiting Advertising, August–September 1971," memorandum to Secretary of Defense, Washington, D.C., July 27, 1971. G0653.pdf.

———, "Recruiting and Reenlistment—Use of Draft the Last Half of FY 73," memorandum to Assistant Secretary of the Army (M&RA), Washington, D.C., September 23, 1972. G0529.pdf.

Furlong, Raymond B., *Impression of the Presentation of Project Volunteer,* Washington, D.C.: Military Assistant to the Deputy Secretary of Defense, November 10, 1970. G0502.pdf.

Gates, Thomas S., Jr., "Concern that Project Volunteer Will Lead to 'Unnecessary Public Controversy'," letter to Melvin R. Laird, Washington, D.C., July 29, 1969. G0278.pdf.

Gates, Thomas S., Jr., Thomas Curtis, Frederick Dent, Milton Friedman, Greenewalt Crawford, Alan Greenspan, Alfred Gruenther, Stephen E. Herbits, John Kemper, Lauris Norstad, and Allen Wallis, "Delay in Submission of Final REPORT," memorandum to the President, Washington, D.C., October 7, 1969. L0010.pdf.

Greenberg, I. M., "Achieving the All-Volunteer Force," memorandum to Roger Kelley, Washington, D.C., December 7, 1972. G0092.pdf.

———, "Technical Comments," memorandum to Bernard Rostker, Washington, D.C., July 2004.

Greene, William M. A., *Navy Inaugurates Three Year Enlistment,* Washington, D.C.: Navy Recruiting Command, March 1, 1972. G0518.pdf.

Griffith, Robert K., Jr., *The U.S. Army's Transition to the All-Volunteer Force 1968–1974,* Washington, D.C.: U.S. Army Center of Military History, 1997. S0186.pdf.

Grissmer, David W., D. M. Amey, R. L. Arms, W. L. Clement, V. W. Hobson, J. D. Lanigan, W. S. Moore, G. P. Sica, and R. Szymanski, *An Evaluation of Army Manpower Accession Programs,* McLean, Va.: General Research Corporation, OADC-R-37, April 1974. S0350.pdf.

Grissmer, David W., V. W. Hobson, and R. W. Rae, *Evaluation of Recruiter Assistant and Unit Canvasser Recruiting Programs,* McLean, Va.: General Research Corporation, Operations Analysis Division, November 1973. S0348.pdf.

Herbits, Stephen E., "Volunteer Army Program for 1972," memorandum to Senator Stafford, Senator Gordon Allott and Dr. George Will, Washington, D.C., February 9, 1972. S0067.pdf.

————, Interview with Bernard Rostker, Washington, D.C., March 6, 2001.

Hershey, Lewis B., "Extension of the Military Selective Service Act of 1971," memorandum to the President, Washington, D.C., January 2, 1973. G1104.pdf.

Hitch, Charles J., and Roland McKean, *The Economics of Defense in the Nuclear Age,* Cambridge, Mass.: Harvard University Press, 1960.

Hittle, James D., "Department of the Navy position on All-Volunteer Force Options," memorandum to Assistant Secretary of Defense (M&RA), Washington, D.C., December 30, 1970. G0314.pdf.

————, "Project Volunteer—Paid Advertising," memorandum to Assistant Secretary of Defense (M&RA), Washington, D.C., February 24, 1971. G0198.pdf.

Hoffman, F. S., and M. R. Fiorello, *The Evaluation of the Transition to a Volunteer Force,* Santa Monica, Calif.: RAND Corporation, WN-7720-SA, December 1971. S0306.pdf.

Janowitz, Morris, and Charles C. Moskos, Jr., "Racial Composition in the All-Volunteer Force," *Armed Forces and Society,* Vol. 1, No. 1, November 1974, pp. 109–123.

Jehn, Christopher, and Hugh E. Carroll, *Navy Recruiting in an All-Volunteer Environment,* Arlington, Va.: Center for Naval Analyses, CRC 235, April 25, 1974. S0342.pdf.

Johnson, James E., "Department of the Army Proposal for Additional Paid TV-Radio Advertising," memorandum to Assistant Secretary of Defense (M&RA), Washington, D.C., June 21, 1971a. S0055.pdf.

————, "Impact of the Army Enlistment Bonus (on the Navy)," memorandum to Assistant Secretary of Defense (M&RA), Washington, D.C., October 19, 1971b. G0236.pdf.

Johnson, John D., *An Analysis of Problems Association with the Establishment of an All-Volunteer (Zero Draft) Force for the United States: Final Report (Saber Volunteer),* Washington, D.C.: U.S. Air Force, Headquarters, Office for Special Studies, Assistant Chief of Staff, Studies and Analysis, December 1, 1971. G1473.pdf.

Kelley, Roger T., "Project Volunteer," memorandum to Secretary Selin, Charles Rossotti, Vice Admiral William Mack, Brigadier General Lee Benade and Harold Wood, Washington, D.C., April 10, 1969a. G0267.pdf.

———, "Notice of Meeting of 'Project Volunteer' Committee," memorandum to Assistant Secretary of Defense (Systems Analysis), Marine Corps and Air Force Assistant Secretaries of the Military Departments or Personnel of the Army, Chief of Naval Operations and J1 Director, Personnel of the Joint Staff, JCS, Washington, D.C., April 15, 1969b. G0326.pdf.

———, "Appointment of Paul Wollstadt as Deputy Assistant Secretary of Defense (Manpower Research and Utilization)," memorandum to Secretary of Defense, Washington, D.C., June 5, 1969c. G0676.pdf.

———, "Research Program in Support of Project Volunteer," memorandum to Director of Defense Research and Engineering, Washington, D.C., June 6, 1969d. G0273.pdf.

———, "Development of Project Volunteer Action Program," memorandum to Deputy Assistant Secretaries (M&RA), Staff Directors, C&CD Director, IAF Director, Project TRANSITION Director and RFPB Military Executives, Washington, D.C., July 16, 1969e. L0005.pdf.

———, "Establishment of Program Evaluation Group, Project Volunteer," memorandum to Assistant Secretary of Defense (Comptroller), Assistant Secretary of Defense (Systems Analysis) (Acting) and Assistant Secretaries of the Military Departments (M&RA), Washington, D.C., July 16, 1969f. G1472.pdf.

———, "Project Volunteer Studies," memorandum to Assistant Secretary of Defense (I&L) and Assistant Secretary of Defense (PA), Washington, D.C., July 16, 1969g. L0007.pdf.

———, "All-Volunteer Force," memorandum to Secretary Melvin R. Laird, Washington, D.C., December 24, 1969h. G0283.pdf.

———, "Project Volunteer," memorandum to Assistant Secretaries of the Military Department (M&RA), Assistant Deputy Chiefs of Staff for Personnel and Director J1 Personnel of the Joint Staff, Washington, D.C., January 22, 1970a. G1139.pdf.

———, "Defense Manpower Needs and Policies—the Department of Defense Program for Zero Draft Calls," slides used with the Hebert Committee to Martin C. Anderson, Washington, D.C., August 20, 1970b. G1148.pdf.

———, Project Volunteer Press Conference, Washington, D.C.: Assistant Secretary of Defense (M&RA), October 14, 1970c. G0307.pdf.

———, "Zero Draft Program," memorandum to Secretary Laird and Secretary Packard, Washington, D.C., December 28, 1970d. G0546.pdf.

———, "Army Zero Draft Requests for FY 71," memorandum to Secretary Packard, Washington, D.C., January 8, 1971a. G0318.pdf.

———, "Conflict Between Systems Analysis and Manpower and Reserve Affairs," memorandum to Secretary Packard, Washington, D.C., January 18, 1971b. G0643.pdf.

———, "Incentive Plan for Army Combat Arms," memorandum to Deputy Secretary of Defense, Washington, D.C., February 19, 1971c. G0581.pdf.

———, "TV/Radio Advertising," memorandum to Secretaries of the Military Department, Washington, D.C., March 2, 1971d. G0199.pdf.

———, "Evaluation System for Project Volunteer," memorandum to Paul Wollstadt, Washington, D.C., April 6, 1971e. G0658.pdf.

———, "Evaluation System for PROJECT VOLUNTEER," memorandum to Mr. Wollstadt, Washington, D.C., May 25, 1971f. G1202.pdf.

———, "Evaluating Actions to Achieve an All-Volunteer Force," memorandum to Members of the Project Volunteer Committee, Washington, D.C., June 8, 1971g. S0061.pdf.

———, "Army's Request for a Six-Week Paid Radio and TV Advertising Program," memorandum to Secretary of Defense, Washington, D.C., June 30, 1971h. G0605.pdf.

———, "Paid Radio/Television Advertising," memorandum to Assistant Secretary of the Army (M&RA), Washington, D.C., June 22, 1971i. S0051.pdf.

———, "FY 1973 Budget Estimates and Legislative Proposals for Volunteers," memorandum to Robert C. Moot, Washington, D.C., November 22, 1971j. G0122.pdf.

———, "Project Volunteer Requests of the Services," memorandum to Melvin Laird, Washington, D.C., December 16, 1971k. G0130.pdf.

———, "All-Volunteer Force," memorandum to Melvin R. Laird, Washington, D.C., January 3, 1972a. G0522.pdf.

———, "Testing The Enlistment Bonus," memorandum to Secretary of Defense, Washington, D.C., May 8, 1972b. G0173.pdf.

———, "Testing The Enlistment Bonus," memorandum to Secretary of Defense, Washington, D.C., May 15, 1972c. G0174.pdf.

———, "(Testing The Enlistment Bonus) Combat Elements Enlistment Bonus," memorandum to Assistant Secretaries of the Military Departments (M&RA), Washington, D.C., May 22, 1972d. G0175.pdf.

———, "Project Volunteer Funds for Navy Recruiting in FY 73," memorandum to Secretary of Defense, Washington, D.C., August 7, 1972e. G0566.pdf.

———, "Recommendations on Systems Analysis Draft on Manpower Issue," memorandum to Mr. Rush, Washington, D.C., August 9, 1972f. G0168.pdf.

———, "Project Volunteer Budget for FY 1974," memorandum to Mr. Moot, Washington, D.C., November 20, 1972g. G0086.pdf.

———, letter to Thomas Gates, Washington, D.C., April 12, 1973. G1204.pdf.

Kester, John G., "Funding of Zero-Draft Programs," memorandum to Assistant Secretary of Defense (M&RA), Washington, D.C., June 11, 1970a. G0299.pdf.

———, "Pay Incentives," memorandum to Assistant Secretary of Defense (M&RA) Staff, Washington, D.C., December 8, 1970b. G0312.pdf.

———, "Volunteer Army Action," memorandum to Assistant Secretary of Defense (M&RA), Washington, D.C., December 10, 1970c. G0315.pdf.

———, "Army Test of Paid Radio and TV Advertising," memorandum to Paul Wollstadt, Washington, D.C., February 12, 1971. G0193.pdf.

Kissinger, Henry A., "Military Manpower," memorandum to Secretary of Defense, Washington, D.C., January 15, 1972a. G1098.pdf.

———, "Ending Reliance on the Draft," memorandum to the President, Washington, D.C., August 22, 1972b. G1112.pdf.

———, "Meeting with Secretary Laird Concerning the All-Volunteer Force; Monday, August 28, 1972," memorandum to the President, Washington, D.C., August 27, 1972c. G1111.pdf.

Laird, Melvin R., "Project Volunteer (Committee)," memorandum to Secretaries of the Military Departments, Chairman of the Joint Chiefs of Staff and Assistants Secretaries of Defense, Washington, D.C., April 10, 1969a. G0269.pdf.

———, "Response," letter to Thomas S. Gates, Washington, D.C., August 7, 1969b. G0279.pdf.

———, "Change in Military Pay for FY 1971," memorandum to the President, Washington, D.C., October 23, 1969c. L0009.pdf.

———, "In response to your letter concerning my statement on Meet The Press," letter to Milton Friedman, Washington, D.C., March 4, 1970a. G0539.pdf.

———, "Future of the Draft," memorandum to the President of the United States, Washington, D.C., March 11, 1970b. G0268.pdf.

———, "Report of 'Project Volunteer' Committee," memorandum to Secretaries of the Military Departments, Washington, D.C., May 4, 1970c. G0513.pdf.

———, "Report of Project Volunteer," memorandum to the President, Washington, D.C., July 18, 1970d. G0302.pdf.

———, "Opposition to Terminating the Draft on July 1, 1971," memorandum to Senator John C. Stennis, Washington, D.C., August 14, 1970e. G1146.pdf.

———, "Zero Draft Calls by July 1, 1973," memorandum to Secretaries of the Military Department and Chairman Joint Chiefs of Staff, Washington, D.C., October 12, 1970f. G0511.pdf.

———, "Programs to Increase Enlistments and Retention," memorandum to the President, Washington, D.C., October 31, 1970g. G0503.pdf.

———, "Third Quarterly Report," memorandum to the President, Washington, D.C., February 27, 1971a. L0030.pdf.

———, "Fourth Quarterly Report," memorandum to the President, Washington, D.C., May 13, 1971b. L0032.pdf.

———, "Fifth Quarterly Report," memorandum to the President, Washington, D.C., August 4, 1971c. L0033.pdf.

———, "Increasing Enlistment and Retention," memorandum to the President, Washington, D.C., August 4, 1971d. G0223.pdf.

———, "All Volunteer Force," memorandum to Assistant Secretary of Defense (M&RA), Washington, D.C., December 27, 1971e. G0134.pdf.

———, "Significant Action," memorandum to the Secretary of the Army, Washington, D.C., January 11, 1972a. G0521.pdf.

———, "Uniformed Services Special Pay Act of 1972," letter to Senator Gordon Allott, Washington, D.C., March 22, 1972b. S0068.pdf.

———, "Project Volunteer Funds for Navy Recruiting in FY 73," memorandum to Secretary of the Navy, Washington, D.C., August 9, 1972c. G0567.pdf.

———, *New Conference at San Clemente, California,* Washington, D.C.: Secretary of Defense, August 28, 1972d. G0531.pdf.

———, "Report to the President: Progress in Ending the Draft and Achieving the All-Volunteer Force," memorandum to the President, Washington, D.C., August 28, 1972e. G1115.pdf.

———, *Progress in Ending the Draft and Achieving the All-Volunteer Force,* Washington, D.C.: U.S. Department of Defense, August 29, 1972f. G1114.pdf.

———, *Prospects for Attaining an All-Volunteer Force,* Washington, D.C.: U.S. Department of Defense, September 28, 1972g. S0091.pdf.

———, "Extension of the Military Selective Service Act of 1971," memorandum to the President, Washington, D.C., January 16, 1973a. G1105.pdf.

———, "Use of the Draft Has Ended," news release Washington, D.C., January 27, 1973b. G0103.pdf.

Lee, Gus C., "Points for White House Meeting on All-Volunteer Force," memorandum to Paul Wollstadt, Washington, D.C., February 19, 1970. G0288.pdf.

———, "OSD Evaluation of Army Advertising Campaign," memorandum to Mr. Wollstadt, Washington, D.C., March 1, 1971a. G0200.pdf.

———, "Evaluation of Project Volunteer," memorandum to Admiral Mack, Washington, D.C., April 1, 1971b. G0203.pdf.

———, "Project Volunteer Accomplishments," memorandum to Roger Kelley, General Taber and Mr. Wollstadt, Washington, D.C., June 29, 1971c. G0219.pdf.

———, "Comments on Interim Report on the Evacuation Process for Project Volunteer," memorandum to General Taber, Washington, D.C., October 14, 1971d. G0235.pdf.

———, "Project Volunteer Problems," memorandum to Roger Kelley, Washington, D.C., December 6, 1971e. G0129.pdf.

———, "HumRRO Studies of Project VOLAR," memorandum to George Daoust, Washington, D.C., February 9, 1972a. G0136.pdf.

———, "Plan for Army Ground Combat Enlistment Bonus," memorandum to Roger Kelley, Washington, D.C., April 19, 1972b. G0153.pdf.

———, "Systems Analysis Study for DPRC: Alternative Options for a Volunteer Force," memorandum to Roger Kelley, Mr. Daoust and General Taber, Washington, D.C., April 21, 1972c. G0206.pdf.

———, "Revised Estimates of True Volunteers," memorandum to Roger Kelley, Washington, D.C., October 17, 1972d. G0179.pdf.

———, "Systems Analysis AVF FY 74 Funding Alternatives," memorandum to Mr. Roger Kelley, Mr. Daoust and General Taber, Washington, D.C., November 15, 1972e. G0087.pdf.

————, "Systems Analysis Priority Ranking of the November 14, 1972 Volunteer Spending Requests," memorandum to Roger Kelley, Mr. Daoust and General Taber, Washington, D.C., November 17, 1972f. G0183.pdf.

Lee, Gus C., and Geoffrey Y. Parker, *Ending the Draft: The Story of the All Volunteer Force*, Washington, D.C.: Human Resources Research Organization, FR-PO-771, April 1977. S0242.pdf.

McKean, Roland N., *Efficiency in Government Through Systems Analysis*, New York: Wiley, 1958.

Meckling, William H., "Comment on 'Women and Minorities in the All-Volunteer' Force," in Rodger Little and G. Thomas Sicilia, William Bowman, ed., *The All-Volunteer Force After A Decade: Retrospect and Prospect*, New York: Pergamon-Brassey's, 1986.

Montague, Robert M., Jr., "Test of Enlistment Bonus in Selected Combat Element Technical Skills," memorandum to Roger Kelley, Washington, D.C., May 25, 1973. G0060.pdf.

Moot, Robert C., "FY 1973 Budget Estimates and Legislative Proposals for Volunteer," memorandum to Roger T. Kelley, Washington, D.C., November 5, 1971. G0117.pdf.

Nixon, Richard M., "Changes in Military Pay for Fiscal Year 1971," memorandum to Secretary of Defense Melvin R. Laird, Washington, D.C., October 16, 1969. L0008.pdf.

————, *Message to Congress on Ending the Draft, April 23, 1970*, Washington, D.C.: The White House, April 23, 1970. G1160.pdf.

————, *Message to the Congress: Ending the Draft*, Washington, D.C.: The White House, January 28, 1971. G0646.pdf.

————, "General Hershey's Retirement," memorandum to General Hershey, Washington, D.C., March 16, 1973. G1064.pdf.

Novick, David, *Program Budgeting, Program Analysis and Federal Budget*, Cambridge, Mass.: Harvard University Press, 1965.

Office of the Assistant Secretary of Defense, Comptroller, *Program Budget Decision All-Volunteer Armed Force*, Washington, D.C.: U.S. Department of Defense, December 23, 1971. G0133.pdf.

————, *Program/Budget Decision Reclama—FY 1974 Budget*, Washington, D.C.: U.S. Department of Defense, December 5, 1972. G0151.pdf.

Office of the Assistant Secretary of Defense [M&RA], *ASD(M&RA) Responsibilities*, Washington, D.C.: U.S. Department of Defense, May 15, 1969. G0675.pdf.

————, *Comparison of Gates Commission and Department of Defense (Project Volunteer) Recommendations on an All-Volunteer Force*, Washington, D.C.: U.S. Department of Defense, February 24, 1970a (Revised August 21, 1970). G0287.pdf.

————, *Comparison of Gates Commission and Department of Defense (Project Volunteer) Recommendations on an All-Volunteer Force*, Washington, D.C.: U.S. Department of Defense, April 9, 1970b. G0300.pdf.

————, *Errors in the Gates Report*, Washington, D.C.: U.S. Department of Defense, April 9, 1970c. G0322.pdf.

————, *Fact Sheet: Project Volunteer Organization within the Military Service,* Washington, D.C.: U.S. Department of Defense, November 12, 1970d. G0119.pdf.

————, *To be Discussed in DPRC Meeting on January 18, 1971,* Washington, D.C.: U.S. Department of Defense, January 1, 1971a. L0028.pdf.

————, "System Analysis Economic Analysis," memorandum to Wollstadt, Washington, D.C., January 21, 1971b.

————, *Department of Defense Proposal for Expenditure of $1,400 M in FY 1972 to Move Toward Zero Draft Calls,* Washington, D.C.: U.S. Department of Defense, January 22, 1971c. G0188.pdf.

————, *Discussions of Paid Radio/TV Advertising,* Washington, D.C.: U.S. Department of Defense, February 12, 1971d. G0197.pdf.

————, *Evaluation System for Project Volunteer,* Washington, D.C.: U.S. Department of Defense, June 2, 1971e. G0210.pdf.

————, *Proposed Six-Week Extension of Army Paid TV/Radio Advertising,* Washington, D.C.: U.S. Department of Defense, July 1, 1971f. G0216.pdf.

————, *Status of FY 73 Funding,* Washington, D.C.: U.S. Department of Defense, December 29, 1971g. G0135.pdf.

————, *Extension of the Combat Arms Bonus,* Washington, D.C.: U.S. Department of Defense, October 1972a. G0171.pdf.

————, *Plan for Testing the Enlistment Bonus for Combat Elements,* Washington, D.C.: U.S. Department of Defense, October 1, 1972b. G0172.pdf.

————, *Approval of $14.2M O&MN Reprogramming for Recruiting,* Washington, D.C.: U.S. Department of Defense, December 11, 1972c. G0526.pdf.

OASD[SA]—*See* Office of the Assistant Secretary of Defense for Systems Analysis.

Odeen, Philip A., "Zero Draft—Systems Analysis Assessment of Zero Draft Proposal," memorandum to Deputy Secretary of Defense, Washington, D.C., December 14, 1970. G0506.pdf.

————, "Zero Draft," memorandum to General Pursley, Washington, D.C., April 5, 1971. G0656.pdf.

————, "Military Manpower and the Zero Draft," memorandum to Henry A. Kissinger, Washington, D.C., July 27, 1972a. G1116.pdf.

————, "Military Manpower and the Zero Draft," memorandum to Henry A. Kissinger, Washington, D.C., August 5, 1972b. G1113.pdf.

————, "Critical Period for Military Manpower Management," memorandum to Henry A. Kissinger, Washington, D.C., August 26, 1972c. G1097.pdf.

————, "All-Volunteer Force Funding for FY 74–78," memorandum to Henry A. Kissinger, Washington, D.C., November 13, 1972d. G1095.pdf.

Office of the Assistant Secretary of Defense for Systems Analysis, *The Volunteer Army: Prospects, Alternatives and Decision Criteria,* memorandum, Washington, D.C.: U.S. Department of Defense, November 23, 1970. G0547.pdf.

————, *Point Paper for DPRC Meeting on Volunteer Army,* Washington, D.C.: U.S. Department of Defense, January 15, 1971. G0184.pdf.

Office of the Special Assistant for the Modern Volunteer Army, *Draft Master Program: Modern Volunteer Army,* Washington, D.C.: U.S. Department of Defense, November 3, 1970.

Packard, David, "Army Zero Draft Requests for FY 71," memorandum to Secretary of the Army, Washington, D.C., January 12, 1971a. G0317.pdf.

————, "DPRC Meeting on Zero Draft," memorandum to Henry A. Kissinger, Washington, D.C., January 15, 1971b. G0321.pdf.

————, "FY 72 All-Volunteer Force Program," memorandum to Assistant to the President for National Security Affairs, Washington, D.C., January 22, 1971c. G0189.pdf.

Project Volunteer Committee, *Plans and Actions to Move Toward an All-Volunteer Force: A Report to the Secretary of Defense by the Project Volunteer Committee,* Washington, D.C.: Office of the Secretary of Defense, August 14, 1970. G0303.pdf.

Pursley, Robert, *Decision from the December 15, 1970, Volunteer Service Meeting with Messrs. Laird and Packard,* Washington, D.C.: Office of the Assistant Secretary of Defense, January 4, 1971. G0645.pdf.

Resor, Stanley R., "Charter of the Special Assistant for the Modern Volunteer Army (SAMVA)," memorandum to Heads of Army Staff Agencies, Washington, D.C., October 31, 1970a. G1201.pdf.

————, "Volunteer Army Action," memorandum to Secretary of Defense, Washington, D.C., November 3, 1970b. G0308.pdf.

————, "Volunteer Army Action," memorandum to Secretary of Defense, Washington, D.C., November 19, 1970c. G0505.pdf.

————, "Army-Funded Zero Draft Actions for FY 1971," memorandum to Secretary of Defense, Washington, D.C., January 4, 1971a. G0316.pdf.

————, "Department of Defense Position on Volunteer Force Plan," memorandum to Secretary of Defense, Washington, D.C., January 20, 1971b. G0639.pdf.

————, "Army Advertising Program," memorandum to Secretary of Defense, Washington, D.C., June 28, 1971c. G0661.pdf.

Richardson, Elliott L., "Expiration of Induction Authority," memorandum to the President, Washington, D.C., February 23, 1973a. G1108.pdf.

————, *Not Necessary to Extend the Draft,* news release, Washington, D.C.: Office of the Secretary of Defense, March 21, 1973b. G0054.pdf.

Roberts, John W., "Project Volunteer FY 1973 Budget Submission," memorandum to Gus C. Lee, Washington, D.C., November 26, 1971. G0124.pdf.

Ryder, Kenneth F., "Volunteer Service Prospects With Higher FY 72 Pay Raise," memorandum to Philip A Odeen, Washington, D.C., March 30, 1971. G0655.pdf.

Selin, Ivan, and Roger T. Kelley, "The Roles of Systems Analysis and Manpower and Reserve Affairs," memorandum of understanding to Secretary Packard, Washington, D.C., October 24, 1969a. G0662.pdf.

———, *The Roles of Systems Analysis and Manpower and Reserve Affairs,* memorandum of understanding, Washington, D.C.: Office of the Secretary of Defense, October 29, 1969b. G0642.pdf.

Shultz, George, "Uniformed Services Special Pay Act of 1972," letter to Senator Gordon Allott, Washington, D.C., March 23, 1972. S0070.pdf.

Srull, Donald W., "Applying the Limited Money to the Tough Part of the Problem," memorandum to Phil Odeen, Washington, D.C., December 4, 1970. S0064.pdf.

———, "Accuracy of Forecasts of the Monthly Supply of Army True Volunteers," memorandum to Assistant Secretary of the Army (M&RA), Washington, D.C., October 30, 1972a. G0180.pdf.

———, "FY 74 Volunteer Force Spending," memorandum to Carl Detwyler, Washington, D.C., November 27, 1972b. G0085.pdf.

Tucker, Gardiner L., "The Volunteer Service: Prospects, Alternatives and Decision Criteria (Second Draft)," memorandum to Roger Kelley, Washington, D.C., November 30, 1970. G0310.pdf.

———, "Army Revised Proficiency Pay Proposal," memorandum to Deputy Secretary of Defense, Washington, D.C., January 9, 1971a. G0644.pdf.

———, "Zero Draft Plan," memorandum to Roger T. Kelley, Washington, D.C., January 9, 1971b. S0059.pdf.

———, "PBD 281. AVF Expansion and New Initiatives," memorandum to Assistant Secretary of Defense (Comptroller), Washington, D.C., December 7, 1972. G0528.pdf.

U.S. Air Force, "Proceedings of the Air Force Industry Conference on the All-Volunteer (Zero-Draft) Force," Washington, D.C., May 4, 1972a. G1306.pdf.

———, *Program/Budget Decision Reclama—FY 1974 Budget,* Washington, D.C., December 15, 1972b. G0150.pdf.

U.S. News & World Report Staff, "Can 'Volunteer Army' End the Draft?" *U.S. News & World Report,* March 9, 1970.

Westmoreland, William C., "Address," Annual Luncheon of the Association of the United States Army, Washington, D.C., October 13, 1970a. G0305.pdf.

———, "Army Actions to Improve Service Attractiveness," press release, Washington, D.C., December 8, 1970b. G0500.pdf.

———, "Alternative Use of Contingency Funds Presently Allocated to the Allott Amendment," memorandum to Secretary of the Army and Secretary of Defense, Washington, D.C., February 16, 1972. G0140.pdf.

White House Press Secretary, *Extension of the Draft and Increase in Military Pay,* Washington, D.C.: The White House, September 28, 1971. G0576.pdf.

White, John P., "Approach to the Establishment of an Evaluation System for the Transition to an All-Volunteer Force," letter to Francis J. Sullivan, Santa Monica, Calif., June 3, 1971. G0211.pdf.

Wollstadt, Paul, "All-Volunteer Force: Report of Program Evaluation Group on Project Volunteer," memorandum to Assistant Secretary of Defense (M&RA), Washington, D.C., January 14, 1970a. G1140.pdf.

———,"All-Volunteer Force: Report of Program Evaluation Group on Project Volunteer," memorandum to Martin C. Anderson, Washington, D.C., February 9, 1970b. G1141.pdf.

———, "Test of Paid TV/Radio Advertising," memorandum to Roger T. Kelley, Washington, D.C., December 3, 1970c. G0195.pdf.

———, "Comments on 'Point Paper for DPRC Meeting on Volunteer Army' dated January 15, 1971," memorandum to Roger T. Kelley, Washington, D.C., January 16, 1971a. L0027.pdf.

———, "Army Test of Paid Radio and TV Advertising," memorandum to Donald W. Srull, Washington, D.C., February 11, 1971b. G0194.pdf.

Wool, Harold, *Minutes of First Meeting, Project Volunteer Committee,* memorandum, Washington, D.C.: Office of the Assistant Secretary of Defense (Manpower and Reserve Affairs), April 12, 1969a. G1206.pdf.

———, "Development on Project Volunteer—Gates Commission," memorandum for the record, Washington, D.C., April 18, 1969b. G0271.pdf.

———, *Minutes of Second Meeting, Project Volunteer Committee,* Washington, D.C.: Director of Procurement Policy and General Research, Office of the Assistant Secretary of Defense (M&RA), April 23, 1969c. G0325.pdf.

———, "Support for Project Volunteer," memorandum to Project Volunteer Service Liaison Officers, Washington, D.C., May 9, 1969d. G0323.pdf.

———, *Steering Committee Meeting on Project Volunteer,* Washington, D.C.: Director of Procurement Policy and General Research, Office of the Assistant Secretary of Defense (M&RA), May 14, 1969e. G0324.pdf.

———, "Development of Project Volunteer Action Programs," memorandum to Assistant Secretary of Defense (M&RA), Washington, D.C., July 16, 1969f. L0006.pdf.

Zech, Lando W., Jr., "Fact Sheets on Recruiting Budgets, FY 74," memorandum to Office of the Assistant Secretary of Defense (M&RA), Washington, D.C., September 22, 1972. G0169.pdf.

Zumwalt, Elmo R., Jr., "Navy Recruiting," memorandum to All Flag Officers, Washington, D.C., March 31, 1972a. G0517.pdf.

———, "Recruiting Z-109," message to Chief of Naval Operations, Washington, D.C., April 26, 1972b. S0069.pdf.

———, *On Watch: A Memoir,* Arlington, Va.: Admiral Zumwalt & Associates, Inc, 1976.

CHAPTER SEVEN

Analytic Studies During the Initial Transition Period (1969–1972)

From the viewpoint of the Project Volunteer Committee there was not enough time . . . . The committee wished to use these funds as efficiently as possible but . . . [was] not persuaded that efficiency meant waiting for the research and analytic community to give them answers. . . . The committee decided to go ahead and try the programs, and then modify or drop them if they were not effective. This approach was oriented to action rather than to experiment in the research sense. . . . But empirical data on which to base new programs or terminate old ones was . . . not definitive.

> —Gus Less
> Director of Procurement Policy
> Director of the Project Volunteer
> Committee[1]

Insofar as OASD/M&RA controls the allocation of Project Volunteer funds among different programs, it should insist such programs being [sic] introduced in a limited and varied way so that they could be evaluated more as real experiments.

> —Stephen Enke
> Consultant to the
> National Security Council and
> Secretary Melvin R. Laird[2]

Estimating the Numbers of "True Volunteers"

One of the most troubling analytic problems the 1964 Pentagon draft study team and the Gates Commission staff faced was how to estimate how the draft affected enlistments.

---

[1] From *Ending the Draft: The Story of the All Volunteer Force* (Lee and Parker, 1977, pp. 474 and 201).

[2] From *Innovation for Achieving an AVAF* (Enke, 1971d, p. 63, n. 1).

Moreover, during the transition to the all-volunteer force, the proportion of true volunteers in each month's accession cohort would be the most important indicator of how well the incentives and program changes were working.

Fortunately, the implementation of the lottery system by Selective Service in 1970 provided a clear indicator of the number of true volunteers. The first-ever random lottery was held on December 1, 1969, to determine the order of selection for 19- to 25-year-olds during 1970.[3] Under this new system, when Selective Service set national random sequence number ceilings, a comparison of the entering cohorts with high numbers to those with low numbers provided an unambiguous measure of the number of true volunteers who were joining. At the Pentagon, Fred Suffa, a senior manpower analyst in Kelley's office, designed a system of reporting enlistments and officer accessions by draft lottery number. This would be key in monitoring the transition to the all-volunteer force (1977, p. 220). An example of the analysis of true volunteers from the Air Reserve Forces—the Air National Guard and the Air Force Reserve—for the second half of 1972 (see Table 7.1) shows how the lottery data were used to estimate a "true volunteer rate." In this case, the rate was about 20 percent.

Table 7.1
Non–Prior Service Enlistments in Air Reserve Forces by Lottery Number, July–December 1972

Lottery Numbers	Number of Enlistments		
	ANG	AFRES	Total
1–40	838	318	1,156
41–80	1,194	387	1,581
81–120	561	171	732
121–160	48	20	68
161–200	41	15	56
201–240	41	18	59
241–280	45	17	62
281–320	32	12	44
321–366	37	16	53
Unknown	285	127	412
Total	3,122	1,101	4,223
Estimated true volunteers (%)	20.6	24.5	21.7

SOURCE: Haggstrom and Rostker (1973, p. 4).

NOTE: The enlistees whose lottery numbers were unknown were less than 19 years of age and therefore had not received their lottery numbers before enlisting.

---

[3] The famous picture of Secretary of War Stimson drawing numbers from a bowl on October 29, 1941, did not show a random lottery. The drawing was to determine the "order of call for the registrants" for the first 10,000 in each draft board area (see Flynn, 1985, p. 73). Tarr discusses the modern random-selection—lottery—process in his account of the time he spent as Director of Selective Service (Tarr, 1981, pp. 44–48).

The Central All-Volunteer Force Task Force

Despite the monitoring of the true volunteer accession numbers, questions were raised about the evaluation of Project Volunteer. As noted, Kelley's philosophy was to emphasize "decentralization," with the services responsible for their own evaluations. In January 1972, however, the Central All-Volunteer Force Task Force was established to respond to a number of criticisms of Kelley's hands-off approach. The task force focused on areas the Gates Commission had raised but that the services had not yet addressed. Kelley charged the task force to undertake a number of studies designed to "evaluate alternative means for maintaining required military force levels in a zero-draft environment" (Central All-Volunteer Force Task Force, 1972a, p. 1). Each study was designed either to decrease the demand for new personnel or to increase the eligible pool of potential recruits.

Civilian Substitution

Attempts to substitute civilians for military personnel were not new and were not uniquely associated with the move to an all-volunteer force. For Congress, civilian substitution had little to do with implementing an all-volunteer force but was a way "to get military personnel from behind desks and back in aircraft, ships and troop units."[4] The Gates Commission, however, saw the substitution of civilians for military personnel as a way to "[reduce] the demand for new recruits" (Gates, 1970, p. 37). The commission's staff argued that, "where non-cost factors do not preclude its use, civilian manpower is generally a less expensive resource from the standpoint of the military manager" than military manpower (Albro, 1970, p. I-5-2). In its analysis, the staff concluded that

> [t]he *maximum* potential for civilian substitution is believed to vary from a low of 173,417 to a high of 237,316 positions across the spectrum of possible post-Vietnam forces considered. . . .
>   The practical limits of civilian substitution are probably about half the maximum levels identified. (Albro, 1970, p. I-5-19; emphasis in the original)

The commission finally suggested that, at a force level of 2.5 million men, about 106,000 positions could be civilianized.

The Project Volunteer Committee "recognized that greater use of civilians for military personnel would assist in achieving the all-volunteer force" (Kelley, 1971a), but recommended no action until after the war in Vietnam had wound down and "military and civilian strengths had leveled out (i.e., FY73-74)" (Kelley, 1971a).

---

[4] House of Representatives Report 92-1389 of the Department of Defense 1993 Defense Appropriations Bill, as cited in Central All-Volunteer Force Task Force (1972a, p. 2).

The Central All-Volunteer Force Task Force took a different tack. It tasked the services to

> determine the theoretical maximum number of military billets which could be civilianized . . . within the constraints of personnel rotation and military requirements. Time phased contingency plans for the civilianization of certain numbers of these billets . . . will then be drawn up. (Central All-Volunteer Force Task Force, 1972a, p. 21)[5]

The number of positions to be civilianized was based on "meeting possible accession shortages" for each of the services. Working from inputs from the military services, the task force accepted 103,000 as the lower bound of the number of military spaces that could be civilianized. Its report, however, notes that "[t]he Services oppose further civilianization" (Central All-Volunteer Force Task Force, 1972a, p. 17), citing their concern for the Pentagon's tendency toward "double dipping," in which the services lose military spaces but, despite the promises to the contrary, do not get new civilian spaces.[6]

A central feature of this and all substitution studies, whether the civilianization study of 1972 or the more recent outsourcing studies of the 1990s, is the lack of any consistent application of a reasonable methodology. The task force's report identified differences by service and ultimately concluded that "the Service submissions appear reasonable," given that the goal, in terms of the number of positions to be civilianized, had been specified at the start.[7]

The concepts, however, are so poorly defined that, in the end, the number of positions civilianized was politically determined and was a fraction of the number the Gates Commission staff originally proposed be civilianized.

Utilization of Women

While the task force's study of the utilization of women used the same "goal assignment" approach used in the civilianization study—each service was asked to present plans to reach a specific numerical goal—the services, with the exception of the Marine

---

[5] The numbers the task force assigned to the services were 10,000 and 20,000 for the Army, Navy, and Air Force and 5,000 and 10,000 for the Marine Corps (see Central All-Volunteer Force Task Force, 1972a, p. 21).

[6] The first "dip" is when military spaces are eliminated before civilian spaces are funded. The second dip is the subsequent cut in civilian spaces. The net result is the reduction in military spaces without any increase in civilian personnel. In early 1971, Kelley told Packard that, when asking about civilianization, he anticipated

> difficulty in generating Service support for such a program in view of their experience with the 1966 to 1968 DoD program which replaced 114,000 military personnel with 90,000 civilians. At that time, DoD was unable to make good its promise to give the Services the full complement of civilian spaces because P.L. 90-364 placed a limitation on civilian employment with the objective of rolling back employment to June 30, 1966 levels. (Kelley, 1971a)

[7] Reasonable, of course, with the exception of the Air Force, which argued that "civilianization potential is considerably larger than the number reported" (Central All-Volunteer Force Task Force, 1972a, p. 37).

Corps, supported this initiative and agreed to meet or exceed the goals the task force had set (Central All-Volunteer Force Task Force, 1972c, p. 45). Besides reporting on the service's plans to meet or exceed the stated goals, the report identified a number of issues that were, and continue to be, central to the debate concerning the appropriate role for women in the military. Table 7.2 summarizes a number of these issues and conclusions. Several of these have become dogma and are the standard answers to critics who question the increased utilization of women in the military. The following were the main points derived from the task force's study:

- The potential supply of women is large enough for the military to expand their use greatly.
- The overall quality of women recruits is better than that of the men.
- The attrition of female recruits is largely driven by policies that treat women differently from they way men are treated, given similar circumstances.

Table 7.2
Issues and Tentative Conclusions Raised by the Central All-Volunteer Force Task Force Concerning the Utilization of Women

Issue	Conclusion
Are enough women available for the services?	Single women in the labor force are more likely candidates for military service.
	Current statutes prohibit enlisting women younger than 18 years old.
	It appears that accession goals are modest and attainable.
	In FY 1973, it would be necessary to attract one out of every 67 qualified women in the full-time labor force to meet accession requirements.
What are the effects of current eligibility standards?	Enlistment standards, which are more restrictive for women than for men, will constrict the available supply of women unnecessarily.
	In all services, women must be high school graduates or have passed the General Educational Development test. Men who have not graduated from high school, however, are acceptable for service.
	None of the services will accept a women who test scores places her in one of the lower mental groups (III or IV).
	In both the Army and Marine Corps, the physical profile at entry required of women is higher than that required of men.
What are the effects of restrictions on marital status at time of entry?	Male enlistees who are married and who have dependent children can enlist with a waiver.
	In the Army and Marine Corps, married women who otherwise meet eligibility standards cannot enlist without a waiver.

Table 7.2—continued

Issue	Conclusion
What is the propensity for females to enlist?	Survey results show that few women have more than scant knowledge of the roles of military women.
	Survey results show, however, that men and women have similar attitudes toward enlisting. The probability of enlisting about one-tenth as many women as men should be very high.
	The potential supply of military women can sustain a substantial increase in accession of military women.
	Supply estimates will improve as recruiting intensifies and as accession goals gradually increase.
How have assignment policies affected the utilization of women?	The services have, in the past, been quite restrictive of the type of occupations open to women.
How has attrition affected the utilization of women?	**The most powerful argument against increasing the use of women has been that attrition rates have historically been significantly higher among military women than among military men.**
	For each month of service and for each military service, the percentage of males remaining in service is higher than the percentage of females remaining in service.
	Policy differences make it easier for women to leave than it is for men. For example, a recently rescinded Air Force policy allowed a woman to request discharge if she married and had completed 18 months of service.
	After the Air Force implemented a policy change that permitted women who were pregnant or had minor children to remain in the services under certain circumstances, retention rates improved.
	As policies change to treat men and women more equally, attrition and turnover rates for women are declining and will decline further.

SOURCE: Compiled from Central All-Volunteer Force Task Force (1972c).

Quality

Of all the work of the Central All-Volunteer Force Task Force, nothing irritated the services more than the conclusions it drew about the quality standards the services applied to entry-level personnel. Following the general line of the Gates Commission, the task force used two different methods to calculate the minimum mental standards for each of the services. The first method "adjusted to the mean mental requirement," and the second method "adjusted to the lowest mental requirement" (Central All-Volunteer Force Task Force, 1972b, p. 4). Without addressing the differences among the services, the task force saw the application of either method as having "the effect of deflating quality requirements" (Central All-Volunteer Force Task Force, 1972b, p. 4). The task force argued that its computations would enable manpower planners in OSD and the Services to compare Service estimates of quality requirements with those developed by the use of a standard method applied to all Services. . . . The Task Force analysis was based on the rationale that all Service requirements should be determined by applying the same standard measure of aptitude for training and job performance. . . . the assumption [is] that for like jobs no Service should require higher aptitude scores than the average score for that occupation. . . . [For] a lower quality bound . . . the lowest aptitude score required for an occupation by any Service was applied to all Services. (Central All-Volunteer Force Task Force, 1972b, p. 15)

The reason the task force was so eager to eliminate excess quality requirements became clear when it estimated how a change would affect the supply of enlisted accessions. According to the task force,

[i]n the case of the Army, there is a projected shortage of 12,000 accessions, assuming Army adheres to its objective of 20% mental category IVs for male accessions. We estimate that this 12,000 accessions shortage can be overcome by increasing male mental category IV input to 25% for FY 1973. (Central All-Volunteer Force Task Force, 1972b, p. 24)

Critiques of Project Volunteer: RAND's Evaluation of the Transition to an All-Volunteer Force and the Enke Study

As Roger Kelley originally envisioned, the transition to an all-volunteer force would be managed on an *ad hoc* basis, largely relying on his existing staff and the staffs of the services. A number of review studies found this arrangement wanting. The most important of these were a RAND study commissioned by the Assistant Secretary of Defense (Systems Analysis), written by Fred Hoffman and Marco Fiorello, *The Evaluation of the Transition to a Volunteer Force* (Hoffman and Fiorello, 1971), and a private report prepared by Stephen Enke for the Secretary of Defense (Enke, 1971a).

The RAND Study

Hoffman and Fiorello focused their assessment on (1) the organizational structure used to monitor and control the transition to the all-volunteer force, (2) designing an evaluation system that could assess the cost and effectiveness of Project Volunteer's many component programs, and (3) the data for these evaluations (Hoffman and Fiorello, 1971, p. iv). The self-described principal conclusion of their report was that "the existing system cannot monitor progress in a way that will adequately support the design of policies and programs to deal with problems that may arise in the transition" (Hoffman and Fiorello, 1971, p. iii). They identified the existing Project Volunteer organization as one shortcoming and the "failure to assign clear and full-time responsibility to offices within OSD that have adequate resources for the development of the [evaluation] process" as another. They argued that, "DoD-wide committees may supplement, but cannot substitute for, strong and substantive leadership by OSD" (Hoffman and Fiorello, 1971, p. iv).

The RAND team also found that there was "inadequate . . . analytical support for the policy selection and resource allocation needed to manage the transition" and recommended a new, "strengthened framework for evaluating the transition" (Hoffman and Fiorello, 1971, p. 14). Probably the authors' most controversial recommendation was to introduce "planned variation in operating programs as a basis for evaluation" (Hoffman and Fiorello, 1971, p. 34). With this recommendation, they took square aim at the psychologists who had dominated the field of military manpower. Hoffman and Fiorello argued that, "[w]ith a few important exceptions, most of the efforts to evaluate component programs have attempted to do so in terms of attitudinal effects rather than in behavioral terms" (Hoffman and Fiorello, 1971, p. iv). The exception they noted was in the area of pay and compensation, which supported the econometric analysis the Gates Commission staff had undertaken. The authors also saw "good prospects for measuring the effectiveness of additions to recruiting resources and various types of enlistment options and bonuses" (Hoffman and Fiorello, 1971, p. iv).

As noted before, the Project Volunteer staff thought these recommendations "ignored the real world" (Lee and Parker, 1977, p. 473). However, within a year, RAND organized the first of what would be many experiments along the lines Hoffman and Fiorello had recommended. The first planned experiment focused on the Air National Guard Recruiter Program. It started in July 1972 with a phased introduction of recruiters and advertising funds to select locations throughout the United States (see Haggstrom and Rostker, 1974).

The Enke Study

After Steve Enke finished the National Security Study Memorandum 78 study for the National Security Council, he wrote Secretary of Defense Melvin Laird's Military Assistant, Brigadier General Bob Pursley, about the possibility of doing a study for the Pentagon. Pursley knew Enke from RAND and his days in Systems Analysis, as well as his more recent work for the National Security Council.[8] In the letter to Pursley, he reminded him that, "some months ago the Secretary asked through you whether I'd do a manpower procurement study on some then undefined topic" (Enke, 1971a). Within days, he sent Pursley a proposal for a Military Manpower Study. He made the case that progress demanded interagency analysis:

> However, the agencies that have sufficient personnel to make these analyses often have special interests of their own, while some more impartial offices in OSD and the Executive Office often have no one available full time to make such studies.

---

[8] At the time, Enke was the Manager of Economic Development Programs for General Electric Company's Center for Advanced Studies (GE TEMPO), in Santa Barbara, California.

This argues for organization of an ad hoc team, directed by someone outside government with experience of the military . . . . This was the arrangement by which the NSC study for the President on draft reform was conducted. It seemed to function satisfactorily at least if the presidential approval of all its 13 recommendations is any test. (Enke, 1971b, p. 1)

By April, Laird had seen and approved a "Draft Statement of Work for GE/Tempo to ASD M&RA" (Enke, 1971c). While, formally, Enke was to provide Kelley "with suggested solutions" to a number of problems, everyone knew the work was being done for Laird.

The Enke report was a problem for Kelley. It came in just as he was trying to fend off Tucker and Systems Analysis and secure the FY 1973 budget. Kelley's staff referred to Enke's study as "a 'Little Gates Report'—pessimistic rather than optimistic and done with less competence than the Gates Report" (Lee, 1971c).

In fact, Enke's findings were pessimistic. He summarized his findings this way:

An AVAF by the end of FY 76 . . . does not seem probable unless current practices are supplemented by additional personnel innovations. As of 15 December 1971, . . . it is . . . considered unlikely that the nation will attain an adequate AVAF. (Enke, 1971d, p. i)

To forestall his projection, which at the time found no support with Kelley's staff (Lee, 1971c), Enke recommended the following: (1) keep draft calls relatively high and induct only those in mental category III or better, that is, draft for quality; (2) pay enlistment bonuses only to those in mental category I or II, that is, pay for quality; (3) increase enlistments of women by an extra 1 percent of accessions for each year for 4 years, that is, enlist more women; and (4) use more civilians in lieu of military, that is, increase civilian to military ratio. Lee, for one, was concerned "the report could be misused to allege that a volunteer force is unfeasible" (Lee, 1971c).

Without naming Kelley, Enke was critical of his major management decisions and the way he was running the transition to the all-volunteer force. He told Laird that

[o]ne of the most important responsibilities of OSD at the present time, perhaps second only to the now-concluding Vietnamization, is to effect a satisfactory transition to the AVAF. The blame should this not transpire will fall more heavily upon OSD than on the Service Chiefs. While the Services can and are making many efforts to increase enlistments, only OSD can initiate the major changes that may be necessary to recruit and retain enough military personnel of sufficient quality. . . . Innovations require OSD leadership, planning or implementation, and sooner rather than later. (Enke, 1971d, p. xvi)

Enke wanted OSD to take a more-active role in managing the transition to the all-volunteer force; while he set out the arguments both for and against centralization, he left little doubt that he was pushing for a more-aggressive, centrally managed program. (Enke, 1971d, pp. 103–106). As he saw it, the absence of conscription would create a new kind of interservice rivalry, with the recruiting actions of one service occasionally reducing the enlistment of another, compelling OSD to intervene:

> [T]here is a real need for OSD to initiate new bonuses and pay structures, new military manpower data series suited to new management functions, and new analyses of effectiveness and impact of different Service expenditures for recruiting. (Enke, 1971d, p. iv)

He thought that,

> [i]nsofar as OASD/M&RA controls the allocation of Project Volunteer funds among different programs, it should insist such programs being [sic] introduced in a limited and varied way so that they could be evaluated more as real experiments. Obviously, this entails delays, and the criticism that the real objective is to collect not statistics but recruits. (Enke, 1971d, p. 63, n. 1)

Enke concluded this way:

> Programs that experienced Service officials believe will be effective relative to their costs should not be blocked simply because the net enlistment effect cannot be precisely estimated. Nevertheless, far more thought, effort, and money should be devoted to quantifying where feasible the effects on each Service of all major recruiting and retention programs. Cost effectiveness analyses of enlistment and retention programs should in the future be undertaken by or for OSD/M&RA, particularly if it is suspected that the program of one Service is reducing the manpower of another. (Enke, 1971d, p. 70)

Evaluations of the Army's Project VOLAR

One of the programs Enke highlighted in his report to Laird was Project VOLAR (Enke, 1971d, pp. 68–69). The Project VOLAR field experiments allocated between $3 million and $5 million each to a number of Army bases in the United States and Europe to enable the base commanders to undertake innovative programs to increase reenlistments. The changes were designed to improve Army life by creating

- a more satisfactory workplace by fostering professionalism, identification with the Army, and greater job satisfaction among officers and enlisted men
- a better living environment by improving the quality of Army life and removing unnecessary sources of irritation and dissatisfaction. (Vineberg and Taylor, 1977, p. v)

F. S. Hoffman and M. R. Fiorello, "The Evaluation of the Transition to a Volunteer Force," Santa Monica, CA.: RAND Corporation, 1971, pp. 34–35

Excerpt:

We [understand] . . . the difficulty and perhaps impossibility of deriving valid measures of cost and effectiveness for each of the many component programs under Project Volunteer. Virtually all of the analysis and experiments undertaken for this purpose that have come to our attention are designed to produce data on proximate measures of effectiveness such as changes in attitude towards the Services, reaction to advertising programs, or stated reasons for re-enlisting or leaving the Service. We know of few analyses that are designed to reflect the effect of programs on key behavioral variables such as recruiting effectiveness or re-enlistment rates. Important exceptions to this observation are the supply analysis that attempts to relate the number of volunteers to a variety of economic and other variables such as draft pressure and compensation.

Attitudinal response, while it falls short of what is needed for resource allocation decisions, does have some value as a filter. A program that has no effect on attitudes presumably will have none on behavior. Such a program can therefore be rejected. It does not, unfortunately, follow that the demonstration of significant attitudinal effects can often be applied to develop measures of effectiveness in determining behavior. It is the latter that ultimately should be reflected in resource allocation decisions.

The isolation of behavioral effects of programs to reduce irritants, to change service images through advertising and public relations, and to change military job content would appear on the face of it to be very difficult. Moreover, account also needs to be taken of changes in external variables such as employment conditions, civilian pay and broad societal attitudes towards national security and foreign affairs.

It is possible that multiple regression analysis can in some cases provide information on program productivities in terms of desired behavioral response. It must be recognized, nevertheless, that the overall aim of Project Volunteer is to change substantially the structure of factors bearing on these aspects of behavior (for example, the elimination of draft inducement). Consequently, regression analysis based on time series going back over a period of years will, at best, encounter substantial problems of shifts in the underlying structural models. This is currently being demonstrated in the use of available time series models.

For this reason cross-section analysis may have a particularly important role to play in making estimates of program effectiveness while avoiding the difficulties encountered in time series analysis. However, cross-section analysis faces a distinct difficulty of its own. To achieve the needed variability for useful cross-section analysis, in many cases it will be necessary to design variation in program content actively and deliberately into operating programs. . . .

Hoffman and Fiorello also used Project VOLAR as an example of the problems they saw with the way Kelley and the Army were approaching needed evaluations, which were critical to informed decisions about the transition to the all-volunteer force. They noted that

> Project VOLAR was deliberately planned as a decentralized activity in which base commanders were given freedom to select the sets of programs they would try. Thus Project VOLAR is less an experiment than an exploration.
>
> A cost of this approach has been the loss of the benefits from controlling and stratifying the large number of variables that bear upon result[s]. . . .
>
> Another aspect of VOLAR that may limit its usefulness is the fact that the activities of SDC and HUMMRO in evaluating the results of VOLAR are almost entirely concerned with attitudinal effects. (Hoffman and Fiorello, 1971, pp. 35–36)

Evaluation by the Human Resources Research Organization

In fact, the Army had planned to evaluate Project VOLAR and had contracted with the Human Resources Research Organization (HumRRO). Unfortunately, this was not the kind of evaluation Hoffman and Fiorello had had in mind. HumRRO's plan was to evaluated Project VOLAR

> by comparing attitudes of officers and enlisted men stationed at the locations where the [Modern Volunteer Army] MVA and funded VOLAR innovations were introduced with the attitudes of officers and [enlisted] men stationed at "control" locations where only MVA innovations were being introduced. (Vineberg and Taylor, 1977, p. v)

Given the design of Project VOLAR, HumRRO concluded that "the most that could be expected of VOLAR during this [the evaluation] period was an increasing awareness of the VOLAR program by the soldiers" (Vineberg and Taylor, 1977, p. 74). This rather unremarkable result reflects, as Hoffman and Fiorello's evaluation of the transition to a volunteer force suggested, a problem with the very design of the Project VOLAR. In its summary report, HumRRO seems to agree. The report explains that one reason for the lack of positive results could be that, given "the short time that many of the innovations were actually in effect before assessment, marked changes in attitudes would hardly be expected" (Vineberg and Taylor, 1977, p. 74).[9]

Evaluation of Paid Advertising Programs

Enke also highlighted the Army's paid advertising test as an example of "how difficult it is to assess the cost effectiveness of a particular program designed to increase enlist-

---

[9] Vineberg and Taylor also noted that "[f]or officers the survey returns were so low and the data so variable that only in a few instances were seemingly stable trends evident" (Vineberg and Taylor, 1977, p. ix).

ments in a single Service" (Enke, 1971d, p. 63). Despite the best efforts of several research companies, he noted, "very little . . . [could] be inferred because this particular advertising program was instituted too rapidly for experimental control groups to be established" (Enke, 1971d, p. 63).

Changes in attitudes and awareness and estimates based on recruiter interviews and a count of the "coupon return rate experiences from print media" (Lee and Parker, 1977, p. 483), as the Army had planned, was also not the kind of evaluation Hoffman and Fiorello had had in mind.[10] Eventually, the Army hired Stanford Research Institute (SRI) to evaluate its paid advertising test, and Kelley's office contracted with a New York company, Audits and Surveys, to do a cost-effectiveness evaluation.[11] Given the poor design of the test, however, these organizations came up with contradictory conclusions.

Stanford Research Institute Study of Paid Advertising

As noted above, there was apparently some miscommunication between the Army and OSD concerning the design of the paid advertising "test." Kelley told his staff that, as long as the evaluation was made by an outside agency, he could support the Army's program (Wollstadt, 1970).[12] However, at some point along the way, the Army told its advertising agency to "forget about the test and go for accessions" (Lee and Parker, 1977, p. 159). This clearly complicated SRI's evaluation. The company noted in its report to the Army that

> An important problem encountered in SRI's assessment was the lack of a control group to serve as a baseline for indicating what enlistments would have occurred in the absence of the paid broadcast media advertising. This lack of a reference base raises many methodological questions, particularly in view of the historical pattern of enlistments that preceded the five-month evaluation period (Ackerman et al., 1971, p. 3).

SRI's evaluation, as a result of "the absence of a control group or area to provide a basis for evaluation," used a time-series analysis (Ackerman et al., 1971, p. 131). To account for seasonal, secular and cyclic factors, they analyzed Army enlistments over a long period, July 1963 to July 1971. In fact, SRI found that enlistment patterns had changed immediately (Ackerman et al., 1971, p. 131). Their analysis shows that, during the program months, an increase of between 2 and 4 percent would have occurred even if there had been no paid advertising program. However, even after enlistment

---

[10] Lee noted that the

> Rome Arnold Study [was] [p]repared for the Army through N.W. Ayer, the Army's advertising agency. [T]he study measures awareness and recall of the advertising messages and attitude changes brought about by the advertising campaign. The method used was to administer questionnaires to young men 17–21 years old and to their fathers before and after the campaign. (Lee and Parker, 1977, p. 482)

[11] Lee provided a summary of the evaluations of the Army's paid television and radio advertising for Kelly (Lee, 1972).

[12] A discussion of the coordination problems between the Army and OSD can be found in Foreman (1972, p. 6).

Ackerman, D., W. Mason, H. Vollmer, A. Baker, and R. Davis. *Effectiveness of the Modern Volunteer Army Advertising Program.* **Menlo Park, CA, Stanford Research Institute, 1971, pp. 131–137**

Excerpt:

In the absence of a control group or area to provide a basis for evaluation of the effect of the Army's three-month (March–April 1971) intensive paid broadcast-media advertising program on Army enlistments, it is necessary to estimate what would have happened during the five-month evaluation period March–July 1971 if the program had not been introduced. If monthly enlistment rates were quite uniform, one could use a simple average of the last few months' enlistment rate preceding the five-month evaluation period as an adequate forecast of what would happen during the evaluation period if no new factors were introduced. However . . . Army [enlistment rates] show a strong and persistent seasonal pattern. Consequently, it would not be appropriate to estimate March–July 1971 enlistment levels by using directly the enlistments in the immediately preceding months. . . .

[A] technique for taking into account seasonal, secular and cyclical factors influencing Army enlistments [while] attempting to forecast March–July 1971 enlistments, in the absence of the Army broadcast-media advertising program, is to analyze a long period of actual Army enlistments preceding March 1971. . . .

The time series was analyzed by means of the U.S. Bureau of the Census Economic Time Series Seasonal Adjustment computer program . . . This program determines the monthly seasonality factors for each year and deseasonalizes and smooths the time series to yield the "trend-cycle" component of the time series. . . .

[F]rom 1968 on there is an increasingly negative secular trend and, during 1970 and early 1971, strong cyclic trends . . . The strong negative trend that is seen for the first half of 1970 was abruptly reversed during August and September and rose sharply through December 1970. In January 1971, this rise had slowed appreciably, by February 1971 it had virtually ceased, and by March 1971 it had begun to decrease slightly. At this time the (normalized) enlistment level was substantially above the falling secular trend curve.

Thus the pattern of deseasonalized and smoothed enlistments immediately preceding the five-month evaluation period signal[s] a turnaround and fall-off from the sharp August–December 1970 rise. To determine an estimate of the continuation of this trend, which would have been expected to occur in the absence of the Army broadcast-media advertising program, a second-order (parabolic) least-squares fit to the normalized October 1970–March 1971 data was made and then used to project normalized enlistments for the five-month evaluation period.

[T]he actual (normalized) enlistments during the evaluation period remain well above the projected levels and there is evidence of a significant upturn beginning in July 1971. The 55,222 enlistments forecast for the five-month evaluation period . . . were considerably less than the 60,630 actual enlistments, or a gain for the latter of 10 percent over those forecast in the absence of the Army advertising program.

data for the program months were "normalized," they found that paid advertising had a significant positive effect on enlistments. The analysis suggests that an increase in enlistments of about 10 percent "should be attributed to the advertising *and other operative factors* introduced during the test period" (Ackerman et al., 1971, p. 108, emphasis added).

The Audits and Surveys, Inc., Study of Paid Advertising

No one but the Army liked the paid advertising test. The other services thought that it gave the Army an unfair advantage and hurt their recruiting efforts. Senior officials in OSD thought the Army had ignored their instructions to treat this as a test or experiment. While the Army suggested that Kelley's office sponsor its own evaluation (Kester, 1971) and while the other services agreed that "it would be desirable for OSD to conduct an independent evaluation of the Army advertising test" (Wollstadt, 1971), things did not work out as planned. Kelley was on the hot seat. He had formally reassured the secretaries of the military departments that his office would "closely monitor" and "make an independent evaluation of the Army's 13-week test" (Kelley, 1971b), but he could not control the Army, and there was little that could be done with a poorly developed "test."

At the start, Kelley's staff was optimistic about the prospects of an independent evaluation. Irv Greenberg was given the task of overseeing the evaluation. He met with the services and "developed a set of objectives for an OSD Evaluation Study" (Lee, 1971a). Several proposals were received, and the services agreed that the proposal from Audits and Surveys, Inc., was best. The Navy remained concerned that "the research task is very difficult and the study may prove to be inconclusive" (Greenberg, 1971a). In addition, some were concerned that paid advertising would produce "negative public reaction." As a result, in June a task was added to the Audits and Surveys contract to "measure the reaction of the 'General Population' to the Army's paid TV/radio advertising" (Greenberg, 1971b).

Preliminary results of the Audits and Surveys, Inc., study were available by early August (Greenberg, 1971c). When the final report came out in November, it focused on the measures of merit of *awareness, recall, attitude change,* and *behavioral change.* Unlike SRI, however, Audits and Surveys found "*no clear evidence* that the campaign had a significant impact on the decision-making process of individuals" (Lee, 1971b).

Evaluating the Army's Bonus, Enlistment Option, and Recruiting Programs

Between 1971 and 1973, the Army initiated a number of bonus programs and enlistment options—unit of choice, stabilized tours at preferred geographic locations, and guaranteed military occupational specialties in the combat arms (later to be extended to noncombat career fields). The service also moved to broaden person-to-person contact by providing recruiters with *canvassers*—soldiers from the unit-of-choice units who helped recruiters enlist prospects for the canvasser's own unit—and *recruiter assistants*—recent graduates of Advanced Individual Training (AIT) who were temporarily sent back to their hometown to help recruiters locate new prospects.

The Army asked the General Research Corporation (GRC), successor to the Research Analysis Corporation (RAC), its former federal contract research center (FCRC), to help monitor monthly enlistment trends and the effects that various programs—bonus, recruiting options, and recruiter resources—had on enlistments. David Grissmer led the GRC team, a physicist turned economist and a person who would become one of the most prolific military manpower researchers over the next 30 years.[13]

Monitoring Monthly Enlistments

Each month, Grissmer and his team prepared an assessment of how "[m]onthly enlistments . . . related to annual requirements and to present enlistment trends" for the Office of the Assistant Secretary of the Army (Manpower and Reserve Affairs) (Grissmer et al., 1974, p. 25). Table 7.3 shows a typical display used to keep Army leaders appraised of projected annual shortfalls and trends in monthly data. Grissmer noted, however, that there were "major variables" that were not in this monthly analysis. The Army asked GRC to do retrospective studies of its bonus programs and of the program to place recruiter assistants and canvassers at a select number of recruiting main stations. Grissmer recalled that, "given the Army's focus on monitoring the program month to month, they did not try these new programs as controlled experiments. Data was collected by the Army Recruiting Command and sent to GRC and regression analysis techniques were applied to these data" (Grissmer, 2002).

Assessment of the Bonus Programs

The Army initiated two bonus programs to complement the nonpecuniary programs: guaranteed unit of choice and guaranteed military occupational specialty. With approval from Congress in May 1972 and programs beginning in June 1972, the Army and Marine Corps were authorized to give a $1,500 enlistment bonus in return for a four-year enlistment in one of the combat arms: infantry, artillery, or armor. The bonus was awarded "upon successful completion of the man's training into his combat arms skill" (Grissmer et al., 1974, p. 314). Timing was critical because the program was implemented at about the same time that several others focusing on combat arms were expanded to include noncombat skills.[14]

---

[13] In July 1977, Grissmer left GRC and moved to RAND, where he took on the job of Deputy Director of Defense Manpower Research Center in Washington.

[14] The special unit enlistment option started in January 1, 1972. It provided the "same basic features (selection of unit, stabilized 16-month tour, and choice of most non-combat MOS [military occupational specialties]) . . . in two CONUS units . . . and by 1 August 1972 had been expanded to 33 CONUS organizations" (Grissmer et al., 1973, p. 3).

Table 7.3
Monitoring and Projections of Monthly Enlistments,
Category I–III Non–High School Graduates

Month	Suggested Requirement	Actual	Difference	Seasonal	Seasonally Adjusted	Average	Projection
Jul	5,730	2,880	−2,850	0.925	3,110		
Aug	6,300	4,720	−1,580	1.017	4,640		
Sep	6,920	5,670	−1,250	1.117	5,080		
Oct	6,160	6,380	+220	0.995	6,410		
Nov	5,970	6,840	+870	0.965	7,090	6,750[a]	
Dec	5,650			0.912			6,160
Jan	8,020			1.295			8,740
Feb	6,830			1.103			7,450
Mar	6,160			0.995			6,720
Apr	5,310			0.858			5,790
May	4,880			0.789			5,330
June	6,370			1.029			6,950
Total	74,300[b]	26,490	−4,590	12.000	26,330		47,140

SOURCE: Grissmer et al. (1974, p. 30).

NOTE: Current projected Category I–IV non–high school graduate total based on present programs: 73,500/1 − 0.187 = 94,800[b]. Requirement is 90,000; surplus is 400.

[a]Average is taken from October through November data only since July through September still reflects effects of 70 percent high school policy.

[b]Assumes non–high school graduates will be 18.7 percent Category IV to balance current 19.3 percent Category IV of high school graduates.

In addition, during 1971 and the first part of 1972, advertising themes centered around the combat arms, and "analysis of combat arms enlistments during this time period showed advertising to be the second major factor in increasing combat arms enlistment during this period" (Grissmer et al., 1974, p. 327). Using regression analysis, Grissmer was able to determine "the effect of the bonus was to reduce what might have possibly been a precipitous 50 percent decline in combat arms enlistments as emphasis and options were changed to other skills to a 20 percent decline" (Grissmer et al., 1974, p. 329). This was confirmed through the analysis of survey responses from recruits in process at several Armed Forces Entry and Examining Stations (AFEES). The survey showed that "17.4 percent . . . of those expecting to receive the bonus would not have enlisted if the bonus had not been available" (Grissmer et al., 1974, p. 319). One feature of the bonus—the requirement to serve four years—proved particularly important over time. Grissmer noted that

> the bonus also reduced the future requirements for combat arms enlistments because of the additional fourth year of commitment made by combat arms bonus enlistees. . . . A measure of this effect would be the number of additional man years of commitment due to the presence of the bonus. (Grissmer et al., 1974, p. 315)

A $2,500 bonus in place during May and June 1973 had a more pronounced positive effect on enlistments into the combat arms. Given the push for "quality," the recipient had to have a high school diploma to receive this bonus. Again, the analysis was performed using both monthly data supplied to GRC by the Army Recruiting Command and AFEES survey responses. Grissmer found that, over the 60-day period the bonus was in effect,

> high school graduate volunteer[s] . . . [increased] by an estimated 1750 over the projected number of enlistees with the old $1500 bonus policy. If the $2500 bonus policy implemented in May and June [1973] were continued for an entire year, the estimated additional enlistees would be 10,700 high school graduate volunteers. (Grissmer et al., 1974, p. 281)

Moreover, he found that the "[t]he additional volunteers who entered the Army as a result of the bonus appear to be primarily people who would not have entered the Service at all as opposed to people who would have entered another Service" (Grissmer et al., 1974, p. 281).

Recruiting Resources

GRC was also asked to evaluate the Army's unit canvasser and recruiter assistant programs in terms of their contributions to the Army recruiting effort and to evaluate their cost effectiveness relative to other programs designed to attract volunteers. Grissmer and his team performed a time series analysis using monthly data for 1970 to 1972. The company performed a number of linear regressions with different aggregations of recruiters "on volunteer enlistments and [the] number of each type of recruiter to determine the relationship between overall changes in volunteer enlistments and changes in each type of recruiter" (Grissmer et al., 1973, p. 7). Breaking out the three different types of recruiters—regular full-time recruiters, recruiter assistants, and canvassers—they showed marginal productivities of 0.84, 3.72, and 1.26 additional recruits per month, respectively. Grissmer et al. noted, however, that the high marginal productivity for the latter two groups might be explained by the fact that

> increases in unit canvassers and recruiter assistants occurred after the pay increase and thus these variables could be measuring part of the pay raise effect. . . . [T]he recruiter assistants and unit canvassers tended to be used in peak recruiting months and thus would absorb a part of the normal seasonal increase. (Grissmer et al., 1973, p. 12)

These problems were not present in the cross-sectional analysis. The cross-sectional data were corrected for reasonable variation and

> appear to indicate that the addition of a unit canvasser or recruiter assistant would be much more effective than the addition of a USAREC [U.S. Army Recruiting Command] recruiter toward increasing NPS [non–prior service] enlistments for each time period. (Grissmer et al., 1973, p. 20)

Two of the researchers' more interesting studies involved pairing similar recruiting main stations, evaluating their performance and following canvassers from a specific unit. Figure 7.1 shows the change in enlistments and the change in canvassers and recruiter assistants.

In most cases, there was a dramatic increase in accessions as canvassers and recruiter assistants increased. The influence canvassers had on accessions for their units was even more dramatic. Grissmer followed the unit canvassers from the 9th Infantry Division, noting the "accessions into that unit and the canvassers assigned by that unit, at each RMS on a monthly basis." As shown in Figure 7.2, "the greater the number of canvassers from a given unit at a RMS [recruiting main station], the greater the number of . . . recruits for that unit" (Grissmer et al., 1973, p. 8). Finally, Grissmer cautioned, "the actual . . . mix of . . . recruiter[s] cannot be determined precisely in this study" (Grissmer et al., 1973, p. xiv). It certainly is evocative to note the higher marginal productivity of canvassers and recruiter assistants. An additional recruiter at the margin seems to be less productive and certainly less cost-effective than augmenting the existing recruiter workforce with canvassers and assistants. However, recruiters have other attributes that are critical to the recruiting process. Their knowledge and training allow them to counsel the enlistee as to the various options available, judge the qualifications of the enlistee for Army service and carry out the actual enlistment procedure.

Figure 7.1
Enlistments and Canvassers and Recruiter Assistants

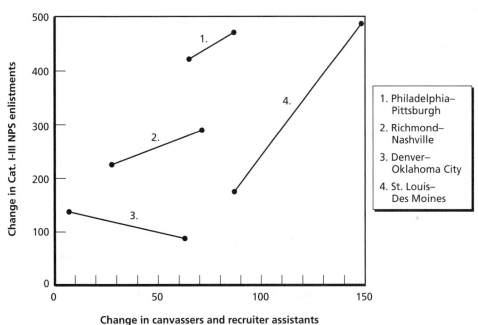

SOURCE: Grissmer et al. (1973, p. 28).
NOTE: 2.0 additional Cat. I–III enlistments per canvasser/assistant per month.
RAND *MG265-7.1*

Figure 7.2
9th Infantry Division Canvassers and Accessions for Selected RMS

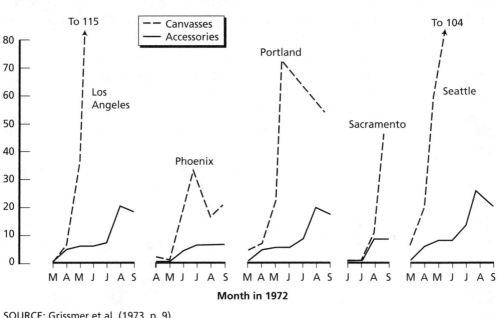

SOURCE: Grissmer et al. (1973, p. 9).
RAND MG265-7.2

Cost-Effectiveness of Alternative Programs

One of the most useful comparisons Grissmer was able to make was the relative cost-effectiveness of a variety of Army programs designed to increase the number of recruits. Using the standard of "additional category I–III volunteers per $1 million," they showed that on average and at the margin, recruiter assistants and canvassers produced 1,100 (plus or minus 320) per $1 million. At the low end, the military pay raise produced only an additional 20 (plus or minus 7) new recruits. Table 7.4 shows the relative cost-effectiveness of several programs the Army used during the transition period.

Grissmer's work was important for several reasons. First, it showed the leadership of the Army that analysis could provide decisionmakers with the information necessary to help manage the recruiting process. While such an analysis would not be a controlled experiment, careful collection and analysis of nonexperimental data could provide valuable insights. Second, this work demonstrated the extent to which nonpecuniary recruiting options could affect the number of people recruited. Clearly, it was possible to raise wages and to "buy" additional recruits through either across-the-board pay changes or specific targeted bonus programs. In fact, in a companion report, Grissmer argued that, "of all programs measured, military pay raises for incoming enlistees is the least cost effective method of attracting additional volunteers" (Grissmer et al., 1974, p. xix).

The success of this program demonstrated that changes in the way the Army goes about recruiting could have the same results as pay raises. In fact, changes in the inter-

Table 7.4
Cost-Effectiveness Measures for Different Army Programs

Program	Additional Category I–III Volunteers per $1 million
Recruiter assistants and canvassers	1,100 ± 320
Print media advertisements	1,200 ± 500
All recruiters	450 ± 200
$2,500 bonus of skill areas to high school graduates	150 ± 45
Paid radio and TV advertisements[a]	150 ± 90
$1,500 bonus to non–high school graduates	110 ± 50
Military pay raise	20 ± 7

SOURCE: Grissmer et al. (1974, p. xvi).

[a]Based on paid campaign of March–June 1971.

nal composition of the recruiter force, with a mix of less-expensive canvassers and recruiter assistants complementing an existing force of professional recruiters, resulted in a cost-effective alternative to pay raises, bonuses, and even the assignment of additional professional recruiters. This study showed that the challenge was better management of the recruiting process.

The Air Force's Saber Volunteer

The Saber Volunteer study was the Air Staff's effort to assess the feasibility of the all-volunteer force for the Air Force. While the Gates Commission, and before it the 1964 Pentagon Draft Study, had addressed these issues, Saber Volunteer came at a particularly advantageous time, when the new lottery data provided, for the first time, a direct way to determine the true volunteer rate and a way to monitor the transition to an all-volunteer force as draft calls were reduced. Up to this point, analysts had relied on responses to survey questions or had constructed "draft pressure" variables in multivariate regression studies to determine how the draft affected enlistments.

Lottery data enabled the Saber Volunteer team to determine the number of volunteers by age, education, and mental quality group. The Air Staff constructed tables and drew graphs that showed the volunteer rates for each military service. The staff found that, of the 463,000 new enlistees between the age of 17 and 22, a little over 39 percent were "true volunteers"; 32 percent volunteered as a result of the draft; and 28 percent were draftees. Unexceptionally, they found that the Army "receive[d] the largest fraction of 'true' volunteers," with the Air Force receiving the smallest (Johnson, 1971b, p. 38). However, some 54 percent of these Air Force accessions were "true" volunteers.

The Saber Volunteer team also looked at the changing demographics of American youth. Would the "task of all-volunteer . . . recruiter[s] . . . be lightened thanks to the population growth" (Johnson, 1971b, p. 66)? The team's answer, based on an analysis of future 17- to 22-year-old cohorts adjusted for their availability to the military, was that

> there appears to be an adequate number of youths. The Department of Defense must be prepared to be an eager competitor when it recruits in the civilian market place males qualified and available for military service, but there is not an over-abundance of personnel. (Johnson, 1972, p. 53)

With regard to wages, the Saber Volunteer team found that "DoD pay levels are reasonably competitive for the very young worker (ages 14–19)" but that, for older workers, who have a lower propensity to volunteer, "military pay prospects do not appear to be attractive to the youth who compares his Service pay proposal with that of his peers in the civilian sector" (Johnson, 1971a, p. 27). The team did argue that "the pay adjustments made possible by Public Law 92-129 [the all-volunteer force pay raise] appear to be a solid step towards comparability between military and civilian wages" (Johnson, 1971b, p. 91).

Special Pays and the Second Quadrennial Review of Military Compensation

In early 1972, with the report of the Second Quadrennial Review of Military Compensation (QRMC) in hand, Laird became convinced that the funds set aside for a second entry-level pay increase should go to solve "special manning problems" (Lee and Parker, 1977, p. 203). The Pentagon recruited Stephen Herbits, a former member of the Gates Commission and a staffer on the Hill, to help persuade Senator Allott to allow the earmarked funds to be used selectively, rather than across the board, and for more than entry-level compensation. Herbits was successful, and that spring, a new proposal was sent forward as the Special Pay Act of 1972.

The final report of the second QRMC was published in December 1971. The QRMC had been chartered by Congress to report on "the effectiveness of . . . [the all-volunteer force pay raise] in increasing the number of volunteers enlisting for active duty in the Armed Forces of the United States" (U.S. Department of Defense, 1971, p. 5). The QRMC staff noted that,

> with the imminent discontinuation of the draft, and with the continuing need for service members with special qualifications, the concomitant flexibility of special pays to attract and retain these members takes on new importance. (U.S. Department of Defense, 1971, p. 5)

The special pays considered covered a wide range of circumstances. Some were based on an individual being a member of a recognized occupation, e.g., health professionals; others on retaining specific skills obtained while serving in the military, e.g., flight and submarine duty pay; some on the conditions of a particular assignment, e.g., hostile fire pay; and still others reflected a more-general concern for attracting and retaining the right skills, e.g., enlistment and retention bonuses and incentive pay. Some were based on meeting the demands of the market place and others to afford "special recognition of the unusual sacrifices and hardships" (U.S. Department of Defense, 1971, p. 8).

While the analytic rigor of the second QRMC pales in comparison with that of the Gates Commission, it did provide a number of valuable insights useful for meeting the challenge of the all-volunteer force. Most important were the arguments against across-the-board reenlistment bonuses. They debunked the long-held arguments against using bonuses to address manning problems, e.g., that restricting payment of the reenlistment bonus to problem skills would cause morale problems. Relying on experience with the variable reenlistment bonus (VRB) that had been in place since 1965, the QRMC argued the following:

- The reenlistment rate in military skills not authorized to use the VRB did not decline.
- Experience gained with the VRB that is paid only in problem skills, reveals that the basic premise leading to the present reenlistment bonus law was faulty.
- The financial impact of continuing reenlistment bonus payments in overmanned skills to overcome minimal morale problems must be recognized.
- Retention problems among military skills do vary over time but the rate of change is small and a problem skill usually remains a problem skill for several years.
- It is true that a selective reenlistment bonus, authorized only in problem skills, would encourage individuals to retrain from non-bonus to bonus military skills. . . . However, this is a desirable rather than an undesirable result (U.S. Department of Defense, 1971, pp. IV.7–IV.8).

In a memorandum to the Secretary of Defense, the authors concluded that "[t]he most attractive way to provide a strong reenlistment incentive to first termers is through a variable reenlistment bonus" (U.S. Department of Defense, 1971, Appendix C). Extension of bonuses for reenlistment of medical personnel, of the Reserve Components, of critical skills not restricted to the combat arms, and the termination of the regular reenlistment bonus program that had been paid to anyone who reenlisted regardless of skill were all features of the proposed Special Pay Act of 1972.

References

Ackerman, D., W. Mason, H. Vollmer, A. Baker, and R. Davis, *Effectiveness of the Modern Volunteer Army Advertising Program,* Menlo Park, Calif.: MSU-1280, December 1971. S0297.pdf.

Albro, Ames S., Jr., "Civilian Substitution," in Gates Commission, ed., *Studies Prepared for the President's Commission on an All-Volunteer Armed Force,* Washington, D.C.: U.S. Government Printing Office, 1970, pp. I-5-1 to I-5-20. G1301.pdf.

Central All-Volunteer Force Task Force, *Civilian Substitution: A Report on Substitution of Civilians for Military Personnel in the Armed Forces,* Washington, D.C.: Office of the Assistant Secretary of Defense (M&RA), AD 764523, October 1972a. G1227.pdf.

———, *Qualitative Accession Requirements: A Report on the Qualitative Accession Needs of the Military Services,* Washington, D.C.: Office of the Assistant Secretary of Defense (M&RA), AD764511, November 1972b. G1226.pdf.

———, *Utilization of Military Women: A Report of Increased Utilization of Military Women, FYs 1973–1977,* Washington, D.C.: Office of the Assistant Secretary of Defense (M&RA), AD764510, December 1972c. S0026.pdf.

Enke, Stephen, "Possible Studies," memorandum to Robert E. Pursley, Washington, D.C., January 20, 1971a. G0641.pdf.

———, "Military Manpower Study," memorandum to Robert E. Pursley, Washington, D.C., January 22, 1971b. G0640.pdf.

———, "Study of Recruit Supply For Volunteer Armed Services," memorandum to Secretary of Defense, Washington, D.C., April 6, 1971c. G0654.pdf.

———, *Innovations for Achieving an AVAF,* Washington, D.C.: GE/TEMPO, December 15, 1971d. G0338.pdf.

Flynn, George Q., *Lewis B. Hershey, Mr. Selective Service,* Chapel Hill, N.C.: University of North Carolina Press, 1985.

Foreman, Robert C., Paid Radio and TV Advertising in Support of a Volunteer Army: A Historical View of the Essential Actions, Washington, D.C.: Industrial College of the Armed Forces, M7211, 1972. S0110.pdf.

Gates, Thomas S., Jr., The Report of the President's Commission on an All-Volunteer Armed Force, Washington, D.C., February 1970. S0243.pdf.

Greenberg, I. M., "Selection of Contractor for OSD Evaluation of Paid TV/Radio Advertising," memorandum for the record, Washington, D.C., April 2, 1971a. G0204.pdf.

———"Advertising Evaluation," memorandum to John W. Devens, Washington, D.C., June 21, 1971b. G0218.pdf.

———, *Audits & Surveys Briefings on 'Impact of the Army's Paid TV/Radio Advertising Campaign',* Washington, D.C.: Office of the Assistant Secretary of Defense (M&RA), August 16, 1971c. G0225.pdf.

Grissmer, David W., "Interview with Bernard Rostker," April 23, 2002.

Grissmer, David W., D. M. Amey, R. L. Arms, W. L. Clement, V. W. Hobson, J. D. Lanigan, W. S. Moore, G. P. Sica, and R. Szymanski, *An Evaluation of Army Manpower Accession Programs,* McLean, Va.: General Research Corporation, OADCR37, April 1974. S0350.pdf.

Grissmer, David W., V. W. Hobson, and R. W. Rae, *Evaluation of Recruiter Assistant and Unit Canvasser Recruiting Programs,* McLean, Va.: General Research Corporation, Operations Analysis Division, November 1973. S0348.pdf.

Haggstrom, Gus W., and Bernard D. Rostker, *Enlisted Strength in the Air Reserve Forces: Recent Trends,* Santa Monica, Calif.: RAND Corporation, WN-8200-PR, March 1973. S0001.pdf.

———, *An Analysis of Recruiter Productivity in the Air National Guard,* Santa Monica, Calif.: RAND Corporation, WN-8880-PR, October 1974. S0296.pdf.

Hoffman, F. S., and M. R. Fiorello, *The Evaluation of the Transition to a Volunteer Force,* Santa Monica, Calif.: RAND Corporation, WN-7720-SA, December 1971. S0306.pdf.

Johnson, John D., *Population Survey Data for Civilian Males Employed Year Around and Full-Time and Comparison of Earnings Survey Data for Civilian and Military Males (14–19 Year Olds and 20–24 Year Olds) for Ten Major Occupational Skill Areas (Saber Volunteer),* Vol. VI, Washington, D.C.: U.S. Air Force, Headquarters, Office for Special Studies, Assistant Chief of Staff, Studies and Analysis, 1971a.

———, *An Analysis of Problems Association with the Establishment of an All-Volunteer (Zero Draft) Force for the United States: Final Report (Saber Volunteer),* Washington, D.C.: U.S. Air Force, Headquarters, Office for Special Studies, Assistant Chief of Staff, Studies and Analysis, Final Report, December 1, 1971b. G1473.pdf.

———, "A Case in Point—Volunteerism in the Military," in U.S. Air Force, ed., *Proceedings of the Air Force–Industry Conference on the All-Volunteer (Zero-Draft) Force; May 4, 1972,* Washington, D.C.: U.S. Air Force, 1972.

Kelley, Roger T., "Replacement of Military Personnel with Civilians," memorandum to Deputy Secretary of Defense, Washington, D.C., February 26, 1971a. G0578.pdf.

———, "TV/Radio Advertising," memorandum to Secretaries of the Military Department, Washington, D.C., March 2, 1971b. G0199.pdf.

Kester, John G., "Army Test of Paid Radio and TV Advertising," memorandum to Paul Wollstadt, Washington, D.C., February 12, 1971. G0193.pdf.

Lee, Gus C., "OSD Evaluation of Army Advertising Campaign," memorandum to Mr. Wollstadt, Washington, D.C., March 1, 1971a. G0200.pdf.

———, "Audit and Surveys Report of Army Paid Radio/TV Advertising," memorandum to Roger Kelley, Washington, D.C., November 2, 1971b. G0114.pdf.

———, "Project Volunteer Problems," memorandum to Roger Kelley, Washington, D.C., December 6, 1971c. G0129.pdf.

———, "Evaluation of Army's Paid TV/Radio Advertising," memorandum to Roger Kelley, Washington, D.C., April 5, 1972. G0152.pdf.

Lee, Gus C., and Geoffrey Y. Parker, *Ending the Draft: The Story of the All Volunteer Force,* Washington, D.C.: Human Resources Research Organization, FR-PO-771, April 1977. S0242.pdf.

Tarr, Curtis W., *By the Numbers: The Reform of the Selective Service System 1970–1972,* Washington, D.C.: National Defense University Press, 1981.

U.S. Department of Defense, *Report of the 1971 Quadrennial Review of Military Compensation,* Washington, D.C.: Office of the Assistant Secretary of Defense (M&RA). G1474.pdf.

Vineberg, Robert, and Elaine N. Taylor, *Summary and Review of Studies of the VOLAR Experiment, 1971: Installation Reports for Forts Benning, Bragg, Carson and Ord, and HumRRO Permanent Party Studies,* Washington, D.C.: Human Resources Research Organization, May 1972. S0383.pdf.

Wollstadt, Paul, "Test of Paid TV/Radio Advertising," memorandum to Roger T. Kelley, Washington, D.C., December 3, 1970. G0195.pdf.

———, "OSD Evaluation of Army Recruiting Advertising Test," memorandum to Lieutenant General George I. Forsythe, Rear Admiral John G. Finneran, Major General John B. Kidd and Major General Earl E. Anderson, Washington, D.C., March 19, 1971. G0201.pdf.

CHAPTER EIGHT

Looking Toward the Future: A New Research Agenda (1969–1972)

> The Defense Department could benefit substantially from improved personnel data bases and research methodologies for designing and accessing alternative policies and programs to deal with the large number of complex manpower and related issues it now confronts or will soon face. . . . Its present research capabilities must be enhanced if it is to find constructive solutions for these difficult problems.
>
> —Task Force on Manpower Research
> Defense Science Board[1]

Introduction

Rigorous and sophisticated research is one of the hallmarks of the all-volunteer force. The questions being asked—Is it feasible to have an all-volunteer force in the middle of a war? What will it cost to introduce an all-volunteer force?—were unprecedented. Almost immediately, even before the Gates Commission reported its recommendations, DoD started to expand its research and analysis capabilities. When the "in-house" and traditional research communities initially proved inadequate to the challenge, the federally funded research centers became the major sources for analytic support. The story of how this came about, with examples of the some of the more-innovative research done for the Air Force National Guard and Air Force Reserves, is the subject of this chapter.

---

[1] From Ginzberg (1971).

Manpower Research in the Office of the Secretary of Defense

When the Gates Commission was chartered in 1969, manpower research was relatively new in the Office of the Secretary of Defense. As late as 1965, Secretary of Defense Robert McNamara noted

> the impressive magnitude of the Five Year Force Structure and Financial Programs for training and education, and the relative negligible funds being spent on innovation, research and development, and new methods and techniques. (OASD[M&RA] 1969, p. 1)

What was being spent was being spent by the services. The Manpower Management Planning Board, to be chaired by the Assistant Secretary of Defense (Manpower), was established on November 15, 1965. An initial research program was formed, starting in FY 1967, for "preparation of a long term program of personnel research" (Dudek, 1966). The major focuses of the board came to be Project 100,000 in 1966 and Project TRANSITION in 1968.[2] In 1970, another task of the board facilitated the study lead by Professor Eli Ginzberg in support of the all-volunteer force.[3]

The Defense Science Board's Report on Manpower Research and Management: The Ginzberg Task Force

In 1970, the Director of Defense Research and Engineering, to be proactive and supportive of the President's initiative to move to an all-volunteer force, established the *Task Force on Manpower Management of the Defense Science Board* "to determine high priority problems in the fields of manpower and personnel planning that the Armed Forces are likely to encounter; and to assess DoD research capabilities and policies" (Ginzberg, 1971, p. v). The distinguished labor economist Professor Eli Ginzberg of Columbia University headed the Task Force. In 1971, they published their landmark study, *Manpower Research and Management in Large Organizations.* The Task Force concluded that

> The Armed Services made important research contributions to manpower selection, classification, training and assignment during and shortly after World War II. Having established a high order of competence in these areas, their research staffs have continued to concentrate on these areas during the past 15 to 20 years so that these efforts are now yielding diminishing returns. This trend was reinforced by the following: the tendency of all researchers to keep working in the fields in which they have acquired specialized knowledge and competence; the relative ease with which

---

[2] Two important members of the Manpower staff who initially worked on Project 100,000 were Irv Greenberg and Eli Flyer. Greenberg had come from the Army in 1965. In 1966, Tom Morris asked that Flyer be "detailed" to his office (Morris, 1966). Also see Flyer (2002, p. 8).

[3] *Author's Note:* In early 1968, Ralph Canter replaced Edmund Dudek as Military Manpower Research Coordinator of the Manpower Management Planning Board (Fitt, 1968). I was the working group representative from Systems Analysis to the Planning Board and helped coordinate the Ginzberg Report.

these problems could be broken up into manageable pieces which lend themselves to experimental design for which approval and funding could be more readily secured; the relative ease with which the research could be conducted and publication credit earned by the principal investigator and his associates. (Ginzberg, 1971, p. 2)

The task force recommended a substantial increase in the manpower research budget for areas in which the "additional sums might profitably be expended" and suggested that "[a]s we move toward voluntary service the Office of the Secretary of Defense and the Services must be in a position to assess anew the validity of the personnel policies and practices on which they have for so long relied" (Ginzberg, 1971, p. 3). They argued for a new emphasis on "macro-studies with broad DoD policy implications" strengthening the leadership role of the OSD, more interchange between military and civilian research and more education of military leaders so they "can be more responsive to the potentialities of manpower research" (Ginzberg, 1971, pp. v–vi). Finally, the Task Force called for an expanded staff with "competence for manpower planning and policy studies" to support the Assistant Secretary in his decisionmaking responsibilities (Ginzberg, 1971, p. 5).

The Ginzberg task force not only commented on the need for more resources and a broader research agenda, it also opined about the organization of personnel research and the academic orientation of personnel researchers. They did not like the "R&D laboratory model" where "funding and control is exercised through the [weapon-system oriented] research and development component" (Ginzberg, 1971, p. 28). They argued that

> senior staff . . . had to . . . respect the fact that the primary mission of the laboratory is to contribute to basic research or to exploratory or advanced development. They did not feel at liberty to assign the laboratory staff to short-term study efforts that would detract from their long-range R&D efforts. (Ginzberg, 1971, pp. 28–29)

As a result, in reviewing the "best of the manpower research" submitted, they found the research to be "narrow in focus, carried out within a straitjacket of quantitative measurement, and [of] marginal impact on manpower management" (Ginzberg, 1971, p. 30).

In a series of comments that some might consider biased, if not self-serving given the academic background of the task force chair, the report spoke frankly about the people doing manpower and personnel research for DoD. While their comments might be considered intemperate for a professional report, they are part of the record and reflect the degree of hostility that had grown up between the several academic communities doing manpower and personnel research at the time. The task force found that

> Throughout the entire Department of Defense, psychologists account for by far the largest number of professional staff. Moreover, they are heavily concentrated within

a relatively narrow sub-sector of psychology; most of them have been trained as experimentalists, predominantly in learning theory and testing.

The professional research staffs do not have broad representation from within the entire field of psychology and they are conspicuously weak when it comes to the allied disciplines of economics, sociology, political science, organizational theory, operations research, computer science and manpower. A long-range program for strengthening military manpower research must give priority to broadening and strengthening the research personnel. (Ginzberg, 1971, p. 35)

Reaction by the Office of the Assistant Secretary of Defense (Manpower and Reserve Affairs)

Neither Kelley nor his senior staff shared Ginzberg's view of an expanded role for the Assistant Secretary of Defense (Manpower and Reserve Affairs) in the design and management of a revised manpower research program. Ralph Canter, Kelley's Director for Manpower Research, initially proposed "a research center directly under ASD(M&RA)." He admitted, however, that there were "inherent difficulties: decentralized policy efforts, civilian position reduction, ambiguity in the role of OASD(M&RA) growth of research activities not under the R&D structure, limited professional talent, and others" (Canter, 1971b).[4] Nothing came of Canter's proposal. An indication of why nothing came of it can be seen several years later in the response prepared by Brigadier General Robert Montague to a query by Rear Admiral Daniel Murphy, Secretary of Defense Richardson's military assistant, concerning why there had never been a positive response to the Ginzberg report. Montague told his boss, Lieutenant General Robert Taber, that the Ginzberg report was excellent, but noted, "Ginzberg's recommendations taken in detail are not very sound" (Montague, 1973a). In the memorandum Taber sent to Murphy in February 1973, he admitted that "manpower research has not been adequately funded nor have coordination procedures been entirely satisfactory" (Taber, 1973, pp. 1–2). Nevertheless, he argued that, while coordination had not been adequate, it was "not clear that centralization to the extent recommended [by Ginzberg] would be desirable" (Taber, 1973, p. 3).

Secretary of Defense Richardson was clearly not satisfied with the response Murphy had gotten. On April 11, 1973, a second memorandum was sent to Richardson, this time signed by Kelley himself. Kelley told Richardson that, "since I have not found our major manpower programs suffering because of insufficient or lack of timely research, I have not singled out our research program for special, priority attention" (Kelley, 1973a). He showed a uniquely nonbureaucratic sensitivity for the "efficient division of responsibility among Assistant Secretaries," explaining that the principal responsibility for managing research, including manpower research, was with the Director of Defense

---

[4] A distinction was always made between a *data center* and a *research center*, although at times the lines seem to be blurred. In 1972, Canter asked for a sole-source contract for the Human Resources Research Organization (HumRRO) as a data center (Canter, 1972a) (Canter, 1972b). Also see Flyer's account of HumRRO in Flyer (2002, p. 12).

Research and Engineering. Despite his office's previous response, he now declared that "the overall Defense manpower research program is being properly managed."

All well and good, but in fact the key managers on Kelley's staff, General Montague, his special assistant for all-volunteer force action, and General Taber, his principal deputy, were much more derisive of manpower research than can be read into the memorandum Kelley sent to Richardson. They told Kelley privately that, if he got "involved in . . . [the] lengthy effort to optimize manpower research activities within the DoD . . . i[t] would be a classic case of sub-optimization, which would not likely produce important results." In their opinion he "should not divert a great deal of additional management effort to the non-critical problem of manpower research" (Montague, 1973b). Their strategy for disposing of this issue is fully reflected in the memorandum Kelley signed and sent to Richardson. As they saw it, the memorandum they asked Kelley to sign and which he did sign was

> designed to convince the Secretary that DDR&E is doing its job, that we are adequately supported by manpower research, and that Service manpower research programs are not unnecessarily duplicative. (Montague, 1973b)

It is not known whether this finally convinced Richardson, but given his short tenure as Secretary of Defense, the issue was moot. In any event, when Bill Brehm replaced Kelley as the Assistant Secretary, one of his highest priorities was developing a manpower research capability for the manpower office. He would eventually establish the Defense Manpower Data Center as an in-house activity, and the Defense Manpower Research Center as an FFRDC at the RAND Corporation. Both centers were within the spirit of Ginzberg's recommendations. The difference Kelley had with the way Ginzberg approached research was the same one he had had with Gardiner Tucker and the Systems Analysis Office. Brehm, of course, had originally come to DoD to work in Systems Analysis and, with his appointment, the manpower office's approach to research changed fundamentally.

The Service's Personnel Laboratories and Research Programs

Lack of action by Assistant Secretary Kelley notwithstanding, each of the services and their respective personnel laboratories responded to the all-volunteer force, each in its own way. As the task force noted, the personnel laboratories had grown up in an era when the central issue was "selection and classification," not "attracting and retaining" personnel. In response to the challenge of this new world, some of the traditional manpower programs diversified and produced important studies that helped the services' transition to the all-volunteer force. Others were slower to act. This may partly be explained by Ginzberg's observation that many senior personnel managers did not recognize that the all-volunteer force required a new approach to manpower management, and therefore to research and analysis (Ginzberg, 1971, p. 57). For example, Kelley had an *ad hoc* approach to the transition to an all-volunteer force. It was not until he was pressured to create the Central All-Volunteer Task Force in January 1972 that he established an analytic staff dedicated to all-volunteer force issues, and then only a temporary staff, for one year.

Air Force Personnel Laboratory

One of the themes of the Ginzberg task force was how "the increasing sophistication of computer science" was opening up new possibilities for research to strengthen manpower management with "dynamic models for manpower analysis and management" (Ginzberg, 1971, p. 19). The task force praised the services for moving "more successfully to use computer-based systems for personnel management," but complained they had "made less use of them to date for forecasting, planning, and simulation for planning policy" (Ginzberg, 1971).[5] It singled out the importance of maintaining personnel records and complimented the Air Force for its repository of longitudinal records. The task force complained, however, that it was difficult to keep the repository up to date and "even more difficult to obtain the research funds to explore how these longitudinal files could be more fully exploited toward the end of better personnel management" (Ginzberg, 1971, p. 20).

In fact, the Air Force led DoD in this area. At a conference in May 1967, John Merck from the Air Force Personnel Research Laboratory explained the Air Force's program:

> In 1957 the Personnel Research Laboratory began the definition and construction of a personnel data system which would provide the kind of transition information to allow projections to be made. . . . By 1960 the progress of defining data records had been completed and we noted that what was needed was a chronologically oriented data file. It took about three years to construct such a file. By 1963 chronological personnel data files were in existence at the Personnel Research Laboratory. Since this file was created it turned out to be useful for very many things. What evolved out of it was a task which probably gives the Personnel Research Laboratory its major reason for existence. This is the Air Force Master Management Model. This is a model which projects the force ahead some years into the future. . . . (Durbin, 1967, pp. 2–3)

This type of data had proven extremely useful in studies even before the advent of the all-volunteer force but would be even more critical in the future. In 1969, Eli Flyer published an analysis of unsuitability discharges among Air Force accessions in 1956 (Flyer, 1969), in which he showed that high school graduation was a more important predictor of success in the Air Force than were mental test scores.[6] Clearly, the ability to work with large personnel files linked over time allowed this kind of research. In 1970, Flyer set up a departmentwide manpower and personnel information center. In 1973, this formally became the Manpower Analysis and Research Data Analysis Center

---

[5] For example, a discussion of personnel models for the Army by RAC is contained in Thomson (1975, p. 33).

[6] Note his earlier work as well (Flyer, 1963).

(MARDAC), which Flyer also headed. MARDAC would later become today's Defense Manpower Data Center.

Flyer's work on attrition, done at the Air Force Human Resources Laboratory, is particularly noteworthy.[7] The Air Force Human Resources Laboratory work on manpower and personnel issues, however, was not so well regarded, and the personnel functions of the laboratory were eventually closed.

Navy

The Navy's Office of Naval Research (ONR), the funding arm of its basic-science program, created an all-volunteer force screening mechanism in 1972. Wallace Sinaiko, who was recruited to support ONR's Psychological Sciences Division to help allocate funds to all-volunteer force projects, noted in his final report that "ONR expected the AVF project to fulfill its objectives and likely go out of business in one year but possibly extend to a second year" (Sinaiko, 1994, p. 4). His contract was extended 22 times and Sinaiko's Manpower Research and Development Committee did not go out of business until 1993. It should also be noted, however, that even when there was a movement to support the all-volunteer force, change could be illusory. In this case, while Sinaiko's committee was very visible to the research community, meeting almost 500 times and considering almost 1,000 proposals over its 23 years (Sinaiko, 1994, p. 5), the funds it was helping to allocate were never more than a small fraction of ONR's human-resources research budget. The vast majority of funds was not made available to the committee and was allocated in the traditional manner, supporting the same line of inquiry, at the same institutions that had done the work before the Navy had to cope with an all-volunteer force.[8]

At the advent of the all-volunteer force, the Navy had two in-house personnel laboratories. On the east coast, the Naval Personnel Research and Development Laboratory was engaged in occupational research and manpower development. On the west coast, the Naval Personnel and Training Research Laboratory had an emphasis on training. Both laboratories reported to the Personnel Research Division of the Bureau of Naval Personnel. In 1973, the east coast laboratory was moved to San Diego, and the entire operation was designated the Navy Personnel Research and Development Center (NPRDC). The center's emphasis was clearly on training and testing research, systems simulation, productivity and incentive measurement, and manpower and personnel data. The research was designed to develop

---

[7] Flyer had also been the driving force behind major data-collection efforts, particularly in creating a database of post-service earnings that would be very helpful in future studies of the supply of prior-service personnel for the reserve component.

[8] *Author's Note:* When I was Principal Deputy Assistant Secretary of the Navy for Manpower and Reserve Affairs (1977–1979) I was briefed a number of times on the Navy's human-resources research program, including the ONR program. It was clear from these briefings and the annual budget reviews that, through Sinaiko's committee, ONR was trying to support the research needs of those charged with managing the all-volunteer force, only a very small fraction of ONR's human resource research budget was "on the table."

the technology needed to improve the acquisition process; to design more effective training programs (at less cost); to optimize personnel management planning and compensation; to increase productivity; to improve morale; and to combat attrition that [was] weakening our operational forces. (Thomas et al., 1999, p. 5)

The center's emphasis was clearly reflected in its 1975 reassignment from the supervision of the Chief of Naval Personnel to that of the Chief of Naval Materiel. In a statement that ran counter to the recommendations of the Ginzberg Panel's report, the center's commanding officer at the time noted that there "seemed to be a great logic in having a scientific organization housed with our principal R&D scientific operations."[9]

Over time, the center would not completely lose its contact with the manpower and personnel community. In the late 1970s, it established "a studies and analysis group to provide analytic studies of a quick-response, short-term nature." The center provided a long series of products to help the Navy staff manage its personnel. Manpower researchers developed mathematical models to predict future personnel losses by occupation and to forecast the future availability of recruits. These models helped in the "distribution, assignment and rotation of personnel" through the Navy. In 1980, the center was assigned additional responsibilities for the "design, development and operation of the Navy personnel system" (Rowe, 1999, p. 5).

In the late 1980s, after the Office of the Chief of Naval Materiel was closed, its hardware-system acquisition functions were moved to the Naval Ocean Systems Command, and the remaining manpower, personnel, and training capabilities were returned to the supervision of the Chief of Naval Personnel. Finally, the center came full circle. In 1998, the training research function was moved to the Naval Air Warfare Center Training Systems Division in Orlando, Florida. And, in 1999, the remainder of the center was moved to Millington, Tennessee, and integrated into the renamed successor organization to the Bureau of Naval Personnel. Today, it is the Navy Personnel Research, Studies, and Technology Department of the Navy Personnel Command, and its technical director is an economist who came up through the force management–manpower side of the center.

Army

The Army Research Institute (ARI) saw its role as helping the Army overcome the most-negative aspects of the all-volunteer force. They viewed the environment of the 1970s as a force made up of "recruits who were socially and economically disadvantaged and who had lower mental abilities" (Zeidner and Drucker, 1983, p. 143) and an Army that was "modernizing its force and . . . formulating new concepts and systems for the Air Land battle 2000" (Zeidner and Drucker, 1983, p. 143). The "challenge," as they saw it, was "operating and maintaining advanced weapon systems to their fullest capability" (Zeidner and Drucker, 1983, p. 143). Army leaders, they believed,

---

[9] Statement by Captain James J. Clarkin in Thomas et al. (1999).

looked to ARI for research results in the following areas: developing new techniques for collective training in the field; performing "front-end analysis" and personnel affordability studies in systems acquisition; designing realistic ways of training while fighting; forging cohesive and committed units; and developing integrated leadership systems at all levels. (Zeidner and Drucker, 1983, p. 143)

ARI's view of the all-volunteer force started to change a little in 1979. In 1979, the soon-to-be head of the Army Recruiting Command, Major General Max Thurman, came to ARI looking for help in addressing the Army's recruiting problems. Thurman was a ferocious consumer of analysis.[10] The timing of Thurman's visit was fortuitous. The ARI leadership had recently changed, with the retirement of its long-serving head, Jay Uhlaner, and the new head, Joseph Zeidner, was eager to become more responsive. He structured ARI into five program areas: Structure and Equip the Force; Man the Force; Train the Force; Develop the Force; and Maintain the Force (Zeidner and Drucker, 1983, p. 156). It was clear that what the Army Chief of Staff, General Shy Meyer, called "the hollow Army" was a very important problem. Joyce Shields, the newly appointed head of the Personnel Utilization Technical Area, was given the job of responding to Thurman. Years later, she remembered calling General Thurman to announce, "I am ARI's answer to your problem" (Shields, 2004). She readily admitted that ARI had not engaged in the things Thurman needed help on, e.g., recruiting, advertising, and recruiter research, but she was willing to learn.

Thurman was also interested in the work that OSD and Congress had commissioned to better tie the entrance examinations and job requirements to documented job performance. As always, he took the broadest view. His job was not just to bring people into the Army, it was to bring the right people into the Army, and a better entrance test was vital. Thurman was eager to engage.[11] Over the next few years, ARI developed plans for and implemented the largest single human-resources research project in DoD history. Called Project A, it was DoD's central effort to meet the congressional mandate to tie the entrance examination and job requirements to performance. When Thurman left the Recruiting Command to become the Deputy Chief of Staff of the Army, ARI established the Manpower and Personnel Laboratory, assigned Shields to head it, and recruited a small group of economists to complement their traditional focus on psychology. As the leadership of ARI saw it, this "provided an economic research complement to the Man the Force research domain" (Zeidner and

---

[10] Besides ARI, he solicited help from RAND and the economics department at the U.S. Military Academy at West Point, resulting in the creation of its Office of Economics and Manpower Analysis.

[11] *Author's Note:* Shields remembers that Thurman started her "education" on recruiting in December 1979 with a trip to the Hoover-Rochester Conference on the All-Volunteer Force Conference at Stanford University, December 13 and 14, 1979 (Anderson, 1982). I also attended that conference, as did Charlie Moskos. It was at that conference that Moskos, looking out at a full house of economists who had been engaged with all-volunteer force issues for almost a decade, paraphrased the famous lines from the movie *Casablanca* and said that they had "rounded up the usual suspects." At least one present, Joyce Shields, was not in that group, but she and her colleagues had certainly been recruited into the cause of the all-volunteer force.

Drucker, 1983, p. 170). The new group was to carry out research in several areas: demographics, economic enlistment and reenlistment modeling, and manpower cost modeling (Zeidner and Drucker, 1983, p. 171). The group was disbanded in 1990, and the ARI budget was cut in half in 1997.

The Federal Contract Research Centers

The most sustained effort to build an analytic capability to support the transition to and management of the all-volunteer force came from the studies and analyses of the federal contract research centers (FCRCs).[12] The Ginzberg task force noted that,

> until the recent past, major military contractors such as RAND, IDA [the Institute for Defense Analyses], [and] CNA [the Center for Naval Analyses] have shown little interest in . . . manpower and manpower-related areas. Recently they have recognized the desirability of undertaking more research in this area. . . .
>
> [T]hese major defense research contractors have the clear advantage of an intimate knowledge of the Services, their problems, and their methods. . . . Hence for the long pull, we believe that it is sound policy for defense funding to facilitate the strengthening of the manpower research capabilities of these proven research establishments. (Ginzberg, 1971, p. 44)

The central role was also indicated when the Office of the Secretary of Defense sponsored a "two-day research coordination conference . . . [that] feature[d] researchers from the Services and the Federal Contact Research Centers" (Canter, 1971a).[13]

In fact, the FCRCs had been heavily engaged in the original work leading up to the Gates Commission's recommendations. IDA supported the original 1964 Pentagon draft study, as well as the Gates Commission. A number of the senior members of the Gates Commission staff came from the University of Rochester and CNA. RAND, with its expertise in Air Force issues, also supported the Gates Commission. RAC, the Army's FCRC, supported the Office of the Assistant Secretary of the Army for Manpower and Reserve Affairs during the transition. HumRRO, another Army FCRC, evaluated Project VOLAR and undertook Project DRAMA to conduct studies on accession patterns, medical standards, and enlistment incentives.[14]

Over time, however, the role of each of these institutions changed. IDA's leading manpower researchers moved on to other research institutions. By May 1972, Alan

---

[12] In later years, they would come to be called *federally funded research and development centers* (FFRDCs). During the transition to an all-volunteer force, both IDA and the Research Analysis Corporation (RAC) provided support to OSD, as indicated in Gus Lee's request for funds to support manpower studies (Lee, 1971).

[13] Canter had been selected in 1968 to be the Manpower Research Coordinator (ASD[PA], 1968).

[14] *Author's Note:* The official history of HumRRO described Lee and Parker's (Lee and Parker, 1977) history of the transition from the draft to the all-volunteer force as one "of the most significant documents to come out of project DRAMA" (Ramsberger, 2001, p. 72). This report has certainly been of great value to me in preparing book.

Fechter, who had worked on both the 1964 Pentagon study and the Gates Commission staff, had moved to the Urban Institute. Gary Nelson, another IDA economist who had also worked on the Gates Commission staff, would soon leave for RAND. Two of DoD's FCRCs ended their special relationships with the Army. HumRRO "delisted" as an Army FCRC in 1971,[15] and RAC did so in 1972.[16] David Grissmer, a leader of RAC's program, initially stayed with the General Research Corporation, the group that bought RAC. He would eventually find his way to RAND. CNA, however, continued its commitment to manpower research and remains a significant provider of manpower research to the Navy and Marine Corps, with a strong focus on issues of manpower supply, the setting of manpower requirements, and the "[i]ncentives, both monetary and non-monetary, [that] connect requirements and supply" (Lockman, 1987, p. 92).[17]

RAND

Over the years, a number of complementary manpower research programs were established at RAND, and it would become the single largest military manpower research organization of the kind recommended by the Ginzberg task force. Since the late 1960s, the Air Force has dedicated a portion of its research program at RAND to manpower, personnel, and training issues. In 1972, the Advanced Research Projects Agency (ARPA) established a Manpower Research Center at RAND. This center was later sponsored by the Assistant Secretary of Defense for Manpower and Reserve Affairs, and his successor, the Under Secretary of Defense for Personnel and Readiness. Today, it still exists as part of the RAND's National Defense Research Institute. In 1984, the Army reestablished its studies and analysis FFRDC at the California Institute of Technology's (Caltech's) Jet Propulsion Laboratory. It was called the Arroyo Center, after the street on which it was located in Pasadena, California. In 1985, when the Caltech faculty senate voted to disinvite the Arroyo Center—they felt that policy research was inconsistent with pure science, or so they said—the center moved across town to RAND. The manpower, personnel, and training program became the Arroyo Center's largest research unit.

RAND (1946–1972)

From its inception in 1946, the RAND Corporation followed a multidisciplinary approach to its staff and research. Early in its history, RAND made a major commitment

---

[15] HumRRO's relationship with the Army is detailed in Ramsberger (2001).

[16] RAC's relationship with the Army is detailed in Thomson (1975).

[17] In 1987, Bob Lockman provided a summary of CNA's manpower research keyed to the tenure of six Chief of Naval Operations. It shows the maturation of manpower issues from the pre–all-volunteer force days starting in 1963 to the stewardship of Admiral James Watkins in 1986 (see Lockman, 1987).

to the development of new training techniques. However, by the mid-1950s, with the spin-off of the Systems Development Division as the Systems Development Corporation, the majority of RAND's psychologists departed, and its commitment to manpower issues waned.[18] By the mid-1960s, a candid assessment admitted that "our present knowledge of Air Force manpower and personnel policies, practices and problems is extremely sketchy" (Durbin, 1966, p. 1).

Military manpower research made a comeback at RAND in the 1960s, with manpower requirement studies and research on the retention of Air Force personnel, the former conducted by a group of operations analysts, the latter by a group of economists. By the end of the decade, a "personnel section" was formed within the Logistics Department—later to become the Project RAND Manpower, Personnel and Training Program—with a research agenda that included manpower requirements, pilot training, and the information and data required to model the movement of people through large personnel systems. Support for the Gates Commission initially came from this group. In addition, several members of the same research staff were also funded by the Office of Economic Opportunity to address civilian labor-market issues and the role that information plays in job search and other sequential employment decisions (McCall, 1968b) (McCall, 1970). This research would find its way back into Air Force personnel studies several years later.

Finally, in 1969, Eugene Durbin, the Head of the Logistics Department, summarized RAND's focus on Air Force personnel issues this way:

> In a time of significant and continuing reduction in the Air Force budget, the manner in which manpower requirements are conceived and developed become quite important. Moreover, the personnel policies adopted to handle transition to a post–Southeast Asia environment affect not only the morale and effectiveness of the Air Force but also the state of the future Air Force. During such turbulent times Rand analysis of important personnel and manpower issues, and Rand assistance to Air Force personnel planners, can help maintain force effectiveness by extending the range of policy options available to the planner and increasing his knowledge of their implications. (Durbin, 1970, p. ii)

During this period—the late 1960s—research on issues of manpower requirements was subordinate to the broader issue of resource allocation.[19] To many, manpower was just another element of cost to be captured and considered when making trade-offs. For example, Gene Fisher, in the landmark book *Cost Consideration in Systems Analysis,* saw manpower requirements as *submodels* to estimate

---

[18] Dickson (1971) provides a history of RAND.

[19] For example, a RAND report on aircraft maintenance explains how its "manpower allocation model . . . takes a systems approach to manpower distribution, using the predicted demands along with manpower costs and effectiveness data to match a base's shop manning with its projected flying program" (Kiviat, 1967, p. iii).

requirements for operations and maintenance personnel as a function of the major equipment characteristics, system operating concepts, and the like. ... In many cases the personnel [costs are] ... very important because total systems cost is often very much a function of the number and type of manpower required to man the system. (Fisher, 1971, p. 175)

Early Personnel Studies at RAND

Complementing RAND's focus on manpower requirements were studies on the economics of personnel. Alain Enthoven, one of the contributors to the *Economics of Defense in the Nuclear Age* and later the Assistant Secretary of Defense for Systems Analysis, had written several "think pieces" in the mid-1950s (Enthoven, 1957), but little came of them. John McCall and Neil Wallace (McCall and Wallace, 1967a) published the first econometric studies of retention done at RAND for the Air Force in 1967. They were interested in the relationship between the investment the Air Force was making in training and the cost of retaining trained personnel through either bonuses or changes in pay. Working with data provided by Eli Flyer at the Air Force's Personnel Research Laboratory, they found "reenlistment rate[s] ... quite sensitive to differences between civilian and Air Force earnings opportunities" (McCall and Wallace, 1967b, p. 27). Later, McCall, with his colleague Glenn Gotz, would do groundbreaking work in this area of retention. McCall and colleague Eugene Durbin were also exploring the use of Markov chains as "simple yet satisfactory approximations to dynamic, probabilistic systems" (Durbin, 1968, p. v). In the late 1960s, John Merck and Kathleen Hall from the Air Force Personnel Research Laboratory joined them at RAND. Their work would be applied in a number of studies over the next decade.

Project RAND Support for the All-Volunteer Force

By 1969, the emphasis on manpower requirements was giving way to concern for the all-volunteer force; it had become the "dominant topic for Air Force personnel planning" (Durbin, 1970, p. 1). RAND was asked to analyze the potential supply of military recruits of "different qualities" and then to participate on the Gates Commission staff. By the end of September 1969, well before the Gates Commission finished its work, RAND reported on its study of the quality and quantity of new, active duty recruits the Air Force was likely to get without a draft to the Air Staff (Cook and White, 1969). RAND was able to reassure the Air Force leadership that

> the cost of a volunteer military may be far less than that postulated in previous DoD studies, and that the quality and quantity of recruits available to the Air Force in the post–Southeast Asia environment may be much greater than manpower planners previously estimated. (Durbin, 1970, p. iii)

It was noteworthy, however, that RAND's work covered only recruits for the regular, active duty Air Force. In 1970, the Air Force asked RAND to address the effects the all-volunteer force might have on the Air Reserve forces—the Air National Guard and the Air Force Reserve. At the time, well over 80 percent of all non–prior service airmen in the Air Reserve were thought to be "draft-induced."[20]

The ARPA Manpower Center at RAND

Motivated by the Ginzberg task force report, which was published in June 1971, and with the Project RAND Manpower, Personnel and Training Program as an example, DoD's Advanced Research Project Agency (ARPA) entered into a dialogue with RAND about establishing a manpower research center in Santa Monica. John White, then Director of the Air Force's Manpower, Personnel, and Training Research Program,[21] led RAND's team. In his presentation to ARPA, he argued that DoD's then-current military manpower research agenda had a number of "serious deficiencies." Echoing Ginzberg's findings, he proposed to ARPA a new center at RAND—"to establish and train a team of analysts in a single location"—that, according to (White, 1971b, pp. 2–3), would focus on

(a) macro-models of manpower flow (utilization) through the services to assess personnel policies
(b) manpower cost estimation and methodologies . . .
(c) . . . manpower requirements . . .
(d) strategies for the cost-effective development of human capital . . .
(e) exploration of civilian/military manpower management . . .
(f) quantitative analysis of factors . . . affecting the supply of manpower to the military services
(g) criteria for determining the appropriate civilian/military mix.

White proposed to recruit a staff that would include economists, cost analysts, operations researchers, and computer scientists and that would, he projected, be funded to support 33 professional man-years of work by 1975. Given that researchers at RAND are not assigned to a single research center or program and almost always work on more than one project at a time, the actual number of researchers working on ARPA-sponsored projects would be much greater.

In early 1972, a more-formal research agenda was presented to ARPA that was built around the paradigm of supply and demand. It committed the new center to a research agenda that, according to Moore (1972), focused on:

• determining manpower requirements
• attracting and retaining the desired quantity and quality of manpower

---

[20] A description of RAND's Air Force Manpower Program in the early 1970s is contained in White (1971a).

[21] *Author's Note:* Before the decade was out, White would be the Assistant Secretary of Defense (Manpower, Reserve Affairs and Logistics), a successor to Roger Kelley, and then the Deputy Director of the Office of Management and Budget. He would later serve as the Deputy Secretary of Defense.

- acquiring and developing skilled manpower—training management
- special studies of social issues.

In September 1972, the ARPA Manpower Research Center was established, paralleling the existing Project RAND Manpower, Personnel, and Training Program.[22]

Analytic Studies in Support of the Transition to the All-Volunteer Force

As noted, the Ginzberg task force saw a need for dynamic models for manpower analysis and management using longitudinal personnel records and highlighted the early work of the Air Force. In fact, these types of activities and modeling had been going on for a very long time.[23]

Early Studies of Personnel Planning

Personnel planning, as we know it today, can be traced to at least 1679, when the Secretary of the Admiralty started to regulate the annual entry of officers into the Royal Navy.[24] By 1779, the Royal Marines were managing career structures, retention rates, and promotion probabilities. The Navy List, a forerunner of the U.S. Navy's Linear List, dates to 1814 and is attributed to John Finlayson, who later became the first Government Actuary of Britain. The systematic collection of statistics that actuaries for the British Navy would find useful for personnel planning dates to this period and enabled the Admiralty to "focus attention on some of the dangerous characteristics of the officer structure in the 1820s—age-blocks leading to promotion stagnation, lack of enough suitable posts in which to gain experience, and so on." By the 1850s, the British Navy had "full fledged even-flow entry, training, appointment, promotion and retirement policies and management practices" (Smith, A. R., 1968, p. 258).

As in many areas, the American Navy followed the Royal Navy. By 1899, to overcome the worst features of the seniority system that characterized the American military,[25] the Navy introduced "plucking boards" to regulate the movement of officers through its personnel system by selecting out a prescribed number of officers each year. This was the first example of the "up-or-out" feature in the American military. Commander Roy C. Smith presented the simple mathematics of personnel planning

---

[22] *Author's Note*: Richard V. L. Cooper and I took over from John White when he was promoted to be a vice president at RAND. Rick headed the ARPA Manpower Center, and I took over the Air Force Manpower, Personnel and Training Program.

[23] A general discussion of human resource modeling can be found in Rostker (1997).

[24] A fuller discussion of early personnel planning is contained in A. R. Smith (1968).

[25] A more-complete discussion of military officer personnel management in America can be found in Hayes (1978).

and up-or-out in his paper *Personnel and Promotion Reduced to its Simplest Term* (Smith, Roy C., 1906). Under the Navy Personnel Act of 1916, promotion boards were directed to select only those who were "best fitted" and established minimum and maximum time-in-grade standards to control the flow of personnel through the system. Our modern personnel systems, particularly for officers—the Defense Officers Personnel Management System—owes much of its form and structure to this pre–World War II Navy system.[26] In the 1970s, the Navy established a formal subspecialty in manpower management and a master's-level graduate program at the Naval Postgraduate School.[27]

The problem with modern personnel-planning systems is not the lack of conceptual planning models. It is the lack of will on the part of senior managers to make the sometimes unpopular short-term decisions to separate personnel from their service to maintain the long-term viability of the force—more on this point later, when examining the draw-down of the American military after the fall of the Soviet Union—and the commitment to collect and manage the mass of data required to "feed" these systems. Collecting the data, storing and archiving the data, and processing the data, which often means matching hundreds of thousands of personnel records to construct the transition probabilities that show how people move through the system, is expensive.

Modeling Personnel Systems as a Markovian Process

The movement of people through very large personnel systems, whether a military system or other "social system," can often be modeled as a Markovian process.[28] By mid-1967, John Merck and Kathleen Hall, who had moved from the Air Force Personnel Research Laboratory to RAND, produced a series of papers and computer models that provided both a theoretical and computational underpinning for the kind of forecasting, planning, and policy simulation that Ginzberg had suggested was needed. An early application of these techniques was the Air Reserve Personnel Study undertaken for the Deputy Chief of Staff for Personnel of the Air Force.

In their 1971 report, *A Markovian Flow Model: The Analysis of Movement in Large-Scale (Military) Personnel Systems* (Merck and Hall, 1971), Merck and Hall illustrated the basic elements of a Markovian system by considering the flow of Air Force pilots and navigators over time. They matched the Air Force Uniform Officer Record file for 1966 with the same file for 1967 to construct the transitional probabilities that a person with particular attributes would move from one state to another state. Figure 8.1 shows several of the tables and figures that best illustrate the type of information that Merck and Hall were able to develop by matching Air Force personnel records. This

---

[26] Early research at RAND on the up-or-out personnel system can be found in Rostker and Gotz (Rostker and Gotz, 1976) and Roy C. Smith (1906).

[27] A rigorous and comprehensive treatment of the mathematics of manpower planning can be found in Grinold and Marshall (1977).

[28] Durbin describes how manpower training programs can be viewed as Markov processes in Durbin (1968, p. v). Teacher mobility was also described as a Markov chain in Greenberg and McCall (1973). McCall proposed using Markovian chains to analyze poverty in McCall (1968a).

**Figure 8.1
Analysis of Movement in Large Personnel System: A Markovian Flow Model**

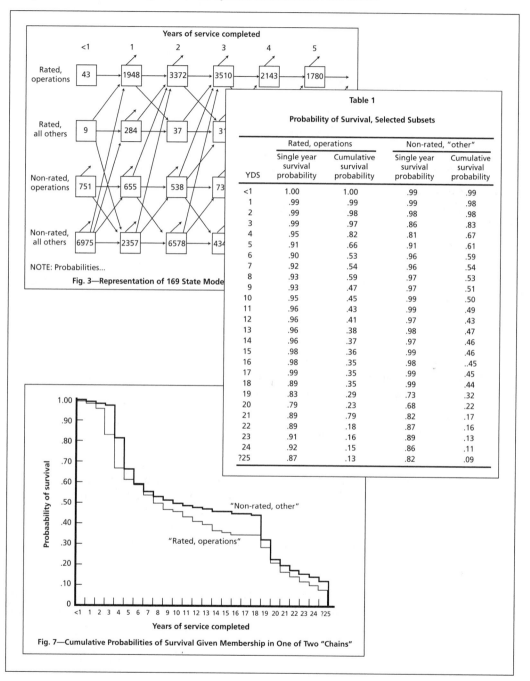

Years of service completed

	<1	1	2	3	4	5
Rated, operations	43	1948	3372	3510	2143	1780
Rated, all others	9	284	37	3		
Non-rated, operations	751	655	538	73		
Non-rated, all others	6975	2357	6578	434		

NOTE: Probabilities...

Fig. 3—Representation of 169 State Model

Table 1

Probability of Survival, Selected Subsets

	Rated, operations		Non-rated, "other"	
YDS	Single year survival probability	Cumulative survival probability	Single year survival probability	Cumulative survival probability
<1	1.00	1.00	.99	.99
1	.99	.99	.99	.98
2	.99	.98	.98	.98
3	.99	.97	.86	.83
4	.95	.82	.81	.67
5	.91	.66	.91	.61
6	.90	.53	.96	.59
7	.92	.54	.96	.54
8	.93	.59	.97	.53
9	.93	.47	.97	.51
10	.95	.45	.99	.50
11	.96	.43	.99	.49
12	.96	.41	.97	.43
13	.96	.38	.98	.47
14	.96	.37	.97	.46
15	.98	.36	.99	.46
16	.98	.35	.98	..45
17	.99	.35	.99	.45
18	.89	.35	.99	.44
19	.83	.29	.73	.32
20	.79	.23	.68	.22
21	.89	.79	.82	.17
22	.89	.18	.87	.16
23	.91	.16	.89	.13
24	.92	.15	.86	.11
?25	.87	.13	.82	.09

Probability of survival

| 1.00 | .90 | .80 | .70 | .60 | .50 | .40 | .30 | .20 | .10 | 0 |

"Non-rated, other"

"Rated, operations"

<1 1 2 3 4 5 6 7 8 9 10 11 12 13 14 15 16 17 18 19 20 21 22 23 24 ?25

Years of service completed

Fig. 7—Cumulative Probabilities of Survival Given Membership in One of Two "Chains"

SOURCE: Merck and Hall (1971).

RAND *MG265-8.1*

information is the mainstay of personnel planning models and was used in the Air Reserve Personnel Study to analyze the movement of people into and out of reserve units. It also provided the raw data used in econometric studies of reenlistment rates.

The Air Reserve Forces Personnel Study

One of the most troubling problems for the Gates Commission was how reserve components would fare under an all-volunteer force. To the exasperation of many in the military community, the commission seemed to beg the question when, in their final report, they argued that, despite survey results that showed that 75 percent of first-term personnel were in the reserves because of the draft, previous studies "significantly overstate[d] the magnitude of the problem" (Gates, 1970, p. 13). Noting that many of the draft-motivated volunteers who had joined the reserve to avoid service in Vietnam were older and better educated than the usual recruit, the commission suggested that "[i]f recruitment is focused on a younger, less well-educated group, the flow of volunteers will be substantially larger than is implied by the draft motivation of the present force" (Gates, 1970, p. 11). The commission did admit that it had no data from which to estimate how pay increases would affect reserve enlistments and that, beyond the recommended pay increase "[a]ny further steps should await the results of experience with higher pay during the next few years" (Gates, 1970, p. 117).

Needless to say, such recommendations and conclusions did not sit well with the military or those representing their interests in Washington. The Association of the United States Army took great exception with the commission's recommendations. In a formal white paper, they argued

> To assume that a modest increase in pay would permit the Reserve Forces to revert to voluntary enlistments flies directly in the face of all of our previous experience.
>
> If we are realistically to give any consideration to reverting only to volunteer enlistments as the only source of manpower for the Reserve Forces there are a whole host of actions, many of them costing considerable sums, that seem to us to be almost as essential as they are for the active establishment. (Association of the United States Army, 1970, p. 7)

It was not just the Army that was concerned about the draft and reserve forces. In 1970, the Deputy Chief of Staff for Personnel asked RAND to examine the likelihood that the two Air Force reserve components could be sustained after the draft ended. What developed over the next five years were a number of studies over a broad range of issues that helped inform and ultimately change the way the Air Force managed its reserve components. These studies quantified the movement of people into and out of the Air Reserve Forces, developed a formal theory of reserve force participation, and analyzed the potential for reserve accessions under a zero-draft system. A number of controlled experiments of recruiter assignment and recruiting options were developed, and recommendations were made on ways to change the personnel structure of the new, all-volunteer reserve forces.

Personnel Posture of the Air National Guard and the Air Force Reserve

What was clear from the start was that nothing was clear. The Air Force did not have even the most basic understanding of how personnel flowed into, out of, or among its component organizations. The Gates Commission had suspected that prior-service airmen were a good potential source of trained personnel for reserve components, but neither they nor the Air Force understood the size or characteristics of that potential source of personnel.

In the winter of 1971, in response to the tasking from the Air Staff, RAND matched almost one million airman records to quantify the flows of personnel during FY 1970. In July 1971, the analysis was briefed to the Air Force.[29] Figure 8.2, taken from that briefing, shows the movement of personnel into and out of the Air Reserve Forces in FY 1970. What is most striking is that, during this period, the active Air Force separated almost 105,000 airmen who were at the ends of their initial terms of

Figure 8.2
Air Reserve Forces: Major Personnel Flows FY 1970

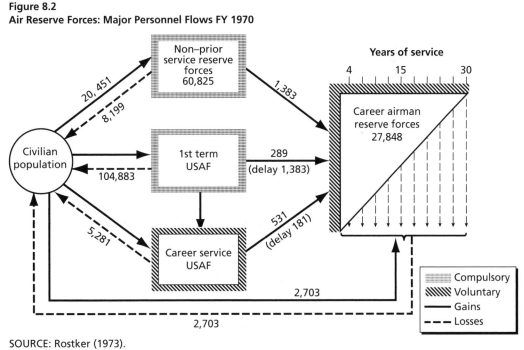

SOURCE: Rostker (1973).
RAND *MG265-8.2*

---

[29] The briefing was given in July 1971. It was documented in a working note in November 1971, and published as a report as part of the study's series in Rostker (1973).

obligated service. Yet, over the following two years, fewer than 700 of this group joined a reserve unit.[30] Moreover, of the almost 10,000 National Guard and Reserve airmen reaching their first-term reenlistment points, only 14.5 percent reenlisted. (See the Markovian flow chart at year of service 6 in Figure 8.3.)

The analysis also showed (Figure 8.4) how the draft had distorted the personnel profiles of the Air National Guard and the Air Force Reserve. For many, joining a reserve component was a way of avoiding service in Vietnam. As a result, even with a requirement to serve six years in a reserve unit, as opposed to two years on active duty, all reserve units had long waiting lists of eligible young men wanting to join. The reserves liked these new recruits because they often were college students, scored well on the AFQT, and were motivated to good behavior and participation under the threat of being called to active service. However, as seen in Figure 8.4, by the end of FY 1970, three-quarters of the Air Reserve Force personnel—73 percent of the Air National Guard and 75 percent of the Air Force Reserve—had six or fewer years of service. This compares with only 58 percent for the active Air Force. RAND projected that sustaining this force profile would take an average of 15,000 new, non–prior service recruits per year. An econometric analysis of the supply of reservists in a zero-draft environment suggested that no more than 4,000 might be willing to join.

Figure 8.3
Air Reserve Forces—Non–Prior Service Continuation

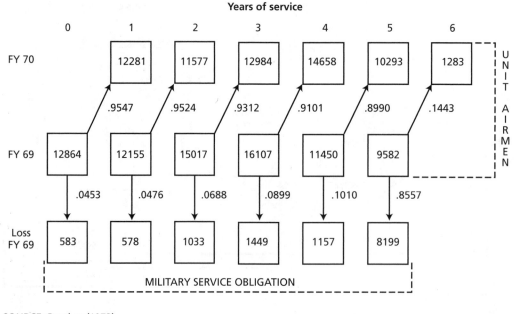

SOURCE: Rostker (1973).

RAND MG265-8.3

---

[30] Over the same period, the reserves also picked up a little over 300 from the career Air Force.

Figure 8.4
Air Force and Air Reserve Forces Personnel Profile, 30 June 1970

	Table 3								
	Airmen of the Regular and Reserve Air Force by Years of Service								
	Air Force[a]			Air National Guard[b]			Air Force Reserve[a]		
Years of Service	Total	Percent	Cumulative Percent[c]	Total	Percent	Cumulative Percent[c]	Total	Percent	Cumulative Percent[c]
0	68,733	10.4	10.4	9,230	12,1	12,1	7,849	20.5	20.5
1	104,904	15.9	26.3	10,354	13.5	25.6	3,808	10.0	30.5
2	79,304	12.0	38.3	8,669	11.3	36.9	3,011	7.9	38.4
3	87,909	13.3	51.6	8,524	11.1	48.0	4,745	12.4	50.8
4	20,462	3.1	54.7	9,795	12.8	60.0	5,130	13.4	64.2
5	12,292	1.8	56.5	9,218	12.0	72.8	4,099	10.7	74.9
6	12,906	1.9	58.4	1,605	2.1	74.9	761	2.0	76.9
7	13,189	2.0	60.4	1,249	1.6	76.5	555	1.5	78.4
8	13,636	2.0	62.4	918	1.2	77.7	528	1.4	79.8
9	13,921	2.1	64.5	877	1.1	78.8	496	1.3	81.1
10	11,666	1.7	66.2	945	1.2	80.0	413	1.1	92.2
11	10,218	1.5	67.7	891	1.2	81.2	488	1.3	83.5
12	10,545	1.6	69.3	901	1.2	92.4	526	1.4	84.9
13	13,985	2.1	71.4	1,085	1.4	83.8	492	1.3	86.2
14	16,598	2.5	73.9	1,124	1.5	85.3	589	1.5	87.7
15	28,675	4.3	78.2	1,266	1.7	87.0	689	1.8	89.5
16	21,909	3.3	81.5	1,545	2.0	89.0	649	1.7	91.2
17	23,348	3.5	85.0	1,539	2.0	91.0	602	1.6	92.8
18	33,005	5.0	90.0	1,178	1.5	92.5	558	1.5	94.3
19	26,193	3.9	93.9	1,026	1.3	93.8	413	1.1	95.4
20	6,675	1.0	94.9	941	1.2	95.0	300	.8	96.2
21	6,807	1.0	95.9	734	1.0	96.0	294	.8	97.0
22	6,436	.0	96.8	674	.9	96.3	224	.6	97.6
23	3,332	.5	97.3	398	.5	97.4	141	.4	98.0
24	2,897	.4	97.7	391	.5	97.9	112	.3	98.3
25	1,827	.2	97.9	374	.5	98.4	78	.2	98.5
26	1,670	.2	98.1	360	.5	98.9	56	.1	98.6
27	1,845	.2	98.3	269	.4	99.3	46	.1	98.7
28	1,267	.1	98.4	160	.2	99.5	22	.1	98.8
29	1,210	.1	98.5	69	.1	99.6	14	.0	98.8
30	--	--	--	33	.0	99.6	5	.0	98.9
>30	--	--	--	61	.1	99.7	9	.0	98.9
Unknown	--	--	--	102	.1	--	548	1.0	--
Total	657,363	100.0		76,505	100.0		38,249	100.0	

[a]As of 30 June 1970.
[b]As of 31 December 1970, reflects "good years for retirement."
[c]Cumulative percent will not add to 100.0 because of rounding.

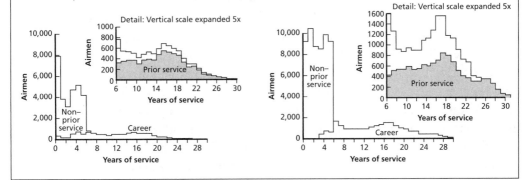

SOURCE: Rostker (1973).

RAND *MG265-8.4*

Estimating the Future Supply of Reservists Without a Draft

In May 1972, RAND briefed the Air Force Deputy Chief of Staff for Personnel on its initial estimates of the number of non–prior service personnel that the Air Force might attract to join the Air National Guard and the Air Force Reserve in the absence of a draft. Given the problems that were expected, considerable time was spent discussing alternatives (Rostker, 1972).

It was clear from the beginning that assessing how the draft affected the reserves was not a simple extension of prior studies. First, more young men were trying to join the reserves than there were positions available. Thus, direct measures of the "true" supply of new, non–prior service airmen were not possible. However, by analyzing the mechanism for rationing the available positions, RAND was able to measure the "true" supply for at least *a portion* of the eligible population. Specifically, in 1967, DoD established a rationing system based on age for "the assignment of applications to vacancies in units of the Ready Reserve." Within the non–prior service class of applicants, priority was given to applicants between the ages of 17 and 18-1/2. DoD Directive 1205.14 stated that older applicants who did not have prior military service could be enlisted only "after the unit commander concerned has determined that qualified applicants in high priority categories are not available" (as quoted in Rostker, 1974, p. 13). In 1968, the policy was revised. A second class of applicants was created, including those between 18-1/2 and 20 years of age, and given priority over applicants older than 20 years of age. Therefore, if stated policy was followed, members of the lowest-priority group or groups would only be allowed to join if the reserve units did not have qualified applicants from a higher-priority group or groups. Thus, the true supply of reservists whose age made them eligible for a high-priority group was revealed as the observed accessions of reservists from that group.[31]

Second, while Altman and Barro argued that draft-eligible individuals faced three options—remaining a civilian, becoming an officer, or being drafted—there was, in fact, a fourth option. A person could instead join a reserve unit, and thousands of draft eligible young men did just that. Countless more put their names on waiting lists, never to be called. RAND modeled reserve participation taking into account the differences between civilian and military incomes, incorporating both the subjective probabilities of being drafted and of having a reserve unit mobilized (Rostker, 1974, p. 5). RAND argued that reserve participation was similar to any moonlighting situation, except that the draft and the chance of reserve mobilization resulted in uncertainty in the calculation of the various expected wage rates. RAND showed that the net benefit of joining the reserves was equal to the expected money payment for participating in the Reserve program and the value of protecting expected future civilian income, since enlistment in the reserves precluded being drafted, less any potential loss of this advan-

---

[31] A more complete presentation of the model for non–prior service priority applicants can be found in Rostker (1974, pp. 27–29).

tage if the reservist thought there was some chance of being mobilized. Thus, "the institution of the draft," RAND noted, "has the effect of encouraging people to join the reserves" (Rostker, 1974, p. 7).

Given this formulation, it was not possible to assume that the regression coefficients in the traditional "reduced form" equation were the appropriate partial derivatives. Now, the partial derivative with respect to expected civilian pay included the probability of being drafted and the probability of being mobilized. RAND was able to estimate the partial derivatives, however, by assuming that, for the relevant priority age group (17- to 20-year-olds in 1968 and 1969), the cumulative probability of being drafted was one. Thus, given the Selective Service policy of draft vulnerability until age 26, young men ages 17 to 20 in 1968 and 1969 thought the draft would eventually catch up with them and that they would eventually be inducted. RAND also argued that given the Johnson administration's policy of not calling up reservists, the probability of mobilization was zero.

A further word on measuring the effects of the draft is in order. Many studies have used periodic draft calls as a real-time measure of immediate draft pressure. The larger the number of calls, it is assumed, the more young men would feel the pressure of the draft and act accordingly. In this case, however, such a measure may not be appropriate. Given the policies Selective Service followed, the priority age group did not face an immediate threat of induction. Moreover, given the priority accession scheme in place at the time, it was more likely that those who joined were loath to give up the opportunity of escaping the draft—with the possibility of being sent to Vietnam—regardless of any immediate fluctuation in draft calls. As a result, an early assessment of the effect of the draft on the supply of non–prior service personnel that was constructed in the usual manner was most certainly incorrect when it suggested that only 28 percent of young men in the priority accession age group in 1968 and 1969 were motivated to join reserve units because of the draft (Rostker, 1972, p. 22). A better measure of the effects of the draft comes from the lottery, and it suggests something very different. In 1970, the lottery provided draft-eligible young men with unambiguous information concerning the likelihood that they would be drafted. RAND estimated that using lottery data (as shown in Figure 8.5), 77 percent of the non–prior service accessions were draft motivated (Rostker, 1972, p. 22).

The resulting report to the Air Force showed that, during the draft period of the late 1960s, both higher reserve income and higher civilian income were positively, and significantly, associated with a greater number of reserve accessions. However, in a zero-draft environment, higher civilian earnings were no longer associated with higher reserve enlistments. This reinforces the notion that, during the draft period, participation in the reserves was a means of avoiding the military draft. Clearly, people with high civilian incomes had a lot more to lose if they were drafted than did people with low civilian incomes. RAND noted that this was consistent with research on the economics of moonlighting—namely that "the [moonlighting] supply curve is forward sloping with respect to the moonlighting wage rate . . . and backward bending with respect to primary earnings." (Rostker, 1974, p. 21)[32]

Figure 8.5
Effects of Information from the Lottery on Air Force Reserve Enlistments 1970

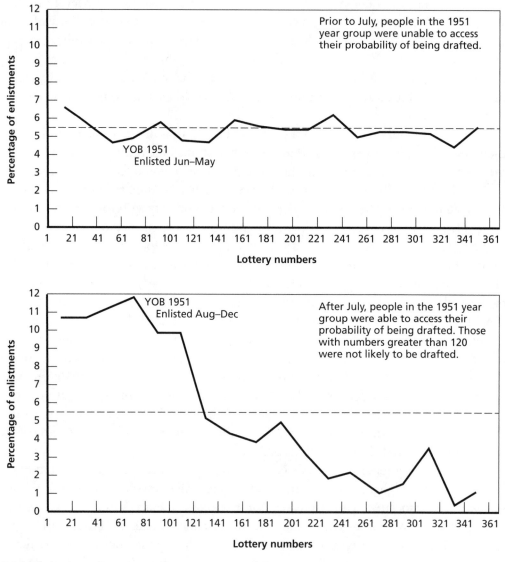

SOURCE: Rostker (1972, pp. 27–29).

RAND *MG265-8.5*

---

[32] The inner quote is from Rostker and Shishko (1973, p. 18).

Rostker, Bernard. *Air Reserve Personnel Study: Volume III. Total Force Planning, Personnel Costs and the Supply of New Reservists.* Santa Monica: RAND, R-1430-PR, 1974

II. The Economics of Reserve Force Participation

The Effects of the Draft

The analysis of the supply of reservists under the military draft is similar to any moonlighting situation except that the draft and the chance of reserve mobilization results in uncertainty in the calculation of the various expected wage rates.

Each individual may be viewed as facing three options: (1) enlisting in the military with earned income M; (2) entering the civilian labor force with expected earned income W; or (3) entering the civilian labor force and joining the reserves with expected total income T. The net income gain (R) from joining the reserves, which is the difference between T and W, can be shown under various assumptions about the probability of being drafted and the probability of the reserves being mobilized. For example, if we assume a single multiyear time period, and if π is the probability of being drafted and δ is the probability of reserve mobilization, then in the present zero draft and zero mobilization situation ($\pi = 0$, $\delta = 0$) the expected income consequence of various employment options is:

Case I $\pi = 0, \delta = 0$

Option	Expected Income
Joining the active military	$M = m$
Taking a civilian job	$W = w$
Taking a second reserve job	$T = w + r$

where m = military active duty money income,
w = civilian money income,
r = reserve money income.

The net gain from joining the reserves (R) is r.

If, as has been true through most of the post-war period, there is a positive probability of being drafted ($\pi > 0$) then:

Case II $\pi > 0, \delta = 0$

Option	Expected Income
Joining the active military	$M = m$
Taking a civilian job	$W = w(1 - \pi) + m\pi$
Taking a second reserve job	$T = w + r$

In this case the net gain from joining the reserves (R) is:

$$(w + r) - [w(1 - \pi) + m\pi] = r + \pi(w - m)$$

For completeness we should also consider that a reserve unit has the possibility of mobilization ($\delta > 0$). In that case

Case III $\pi > 0, \delta > 0$

Option	Expected Income
Joining the active military	$M = m$
Taking a civilian job	$W = w(1 - \pi) + m\pi$
Taking a second reserve job	$T = (w + r)(1 - \delta) + m\delta$

In this case the net gain from joining the reserves (R) is:

$$(1 - \delta)r + (\pi - \delta)(w - m)$$

In sum, the net benefit a person derives from joining the reserves is made up by (a) the money payment he gets from participating in the program (r), (b) the value from protecting his civilian income, since enlistment in the reserves precludes being drafted ($\pi[w - m]$), (c) an adjustment for the probability of reserve mobilization ($\delta[m - w - r]$).

In general, the institution of the draft has the effect of encouraging people to join the reserves. Presumably, people's behavior results from consideration of expected, rather than nominal values. Even though young men are not drafted directly into the reserves since w > m and $\pi > \delta$ in the late 1960s, in that period the presence of the draft resulted in w > W and R > r. An increase in w resulted in an increase in both W and R. In effect, the

Rostker, Bernard. *Air Reserve Personnel Study: Volume III. Total Force Planning, Personnel Costs and the Supply of New Reservists.* Santa Monica: RAND, R-1430-PR, 1974—continued

draft discounted the effect of civilian earnings and inflated the effect of reserve pay.

Estimating the Reserve Supply Curve

The effect of changes in the supply of military personnel with respect to changes in civilian and military incomes has generally been estimated using data generated in a period when there was a positive probability of being drafted. Characteristic of earlier studies of active duty enlistment is the following equation:

$$E = b_0 + b_1 r + b_2 w + b_3 \pi$$

E = enlistments/population.

Most studies assume that the effect of the draft is simply b_3 ($\partial E/\partial \pi$) and b_1 and b_2 ($\partial E/\partial r$ and $\partial E/\partial w$) are constant regardless of the level of π. However, it can be shown that, based upon the expected values as formulated above, $\partial E/\partial w$ is not invariant with respect to π. Therefore, the method used to analyze active duty enlistments would be inappropriate for analysis of reserve enlistments.

The relationship between π, $\partial E/\partial r$ and $\partial E/\partial w$ can be developed as follows: If the underlying reserve supply curve

$$(1) \qquad E = F(R, W)$$

where $R = (1 - \delta)r + (\pi - \delta)(w - m)$,
$\qquad W = w(1 - \pi) + m\pi$

can be approximated by

$$(2) \qquad E = a_0 + a_1 w + a_2 R$$

then $\partial E/\partial W$ and $\partial E/\partial R$ are independent of π. However

$$(3) \qquad \frac{\partial E}{\partial w} = \frac{\partial E}{\partial R}(\pi - \delta) + \frac{\partial E}{\partial W}(1 - \pi)$$

is not independent of π, while

$$(4) \qquad \frac{\partial E}{\partial r} = \frac{\partial E}{\partial R}(1 - \delta)$$

is independent of π. Moreover, if one can estimate $\overline{\partial E}/\partial r$ and $\overline{\partial E}/\partial w$ for some value of π ($= \pi_0$) and δ ($= \delta_0$) then one should be able to solve for $\hat{\partial E}/\partial r$ and $\hat{\partial E}/\partial w$ in a zero draft situation ($\pi = 0$).

For example, if we estimate

$$(5) \qquad E = b_0 + b_1 w + b_2 r$$

during a draft period when $\pi = \pi_0$ and $\delta = \delta_0$, then from (3) and (4)

$$(6) \quad b_1 = \frac{\overline{\partial E}}{\partial w} = \frac{\partial E}{\partial R}(\pi_0 - \delta_0) + \frac{\partial E}{\partial W}(1 - \pi_0)$$

$$(7) \qquad b_2 = \frac{\overline{\partial E}}{\partial r} = \frac{\partial E}{\partial R}(1 - \delta_0)$$

Solving for $\partial E/\partial R$ and $\partial E/\partial W$ in terms of $\overline{\partial E}/\partial w$ and $\overline{\partial E}/\partial r$,

$$(8) \qquad \frac{\partial E}{\partial R} = \frac{1}{1 - \delta_0}\left[\frac{\overline{\partial E}}{\partial r}\right]$$

$$(9) \qquad \frac{\partial E}{\partial W} = \frac{1}{1 - \pi_0}\left\{\frac{\overline{\partial E}}{\partial w} - \left[\frac{\overline{\partial E}}{\partial r}\left(\frac{\pi_0 - \delta_0}{1 - \delta_0}\right)\right]\right\}.$$

Then since $\partial E/\partial R$ and $\partial E/\partial W$ are independent of π and since we know $\overline{\partial E}/\partial r$ and $\overline{\partial E}/\partial w$ for $\pi = \pi_0$, then for $\pi = 0$

$$(10) \qquad \frac{\hat{\partial E}}{\partial r} = \frac{\partial E}{\partial R}(1 - \delta_0),$$

and substituting (8)

$$(11) \qquad \frac{\hat{\partial E}}{\partial r} = \frac{\overline{\partial E}}{\partial r}.$$

In addition, since

$$(12) \qquad \frac{\hat{\partial E}}{\partial w} = \left(\frac{\partial E}{\partial R} \times -\delta_0\right) + \frac{\partial E}{\partial W}$$

and substituting (8) and (9)

$$(13) \qquad \begin{aligned} \frac{\hat{\partial E}}{\partial w} = &-\frac{\overline{\partial E}}{\partial r} \times \frac{\delta_0}{1 - \delta_0} \\ &+ \frac{1}{1 - \pi_0}\left[\frac{\overline{\partial E}}{\partial w} - \left(\frac{\overline{\partial E}}{\partial r} \times \frac{\pi_0 - \delta_0}{1 - \delta_0}\right)\right]. \end{aligned}$$

> **Rostker, Bernard. *Air Reserve Personnel Study: Volume III. Total Force Planning, Personnel Costs and the Supply of New Reservists.* Santa Monica: RAND, R-1430-PR, 1974—continued**
>
> Or in terms of Eq. (5) for $\pi = 0$ however, for $\pi = 0$
>
> $$\frac{\partial E}{\partial w} = b_1 \quad \text{and} \quad \frac{\partial E}{\partial r} = b_2; \qquad\qquad \frac{\partial E}{\partial w} \neq b_1 \quad \text{and} \quad \frac{\partial E}{\partial r} = b_2.$$

Moonlighting as a Model for Reserve Participation

One of the most enduring and widely cited publications that came from the Air Reserve Personnel Study project dealt with the economics of secondary labor-market participation, or moonlighting.[33] Originally published as a report for the Air Force in 1973 (Rostker and Shishko, 1973),[34] a revised version was published in the *American Economic Review* in 1976 (Shishko and Rostker, 1976).[35] This study differed from *all other* studies done to support the transition to the all-volunteer force in that it did not estimate a reserve supply curve, or even incorporate military personnel data, and yet it has been cited as "the primary theoretical basis for most studies of Reserve labor supply" (Regets, 1989). The study used civilian data from the Income Dynamics Panel and Tobit econometric techniques to examine the major economic features of the secondary labor market, a market the Air Force participates in when it recruits men for part-time employment in the Air National Guard or the Air Force Reserve. The authors noted that, "[a]lthough specific results cannot be directly applied to the Air Reserve Forces . . . [their] report provided a benchmark" (Rostker and Shishko, 1973, p. iii). The results from the analysis suggest that

> [T]he supply of moonlighting labor increases with the moonlighting wage rate . . . and falls with primary job earnings . . . An increase in the moonlighting wage rate will increase the labor supplied by moonlighters and cause previous nonmoonlighters to enter the secondary market. To put this in quantitative terms . . . a 10 percent increase in the moonlighting wage rate results in moonlighters increasing their hours worked by 26.0 percent. . . . More importantly, unconditional expected moonlighting hours worked increase 17.7 percent while the probability of entering the secondary labor market increases by 9.6 percent.
>
> A given increase in first-job earnings will have a negative effect, as seen by the [negative sign] on the primary wage, primary hours, and [the] interaction terms. However, the magnitude of the change depends upon whether the increase was

---

[33] For example, Regets stated that "[t]he most theoretical, and most cited, [moonlighting study]. . . was Rostker and Shishko which considered participation in the Air Force Selected Reserve analogous to civilian moonlighting" (Regets, 1989).

[34] *Author's Note:* My co-author was Robert Shishko, a Yale-trained economist. Bob moved to the Jet Propulsion Laboratory and became a resident economist, working on the economics of the space shuttle program.

[35] Shishko extensively revised the econometrics based on comments from a reviewer. In recognition of this additional work, the order of names was reversed in the final version (see Shishko and Rostker, 1976).

affected by a change in the primary wage rate or by a change in hours worked on the primary job. The negative elasticity with respect to primary hours appears to be greater in absolute value than the negative elasticity with respect to primary wage[s], because a change in the latter affects only earnings but a change in the former also reduces the time available to moonlight. (Shishko and Rostker, 1976, p. 307)

Family size (a proxy for consumption) is significantly and positively related to moonlighting hours. Furthermore, as is consistent with the life-cycle consumption hypothesis, age, which can be considered an inverse proxy for unmet family needs, shows a significantly negative relationship to moonlighting hours (Shishko and Rostker, 1976, pp. 307–308).

Shishko, Robert, and Bernard Rostker. "The Economics of Multiple Job Holding." *American Economic Review* 66, no. 3 (June 1976): 298–308

A person holding two or more jobs is said to be moonlighting, or participating in a secondary labor market. This study investigates the determinants of the moonlighting supply function in terms of demographic and market factors and describes the relationship between primary and secondary employment.

Economic literature has treated moonlighting in two ways. First, there have been several attempts to extend traditional microeconomic theory to explain the individual moonlighter's supply curve. Second some researchers have presented demographic

Figure 1. Utility maximization in income and leisure with and without restricting hours worked on primary job

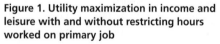

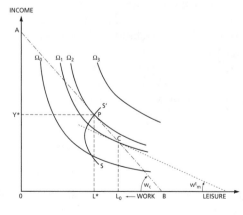

profiles of the typical moonlighter. To our knowledge, no one has combined these two approaches to estimate a moonlighting supply curve. In this paper we attempt to estimate the moonlighting supply curve with data from the Income Dynamics Panel (*IDP*) using the Tobit technique for estimating relationships with limited dependent variables.

I. The Economics of Moonlighting

Traditionally, an individual receives purchasing power, income, as payment for work. Time spent to obtain this income can be viewed as forgone leisure. In Figure 1, which shows a representative set of indifference curves indicating equal utility combinations of income an leisure, point *B* represents the maximum amount of leisure available per period. The slope of the line *AB* is the negative of the prevailing wage rate, i.e., the rate at which leisure can be traded for income in the labor market. If an individual is assumed to maximize utility, he will choose a contract such that the prevailing wage rate is equal to his marginal rate of substitution of leisure for income. Such a contract is point *P*, the point of tangency between the indifference curve Ω_2 and the wage line *AB*. The locus of all such tangency points *SS'*, i.e., the price expansion path, can easily be translated into the individual supply curve.

Shishko, Robert, and Bernard Rostker. "The Economics of Multiple Job Holding."
American Economic Review **66, no. 3 (June 1976): 298–308—continued**

A. Multiple Job Holding—A Geometric Treatment

An individual's willingness to take a second job depends on whether he can work enough hours at his prevailing primary wage rate to satisfy his income goals. Consider an individual whose primary job allows him to work only L_0 hours but who would like to work $L* - L_0$ additional hours. This restriction forces the individual to indifference curve Ω_1 at point C. Ignoring any additional costs of securing the second job, or any additional job-related costs (such as transportation), an individual will accept a second job as long as it pays a wage above the marginal rate of substitution of income for leisure at point C—the intersection of the primary wage line and the allowable hours on the first job.[4] If the wage rate on the second job lies between this minimum, $w^T m$, and the primary wage rate w_0, he will take a second job, and the total hours worked will be somewhat fewer than the number he desired to work on his first job. If the wage rate on the second job exceeds that on his first job, depending on his preference pattern, he may decide to work even more hours than he originally desired. Moreover, if there are no limits on the amount of time he can spend on the second job, he may even substitute it for his primary employment—as sometimes occurs when people make their avocation their vocation. However, the general character of second jobs often limits the number of hours that can be worked to less than "full time" (for example, seasonal work), or is contingent upon or complementary to the primary employment (for example, when a school teacher tutors students after class), or has an unacceptable uncertainty of income given the person's risk aversion. If an individual is completely free to deter-mine the number of hours he wants to work, at a high enough secondary wage he may develop a backward bending supply curve; and an increase in his secondary wage might result in a decrease in the number of hours worked.

Changes in the primary wage alter the minimum wage necessary to induce people to take a second job. In theory, an increase in the primary wage rate can result in an increase or a decrease in the minimum acceptable second-job wage rate. Moreover, an increase in the primary wage can increase or decrease the hours offered on the secondary labor market.

Just as a change in the primary wage rate affects both the reservation wage for moonlighting and the hours offered in the secondary labor market, so will a change in the primary job hours affect these two variables. An increase in the first-job hours L_0 can result in an increase or a decrease in the moonlighting reservation wage, though a large increase in L_0 will probably result in an increase in that wage. An increase in L_0 can result in an increase or a decrease in the moonlighting hours offered to the market, depending only on whether the moonlighting wage is greater or less than the primary job wage, and on whether leisure is a superior good. If the primary wage rate exceeds the moonlighting wage rate *and* leisure is a superior good, moonlighting hours offered will unambiguously decrease. If the primary wage rate equals the moonlighting wage rate, then the situation depicted in Figure 1 prevails, and moonlighting hours offered will be decreased on a one-for-one basis as primary hours increase. Only if the primary wage rate is less than the moonlighting wage rate could an increase in primary hours result in a increase in moonlighting hours offered.

Projections and Results: Overcoming Personnel Shortages

In 1972, RAND provided the Air Force with a range of projections. The most likely, and most pessimistic, suggested that the Air Reserve forces would only be able to recruit 40 percent of their non–prior service goal (Rostker, 1972, p. 37). In fact, after Secretary Laird announced the end of the draft on January 27, 1973, non–prior service accessions plummeted. During the third quarter of FY 1973, the Air Reserve Forces recruited 34 percent of their goal (an actual 1,064 out of a goal of 3,142). During the fourth quarter the numbers went down further to 17 percent of goal (an actual 628 out of a goal of 3,795) (Morgan et al., 1974).

Given the projections, which would prove prophetic, and armed with a better understanding of the basic economics of moonlighting, RAND made a number of suggestions to the Air Force on ways to cope with the all-volunteer force. These suggestions emphasized the productivity of prior-service personnel and how they might be utilized and recruited. Ongoing research at RAND suggested that non–prior service personnel contributed little to the maintenance capabilities of Air Reserve flying units and that, despite lower pay scales for non–prior service personnel, their direct costs were approximately equal to those for prior service personnel because of the larger initial training costs incurred (Morgan et al., 1974, p. viii).

First, RAND suggested that the Air Force consider the total manpower resources of both active duty and reserve forces when considering how to adjust to the new all-volunteer force. This led to the "Palace Chase" program. Next, RAND suggested a number of recruiting initiatives and ways to test their cost-effectiveness.

The "Palace Chase" Program

At RAND's request, the March 1971 Air Force Personnel Sample Survey included a set of questions directed to active Air Force personnel concerning their attitudes, knowledge, and intentions concerning participation in the Air National Guard or the Air Force Reserve. The survey showed that less than 5 percent of those nearing the ends of their terms of obligated active service intended to join a reserve unit. While RAND found evidence that pay increases might induce some increase in accessions, the levels being discussed would not likely produce enough new recruits to eliminate the problem.

The survey also revealed that there was "a large pool of regular enlisted men who were willing to trade time in [a reserve unit] for active duty time in the regular Air Force" (Rostker, 1972, p. 64), even if the trade was more than one for one, e.g., two or three years with a reserve unit for every year they could get out of serving. Responses to the survey questions suggested the Air Force would have a *net man-year gain* if active-duty airmen who wanted to leave early were allowed to do so on a two-for-one basis. The two-for-one trade was projected to produce a 900-percent increase in the number of prior-service personnel joining reserve units. The Air Force put this concept into action on July 1, 1973, calling the program "Palace Chase." Between July 1973 and February 1974, over 4,000 airmen took the Palace Chase option.

Recruiting Prior-Service Airmen

Surveys also pointed to the possibility that better recruiting might be cost-effective in meeting the demand for new personnel, both non–prior service and prior service. The survey suggested almost 70 percent of Air Force airmen on active duty who were nearing the ends of their obligated active service knew nothing about what the Air National Guard or the Air Force Reserve had to offer, and only about 10 percent said they had received information about reserve programs (Rostker, 1972, p. 70). Recruiting was clearly an untried and potentially productive way to proceed.

The Air National Guard Full-Time Recruiter Experiment

In August 1971, RAND was asked to assist the Air National Guard in evaluating its new full-time recruiter program. RAND proposed "an experimental design [that] phase[d] in the recruiters and advertising funds . . . over time in such a way as to permit reliable estimates of the effectiveness of the recruiters and advertising, both separately and jointly" (Haggstrom and Rostker, 1973, p. 6). The original plan called for a base period from September 1972 to June 1973 when no recruiters were to be assigned. However, due to the popularity of the program, units requested recruiters, and they were assigned without regard for the formal experimental design. (So much for experimental design discipline.) While this complicated the analysis, there was still a great deal of variation in the way the program was implemented, and much was learned by analyzing the resulting *nonexperimental* data.[36]

The program actually got started in July 1972, when the first two dedicated, full-time recruiters arrived at their unit. The first group of trained recruiters, those who had completed a four-week training program, began arriving at their units in December 1972. The distribution of recruiters, however, was not uniform, and the resulting variation produced a natural experiment that was analytically tractable. By January 1973, 89 recruiters were assigned, but only 25 percent had completed training. Most bases had one recruiter, but seven had more than one, and 26 bases still did not have any recruiters. By December 1973, over 184 recruiters were at work—72 percent having completed training. The majority of bases—87 percent—had more than one recruiter (Haggstrom and Rostker, 1974, p. 3).

The multivariate regression analysis of the Air National Guard full-time recruiter program showed that

> on average for the entire eighteen-month period, units with only one recruiter had only a slight increase in their enlistment rate, while those with two recruiters had a more pronounced increase. Units with three or more recruiters showed only a very small gain in the non–prior service enlistment rate, but a sizeable gain in prior

---

[36] A discussion of the Army's In-Service Recruiter Program can be found in Griffith (1997, p. 273).

service enlistments over units with only two recruiters. In total, recruiters seem to have a significant and positive effect on enlistment. . . .

The regression coefficients on the variables which indicate the amount of recruiter activity conducted by recruiters who had completed the special four-week training program were not significant. The results therefore do not support the hypothesis that recruiters who had completed training are able to outperform their untrained counterpart. (Haggstrom and Rostker, 1974, pp. 8–10)

The ultimate test of the recruiter program was how recruiters performed relative to the cost and effectiveness of other programs designed to attract new prior-service and non–prior service personnel. In this regard, recruiters appeared to do very well, especially when compared to the projected costs and effectiveness of a bonus program. RAND's assessment of the cost-effectiveness of recruiters versus a bonus program was that at equal costs, given the almost $2 million spent on recruiters, the "bonus program would be only about 11 percent as effective as an equal cost recruiter program. . . . [Thus,] the recruiter program appear[ed] to produce the same output as a bonus program costing almost 14 million dollars more" (Haggstrom and Rostker, 1974, pp. 13–14).

The Air Reserve Forces Variable Tour Length Experiment

Even as the Air National Guard recruiter experiment was getting under way in summer 1972, RAND was engaged in designing a second experiment. The second test was to determine whether "certain recruiting incentives can significantly increase the number of enlistments" (Haggstrom and Rostker, 1973). This was the first formal experiment designed to test an all-volunteer force program, and it represented an example of what the critics of the Project Volunteer Committee's approach to managing the all-volunteer force wanted.[37] Unlike the previous recruiter experiment, which was really an evaluation of an existing program, the variable-tour experiment was a true controlled experiment. A "treatment" was to be applied for a limited period of time, in a limited number of places, that had been carefully selected based on a research design.

At the time, the proponents at RAND argued there were at least three reasons to undertake a controlled experiment:

[T]he cost in dollars and resources may be so high that a service-wide implementation of certain recruiting efforts and incentives without a clear indication of the criteria would be unwise.

[I]f . . . instituted service-wide one important dimension of evaluation is lost. [A] failure to achieve desired results could lead to a major loss of organizational effectiveness. (Haggstrom and Rostker, 1973, pp. 3–4)

---

[37] Lee noted that "there was strong advocacy by ASD (Systems Analysis) and by members of the research community generally for a program approach of controlled experimentation." He argued, however, that the "advocates of the experimental approach sometimes ignored the real world." Lee and Parker (1977, p. 473) noted that the "ideal situation is described by a RAND study" (referring to Haggstrom, 1973).

In a more complete treatment on the subject of experimentation, Gus Haggstrom, a statistician at RAND who was instrumental in the design and evaluation of a number of experiments, considered the alternatives to experimentation—expert opinion, anecdotal evidence, sample surveys, analysis of nonexperimental data, simulation—and found that they could well complement experiments. He argued, however, that

> [a] well-designed pilot study [experiment] can test the relative effectiveness of several alternative proposals simultaneously. . . .
> In addition to providing more reliable information than one can usually acquire through alternative methods, a pilot study often uncovers some negative side effects that might not be foreseen before experimentation. (Haggstrom, 1973, pp. 4–5)

The variable-tour experiment began on June 1, 1973, to test whether reducing the term of enlistment for new recruits would substantially affect the propensity of young men to join National Guard and Air Force Reserve units. Unlike the regular Air Force, which generally enlisted personnel for four years of service, an enlistment with a reserve unit was for six years. Before the advent of the all-volunteer force, this did not seem to be much of a deterrent, as units had long waiting lists of young men ready to join. When the draft ended, so did the waiting lists. Many were concerned that the six-year tour of service was a significant disincentive. If they were right, a reduced commitment might *significantly* increase both the number of young men willing to join, and the total man-years this cohort would provide might increase. However, if the response was not substantial and only a few additional enlistments resulted, a shorter tour could result in a loss in total man-years served. Therefore, a test was conducted at a small number of bases where potential recruits could enlist for either three or four years, with the remainder of their six-year military service obligation being served in the Individual Ready Reserve.[38]

The initial results, which were presented to the Air Force in January 1974, showed that "the shortened enlistment options have had little effect upon recruiting performance in the Air Reserve Forces. . . . [A]dopting either option would result in a man-year loss" (Haggstrom and Rostker, 1974, pp. 6–8). RAND concluded that, on the whole,

> [units] that were recruiting well before the experiment began continued to do so during the experimental period, whether they had an experimental option to offer or not.
> In conclusion, implementing with the [3 year] or [4 year] option, in itself, would have little effect upon NPS recruiting in the short run and will lead to more serious manning problems later. (Haggstrom and Rostker, 1974, p. 10)

---

[38] Everyone who joined the military accepted a six-year "military service obligation." It could be met with a combination of service in the regular component or a reserve component. Some of the reserve time could be with a reserve unit, with up to the final two years being in the Individual Ready Reserve. Members of this reserve did not have to drill but were subject to recall in time of national emergency.

The Army Variable Tour Length Test

In spring 1973, all reserve components thought that the six-year enlistment was a disincentive. The Air Force, working with RAND, planned for a limited test. Based on a recommendation from General Montague (Special Assistant for All-Volunteer Force Action), Kelley required the Army Reserve Components to conduct a "similar" experiment in lieu of implementing a three-year enlistment across the board.[39] Since RAND was already monitoring the Air Force experiment, RAND was asked to also monitor the Army test (Haggstrom, 1975, p. 7). The test started on July 1, 1973, and was to last for 90 days. In late August, Herbits argued for an extension: "We know from RAND and our own data that we will know virtually nothing after three months" (Herbits, 1973). The test was extended until the end of the year.

Unlike the Air Force experiment, RAND did not design the Army program. In the judgment of the RAND monitor

> the experiment had certain shortcomings, both in design and execution, that not only made the experiment less informative than it could have been but jeopardized the credibility of the experimental results. (Haggstrom, 1975, p. 65)

This judgment was apparently shared by some in the Army who questioned if, "the ongoing test will . . . prove anything about the effectiveness of the . . . enlistment [options]."[40]

In his own assessment, Haggstrom noted a number of major flaws. He was critical of the design decision to offer the options "on such a wide scale and simultaneously" (Haggstrom, 1975, p. 67). He also argued that there was

> [a]nother serious flaw in the execution of the experiment was to permit the recruiting campaigns to confound the experiment. Each of the three groups should have received approximately the same level of recruiting effort, and the amount of recruiting activity in each campaign should have been monitored carefully. By conducting the intensive recruiting campaign primarily in the [3 year option] states, the Guard effectively destroyed the credibility of the experiment insofar as establishing the worth of the shorter enlistment options is concerned. (Haggstrom, 1975, p. 69)

---

[39] Montague told Kelley that

> the plans for test[ing] and later evaluating the test of shorter reserve enlistments should be fully reviewed before the test begins. The RAND plan covering the Air Force is good. An Army plan, worthy of the name, doesn't exist to my knowledge. (Montague, 1973c, p. 2)

Kelley was also concerned that there had been "minimal consideration of the adverse impact on mobilization readiness which may result from large numbers of short-term non–prior service enlistees" (Kelley, 1973b, p. 1).

[40] These are the comments of Colonel Robert S. Young, Chief of the Manpower Systems Division of the Office of the Assistant Secretary of the Army (M&RA), as quoted in Haggstrom (1975, p. 65).

Probably the greatest flaw was the mind set of the personnel managers in the Army and the Office of the Secretary of Defense who confused experimentation with inaction and who were so confident in their ability to understand the effects of a policy change in the absence of data that they risked implementing a potentially harmful policy. The Army's decision to load the new recruiting option on the states that were already doing poorly not only confounded the analysis, it was nothing short of reckless. As Haggstrom noted that

> [i]t was no secret that many Army recruiters and officials wanted to see the experiment confirm their claims that the three-year enlistment tour would increase NPS enlistments substantially, and many of them regarded the experiment as a nuisance to be barely tolerated. . . . (Haggstrom, 1975, p. 26)

Clearly this is a well-ingrained mindset. Two years *after* the RAND report, *The Variable Tour Experiment in the Army Reserve Components,* was published, the former Staff Director of the Project Volunteer Committee was still attacking the use of experimentation. On this subject, Lee wrote in 1977 that

> The advocates of the experimental approach sometimes ignored the real world. . . .
> It is true that experimental designs could have been adopted. . . . New programs could have been put into effect on a small scale . . . . The exact data needed for measurement could have been specified and provided in advance. . . . However, controlled conditions were not established to insure precise evaluations of these experiments; the emphasis was placed on getting results.
> [the Project Volunteer Committee did not want to wait] for the research and analytical community to give them answers on the basis of experimentation. Over a year of study and analysis had preceded the formulation of the programs. The committee decided to go ahead and try the programs, and then modify or drop them if they were not effective. The approach was oriented to action rather than to experiment in the research sense. (Lee and Parker, 1977, pp. 473–474)

In the case at hand, experimentation provided results and led to action. On December 31, 1973, with the experimental results in hand, the variable-tour experiment for reserve force units was suspended.[41] Haggstrom estimated that, in 1973 alone, by not implementing the options across the board, the Army and Air Force reserve components saved 14,000 man-years (Haggstrom, 1975, p. 73).

Lessons to Be Learned

RAND's initial assessment well illustrated the need for a carefully designed experiment. At the outset, everyone was convinced of the logic that tour length was a

---

[41] On April 1, 1974, OSD authorized the option limited to no more than 20 percent of accessions, and then only to applicants in the higher mental categories (Marris, 1974).

significant disincentive. In fact, the Army and Marine Corps were so convinced that they initiated a "large scale" program to shorten enlistments. The Army allowed all units in 38 states and the District of Columbia—76 percent of the country—to offer shortened enlistments. Moreover, Army officials freely admitted that their program put the states with the biggest shortfalls into the experimental group (Haggstrom, 1975, p. 7). The analysis indicated, however, that if these policies were adopted across the board, they would have made a bad situation worse. As it turned out, after "allowances" were made for a number of

> factors that tended to confound the experimental results, it appears that [for the Army National Guard] the [3-year] option resulted in a 20–40 percent increase in nonprior service enlistments during the experimental period, and the [4-year] option yielded a 10–30 percent increase. (Haggstrom, 1975, p. v)

This was not enough to offset future man-year losses. Little can be said about the Army Reserve since "the effects of the shorter enlistment options in the [Army Reserves] could not be analyzed as they were in the [Army National Guard] because of inadequate data" (Haggstrom, 1975, p. 70).

References

Anderson, Martin C., ed., *Registration and the Draft,* Stanford, Ca.: Hoover Institution Stanford University, 1982.

ASD[PA], "Dr. Ralph Canter Appointed Military Manpower Research Coordinator," news release, Washington, D.C., May 17, 1968. G0963.pdf.

Association of the United States Army, *Protecting the Free Society: An AUSA White Paper on Proposals for an All-Volunteer Armed Force,* Washington, D.C.: Association of the United States Army. S0081.pdf.

Canter, Ralph R., "Review of Econometric-Oriented Manpower Research in Relation to CY 1972–73 Program Needs," memorandum to Assistant Deputy Chiefs of Staff for Personnel, Washington, D.C., September 2, 1971a. G0230.pdf.

———, "Proposed Implementation Plans for the Recommendations of the Defense Science Board Task Force on Manpower Research—the Ginzberg Report," memorandum to General Taber, Washington, D.C., October 21, 1971b. G0237.pdf.

———, "FY73 Funding for the Department of Defense Manpower Data Analysis Center," memorandum to George Daoust, Washington, D.C., July 3, 1972a. G0723.pdf.

———, "Selected Source Procurement for a Contract Entitled 'Research Studies and Analyses on Procurement, Utilization, Performance, Retention, and Separation of Military Personnel'," memorandum to Defense Supply Service, Washington, D.C., July 3, 1972b. G0722.pdf.

Cook, Alvin A., Jr., and John P. White, *A Briefing to the Air Staff (AFPDP): The Supply of Air Force Recruits in a Post-Southeast Asia Environment,* Santa Monica, Calif.: RAND Corporation, D-19610-PR, November 5, 1969. S0283.pdf.

Dickson, Paul, *Think Tanks,* New York: Atheneum, 1971.

Dudek, Edmund E., "High Priority Projects Suggestions for 1967," memorandum to Assistant Secretary of Defense (M&RA), Washington, D.C., November 30, 1966. G0716.pdf.

Durbin, Eugene P., *Thoughts of USAF Manpower and Personnel Research,* Santa Monica, Calif.: RAND Corporation, D-15098-PR, September 27, 1966. S0266.pdf.

———, *Summary of the Manpower Planning Seminar, May 25, 1967,* Santa Monica, Calif.: RAND Corporation, D-15937-PR, July 27, 1967. S0267.pdf.

———, *Manpower Programs as Markov Chains,* Santa Monica, Calif.: RAND Corporation, RM-5741-OEO, October 1968. S0268.pdf.

———, Project RAND Semiannual Progress Report: Manpower, Personnel and Training, July–December 1969, Santa Monica, Calif.: RAND Corporation, D-19861-PR, January 23, 1970. S0272.pdf.

Enthoven, Alain C., *The Mathematics of Military Pay,* Santa Monica, Calif.: RAND Corporation, P-1100, November 11, 1957. S0005.pdf.

Fisher, Gene H., *Cost Consideration in Systems Analysis,* New York: American Elsevier Publishing Company, Inc., 1971.

Fitt, Alfred B., *Dr. Ralph Canter Appointed Military Manpower Research Coordinator,* Washington, D.C.: Assistant Secretary of Defense (M&RA), May 17, 1968. G0714.pdf.

Flyer, Eli S., *Factors Relating to Discharge for Unsuitability Among 1956 Accessions to the Air Force,* Lackland Air Force Base, San Antonio, Tex.: U.S. Air Force Personnel Research Laboratory, WADC TN 59201, December 1959.

———, *Prediction of Unsuitability Among First-Term Airmen from Aptitude Indexes, High School Reference Data and Basic Training Evaluations,* Lackland Air Force Base, Tex: U.S. Air Force Personnel Research Laboratory, PRLTDR6317, June 1963.

———, "Abridged History of Personnel Research in the Department of Defense," interview with Bernard Rostker, Monterey, California, August 13 and 15, 2002. S0633.pdf.

Gates, Thomas S. Jr., The Report of the President's Commission on an All-Volunteer Armed Force, Washington, D.C., February 1970. S0243.pdf.

Ginzberg, Eli, *Manpower Research and Management in Large Organizations,* Washington, D.C.: U.S. Department of Defense, Defense Science Board, June 1971. S0145.pdf.

Greenberg, David, and John J. McCall, Analysis of the Educational Personnel System, Vol. II: A Theory of Labor Mobility with Application of the Teacher Market, Santa Monica, Calif.: RAND Corporation, R-1270-HEW, 1973.

Griffith, Robert K., Jr., *The U.S. Army's Transition to the All-Volunteer Force 1968–1974,* Washington, D.C.: U.S. Army Center of Military History, 1997. S0186.pdf.

Grinold, Richard C., and Kneale T. Marshall, *Manpower Planning Models,* New York: Elsevier North-Holland, 1977.

Haggstrom, Gus W., *The Role of Experimentation in Manpower Planning,* Santa Monica, Calif.: RAND Corporation, R-1348-ARPA, December 1973. S0484.pdf.

———, *The Variable Tour Experiment in the Army Reserve Components,* Santa Monica, Calif.: RAND Corporation, R-1568-ARPA, May 1975. S0128.pdf.

Haggstrom, Gus W., and Bernard D. Rostker, *Testing the Effectiveness of Recruiting Incentives in the Air Reserve Forces,* Santa Monica, Calif.: RAND Corporation, 1973, WN-8094-PR. S0292.pdf.

———, *The Variable Tour Experiment in the Air Reserve Forces: Preliminary Report,* Santa Monica, Calif.: RAND Corporation, WN-8590-PR, January 1974a. S0293.pdf.

———, *An Analysis of Recruiter Productivity in the Air National Guard,* Santa Monica, Calif.: RAND Corporation, WN-8880-PR, October 1974b. S0296.pdf.

Hayes, James H., The Evolution of Military Officer Personnel Management Policies: A Preliminary Study with Parallels from Industry, Santa Monica, Calif.: RAND Corporation, R-2276-AF, August 1978. S0685.pdf.

Herbits, Stephen E., "Reserve Enlistment Experiment," memorandum to Acting Assistant Secretary of Defense (M&RA) Lieutenant General Taber, Washington, D.C., August 24, 1973. S0129.pdf.

Kelley, Roger T., "Action on Report on *Manpower Research and Management in Large Organizations,*" follow-up to Secretary of Defense, Washington, D.C., April 11, 1973a. S0122.pdf.

———, "Test of Reduced Terms of Selected Reserve Participation as a Recruiting Incentive," action memorandum to Deputy Secretary of Defense, Washington, D.C., May 28, 1973b. G0333.pdf.

Kiviat, P. J., Manpower Requirements Prediction and Allocation for Unscheduled Maintenance on Aircraft, Santa Monica, Calif.: RAND Corporation, RM-5215-PR, February 1967.

Lee, Gus C., "Request for Additional Research Support," memorandum to Ralph Canter, Washington, D.C., January 29, 1971. G0191.pdf.

Lee, Gus C., and Geoffrey Y. Parker, *Ending the Draft: The Story of the All Volunteer Force,* Washington, D.C.: Human Resources Research Organization, FR-PO-771, April 1977. S0242.pdf.

Lockman, Robert F., *Trends and Issues in U.S. Navy Manpower,* Alexandria, Va.: Center for Naval Analyses, 1987. S0836.pdf.

U.S. Congress, Testimony of Theodore C. Marris on Military Personnel, hearing before the Committee on Armed Services, House of Representatives, 93rd Cong., 2nd Sess., Washington, D.C., U.S. Government Printing Office, January 30, 1974.

McCall, John J., *An Analysis of Poverty: A Suggested Methodology,* Santa Monica, Calif.: RAND Corporation, RM-5739-OEO, 1968a.

———, *Economics of Information and Job Search,* Santa Monica, Calif.: RAND Corporation, RM-5745-OEO, 1968b. S0424.pdf.

———, *Racial Discrimination in the Job Market: The Role of Information and Search,* Santa Monica, Calif.: RAND Corporation, RM-6162-OEO, 1970. S0422.pdf.

McCall, John J., and Neil Wallace, *A Supply Function of First-Term Reenlistees to the Air Force,* Santa Monica, Calif.: RAND Corporation, P-3653, 1967a. S0425.pdf.

———, *Training and Retention of Air Force Airmen: An Economic Analysis,* Santa Monica, Calif.: RAND Corporation, RM-5384-PR, 1967b. S0798.pdf.

Merck, J. W., and Kathleen Hall, *A Markovian Flow Model: The Analysis of Movement in Large-Scale (Military) Personnel Systems,* Santa Monica, Calif.: RAND Corporation, R-514-PR, 1971. S0368.pdf.

Montague, Robert M., Jr., "On the Ginzberg Report," memorandum to Principal Deputy Assistant Secretary of Defense (M&RA) Lieutenant General Taber, Washington, D.C., February 15, 1973a. S0120.pdf.

———, "Action on Report on *Manpower Research and Management in Large Organizations,*" follow-up to Assistant Secretary of Defense (M&RA) Roger Kelley, Washington, D.C., April 4, 1973b. S0127.pdf.

———, "Test of Enlistment Bonus in Selected Combat Element Technical Skills," memorandum to Roger Kelley, Washington, D.C., May 25, 1973c. G0060.pdf.

Moore, Arnold B., *Suggestions for an ARPA Manpower Research Program,* Santa Monica, Calif.: RAND Corporation, WN-7771-ARPA, 1972. S0166.pdf.

Morgan, F. J., L. V. Scifers, and D. K. Shelton, *Air Reserve Forces Personnel Study,* Vol. IV: *Personnel Shortages and Combat Capability,* Santa Monica, Calif.: RAND Corporation, R-1459-PR, 1974. S0799.pdf.

Morris, Thomas D., "Special Study Group on Standards for Selection, Manning and Assignment for New Enlisted Personnel," memorandum to Dr. Ferraro, Washington, D.C., September 23, 1966. G0715.pdf.

OASD[M&RA], *Administrative Histories Project: Research and Development Items,* Washington, D.C.: U.S. Department of Defense, January 16, 1969. G0493.pdf.

Ramsberger, Peter F., *HumRRO: The First 50 Years,* Alexandria, Va.: Human Resources Research Organization, 2001.

Regets, Mark C., *Labor Supply in the Naval Reserve: Moonlighting or Voluntarism?* Binghamton, N.Y.: State University of New York, 1989.

Rostker, Bernard D., *Air Reserve Forces Personnel Study: Non-Prior Service Airmen—A Briefing,* Santa Monica, Ca.: RAND Corporation, WN-7902-PR, 1972. S0903.pdf.

———, *The Personnel Structure and Posture of the Air National Guard and the Air Force Reserve,* Santa Monica, Calif.: RAND Corporation, R-1049-PR, 1973. S0794.pdf.

———, *Total Force Planning, Personnel Costs and the Supply of New Reservists,* Santa Monica, Calif.: RAND Corporation, R-1430-PR, 1974. S0796.pdf.

———, "Human Resource Models: An Overview," in Wayne P. Jr. Hughes, ed., *Military Modeling for Decision Making,* 3rd ed., Washington, D.C.: The Military Operations Research Society, Inc., 1997. S0843.pdf.

Rostker, Bernard D., and Glenn A. Gotz, *Officer Personnel Management Systems: The Up-or-Out Promotion and Tenure Policy,* Santa Monica, Calif.: RAND Corporation, WN-9472-PR, October 1976. S0845.pdf.

Rostker, Bernard D., and Robert Shishko, *The Air Force Reserve and the Economics of Secondary Labor Market Participation,* Santa Monica, Calif.: RAND Corporation, R-1254-PR, August 1973. S0797.pdf.

Rowe, Murray W., *Command History: Calendar Year 1998,* San Diego, Calif.: Navy Personnel Research and Development Center, 1999.

Shields, Joyce L., "Interview with Bernard Rostker," March 5, 2004.

Shishko, Robert, and Bernard D. Rostker, "The Economics of Multiple Job Holding," *The American Economic Review,* Vol. 66, No. 3, June 1976, pp. 298–308. S0159.pdf.

Sinaiko, H. Wallace, *Smithsonian's Manpower Research and Advisory Services: A 22-Year Partnership with the Office of Naval Research,* Washington, D.C.: Smithsonian Institution, April 1994. S0381.pdf.

Smith, A. R., "Defense Manpower Studies," *Operations Research Quarterly,* Vol. 19, No. 3, September 1968. S0009.pdf.

Smith, Roy C., "Personnel and Promotion Reduced to Its Simplest Terms," *Proceedings: The U.S. Naval Institute,* 1906, pp. 801–859. S0020.pdf.

Taber, Robert, "Action on *Manpower Research and Management in Large Organizations,*" follow-up to Military Assistant to the Secretary of Defense Daniel J. Murphy, Washington, D.C., February 15, 1973. S0121.pdf.

Thomas, Edmund D., Ted M. Yellen, and Sam J. Polese, Voices From the Past—Command History Post WWII to November 1999: An Historical Account of the Navy Personnel Research & Development Center (NPRDC), San Diego, Calif.: Navy Personnel Research and Development Center, NPRDCAP994. S0025.pdf.

Thomson, Charles A. H., *The Research Analysis Corporation: A History of a Federal Contract Research Center,* McLean,Va.: Research Analysis Corporation, June 1975. S0083.pdf.

White, John P., RAND's Manpower, Personnel and Training Research Program: An Overview, Santa Monica, Calif.: RAND Corporation, WN-7712-PR, 1971a.

———, "A Proposed ARPA Manpower Research Program at RAND," letter to Director Dr. Stephen J. Lukasik, Advanced Research Projects Agency, Santa Monica, Calif., October 29, 1971b. S0260.pdf.

Zeidner, Joseph, and Arthur J. Drucker, *Behavioral Science in the Army: A Corporate History of the Army Research Institute,* Alexandria, Va.: United States Army Research Institute for the Behavioral and Social Sciences, 1983.

CHAPTER NINE

The Second Inning (1973–1976)

> We interpret our experience to date as highly promising and I can assure you that there is no lack of commitment in the Department of Defense in implementing the Nation's policy of an All-Volunteer Force in time of peace.
>
> —William K. Brehm
> Assistant Secretary of Defense
> (Manpower and Reserve Affairs)[1]

The Quality War

At the end of 1972, and with a change of leadership at the Pentagon imminent, the prospects for an all-volunteer force looked bright.[2] So bright, in fact, that within weeks of the New Year—January 27, 1973—the departing Secretary of Defense, Melvin Laird, announced that the draft had ended (1973). Unfortunately, this optimism would soon turn sour amidst charges that the Army was sabotaging the all-volunteer force. Here is what happened.

The Army Changes Quality Standards

In fall 1972 the Central All-Volunteer Force Task Force pressed forward on its study of "quality." Like the Gates Commission before it, the task force concluded that the "quality requirements for accessions exceed minimum needs" (Central All-Volunteer Force Task Force, 1972, p. ii). Its conclusion, however, was at odds with the Army's own assessment. Paul Phillips, the acting Assistant Secretary of the Army for Manpower and Reserve Affairs, and his Deputy Assistant Secretary, Clay Gompf, believed that by the

---

[1] From *Commanders Digest,* February 28, 1974 (Brehm, 1974d).

[2] In early 1973 General Montague provided the House Appropriations Committee with an upbeat account of "military recruiting and advertising as they affect movement toward the All-Volunteer Force" (Montague, 1973a).

end of 1972, "[t]he problem was no longer quantity but quality" (Griffith, 1997, p. 186).[3] They were convinced that the Army was not getting volunteers who had the skills to man critical occupations. Backing Phillips, the departing Secretary of the Army, Robert Froehlke, instructed the Army Secretariat and staff "not to lower quality in order to reach a volunteer force" (Lee and Parker, 1977, p. 205). In fact, the Army went in the other direction. They raised quality standards.

In October, as the debate with the task force continued, the Army raised the level of AFQT scores below which recruiters would not earn credit for an enlistment.[4] Kelley's staff urged him to "direct [the] Army to cancel the directive which changes the recruiter credit system . . . [and] request [the] Army to consider increasing the input of CAT IV's" (OASD[M&RA], 1972). What happened next is not clear.[5] The Army's official history of the period states that the "Army ignored Kelley's request and went ahead with Philips' proposed action to reorient recruiting" (Griffith, 1997, p. 188). Years later, Gus Lee, Kelley's Director of Procurement Policy, believed that "Kelley reluctantly 'went along' with the Army" (Lee and Parker, 1977, p. 383). If Kelley was reluctant, it was with Lee's recommendation to let the Army proceed. Lee told Kelley's deputy that "[t]he Army is giving more emphasis to critical skill enlistments. In the long run this emphasis is needed and we should support the Army in spite of a possible short run disadvantage of losing 3,000 enlistments in FY73" (Lee, 1972a).

An Initial Setback

At the beginning of 1973, Phillips and Gompf pressed on. Seeing no immediate reduction in recruiting[6]—in fact, January 1973 was an outstanding recruiting month—they next removed all credit recruiters received for enlisting a Category IV recruit who did not have a high school diploma and reduced the Category IV ceiling from 19 percent

---

[3] *Author's Note:* Several years later, in 1977, Paul Phillips and I held parallel positions. He was the Principal Deputy Assistant Secretary of the Army for Manpower and Reserve Affairs, and I was the Principal Deputy in the Navy.

[4] This was not the first time that the Army had changed quality standards. As Odeen noted in a memorandum to Kissinger on July 27, 1972,

> [b]etween November of 1971 and March of 1972, the Services increased the number of high school graduates inducted and decreased the percent of low mental category enlistees compared with previous years. . . . This was the result of an Army policy not to give recruiters "credit" for inducting non–high school graduates or lower mental category recruits—a policy that has since been softened. (Odeen, 1972, p. 4)

[5] Kelley's staff told him

> The Army apparently has not respected its verbal commitment to you to discuss changes in quality criteria with you prior to putting them into effect. . . . The Army, however, has not violated standing instructions regarding changes in quality criteria. . . . It would be desirable from a management point of view for the Services to announce to you, well in advance, their plans to change enlistment quality criteria, either up or down. (Richardson, 1973)

[6] David Grissmer has estimated that "[t]he policy implemented in October 1971 of withdrawing recruiter credit for Category III non–high school graduates resulted in a net average monthly loss of an estimated 1540 and 2100 for non–high school graduate Category III" (Grissmer et al., 1974, p. 58). He noted that his high and low estimates were "developed from different regression equations and reflect uncertainty due to multicollinearity of variables" (Grissmer et al., 1974, p. 56).

of accessions to 15 percent. They also, for the first time, limited the percentage of new recruits without a high school diploma to 30 percent of total non–prior service accessions (Griffith, 1997, p. 200).[7] This time, there was an immediate and negative reaction.[8] Enlistments fell sharply. In March, despite the rosy picture the new Secretary of Defense, Elliott Richardson, painted (Richardson, 1973), the Army missed its goal by 29 percent. In April, it missed "a modest 9,000 objective" by 51 percent. While the Army did recruit about 4,000 more high school graduates in the first five months of 1973 than it had previously, it also recruited 12,000 fewer high school dropouts. By May, the cumulative shortfall had reached 12,000, or almost 33 percent under goal (Griffith, 1997, p. 199).[9]

In retrospect, it was unfortunate that the changes to the standards came when they did. The February through May period is traditionally a low point in the yearly recruiting cycle. In addition, the Army Recruiting Command was having serious internal problems. A decision to move its headquarters from Fort Monroe to Fort Sheridan was disruptive. The number of field recruiters was down. The Army had filled only 80 percent of its authorized recruiter positions. To make matters worse, the Army Audit Agency released a report that there was "evidence of extensive recruiter malpractice" (Griffith, 1997, pp. 205–209), resulting in widespread dislocations as the Army's Criminal Investigation Command moved in to investigate.[10] Finally, the Army's commitment to the all-volunteer force came into question when its uniformed leadership proposed to disestablish the last vestige of their dedicated Modern Volunteer Army Program office (Jacoby, 1973),[11] integrating what was left into the regular Army Staff—into the Office of the Deputy Chief of Staff (Personnel) (Chief of Staff, 1973).

The Army's position on quality got some support from an unexpected source. In June, the Procurement Policy office under Kelley produced three staff papers on quality. While the studies clearly tied the recruiting quality mix to the high school graduation goal and projected continuing Army recruiting shortfalls, they also "verified the

---

[7] Gompf would later tell Griffith that this was a device to force the recruiters further into the high school market (Griffith, 1997, p. 200).

[8] Grissmer found that "[t]he estimated effect of the 70 percent policy on high school graduates group was to increase Category I–III high school graduates by between 0 and 750 per month, while an estimated 3,000 to 5,700 Category I–III non–high school graduates were lost during those months the policy was in effect" (Grissmer et al., 1974, p. 58).

[9] In the official Army history, Griffith singled out Phillips and Gompf for blame. He refers to their actions as an "unintentional self-inflicted wound administered by the manpower managers in the Office of the Assistant Secretary of the Army for Manpower and Reserve Affairs, Paul Phillips and Clayton Gompf" (see Griffith, 1997, p. 199).

[10] Between January 1972 and October 1973, the Army investigated "approximately" 1,600 recruiters for malpractice, resulting in 298 proven cases of malpractice. In the same period, the other three services together investigated 213 cases of malpractice, with 31 cases proven (Huck, 1973). The numbers do not necessarily reflect actual incidents of malpractice but do illustrate the scope and intensity of the Army effort and the pressure being put on Army recruiters. After General Montague left OSD, he was appointed Deputy Commanding General of the U.S. Army Recruiting Command, then provided Herbits a summary of the policies, procedures, and problem areas related to the recruiting and processing malpractice he found (Montague, 1973e).

[11] The fact that Kelley "strongly disagree[d]" with this action was communicated to the Army through a number of channels (Montague, 1973c).

desirability of recruiting high school graduates" (Lee and Parker, 1977, p. 386). Jeanne Fites found that "[t]he best predictors of unsuitability discharge are educational level at entry into Service, age at entry into Service and AFQT [score]" (Lee and Parker, 1977, p. 386).[12] Nevertheless, pressure was mounting on the Army as Congress and the press zeroed in on the Army's continuing problems and credibility.

Charges of Sabotage

What had brought about the sudden change in the fortunes of the all-volunteer force? The Army blamed the falloff in recruiting on Laird's announcement that the use of the draft had ended. Those favoring the all-volunteer force charged the military leadership with "bolder and more frequent acts of sabotage" (Franklin, 1973). The official Army history of the period steadfastly maintained that "[n]one of the policy changes or actions initiated in early 1973 . . . was intended to subvert the objective of attaining the zero-draft goal" (Griffith, 1997, p. 209). Gus Lee agreed. Several years later, he wrote that the Army's poor performance in 1973 was the result of "untimely judgments, rather than a deliberate effort to defeat the programs" (Lee and Parker, 1977, p. 207). Irv Greenberg also agreed. He would later remark,

> I find it hard to believe that senior Army leaders could think Army had the ability to bring back the draft so soon after it was abolished. The draft was ended because it was politically untenable at the time. Recruiting failure could only lead—as the Army Deputy Chief of Staff for Personnel would find out during summer 1973— to reducing the size of the Army. (Greenberg, 2004)[13]

There were those in Kelley's office who saw things differently, however. The Special Assistant for All-Volunteer Force Matters, Army Brigadier General Robert Montague, in preparing Kelley for his final meeting with Deputy Secretary of Defense William Clements, told him that the

> Services [had] used [t]he quality issue to defeat the previous effort to end the draft in 1948. In effect, they priced themselves out of the market. Events are repeating themselves. . . . [The] Services are expected to defend their inflated quality needs before Congress. . . . [The] quality issue now is a strong rallying point for opponents of the AVF. . . . The Army appears to be drawing a hard line which will be fully exposed after your departure. (Montague, 1973d)

A further problem Montague had with the Army was the decision to terminate the Modern Volunteer Army Program. He had told the Army staff that "[a]ny change

---

[12] *Author's Note:* Fites would rise to become the Deputy Under Secretary of Defense for Program Integration with responsibilities for the personnel research and data management programs, including RAND's Defense Manpower Research Center. She would later work for me when I was Under Secretary of Defense for Personnel and Readiness.

[13] Greenberg believes that "Phillip and Gompf . . . misjudged the capabilities of the Army Recruiting Command. [And] the issue was aggravated by the emotional personalities of some of the protagonists in OSD and Army" (Greenberg, 2004).

which appears to lessen the priority and emphasis the Army attaches to its all-volunteer force effort is not acceptable" (Montague, 1973c). Lee also told the Army that "the termination of the MVA [Modern Volunteer Army] . . . might be subject to misinterpretation and could suggest that aggressive actions to sustain the volunteer force are no longer necessary" (Lee, 1973).[14]

In his final memorandum to Clements, Kelley said:

> There is one thing only that can keep the All-Volunteer Force from being a success, and that is a lack of complete and positive commitment on the part of those responsible for its operation. I appreciate your exceptional leadership in encouraging the essential commitment to cause, and I hope that any who are incapable of following your lead would disassociate themselves from the effort altogether. (Kelley, 1973c)

The implication of Kelley's memorandum was not lost on the Secretary of the Army. Within days Callaway wrote Clements to assure him that

> the Army is completely and positively committed to the zero draft Army. I, and the Army, accept totally that the decision to end induction authority is final. . . . I disagree strongly with several basic points in Roger [Kelley]'s paper. (Callaway, 1973a)

Shortly after leaving DoD, Kelley publicly charged the Army with "sabotage" (Lee and Parker, 1977, p. 207). His new "special assistant," Stephen Herbits, late of the Gates Commission and service on the Hill, believed the word *sabotage* was appropriate. He told the tenth anniversary conference held at the U.S. Naval Academy in 1983 that, "in the nine months that followed . . . [Kelley's] departure from the Pentagon . . . [he had] tracked and found such a pattern [of sabotage]" (Herbits, 1986). Milton Friedman also used the word *sabotage* in a signed column in *Newsweek*. Friedman charged the Army leadership with "either gross incompetence or deliberate sabotage" and noted that, out of 129 officers engaged in recruiting who were either eligible for promotion to senior ranks or for assignment to a senior service school, "not a single one was either promoted or sent to a service school" (Friedman, 1974).[15]

A New Special Assistant for All-Volunteer Matters

While Kelley despaired for the future of the all-volunteer force, he put in place two bulwarks against the tide of opposition. First, he got Clements to personally get involved and to take the lead of a new "special task force on the All-Volunteer Force to

---

[14] The Office of the Special Assistant for the Modern Volunteer Army was disestablished on June 20, 1972. The program was further decentralized when the services were notified in spring 1973 that Project Volunteer funds would be "integrated into the regular budget beginning with the formulation in 1973 of the fiscal year 1975 budget" (Bell and Cocke, 1977, p. 61).

[15] Brehm told Schlesinger that Friedman's "information, . . . is basically factual, but I don't share his interpretation," and that whether Army shortfalls resulted from incompetence or sabotage is a matter of opinion (Brehm, 1974b). He wrote to Friedman that "I think that the Army has received more abuse than it really deserves for mistakes it may have made in launching its volunteer force effort. . . . I know the Army well enough to be certain that they are committed to this program" (Brehm, 1974c).

meet . . . weekly" (Clements, 1973a). Second, he hired Herbits as the new Special Assistant for All-Volunteer Force Matters, replacing Bob Montague, who was being reassigned as the Deputy Commander of the Army Recruiting Command.[16]

Now Herbits was on the inside, and for the next year he would drive the all-volunteer force issue as hard as he could. He constantly prodded and pushed his superiors—first, the acting assistant secretary, General Taber; Deputy Secretary of Defense William Clements; and, later, Assistant Secretary William Brehm—for more action on behalf of *his* all-volunteer force. On June 4, he argued for more effort on reserve enlistments; on June 5, the issue was prior clearance for changes in mental standards. On June 7, he focused on the shortage of army recruiters while pressing the issue of medical standards.[17]

Herbits' depth of concern can be seen in the "bill of particulars" against the Army he prepared and sent to Taber at the end of June. Herbits complained that the Army was

> no longer emphasizing the all-volunteer force sufficiently to overcome the problems it faces in the immediate future. . . . Because of . . . negative statements by Army officials, the Congress, the press, and the public are apprehensive about the success of the program. . . . [T]hese signals have led to an attitude . . . that the Army is willing and actually desires to return to past practices. (Herbits, 1973f)

Under pressure from Herbits, Taber told the deputy secretary that

> Some recent statements by Service officials casting doubt on the feasibility of the all-volunteer concept, and a growing number of stories in the media about all-volunteer force difficulties [make it imperative] that you call a Task Force meeting [within the next several days]. (Taber, 1973b)

Moreover, in June, the Army missed its recruiting goals by 9 percent.[18] The talking points prepared for Clements to use at the July 2, 1973, meeting of the Armed Force Policy Board were direct and forceful, for instance, "I want more positive and timely action to meet the President's All-Volunteer Force objective" (Taber, 1973, p. 3).

Pressure on the Army

Pressure on the Army from the Office of the Secretary of Defense was matched by pressure from Congress. On June 11, 1973, the Senate Armed Services Committee held hearings on the authorization of military personnel for FY 1974. The Senate Armed

---

[16] On May 30, 1973, Kelley's last day in office, he and Herbits agreed on a charter for the special assistant (Herbits, 1973a).

[17] See the memoranda by Herbits: (1973d), (1973c), (1973e), and (1973b).

[18] A Manpower Office report providing information on the all-volunteer force concluded that the

> Army shortage occurred because Army recruiters greatly exceeded the quality goals established for them. Army's strength shortfall at the end of FY 1973 was primarily due to its decision to limit non–high school graduates to 30% of total enlistments. . . . Army could have exceeded its objectives by 1,350 if it had accepted 30% non–high school graduates. (OASD[M&RA], 1973)

Services Committee, never a friend or supporter of the all-volunteer force, pressed the Army. They were armed with two new studies from the General Accounting Office (GAO)[19] and the Brookings Institution that predicted that the all-volunteer force was feasible. The Senators wanted to know what had happened. The Army's Deputy Chief of Staff for Personnel, Lieutenant General Bernard Rogers, later to become the Chief of Staff of the Army, was convinced that Congress was prepared to reduce the Army's end strength because of its "apparent inability to achieve its stated quantitative manpower goals and its apparent unwillingness to reduce qualitative standards" (Griffith, 1997, p. 213).[20] Lee, citing a conversation with General Rogers, would later agree that this was a critical factor in the Army's decision to reduce quality standards (Lee and Parker, 1977, p. 388).[21] Coverage of the Army shortfall in the popular press, most notably an article in the *New York Times* (Franklin, 1973), also pushed the Army to act, or more important, pushed the new Secretary of the Army, Howard Callaway, to act (Griffith, 1997, p. 225).[22]

Callaway Acts

On July 6, 1973, Callaway "preempted" Clements's pending action by changing the Army policy from a 70:30 high school graduate to nongraduate ratio to 50:50.[23] The Army's new approach to quality was laid out in a press release in July. In it, the Army explained that the "new program . . . will permit a greater number of non–high school graduates to enlist. . . . [The] program provides non–high school graduates the opportunity to prove themselves by their performance in training" (Callaway, 1973b). Calloway noted that, "[e]ven though it's true that the non–high school graduates give us most of our drug problems, most of our discipline problems, still four out of five non–high school graduates make fine soldiers" (Callaway, 1973c).

Callaway also launched a personal campaign to shore up support for the volunteer Army from key groups within and outside the service. On October 10, 1972, he

---

[19] Known these days as the Government Accountability Office.

[20] The following spring, General Rogers was still smarting over the way Congress was handling the Army's requested end strength. He asked Congress not base end strength on an "estimate of the Army's capability to recruit toward an end strength. Rather, you [should] set end strength to meet the requirements as we see them and you see them, and then give us the target and let us recruit toward that target" (Rogers, 1974).

[21] In fact, on August 28, 1973, the Senate Armed Services Committee voted to cut Army end strength by 9 percent (Griffith, 1997, p. 229).

[22] Senator Stuart Symington, Acting Chairman of the Senate Armed Services Committee, citing the *New York Times* article, asked Secretary of Defense James Schlesinger for his "comments on the issues raised in this article; also on the prospects for the All-Volunteer Force" (Symington, 1973). For Clements's response to Schlesinger, see Clements (1973c).

[23] On July 11, 1972, Clements thanked Callaway for his "decision . . . to adjust quality of Army new entries so as to meet both quality and quantity requirements." Clements called the decision "timely" (Clements, 1973b). The Army went public with the new program on July 27, 1973 (Callaway, 1973b).

reported to Clements that, while recruiting results were not good—the Army had achieved 82 percent of its non–prior service objectives (Clements, 1973d)—"we know the problems and the entire Army is energized to attack them. We cannot yet assure you of success, but we can assure you of a maximum effort to that end" (Callaway, 1973e). The following day, he wrote all general officers on active duty "eliciting support for the volunteer concept" (Callaway, 1974a). His October 15, 1973, speech before the Association of the United States Army (Callaway, 1973f) even drew praise from Herbits as "probably one of the strongest statements coming out of the United States Army since we began the move to end the draft" (Herbits, 1973h). In early February, Callaway again wrote all general officers asking for their

> support in seeking out and implementing locally those ideas for improving both the qualitative and quantitative aspects of the Army. . . . We are now completing a report on the first year of the volunteer Army. The tone is upbeat, but problem areas are also candidly identified. (Callaway, 1974a)

Just one day later, in a letter to the President, Callaway reported, "the Volunteer Army is a reality" (Callaway, 1974b, p. 1).[24]

The generals, at least publicly, seemed to agree. In March 1974, General Rogers told Congress that, given the adjusted end strength as a result of the congressional reduction of 43,000 "for the program which we are now on, we are achieving . . . 97 percent of required enlistments. . . . I think 97 percent is a pretty significant figure" (Rogers, 1974, p. 1,627). By the end of the fiscal year, the Army had recruited over 199,000 volunteers and, through high reenlistments, had exceeded its authorized end strength of 781,600. Callaway told the press that the "Volunteer Army is a success . . . and I am proud to be a part of it" (Callaway, 1974c). An Army report describing the highlights of FY 1974 called it an "unqualified success" (Department of the Army, 1974).

Section 718 Restrictions on Non–High School Graduates

The change in the Army's quality program did not go down well in Congress. The Defense Appropriations Act for FY 1974 that passed in December 1973 contained Section 718, which set restrictions on who could be recruited—no more than 45 percent of new recruits could be non–high school graduates, and only 18 percent could score at the Mental Category IV level.[25] To make things even worse, these restrictions applied separately to each service. This congressional action did not go down well with the generals in the Pentagon either. Admiral Elmo Zumwalt, writing for the Joint Chiefs of Staff, told Schlesinger that they were

---

[24] The President thanked Callaway, telling him that he could "take special satisfaction in the transitional progress already made. . . . Keep up the fine work!" (Nixon, 1974).

[25] Congress had asked DoD to report on its "quality requirements," but did not wait to receive the report when it acted to pass the Section 718 restrictions. The report was sent to the Senate Armed Service Committee in January 1974 (Kelley, 1972).

becoming increasingly concerned over the inconsistent congressional actions which have approved the All-Volunteer Force concept by allowing the military induction authority to expire but, in the same timeframe, have curtailed needed executive authority to recruit, train and retain the qualified personnel needed to man such a force. (Zumwalt, 1973)

The following March, General Rogers told Congress that the traditional measures of mental category scores and high school graduation status were not necessarily the best measures of quality:

> Failing to enlist non–high school graduates or Category IV personnel would result in a substantial number of potentially successful soldiers being rejected. . . . In the end, the true test of quality of a soldier is his performance on the job in his unit. (Rogers, 1974, p. 1,358)

He also complained of the "new constraints" placed on the Army in December 1973 in Section 718 of the appropriations act. He told Senator John Stennis (D-Mississippi) that Congress had made it "more difficult . . . for us to achieve our objectives" and asked that the Army be allowed to "establish its own standards of quality" (Rogers, 1974, p. 1,628).[26] In fact, at the time, the Army was up against the ceiling, with only 54 percent of its recruits during the fiscal year having graduated from high school. The Marine Corps also saw this as presenting "an additional problem." Lieutenant General Samuel Jaskilka, the Marine Corps Deputy Chief of Staff for Manpower and later the Assistant Commandant of the Marine Corps, reminded Stennis that the Marine Corps had "not achieved that level [55 percent high school graduates] even with the draft, since 1969" (Jaskilka, 1974). The previous year, only 53.3 percent of Marine Corps recruits had been high school graduates. This prompted a formal request from Navy Secretary John Warner to the Armed Services Committee Chair John Stennis—Warner would later chair the same committee—asking that the "Section 718 be removed or that the services be required to adhere only to the Mental Group IV provision" (Warner, 1974).

Quality or Race?

While the Army's actions at the end of 1972 and the beginning of 1973 were couched in terms of quality, others have suggested that the real issue was race. The Office of the Assistant Secretary of Defense closely monitored the racial composition of the force. A report compiled for Kelley noted that

> the proportion of non-white enlistees recruited by the Army and Marine Corps is continuing to increase. 26.5% of the Marine Corps enlistees and 21.5% of the Army's enlistees in November were non-white. Both of these percentages are

---

[26] For an expanded discussion of the quality and Congress, see Griffith (1997, pp. 243–245).

substantially above 13.5%—the proportion of 17–20 year old non-white males to the total 17–20 year old male population. (Lee, 1972b)

The official Army history of the period acknowledged that "the future racial balance of the MVA [modern volunteer Army] was a matter of deep concern to many of the Army's leaders," and noted that this "sensitive subject . . . played a part in the Army's approach to the transition" (Griffith, 1997, p. 235). With the race riots on the USS *Constellation* and the USS *Kitty Hawk* fresh on people's minds,[27] some in the Army believed that, if the service became too black, it would become difficult to attract white recruits.[28]

In August, with the Army in retreat on the quality front, a more-direct approach to the racial question seemed needed. On August 17, 1973, Secretary Callaway asked the Army Chief of Staff for "a recommendation as to whether or not any type or degree of controls should be established on black accessions" (Callaway, 1973d).[29] The secretary also asked that any recommendation be supported by "logical reasons." He said that "[i]f the recommendation is to establish controls," he wanted "the rationale for such action . . . recommendation[s] on how this would be done, [and] . . . a plan for explaining it frankly and positively to the public as a whole, to blacks, to the Congress as a whole, and to the [Congressional] Black Caucus" (Callaway, 1973d).

While the record is not clear on what, if any, recommendation the Chief of Staff provided the Secretary of the Army, the Army adopted a "self-imposed goal" to produce a force that was "representative" of the American people (Binkin et al., 1982, p. 3). In fact, the Army was recruiting almost twice as many black soldiers as it had before the end of conscription and almost twice as many as existed in the general population. This clearly was a point of concern for General William Westmoreland, the

---

[27] The racial problems in the Navy were the subject of a inquiry by a special subcommittee of the House Armed Services Committee (1973).

[28] Herbits recalls this argument being put forward by members of the Secretary of the Army's manpower office. Griffith refers to this as the "tipping point" argument in Griffith (1997, p. 235). The argument was given a degree of legitimacy when it was apparently endorsed by the two leading military sociologists of the day, Morris Janowitz and Charles Moskos (Janowitz and Moskos, 1974). Years later, in 1981, Moskos would admit that

> to what degree the changing racial composition of the Army reflects white reluctance to join an increasingly black organization, one does not know. . . . The fact that the disproportionately white navy and the racially balanced Air Force also face recruiting problems indicates that there is more than racial content at work in recruiting an all-volunteer force. (Moskos, 1981, p. 230)

Later, he also indicated that he preferred to shift the issue. He told Congress in 1978 that, "[r]ather than focus on minority representation, I would prefer to shift attention to the white middle class participation" (see Moskos in Nunn, 1978, p. 46).

[29] Griffith noted that "the sensitive subject [of race] was rarely if ever raised in formal deliberations" and that the staff documents he examined "never ever address the subject" (Griffith, 1997, pp. 235, 238, n. 22). In fact, on August 17, 1973, the Secretary of the Army addressed the subject in a "close hold" memorandum to the Chief of Staff. The secretary apparently ordered that the memorandum be shared with the Acting Assistant Secretary of Defense (Manpower and Reserve Affairs), as noted in Phillips (1973). One can only wonder, given the sensitivity of the subject, if this was a defensive bureaucratic move to share responsibility in case the memorandum leaked to Congress or the press.

recently retired Army Chief of Staff. In an interview, he told a *New York Times* reporter that "the social composition . . . [of the all-volunteer Army] bothers me. I deplore the prospect of our military forces not representing a cross-section of our society" (Franklin, 1973, p. 20). In a similar vein, Secretary of the Army Callaway explained to Congress in 1975 that, "[o]ur obligation to the American people is to strive to field an Army which is both representative of them and acceptable to them" (Binkin et al., 1982, p. 4). This apparently extended to—what was referred to as the "Callaway Shift"—transferring some recruiters out from areas with a heavy black population.[30]

The issue of "selective" recruiting, however, was not limited to the Army or to the early 1970s. The Navy and Marine Corps would have a similar problem later in the decade as noted by Eitelberg (1979, p. 250) and Wilson (1979).[31] Neither did the issue suffer from a lack of analytic attention. A number of studies reported on the changing demographics of the military. By early 1974, however, the Secretary of the Army reported to the President that concerns that the Army would become "all black" were unfounded and that, "while 1973 saw an overall increase in the percentage of black male enlistees, it appears this trend may have peaked" (Callaway, 1974b, p. II-4).

New Leadership in the Office of the Assistant Secretary of Defense

The end of the "quality war" between the Army and the Office of the Assistant Secretary of Defense was also hastened by the arrival of a new player or, more appropriately,

---

[30] Coffey noted that, in

> FY 1975, the Army redistributed its recruiting force with a stated objective of achieving better geographical representation among recruits. . . . This move, which transferred some recruiters out of heavily black areas, also resulted in a reduction in black enlistments, although the impact on black enlistments was not a stated goal of the redistribution program. (Coffey and Reeg, 1975, pp. 16–17)

Griffith also noted "[s]ome recruiting offices were moved out of the ghettos and into the suburbs" (Griffith, 1997, 236). The issue was also highlighted in a June 8, 1976, Associated Press report, which noted that the Defense Manpower Commission's final report "mentioned discriminatory practices generally but does not specify which service employed them or the extent of their use." The commission's executive director, retired General Bruce Palmer, Jr., was reported as telling the *Washington Post* that "'it would be wrong to kick the services in the teeth' by describing alleged discriminatory practices" (Associated Press, 1976). In 1975, in response to a question from Congressman Ron Dellums, Callaway denied transferring recruiters. He told the congressman that

> [r]ecruiters are presently assigned throughout the United States on the basis of the number of qualified potential enlistees in the various sections of the Country. The opportunity to enlist is not reduced in an area. There has been very little change in assignment patterns from two years ago. Essentially, most changes are keyed to population shifts, traffic flow and areas offering quality enlistments. (Callaway, 1975c)

[31] In 1974, Brehm noted that "the Marines were using a quota device in their recruiting program which, though well-intended, was questionable on the grounds that it did not afford equal opportunity for blacks" (Brehm, 1974a, p. 1). The Navy's program, initiated in July 1976 to limit the number of minorities, was called "parity." While it was designed to ensure "that a particular group does not shoulder the burden of the less desirable jobs on a proportional basis" (Woolsey, 1979a), it also limited the opportunity of blacks to join the Navy. In 1979, "because it [the parity program] led to perceptions that the policy was discriminatory, the Department of the Navy . . . discontinued the parity recruiting program" (Tice, 1979). The Navy initiated an upward-mobility program to address the issue of stagnation of minorities in the lower ranks (Woolsey, 1979b).

an old player in a new role, when William K. Brehm took office on September 1, 1973.[32]

William K. Brehm

Brehm had been the Director and later the Deputy Assistant Secretary of Defense for Land Forces Programs in the Systems Analysis Office (1964–1968). Then, in 1968, after the Reserve Forces Bill of Rights and Vitalization Act of 1967 created the position of Assistant Secretary for Manpower and Reserve Affairs in each military department, Secretary of the Army Stanley Resor selected him to be the first Assistant Secretary of the Army for Manpower and Reserve Affairs. The new position "was designed to strengthen the management structure of the reserve forces in order to make them more effective" (ASD[PA], 1968).

Brehm joined the Army Secretariat at a time when the Army was struggling to manage the buildup of forces for Vietnam and to control the monthly draft calls forwarded to the Selective Service System. He initiated a number of "analytic" efforts that allowed the Army to deal with the manpower-planning demands of a rapidly changing personnel situation to rationalize draft calls. Years later, Brehm pointed out how important the overall "analytic maturing" of the Army had been to its effective transition to an all-volunteer force. Brehm recounted that in 1965,

> as the Viet Nam build-up and deployment began in earnest, it became apparent that the US Army Headquarters did not have the analytic skills necessary to manage manpower and force structure or, for that matter, its overall readiness posture. The Secretary of Defense was, for good reason, very concerned about this weakness. . . . Outreach to the Army staff in 1966, when Systems Analysis (Land Forces Division) helped the Army organize a new entity—the Force Planning and Analysis Office, which initially reported to the Army Chief of Staff and to the Secretary of the Army. . . . [Later it] became an integral part of the office of the new Assistant Vice Chief of Staff, a three-star position. [It built] a solid analytical capability combined with a dominant understanding of the Army. In due course, the Army Staff began to hold its own in analytical dialog with the Office of the Secretary of Defense. (Brehm, 2002)

He was one of the chief architects of the initial Modern Volunteer Army program and saw this program through the first year, until he left government service in December 1970.[33]

With his background in Systems Analysis, no one should have been surprised when Brehm moved to improve the analytic capabilities of the office he had inherited from Kelley. One of his first moves, even before he formally took over the manpower

---

[32] The White House had announced Brehm's nomination on July 30, 1973 (White House Press Secretary, 1973).

[33] Between 1970, when he left federal service and his return in 1973, Brehm was Vice President for Corporate Development of Dart Industries. Brehm's relationship with his inherited Special Assistant, Stephen Herbits, was never good and certainly did not get off to a good start when, within days of taking office, he received from Herbits an accounting of "how the Army has mismanaged their entire accession program" (Herbits, 1973g, p. 2).

office, was to eliminate the bureaucratic squabbles that had infected the relationship between the Manpower and Reserve Affairs office and the Systems Analysis office. He convinced the new Secretary of Defense, James R. Schlesinger, to reassign the manpower requirements function from Program Analysis and Evaluation (PA&E)—the new name for Systems Analysis—to his new office.[34] In addition, during his tenure, the importance of manpower data was recognized and the Defense Manpower Data Center was established as a field activity reporting directly to the assistant secretary. He also picked up the funding of the Manpower Research Center at the RAND Corporation, which had been funded by the Advanced Research Projects Agency since 1972. The center was renamed the Defense Manpower Research Center.

From his new position, Brehm was also able to move the all-volunteer force program forward. He pressed Congress for final approval of special pays, including bonuses. He improved the effectiveness, efficiency, and veracity of recruiting in a way that would eventually lead to an overhaul of recruit processing and the establishment of the new Military Enlistment Processing Command. He fielded a new, common screening test. On January 1, 1976, the Armed Services Vocational Aptitude Battery (ASVAB) became the single screening test used by all services. This new test, however, would again raise the issue of quality in new and totally unexpected ways and would put the all-volunteer force through one of its most difficult periods.

Leadership

Probably the most-important thing Brehm provided was a high level of leadership when it was most needed. This was especially important given the lukewarm endorsement his boss, Secretary of Defense Schlesinger, gave the all-volunteer force at his confirmation hearing and against the backdrop of a much-weakened White House, as President Nixon faced Watergate.[35] Years later, Lee reflected on Brehm's role:

> Brehm deserves much of the credit for the press turn-around. Taking office in September 1973 at the peak of press and media stories of failure [he] immersed himself in analysis of the measures for evaluation of implementation. He concluded that the facts would speak for themselves if they were made available to the public in a logical manner. Month after month he presented the recruiting results and strength data, good and bad, in an accurate manner without rhetorical interpretation. When the results showed 100 percent accomplishment, the press was willing

---

[34] Within days of Brehm taking office, Schlesinger transferred the manpower requirements office from PA&E to Brehm (Schlesinger, 1973). It would not be until December that Brehm created the Office of the Assistant Secretary of Defense (Manpower Requirements and Analysis). Don Srull, his previous deputy when he had been the Assistant Secretary of the Army and lately the Deputy Assistant Secretary of Defense (Resources Analysis) in PA&E, had "agreed to head up this new office" (Brehm, 1973, p. 2). The role of the new office and the manpower functions that would remain with PA&E were spelled out in a memorandum Schlesinger's special assistant to the senior administrator at the Pentagon, David O. (Doc) Cook in March 1974. PA&E would continue to "focus on the program evaluation/resource allocation aspects of the total DoD Program" (Latimer, 1974).

[35] Friedman thought Watergate may have emboldened the Army leadership to "attempt to reverse the decision" to go to an all-volunteer force (Friedman, 1974, p. 82; Lee and Parker, 1977, p. 213).

to recognize the achievement. By the end of December 1974, the facts were clear: In general, officer and enlisted strengths in all Services could be maintained on a volunteer basis. (Lee and Parker, 1977, pp. 214–215)

Brehm's single most important act of leadership may have been when he directly "spoke" to DoD "commanders and key personnel." His forum was the widely circulated *Commanders Digest,* which provided "official and professional information to commanders and key personnel on matters related to Defense policies, programs and interests," and was designed "to create better understanding and teamwork within the Department of Defense." In a February 28, 1974, special report, he told commanders in blunt language that whatever shortfall existed in the all-volunteer force, it was "not enough to cause us to think about returning to the draft" (Brehm, 1974d, p. 3).[36]

He endorsed the Army's new quality-standards program, pointing out that "the Army's experience shows that four out of five non–high school graduates make good soldiers" (Brehm, 1974d, p. 4). He chided Congress for limiting new entrants to a maximum of 45 percent non–high school graduates and argued that, when "the number of high school graduates available is not enough to meet requirements, then the Services should have the option of recruiting non–high school graduates." On the issue of race, he refuted Westmoreland and Callaway's proposition concerning "representativeness" and reminded commanders that, while the Army's percentage of blacks had increased from 14 percent in 1970 to over 20 percent in 1974, "[p]erformance is the sole basis upon which the Department of Defense seeks to accept or exclude any individual. We are an equal opportunity employer" (Brehm, 1974d, p. 5).

Brehm's strong stance was clearly helped by improving numbers. At the time of the *Commanders Digest* article in February 1974, he could report that the services had made 93 percent of their non–prior service recruiting goals for that January (ASD[PA], 1974). By the time of his last appearance before Congress, in spring 1976, he reported that, in FY 1975, all active components had exceeded their recruiting goals, with substantial increases in the numbers that had graduated high school—68 percent in FY 1974, as opposed to 79 percent during the first half of FY 1976—and that there was a similar increase in those with "average or above mental ability" (categories I to III)—90 percent versus 96 percent (Brehm, 1976c, p. 31). Even in the Army, the percentage of mental category IVs dropped from 17.8 percent in FY 1974 to 6.6 percent for the first half of FY 1976 (Moore, 1976, p. 43). However, in what would be a harbinger of things to come, Brehm added that, in the future, "we plan to limit [the] use of . . . bonuses to the combat arms in the interest of reducing manpower costs" (Brehm, 1976c, p. 31).

---

[36] In fact, that February, DoD announced that there had been recruiting shortfalls in January. The services had recruited only 93 percent of their objectives, but since the 39,710 recruited were "the largest monthly total since January 1973, exceeding even the results obtained last June [1973], which is normally the best recruiting month of the year" (ASD[PA], 1974, p. 1), things seemed to be looking up.

Research and Analysis

When Brehm was asked to fill the position that Kelley had vacated in summer 1973, he was well aware of the tensions that had existed between the Manpower and Systems Analysis offices. He was determined to do something about it and to improve the capabilities of his new office. His initial efforts centered on recruiting Don Srull to be his Deputy Assistant Secretary of Defense for Manpower Requirements and Analysis and consolidating the manpower requirements function in his office.[37] At the time, Srull was a deputy director in the Office of the Director, PA&E, and was responsible for analysis of cost and manpower requirements. This was the old Systems Analysis office under a new name. In fact, Srull had a long history both with Brehm and in the manpower and personnel analysis business. He and Brehm had gone to high school together. They had both attended the University of Michigan and had worked at CONVAIR together. In 1969, Brehm had recruited Srull to be the Deputy Assistant Secretary of the Army for Manpower. Srull was instrumental in bringing analytic tools to bear on the Army's draft-call and loss-management problems. He worked with Research Analysis Corporation [RAC] on the development of a family of manpower-projection models (known as the Enlisted Loss Inventory Model–Computation of Manpower Programs Using Linear Programming). He served as Acting Assistant Secretary after Brehm left federal service in December 1970. In 1971, Srull moved to Systems Analysis, replacing Don Rice, who had left to become the Deputy Director of the Office of Management and Budget (OMB) for National Security Affairs, as the Deputy Assistant Secretary for Resource Analysis.[38] He was well engaged in the Roger Kelley–Gardner Tucker wars in late 1971. Most important for Brehm, Srull was an analyst who knew the issues. He had once complained to Phil Odeen about the need for data "to start measuring effects" (Srull, 1970). It was now his job to produce the analysis that Brehm would use to "save" the all-volunteer force. Since the press was questioning the all-volunteer force, Brehm decided to give them a steady diet of the facts. Scull's job was to produce the numbers. Brehm's job was to feed them to a skeptical press until they could take no more.

---

[37] With the manpower requirements office came the Manpower Requirements Report to Congress. Brehm assigned the report to Irv Greenberg. Greenberg had problems getting the report out on time—45 days after the budget went to Congress—given the yearly programming and budgeting cycle. Eventually, in August 1975, Greenberg obtained the assistance of a young Army officer on temporary assignment after a year-long White House Fellowship at OMB. Brehm told the newly assigned Lieutenant Colonel Colin Powell that it was his job to see to it that the report was on time. Powell approached the problem by getting points of contact in the services and meeting with them at the Fort Myers officers' club after work. Through this informal network, Powell got the job done. Powell also used his OMB contacts to make sure the report sailed through the review process. This incident apparently was meaningful for all concerned. It came up independently and consistently in interviews with Brehm (2002), Irv Greenberg (2002) and Tom Stanners (2002). Powell recounts the same story, referring to Greenberg as a "thoroughgoing professional" in Powell and Persico (1995, p. 206).

[38] *Author's Note:* Rice had been the Director of the Cost Analysis Office in Systems Analysis before taking over as the Deputy Assistant Secretary for Resource Analysis in 1969. I worked for him when I served in Systems Analysis and again after he left OMB to become president of the RAND Corporation.

Brehm and Srull did not share Kelley's negative view of the importance of and need for manpower research. In fact, one of the places Brehm visited after he was confirmed but before he assumed his new responsibilities as Assistant Secretary of Defense was RAND. The president of RAND, Don Rice, a former colleague at Systems Analysis and the person that Srull had replaced in Systems Analysis in 1971, arranged a day of briefings to showcase the manpower, personnel, and training programs sponsored by the Air Force and Advanced Projects Research Agency (ARPA). Brehm talked about the major effort he wanted to put forward in the area of compensation reform and asked RAND for help with the next Quadrennial Review of Military Compensation (QRMC), which was scheduled to begin during his tenure.

Both Brehm and Srull, contrary to Kelley's view, believed that the Manpower Office had suffered because of "insufficient [and not] timely research." Moreover, they did not share Kelley's concern for "an efficient division of responsibility among Assistant Secretaries" (Kelley, 1973b), with DDR&E and ARPA responsible for manpower and personnel research. Srull told Brehm that, in fact, he did not have sufficient resources, either in house or on retainer, to provide the analysis that Brehm needed (Srull, 2001). When ARPA decided to phase out its support for manpower, personnel, and training research at RAND, Brehm and Srull were ready to pick it up. In January 1976, Greenberg prepared a description of the Defense Manpower Studies Center, which was "to engage in high-priority studies and analysis to support DoD-wide manpower policy decisions" (Greenberg and Flyer, 1976, p. 1). The center, as he saw it, would "be located in an existing non-profit corporation currently performing studies and analysis for OSD . . . with diverse academic backgrounds (e.g., economics, operations research, psychology, math, etc.) and experience in manpower and personnel studies and analysis" (Greenberg and Flyer, 1976, p. 2). The "description" seemed ready made for RAND, and RAND was awarded the contact.[39]

Manpower Data

Brehm and Srull saw the need for manpower data that could stand the test of press inquiry and public scrutiny. Originally concerned with monitoring and reporting on Project 100,000, DoD had established a Manpower Data Analysis Center at HumRRO in FY 1971. The center had maintained "a number of separate, computerized manpower files . . . for OSD usage, integrated on a DoD and inter-agency basis, and utilities for analysis and reporting" (Flyer, 1971). Brehm, however, wanted more-direct control and so created the Manpower Analysis and Research Data Analysis Center (MARDAC). As originally conceived by Eli Flyer and approved by Srull and Brehm, MARDAC would also have a capability to do manpower research.[40]

---

[39] Greenberg was also given the task of finding $2 million to fund the center for the following year (Greenberg, 2004).

[40] DoD Directive 5100.75 created MARDAC on July 8, 1974 (Clements, 1974). Flyer describes the building of MARDAC in Flyer (2002, pp. 12–15).

Part of Flyer's plan was that MARDAC be located at the Naval Postgraduate School at Monterey, California. The school had the computing power and capabilities to manage large data files. The prospect of research funding for the school's staff was enticing, and they were eager to have some of their excess computer capability used.[41] Almost immediately, however, the Senate Appropriations Committee moved to eliminate MARDAC in its budget mark. While Greenberg and Flyer finally convinced the committee staff to restore some of the funds it had proposed to cut, earmarking the restored funds for data collection, MARDAC was stripped of its research capabilities (Greenberg, 2004). The research function went to RAND, and MARDAC became the Defense Manpower Data Center (DMDC), which is still housed at the Naval Postgraduate School.

Market Research and Analysis

If there was one area that Brehm and Herbits agreed on, it was the need for professional marketing research. Lee recalled that, on the new assistant secretary's first day in office, Brehm asked who the "market expert" was on the staff. In January, Herbits pressed for a "Director of Recruiting . . . with expertise to supervise and manage adequately the broad range of functions which come under the heading of recruiting" (Herbits, 1974). The following September, Dr. Al J. Martin was appointed Special Assistant for Accessions Policy.

Martin was not new to the Pentagon. A graduate of the Reserve Officer Training (ROTC) program, he had taken a "delay of call to active duty" to pursue a doctorate in marketing at the Ohio State University. When his delay-of-call ran out—delays were granted for a maximum of four years—and with the degree in hand, he was assigned to teach at the Naval Postgraduate School and then was deployed to Vietnam, where he completed his two years of obligated service. Before he left for Vietnam, however, Don Rice, the Deputy Assistant Secretary of Defense for Resource Analysis, recruited him for the Systems Analysis office, after he completed his military service, to work on all-volunteer force marketing issues. Rice had himself taught at the Naval Postgraduate School, when he was a junior officer, and had started the program in which Martin was an instructor.

By the time Martin finally took up that position in Systems Analysis in September 1971, Rice had left for OMB. To Martin's chagrin, he found himself in a difficult situation. With Rice gone, there was little interest in the Systems Analysis office in his particular view of how to "market" the all-volunteer force. In spring 1972, after writing a paper arguing for an integrated marketing approach, he left Systems Analysis for an associate professorship at the new American International University in Miami, Florida. Now, two years later, when Brehm asked who on his staff was his "marketing expert"

---

[41] *Author's Note:* When I was Director of Selective Service, our "secret" backup computer capability was also at the Naval Post Graduate School. Every night during the registration, computer files were mailed to Monterey. If something happened to the primary center in Washington, we could restore operations in California in a matter of hours.

(Lee and Parker, 1977, p. 462), Martin's former colleagues, who had moved with Don Srull to the Manpower Office, remembered his long-neglected report and called him in Florida to see if he might be interested in coming back. Martin met with Brehm and agreed to take the special assistant's job formerly held by Steve Herbits. Eventually, this was made into a permanent career position, with the title of Director of Accessions and Retention Programs. Martin would explain years later that it was very important that the new office consider both accessions and retention policy. As he saw it, "having both parts was the essence of the marketing approach" (Martin, 2002).

Martin's approach was controversial from the start. His focus on joint advertising was not viewed favorably by the individual services, which saw themselves in deadly combat for quality recruits. His focus on research, sales promotion directed at the educational community, and advertising encroached on the traditional turf of the services. While he established a number of joint committees to ensure the involvement of the services and their recruiter commanders, they worked together begrudgingly.

One of Martin's most important initiatives was to get Brehm to resurrect the long-dormant issue of paid radio and television advertising. Paid advertising had been one of the first initiatives that Brehm had undertaken at the advent of the all-volunteer force in 1970, when he was the Assistant Secretary of the Army. It had run afoul of the powerful Chairman of the House Armed Services Committee, F. Edward Hebert. Hebert had made it plain that he thought the broadcasting networks should provide free airtime and had initiated a one-year ban on paid advertising. Unfortunately, free public-service advertisements were almost never shown in prime time but late at night, when radio and television stations had few paying advertisers—or listeners or viewers. The old adage that you "get what you pay for" was certainly true for the services. While the ban had not been extended in law, DoD decided it would not cross the powerful chairman of its authorizing committee.

Subsequent efforts to get a more favorable resolution of the issue had not been successful. In spring 1972, General Montague tried to interest Steve Herbits, then a staffer for Senator Robert Stafford (R-Vermont), in pressing the case for paid radio and television advertising as "an excellent way to stimulate actions and interest in AVF . . . [by] sponsor[ing] a powerful campaign to advertise the new, ample military pay." As he saw it, "[u]se of paid radio/TV would be essential. Except for newspapers (which are not efficient) they are the only media which could be used on such short notice" (Montague, 1972). Herbits saw no way around Hebert. Again that fall, in a report to John Stennis, Chairman of the Senate Armed Services Committee, the Secretary of Defense complained of the "current limitations, imposed by the Congress." Citing paid media as being "highly efficient and effective," he told Senator Stennis that

> [e]stimates indicate that by using paid television and radio advertising and without increasing its FY 1973 expenditure for advertising, the Army could obtain more than 10,000 additional male enlistments. . . . We believe that we should have the flexibility to test this option if necessary under careful control by the Office [of the] Secretary of Defense. (Secretary of Defense, 1972, p. 17)

By mid-January 1975, Hebert was no longer a problem. Having run afoul of a reform movement in the post-Watergate Democratic Caucus, he lost the chairmanship of the Armed Services Committee when the Democrats gathered to organize the new House of Representatives (Hebert and McMillan, 1976, p. 447). Martin would remember that "Brehm did not ask the new Chairman, Melvin Price, for his permission, but told his staff that he was going to 'test' the concept to see if it had any place in the future" (Martin, 2002). Brehm believed that "In our long-run recruiting effort, we will want a full spectrum of advertising including a paid broadcast program," and, on March 19, 1975, he "approved an OSD media study designed to analyze the cost-effectiveness of DoD use of paid broadcast advertising and to estimate its cross-Service and public service impacts" (Brehm, 1975b).

For Martin, the notion of a test was both a way to ease back into paid advertising and a way to gain critical proof of the "efficiency and effectiveness" of paid media that, in his judgment, was still lacking. The 1971 test by the Army had been flawed, and this was his opportunity to do a test right. In fact, there were two tests in 1975. The Army, repeating what had happened in 1971, moved ahead without Brehm's permission and fielded a limited paid media program.[42] Years later, when Martin remembered the Army's action, he admonished that the Army's 1975 program should not be called a test:

> The Army moved out without much thought to research design or controls. In the end, they could not tell if their program worked or if it didn't work. Our test of paid radio was carefully constructed and ground breaking. (Martin, 2002)

At the end of that test, Martin reported, "on the basis of the DoD test results, . . . the military services have been permitted to use paid broadcast recruiting advertising since October 1976" (Martin, 1980, p. 18).

Compensation, Special Pay, and Manning Problems

When Brehm took office in September 1973, one of the most important management initiatives of the all-volunteer force was bogged down in Congress, the Uniformed Service Special Pay Act. This bill provided bonus authorization to address a number of special manning problems. Most significant were bonuses for the reserve components—the National Guard and the Reserve—and for health professionals. In addition, it allowed the services to pay bonuses for initial enlistments in critical shortage occupations, other than the combat arms. It also sought to repeal the regular enlistment bonus

---

[42] Brehm asked Callaway to "delay use of paid broadcast advertising until we complete the OSD media study" (Brehm, 1975b). Callaway agreed only if the OSD study was in place by May 1, 1975; if not, the Army would "proceed with its paid radio advertising test" (Callaway, 1975a). Brehm thought July 1, 1975, was the earliest possible start date (Brehm, 1975c). Callaway decided to move ahead anyway, and told Brehm he had "instructed USAREC to proceed with the paid broadcast plan. We will begin to obligate funds today" (Callaway, 1975b).

that was paid to all personnel and the expansion of the variable enlistment bonus beyond the first term in a new Selective Reenlistment Bonus Program.

Enlistment and Reenlistment Bonuses

In recognition of a problem in attracting men to the combat arms of infantry, armor, and artillery, the Pentagon had, in 1971, proposed to Congress an enlistment bonus of up to $3,000 for those who enlisted for three years in one of the combat branches of the Army or Marine Corps. Congress approved the request in September 1971, and a test of $1,500 for a four-year enlistment in the combat elements of the Army and Marine Corps began on June 1, 1972. Between June and the following May, over 23,000 men took advantage of this program and signed on for a four-year enlistment contract.

The General Research Corporation told the Army that "about 83 percent of the bonus enlistees would have entered the Army without the bonus; most of the others would have entered one of the other Services" (Lee and Parker, 1977). They argued that the main effect was to channel those who would have joined into longer terms of service and into the combat arms. This was not insignificant, however, since the longer enlistments provided a 36-percent gain in the projected man-years of service that each new recruit would provide. This translated into a reduction in future accessions, which was estimated to be about 28,000, and made the entire program very cost-effective.

One disturbing aspect of the bonus was the large number of non–high school graduates it brought into the Army. Only 39 percent of those who signed up for the bonus had completed high school. As a result, the program was changed in May 1973. Although the Army did not use all the authority granted by Congress, it did increase the bonus to $2,500, but only high school graduates that scored at or above average on the AFQT were eligible. Over time, this had the desired effect of channeling manpower into particular skills, increasing the man-years of service from each new recruit, and increasing the quality of the recruits. On June 1, 1974, a new expanded enlistment bonus that Congress had passed went into effect, replacing the combat arms bonus with a broader program for all services and for any critical skill suffering from inadequate accessions, as long as the recruit agreed to serve a minimum of four years. At the same time, a new selected reenlistment bonus replaced the across-the-board regular reenlistment bonus and extended the variable reenlistment bonus to "any problem reenlistment point within the member's first ten years of service. The amount paid depends on the severity of the retention problem . . . and the amount of additional obligated service to which the member agrees" (Brehm, 1975a). In February 1975, with an "improved recruiting environment," the then-current programs for enlistment terms and enlistment bonuses were modified (Brehm, 1975a). Short-term enlistments were ended (Schlesinger, 1975), and the maximum enlistment bonus was reduced to $2,000.

Manpower for Mobilization and the Standby Draft

One area of increasing concern to the administration and Congress was how the armed services would meet their manpower needs in the face of the most demanding contingency, an attack by the Soviet Union and its Warsaw Pact allies on Western Europe and NATO. Brehm told the Senate that this would require recalling "previously trained veterans of the peacetime volunteer force to fill units and sustain forces in combat, and a draft oriented toward a protracted conflict" (Brehm, 1976a, p. 1,520). This meant a new focus on trained individuals who left active service but did not join a selected reserve unit, yet still had a military service obligation under the terms of their initial enlistment (the military service obligation for all new recruits was six years). Analysis showed that, even with a postmobilization draft and a "fully structured Selective Service System" and with the then-current sources of trained and untrained manpower, there would be "a major manpower shortfall in the early months of a [future] war" (Brehm, 1976a, p. 1,524).

Congress found the fixes for this problem to be alarming. Brehm suggested that the active armed forces might have to be increased by as much as 400,000 men at a cost of $12.5 billion per year. Astonished, Senator Sam Nunn (D–Georgia) noted that 62 percent of the total DoD budget would go to personnel. As Brehm saw it, however, being more aggressive with a standby draft would not help because the Armed Forces did "not have units to absorb them once we have taken care of the earlier requirements with trained personnel" (Brehm, 1976a, p. 1,527). While the issue was not resolved, the termination of draft registration in 1975 led to a debate on how best to structure the Selective Service System to meet its postmobilization schedule to deliver untrained personnel to the DoD. This debate was not resolved until President Carter reinstated peacetime draft registration in 1980.[43]

Reserve Components

If issues of manning, quality, and race punctuated the continuing debate over the all-volunteer force, the problems the Reserve components were having received little attention. The Army's official history characterized the concern for the "reserve manning problem" as receiving "little more than lip service in the early days of the transition and only piecemeal attention thereafter" (Griffith, 1997, p. 255). This was no better

---

[43] Greenberg felt Brehm's testimony was "a big mistake." He recalls that Brehm was

> misled by a faulty casualty estimating model. The testimony did not result in any immediate policy or budget changes but was used for many years by opponents of the all-volunteer force as an argument for returning to the draft. A draft would increase the inventory of the Individual Ready Reserve because 2-year draftees would be in the IRR for four more years while 2-year volunteers would be in the IRR for only 3 years. The issue became moot when the Military Service Obligation (MSO) was increased from 6 to 8 years as recommended by the Military Manpower Task Force Report in 1982. (Greenberg, 2004)

dramatized than when, on December 13, 1973, Brehm told Congress that DoD no longer supported a bonus package for the reserve components, even though they were not meeting their recruiting goals. His rationale, he explained, was that the necessary size of the reserve components was "uncertain" (Lee and Parker, 1977, p. 316). Brehm's action made it clear the reserve components were on their own: Any initiatives to improve the prospects of meeting their all-volunteer force manpower goals would rest solely in their own hands.

Their first self-help initiative was the successful full-time recruiters program. In 1971, the reserve components funded 767 recruiter man-years. That number doubled the next year and doubled again until, by fiscal 1974, the number reached 4,140. In 1973, the reserve components flirted with the notion that the six-year commitment to serve in a unit was a significant deterrent to joining the reserves and wanted to change policy across the board. However, careful assessment of an initial test proved that this was not the case. Eventually, Kelley allowed limited numbers of enlistment contracts to be written for less than six years. In the final analysis, however, reserve components achieved their goals by successfully recruiting from groups that they had not previously drawn on: women; blacks; and, especially, prior-service personnel recently separated from active duty (Griffith, 1997, p. 275).

In 1975, Brehm was still lamenting the falling numbers of non–prior service personnel being recruited into selected reserve units. He noted his "concerns about not getting enough non–prior service enlistees. Moreover, those that we are getting do not have the quality characteristics that we would like" (Brehm, 1975b). Almost begrudgingly, he told Congress that "[w]e do not object to having prior-service people since they are trained and have experience, but we must have the correct balance." By 1976, Brehm was touting the reserve components' success in shifting their focus from non–prior service to prior-service accessions:

> In 1970, during the draft era, about two-thirds of reserve accessions were non–prior service. Recently, however, the proportions have changed, and for FY 1974 and FY 1975 only about one-fourth of the accessions were non–prior service.
>
> Prior Service personnel are generally of high quality. They are already trained and have served successfully in an active component. (Brehm, 1976b, p. 37)

Health Professionals

If the reserve manning problem could be ignored, the other major problem area— medical personnel—could not be. The Gates Commission had highlighted "medical" as a problem area but had argued that

> given the reduction in forces now planned and the students already committed to military service, there is time not only for further study, but for experimentation with some of the measures suggested, such as increased compensation for military physicians and fellowship programs for medical students. (Gates, 1970, p. 87)

The "students now committed" was a reference to the "Berry Plan,"[44] a program wherein participants accepted a Selective Service deferment that allowed them to complete their medical education in exchange for agreeing to enter military service for two years once they had completed their medical training. Medical students, as special registrants under Section 5(a) of the Military Selective Service Act, were subject to the "doctor draft" and were treated differently from other graduate students. Other graduate students received yearly deferments with the understanding that, if they remained in school past their 28th birthdays, Selective Service policy was that they would not be called. As a matter of the same policy, special registrants were subject to being called until age 35. Under the Berry Plan, medical students received multiyear deferments with the option to apply for a variety of intern and residency options. Those who were offered the longest training programs, ones that might take them past the 35 age limit, were given reserve commissions and were placed on delay-of-call status until they had completed their medical training. As commissioned officers, there was no limit on when they might be called to active duty. Thus, when Secretary Laird announced an end to the draft and after induction authority had expired in 1973, all nonmedical graduate students were free from the threat of being drafted. However, medical students who had signed up for the Berry Plan exemption or who had accepted reserve commissions still had to honor their commitments and continued to staff military medical departments well into the 1980s.[45]

A long-range program to address the medical problem focused on medical scholarships and bonuses for physicians and other critical health professionals. It also included the establishment of the military's own medical school, the Uniformed Services University of the Health Sciences, attempts to reduce the demand for physicians through the use of physician's assistants, other "extenders," and the direct recruiting of older physicians from private civilian practice.[46]

On September 21, 1972, Congress passed the Armed Forces Health Professional Revitalization Act. The act contained authorization for the Armed Forces Health Professions Scholarship Program and the establishment of the uniformed services' medical school. On May 4, 1974, Congress also approved a program of internal incentives—the Uniformed Services Variable Incentive Pay Act for Physicians. After some delay, a program of incentive pays was initiated on September 12, 1974. By the end of FY 1976, the number of new physicians was almost three and one-half times that of the previous year. Moreover, physician losses were down by 27 percent. While Lee argued that, "with the implementation of the physician's bonus it appeared that the last remaining manning problem of the volunteer force was virtually solved" (Lee and Parker, 1977, p. 334),

---

[44] This plan, known more formally as the Armed Forces Physician's Appointment and Residency Consideration Program, was established in 1954 and named after Dr. Frank Berry, Assistant Secretary of Defense (Health and Medical).

[45] A discussion of the doctor draft and the Berry Plan is in Brooke (1979, pp. 23–27).

[46] Lee and Parker (1977, p. 333) and Griffith (1997, p. 258) discuss the use of physician assistants in the context of the overall strategy.

problems would in fact remain until the higher retention from Uniformed Services University of the Health Sciences graduates became apparent in the late 1980s.

Managing the Recruiting Process

As the all-volunteer force moved forward, DoD officials and Congress became increasingly concerned about the effectiveness, efficiency, and veracity of the recruiting process. In spring 1973, the Army Audit Agency reported on widespread recruiter malpractice. GAO also saw widespread malpractice (Comptroller General of the United States, 1976b). It found that recruits were "improperly helped through AFEES [Armed Forces Examining and Entrance Station] processing by recruiters" (Comptroller General of the United States, 1976b, p. 4). This included coaching applicants who had failed tests at one AFEES and were sent to another, to give them additional chances to pass the entrance examination. GAO also found that medical examinations and police record checks were not adequately performed, adding to stress and costs at the basic-training reception centers. In FY 1974, 10.5 percent of the enlistees sent to the basic-training reception centers were discharged for causes GAO felt should have been identified at the AFEES.

GAO attributed much of the problem to the fact that, while AFEES were joint-service facilities operated by the U.S. Army Recruiting Command, they were really subordinate to the recruiting commands of the individual services. In GAO's words, the stations "[perform] as a supporting agency to the recruiter" (Comptroller General of the United States, 1976b, p. 7). GAO concluded that

> [t]he AFEES, because they do not have a recruiting mission, are better suited than the recruiting services to perform quality control over mental and medical examinations, moral fitness, and enlistment paperwork. Subordination to the recruiting services, fragmented and incomplete procedural controls, noncompatible recruiting service boundaries, service-administered mental examinations, and operational inefficiencies have precluded the AFEES from acting as a central, independent monitoring agent. These problems have probably resulted in a considerable number of recruits entering the military services who do not meet recruiting standards. (Comptroller General of the United States, 1976b, p. 7)

Of particular concern to GAO were the failure of the AFEES to administer mental examinations adequately and the disparate mental qualifying tests the individual services used. At the time, the Navy and Air Force did not give their mental qualifying examinations at the AFEES. The Marine Corp and Army did give the test at the AFEES. The Marine Corps, however, retested almost all its recruits at its training center. The other services retested to a lesser extent. What concerned GAO was that, in all the services, retesting produced a substantial increase in category IV personnel (Comptroller General of the United States, 1976b, p. 13). GAO recommended that "a single test should be given at the AFEES for all services under circumstances that make compromising it difficult or impossible" (Comptroller General of the United States, 1976b, p. 14).

Enlistment Processing

DoD responded to the increasing dissatisfaction with the AFEES system in a number of ways. In November 1974, Brehm established a task force under the leadership of Air Force Major John Johnson to streamline enlistment documents and processing. Johnson had a reputation as a very tenacious staff officer. He previously organized the Air Force's Saber Volunteer Study and the 1972 Air Force-Industry Conference on the All-Volunteer Force. As an Air Force Fellow at the Brookings Institution, he coauthored an important study for the Senate Armed Services Committee, *All Volunteer Armed Forces: Progress, Problems and Prospects* (Binkin and Johnson, 1973).

The often-used quip about "herding a bunch of cats" was never more apt than for getting the services to agree on common recruit processing. Bringing some semblance of order to recruit processing would take all Johnson's considerable talents. His task force would standardize data and standardize recruiting forms. GAO would credit DoD, after the implementation of new documents and procedures on July 1, 1975, with millions of dollars of savings per year. Eventually, these efforts would lead to the creation of a new, independent Military Enlistment Process Command reporting to the Assistant Secretary of Defense for Manpower and Reserve Affairs.

Qualification Testing

Brehm also addressed the issue of multiple entrance examinations and the need to standardize both the test and its administration. The proliferation of quality testing took off after May 1972 when, following his basic philosophy of giving each military department maximum freedom in implementing the all-volunteer force, Kelley decided that, in addition to setting its own qualification standards, each service should be free to choose its own qualification tests.[47] He required only that, whatever the test it selected, the service be capable of "expressing" test results in terms of the familiar mental categories. Lee reported that, in making his decision, Kelley was influenced by his visits to recruiters in the field. Apparently, "some recruiters had reported to him that many qualified applicants were lost because they 'flunked' the AFQT" (Lee and Parker, 1977, p. 370). As it would turn out, this was akin to taking the foxes seriously when they complain that the lock on the henhouse door is difficult to open.

There is no question that one of the most difficult jobs in the military is recruiting. Nowhere else in the military do you get a report card every month. Despite formal training, it often appears that recruiters are born and not made. Why, for instance, would one recruiter be able to recruit three or four people per month, while another has problems recruiting even one, *in the same district*? Recruiters are often not volunteers.

---

[47] Kelley also flirted with the notion during November 1972 of closing the AFEES in favor of each service going it alone. All the services opposed this idea.

Recruiting duty is hardly what they joined the military to do. While there are rewards for being a successful recruiter, there are also severe penalties for not succeeding. No wonder recruiters sometimes cut corners. GAO believed that independent AFEES with a common entrance test was the means of maintaining quality control over the enlistment processing system (Comptroller General of the United States, 1976a).

The Move to a New Common Test

Just as the services were freed from the common AFQT, the realities of the all-volunteer force pushed them back together because the high school recruiting and testing program became an important source of "qualified" leads. Under this program, the military provided a valuable service to high schools. Their students were given, free of charge, a well-recognized vocational aptitude test—the ASVAB—that they found useful for career planning and counseling. In November 1972, a DoD-wide task force recommended all the services begin using the ASVAB by January 1, 1973. The task force believed that a common test would eliminate the need for multiple tests as prospective enlistees compared service options, simplify referrals among services, broaden the recruiting market, and eliminate the wide variance in entry standards for similar jobs (Central All-Volunteer Force Task Force, 1972).

Movement toward a common test, however, was not smooth. The Joint Service Working Group charged with the task of creating a battery of tests that would meet the needs of all the services reported dissension among the services. In May 1974, Brehm personally took charge of the program to implement the common aptitude test.[48] Bowing to concerns from the Navy, he slipped the implementation date from September 1, 1975, to June 1, 1976. Even with that delay, the test as finally fielded was "not ready for prime time," as would become clear during the Carter administration.

Physical Standards

In June 1973, Herbits endorsed Gus Lee's recommendation for a review of medical standards, citing the April 1972 RAND study (Chu, 1972), calling it "an important untapped resource that should be studied in depth" (Herbits, 1973d). A week later, General Taber, as the acting Assistant Secretary of Defense (Manpower and Reserve Affairs), asked the Army to take the lead in examining medical standards in five areas and "review . . . differences in medical standards and examination procedures" among the services (Taber, 1973a). In April 1974, David Chu delivered a well received and often quoted RAND report on physical standards (Chu et al., 1974).

---

[48] GAO noted that, in "May 1974, the Defense Manpower Policy Council established a steering committee chaired by the Assistant Secretary . . . to develop and implement a common aptitude test by September 1, 1975" (Comptroller General of the United States, 1976a, p. 19).

The Cost of the All-Volunteer Force, the Third QRMC, and the Defense Manpower Commission

The progress toward an all-volunteer force came at a cost, which became an important political issue during spring 1973. While the Gates Commission had been forceful in the distinction it made between the "true" or social costs of the all-volunteer force and its budget costs, the effects on the budget were foremost in policymakers' minds. GAO raised the issue in a May 1973 progress report to Congress, which struck a chord of concern by stating that "pay and related costs increased from about 42 percent [of the total DoD costs] in fiscal year 1968 to 56 percent in fiscal year 1973" (Comptroller General of the United States, 1973, p. 63). GAO estimated that "DoD programs for the AVF have contributed about 23 percent of the increase in personnel costs" (Comptroller General of the United States, 1973, p. 63). The argument was that personnel costs were pushing hardware procurement out of the defense budget.

In the popular press, Joseph A. Califano Jr., who had been President Johnson's Special Assistant for Domestic Affairs, led the charge with an editorial in the *Washington Post* complaining that the "all-volunteer military is a very expensive proposition" (Califano, 1973). While it drew an immediate response from Kelley (1973a) to the editors of the *Washington Post*, and a rebuttal by Congressman William Steiger (R-Wisconsin) (Steiger, 1973), also in the *Washington Post*, it was an argument that would not go away. Even though DoD showed that, in FY 1974, the all-volunteer force added only 7.1 percent to the personnel budget and only 4 percent to the total budget (Montague, 1973b), this was a prominent topic at the authorization hearings in early summer 1973 and again at Brehm's confirmation hearings in August.

Defending the All-Volunteer Force

Brehm defended the all-volunteer force on the issue of costs when he addressed commanders in February 1974. He argued that most of the cost increase was attributable to pre–all-volunteer force legislation in 1967 that had moved the services toward "full comparability between Federal civilian salaries and those found in the civilian sector . . . [and the] special 'catch-up' pay increase for junior officer and enlisted personnel" (Brehm, 1974d, p. 6). He held that these increases were "deserved in the interest of fairness and equity, and should have been done whether we moved to an All-Volunteer Force or not." He directly addressed those in Congress who were using the increase in cost as a stalking-horse for their agenda of returning to a draft by pointing out that "one who contemplates a return to the draft should not count on rolling back the wages of the first-termer to reduce personnel costs. It simply will not happen" (Brehm, 1974d, p. 6).[49]

---

[49] A *stalking-horse* is a screen bearing a figure of a horse that a hunter can hide behind while stalking game.

In a letter to Senator Jacob Javits (R-New York) on the same subject, Brehm told the Senator that, while

> Defense manpower costs represent about 53% of the FY 1976 Defense Budget Request, . . . [m]ilitary personnel costs represented 29.1% of the FY 1976 Budget, compared to 26.6 percent in FY 1964 [an increase of a little over 9 percent . . . [and] [c]ivilian personnel costs and military retired pay represent 24.0% of the FY 1976 budget, compared to 16.8% in FY 1964 [an increase of over 43 percent]. (Brehm, 1975d, p. 1)

He reminded Senator Javits that

> [t]he extent to which "Military Personnel Costs" would be reduced by a return to the draft would depend on two judgments which would probably have to be made by Congress. The first is the degree to which the pay of first-termers (i.e., draftees) would be reduced; the second is whether or not the principle of pay comparability for careerists—established by the Congress in 1967 (three years before the President proposed the All-Volunteer Force)—would be turned aside. (Brehm, 1975d, p. 3)

Brehm also responded to the issue of how a return to the draft would affect the readiness and the ability of the Armed Forces to perform their assigned missions, concluding that "a return to the draft would be counterproductive" (Brehm, 1975d, p. 5).

Brehm was not without allies in Congress who were willing to speak out. Representative William Steiger (R-Wisconsin), a long-standing friend of the all-volunteer force, wrote the syndicated columnists Roland Evans and Robert Novak to complain of their discussion of the "impact of the volunteer force on the defense budget." He told them "it is illusory to think that there are savings to be achieved from a return to the draft" (Steiger, 1974). But he and Brehm were up against formidable foes in Congress. The most outspoken was the Chairman of the Senate Armed Services Committee's Manpower and Personnel Subcommittee, Senator Nunn.

Senator Sam Nunn of Georgia

Senator Nunn was one of the most ardent opponents of the all-volunteer force. No one in Congress before or since has been so focused on issues of military manpower. On an early trip home, soon after becoming a U.S. Senator, he warned his former colleagues in the Georgia General Assembly about "skyrocketing manpower costs and failing popular support and appreciation of our defense needs" (Nunn, 1973, pp. 4–7):

> The hardest reality of all has not been squarely faced by our government and has not been fully recognized by our people. This reality, the problem of military manpower, is on the verge of getting completely out of control.
> The military draft has never been popular and all of us hope that conditions will not require its large scale use again.

Realistically, however, it is time for us to take another look at the results of the all out push for the so-called "volunteer force." This concept is a clear result of the Vietnam war which because of its unpopularity caused the President and Congress to yield to the tremendous pressure to end the draft at almost any price. . . .

Most of this phenomenal rise in the costs of manpower can be laid at the door of the all-volunteer force concept. . . .

I am not opposed to a fair system of pay and allowances for our servicemen. But . . . we cannot afford to see manpower costs escalate. . . .

I do not dogmatically oppose the volunteer concept, but I feel that it is imperative for our government and our people to ask some hard cold realistic questions as to where this road leads. . . .

Although the draft system contains many inequities, it is still a better means of providing an armed force more representative of the American society as a whole than is possible under the all volunteer system. . . .

No mercenary in history has ever been a match for free and dedicated men fighting to preserve their stakes in a free society.

Eight months after his speech, his view that it "is imperative for our Government and our people to ask some hard cold realistic questions as to where this road leads" took voice when Congress created the Defense Manpower Commission.[50]

Senator John Stennis of Mississippi

The effectiveness of Nunn's opposition to the all-volunteer force was somewhat tempered by the position taken by Senator Stennis, Chairman of the Senate Armed Services Committee. Stennis, to say the least, had always been "skeptical" that the nation could achieve an all-volunteer force in the numbers and at the quality levels required. While he had once called the whole concept "a flight from reality," Herbits thought "he does understand and will promote good policy." Herbits wrote him down as "the most wily of them all," who "must be watched like a hawk." Whether it was guile or not, in the hour of maximum despair for the all-volunteer force—in Herbits's view "the AVF is in more danger today than at any time"—Stennis took to the floor of the Senate on September 24, 1973, to say that,

[h]aving gone as far as we have, we must be certain that this plan is given a real chance. . . . The facts are that the plan has not been sufficiently tried, not by any means. . . . Congress is certainly obligated to see that the plan is given a fair trial and not dropped at least until it has been given an exhaustive trial. (Stennis, 1973, p. 31,070)

---

[50] In fact, Senator Nunn delivered the same speech on the floor of the Senate on September 26, 1973, during the floor debate concerning the establishment of the Defense Manpower Commission (see Nunn et al., 1973, pp. 31,597–31,598).

Senator Nunn clearly did not share his views on cost. Senator Stennis argued that "from 80 to 90 percent of the $3 billion [in additional costs] will remain as an annual cost, whether this all-volunteer plan is retained or not" (Stennis, 1973, p. 31,070).

The Defense Manpower Commission

On November 16, 1973, Congress created the Defense Manpower Commission with a charter to "focus on the substantial increase in the costs of military manpower" (Tarr, 1976, p. vii).[51] In the Senate, the bipartisan sponsors of the commission were Senators Howard Baker (R-Tennessee) and Lloyd Bentsen of Texas (D-Texas).[52] They and their colleagues left no doubt of their "firm belief that unless the Congress and the President can find a better means to control the expense of personnel for the defense establishment, the security of this country will be seriously jeopardized" (Nunn et al., 1973, p. 31,595). In what seems a direct rejection of Brehm and Steiger's arguments, the commission noted that "[t]he fact that a major share of these high and rising manpower costs could be explained by such causes as inflation and pay comparability, which do not involve ineffective management, did not make the effect any more palatable" (Tarr, 1976, p. viii). The commission knew it was on notice of Congress's "deep, albeit varied, concern about the effectiveness of the All-Volunteer Force" (Tarr, 1976, p. viii)—a concern reflected in Senator Nunn's suggestion to Brehm that the government should "abolish the Volunteer Force and go back to the draft and freeze manpower costs for the next five years" (Nunn, 1976, p. 1,528).

As a joint presidential and congressional commission, the Defense Manpower Commission was made up of seven commissioners, four appointed by Congress and three by the President. Curtis Tarr, the former Director of Selective Service and then–Vice President of Deere & Company, agreed to serve as chairman. The White House appointed Martin Anderson, who had left government service for a position at the Hoover Institution at Stanford University. Retired Army General Bruce Palmer Jr. was selected to be the executive director.[53]

The Defense Manpower Commission reported on April 19, 1976. A summary prepared for the Secretary of Defense by his staff called the report "very positive. . . .

---

[51] Tarr provided Brehm a summary background description of the commission's "current and planned activities" in Tarr (1974).

[52] As Senator Baker saw it, Congress neither had the time nor the resources to undertake the sort of fundamental but comprehensive examination of defense manpower required to deal effectively with this complex matter (Nunn, 1973, p. 31,587).

[53] Senator William Proxmire (D-Wisconsin) for one was concerned about the composition of the commission and its staff:

> [T]he Commission, its staff, and the AMC Advisory Panel are so overwhelmingly composed of former Pentagon employees that I fail to see how the Commission can possibly offer the "uninvolved, objective perspective" so necessary in tackling this massive manpower problem in the Defense Department. (Proxmire, 1974)

The report is very much a blueprint for the future and recognizes that there is no immediate action available to substantially reduce manpower costs" (Murray, 1976).[54] The report must have been a disappointment to Senator Nunn and those in Congress who opposed the all-volunteer force.[55] It certainly was a disappointment to the *New York Times* editorial staff. As they saw it,

> the real problem is the volunteer army. . . . To keep a mass army in being by volunteer recruitment—something no other country has attempted in recent memory—may even require lifting military pay significantly above civilian levels once economic recovery takes hold. (*New York Times* Editorial Board, 1976)

The *Times* complained that "all of the economies proposed by the administration and the commission are marginal compared to the excruciating costs imposed on the defense budget by the volunteer army" (*New York Times* Editorial Board, 1976). In fact, one commissioner had resigned the previous year, complaining the commission had fallen under the influence of the military and did not seriously look at the benefit package enjoyed by service members (Finney, 1976).

As for the all-volunteer force, the question Nunn posed during his speech to the Georgia General Assembly in March 1973—"Where [does] this road lead?"—was answered by the commission in April 1976:

> The prospects for sustaining peacetime All-Volunteer Force during the next ten years (1976–85) will be determined basically by the economic situation. . . . If rapid economic growth is realized the supply of recruits will probably not be large enough to support Service needs under current policies and programs. However, a range of actions is available which, if implemented, should avert a major recruiting shortfall without resorting to pay increases beyond those required to maintain the current competitive nature of military compensation. (Tarr, 1976, p. 417)

The commission made one pointed and specific recommendation that found favor with Senator Nunn, concerning the need for a standby draft. They expressed their "grave concern" that "[r]ecent administrative actions have already emasculated any semblance of a viable standby Selective Service System" (Tarr, 1976, p. 427) and recommended that the "Standby Draft System should be reconstituted with adequate funding to provide a capability to commence inductions within 30 days" (Tarr, 1976, p. 431). Martin Anderson was the lone commissioner to dissent from the commission's recommendations concerning a standby draft. He argued that "[c]linging to a standby draft will . . . give false hope to those who wish to dodge the managerial difficulties and

---

[54] On November 20, 1975, White House Chief of Staff Donald Rumsfeld became the 13th and youngest Secretary of Defense. In August 1976, he sent DoD's "tentative position" on the Defense Manpower Commission to the President's National Security Advisor (Rumsfeld, 1976b).

[55] A search of the Congressional Information Service, Inc., index of witnesses shows that the Defense Manpower Commission's Chairman, Curtis Tarr, never testified before Congress after the commission's report was published in 1976.

cost of sustaining an all-volunteer force" (Tarr, 1976, p. 462). In fact, the arguments and actions concerning the standby draft would be a major issue for the next (Carter) administration.

When all was said and done, the commission had little influence on defense policy and programs. In fact, seven months after the commission presented its findings to the President and Congress, and after they had "informally requested a status report from the Department," Senators Baker and Bentsen asked GAO to "follow up on the contents of the report [and to provide] an evaluation of the Department of Defense's decision process involved in considering and acting upon the Commission's recommendations."[56] GAO reported to Congress that DoD's

> responses lacked specific details . . . did not indicate the organization with the specific responsibility for taking action or a time frame for completing any action . . . [and] in most cases . . . stated that no further action was necessary. (Comptroller General of the United States, 1977, p. i)

It would fall to the Carter administration to "formally" respond in January 1978 (U.S. Department of Defense, 1978). This was not, however, the only thing that would fall to the new administration. Reform of the compensation system would also be passed along as the Third QRMC failed to move the cause of reform forward.

The Third Quadrennial Review of Military Compensation

In January 1975, with growing concern about the rising cost of military manpower, DoD started the Third QRMC.[57] This was the first comprehensive look at the principles and concepts of military compensation in almost a decade and the first since the advent of the all-volunteer force.[58] Brehm selected his Director of Compensation, Navy Captain James Campbell to be the staff director. In June, Navy Captain James Talbot succeeded him.[59] A study group was established that included the assistant secretaries of defense, the deputy chiefs of staff for personnel of each of the services, the assistant secretaries of the military departments, and OMB's Associate Director for National Security Programs. A coordination committee representing the principals, chaired by

---

[56] From a letter from Senators Baker and Bentsen to Elmer Staats, November 9, 1976 in Comptroller General of the United States (1977).

[57] Senator Dewey Bartlett (R-Oklahoma), calling for a "curb on military benefits," told Brehm in February 1976 that he hoped "this is the last year we would have such a package [commissary subsidies and things of that nature] in the budget, and that we would take care of that particular group of issues within the framework of the quadrennial review of military compensation" (Bartlett, 1976, p. 1,529).

[58] Brehm had looked forward to taking on the military compensation system even before he returned to the Pentagon. This was one of the topics he asked RAND for help with when he visited in late summer 1973.

[59] *Author's Note:* After his retirement from the Navy in 1977, Jim Talbot would work for me when I was Principal Deputy Assistant Secretary of the Navy (Manpower and Reserves Affairs) as my Director of Personnel Programs. He would hold that position until his retirement from the civil service in 1992.

Talbot, carried on most of the work of coordination. The committee maintained a liaison with the other uniformed services, the National Oceanic and Atmospheric Administration (NOAA), the Coast Guard, and the Defense Manpower Commission. Talbot also headed a professional and administrative staff drawn from the military services that, over time (early 1975 to late 1976), employed 50 people.

The QRMC was set against the same cost-cutting mood that had spawned the Defense Manpower Commission and would shape the manpower and personnel program that Brehm would present to Congress. In the preface to the QRMC report, Secretary of Defense Donald Rumsfeld commented that

> [p]ressures to reduce the Defense budget after the war in Southeast Asia have not spared the manpower segment of the Defense budget; on the contrary, they have focussed [sic] on manpower costs more sharply than on any other area of Defense resources. At the same time, countervailing pressures to improve military pays and benefits in order to maintain the quality and quantity of manpower for an all-volunteer armed force have been coupled with other demands . . . .
>
> reducing manpower levels or reducing pay are effectively closed to us, at least in the short run. . . . the one avenue of exploration open is that of management efficiency of the compensation system. (Rumsfeld, 1976a, p. 1)

Rumsfeld chose not to ponder the word "efficiency" and noted the QRMC's "attempt to identify, cost and value all the various elements of the military compensation in a way that would facilitate comparisons with other segments of society" (Rumsfeld, 1976a, p. 2). He observed that "[t]his effort was not entirely successful" and that "[e]fforts to deal with total compensation were severely limited by" the valuation methodologies used (Rumsfeld, 1976a, p. 2). What Secretary Rumsfeld did not mention was the bitter debate over how to set compensation levels and the form that the compensation system should take. These issues were often spoken about as "comparability or competitiveness" and "a pay and allowance system versus a salary system." It pitted those who believed that "[m]ilitary compensation can be set and adjusted on the basis of a military pay standard" (Rumsfeld, 1976a, p. 11) against those who favored a competitive system in which compensation was set to "attract and retain" needed personnel. In general, the former also believed in a traditional pay and allowance structure, and the latter group tended to favor a salary system, although the two issues were technically separable.

The First QRMC—the Hubbell Study—had proposed a salary system for the career force that was pegged to changes in the level of compensation for the federal civilian workforce. This was rejected early in the Nixon administration as being inconsistent with the market orientation implicit in the Gates Commission's recommendations for ending the draft. Now, in 1975, the Third QRMC once again saw the Hubbell "comparability" standard that linked military pay to the pay of the Civil Service as a responsible choice. Not all members of the study group or the coordination committee shared this opinion.

Members of the study group and the coordination committee broke into two camps, one favoring reform in the form of a competitive salary system, the other favoring the familiar pay and allowance system. Those in the first group thought that military compensation should be set and adjusted solely on the basis of economics (that is, the supply of and demand for personnel) and thought that this could best be accomplished by converting to a salary system. For them, there was only one standard for military personnel and that was to "attract and retain the people needed to staff the military" (Hix, 2002). This group included John Ahearne, Brehm's Principal Deputy, and the representatives from the PA&E office (formerly the Systems Analysis office), John Christie and George Hall on the study group and Major William (Mike) Hix on the coordinating committee. Tom Stanners from OMB joined them. They, however, faced a united front from the services and military departments, which favored the status quo of a pay and allowance system under the banner of "comparability."

The prevailing view of the majority of the QRMC was that, while a competitive system was

> an internal supply-and-demand adjustment method . . . [and had] obvious theoretical appeal, its overwhelming disadvantage is that it does not take [into] account the history of American labor relations for the last 100 years . . . [that] resulted in large scale unionization. (Rumsfeld, 1976a, p. 13)[60]

Favoring the *status quo*, they argued that such a system would be "too complex" and would "effectively destroy the 'rank in the man' concept of the armed forces and replace it with the 'pay for the job' concept of the civilian sector" (Rumsfeld, 1976a, p. 14)—that is, it would destroy a basic feature of military compensation systems, in which personnel of the same grade and years of service receive the same basic level of compensation regardless of skill. They argued that

> a comparability system . . . through administrative personnel actions, supported by bonuses and special pays when required, . . . will ensure that military pay remains competitive with pay in the private sector. (Rumsfeld, 1976a, p. 14)[61]

Hix would later argue that "comparability" was a slippery slope into arguments about the uniqueness of the military and the value that should be placed on the unique dangers military personnel face. These arguments could be avoided if the sole focus

---

[60] Members of the QRMC wrote extensively about their fear of unions. They acknowledged that "most of the causes of unionism in civilian employee groups . . . are present in the armed forces today," but inexplicably argued that their proposals would "defuse the underlying motivations causing them [service members] to seek representation through union organization" (Rumsfeld, 1976a, p. 110). The commission never explained how a salary system was tied to unionization or why the vast majority of white-collar workers in this country are not unionized.

[61] The report of the Third QRMC (Rumsfeld, 1976a) is devoid of any analysis. Brehm had, however, asked RAND to help when the QRMC started. They produced a paper that dealt with an "adjustment mechanism for military pay." They argued that the current system "should be replaced by an approach based on 'competitiveness'" (Chu et al., 1976, p. 53).

were on whether a given compensation system—such as salaries—were adequate for attracting and retaining personnel most efficiently and effectively.

From the start, the QRMC knew that agreeing on measures of "comparability" would be a problem. They knew that Hubbell's recommendation that a military pay standard be based on "comparability" with the Civil Service had brought forth an "emotional reaction of many military personnel and others" (Rumsfeld, 1976a, p. 11). Many in the military argued that "it is insulting and demeaning to compare a combat soldier, on duty for 24 hours a day and potentially subject to death or injury, with a '9-to-5' civilian" (Rumsfeld, 1976a, p. 12). The QRMC decided that they could use "job factor value analysis," as developed by Hay Associates,

> to establish equivalencies between fixed grades of two differing compensation systems. The "relative positioning" method of work level linkage permit[ed] relatively precise identification of the location of a military grade between two Civil Service grades in terms of job difficulty when the work level does not exactly match a GS [General Schedule] grade. (Rumsfeld, 1976a, p. 19)

The QRMC decided that the military, or "X-Factor," while not explicitly quantified in pay, should be addressed by excluding certain traditional benefits of the armed forces from inclusion in the calculations that would be used to establish "comparability." Access to the commissary and exchange systems, a portion of the health benefit, and "perhaps a part of the military welfare and recreation benefit" were identified as "institutional benefits" that would not be counted as part of compensation for the purposes of setting or adjusting military compensation. In addition, it determined that payments of such "individual military liabilities" as hazardous duty should be made "through the existing system of special and incentive pays tailored to the particular situational liability" (Rumsfeld, 1976a, p. 31) and would not be considered to be part of regular compensation.

Unfortunately, notwithstanding the claim of the QRMC that it had dealt with the X-Factor, their declaration that the X-Factor was equal to "institutional and individual benefits" and should not be counted as a part of compensation for the purposes of comparability did not address the adequacy of the then-current level of these benefits or how they should be adjusted in the future. Moreover, while endorsing the Hay system for "job factor value analysis," the QRMC inexplicably concluded that its "effort was not entirely successful in that we found compensation valuation methodologies neither well developed nor standardized to a useful extent" (Rumsfeld, 1976a, p. 2).

In the final analysis, the QRMC was more about giving a voice to the anti–all-volunteer force elements in the military than in determining the structure of military compensation or how pay levels would be set and adjusted. The draft final report of the QRMC endorsed

> the concern[s] of some of our military leaders over the progressive "civilianization" of the armed forces, and . . . the introduction of a salary form of military compensation would contribute to such a trend. (Rumsfeld, 1976a, p. 23)

In statements that echoed the anti all-volunteer force arguments being put forward by Charles Moskos,[62] the QRMC rejected the salary proposals because

> military life is "institutional" rather than "occupational," and characterized by an entire way of life rather than a transitory "job" or "work." The "paternalistic" aspects of the military compensation system . . . should be retained. . . . The compensation system chosen should reinforce and enhance the military values and the special features of the military way of life. (Rumsfeld, 1976a, pp. 23–24)

Finally, the unsigned draft final report of the QRMC noted:

> The strong arguments of the military departments against the salary system are matched by the strength of their case for a version of the pay and allowances system. The current system has been under heavy criticism for years,[63] although it has worked well in both peace and war. It is familiar to and liked by the armed forces, who must eventually "live" with whatever compensation system is adopted; and it is somewhat cheaper than a salary approach in the event of mobilization for war. (Rumsfeld, 1976a, p. 24)

To the chagrin of many who worked on the Third QRMC—Brehm's staff, the PA&E representative, and the representative from OMB—the final report was a total endorsement of the existing system. While the report did represent the views of the service chiefs, PA&E and OMB's opposition ensured that it went unsigned by the departing Secretary of Defense. Moreover, for those interested in reforming the system, it was taken as proof that DoD was not capable of reforming itself. Within months, the new Carter administration chartered a new blue ribbon panel of civilian experts from outside DoD as the President's commission on Military Compensation. One holdover was Major William M. (Mike) Hix,[64] the reform-minded Army officer who became the deputy executive director of the new commission and provided the civilian outsiders with a window on the inner working of the Pentagon.

---

[62] Moskos has argued that he was not anti–all-volunteer force, just against the use of economic incentives as a way of achieving the all-volunteer force. In 1978, he told a congressional committee that

> [the] problems of the All-Volunteer Force are not found in the end of conscription, or in the efforts of service recruiters. The grievous flaw has been a redefinition of military service in terms of the economic marketplace. . . . The Gates Commission . . . set the rationale for the All-Volunteer Force in terms of econometric models, the economic animal type of philosophy. The Gates Commission largely moved the military from an institution to an occupation. (Moskos, 1973)

[63] For example, the Brookings Study by Martin Binkin (1975).

[64] *Author's Note:* Mike Hix also served in the Systems Analysis Office; when the Manpower Requirements office was moved under Bill Brehm, he moved to the Manpower and Reserve Affairs Office. Besides serving as the Deputy Director of the President's commission on Military Compensation, Mike also worked on the Defense Resource Management Study. After retiring from the Army as a Colonel in 1990, he joined RAND and served for a time as the Associate Director of the Arroyo Center, the Army's study and analysis federally funded research and development center at RAND. He retired from RAND in 2006.

Cost-Cutting in the FY 1977 Program

When the Defense Manpower Commission reported to the President and Congress in spring 1976, Assistant Secretary Brehm was also reporting to Congress on the FY 1977 manpower program. If the commission, which itself had been born out of concern for rising personnel costs, did not prove to be the cost-cutting zealot that some had hoped, Assistant Secretary Brehm proved to be the cost-cutting convert whose actions imperiled the all-volunteer force, actions that would be carried into the Carter administration. In a statement to the House Armed Service Committee, Brehm said three factors were shaping the manpower program and that they had to be faced squarely:

> First, . . . we must have strong conventional forces. . . . Second, *our military strength is now measured by our forces in being, including the Reserve Components.* . . .
>
> Third, *we must deal successfully with the problem of escalating manpower costs.* We must meet our minimum manpower needs without creating an unbalanced defense program—this is, without starving R&D, procurement, and operating accounts to pay and support people. Thus we are putting forth a package of proposals to restrain the growth of the average cost per person. . . . We need to be more careful, however, in conveying [to our people] the reasons for our decisions. (Brehm, 1976b, pp. 4, 5, emphasis in original)

Clearly, Brehm was concerned that

> the increase of 12.9 [percent] in payroll and personnel and support costs . . . represent[ed] a shift [of funds] from RDT&E procurement, maintenance, and operations to manpower, in spite of the fact that there are 19 [percent] fewer active military and civilian personnel on the payroll. (Brehm, 1976c, p. 12)

While defending the cost growth as the result of "pay comparability," he proposed a number of initiatives to "restrain" manpower costs. These included restraints on increases in civilian and military pay, enactment of military retirement reform, reductions in special pay and entitlements (such as elimination of commissary subsidies), and civilian and military grade controls. He even proposed cutting the pay of cadets and midshipman at the military academies (Brehm, 1976a, p. 1,440). It seemed that no cost was too small to be considered.

Reducing Recruiting Resources

Clearly, the most problematic cost-cutting came in the sensitive area of recruiting. On reflection years later, General Max Thurman, the legendary commander of the U.S. Army Recruiting Command, called this period "the Second All-Volunteer Army," noting that "missing recruiting objectives [became] the norm" (Thurman, 1986, p. 270). As Thurman saw it, "recruiting resources as a whole were thought to be at least adequate, if not excessive, and those became targets for cost-cutting" (Thurman, 1986, p. 269). Brehm's proposed FY 1977 budget for enlistment bonuses of $29 million was a sharp reduction from the $72 million of the previous year, or even from the $41 million when the program started in FY 1973.

But Brehm's actions were made with forethought. In 1976, he told Congress that it was his view

> that adjustments to Service recruiting resources should be made to reflect changes in the recruiting market, and should take into consideration changes in recruiting incentives, such as the enlistment bonus, educational opportunities, veteran's benefits, and changes in terms of service. I believe that adjustments should first be made in those resources which can most easily be increased or decreased—advertising and enlistment bonuses. (Brehm, 1976b, p. 35)[65]

Thurman would later point out that these cuts were also accompanied by the end of the Vietnam-era GI Bill, a lapse in pay comparability, and increases in federal education assistance not tied to military service (Thurman, 1986, p. 269). At the time, Brehm acknowledged that his cost-cutting scheme represented "a slight risk . . . because we're doing a lot of other things that make recruiting more difficult," e.g., the elimination of the two year enlistment, and the "prospective loss of the GI bill" (Brehm, 1976b, p. 67). When asked to explain his recommendations during congressional hearings on March 4, 1976, on why recruiting bonuses were being significantly reduced "despite the fact that it is generally agreed that fiscal year 1977 will be a more difficult recruiting year than fiscal year 1976," Brehm explained that he was

> not necessarily among those who believe that fiscal year 1977 is going to be a much more difficult recruiting year than fiscal year 1975, or fiscal year 1976. . . . If, at any time we detect a drop in quality which we consider to be unacceptable, we will immediately move to expand such things as the enlistment bonus in order to be sure that we get the quality we need. Obviously, that would require reprogramming authority. . . . I think that while what we are doing here has a certain risk attached

---

[65] At the 30th anniversary of the all-volunteer force, John White referred to this kind of thinking as showing a "supply side bias." He wrote

> The emphasis on recruiting and retention metrics carries with it an over-emphasis on supply side changes at the expense of parallel assessments of demand side program performance such as the effectiveness of advertising, the efficiency of the recruiting organization, the value of Quality of Life programs and the magnitude of first-term attrition rates.

> Shortfalls in recruiting and retention are usually first defined in terms of exogenous events. The failure to meet DoD goals is attributed to market forces such as civilian wage increases, expanding civilian employment and so on. Consequently, the proposed remedies stress compensation adjustments while leaving DoD's human resources management programs largely unexamined.

> This problem is exacerbated by two lags in remedial action. First, it takes some time for the system to detect any important shifts in program effectiveness. Monitoring mechanisms are "weak and imperfect, leading to an unfortunate lag between changes in conditions and changes in policy." [quoting Chu and White, 2001, p. 213] . . .

> Second, once the remedies are fashioned there is a further, inevitable, lag in the time it takes to make either internal, programmatic adjustments or legislative changes such as authorizing pay increases. (White, 2003, p. 5)

to it, however, given the overall need to restrain manpower costs, it is appropriate. (Brehm, 1976c)

One can only wonder if, in retrospect, Brehm would have still considered the risk "appropriate," given that, when recruit quality did begin to go down, DoD would not be allowed to reprogram funds to increase advertising and enlistment bonuses.

A Downturn in Recruiting

During his time as Assistant Secretary of Defense, Brehm had more on his bureaucratic plate than the all-volunteer force. He was deeply involved with a number of initiatives to reform the management of the Pentagon, particularly the Office of the Secretary of Defense. When the Assistant Secretary of Defense for Legislative Affairs decided to leave, Secretary Rumsfeld thought that the best person on his team to fill that critical vacancy was Bill Brehm. The manpower office and the all-volunteer force seemed to be doing well, and, despite the fact that Brehm had no particular legislative experience, Rumsfeld thought he was the right person for the job. Brehm recommended the Assistant Secretary of the Air Force, David Taylor, to be his replacement. No sooner had Taylor moved over from the Air Force, cracks started to appear in the performance of the all-volunteer force. The services were making their numbers all right, but quality was slipping to the extent that the services asked, and the Secretary of Defense agreed, to "reprogram" funds from the general personnel account to the advertising account. This was just the strategy that Brehm suggested in February 1976. Now, later in the year, however, it turned out that resources, once reduced, were not so easily reinstated.

The Legacy

In his last appearance before Congress as the Assistant Secretary of Defense for Manpower and Reserve Affairs, Brehm suggested the legacy of the Nixon and Ford administrations:

> The Peacetime Volunteer Force is a reality, and it is working. . . . The challenge faced by the Department of Defense in making the Volunteer Force concept work was to attract Service members in sufficient quantity and quality to meet national security needs. To date, the Department has been successful in this effort, and we expect to be able to maintain our peacetime force on a volunteer basis. (Brehm, 1976a, p. 1,457)

Unwittingly, however, there was more to the Nixon-Ford legacy. While Brehm and his team had rescued the all-volunteer force in 1974, the obsession with the rising costs of personnel, reductions in recruiting resources, and early fielding of the ASVAB proved a poor foundation for the new Carter administration. So poor, in fact, that, by the end of the Carter term, former President Nixon pronounced the all-volunteer force a failure and "reluctantly concluded that we should reintroduce the draft" (Nixon, 1980, p. 201).

References

ASD[PA]—*See* Assistant Secretary of Defense for Public Affairs

Assistant Secretary of Defense for Public Affairs, *William K. Brehm Assumes Duties as Assistant Secretary of the Army for M&RA,* Washington, D.C.: U.S. Department of Defense, April 11, 1968. G1051.pdf.

———, "Department of Defense Recruiting Results," fact sheet, February 15, 1974a. G0603.pdf.

Associated Press, "Military Accused of Bias in Recruiting," *New York Times,* June 2, 1976, p. 10.

Bartlett, Dewey, Statement by Senator Dewey F. Bartlett on S.2965, Part 3: Manpower, hearing before the Committee on Armed Services, Subcommittee on Manpower and Personnel, 94th Cong., 2nd Sess., Washington, D.C., U.S. Government Printing Office, February 1976.

Bell, William G., and Karl E. Cocke, eds., *Department of the Army Historical Summary: Fiscal Year 1973,* Washington, D.C. : U.S. Army Center of Military History, 1977.

Binkin, Martin, *The Military Pay Muddle,* Washington, D.C.: The Brookings Institution, 1975.

Binkin, Martin, Mark Jan Eitelberg, Alvin J. Schenider, and Marvin M. Smith, *Blacks and the Military,* Washington, D.C.: The Brookings Institution, 1982.

Binkin, Martin, and John D. Johnson, *All Volunteer Armed Forces: Progress, Problems, and Prospects,* Washington, D.C.: Senate Armed Service Committee, June 1, 1973. S0148.pdf.

Brehm, William K., "Actions to Consolidate OSD Manpower Requirements Function into M&RA," memorandum to Secretary of Defense, Washington, D.C., December 7, 1973. G0648.pdf.

———, "Marine Corps Minority Procurement Policy—Chronology of Events," memorandum to Deputy Secretary of Defense, Washington, D.C., February 14, 1974a. G0548.pdf.

———, "Reply to Milton Friedman's Letter to the Secretary of Defense of January 28, 1974," letter to Secretary of Defense, Washington, D.C., February 19, 1974b. G0562.pdf.

———, "Reply to Milton Friedman's Letter to the Secretary of Defense of January 28, 1974," letter to Milton Friedman, Washington, D.C., February 19, 1974c. G0560.pdf.

———, "A Special Status Report: All Volunteer Force," *Commanders Digest,* Vol. 15, No. 9, February 28, 1974d. G0040.pdf.

———, "Adjustment to Enlistment Terms of Service and Enlistment Bonus Programs," memorandum to Deputy Secretary of Defense and Secretaries of the Military Department, Washington, D.C., February 14, 1975a. G0685.pdf.

———, "Paid Broadcast Advertising and the Army's Test Radio Campaign," memorandum to Secretary of the Army, Washington, D.C., March 19, 1975b. G0688.pdf.

———, "Paid Broadcast Advertising and the Army's Test Radio Campaign," memorandum to Secretary of the Army, Washington, D.C., April 7, 1975c. G0687.pdf.

————, "Response to Letter from Senator Javits, February 12," letter to Senator Jacob K. Javits, Washington, D.C., Undated (1975d). S0269.pdf.

Brehm, William K., Testimony of William K. Brehm on Manpower, hearing before the Committee on Armed Services, U.S. Senate, 94h Cong., 1st Sess., Washington, D.C., U.S. Government Printing Office, February 24, 1975a. G1312.pdf.

————, Testimony of William K. Brehm on Military Posture, hearing before the Committee on Armed Services, House of Representatives, 94th Cong., 1st Sess., Washington, D.C., U.S. Government Printing Office, March 5, 1975b. G1303.pdf.

————, Briefing by Assistant Secretary William K. Brehm at Hearings on S.2965, Part 3: Manpower, hearing before the Committee on Armed Services, Subcommittee on Manpower and Personnel, 94th Cong., 2nd Sess., Washington, D.C., U.S. Government Printing Office, February 1976a. G1300.pdf.

————, Statement of William K. Brehm on Military Posture before the House Armed Service Committee, hearing before the Committee on Armed Services, House of Representatives, 94th Cong., 2nd Sess., Washington, D.C., U.S. Government Printing Office, February 17, 1976b. G1308.pdf.

————, Fiscal Year 1977 Defense Manpower Overview, hearing before the House Appropriations Committee: Subcommittee on Defense, Washington, D.C., U.S. Government Printing Office, March 4, 1976c. G1313.pdf.

————, Interview with Bernard Rostker, January 31, 2002.

Brooke, Paul P., *The Impact of the All-Volunteer Force on Physician Procurement and Retention in the Army Medical Department, 1973–1978*, Master of Military Art and Science, Ft. Leavenworth, Kan.: United States Army Command and General Staff College, June 8, 1979. S0146.pdf.

Califano, Joseph A., Jr., "A Costly Army of Volunteers," *Washington Post,* March 23, 1973, p. A26.

Callaway, Howard H., "The All-Volunteer Force: 'As leave my job today,'" memorandum to Deputy Secretary of Defense, Washington, D.C., June 8, 1973a. G0063.pdf.

————,"Army Establishes Quality Recruiting Program for Non-High School Graduates," press release, Washington, D.C., July 27, 1973b. G0586.pdf.

————, *News Brief—On All-Volunteer Force,* Washington, D.C.: Office of the Assistant Secretary of Defense (M&RA), July 27, 1973c. G0573.pdf.

————, "Recruiting for the Zero-Draft Army," memorandum to Chief of Staff of the Army, Washington, D.C., August 17, 1973d. S0107.pdf.

————, "Army Recruitment," memorandum to Deputy Secretary of Defense, Washington, D.C., October 10, 1973e. G0617.pdf.

————, "Army Secretary Confident that Volunteer Army is Working (Keynote Address)," Association of the United States Army, Washington, D.C., October 15, 1973f. G0615.pdf.

————, "Support for the Volunteer Concept (Letter to General Officers)," letter to Military Assistant to the Deputy Secretary of Defense, Washington, D.C., February 11, 1974a. G0549.pdf.

————, "The Volunteer Army—One Year Later," memorandum to the President of the United States, Washington, D.C., February 14, 1974b. G0039.pdf.

————, *Secretary Callaway's Statement on Volunteer Army Success,* Washington, D.C.: Office of the Assistant Secretary of Defense (Public Affairs), 28474, July 1, 1974c. G0043.pdf.

————, "Paid Broadcast Advertising and the Army's Test Radio Campaign," memorandum to Assistant Secretary of Defense (M&RA), Washington, D.C., March 20, 1975a. G0692.pdf.

————, "Paid Broadcast Advertising and the Army's Test Radio Campaign," memorandum to Assistant Secretary of Defense (M&RA), Washington, D.C., April 9, 1975b. G0689.pdf.

————, "Response to Congressman Dellums on Quality Standards and Discrimination," memorandum to Deputy Secretary of Defense, Washington, D.C., May 31, 1975c. G0665.pdf.

Central All-Volunteer Force Task Force, *Qualitative Accession Requirements: A Report on the Qualitative Accession Needs of the Military Services,* Washington, D.C.: Office of the Assistant Secretary of Defense (M&RA), AD764511, November 1972. G1226.pdf.

Chief of Staff, U.S. Army, "Concluding Phases of the Modern Volunteer Army (MVA) Program," memorandum to Heads of Army Staff Agency, Washington, D.C., May 14, 1973. G0058.pdf.

Chu, David S. C., *Physical Standards and the Supply of Enlisted Volunteers,* Santa Monica, Calif.: RAND Corporation, WN-7816-SA, April 1972. S0135.pdf.

Chu, David S. C., Richard V. L. Cooper, and Robert Shishko, *The Adjustment Mechanism for Military Pay: Present Policy and Alternative Approaches,* Santa Monica, Calif.: RAND Corporation, WN-9401-ARPA/MRA, August 1976. S0351.pdf.

Chu, David S. C., Eva Norrblom, Kent Brown, and Alfred MacInnes, *Physical Standards in an All Volunteer Force,* Santa Monica, Calif.: RAND Corporation, R-1347-ARPA/DDPAE, April 1974. S0132.pdf.

Chu, David S. C., and John P. White, "Ensuring Quality People in Defense," in Ashton B. Carter and John P. White, eds., *Keeping the Edge: Managing Defense for the Future,* Cambridge, Mass.: MIT Press, 2001.

Clements, William P., Jr., "The All-Volunteer Force," memorandum to Secretaries of the Military Department, Chairman Joint Chiefs of Staff and Assistant Secretaries of Defense, Washington, D.C., May 7, 1973a. G0613.pdf.

————, "Adjust Quality of Army Entries," memorandum to Secretary of the Army, Washington, D.C., July 11, 1973b. G0571.pdf.

————, "Attainability of the All-Volunteer Force," memorandum to Stuart Symington, Washington, D.C., August 14, 1973c. G0623.pdf.

————, "Department of Defense Announces Recruiting Results for September; Recruiting Objectives for October Set at 32,910," press release Washington, D.C., October 12, 1973d. G0616.pdf.

————, Department of Defense Directive: Manpower Research and Data Analysis Center (MARDAC), Washington, D.C.: Deputy Secretary of Defense, July 8, 1974. G0724.pdf.

Coffey, Kenneth J., and Frederick J. Reeg, *Representational Policy in the U.S. Armed Forces,* Washington, D.C.: Defense Manpower Commission, February 1975. S0162.pdf.

Comptroller General of the United States, *Problems in Meeting Military Manpower Needs in the All-Volunteer Force,* Washington, D.C.: General Accounting Office, B177952, May 2, 1973. S0156.pdf.

————, *An Assessment of All-Volunteer Force Recruits,* Washington, D.C.: General Accounting Office, February 27, 1976a. S0077.pdf.

————, *Improving the Effectiveness and Efficiency of Recruiting,* Washington, D.C.: General Accounting Office, FPCD75169, March 5, 1976b. S0011.pdf.

————, *What Defense Says About Issues in Defense Manpower Commission Report—A Summary,* Washington, D.C.: General Accounting Office, May, 3 1977. S0195.pdf.

Department of the Army, *FY 74 Volunteer Army Highlights,* Washington, D.C., July 31, 1974. G0553.pdf.

Eitelberg, Mark Jan, *Military Representation: The Theoretical and Practical Implications of Population Representation in the American Armed Forces,* dissertation, New York: New York University, 1979. S0221.pdf.

Finney, John W., "Congress Is Told Defense Forces Can't Be Reduced," *New York Times,* April 18, 1976, pp. 1, 6.

Flyer, Eli S., *Department of Defense Manpower Data Analysis Center,* Washington, D.C.: Office of the Assistant Secretary of Defense (M&RA), June 1, 1971. G0721.pdf.

————, "Abridged History of Personnel Research in the Department of Defense: From an Interview with Bernard Rostker, Conducted at Dr. Flyer's office in Monterey, California, August 13 and 15, 2002," 2002. S0633.pdf.

Franklin, Ben A., "Lag in a Volunteer Force Spurs Talk of New Draft," *New York Times,* July 1, 1973.

Friedman, Milton, "Volunteer Armed Force: Failure or Victim?" *Newsweek,* Vol. 83, No. 6, February 11, 1974, p. 82.

Gates, Thomas S. Jr., *The Report of the President's Commission on an All-Volunteer Armed Force,* Washington, D.C., February 1970. S0243.pdf.

Greenberg, I. M., Interview with Bernard Rostker, February 18, 2002.

————, "Technical Comments," memorandum to Bernard Rostker, Washington, D.C., July 2004.

Greenberg, I. M., and Eli S. Flyer, *Proposal for an Inhouse Defense Manpower Studies Center— FY 1977,* Washington, D.C.: Office of the Assistant Secretary of Defense (M&RA), January 1, 1976. G0717.pdf.

Griffith, Robert K., Jr., *The U.S. Army's Transition to the All-Volunteer Force 1968–1974,* Washington, D.C.: U.S. Army Center of Military History, 1997. S0186.pdf.

Grissmer, David W., D. M. Amey, R. L. Arms, W. L. Clement, V. W. Hobson, J. D. Lanigan, W. S. Moore, G. P. Sica, and R. Szymanski, *An Evaluation of Army Manpower Accession Programs,* McLean, Va.: General Research Corporation, OADCR37, April 1974. S0350.pdf.

Hebert, F. Edward, and John McMillan, *'Last of the Titans:' The Life and Times of Congressman F. Edward Hebert of Louisiana,* Lafayette, Louisiana: Center for Louisiana Studies, The University of Southern Louisiana, 1976.

Herbits, Stephen E., "Charter: Special Assistant for AVF," memorandum to Secretary Kelley, Washington, D.C., May 30, 1973a. G0067.pdf.

———, "Three-Year Reserve Enlistment," memorandum to Acting Assistant Secretary of Defense (M&RA) Lieutenant General Taber, Washington, D.C., June 4, 1973b. S0098.pdf.

———, "Prior Clearance for Mental Standards Changes," memorandum to Acting Assistant Secretary of Defense (M&RA) Lieutenant General Taber, Washington, D.C., June 5, 1973c. S0099.pdf.

———, "Medical Standards in a Volunteer Environment," memorandum to Director of Procurement Policy Gus Lee, Washington, D.C., June 7, 1973d. S0101.pdf.

———, "Shortage in Army Recruiters," memorandum to Acting Assistant Secretary of Defense (M&RA) Lieutenant General Taber, Washington, D.C., June 7, 1973e. S0100.pdf.

———, "Current Army Approach to the All-Volunteer Force," memorandum to Acting Assistant Secretary of Defense (M&RA) Lieutenant General Taber, Washington, D.C., June 21, 1973f. S0126.pdf.

———, "Department of Defense Leadership on the All-Volunteer Force," memorandum to Assistant Secretary of Defense (M&RA) Secretary Brehm, Washington, D.C., September 4, 1973g. S0109.pdf.

———, "Secretary Callaway's Address to AUSA," memorandum to Secretary Brehm, Washington, D.C., October 17, 1973h. S0106.pdf.

———, "The Need for a Director of Recruiting Within OASD (M&RA)," memorandum to Assistant Secretary of Defense (M&RA) Secretary Brehm, Washington, D.C., January 14, 1974. S0153.pdf.

———, "Comments," in William Bowman, Roger Little and G. Thomas Sicilia, eds., *The All-Volunteer Force After a Decade: Retrospect and Prospect,* New York: Pergamon-Brassey's, 1986.

Hix, William M., "Interview with Bernard Rostker," April 18, 2002.

House Armed Services Special Subcommittee, *Report by the Special Subcommittee on Disciplinary Problems in the US Navy,* Washington, D.C.: Government Printing Office, H.A.S.C. 9281, January 2, 1973. G1322.pdf.

Huck, Daniel F., *Recruiter Malpractices,* Washington, D.C.: Office of the Assistant Secretary of Defense (M&RA), November 9, 1973. G0082.pdf.

Jacoby, LTC, "Concluding Phrases of the Modern Volunteer Army (MVA) Program," memorandum to Heads of Army Staff Agency, Washington, D.C., May 14, 1973. G0332.pdf.

Janowitz, Morris, and Charles C. Moskos, Jr., "Racial Composition in the All-Volunteer Force," *Armed Forces and Society,* Vol. 1, No. 1, November 1974, pp. 109–123.

U.S. Congress, Testimony of Samuel Jaskilka on Manpower, hearing before the Committee on Armed Services, U.S. Senate, 93rd Cong., 2nd. Sess., Washington, D.C., U.S. Government Printing Office, March 21, 1974.

Kelley, Roger T., "Project Volunteer Budget for FY 1974," memorandum to Mr. Moot, Washington, D.C., November 20, 1972. G0086.pdf.

———, "Mr. Joseph Califano's OPED," letter to the editor of the *Washington Post,* March 30, 1973a. G0107.pdf.

———, "Action on Report on *Manpower Research and Management in Large Organizations,*" follow-up to Secretary of Defense, Washington, D.C., April 11, 1973b. S0122.pdf.

———, "The All-Volunteer Force: As I Leave My Job Today, . . ." memorandum to Deputy Secretary of Defense, Washington, D.C., May 31, 1973c. G0609.pdf.

Laird, Melvin R., "Use of the Draft Has Ended," news release, Washington, D.C., January 27, 1973. G0103.pdf.

Latimer, Thomas K., "Functional Transfer of Manpower Requirements: M&RA/PA&E," memorandum to David O. Cooke, Leonard Sullivan and William K. Brehm, Washington, D.C., March 19. 1974. G1476.pdf.

Lee, Gus C., "Changes in Army Recruiting Policies and Standards," memorandum to General Taber, Washington, D.C., October 2, 1972a. G0176.pdf.

———, "Trends in Non-White Enlistments," memorandum to Roger Kelley, Washington, D.C., December 11, 1972b. G0094.pdf.

———, "Concluding Phase of the Modern Volunteer Army Program," memorandum to Volunteer Army Office Chief, DCSPER, Washington, D.C., April 19, 1973. G0055.pdf.

Lee, Gus C., and Geoffrey Y. Parker, *Ending the Draft: The Story of the All Volunteer Force,* Washington, D.C.: Human Resources Research Organization, FR-PO-771, April 1977. S0242.pdf.

Martin, Albert J., *Design Considerations and Objectives: The Department of Defense Paid Radio Test of 1975,* unpublished, Washington, D.C.: Office of the Assistant Secretary of Defense (MRA&L), 1980. S0327.pdf.

———, Interview with Bernard Rostker, January 15, 2002.

Montague, Robert M., Jr., "Advertising the Military Pay Raise," memorandum to Steve Herbits, Washington, D.C., May 2, 1972. S0251.pdf.

———, Statement on AVF, hearing before the House Appropriations Committee, Defense Subcommittee, Washington, D.C., Special Assistant to the ASD (M&RA) for AVF Action, January 17, 1973a. G0096.pdf.

———, "Comparison of AVF Costs with Total Personnel Costs," memorandum to Roger Kelley, Washington, D.C., April 9, 1973b. G0053.pdf.

———, "Army Paper: Concluding Phases of the Modern Volunteer Army Program," memorandum to Lieutenant Colonel Wright, Washington, D.C., April 17, 1973c. G0056.pdf.

————, "Meeting with Deputy Secretary Clements," memorandum to Secretary Kelley, Washington, D.C., May 7, 1973d. S0095.pdf.

————, "Summary of Policies/Procedures/Problem Areas Related to Recruiting/Processing Malpractice," memorandum to Stephen Herbits, Fort Sheridan, Ill., August 6, 1973e. G0072.pdf.

Moore, H, G., Statement of H. G. Moore, Deputy Chief of Staff for Personnel, Department of the Army, hearing before the House Appropriations Committee, 942, Washington, D.C., U.S. Government Printing Office, 76-H1817-2, March 4, 1976.

Moskos, Charles C., Jr., Continuing Review of the All-Volunteer Force, hearing before the Military Personnel Subcommittee of the Committee on Armed Services, House of Representatives, 95th Cong., 2nd Sess., Washington, D.C., U.S. Government Printing Office, July 11, 1978. S0408.pdf.

————, "Making the All-Volunteer Force Work," in William J. Jr. Taylor, Eric T. Olson and Richard A. Schrader, eds., *Defense Manpower Planning: Issues for the 1980s,* New York: Pergamon Press, 1981.

Murray, J. E., Jr., "Defense Manpower Commission Final Report," information memorandum to Secretary of Defense, Washington, D.C., April 27, 1976. G0241.pdf.

New York Times Editorial Board, "Defense Payload," editorial, *New York Times,* May 10, 1976, p. 26.

Nixon, Richard M., "First Year Report on the Volunteer Army," memorandum to Howard H. Callaway, Washington, D.C., February 25, 1974. G0604.pdf.

————, *The Real War,* New York: Warner Books, 1980.

Nunn, Sam, "Remarks by US Senator Sam Nunn before the George General Assembly," news release, Washington, D.C., March 5, 1973. S0118.pdf.

————, Fiscal Year 1977 Authorization for Military ... Personnel, hearing before the Senate Armed Services, 94th Cong., 2nd Sess., Washington, D.C., U.S. Government Printing Office, February 6, 1976.

————, Status of the All-Volunteer Force, hearing before the Senate Armed Services Subcommittee on Manpower and Personnel, 95th Cong., 2nd Sess., Washington, D.C., U.S. Government Printing Office, June 20, 1978. S0444.pdf.

Nunn, Sam, Howard Baker, Thomas Eagleton, and Edward Kennedy, *Remarks on the Charter of the Defense Manpower Commission,* Washington, D.C.: United States Senate, September 26, 1973. S0271.pdf.

OASD[M&RA]—*See* Office of the Assistant Secretary of Defense for Manpower and Reserve Affairs.

Odeen, Philip A., "Military Manpower and the Zero Draft," memorandum to Henry A. Kissinger, Washington, D.C., July 27, 1972. G1116.pdf.

Office of the Assistant Secretary of Defense for Manpower and Reserve Affairs, "All-Volunteer Force Information," 1973. G0065.pdf.

Phillips, Paul D., "Recruiting for the Zero Draft Army," memorandum to Acting Assistant Secretary of Defense (M&RA) Lieutenant General Taber, Washington, D.C., August 20, 1973. S0108.pdf.

Powell, Colin L., and Joseph E. Persico, *My American Journey,* New York: Random House, 1995.

Proxmire, William, "Concerns About The Defense Manpower Commission," memorandum to Curtis W. Tarr, Washington, D.C., December 23, 1974. G0050.pdf.

Richardson, Elliott L., *The All-Volunteer Force and the End of the Draft: Special Report of the Secretary of Defense Elliot L. Richardson,* Washington, D.C.: U.S. Department of Defense, March 1973. S0130.pdf.

Rogers, Bernard, Testimony of Bernard Rogers on Manpower, hearing before the Committee on Armed Services, U.S. Senate, 93rd Cong., 2nd Sess., Washington, D.C., U.S. Government Printing Office, March 21, 1974.

Rumsfeld, Donald H., *Report of the Third Quadrennial Review of Military Compensation: Military Compensation—A Modernized System,* Washington, D.C.: U.S. Department of Defense, 1976a. S0168.pdf.

———, "Summary of Issues in the Defense Manpower Commission Report and Tentative Department of Defense Positions," memorandum to Assistant to the President for National Security Affairs, Washington, D.C., August 8, 1976b. G0243.pdf.

Schlesinger, James R., "Consolidation of Manpower Requirement in ASD (M&RA)," memorandum to Chairman of the Joint Chief of Staff Secretaries of the Military Departments, Director of Defense Research and Engineering, Assistant Secretaries of Defense, General Counsel, Director of Defense Program Analysis and Evaluation, Assistants to the Secretary of Defense, Directors of Defense Agencies, Washington, D.C., September 3, 1973. G0652.pdf.

———, Secretary Schlesinger Announces Elimination of Two-Year Enlistments, Washington, D.C.: U.S. Department of Defense, February 24, 1975. G0686.pdf.

Secretary of Defense, *Report to the Committee on Armed Services, U.S. Senate: Prospects for Attaining an All-Volunteer Force,* Washington, D.C.: U.S. Department of Defense, September 28, 1972. S0252.pdf.

Srull, Donald W., "Applying the Limited Money to the Tough Part of the Problem," memorandum to Phil Odeen, Washington, D.C., December 4, 1970. S0064.pdf.

———, Interview with Bernard Rostker, November 20, 2001.

Stanners, Thomas, Interview with Bernard Rostker, February 18, 2002.

Steiger, William A., "The Case for a Volunteer Military," *Washington Post,* March 31, 1973. G0610.pdf.

———, "Impact of the All-Volunteer Force on the Defense Budget," letter to Roland Evans and Robert Novak, Washington, D.C., January 22, 1974. S0116.pdf.

Stennis, John, Enlistments in the All-Volunteer Force, hearing before the Enlistments in the All-Volunteer Force, 93rd Cong., 1st Sess., September 24, 1973. S0150.pdf.

Symington, Stuart, "Attainability of the All-Volunteer Armed Force," memorandum to James R. Schlesinger, Washington, D.C., July 5, 1973. G0622.pdf.

Taber, Robert, "Agenda Item on the All-Volunteer Force for the July 2 Armed Force Policy Council," information memorandum to Deputy Secretary of Defense, Washington, D.C., Undated (circa July 1, 1973). S0103.pdf.

———, "Medical Standards in the Volunteer Environment," memorandum to Assistant Secretaries of the Military Departments (M&RA), Washington, D.C., June 11, 1973a. S0125.pdf.

———, "All-Volunteer Task Force Meeting," action memorandum to Deputy Secretary of Defense, Washington, D.C., June 27, 1973b. S0102.pdf.

Tarr, Curtis W., "Background of the Defense Manpower Commission," memorandum to William K. Brehm, Washington, D.C., December 19, 1974. G0049.pdf.

———, *Defense Manpower: The Keystone of National Security—Report to the President and Congress,* Washington, D.C.: Defense Manpower Commission, April 1976. S0113.pdf.

Thurman, Maxwell R., "Sustaining the All-Volunteer Force 1983–1992: The Second Decade," in William Bowman, Roger Little and G. Thomas Sicilia, eds., *The All-Volunteer Force After a Decade: Retrospect and Prospect,* New York: Pergamon-Brassey's, 1986.

Tice, R. Dean, "Navy Recruiting Policy," memorandum to Joseph Addabbo, Washington, D.C., September 17, 1979. G0457.pdf.

U.S. Department of Defense, *Department of Defense Response to the Report to the President and the Congress by the Defense Manpower Commission,* Washington, D.C.: U.S. Department of Defense, January 1978. S0219.pdf.

Warner, John T., "Section 718 of the Defense Authorizations Act of 1973," memorandum to Committee on Armed Services Chairman John Stennis, U.S. Senate, Washington, D.C., March 19, 1974. S0154.pdf.

White House Press Secretary, *Nomination of William Keith Brehm,* Washington, D.C.: The White House, July 30, 1973. G0649.pdf.

White, John P., "Comments," 30th Anniversary Conference, Washington, D.C., September 2003. S0717.pdf.

Wilson, George C., "Navy Is Accused of Bias in Entrance Standards," *Washington Post,* June 15, 1979, p. A3.

Woolsey, R. James, "Parity Policy for Navy Recruiting," information memorandum to Secretary of Defense, Washington, D.C., June 21, 1979a. G0446.pdf.

———, "(New) Navy Recruiting Policy," information memorandum to Secretary of Defense, Washington, D.C., September 21, 1979b. G0364.pdf.

Zumwalt, Elmo R., Jr., "All-Volunteer Force," memorandum to Secretary of Defense, Washington, D.C., December 8, 1973. G0630.pdf.

CHAPTER TEN

The Second Inning:
Analytic Studies (1973–1976)

> In a managerial sense, the elimination of the draft was a major shock. The draft had set up many internal behavioral and organizational responses that have had to be altered in the zero draft world.
>
> —Richard V.L. Cooper and
> Bernard Rostker[1]

Introduction

The "second inning" of the all-volunteer force saw the increased use of analysis to *inform* managers and decisionmakers in DoD, as well as Congress. By the end of the Ford administration, the investments in manpower research that had began in the early 1970s started to pay off with a steady flow of studies and analysis. Research focused on reducing the demand for medical personnel while increasing the supply of doctors and the development of more-efficient compensation systems helped OSD and the services address all-volunteer force cost issues. There was a new focus on the value of paid advertising for recruiting as Congress relented in its opposition to anything other than public-service advertising. The analytic question *du jour* was no longer the feasibility of the volunteer force. It was generally agreed, with the exception of a few lingering problems with attracting reserve and medical personnel, that a force could be recruited. The debate now centered on the cost of the all-volunteer force, the issue of "quality" (both cognitive and physical), how representative this new force was of American society, and the degree to which a "market based" all-volunteer force would move the military from a profession to an occupation, with what some believed would be harmful consequences for the military.

---

[1] From an essay entitled "Military Manpower in a Changing Environment" in a volume celebrating the RAND Corporation's 25th anniversary (Cooper and Rostker, 1973).

Analytic Support for Congress in Spring 1973

In spring 1973, Congress was impatient to know how the new all-volunteer force was doing. While Laird had optimistically announced the end of the draft days before he departed DoD in January, reports of new shortfalls abounded, together with concerns about the quality of the recruits, the representativeness of the force, and the rising cost of personnel.

Two comprehensive assessments of the all-volunteer force were important to Congress (Comptroller General of the United States, 1973) as it considered the FY 1974 budget and whether to let induction authority expire on June 30, 1973. In May 1973, the General Accounting Office (GAO) published a study titled *Problems in Meeting Military Manpower Needs in the All-Volunteer Force* (Comptroller General of the United States, 1973).[2] In June 1973, the Brookings Institution released a report prepared for the Senate Armed Services Committee: *All-Volunteer Armed Forces: Progress, Problems and Prospects* (Binkin and Johnson, 1973).

The GAO Study

GAO's principal concern was "the [S]ervices' abilities to obtain and retain a sufficient quantity of qualified enlisted personnel to support desired force levels" (Comptroller General of the United States, 1973, p. 9). Working with data provided by the Research Analysis Corporation (RAC), GAO looked at the limitations quality standards placed on accessions. It concluded that the "Service quality goals have been set at levels difficult to obtain" (Comptroller General of the United States, 1973, p. 2). They pointed out that the problem was not that the services prescribed a maximum percentage that could be recruited from mental category IV, but the insistence that 60 percent of recruits come from categories I, II or IIIAs, *and* that 70 percent be high school graduates[3]. The Army had met that standard only one month since January 1970. Neither the Marine Corps, with a 65-percent high school goal, nor the Navy, with an 80-percent goal, had ever achieved these levels of recruiting.

Finally, in the area of the cost of the all-volunteer force, one issue of great concern to Congress and one that would eventually lead to the establishment of the Defense Manpower Commission, GAO noted that "DoD programs for the AVF have contributed about 23 percent of the increased manpower costs which have occurred since 1968" (Comptroller General of the United States, 1973, p. 4) and that "[i]f force levels need to be increased in the future, the cost of volunteers may increase sharply" (Comptroller General of the United States, 1973, p. 5).

---

[2] The Chairman of the House Armed Services Committee requested the study on January 18, 1973. Many in DoD were nervous about the report and the testimony of the Assistant Comptroller General, Tom Morris—the same Tom Morris who had been the Assistant Secretary of Defense (Manpower and Reserves Affairs) in the previous administration and who had spoken against the all-volunteer force in 1966.

[3] Mental *categories* refer to scores on the Armed Forces Qualify Test, an IQ test. Those from categories I, II, and IIIA are above average, having an IQ of 100 or above.

The Brookings Study

Martin Binkin and Major John Johnston did the Brookings Institution study under contract to the Senate Armed Services Committee. Binkin had joined the Brookings staff in 1970 after a career in the Air Force, serving last in the Manpower Requirements Directorate of the Systems Analysis office.[4] Johnston was on a fellowship at Brookings, arranged by his former boss, Major General Glenn Kent, Assistant Chief of Staff of the Air Force for Studies and Analysis. Kent thought that Johnston's time at Brookings would broaden him, allow him to meet others in official Washington, and let him make contacts that would serve the Air Force well in the future (Kent, 2001). When Johnston arrived at Brookings, he found Binkin had just started working on the report for the Senate Armed Services Committee. They agreed to collaborate.[5]

As Binkin and Johnston saw it, "[o]n balance, the 1970–73 transition experience is promising" (Binkin and Johnson, 1973, p. 2). In an analysis that was reminiscent of the approach Johnston had used in the Air Force's Saber Volunteer study, they pointed out that

> existing manpower policies will require that one of every three qualified and available [noncollege] men eventually volunteer for active military service. . . .
>
> Given no unforeseen changes in present trends and circumstances, the rate at which qualified volunteers enlisted in fiscal 1973, if continued, should be adequate to meet average long-term *quantitative* needs without any further real increase in costs. (Binkin and Johnson, 1973, p. 3, emphasis in the original)

Like the GAO study, the Brookings study emphasized the issue of quality. The authors noted that "the quality of volunteers, as measured by the Armed Forces Qualification Test (AFQT) has generally improved since fiscal 1970" (Binkin and Johnson, 1973, p. 2), with "modest declines in the proportion of Army and Navy enlistees that have completed high school" (Binkin and Johnson, 1973, p. 2). They did conclude that

> [d]espite success in achieving high volunteer rates, it appears that a manpower scarcity could develop in three areas: critical skills (including combat arms), reserve

---

[4] *Author's Note:* Marty Binkin had been a Colonel in the Air Force. His last assignment was to the Manpower Requirements Directorate in the Office of the Assistant Secretary for Systems Analysis, where we were colleagues. In 1970, he retired, taking a position at the Brookings Institution, where he authored numerous important monographs on military manpower issues. The totality of his work while at Brookings is an outstanding chronicle of evolving manpower issues during the 1970s and 1980s.

[5] When the report was finished, Johnston was concerned about putting his name on it, given his status as an Air Force officer, lest someone might take it for the official position of the United States Air Force. He submitted a copy to the Air Force Deputy Chief of Staff for Personnel, Lieutenant General John Roberts—Johnston would later work for him—who decided that Johnston could sign the report but should not indicate that he was a major in the Air Force. In fact, the Pentagon favored the Brookings study. In a staff assessment prepared for the Deputy Secretary of Defense, Kelley's Manpower Office characterized the report as "helpful." General Montague said that "Brookings generally agrees with the DoD approach to the all-volunteer force and validates our assessment of progress" (Montague, 1973).

forces, and health professionals (such as physicians and dentists). (Binkin and Johnson, 1973, p. 2)

Unlike GAO, however, they were skeptical about how much "quality" the services really needed. They seemed to take the edge off the quality issue and implicitly challenged the Army's decision to raise quality standards at the cost of imperiling the quantitative goals of the all-volunteer force. They argued that the two measures of quality, test scores and educational attainment, had not been "rationalized" or related to performance on the job, and until they were, "undue concern about shortfalls in certain skills would be premature" (Binkin and Johnson, 1973, p. 2).

Binkin and Johnston also provided a more-favorable accounting of the issue of the cost of the all-volunteer force. They noted that the GAO estimates were based on the assumption "as to whether the improvements in fact were tied to an all-volunteer service or whether they would have been made in any event." They argued that, "What is clear from these data, however, is that the large growth in the manpower-related component of the defense budget should not be attributed to the implementation of the all-volunteer concept" (Binkin and Johnson, 1973, p. 24). They wrote, "Taken together, these achievements suggest that this nation can accomplish what no other nation has ever attempted—to maintain an active armed force of over two million men and women on a voluntary basis" (Binkin and Johnson, 1973, p. 25).

Looking toward the future, Binkin and Johnston endorsed the need for a scholarship program for needed health professionals and the need to offload military and dependent patients to the civilian medical community or substitute civilian health professionals for military health professionals in military medical facilities. They encouraged the reevaluation of the requirement for personnel based on changes in support, personnel assignment, and training polices, although they thought the results of such changers were far from clear and would need further study (Binkin and Johnson, 1973, p. 47). They also stressed the importance of additional research to address a number of critical problems: critical skill shortages, reserve manning, and the supply of physicians. Despite the General Research Corporation's analysis of the Combat Arms Bonus, Binkin and Johnston concluded that

> [m]easuring the success of this initial attempt [at using a bonus] is difficult because several other influences were simultaneously at work. . . . How much each of these [other factors] affected recruitment is unclear and the precise effect of the bonus program is therefore difficult to measure. (Binkin and Johnson, 1973, p. 27)

For them, because of this lack of a "central, integrated, experimental design and data collection program. . . . Assessing future options in moving towards an all-volunteer force in the most efficient way was thus much more difficult" (Binkin and Johnson, 1973, p. 27, n. 1).

Binkin, Martin and John D. Johnston. 1973. "All Volunteer Armed Forces: Progress, Problems and Prospects." Brookings Institution: Washington, DC, pp. 21–22

A Successful Transition: Rationale

The number of appropriately qualified true volunteers rose during this period because of a wide variety of measures, chief among which were substantial pay increases at the entry level and greater emphasis on recruiting.

The Military Selective Service Act of 1971 provided incentive increases in military pay and allowances similar to those recommended by the Gates Commission. These were mainly for enlisted personnel, especially those just entering the service. The disproportionately low pay for new recruits was increased by roughly 60 percent. By raising military pay levels to those prevailing in the private sector, it was expected that the military services wold be able to compete in the labor market.

Figure 16 shows the effect of that pay legislation and subsequent annual comparability increases in January 1972 and January 1973. Average weekly earnings of new recruits,

which had lagged behind those of 19-year-old civilian male workers by about 30 percent in 1970, had attained reasonable comparability by fiscal 1972.

Beyond the entry level, men's earnings, enlisted and civilian, roughly corresponded for all groups; enlisted earnings were higher for women than in civilian jobs, as seen in Figure 17. These data probably understate military compensation. If fringe benefits such as retirement, commissary and exchange privileges, and medical services are included, the military pay advantages would be even more pronounced.

Figure 17
Comparison of Median Weekly Earnings of Civilian Full-time Wage and Salary Workers and Military Enlisted Personnel on Active Duty, by Age and Sex, May 1972

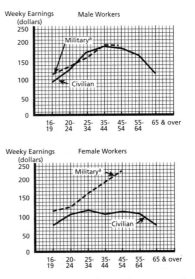

Figure 16
A Comparison of Median Weekly Earnings of Civilian Full-time Wage and Salary Workers (Ages 18, 19, and 20) and Weekly Earnings of Enlisted Males during the First Year of Military Service, Fiscal Years 1967–73[a]

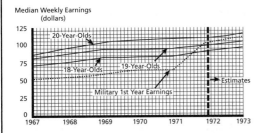

SOURCES: 1967, 1969–72, Department of Labor, Bureau of Labor Statistics (March 1973); and Department of Defense, Office of the Assistant Secretary of Defense, Manpower and Reserve Affairs (March 1973); 1968, authors' estimates.

[a]Military earnings refer to base pay, plus allowances for subsistence and housing and tax advantage. First year earnings are based on a weighted combination of the pay grades normally attained during the first year of service. Estimate of civilian earnings for fiscal 1973 assumes 5.5 percent increases; estimate of military earnings includes the January 1973 pay raise.

SOURCES: Undated material provided by Department of Labor, Bureau of Labor Statistics (March 1973); and Department of Defense, Manpower and Reserve Affairs (February 1973).

[a]Military earnings are not given beyond age 54 since almost all of the military personnel are retired by this age. Estimates of median military salaries are based on age, pay grade, and representative salaries for each grade. However, years of service for each age group was not available so that a more rigorous calculation has not been possible.

Physical Standards[6]

While much attention was focused on mental aptitude as the measure of quality, Binkin and Johnston reminded Congress that the "quality of military manpower can also be viewed from the perspective of physical requirements" (Binkin and Johnson, 1973).[7] They cited data compiled by Bernard Karpinos at HUMMRO and a study by David Chu[8] and others at RAND that showed that 41 percent of those rejected for military service were rejected for physical problems (Karpinos) and that 54 percent of those so disqualified had physical limitations that were only marginal.

Chu's paper, published in April 1972 (Chu, 1972), was prepared for the Assistant Secretary of Defense for Systems Analysis. It was very much in the same vein as several reports from the Central All-Volunteer Force Task Force. They all shared the goal of finding ways to increase the number of recruits entering the military by increasing the pool of eligible personnel, improving the recruiting process, or reducing demand through civilian substitution. This particular paper was evocative and helped focus interest on the possibilities of changing physical standards, which led to a much-more-complete study that was published in 1974 (Chu et al., 1974). Action in the Pentagon, however, is not always rapid, and it was not until June 1973 that the services were asked to review current standards for a number of common disqualifying conditions to see "if they are appropriate in the volunteer environment" (Taber, 1973).

The follow-up study by Chu was cosponsored by the Advanced Research Projects Agency and the Director of Defense Program Analysis and Evaluation, the successor organization to the Systems Analysis Office, and was one of the first studies completed under the auspices of RAND's new Manpower Research Center. In their report, Chu and his colleagues first examined the physical disqualification rate to establish a base rate that might be expected from an all-volunteer force. They reported the "unexpected" result that physical disqualification rates had actually increased as the draft was being phased out. Their analysis showed an expected physical disqualification for the zero-draft environment between 14 and 17 percent, with three-quarters resulting from being overweight.

Next, they considered the relationship between military standards and the ability to perform in a military environment. They found that "unfortunately, direct evidence is lacking on the relationship between the kind of standards now set and military job performance." To get at the relationship "indirectly," they compared the physical standards for our military with those of seven "advanced" countries. They found a general tendency for U.S. standards to be more stringent. They noted that foreign standards

---

[6] In 1980, the Pentagon provided Senator S. I. Hayakawa (D-Hawaii) a short review of the studies concerning physical standards that had occurred over the previous 15 years (Tice, 1980).

[7] In 1973, the new Assistant Secretary of Defense (Manpower and Reserve Affairs) sent the Special Assistant to the Secretary of Defense "a summary of major studies of physical standards since 1971" (Taylor, 1976).

[8] *Author's Note:* David Chu, a long-standing RAND colleague, later became the Director of Defense Program, Analysis and Evaluation. More recently, he replaced me as the Under Secretary of Defense for Personnel and Readiness.

were more often written as guidelines and were often based on requirements for the specific jobs an enlistee might be called to do. A comparison of physical standards in private industry and nondefense government agencies showed similar results. Their analysis suggested that military standards were dominated by the requirements for combat occupations and were thus more stringent than might be necessary for the vast majority of jobs in the military. For example, 95 percent of the Navy jobs were categorized as "support" rather than combat, and even 75 percent of the Army and Marine Corps jobs were in the support category.

Chu thought that the differences in standards between U.S. and other militaries, the private sector, and non-Defense agencies might "reflect post–World War II history of the U.S. armed forces, in which a draft has usually been available to supply all necessary manpower" (Chu et al., 1974, p. 18). While this might have made sense with a large pool of draft-eligible men ready to be conscripted for a limited number of positions, it might not make sense in a zero-draft environment. In fact, there was already a significant break with the logic of the "one standard fits all" policy. The military had already established a two-tier system when it came to gender. Men had to pass one set of standards and were assumed physically fit for all jobs. Women were required to pass another set of standards and were assumed physically fit only for noncombat jobs. In reality, however, the services already used assignment systems that took into account a multitude of restrictions. Guaranteed choice of training, training assignments based on the results of mental and aptitude batteries, and the requirements to place only trained technicians in certain jobs showed that the myth of the universally assignable soldier was not reality. It was, however, a myth that would, in the future, be central to a Supreme Court case. The argument that the draft was associated with providing only personnel capable of being assigned to one of the combat arms, an assignment for which women were excluded, was the argument the Supreme Court relied on when it upheld a male-only draft in 1981 (see Rehnquist, 1981).

In the final analysis, comparisons among foreign militaries, private companies, and nondefense government agencies was only suggestive that military standards had been set too high and could be lowered. Chu's groundbreaking work came in his analysis of time lost from work and the demands placed on the health care system associated with chronic physical impairments. Using data from the Health Interview Survey, a national survey of approximately 134,000 persons living in 42,000 households, his team "adjusted" the sample to match the profile of men in the military. They too identified "conditions that meet the objectives of minimizing health care demands and time lost from work" (Chu et al., 1974, p. 31). Next, using data from the files of those who had failed their physical examinations, the researchers estimated how specific changes in physical standards might affect the supply of new recruits. For example, they found that changing the systolic blood pressure standard from 139 mm to a limit of 150 mm, a level commonly observed among foreign militaries and in the civilian sector, would reduce the physical disqualification rate by 2 percent. Relaxing weight standards by 5 percent decreased the disqualification rate by almost 10 percent. Table 10.1 shows

Table 10.1
Effects on Disqualification Rate of
Changes in Selected Standards

Area of Change	Change (%)
Systolic blood pressure cutoff raised to 150 mm	–2.0
Weight standards relaxed 5 percent	–9.9
Weight standards relaxed 10 percent	–16.8
Lungs and chest (including X-ray)	–2.5
Abdomen	–2.3
Genitourinary system	–1.8
Upper extremities	–1.7
Spine	–1.0
Skin	–2.7
Audiometer	–2.6

SOURCE: AFEES records as noted in Chu et al. (1974, p. 35).

the effects of changes in these and other conditions on the disqualification rate. Relaxing all the standards in Table 10.1, plus relaxing weight standards by 10 percent, decreases the volunteer disqualification rate by 35 percent, which translates into approximately 10 percent more enlistments.

Chu et al. next tried to compare changes in physical standards and the resulting gains in enlistments to other means of increasing enlistments using bonuses and across-the-board pay raises. His conclusion was that

> the [expected attrition] cost of additional volunteers from relaxing physical standards is substantially less [in the range of several hundred dollars] than the $2,500 that the Army and Marines are currently paying as a bonus to enlist men in the combat arms.
>
> Likewise, the estimated marginal cost of volunteers from relaxing physical standards is much lower than the marginal cost using a general pay increase in first-term pay. If the pay elasticity is 1.5, then the marginal cost of a pay increase would exceed $10,000 per volunteer" (Chu et al., 1974, pp. 45, 48).

Representativeness of the All-Volunteer Force

The issue of representativeness had surfaced during the early debates about the all-volunteer force, the deliberations of the Gates Commission, and the Army's transition to the all-volunteer force. Despite the Gates Commission's pronouncements that "blacks do not serve disproportionately to their numbers in the population" (Gates, 1970, p. 145), its members clearly understood that "[b]ecause of racial differences in civilian earnings, even the [pre-1970] levels of military pay are more attractive to blacks than to whites" (Gates, 1970, p. 143). After the Gates Commission report, I. M. (Irv) Greenberg

> found in discussions with [the] Army that they are concerned about the concentration of blacks in line companies of the combat arms. For example, if 20% of the Army is black, it may result in a 50% or more black proportion in Infantry companies. (Greenberg and Saben, 1970, p. 2)

The Army historian Robert Griffith reports that, by 1974, concerns "over racial balance . . . played a part in orienting the Army's revamped recruiting and retention program" (Griffith, 1997, p. 236).

Racial Composition and the Tipping Theory

In 1974, the two leading American military sociologists, Morris Janowitz and Charles Moskos, legitimized the Army's concerns about race by endorsing the so-called *tipping theory*. Moreover, this was not a view that they reserved just for academic journals. Pre-publication copies of their article were circulated at the White House, and the White House Chief of Staff, Donald Rumsfeld, the former congressman from Illinois, made sure that the Secretary of the Army had a copy (Rumsfeld, 1974).

In a policy paper published in the first issue of the journal *Armed Force and Society* (Janowitz and Moskos, 1974), Janowitz and Moskos expressed their concerns about the large number of blacks who had joined the volunteer Army:

> Can a political democracy have a legitimate form of government if its military is not broadly representative of a larger society? Can a military force whose combat units are overweighed with a racial minority have credibility in the world arena? (Janowitz and Moskos, 1974, p. 110)

They lamented "[t]he absence of public discussion on the racial make-up of the military" (Janowitz and Moskos, 1974, p. 114).

While a number of observers made the point that a force could be representative of the American people in a number of ways—geographic,[9] socioeconomic, and racial[10]—there seemed to be more interest in the racial composition of the force than in any other measure. For Congressman Ronald Dellums (D-California), the "sudden concern for 'representativeness' turns out to mean only one thing: there are too many blacks in the military" (Dellums, 1975, p. 6). There were many in the military who "view[ed] a large concentration of blacks as exacerbating race tensions and management problems within the services" (Janowitz and Moskos, 1974, p. 109).

---

[9] For example, in the 1840s, Congress determined that cadets should be admitted to the U.S. Military Academy at West Point in such a way as to ensure that the school's enrollment was geographically representative of the country. Each senator and each congressman was allowed to nominate one prospective cadet in each year's freshman or plebe class.

[10] Brehm (1974) reported to the Senate Armed Services Committee statistics on the "population representation of the All-Volunteer Force" showing geographic, educational, economic, and racial composition.

Fear of a disproportionately black military centered on several arguments, including military effectiveness, social equity, and political legitimacy. For the left, the social equity proved most persuasive. In fact, Senators Thomas Eagleton (D-Missouri) and Edward Kennedy (D-Massachusetts) introduced an amendment to the legislation chartering the Defense Manpower Commission requiring the commission to study "the implication [of] . . . the ability of the Armed Forces to fulfill their mission as a result of the change in the socio-economic composition of military enlistees" (Coffey and Reeg, 1975, p. 9). For the right, Eitelberg noted there were concerns that

> a disproportionately Black Army would lead to increased racial tensions and polarization, as well as an unreliable and less effective military force. . . . The racial unrest of the late 1960s [and unrest within the military in the early 1970s] can be said to have contributed to these fears—fears which even viewed the training of Black servicemen as a way of preparing a potential enemy for war in the streets of urban America. (Eitelberg, 1977, pp. 12–13)

The tipping theory was popular among those who argued for a limit on the numbers of blacks entering the military. Griffin noted that the Army's senior leaders of the period were concerned about this (Griffith, 1997, p. 235) and that it was also reflected in the Navy's recruiting policy, called *parity*, which was developed in the wake of race riots abroad an aircraft carrier, the USS *Kitty Hawk,* in October 1972. For those who believed in this theory, Janowitz and Moskos's endorsement of it only added to the perceived correctness of the argument. They chastised the uniformed leadership for "uncritical acceptance of a mission without sufficient professional dissent" and derided them because "[t]here has been repeated emphasis on the fact that the armed forces are an equal opportunity employer" (Janowitz and Moskos, 1974, p. 115). They singled out for praise Army Secretary Howard "Bo" Callaway, praising him because he, "shortly after becoming Secretary of the Army, boldly and clearly stated the Army goal to recruit from a relatively representative cross-section of the civilian population" (Janowitz and Moskos, 1974, p. 115).

Janowitz and Moskos supported the tipping theory:

> By tipping we refer to the point at which the proportion of blacks becomes so high that large numbers of whites are no longer prepared to enter the particular service or branch involved. Such an occurrence could be engendered by factors including the perceived status decline of units overproportionately black, or the very real fear of black "hooliganism" on the part of many lower-ranking white enlisted men. It can be expected that the tipping point will operate in a gradual fashion in the military rather than in the dramatic threshold fashion of residential communities. But the end result, nevertheless, could well be a significant diminishment of white recruits for the ground force units involved. (Janowitz and Moskos, 1974, p. 113)

Janowitz and Moskos recognized that it was unlikely that the government would install racial quotas to limit the number of blacks entering the military. Their preferred solution was to reduce the size of the military and station its members at home because, as they speculated, "the attractiveness of military service for a wider representation of the American population will probably increase to the degree U.S. forces are stationed at home" (Janowitz and Moskos, 1974, p. 117). They also argued for increased use of women and civilians because they thought it would "generally work toward more racial balance," but warned that "it is especially important that civilianization be monitored for its precise impact on the racial composition of uniformed military personnel" (Janowitz and Moskos, 1974, p. 118). They saw the need for internal reforms to strengthen the social cohesion of units, implying members of different races are unlikely to achieve "group cohesion."[11] Finally, they argued that, by emphasizing educational benefits and the GI Bill for the combat arms, the black problem would take care of itself. As they saw it, "a major outcome [of a civilian educational program] would be the reintroduction of white middle class males into the ground combat forces" (Janowitz and Moskos, 1974, p. 122).

By the mid-1990s, and notwithstanding these initial negative views of blacks and concerns about the harm that they would do to the Army as an institution, Moskos saw a very different picture. In 1996, he wrote that the U.S. Army

> is an organization unmatched in its level of racial integration. It is an institution unmatched in its broad record of black achievement. . . . The Army stands out, even among governmental agencies, as an organization in which blacks often do better than their white counterparts. (Moskos and Butler, 1996, p. 2)

Most telling, given his original concerns, Moskos now found that "the Army does not lower its standards in order to assure an acceptable racial mix" (Moskos and Butler, 1996, p. 9).

The Defense Manpower Commission

Even while fear and stereotyping typified the debate about race, a number of serious studies addressed the issue of representativeness. In 1976, the Defense Manpower Commission staff carefully looked at the representativeness of the new volunteer force from a number of view points; educational status, mental group, gender, economic status, geography—and race.

First, they considered the representativeness, in terms of education and mental group, of recent accessions to the armed forces. They found that "the overall pattern of accessions into the Total Force for non–high school graduates did not change significantly during the AVF years" (Coffey et al., 1975). By FY 1975, for the active components, about 28 percent of all accessions were non–high school graduates. This compares with a civilian rate of 23 percent and a pre–Vietnam War rate of 32 percent in 1964. The reserve component, which had been a haven for draft-motivated volunteers

---

[11] Fifteen years later, members of the Presidential Commission on Women in the Military used the same argument about unit cohesion to limit the role of women in military units, and it was used again when the issue of homosexuals was raised in 1993 (see Rostker et al., 1993).

during the Vietnam War did, however, experience a sharp increase in non–high school graduates. The commission noted, however, that

> due both to in-service education programs and G.E.D. testing, the overall proportion of non–high school graduates among all in-service active duty personnel has steadily decreased from 27 percent in FY 64 to 13 percent in FY 75. (Coffey et al., 1975, p. 7)

Moreover, the proportion of the active force with high school diplomas rose from 73 percent in FY 1964 to 87 percent in FY 1975. The commission also found that, in FY 1970, 18 percent of the force's accessions were classified as belonging to mental group IV; by FY 1975, that number had been reduced to 6 percent.

Second, the commission considered gender. While there had been a sharp increase in the number of women in the armed services—from 1.9 percent in FY 1972 to 4.6 percent in FY 1975—women were still underrepresented relative to the total population, not only in the total military population but also in noncombat career fields. Over time, the percentage of career fields that women were allowed to join increased, and the total number of positions for which they could qualify also increased. For example, by FY 1975, 94 percent of all Army, 80 percent of Navy, 70 percent of Marine Corps, and 97 percent of Air Force career fields were open to women. The actual number of positions was significantly less because the few career fields that were closed to women were in the combat arms, which were the largest career fields. Nevertheless, over half the positions in the armed services were ostensibly open to women. In FY 1975, however, women filled less then 5 percent of them. When this is compared with the less than 2 percent earlier in the decade, it shows how far women had come. It also shows how far they still had to travel to achieve their representative numbers even in noncombat career fields.

Next, the staff of the Defense Manpower Commission considered the economic status of those joining the military since the end of conscription. This issue addressed the concerns of Senators Eagleton, Kennedy, and Nunn. The senators wanted the issue of representativeness "resolved not only with regard to the black and Spanish-speaking but also with regard to the poor" (Nunn et al., 1973, p. 31,596). Senator Eagleton, noting his support for the Defense Manpower Commission and his earlier opposition to the all-volunteer force, said he

> believed that an All-Volunteer Army would be a poor man's Army, that it would be composed of young men and women from the lower end of the socioeconomic scale who, because of lack of formal education, lack of training, lack of opportunities, and lack of money would accept military service as a means of economic survival. (Nunn et al., 1973, p. 31,587)

He told the Senate he now wanted the issue studied. So did Senators Kennedy and Nunn. They went to the floor of the Senate to cosponsor an amendment to ensure that the commission examine[d] the implications for the Armed Forces of the shift in the number of poor, the number of less educated, and the number of minority persons who have enlisted since the end [of] the use of the induction authority. (Senator Kennedy in Nunn et al., 1973, p. 31,596)

Senator Kennedy noted that he was from a group

who had serious concern about the volunteer Army [and] . . . stress[ed] that those of us who opposed it . . . thought it would end up being a poor man's Army to fight the rich man's war. [He expressed his] hope this commission would better enlighten Congress and the American people as to the danger of this happening. (Nunn et al., 1973, p. 31,596)

Senator Nunn, who had not been in the Senate in 1971 when the Selective Service and the All-Volunteer Force had been debated and voted on, saw his cosponsorship of the amendment with Senator Kennedy as a way to "further emphasize the concern of this body [the Senate] on the workings or failures of the all-volunteer force" (Nunn et al., 1973, p. 31,596).

The commission staff noted that the economic status of enlistees had generally been examined by looking at the earnings of a recruit's parents or by comparing the average wages from the enlistee's home area of record. In terms of the latter, they cited the work of Dr. Richard V.L. Cooper of RAND "to indicate that there has been no significant shift in the levels during the pre- and post-AVF years" (Coffey et al., 1975, p. 29). Cooper had undertaken a major study using Zip code data from the 1970 Census. He concluded that not only had there been

little difference between the overall draft and AVF periods in the area distributions [Zip codes] of enlisted accessions, there [had] in general been an almost remarkable stability over time, even over such short time intervals as six months. (Cooper, 1977, p. 235)

Finally, the commission staff examined the issue of race. The numbers showed that accessions of blacks had grown in all services and all components. The percentage of black accessions in the Army had grown from 14 percent in FY 1970 to 23 percent in FY 1975; in the Navy, from 8 percent to 10 percent; in the Marine Corps, from 15 percent to 19 percent; and in the Air Force, from 13 percent to 18 percent. The biggest increase, however, was in the reserve components. In FY 1970, only 1.8 percent of all accessions in the reserve components were black. By FY 1975, that number had grown to 27.5 percent. The corresponding number for the Army Reserve was 42.4 percent. The number of black officers joining the services had also increased, but blacks were still underrepresented in the officer corps.

To get at the question of "impact," the commission staff conducted a survey of 154 military field commanders to gain their "perceptions of how changes in the socio-economic composition of their units impacted upon the ability to perform their mission." Using the results of field visits and their survey, the commission staff concluded that

> to date an increased number of Blacks has not degraded [the] ability [of] units to perform their mission. However, as with *any* change . . . a true evaluation can only be arrived at after a unit is committed to actual combat. (Coffey et al., 1975, p. 51, emphasis in original)

In that regard, the all-volunteer force would undergo a major test during Desert Storm.

Cooper, Richard V.L. Military Manpower and the All-Volunteer Force. Santa Monica, CA: RAND, 1977

Has there in fact been a disproportionate increase in the numbers of individuals from poor families? Or are members of more well-to-do families no longer serving in the same numbers as they did under the draft? The remainder of this section focuses on these questions.

Historically, it has been difficult to deal with these types of questions because of a lack of data. As a results, analysts were forced to rely on such measures as the proportion of recruits that were black as a proxy for changes in the socioeconomic composition of the force, under the assumption that because blacks on average are poorer than whites, a larger proportion of blacks in the force implies a larger representation of the poor in the military. Indeed, the rising percentage of blacks in the force has been cited over and over again as "evidence" of the fact that the poor are bearing a disproportionately large share of the burden of military service, an assumption that will be shown to be incorrect in the discussion below.

The 1970 Census of the United States provides us with an alternative way of examining the questions raised above. In particular, the "fifth count" census data files contain detailed information on a random subset of the American population living in standard metropolitan statistical areas (SMSAs). This information includes such statistics as income, education, and the like, both for individuals and for families. Fortunately, the data files include the postal Zip codes of the individuals and families, so that we are able to reconstruct some of the key socioeconomic characteristics of the population living within each Zip code located in an SMSA.

Using the enlisted accession data files maintained by the DoD, which include the home address Zip code for nearly every enlisted accession since fiscal 1971, we can match each enlisted accession with his home address Zip code and, hence, with its corresponding socioeconomic characteristics. These matches then provide us with a measure of the distribution of enlisted accessions according to the various socioeconomic measures available from the census data files.

The results of this procedure, using average family income for Zip codes, are illustrated in Table 10-16. The within-Zip code average family income was first estimated for each of the approximately 12,000 SMSA Zip codes in the census file. As shown in Table 10-16, these Zip codes were marked and grouped according to average family income, with the result, for instance, that Zip codes reporting an average family income of $24,500 or more in the 1970 Census fell into the upper 1 percent (i.e., the 99th percentile or greater) of all Zip codes located in SMSAs; Zip codes showing average family incomes of between $17,000 and $24,500 fell between the 95th and 99th percentiles; and so forth. In other words, by ranking Zip codes in this fashion, we are able to identify high-income areas (e.g., those falling in or

Cooper, Richard V.L. Military Manpower and the All-Volunteer Force. Santa Monica, CA: RAND, 1977—continued

above the 95 or 99th percentiles), medium income areas (e.g., the 50th to 75th percentiles), and the like.

Also shown in the table are the distributions of all enlisted accessions with these Zip code groupings for the two years preceding the removal of the draft, as well as the first 2-1/2 years of the AVF. The remarkable fact is that there has been virtually no change in the distribution of enlisted accessions according to the average family income of their home address Zip codes. In fact, whatever changes have occurred can be measured in tenths of a percentage point. For example, during the last two years of the draft, about 3.22 percent of all enlisted accessions (i.e., inductees and enlistees) came from the highest-income areas—i.e., those falling in the upper 5 percent of all Zip codes according to average family income. Since the removal of the draft, the proportion has been about 3.01 percent coming from these same Zip codes, a scant 0.21 percentage point difference.

Also shown in the table are the distributions of all 16 to 21 year old males and 16 to 21 year old males not enrolled in school according to these Zip code groupings. As is evident from these results, the Services have historically drawn a disproportionately small number of enlisted accessions from the upper-income areas, at least as reflected by the percentage of all 16 to 21 year old males living in these higher-income areas. It is interesting to note, however, that although the distribution of enlisted accessions, both before and since the volunteer force, is somewhat skewed toward the lower-income groups relative to the distribution of all 16 to 21 year old males, it actually exceeds somewhat the distribution of 16 to 21 year old males not enrolled in school. Thus the Services have and are continuing to draw a "socially representative" sample of those young men not enrolled in school, which, recognizing the blue collar nature of the majority of jobs in the enlisted ranks, is probably the appropriate basis for comparison.

It is clear, therefore, from Table 10-16 that there has not been a systematic reduction in the proportion of new recruits accessed from high-income areas, just as there has been little change in the proportion of new recruits coming from very low-income areas.

Table 10-16
Distribution of Male Enlisted Accessions by SMSA Zip Codes
Ranked According to Average Family Income
(percent)

Percentile	Income Range ($000s)	Enlisted Accessions		16-21 Male Population	
		Draft	AVF	All	N.S.
≥99	≥$24.5	0.38	0.34	1.06	0.43
95–99	$17.0–$24.5	2.84	2.67	5.13	2.59
90–95	$14.7–$17.0	5.08	4.93	7.36	4.61
75–90	$12.2–$14.7	19.33	18.95	20.83	16.65
50–75	$10.3–$12.2	29.88	29.70	28.56	28.01
25–50	$8.4–$10.3	25.17	25.23	22.63	27.70
10–25	$6.3–$8.4	13.21	13.99	12.13	16.70
5–10	$1.3–$6.3	2.88	3.02	2.10	2.91
<5	<$1.3	1.24	1.18	0.19	0.42

In their final report, the commissioners, noting that their charge from Senators Kennedy and Eagleton was "based on the premise that socioeconomic composition of a force affects its performance," concluded that they had "found no evidence that such is the case" (Tarr, 1976, p. 156).

Eitelberg's Evaluation of Army Representation

Possibly the most rigorous assessment of representativeness came in a 1977 report by Mark Eitelberg of the Human Resources Research Organization for the Army Research Institute (Eitelberg, 1977). Eitelberg used a "convergent-divergent" model first suggested by Charles Moskos in his 1970 book, *The American Enlisted Man* (Moskos, 1970). What set Eitelberg's study apart from others of the day was his treatment of "representati[ve] policy . . . [with] total objectivity . . . as a mathematical problem" (Eitelberg, 1979, p. 32) and the number of data sources he used to make his "mathematical" comparisons of representativeness.[12] His study provided a more-robust perspective on patterns of Army representativeness than any other. His analysis of demographic factors relied on the November 1975 Army Quarterly Survey and reports from the bureaus of the Census and Labor Statistics. Here are the "generalizations" Eitelberg made concerning demographics, based on his review of available studies and data:

> Blacks are overrepresented, but there is a trend downward. . . . The lower economic classes are not overrepresented to any substantial degree. More high economic classes were enlisted during the draft years than the AVF, and are now underrepresented—but not *un*represented. The bulk of accessions are coming from the middle-income segment of society, and there is reason to believe that the present system may somewhat *favor enlistment from the middle range*. . . . Regional representation is improving, though large cities are underrepresented and rural areas are over represented. . . . The lowest level of mental aptitude is unrepresented due to quality restrictions on enlistments. . . . By educational attainment, the Army compares favorably with age-similar civilians. . . . Overall there has been a steady decline in the number of non–high school graduates and Category IV's, a decrease [since the draft] in the number of college-trained accessions, and an increase in the number of high school graduates. Army high school graduates are overrepresented in every age category among newly enlisted accessions. (Eitelberg, 1977, pp. 51–52)

Eitelberg also reports on analysis using the National Longitudinal Study (NLS) of the High School Class of 1972. He concluded, "The NLS group of Army entrants does not appear to be radically different from its civilian counterparts" (Eitelberg, 1977,

---

[12] Eitelberg would later argue that " '[r]epresentation' clearly extended far beyond numbers and ratios and statistical summaries; simple comparisons of military and civilian populations were often inappropriate and generally inadequate" (Eitelberg, 1979, p. xiv). He saw statistical evaluations of representation as

> fraught with ambiguity, conflicting methods, standards and measurement criteria, persistent controversies, a wide array of competing values and emoti[onal] generalities, and often contradictory conclusions derived from the same statistical evidence. (Eitelberg, 1979, pp. xiii–xiv)

p. 84). Using the NLS data, he was also able to address some of the fears that critics had concerning the nature of an all-volunteer force:

> Army tendencies toward isolation or alienation from society do not appear to be evident in these data. In fact, Army entrants profess greater acceptance of community standards and political processes than their civilian peers. . . . Attitudinal data on the "mercenary" bent of Army entrants are inconclusive. (Eitelberg, 1977, p. 116)

In his final analysis, Eitelberg noted that,

> [s]tatistically, the Army never achieved proportional representation under the draft. . . . *Perfect representation* under the all-volunteer format is an unrealistic concept . . . which, from the perspective of *organizational goals,* is probably not advantageous. . . . it may be concluded that, generally, *Army entrants are not exceptionally divergent from their civilian counterparts.* (Eitelberg, 1977, pp. 160–161, emphasis in the original)

It is interesting to note that none of the studies reviewed presented any data or analysis that supported the tipping theory. In fact, given the sharp increase in black enlistments in the Army between FYs 1970 and 1974—black accessions as a percentage of the total doubled from 14 to 28 percent—it is noteworthy that white accessions, as a percentage of the total, actually *increased* during every month of FY 1975 over the previous year. Eitelberg summed it up best when he wrote the following:

> The data of this evaluation support the hypothesis that the All-Volunteer *system* somehow *favors* the enlistment of "average" young men and women—that is, those individuals from the middle-ranges of socioeconomic achievement, those from the rural "heartlands" of America, those whose fathers are employed in "average" working-class jobs, and those who appear to possess attitudes and feelings which are somewhat categorized as "middle-American." The corollary to this observation might be that the system also somehow acts in opposition to the enlistment of individuals at the extreme ends of representational scales—that is, those who are either rich or poor, those who are above or below average intelligence, those who never finished high school or those who finish college, those whose fathers are unemployable or those whose fathers are company executives, and so forth. (Eitelberg, 1977, p. 164, emphasis in the original)

The Institution-Occupation Thesis

Opposition to the all-volunteer force crystallized in the institution-occupation (I/O) thesis Charles Moskos developed. It resonated not only with sociologists but also with military leaders who feared recruiting was disproportionately from minorities and was producing a force that was poorly disciplined and difficult to train. Moskos even held out the prospect that the all-volunteer force could not be counted on to fight on a future battlefield.[13] Pressure from their civilian bosses at the Pentagon and from the Office of Management and Budget for further reforms in military compensation and the threat that labor unions might try to organize the enlisted ranks worried them. In Moskos's view, as expressed in his theory, the market orientation of the Gates Commission was to blame and was moving the military away from an institution toward an occupation resulting, as one colleague wrote, in "changes [that] were harmful to both the military profession and the organization" (Sorensen, 2003, p. 176).[14]

The I/O thesis provided the intellectual underpinning for the service chiefs' concerns and told them they were right to worry—but they did more than worry. They rejected the results of the Third Quadrennial Review of Military because the I/O thesis told them such a system would move them even further from being an *institution* to becoming an *occupation*.[15]

Formally put forward in October 1976 at the Regional Conference of the Inter-University Seminar on Armed Forces and Society in Alabama, the I/O thesis drew a sharp distinction between the military as an institution and the military as an occupation. Moskos defines an institution as "transcending individual self-interest in favor of a presumed higher good. . . . " and notes that its members "are often viewed as following a calling;" he defines an occupation "in terms of the marketplace, i.e., prevailing monetary rewards for equivalent competencies" (Moskos, 1977, pp. 42–43).

Moskos argued that the military was being transformed from an institution to an occupation with "consequences in the structure and, perhaps, the function of the armed forces"; these consequences most notably included "the growing likelihood of unionization" (Moskos, 1977, p. 45). As Segal et al. (1983, p. 112) noted, "the growth of an occupational orientation in the military is antithetical to the integration and commitment required to maintain minimum levels of motivation to perform effectively." Moskos put it this way: "institutional identification fosters greater organizational commitment and performance than does occupational [identification]" (Moskos and Wood, 1988, p. 5).

---

[13] Although he held this view, it was not consistent with his own empirical research. In 1977, Moskos coauthored an article in the *Military Review* that concluded that the "transition to the volunteer Army has been generally successful. The volunteer combat soldier in today's Army [1975] can be expected to perform as well if not better than his counterpart of the early 1970s" (Brown and Moskos, 1997).

[14] Moskos's criticism of the all-volunteer force was based on his opposition to the "marketplace philosophy" that "underpinned the rationale of the 1970 Gates Commission" (Moskos and Wood, 1988, p. 19). He suggested that this is a debate between economists and sociologists and is a conflict between those "with the econometric mindset that had become dominant in the Office of the Secretary of Defense and in sponsored research on military manpower" (Moskos and Wood, 1988, p. 4).

[15] One of Brehm's biggest disappointments during his tenure as the Assistant Secretary of Defense was the service chiefs' rejection of the work of the Third Quadrennial Review of Military Compensation. Brehm had come into office with high hopes of resurrecting the work of the Hubbell commission and of moving the military to a modern salary system. In 1975, he told Congress that there had been a "number of significant changes" that called for a "fresh comprehensive look at the workings of the entire compensation system" (Brehm, 1975, p. 913). The review was completed in the last days of the Ford administration, but departing Secretary of Defense Donald Rumsfeld left the final report unsigned. Rather than being an instrument for reforming the military compensation system, as many in Congress and in the administration had demanded, the unsigned draft report reflected the anti all-volunteer force arguments being put forward by Charles Moskos, as rationalized by his I/O thesis.

While Moskos's formulation of the I/O thesis attracted nationwide attention, Janowitz, founder of the Interuniversity Seminar and editor of *Armed Forces and Society* thought the I/O thesis was based on neither sound logic nor empirical observation. In the November 1977 issue of *Armed Forces and Society*, he wrote an article to accompany Moskos's "From Institution to Occupation: Trends in Military Organization" that chided Moskos for his reformulation of the old arguments about professionalism.[16] Janowitz argued that

> there is no basis—analytic and empirical—to apply such a formulation [the new I/O thesis], for either the short-term or long-term trends in military organizations and military profession in the United States. (Janowitz, 1977, p. 52)

He noted that while Moskos's arguments "resonated" with "a variety of military officers and elected officials and administrators concerned with defense management and the impact of the all-volunteer force" (Janowitz, 1977, p. 52), Moskos had an obligation to use language and concepts carefully, particularly when dealing "with politically and emotionally charged topics" (Janowitz, 1977, p. 51). Janowitz argued that the "formulation of the shift from institution to occupation . . . [has] overtones of an ideological appeal to return to the 'good old days.' But there is no return" (Janowitz, 1977, p. 54).

Researchers have tried to empirically test the I/O theory. Michael Stahl, Roger Manley, and Charles McNichols tried to test Moskos's hypothesis using responses to a survey given to almost 1,100 Air Force personnel. Their factor analysis of the responses produced two independent dimensions of four questions each. They labeled the two dimensions the *institution* measure and the *occupation* measure. They found that, since

> the two dimensions [were] weakly associated with each other . . . a respondent could score high on both dimensions or low on both. This corresponds well with Janowitz's . . . conceptualization that "we are not dealing with a 'zero sum game'" (Stahl et al., 1978, p. 426),

as implied by the I/O thesis. Segal and his colleagues found that the I and the O are "two independent . . . [and] potentially covariant orientations . . . [that] could also be an indicator of very positive development and stability in the new military" (Segal et al., 1983, p. 113). Their assessment of survey data of Army personnel divided between combat and noncombat units resulted in conclusions that were at odds with the I/O thesis:

> This analysis seems to suggest that the Army may not need to choose between institutional and corporate models but, rather, may be able to use both models effectively. Personnel accession, retention, and management policies [are] incentives that have prove[n] effective in the civilian sector [and] can be adapted for use

---

[16] Sorensen (2003) suggested there were "nine angles" from which to view the Janowitz and Moskos disagreement.

in the military setting regardless of the extent to which these practices make the conditions of military service increasingly similar to civilian employment. There may be no harm in making service in the Army a job, as long as it is not just a job. The difference lies in the sense of calling, or mission, that can also be nurtured and, indeed, is essential if the uniformed federal employee is to perform effectively in combat situations. (Segal et al., 1983, p. 125)

More recently, the sociologist James Burk considered whether "the move to an all-volunteer force . . . reflects a shift in American culture away from an emphasis on the duties of citizenship to an emphasis on the rights of citizenship and the pursuit of individual interests" (Burk, 2002, p. 2). He noted that this is an empirical question, and asked, "has there been a withering of civic virtues"? The

evidence [he found] casts doubt on the proposition that members of the current generation suffer from a deficit of civic virtue . . . citizen-soldiers in the all-volunteer force [he found] possess civic virtues and political beliefs that are largely indistinguishable from those held by their civilian counterparts who failed to volunteer for military service. (Burk, 2002, pp. 3–4)[17]

A look back over the last 30 years of the all-volunteer force shows that the dire outcomes from high pay and recruitment and reenlistment bonuses that Moskos predicted have not come to pass.[18] The force today does not suffer from "lack of motivation, low commitment, a loss of professionalism and a drop in the overall performance" (Moskos, 1977, p. 44), as predicted. Performance has improved, which even Moskos seems to acknowledge. In 2003, after a visit to the Middle East, he told the acting Secretary of the Army that soldiers in Iraq had achieved "exceptional levels of performance under very demanding conditions" (Moskos, 2003). Either the all-volunteer force did not move the Army toward an occupation, as Moskos feared it would, or his contention that "institutional identification fosters greater organizational commitment and performance than does occupational commitment" (Moskos and Wood, 1988, pp. 4–5) was wrong. What has come to pass as a direct result of the all-volunteer force is the professionalization of the military, an increase in the "commitment" of service by men and women, as has been demonstrated by their sterling performance on battlefields worldwide. There

---

[17] Burk found that "[t]he rate of participation has fluctuated. But these fluctuations are better explained by changing political judgments about how large a military was needed to meet current threats than by a long-term decline in the virtue of the citizenry" (Burk, 2002, p. 10). He also thought that there was "no reason to conclude that enlistment in the all-volunteer force is driven by social inequalities of sufficient strength that they would undermine the civic virtue of those who do not serve" (Burk, 2002, p. 12).

[18] In 1978, Moskos testified before Senator Nunn's Manpower and Personnel Subcommittee of the Senate Armed Services Committee that raising pay would be ineffective in recruiting the right kind of people into the military, that the white middle class was not interested in pay. He argued,

The volunteer concept can be made to work. . . . [If it] track[s] into the main stream of the youth population by less emphasis on marketplace economics, more emphasis on national service coupled with shorter tours and postservice educational benefits. (Moskos, as quoted in Nunn, 1978, p. 72)

Nunn seemed to go along, but in 1980, he and Senator John Warner (R-Virginia) co-sponsored the largest military pay increase since the founding of the all-volunteer force.

has been an explosion in the size of the career military. More people than ever—officers and enlisted—have decided to make the military their career. Today, during the war in Iraq, while enlistments are down, retention remains high, even above stated goals.

In 1969, when President Nixon established the Gates Commission, only 18 percent of the Army had more than four years of service. The corresponding numbers for the Navy, Marine Corps, and Air Force were 31, 16, and 46 percent, respectively (ASD[M&RA], 1978, p. 82). In 2001, with a fully achieved all-volunteer force, the numbers stand at 51 percent for the Army, 49 percent for the Navy, 35 percent for the Marine Corps, and 66 percent for the Air Force (DASD[MPP], 2001). In the early 1970s, before the all-volunteer force, the services routinely retained about 15 percent of the cohort of true volunteers, draft-motivated volunteers, and draftees who were eligible to reenlist (Lee and Parker, 1977, p. 358). In 2001, the corresponding number was about 53 percent.

Reducing the Demand for and Increasing the Supply of Medical Personnel

To the Gates Commission, manning medical and dental services was a "very troublesome problem . . . [and] the subject of independent inquiry by the Commission" (Gates, 1970, p. 87).[19] The commission noted a number of points that shaped its view:

- As of 1970, 80 percent of all male physicians in the United States under 35 had served in the military.
- As of 1970, only 4 percent of male physicians under 35 who were eligible for the military had not yet served.
- Physicians suffered the greatest financial loss having to serve.
- A large centralized health organization had been developed, not just to serve active-duty military personnel, but to serve a broad clientele.
- The professional manpower required to provide these services was drawn from a wide variety of sources, but virtually none of the entrants were true volunteers.

As far as the commission was concerned, there were

two courses of action open in converting the system to volunteers. One is to decrease the requirements for military physicians by substituting civilians in their stead. The other is to increase the number of physicians willing to volunteer by improving earnings and other conditions of employment. (Gates, 1970, p. 90-1)

The commission staff envisioned a civilian medical group, perhaps a health maintenance organization, providing medical care in the United States, with a small uniformed

---

[19] See the Gates Commission staff study (Lando, 1970).

medical corps. The staff suggested that such the uniformed medical corps "[w]ould be composed primarily of people who prefer military life and who are not fazed by the non-pecuniary disadvantages of such a life" (Lando, 1970, p. IV-3-28). As they saw it,

> [t]he primary need for the uniform corps will be at sea and in foreign countries where the level of medical care is below American standards. In other countries, such as Western Europe, civilian group practice should prove . . . feasible. (Lando, 1970, p. IV-3-28)

In fact, DoD addressed the medical manpower problem along more-traditional lines: medical scholarships and a new uniformed-services medical school, special pays to encourage retention and the use of physician extenders (PEs), such as physician's assistants (PAs) and primary-care nurse practitioners (PCNPs), to reduce the need for new physicians.

Military Medical Manpower Research at RAND

In early 1973, the Air Force Deputy Chief of Staff for Personnel and the Air Force Surgeon General asked RAND to develop a broad-based research program to help the Air Force cope with the end of the draft and the expected sharp decline in the uniformed medical corps.[20] RAND was in a particularly strong position to undertake this additional assignment. The largest program in RAND's domestic portfolio was its health system research program. At that time, RAND was managing the National Health Insurance Experiment. The locus of this activity provided staff and expertise that the Air Force Manpower Program at RAND was able to use to focus on the problems of the Air Force and DoD.

While the new research program was formally part of the Project AIR FORCE Manpower, Personnel, and Training program, the new health-care system research effort had all the attributes of a stand-alone program. It was a large, multitask effort designed to help the Air Force in three broad areas: the supply of health professionals, understanding and controlling the demand for health services, and evaluating alternatives in the delivery of health services. Just as its parent program had tried to focus its efforts on an important policy question of military manpower and to provide answers from a broad base, the set of health delivery projects made up an integrated whole that proved more valuable to the Air Force than if it had been just three individual projects.

To set the stage, when the Air Force asked RAND for help, Congress had already passed the Health Professions Scholarship Program (HPSP) and had authorized the creation of the Uniformed Services University of the Health Sciences (USUHS). The bonus and incentives programs would follow the next spring (1974), with implemen-

---

[20] *Author's Note:* I was the head of the Project AIR FORCE Manpower, Personnel, and Training program at the time. David Chu agreed to lead the Air Force health work. Eighteen years later, David would follow me as Under Secretary of Defense for Personnel and Readiness. In that job, both of us in turn were responsible for DoD's health delivery system. Our initial exposure to military health delivery system problems came as a result of these Air Force projects, which started in 1973.

tation in the early fall. PEs were already in the field. The question was how, in practice, would this new class of health professionals be employed, and how effective would they prove as a way to alleviate the pending shortage of military physicians?

Analysis of the Bonus Program

In February 1974, Bill Albright and David Chu reported to the Air Force Deputy Chief of Staff for Personnel and the Air Force Surgeon General on the initial progress of RAND's research examining the retention of physicians based on the new Special Pay Act of 1974 and HPSP (Albright and Chu, 1974). Some time later—April 1975—they published their initial results, modeling the retention decision of physicians at the end of their initial service obligation as a

> function of the amount of income (the physician) expects to earn if he remains in the military, the amount of income he can earn in his best alternative, and the relative nonpecuniary aspects of the two alternatives. (Albright et al., 1975, p. 9)

Using an occupational choice model first suggested by Anthony Fisher (1970) and used by Stuart Altman and Robert Barro (1971), they examined the retention decision of Air Force physicians for the five years between 1967 and 1971. They noted that, while the absolute retention was low compared with other categories of military manpower, ranging from 6 percent for general practitioners to less than 1 percent for surgeons, the "variation both among specialty groups and among year groups . . . exceeds what can be explained by mere randomness in the observations" (Albright et al., 1975, p. 15). Moreover, they also observed that there had "been substantial variation in the ratio of military and civilian earnings both among specialty groups and among year groups" (Albright et al., 1975, p. 17).

They paid particular attention to conditions of service, such as the size of the hospital to which physicians were assigned and the stage that each physician was at in his or her professional development. The results suggested that "physicians who have not had any specialty training before entering the Air Force are less likely to remain beyond initial obligation, other things equal, than board certified or board eligible physicians." Surprisingly, given the raw data, they found that "physicians in the surgical group are significantly more likely to remain beyond initial obligation than those in the medical group" (Albright et al., 1975, p. 25), as shown by the vertical differences between the supply curves in Figure 10.1. They attributed this to the "kinds of medical problems that are presented to these types of practitioners" (Albright et al., 1975, p. 31). Finally, they noted that, for

> all physician groups the response to changes in relative military/civilian compensation is impressive, with an increase in annual military compensation of $10,000 more than tripling retention beyond initial obligation. . . .
>
> From the point of view of establishing an all-volunteer physician force, the results are encouraging. Not only do they suggest a higher initial retention, but also for the first time the military services may be successful in recruiting physicians directly from the civilian market. (Albright et al., 1975, pp. 30–31)

Figure 10.1
Initial Supply Curve

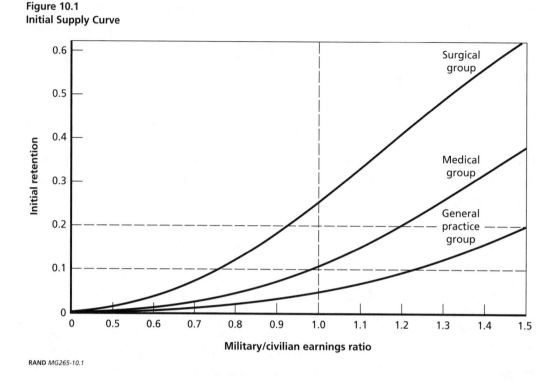

RAND *MG265-10.1*

Analysis of the Scholarship Program

Albright and Chu's analysis of the scholarship program was initially based on two RAND-administered surveys. In September 1973, the first survey was sent to all Air Force HPSP scholarship holders who were either in their first or second year of medical school. The following May, a second survey was sent to 2,000 randomly selected first- and second-year medical students inquiring about their attitudes toward military service, their knowledge of the scholarship program, their potential response to the then–currently authorized program, and a number of alternatives.[21]

In the second survey, 2,000 randomly selected medical students were asked to answer a hypothetical question concerning their willingness to accept a scholarship that came with various levels of a monthly stipend and a variety of postgraduation military commitments and residency restrictions. Answers were recorded by marking a table, as

---

[21] It should be noted that, among economists, the use of survey data is controversial. It is usually held that you cannot trust what people tell you they are going to do. This is often captured in the axiom that "people vote with their feet," which means that you need to collect data on actual behavior and not on individuals' conjectures about what they might do in the future. In this case, however, there was no actual behavior to observe, and the option of simply waiting for the policy to take hold before doing any analysis was not acceptable. This does not mean that simple descriptive statistics from the survey or tables that compare only two variables are an appropriate means of analyzing the survey response. The case of the May 1974 survey of medical students is instructive.

shown in Figure 10.2. "Rational" and consistent behavior is indicated by the upward-sloping series of marks, which represents the respondents' "participation frontier." The responses of all the individuals were aggregated, as shown in Table 10.2, with a similar table constructed for each option available to a respondent, e.g., each year of total commitment and each alternative residency policy. The resulting data were fitted to a logistics function using weighted least squares, and projections were made of the number of students who would take the scholarship under different scenarios. Where data were available—academic years 1973, 1974, and 1975—a scenario was constructed that

Figure 10.2
Sample Question from the 1974 RAND Survey of All Medical Students

The following table asks how you would trade off TOTAL military commitment and monthly scholarship stipend. For *EACH TOTAL MILITARY COMMITMENT* please indicate the minimum monthly stipend you would have required to accept an Armed Forces Health Professions Scholarship at the start of this year. The Scholarship could cover all tuition and fees from September 1973 until your graduation from medical school. In answering the question, make the following assumptions:

- Tuition, fees, and stipend are not taxable.
- 50 percent of the graduates would not be able to complete residency training prior to being called for active duty.
- Military physicians are paid according to the schedule on page 5.

For *EACH TOTAL MILITARY COMMITMENT (EACH COLUMN)* please indicate with an "X" the minimum monthly stipend you would require.

		TOTAL MILITARY COMMITMENT							
		1 yr	2 yrs	3 yrs	4 yrs	5 yrs	6 yrs	7 yrs	8 yrs
	Would not accept at any stipend level	( )	( )	( )	( )	( )	( )	( )	( )
	Above $1500	( )	( )	( )	( )	( )	( )	( )	( )
	1400	( )	( )	( )	( )	( )	( )	( )	(X)
	1300	( )	( )	( )	( )	( )	( )	( )	( )
	1200	( )	( )	( )	( )	( )	( )	(X)	( )
	1100	( )	( )	( )	( )	( )	( )	( )	( )
	1000	( )	( )	( )	( )	( )	(X)	( )	( )
Monthly stipend	900	( )	( )	( )	( )	( )	( )	( )	( )
	800	( )	( )	( )	( )	(X)	( )	( )	( )
	700	( )	( )	( )	( )	( )	( )	( )	( )
	600	( )	( )	( )	(X)	( )	( )	( )	( )
	500	( )	( )	(X)	( )	( )	( )	( )	( )
	400	( )	(X)	( )	( )	( )	( )	( )	( )
	300	(X)	( )	( )	( )	( )	( )	( )	( )
	200	( )	( )	( )	( )	( )	( )	( )	( )
	100	( )	( )	( )	( )	( )	( )	( )	( )
	0	( )	( )	( )	( )	( )	( )	( )	( )

SOURCE: Albright (1976, p. 7).
RAND *MG265-10.2*

Table 10.2
First-Year Students in Four-Year Medical Schools
Who Would Participate in HPSP if the
Total Commitment Were Four Years

After-Tax Stipend Level Per Month[a]	Proportion Indicating HPSP Participation[b]
1,000	0.32
900	0.26
800	0.21
700	0.16
600	0.12
500	0.08
400	0.05
300	0.02
200	0.01

[a] In 1974 dollars.

[b] With a 50-percent residency policy and total commitment of four years.

allowed direct comparison between the predicted and actual numbers of first-year scholarship students in the four-year program. The prediction error for three academic years ranged from a high (overprediction) of 10 percent to a low (underprediction) of 3 percent. The statistical model was also used to project the net number of "new participants" in the program, showing how components of the program influenced enrollment. An average elasticity of 1.75 was observed, making "participation [in the program] very sensitive to the effective level of the stipend" (Albright, 1976, p. 14).

Daubert, Victoria, Daniel Relles, and Jr. Charles Roll. Medical Student Financing and the Armed Forces Health Professional Scholarship Program. Santa Monica, CA: RAND, 1982

It is useful to indicate where this survey study falls along the spectrum of empirical research. At one end there is the "back of the envelope" analysis on what most policy decisions are probably justified. In the best of circumstances, this type of analysis is based on economic theories that have been subjected to repeated tests, and the predicted sign of the changes resulting from the recommended policy should be correct. At the next level are decisions that require more than qualitative guidance even when there are no historical data, A survey is conducted and with good luck a careful study emerges. Now we have quantitative estimates, but they must be treated gingerly until the appropriate historical data are collected, especially when the survey data are based on answers to hypothetical rather than retrospective questions. Next, there are studies based on historical data that are, as a rule, superior to studies that rely on hypothetical survey data. Finally, there are the "experimental studies" that are presumably the most informative of all empirical research in the social sciences.

Increases in medical-school enrollment and the effects of removing tax liability from the monthly stipend were also shown to encourage participation in the program, while inflation was shown to have a deleterious effect on participation.

The scholarship program was again in the spotlight in 1976, when the new Health Professions Educational Assistance Act was enacted. This provided

> equally (or more) attractive scholarships to medical students [not already committed to the armed services] on a sufficiently large scale. As a result, the continued success of the AFHPSP [Armed Forces HPSP] in meeting DoD physician requirements was seriously jeopardized. (Daubert et al., 1982, p. iii)

In late 1977, RAND fielded a new sample survey to 3,400 first- and second-year medical students randomly selected by the American Medical Association "to evaluate student preferences regarding several alternative financing methods" (Daubert et al., 1982, p. 8). The survey data were analyzed using a conditional logit model designed to analyze "the choice behavior of individuals confronted with a finite set of mutually exclusive alternatives." A typical question is shown in Figure 10.3. The resulting estimates allowed predictions for each alternative based on the demographic characteristics of medical students and the characteristics of all the other alternatives, thus providing, in effect, the cross-elasticities of supply, including the differential effect of student stipends and compensation after graduation from medical school during periods of mandatory (payback) service.

The analysis found that HPSP faced a significant shortfall in its recruiting objectives and "suggested that increasing service compensation was the most cost effective policy option to achieve the desired number of AFHPSP recruits" (Daubert et al., 1982, p. 1). When these results were briefed to the staff director of the House Armed Services Committee, Kim Wincup, he made sure the new physician pay bill passed in June 1980 provided a 50-percent increase in the pay of HPSP physicians with one year of postgraduate training and up to a 100-percent increase for those in advanced residency training. Medical students saw a 33-percent increase in their stipend. The study also found that "the residency option was probably the most powerful of all the nonpecuniary options open to the military services" (Daubert et al., 1982, p. 22). This presented a difficult problem to the military medical manpower managers. They could increase the number of medical students who enrolled in HPSP by allowing all graduates the opportunity to take residency training immediately after their internships. However, as the study noted, this would "[exacerbate] the physician supply problem in the short run . . . [and] would have made control over the specialty mix in the services difficult" (Daubert et al., 1982, p. 22).

Figure 10.3
Sample Question from the 1977 RAND Survey of All Medical Students

9. Consider the three programs for financing your medical school education described on the opposite page *and* the way you are financing your medical school education *this year* (76–77). Assure that you were eligible and that each of these alternatives had been available to you at the beginning of this academic year. How would you have rated these on a scale from 0 to 100?

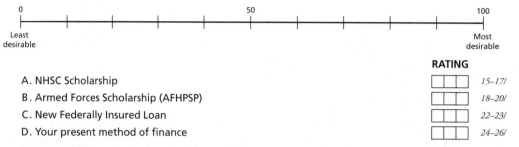

RATING

A. NHSC Scholarship ☐☐☐ *15–17/*

B. Armed Forces Scholarship (AFHPSP) ☐☐☐ *18–20/*

C. New Federally Insured Loan ☐☐☐ *22–23/*

D. Your present method of finance ☐☐☐ *24–26/*

How would your ratings in Question 9 change if the following modifications in the respective programs were made? *Please consider these changes individually and make your ratings relative to those in Question 9.* (Ratings may exceed 100)

10. How would you rate the NHSC Scholarship:
    - If the 3 year limit on post graduate training were removed? ☐☐☐ *27–29/*
    - If the monthly stipend were increased to $800 and the service compensation were increased to $29,000/year? ☐☐☐ *30–32/*
    - If the monthly stipend were increased to $600 and the service compensation were increased to $37,000/year? ☐☐☐ *33–35/*
    - If the 3 year limit on post graduate training were removed, the monthly stipend were increased to $600, and the service compensation were increased to $37,000/year? ☐☐☐ *36–38/*

11. How would you rate the AFHPSP Scholarship:
    - If there were no annual cost of living adjustment in the stipend? ☐☐☐ *39–42/*
    - If the residency opportunity were increased to 100% and the monthly stipend were increased to $600? ☐☐☐ *42–44/*
    - If the residency opportunity were increased to 100%, the monthly stipend were increased to $600, and the service compensation were increased to $29,000/year? ☐☐☐ *45–47/*
    - If the residency opportunity were increased to 100%, the monthly stipend were increased to $600, and the service compensation were increased to $37,000/year? ☐☐☐ *48–50/*

12. How would you rate the New Federally Insured Loan:
    - If interest payments were deferred until graduation from medical school? ☐☐☐ *52–53/*
    - If interest payments were deferred until 3 years after medical school? ☐☐☐ *54–56/*

SOURCE: Daubert et al. (1982, p. 39).

RAND *MG265-10.3*

Daubert, Victoria, Daniel Relles, and Jr. Charles Roll. Medical Student Financing and the Armed Forces Health Professional Scholarship Program. Santa Monica, CA: RAND, 1982

The Conditional Logit Model

The problem of analyzing the choice behavior of individuals confronted with a finite set of mutually exclusive alternatives arises in a wide variety of contexts. The conditional logit technique, recently popularized by McFadden, has become a widely accepted approach. Recent applications include studies of choice among institutions of higher education (Radner and Miller), transportation modes (Charles River Associates), and occupations (Schmidt and Strauss).

The conditional logit model focuses on dependent variables that identify which of a set of alternatives was chosen by each individual in a group. It postulates that every individual first evaluates the utility of each alternative available to him, then selects the alternative for which the utility is largest. In practice, the utility function is assumed to be linear in parameters that describe the individual and the alternatives; it also incudes an additive random disturbance term from a specific family of distributions. Such restrictions are necessary for tractable estimation procedures.

In our case, there are four alternatives, each defining a different method for medical school financing: NHSC, HPSP, LOAN, and OTHER. The utility functions depend on the projected income streams under each program, additional program incentives, and the individual's wealth, race, sex, and marital status:

$$U_{ij} = b'X_{ij} + e_{ij},$$

where i = an index of individuals,

j = an index of alternatives, identifying NHSC, HPSP, LOAN, and OTHER,

U_{ij} = utility (or score) of jth alternative to ith person,

b = (p by 1) vector of unknown coefficients,

X_{ij} = (p by 1) vector of attributes of jth alternative to ith person,

e_{ij} = random error.

The goal of the analysis is to estimate b, thereby identifying the attributes of alternatives that affect choices and quantifying the magnitude of their effects. We also seek a method for simulating future choices which is consistent with the above formulation.

General principles of statistical analysis prescribe that one first write down the likelihood function of the observed data. The maximum likelihood estimates generally have good classical and Bayesian properties, and the inverse of the log likelihood function's second derivatives matrix approximates the estimates' variances and covariances.

In conditional logit estimation, the only distribution on the random disturbances that leads to a closed form and tractable likelihood function is the Weibull distribution:

$$\text{Prob}(e < t) = \exp[- A*\exp(- Bt)], \quad A, B > 0.$$

The class of Weibull distributions is quite rich, admitting a variety of error density function shapes for various choices of A and B.

Given the Weibull assumptions, McFadden derives an expression for the probability that individual i chooses alternative j:

$$P_{ij} = \text{Prob}(\text{individual i chooses j})$$
$$= \exp(b'X_{ij}) / \sum_k \exp(b'X_{ik}).$$

Hence, a sample of n students making choices c(1), c(2), . . ., c(n) yields the closed-form likelihood function

$$L(b) = \prod_1^n [\exp(b'X_{i,c(i)}) / \sum_k \exp(b'X_{ik}).$$

This function has been studies extensively by many authors besides McFadden (cf. Theil, Haberman, Nerlove and Press), and its numerical properties are well-known. It has a unique maximum, and the Newton-Raphson iteration technique generally finds the maximum quickly. Inference statistics include the maximum likelihood values themselves, the log likelihood function (useful in tests of hypotheses), and the

---

Daubert, Victoria, Daniel Relles, and Jr. Charles Roll. Medical Student Financing and the Armed Forces Health Professional Scholarship Program. Santa Monica, CA: RAND, 1982—continued

inverse of the second derivatives matrix (for confidence intervals).

In our empirical work, we postulated several alternative formulations for the X's, fit the parameters by the maximum likelihood methods, and tested for the importance of terms using likelihood ratio tests. We examined signs of fitted coefficients to verity that the fits were compatible with theory; for example, income elasticities had to be positive. Finally, we used the fitted models to simulate choices of individuals, and verified that the percentages predicted for each option were roughly compatible with empirical flows.

Analysis of the Use of Physician Extenders

One of the first projects the Air Force Surgeon General requested in 1973 was an assessment of the new Air Force PA program. The program was started in 1971 as a means of reducing the demand for physicians, given the new all-volunteer force. PAs were trained at Sheppard Air Force Base in an in-house program modeled after the PA training program at Duke University. Each PA was a former enlisted corpsman who received two years of instruction: one year of classroom work in the basic sciences and a second on rotation through the outpatient department of one of several large Air Force hospitals. PAs were trained to diagnose and treat common illnesses and could also help manage complex patient problems under the supervision of a physician. Graduates of the program received a Bachelor of Science degree, and almost all took and passed the certification exam given by the National Commission on Certification of Physician Assistants (Buchanan and Hosek, 1983, p. 5).

When the first class of PAs graduated in 1973, there was no definitive plan for how they might be employed to best advantage, no scheme to collect data on their utilization or performance, and no program to provide feedback to the school that had trained them. RAND initiated an ambitious data-collection program at the primary-care outpatient clinics of nine Air Force hospitals that received the new graduates. Typically, these were general practice, internal medicine, and pediatric outpatient clinics at a "community hospital" in the relatively small, 50-bed range. A each health care provider filled out a "patient contact record" (Chu, 1974) for every visit for two weeks at seven of the nine clinics and, to better understand issues of continuity of care, at the other two clinics for six months.[22] In total, approximately 30,000 patient visits were recorded, each record showing the health provider, the diagnosis or diagnoses made, the treatment given and the amount of time spent with each patient.

---

[22] The patient contact record was a checklist "encounter form" filled out partly by the patient (or the parent of a child) and partly by the medical provider. At the time of the visit, the patient filled out requested demographic information, while the provider of care checked off diagnostic and therapeutic information, as well as time stamping the start and finish of each visit.

Using these data, RAND "constructed a simple activity analysis model to identify the most cost-effective mix of providers to treat the conditions seen in the primary care clinics" (Hosek and Roll, 1979, p. 7). The analysis was briefed to the Air Force Surgeon General in February 1976. It suggested that, based on the mix of conditions typically presented by the populations, a ratio of two or three PAs to one physician would be cost-effective in primary-care clinics, such as the ones studied. At the time these results were presented to the Surgeon General, the Air Force had never staffed a clinic with more than one PA for each physician (Hosek and Roll, 1979, p. 8). The concern, of course, was quality of care. The RAND recommendation was made with full regard for the quality of care this initial group of PAs provided.

Borrowing some of the techniques and staff from the RAND-managed National Health Insurance Experiment Study, a "comparative method" was used in which "the technical process of care [of PAs]" was weighed against "the care rendered by physicians in the same settings . . . us[ing] data collected with a patient contact record at nine Air Force bases in 1974" (Goldberg et al., 1979, p. v).

In addition to technical comparisons of care, the "degree of misordering or over-utilization of tests or procedures, in which a pattern of ordering, suggestive of wasteful or unnecessary testing, was sought" (Goldberg et al., 1979, p. 2). The study concluded that

> [T]he Air Force *can* deliver the same quality of medical care when physician assistants treat some of the patients formerly treated by physicians, and that no quality bar exists to the continued training and employment of physician assistants in Air Force outpatient clinics. . . . We find the quality of care they deliver to be acceptable when they are providing care for the types of problems they have been trained to treat.
>
> Insofar as we can measure with our criteria, for routine, outpatient conditions, physician assistants are safe, and they deliver a technical process quality of care at least equal to that of physicians. Our finding that physician assistants treat at least as well as physicians for the problems we were able to study is consistent with other published evidence.[23] . . .
>
> The performance of physician assistants, as measured by these 1974 data, constitutes a strong endorsement of the Air Force's in-house physician assistant training program. (Goldberg et al., 1979, p. 26, emphasis in the original)

In February 1976, the Air Force Surgeon General authorized a demonstration project to test the feasibility of intensive use of PEs—PAs and/or PCNPs—in primary medical clinics (Buchanan and Hosek, 1983, p. 1). The test began in fall 1976. It ran for two years at four Air Force hospitals—Chanute, Dyess, Fairchild and Nellis Air Force bases—between 1976 and 1978.[24] The outpatient clinics were staffed by teams,

---

[23] See Appendix B, "Previous Research into Physician Extenders' Quality of Care" in Goldberg et al. (1979).

[24] Preliminary results were presented to the Air Force Surgeon General on March 2, 1978. See Chu et al. (1978) for the briefing.

each consisting of two extenders supervised by a physician, at three bases. At one base, three extenders were assigned to each physician. In addition to the new manning, RAND developed a comprehensive set of guidelines for clinic operations that, among other things, created panels of patients who would be seen by a specific provider team and changed the way appointments were made by patients at the clinics (Armor et al., 1976). The guidelines were "distributed widely in the demonstration base clinics" (Buchanan and Hosek, 1983, p. 51).

Approximately six months after the program started, a revised patient contact record was fielded, recording every visit at each hospital for over one month (Chu et al., 1978, p. v). In addition, two surveys were used to judge patient reactions: the first at the beginning of the demonstration in fall 1976 to measure initial reactions, and the other one year later to measure reactions after the system had been operating for a while (Chu et al., 1978, p. 27). Staff and line reactions were assessed through a series of structured interviews with commanders, hospital administrators, physician supervisors, PEs, and senior corpsmen in fall 1977.

While the PAs were originally seen as a way to resolve the manning problem caused by the end of the draft, the Air Force had, with the help of the scholarship program and increases in physician pay, the Air Force had "eliminated the primary care shortage . . . [and] was more concerned about maintaining service levels [and patient satisfaction] than about decreasing costs" by 1976 (Buchanan and Hosek, 1983, p. 2). The research plan therefore called for the test to be evaluated, in terms of both cost-effective personnel utilization, the quality of care patients received, and patients' acceptance of the new manning model of physicians and extenders.

As in the case of the 1974 study of PAs, RAND used a "process" measure of quality of care that focused on "procedures, methods and strategies of care." The RAND team also noted that it had

> relied on the process measures that we could easily estimate from our [patient] encounter form data. These measures of "technical process of care" make sense in the outpatient setting, where many of the conditions treated, though perhaps ill-defined, are common and conventionally managed. (Goldberg et al., 1981, p. 953)

As before, the team found that there were

> [v]ery few significant differences between provider groups. . . . [For] 25 of 28 criteria, [the] PAs' performance statistically equaled or exceeded the performance standards set by physicians. . . . PAs' compliance on criteria were found to be stable over time. . . . When we compared our 1977 results with those of 1974, there was no evidence of any worsening in PAs' performance. (Goldberg et al., 1981, p. 955)

Some differences among providers were noted in terms of the "ordering" rate for x-rays and other diagnostic tests, but there was no consistent evidence that extenders disordered and overburdened the Air Force's care delivery system. Likewise, . . . [the data] showed that PAs are not generating an inordinate number of return visits, referrals or hospital admissions. We believe that the Air Force can deliver the same quality of medical care when PEs [PAs and PCNPs] treat a sizable proportion of the patients formerly treated by physicians, and that no quality bar exists to the continued training and employment of PAs and PCNPs in Air Force outpatient clinics. (Goldberg et al., 1981)

Productivity was measured using econometric, production function, and activity analyses and linear programming techniques. The production-function approach provided a functional relationship between the number of patients a clinic saw over a given period, the inputs of physicians' and extenders' time, and other variables. The activity-analysis approach allowed the team to evaluate the alternative provider combinations that were competent to treat each class of patient visits and to identify the least costly combination. Together with a detailed "billet" or manpower cost model, the activity analysis results allowed the team to infer whether the demonstration project's physician extender ratio was too high or too low (Buchanan and Hosek, 1983).

At the end of the demonstration period, and for the four hospitals included in the study, the RAND team concluded the following:

In performing their outpatient care duties; PAs . . . were as productive as the physicians with whom they worked. Whether based on estimated production functions or activity analysis, we find that at current relative personnel costs the Air Force should use PAs to treat as many primary medicine patients as the PA's training and patient acceptance allow. This conclusion also rests in the PA's documented quality of care. . . . Allowing for enough physicians to supervise the PAs, treat more complex problems, and satisfy patient preferences for physician treatment, we calculate that this workload is most efficiently handled with three physicians and eight or nine PAs, depending on case mix complexity. (Buchanan and Hosek, 1983, p. 45)

The RAND team also noted that "PAs currently entail significantly lower personnel costs than either the Armed Forces Health Professions Scholarship Program (HPSP) or volunteer physicians" (Buchanan and Hosek, 1983, p. v). One can only imagine what they would have said if they had compared the cost of PAs with the cost of physicians who graduated from the DoD's own USUHS.

The Uniformed Services University of the Health Sciences

The 1972 legislation that had authorized the scholarship program also chartered USUHS as a "degree-granting Federal University for the education of physicians and members of other health professions within 25 miles of the District of Columbia."[25]

---

[25] See The Uniformed Services Health Professions Revitalization Act of 1972 (Chapter 104—Uniformed Services University of the Health Sciences—of Public Law 92-428, September 21, 1972).

The sponsor and acknowledged father of the new university was the chairman of the House Armed Services Committee, Congressman F. Edward Hebert (D–Louisiana). In appreciation for his vision, the main building of the university, which is located on the grounds of the National Naval Medical Center in Bethesda, Maryland, is named after the congressman.

While the university was created ostensibly to respond to the shortage of physicians accompanying the all-volunteer force and the end of the Berry Plan, Congressman Hebert had in fact been pressing for the establishment of the school for some time. At least as early as 1968, well before there was an all-volunteer force, he had proposed that a federal medical school be created that could, he believed, take advantage of the concentration of federal medical institutions near Bethesda, Maryland. These included, besides the National Naval Medical Center, the laboratories and hospitals of the National Institutes of Health and the National Medical Library. An assessment at the time by the Office of the Assistant Secretary of Defense (Systems Analysis) showed none of the federal institutions that Hebert was counting on to form the core of the University complex was well suited to be part of a medical school, and each of the institutions opposed the creation of the new school.[26] There was not enough free space to be turned into classrooms, and even the National Medical Library did not have the reading rooms to support the more than 400 medical and other students that were envisioned. Most importantly, in 1968, with the draft and Berry Plan in full sway, the services had more medical staff onboard than they were authorized to have in their approved manning documents.

By 1971 several things had changed that affected Congress' decision to establish a DoD medical school: the all-volunteer force was enacted, which ended the Berry Plan; Congressman Hebert had "ascended" to the chairmanship of the House Armed Services Committee; and Secretary of Defense Melvin Laird had withdrawn the opposition of DoD in a "private agreement" with Hebert to move the all-volunteer force legislation through his committee (Laird, 2003). One thing, however, had not changed: The new school made little "analytic" sense. The numbers just did not add up. Working against the arguments for the need for a dedicated DoD medical school was the sharp increase in the number of medical students enrolled nationally. In 1968, the American Medical Association changed its long-held position and agreed to support efforts to expand medical school enrollment at existing schools and even the development of new medical schools. Between 1965 and 1975, 28 new medical schools opened, and medical school enrollment at all schools increased by 55 percent.[27] An assessment of the USUHS and "alternatives" done by the staff of the Defense Manpower Commission showed that

---

[26] *Author's Note:* This was one of the first studies I did when I joined the Systems Analysis staff in 1968.

[27] E. J. Devine noted that in February 1975 the U.S. Department of Health, Education and Welfare had told Congress that "a surplus of physicians is likely to result if the Federal government continues its financial aid to expand the output of medical schools" (Devine, 1975, p. 11).

accessions cost per medical graduate [of USUHS] will be no lower than $150,000 and may well exceed $200,000. . . . This is about four or five times the $34,000 cost to the government of obtaining a graduate through the scholarship program and is also far more expensive than procuring trained physicians through the use of the bonus. (Devine, 1975, p. 32)

Even the presumed higher retention projected for USUHS graduates proved to be less of an advantage when the analysis included the substantial retirement payments that a full-career physician would earn after serving out a nominal 20-year career. In May 1975, the Defense Manpower Commission made the following recommendation to the President and Congress:

Notwithstanding the minimal start-up expenditures that have already been made, the Commission recommends that: (1) the Uniformed Services University of the Health Sciences approach be terminated; and (2) utilization be made of existing scholarship, subsidies and bonus programs as a more cost-effective way to meet current and future procurement and retention goals for military professional medical personnel of high quality. (Tarr, 1975, p. 57)

While the staff's analysis obviously convinced the Defense Manpower Commission that USHUS was unnecessary, and despite a strong statement in both their interim and final reports arguing that the University not be built, the USHUS exists to this day—including a recent decision to renovate and expand its facilities. One can only wonder what factors the staff left out of their analysis and what considerations the commissioners neglected for both to have gotten it so wrong. The answer, of course, was the private arrangement between the administration and Congress at the highest levels that traded support for the school for consideration of the all-volunteer force legislation.[28]

Assessing the Effectiveness of Paid Advertising

When Bill Brehm returned to the Pentagon as the Assistant Secretary of Defense (Manpower & Reserve Affairs), he asked who the "market expert" on the staff was. By the following September, he had hired Al J. Martin as his Special Assistant for Accessions Policy. He and Martin set out to raise anew with Congress the issue of paid advertising. They knew that House Armed Services Committee Chairman F. Edward Hebert's antipathy to paid advertising had prevented progress in this area since 1971. After Hebert lost the chairmanship of the House Armed Services Committee in January 1975 (Hebert and McMillan, 1976, p. 447), they reasoned that if they could definitively demonstrate

---

[28] In 2003, at the All-Volunteer Force Conference, former Secretary of Defense Laird recalled the opposition of the Office of Manpower and Budget to the idea of the medical school and his appeal directly to President Nixon. Laird said that Nixon understood his argument that support for the school was tied to the end of the draft and told Laird to "do what you have to do" (Laird, 2003).

the advantages of paid radio or television, they could convince Congress to allow them to move forward. In early 1975, they sponsored a study of and decided

> the cost efficiency of including paid broadcasts in service advertising media schedules . . . a decision was made in the spring of 1975 to carry the investigation further by testing the capability of paid radio advertising to convey service advertising messages and to accomplish advertising objectives. All four services agreed to participate simultaneously in the test. (Schucker, 1976, pp. 1–2)

The test that was to constitute the "rationale in requesting the consent of Congress for all components . . . to employ paid broadcast recruit advertising" (Martin and Haley, 1978, p. 151) was to be a "true experiment." Martin was mindful that the Army's 1971 media test "was not conclusive enough to justify a return to unrestricted paid broadcast advertising . . . primarily due to the lack of a detailed experimental design and to insufficient time within the paid broadcast media" (Martin and Haley, 1978, p. 149). The analysis that had been completed had relied on trend or time-series regression analyses to untangle the effects of the many variables that interact in any real-world situation. Martin argued, however, that

> the assumptions of the regression model are rarely met. Moreover, time series analyses usually raise problems of multicollinearity, and if cross-sectional analysis is introduced to circumvent such problems, the criterion effect are frequently confounded with variables that are mismatched across markets with high levels of the variable of interest (i.e., test markets) and those with low or zero levels (i.e., control markets). (Martin and Haley, 1978, p. 150)

Martin wanted a "true experiment" where the "integral part of [his] controlled experiment" would be "the random assignment of individual markets to the test and control conditions." He argued that, while "experiments are more expensive and more time-consuming than most alternative approaches, experimental results are almost always more valid and more reliable than the results of other methods" (Martin and Haley, 1978, p. 150).

From the beginning, however, Martin ran into some "constraints" that prevented him from "modeling any specific relationship between radio and market performance." Thus,

> [t]he central research question was how radio would perform when gross impressions against young men between the ages of 17 and 24 are equalized for a schedule containing a mix of radio and other media versus a schedule containing other media alone. (Martin, 1980, p. 2)

While it was argued that the goals of the test were "relatively modest," it was also argued that given the generally negative experience of past media tests in other areas . . . it would be unwise to be more ambitious in the first experiment for the armed services. It was hoped that one solid clean experiment would lay the groundwork for future work with controlled experiments. (Schucker, 1976, p. 3)[29]

The basic experimental design was a standard before-and-after comparison in carefully matched test and control markets. Researchers examined 175 metropolitan areas—Standard Metropolitan Statistical Areas (SMSAs)—and pared them down to 138 markets, which they thought would not be too large for the type of test that was being run, did not contain a large military base, and did not have other "media problems." They then analyzed these markets using stepwise multiple regression analysis to determine the market characteristics that best predicted "quality" male accessions. The markets were then grouped "to form market subgroups using the accessions measure and associated predictor variables from the regression analysis" (Martin, 1980, p. 6). Finally, researchers developed "triads of matched markets," and "markets within triads were randomly assigned to the test and control conditions" (Schucker, 1976, p. 25).

Each service had two test markets and one matched control market for each of its own service-specific advertising schemes. To "obtain more precision on the joint radio advertising condition," Martin allocated six tests and three controls to the "simultaneous advertiser condition" (Martin, 1980, p. 6). A telephone survey was taken in three waves; each wave involved approximately 2,400 interviews, with an average of 150 per test and control market. The interviews were conducted in late summer 1975, before advertising started; again in October; and finally in December, after the advertising was completed. The services' advertising agencies provided detailed information on the media delivered in each of the 24 test and control markets.

Broadly, the study considered five measures:

- audits of recruiting stations to determine the number of signed contracts
- audits of recruiting stations to determine the level of inquiries by mail, telephone, and in person
- interview results that showed a predisposition toward joining a service
- interview results concerning awareness and knowledge of specific programs and benefits offered by individual services
- interview results indicating awareness of Armed Forces advertising.

---

[29] Martin provides an alternative explanation:

> A principal constraint was that the test be completed quickly. An improving economy had led policy makers in DoD to believe that future recruiting would become increasingly difficult. Also, lead-time would be required to get Congressional approval to use broadcast advertising and for Services to incorporate paid radio into their media plans should the test prove successful. Consequently, the decision was made to execute a 13-week screening test of gross market response to radio, and in so doing it was recognized that the shortness of the test precluded modeling any specific relationship between radio and market performance. (Martin, 1980, p. 1)

Generally, the test showed that "accessions were larger during the test period than during the base period in both the test and control markets. However, the test markets showed larger increases than control markets" (Schucker, 1976, pp. 37–38). In terms of inquires, there were "larger gains for the radio market" (Schucker, 1976, p. 40). Statistics on the "recall" variables were "somewhat erratic" (Schucker, 1976, p. 46), with responses on the "likelihood of joining" measures "all indicating slightly higher net changes for the control market" (Schucker, 1976, pp. 51–52). Finally, "the awareness statistics reflected favorably on the use of radio. Both awareness of service advertising and recall of radio advertising are higher in radio markets than in control markets" (Schucker, 1976, p. 61). The final report made the relatively low-keyed conclusion that

> [e]nough statistically significant results were found in excess of the number expected by chance to warrant the conclusion that paid radio made an incremental contribution to the advertising and recruiting programs of the Services as a whole in test markets where used in conjunction with other media advertising. (Schucker, 1977, p. 4)[30]

At the end of the test, Martin concluded that, "on the basis of the DoD test results, . . . the military services have been permitted to use paid broadcast recruiting advertising since October 1976" (Martin, 1980, p. 18).[31] He also made the more general point about experimentation:

> This particular media study should serve to illustrate the demands on management and researchers alike required to measure recruiting advertising effectiveness. Multivariate experimental design (quasi-experimental at best) is the research tool that can accomplish this but it is demanding, complex, time-consuming, and costly. . . . Measurement of advertising effectiveness for recruiting is a challenging task in and of itself. DoD managers should attempt to improve his [sic] understanding of advertising productivity through the judicious use of experimentation to provide data for modeling the relationships between advertising and quality accession effects. Experimentation can be combined with tracking (descriptive studies) of such intermediate criteria as awareness, attitude, and inquiries. The tracking results can then be used to estimate accession effects based on the models developed through experimentation. (Martin and Haley, 1978, p. 162)

---

[30] A review of the study at the time seemed more definitive, finding the "results lead to the clear conclusion that paid radio advertising is a worthwhile addition to the media mix." The reviewer seemed particularly pleased because

> from an academic theoretical viewpoint, the results indicated that, contrary to a lot of "conventional wisdom" advertising effectiveness—even of relatively minor subelement (media)—can be measured. The results further indicate that "sales" (accession contracts) can be a sensitive measure of advertising effectiveness. (Sawyer, 1977, p. 1)

[31] It should also be noted that Congressman F. Edward Hebert, who had opposed paid advertising, was preoccupied by a political scandal in New Orleans and did not stand for reelection in fall 1976.

Officer Retention: Development of Dynamic Officer Retention Models

One of the most important advances in military personnel analysis came in the mid-1970s when Glenn Gotz, working at RAND, challenged the conventional wisdom concerning the appropriate way to think about and estimate the effects that personnel policies—the promotion and tenure system and changes in compensation—had on the propensity of service members to remain in the military. Gotz questioned the conceptual underpinnings of the traditional retention models that the Gates Commission and DoD had used and moved the field to an entirely new understanding of how compensation and personnel policies should be considered in the continuation-and-retention analysis.[32] He provided the central links that allowed personnel planners to incorporate the expected behavior of service members in their personnel plans. While his initial work focused on Air Force officers, it was applicable to both officers and enlisted personnel of all services. His breakthrough in understanding that the continuation-and-retention decision can be modeled as a dynamic programming problem is a classic example of how progress is made in science—small steps building on the base of what has gone before. In much the same way, his work is a more general and logically complete case of the more tractable annual cost of leaving (ACOL) retention models used by the Fourth Quadrennial Review of Military Compensation and is today the methodology employed to manage the retention bonus program. His work remains the basis for contemporary research into alternative retirement and compensation systems.

Historically, the development and maturation of the dynamic retention modeling[33] approach is documented in a series of working and internal notes used to communicate Gotz' evolving ideas with his Air Force sponsors and colleagues. It is a story that starts well before the models and results were formally published, either in RAND reports or in academic journals. Here is the story.

Project RAND's Officer Supply and Retention Study

In spring 1972, the Air Force Deputy Chief of Staff for Personnel, Lieutenant General Robert Dixon, asked RAND to initiate a series of studies designed to help the Air Force better manage its officer corps. The year before, the Air Force had published a new personnel plan. The "Total Officer Personnel Objective Structure for the Line Officer Force" (TOPLINE) was the portion of the plan that covered officers. TOPLINE projections had been developed using a steady-state Markovian flow model that incor-

---

[32] John Enns provides a review of retention modeling in Enns (1977).

[33] Richard Bellman invented dynamic programming at RAND in the 1950s, A particular version of dynamic programming, namely, dynamic stochastic programming, provided a sophisticated way of handling future uncertainty as the decision maker tried to make optimal decisions over time, i.e., dynamically. This was a powerful addition to the inclusion of a "taste" factor to allow for persistent individual differences in the strength of their attachment to military service.

porated an historical set of transition rates to project a fully structured officer corps by grade and year of service (Miller and Sammis, 1973). The models "treat[ed] the retention rates of the various categories of officers as fixed, that is, policy changes are not allowed to influence retention rates" (Gotz, 1974a, p. 1).

Dixon was concerned that officer accessions and, ultimately, retention might be different under the all-volunteer force.[34] He wanted to know whether the Air Force would be able to attract the number and quality of officers that it had been able to attract in the past and whether the new cohorts would exhibit the same propensity to make the Air Force a career that had been incorporated into TOPLINE projections and the Air Force Personnel Plan. RAND initiated several research projects to examine and extend the personnel planning models used in TOPLINE (see, for example, Sammis et al., 1975) to study the effects that the all-volunteer force were likely to have on Reserve Officer Training Corps (ROTC) and Officer Candidate School accessions, and to estimate new retention functions that would be sensitive to the new all-volunteer environment.

Initially work focused on the accession problem. William Albright and Gertrude Brunner took on the ROTC problem (see Albright and Brunner, 1973), and Glenn Gotz, a graduate student at University of California, Los Angeles, and a consultant at RAND, set out to examine the determinants of Officer Candidate School accessions. In a series of working notes, Gotz reviewed the economic literature on the accession of officers and raised a critical issue that would eventually change the whole field of military manpower research. Gotz noted that, with one exception, "none of the supply studies in the literature used a time horizon for discounting longer than the length of the initial commitment" (Gotz, 1972, pp. 6, 8) and, in his study plan, promised to "investigate whether the proper horizon for measuring pecuniary returns is six years, the usual length of the initial commitment for a flight rated officer, or a longer period of time" (Gotz, 1972, p. 5).

Before Gotz was able to carry out the analysis of Officer Candidate School accessions, the Air Force asked RAND to move up the retention study. The Air Force's interest in further studies of initial accessions of officers waned with the initial success of the all-volunteer force. Moreover, given the additional attention that OSD was placing on reforming the retirement system, the Air Force wanted to better understand how the all-volunteer force was likely affect retention and the future structure of its officer corps.[35] As Gotz started to think about the retention decision, it became clear that the

---

[34] Studies of the accession and retention of Air Force officers had been largely overlooked during the initial efforts of the Gates Commission. While Cook and White (1970) provided the Air Force with estimates of how the all-volunteer force would affect the quality and quantity of new enlisted accessions, no work had been done on the supply of Air Force officers. Moreover, no work had been done on the retention decision of officers at all. The retention work that had been done focused on Army enlisted personnel.

[35] Gotz noted that

> there is a strong possibility that two distinct policy changes will occur in the next few years. First, partial vesting of pension rights . . . . The second change might be an increase in the promotion phase point to colonel, the phase point being the modal year of service during which promotion occurs. (Gotz, 1974a, p. 1)

question he was asking about the appropriate time horizon for the analysis of new officers was still germane.[36]

Gotz's work focused on "estimat[ing] the effects of promotion and pay policies on the retention of Air Force officers [through] a behavioral model of retention" (Gotz, 1974b, p. v), e.g., the promotion opportunities (probability of being promoted) and the phase point (when the officer is selected for promotion), as well as the structure and amount of pay. He split his analysis into two parts: first, the analysis of the retention of captains between the fifth and 30th year of service and, second, the retention of officers who were eligible to retire. These were officers between the 21st and 31st year of service. Other officers were excluded—majors and other officers before 21 years of service—because the structure of the retirement system resulted in very little variation in retention rates for those officers.

Retention of Captains

A major feature of Gotz's work was the explicit treatment of the promotion system. Gotz modeled retention assuming that "officers base their expectations about the promotion system on the current experiences of officers more senior in years of service" (Gotz, 1974b, p. v). That is, Gotz assumed that Air Force officers made the decision to leave or remain in the Air Force by evaluating expectations about future events. According to Gotz,

> [t]he individual, looking forward in time, does not know precisely which direction his career will take should he remain in the Air Force. We assume that he chooses to remain or leave based in part upon probabilities that he can assign to each of the possible career paths. (Gotz, 1974b, p. 2)

These probabilities, however, are not constant. Gotz notes "promotion timing and probabilities vary by fiscal year, rating and source of commission," as well as "the size of [the] cohort relative to the sizes of preceding and following cohorts" (Gotz, 1974b, p. 10). In a series of internal notes meant to facilitate communication with his colleagues, Gotz shows the evolution of his thinking. In summer 1974 he wrote the following:

> Knowing the state the officer currently occupies, having estimates of the transition probabilities he faces in the next and following years, and having estimates of his military earnings in each state and his civilian earnings we wish to predict the probability that he will remain one more year in the military. This seems to be a *dynamic programming problem*. (Gotz, 1974a, p. 2, emphasis added)

---

[36] Gates Commission staffer Gary Nelson had modeled the decision to reenlist in the same way that the initial decision to enter the military had been modeled. Using a cross-sectional approach, Nelson provided

> statistical estimation of the supply-of-reenlistments function . . . based on the reenlistment behavior of nearly 300 subgroups of Army enlisted men who initially enlisted in calendar year 1964" with "expected pay . . . discounted over a three-year time horizon . . . in order to reflect the relative earnings facing the marginal or most uncertain reenlistee. (Nelson, 1970, p. II-6-3)

Gotz, Glenn A. "The Supply of OTS Officers in the Absence of the Draft," Santa Monica, CA: RAND, October 1972

None of the supply studies in the literature used a time horizon for discounting longer than the length of the initial commitment. The pay rate beyond the initial obligation does affect supply, however. If the government raises the wage rate for, say, majors and higher-ranking officers, not only has the incentive to remain in the Air Force increased, but also the total benefits to becoming an officer increase. For each individual considering a tour as an officer in the Air Force there is some positive probability that he will remain in that service after his initial obligation. The increase in the pay of majors and higher ranking officers is multiplied times the probability of remaining in the Air Force and the discounted value of the product is approximately the expected increase in pecuniary benefits to becoming an officer.

If the pay rates beyond the initial commitment do positively influence supply, then the omission of the expected present value of that future pay in a regression analysis will generally result in a biased estimate of the elasticity of supply with respect to first term pay. . . .

The time horizon starts at the point in time when the individual is faced with the choice between military and civilian occupations and ranges over the interval during which he receives benefits from either occupation. For the purposes of this study we assume that the individual makes his occupational choice at the point of graduation from college with a bachelor's degree. As an empirical matter, 20 years of military service is the maximum for almost all reserve officers and the small amount of evidence available indicates that a veteran's earning and a civilian's earnings roughly coincide. Also, the present value of small differences in earning more than 20 years in the future will be vary small at any discount rate over, say, 10 percent. Twenty years then may be the appropriate time horizon although account should be taken of any lump sum retirement benefit.

By early 1975, he had laid out the dynamic program. He argued that

> from the officer's point of view, this is a sequential decisionmaking problem, assuming that the officer's utility of income function is cardinally additive, the problem can be formulated as a dynamic program [in which] the individual receives utility from achieving successively higher grades as well as from the income received in those grades. (Gotz, 1975, p. 5)

His initial empirical results were incorporated into RAND's version of the TOPLINE model. Through a series of simulations, he showed how the analysis of a personnel policy change, in this case a change in the promotion phase point to major from 10 to 11 years of service, would affect retention and the number of pilots the Air Force needed to train each year.

The Retirement Decision

When Gotz took on the officer accession work, he was also looking for a topic he could use as the subject of his doctoral dissertation in the Department of Economics at UCLA, where he was a graduate student. With the shift in focus in the project, he decided to base his dissertation on the retention work he was doing at RAND. As the work progressed, he reviewed some of the early RAND work by John McCall on job search and information (McCall, 1968). He asked McCall, then a consultant to RAND and a full professor at UCLA, if he would become his dissertation advisor. Eventually, they would become collaborators as the work on captain retention morphed into the retirement work and then into the more-general model of "sequential decision-making." McCall would tie things together as the "life cycle model of optimal decision-making," in which

> [t]he life cycle can be decomposed into several stages including human capital formation and occupational choice, the working period where individuals are subject to layoffs and may find it desirable to quit and change jobs or occupations, and the retirement period. (McCall, 1977, p. 1)

Over the next several years, they developed and then embellished the Dynamic Retention Model (DRM). In July 1976, they circulated among their colleagues at RAND the first formulation of an "elementary model" (Gotz and McCall, 1976). In March 1977, they prepared a working note for their Air Force sponsors that extended the elementary model by incorporating the details of the Air Force promotion system (Gotz and McCall, 1977). In fall 1979, the latter work, updated by including separate models for risk-neutral and risk-averse officers, was published as a RAND note (Gotz and McCall, 1979a). It was then used to prepare a manuscript that they submitted to *Management Science,* where it was finally published in March 1983 (Gotz and McCall, 1983).

Gotz and McCall continued to press forward. In a 1979 working draft, they noted that, "[i]n the dynamic model of retirement, it was assumed that individuals are identical and not affected by any exogenous uncertainty." They now acknowledged that "characteristics that influence retirement will differ across individuals and, furthermore, each individual will be affected by transient variables that are beyond his control" (Gotz and McCall, 1979b, p. 19).[37] In June 1980, the Dynamic Econometric Retention Model was presented in a RAND report (Gotz and McCall, 1980).[38]

The Dynamic Retention Model (DRM) incorporated insights from two developing fields of economics; advances in modeling individual behavior, e.g., rational economic behavior under uncertainty, and the new, econometric procedures that were being developed to deal with the panel or longitudinal data generated by such studies as the Income Dynamics Study and the National Longitudinal Education Study, i.e., data sets that contained observations of a given individual over time. From the former came the sequential decisionmaking concepts pioneered by McCall since the 1960s,

---

[37] That is, "[p]opulation heterogeneity causes individuals to respond differently to identical environmental changes, whereas transient variables are themselves the generators of differential behavior" (Gotz and McCall, 1979b, p. 19).

[38] The name of this model would later be shortened to Dynamic Retention Model, as it is most often referred to in the economic literature.

starting with his work on the economics of job search (McCall, 1968). From the latter came econometric methods to estimate persistent and transient stochastic factors. Instead of separating the calculation of the cost of leaving and the resulting binary stay-leave decisions from the econometric procedures to estimate the parameters of the stochastic process, which had been done before, Gotz and McCall embedded them in their sequential decisionmaking model. They argued that the stochastic process

> directly affect[ed] the calculation of optimal retirement policy [and the estimates of the stochastic parameters] should occur with the optimization setting, i.e., the estimation should be imbedded in the dynamic program. (Gotz and McCall, 1980, p. 4)

A unique DRM contribution to the study of retention is that "retention rates by year of service are dependent on both the future and the past" (Gotz and McCall, 1980, p. 23). Some would call this *forward looking* and *backward looking*. The traditional way of estimating retention was to look *forward* and argue that the retention decision was based on a comparison of the present value of alternative income streams. DRM allowed analysts to take into account the transient nature of a change in the income stream and account for the fact that those induced to remain in service by a bonus, for example, are more likely to leave after their term of obligation is completed than those who had not taken the bonus, who showed a higher propensity to stay in the first place. In this way, the cohort that makes a decision today is the result of *past* decisions to stay and leave. In this way, the model looks *backward*.[39] They argued that by not taking these factors into account, the traditional regression model analysis of the comparison of future income streams to calculate the cost of leaving resulted in "omitted variable bias in the regression, and the coefficient of the cost of leaving is biased upward," and thus, "a regression model should overpredict early year of service retention rates and underpredict later ones" (Gotz and McCall, 1980, p. 31).

The Legacy

The research and analysis reported here not only helped those charged with managing the all-volunteer force in the 1970s, they also left a rich legacy for the decades to come. The HPSP scholarship program, medical bonuses, and USUHS solved one of the most troublesome problems the all-volunteer force faced. Further research on medical benefits programs would shape the health programs of DoD. The paid advertising experiments of the late 1970s lead to a number of further tests during the 1980s, discussed in later chapters. Finally, the work of Gotz and McCall provided the theoretical underpinnings for research on military compensation for decades.

---

[39] A nontechnical discussion of the Dynamic Retention Model and the forward and backward looking features can be found in Fernandez et al. (1985).

References

Albright, William H., *Medical Student Participation in the Health Professions Scholarship Program: The Influence of the Stipend, Postgraduate Training Opportunity and the Obligated Service Commitment,* Santa Monica, Calif.: RAND Corporation, WN-9471-PR, April 1976. S0208.pdf.

Albright, William H., and G.L. Brunner, *Determinants of AF/ROTC Enrollment: The Four-Year Program,* briefing, Santa Monica, Calif.: RAND Corporation, WN-8136-PR, February 1973. S0304.pdf.

Albright, William H., and David S. C. Chu, *Air Force Health Delivery Services: First Progress Briefing,* Santa Monica, Calif.: RAND Corporation, WN-8725-PR, June 1974. S0137.pdf.

Albright, William H., David S. C. Chu, and Lawrence S. Bacow, *The Supply of Air Force Physicians: Response to the Bonus and Scholarship Programs,* Santa Monica, Calif.: RAND Corporation, WN-9057-PR, April 1975. S0191.pdf.

Altman, Stuart H., and Robert J. Barro, "Officer Supply: The Impact of Pay, the Draft, and the Vietnam War," *The American Economic Review,* Vol. 61, No. 4, September 1971, pp. 649–664. S0193.pdf.

Armor, David J., David S. C. Chu, and George A. Goldberg, *Guidelines for a Demonstration Project on the Organization of Air Force Outpatient Care,* Santa Monica, Calif.: RAND Corporation, WN-9527-PR, December 1976. S0203.pdf.

ASD[M&RA], *America's Volunteers: A Report on the All-Volunteer Armed Forces—Summary,* Washington, D.C.: Office of the Assistant Secretary of Defense (M&RA), December 31, 1978. S0194.pdf.

Binkin, Martin, and John D. Johnson, *All Volunteer Armed Forces: Progress, Problems, and Prospects,* Washington, D.C.: Senate Armed Service Committee, June 1, 1973. S0148.pdf.

Brehm, William K., "Report on Population Representation in the All-Volunteer Force," memorandum to John C. Stennis, Washington, D.C., December 17, 1974. G0048.pdf.

———, Statement by Assistant Secretary of Defense William K. Brehm at Earnings on S.920, Part 3: Manpower, hearing before the Committee on Armed Services, Subcommittee on Manpower and Personnel, First, Washington, D.C., U.S. Government Printing Office, February 1975. G1314.pdf.

Brown, Charles W., and Charles C. Moskos, Jr., "The American Soldier: Will He Fight?" *Military Review,* Vol. LXXVII, No. 1, 1997, pp. 1–9. S0655.pdf.

Buchanan, Joan, and Susan D. Hosek, *Costs, Productivity, and the Utilization of Physician's Extenders in Air Force Primary Medicine Clinics,* Santa Monica, Calif.: RAND Corporation, R-2896-AF, June 1983. S0207.pdf.

Burk, James, *The Civic Virtue, Rights and Opportunities of Citizen-Soldiers,* unpublished RAND research, 2002. S0478.pdf.

Chu, David S. C., *Physical Standards and the Supply of Enlisted Volunteers,* Santa Monica, Calif.: RAND Corporation, WN-7816-SA, April 1972. S0135.pdf.

———, *Patient Contact Record,* Santa Monica, Calif.: RAND Corporation, 1974. S0204.pdf.

Chu, David S. C., George A. Goldberg, Naomi Ainslee, Leona Cutler, David Jolly, and Kathy Scofield, *The Organization of Air Force Outpatient Care: A Briefing for the Surgeon General,* Santa Monica, Calif.: RAND Corporation, WN-10250-AF, September 1978. S0202.pdf.

Chu, David S. C., Eva Norrblom, Kent Brown, and Alfred MacInnes, *Physical Standards in an All Volunteer Force,* Santa Monica, Calif.: RAND Corporation, R-1347-ARPA/DDPAE, April 1974. S0132.pdf.

Coffey, Kenneth J., and Frederick J. Reeg, *Representational Policy in the U.S. Armed Forces,* Washington, D.C.: Defense Manpower Commission, February 1975. S0162.pdf.

Coffey, Kenneth J., Edward Scarborough, Frederick J. Reeg, Audrey Page, and James A. Abellera, *The Impact of Socio-Economic Composition in the All-Volunteer Force: A Staff Paper for the Defense Manpower Commission,* Washington, D.C.: Defense Manpower Commission, November 1975. G1298.pdf.

Comptroller General of the United States, *Problems in Meeting Military Manpower Needs in the All-Volunteer Force,* Washington, D.C.: General Accounting Office, B177952, May 2, 1973. S0156.pdf.

Cook, Alvin A., Jr., and John P. White, *Estimating the Quality of Air Force Volunteers,* Santa Monica, Calif.: RAND Corporation, RM-630-PR, September 1970. S0301.pdf.

Cooper, Richard V. L., *Military Manpower and the All-Volunteer Force,* Santa Monica, Calif.: RAND Corporation, R-1450-ARPA, September 1977. S0177.pdf.

Cooper, Richard V. L., and Bernard D. Rostker, "Military Manpower in a Changing Environment," in RAND Corporation, ed., *25th Anniversary Volume,* Santa Monica, Calif., 1973. S0904.pdf.

DASD[MPP], *Department of Defense Personnel Update,* Washington, D.C.: Office of the Under Secretary of Defense (Personnel and Readiness), May 1, 2001. S0654.pdf.

Daubert, Victoria, Daniel Relles, and C. Robert. Roll, Jr., *Medical Student Financing and the Armed Forces Health Professional Scholarship Program,* Santa Monica, Calif.: RAND Corporation, R-2414-HA, January 1982. S0165.pdf.

Dellums, Ronald, "Don't Slam Door to Military," *Focus,* June 1975, pp. 6–8. S0170.pdf.

Devine, E.J., "The Uniformed Services University of the Health Sciences and Alternative Methods of Procuring and Retaining Military Physicians," in Defense Manpower Commission, ed., *Defense Manpower Commission Staff Studies and Supporting Papers,* Washington, D.C: U.S. Government Printing Office, 1975. S0190.pdf.

Eitelberg, Mark Jan, *Evaluation of Army Representation,* Alexandria, Va.: Human Resources Research Organization, August 1977. S0196.pdf.

———, *Military Representation: The Theoretical and Practical Implications of Population Representation in the American Armed Forces,* dissertation, New York: New York University, 1979. S0221.pdf.

Enns, John H., *Reenlistment Bonuses and First Term Retention,* Santa Monica, Calif.: RAND Corporation, R-1935-ARPA, September 1977. S0410.pdf.

Fernandez, Richard L., Glenn A. Gotz, and Robert M. Bell, *The Dynamic Retention Model,* Santa Monica, Calif.: RAND Corporation, N-2141-MIL, April 1985. S0435.pdf.

Fisher, Anthony C., "The Cost of Ending the Draft: Reply," *The American Economic Review,* Vol. 60, No. 5, December 1970, pp. 979–983. S0234.pdf.

Gates, Thomas S. Jr., *The Report of the President's Commission on an All-Volunteer Armed Force,* Washington, D.C., February 1970. S0243.pdf.

Goldberg, George A., David Maxwell Jolly, Susan D. Hosek, and David S. C. Chu, "Physician's Extenders' Performance in Air Force Clinics," *Medical Care,* Vol. XIX, No. 9, September 1981, pp. 951–965.

Goldberg, George A., Andrew F. Siegel, David S. C. Chu, and David G. Jolly, *The Quality of Air Force Outpatient Care: How Well Do Physician Assistants Perform?* Santa Monica, Calif.: RAND Corporation, N-1184-AF, June 1979. S0131.pdf.

Gotz, Glenn A., *The Supply of OTS Officers in the Absence of the Draft,* Santa Monica, Calif.: RAND Corporation, WN-7977-PR, October 1972. S0414.pdf.

———, *The Retention of Air Force Offices Eligible to Retire,* Santa Monica, Calif.: RAND Corporation, IN-23017-PR, July 10, 1974a. S0805.pdf.

———, *An Analysis of the Retention of Air Force Offices: An Empirical Model,* Santa Monica, Calif.: RAND Corporation, WN-8796-PR, August 1974b. S0176.pdf.

———, *The Retention of Air Force Captains,* Santa Monica, Calif.: RAND Corporation, IN-23263-PR, February 1975. S0426.pdf.

Gotz, Glenn A., and John J. McCall, *The Retirement Decision: 1. An Elementary Model,* Santa Monica, Calif.: RAND Corporation, IN-23610-PR, July 1976. S0423.pdf.

———, *The Retirement Decision: A Numerical Analysis of a Dynamic Retirement Model,* Santa Monica, Calif.: RAND Corporation, WN-9628-AF, March 1977. S0436.pdf.

———, *A Sequential Analysis of the Air Force Office's Retirement Decision,* Santa Monica, Calif.: RAND Corporation, N-10131-AF, October 1979a. S0437.pdf.

———, *Estimating Military Personnel Retention Rates: Theory and Statistical Method,* Santa Monica, Calif.: RAND Corporation, WD-375-PR, October 1979b. S0175.pdf.

———, *Estimating Military Personnel Retention Rates: Theory and Statistical Method,* Santa Monica, Calif.: RAND Corporation, R-2541-AF, June 1980. S0428.pdf.

———, "Sequential Analysis of the Stay/Leave Decision: U.S. Air Force Officers," *Management Science,* Vol. 29, No. 3, March 1983.

Greenberg, I. M., and Sam Saben, "Comments re Chapter XII—An Army of the Black or Poor," memorandum to Gus C. Lee, Washington, D.C., February 11, 1970. G0286.pdf.

Griffith, Robert K., Jr., *The U.S. Army's Transition to the All-Volunteer Force 1968–1974,* Washington, D.C.: U.S. Army Center of Military History, 1997. S0186.pdf.

Hebert, F. Edward, and John McMillan, *'Last of the Titans:' The Life and Times of Congressman F. Edward Hebert of Louisiana,* Lafayette, Louisiana: Center for Louisiana Studies, The University of Southern Louisiana, 1976.

Hosek, Susan D., and C. Robert. Roll, Jr., *Military Utilization of Physician's Assistants,* Santa Monica, Calif.: RAND Corporation, N-1019-HA, April 1979. S0205.pdf.

Janowitz, Morris, "From Institutional to Occupational: The Need for Conceptual Continuity," *Armed Forces and Society,* Vol. 4, No. 1, November 1977, pp. 51–54.

Janowitz, Morris, and Charles C. Moskos, Jr., "Racial Composition in the All-Volunteer Force," *Armed Forces and Society,* Vol. 1, No. 1, November 1974, pp. 109–123.

Kent, Glenn, "Interview with Bernard Rostker," November 27, 2001.

Laird, Melvin R., "Statement by Former Secretary of Defense Melvin Laird," Conference Celebrating the 30th Anniversary of the All-Volunteer Force, Washington, D.C., September 16, 2003.

Lando, Mordechai, "Health Services in the All-Volunteer Armed Force," in President's Commission on an All-Volunteer Armed Force, ed., *Studies Prepared for the President's Commission on an All-Volunteer Armed Force,* Washington, D.C.: U.S. Government Printing Office, 1970, pp. IV-3-1 to IV-3-45. S0182.pdf.

Lee, Gus C., and Geoffrey Y. Parker, *Ending the Draft: The Story of the All Volunteer Force,* Washington, D.C.: Human Resources Research Organization, FR-PO-771, April 1977. S0242.pdf.

Martin, Albert J., *Design Considerations and Objectives: The Department of Defense Paid Radio Test of 1975,* unpublished, Washington, D.C.: Office of the Assistant Secretary of Defense (MRA&L), 1980. S0327.pdf.

Martin, Albert J., and Russell I. Haley, "A Media Mix Test of Paid Radio Advertising for Armed Services Recruitment," in Richard V. L. Cooper, ed., *Defense Manpower Policy: Presentation from the 1976 RAND Conference on Defense Manpower,* Santa Monica, Calif.: RAND Corporation, 1978. S0215.pdf.

McCall, John J., *Economics of Information and Job Search,* Santa Monica, Calif.: RAND Corporation, RM-5745-OEO, November 1968. S0424.pdf.

———, *Sequential Decisionmaking: Applications to Retirement and Welfare Participation,* Santa Monica, Calif.: RAND Corporation, P-5775, January 1977. S0416.pdf.

Miller, Louis, and Laura Critchlow Sammis, *Planning in Large Personnel Systems: A Reexamination of the TOPLINE Static Planning Model,* Santa Monica, Calif.: RAND Corporation, R-1274-PR, July 1973. S0419.pdf.

Montague, Robert M., Jr., "Brookings Institution Report, *Volunteer Armed Forces: Progress, Problems, and Prospects,*" memorandum to Deputy Secretary of Defense William Clements, Washington, D.C., Undated.

Moskos, Charles C., Jr., *The American Enlisted Man: The Rank and File in Today's Military,* New York: Russell Sage Foundation, 1970.

———, "From Institution to Occupation: Trends in Military Organization," *Armed Forces & Society,* Vol. 4, No. 1, November 1977, pp. 41–50.

———, "Preliminary Report on Operation Iraqi Freedom (OIF)," memorandum to Acting Secretary of the Army, Evanston, Ill., December 14, 2003. S0656.pdf.

Moskos, Charles C., Jr., and John Sibley Butler, *Be All You Can Be: Black Leadership and Racial Integration the Army Way,* New York: Basic Books, 1996.

Moskos, Charles C., Jr., and Frank R. Wood, "Introduction—'The Military: More than Just a Job?'" in Charles C. Moskos and Frank R. Wood, eds., *The Military: More Than Just a Job?* New York: Pergamon-Brassey's International Defense Publishers, Inc., 1988, pp. 3–14.

Nelson, Gary R., "Economic Analysis of First-Term Reenlistments in the Army," in Gates Commission, ed., *Studies Prepared for the President's Commission on All-Volunteer Armed Force,* Washington, D.C.: U.S. Government Printing Office, 1970, pp. II-6-II to II-6-31. S0715.pdf.

Nunn, Sam, "Remarks by US Senator Sam Nunn before the George General Assembly," news release, Washington, D.C., March 5, 1973. S0118.pdf.

———, Status of the All-Volunteer Force, hearing before the Senate Armed Services Subcommittee on Manpower and Personnel, 95th Cong., 2nd Sess., Washington, D.C., U.S. Government Printing Office, June 20, 1978. S0444.pdf.

Nunn, Sam, Howard Baker, Thomas Eagleton, and Edward Kennedy, *Remarks on the Charter of the Defense Manpower Commission,* Washington, D.C.: United States Senate, September 26, 1973. S0271.pdf.

Rehnquist, Justice, *Rostker v. Goldberg 453 U.S. 57* U.S. Supreme Court, June 25, 1981. S0610.pdf.

Rostker, Bernard, Scott A. Harris, James Kahan, Paul Koegel, Sandy H. Berry, Steven Schlossman, Peter Tiemeyer, Robert MacCoun, Janel Lever, Mark A. Schuster, Gail L. Zellman, Peter D. Jacobson, Roger Brown, John Winkler, Karl Builder, and James A Dewar, *Sexual Orientation and U.S. Military Personnel Policy: Options and Assessment,* Santa Monica, Calif.: RAND Corporation, MR-323-OSD, 1993. S0800.pdf.

Rumsfeld, Donald H., "Janowitz Study on Racial Composition," memorandum to Secretary of the Army, Washington, D.C., November 15, 1974. G0555.pdf.

Sammis, Laura Critchlow, Sidney H. Miller, and Herbert J. Shukiar, *The Office Grade Limitations Model: A Steady-Mathematical Model for the U.S. Air Force Officer Structure,* Santa Monica, Calif.: RAND Corporation, R-1632-PR, July 1975. S0420.pdf.

Sawyer, Allen, *Comments on "A Media Mix Test of Paid Radio Advertising for Armed Services Recruitment,"* 1977. S0329.pdf.

Schucker, Raymond E., *A Media Mix Test of Paid Radio Advertising For Armed Services Recruitment,* Vol. 1, New York: Russ Haley & Associates, Inc., 1976. S0143.pdf.

———, Further Analyses of the Test of Paid Radio Advertising for Armed Services Recruitment, Washington, D.C.: Office of the Assistant Secretary of Defense (M&RA), March 1977. S0322.pdf.

Segal, David R., John D. Blair, Joseph J. Lengermann, and Richard C. Thompson, "Institutional and Occupational Values in the U.S. Military," in Franklyn D. Margiotta, James Brown and Michael J. Collins, eds., *Changing U.S. Military Manpower Realities,* Boulder, Colo.: Westview Press, 1983.

Sorensen, Henning, "The I/O Model: Institution vs. Occupation," in Jean Callaghan and Franz Kernic, eds., *Armed Forces and International Security: Global Trends and Issues*, New Brunswick, Conn.: Transaction, 2003.

Stahl, Michael J., T. Roger Manley, and Charles W. McNichols, "Denationalizing the Moskos Institution-Occupation Model: An Application of Gouldner's Cosmopolitan-Local Research," *Journal of Applied Psychology*, Vol. 63, No. 4, 1978, pp. 422–427. S0227.pdf.

Taber, Robert, "Medical Standards in the Volunteer Environment," memorandum to Assistant Secretaries of the Military Departments, Washington, D.C., June 11, 1973. S0160.pdf.

Tarr, Curtis W., *Interim Report to the President and the Congress*, Washington, D.C.: Defense Manpower Commission, May 16, 1975. S0216.pdf.

———, *Defense Manpower: The Keystone of National Security—Report to the President and Congress*, Washington, D.C.: Defense Manpower Commission, April 1976. S0113.pdf.

Taylor, David P., "Physical Standards for Enlistment," memorandum to Special Assistant to the Secretary of Defense, Washington, D.C., September 1, 1976. G0598.pdf.

Tice, R. Dean, "Physical Standards," memorandum to S. I. Hayakawa, Washington, D.C., April 28, 1980. G0440.pdf.

CHAPTER ELEVEN

The Carter Years:
The All-Volunteer Force in Distress (1977–1980)

I considered the end of the draft in 1973 to be one of the major achievements of my administration. Now seven years later, I have reluctantly concluded that we should reintroduce the draft. . . . The volunteer army has failed to provide enough personnel of the caliber we need.

—Richard Nixon
President of the United States[1]

Introduction

For proponents of the all-volunteer force, the years of the Carter presidency were ones of frustration. When President Carter replaced President Ford in January 20, 1977, the prevailing view was optimism, as reflected in Bill Brehm's final assessment to Congress in 1976 that "we expect to be able to maintain our peacetime force on a volunteer basis" (Brehm, 1976, p. 34). By the time President Reagan replaced President Carter in 1981, the prevailing view was one of pessimism, as reflected in President's Nixon's published statement that our military forces had sharply deteriorated in quality under Carter and that he saw no way forward "except by reinstituting of the draft" (Nixon, 1993).[2]

Over the four years the Carter term fought hard to save the all-volunteer force. Unfortunately, the fight often pitted one part of the administration against another, and often against the Congress, despite the fact that it was controlled by the President's own party. It was a fight that saw protagonists often change sides, with the final act of

---

[1] *The Real War 1980* (Nixon, 1980, p. 201). By 1993, Nixon again had a change of heart, concluding that there had been "a dramatic improvement in the quality of the men and women who joined the Armed forces" in the 1980s and that he could "endorse the all-volunteer Army approach without qualification today" (Nixon, 1993).

[2] Just before leaving office, the Ford administration published a report on the current status and prospects of the all-volunteer force. The report concluded that "the AVF has been successful and can be sustained in the future through committed, competent and flexible leadership" (OASD[M&RA], 1976).

salvation coming from the leading congressional critic of the all-volunteer force, Senator Sam Nunn, in the form of a significant pay increase—the Nunn-Warner Amendment to the Defense Appropriation Act of 1981. It was a fight that, by the end of Carter's four-year term, saw the all-volunteer force on firmer ground than it had been on when Carter took office on January 20, 1977.

In truth, the Carter administration had not inherited as strong an all-volunteer force as Brehm's assurances to Congress in 1976 had implied,[3] and it did not leave the all-volunteer force in dire enough straits to warrant President Nixon's conclusion that the country should reinstate conscription. Unappreciated at the time, it provided a base on which the Reagan team built an effective program, with the ultimate result that President Nixon again "endorse[d] the all-volunteer Army approach without qualification" (Nixon, 1993).

The Carter Team

There should be no question as to the dedication to the principles of the all-volunteer force shared by the group of people President Carter recruited to manage defense personnel issues. The first person on board was Secretary of Defense Harold Brown. Alarmed by the drop in recruit quality that had already been noticed in the closing days of the Ford administration, he asked his manpower office for a complete assessment of the prospects of an all-volunteer force within days of taking office (Brown, 1977). Not satisfied with the White House's designated Assistant Secretary of Defense for Manpower, Reserve Affairs and Logistics, he successfully pressed for his own candidate, Dr. John White, Senior Vice President of the RAND Corporation. White had supported the Gates Commission, had run the Air Force's manpower, personnel and training program at RAND, and successfully orchestrated ARPA's sponsorship of a new manpower research center at RAND to support the transition to the all-volunteer force at a time when Assistant Secretary of Defense Roger Kelly was not interested in manpower research.

White recruited a first-rate team. His Principal Deputy was Robert (Robin) Pirie, Jr., a graduate of the Naval Academy and former Rhodes scholar who had retired from the Navy after serving as commanding officer of the USS *Skipjack*. He had served in the Pentagon on the staff of the Secretary of Defense and later on the National Security Council staff. His most recent experience had been as the first Deputy Assistant Director for National Security of the new Congressional Budget Office (CBO). Richard Danzig, similarly a Rhodes scholar and Yale-trained lawyer who had clerked for Justice Byron White on the U.S. Supreme Court, joined Pirie on the John White team. While

---

[3] In fact, in 1981, Senator William Cohen (R-Maine) recalled,

> We started losing people in 1976. . . . It came at the time Congress was participating in some of the cuts, the GI bill, advertising budgets, and so forth. We actually contributed to a decline in the ability of the All-Volunteer Force to work successfully. (Cohen, 1981)

Danzig had not served in the military and was not a manpower expert, he was a student of organizational behavior. White was confident that Danzig, as Deputy Assistant Secretary for Program Integration—a deputy without portfolio—would figure out how to be useful, and he did.

Two other former RAND colleagues also joined the White team and would be instrumental in the efforts to save the all-volunteer force. Gary Nelson had been at the Institute for Defense Analysis and, like White, had supported the analytic efforts of the Gates Commission. Nelson had moved to RAND to help start the ARPA-sponsored manpower program, then had moved back to Washington to establish the military manpower section in the CBO. Nelson became the Deputy Assistant Secretary of Defense for Requirements, Resources and Analysis in the Manpower Office—White's chief analyst. This was a position he was well suited for, both by training and experience, having just completed a CBO assessment entitled *The Costs of Defense Manpower: Issues for 1977* (Nelson, G., 1977). Having already raised questions about defense manpower, it would now be his job to answer them.

The last member of the team, one somewhat removed from White's day-to-day inner circle because he officially worked for the Secretary of the Navy, was Bernard Rostker. Rostker succeeded White as head of RAND's Project Air Force Manpower, Personnel, and Training Program after White had moved up to be a Vice President at RAND. Rostker had been recruited by the Carter transition team to be the Principal Deputy Assistant Secretary of the Navy for Manpower and Reserve Affairs.

It should be noted that, while this was the starting lineup in 1977, everyone had changed jobs by the latter years of the Carter presidency. All were, however, still serving White and the cause of the all-volunteer force. White left DoD first to become Deputy Director of the Office of Management and Budget. Robin Pirie replaced him as Assistant Secretary, and Richard Danzig replaced Pirie as Principal Deputy Assistant Secretary. Nelson moved to the Office of Personnel Management to serve as the Associate Director for Compensation for the federal government, soon followed by Rostker who became the Director of Selective Service.

Greetings from Congress

Within weeks of becoming the Assistant Secretary of Defense for Manpower, Reserve Affairs and Logistics,[4] White was before the Budget Committee of the House of

---

[4] At the beginning of the Carter administration, Secretary Brown decided to add logistics to the manpower and reserve affairs portfolio and eliminate an assistant secretary in the Office of the Secretary of Defense (OSD) and each of the military departments. The rationale was that due consideration of manpower issues was critical to the proper management of logistics and that, by combining the two offices, OSD would be in a better position to manage logistics. This view was reflected in the Defense Resource Management Study: "Over one-third of the Defense budget is consumed, and a similar fraction of Defense manpower is employed, in the delivery of logistics support" (Rice, 1979, p. xii). It was a view that ultimately proved incorrect, and almost a decade later, logistics was striped out from the manpower office.

Representatives on July 13, 1977, explaining the status of and prospects for the all-volunteer force. The budget committee did not focus on the philosophical arguments about social costs or the burden of hidden taxes of conscription that were so important to the Gates Commission. It made no distinction between social and budget costs, arguments that had been carefully worked out by economists a decade before. As the budget committee saw it, there were three reasons for them to be holding hearings on the all-volunteer force at this time, and they all came down to the fact that over half of defense spending was on people. They were concerned that

> if we continue allocating increasing amounts of funds to defense manpower, we may not be able to modernize and increase our weapons systems, [and] . . . if we continue with our present manpower management practices, we will need to recruit one of every three qualified and available males by the mid- to late 1980s to meet the total Active and Reserve Force requirements. (Leggett, 1977, p. 1)

Robert Hale, who succeeded Gary Nelson as Director of Military Manpower Analysis at the CBO, and Richard V. L. Cooper, Director of Defense Manpower Studies for the RAND Corporation, set the stage. Hale led off by arguing that the "costs of Defense manpower really depend quite critically on how we decide to meet our needs for recruits. . . . If we raise pay to meet [likely] shortfalls, costs could go up, perhaps by $2 billion, maybe by as much as $8 billion per year." Despite the conclusions of the recently completed congressionally chartered Defense Manpower Commission, he saw that "there are changes in policy that we believe could meet the need for Active recruits and avoid those increases" (Hale, 1977, p. 16).

In his testimony before the House Budget Committee, Cooper carried on Hale's theme. He argued that the "AVF can be made to fail. But it can also be made to work—and perhaps much better than its draft-dependant predecessor" (Cooper, 1977a, p. 34). Cooper started his testimony by bringing the committee members back to the foundations of the all-volunteer force, recalling that the Gates Commission "persuasively" argued that "those forced to serve should not have to pay a large financial price in addition to the other burdens of involuntary servitude" (Cooper, 1977a, p. 22). He argued that, to hold down costs for the all-volunteer force, it was "not manpower supply" that caused the problem but rather "enlisted accession requirements," and that "reducing personnel turnover rates" would help the most (Cooper, 1977a, p. 23). He singled out reform of the compensation system and changes to the up-or-out promotion and tenure system then being considered for officers as part of the pending Defense Officer Personnel Management Act.

Cooper's testimony in July 1977 and again the following February proved to be very useful to the new administration (Cooper, 1978b, pp. 48–123). He presented a comprehensive set of arguments, well grounded in research, that presented the all-volunteer force in a very favorable light. While in July he could only point to his extensive study of the all-volunteer force as "forthcoming," the next time he appeared before

Congress it was fully available to back up his analysis (Cooper, 1977b).[5] While it would be almost a year before DoD produced its own report on the all-volunteer force (Nelson, G., 1978b)—*America's Volunteers: A Report on the All-Volunteer Armed Forces*—Cooper's work filled the void and helped keep the critics at bay. For example, his analysis of the costs of the all-volunteer force differed from those suggested by the General Accounting Office (GAO).[6] Cooper prepared a detailed analysis (Cooper, 1978a, pp. 1,695–1,741) to back up his contention that the cost of the all-volunteer force was minimal, about one-tenth of the costs GAO had estimated (Comptroller General of the United States, 1978) and that returning to conscription would not save very much money. Cooper's report analyzed such issues as the social representativeness of the post-draft force and the relevant costs; it also highlighted the full range of research that RAND had undertaken as part of its ARPA-sponsored research program. This was the kind of policy research that Ginzberg had called for in the early days of the all-volunteer force and others had also recommended (Ginzberg, 1971).[7]

White followed Hale and Cooper and, in his first review before Congress, set the outlines of his approach to managing the all-volunteer force. He started with the observation that, with the all-volunteer force,

> we have been successful over the past several years in meeting the challenge of the Active Force with reference to having enough accessions and enough reenlistments in order to essentially obtain 99 percent of our requirements. (White, 1977, p. 119)

He praised the services for the "remarkable job" they had done recruiting first-term enlistees and acknowledged that there were some problems: "We do have some indications that recruiting is tougher, particularly in the Army, with respect to high school graduates." He did promise "to continue to try to maintain quality" (White, 1977, p. 120).[8] He criticized those who argued that the way to control costs was to reinstate the draft. He told the House Budget Committee that a

> return to the draft would not, in and of itself, save much money. If one accepts the premise that equity requires payment of wages to all Service members that are comparable and competitive with private sector wages, then the annual budget savings

---

[5] Cooper provided an excellent summary of the report to Congress (Cooper, 1978b, pp. 50–113), which was later published in *International Security* as "The All-Volunteer Force: Five Years Later" (Cooper, 1978c).

[6] Today, the organization is known as the Government Accountability Office.

[7] Several studies for the Pentagon called for increased policy research (Enke, 1971; Hoffman and Fiorello, 1971).

[8] In his prepared statement, White noted that

> Most recently, however, the Services have faced increased difficulty in attracting high school diploma graduates. In FY 1976, 69% of the non–prior service accessions were high school diploma graduates. For the twelve months ending 30 June 1977, this percentage was 67%. The high school diploma graduate percentages among non–prior service accessions dropped for every Service during this last year, with the exception of the Marine Corps. . . . It takes more recruiting effort to recruit high school diploma graduates. A prime reason that the Services are requesting added recruiting resources in FY 1978 is to increase the enlistment of these quality volunteers. (White, 1977, pp. 76–77)

would be about $500 million. This savings results from smaller expenditures for Active and Reserve recruiting and enlistment bonus programs.

A reduction of junior enlisted wages to the current Federal minimum wage would avoid an additional $2 billion in Active and Reserve pay for a total of $2.5 billion, or only about 2% reduction of the FY 1978 defense budget.

Those who argue that a return to compulsory service will greatly reduce manpower's share of the defense budget are simply wrong. The volunteer force is not a major cause of the magnitude of manpower's portion of the defense dollar. I do not believe that the American people would favor a return to the draft to achieve dollar savings ranging from $.5 billion to $2.5 billion and accounting for, at most, 2% of the total defense budget. (White, 1977, pp. 82–83)

White also highlighted the need to reform the military compensation system as "of major importance to this Administration" (White, 1977, p. 90). He told the committee that he was concerned that the conclusions and recommendations of the analyses presented in a number of recently completed studies, the unsigned Third Quadrennial Review of Military Compensation, and the Defense Manpower Commission, as well as GAO studies, were inconsistent. In fact, just several weeks before the July hearings, the President had issued an Executive Order (EO 11998, dated June 27, 1977) creating a new nine-member group, the President's Commission on Military Compensation (PCMC), that was to report by March 15, 1978.[9] Given the recent experience with the Third Quadrennial Review and its inability to overcome the interests of the services, the new administration had decided to follow President Nixon's example and create a commission outside the Pentagon.[10] White told the committee that the commission would be under the chairmanship of Charles J. Zwick of Miami, a former Director of the Office of Management and Budget in the Johnson administration, Chairman of the Southeast Banking Corporation, and an economist.[11]

In subsequent testimony during his first "hearing season" the following winter, White and his boss, Secretary of Defense Harold Brown, laid out the new administration's all-volunteer force program. They highlighted

- the need for an effective wartime draft system: White and Brown noted that, in 1976, the former Director of Selective Service had testified that it would take the system 110 days after mobilization to deliver the first inductees to the Army, against DoD's requirement of 30 days. White told the committee that the FY 1979 budget they were considering would increase the Selective Service budget

---

[9] The historical documents surrounding the formation of the PCMC can be found in Zwick (1978a).

[10] The White House press announcement of the creation of the PCMC on June 27, 1977, highlighted the recommendation of the Defense Manpower Commission that "the armed forces be paid in the form of a fully taxable salary" and the opposition of the Third Quadrennial Review, which said that "members should continue to be paid through a modified pay and allowance system." The press office noted that President Carter "expects the [new] Commission to resolve these differences and to propose one integrated, long-term solution to military compensation" (Zwick, 1978a).

[11] White did not point out to the committee Zwick's RAND connection. Earlier in his career, Zwick had been on the RAND staff and was also a member of its Board of Directors.

by 40 percent and that this would "assure that the required delivery schedule can be met . . . without peacetime registration" (White, 1978, pp. 172, 216). He also noted that Selective Service would test its new capabilities by participating in the upcoming Joint Chiefs of Staff–directed mobilization exercise, Nifty Nugget, scheduled for fall 1978.

- the critical role that women were and increasingly could play in manning the force: In FY 1973, women made up less than 2 percent of total enlisted strength. Now, under the volunteer force in FY 1977, that number had almost doubled. Brown indicated that there was

> a potential to increase the number of women in the military even further—in part because more women want to enlist than we now accept. . . . We are studying all these issues in the context of a positive program to enlarge the role of women in the military service. (Brown, 1978, p. 329)

- the need to control first-term attrition, particularly in the Army: Brown noted that, between FY 1971 and FY 1974 (the last year for which there were complete data), first-term attrition in the Army had risen from 25 percent of the entering cohort to 40 percent, with the other Services showing similar, but smaller increases (Brown, 1978, p. 338).
- the need to review physical and mental standards: Brown expressed concern that "standards [may] exclude many persons who would perform well if permitted to enlist." He told the Congress that, "[i]f we do have recruiting shortages during the 1980s, we could vary enlistment standards to increase the number of eligible recruits . . . [yet still] maintain standards consistent with those in effect under the draft" (Brown, 1978, p. 339).
- his commitment to review the mix of first-term and career enlisted personnel: One element of this would be developing "a better understanding of the age and experience mixes which will yield a cost/effective military force" (Brown, 1978, p. 339). Cooper made this proposal in his study of the all-volunteer force, and it was one of the topics the Defense Resource Management Study that he had commissioned the previous November (1977) was to address.[12]

Senator Nunn and the Senate Subcommittee on Manpower and Personnel

The most outspoken critic of the all-volunteer force was Sam Nunn, the junior Democratic Senator from Georgia. He focused his criticism in two areas: the cost of the all-volunteer force and the quality of the people it attracted. For Nunn, the all-volunteer

---

[12] Cooper had pressed the point in his July appearance before the House Budget Committee (1977) and in his book (1977, pp. 303–318). The Director of the Defense Resource Management Study was Donald B. Rice, President of the RAND Corporation. C. Robert Roll, Jr., and Glenn Gotz, both from RAND, prepared the chapter on career mix (Roll and Gotz, 1979, pp. 63–77).

force was wanting on both counts. The opening round focused on the costs of the all-volunteer force.

As Nunn saw it, the issue of the rising costs of the all-volunteer force was primarily about the transfer of funds from the nonpersonnel side to the personnel side of what he viewed as a fixed defense budget and the consequences this would have on the ability to fund needed nonpersonnel improvements. As he saw it, if the country really wanted an all-volunteer force, it should be prepared to pay for it by adding funds to the already overextended budget. For Nunn, the issue of how much the all-volunteer force cost was not an academic exercise. He was concerned that the day would come when the United States would face Soviet forces in Europe with a well-paid Army that lacked the equipment to be effective. Was it true that the all-volunteer force had merely cost several hundred million dollars, or had it cost billions? Nunn believed that "[o]ne of the major problems in evaluating the All-Volunteer Force is trying to estimate its cost." On May 4, 1977, he requested GAO's assistance in evaluating the DoD position that, if "we were to return to the draft today, we could save about $500 million by making substantial cuts in recruiting, advertising, and enlistment bonuses."[13] GAO gave him the answer he was looking for in a lengthy study that it published on February 6, 1978—the same day Nunn held hearings.

The lines were clearly drawn. Rather than the $500 million DoD had cited, GAO found that "[t]he move from a conscripted to an all-volunteer force caused substantial annual cost increases of more than $3 billion since 1973" (Comptroller General of the United States, 1978, cover). GAO explained that it had used a "budget approach . . . [to] represent a reasonable assessment of costs associated with creating and establishing the All-Volunteer Force" (Comptroller General of the United States, 1978, p. ii). GAO devoted a whole chapter in its study to previous studies of the cost of the all-volunteer force, including a discussion of economic and social costs as expounded by economists associated with the Gates Commission. GAO explained why these alternative measures were not appropriate ways to measure the cost of the all-volunteer force. They reviewed in detail the costs the Gates Commission had projected and highlighted a number of RAND estimates.[14]

With GAO's estimates in hand, Nunn wasted no time in jumping on the latest RAND report, prepared by Cooper. Nunn asked the GAO witness if he agreed with Cooper's conclusion that the "Volunteer Force has added less than $300 million to the budget costs of defense manpower—about two-tenths of 1 percent of the defense budget" (Nunn et al., 1978, p. 12). When the GAO witness said that Cooper's numbers

---

[13] Letter from Senator Sam Nunn to Elmer Staats, the Controller General of the United States and head of GAO, reproduced in Comptroller General of the United States (1978, pp. 79–80). This was the same position White took before the House Budget Committee in July 1977 (White, 1977, pp. 82–83).

[14] GAO made constant reference to the RAND study. They noted in a table on page 65 that they were referring to the Canby and Klotz study (Canby and Klotz, 1970) as the RAND study. Later they refer to "the most recent study of the AVF . . . issued by RAND in September 1977," which was the study by Cooper (Cooper, 1977b). Using the same term, *RAND study*, is a bit confusing, but somewhat less since they did not like either of the RAND reports.

were annual costs and incorporated a number of savings that GAO did not feel were appropriate, Nunn lashed out:

> Senator Nunn: The RAND report has been quoted over and over again. I have a very high regard for RAND and they do a lot of very good work, but this report I found to be absolutely incredible when I read it because it defied everything that was so apparent from having testimony over the years. . . .
> GAO Witness: I believe a lot of the things which RAND states as management savings from the other side of the coin are costs of the way we have done the All-Volunteer Force. (Nunn et al., 1978, p. 13)

Then it was White's turn to defend DoD estimates and, by implication, Cooper's report. White stressed that "the GAO estimate for the budget cost of the All-Volunteer Force is not too different from the costs predicted by the Gates Commission in its 1970 report" (Nunn et al., 1978, p. 35). Nunn immediately called White on his statement, countering that "the best estimate GAO has is the Gates Commission report . . . [which understates the real costs] by 80 to 100 percent. It seems to me that this is substantially different from the Gates Commission" (Nunn et al., 1978, p. 35). Illustrating the esoteric nature of these cost calculations, White responded that the differences were related to the use of "constant versus current dollars." In responses for the record, DoD and GAO would finally agree that the all-volunteer force had cost only 21 percent more than the Gates Commission's projection for 1976, and only 8 percent more than the projection for 1977.[15]

In his final statement, Nunn was undeterred and reiterated his concerns about the all-volunteer force. He rejected the previous DoD and RAND estimates: "I think many people will be surprised that the AVF has cost $18.4 billion" (Nunn et al., 1978, p. 48). He tried, however, to move the debate to higher ground. Recognizing the conundrum that he faced, he concluded that no one could

> turn back the clock and the GAO report does not imply that these amounts of money could now be saved by returning to the draft. . . . There is little point in speculation about what decision or structural changes would have been made if early AVF planners knew that they were dealing with an $18 billion program.
>   The real question we must face is the future capability to meet our national security problems. . . . Do we choose to continue increases in manpower costs? . . . Instead of adding potentially larger costs for the current structure of the AVF,

---

[15] Gary Nelson remembers being in the room that day:

> Having prepared his [John White's] testimony, I was at the hearing on the cost of the all-volunteer force. For GAO, Elmer Staats himself appeared as head of their team. Everyone from GAO left when Staats finished. Once John [White] said we found the costs of the all-volunteer force to be consistent with the Gates Commission, Senator Nunn sent his staff out to find Staats and Co. and bring them back into the hearing room—but to no avail. What GAO had failed to do was provide a meaningful comparison between Gates Commission and actual spending. It was a rookie mistake and was politically highly useful to John [White] and me in giving us a political platform to point out consistency of actuals with the Gates Commission forecasts. (Nelson, G., 2004)

shouldn't we recognize that . . . alternative structures should be examined? The only alternative is not a return to the draft as previously constituted. Management initiatives by DoD can help, at least in the short term. National service alternatives should be explored. I am hopeful that this report [the GAO report] on costs will give impetus to the examination of alternatives to meet our future needs. (Nunn et al., 1978, p. 49)[16]

Nunn's statement that the clock could not be turned back and his focus on alternatives, rather than adding to the cost of the all-volunteer force, is particularly important in light of later events. Within two years, he and Senator John Warner (R-Virginia) would cosponsor an amendment to the FY 1981 Defense Appropriation Act providing the largest pay increase since the original all-volunteer force pay increase of 1971. While their actions substantially added to the cost of the all-volunteer force, it most likely averted a crisis in our ability to staff the military.[17] Moreover, by 1980, there had been a reversal in roles. Nunn and Warner, two senators who were hostile to the very concept of an all-volunteer force, pushed their pay raise through Congress over the initial objections of the pro–all-volunteer force White House.[18] For them, ensuring that the manpower needs of the military were being met was more important than the associated increase in manpower costs in the defense budget.

The Administration Develops a Strategy

Well before first congressional hearing in July 1977, the new administration took steps to assess the current situation and develop its policy options. There would be a study of the all-volunteer force—in fact, there would be two studies of the all-volunteer force, one by the staff of the Office of Management and Budget and the other by John White's office at the Pentagon.

Even before White arrived at the Pentagon, the Office of Management and Budget (OMB) had proposed, in April 1977, a comprehensive study to be completed by September 1977. While OMB did not meet that goal, Peter Linn completed a "draft" report on December 8, 1977 (Linn, 1977). In a summary of the report sent to President Carter on April 13, 1973, OMB Director James McIntyre suggested that

some modifications in the management of the AVF appear to be necessary to avoid very large cost increases in future budgets as the size of the prime recruiting pool of military-age males starts to decrease in 1980. Unless policy changes reduce present standards and allow larger numbers of enlistments from lower entrance test

---

[16] Nunn's concepts for national service were articulated in a study he commissioned (King, 1977).

[17] Nunn's position on the "adequacy of military pay" can be found in Nunn (1980).

[18] For a discussion of congressional and White House issues relating to the Nunn-Warner Amendment, see Nunn (1980).

score categories, we estimate that an additional budgetary cost of $14 billion per year cold be required by 1985 to maintain the current quality and quantity of military manpower through voluntary enlistments. Other than the areas where DOD is already moving forward (e.g., increased use of women), our principal suggestion would be to gradually reduce active duty military force levels, substituting increased contracting out of support functions at bases within the U.S. (McIntyre, James T., 1978, p. 1)

The report created something of a stir at the Pentagon. Gary Nelson, the leader of the Pentagon team preparing the Pentagon's own report, however, thought it was the proverbial tempest in a teapot. The report, he told official at OMB was "a valuable and illuminating study of the AVF policy options" (Nelson, G., 1978a). He did, however, want to make sure the President was aware that

since the Secretary of Defense adopted your recommended option of a better-managed AVF . . . last summer, many of the actions needed to ensure success of the AVF during the early 1980s have already been taken. (Nelson, G., 1978a)

While Nelson's own study was well along—an Interim Report of the Study of the All-Volunteer Force had been sent to OMB earlier in the winter—it would be eight months before *America's Volunteers* (Nelson, G., 1978b) would be published. At this stage in the process, the OMB staff was concerned that the Pentagon's report did not "specify in detail exactly what additional steps [would] need to be taken by each organization with a specific timetable for accomplishment of required implementation activities" (Taft, 1978). In general, however, staff members were "favorably impressed with the quality of the analysis contained in the Interim Report and also with the balance and moderation of the report" (Taft, 1978). OMB's endorsement notwithstanding, the delay in finishing the DoD report—it would not be out until the end of December—meant that Senator Nunn would continue to control the all-volunteer force debate and DoD would continue to be on the defensive.

Senator Nunn and the Status of the All-Volunteer Force

In June 1978, Senator Nunn held more hearings on the *status* of the all-volunteer force. He started with an observation John White certainly did not share:

There now appears to be a growing consensus that the All-Volunteer Force, as currently constituted, may fail to provide an adequate foundation for the future national security needs of our Nation. (Nunn, 1978, p. 1)

The tone of the hearings was set with the testimony of Congressman Robin Beard (R-Tennessee). A member of the House Armed Services Committee, Beard had commissioned a study of the state of military preparedness (Beard and Reed, 1978). Jerry

Reed, a DoD employee on detail to Congress, did the study for Beard.[19] The study incorporated extensive field interviews, was critical of "the poor state of mobilization and the weakened posture of our reserves" (Nunn, 1978, p. 4), and was critical of the state of the Selective Service System. The study charged that, to get people into the military, "recruiters are making unrealistic promises" about training, occupational assignments, and the demands of military life. It found that "mental qualification scores for new recruits are declining each year" and that the shortage of physicians and support medical staff would result in unnecessary deaths on any future battlefield. In his testimony, Congressman Beard was particularly critical of the Army, telling Nunn that "the Army's can do attitude has resulted in its minimizing its problems to the point that the picture of our Army presented to the American public has been totally distorted" (Congressman Beard in Nunn, 1978, p. 4). He was alarmed by the "social problems" he saw the military dealing with, e.g., single and unmarried parents, and asked: "Is the Army a fighting machine or a social institution?"

Defense of the all-volunteer force fell to Assistant Secretary John White and Army Deputy Chief of Staff for Personnel Lieutenant General DeWitt C. Smith, Jr. While admitting that the all-volunteer force had some problems, White's general conclusion was that "[i]n fact, a strong case can be made that our Active Forces are stronger and better manned than at any time in our history." White went on to say that, "with the help of Congress, we can solve our very real problems in our organized and individual Reserve Forces" (White in Nunn, 1978, p. 55). Smith, indirectly criticizing the field visits Reed made in preparing the Beard report, told the committee of his concern for "anecdotal gossip, not accurate or helpful reporting." He added, "It is important, of course, to hear those perceptions, to sense them and pull out whatever reality they have" (Smith in Nunn, 1978, p. 58). He illustrated his point with the following story:

> Recently, some young officers told me—and I take the chance to speak to them whenever I get a chance—that the draftees were much better than the soldiers in the Army today. I asked them how they knew. They really didn't. They had not been in the Army when draftees were coming in. (Smith in Nunn, 1978, p. 58)

Two additional witnesses filled out the hearing lineup. Professor Charles Moskos spoke in familiar terms. He deplored

> the grievous flaw [that] has been a redefinition of military service in terms of the economic market place [that] has contributed to moving the American military away from an institutional format to one more and more resembling that of an occupation. (Moskos in Nunn, 1978)

He emphasized, however,

---

[19] Reed was the 1978 federal fellow sponsored by the American Political Science Association. He later served as Associate Department Head for Test Ranges, Naval Weapons System, at China Lake, California.

the volunteer concept can be made to work. . . . [If it tracked] into the main stream of the youth population by less emphasis on marketplace economics, more emphasis on national service coupled with shorter tours and post service educational benefits. (Nunn, 1978, p. 72)

Moskos also noted that "[w]e have heard some talk about bringing the draft back in recent months, but I think the possibility is remote. The most popular thing Richard Nixon ever did was to end the draft" (Nunn, 1978, p. 41).[20] Congressman William Steiger (R-Wisconsin) expressed similar views. Steiger was one of the all-volunteer force's most ardent supporters. A frequent commentator and writer of letters to the editor to keep reporting on the all-volunteer force "honest, " he was the counter to Congressman Beard's viewpoint. He praised the Beard report because, as he told the committee,

[t]here is much in his report that I can agree with, because it reflects my own study of the Army during the draft. . . . [T]he point to remember is that because such difficulties predate the AVF, they cannot be cured by a return to the draft. . . . The AVF is blamed for problems that are not related to it and that are, in fact, symptomatic of society as a whole. (Nunn, 1978, pp. 75–76)[21]

At the end of the day, it seemed that White, Smith, and Steiger had fought Nunn, Beard, and Moskos to a draw. All agreed that the all-volunteer force had problems. All agreed that physicians, reserve forces, and the state of the standby draft and the Selective Service System were problems. They even agreed that the postservice educational benefits Professor Moskos suggested were worth trying.[22] They did not seem to agree on much else. They did not agree on the cost of the all-volunteer force. They could not agree on the quality of the force relative to that of the pre-Vietnam draft force. They could not even agree about whether higher wages encouraged better "quality" people to join—the economists' view, as expressed by John White—or poorer "quality" people to join—the sociologists' view, expressed by Charlie Moskos. Moskos believed that it was "indisputable that public opinion strongly supports the all-volunteer concept. A return to the draft would also pose again the question of who serves when not all serve" (Moskos

---

[20] Gary Nelson, who was at this hearing recalls, "Moskos's testimony was a complete surprise to Nunn because Charlie . . . did not advocate a return to the draft" (Nelson, G., 2004).

[21] Steiger also had a reminder for the committee:

Before we cast stones at DoD manpower managers, we should consider the degree to which we have complicated their job. . . . Congress's record in handling the Pentagon's appropriations requests for AVF recruiting and retention resources is not one of which we can be proud. (Steiger in Nunn, 1978, p. 78)

He then placed in the hearing record a bill of particulars of how Congress undercut DoD—"The committee . . . continues to have reservations about the attainability and the desirability of an All-Volunteer Force and especially an All-Volunteer Army" (Steiger in Nunn, 1978, pp. 78–81)—starting with the fiscal 1972 defense appropriation at the very beginning of the all-volunteer force.

[22] White, however, complained about "this continually picking on our people with respect to the so-called marketplace. . . . Education is a form of pay. If that is more attractive to a youngster and we get higher quality that way, that is all to the good." (White in Nunn, 1978, pp. 72–73)

in Nunn, 1978, p. 41). Not everyone shared that view. Peter Szanton, of the President's Reorganization Project, told his colleagues in the administration that Senator Nunn had told him that, by the end of 1979, "Congress will approve a return to peacetime registration, and that it will reinstate the draft within three years" (Pirie, 1979b).

DoD's All-Volunteer Force Initiatives

While OMB's recommendation to cut standards and increase civilianization had a familiar ring, the Pentagon was trying several new things to improve the fortunes of the all-volunteer force. It was experimenting with recruiting options, aggressively moving to test the effects of advertising so neglected during the early 1970s, and fielding a new bonus program. Of the old menu of all-volunteer force policy and management options, the Pentagon was moving out most aggressively on opening up the services to women.

Increasing the Use of Women in the All-Volunteer Force

Within a week of taking office, Secretary of Defense Brown called for a special study of "military manpower utilization, including the utilization of women in the military" (Hunter, 1977, p. iii). As Jeanne Holm later pointed out, this report, together with the appointment of Sarah Lister as Deputy General Counsel, Metzi Wertheim as Deputy Under Secretary of the Navy, and Kathleen Carpenter as the Deputy Assistant Secretary of Defense (Equal Opportunity) demonstrated that "the new administration's decision not to back off the women issue" (Holm, 1992, p. 253).

Dick Hunter, a Navy pilot with a distinguished flying record over Vietnam who just happened to have a Ph.D., prepared the report.[23] The report presented a number of important "findings" that would shape the policy of the new administration. Specifically,

> The number of women on active duty more than tripled from 1971 through 1976. . . .
>
> The Navy and Marine Corps are planning significant increases in the number of enlisted women on active duty in the 1978 to 1982 period. The Army's current plan, however, calls for no growth in enlisted women after 1979. The Air Force has not formally submitted a new program past 1978. . . .

---

[23] *Author's Note:* Hunter had studied the issues as a research fellow at the Brookings Institution, working with Marty Binkin and Shirley Bach as they prepared their report on women (Binkin and Bach, 1977). As I was writing this section, I received an email reporting Dick's untimely death. The emails that followed recounted his many contributions to the AVF; as one of his friends noted, "Among his many accomplishments, he successfully punched out of his A-4 , after being shot over North Viet Nam and losing rudder control, executing barrel rolls until he was over the ocean." Another former colleague recalled this about him:

> Dick was among the first to recognize the disconnect between what we thought were valid test results and the reports coming back from the field, and his persistence in uncovering the source of the inconsistency was perhaps the key factor in resolving the problem and, in all likelihood, saving the all-volunteer force from its opponents and skeptics in both the services and Congress.

Significant dollar savings and quality improvement are possible through the expanded use of enlisted women. Cost avoidance could exceed $1 billion annually by 1982. . . .

Continued expansion of the number of enlisted women used in the military can be an important factor in making the all-volunteer force continue to work. (Hunter, 1977, pp. iii–iv)

Foreshadowing future events, Hunter realized that the problem was the Army, concluding that the "Army should pursue a more ambitious program to find ways to use more of the high quality women to meet their enlisted requirements" (Hunter, 1977, p. 49). However, the previous November, outgoing Secretary of the Army Martin Hoffman concluded from a newly Women in the Army Study that the number of women should remain at 50,400. The Director of the Women's Army Corps, Brigadier General Mary Elizabeth Clarke, disagreed with the Army's findings and with its subsequent studies to evaluate the goal of 100,000 women in the Army (which was the number leaders believed Brown would force on them) and complained: "This has not been an effort to see if we could use 100,000 women; the effort has been to prove that we could not" (as quoted in Morden, 1989, p. 375).[24] Eventually, Brown did direct that the number of enlisted women in the Army be doubled to 100,000 by 1983.

There was, however, substantial push back. In January a "seminar" to examine the "leadership problems and challenges caused by increased number of women" (Cocke et al., 1980, p. 82) identified many areas of concern. In June 1978, Secretary of the Army Clifford Alexander ordered a reexamination of the units and specialties closed to women because of the combat-exclusion policy. "Feedback" from field commanders reported "negative effects on deployability, morale, operational readiness, field training, time on the job, and harmonious relations among unit members" (Cocke et al., 1980, p. 82). For the time being, at least, the Army leadership was not willing to face its clearly unhappy field commands and "concluded that women provide meaningful contribution to the all-volunteer Army (Cocke et al., 1980, p. 82). But the stage was set for change, which would come with the departure of the Carter team on January 20, 1981.

The Multiple Option Recruiting Experiment

One of the recurring issues the managers of the all-volunteer force faced was the initial service obligation that would be required of new recruits.[25] The services had bounced

---

[24] The Army Research Institute had recently completed a study known as MAX WAC. It was designed to analyze the effects of varying the proportion of women soldiers from 0 to 35 percent in five types of combat service and combat service support units. It showed that "up to 35 percent of total strength—the limits of the test—the number of women had no significant effect on the capability of a unit to perform its mission for short periods of time" (Cocke et al., 1980, p. 79).

[25] Congress also directed a program be tested for "direct enlistment . . . into the Individual Ready Reserve (IRR). . . . The recruiting to begin no later than March 1, 1979" (Pirie, 1978a). RAND was to assist with the "development of parameters for this test" (Pirie, 1978a). The Army, of course, wanted additional funds to carry out the test (Yerks, 1978).

back and forth between short and long initial service obligations. Those who favored the former thought that having a shorter service obligation would encourage more people to try the military.[26] At the least, they argued, having young men and women serve, even for a short period, then return to civilian life would provide a benefit to society, if not an immediate return on the training investment to the military. Others argued that a short obligation would result in the services either not making an appropriate training investment in the new recruit or, if they did make the investment, not being able to enjoy the benefits of it as recruits returned to the civilian sector.

The various options had been tried several times in both the active and reserve forces. In fact, in the reserve forces, a number of experiments had been run that showed the shorter enlistments failed to generate enough response to justify the investment. In early 1975, Secretary of Defense James Schlesinger terminated the two-year enlistment options "to minimize turnover, to reduce training costs, and to increase stability, assignment flexibility and experience levels within the force" (Schlesinger, 1975). At the time, it was estimated that this would "permit a total reduction of about 35,000 to 40,000 in recruiting requirements by the end of 1978" (Schlesinger, 1975). Now, in 1978, with accessions falling and at the prodding of such outside critics as Charlie Moskos, Congress directed a test of a two-year enlistment option. The Army wanted White to approve such a test no later than November 1978 so that it could "provide advertising and recruiter orientation lead time and an opportunity for the recruiters to tap a new market [and to] reach the high school seniors prior to graduation" (Nelson, R., 1978a).[27] In late October, White moved to the Office of Management and Budget as its Deputy Director, leaving further action to Robin Pirie, for the time being the Acting Assistant Secretary. In December, Pirie finally agreed to the Army proposal, making the points that,

> should the new shorter enlistment options result in only a shifting of high quality enlistees from three and four-year enlistments (i.e., a significant net loss of quality manyears to the active Army), it may be necessary to terminate the options during the test year. . . . [And these] tests must be carefully implemented, monitored, and evaluated. (Pirie, 1978h)

The Navy and Marine Corps were authorized to undertake a 12-month test, along similar lines, starting March 1, 1979 (Pirie, 1979e).[28]

Advertising

As had occurred years earlier with the first paid radio and TV advertising test in 1970, the Army undercut the test aspect of the program by trying to gain the maximum

---

[26] For example, in 1973, Assistant Secretary of the Air Force Richard Borda laid out the arguments for and against shortening the terms of initial service. He concluded, however, that there was a need to test "the effectiveness of variable terms of enlistment prior to a firm decision to effect a definite change" (Borda, 1973).

[27] In fall 1978, the Army and Pirie's office worked together to agree on the test protocols, e.g., "My people and yours have gotten together on the outline of a more detailed, complex test" (Nelson, R., 1978b).

[28] The Marine Corps test did not start until April 15, 1979 (Haggstrom et al., 1981, p. 1).

advantage for solving their immediate problems. In this case, the Army had agreed to a test design that "established 'test areas' in about three quarters of the country and 'control areas'—in which the option was to be neither advertised nor offered—in a quarter of the country." Pirie reported to Brown that, "despite the quarantining of test areas—which the Army agreed to—the Army recently started a national campaign advertising the availability of the two-year option" (Pirie, 1979g). The Army very reluctantly agreed to stop the national campaign and Pirie thought "their efforts thus far have [not] unduly affected the validity of the test" (Pirie, 1979g).

The Army, never happy about being forced to test the two-year option rather than simply offering it, pressed Secretary Brown and got the authority to terminate the test on September 30, 1979, allowing the service to undertake a national and regional advertising campaign. In an argument that closely followed those Moskos used in his testimony before Congress and that Congress had relied on when it ordered DoD to undertake the test, the Army maintained that the two-year option was central to "refocusing [its] recruiting efforts on the upper mental category, high school diploma graduate market, and at the same time meeting . . . first term replacement requirements in critical skills with soldiers who would serve about an eighteen-month tour" (Alexander, 1979). Secretary of the Army Clifford L. Alexander, Jr., told Brown, that the "[w]ider use of the alternative two-year option is a key element of the Army's recruiting strategy for FY 80" (Alexander, 1979).

Conspicuously absent from the Army's request, however, was any analysis of the test results to date. Pirie provided that analysis for Brown's consideration. He told Brown that "[p]reliminary results to date show very little high quality supply effects—nowhere near the levels needed to justify an Army two-year enlistment program. . . . The low two-year response may be the result of low appeal among high quality prospects for unpopular skills and mandatory European assignment" (Pirie, 1979m). The new Deputy Secretary of Defense, Graham Claytor, writing for Brown, rejected the Army's request (Claytor, 1979). Pirie was concerned, however, that the results "may have been biased by poor execution" on the part of the Army and ordered "a retest using a simpler design" (Pirie, 1979n). He told Brown and Claytor that

> [i]n spite of strong appeals from the Army to drop the control group, . . . Congress has required us to test two-year enlistments, and we need a means of knowing whether they in fact bring us more man-years than they cost us. Every present indication is that a two-year program will cost more in lost man-years than it will gain in added recruitment. (Pirie, 1979n)[29]

---

[29] In fact, in December RAND had provided Pirie a preliminary report that concluded the following:

> None of the . . . options under test in the Army has elicited a sizable enlistment response among high-quality males. In particular, the two-year option has yielded no apparent increase whatsoever in the number of high-quality male enlistments. (Haggstrom, 1979, p. 29)

Enlistment Bonuses

While Pirie thought the Army was too aggressive in wanting to move immediately to implement a two-year enlistment program across the nation, he also felt that it was not aggressive enough in using "tools which are most valuable in increasing the supply of new accessions, especially the enlistment bonus" (Pirie, 1980d). In spring 1979, he told the Secretary of the Army he was concerned "that the effectiveness of the bonus program may have been suppressed by a lack of youth awareness" (Pirie, 1980d). Citing the results of the fall 1978 Youth Attitude Tracking Survey (YATS), he noted that "only 28% of the sample was aware that cash bonuses were offered for enlistment and those who were aware significantly underestimated the value of the bonus" (Pirie, 1980d). The following year, he again expressed his concern that prospective recruits were still not aware of the bonus program and told the Army that DoD was proposing a more-flexible enlistment bonus program to Congress that would increase the maximum award to $5,000. He wanted to know what changes they had made or were planning to make "designed to highlight enlistment bonuses" (Pirie, 1980d).

Compensation Reform and the President's Commission on Military Compensation

One of the early initiatives of the Carter administration was the creation of the PCMC. As noted before, the PCMC was born out of the frustration and failure of the Third Quadrennial Review of Military Compensation (3rd QRMC). As far as the administration was concerned, the 3rd QRMC demonstrated the unwillingness of the military services to agree to reforms in the compensation system. What Kermit Gordon, president of the Brookings Institution, had called "a costly anachronism" had become the center of the administration's efforts to control the rising cost of defense manpower (Binkin, 1975, p. vii).

Charlie Zwick, chairman of the commission, understood the role that the service chiefs had played in thwarting earlier attempts at reform. He thought that he had cut a deal with the service chiefs that, if he steered the commission away from recommending a salary system, they would support the commission's recommendations to reform the retirement system. As Zwick saw it, the reforms were a "substantial revision of the present compensation system" (Zwick, 1978b). When it was time to be counted, the service chiefs were not prepared for such changes and opposed the commission's recommendation.[30]

On April 10, 1978, the commission reported to the President (Zwick, 1978c). The *New York Times,* noting the "conservative opposition within the armed forces" called the commission recommendation "a reform package worth fighting for":

---

[30] According to Mike Hix, the Deputy Director of the Commission Staff (Hix, 2002).

The Presidential commission's solution was as bold as it was simple: first abolish the half-pay bonanza for 20-year veterans who retire long before their productive working lives are over; allow everyone with just 10 years of service to build credits toward pensions that do not begin until age 60; and provide hefty lump-sum payments for long-termers who decide to go back to civilian careers in midlife. This would give short-termers a fair shake and eliminate the wasteful incentives to stay in the military past the point when either the soldier or the service benefits. (*New York Times* Editorial Board, 1978)

In fact, there had been widespread opposition to the commission's recommendations, as the *Times* noted: "Senior officers with powerful friends on Capitol Hill oppose any break with this tradition—the 20 year voluntary retirement—even though the change would have no effect on their benefit rights" (*New York Times* Editorial Board, 1978). Pirie had tried to fashion a compromise in fall 1978.[31] (Officially, the crafting of DoD position on the PCMC constituted the Fourth Quadrennial Review of Military Compensation.) In late November, he told Brown,

The Services comments on our decision paper . . . are in. Not surprisingly, their responses give little evidence of wild enthusiasm concerning possible modifications of the military retirement system. The Air Force and Army want the current system but appear willing to settle for the highest two-tier plan. The Navy would like to retain the same level of benefits as the current system but restructure them to provide more money up front. (Pirie, 1978c)

There were, however, a number of design questions outstanding. Five in particular he wanted Brown to answer. He told the Secretary, "We will use the decisions you make . . . to construct a detailed retirement plan" (Pirie, 1978d).

Under pressure from the President, who wanted "to propose in the FY 1980 budget a comprehensive reform of the compensation systems now in place for federal civilians, both white and blue collar, and for military personnel" (Carter, 1978), Brown suspended the agreed-to schedule and asked Pirie to circulate his own—Pirie's—recommendations to the services and the Joint Chiefs to "solicit any comments you may have on it and any further thoughts you may have on this question" (Pirie, 1978e). On December 11, 1978, the day the President had asked Brown to submit DoD's position to the White House, there was still no agreement on that position. Pirie told Brown that the Joint Chiefs had considered his recommendations, and "[m]y proposal came in dead last and my suggestion that it is important to save money aroused resentment. The Services are strongly of the view that whatever new system is devised, the

---

[31] In August, White had conveyed to the secretaries of the military departments Brown's desire "that over the next several weeks we make a further effort to reach agreement on a proposed DoD position" (White, 1978). In November, Pirie, now the Acting assistant secretary, sent a draft decision memorandum for the secretary of defense to the secretaries of the military departments and the chairman of the Joint Chiefs of Staff for their consideration. The memorandum asked Secretary Brown to make a "decision on a number of specific retirement issues that will permit OSD and the Services to develop a detailed DoD retirement proposal and to integrate it with the non-retirement compensation issues still to be decided" (Pirie, 1978b).

more it is a reduction in benefits . . . , the worse it is" (Pirie, 1978g).[32] In preparing for a final meeting with the Service Chiefs, Pirie "in accordance with . . . instructions [from the Deputy Secretary constructed] . . . an early withdrawal plan that is a modification of my two-tier plan using several of the Chairman's ideas" (Pirie, 1978g).[33]

On December 12, 1978, Brown sent his revisions to the commission's recommendation to the President. He told the President that, while "we differ from the Commission on some particulars . . . the Commission's call for restricting the military retirement system . . . seems to us to be right" (Brown, 1978). Unfortunately, this did not sit well with the commission chairman. In a letter to the editor of the *New York Times* commenting on their editorial of December 28, 1978, which praised Brown's approach as "meeting the Commission's reform objectives," Zwick argued that "the Pentagon's proposal, *as reported,* falls short of the reform that the system requires and the country expects" (Zwick, 1979, emphasis added).[34] Zwick wrote the *Times* that he believed

> that two key recommendations of the Presidential commission should not be compromised. First, the existing half-pay pension for 20 years of service should be eliminated as wasteful and counterproductive to the maintenance of a truly high-quality armed force. Second, we must provide adequate up-front financial incentives for competent and ambitious short-term personnel and adequate transition payments to them when they return to civilian status. (Zwick, 1979)

In fact, while Zwick's use of the words "as reported" conveys his hope that DoD would fully back the commission's recommendations, Pirie's testimony to Congress late that spring left little doubt that reform was in deep trouble, if not dead:

> After careful review we have decided that we do not want totally to abandon the jump in benefits at the twenty-year point. Service personnel chiefs make a convincing case that a step up in benefits at that point serves as an important magnet to encourage senior personnel to continue military service in the face of assignments that are more arduous and often less lucrative than civilian alternatives. We think, however, that we can capture many of the benefits of the Commission's graduated trust fund recommendation. . . . [W]e have very much taken the recommendations

---

[32] Pirie remembers the strong position that Tom Hayward, the Chief of Naval Operations, took: Haywood would not accept any reduction in the *net present value* of the income stream (Pirie, 2004).

[33] In a separate memorandum, Pirie told Brown that he did not favor this final system: "I value the 10 YOS [years of service] old age vesting. . . . I would not compromise it away in a two-tier system, nor . . . would I favor permitting its early withdrawal through a hybrid Two-Tier Individual Choice Plan" (Pirie, 1978f) recommended by the chairman.

[34] Pirie remembers that Zwick lobbied him very hard not to compromise the PCMC recommendations (Pirie, 2004). He told Brown, before Zwick's letter was published by the *Times*, that "Charlie Zwick thinks the package is 'quite good, quite clever,' but he fears that it will be compromised away" (Pirie, 1979a). Zwick's letter to the *Times* leaves a different impression, but that may have been part of Zwick's game plan. Gary Nelson recalls a conversation with Zwick "after the tortured Pentagon decision process. . . . He said he liked the proposal but was going 'to help' us by attacking it as not going far enough" (Nelson, G., 2004).

of the President's Commission to heart, and will recommend a system that I think captures the best of both the old and the new. (Pirie, 1979f, p. 17)

What the administration eventually proposed was "a system of permissive early withdrawals." What the *New York Times* had characterized "as *bold* as it was *simple*" (*New York Times* Editorial Board, 1978, emphasis added), Pirie would describe as a system in which

> a member in or beyond his tenth year of service will be entitled to draw advances against his prospective twenty year retirement benefits. If he leaves the Service before twenty years, these advances would substitute for his old age retirement benefits. (Pirie, 1979f, p. 17)

It may have been bold, but it was hardly simple. Over the next several months it became clear that reform was dead.[35]

At the Half-Way Point

The results of the then–newly released (December 31, 1978) comprehensive report—*America's Volunteers: A Report on the All-Volunteer Armed Force* (Nelson, G., 1978b)—on the all-volunteer force not withstanding, things were not looking good as the administration reached its half-way point. While the report had concluded that the "AVF has provided the military services with a full-strength active force of a quality equal to or superior to that achieved under the draft" (Nelson, G., 1978b, p. 10), recruiting had turned down, the quality of recruits had turned down, the state of mobilization planning and the status of the Selective Service System had not improved, and the services had successfully pushed back the retirement reforms the PCMC had recommended. In fact, Pirie told Brown within weeks of releasing *America's Volunteers* that "[n]one of the Services achieved their December [1978] or first quarter FY 1979 recruiting objectives. This was the first quarter since the draft ended in which no Service made its objective" (Pirie, 1979c). He further told Brown that "[r]ecruiting prospects for the balance of the year are highly uncertain. The entire situation causes us great concern. Without sustained improvement, significant quantity and quality shortcomings are likely" (Pirie, 1979d). While first-term attrition was down, it seemed that the services were being

---

[35] Pirie had a moment of vindication: "The recalcitrance of the Chiefs in 1978 led to changes being rammed down their throats in 1986" (Pirie, 2004). Congress finally made changes in the military retirement system unilaterally in 1986, reducing the immediate annuity at 20 years of service from 50 percent of base pay to 40 percent of base pay. The Acting Assistant Secretary of Defense at the time, David Armor, observed that, "[o]ver the objections of DoD, Congress has passed an act revising military retirement for new entrants" (Armor, 1986). It was restricted to "new entrants" because Congress could not take the heat of imposing changes on "current and retired members." Even then, Joint Chiefs Chairman Henry Shelton successfully led a move 14 years later to repeal even these moderate reforms: "Restoring an attractive retirement program for all active duty members is . . . my top legislative priority in the FY 2000 Budget" (Shelton, 1999).

forced to keep recruits that they would have preferred to let go. It now fell to Robin Pirie, the acting Assistant Secretary, to bring the bad news to Congress.

Recruiting

More than anything else the all-volunteer force was about recruiting. As the Carter administration started its third year, the manning of reserve forces and medical services, particularly physician manning, had not improved. Now, recruiting for the active force was sliding.[36] This trend had been noticed during the last days of the Ford administration, but it was obvious now across the board.[37] On March 27, 1979, Pirie addressed the Senate Armed Services Committee:

> I note that the Services had difficulty meeting recruiting goals during FY 1978 and that in the first quarter of FY 1979, for the first time since the inception of the AVF, none of the Services met its objectives fully. As a group they met only 90 percent of their enlistment objectives compared with 97 percent of slightly larger objectives in the first quarter of FY 1978. We do not now have a complete explanation for this experience. Generally speaking, we expect that it is attributable to such varied factors as the constraints we have imposed on ourselves by adopting very high recruiting goals, an abrupt increase in youth enrollment in the CETA [Comprehensive Education and Training Act] public service program, a decline in the entry salaries of servicemen when compared with civilian workers, the termination of the GI bill for new recruits, and a decline in the unemployment rate for 18 to 19 year old males. We do not yet know whether our recent experience represents merely an isolated deviation from our strong recruitment experiences or whether it signals the beginning of a disturbing trend. . . . Among management actions we are considering are such steps as offering a two year enlistment in the Army combat arms combined with enhanced educational benefits. (Pirie, 1979f, p. 8)[38]

Moreover, as recruiting slipped, DoD got little help from Congress. While the accession requirements for FY 1978 had grown by 11 percent and the "recruiting and advertising resources available to the Services . . . are only 1% above the FY 1977 levels, in real terms" (Pirie, 1979i), Congress denied the services' requests to reprogram resources. The House Appropriations Committee (HAC) completely rejected the Navy

---

[36] One of Pirie's frustrations was that the Army was not aggressively using enlistment bonuses. He told the Secretary of the Army of his concern that "we are not achieving maximum results from some of our tools which are most valuable in increasing the supply of new accessions, especially the enlistment bonus" (Pirie, 1980f). He noted that only 28 percent of those who responded on the Youth Attitude Tracking Survey in fall 1978 were "aware that cash bonuses were offered for enlistment and those who were aware significantly underestimated the value of the bonus" (Pirie, 1980f). He wanted the Army 's advertising program to "highlight enlistment bonuses" and reminded the Army Secretary that there was "also flexibility in bonus management which has not been tested" (Pirie, 1980d).

[37] Pirie told Brown in late 1978 that there had "been a perceptible tightening of the enlisted recruiting market in the past 12 months. While I suspect this is a transitory phenomenon, it could conceivably be connected to elimination of the G.I. Bill incentive or to other non-transitory factors" (Danzig, 1978). The termination of the G.I. Bill program was one of the cost-saving actions during the Ford administration.

[38] He could have added that the actions under consideration had previously been recommended by Professor Moskos.

and Air Force requests to reprogram funds to recruiting, and both the Senate and House Appropriations Committees "approved only about forty percent of the Army's request to reprogram resources to recruiting and advertising" (Pirie, 1979i). It took a personal appeal from Graham Claytor, when he was Navy Secretary, before the HAC would even allow the Navy to add personnel to its chronically undermanned recruiter force.

Desperately looking for some little piece of good news, Pirie still maintained that recruiting was representative of the American people "as to geographical distribution and as to family income distribution," citing the results of the long-awaited and recently completed report, *America's Volunteers: A Report on the All-Volunteer Armed Force* (Nelson, G., 1978b). When he argued that the percentage of Army recruits with high school diplomas had increased from a pre-Vietnam level of 68 percent to an FY 1978 level of 77 percent, he was challenged that the number of white male high school graduates had actually declined.[39] In fact, blacks accounted for 34 percent of all Army active-duty accessions. He took pride in the fact that

> under the AVF the percentage of recruits scoring significantly below average in mental tests (mental group IV) has decreased from a pre-Vietnam level of 15% and a high of 25% in FY 1968 to about 5% in FY 1977 and FY 1978. The average test scores of recruits have increased in spite of a somewhat smaller proportion scoring well above average (mental groups I and II). (Pirie, 1979f, p. 8)[40]

But a closer look revealed some disturbing numbers. The entire improvement in the average score was the result of the services taking fewer people who scored in the category IV range and more who scored in category IIB. In fact, the drop-off in higher-quality recruits was not just in the top two categories (I and II). The number of category IIIAs was also down.[41] As it would turn out to the embarrassment of Pirie and the

---

[39] In fact, Moskos claimed that

> [s]ince the end of the draft, the proportion of black high school graduates entering the Army has exceeded that of whites, and this is a trend that is becoming more pronounced. In point of fact, today's Army is the only major arena in American Society where black educational levels surpass that of whites, and by quite a significant margin. . . . A strong argument could be made that it has been the female entrants, virtually all of whom possess a high school diploma, that are the margin of success in the All-Volunteer Force. (Moskos in Nunn, 1978, p. 40)

[40] As a point of reference, Pirie examined the "mental ability scores of all male accessions during WW II, including officers and enlisted" (Pirie, 1980c), determining the percentages falling into each mental category. The top 8 percent of the accession pool fell into category I, the next 28 percent into category II, the next 34 percent into category III, the next 21 percent into category IV, and the bottom 10 percent into category V. Moskos recently commented on the World War II numbers, pointing out that

> accessions category I in WW II [was 8%, compared with] 3% today. Historically, starting in 1944, no one could volunteer for the military because the volunteers were seeking to join the Army Air Corps or Navy and stay out of combat arms. Thereafter, all those who entered the military were drafted. (Moskos, 2004)

[41] The disaggregated numbers were presented in the Beard study (Beard and Reed, 1978, pp. 151–154), which noted that the "Army position regarding the downswing in high school diploma accessions and mental category I–IIIA personnel is stated as directly related to a cut by Congress of $50 million and reduction of 800 recruiting personnel in fiscal year 1976" (Beard and Reed, 1978, p. 184).

whole Defense establishment, the apparent reduction in category IV recruits and the increase in category IIIB personnel was the result of misnormed Armed Services Vocational Aptitude Battery (ASVAB) that had been introduced in 1976. Recruit quality had, in fact, fallen, and the trend was down.

In late August, Brown asked Pirie for his views on recruiting and retention and his end-strength projections for that and the following year (Pirie, 1979j). It was not a pretty report. Pirie characterized the situation as "a matter of serious concern to us and all of the Services" (Pirie, 1979j, p. 1). He told the secretary that, through the first three quarters of the fiscal year, all "four Services had recruited 22,500 fewer men and women than they had planned. . . . the Army and Navy had the largest shortfalls" (Pirie, 1979j, p. 1). Most importantly, retention had improved, so the effect on end strength was only a shortfall of about 1 percent. Pirie focused on four specific recruiting problems: the decline in the youth population, a reduced share of the high school graduate market, a loss in recruiter productivity in the non–high school graduate market, and unfavorable publicity. His approach to solving the problems, he told Brown, was to try to reduce accession requirements but also considered it important to maintain "our relative competitiveness against the options available to employable young people" (Pirie, 1979j, p. 5). He reminded Brown that they had a "study of the adequacy of military compensation under way" (Pirie, 1979j, p. 6), and later noted that this would "be a contentious issue in FY 81"(Pirie, 1979k, p. 2).

Recruiting and the "Thurman Effect"

By the beginning of 1980, things seemed to be looking up. Pirie reported that the first quarter of FY 1980 (October–December 1979) was "encouraging" (Pirie, 1980g, p. 4). The services had enlisted 19,000 more non–prior service personnel than they had during the same period the previous year. Almost all the services were at or above the percentages of their objectives that they had attained the previous year. The exception was the Army, which was still reporting that it had achieved 94 percent of its goal. The Army's requirements for the last quarter of calendar 1979, however, had increased by almost 64 percent from the previous year. In fact, the Army had recruited over 15,000 more recruits during the last quarter of calendar 1979 than it had during the last quarter of calendar 1978.

Pirie's use of the word "encouraging" to describe the last quarter of 1979 might have also extended to the assignment of Major General Maxwell (Max) Thurman as the new Commander of the Army Recruiting Command. While the Army had recruited more people at the end of 1979 than it had the previous year, the Army's new recruiting boss was far from satisfied. For Thurman, the issue was not just numbers, or what he called the "volumetric mission," the issue was high school graduates, and he did not see the improvement in this area that he wanted. In April 1980, Thurman told Congress that the Army was "on track in volume. However, there is a content side of the mission where we are clearly not on track, and many of the resources" they were asking for were "headed for the content . . . side of that mission" (Thurman, 1980b, p. 75).

Before he was finished in 1981, Thurman and the Army Recruiting Command would turn the corner on content and be on track.

Army General Maxwell Reid Thurman

General Thurman arguably was the single most important person in the history of the All-Volunteer Force—as one commentator put it, he "taught the Pentagon how to recruit, and by dint of personality and intellect he made the all-volunteer concept work throughout the 1980s" (Davis, 2000).[42] The reverence that those engaged in managing the all-volunteer force held for Thurman was captured in the dedication of the book

Figure 11.1
Dedication of *Professionals on the Front Line: Two Decades of the All-Volunteer Force*

This book is dedicated to General Maxwell R. Thurman, who succumbed to leukemia at Walter Reed Army Medical Center, Washington, D.C., on 1 December 1995. Max Thurman held some of the most important positions in the U.S. Army, but it is in the context of the All-Volunteer Force that most will remember him. An ardent supporter of the AVF from its inception, he kept the faith even when the administration, members of Congress, and the public began to lose theirs during the difficult years of the late 1970s and early 1980s. He maintained that higher investments in "human Capital" early on would provide great returns later in an efficient and well-trained fighting force, and in this effort he challenged both the Department of Defense and Congress to provide the resources necessary to recruit and retain high-quality personnel. He lobbied Congress for higher military pay, instituted a rigorous systems approach to personnel decision making for the Army, and established one of the most successful and memorable advertising campaigns in history—"Be All You Can Be." In turning Army recruiting around, most believe he saved the All-Volunteer Force, or as he preferred to call it, the "All Recruited Force." In his last assignment, as Commander in Chief, U.S. Southern Command, Thurman put the All-Volunteer Force, which he was so instrumental in building, to its first test; the result was overwhelming victory in Operation Just Cause in Panama.

Max Thurman was especially admired for his analytic approach to problem solving; he placed a high value on research and extraordinary emphasis on the technical competence, at all levels, of those around him. He also was noted for his thoroughness, excellence, zeal, and mission accomplishment—qualities that earned him the utmost respect from the President, members of Congress, and the Department of Defense.

He stated that he would like to be remembered as one who could make things happen, but his impact is much greater than that. His legacy is best characterized not by what he did while he served, but rather by the Army itself—the organization, the values, and, most important, the people who remain after his departure.

---

[42] Thurman's official obituary at Arlington National Cemetery credits him with being "a principal architect of the all-volunteer Army" (Staff of Arlington National Cemetery, 2005). It notes he "headed the Army's Recruiting Command at Fort Sheridan, Illinois, where he worked to develop the service's 'Be all that you can be' campaign . . . [and] vastly improving the quality of the average soldier. Under Thurman's guidance … the modern professional Army we now possess came into existence" (Staff of Arlington National Cemetery, 2005).

that presented the proceedings of the conference held at the U.S. Naval Academy in September 1993 commemorating the 20th anniversary of the end of the draft.

Even before he got involved with the all-volunteer force, Thurman was a formidable figure in the Army, holding the critical position of the director of the Army's Office of Program Analysis and Evaluation (PA&E). As the Army's programmer, Thurman had been peripherally involved with the Army recruiting program. In an oral history recorded by the Army's Military History Institute after Thurman retired from the Army, he recounted how he and the Army's Deputy Chief of Staff for Personnel took "the abuse from General [Bernard] Rogers [the Army Chief of Staff] over the fact that the recruiting command could not recruit enough people" (Thurman, 1992, p. 181). Thurman recalled that when he was in PA&E

> I was heavily involved in the recruiting. That was one thing that wasn't going well. So as a programmer, I was trying to figure out what the hell was going on. . . . (p. 182)
> The Recruiting Command said that we had to expand the market. We had to keep expanding the market! They were expanding the market to the bottom fish. They wanted to recruit down to 17-year-olds who were non–high school graduates. They kept lowering their sights in order to increase what they thought was a volume operation. (p. 181)
> I got called up one day by a guy who did me a great turn. He was Dr. Al Martin. Al was the accession policy guy. He was up at OSD. He called me up and said he wanted to introduce me to . . . three advertising consultants that the Defense Department had hired out of New York. [He] had taken a liking to me and introduced me to the advertising side of things as the PA&E. (Thurman, 1992, pp. 182–183)

In November 1979, with two weeks notice, the new Chief of Staff, General Shy Meyer, told Thurman he was being reassigned as the commander of the troubled Army Recruiting Command.[43] The command was troubled not only because it was not meeting its recruiting goals but also because of charges that Army recruiters were cheating.[44] After taking command, the first thing that Thurman did was travel around the country

---

[43] Gary Nelson recalls how this came about:

> Max Thurman told me, when he was asked to go to USAREC [U.S. Army Recruiting Command], he told Meyer that he wasn't going to work for Munson, the Army DCSPER [Deputy Chief of Staff for Personnel], because of the way Munson had been trashing the USAREC commander in the regular meetings on recruiting back in the Pentagon. So they worked out a face-saving arrangement whereby Max would come back every month for a joint meeting with the Under Secretary and the DCSPER. Also, I believe the decision to send Max to USAREC came from the Secretary of the Army more than from Meyer. (Nelson, G., 2004)

[44] In March 1980, Pirie reported to Nunn that 319 Army recruiters had been removed for malpractice during the first three months of FY 1980. That was 5.5 percent of all Army recruiters. The numbers for the Navy (1.00 percent), the Air Force (0.50 percent), and the Marine Corps (0.70 percent) were much lower (Pirie and Danzig, 1980, p. 1,325).

to meet with all 57 battalion commanders and their brigade commanders. Years later, he remembered it as a

> 7-day a week schedule with 5 days on the road and 2 days at home. The 2 days at Fort Sheridan were to handle cases [the recruiter scandal] with the legal staff. The 5 days on the road were used to find out who the guys were commanding units and who were either failing to do their work or doing their work. (Thurman, 1992, p. 186)

Thurman quickly came to a conclusion about what was wrong with the Recruiting Command, repeating what he had told his staff at the time:

> You know, it strikes me that what is wrong with the recruiting command at the moment is that the officers are not running it—sergeants are. All of you guys are doing what sergeants are telling you to do and that is not the way to run military units. (Thurman, 1992, p. 187)

That Christmas (1979), Thurman gave all the officers in his command a very special present. He told them, "all of the officers of the Recruiting Command have 60 days to put a guy in boots" (Thurman, 1992, p. 191). Thus, he wanted every officer in the command to go out and actually recruit at least one soldier. This was Thurman's way of making sure that the officers of the Recruiting Command would learn the job of recruiting themselves, not just sit in an office pushing papers.

Thurman had a hands-on style. In his oral history he tells how he would have each one of the regions gather and would directly interact with the battalion commanders and assign them their missions—the accumulation of which became the brigade commander's mission:

> People thought I had violated the chain of command by not giving it to the brigade commander, but I did that for a purpose. The purpose was to reinforce, two echelons down, what was going on so there would be no misconstruing what the operative orders were. (Thurman, 1992, p. 188)

Thurman also saw the need to "take charge of advertising." NW Ayer had been the Army's advertising agency since the first days of the all-volunteer force, when the agency had been involved in the first advertising experiment. Thurman remembers them as the people who had given the Army the famous slogan, "The Army Wants to Join You." He decided that he

> would grab hold of the advertising business. . . . We were running a 65 million dollar advertising budget in 1979. . . . Not a single officer had been sent to advertising school to find out what the principles of advertising were. . . . I fired the account manager. . . . I got it straight with them that I was in charge of the advertising. They weren't in charge of it, I was. That was a major watershed for them, to get inside of my head and understand my objectives. (Thurman, 1992, pp. 192–194)

Thurman describes how he worked with the agency to build the "Be All You Can Be" campaign and the interactive partnership they forged (Thurman, 1992, pp. 200–209). The "Be All You Can Be" slogan became one of the most recognized tag lines in the history of advertising and stayed in place until 2000, when the "Army of One" replaced it.[45]

Thurman appreciated numerical analysis, sponsored it and used it. He loved the "operations research and system guys." He created a ten-man analysis cell at his headquarters. Its job was to determine the relative market potential around the country and to translate that into a mission each and every recruiter would know he was responsible for accomplishing. That mission was to be defined not just in terms of numbers; it would also, most important, include the quality of the recruits they were expected to sign up. Thurman wanted to move the command from an emphasis on volume to a stress on quality. He commissioned research from four organizations. The first two were the RAND Corporation and the NW Ayer agency. The third was Thurman's own research, with Colonel Tom Faggan of the U.S. Military Academy as principal driver (Thurman, 1992, p. 200).[46] The fourth was the Army Research Institute (ARI), which he enlisted to help "[identify] good soldiers who could be good recruiters if they just got through the school system and applied themselves" (Thurman, 1992, p. 212).[47]

When Thurman was promoted to lieutenant general and returned to Washington in 1981 to take the position of Deputy Chief of Staff for Personnel (DCSPER) on the Army staff, he asked ARI, an organization that mainly employed psychologists, to create an economic analysis cell that would support him directly. This cell became part of Joyce Shields' Manpower and Personnel Research Laboratory. Curtis Gilroy, an economist, was brought in from outside the military community to head the group. When Shields left ARI, Gilroy formally reported to the ARI Commander, but in fact, worked directly for the DCSPER and the Commander, USAREC. He and his group continued working directly for Thurman after he got his fourth star and took over the Army's Training and Doctrine Command (TRADOC) and later when he was the Army Vice Chief Staff. Gilroy also directly supported a long line of Thurman protégées who

---

[45] *Authors Note:* I was Undersecretary of the Army when the slogan was changed. To this day, I think the Army made a big mistake changing slogans. I still do not understand what "An Army of One" means. I have been told, however, that it is very popular and that changing slogans has had positive results on Army recruiting camaraderie.

[46] The group he set up was formally commissioned as the Office of Economic and Manpower Research (OEMA) and is still operating at West Point. Thurman recounts how he "established . . . a cell at West Point to review demographic research data to act as a counter-weight to RAND. RAND at that time was the Daddy Rabbit in all matters pertaining to demographic research" (Thurman, 1992, p. 200).

Author's Note: In 1984, as the Army Vice Chief of Staff, Max Thurman selected RAND to host the Arroyo Center, the Army's federally funded research and development center for studies and analysis. I was the first deputy director of the center at RAND. I had previously worked with Thurman when he commanded the Recruiting Command and I was the Director of Selective Service.

[47] In his oral history, Thurman singled out Joyce Shields and the ARI study on recruiting and retention practices as being a "tremendous assist" (Thurman, 1992, p. 212).

succeeded Thurman as the Army's DCSPER—lieutenant generals Elton, Ono, Carney, Reno, and Stroup—until 1992, when Gilroy left and ARI dissolved the group.[48]

One of the earliest products from Gilroy's group was a regular forecast of high-quality Army enlistments. Thurman thought this was useful to provide early warning of recruiting difficulties.[49] Typical of Thurman, he compared Gilroy's forecasts with those from OEMA to see which would come closest. It was a game to him and one way to foster friendly competition between the two analytic groups.

While Thurman would be the first to credit the increasing pay levels and educational bonuses for selling the Army, the period is most noted for his leadership. There were no "school solutions" before Max Thurman. He was the school. He wrote the book and delivered the lessons for the Army and all to see. For generations to come, students of the all-volunteer force would note the remarkable change in Army recruiting during his tenure as commander of the Army Recruiting Command by formally accounting for the "Thurman Effect."[50]

In 1983, with the all-volunteer force in relatively good health, Thurman reflected on his time as recruiting command boss. He addressed the commemorative tenth anniversary conference on the all-volunteer force held at the U.S. Naval Academy:

> From the depths of the FY1977–FY1979 period, there was no way to go but up. The . . . volunteer army began in 1980. We had seen that lapsed pay comparability cost us quality new recruits and continued to drive mid-career NCOs out. It was time to regain comparability. . . . The 11.1 percent pay increase in 1981 and the 14.3 percent pay increase in 1982 gave a big boost towards that goal. Retention increased across the board, but most noticeably among the best of our Soldiers. We saw that education incentives drew smart, college-bound or college-capable soldiers. . . .
>
> We saw that our recruiters were struggling, unaided by knowledge of the marketplace and by the influence of advertising. . . . We assigned recruiters missions by education level and test category. Our recruiters rose to the occasion. They knew their mission, and it was not to fill quotas. It was to recruit high-quality soldiers. (Thurman, 1986, p. 271)

---

[48] *Author's Note:* During the decade it was in existence, the ARI group published eight articles on Army military manpower in refereed journals, as well as numerous book chapters and technical reports. Giloy edited two important book on Army manpower: Gilroy (1986) and Gilroy et al. (1991). After leaving ARI, Gilroy headed the Office of Special Projects for the Assistant Secretary, and later Under Secretary, for Personnel and Readiness. In 2003, he succeeded Steve Sellman as the Director of Accessions Policy. This is the job Harold Wool, Gus Lee, Al Martin, and Tom Sicilia had held. For almost 40 years, this has been *the* central job in the successful evolution of the all-volunteer force.

[49] An early version of that model appears as a short paper in the *American Economic Review* (Dale and Gilroy, 1985). It rebutted an article that took a naïve view of forecasting enlistment supply.

[50] Gilroy recalls trying to describe the "Thurman Effect" using

> an enlistment equation showing the importance of Thurman's leadership during the time he was at USAREC (Dale and Gilroy, 1984). When I briefed this to Thurman, he quickly told me in a firm voice that he was not into self-aggrandizement—then he thought a few seconds, squinted his eyes and said, "But I like it!" We never briefed it again, though. (Gilroy, 2004)

A decade later, at the 20th anniversary conference, Thurman catalogued 13 major actions that he believed had turned the Army's 1979 recruiting failure into a success story in the 1980s (Thurman, 1996, p. 59). As he saw it, there were "nine internal management changes" and "four that required action by Congress." The thirteen changes are recorded in Table 11.1.

The fact that so many of these "actions" had, in Thurman's judgment, "turned the Army's 1979 recruiting failure into a success" reflects how far the all-volunteer force had come from the days of the Gates Commission. While improved compensation was part of the external changes that Congress made and had been the focus of the Gates Commission, such changes were not, by themselves, sufficient to ensure a voluntary military—or as Thurman would call it, a *recruited* armed force (Thurman, 1996, p. 53). More than a decade after he left the Army Recruiting Command and after leading the troops he had recruited as the U.S. commander of Operation Just Cause (the invasion of Panama), Thurman argued that the "Army recruiting turnaround was a leadership and managerial metamorphosis" (Thurman, 1996, p. 59).

Quality and the Misnormed Armed Services Vocational Aptitude Battery

In 1979, the quality of new enlistees was one of the few bright spots to which proponents of the all-volunteer force could point. Whether it was in testimony or reports to Congress, administration officials touted the rising quality of volunteers—quality that these officials saw largely in terms of the ability of the services to attract volunteers who scored in the upper mental categories. In 1979 Pirie told Congress that the number of recruits in category IV had decreased "from a pre-Vietnam level of 15 percent and a high of 25 percent in FY 1968 to about 5 percent in FY 1977 and FY 1978" (Pirie, 1979f, p. 8). The claims were repeated in the benchmark report, *America's Volunteers,* but with what would turn out to be a prophetic caveat that "the Army had about 45 percent of recruits in mental category IIIB while the normal military eligible population has only about 32 percent in this group" (Nelson, G., 1978b, pp. 25–26). Senator Nunn, however, was not convinced and repeatedly challenged administration witnesses, citing discussions he had with senior enlisted leaders that questioned the quality of those entering the military. For example, Nunn argued that another reason that petty officers and sergeants were becoming discouraged was "the quality of the personnel they are being called on to train and work with. That quality, according to everybody who is out there in the field, is deteriorating very, very rapidly" (Nunn, 1980a, p. 9).

On March 10, 1980, Pirie, together with his principal deputy, Richard Danzig, and accessions policy chief, Al Martin, went before Nunn's Manpower and Personnel Subcommittee to tell the senator that he had been right all along. Quality had not increased; in fact, it had decreased. The problem, they explained, had been with the

Table 11.1
Thurman's 13 Major Actions That Turned Recruiting Failure into a Success Story

Major Action	Discussion
Internal	
1. Establishing "quality goals" for recruiting	Standards were raised to attract quality recruits, keeping in mind that it is easy to lower standards and even easier to achieve mediocrity if you set your sights on it. If leadership does not set standards, subordinates will, and the standards set may not be congruent with leadership's desires.
2. Inventing the "mission box"— a simple device carried by each recruiter to identify whom, in terms of quality and numbers, to recruit each month	The goal was to concentrate on quality, not quantity; no credit was given for more recruits unless the recruiter brought on the designated high school graduate with above-average aptitude
3. Establishing the "mission adjudication" —face-to-face meetings between the recruiting chief and each of his 57 battalion commanders every three months to identify the quality and numbers to be recruited	This technique carried down to the recruiter level and promoted congruence of goals, while feedback improved understanding, at all levels, of the complexity of recruiting on the street.
4. Assigning a "quality recruiting force"	Rather than depending on professional recruiters, who sometimes forgot the arduousness of field service, the Army selected the very best soldiers as recruiters and provided them substantial training.
5. Developing a "research program"	This involved the Army's advertising agency, the RAND Corporation, the DoD, the U.S. Military Academy at West Point, and the Army Research Institute and led to a normative approach. Understanding the market is crucial to business success.
6. Instituting the "Be All You Can Be" campaign	The Army was sending a very positive message by telling prospective recruits that the Army was a place where they could grow and achieve.
7. Curing the "NCO shortage" of 1979	This shortage had exacerbated the recruiting problem and denuded the Army of leadership.
8. Putting in place a "training revolution" in the U.S. Army	Soldiers join the Army to soldier. So, providing rigorous and demanding training instilled pride, improved retention, and took the pressure off the recruiting force.
9. Building a sophisticated "information system" for job assignment that rivaled airline reservation systems	This system could forecast requirements a year in advance; inventory vacancies "sold" by AFQT category, gender, and age; match applicant talents with residual needs; and allowed the recruiter to show the applicant, via video, the top 15 positions for which he or she was most suited.
External	
1. Passage of the Nunn-Warner bill	The bill thrust temporary pay equality on DoD. Together with the Reagan pay increases two years later, this led to a total pay increase of 25.5 percent.
2. Recruiting resources	Funds provided by a sympathetic Congress.
3. College funds	Allowed the Army to attract recruits that were of college caliber but who needed money to attend college. A very important and positive program.
4. GI Bill	Championed by Congressman Sonny Montgomery over the objections of OSD and OMB; the new GI Bill became law in 1984.

new ASVAB introduced in 1976.[51] The test had not been properly "normed"—a process in which a test's raw score is transformed into a score that could be compared to a representative sample of young Americans. The "misnorming" allowed large numbers of unqualified, non–high school graduates to enter the services. Pirie, Dazing, and Martin were now on the hot seat, and Nunn was going to make it even hotter before he would let them go.

Nunn, with a tone of vindication in his words, started the hearing:

> It has been very difficult to reconcile statements by the administration about continuing high quality of the volunteer force with the difficulties expressed by supervisors in the field about personnel who could not perform the jobs they were given. . . . It now appears that reconciliation is possible. . . . [T]he reported mental test scores of recruits at the lower ability levels have, in fact, been inflated and that as many as 28 percent of DoD accessions may be in the category IV mental group instead of the 5 percent previously reported. . . . For fiscal year 1978, we have been told that only 11 percent of the Army recruits fell into this category. Now it turns out that as many as 40 percent of the Army recruits may be in this low mental group. (Nunn, 1980b, pp. 1,286–1,287)

It was now Pirie's turn. In a prepared statement and then under questioning by Senator Nunn, Pirie laid out the story.[52] He described how, in April 1978, the Center for Naval Analyses brought to his attention a study by Dr. William Sims that "suggested that the [ASVAB] test was, in fact, misnormed, but in a highly tentative way" (Pirie and Danzig, 1980, p. 1,306). Pirie went on to explain:

> Because the data was uncertain and collected for purposes other than norming, Dr. [William] Sims [of the Center for Naval Analyses, CNA] was asked by my office, on the advice of the working group charged with the development of these tests to replicate more systematically his study. Dr. Sims did and that yielded a second study. . . . The two studies were noticeably at variance. Why was it that in his first study there is one set of results and in the second the more severe of those results? One of the difficulties was that he was testing only Marine recruits after enlistment. In other words, people we had already accepted and that was a source of considerable concern to us. Since the norming error appeared to be mostly in the lower mental categories, to the extent that the Marines had already screened out many lower ability applicants. Dr. Sims was working, in both his efforts, with a less than fully complete database.
>
> When the preliminary findings of the second CNA study came in, my office asked the Army Research Institute [ARI] to do a third study on behalf of the ASVAB

---

[51] A very readable history of the misnorming can be found in Laurence and Ramsberger (1991).

[52] Pirie's statement was not printed in the subcommittee's hearing records. The transcript noted that the statement "is retained in the files of the committee." (Nunn, 1980b, p. 1,288) It was, however, part of the Appropriations Committee's hearings on April 2, 1980 (Pirie, 1980g) and was included as an attachment to a memorandum to the Secretary of Defense on March 28, 1980 (Pirie, 1980f). Pirie also summarized "what we are doing" for the secretary in another attachment to the March 28, 1980, memorandum.

Steering Committee which would consider DoD applicants as a whole, not just Marine recruits. . . . That study was done, and it is the receipt of the first information from that study that has motivated us to share our concerns with you.

One of the reasons I am inclined to put more faith in that study than I might otherwise is that its preliminary results fell between the two studies done by Dr. Sims. (Pirie and Danzig, 1980, pp. 1,306–1,307)

Pirie and his team tried to explain to Senator Nunn what this all meant. Richard Danzig, Pirie's principal deputy, told Nunn that "for all recruits of all services in fiscal year 1978 we found that 29 percent of [recruits] . . . fell into mental category IV or below" (Pirie and Danzig, 1980, p. 1,307). Nunn pressed for the Army figures. Pirie told him the number was 41 percent. Nunn asked about the "originally reported category IV's in 1978" (Pirie and Danzig, 1980, p. 1,312). Al Martin, Pirie's director of accession policy, responded: "Originally category IV in 1978 was 12 percent for males. So in 1978 it is 12 to 41 percent, in 1979 it is 11 to 45, which we are using to give you a perspective on the degree of the problem" (Pirie and Danzig, 1980, p. 1,312). Pirie went on to admit that these numbers were worse than the benchmark pre–all-volunteer force draft-era numbers from 1964. In that year, only 19.9 percent of Army accessions were category IV. Nunn noted that, since 1964 and under the all-volunteer force, the Army had seen an increase of about 50 percent in the lower categories (III and IV) and had a 50-percent reduction, from 34 percent to 16 percent, in the higher categories (I and II). He summed up the situation this way:

> If this information holds up, that is an astounding change in the quality of the enlisted force in the U.S. Army, is it not? I mean you are talking about very significant deterioration in [the] quality of the U.S. Army. (Nunn, 1980b, p. 1,313)

Pirie could only respond, "the accession statistics speak for themselves. These shifts . . . are something about which we need to be profoundly concerned" (Pirie and Danzig, 1980, p. 1,313). Within a week, GAO, the investigative arm of Congress, had a full inquiry under way. Martin turned over all the ASVAB Working Group Meeting minutes and told Pirie the initial meeting with GAO had been "candid and constructive. . . . However, there was a certain GAO aura that the norming problem was a conspiracy on the part of the ASVAB Working Group to ensure the viability of the AVF" (Martin, 1980a).[53]

Not only had Pirie commissioned a DoD-wide study from ARI, he had also contracted with the Educational Testing Service (ETS) to administer the AFQT portion of the ASVAB to a sample of high school students from schools where it could reasonably be expected the students had not been coached to determine the extent to which these

---

[53] Danzig had asked the working group to prepare a comprehensive history of the development and fielding of the ASVAB from 1974 to 1980. On March 10, the day he and Pirie testified before Senator Nunn's Manpower and Personnel Subcommittee, "current and past members of the ASVAB Working Group" presented their report (ASVAB Working Group, 1980).

results are confounded by test compromise[54] By June 1980, several months after Pirie had first raised the issue with Congress, the ETS study confirmed the results of the study Bill Sims had previously done. The problem, however, was that all three studies "differed significantly in their suggestion of a new 'correct' score" (Laurence and Ramsberger, 1991, p. 76). An outside group of experts, dubbed the "three wise men" confirmed "that the current norms are too easy and are inflating the scores of individuals in the lower AFQT categories" (Martin, 1980d). They noted, however, that there was

> no criterion for selecting one of the four calibration tables (the operational table and plus the ones suggested by the three studies [CNA, ARI and ETS]) . . . as being clearly best for all purposes. Any recommendation must be somewhat tenuous because the tests are not parallel and therefore a unique calibration cannot be expected. . . . For practical purposes, there would be little difference in a choice between the CNA and ARI conversion tables for the score regions defining the boundaries of Category IV. . . .
>
> We do not recommend using the ETS results . . . because the population on which the ETS results are based differs from the population of applicants to the Services. (Jaeger et al., 1980, p. 18)

In their final analysis they found

> the ARI calibration table . . . to be more defensible than any of the other alternatives. In the future, the analytic procedures used for test calibration should be . . . routinely conducted prior to using calibration results operationally. (Jaeger et al., 1980, p. 41)

Ultimately, a new, properly calibrated test was introduced on October 1, 1980, and "the new norms for [the old] ASVAB 6/7 were used only retrospectively to correct the inflated scores" (Laurence and Ramsberger, 1991, p. 76). But herein lies a tale, because the idea of *correcting inflated scores* became a major controversy within the Pentagon.

The misnorming had caused Pirie to focus on more than just the calibration of the raw ASVAB data. As he and Danzig got into the details of testing, they found to their surprise that the reference population was not the male youth population that the services were trying to recruit but the individuals who had served in the armed forces during World War II.[55] Pirie ordered that a new reference population be constructed. In summer and fall 1980, DoD "subsidized the testing of a nationally representative

---

[54] The ETS testing started on January 21, 1980 (Maier, 1980).

[55] Pirie noted,

> There have been significant changes in the various . . . tests that have been in use since 1951. These changes involve test content, motivation of the population being tested, and calibration to previous forms of the test. Each time the Services have developed a new form of the . . . test, they have tried to maintain the capability to relate an individual's score to that WW II reference population. But our ability to track back to the World War II population has suffered from these changes. (Pirie, 1980g, p. 7)

sample of almost 12,000 youths, ages 16 through 23, with the ASVAB" (Laurence and Ramsberger, 1991, p. 82). This sample became part of the Department of Labor's National Longitudinal Survey of Youth Labor Force Behavior and resulted in the *Profile of American Youth* report.[56] As a result of the misnorming, and for the first time since World War II, when DoD talked about "recruit quality [it] could be described relative to today's youth population" (Laurence and Ramsberger, 1991, p. 82).

Pirie also focused on the fact that the old test had been "validated against training success, not job performance" (Laurence and Ramsberger, 1991, p. 83). He noted that, between January 1976, when the new test was put in place, and September 1980, thousands of youths who would normally not have been eligible to enter the military were recruited. He ordered a research program to "determine how those individuals who would have been ineligible for enlistment were in fact performing their military duties" (Pirie, 1980p, p. 9).[57] Pirie's concerns should be noted against the fact that, during World War II, a large number of category IV and V men were inducted. The category IV soldiers were "expected to cope with . . . basic and some advanced training." Category Vs (or class Vs, as they were referred to then) were considered "definitely handicapped men," who would receive only basic training. In some branches of the Army (i.e., armored force and infantry), over 40 percent of the men assigned were from class IV or V. The branch with the largest proportion of personnel in the classes IV and V was combat engineers, where 50.5 percent came from these lowest classes (Creveld, 1982, pp. 70–71).

The practical problems that the misnorming caused were evident when Nunn proposed that the proportion of recruits scoring in category IV not exceed 20 percent. Martin noted the following:

> Renorming of the AFQT is expected to result in the determination that nearly half of the Army's FY 1980 NPS [non–prior service] male enlistees are in test Category IV.
>
> It is estimated that the 20% Category IV limitation in 1981 would result in denial of enlistment to 15,600 male high school diploma graduates who would have been able to enter under the current norms. In addition, it could also result in an overall recruiting or strength shortfall of 27,000. (Martin, 1980c, p. 1)

Moreover, in a response to an inquiry by Senator Levin, Pirie pointed out there was no historical basis for the proposed 20-percent reduction:

> What is the "proper" percentage of Category IVs for a Service to take? No reasonably clear answer to this question has yet emerged. The Selective Service Laws

---

[56] The official *Profile of American Youth* report (Korb, 1982) was published by Pirie's successor as Assistant Secretary of Defense Lawrence Korb in March 1982. In addition Accessions Policy compiled an annotated bibliography of related publications (Waters, 1982). A number of papers were also presented at a special Symposium at the Ninetieth Annual Convention of the American Psychological Association (Directorate of Accession Policy, 1982).

[57] Pirie laid out his plan for validating enlistment standards by using job performance in a memorandum to secretaries of the military department on July 7, 1980 (Pirie, 1980k).

provide some insight into this question by their provision that *no* Category IV personnel shall be refused in the event of War. The World War II force provides a measuring stick where 30% of all personnel—including officers—were at the Category IV level or below. The Korean War provides a measure, when some 44% of Army accessions (in 1952) were at the Category IV level. The Viet Nam War period provides another measure, when some 19 to 28% of Army accessions (an average of 24.4%) were in Category IV.

In sum, our experience suggests no basis for a 20% cap on Category IV enlisted accession to any Service. (Pirie, 1980j, emphasis in the original)

On August 13, 1980, the ASVAB Steering Committee, looking toward the fall and the introduction of the new ASVAB, recommended that individuals previously tested on the misnormed tests have their test scores renormed. If the renormed score was not high enough to qualify "they would be offered the opportunity to retest with the new normed test. Only DEP [Delayed Entry Pool] members will be enlisted, after introduction of the new test, with misnormed scores" (Martin, 1980f). Potentially, thousands of people recruited by the services would no longer be eligible, making recruiting that much harder.

Each of the services responded differently. The Air Force maintained its recruiting standards even as it recognized that it would have to work even harder to meet its goals. The Air Force recruiting chief's concern was that recruiters in urban areas would be the hardest hit (Martin, 1980h). By contrast, the response of the Chief of Naval Operations approved "a lowering of Navy's enlistment standards to occur with the introduction of the new ASVAB" (Martin, 1980g). The "character of Navy accessions" would largely go unchanged. The service would bring in about 95 percent of recruits who had been part of the misnormed, now category IV, population.

Thurman described the misnorming as a "calamity." Years later, he noted that they had ended the year "thinking we were in good shape," when in reality, they

took more non–high school graduates than we would have liked; 54 percent. . . . We thought that we had accessed only 28 percent mental category IV. We find out later, we accessed 54 percent mental Category IV. (Thurman, 1992, pp. 213–214).

The response of the Army, and General Max Thurman, was to continue to push for high-quality (category I, II, and IIIA) high school graduates. He wanted no part of the unqualified population. He had already started to "twist the volume, which is what the accession mission was all about, into a quality mission" (Thurman, 1992). Under Thurman, there would be no "bottom fishing."[58] From now on, recruiters would carry

---

[58] *Bottom fishing* was Thurman's expression for what the Recruiting Command was doing before he got there: "They wanted to recruit down to 17-year-olds who were non–high school graduates. They kept lowering their sights in order to increase what they thought was a volume operation" (Thurman, 1980b, p. 181).

a "mission card" (Thurman, 1980b, p. 219), a card that told them to concentrate on upper mental category, high school graduates.[59]

At the end of December 1980, just weeks before leaving office, Pirie formally presented his report to Congress, entitled *Implementation of the New Armed Services Vocational Aptitude Battery and Actions to Improve the Enlistment Standards Process* (Pirie, 1980p). He told Congress of the use of a new ASVAB, the creation of an independent board to oversee test development, and the first reports on the results of the "natural experiment" caused by the misnorming. These first results, however, were related to things that could readily be measured, such as attrition, time to promotions, and graduation from training. It would take another five years before the research community could talk about the relationship between test scores and actual job performance.

Rescoring the Misnormed Records

One of the more bizarre incidents surrounding the misnorming fiasco was the internal fight in the Pentagon between Pirie and Secretary of the Army Clifford Alexander. Alexander was the first black Secretary of the Army and the highest ranking black at the Pentagon. He saw the misnorming issue as an attack on the advances blacks had made in the Army. Despite the information coming out of Pirie's office throughout the spring, the Army continued to brief Congress that, in FY 1980, "less than 10 percent of Army recruits scored in Category IV on the Armed Forces Qualifying Test" (Pirie, 1980h). Pirie tried to explain to Senator Stennis that the Army's statement was "accurate, given the current test scoring system, and restated" and that he was uncertain about "the validity of the test scoring system" (Pirie, 1980h). Pirie believed the real number was about 45 percent. Secretary Alexander did not agree, as Pirie told Brown, because he was "concerned that Army recruits are being maligned through our public discussion of test scoring problems." Brown apparently was sympathetic to both positions, and told Pirie, "they probably are [maligned], but that doesn't invalidate the statement" that 45 percent of Army recruits were category IVs (Pirie, 1980h).

In April 1980, Pirie's office signed a contract with ETS to administer the current version of the ASVAB in high schools to calibrate the test definitively for rescoring the records of those already in the military (Martin, 1980b), a task the Army bitterly resisted. Danzig received periodic updates from his staff.[60] In late June, Alexander launched an inquiry into the ASVAB situation, which was conducted by the Army's general counsel,

---

[59] Thurman later wrote:

> We saw that our recruiters were struggling, unaided by knowledge of the marketplace and by the influence of advertising. It was time to learn more about the people who we wanted to serve in the Army. We used academia to help us focus on smart, college-bound youth. We assigned recruiters missions by education level and test category. Our recruiters rose to the occasion. They knew their mission, and it was not to fill quotas. It was to recruit high-quality soldiers. (Thurman, 1986, p. 271)

[60] Danzig was given a comprehensive report on June 4. Pat Larro prepared notes and "talking points" (Larro, 1980).

Sara Lister.[61] In a meeting with ETS on July 2, 1980, she wanted to know "(a) is there really a norming problem; (b) how is AFQT presently used; and (c) how should AFQT be used in the future?" (Martin, 1980e). When Pirie told the services that he wanted them to develop a research program "to establish standards for enlistment and assignment to training that are validated against eventual job performance" (Pirie, 1980k), Alexander reacted in what was a very direct memorandum for the usually genteel Pentagon. He told Pirie that he, "advised by the Chief of Staff," was "in the best position to establish standards for enlistment into the Army." In addition, if Pirie, "on reflection," did not change his position, "the Chief of Staff of the Army and I will be happy to discuss this matter with Secretary Brown" (Alexander, 1980). Deputy Secretary Claytor tried to settle things down, but had to admit to Brown, that, after

> unsuccessfully attempting to get Robin [Pirie] and Cliff [Alexander] to agree on an appropriate program, I have tried my own hand at a memo to Service Secretaries, setting out a summary of our policy and program with respect to ASVAB revisions and development of enlistment standards. (Claytor, 1980, cover memo)

The problem, as he explained to Brown, was that Alexander does not agree that standards should be subject to review and approval or revision by the Secretary of Defense:

> He thinks they should be set exclusively by Service Secretaries and Chiefs. . . . He opposes having any validation projects initiated by OSD . . . [and] any rescoring of test scores . . . [he] wants to eliminate altogether the five mental categories resulting from AFQT scores. (Claytor, 1980, cover memo)

Brown agreed with Claytor's assessment that the "primary responsibility for determining standards for enlistment and assignment is in the Military Services, subject to review and approval or revision of the Secretary of Defense" (Claytor, 1980, p. 1 of draft). He sided with Claytor on the issue of rescoring—in Claytor's words, "rescoring is required if we are to maintain any credibility of decent relationship with the SASC [Senate Armed Services Committee]" (Claytor, 1980, p. 2 of draft)—but told Claytor, "I'd do as little as possible" (Claytor, 1980, p. 1). On the issue of OSD's research program, Brown thought, "OSD should do some because relating these cross-service issues is important" (Claytor, 1980, p. 1). On the final issue of eliminating the AFQT categories, Claytor thought such a move "would be very unwise . . . and would be interpreted by Committee and staff people as an attempted cover-up," (Claytor, 1980, p. 1) and Brown did not disagree. Clayton's draft, appropriately signed by Pirie, was sent to the Service Assistant Secretaries on September 11, 1980 (Pirie, 1980m).

---

[61] *Author's Note:* Sara Lister and I had been colleagues when I was Principal Deputy Assistant Secretary of the Navy for Manpower and Reserve Affairs and she had been the Navy's principal deputy general counsel. In 1994, we would again have parallel positions. She served in the Clinton administration as the Assistant Secretary of the Army for Manpower and Reserve Affairs, and I held the same position in the Navy.

Compensation

By late 1979, there was a growing realization in the Pentagon and in Congress that the level of military compensation was inadequate to attract and retain personnel to staff the services with the numbers and quality of people they needed. The lone holdout was the White House, which was more concerned about double-digit inflation and holding down the overall size of the federal budget.[62] During 1980, the split within the administration, particularly between the President and his military leadership, became more evident. The Joint Chiefs let it be known that they supported the Nunn-Warner Amendment. The civilian leaders at the Pentagon were caught in the middle. Privately, they supported the chiefs and the efforts to increase pay.

All through 1979—in memorandum after memorandum through January, June, and November—the Joint Chiefs told Secretary Brown of their concern "about the adverse impact of inflation and pay caps on the way active duty personnel view the desirability of a military career" (Allen, 1979). In June, they suggested that the civilian leadership was derelict in using the Fourth QRMC to "prepare legislative proposals that resulted from the review of the recommendations of the President's Commission on Military Compensation" (Allen, 1979), rather than convene a review of the adequacy of active-duty compensation.

In July, noting that the service chiefs had "asked in the strongest terms for a comprehensive review of overall pay adequacy and comparability," Pirie told Brown that he was "inclined to expand a planned study . . . to include the broader questions of the overall adequacy of compensation levels and their relation to appropriate standards of comparability" (Pirie, 1979h). Pirie clearly knew he was skating on thin ice when he told Brown that the probable "result would be to sharpen the case for substantial FY81

---

[62] John White, President Carter's Deputy Director at the Office of Management and Budget, later called this a "major policy decision . . . [a] policy error." In a review prepared for the 30th anniversary of the all-volunteer force, he wrote the following:

> The policy error was the result of President Carter's strategy for fighting inflation, which included limiting all federal pay raises, including that for the military. I have a clear recollection of the anti-inflation policy debate, having been an active participant as the Deputy Director of the Office of Management and Budget. First, the President felt very strongly about his anti-inflation stance and was not open to considering major exceptions. Second, those of us involved in the AVF transition did not appreciate the magnitude and rapidity of the damage that would be done. The force was already in a much more fragile state than we realized because of the general difficulties in making the transition from a draft compounded by the mis-norming errors. . . .

> I believe that the country would have returned to conscription if the recruiting difficulties had persisted into the 1980s. Fortunately, the commitment and professionalism of those responsible for managing the AVF saved it. The central issue was always the Army's ability to attract recruits of the numbers and quality required. Success there meant success everywhere. That success was engineered by General Maxwell Thurman at the Army recruiting command during the late 1970s and early 1980s. If the AVF has a hero in its past, the hero was Max.

> The Congress also played a key role in solving the problem; as it has done so often in support of the AVF. It increased the administration's pay raise recommendations in 1980 and provided an added raise in 1981. The percentage increases for those years were 11.7 and 14.3 percent, respectively. (White, 2003, p. 3)

pay raises" and noted that he was afraid that this would "increase the FY81 pressure on you" (Pirie, 1979h, p. 1). Pirie then asked, "Does this disturb you?" Brown's answer, "I think we should go ahead with such a study despite the increased . . . pressure it would bring" (Pirie, 1979h, marginal note).[63] Pirie then commissioned a study on the adequacy of military compensation.[64] In October, when Pirie met with reporters to review the final numbers for fiscal year 1979, his study was complete and out for review. Pirie told reporters that, for fiscal 1979, "recruiting results show the Services achieving 93 percent of their total recruiting objectives." He told them his office had a study under way

> looking at the general level of military pay with respect to a number of criteria— cost of living, comparable pay for people in comparable professions at comparable periods in their lives and things of that kind. (Pirie, 1979p, p. 7)

He told the press that he expected the results of this study to "play some role in the formulation of the fiscal '81 budget." He was evasive, however, when asked if he had assurances from OMB or the White House that they would be sympathetic to DoD's proposal for a pay increase. All he would say is that "we have had discussions with other parts of the Administration" (Pirie, 1979p, pp. 10, 13). In fact, that fall, the Pentagon sent to the White House a proposal to spend an additional $650 million in FY 1981 to fund a larger housing allowance program and provide extra pay to enlisted personnel and junior officers.[65] The *Washington Post* reported that, "as with the 7 percent general pay increase, the chiefs . . . [concluded] that the $650 million package is a good start but not enough" (Wilson, 1979). It might have been a good start if the White House had agreed to support the Pentagon's request, but it did not.

As 1979 flowed into 1980, the focus of actions to improve compensation shifted from the Pentagon to Congress. On the first day of business for the new year—January 22, 1980—Senator Nunn opened hearings before his Manpower and Personnel Subcommittee on the growing problem with military compensation. For years, Nunn had complained about manpower costs and the growing share of the defense budget that

---

[63] Pirie remembered that Brown had initially been skeptical and had asked for a special study on military pay and comparable civilian wages. With the study in hand, Pirie asked for $850 million, which the DoD Comptroller reduced to $650 million. Brown forwarded this request to the White House. OMB opposed Brown's request, despite the fact that Deputy Director John White had previously served in DoD. The administration's focus at the time was on "fighting inflation, which included limiting all federal pay raises, including that for the military" (White, 2003). When President Carter got the memorandum asking for the funds, he wrote in its margin, "too costly." The memorandum, together with Carter's comments, was eventually leaked to the press and proved to be very embarrassing to the White House. After it broke in the press, Brigadier General Colin Powell, one of Secretary Brown's military aides, showed Pirie the memorandum and the President's comments but was under orders not to leave a copy with him (Pirie, 2004).

[64] This study was later used by Senators Nunn and Warner as the basis for the pay rise they sponsored (Pirie, 2004).

[65] On November 9, 1979, Pirie sent Secretary Brown the *Study of Military Pay Adequacy*. It documented "an apparent lag in overall military compensation since 1972 of . . . 20 percent" (Pirie, 1979q). Four days later, he sent a copy of the study to John White at OMB that included the $650 million compensation proposal (Pirie, 1979r).

was going to people. He now made it clear that he did not begrudge service members' higher pay, but thought that, if there was to be an all-volunteer force, it should be paid for with additional funds, not by transferring funds from nonpersonnel accounts, an amount he placed at $100 billion.[66] He opened the hearings by stating that, despite "large increases in manpower costs, the military faces severe problems in the recruiting and retention of sufficient numbers and quality of active duty people and reserve personnel" (Nunn, 1980a, p. 1).

Senator Bill Cohen (R-Maine), who 16 years later would himself become Secretary of Defense, added that "much more can be done to fulfill our obligation to our men and women" and complained that OMB "has too much authority and the military leadership too little when it comes to personnel and compensation policies" (Cohen, 1980, p. 6).

Before Nunn's subcommittee were two competing amendments that focused the debate on the level and structure that proposed changes in military compensation might take.[67] An amendment proposed by Senator William Armstrong (R-Colorado) would increase military pay across the board 3.41 percent in addition to the 7 percent proposed by the administration, authorize a variable housing allowance, and provide additional funding for reimbursement of permanent change of station moving expenses. An alternative proposed by Senator Warner targeted the career force. He recognized the problems the services were having with recruiting but thought it best if it were left to a more-general discussion of the all-volunteer force. Warner explained he had omitted from the "bill additional pay for the first three enlisted grades . . . to take out of the context of this hearing . . . the greater problem of how we deal with the All-Volunteer Force" (Warner, 1980, p. 10).

The hearings were ostensibly to get the administration's position on the two amendments that the full Senate would be voting on in early February. As Senator Warner put it, he wanted to ask the administration what guidance it wished "to give this committee in changing the present proposal before the Senate" (Warner, 1980, p. 10). What the hearings also did was build a record that exposed the fissure within the administration and undermined the White House position. The DoD witnesses were Assistant Secretary Robin Pirie and the services' personnel chiefs.

The hearings were very uncomfortable for Pirie. For months, he had led the charge for better pay within the administration. At the request of the Joint Chiefs and with Secretary Brown's concurrence he had commissioned a study on the adequacy of

---

[66] For years, Charles Moskos had been a frequent witness before Nunn's subcommittee. In 1978, Moskos had complained to Nunn that "large [l]arge raises in military pay were the principal rationale to induce persons to join the All-Volunteer Force, " but that "high pay motivates less qualified youths," such as high school dropouts and those with poor grades. He further stated that using "salary incentives as the primary motivating force to join and remain in the military can also lead to grave morale problems." See Moskos in Nunn (1978, p. 42). Now, in 1980, Nunn was at the forefront of moves to increase military pay to save the all-volunteer force.

[67] The two were technically amendments to the personnel management bill already before the Senate (Halloran, 1980).

military compensation and raised popular expectations through a number of interviews that were reported in the press. Unfortunately, he had lost the battle for higher pay within the administration. Now he had to defend an administration position that he privately disagreed with. For him, the hearings were a trap, one that he barely escaped with his political life.

He started his testimony by trying to limit his response to the issue of the Armstrong amendment:

> While more [pay] is always better in at least some sense, and while increases in military pay are of particular interest to me, I must tell you that the Department of Defense opposes the additional expenditure promised in the Armstrong amendment. We do so for two reasons:
>
> First, the amendment would violate the President's wage guidelines. Second, it would add some $800 million on an annual basis to the President's budget, some smaller, but still considerable amount to the fiscal year 1980 budget deficit. . . .
>
> The long-term interest of the people of the Armed Forces, and of all their fellow citizens, will be best served by a return to lower inflation levels.
>
> I have no doubt that the problems we are having with accession and retention are related in some significant measure to compensation. The manner and extent to which funds are devoted to dealing with this issue must, however, take account of a range of competing priorities. (Pirie, 1980a, p. 6)

This response was not adequate for Senator Warner. He asked which of the two bills Pirie preferred. Pirie responded that he could not "make a choice between the two bills which did not meet the criteria that I mentioned" (Pirie, 1980a, p. 10). Senator Warner pushed further. He reminded Pirie that, at his confirmation hearings, Chairman Stennis had

> put to you the question he puts to every single member of the Department of Defense who comes before this committee: "There will come a time when we as a committee will ask you for your personal opinion, irrespective of those criteria which you have to follow as a loyal supporter of the Commander in Chief and Secretary of Defense."
>
> And your answer . . . was "Yes, Mr. Chairman, I will always provide the committee with my personal opinion." (Pirie, 1980a, p. 10)

In a classic Washington move, Warner was calling in the promise. He had Pirie in the trap, and he was squeezing.

Pirie responded honestly and with a candor that could well have cost him his job:

> Recognizing, as I have said before, the broader context in which the President must make many difficult decisions in putting together his budget, my own personal perspective, narrow and limited in this case, leads me to conclude there is much merit in both of these proposals that attack the problems that we see facing us.
>
> I am, I think, on balance, more concerned about retention of the career force than I am about the admitted problems that we have with accession. I believe that

in priority order that will be my judgment. To the degree then that one bill favors that set of priorities, I would personally be inclined to accept that bill. (Pirie, 1980a, p. 10)

Warner put each of the service personnel chiefs through the same questioning. When all was said and done, the Army and the Marine Corps favored the Armstrong amendment, and the Navy and Air Force personnel chiefs indicated a preference for the Warner amendment. When the vote came before the Senate on February 4, 1980, the Nunn-Warner amendment passed by a vote of 87 to 1 (Halloran, 1980). The stage was now set for the big battle over the FY 1981 budget.

On March 10, 1980, former Secretary Melvin Laird, in an op-ed article in the *Washington Post,* noted that, "since 1972, the consumer price index had risen 75 percent, while military compensation had risen only 51 percent" (Laird, 1980). He called for a 17-percent across-the-board pay raise. In a move that signaled the White House's insistence on holding the line on pay and government costs, the next day—March 11, 1980—and against DoD recommendations, the President vetoed the Uniformed Services Health Professional Special Pay Act of 1980.[68] While the shortage of physicians had been one of the major concerns with the all-volunteer force since the original proposal by the Gates Commission, the President vetoed the doctor pay bill because it included an additional five-year total cumulative cost of $171 million.[69]

By late spring the service chiefs—the entire Joint Chiefs of Staff—were in open revolt. Using the same ploy that had trapped Pirie in January, Congressman Sam Stratton (D-New York) had pushed the chiefs for their personal opinions. One after another, they declared that the defense budget before Congress "is not big enough to meet the Soviet threat" (Wilson, 1980a).[70] Within the Pentagon, the Chiefs kept the pressure on Brown and in a memorandum the Chairman told him, "The Joint Chiefs of Staff are concerned over prospects for the Nunn-Warner Amendment, particularly in light of the position being developed with the Office of Management and Budget" (Jones, 1980). In exceptionally strong language, the chairman "requested" that he "inform the President of our deep concern in this matter which fundamentally affects the nation's defense capabilities." They told him that they stood ready "to meet with you, or the President if you should desire, to provide supporting rationale for our position" (Jones, 1980).

In a May study, the CBO found that "[t]he Administration's pay proposals for fiscal year 1981, despite pay increases, would be insufficient to meet the service needs for enlisted recruits and maintain recruit quality in 1980 and 1981" (Hale and Slackman,

---

[68] Pirie would call later this "[o]ne of the stupidest decisions ever made" (Pirie, 2004).

[69] DoD recommended that the President sign the bill. The department was concerned because the 5,600 military physicians (out of a population of 11,300) who had joined under the provisions of the Berry Plan would be eligible to leave the military that summer and would be making career decisions (Nunn, 1980b, p. 1,321).

[70] These were technically amendments to the personnel management bill already before the Senate (Halloran, 1980).

1980, p. ix). On May 15, Pirie proposed to Brown that the secretary "call John White and/or the President" and tell them he was "prepared to reprogram whatever is necessary to fund these actions after completion of the congressional appropriation process" (Pirie, 1980i). Brown agreed, and four days later the OMB Director Jim McIntyre told the President,

> Harold . . . considers the amendment so important to the military community, and to our military capability and readiness, that he is prepared to reprogram whatever is necessary to fund it after completion of the Congressional appropriation process. (McIntyre, James A. Jr., 1980)

When the Senate passed the Nunn-Warner amendment, which provided $527 million in 1980 and additional $720 million in 1981 for the military and "included several provisions proposed in . . . [the administration's] 1981 budget but also added some $500 million in new features," the White House knew the game was up.

The White House now tried to put the best face it could on a policy and political disaster. While Pirie thought it was too late for President Carter to get any credit in the upcoming election (Pirie, 2004), and White would later remember President Carter's long months of opposition to the pay raise as a "policy error" (White, 2003), McIntyre and Brown recommended to Carter that it was

> extremely valuable for you to become involved personally at appropriate times in expressing your commitment that a career in the military should be as rewarding as a career elsewhere in our society.
>
> It is important for you to emphasize that Warner/Nunn is an augmentation to, and not a substitute for, your own legislative initiative outlined in the January budget. . . . [This would] put you in a positive position rather than being seen as acquiescing to Congressional pressure. (McIntyre, James A. Jr., 1980)

On May 23, 1980, following the line suggested by McIntyre, Carter told Brown that he could now support the Warner/Nunn amendment, and stressed that it "incorporates a number of the initiatives first proposed in our January budget" (Carter, 1980a).[71] Three days later, White and Pirie were told to get on a plane and fly to Norfolk for a presidential announcement. On the decks of the aircraft carrier *Nimitz,* the President announced a new $1 billion "Fair Benefits Package" with these words:

> I'm committed to the principle that a career in the military should be as rewarding personally for those who serve as a career in any pursuit in the society I represent. We will therefore ask that Congress move without delay to appropriate compensation in addition to what's already provided. (Carter, 1980b)

In hearings the following week, Nunn grilled Pirie for details on the President's announcement (Wilson, 1980b). "Where is the money going to come from?" Nunn

---

[71] The modifications were in the area of the housing allowance (Pirie, 1980b).

pushed Pirie. Pirie could not tell him because he did not know; the "details" had not been worked out. Even the answer that DoD and OMB provided for the record was unsatisfactory. The amended fiscal year 1981 budget—the FY 1981 budget submission had already been amended by the administration four times—included only $300 million of the needed $1 billion. The insert for the record admitted that the "decision on how to finance the remaining costs in fiscal year 1981 has not been made. . . . The precise timing of the submission of detailed appropriation requests is not yet known" (Nunn, 1980c, p. 15). Senator Cohen eloquently summed up the frustration of the committee

> trying to comprehend the policy of the administration with respect to pay of military personnel is the equivalent of walking through a maze of mirrors, where you can't distinguish reality from reflection and where multiplication of reflection produces a sense of disorientation and confusion. (Cohen, 1980, p. 15)

Reality or reflection, on July 2, 1980, the Senate voted an 11.7-percent pay raise for members of the armed services, effective October 1, 1980 (Wilson, 1980c). That August, Major General Max Thurman, the head of the Army Recruiting Command, told reporters that "if Congress comes through with promised military pay raises and restores the GI bill, a quality All-Voluntary Force is definitely 'recruitable'" (Wilson, 1980d). Moreover, whether it was the passage of a pay bill by itself, even though the pay increase had not yet taken effect, or a combination of other factors, such as Thurman's taking charge of the Army's recruiting command, the services exceeded their recruiting target for September 1980. In fact, Pirie announced that all four services had "met or exceeded their FY 1980 recruiting objectives" and that each had "enlisted more recruits this year [FY 1980] than in FY 1979," to the tune of almost 52,000 more recruits. Pirie told the press that the Army had made the largest increase, "recruiting 31,000 or 22% more enlistees in FY 1980" (Pirie, 1980n). Even more importantly, retention was up.

References

Alexander, Clifford L., Jr., "Army Two–Year Enlistments," action memorandum to Secretary of Defense, Washington, D.C., September 25, 1979. G0431.pdf.

———, "Plan for Validating Enlistment Standards Against Job Performance," memorandum to Assistant Secretary of Defense (M&RA), Washington, D.C., July 15, 1980. G0443.pdf.

Allen, Lew, Jr., "Military Compensation," memorandum to Secretary of Defense Harold Brown, Washington, D.C., June 14, 1979.

Armor, David J., "Military Retirement," information memorandum to Secretary of Defense, Washington, D.C., July 27, 1986. G0981.pdf.

ASVAB Working Group, *History of the Armed Services Vocational Aptitude Battery (ASVAB) 1974–1980,* Washington, D.C.: Assistant Secretary of Defense (MRA&L), March 10, 1980. S0585.pdf.

Beard, Robin, and Jerry L. Reed, The Beard Study: An Analysis and Evaluation of the United States Army (April 1978), hearing before the Senate Armed Services Subcommittee on Manpower and Personnel, 95th Cong., 2nd Sess., Washington, D.C., U.S. Government Printing Office, June 20, 1978. S0445.pdf.

Binkin, Martin, *The Military Pay Muddle,* Washington, D.C.: Brookings Institution, 1975.

Binkin, Martin, and Shirley J. Bach, *Women and the Military,* Washington, D.C.: Brookings Institution, June 1977.

Borda, Richard J., "Testing the Effectiveness of Variable Terms of Enlistment in the Air Reserve Forces," memorandum to Assistant Secretary of Defense (M&RA), Washington, D.C., March 12, 1973. G0101.pdf.

Brehm, William K., Statement on Military Posture, before the House Armed Service Committee, hearing before the Committee on Armed Services, House of Representatives, 94th Cong., 2nd Sess., Washington, D.C., U.S. Government Printing Office, February 17, 1976. G1308.pdf.

Brown, Harold, "All Volunteer Force," memorandum to Assistant Secretary of Defense (M&RA), Washington, D.C., January 27, 1977. G0427.pdf.

———, Department of Defense Authorization for Appropriations for Fiscal Year 1979, hearing before the Committee on Armed Services: United States Senate, 95th Cong., 2nd Sess., Washington, D.C., U.S. Government Printing Office, February 7, 1978. S0451.pdf.

———, "Recommendations of the Commission on Military Compensation," memorandum to the President, Washington, D.C., December 12, 1979. G0009.pdf.

Canby, Steven L., and Ben Klotz, *The Budget Cost of a Volunteer Military,* Santa Monica, Calif.: RAND Corporation, RM-6184-PR, August 1970. S0793.pdf.

Carter, Jimmy, "Compensation Reform," memorandum to Secretary of Defense, Washington, D.C., November 30, 1978. G0008.pdf.

———, "Benefits for Members of the Armed Forces," memorandum to Secretary of Defense, Washington, D.C., May 23, 1980a. G1161.pdf.

————, *Remarks on Board the USS* Nimitz *on the Battle Group's Return to the United States May 26. 1980,* Norfolk, Va.: the President, May 26, 1980b. G1162.pdf.

Claytor, W. Graham, Jr., "Two–Year Enlistment Test," memorandum to Secretary of the Army, Washington, D.C., October 4, 1979. G0433.pdf.

————, "Unsuccessful Attempts to Get Robin and Cliff to Agree on an Appropriate Program," memorandum to Secretary of Defense, Washington, D.C., July 30, 1980. G0368.pdf.

Cocke, Karl E., William Gardner Bell, Romana M. Danysh, Detmar H. Finke, Walter G. Hermes, James E. Hewes, Jr., Vincent C. Jones, and B. C. Mossman, eds., *Department of the Army Historical Summary: Fiscal Year 1978,* Washington, D.C.: U.S. Army Center of Military History, 1980.

Cohen, William S., Military Compensation, hearing before the Subcommittee on Manpower and Personnel of the Committee on Armed Services, U.S. Senate, 96th Cong., 2nd Sess., Washington, D.C., U.S. Government Printing Office, June 2, 1980.

————, Proposed Changes to Military Compensation, hearing before the Senate Armed Services: Subcommittee on Manpower and Personnel, 96th Cong., 2nd Sess., Washington, D.C., U.S. Government Printing Office, January 22, 1980. S0447.pdf.

Cohen, William S., *Roll Call: One Year in the United States Senate,* New York: Simon and Schuster, 1981.

Comptroller General of the United States, *Additional Cost of the All-Volunteer Force,* Washington, D.C.: General Accounting Office, February 6, 1978. S0487.pdf.

Cooper, Richard V. L., Defense Manpower and the All-Volunteer Force, hearing before the Committee on the Budget: House of Representative, 95th Cong., 1st Sess., Washington, D.C., U.S. Government Printing Office, July 12, 1977a. S0491.pdf.

————, *Military Manpower and the All-Volunteer Force,* Santa Monica, Calif.: RAND Corporation, R-1450-ARPA, September 1977b. S0177.pdf.

————, Additional Cost of the All-Volunteer Force: Comment, hearing before the Committee on Armed Services: House of Representatives, 95th Cong., 2nd Sess., Washington, D.C., U.S. Government Printing Office, February 15, 1978a. S0489.pdf.

————, Hearings on Military Posture, hearing before the Committee on Armed Services: House of Representatives, 95th Cong., 2nd Sess., Washington, D.C., U.S. Government Printing Office, February 15, 1978b. S0490.pdf.

————, "The All-Volunteer Force: Five Years Later," *International Security,* Vol. 2, No. 4, Spring 1978c, pp. 101–131.

Creveld, Martin van, *Fighting Power: German and U.S. Army Performance, 1939–1945,* Vol. Number 32, Westport, Conn.: Greenwood Press, 1982.

Dale, Charles, and Curtis Gilroy, "Determinants of Enlistments: A Macroeconomics Time-Series View," *Armed Forces and Society,* Vol. 10, No. 2, Winter 1984, pp. 192–210.

————, "Enlistments in the All-Volunteer Force: Note," *American Economic Review,* June 1985, pp. 547–551. G0853.pdf.

Danzig, Richard, "Report on the All-Volunteer Force," memorandum to Secretary of Defense, Washington, D.C., December 22, 1978. G0402.pdf.

Davis, M. Thomas, *Operation Dire Straits: Here's Why the Military Is Failing to Attract the Right Recruits,* Arlington, Va.: Northrop Grumman Corporation Analytic Center, January 2000. S0804.pdf.

Directorate of Accession Policy, *The Profile of American Youth Study: Results and Implications,* Washington, D.C.: Accessions Policy Office of the Secretary of Defense, Technical Memorandum 822, September 1982.

Enke, Stephen, *Innovations for Achieving an AVAF,* Washington, D.C.: GE/TEMPO, December 15, 1971. G0338.pdf.

Gilroy, Curtis L., ed., *Army Manpower Economics,* Boulder, Colo.: Westview Press, 1986.

————, interview with Bernard Rostker, September 15, 2004.

Gilroy, Curtis L., David K. Horne, and D. Alton Smith, eds., *Military Compensation and Personnel Retention: Models and Evidence,* Washington, D.C.: U.S. Army Research Institute for the Behavioral and Social Sciences, 1991. S0595.pdf.

Ginzberg, Eli, *Manpower Research and Management in Large Organizations,* Washington, D.C.: U.S. Department of Defense, Defense Science Board, June 1971. S0145.pdf.

Haggstrom, Gus W., *The Multiple Option Recruiting Experiment: A Preliminary Report,* Santa Monica, Calif.: RAND Corporation, WD-4261-MRAL, December 1979. S0307.pdf.

Haggstrom, Gus W., Thomas J. Blaschke, Winston K. Chow, and William Lisowski, *The Multiple Option Recruiting Experiment,* Santa Monica, Calif.: RAND Corporation, R-2671-MRAL, 1981. S0673.pdf.

Hale, Robert F., Defense Manpower and the All-Volunteer Force, hearing before the Committee on the Budget: House of Representative, 95th Cong., 1st Sess., Washington, D.C., U.S. Government Printing Office, July 12, 1977. S0491.pdf.

Hale, Robert F., and Joel N. Slackman, *Costs of Manning the Active-Duty Military,* Washington, D.C.: Congressional Budget Office, U.S. Congress, May 1980. S0457.pdf.

Halloran, Richard, "Military Incentives and Bonuses of $3.2 Billion Cleared by Senate," *New York Times,* February 5, 1980, p. 16.

Hix, William M., interview with Bernard Rostker, Arlington, Va., December 10, 2002.

Hoffman, F. S., and M. R. Fiorello, *The Evaluation of the Transition to a Volunteer Force,* Santa Monica, Calif.: RAND Corporation, WN-7720-SA, December 1971. S0306.pdf.

Holm, Jeanne, *Women in the Military: An Unfinished Revolution,* rev. ed., Navato, Ca.: Presidio, 1992.

Hunter, Richard W., *Use of Women in the Military: Background Study,* Washington, D.C.: Office of the Deputy Secretary of Defense (Programs and Requirements), May 2, 1977. G1440.pdf.

Jaeger, Richard M., Robert L. Linn, and Melvin R. Novick, *A Review and Analysis of Score Calibration for the Armed Services Vocational Aptitude Battery,* Washington, D.C.: Office of the Secretary of Defense, June 1980. S0581.pdf.

Jones, David C., "Military Compensation," memorandum to Secretary of Defense, Washington, D.C., April 10, 1980.

King, William R., *Achieving America's Goals: National Service or the All-Volunteer Armed Force? A Study Prepared for Senator Sam Nunn,* Washington, D.C.: Senate Armed Service Committee, February 25, 1977. G1295.pdf.

Korb, Lawrence J., *Profile of American Youth: 1980 Nationwide Administration of the Armed Services Vocational Aptitude Battery,* Washington, D.C.: Office of the Assistant Secretary of Defense (MRA&L), March 1982. S0576.pdf.

Laird, Melvin R., "The All-Volunteer Force: It's Time for a Big Pay Raise," *Washington Post,* March 10, 1980.

Larro, Pat, "Significant Events—Week of 2 June 1980 and Fact Sheet: Development of ASVAB-8/9/10," memorandum to LTC Chelberg, Washington, D.C., June 5 1980. S0531.pdf.

Laurence, Janice H., and Peter F. Ramsberger, *Low-Aptitude Men in the Military,* New York: Praeger, 1991.

Leggett, Robert L., Defense Manpower and the All-Volunteer Force, hearing before the Committee on the Budget: House of Representatives, 95th Cong., 1st Sess., Washington, D.C., U.S. Government Printing Office, July 12, 1977. S0491.pdf.

Linn, Peter C., *Report on the All-Volunteer Force,* Washington, D.C.: National Security & International Affairs Special Studies Division, Office of Management and Budget, December 8, 1977. G1436.pdf.

Maier, Milton H., "ASVAB Steering Committee Meeting on January 22, 1980," memorandum for the record, Washington, D.C., January 29, 1980. S0518.pdf.

Martin, Albert J., "Weekly Activity Report—Week of March 17 1980—Military Personnel Policy," memorandum to General Tice, Washington, D.C., March 20, 1980a. S0520.pdf.

———, "Significant Events—Week of 31 March 1980," memorandum to Major General Dean Tice Jr., Washington, D.C., April 4, 1980b. S0529.pdf.

———, "Significant Events—Week of 16 June1980," memorandum to Major General Dean Tice Jr., Washington, D.C., June 20, 1980c. S0527.pdf.

———, "Significant Events—Week of 23 June 1980," memorandum to LTC Chelberg, Washington, D.C., June 26, 1980d. S0521.pdf.

———, "Significant Events—Week of 14 July 1980," memorandum to Major General Dean Tice Jr., Washington, D.C., July 10, 1980e. S0535.pdf.

———, "Significant Events—Week of August 11 1980," memorandum to Major General Dean Tice Jr., Washington, D.C., August 15, 1980f. S0522.pdf.

———, "Significant Events—Week of 1 September 1980," memorandum to COL Chelberg, Washington, D.C., September 4, 1980g. S0528.pdf.

———, "Significant Events—Week of 3 November 1980," memorandum to Major General Dean Tice Jr., Washington, D.C., November 6, 1980h. S0526.pdf.

McIntyre, James A. Jr., "Warner/Nunn Amendment on Military Pay," memorandum to the President, Washington, D.C, May 19, 1980. C0017.pdf.

McIntyre, James T., "Report on the All-Volunteer Force (AVF) " memorandum to the President, Washington, D.C., April 13, 1973. G1437.pdf.

Morden, Bettie J., "Chapter XIII: Women in the Army," in *The Women's Army Corps, 1945–1978*, Washington, D.C.: U.S. Army Center of Military History, 1989. G1441.pdf.

Moskos, Charles C., Jr., interview with Bernard Rostker, September 4, 2004.

Nelson, Gary R., *The Costs of Defense Manpower: Issues for 1977*, Washington, D.C.: Congressional Budget Office, January 1977. S0458.pdf.

———, "OMB Study of the All-Volunteer Force (AVF)," memorandum to Associate Director for National Security and International Affairs Edward R. Jayne, Office of Management and Budget, Washington, D.C, April 21, 1978a. G1438.pdf.

———, *America's Volunteers: A Report on the All-Volunteer Armed Forces*, Washington, D.C.: Office of the Assistant Secretary of Defense (M&RA), December 31, 1978b. S0194.pdf.

———, interview with Bernard Rostker, September 7, 2004.

Nelson, Robert L., "Two Year Enlistment Option," action memorandum to Assistant Secretary of Defense (MRA&L), Washington, D.C., October 26, 1978a. G0005.pdf.

———, "Army Enlistment Tests," memorandum to Acting Assistant Secretary of Defense (MRA&L), Washington, D.C., November 20, 1978b. G0006.pdf.

New York Times Editorial Board, "Armistice on Military Pensions," *New York Times*, December 28, 1978, p. A16.

Nixon, Richard M., *The Real War*, New York: Warner Books, 1980.

———, "Volunteer Army," letter to John C. Whitaker, Wookcliff Lake, N.J., November 4, 1993. S0481.pdf.

Nunn, Sam, Status of the All-Volunteer Force, hearing before the Senate Armed Services Subcommittee on Manpower and Personnel, 95th Cong., 2nd Sess., Washington, D.C., U.S. Government Printing Office, June 20, 1978. S0444.pdf.

———, Proposed Changes to Military Compensation, hearing before the Senate Armed Services: Subcommittee on Manpower and Personnel, 96th Cong., 2nd Sess., Washington, D.C., U.S. Government Printing Office, January 22, 1980a. S0447.pdf.

———, Department of Defense Authorization for Appropriations for Fiscal year 1981: Active Duty, Reserve, Civilian Manpower, hearing before the Senate Armed Services Committee, Washington, D.C., U.S. Government Printing Office, March 10, 1980b. S0567.pdf.

———, Military Compensation, hearing before the Subcommittee on Manpower and Personnel of the Committee on Armed Services, U.S. Senate, 96th Cong., 2nd Sess., Washington, D.C., U.S. Government Printing Office, June 2, 1980c. S0564.pdf.

Nunn, Sam, et al., Costs of the All-Volunteer Force, hearing before the Senate Armed U.S. Services Subcommittee on Manpower and Personnel, 95th Cong., 2nd Sess., Washington, D.C., U.S. Government Printing Office, February 6, 1978. S0443.pdf.

OASD[M&RA]—*See* Office of the Assistant Secretary of Defense for Manpower and Reserve Affairs.

Office of the Assistant Secretary of Defense for Manpower and Reserve Affairs, *The All-Volunteer Force: Current Status and Prospects,* Washington, D.C.: U.S. Department of Defense, December 17, 1976. G0353.pdf.

Pirie, Robert B., Jr., "Army IRR Direct Enlistment Test," memorandum to Assistant Secretary of the Army (M&RA), Washington, D.C., October 28, 1978a. G0002.pdf.

———, "Draft for the Secretary of Defense," decision memorandum to Secretaries of the Military Department and Joint Chiefs of Staff Chairman, Washington, D.C., November 9, 1978b. S0505.pdf.

———, "Weekly Activity Report (20–24 November 1978)," information memorandum to Secretary of Defense, Washington, D.C., November 30, 1978c. G0370.pdf.

———, "Military Retirement," decision memorandum to Secretary of Defense, Washington, D.C., December 4, 1978d. G0375.pdf.

———, "Military Retirement," memorandum to Secretaries of the Military Department and Chairman Joint Chiefs of Staff, Washington, D.C., December 7, 1978e. G0499.pdf.

———, "New Early Withdrawal Retirement Option," memorandum to Secretary of Defense, Washington, D.C., December 11, 1978f. G0378.pdf.

———, "State of Play on PCMC," memorandum to Secretary of Defense, Washington, D.C., December 11, 1978g. G0377.pdf.

———, "Two-Year Enlistment Test," memorandum to Assistant Secretary of the Army (M&RA), Washington, D.C., December 19, 1978h. G0004.pdf.

———, "Weekly Activity Report (2–5 January 1979)," information memorandum to Secretary of Defense, Washington, D.C., January 8, 1979a. G0482.pdf.

———, "Weekly Activity Report (15–19 January 1979)," information memorandum to Secretary of Defense, Washington, D.C., January 20, 1979b. G0449.pdf.

———, "Active Force Enlisted Recruiting—Trends and Outlook," memorandum to Secretary of Defense, Washington, D.C., February 7, 1979c. G0483.pdf.

———, "Weekly Activity Report (5–9 February 1979)," information memorandum to Secretary of Defense, Washington, D.C., February 14, 1979d. G0491.pdf.

———, "Two-Year Enlistment Tests in the Navy and Marine Corps," memorandum to Assistant Secretary of the Navy (MRA&L), Washington, D.C., February 28, 1979e. G0365.pdf.

———, Manpower Overview, hearing before the Senate Appropriations Committee, 96th Cong., 1st Sess., Washington, D.C., U.S. Government Printing Office, March 27, 1979f. S0452.pdf.

———, "Weekly Activity Report (10–23 March 1979)," information memorandum to Secretary of Defense, Washington, D.C., March 27, 1979g. G0447.pdf.

———, "Weekly Activity Report—18–29 June 1979," information memorandum to Deputy Secretary of Defense Secretary of Defense, Washington, D.C., July 9, 1979h. G0488.pdf.

———, "Active Force Recruiting Reprogramming," action memorandum to Secretary of Defense, Washington, D.C., July 10, 1979i. G0420.pdf.

———, "Active Force Enlisted Recruiting, Retention and Strength—Trends and Outlook," information memorandum to Secretary of Defense, Washington, D.C., August 28, 1979j. G0419.pdf.

———, "MRA&L Planning for the Year Ahead," information memorandum to Secretary of Defense, Washington, D.C., August 31, 1979k. G0486.pdf.

———, "Army Request to Terminate the Two–Year Enlistment Test and Offer Two–Year Enlistments Nationwide," action memorandum to Secretary of Defense, Washington, D.C., September 28, 1979m. G0432.pdf.

———, "MRA&L Activity Report," information memorandum to Deputy Secretary of Defense Secretary of Defense, Washington, D.C., October 22, 1979n. G0577.pdf.

———, News Brief, Washington, D.C.: Office of the Assistant Secretary of Defense (MRA&L), October 25, 1979p. S0507.pdf.

———, "Study of Military Pay Adequacy," memorandum to Secretary of Defense, Washington, D.C., November 13, 1979q. G0354.pdf.

———, "Study of Pay and Compensation Adequacy," memorandum to John P. White, Washington, D.C., November 13, 1979r. G0398.pdf.

———, Proposed Changes to Military Compensation, hearing before the Senate Armed Services: Subcommittee on Manpower and Personnel, 96th Cong., 2nd Sess., Washington, D.C., U.S. Government Printing Office, January 22, 1980a. S0447.pdf.

———, "The Variable Housing Provision in the Nunn-Warner Bill," memorandum to Secretary of Defense, Washington, D.C., February 19, 1980b. G0387.pdf.

———, "More Data on ASVAB Norming Problem," memorandum to Deputy Secretary of Defense, Washington, D.C., February 23, 1980v. G0366.pdf.

———, "Enlistment Bonus Management," memorandum to Secretary of the Army, Washington, D.C., March 8, 1980d. G0382.pdf.

———, Testimony on the ASAVB Misnorming, hearing before the Subcommittee on Manpower and Personnel, Senate Armed Services Committee, Washington, D.C., U.S. Government Printing Office, March 10, 1980e. S0567.pdf.

———, "Enlistment Mental Testing," memorandum to Secretary of Defense, Washington, D.C., March 28, 1980f. G0439.pdf.

———, Prepared Statement of Assistant Secretary of Defense, MRA&L, hearing before the Senate Appropriations Committee, 96th Cong., 2nd Sess., Washington, D.C., U.S. Government Printing Office, April 2, 1980g. S0568.pdf.

———, "ASVAB Norming," memorandum to Secretary of Defense, Washington, D.C., May 9, 1980h. G0441.pdf.

———, "Warner/Nunn," draft memorandum for the President to Secretary of Defense, Washington, D.C., May 15, 1980i. G0381.pdf.

———, "Limits on Category IV Accessions," memorandum to Carl Levin, Washington, D.C., June 28, 1980j. G0448.pdf.

———, "Plan for Validating Enlistment Standards Against Job Performance," memorandum to Secretaries of the Military Departments, Washington, D.C., July 7, 1980k. G0371.pdf.

———, "Enlistment Standards," memorandum to Assistant Secretaries of the Military Departments (M&RA), Washington, D.C., September 11, 1980m. G0477.pdf.

———, *Military Manpower Strength Assessment, Recruiting and Reenlistment Results for Fiscal Year 1980 (Active Force)*, Washington, D.C.: Office of the Assistant Secretary of Defense (Public Affairs), October 31, 1980n. G0464.pdf.

———, *Implementation of New Armed Services Vocational Aptitude Battery and Actions to Improve the Enlistment Standards Process: A Report to the House and Senate Committees on Armed Services*, Washington, D.C.: Office of the Assistant Secretary of Defense (MRA&L), December 31, 1980p. S0338.pdf.

———, interview with Bernard Rostker, September 27, 2004.

Rice, Donald B., ed., *Defense Resource Management Study: A Report Requested by the President and Submitted to the Secretary of Defense—February 1979*, Washington, D.C.: U.S. Government Printing Office, 1979. S0488.pdf.

Roll, C. Robert., Jr., and Glenn A. Gotz, "The First-Term/Career Mix of Enlisted Military Personnel," in Donald B. Rice, ed., *Defense Resource Management Study: A Report requested by the President and Submitted to the Secretary of Defense—February 1979*, Washington, D.C.: U.S. Government Printing Office, 1979.

Schlesinger, James R., *Secretary Schlesinger Announces Elimination of Two-Year Enlistments*, Washington, D.C.: U.S. Department of Defense, February 24, 1975. G0686.pdf.

Shelton, Henry, *Statement of Chairman of the Joint Chiefs of Staff, Senate Budget Committee Hearing*, Washington, D.C.: Joint Chiefs of Staff, March 3, 1999.

Staff of Arlington National Cemetery, "Maxwell Reid Thurman," 2005. Online at http://www.arlingtoncemetery.net/mthurman.htm.

Taft, Daniel H., "Comments on the (DOD) 'Interim Report of the Study of the All-Volunteer Force'," memorandum to Thomas Stanners, Washington, D.C., March 17, 1978. G1439.pdf.

Thurman, Maxwell R., Proposed Changes to Military Compensation, hearing before the Senate Armed Services: Subcommittee on Manpower and Personnel, 96th Cong 2nd Sess., Washington, D.C., U.S. Government Printing Office, January 22, 1980a. S0447.pdf.

———, Fiscal Year 1980 Army Supplemental Request, hearing before the House Appropriations Committee, 96th Cong., 2nd Sess., Washington, D.C., U.S. Government Printing Office, April 22, 1980b. G1292.pdf.

———, "Sustaining the All-Volunteer Force 1983–1992: The Second Decade," in William Bowman, Roger Little and G. Thomas Sicilia, eds., *The All-Volunteer Force After a Decade: Retrospect and Prospect*, New York: Pergamon-Brassey's, 1986.

———, *Oral History*, unpublished RAND research, 1992.

———, "On Being All You Can Be: A Recruiting Perspective," in J. Eric Fredland, Curtis L. Gilroy, Roger D. Little and W.S. Sellman, eds., *Professionals on the Front Line: Two Decades of the All-Volunteer Force*, Washington, D.C.: Brassey's, 1996.

Waters, Brian K., Defense Manpower and the All-Volunteer Force, hearing before the Committee on the Budget: House of Representatives, 95th Cong., 1st Sess., Washington, D.C., U.S. Government Printing Office, July 12, 1977. S0491.pdf.

———, Military Posture: Military Personnel, hearing before the Committee on Armed Services: House of Representatives, 95th Cong., 2nd Sess., Washington, D.C., U.S. Government Printing Office, February 22, 1978.

———, The Profile of American Youth: Annotated Bibliography of Department of Defense Related Publications, Washington, D.C.: Directorate of Accession Policy Office of the Secretary of Defense, Technical memorandum 821, March 1982. S0575.pdf.

White, John P., "President's Commission on Military Compensation," memorandum to Secretaries of the Military Departments, Washington, D.C., August 14, 1978. G0032.pdf.

———, "Comments," 30th Anniversary Conference, Washington, D.C., September 2003. S0717.pdf.

Wilson, George C., "More Pay Urged to Keep Skilled People in Military," Washington Post, November 13, 1979, p. A6.

———, "Joint Chiefs of Staff Break with Carter on Budget Planning for Defense Needs; Joint Chiefs Break With Carter on Defense Budget," Washington Post, May 30, 1980a, p. A1. S0494.pdf. [671]

———, "Nunn Raps Carter on Defense Flip-Flops," Washington Post, June 3, 1980b, p. A2.

———, "Senate Authorizes 11.7 Percent Increase for Military Pay; 11.7 Boost for Military is Voted," Washington Post, July 3, 1980c, p. A1.

———, "General Favors Volunteer Army Over Draftees," Washington Post, August 8, 1980d, p. A7.

Yerks, Robert G., "Army IRR Direct Enlistment Test," action memorandum to Assistant Secretary of the Army (M&RA), Washington, D.C., December 4, 1978. G0007.pdf.

Zwick, Charles J., President's Commission on Military Compensation: Background Papers, Washington, D.C.: President's Commission on Military Compensation, 1978a. S0580.pdf.

———, "Preliminary Report of the President's Commission on Military Compensation," memorandum to James T. Jr. McIntyre, Washington, D.C., March 14, 1978b. G0017.pdf.

———, Report of the President's Commission on Military Compensation, Washington. D.C.: President's Commission on Military Compensation, April 10, 1978c. S0565.pdf.

———, "On Military Pensions—Flaws in the Pentagon Proposal," letter, New York Times, January 11, 1979. S0504.pdf.

CHAPTER TWELVE

The Selective Service Sideshow (1979–1980)

The Soviet Union has taken a radical and aggressive new step. It's using its great military power against a relatively defenseless nation. The implications of the Soviet invasion of Afghanistan would pose the most serious threat to the peace since the Second World War. . . . For this reason, I have determined that the Selective Service System must be revitalized. I will send legislation and budget proposals to the Congress next month so that we can begin registration and then meet future mobilization needs rapidly if they arise.

—Jimmy Carter
President of the United States[1]

Introduction

One of the more bizarre episodes in the history of the all-volunteer force was the machination that surrounded the debate about the status of the Selective Service System and the call for the resumption of draft registration. Ostensibly, the issue was the ability of the nation to mobilize its manpower for a major conflict with the Soviet Union. The hidden agenda, however, for those who opposed the all-volunteer force, was a return to the draft. Those opposed to the all-volunteer force saw the lack of a credible emergency induction system, especially since the original report of the Gates Commission had called for one, as a ready-made issue that, if they played it right, would inevitably lead to the return of the draft. The facts that, at the time, the Army did not consider conscripts to be an important part of its mobilization strategy or that DoD could not have absorbed large numbers of new inductees did not prevent those opposed to the all-volunteer force from pushing the issue of draft registration.

---

[1] The State of the Union Address, January 1980 (Carter, J., 1980a).

While the proponents of the all-volunteer force understood this strategy, they at times seemed unable to put a credible postmobilization registration plan in place, thus playing into the hands of their opponents. When President Carter called for registration in early 1980 in response to the Soviet Union's invasion of Afghanistan, the much-held belief that registration would be a slippery slope leading to the end of the all-volunteer force was put to the test. Registration was not the slippery slope that some had feared and that others hoped for. In retrospect, even though during much of the last two years of the Carter administration Selective Service registration was the central issue concerning mobilization, military preparedness, and the all-volunteer force, it was a sideshow that added little either to military preparedness or to the ultimate efficacy of the all-volunteer force.[2]

Mobilization, the Standby Draft, and the Decision to Terminate Draft Registration

The Gates Commission thought having a standby draft so important that it devoted an entire chapter (10) to the subject (Gates, 1970, pp. 119–124). The rationale they presented stressed

> the possible urgent need for the nation to act quickly . . . [to] provide a basis for acquiring eligible manpower who must be trained, organized and equipped. . . . The function of a standby draft is to provide manpower resources for the second stage of expansion in effective forces. (Gates, 1970, p. 120)[3]

Soon after the Gates Commission submitted its report, it became clear there were several concepts of what a standby draft would look like (OASD[M&RA], 1970).

By fall 1972, with induction authority scheduled to expire the following July and with no resolution concerning the future status of a standby draft, the administration started to focus on the issue. The White House saw "value to be gained by a . . . low profile for Selective Service" (Pepitone, 1972, p. 1). Byron Pepitone, the acting director after Curtis Tarr's move to the Department of State, wanted a "Selective Service structure" that would "remain active and viable" and that would require "well-qualified, dedicated civilian employees for the foreseeable future" (Pepitone, 1972, p. 1). DoD wanted "the

---

[2] Pirie told Secretary Brown that, as "far as active military manpower is concerned, the national debate over the efficacy of the all-volunteer force and the calls for peacetime registration . . . command much of our attention" (Pirie, 1979c, p. 1).

[3] In September 1971, the Military Selective Service Act was amended to provide for a "standby draft." Section 10(h) of the act required

> that the structure and organization of the Selective Service System and procedures for registration and classification remain intact, even in a period when induction calls might be suspended, so that the System can react immediately in the event of a national emergency. (Marrs, 1974)

establishment of a 1-A qualified and examined pool of men under a standby draft" (Daoust, 1972a). Options, however, ranged from "a standby pool of 100,000 examined men" to "50,000 examined men [and even] no standby pool" (OASD[M&RA], 1970).

By November 1972 the National Security Council took the initiative to "plan and coordinate a government-wide study of the standby draft machinery" (Lee, 1972). Phil Odeen told National Security Advisor Henry Kissinger that there was "a need for Presidential guidance to cover planning for the Selective Service System after July [1973]" (Odeen, 1973), when induction expired. Odeen thought it important because none of the interagency planning had "consider[ed] strategic requirements such as likely future mobilization requirements of the capacity of the training establishment to accept personnel during mobilization" (Odeen, 1973, p. 1). With Selective Service continuing to plan for a pool of 100,000 "physically examined potential inductees," Odeen asked, "should the current local board system be preserved or should a centrally located, computer run registration system be kept?" He noted, however, that "doing away with local boards requires new legislation and a new Selective Service Act next July. The reception this would receive on the Hill is doubtful" (Odeen, 1973). Kissinger agreed, and on December 3, 1972, signed National Security Study Memorandum (NSSM) 165 to study the standby draft and to "investigate potential manpower mobilization needs in future crises and alternative ways of fulfilling those requirements" (Kissinger, 1972c). Because of the very short deadlines—Kissinger wanted to report back to the President on December 20, 1972—DoD decided to use existing Joint Chiefs of Staff (JCS) planning documents and asked the military departments to "comment on the criticality of delivery of the first group of inductees. . . . [I]f the first inductees are not critically needed until M+45 to M+60 days, a standby pool may not be necessary" (Daoust, 1972b). The fact that the mobilization numbers had not been updated or validated by the Systems Analysis office brought the requirement numbers into question and opened up the President's decision for further debate over the following year.

Rather than bring things together, NSSM 165 showed that the administration was split over what to do about the standby draft. DoD, Selective Service, and the Office of Emergency Preparedness wanted a system that would include

> registration and full processing by local boards using the present organization with reduced numbers of administrative sites and compensated employees. Complete classification of a pool of physically and mentally examined individuals would permit induction to begin 10 to 15 days after mobilization. (Laird, 1972, p. 1)

Caspar Weinberger, Director of the Office of Management and Budget (OMB), did not agree. His office thought that "a more rapid induction procedure . . . [could] be developed which would shorten delivery time under a more austere Selective Service System to meet or reduce the induction time . . . recommended" (Laird, 1972, p. 1). Kissinger did not agree with either position, preferring something in the middle, what he called a "quick reactivation" option (Kissinger, 1973b).[4] In March 1973, the President, in National Security Decision Memorandum (NSDM) 208, opted for "a standby draft structure similar to that of the Office of Selective Service Records which existed in 1947 and 1948" (Kissinger, 1973a, p. 5), leaving the details to be worked out by the respective staffs. However, as so often happens, the devil was in the details.

In July 1973, the Director of Selective Service initiated a study with representation from DoD, OMB, and Selective Service "to examine and make recommendations as to alternatives concepts of operation for fiscal year 1975" (Selective Service System Staff, 1975, p. 3).[5] The informal group crafted three alternatives, and Selective Service reported that

> [g]eneral agreement was reached among the agencies as to the alternatives and concurrence was given to Concept A . . . to [make no] major alterations in the structure of the Selective Service System until the success of the all-volunteer force had been proved. . . . [This] had the effect of postponing the President's earlier decision to place Selective Service System in a deep standby status. (Selective Service System Staff, 1975, p. 4)

That year, Congress provided sufficient funds to continue operations at the Concept A level.

During 1974, the future of Selective Service was again the subject of another study group as the administration worked to develop the FY 1976 program. Meanwhile pressure mounted to reduce the Selective Service budget, despite an endorsement by Secretary of Defense James Schlesinger, who "testified . . . 'it is essential' that the Selective Service operation remain in place. Although no one is being drafted, they still must register, classify and maintain an active stand-by force" (Loen, 1974, p.1). As the final budget was being prepared in the fall it became clear the OMB's position had changed. The OMB staff argued that the "best evidence to date suggests that induction authority will not be required to meet peacetime force objectives" and that "maintenance of the existing system can no longer be justified" on the basis of the questionable "viability of the volunteer force" (Sitrin and Hannon, 1974, p. 1). OMB rejected

---

[4] Kissinger told Nixon that, if

> the current laws and procedures were changed, reactivation and processing times could be reduced to as little as one month. . . . Under this assumption, . . . [the Selective Service System] would be capable of satisfying the services' manpower requirements contained in the NSSM 165 study. (Kissinger, 1973b)

[5] There is some dispute about who commissioned the working group. The Selective Service Staff summary says the study group was "at the instigation of the Director of Selective Service" (Selective Service System Staff, 1975, p. 3), while DoD staff reports that "NSC verbally instructed Tom Stanners [of OMB] to chair a working group on the standby draft" (Wright, 1973, p. 1). In any event, Stanners chaired the initial meetings of the working group, which apparently examined the mobilization requirements and revealed the disagreement between the M&RA and PA&E staffs. On October 24, 1973, Bill Brehm confirmed that Tom Stanners "intends ... to support a Selective Service structure for FY75 at the 'Concept A' level" (Brehm, 1973, p. 1).

the Concept A option of the previous year and came down in favor of a new option that would suspend

> local board operations and all standby classification processing. Nineteen year olds would be registered on a once-a-year basis. Four-hundred compensated employees would account for the bulk of the estimated $18 million annual operating costs. Local board members would continue to be appointed during the standby in order to minimize the time (about 30 days) required to reconstitute local board operations in a crisis. Planned mobilization processing procedures would deliver the first inductees about 55 days after draft authority is restored. (Sitrin and Hannon, 1974, p. 2)

Byron Pepitone, the recently confirmed Director of Selective Service, did not agree with the OMB position, and so told Roy Ash, the new OMB Director.[6] Pepitone's objections notwithstanding, Ash conveyed the President's decision to Pepitone on December 19, 1974 and asked him to prepare a presidential proclamation terminating the registration of men under the Military Selective Service Act. The proposed proclamation was sent to OMB on January 17, 1975, with Pepitone's note that "[a] suitable proposed Proclamation announcing the 'annual registration' procedure will be forwarded for signature . . . at the appropriate time" (Pepitone, 1975a).[7]

Pepitone initially found several allies in his objections to suspending registration. Jeanne Davis at the National Security Council argued against the proclamation on the grounds that "it would be unwise to begin dismantling the current mobilization structure until a complete new process is thought through and formulated, and until we know that the new process will work" (Davis, 1975a). In an argument that would resonate in the debate about registration that would take place at the end of the decade, she felt that terminating registration "could be misinterpreted as a weakening of America's willingness to mobilize in a crisis . . . [and] a sign of ambivalence concerning what we need in the way of level of preparedness" (Davis, 1975a). Bill Casselman thought it

---

[6] Pepitone told Ash that

> it would not be possible to meet DoD manpower requirements . . . without the adoption of new procedures which . . . will without question require major changes in the Military Selective Service Act [and] the Chairmen of the Armed Services Committees of both Houses of Congress have each advised me personally that they are not in favor of considering a modification of the Act at this time. (Pepitone, 1974)

Pepitone even thought that, if the OMB proposal were accepted by the President, "serious consideration should be given to assigning to some other agency the functions now entrusted to the Selective Service System" (Pepitone, 1974).

[7] OMB sent the proposed proclamation to the Department of Justice for review on February 11, 1975 (Nichols, 1975). The Assistant Attorney General and the head of the Office of Legal Counsel, Antonin Scalia, approved a revised proclamation. It was returned to the White House several days later with the clarification that a registration procedure was being changed, not the statutory requirement to register (Scalia, 1975). Even so, some in the White House thought that confusing and questioned "the wisdom and effectiveness of the proposed proclamation" (Casselman, 1975a).

in conflict with Section 10(h) of the Military Selective Service Act (Casselman, 1975b), although he later softened his objections to a recommendation that "certain policy guidance received by OLC [Office of Legal Council], and upon which it based part of its opinion, be carefully reviewed as to its sufficiency" (Casselman, 1975b). Davis would also change her position after a "fact sheet" made it clear that "this action . . . did not affect the liability for young men to register . . . [it] only results in the change in methods by which young men register" (Davis, 1975b). President Ford signed the proclamation, "Terminating Registration Procedures Under the Military Selective Service Act, as Amended," on March 25, 1975 (Ford, 1975).

The proclamation clearly stated that registration was being terminated "to evaluate an annual registration system" and that it would "be replaced by new procedures which will provide for periodic registration" (Ford, 1975), but by the fall, National Security Advisor Brent Scowcroft was questioning whether, "because of its visibility, such a procedure might have domestic implications worth considering before the plan is finalized" (Scowcroft, 1975). Again the various parts of the administration could not agree on how to proceed. DoD preferred "a mail-in registration conducted over a one-month period. . . . Selective Service rejected the mail-in registration as unsuitable" (Lynn, 1975). OMB argued that there "would appear to be relatively little national security risk in moving to a much deeper standby system than now planned," even transferring "responsibility to the Department of Defense with no independent agency" (Lynn, 1975). Pepitone lobbied his friends in the White House for guidance and support even as support from the DoD evaporated[8]:

> Selective Service does not base its advocacy for the maintenance of a viable standby system upon the merits of DoD requirements but rather on the requirements themselves. I believe that as Director of Selective Service, I have a clear responsibility for determining and starting the posture and functions of the structure necessary to meet these requirements. I solicit your assistance in having my views considered. (Pepitone, 1975b)

When Pepitone signed his semiannual report to Congress on December 31, 1975, he had to admit that he had not been successful in achieving his vision of what the standby draft system should look like. He told Congress that the President had decided on December 12, 1975,

> that a $6.8 million budget for fiscal year 1977 would satisfy the requirements of the Selective Service System. This extremely austere budget was based on a current

---

[8] While only a month before Pepitone told supporters that DoD "strongly support[s] a standby draft mechanism to call up Standby Reservists needed under a mobilization scenario, and to draft new personnel needed principally as a hedge against protracted major combat" (Pepitone, 1975b), he now admitted in his report to Congress that it was "quite evident that the System will adopt by the end of fiscal year 1976 a much more deepened standby posture than I had anticipated" (Pepitone, 1975c, p. 13).

analysis by the Department of Defense of their mobilization manpower requirements in the event of a national emergency. The President's decision necessitates a complete change to the operational concept contained in the agency fiscal year 1977 budget request of $27.2 million. . . . The Selective Service System will move into a greatly deepened standby posture. (Pepitone, 1975c, pp. 12–13)

In a very important way, the move of the Selective Service System into deep standby was simply catching up with the realities of a changing Army posture after the Vietnam War. From the end of World War II through the mid-1970s the official military doctrine of the Army in defense of Western Europe against the Soviet Union was mobilization. Starting in 1973, the Army moved away from mobilization with a new "come-as-you-are" doctrine of active defense.[9] The recommendations of the Gates Commission and later the Defense Manpower Commission that had incorporated the older mobilization paradigm were rejected by an Army that now expected to fight with forward-deployed regular Army formations in Europe that could be quickly augmented with existing National Guard and Army Reserve units and with the fully trained Individual Ready Reserve.[10] Assistant Secretary of Defense Bill Brehm summed up the new realities for Selective Service:

> There was a need for a pool of trained and experienced military personnel who, together with our active duty and selected Reserve paid drill personnel, would man and sustain our existing combat force structure in the initial months of an intense conflict. Untrained people coming to active duty, whether volunteers or draftees, would be of little use to the services during this period since they could not be trained in time. (Pepitone, 1975c)[11]

This new understanding of mobilization, however, did not seem to extend across administrations as the Carter administration and Congress continued to treat mobilization of untrained manpower as a critical issue of national defense leading to a decision in 1980 to reinstate registration.

---

[9] John Romjue has noted that the AirLand Battle "doctrine of 1976 . . . laid great stress on the demise of the old mobilization concept as a strategic factor. . . . Facing expected superior forces [in Central Europe], *'The U.S. Army must prepare its units to fight out-numbered, and to win'*" (Romjue, 1984, p. 6).

[10] The Gates Commission had concluded that the country should maintain a viable standby draft that included "a register of all males who might be conscripted when essential for national security" (Gates, 1970, p. 119). The Defense Manpower Commission thought that the need for a standby draft was a significant shortcoming of the all-volunteer force and, with one dissenting vote, recommended immediate reform: "The standby draft system should be reconstituted with adequate funding to provide a capability to commence inductions within 30 days" (Tarr, 1976, p. 431).

[11] Pepitone quoting Brehm's testimony before the House Armed Services Committee, January 21, 1976 (Pepitone, 1975c, p. 1).

The Carter Administration

When President Carter took office, one of his first acts was to establish the Presidential Reorganization Project to recommend changes that needed to be made to reduce cost and increase efficiency. One of the issues the project considered was what to do with the small Selective Service System headquarters that remained after registration was suspended, as well as what to do about registration itself. They concluded that plans should be developed to

> relocate the standby SSS [Selective Service System] into the Department of Defense such that upon Presidential proclamation or declaration of war or resumption of registration the SSS will become independent in its active mode, and return to DoD again by Executive Order when registration ceases. (President's Reorganization Project, 1978, p. 34)[12]

Importantly, they also concluded that "while effectiveness might be enhanced through merger, additional steps should be taken as well to insure that [the Selective Service System] is able to meet the requirements which may be laid upon it" (President's Reorganization Project, 1978, p. 1).[13] They did not see, however, that active registration was necessary.

In DoD, Assistant Secretary of Defense John White and then his successor Robin Pirie were caught in the middle on the question of registration. The Joint Chiefs, never very favorable toward the all-volunteer force, pressed for peacetime registration. The director of the Joint Staff wrote to Pirie that the Joint Chiefs

> are convinced that peacetime registration will make a substantial contribution to national security by providing a continuous inventory of potential inductees, thereby insuring early arrival of inductees for training if mobilization is required. . . . Peacetime registration would also . . . permit early processing of the Standby

---

[12] White told Secretary Brown,

> The more I work on the problem of improving the [Selective Service System] the more I am convinced that this [the so-called "fold-in, fold-out option"] is the best approach if we are going to make it an effective organization that will be able to respond to future mobilization needs without reintroducing peacetime registration. (White, J., 1978b)

A DoD position paper noted the proposal that

> SSS should be collocated in DoD . . . was, in part, based on historical precedent, since the SSS mobilization planning function was a part of the War Department from the early 1920s until 1940 when registration was mandated by Congress. (OASD[M&RA], 1979)

In spring 1979 the House Armed Services Committee took action to bar transfer of the Selective Service to DoD (Suffa, 1979).

[13] DoD thought the study was "an excellent analysis [and] generally supports the major recommendations in the report." The department's main reaction was to "strongly urge OMB to take immediate action to improve the Selective Service System's mobilization capability" (White, J., 1978c, p. 1).

Reserve and insure maximum utilization of the Services' training capability. . . . [T]he JCS believe peacetime registration and initial screening are warranted. (Wickham, 1979)

Pirie had another view. He thought that "peacetime registration [was] not likely to make a substantial contribution to the national security" because, as he saw it "the soundest planning assumption is that there would be no room" at training bases "for inductees that, as a result of peacetime registration, might be made available" (Pirie, 1979b, pp. 6, 8).[14]

Others in the administration thought registration was the "slippery slope" that would return the nation to peacetime conscription.[15] While they told Congress they recognized an increasing need for conscripts in case of mobilization and the inability of the Selective Service System to deliver the inductees on the schedule they had published, they also actively resisted calls for registration. They desperately wanted to find a way to demonstrate to Congress that they had a plan to meet the ambitious timetable without resorting to peacetime draft registration.

The Nifty Nugget Mobilization Exercise and the New Call for Draft Registration

In 1978, Assistant Secretary White told Congress that the projected capability of the Selective Service System to deliver the first inductees on M+100 days and the 100,000th at M+150 days, with a total of 390,000 within six months did not meet the revised DoD wartime requirement. That requirement was that the first inductee arrive at M+30 and the 100,000th by M+60, with a total of 650,000 within six months.[16] He promised that the budget for FY 1979 would provide an increase of $2.9 million (40 percent) and that Selective Service would participate in a JCS-directed mobilization

---

[14] Pirie later (March 3, 1980) told Brown that the "Army has made a detailed review of its training base potential for rapidly accepting new trainees after mobilization. That review shows that its training base could expand more rapidly" (Pirie, 1980e). Pirie was probably right the first time. In 1983, the General Accounting Office (GAO; now known as the Government Accountability Office) found that, "[a]lthough the Army had made some progress, . . . it still needs to do much more" and provided a number of specific recommendations (Gould, 1983).

[15] One 1982 report noted that,

> [i]n truth, Selective Service is both a complement to the AVF, as well as its substitute. As its complement, a strong and responsive Selective Service System adds to the viability of the AVF by insuring the ability of the Nation to mobilize during an emergency. As its substitute, it is an alternative means of procuring military manpower during peace and war. (Rostker, 1982, p. 2)

[16] As noted, these new requirements came at a time when the Army in Europe was moving away from reliance on mobilization to defend NATO to a new "come-as-you are" defense (Romjue, 1984, p. 6). Apparently, the reality of the new Airland Battle Doctrine as applied to Europe was not shared with the Pentagon. One can speculate if this was part of a deliberate program to demonstrate the failings of the all-volunteer force and to bring back the draft.

exercise, Nifty Nugget,[17] scheduled for fall 1978 to test its new capabilities (White, J., 1978a, pp. 172, 216).[18]

The results of the Nifty Nugget mobilization exercise did not cool but instead intensified the concerns of some in Congress who saw the mobilization issue as one of the most critical indictments against the all-volunteer force.[19] In testimony before the House Armed Services Committee and in a lengthy statement he had included in the record, Congressman Robin Beard (R-Tennessee) charged that the post-hostilities man-power situation was so desperate that "if we are attacked by major conventional forces, our only alternative would be the use of nuclear weapons—an irresponsible and danger-ous national policy" (Beard, 1979, p. 1,300). He called for a Joint Select Committee "to conduct a complete analysis of our military manpower system" (Beard, 1979, p. 1,301). Congressman Sonny Montgomery (D-Mississippi) went even further. He introduced legislation to "provide for reactivation of registration and classification under the Mili-tary Selective Service Act" (Montgomery, 1979, p. 54). His bill also mandated a return to conscription and the induction of 200,000 men a year for three months of active duty for training, with subsequent service in the Individual Ready Reserve. The power-ful National Guard Association of the United States, and its well-regarded Executive Vice President, Fran Greenlief, supported his call (Greenlief, 1979).

Given the then-current state of the Selective Service System and its recognized inability to meet the mobilization needs of DoD, there were options other than the peacetime registration that Montgomery's bill would have instituted. The most candid assessment and evenhanded presentation of options did not come from the administra-tion but from the Congressional Budget Office (CBO). In a presentation to the House Armed Services Committee, the Assistant Director of the National Security and Inter-national Affairs Division, David S.C. Chu, and his Principal Analyst, Dan Huck, laid out the options.[20] They started their review by noting that

---

[17] As a prelude to Nifty Nugget, a premobilization game called Exercise Petite Nugget which examined options appropriate to improve readiness during a period of heightened tension. One of the options considered was draft registration. In a report to Secretary Brown, White noted that there was "[a] strong preference on the part of most of the players to initiate mobilization steps (e.g., Selective Service registration . . .) even if they are *not* fully warranted by the scenario because they are actions 'that ought to be done anyway'" (White, J., 1978d, emphasis in original).

[18] *Author's Note:* Richard Danzig organized the Petite Nugget geopolitical game. I played the Secretary of the Navy during the game. The Selective Service System's capabilities to reinstate the draft and begin inducting young men was also played. At the time I would never have imagined that before the next year was over I would be the Director of Selective Service—not for a game, but for real.

[19] Pirie told Brown that after the exercise, "interest . . . remain[ed] high" in Nifty Nugget (Pirie, 1978c). Soon after Pirie initiated a number of actions to "resolve particular issues . . . [and] to keep mobilization issues on the forefront of DoD concerns." This included establishing a mobilization directorate within his office. Brown told him that these steps were "a good start. They need to be integrated within an overall policy [to be] derived from the interac-tion between mobilization capabilities/costs and full objectives/operational plans & needs" (Pirie, 1978a).

[20] Huck was reporting on a study CBO had released the previous November (Huck, 1978).

there is no reliable plan for a quick, mass registration, . . . the computer support . . . available to Selective Service is neither adequate nor appropriate . . . [P]lan[s] to reconstitute a field structure . . . upon mobilization [a]re complex, cumbersome, and outdated. (Chu and Huck, 1979, pp. 68–69)

They noted that the administration had three options: create a credible post-mobilization registration plan; reinstate the peacetime registration suspended by the Ford administration on March 29, 1975; and not only register but classify young men who would be eligible for induction in an emergency. As they saw it, providing

even minimal assurance that Selective Service can meet DoD's current wartime induction schedule will require at least a year and possibly two years of development and testing of equipment and procedures. If such development and testing is funded in the fiscal year 1980 and 1981 appropriations for Selective Service, a capable system could be in place at the start of fiscal 1982. (Chu and Huck, 1979, p. 106)

What they did not say, but what Pirie did say at his confirmation hearing on April 6, 1979 (Pirie, 1979a, p. 4), was that the administration did not favor registration. What also could be read into Pirie's manpower overview was that the administration did not have a plan or even a clear path to a plan to create a viable postmobilization registration and draft. One of the first actions during that spring (1979) by John White, after leaving DoD to become the Deputy Director of OMB, was to recruit and install a new Director of Selective Service.

Dear Colleague and the Registration Debate

As White was searching for a new Director of Selective Service, Congress was moving toward a vote on draft registration. *Dear Colleague* letters flew through the halls of Capitol Hill. Some urged members to support the provision of the Defense Appropriations Bill for Fiscal Year 1980 (Section 812 of H.R. 4040) that required mandatory registration; others argued that it be stricken from the bill. Congressmen Montgomery and Beard argued that "[s]trengthening the existing system and mandating registration are now a necessary step we must take" (Montgomery and Beard, 1979). A coalition of members of varying views on the all-volunteer force and national service united in opposition to registration *at this time*. They favored an amendment that would "require the President to include registration in a thorough study of alternatives, to be submitted by January 15, 1980" (Aspin et al., 1979).

The administration weighed in with letters to the leadership and key supporters. On June 6, 1979, the Director of the OMB wrote the chairman of the House Committee on Rules telling him that the administration objected "to the provisions [of the bill] regarding reinstatement of registration for the draft. The Administration is opposed to registration" (McIntyre, 1979). On June 8, 1979, the day after Senator Nunn's sub-committee approved a "Selective Service Registration Bill" (Nunn, 1979a), Secretary Brown wrote Senator William Cohen (R-Maine) arguing for more resources rather than a move to registration:

> the critical step towards achieving our goals is not immediate collection of names through registration, but rather the immediate improvement of our ability to prepare for processing people, and in the case of mobilization actually to process them, through the Selective Service. (Brown, 1979)

On July 23, 1979, President Carter's views were communicated to the Hill by Stuart Eizenstat, Assistant to the President for Domestic Affairs and Policy. In a letter to Congressman John Seiberling (D-Ohio), Eizenstat said that the "Administration opposes new legislation to reimpose peacetime registration for the draft. The President already has adequate authority to require registration if circumstances warrant" (Eizenstat, 1979). On the same day Brown wrote Congressman Charles Bennett (D-New York) to say he

> oppose[s] peacetime registration at this point. I believe the Selective Service System could be able to meet the Department of Defense requirement for delivery of new inductees without peacetime registration. Emergency plans are under preparation. The Administration has asked for the necessary funds. Appropriates of those funds is the correct next step. (Brown, 1979)

But Senator Nunn was not to be put off. On July 27, 1979, the *Washington Post* published his op-ed piece, "The Case for Peacetime Registration." In his judgment, Secretary Brown's arguments in support of the "current unworkable scheme [were] . . . politically motivated nonfeasance." In very strong language even for political Washington, Nunn wrote that, if

> we have a war or emergency mobilization during this period, those in the chain of command responsible for basing our nation's security on this hoax and those who know better but sit silently by will be held accountable, by an enraged nation, for their gross negligence. (Nunn, 1979b)

On September 12, 1979, the vote in the House went against a registration amendment put forward by Congressman Montgomery, by a margin of 163 to 259. The requirement for draft registration was stricken from the bill. The requirement for the President to report stood, and just days before the vote, President Carter nominated me to become the new Director of Selective Service. It would be my job, once confirmed, to develop the recommendations the President would forward to Congress on January 15, 1980.[21]

---

[21] *Author's Note:* Given the degree of my involvement in these events, I will be writing here in the first person.

In the Senate, Nunn pressed forward. Taking to the floor of the Senate on September 21, 1979, he told his colleagues that "[o]nly peacetime registration will address our real manpower needs" (Nunn, 1979c, p. 9). He requested a closed session of the Senate to discuss the results of Nifty Nugget. Cohen would later reflect that Senator Nunn's actions "served the purpose of [not only] preparing a foundation for the need to return to a system of face-to-face registration of young males . . . [but] ultimately, the draft" (Cohen, 1981, p. 279).

It was clear all summer that the administration had turned back registration only by agreeing to bring Congress a new plan for Selective Service. In short, Congress was giving the administration one more chance to make things right. Even before the final report language became law on November 9, 1979, as Section 811 to the 1980 Defense Authorization Act (Public Law 96-107), White was gearing up for the report.

Search for a New Director of Selective Service

For the administration, after the decision was made to keep Selective Service, it was important to nominate and confirm a new Director of Selective Service as soon as possible. In November 1978, Secretary Brown's Special Assistant, John Kester suggested Pirie help the White House Reorganization team "identify and evaluate a potential director . . . for the Selective Service System" (Pirie, 1978b).[22] Richard Danzig led the search. Several candidates were interviewed, but no one was selected. Sometime the following spring, I mentioned to Danzig my desire to move on and do something else within the administration. I explained that I had just finished the successful implementation of Civil Service Reform in the Navy and the establishment of the Navy's Senior Executive Service, and I thought that it was time to do something else. Danzig asked me whether I would consider becoming the next Director of Selective Service. I asked him if he was kidding: "Why should I be interested in moving from the Navy and the Department of Defense to a backwater agency in deep standby?" I clearly did not understand how this fit into the big picture of the

---

[22] Earlier in 1978, Pirie told Brown,

> I must confess my own view of the criteria generate some sense of contradiction: the optimal candidate would not be associated with the military, but would be experienced in the Pentagon; committed and active enough to repair Selective Service deficiencies, but not a zealot who may preach a draft and undercut the AVF; a young person because that would make him or her more acceptable to youth, but an older person because the job requires an established track record and a reputation for fairness—and it should not be seen as a stepping stone to other things. (Pirie, 1978b, pp. 1–2)

He asked Brown if he had "[a]ny comments . . . on [the] criteria, likely arenas for search, or candidates." Brown responded by writing "some President of a small college?" in the margin (Pirie, 1978b, p. 2).

all-volunteer force.[23] Danzig did not try to sell the idea, but suggested we speak about it again some time in the future.

I went back to my office and told my executive assistant, Commander Mike Boorda[24]: "Can you imagine what Danzig just suggested?" Boorda thought that I should have said yes immediately: "Remember, it is better to be the captain of a tug boat than the executive officer on an aircraft carrier." He then told me to "go right downstairs and tell Danzig you will take the job if it is not too late," in his most direct, but respectful, voice.

The next day, I did just that and was interviewed several weeks later by the White House Director of Personnel, Arnold Miller. The interview went very well—Miller and I had actually gone to the same junior high school in the Bronx—but then nothing seemed to happen. White later explained that, while Miller had no doubt that I could do the job, he was holding out for someone with a better political pedigree. But pressure was mounting in Congress, and White was losing patience. In early July, he told Miller he had one week to either find another candidate who was acceptable to him or get behind his candidate; otherwise, he would take the disagreement to the President. Miller finally agreed. On August 9, 1979, the White House announced my nomination to be the Director of Selective Service (Carter, J., 1979).

Being nominated by the President is one thing; being confirmed by the Senate is something altogether different. Senator Stennis, the Chairman of the Senate Armed Services Committee, delayed the confirmation hearing for almost three months. It was finally scheduled for October 17, 1979. Just minutes before the hearing was to take place, I was told by one of Stennis's aides, Frank Sullivan, that the committee would not be considering my nomination that day.[25] Congressman Montgomery had raised some questions, and more information would be needed. In *Roll Call: One Year in the United States Senate,* Senator Cohen recalled the events of that day:

---

[23] I also did not realize how vulnerable I was on this issue. On December 13, 1978, JCS wrote to the Secretary of Defense recommending

> that the Selective Service System be reinstituted without delay, with provisions for registration and initial screening. We request your support with the President and Congress for this important action. (Jones, 1978, p. 2)

Danzig asked for comments on a decision memo for the Secretary of Defense (Danzig, 1978). Secretary of the Navy Graham Claytor asked me for a review. In what surely would have disqualified me for the job, if it had been known, I had written that I concurred

> with the JCS recommendation. This alternative, reinstating peacetime registration and classification, would insure that the Nation could mobilize in the event of need. Readiness should be, in my opinion, the deciding factor. (Rostker, 1979a, p. 3)

[24] *Author's Note:* Mike Boorda would eventually rise to the rank of admiral and the position of Chief of Naval Operations, the highest ranking naval officer in the country.

[25] *Author's Note:* Frank Sullivan was my boss in the Manpower Requirements Directorate of Systems Analysis from 1968 to 1970.

Everyone was confirmed except Rostker, on whom Chairman Stennis deferred a vote on grounds that more information had to be furnished by the nominee before the Committee could give him full consideration. The fact was that no additional information was needed. . . .

Delay could only work to the disadvantage of Rostker. Selective Service was under a mandate to report to Congress by the end of January 1980, and to provide a viable program for meeting the nation's mobilization needs. The longer Rostker was denied a position of authority with which he could carry out the mandate, the lower the odds he would be able to meet the deadline with anything resembling a thoughtful program. (Cohen, 1981, p. 287)[26]

My new hearing was finally scheduled for November 16, 1979. The White House staff had hoped that I could be confirmed in September because they faced a January deadline for the President to submit a viable mobilization and standby draft plan to Congress. They were outraged when my confirmation hearing was postponed without any indication of when a new hearing would be scheduled.

Now, as they faced a November hearing, they had a new problem. They wanted me to endorse the post-mobilization plan that the acting Director of Selective Service, Robert Shuck, had developed. Shuck had told Congress of his intent to use the state election machinery, as had been done in 1917, 1918 and 1940.[27] I however, refused to endorse Shuck's plan. Having been briefed by Shuck, I found the plan inadequate.[28] Since Congress did not require the administration to submit a plan until January, it did not seem necessary to endorse any plan during my confirmation hearing. I told my White House handlers that, if asked, I would "tell the Senators that I have an open mind and will respond at the appropriate time." And it was a very good thing that I took that position.

---

[26] Senator Cohen also wrote of his concern that "registration . . . would be seen by many as the first step toward a return to the draft" (Cohen, 1981, p. 231).

[27] Shuck observed that, on

> October 16, 1940, this Nation registered 16 million men using the election machinery and began the induction process in November 1940. In 1917 and again in 1918, the election process was used for an emergency registration. We have evaluated that process. We have now contacted the State election officials in all 50 States, and are in the final stages of developing an emergency registration program. (Shuck, 1979a, p. 128)

[28] *Author's Note:* I had serious misgivings about Shuck's plan to use the state election machinery. I thought his plan overly complicated, requiring thousands of state workers to be employed at considerable expense. I knew we could do a better job if we used the U.S. Postal Service, an organization already in the field with thousands of retail outlets all over the United States. I was sure , if we paid the normal cost for a "transaction," we could do the job at a fraction of the cost Shuck proposed. In fact, that is the way it turned out. We eventually registered the entire nation for less than Shuck thought it would cost to register the state of California, $20 million. At the time of my confirmation hearings, however, I was already in trouble on this point. In September, I met with a group of Congressmen and in a fit of candor I expressed my doubts about Shuck's plan. In the hard ball that is Washington, these "private" remarks were circulated in a *Dear Colleague* letter. Congressman White told his colleagues, "Dr. Rostker told us that he has reviewed the current plan . . . [and] [h]e stated unequivocally that the plan is not credible and cannot be relied upon" (White, R., 1979). To say the least, the White House was not happy.

Just before the confirmation hearing on November 16, 1979, I went to pay a courtesy call on Frank Sullivan. Sullivan thanked me for coming and quickly escorted me out of his office, which was directly connected to the hearing room. Out of the corner of my eye, I caught a glimpse of large wallboards with Shuck's plan laid out and with attached illustrations and comments.[29] It was a trap. If I had endorsed Shuck's plan, Senator Nunn, armed with the critical GAO study,[30] was prepared to bring the wall boards into the hearing rooms and force me to defend each and every detail. It would have been tough going because Nunn had already characterized the Shuck plan: "At best, it is a pipedream. At worst, it is a fraud on the Nation. It is placing the foundation of our mobilization capability in a bed of quicksand" (Nunn, 1979c). I would not take the bait, although a number of Senators dangled it before me:

> Senator Thurman: [D]o you feel that there is a need to have registration at this time. . . .
>
> Rostker: Senator, I don't feel qualified at this point to make a judgment. I am fully aware of the requirement in the law for the President to report to Congress in the January timeframe. . . . I have not had the opportunity to avail myself of the best reasoning. I would like to defer that until I can bring a more reasoned opinion to this committee.
>
> Senator Cohen: Dr. Rostker, I assume you have had an opportunity to at least review the existing Selective Service System, the apparatus, the regulations, and have made some initial determinations of its strengths and weaknesses. . . .
>
> Rostker: Senator, I wish I had had the opportunity to become as familiar with the Selective Service System as, I guess, I will in the weeks and months ahead if it is the pleasure of the committee. . . .
>
> Senator Cohen: Do you have a problem so far as that January deadline? . . .
>
> Rostker: . . . I think we can bring a reasonable approach to the Congress in that timeframe. Certainly that is the requirement, and that is what I am prepared to try to do. . . .
>
> Senator Nunn[31]: . . . Do you think Mr. Shuck's present . . . plan endorsed by the Secretary of Defense and endorsed by the President of the United States and . . . used extensively in the debate to try to defeat the efforts to have peacetime registration [will work]? The question is: Will that plan work in your opinion?

---

[29] *Author's Note:* Twenty-three years later, on October 11, 2002, at Frank Sullivan's 70th birthday party, Arnold Punaro, Nunn's long-serving legislative assistant, still remembered and could describe those charts. Punaro said George Travis, Nunn's staff assistant on the Manpower and Personnel subcommittee, had drawn them. (George Travis and I had served together as junior officers in Systems Analysis under Frank Sullivan.) With a laugh in his voice, Punaro described to me the "bombs" and other illustrations with which George had adorned the charts.

[30] The GAO had concluded "the emergency plan has shortcomings which make it doubtful that the plan will ever be implemented. A national peacetime registration program, in GAO's view will best meet DoD's current mobilization program" (Comptroller General of the United States, 1979b). Of course, Shuck disagreed and wrote to the head of GAO complaining that, "Since history reveals the use of election assistance has been successful in the past, we certainly have difficulty in understanding why there is any doubt as to its value or capability, in this connection, in the future" (Shuck, 1979b).

[31] Senator Nunn arrived late, but now bore in for the kill, with the GAO study in hand and the wall charts ready to go in the next room.

Rostker: I don't know, Senator. It is one of many options we have to look at. Certainly the time is short to look at all the options, but I am prepared to report back to the Congress in January on the recommendation for the best possible plan.

Senator Nunn: Mr. Shuck says that plan will work. Does that mean you differ from Mr. Shuck at this stage?

Rostker: I will neither accept or refute that plan. I have no basis for criticizing it. I would like the option to approach it in an evenhanded way as I would approach the other options that have been spoken about. . . .

Senator Nunn: . . . [W]e have a plan that the President of the United States says will work, the Secretary of Defense says it will work, Mr. Shuck says it will work. Now we are getting a new Director. You say you don't have any idea whether you differ or not. What needs changing if everything is fine?

Rostker: The requirement to report back to the Congress in January is for the President to present the plan. I would like the option to look at a whole range of possibilities. What you refer to as the Shuck plan is just one of them. (Rostker, 1979b, pp. 7–10)

Nunn never brought out the wallboards on which Shuck's plan was mockingly depicted. The committee voted for confirmation. The nomination passed the Senate and on November 26, 1979, I was sworn in as Director of Selective Service.

Development of the Selective Service Revitalization Plan and the President's Decision to Resume Draft Registration

During the fall, with the mid-January date for the President to report to Congress on his plans for the Selective Service System and with the delay in getting a confirmation date for a new director, the OMB staff working the registration issue became very anxious.[32] In a breach of etiquette, they pressed me to get involved.[33] "At least pick a staff so that once you are confirmed you can hit the ground running," Tom Stanners from OMB told me. In September, on an orientation visit to Selective Service headquarters, Acting Director Shuck told me that he had some extra money left over at the end of the fiscal year and asked me if I had any suggestions for how he might productively use it. I immediately suggested that Shuck hire a consulting firm to help prepare the report due to Congress in January. I told him that Phil Odeen, now of the firm of Coopers & Lybrand, had offered his services. Moreover, Rick Cooper had recently left RAND and had gone to work for Odeen. Shuck thought it a good idea but did not know how he could bring them under contract. I suggested he contact Johnny Johnson, who had recently retired from the Air Force after serving in White and Pirie's office at DoD.

---

[32] The staff members most involved were Tom Stanners from OMB and Bill Jones from the President's Reorganization Project.

[33] The Senate insists that a nominee do nothing that in any way assumes the outcome of its prerogative to "advise and consent" through the confirmation process.

Johnson knew how to get things done. By October, the Selective Service System had a stable of contractors at work.

Under pressure from Congress and with a new report due in January 1980, on October 3, 1979, the President approved the establishment of a "policy level steering committee . . . chaired by John White" (White, J., 1979, p. 2) to address the 10 specific points set out in the authorization bill.[34] Although the President agreed that I should have "specific responsibilities" for the "mandated tasks deal[ing] with the ability of the Selective Service System to meet DoD requirements for inductees upon mobilization," and he was told that I had "already started work on them" (White, J., 1979, p. 2), the problem I was having getting confirmed dictated that I be very circumspect in my involvement and do nothing to give the Senate committee the impression that I was presuming that they would eventually confirm me. As a result, Bill Jones of the President's Reorganization Project staff took the lead in chairing the group working on the President's formal plan for reforming the Selective Service System. After I was confirmed by the Senate and even before the President had signed my commission, I was at work. During the first three days after I became director, I reviewed a number of concept papers. Some of them need reworking, and several new taskings were given out and new deadlines set.

By December 21, 1979, I reported to John White that we had a

> "new" *POST-MOBILIZATION PARTICIPATORY REGISTRATION* option . . . [that is] markedly different from previous Selective Service plans. . . . The major changes are (1) reliance on the U.S. Postal Service (USPS) for registration, (2) the pre-sorting of registration data to facilitate the promulgation of induction notices, and (3) the reliance on operating, in place, testable federal infrastructures to support the Selective Service in an emergency. (Rostker, 1979c, pp. 2–3)

I also provided White "a list of items which will be covered between now and mid-January in our next report to you. The report is [now] due to the Congress on February 9, 1980" (Rostker, 1979c, p. 3). This report to White included several draft memoranda of understanding with the Postal Service for registration and with the Internal Revenue Service (IRS) and the Social Security Administration for data entry, as well as a new plan for computer support. The revitalization plan also included a new level of coordination between DoD and the Selective Service System.[35] To Pirie's delight, I recommended that Deputy Secretary Clayton sign the memorandum of understanding that formalized the joint policy in place since November 28, 1979, two days after I took office. Under the agreement

---

[34] The program formally became known as PRM-47 (Brezinski, 1979).

[35] The most important agreement was with the Postal Service because it, rather than local draft boards, would be handling the face-to-face contact with registrants. The postmaster general signed the agreement just days before President Carter's scheduled State of the Union address. After President Carter called for registration, the agreement was amended to show the costs of the 1980 registration (Rostker and Bolger, 1980).

DoD and Selective Service agree to collocation and joint use of facilities and resources, to establishment of a joint computer center in the Chicago area to be operated by the Military Enlistment Processing Command (MEPCOM), and to develop the architecture for a joint manpower mobilization system. Security, privacy, cost sharing, backup, joint readiness exercises, and continuity of operations plans are also covered. (Pirie, 1980b)

Central to this new working relationship was the joint computer center. The previous plan addressed only Selective Service computer needs. It did not address the total preinduction requirements—requirements Selective Service shared with MEPCOM. The new joint Selective Service–MEPCOM Computer Center would, for the first time,

reinforce the link between the two organizations . . . [and] put Selective Service on a computer fully dedicated to the military manpower procurement mission. It would help insure coordination of manpower flows from Selective Service to the AFEES [Armed Forces Entrance and Examining Stations]. It would provide the critical mass [r]equired to insure that the computer needs of both organizations are met. (Rostker, 1979c, p.13)

Building on the late December progress report to White, I drafted an updated report, *Improving Capability to Mobilize Military Manpower: A Report by the Director of the Selective Service,* to be the basis of the President's report to Congress (Rostker, 1980a). The final document presented to White's staff, dated January 16, 1980, was marked as "a draft working document." In words that at the time represented administration policy, I stated that

our analysis of the various face-to-face registration options suggests that the post-mobilization plan is preferable. . . .The post-mobilization option should substantially exceed Defense requirements, employs the fewest number of full time personnel, and costs the least. While costs and staffing should not be the determining factor, the reduced delivery time provided by the other options [such as active peacetime registration] is redundant and unnecessary. The post-mobilization option, subject to field testing later this year, and the international situation at any time, is recommended as the basis for an effective Standby Selective Service. (Rostker, 1980a, p. 13)

The phrase "subject to . . . the international situation" was added just before this draft paper was released on a hunch and in deference to the heightened tensions between the United States and the Soviet Union after the influx of Russian troops into Afghanistan after the coup on December 27, 1979.

President Carter's State of the Union Address

With Afghanistan all the buzz in Washington, I approached my White House liaison, Bill Jones, with a suggestion. I proposed that the President include in the upcoming

State of the Union address some reference to the standby draft and the state of the Selective Service System. After all, the President would be sending a report to Congress in two weeks that would outline the new look at Selective Service, it seemed to be timely to make the announcement in this important policy address. It could also head off the criticism that would surely follow if the President said nothing. Jones was non-committal: "This was not a good time to raise the issue at the White House."

In the inner circles at the White House, Lloyd Cutler, the Counsel to the President, was more than raising the issue of a revitalized Selective Service, he was pressing for the resumption of draft registration, the very policy the administration has been resisting for months. His argument was that, in 1940, the fact that the continuation of the draft passed by only one vote in the House of Representatives signaled the Japanese that America was not willing to fight. Now, 40 years later, the failure to press for registration would send the same signal to the Soviet Union. Lined up against Cutler were John White and the President's domestic policy advisor, Stuart Eizenstat. The decision to change policy and move to registration was made by the weekend before the State of the Union Address was to be given. Robin Pirie remembers being in his office at the Pentagon the Saturday afternoon before the State of the Union—January 19, 1980—when the hotline that connected his office with Harold Brown's rang. Some years later, he told an interviewer that this was

> one of the two times I think that Harold rang me on the hot line. Harold said, "Come down, I want to talk to you." I came down, and he said, "Write up a paragraph for the President's State of the Union address that says that we are reinstating registration." I said "that's a really crummy idea" and he said, . . . "Go write the paragraph." (Kerber, 1998, p. 280)

Pirie prepared the paragraph and asked Brown for permission to tell me what was going on.

In the meantime, White desperately tried to change the President's mind. On January 22, 1980, the day before the State of the Union address, he wrote the President to remind him that

> [t]he interagency task force . . . has been working since last October . . . [and] there is no justification for peacetime registration. Given the system enhancements called for in the plan, SSS [Selective Service System] can meet and exceed the agreed upon DoD requirement. (White, J., 1980a)

He told the President that the new plan involved "interagency agreements which are already negotiated and signed" and that the President stressed his commitment to "[a]ccelerate the upgrading of SSS" (White, J., 1980a). Foreshadowing the difficulties that the administration would face in the spring, White warned of the "volatile issues of registering women and legal enforcement . . . [and] the costs associated with having to debate the 'draft-related' issues of registration, women, conscription, etc., in the present environment" (White, J., 1980a). The President was unmoved.

It was not until the morning of the State of Union address that I was told of the President's change of direction from opposing registration to calling for it.[36] My account of the events of that day is recorded in Linda Kerber's book on women and the Constitution:

> Early Wednesday morning, Rostker "got a phone call about eight o'clock from John White . . . that said stop everything you're doing, come over here [to the Old Executive Office Building], don't tell anybody where you are going. And I came to his office. He said 'I need you to start writing paragraphs [about] why this is a bad idea.' He stuck me into somebody's office, and I sat there scribbling, sending pieces of paper out. . . . Then about four o'clock he came back and said it's lost, stick around here and the President's going to announce it." (Rostker, as quoted in Kerber, 1998, p. 376)

That evening, January 23, 1980, President Carter addressed the American people (Carter, J., 1980b):

> The Soviet Union has taken a radical and aggressive new step. It's using its great military power against a relatively defenseless nation. The implications of the Soviet invasion of Afghanistan would pose the most serious threat to the peace since the Second World War. . . .
>
> The men and women of America's Armed Forces are on duty tonight in many parts of the world. I'm proud of the job they are doing, and I know you share that pride. I believe that our volunteer forces are adequate for current defense needs, and I hope that it will not become necessary to impose a draft. However, we must be prepared for that possibility. For this reason, I have determined that the Selective Service System must be revitalized. I will send legislation and budget proposals to the Congress next month so that we can begin registration and then meet future mobilization needs rapidly if they arise. (Carter, J., 1980a)[37]

"Legislation and Budget Proposals . . . so that We Can Begin Registration"

Not only was I unprepared for the change of policy President Carter announced on January 23, so was the White House staff. The White House rushed to put out a set of questions and answers to try to explain why the administration had changed direction

---

[36] On January 22, Danzig reminded Pirie (and Brown) that Tom Ross, DoD's press chief, the Postmaster General, and I had not been informed that the President was even considering draft registration. Danzig worried that if they did not have a chance to prepare their reaction, the administration might "look ill-coordinated and unprepared." Brown told Pirie he would leave it to him and John White "to bring Rostker and the P.O. in" (Danzig, 1980a). The next morning, Pirie reported to Brown that "Rostker was wired in, Ross has a press plan" (Pirie, 1980a). In fact, the Postmaster General did not have any warning. After watching the President deliver the State of the Union with John White in his office, I called the Postmaster General at his home. I told the Postmaster General that the contingency memorandum of understanding he had signed just the week before was being implemented and the Selective Service System would put its new revitalization plan, a plan that featured registration at post offices throughout the United States, into effect.

[37] A video recording of the portion of the State of the Union (Carter, J., 1980b).

(White House Press Secretary, 1980). After the decision was announced, John Royer prepared an overall assessment detailing the very difficult situation the administration now found itself in (Ryor, 1980), with specific assignments given to Anne Wexler, John White, and me. Harrison Wellford of White's OMB staff took the lead to make sure that a new revised PRM-47, the report the administration still owed to Congress, was prepared with a new conclusion (Wellford, 1980). The report was sent to Congress on February 13, 1980 (Carter, J., 1980d). Several days before sending the report to Congress, the White House went on the offensive to explain to the American people that the President's actions were designed to strengthen "this nation's capability for rapid personnel mobilization in an emergency" (Carter, J., 1980c).[38] In a "statement" released to the press, Carter argued that "[r]egistration for the draft is needed to increase our preparedness and is a further demonstration of our resolve as a nation." Following the line that Cutler had articulated in the days leading up to the State of the Union, the President said that a "vigorous effort to improve our current capabilities will help . . . to deter Soviet aggression." He stressed that this decision to renew registration was "is in no sense a move away from the volunteer force" but that "we have always recognized that [the volunteer force] . . . would have to be supplemented by the draft at a time of national emergency and mobilization" (Carter, J., 1980c). In what would become the most controversial part of his announcement, and a subject he had not broached in the State of the Union address, he announced his "decision to register women" (Carter, J., 1980, p. 2). In an adamant tone he said, "There is no distinction possible, on the basis of ability or performance, that would allow me to exclude women from an obligation to register" (Carter, J., 1980c).[39]

---

[38] *Author's Note:* The events in this section were also covered in a seminar I gave at West Point on December 11, 1980 (Rostker, 1980f).

[39] The decision to register women was controversial even in the White House. On February 2, 1980, OMB Director McIntyre laid out for the President the "sensitive issues on which we will request your decision" (McIntyre, 1980, p. 1). These included the present law, likely equal-protection challenges, DoD's needs, and Equal Rights Amendment issues. He presented three options: peacetime registration of men only; expeditious registration of men while seeking prompt enactment of authority to register women; and peacetime registration of men only, but with a statement of intention to register women upon mobilization. He told the President that most of the staff favored the second option, with the National Security Council favoring the last options. For examples, see Wexler, 1980 and Weddington, 1980. He reported that "there is significant support in both Houses" of Congress but warned that "the bill would probably encounter a filibuster in the Senate" (McIntyre, 1980, p. 5) with further opposition from the House Armed Services Committee and the Speaker of the House. McIntyre conveyed the request that Senator Sam Nunn had made to me and John White when we visited him after the State of the Union address, "that he have a chance to talk with the President before any final decision is made" (McIntyre, 1980, p. 6). The President chose the second option with a "J" in the appropriate check-off box (McIntyre, 1980, p. 6).

President Carter's domestic policy advisor, Stu Eizenstat, was not at all happy about the President's decision and was not shy in telling him: "I, frankly, have some serious concern, both philosophically and politically, with registering women . . . I believe the registration of women will hurt you badly" (Eizenstat, 1980), correctly predicting that "a decision to register women will be highly unpopular among many of your moderate-to-conservative supporters" (Eizenstat, 1980). Eizenstat was right, and his views were reflected by the phone calls being received by the White House Comment Office, which for the week of February 1, 1980, were mainly about the registration of women and were running 98 to 2 percent against the option the President had chosen (Shoob, 1980). On February 6, 1980, the President was informed that, of 4,002 calls the White House had received, over 97 percent were against the registration of women (Carter, H., 1980).

On February 11, 1980, the White House sent the congressionally mandated report to Congress (Carter, J., 1980d). The report, obviously, did not carry the conclusions and recommendations that up until the evening of the State of the Union address had been the steadfast position of the administration. In a strange way, however, it resembled the draft working document I had sent to White on January 16, 1980. The postmobilization registration plan would be implemented as envisioned, but with two "catch-up" registrations in summer 1980 and January 1981 and then with an ongoing system of continuous registration to be carried out at local post offices throughout the country. The report correctly noted that the President's decision "substitute[s] an actual registration system for a registration contingency plan and accelerate the process of improving the other components of the Selective Service System" (Rostker, 1980b).

Reinstating draft registration was simple. It could be done by Presidential proclamation. The problem, however, was that the Selective Service System did not have the funds to carry out the summer "catch-up" registration for those born in 1960 and 1961 that was scheduled for the last week of July and the first week of August (Rostker, 1980c). Congress would have to act; therefore, a majority of members of the House of Representatives would have to agree, and 60 senators would be needed to end the filibuster threatened by Senator Mark Hatfield (R-Oregon). While the battle was technically over with the President's decision to reinstate registration, Congress would have the last word through the power of the purse. As a result, the critical fight would not be about registration per se but about the transfer of a relatively small amount of funds—$13,285,000—from the military personnel account of the Air Force to the Selective Service System. It was not until June 27, 1980, when the House passed Joint Resolution 521 (U.S. Congress, 1980), that the final pieces fell into place. President Carter signed the Joint Resolution in a formal ceremony at the White House on July 2, 1980.

In an interview years later, Pirie recalled the events of that spring:

> During the congressional campaign to reinstitute registration . . . we had been beaten up one side and down the other by prodraft forces without the appearance of any congressional allies whatsoever. However, when the tables turned, and the President wanted to reinstitute registration, the antidraft force in Congress came out of the woodwork, and they beat us up. So we got it coming and going. (Kerber, 1998, p. 376)

Three things made President Carter's call for draft registration problematic: First, many on the political left opposed registration, citing the strong case the administration had been making for years that draft registration was not necessary.[40] Second, these arguments and the draft working document that had been leaked to the press

---

[40] The registration battle is reported in Wilson (1980b).

provided support for the antiregistration forces.[41] Third, the very arguments that Lloyd Cutler had made that had swayed the President that the creditability of the United States was on the line with the Soviet Union if he did not reinstitute registration were not selling on Capital Hill.[42] For example, after the administration's request for funds to implement Selective Service registration lost a critical vote in a subcommittee of the House Appropriations Committee, Congressman Norm Dicks (D-Washington), one of the administration's staunchest allies, told Secretary Brown,

---

[41] *Author's Note:* I listened to President Carter give the State of the Union address with John White in his office in the Old Executive Office Building. When I returned to my office at Selective Service Headquarters that night, a handful of senior staff were waiting. We reviewed the day's events and made plans for the next morning. I asked them to give me all copies of the draft working document and locked them in my desk. Technically these were "pre-decisional" documents that I knew were not subject to the Freedom of Information Act. However, as a government document it needed to be safeguarded. I was sure that, if it were ever made public, it would prove very embarrassing to the administration because it laid out the case why registration was not necessary. On the other hand, the decision was the President's, not mine, to make. If the issue ever came to a head, others would make the decision concerning release of the draft. One thing I was sure of: I was not going to destroy any documents. In fact, on February 23, 1980, George Wilson of the *Washington Post* reported the whole story under the headline, "Selective Service Told Carter Registration is 'Unnecessary'" (Wilson, 1980a). To this day, I don't know how he got the draft. I certainly did not have all the copies; a number had been sent to the OMB and the White House in early January. Eventually, the White House formally released the draft working document.

When the draft working document became public, the administration's first inclination was to attack the plan as unworkable, even though it was the plan that was being implemented to carry out the registration. Secretary of Defense held an open meeting with interested Congressmen in the Blue Room of the White House. Now not only did the argument center around the strong signal registration would send the Soviets, Brown's point paper for the meeting stressed that, if Congress reversed the President's registration decision, it would send "a far more dramatic symbol" (Powell, 1980). When asked about the draft working document, Brown derided the plan that only weeks before had had the strongest backing within the administration, calling it naive. Right after the meeting, I told White, that if the President

> felt . . . it was important to [have an] extra level of security to have the registration, I can support that. I can support submitting a plan and having the President rationally say that he wants more than the plan gave him, but I am not going to be dragged through the mud of Washington about how I had produced a lousy plan. If the original plan is vilified, I will resign and defend it. (As told to Kerber, 1998, p. 282)

The "discussion" with White seemed to have made a difference. In any event, the tone changed. I was asked to help structure a "defensible" argument. Pirie forwarded my position to the White House that

> the small difference in time that registration buys . . . can't justify registration. The justification . . . [should] be based only on the question of how certain we would be that our requirements could be met in an emergency. (Pirie, 1980c)

As I saw it, registration was "insurance against the possible failure of the system in the event of a national emergency" (Pirie, 1980c, p. 3). Eventually, Pirie and White

> agreed to use two arguments: . . . If Congress denies or even comes close to denying the President's request . . . it will send a signal to the Soviets . . . [and] a draft paper prepared by the Selective Service System . . . has already proved to be overly optimistic as Selective Service begins more detailed planning with the other Federal agencies. (Pirie, 1980d, pp. 1, 4)

[42] White found that

> from his contacts on the Hill . . . the argument that registration is a symbol of resolve threatens to irritate the conservatives. Their view is that with all the other real problems we have, we shouldn't be focusing on a symbol. (Office of the Secretary of Defense, 1980)

It was apparent in the Subcommittee's hearings that confusion exists concerning the substantive effect of implementing registration to meet mobilization requirements. There is a perception among some members that registration is simply a symbolic action, and is not tied to real defense requirements. (Dicks, 1980)[43]

Eventually, the full Appropriations Committee approved the transfer of $13.3 million from the Air Force to Selective Service by a vote of 28 to 21. Danzig told Brown, "The vote was closer than we expected even after allowances for some losses as a result of local pressures by anti-registration groups" (Danzig, 1980b). The first critical hurdle had been jumped, even if support was less than impressive. The final House vote came on April 22, 1980, and passed the recommendation of the Appropriations Committee 218 in favor, and 186 against.[44] In the Senate, on May 13 the full Armed Services Committee rejected an amendment by Senator Hatfield to eliminate funds for the revitalization of the Selective Service System by a close vote of 13 to 11, and then the full Senate passed the reprogramming proposal by a voice vote.[45] The issue, however, was still not resolved. In early June, Brown was still lobbying the Senate hard. On June 5, 1980, he told Senator Stennis that he "would like to reemphasize in the strongest terms my judgment, and that of the Joint Chiefs of Staff, that a favorable vote on this measure [registration] is of special importance to the national security" (Brown, 1980b).

The opposition to draft registration received a boost when the leading Republican candidate for President, Ronald Reagan, wrote to Senator Mark Hatfield (R-Oregon) confirming his "concern over the proposal to register young men for the draft." He went on to say that he believed "this proposal is an ill-considered one, and should be rejected. Advanced registration will do little to enhance our military preparedness." Reagan, citing the much-maligned draft Selective Service report argued, "The President's Selective Service Director himself admits that registration will save a scant seven days of the six-month mobilization period" (Reagan, 1980), proving how hard it is for an administration to turn a policy position without proper preparation.

Finally, those on the right who had fought for registration were against the President's decision to register women. Senator Nunn saw it as a potential "show stopper" and warned White and me in a meeting in his office shortly after the State of the Union address that the women's registration issue would have to be separated from registration if the President was serious about getting the reprogramming proposals through Congress.

---

[43] Brown responded by telling Dicks that the "assumptions of the post-mobilization registration plan contained in the January 16th Selective Service draft paper are, in my opinion, unduly optimistic" (Brown, 1980a).

[44] Assistant Secretary of Defense for Legislative Affairs Jack Stempler reported to Secretary Brown that he thought overwhelming defeat of the amendment, which called not only for registration but also examination and classification, by a margin of 45 for and 363 against was "of interest" (Stempler, 1980).

[45] The OSD staff prepared a "sequence of events" detailing "DoD's efforts to promote the President's proposal for reinstitution of peacetime registration" (OASD[MRA&L], 1980) from early February 1980 to the vote of the Senate Appropriations Committee on May 13, 1980.

Registration of Women

The role of women in the military changed remarkably during the 1970s. When Richard Nixon became President, women constituted less than 1 percent of the force. They were either nurses or members of specific women's corps, and, while they held military rank, they were more akin to women's auxiliaries than full members of the armed forces. Under pressure of a changing society and the needs of the all-volunteer force, they had gained emancipation and had become fully integrated into their respective services. Women had even obtained flag and general officer rank in the unrestricted line organizations and had commanded men in gender integrated units. By 1980, women were graduating from the three service academies, and the promise of passage of the Equal Rights Amendment to the United States Constitution seemed to foretell full equality.

After Secretary Brown directed the Services to double the number of women in their ranks by 1983, the inclusion of women in any future draft, even if their numbers might be limited by the gender-based combat restrictions Congress had placed on the Armed Forces, seemed a foregone conclusion. Preliminary plans for a standby draft had contemplated the registration and limited induction of women. Staff papers circulated within the administration argued that the Supreme Court was likely to hold an all-male registration unconstitutional. The Air Force General Counsel's office argued that

> [a]ny selective service law limited to men that would deploy draftees in military positions from which women are not legally barred and to which they are currently assigned would fail to satisfy the substantial relationship branch of the equal protection analysis now required by the Supreme Court. Thus . . . such a law would be held unconstitutional. (Teichler, 1979, p. 53)[46]

The Selective Service System General Counsel expressed similar views when he prepared "a draft bill to amend the Military Selective Service Act to provide for the registration and induction of both men and women" as part of the new postmobilization registration plan being developed during December 1979 (Williams, 1979).

There were opposing views. During the registration debate the previous spring, the Congressional Research Service (CRS) had argued that Congress could order a male-only registration based on its decision to exclude women from combat (Lewis, 1979).[47] Since those drafted would likely be assigned to both combat and noncombat positions, the Air Force General Counsel argued that it was not "constitutionally permissible to register and induct only men to meet noncombat personnel requirements, particularly when women may serve in these positions on a voluntary basis" (Chayes,

---

[46] The American Civil Liberties Union also provided a legal memorandum on the subject (Landau, 1979).

[47] CRS, a part of the Library of Congress, found the existing law constitutional (Lewis, 1979). I asked the Under Secretary of the Air Force to have her General Counsel review the CRS opinion, given its brief of the previous summer.

1980, p. 10). The Department of Justice gave this view some support in an opinion it provided to John White on January 31, 1980. The Office of Legal Counsel found that

> the linchpin of a successful argument supporting the constitutionality of an all-male registration under a stricter standard is the proposition that Congress may, as a matter of substantive constitutional law, prohibit the service of females in actual combat. (Harmon, 1980, p. 8)

The office concluded, however, that if it were possible to

> fashion the registration/conscription process in such a way as to conscript separately for combat and noncombat positions, the rationale for the constitutionality of the Act might as a factual matter be reduced to one of administrative convenience. (Harmon, 1980, p. 9)

In fact, this was exactly what DoD intended to do. In early January 1980, the Assistant General Counsel assigned to Pirie's office observed that

> [i]f conscription is reinstated and the induction of women is authorized, separate draft calls would be necessary as a result of the combat exclusion and related policies based upon rotational and replacement requirements for combat personnel. . . . If women are conscripted, the most reasonable means of selecting and inducting the appropriate number of women would be through separate draft calls for men and women. . . . [T]here is no legal impediment to separate draft calls for men and women. (Gilliat, 1980, p. 5)

The issue of registering women was joined in Congress in a series of hearings in both the House and Senate. The enthusiasm in the administration for including women in registration was certainly not shared by members of Congress. The first hearing before the House Armed Services Committee set the tone for the whole debate. While the usual antagonists were present and took familiar positions, the first witness, from Haleyville, Alabama, framed the issue simply as one of providing equal opportunity, for which she was all in favor, rather than enforced equality, to which she was opposed. She explained it this way:

> I think that the majority of American girls, including my daughter, are unfit both physically and emotionally to serve in the Armed Forces. . . . I am not saying military is not for every American woman. I am saying it is not for the majority. It would take my daughter—and I am thinking of her close friends—2 days in basic training before I know there would be total havoc in that camp. I can see her saying, "Oh, you have got mud on my pants. I can't fix my hair." This is the type of girls they are. (White, R., 1980, pp. 3–4)

Congresswoman Marjorie Holt (R-Maryland) agreed, and noted that

> the majority of the American women want to stay out of the military. This is not taking anything away from the very fine women who are doing a great job in the

military, who want to be there voluntarily, and we do need them. They are doing a splendid job. We want to open up every opportunity for them . . . [but] this Nation is not ready to send its women into combat. (White, R., 1980, p. 3)

By the end of the day, the committee voted eight to one to table the bill that would have amended the Military Selective Service Act to permit the registration of women.[48]

Between the legislative and executive branches, the issue was settled. While, as a matter of policy, the Carter administration would have liked to register women and to hold a limited draft to fill noncombat jobs, it was not prepared to call off registration over that issue. The constitutionality of a male-only draft, however, was not settled until the decision in the Supreme Court case of *Rostker v. Goldberg*. The majority of the court found a compelling governmental interest and upheld the right of Congress to discriminate on the basis of gender. Both the tone of the hearings and the majority opinion by Justice Rehnquist were instructive of the mood of the country and the rising conservative attitude toward women in the military.

The Constitutionality of a Male-Only Draft

While congressional action prohibited me from registering women, it did not prevent a constitutional challenge to the all-male draft. Karen J. Lewis's opinion of the previous summer laid out the logic of such a case:

If there is a challenge to the exclusion [of women], it will probably [be] brought by a male claiming that his Fifth Amendment guarantees for equal protection and due process have been violated. He will assert he has been burdened by the exclusion of women from the registration system because his individual chance of being drafted has thereby increased because the pool is smaller. (Lewis, 1979, p. 34)

In fact, the name of the male making such a claim was Robert L. Goldberg. His case was left over from the Vietnam draft days. It had become moot with the end of conscription in 1973. In 1980, it was no longer moot. On February 19, 1980, soon after President Carter's decision to resume draft registration, Goldberg filed in the United States District Court for the Eastern District of Pennsylvania to reactivate the case. With the first round of registrations quickly approaching, the court granted Goldberg's motion for "class certification." On July 1, 1980, the three-judge panel heard oral arguments. On the Friday before registration was to start—as a result of the Presidential proclamation of July 2, 1980, registration of males born in 1960 and 1961 was to begin on Monday, July 21, 1980—the court found that

the exclusion of women from the pool of registrants does not serve "important government objectives" and is not "substantially related" . . . to any alleged

---

[48] A full account is provided in Foley and Davidson (1980).

government interest. Thus, the MSSA [Military Selective Service Act] unconstitutionally discriminated between males and females. (Rosenn, Lord, and Cahn, 1980, p. 41)

They issued an order stopping the registration that was scheduled to start in less than three days.[49]

The following day, Saturday, July 19, 1980, Justice Brennan, acting in his capacity as the Circuit Justice of the Third Circuit, responded favorably to a request to stay the decision of the district court, determining that any "inconvenience" caused by imposing registration on males born in 1960 and 1961, even if the Supreme Court eventually upheld the district court's order, did not outweigh the "gravity of the harm to the United States" (Brennan, 1980). He allowed the registration to proceed as scheduled. On March 24, 1981, however, the appeal of the district court's ruling, now known as *Rostker v. Goldberg,* was argued before the Supreme Court.

On June 25, 1981, Justice Rehnquist delivered the opinion of the court (Rehnquist, 1981). The majority upheld the constitutionality of excluding women from the draft. The opinion started with a restatement of the "exclusive" authority of Congress "to raise and support Armies [and] to provide and maintain a Navy, [and] to make Rules for the Government and Regulation of the land and naval forces." Rehnquist, citing the "healthy deference" the Court had given "to legislative and executive judgments in the area of military affairs," noted that "it is difficult to conceive of an area of governmental activity in which the courts have less competence." His main arguments, however, were based on the carefully laid out proposition developed in the Senate's report that "Congress determined that any future draft, which would be facilitated by the registration scheme, would be characterized by a need for combat troops."[50] And, thus, he concluded, "[t]he existence of the combat restrictions [on women] clearly indicates the basis for Congress' decision to exempt women from registration." In a bold statement that belied DoD's direct testimony, Rehnquist declared that the "purpose of registration was to prepare for a draft of combat troops."

In the disagreement between Congress and the President, Rehnquist took the side of Congress, noting that Congress had considered a gender-specific draft, with women draftees filling noncombat jobs, and rejected it as "inflexible . . . not worth the added burden . . . confusing . . . and insignificant in the context of military preparedness and the exigencies of a future mobilization." He drew on a statement from Senator Nunn to the effect that equality issues, while "legitimate," were far less important than "military needs" and that "considering . . . the overall registration bill, there is no military necessity" to register women. Finally he argued that the district court had been "quite

---

[49] Their order "permanently enjoined [the government] from requiring the registration under the Military Selective Service Act of any members of the plaintiff class" (Rosenn, Lord, and Cahn, 1980b).

[50] The Chief Justice held "The Senate Report . . . is considerably more significant than a typical report of a single House, and its findings are in effect the findings of the entire Congress" (Rehnquist, 1981).

wrong in undertaking an independent evaluation of the evidence" on the military need to register women, "rather than adopting an appropriate deferential examination of Congress' evaluation of that evidence."

If the facts—at least the facts as administration witnesses representing the Executive Office of the President, DoD, and the Selective Service System had presented them—were lost on Justice Rehnquist and the majority of the court, they were fully appreciated by justices Marshall and White, as reflected in their dissenting opinions. Marshall chided the court for "placing its imprimatur on one of the most potent remaining public expressions of 'ancient canards about the proper role of women'" (Rehnquist, 1981, p. 13).[51] He noted

> nothing in the [much cited] Senate Report supports the Court's intimation that women must be excluded from registration because combat eligibility is a prerequisite for all the positions that would need to be filled in the event of a draft. . . . All four Service Chiefs agreed that there are no military reasons for refusing to register women. (Rehnquist, 1981, p. 15)

White also argued that, even given the combat exclusion, which would limit the future induction of women to noncombat jobs, "administrative convenience," as suggested in the Senate Report, "has not been sufficient justification for the kind of outright gender-based discrimination involved in registering and conscripting men but no women at all."

Results of the Draft Registration and Its Effects on the All-Volunteer Force

The summer catch-up registration of males born in 1960 and 1961 went very smoothly. If there was to be any trouble, it was expected to happen the first day. As reported widely in the press and media, however, the day went largely without incident. The

---

[51] Justice Marshall may have had in mind the positions that Phyllis Schlafly, Elaine Donnelly, and other activists took when they lobbied Congress against extending the role of women in the military. They were opposed to any involuntary service for women, even if it were to fill noncombat jobs releasing men for combat duty. Kathleen Teague, speaking for the Coalition Against Drafting Women, told Congress that compulsory service for women was contrary to

> American traditions, laws, morals, and the wishes of the majority of the American people. We don't want our daughters taught to kill. Women's mission is to participate in the creation of life, not in destroying it. We expect our servicemen to be tough enough to defend us against any enemy—and we want our women to be feminine and human enough to transform our servicemen into good husbands, fathers, and citizens upon their return from battle. . . . Have we sunk so low that the men of America are willing to send their daughters and sisters and wives out to fight for them in the Persian Gulf, or wherever we face a crisis? (Schlafly and Teague, 1980, p. 103)

Both Schlafly and Donnelly continued to be frequent critics of the role of women in the all-volunteer armed forces. They received a sympathetic ear in the Reagan and Bush administrations, culminating in the Presidential Commission on the Role of Women in the Military after Operation Desert Storm (as discussed in Chapter Fifteen).

following evening, after the second day of the registration, the entire MacNeil/Lehrer Report on the Public Broadcasting System was devoted to draft registration, with commentary from myself and from antidraft activist Barry Lynn.[52] This is the way Robert MacNeil and Jim Lehrer saw the first two days of the registration:

> Thousands of 20-year-old men have been registered for the draft, despite efforts at a nation-wide protest and uncertainty about whether the registration law is constitutional. . . . Demonstrations against registration were scattered around the country and they were mostly small and quiet affairs. Young people picketed post offices and government buildings, carrying placards, chanting slogans, and handing out leaflets. But there were few incidents of violence. ("Draft Registration," 1980)

On September 2, 1980, the Selective Service System Headquarters received the final shipment of keypunched registration forms from the IRS (which had used its off-tax-season capability to support the summer registration). The shipment contained all registration forms received through August 22, 1980—3,593,187 of them. These were keypunched, and individual records were entered into Selective Service computers. On September 3, 1980,[53] I told President Carter that I estimated this to be "93% of the eligible population" (Rostker, 1980e).[54] By comparison, I told the President, in 1975—the last year of the registration during the Ford administration—the comparable number was 83 percent. I also added that the President's decision to reject the postmobilization plan had been correct:

> Our experience over the last nine months clearly indicates the need for a system of continuous registration. Even with six months of intense planning and prepositioning of registration materials, it still took us four weeks, after Congressional approval, to mount the registration. The processing of completed registration material is still underway. If these actions were not accomplished before a mobilization it would not be possible for Selective Service to meet its obligations to the Department of Defense. (Rostker, 1980e)

---

[52] Lynn was the chairman of the Committee Against Registration and the Draft (CARD), an ordained minister in the United Church of Christ, and a lawyer.

[53] My memorandum was forward to the President with a cover memorandum from John White (White, J., 1980b).

[54] *Author's Note:* On October 21, 1980, President Carter acknowledged the success of the military registration program and his personal appreciation to me and my staff;

> our Nation owes you and your staff a debt of gratitude for your hard work and for the foresight which led you, as the newly appointed director, to take steps to increase our mobilization readiness even prior to my announced decision to revitalize the Selective Service System. (Carter, J., 1980e)

Senator Bill Cohen, even though he had opposed the registration, was the only member of Congress to personally acknowledge the results of the registration. In a letter he congratulated me and my staff "on the successful implementation of the President's peacetime registration plan. The level of compliance and smooth manner in which the registration process was carried out are a tribute to you and the plan you developed" (Cohen, 1980). His parting thought was prophetic; "I look forward to continuing to work with you for a strong national defense capability" (Cohen, 1980). Sixteen years later, Secretary of Defense Bill Cohen and I would work together in the Pentagon.

The results of the registration were made available to the public through an announcement and press conference on September 4, 1980 (Rostker, 1980d). The day before the press conference, Richard Halloran of *The New York Times* reported that someone in the administration had told him that, "[d]uring the war in Vietnam . . . 75 to 77 percent of the nation's young men registered when they were legally required to do so" (Halloran, 1980a). He apparently took this to be some kind of a bar the administration wanted to be judged by as it prepared the public for a result well below the numbers that had been talked about since January. He speculated that "Selective Service System expects to announce that more than 80 percent of the young men subject to draft registration" had signed up. In fact, the number reported was well above 80 percent. Two days later, the headline in the *Times* over Halloran's byline was "compliance with draft registration is put at 93%" (Halloran, 1980b). He reported, however, that Barry Lynn of CARD "doubted the accuracy of the base population figure . . . and the number who signed, and contended that many of those counted have given false names or addresses" (Halloran, 1980b).

It fell to GAO to certify the results of the 1980 draft-registration program. On December 19, 1980, the Director of GAO's Federal Personnel and Compensation Division wrote to tell me that GAO was "impressed by the thoroughness, completeness, and accuracy with which this program [draft registration] was conducted" (Krieger, 1980b).[55] The details of their monitoring of registration were contained in a report sent to the chairmen of Selective Service's oversight congressional committees. GAO told the chairmen that the system had "been subject to challenge by a variety of critics and organizations" (Krieger, 1980a). To check on the veracity of the system, GAO randomly called 378 of the more than 3.6 million registrants. From this random sample, GAO was able to conclude that less than 1,000 registrations had "obviously fictitious" names or addresses and that a "final accuracy levels of 98 percent do not appear to be unreasonable expectations" (Krieger, 1980a, p. 3).

If GAO was now pleased with the way registration had proceeded, it was less so with the rest of the mobilization system, as indicated by the title of one of its reports, *Problems in Getting People Into the Active Force After Mobilization*. This report, written before the new registration was put in place, not only highlighted bottlenecks in the Selective Service induction process but also noted that "training centers may be hindered in housing and will be unable to train these draftees" (Comptroller General of the United States, 1979a).

With the Selective Service part of the problem successfully out of the way, GAO now focused on DoD's failure to build and sustain a mobilization infrastructure. In

---

[55] *Author's Note*: Krieger later told me that the words, "impressed by the thoroughness, completeness, and accuracy," which had been included in a previous draft of his report and contained in his letter to me, had been edited out of the final report as being too exalting in tone and not in keeping with the usual GAO rhetoric. The more subdued words, "[o]verall, we did not find any major problems with the manner in which registration was organized or conducted," had been substituted. Nevertheless, six months later, when I visited Senator Nunn for the last time as Director of Selective Service, he commented that he had never seen a more favorable report from GAO.

1983, GAO estimated that the Army could "accommodate only about 50 percent of the personnel it needs to begin training within 180 days following mobilization, due to shortages in equipment, trainers and training units" (Gould, 1983). What was more troubling, GAO now questioned the whole mobilization requirement that had been at the heart of the draft registration debate. Five years after the "great debate" over the future of the all-volunteer force and after the start of the Selective Service draft registration, GAO told the Secretary of Defense that

> DoD has not analyzed systematically the military services actual need for inductees. Even though the data exist, the system that DoD uses for making wartime manpower planning decisions collects insufficiently detailed data on each service's wartime needs and expected manning shortages and surpluses to enable it to validate the accuracy of the current inductee request schedule. (Conahan, 1984, cover)

While DoD strongly disagreed that it did not have a "systematic method for validating induction requirements," we can only wonder if GAO's conclusions had been brought forth in 1979 rather than 1984, if draft registration would have gone on.

Finally, while the GAO report on the 1980 draft registration was forwarded to President-elect Ronald Reagan's defense transition team (Krieger, 1980b), this was an issue that the team did not want to deal with, at least at the time. In fact, it is not clear who on the transition team would have received the report, since the Selective Service System was the only agency in government not to have a designated transition official.[56]

---

[56] *Author's Note:* Two weeks before the end of President Carter's term and the Reagan inaugural, a deputy in the White House General Counsel's office called me. He said, "If I had not heard otherwise from my transition coordinator on the Reagan Transition team I should clear out my desk by noon on the day of President Reagan's inaugural." I told him the Reagan transition organization had never appointed a transition coordinator. He told me that was impossible and that he would get back to me. Several days later he called to explain that I was correct that no transition coordinator had been appointed but that he was talking to his counterpart on the transition team, and would get back to me. I kept calling and he kept telling me that they had not made up their minds and that he would let me know what was to happen.

Finally, the night before the inaugural he asked for my home phone number and promised to call me the next morning to let me know if I should come to work the following day—the first work day of the new administration. I never received a call. I decided to go to work as usual. I did that for three days not knowing whom to call in the new White House. Finally, on the third day, I received a call from the new deputy general counsel. He explained that the whole issue was up in the air, that I should proceed with the second phase of the mass registrations, and that the White House wanted me to stay in place and continue to do what ever I had been doing. He made it clear, however, that this arrangement was temporary.

In fact, it lasted until the end of July, when the new administration named California National Guard Major General Tom Turnage as the new Director of Selective Service, and I resigned to take a position at the Center for Naval Analyses.

Transitioning to the New Administration

On the evening of November 4, 1980, NBC news was the first to declare Ronald Reagan the winner of the Presidential election. The time was 8:15 P.M., Eastern Standard Time, and most of the nation's polling places were still open and people were still voting.[57] The transition started the next morning. Agencies throughout the federal government were asked to send a senior representative to the White House to get instructions on the transition to a new administration.[58] The outgoing administration asked each department or agency to appoint a transition coordinator to be paired with one from President-elect Reagan's transition team.

At least that was the way it was supposed to be. The Reagan team never named a transition team for Selective Service. This was not an oversight but a deliberate act reflecting the deep divisions within the new administration concerning both the all-volunteer force and the recent draft registration. Moreover, within weeks of the pending inaugural, Selective Service had scheduled the second catch-up registration, after which the system would transition to continuing registration of men as they turned 18. Not having agreed on what course of action to follow—whether or not to support the January registration or what to do about the all-volunteer force—the new administration thought it best not to name anyone to the transition team whom the press could corner. By the end of the first week in office, however, the new administration had decided to support the status quo, at least temporarily, until it could sort things out. I was asked to *temporarily* remain in my post as Director of Selective Service and to proceed with the second mass registration. All other decisions were put on hold.[59]

---

[57] *Author's Note:* Many of those who were engaged in the management of the all-volunteer force during the Carter administration gathered at my house to watch the election returns. Those in attendance included Richard Danzig and Robin Pirie from DoD, Bob Murray (the Under Secretary of the Navy) and Phil Odeen, formerly of Systems Analysis and the National Security Council staff, and more recently a member of the President's Commission on Military Compensation. No one was expecting President Carter to win. The polls for the last week all pointed to a defeat. What was more ominous was the poor morale of those in the administration. The lack of support for the military and the all-volunteer force, the draft registration debates and flip-flop and the Iranian hostage situation had taken their toll. This was an administration that had lost confidence in itself, just as the American people had lost confidence in it. In anticipation of a defeat I had gotten unemployment insurance claim forms from each of the three political areas that made up the Washington metropolitan area and expected to hand them out sometime during the evening when it was clear that Carter had lost. I did not expect that I would hand them out as my guests arrived, but that was what happened as most arrived after the networks declared Reagan the winner. For a discussion of the early call see Weinraub (1980).

[58] *Author's Note:* Because Selective Service was such a small agency and because I was curious about what was unfolding, I nominated myself to be the Selective Service transition coordinator. I believe that I was the only head of an executive agency that was so designated.

[59] Senator Mark Hatfield was not happy with this arrangement and told President Reagan he wanted to "move promptly to end the [draft registration] program . . . [before] the debate . . . evolve[s] beyond the registration issue toward a discussion of the pros and cons of the draft" (Hatfield, 1981). He told the President that, in his view, "Dr. Rostker should be replaced with an individual who is prepared to carry forth your policy, not that of the last Administration. I have no doubt that the most effective way to lay the draft issue to rest is to dismantle the Carter registration program" (Hatfield, 1981).

Figure 12.1
Bernard Rostker, Director of Selective Service, meets President Carter in the Oval Office while John P. White, Deputy Director of OMB, looks on, March 4, 1980 (White House Staff, 1980).

Photo Courtesy Jimmy Carter Library

Figure 12.2
President Carter calls for draft registration at the State of the Union, January 21, 1980 (Carter, J., 1980b).

Video Image Courtesy Jimmy Carter Library

Figure 12.3
President Carter and Senator Sam Nunn of Georgia at the signing ceremony for the bill transferring money to the Selective Service System that would allow registration to proceed. Senior members of the House Armed Services Committee look on, as well as Bernard Rostker, Director of Selective Service.

Photo Courtesy Jimmy Carter Library

Figure 12.4
Rostker briefs the press on the results of the 1980 draft registration, September 4, 1980.

Photo Courtesy Jimmy Carter Library

Figure 12.5
World War I Draft Registration Cards for Bernard Rostker's grandfathers. Despite Frederick Cutler's (1923, p. 174) description of registration day—"a feeling of solemnity possessed all hearts; a holiday was declared; at the stated hour, church bells rang as though summoning men to worship,"—it is doubtful that on September 12, 1918, the day when men between the ages of 31 years and 45 registered, Rostker's grandfathers were very pleased. Both had fled Europe to escape the draft and now, at an advanced age, they were being asked to register for possible service in a European war. As it turned out, neither was called to serve.

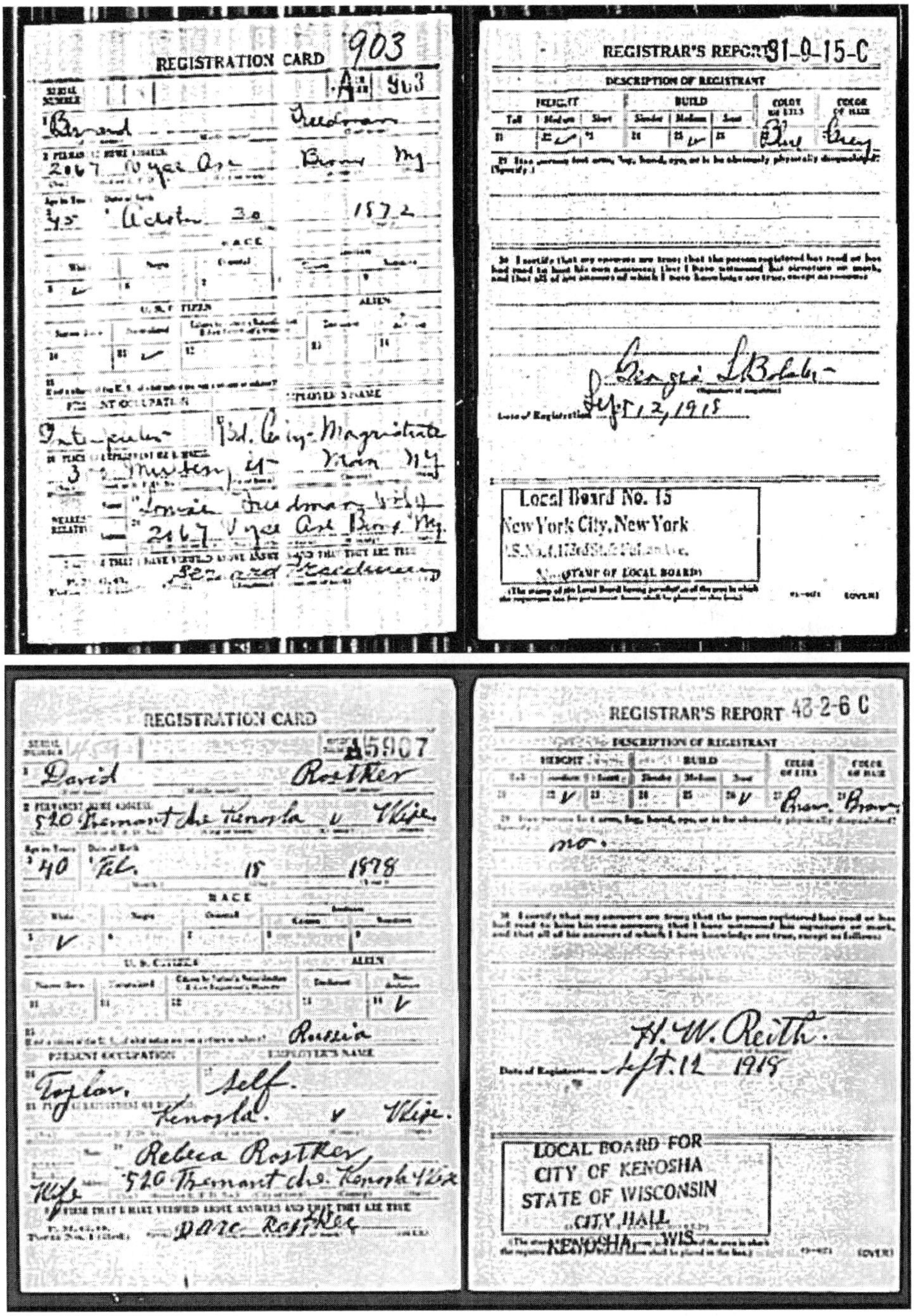

REGISTRATION CARD 903

A 903

REGISTRAR'S REPORT 31-9-15-C

DESCRIPTION OF REGISTRANT

Sept 12, 1918

Local Board No. 15
New York City, New York

REGISTRATION CARD

A5907

David Rostker

40 Feb. 15 1878

RACE

U. S. CITIZEN

ALIEN

Russia

PRESENT OCCUPATION

EMPLOYER'S NAME

Self

Rebeca Rostker

Wife

REGISTRAR'S REPORT 43-2-6 C

DESCRIPTION OF REGISTRANT

H. W. Reith

Sept. 12 1918

LOCAL BOARD FOR
CITY OF KENOSHA
STATE OF WISCONSIN
CITY HALL
KENOSHA, WIS.

SOURCE: National Archives

References

Aspin, Les, et al., "Dear Colleague (on draft registration)," to Members of the U.S. Congress, Washington, D.C., Undated (June 1979). S0544.pdf.

Beard, Robin, Testimony and Statement Concerning the Selective Service System, hearing before the House Committee on Armed Services, 96th Cong., 1st Sess., Washington, D.C., U.S. Government Printing Office, April 9, 1979.

Brehm, William K., "Standby Draft," memorandum to Gus C. Less, Washington, D.C., October 24, 1973. G0080.pdf.

Brennan, William J., *Bernard Rostker et al. v Robert Goldberg et al.,* on Application for Stay N. A-70, Decided July 19, 1980, Washington, D.C.: U.S. Supreme Court, July 19, 1980.

Brezinski, Zbigniew, "President's Plan for Selective Service Reform: Presidential Review Memorandum (PRM)/National Security Council-47," memorandum to the Vice President, the Secretary of State and the Secretary of Defense, Washington, D.C., October 12, 1979. C0019.pdf.

Brown, Harold, "Department of Defense Position on Registration," letter to Senator William Cohen, Washington, D.C., June 8, 1979. S0548.pdf.

———, "Proposed Legislation for Peacetime Registration," letter to Congressman Charles E. Bennett, Washington, D.C., July 23, 1979. G1480.pdf.

———, "Draft Registration," memorandum to Norman D. Dicks, March 6, 1980a. G0349.pdf.

———, "Draft Registration," memorandum to John C. Stennis, Washington, D.C., June 5, 1980b. G0445.pdf.

Carter, Hugh, "Draft Registration Mail and Calls (Per Your Request)," memorandum to the President, Washington, D.C., February 6, 1980a. C0008.pdf.

Carter, Jimmy, "Nomination of Bernard Daniel Rostker to be Director of the Selective Service System," *Weekly Compilation of Presidential Documents,* Vol. 15, No. 32, August 13, 1979, pp. 1,419.

———,"State of the Union Address 1980," address to the Congress of the United States, Washington, D.C., January 23, 1980a. G1485.pdf.

———, "State of the Union Address," video of address to the Congress of the United States, Washington, D.C., January 23, 1980b. S0589.mov.

———, *Statement by the President: Selective Service Registration and Revitalization,* Washington, D.C.: The White House, February 8, 1980c. G1186.pdf.

———, *Presidential Recommendations for Selective Service Reform: A Report to Congress Prepared Pursuant to P.L. 96-107,* Washington, D.C.: The White House, February 11, 1980d. S0561.pdf.

———, "Congratulations," letter to Bernard D. Rostker, Washington, D.C., October 21, 1980e. G1190.pdf.

Casselman, Bill, "Proclamation Terminating Selective Service Registration," memorandum to Phil Buchen, Washington, D.C., February 18, 1975a. F0003.pdf.

———, "Proposed Proclamation," memorandum to Judy Johnson, Jerry Jones and Phil Buchen, Washington, D.C., March 4, 1975b. F0008.pdf.

Chayes, Antonia Handler, "Registration and Induction of Women for Military Service," memorandum to Bernard D. Rostker, Washington, D.C., January 8, 1980. S0606.pdf.

Chu, David S. C., and Daniel F. Huck, Testimony and Statement Concerning the Selective Service System, hearing before the House Committee on Armed Services, 96th Cong., 1st Sess., Washington, D.C., U.S. Government Printing Office, February 14, 1979. S0498.pdf.

Cohen, William S., "Congratulations," letter to Bernard D. Rostker, Washington, D.C., September 5, 1980. G1191.pdf.

———, *Roll Call: One Year in the United States Senate,* New York: Simon and Schuster, 1981.

Comptroller General of the United States, *Problems in Getting People Into the Active Force After Mobilization,* Washington, D.C.: General Accounting Office, May 17, 1979a. S0285.pdf.

———, *Weaknesses in the Selective Service System's Emergency Registration Plan,* Washington, D.C.: General Accounting Office, FPCD7989, August 29, 1979b. S0563.pdf.

Conahan, Frank C., "Better Use of Available Data Would improve Mobilization Planning for Inductees," memorandum to Caspar W. Weinberger, Washington, D.C., October 22, 1984. G1164.pdf.

Danzig, Richard, "Improved Selective Service System," memorandum to Assistant Secretaries (M&RA) & Director Joint Staff, Washington, D.C., December 27, 1978. S0552.pdf.

———, "Arrangements Should Be Made to Inform Ross, Rostker and the Head of the Post Office," memorandum to Robin Pirie, Washington, D.C., January 22, 1980a. G0341.pdf.

———, "Funding for Peacetime Registration," information memorandum to Secretary of Defense, Washington, D.C., April 18, 1980b. G0343.pdf.

Daoust, George A., Jr., "Standby Draft Procedures," memorandum to Assistant Secretary of the Army (M&RA), Washington, D.C., October 10, 1972a. G0177.pdf.

———, "Standby Draft," memorandum to Assistant Secretaries of the Military Departments (M&RA), Washington, D.C., December 11, 1972b. G0093.pdf.

Davis, Jeanne W., "Proclamation Terminating Registration Procedures Under the Military Selective Service Act," memorandum to Warren Hendriks, Washington, D.C., February 24, 1975a. F0016.pdf.

———, "Proclamation 'Terminating Registration Procedures Under the Military Selective Service Act, as Amended'," memorandum to Warren Hendriks, Washington, D.C., March 21, 1975b. F0019.pdf.

Dicks, Norman D., "Draft Registration," memorandum to Harold Brown, Washington, D.C., February 28, 1980. G0348.pdf.

Eizenstat, Stuart E., "Draft Registration," letter to Congressman John Seiberling, Washington, D.C., July 23, 1979. S0543.pdf.

———, "Selective Service Reform and Registration," memorandum to the President, Washington, D.C., February 2, 1980. C0010.pdf.

Foley, Joe, and Marjorie Davidson, "The Registration of Women Legislation During the 96th Congress," memorandum to Director of Selective Service Bernard D. Rostker, Washington, D.C., December 18, 1980. S0609.pdf.

Ford, Gerald R., *Proclamation Terminating Registration Procedures Under the Military Selective Service Act, as Amended,* Washington, D.C.: The White House, Proclamation No. 4360, March 29, 1975. F0020.pdf.

Gates, Thomas S., Jr., *The Report of the President's Commission on an All-Volunteer Armed Force,* Washington, D.C., February 1970. S0243.pdf.

Gilliat, Robert L., "PRM 47 (Selective Service Systems comments, dated December 12, 1979)," memorandum to Deputy Assistant Secretary of Defense for MRA&L (Program Management), Washington, D.C., January 2, 1980. S0608.pdf.

Gould, Clifford I., "Army's Ability to Expand Training Base Upon Mobilization Remains Limited," memorandum to John O. Jr. March, Washington, D.C., February 2, 1983. G1163.pdf.

Greenlief, Francis S., Testimony and Statement Concerning the Selective Service System, hearing before the House Committee on Armed Services, 96th Cong., 1st. Sess., Washington, D.C., U.S. Government Printing Office, April 15, 1979. S0510.pdf.

Halloran, Richard, "U.S. Is Expected to Announce 80% Signed Up for Draft," *New York Times,* September 4, 1980a, p. A18.

———, "Compliance with Draft Registration Is Put at 93%," *New York Times,* September 5, 1980b, p. A14.

Harmon, John M., "Constitutionality of All-Male Draft Registration," memorandum to John White, Deputy Director of Office of Management and Budget, Washington, D.C., January 11, 1980. S0607.pdf.

Hatfield, Mark O., "Opposition to Continued Registration, Together with Draft Response," letter to the President, Washington, D.C., April 3, 1981. R0007.pdf.

Huck, Daniel F., *The Selective Service System: Mobilization Capabilities and Options for Improvement,* Washington, D.C.: Congressional Budget Office, November 1978. S0562.pdf.

Jones, David C., "Improved Standby Draft," memorandum to the Secretary of Defense, Washington, D.C., December 13, 1978. S0554.pdf.

Kerber, Linda K., *No Constitutional Right to Be Ladies: Women and the Obligations of Citizenship,* New York: Hill and Wang: A Division of Farrar, Straus and Giroux, 1998.

Kissinger, Henry A., "National Security Decision Memorandum 208: Standby Draft," memorandum to Secretary of Defense, Office of Management and Budget Director and Selective Service System Director, Washington, D.C., March 16, 1973a. F0014.pdf.

———, "Standby Draft," memorandum to the President, Washington, D.C., August 16, 1973b. G0071.pdf.

————, "National Security Study Memorandum 165—Standby Draft," memorandum to Secretary of Defense, Director of Selective Service, Director of the Office of Management and Budget and Director of the Office of Emergency Preparedness, Washington, D.C., December 3, 1972v. G1228.pdf.

Krieger, H. L., "Evaluation of the Recent Draft Registration (FPCD-81-30) B-201499," memorandum to William Proxmire, Sam Nunn, Edward P. Boland and Richard C. White, Washington, D.C., December 19, 1980a. G0024.pdf.

————, "GAO Report on Draft Registration," memorandum to Bernard D. Rostker, Washington, D.C., December 19, 1980b. G0023.pdf.

Laird, Melvin R., "National Security Study Memorandum 165 on the Standby Draft," memorandum to Henry A. Kissinger, Washington, D.C., December 12, 1972. G0095.pdf.

Landau, David E., *Males-Only Draft Registration Requirements: An Equal Protection Analysis,* memorandum, Washington, D.C.: American Civil Liberties Union. S0605.pdf.

Lee, Gus C., "Study of Standby Draft Machinery," memorandum to Roger Kelley, Washington, D.C., October 11, 1972. G0178.pdf.

Lewis, Karen J., *A Legal Analysis Regarding the Constitutionality of Excluding Women from Registration and Classification Procedures Under the Selective Service Act,* Washington, D.C.: The Library of Congress, Congressional Research Service, Legislative Law Division, June 14, 1979. S0604.pdf.

Loen, Vern, "Selective Service Budget Cuts," memorandum to Max L. Friedersdorf and Tom C. Korologos, Washington, D.C., August 19, 1974. F0001.pdf.

Lynn, James T., *The Selective Service System: Draft of 10/17/75,* Washington, D.C.: Office of Management and Budget, October 17, 1975 (draft). F0027.pdf.

MacNeil, Robert, Jim Lehrer, Barry Lynn, and Bernard D. Rostker, "Draft Registration," *The MacNeil/Lehrer Report,* transcript, July 22, 1980. S0643.pdf.

Marrs, Ted, *The Selective Service System,* Washington, D.C.: The White House, August 27, 1974. F0021.pdf.

McIntyre, James T. Jr., "Consideration of FY'80 Department of Defense Authorization Bill," letter to Chairman of the House Committee on Rules, Washington, D.C., July 6, 1979. G1479.pdf.

————, "Registration of Women for Selective Service," memorandum to the President, Washington, D.C., February 2, 1980. C0005.pdf.

Montgomery, Gillespie V., Testimony and Statement Concerning the Selective Service System, hearing before the House Committee on Armed Services, 96th Cong., 1st Sess., Washington, D.C., U.S. Government Printing Office, April 15, 1979. S0511.pdf.

Montgomery, Gillespie V., and Robin L. Beard, "Dear Colleague (on draft registration)," Dear Colleague letter to Member of the U.S. Congress, Washington, D.C., July 3, 1979. S0550.pdf.

Nichols, William M., "Department of Justice Review of Proposed Proclamation," memorandum to Attorney General, Washington, D.C., February 11, 1975. F0005.pdf.

Nunn, Sam, *News Release: Subcommittee Approves Selective Service Registration Bill,* Washington, D.C.: Office of Senator Sam Nunn, June 7, 1979a. S0542.pdf.

———, "The Case for Peacetime Registration," *Washington Post,* July 27, 1979b. S0556.pdf.

———, *Floor Statement: The Need for Registration,* Washington, D.C.: United States Senate, September 21, 1979c. S0541.pdf.

OASD[M&RA]—*See* Office of the Assistant Secretary of Defense for Manpower and Reserve Affairs.

OASD[MRA&L]—*See* Office of the Assistant Secretary of Defense for Manpower, Reserve Affairs, and Logistics.

Office of the Assistant Secretary of Defense for Manpower and Reserve Affairs, *Mohn's Paper on Standby Draft,* Washington, D.C.: U.S. Department of Defense, October 20, 1970. G0170.pdf.

———, *Proposed Department of Defense Position on the Transfer of the Selective Service System to the Department of Defense,* Washington, D.C.: Office of the Assistant Secretary of Defense (M&RA), May 9, 1979. G0358.pdf.

Office of the Assistant Secretary of Defense for Manpower, Reserve Affairs, and Logistics, *Registration/Selective Service Reform,* Washington, D.C.: U.S. Department of Defense, May 20, 1980. G0346.pdf.

Odeen, Philip A., "Standby Draft," memorandum to Henry A. Kissinger, Washington, D.C., November 24, 1972. G1110.pdf.

Office of the Secretary of Defense, "John White Called," note to Secretary of Defense, Washington, D.C., March 3, 1980. G0344.pdf.

Pepitone, Byron V., "The Ill-Described Posture of 'Standby'," memorandum to Jonathan Rose, Washington, D.C., July 14, 1972. G1062.pdf.

———, "Comments on Alternative Funding Levels," memorandum to Director Office of Management and Budget, Washington, D.C., December 4, 1974. F0022.pdf.

———, "Proposed Proclamation Terminating Registration," memorandum to Roy Ash Director Office of Management and Budget, Washington, D.C., January 17, 1975a. F0004.pdf.

———, "Concerns About the OMB Paper on Registration," memorandum to Theodore C. Marrs, Washington, D.C., October 22, 1975b. F0013.pdf.

———, *Semiannual Report of the Director of Selective Service: July 1, 1975–December 31, 1975,* Washington, D.C.: Selective Service System, December 31, 1975c. F0002.pdf.

Pirie, Robert B., Jr., "Weekly Activity Report (23–27 October 1978)," information memorandum to Secretary of Defense, Washington, D.C., November 1, 1978a. G0414.pdf.

———, "Weekly Activity Report (13–17 November 1978)," information memorandum to Secretary of Defense, Washington, D.C., November 21, 1978b. G0411.pdf.

———, "Activity Report (27 November–8 December 1978)," information memorandum to Secretary of Defense, Washington, D.C., December 9, 1978c. G0409.pdf.

————, The Nomination of Robert B. Pirie, Jr. to be Assistant Secretary of Defense for Manpower, Reserve Affairs and Logistics, hearing before the Subcommittee on Manpower and Personnel, Committee on Armed Services, United States Senate, First, Washington, D.C., U.S. Government Printing Office, April 6, 1979a. S0492.pdf.

————, "Peacetime Registration," action memorandum to Secretary of Defense, Washington, D.C., June 11, 1979b. G0359.pdf.

————, "MRA&L Planning for the Year Ahead," information memorandum to Secretary of Defense, Washington, D.C., August 31, 1979c. G0486.pdf.

————, "Prepared Whichever Way the President Wants to Go Tonight," memorandum to Secretary of Defense, Washington, D.C., January 23, 1980a. G0342.pdf.

————, "Memorandum of Understanding Between the Department of Defense and Selective Service," memorandum to Deputy Secretary of Defense, Washington, D.C., February 5, 1980b. G0385.pdf.

————, "Selective Service Alternatives," memorandum to Peter Hamilton, Washington, D.C., February 27, 1980c. G0383.pdf.

————, "Peacetime Registration," action memorandum to Secretary of Defense, Washington, D.C., February 29, 1980d. G0350.pdf.

————, "One More Thought on Registration," memorandum to Secretary of Defense, Washington, D.C., March 3, 1980e. G0351.pdf.

Powell, Colin L., "Point Paper on Registration Used at White House on March 3, 1980," memorandum to Mr. C, Washington, D.C., March 4, 1980. G0357.pdf.

President's Reorganization Project, *Selective Service System Reorganization Study: Report of the Study Team,* Washington, D.C.: Executive Office of the President, Office of Management and Budget, December 1978. S0546.pdf.

Reagan, Ronald, "Draft Registration," letter to Mark O. Hatfield, Los Angeles, Ca., May 5, 1980. G0352.pdf.

Rehnquist, William H., *Rostker v. Goldberg 453 U.S. 57* U.S. Supreme Court, June 25, 1981. S0610.pdf.

Romjue, John L., *From Active Defense to AirLand Battle: The Development of Army Doctrine, 1973–1982,* Fort Monroe, Va.: United States Army Training and Doctrine Command.

Rosenn, Max, Joseph S. Lord, and Edward N. Cahn, *Memorandum Concerning Robert L. Goldberg v. Bernard Rostker, et al.,* memorandum, Philadelphia, Pa.: U.S. District Court for the Eastern District of Pennsylvania, Civil Action No. 71-1480, July 18, 1980a. S0611.pdf.

————, *Order Concerning Robert L. Goldberg v. Bernard Rostker, et al.,* Philadelphia, Pa.: U.S. District Court for the Eastern District of Pennsylvania, Civil Action No. 71-1480, July 18, 1980b.

Rostker, Bernard D., "Selective Service System," memorandum to the Secretary of the Navy, Washington, D.C., January 17, 1979a. S0549.pdf.

————, Nomination of Bernard D. Rostker to be Director of Selective Service, hearing before the Senate Armed Services Committee, 96th Cong., 1st Sess., Washington, D.C., U.S. Government Printing Office, November 16, 1979b. S0499.pdf.

————, "Selective Service Progress Report on PRM-47," memorandum to Deputy Director of OMB John White, Washington, D.C., December 21, 1979c. S0557.pdf.

————, *Improving Capability to Mobilize Military Manpower: A Report by the Director of the Selective Service (draft)* draft working document, Washington, D.C.: The Director of the Selective Service System, January 16, 1980a. S0560.pdf.

————, *Presidential Recommendations for Selective Service Reform: A Report to Congress Prepared Pursuant to P.L. 96-107,* Washington, D.C.: Selective Service System, February 11, 1980b.

————, *Selective Service System Budget Justifications: Fiscal Year 1981,* Washington, D.C.: Selective Service System, February 11, 1980c.

————, *News from Selective Service: Registration Results,* Washington, D.C.: Selective Service System, September 4, 1980d. G1189.pdf.

————, "Selective Service Registration," memorandum to the President, Washington, D.C., September 4, 1980e. G1188.pdf.

————, *1980 Draft Issues,* West Point, New York: U.S. Military Academy at West Point, December 11, 1980f. G1390.mov.

————, *Selective Service and the All-Volunteer Force,* Alexandria, Va.: Center for Naval Analyses, Professional Paper 346, March 1982.

Rostker, Bernard D., and William F. Bolger, *Agreement Between United States Postal Service and Selective Service System,* Washington, D.C.: United States Postal Service and Selective Service System, January 21, 1980. G1481.pdf.

Ryor, John, "Outreach Strategy for President's Registration Legislation," memorandum to Anne Wexler and Mike Channin, Washington, D.C., undated. C0004.pdf.

Scalia, Antonin, "Proposed Proclamation," memorandum to the President, Washington, D.C., February 13, 1975. F0006.pdf.

Schlafly, Phyllis, and Kathleen Teague, Coalition Against Drafting Women, Statement, hearing before the Military Personnel Subcommittee, House Armed Service Committee, 96th Cong., 2nd Sess., Washington, D.C., Hearings on H.R. 6569, March 5, 1980. S0614.pdf.

Scowcroft, Brent, "Selective Service Annual Registration," memorandum to Phil Buchen, Washington, D.C., September 1, 1975. F0012.pdf.

Selective Service System Staff, *Events Leading to the Signing of Proclamation 4360,* Washington, D.C.: Selective Service System, October 1, 1975. G1478.pdf.

Shoob, Steven, "Comment Office Week-Ending Report," memorandum to Hugh Carter, Washington, D.C., February 8, 1980. C0007.pdf.

Shuck, Robert E., Acting Director of Selective Service, Statement, hearing before the House Armed Services, 96th Cong., 1st Sess., Washington, D.C., U.S. Government Printing Office, February 14, 1979a.

———, "Response to GAO Report, 'Weakness in the Selective Service System's Emergency Registration Plan.'" letter to Elmer B. Staats Comptroller General of the United States, Washington, D.C., September 13, 1979b. S0547.pdf.

Sitrin, David, and William W. Hannon, *OMB Paper 'Discussion of Recommendations'*, Washington, D.C.: Office of Management and Budget, October 11, 1974. F0023.pdf.

Stempler, Jack, "House Vote on Registration," memorandum to Secretary of Defense, Washington, D.C., April 22, 1980. G0663.pdf.

Suffa, Frederick W., "Significant Events—Week of 28 May 1979," memorandum to Major General Stan Umstead, Washington, D.C., June 1, 1979. S0514.pdf.

Tarr, Curtis W., *Defense Manpower: The Keystone of National Security—Report to the President and Congress,* Washington, D.C.: Defense Manpower Commission, April 1976. S0113.pdf.

Teichler, Stephen L., "Constitutionality of an All Male Draft," memorandum to U.S. Air Force General Counsel, Washington, D.C., May 9, 1979. S0602.pdf.

U.S. Congress, Joint Resolution 521: Making Additional Funds Available by Transfer for the Fiscal Year Ending September 30, 1980 for the Selective Service System, June 27, 1980.

Weddington, Sarah, "Registration of Women," memorandum to the President, Washington, D.C., February 4, 1980. C0014.pdf.

Weinraub, Bernard, "Networks in Dispute on Fast Projections," *New York Times,* November 6, 1980, p. 32.

Wellford, Harrison, "Plan for Project Completion: SSS Reform," memorandum to Al McDonald, Washington, D.C. , January 30, 1980. C0003.pdf.

Wexler, Anne, "Presidential Decisions on Selective Service Reform," memorandum to Jim McIntyre, Washington, D.C. , February 2, 1980. C0012.pdf.

White House Press Secretary, *Military Registration: Questions and Answers,* Washington, D.C. : Office of Media Liaison January 24, 1980. C0002.pdf.

White House Staff, *The White House Daily Diary of President Jimmy Carter: March 4, 1980,* Washington, D.C.: The White House, March 4, 1980. C0020.pdf.

White, John P., Military Posture: Military Personnel, hearing before the Committee on Armed Services: House of Representatives, 95th Cong., 2nd Sess., Washington, D.C., U.S. Government Printing Office, February 22, 1978a.

———, "Weekly Activity Report (10–14 July 1978)," information memorandum to Secretary of Defense and Deputy Secretary of Defense, Washington, D.C., July 17, 1978b. G0412.pdf.

———, "Review of the Draft Study on the Selective Service System Reorganization," letter to Peter L Stanton. Associate Director for Organization Studies. President's Reorganization Project. Office of Management and Budget. Executive Office of the President, Washington, D.C., October 6, 1978c. S0555.pdf.

———, "Weekly Activity Report (2–13 October 1978)," information memorandum to Secretary of Defense, Washington, D.C., October 16, 1978d. G0413.pdf.

————, "Presidential Plan for Reform of the Selective Service System," memorandum to the President, Washington, D.C., October 3, 1979. C0015.pdf.

————, "Peacetime Registration," memorandum to the President, Washington, D.C., January 22, 1980a. C0001.pdf.

————, "Release of Interim Registration Data," memorandum to the President, Washington, D.C., September 3, 1980b. G1187.pdf.

White, Richard C., "Dear Colleague (on Registration and Dr. Bernard Rostker's views)," Dear Colleague letter to Members of the House of Representatives, Washington, D.C., September 11, 1979. S0551.pdf.

————, Testimony on the Registration of Women, hearing before the Military Personnel Subcommittee of the House Committee on Armed Services, 96th Cong., 2nd Sess., Washington, D.C., U.S. Government Printing Office, March 5, 1980. G1175.pdf.

Wickham, John, Jr., "Peacetime Registration," memorandum to Assistant Secretary of Defense (M&RA), Washington, D.C., May 25, 1979. G0356.pdf.

Williams, Henry N., "Legislation to Authorize the Registration and Induction of Women," memorandum to The Director of Selective Service, Washington, D.C., December 4, 1979. S0603.pdf.

Wilson, George C., "Selective Service Told Carter Registration Is 'Unnecessary'," *Washington Post,* February 23, 1980a, p. A11.

————, "Registration in Trouble in Congress," *Washington Post,* March 2, 1980b.

Wright, William J., "Standby Draft Structure for FY 1975," memorandum to Gus C. Lee, Washington, D.C., August 10, 1973. G0069.pdf.

CHAPTER THIRTEEN

The Carter Years:
Analytic Studies (1977–1980)

> I considered the end of the draft in 1973 to be one of the major
> achievements of my administration. Now seven years later, I have
> reluctantly concluded that we should reintroduce the draft. . . .
> The volunteer army has failed to provide enough personnel of the
> caliber we need.
>
> —Richard Nixon
> President of the United States[1]

Introduction

The renaissance in analytic studies that Bill Brehm had started paid dividends during
the Carter years. Early in the administration, Assistant Secretary John White used
Richard Cooper's report extensively to defend the all-volunteer force with Congress.
Reducing attrition was a major goal of the new administration. While White and
Deputy Secretary Charles Duncan pressed the services to look at their internal policies
and procedures, the major focus of the services was trying to screen out groups with a
high propensity not to complete training or their first terms of service. The Navy
extensively used the work of Bob Lockman from the Center for Naval Analyses (CNA)
to create a new set of selection tools, such as "procedures used to select enlisted personnel for the Navy and for school, job and advancement" (Lockman, 1974). The work of
the President's Commission on Military Compensation (PCMC) and the follow-up
Fourth Quadrennial Review of Military Compensation (QRMC) pushed the practical
frontiers of knowledge about retention behavior and the design of compensation systems. The freedom to look at all forms of advertising, paid and free, led to new efforts
to optimize recruiting programs through large-scale advertising experiments. Finally,
the central role that analysis played in identifying the Armed Services Vocational

---

[1] *The Real War: 1980* (Nixon, 1980).

Aptitude Battery (ASVAB) misnorming and then in addressing the link between a screening test and job performance provided a firm base for the Reagan administration that followed.

Attempts to Control Attrition

One area that Congress and the Congressional Budget Office had highlighted as substantially adding to the cost of the all-volunteer force was attrition of first-term accessions (Nelson, 1977, p. 26). *Attrition* is the term used to describe the loss—separation from the military—of a service member during the first term of service. The majority of losses tend to occur during basic training, but significant numbers of new service members leave after advanced individual and specialty training. While some new service members were separated through judicial proceedings, most losses were administrative and characterized as "for the good of the service" actions. Presumably, the services could develop programs that could better equip new recruits for the transition from civilian life to the life of a junior service member to reduce first-term attrition. Any reductions would, of course, mean fewer replacements would have to be recruited in the future.

Reducing first-term attrition became a goal of Assistant Secretary John White. By early November 1977, however, White had concluded that the services "had not designed any meaningful programs to reduce . . . high first-term attrition rates [because] [t]hey all viewed high attrition rates as simply a result of low recruit quality" (White, 1977, p. 1). White asked Secretary of Defense Harold Brown to direct the services "to program for reduced first-term attrition rates in order to reduce accession requirements" (White, 1977, p. 2). As White saw it, efforts in his office to improve the administrative discharge process and to study what caused attrition were likely to produce "small improvements at best." He believed the services were key and that they needed to "develop programs to reduce the attrition of potentially productive individuals," and to "encourage commanders at all levels to reduce unnecessary attrition" (White, 1977, p. 1). Brown's personal staff had "reservations" about White's approach since it asked the services not to "retain poor performers, but [to] reduce attrition."[2] Brown asked his deputy, Charles Duncan, to work with White to "clarify" what was needed and then to "send out whatever should be sent out." In February 1978, he sent a memorandum to the Secretaries of the Military Departments. In the memorandum he wrote:

> I would like the Services to take the lead in developing broad-gauged programs to meet the attrition goals of 23 percent for high school graduates and 44 percent for

---

[2] White's memorandum to the services was not well received in the front office. Secretary Brown's Special Assistant, John Kester, had "reservations" about Brown sending the memorandum White had prepared to the services. Brown's senior military assistant, Rear Admiral Thor Hanson, also was "not sure what the proposed memo is asking the Services to do—i.e., don't retain poor performers but reduce attrition" (attachment to White's file memorandum, White, 1977).

non-graduates. The emphasis should be placed on improving those personnel prac- tices that contribute to high "failure" rates and not on raising enlistment standards to unrealistic levels. While I do not advocate the retention of individuals who have proven themselves unproductive and who do not respond to positive management actions, I am convinced that we are discharging some individuals who, with some additional support or direction, could be developed into effective performers.

I ask that you reemphasize to commanders at all levels that manpower is not unlimited and that they must, through the use of discipline, guidance, counseling, and good leadership techniques, reduce the attrition of those individuals who offer potential for being productive members of the Armed Forces.

Please advise me within sixty days of the actions you will be taking to lower attrition. (Duncan, 1978)

By October 1978, White's Principal Deputy Robin Pirie reported to Brown and Duncan that "three of the four services have not achieved . . . attrition goals for either high school or non–high school graduate accessions." He noted that only the Army had met the goal, and then only for "non–high school graduate accessions" (Pirie, 1978).

Over the ensuing years, attrition remained troublesome for all the services. Efforts to reduce it, such as denying recruiters credit for recruits who did not complete train- ing or who failed to remain in service for a specific period, were met with hostility. Pressure on the basic training commands to reduce dropouts was mistakenly viewed as a numbers game at the expense of a quality force. In the long term, attrition remained a constant, with the only effective screening program being limits on the number of nondiploma high school graduates the services were permitted to take.

Attrition Research

First-term attrition had become a significant topic for researchers even before it became the focus of White's actions to improve the performance of the all-volunteer force. In early April 1977, just months after the Carter team took over, the Office of Naval Research hosted a four-day conference to "review what is known about attrition in the Services—its magnitude, current trends and costs, and how it is managed . . . to learn about relevant research—both inside and out of DoD—that deals with attrition and to identify gaps in our knowledge that could be addressed by new R&D" (Sinaiko, 1977).

There were at least two approaches to reducing attrition. White's approach, artic- ulated in Deputy Secretary Duncan's memorandum to the service secretaries, was to improve "personnel practices that contribute to high failure rates." He asked that the services not "raise enlistment standards to unrealistic levels" (Duncan, 1978). In fact, Charlie Moskos highlighted this view in the keynote address at the ONR conference. Moskos thought that the problem was the way the services recruited under the all- volunteer force. He noted that, under the peacetime draft, new accessions "entered military service reluctantly and thereby [were] not subject to profound disillusionment after service entry; accepting military service on its own terms" (Moskos, 1977, p. 1).[3] By comparison, Moskos argued that high attrition occurred when the new volunteers found life in the military not as they expected, and they were subject to "post-entry disillusionment if expectations not met [and] . . . [want] out regardless of type of discharge" (Moskos, 1977, p. 1). An alternative approach the services had been using was to screen out prospective members who, based on historical data, had a higher probability of not completing their first terms of service. At the ONR conference, Bob Lockman and John Warner from the Center for Naval Analysis (Lockman and Warner, 1977, p. 1) presented a paper having this viewpoint. They noted that this type of analysis went back to at least the early 1960s. In fact, it went back further.

One of the axioms of defense manpower research is that non–high school graduates attrit at a significantly higher rate than do high school graduates. Credit for discovering this relationship is generally given to Eli Flyer. In a recent interview (Flyer, 2002), Flyer recounted how he first identified the enlistment of non–high school graduates as a significant contributor to later attrition:

> I became increasingly distressed with the research I was doing on the Air Force's officer population [in the late 1950s]. Retention studies in particular showed all sorts of uncontrollable factors and events that made predictive research very difficult. So I switched the focus of my research studies from the officer population to the enlisted population. What helped to make this happen was that General White, the Air Force Chief of Staff, had heard from his field commanders that they had large numbers of enlisted people who were behaving and performing poorly, and they needed some relief. [This was mulled over at the staff level, and] [t]he Air Force decided it would ease up on its discharge procedures for unsuitable behavior and substandard performance. This led to the discharge of over 18,000 airmen during the first ten months of 1958.
>
> I was sent a set of punch cards with some individual information on each of them to see if they had any factors in common. When I ran off some distributions it was clear that unsuitability discharges were disproportionately non–high school graduates, when compared to the total force. Then, with the computer capability [then] available, I was able to do a cohort or longitudinal analysis as well. Using all

---

[3] *Authors Note:* In 1978, when I was the Principal Deputy Assistant Secretary of the Navy for Manpower and Reserve Affairs, I went to Norfolk Naval Base with my executive assistant, Commander Mike Boorda, to interview sailors who were being separated from the Navy. My escort officer asked why we were interviewing these "bad apples." I explained that if we were going to reduce attrition, these were the very sailors we would have to keep in the Navy, and it was important to understand why they were leaving.

After spending the day with these sailors, I came back to Washington and reported to Secretary of the Navy Graham Clayton and Vice Admiral James Watkins, the Chief of Naval Personnel. I told them that the rage these sailors had against the Navy was palpable. Many of the women complained about sexual harassment. A common complaint was that their actual job assignments were very different from the jobs their recruiters had promised. Watkins did not believe that the Navy Recruiting Command was doing a "bait and switch," but after reviewing the standard recruiting contract and finding that his experts at the Naval Personnel Research Development Center assessed it as "unintelligible at the sixth grade reading level," he ordered reforms. The visit had a profound effect on Commander Boorda. For the first time, he came face to face with what Moskos called "post-entry disillusionment of expectations." A decade later, it would affect the way he approached his senior assignments as Chief of Naval Personnel and Chief of Naval Operations.

Air Force enlisted accessions during 1956, I did an entry cohort follow up study that clearly established the value of high school grad status, AFQT, and age as predictors of first-term attrition. [I] even developed an actuarial table showing attrition rates when all three variables were taken into account. This came out as a report in 1959.

Colonel Fred Holdrege, Personnel Research Lab commander, and also a Ph.D. psychologist, was very innovative. He took the attrition findings we had and developed a kind of cardboard compass—a spin wheel on wheels. Spin one wheel to an educational level, another to an AFQT score, and one to age, and an arrow pointed to a probable first term attrition rate for the combined factors. [I] had them made in a form to be distributed to all Air Force recruiters to emphasize quality procurement. The tables Fred and I worked up were first of their kind. Then . . . the Navy Health Research center built one [the Odds for Effectiveness Table] for the Navy. . . . However, they all stem from the original report on Air Force recruits identifying the key factors associated with attrition.

Under pressure to cut attrition during the transition to the all-volunteer force, the Navy asked CNA "to develop a model for estimating premature losses that could be used to plan recruiting policy and screen applicants for enlistment, and a model of recruiting district productivity that could be used to allocate quotas and canvassers and evaluate recruiting results" (Lockman, 1975, p. 1). Bob Lockman obtained data on 98 percent of Navy non–prior service recruits who entered active duty in calendar year (CY) 1963. He tracked recruits through the first year of service, computed loss rates, and related the loss rates to background and test data. On October 1, 1977, the Success Chances of Recruits Entering the Navy (SCREEN) tables replaced the Odds for Effectiveness tables as the primary tool the Navy Recruiting Command provided recruiters to determine who should or should not be enlisted in the Navy. In 1977, Lockman revised the SCREEN tables (Lockman and Gordon, 1977) to reflect his work with John Warner on alternative approaches (Lockman and Warner, 1977). He noted that "the best fitting as well as the cheapest statistical model to use with very large numbers of observations was the grouped logit model" (Lockman and Gordon, 1977, p. 1). He also noted that, since his original research, only 75 percent of non-Caucasians were blacks, reflecting an increase in the number of recruits of Hispanic heritage, and revised the scale for the level-of-education variable.

Table 13.1 is the revised first-year SCREEN table (Lockman and Gordon, 1977, p. 6). Lockman noted that a cut or "qualifying score of 72 would have excluded 28 percent of the blacks in CY 1973 and 31 percent in CY 1974, compared to 16 and 24 percent in their total cohorts" (Lockman and Gordon, 1977, p. 7). To reduce attrition, the Navy was considering moving the cut score to 76. The SCREEN table, however, reflected the difficulty in rejecting recruits based on their demographic characteristics. Increasing the cut off score to 76 would surely reduce attrition (the "false negatives" would drop). However, it would also screen out a large number of recruits because for demographic reasons—recruits that would have completed their first terms (the number of "false positives" would increase). Lockman and Warner counseled the Navy that, "since the supply of manpower is limited and growing more so all the time," they should

> not want to reject more applicants than is absolutely necessary to achieve some desired attrition rate. . . . This way of reducing attrition should be pursued only if the marginal costs of attrition exceed the cost imposed because end-strength goals are not met. (Lockman and Warner, 1977, p. 21)

Retention Research

Answering an inquiry from the President and mentioning that DoD had, in recent years, "collected and analyzed a great amount of data on retention factors" (Pirie, 1980c), Pirie told Brown that "our analyses indicate that, at the first-term point, pay dominates nonpay factors [and] . . . nonpay factors play a considerably larger role in enlisted career force retention in the critical 6 to 10 years-of-service period" (Pirie, 1980c). Pirie was able to answer these types of inquiries because of the investments the manpower office had made in its in-house capabilities and in establishing the Defense Manpower Analysis Center at the RAND Corporation. Increasingly, studies from these

Table 13.1
First Year SCREEN

AFQT	Age	No Dependents Years of Education Over 12	12	11	Under 11	Dependents Years of Education Over 12	12	11	Under 11
95–100	18–19	96	95	90	89	94	93	87	84
	17	96	94	90	88	94	92	86	83
	20+	95	93	88	86	93	90	83	80
67–94	18–19	92	90	82	79	89	86	76	72
	17	92	89	81	78	88	84	74	70
	20+	90	87	78	74	86	82	70	66
50–66	18–19	91	88	79	76	87	83	72	78
	17	90	87	77	74	86	82	70	66
	20+	88	84	74	70	84	79	66	62
35–49	18–19	87	83	72	68	82	77	63	59
	17	86	81	70	66	81	75	61	57
	20+	83	78	66	62	78	71	57	52
21–34	18–19	85	80	68	64	79	73	59	55
	17	84	79	66	62	78	72	57	52
	20+	81	75	62	57	74	68	52	48

SOURCE: Lockman and Gordon (1977, p. 6).
NOTE: Revision of May 1977.

activities found their way into policy discussions and were used when decisions were being made.

Reforming the Compensation System: Analytical Work in Support of the PCMC and the Fourth QRMC

One of the first initiatives of the Carter administration was the creation of a new commission to undertake a

> fresh review of pay, benefits, and the military retirement system since previous attempts to provide an equitable and efficient total military compensation system failed to achieve general agreement. (White House Press Secretary, 1977)

The White House Press Secretary's office noted in the news release accompanying the appointment of the PCMC the differences between the recommendations of the Defense Manpower Commission and the Third QRMC, and President Carter's expectation that the commission would "resolve these differences" and "propose one integrated, long-term solution to military compensation" that would "be fair to the taxpayers of the United States, as well as members of the armed forces" (White House Press Secretary, 1977).

The Work of John Warner

Critical to the commission's focus on retirement reform were "estimates of the effects on retention of the retirement system proposed" (Warner, 1978, p. 1). John Warner from CNA undertook this work for the commission. Warner had joined the CNA staff several years before being loaned to the commission in 1977. Starting with this work for PCMC, he would establish himself over the next quarter century as one of the leading experts on defense manpower and compensation systems. He would leave CNA in 1980 to take a full-time teaching position at Clemson University but collaborated with colleagues at a number of institutions and took several leaves of absence to work on the staffs of several Assistant and Under Secretaries of Defense. His contributions through sponsored research; academic publications; and, most important, direct participation in the support of DoD's own analytic efforts are noteworthy.

In 1977, when Warner went to the PCMC staff, he faced a number of difficult problems. In his report on the retention work for the commission, he observed that the "future is difficult to predict," especially when there is a "lack of empirical data," and that "analytical models which could be used to predict these effects have been limited" (Warner, 1978, p. 1). Warner based his approach on the work of Glenn Gotz and John McCall, particularly that reported in *The Retirement Decision: A Numerical*

Analysis of a Dynamic Retirement Model (Gotz and McCall, 1977).[4] Warner noted the following:

> To empirically implement this model, we need data on expected future military earnings and retirement pay, the distribution of civilian opportunities available at each year, tastes, and the discount rate. To compute expected future military earnings and retired pay, we constructed . . . different career paths. . . . The effect of a change in the retirement system on the optimal leaving time of individuals on these different paths is examined [and] . . . collapsed into one average path for officers and one average path for enlisted personnel. . . . Knowledge of the distribution of civilian offers available to the individual presents the most severe data difficulty. . . . Estimates of personal discount rates do exist.
>
> The retirement system proposed by the PCMC represents a significant change in the pattern of incentives from the current retirement system.[5] . . . It is . . . evident that the pull to 30 years of service under the PCMC proposal is likely to depend crucially upon the individual's discount rate. . . . The PCMC proposal is not expected to adversely affect retention prior to the 10th year of service. . . . Retired pay benefits at 10 years of service are like a bonus and will serve to retain some of the people who would otherwise leave before 10 years of service. . . .
>
> The cost of leaving at the beginning of a given year of service is the individual's RMC [regular military compensation] for the year plus the contribution into his deferred compensation trust fund. . . . [In terms of] the fraction of an accession cohort that is expected to reach various years of service . . . under the PCMC proposal, a larger fraction is predicted to reach 10 years, a smaller fraction is predicted to reach 20 years, and a larger fraction is predicted to reach 30 years. (Warner, 1978)

After PCMC published its report to the President, responsibility for assessing its work and developing a DoD position fell to Assistant Secretary John White's staff. Richard Danzig, the Deputy Assistant Secretary of Defense for Program Development, was given "responsibility for residual action of the Commission . . . [and] to coordinate review of the [commission's] Report" (Zwick, 1978). The analytic work, however, fell to the senior economist on White's staff, Gary Nelson, the Deputy Assistant Secretary of Defense for Requirement, Resources and Analysis. Nelson immediately asked Danzig to secure Warner's services from CNA. He told Danzig that Warner had done "all the work on the relationship between retirement and retention for the President's Commission on Military Compensation, . . . the heart of the analysis in judging any proposed new compensation system" (Nelson, 1978). He argued that they needed Warner

---

[4] Warner noted, however, that

> by focusing only on predicted optimal leaving time for the average officer, Gotz and McCall fail to explore the essence of the problem addressed here [by the PCMC] namely, determining how the offer required to induce individuals with given years of service to leave changes with the retirement system and how this in turn changes the probability of leaving. (Warner, 1978, p. 34)

[5] The traditional military retirement system requires a minimum of 20 years of service both for vesting and to receive an immediate annuity for life. PCMC proposed an early vesting system with increasing levels of transition pay when a service member leaves and an old-age retirement system at 65 years of age.

to do our own analysis . . . with respect to new bonus policies, differential pay raises and other special pays . . . to apply the various compensation proposals to the individual services . . . and . . . [to] be in a position to evaluate the Services' comments on the PCMC proposal and any alternatives the Services might propose. (Nelson, 1978)

Most important, Nelson noted that Warner continued "to improve the work he did for the Commission" (Nelson, 1978).

Warner had, in fact, been working with Nelson and John Enns to improve the techniques he had used while supporting PCMC. The model they developed was called the Annualized Cost of Leaving (ACOL) model. The ACOL model considered the "individual's yearly 'taste for service' . . . (as) the monetary value the individual places on the nonpecuniary aspects of military versus civilian life" (Warner, 1979b, p. 7). Warner noted that "there has been some confusion about similarity or difference between this model and models, such as the original dynamic programming model of Gotz and McCall" (Warner, 1979b, p. 9). Previously, he had referred to their 1977 specification as a Present Value of Cost of Leaving (PVCOL) and noted that "the original dynamic programming model did not have a taste factor in it" (Warner, 1979b, p. 10).[6] Citing "useful discussions" he had with Gotz, he wrote that "the ACOL model is really a PVCOL model with a taste factor included." The ACOL model, he determined, was "really just a way of calculating" the taste-for-service factor "analytically rather than searching over various possible values of the dynamic program" (Warner, 1979a, p. 9). Under his formulation, retention rates could be estimated using cohort data as a logit or probit function, rather than using the more cumbersome techniques of dynamic programming.[7]

ACOL and the Dynamic Retention Model[8]

As discussed earlier, Gotz and McCall had, in fact, moved past their original model, incorporating not only permanent taste but also, as Warner noted, "by making a distinction that has been made in the econometrics literature between transitory and permanent components of variation" (Warner, 1979a, p. 11). To keep the model tractable and relatively easy to estimate, Warner's ACOL model specified a "logistics regression

---

[6] That is, the PVCOL model lacked an error term. The model only explained the behavior of those who were "taste neutral"; therefore, there was "no source of variation in the model to explain [actual] retention" (Warner, 1979a, p. 5).

[7] In 1979, Warner noted that, in practice, dynamic program's estimation procedures were "quite complicated. It is nowhere as easy as estimating a regression or a logit or probit" (Warner, 1979a, p. 21). The situation has changed with the advent of more powerful computers and new statistical tools.

[8] The issues surrounding ACOL and Dynamic Retention are technical and contentious but important to the continuous management of the all-volunteer force. A side bar cannot do it justice, and the reader is referred to the excellent discussion in Ausink et al. (2003).

equation that purported to capture the essence of the [transitory error term]" (Warner, 1979a, p. 12). He noted, however, that his approach "still has the problem that it is a forward-looking model" and was "not as good as the Gotz-McCall methodology," in which both the transitory and permanent disturbances are embedded in the dynamic program. This "means that the calculation of the future costs of staying or leaving becomes probabilistic, rather than certain; a condition which may more accurately describe behavior" (Warner, 1981, p. 36). The new model by Gotz and McCall— a model Warner dubbed the Stochastic Cost of Leaving Model (SCOL), but which is generally referred to in the economics literature as the Dynamic Retention Model— "makes the link between pay in one term and retention in future terms as part of the model, rather than an ad hoc procedure, [and] retention by term of service is endogenous to the model, not exogenous" (Warner, 1981, p. 36).

Warner was concerned about the differences between the new Gotz and McCall model, the so-called SCOL or Dynamic Retention Programming Model, and the ACOL model and the fact that the latter was only "forward-looking," while the former was "backward-looking." He tested the differences using "simulate[d] retention rates for alternative pay regimes using a 'reasonable' set of parameter values for the new model" (Warner and Lurie, 1979, p. 1).[9] Warner found that the

> SCOL model simulations of alternative retirement plans provide estimates that are reasonably consistent with those from the ACOL model. . . . The main difference is that the SCOL model predicts a smaller change in second-term retention than does the ACOL model, but a larger drop in third-term retention. (Warner, 1981, p. viii)

He also noted "a tendency for the [ACOL] logistics supply equation model to overpredict the third-term rate since it is essentially a forward-looking model" (Warner and Lurie, 1979, p. 11).[10]

The debate about the efficacy of the ACOL Model and the Dynamic Retention Model (SCOL) in terms of computational tractability and policy analysis lived on well after the work of the PCMC or the Fourth QRMC had been largely forgotten. In the 1990s, almost a decade after Warner's *Analysis of Alternative Models* (Warner, 1981), the issues were joined again in an exchange of papers in the *Journal of Applied Econometrics*. The editors of the journal obviously thought the debate important enough to include the paper by Matthew Black, Robert Moffitt, and John Warner (BMW), *The Dynamics of Job Separation: The Case of Federal Employees* (Black et al., 1990b); Gotz's

---

[9] Warner noted that

> The major improvement of the new model [Gotz and McCall's SCOL] over existing models is that retention rates in *future* LOS [length of service] cell as well as current cells retention rates are dependent upon pay in the current cell. Ceteris paribus an increase in military pay in the current LOS cell (e.g., a bonus) serves to reduce retention in future LOS cells. (Warner and Lurie, 1979, p. 1, emphasis in the original)

[10] Warner (1981) further discusses the simulation of the new Gotz-McCall model.

comments (Gotz, 1990); and a reply by the authors of the paper (Black et al., 1990a). Gotz characterized the model used in the paper as a "fairly straightforward extension of the ACOL model."[11] He argued that, while the model was easier to estimate than the Dynamic Retention Model, this specification raised "doubts about its usefulness for analyzing changes in retirement benefits and the experience structure of pay" because the model was "not a structural model"; did not "estimate the underlying parameters of individuals' preference functions"; and "under a plausible assumption about individual behavior in the presence of uncertainty due to random shocks," was "not consistent with utility maximization" (Gotz, 1990, pp. 263–264). Specifically

> The ease with which BMW's model may be estimated comes at a substantial price. The model assumes away optimal behavior with respect to future time-varying factors, including random shocks, thereby limiting the types of policies that may be analyzed. Specifically, it is easy to construct examples of compensation, personnel policy, and retirement system changes that would affect predicted quit rates in a model of rational decision-making but that will not cause changes in BMW's quit rate predictions.
>
> The policy analysis problem exists because the [BMW] econometric model . . . treat[s] random shocks and the unemployment rate as *ad hoc* additions to the statistical model instead of developing their implications for behavior. . . . [M]ost changes in personnel, compensation, and retirement policy are structural changes to BMW's model. (Gotz, 1990, pp. 266–268)

In their reply, Black, Moffitt, and Warner argued that they had "no major disagreement with Gotz on what the advantages" of the Dynamic Programming Model were but pressed "the advantages of computation that largely motivated our model choice," and the value of a more complete delineation "for the practitioner of the trade-offs that must be faced by any analyst" (Black et al., 1990a, p. 269). After a very useful comparison of the various features and specifications of the Dynamic Program and ACOL models, they concluded that

> For government policy-makers interested in quickly obtaining approximate effects of policy measures, the ACOL model has considerable appeal. The trade-offs may lessen as technological improvements reduce the burden of computing estimates and policy simulation of the DP [Dynamic Program] Model. . . . [A]t the present state of technology ACOL model represents an alternative which is considerably

---

[11] Gotz noted that the

> underlying economic model of stay-leave decision-making presented in BMW first appeared in the professional literature in 1984 (Warner and Goldberg). . . . [T]he model was initially developed by Warner and others in the late 1970s, albeit with a much simpler stochastic structure. The simpler version . . . (was) called the ACOL . . . model. . . . [I]t is widely used by DoD analysts and by other military manpower researchers to predict changes in turnover rates by length of experience given changes in military pay, the military retirement system, and changes in other elements of military compensation. (Gotz, 1990, p. 263)

Gotz clearly thought these uses were inappropriate.

simpler to compute, and from which to simulate and whose behavioral assumptions may not worsen the model fit. (Black et al., 1990a, pp. 271–272)

In later work, however, when considering alternative retirement systems, Warner found the Dynamic Retention Model approach useful because "it allows us to investigate the force structure implication of policies that depart significantly from current policy" (Asch and Warner, 1994, p. 2). He did note, that "[t]he ACOL model is [still] better suited for examining the implications of marginal changes from current policy" (Asch and Warner, 1994, p. 2).[12]

Testing Recruiting Options

From the beginning of the Carter administration, testifying before Senator Nunn's Manpower and Personnel Subcommittee of the Senate Armed Services Committee always meant one thing for Assistant Secretary John White and his successor Robin Pirie: a battle. The June 1980 hearing on the status of the all-volunteer force (Nunn, 1978) was a case in point. This time, however, something productive came out of it. White agreed to a test of some of the proposals being put forth by Charles Moskos with regard to changes to the newly enacted, and not very effective, postservice educational benefit.

The Veterans' Education and Assistance Act of 1976 was passed on October 1, 1976, to replace the "old" GI Bill, which was to expire on December 31, 1976. Chapter 32 of the Act (PL 94-502) established the Veterans' Education Assistance Program (VEAP) as a cost-cutting measure.[13] And with these benefits greatly reduced, relatively few signed up.[14] In 1978, less than 25 percent of those eligible enrolled (Fernandez, 1982, p. 72). Even though such a benefit would be an incentive for service members to quit after their first terms, since the benefits could only be used after leaving the military, Moskos had convinced Senator Nunn that an enhanced education benefit would

---

[12] In 2005, James Hosek, when reviewing a draft of this section, made the following comment:

> The debate about the efficacy of the ACOL model and the dynamic retention model in my opinion ultimately proved to be moot because of the advance of computing power and statistical methods needed to estimate dynamic programming models. The ACOL was indeed easier to estimate, it simply was not as rich a model. It did a much poorer job of handling future uncertainty and it led to time inconsistent decision making, as the published exchange of comments between Gotz and Black, Moffitt, and Warner made clear [as discussed above]. Today in economics, dynamic decision making under uncertainty is modeled with dynamic programming.

[13] In letting the old GI Bill expire, Congress was determined to reduce the cost of military personnel. According to Richard Fernandez, "[b]enefit levels were reduced; instead of the $270 per month or more, for up to 45 months, that the GI Bill was offering in 1976, the new Veterans Educational Assistance Program (VEAP) offered a maximum of $150 per month for 36 months" (Fernandez, 1982, p. 72).

[14] By one account, "[m]easured in present discounted value terms at the time of enlistment, the GI Bill was worth at least two and one-half times, and perhaps ten or more times, as much as VEAP" (Fernandez, 1980, p. 32).

help the services by attracting high-scoring middle-class youths. White, exasperated about the "continually picking on our young people with respect to the so-called marketplace . . . [knew] education is a form of pay" (White in Nunn, 1978, pp. 72–73). He knew Moskos's proposal could be empirically tested and told Senator Nunn that if "that is more attractive to a youngster and we get higher quality that way, that is all to the good" (White in Nunn, 1978, p. 73).

On January 1, 1979, the Multiple Option Recruiting Experiment (MORE) began for the Army, with the Navy following on March 1, 1979, and the Marine Corps 45 days later. Consistent with the Army's often-demonstrated aversion to testing recruiting options, and even before the analysis of the congressionally mandated test was completed, the Army extended the enhanced benefit option nationwide and the two-year enlistment option "to all but a small part of the country" on December 4, 1979 (Fernandez, 1980, p. 2).

MORE was the kind of carefully controlled experiment that analysts had been wanting to undertake since the beginning of the all-volunteer force. Its design was elaborate, incorporating the many proposals that had gained support among various parties in Congress, the services, and academia. There was the two-year enlistment option Moskos favored. There were varying levels of educational benefits. There was an Individual Ready Reserve option that allowed "Army enlistees to choose between active service and reserve duty after they completed initial training—about four months" (Haggstrom et al., 1981, p. v). The value of the experiment as a tool to test alternative options was borne out. RAND's assessment noted that "[a]lthough the MORE options had little effect on recruiting, the experiment itself was a success because it produced some valuable information. Most notably, it refuted the hypothesis that a shorter term of enlistment would attract large numbers of high-quality recruits into hard-to-fill occupational specialties" (Haggstrom et al., 1981, p. vi).[15]

The design of the Army experiment is reflected in Table 13.2. The two-year option was offered only to high-quality recruits who agreed to serve primarily in the combat arms. An enhanced educational benefit added money to the current postservice educational benefit plan. The "kicker" referred to the additional lump-sum payment the Army could make to the VEAP fund for high-quality enlistees in certain occupations. The "super VEAP kicker" was a doubling of the regular kicker in certain areas after June 1, 1979.

---

[15] Moskos continued to press the advantages of short-term enlistments. In the late 1980s, Congress authorized the test of a two-year option as part of the so called 2 + 2 + 4 program—two years on active duty, two years in the ready reserve, and for years in the Individual Ready Reserve—and Army College Fund payments in addition to the regular GI Bill educational benefit. A study by Richard Buddin at RAND gave some support to Moskos's claims. Buddin found a small expansion effect. While the experiment was small, he estimated that 25 to 30 percent of the men opting for the 2 + 2 + 4 option were enlisting because of the new option (Buddin, 1991). (See Chapter Sixteen for a more complete discussion.) More recently, Moskos has pressed for even shorter enlistments to support deployments to Iraq to fill low-skill jobs.

Table 13.2
Army Test Design

	Two-Year Option	No Two-Year Option
VEAP kicker (2, 3, or 4 years)	Area 1 (Europe only) Area 2	Area 3 (Europe only) Area 4
VEAP kicker (3 or 4 years only)	Area 5 (Europe only)	
No VEAP kicker		Area 6

SOURCE: Haggstrom et al. (1981, p. 3).

NOTES: Area 7 offered the same options as Area 1 from January 1, 1979, to March 31, 1979, and began offering the Individual Ready Reserve option on April 1, 1979. Area 1A (part of Area 1) offered the super-VEAP kicker beginning June 1, 1979.

The "primary unit of analysis" was the Armed Forces Entrance and Examination Stations (AFEES) groups, so that "(a) each test area would contain a number of geographic dispersed AFEES, and (b) the test areas would be relatively well balanced in terms of pre-experimental recruiting performance" (Haggstrom et al., 1981, p. 4). Figure 13.1 shows how the United States was divided and, in conjunction with Table 13.2, shows which areas were selected to offer which options. The experimental design produced a robust set of data with wide variation in the incentive packages offered in the various regions and over time. After December 4, 1979, two levels of VEAP kickers were offered both to treatment areas and to the control areas that did not have VEAP kickers for the first 12 months of the experiment.

The Navy and Marine Corps' experimental design was different from the Army's. The programs were different, as were the geographic areas selected. In addition to the VEAP and term-of-enlistment options, the Navy "tested whether guaranteed Class 'A' [technical training] school assignments would be effective enlistment or reenlistment incentives" (Haggstrom et al., 1981, p. 7). The Marine Corps offered the two-year option in only two areas and, for budgetary reasons, did not offer the VEAP.

The analysis showed that these recruiting options did not produce the results the proponents had hoped for. Gus Haggstrom, the principal investigator for these tests, who had been involved with such efforts going back to the original Air Reserve Forces "experiments" in 1972, found for the Army:

> [N]o discernable increase in high-quality male enlistments in response to the option. [W]e infer that the two-year enlistees were mainly drawn away from three- and four-year enlistments. As a consequence of this lowering of enlistment obligations, the Army will lose many of the two-year enlistees at the two-year point and find recruiting problems worsened beginning in 1981. . . .
>
> MORE did not reveal promising solutions to the military recruitment problems, but it has forestalled the implementation of some options that would exacerbate the problems, and it has provided valuable information for structuring future recruitment strategies. (Haggstrom et al., 1981, pp. 29, 54)

Figure 13.1
Army Areas Offering Two-Year Enlistments

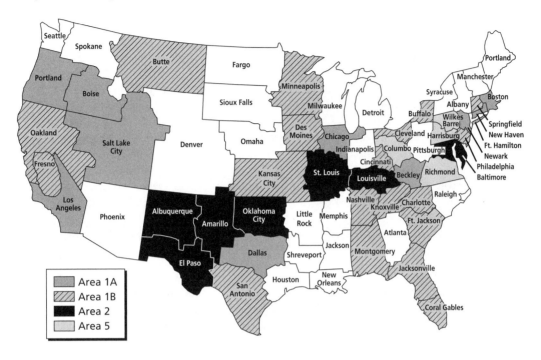

SOURCE: Haggstrom et al. (1981, p. 5).
RAND *MG265-13.1*

The Navy Research on Recruiters and Advertising Effectiveness

While the Army was the focus of attention concerning the viability of the all-volunteer force, Navy recruiting was even more problematic. In FY 1977, the Navy enlisted only 95.0 percent of its goal. When Navy Assistant Secretary Edward Hidalgo testified for the first time before Congress, the Navy had, through the first quarter of FY 1978 (October through December), achieved only 91 percent of its accession goal (Hidalgo, 1978).[16]

Within months, the Navy had in place several research efforts to look at ways to increase the effectiveness of its recruiting force. CNA undertook an econometric study of recruiters, advertising, and Navy enlistments. The Office of Naval Research contracted with the Wharton Applied Research Center at the University of Pennsylvania for a controlled test to "estimate the impact of changes in the Navy advertising budget

---

[16] *Author's Note:* Assistant Secretary of the Navy (Manpower) Edward Hidalgo reported to the House Armed Services Committee that the Navy's "failure to meet recruiting objectives resulted in significant manpower shortfalls" (Hidalgo, 1978, p. 621). As his Principal Deputy Assistant Secretary, I accompanied him to those hearings.

and in the size of the Navy recruiter force on Navy enlistment contracts of various quality and types" (Carroll et al., 1985, p. 355).[17]

The Navy Enlistment Marketing Experiment

Wharton proposed a one-year experiment:

> Advertising and recruiters were to be varied in a systematic and controlled way, independent of sales in prior periods and with treatments independent of one another.
>
> A broad range of each treatment variable was to be tested and treatments were to be replicated in multiple markets.
>
> A substantial body of supplemental data was to be collected for each market involved in the experiment. These included both sales and marketing data for the other (competing) branches of the Armed Forces. (Carroll et al., 1985, pp. 356–357)

The critical issues in Wharton's experimental design were the selection of media markets and what data would be collected. Data were collected on enlistment contracts (direct ship and delayed-entry program contracts), as well as on educational attainment, race, gender, mental category, recruiters, advertising characteristics (joint, national versus local, and type of advertising), and environmental variables, for a number of markets, each described as an area of dominant influence (ADI). Under the Wharton design, individual counties

> [were] assigned to ADIs by the electronic media-rating services based on media-use patterns of sample households. ADIs offered the most reliable way of executing and measuring the changes in electronic advertising incorporated in the experiment. Of the 200 ADIs in the United Sates, a subset of 26 ADIs was selected for experimental treatment [e.g., more or less advertising funds and more or fewer recruiters]. . . . After excluding from consideration markets in which special enlistment programs were being tested [e.g., the VEAP and two-year enlistment option test] and those where substantial amounts of advertising "spilled" in from neighboring markets . . . individual markets were assigned to treatment conditions. (Carroll et al., 1985, pp. 357–358)

Figure 13.2 illustrates the results.

---

[17] *Author's Note*: I originally proposed an experiment following the successes we had at RAND with the test of recruiting options for the Air Reserve Forces. An experiment involving advertising and recruiters throughout the nation would be much more complicated. The possible became reality when, after a hearing before the House Armed Services Subcommittee on Military Appropriation, Congress Joseph Addabbo (D-New York) complained that we did not know anything about the value of advertising. I said that the Navy could do a test, but it would be very expensive. He asked, how much. I remember I said about a million dollars. He laughed and said that should not be a problem. The Navy budget office had the Office of Naval Research provide the money. The Deputy Assistant Secretary of the Navy for Manpower, Mary Snavely, orchestrated the competitive selection of a contractor and oversaw the research. Vice Admiral Jim Watkins, Chief of Naval Personnel, and Rear Admiral Ed Briggs, commander of the Navy Recruiting Command, were very supportive, especially since they were under constant pressure to make their recruiting goals and since enforcing the research design was not always easy. Their cooperation was essential.

Figure 13.2
Experimental Markets and Treatment Conditions

	Recruiters –20%	Recruiters Same	Recruiters +20%
AD +100%		Davenport-Rock Island	
AD +50%	Tulsa Roanoke Syracuse	Washington Indianapolis Richmond	Boston St. Louis Charleston-Huntington
AD Same	Baltimore Cheyenne, WY Laurel, MS	Providence Terre Haute Springfield, IL*	Harrisburg South Bend Grand Junction, CO
AD –50%	Wilkes Barre Phoenix Odessa-Midland	Chicago Pittsburgh Columbus, OH	Dallas Louisville Lansing
AD –100%		Johnstown-Altoona	

*Additional control markets: Nashville   Greenville   Youngstown   Huntsville   McAllen
                             Los Angeles   Knoxville   West Palm Beach   Waco   Anniston
                             Charlotte   Des Moines   Chattanooga   Sioux City

SOURCE: Carroll et al. (1985, p. 357).

RAND *MG265-13.2*

Wharton showed that more "Navy recruiters and Joint advertising [were] effective across all types of contracts while Navy national advertising is not even marginally significant" (Carroll et al., 1985, pp. 362–363). They found that "local advertising was effective in obtaining High School contracts" (Carroll et al., 1985, p. 365). Their results were important because they provided "marginal costs for achievement of enlistment contracts" (Carroll et al., 1985, p. 369), as well as "a context for decision making initiatives" (Carroll et al., 1985, p. 370).

The CNA Study

On June 13, 1979, I, as the Principal Deputy Assistant Secretary of the Navy (Manpower and Reserve Affairs), and Rear Admiral Edward Briggs, Commander of the Navy Recruiting Command, went before the Defense Appropriation Subcommittee to ask for approval of the Navy's request to reprogram funds and assign an additional 531 recruiters over the currently funded FY 1979 level of 3,496 (Rostker, 1979, p. 621). In support of the reprogramming request, I told the subcommittee the following:

> We have been concerned with the productivity of our additional recruiters. The Center for Naval Analyses, as part of their continuing program of research and development in military manpower matters, has undertaken an extensive study on recruiters and . . . advertising. (Rostker, 1979, p. 625)

The CNA study had

> found that additional recruiters will indeed result in the reduction of our [recruit-
> ing] shortfall. . . . We are far from the flat part of the recruiter productivity curve—
> that is, individual recruiters will not be competing with each other for the potential
> enlistees. There is a substantial portion of the market yet to be tapped—the addi-
> tional 531 recruiters will enable us to reach some of it. (Rostker, 1979, p. 623)

The Navy's decision to ask for more recruiters was based on a study by Lawrence
Goldberg at CNA. Goldberg estimated a statistical regression model using quarterly
data from the third quarter of 1971 to the end of 1977. He estimated separate equations for the supply of high school graduates and for the supply of recruits in the upper
mental categories (I–IIIA). He modeled the expenditure of funds on advertising as an
investment in awareness and depreciated its value (effect) over time, measuring both
the short- and long-term effects of advertising. He accounted for changes in relative
military pay; unemployment; the eligible population of potential recruits; a number of
policies, such as the end of the GI Bill benefits; the number of recruits; the Recruiting
Command's change in recruiting policy to focus on high school graduates; and the end
of the draft. Unlike the results of the Wharton experiment, Goldberg reported that

> [recruiters] and [advertising] both affect [high school graduates], but the effects
> differ in two important respects which make advertising less attractive; unlike
> recruiters, advertising predominately affects [high school graduates] in the lower
> mental groups; and rather than this year, most of its effects are felt in the future.
> (Goldberg, 1982, p. 396)

During the years that followed, a number of additional studies would look at
recruiters and advertising using both experimental data, as Wharton had done, and
nonexperimental data, as Goldberg had done.

The ASVAB Misnorming

This book was written to examine the proposition that the development and implementation of the all-volunteer force is the "classic marriage between political decisionmaking and policy analysis." Implied in these words is the idea that the all-volunteer
force benefited from the use of analysis. While the examples in this and other chapters
tend to validate this conclusion, the case of the ASVAB misnorming is strikingly different.[18] The author of one of the more cogent accounts of the misnorming made the
following observation that justly summed up the experience:

---

[18] While the term *misnorming* is widely used, the issue is more correctly *miscalibration*. The problem was converting
raw scores, or the number of correct items on the test, to percentiles and standard scores of a reference population.
The World War II reference population and score scales were the standard for calibrating the AFQT and service classification batteries. By using the World War II reference population, the test "would retain the traditional meaning
of the test scores and would enable use of existing qualification standards" (Maier, 1993, p. 70).

> The ASVAB Misnorming was a "tragedy of errors." A travesty of sound psychometric practices and common sense. Rather than being attributable to one technical mistake, this five-year period was nurtured by reactionary decisions, Service disagreements, haste, a multitude of testing and sampling mistakes, test compromise, and inexperience with what the results of the recruiting of volunteers should look like. (Laurence and Ramsberger, 1991, p. 72)

The story of the misnorming starts at the very being of the modern military with the development of a screening test during World War I (Wigdor and Green, 1991, pp. 20–21). Aptitude tests were used extensively during World War II, and each service set up its own psychological research laboratories to develop specific tests for its own use. These tests were used for *selection, classification,* and *assignment* purposes. *Selection* was for determining whether the person met minimum standards, *classification* for assessing what job the person might qualify for, and *assignment* for placing the person in a specific job. Milton Maier has noted that,

> with the inception of the peacetime draft in 1948, the need for a joint service selection test to test potential inductees became apparent. The Armed Forces Qualification Test (AFQT) was introduced on January 1, 1950, and taken by millions of registrants for the draft and applicants for enlistment until 1973. (Maier, 1993)

The last date was the year Assistant Secretary of Defense Roger Kelley allowed each service to administer its own test, as long as it could link its test scores to the AFQT for reporting purposes. Kelley was reflecting the views of many recruiters he had met on visits to the field, who complained that the AFQT denied many potential volunteers the opportunity to serve. In the middle of a recruiting scandal that saw recruiters coaching prospective recruits on how to pass the AFQT, Kelley sided with the recruiters.[19] It was not the recruiters or the low caliber of recruits that was causing the problem, they argued, it was the test. If there was no test, they could use their "professional judgment" in determining who should be enlisted.

As noted before, things changed when Bill Brehm became the Assistant Secretary several months after Kelley left. Brehm initiated a number of reforms of the recruitment process, such as standardization of paperwork, creation of a joint command reporting to the Office of the Secretary of Defense, and reinstitution of a joint test. The test was to be the ASVAB, which had been developed by a joint-service committee, with the Air Force as the follow-on executive agent for DoD. This test had a distinct advantage over other candidates in that it was known to high school guidance counselors, who used it for counseling students. The cost, of course, was having to share the

---

[19] The Army was the executive agent for the AFQT. By the time of the Vietnam War, the program had become "a problem and embarrassment" (Maier, 1993, p. 31). As Maier noted, "[f]rom 1966 through 1972, the existence of only two operational forms of the AFQT became a problem" because, with "the limited number of items in use, recruiters could . . . learn their content and [so could] coach examinees on the test. The embarrassment arose because there was no adequate response by the research community to pleas from personnel managers for new items that could help reduce coaching" (Maier, 1993, p. 31).

students' results with the military.[20] All through 1974 and 1975 the services worked, but not always together, to come up with a common ASVAB that would meet everyone's needs.[21] At the time, each service administered its own test, and an applicant interested in more than one service would have to take multiple tests. Maier summed up the situation: "[M]ilitary selection and classification testing and personnel decisions in the mid-1970s were chaotic" (Maier, 1993, p. 37). Finally, in desperation, Brehm set a new firm implementation date: "Effective 1 January 1976, the AFEES will be given the responsibilities and necessary resources to centrally manage the administration of the ASVAB" (Brehm, 1975).

The misnorming problem was suspected within months of the test being fielded and reported by the Navy. In April 1976, the Navy found that too many enlistees were scoring in the top mental group categories (I and II).[22] The personnel research laboratories agreed, and a recalibration was developed, but "only for the upper end of the distribution" (Laurence and Ramsberger, 1991, p. 75). The Marine Corps disagreed. In July 1976, the Corps brought a complaint to the ASVAB Working Group that the test was misnormed over the entire range. Given the approved conversion tables, which translated raw scores into AFQT groupings, the tables were systematically reporting higher AFQT scores than were warranted. Unfortunately, the other services did not agree. In their account of these events, Janice Laurence and Peter Ramsberger observed that the other services had not yet noted any anomalies in their accession data. So, a conversion table was adopted in September 1976 that fixed only the high-end problem (Laurence and Ramsberger, 1991, p. 75). It was not until the analysts at CNA working for the Marine Corp compared actual the test results of individual test-takers on different tests that the charge of misnorming on the lower end of the distribution became credible.

Should a careful review of "accession data" have set off alarms? David Armor, a distinguished social psychologist and new RAND analyst at the time—he would later serve as the Principal Deputy Assistant Secretary of Defense (Manpower, Reserve Affairs and Logistics) in the Reagan administration—thought that they should have. Armor recalls that, in 1977 and 1978, even before the misnorming problem was known, he had heated discussions with Rick Cooper over the issue of quality as Cooper was preparing his study on the all-volunteer force (Armor, 2002). As Armor saw it, Cooper and others in DoD were caught up in the euphoria of rising all-volunteer force

---

[20] The initial ASVAB had been developed in 1966 in response to educators' complaints about the "burden of being approached by recruiters from all Services offering to administer their Service test batteries" (Maier, 1993, p. 36). The Assistant Secretary of Defense at the time ordered that only one military test would be given in high schools. A joint-service committee was established to oversee the development of the test.

[21] Years later Maier noted that, in "1974 and 1975 . . . the technical community was not accustomed to this kind of pressure and scrutiny. In earlier times schedules were taken more lightly by researchers; the prevailing attitude was that new tests would be introduced when they were ready" (Maier, 1993, p. 37).

[22] It would later become clear that cheating on enlistment tests in the period prior to the introduction of the joint service ASVAB played an important role in disguising the effects of the misnorming in other mental categories (Maier, 1993, p. 76).

quality numbers and the falling proportion of recruits scoring in the lower category (IV).[23] Armor argued that this could not be possible at the same time that the number of blacks was increasing sharply. It was true, as Moskos had reported, that

> [s]ince the end of the draft, the proportion of black high school graduates entering the Army has exceeded that of whites, and this is a trend that is becoming more pronounced. . . . [H]igh school graduates accounted for 65 percent of entering blacks, as compared with 54 percent of entering whites. (Moskos, 1982, p. 384)

From what was known at the time, however, even higher numbers of black high school graduates could not explain the corresponding drop in the number of category IV recruits. As it turned out, the explanation was not a shift in the propensity of high-scoring blacks wanting to join the military but a shift to the new ASVAB on January 1, 1976, and the poorly calibrated AFQT conversion tables.

The CNA Study

During the 1970s, the Center for Naval Analyses (CNA) conducted a series of studies for the Marine Corps intended to improve the reliability of the existing estimates of mental aptitude. Two of these studies focused on the misnorming of the ASVAB; several others focused on compromise (cheating) on the test. These issues had separate origins but became analytically intertwined. Fortunately for the manpower community, the Marine Corps had a "secret weapon": It retested all recruits within a few days of their arrival at the Marine Corps Recruit Depot (MCRD). This gave the Marine Corps a unique window into the real state of manpower quality. Differences between the scores recorded at AFEES and the retest scores at MCRD were a source of considerable concern.

The analysis of the misnorming issue was fraught with difficulties. Ideally, to analyze norms on a new test, one would give a correctly normed reference test and the new test to a group of military applicants who were motivated to do well on both and who had been coached on neither. This was difficult to do, given concerns about interfering with hard-pressed recruiters and AFEES personnel. It was also problematic in that CNA knew, from some closely held analyses, that cheating on tests was a very serious problem and would distort norming results. The result was that analysts sometimes used the best data *available,* rather than the best data.

---

[23] Even after the misnorming became widely known, Cooper still argued that,

> for the most part . . . quality seems to have held up reasonably well under the volunteer force. It is almost certainly better than . . . what the Gates Commission forecast it would be. Their original forecast was the Services might have to accept up to 20 percent category IV personnel. (Cooper, 1981, p. 103)

In fact, Pirie told Congress that, for DoD as a whole, the proportion of category IV accessions was 28.7 percent in FY 1979 and 25.1 percent in FY 1980. The numbers for the Army were worse. In FY 1979, 44.7 percent of new Army recruits came from category IV. In FY 1980, the numbers were slightly better, at 40.7 percent (Pirie and Danzig, 1980, p. 1,311).

The first of two CNA studies on misnorming began in spring 1976, when the Marine Corps asked the Marine Corps Operations Analysis Group at CNA to examine the issue of possible misnorming of the ASVAB. CNA issued a preliminary report on July 27, 1976, that formed the basis of the Marine Corps position that the ASVAB was misnormed over the entire range of the test. Formal tasking would come later, on September 7, 1976, when the Marine Corps asked CNA to

> analyze ASVAB area aptitude norms, determine the effect of AFEES environment vice recruit depot environment upon classification scores, and to develop an analytical procedure for detecting compromise of the ASVAB at AFEES. (Headquarters, 1976)[24]

The data the CNA team used were from different versions—forms—of the ASVAB and the "Army Classification Battery 1961" (ACB-61). The new form of the ASVAB and the ACB-61 were given to 3,134 recruits within two days of their arrival at the MCRD in December 1975 and January 1976. Effects due to test compromising were eliminated because these recruits had not previously seen either test. Additional data were obtained from 6,687 recruits who took older forms of the ASVAB and the ACB-61 in June 1974. Another data set containing the records of 5,768 recruits who took an earlier version of the AFQT at the AFEES and the ACB-61 at the MCRD filled out the total set of data available to the CNA analyst, William Sims.

Sims's first ASVAB misnorming study was formally published in April 1978. He found that

> the original[ly] normaliz[ed] ASVAB . . . used from 1 January 1976 through 29 July 1976 was much too easy. The AFQT percentile scores derived from ASVAB during this period were typically 6 to 10 percentile points too high. (Sims, 1978, p. v)

The ASVAB then in use was also incorrect. He found that "the revised normalization is not based upon any self-consistent analysis, but represents a negotiated position between divergent analyses, the most important of which remain unpublished" (Sims, 1978, p. v). In devastatingly simple language he concluded:

> The inaccuracies in both the original and revised normalizations will make historical comparisons of mental test scores subject to considerable uncertainty. These inaccuracies also dictate that ASVAB . . . as presently normalized, should never be used as a reference test for normalizing subsequent versions of ASVAB. (Sims, 1978, p. v)

---

[24] The resulting procedure became known as the Pseudo AFQT and was used by the Marine Corps and eventually by AFEES to help identify recruits and recruiters who had a high probability of being involved in test compromise.

As late as June 1979 test score discrepancies were associated with "test coaching," as shown by a talking paper prepared by the staff of the Assistant Secretary of Defense for Manpower, Reserve Affairs and Logistics (OASD[M&RA], 1979).

Sims remembers that "our results were generally ignored. We had little standing in the DoD aptitude testing arena and, in retrospect, our data were not fully adequate to addressing the issue" (Sims, 1995, p. 8).[25] In fact, Pirie would characterize the results of Sims's first study as "highly tentative" and noted that

> [b]ecause the data were uncertain and collected for purposes other than norming, Dr. Sims was asked by my office, on the advice of the working group charged with development of these tests to replicate more systematically his study. (Pirie and Danzig, 1980, p. 1,306)

In fact, there were good reasons to be suspicious of Sims's results. First, the Marine Corps data were truncated because of the selection standards the Marine Corps used— "relatively few people had AFQT scores below 30, and none had scores below 20" (Maier, 1993, p. 75). In addition, the ACB-61, although it had been around for many years, was itself not well normed[26]:

> [T]he accuracy of the score scale of the ACB-61 was not known [and] the scaling of Service classification batteries, especially at the low end, was not as precise as the testing community demands. (Maier, 1993, p. 75)

At a meeting of the joint service ASVAB Working Group in November 1978, Sims proposed to conduct a second norming study. The offer was endorsed by the working group and, as noted above, by Pirie. The main difference between the first and second CNA studies was that the second used an unimpeachable reference test, AFQT form 7A. Preliminary results were briefed to the working group on May 7, 1979. Al Martin recorded the startling results of that meeting:

> The results from this [the Sims CNA] study were that the norms were apparently correct at the upper ability levels but off by as much as 15 percentile points at the lower ability levels—a finding, which if accepted, would indicate that many AFQT III recruits were actually IVs. (Martin, 1979)

Sims's charts clearly showed (Figure 13.3) that the normalization was "too easy in the lower-ability ranges" (Sims, 1995, p. 8) and, given "true and reported percentages of recruits" (Sims, 1995) (Figure 13.4), "the quality of recruits reported by OSD had been inflated since 1976" (Sims, 1995, p. 8).

---

[25] An internal memorandum asserted that the Sims study was published in July 1978. In fact, it was published in April 1978 (Martin, 1979).

[26] Sims has discounted the truncation argument, noting that his primary sample of 3,134 recruits had enlisted on the basis of scores from a heavily compromised enlistment test. They were all retested at MCRD on the new ASVAB and a reference test. As a result, there was a fully adequate supply of persons with low true scores. He ascribes the shortcomings of the first CNA study to the use of a reference test (ACB-61) which itself was not well normed.

Figure 13.3
Comparison of Operational and Correct AFQT Normalizations for ASVAB Forms 6 and 7

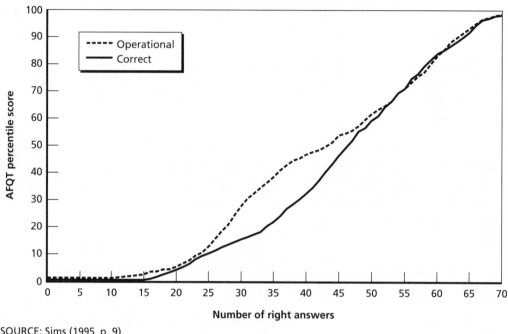

SOURCE: Sims (1995, p. 9).

Figure 13.4
Comparison of True and Reported 1979 Accessions by AFQT Category (all DoD)

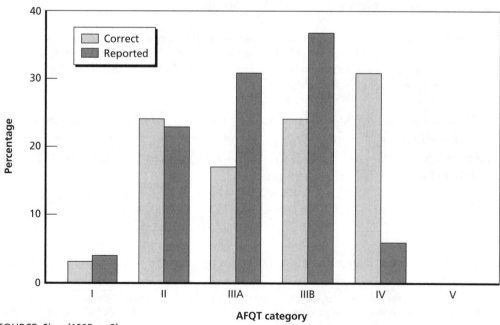

SOURCE: Sims (1995, p. 9).

Martin was still not convinced and told his bosses on May 11, 1979, that

[t]here are reasons to suspect the validity of the findings due to the nature of the potentially biased respondent set. The [ASVAB] Steering Committee has directed that a major study be undertaken immediately, which would involve applicants for all the services, to determine the accuracy of current AFQT norms and specify the potential supply impact. (If feasible, during this summer, an independent and parallel norming study would also be performed using high school students—a cleaner respondent pool from a test compromise viewpoint.) A study plan is being developed by the Army Research Institute and my staff and will be submitted to the ASVAB Steering Committee. (Martin, 1979)

Two independent studies, one by the Army Research Institute (ARI) and the other by the Educational Testing Service (ETS), were commissioned to verify the second CNA study. Preliminary results from the ARI study in September 1979 "essentially confirmed the amount of [score] inflation reported by the Marine Corps [second CNA study] earlier in 1979" (Maier, 1993, p. 76). ETS reported similar results.

Finally, DoD had three studies with consistent answers. In 1980, the department convened a panel of three eminent testing psychologists to decide which study to use. The panel chose the ARI study, and the case was closed.

Pirie's office had the "preliminary ARI tables showing 'order of magnitude' supply implications associated with the misnorming of ASVAB 6 and 7" by mid-November 1979. Danzig and his staff met with Milton Maier of ARI and William Sims of CNA on November 16 and 19 to discuss the misnorming (Martin, 1979). On February 13, 1980, Pirie believed that he had enough information, and "its significance is so apparent" that he told Secretary Brown he felt it "warrant[ed] alerting Congress as soon as possible" (Pirie, 1980a). While Brown believed that "the effect exists in the direction you say," he challenged the statement that, "when compared with the draft of the early 1960s, instead of taking markedly fewer of those from the lower end of the acceptable range, we are in fact taking more" (Pirie, 1980a). Pirie laid out the numbers for him. On February 19, 1980, he wrote to Pirie: "As I read this, the Cat IVs have stayed nearly constant since the late 60s (e.g., 25% or so) instead of going down to 5%, as we had claimed" (Pirie, 1980b). Congress was notified, and Senator Nunn scheduled hearings for March 10, 1980.[27]

---

[27] Sims remembers,

Pirie was only about half a step ahead of the General Accounting Office (GAO). The GAO was on a mission from Sam Nunn and interviewed me in late January or early February 1980 about rumors they had heard about the ASVAB misnorming. They showed me a copy of a slide that described my results and asked what it was all about. As soon as they left my office I called Al Martin (OSD, AP) and told him that the "jig was up." A briefing for Senator Nunn was quickly scheduled. (Sims, 2004)

The Profile of American Youth

Several good and lasting reforms came out of the misnorming debacle. One was the renorming of the ASVAB. When Pirie reported the misnorming to Senator Nunn, Pirie was clearly disturbed that AFQT categories were not normed to the 1980 youth population but to the population that "was under arms in World War II" (Pirie and Danzig, 1980, p. 1,291). Nunn agreed "that this is not commonly understood," and Pirie told him that "[w]e are going forward with an effort which will measure the profile of the present youth population from which we draw our new recruits today" (Pirie and Danzig, 1980, p. 1,292). Al Martin, Pirie's Director of Accession Policy, then proceeded to provide the details:

> We have developed a working relationship with the Department of Labor. They have an excellently designed sample of the current youth population. They use it in a study called the national longitudinal survey of youths. What we intend to do is to give our aptitude test to that sample of young people; and in effect, norm the test against the current youth population. This would, as Mr. Pirie said, for the first time allow us to gage [sic] how well we are doing in terms of accessions relative to young people in the current population. (Al Martin in Pirie and Danzig, 1980, pp. 1,292–1,293)

By the end of March, Pirie's office signed a contract with the National Opinion Research Center (NORC) "to administer the ASVAB to a representative sample of American youth" (Tice, 1980). By the first week in August, NORC had administered 8,887 (70 percent) of the tests that were to be administered (Martin, 1980b). By September 6, the testing was 92-percent complete, and Pirie's office was discussing "analytic plan and milestones" with NORC and RAND (Martin, 1980c). On September 30, 1980, all the tests had been administered, "with an overall sample completion rate of 95 percent" (Martin, 1980a). In fact, this was not the first time DoD had worked with NORC or the National Longitudinal Survey (NLS).[28] In 1979, the NLS's national representative sample of 12,693 (14 to 21 years of age as of January 1, 1979) was augmented by "an additional sample of 1,281 persons within the age group who were serving in the Armed Forces" (Kim et al., 1980, p. 1). When NORC compared the responses of the military-age population who were employed full time, the most relevant comparison the researchers could make, they found that "in the aggregate there were no differences between military and full-time employed youth, [but] there [were] Service differences. . . . The Army is recruiting youth who appear somewhat less qualified than the full-time employed and less qualified than the other Services" (Kim et al., 1980, p. 4).[29]

---

[28] The Department of Labor maintains a web site that provides information about the survey, one page of which references "the ASVAB" (Bureau of Labor Statistics, 2002).

[29] The comparisons showed that

> eighteen measures of different job aspects clearly shows that Armed Forces personnel are *less* satisfied than their civilian labor market counterparts. . . . Of the 18 job measures, by far, the most significant difference between military and civilian personnel was in pay satisfaction. Military youths are significantly more dissatisfied with pay than their civilian counterparts. Other measures which show large significant differences were job comfort, job challenge, job autonomy and relation with coworkers. (Kim et al., 1980, emphasis in original)

Table 13.3
AFQT Distributions in the World War II and 1980 Populations

AFQT Category	Percentile Score Boundaries	Percentage in Category[a]				
		WWII Population[b]		1980 Youth Population		
		Nominal	Actual	Males	Females	Total
I	93–100	8	7.1	6.5	5.0	5.8
II	65–92	28	30.0	35.9	33.3	34.6
III	31–64	34	31.9	28.1	33.4	30.7
IV	10–30	51	22.9	22.0	22.6	22.3
V	1–9	9	8.1	7.5	5.7	6.6
I–IIIA	50–100	51	54.1	55.9	53.5	54.7

SOURCE: Maier and Sims (1986, p. 1-19).

[a]World War II AFQT score scale. AFQT is defined as WK + PC + AR + NO/2.

[b]The World War II population contains only males. The nominal column lists the smoothed values traditionally ascribed to the World War II score scale. The actuals column contains the unsmoothed values observed in the World War II population. Chapter 3 of the source discusses the actual values and precautions for comparing the percentages in each AFQT category.

It was not until October 1984, with the introduction of new ASVAB forms that the "contemporary population replaced the mysterious World War II referent" (Laurence and Ramsberger, 1991, p. 82). The comparison between the 1980 and the World War II populations proved to be very interesting because, despite Pirie's concerns, there was not very much difference between the two populations. First, it should be noted that the so-called "World War II reference population" was not a representative sample of American youths at the time of World War II. The population might better be called the "World War II mobilization reference population" because it did not include males who had been disqualified for service, males who had received occupational deferments, or any females (Maier and Sims, 1986, p. 1-5). When the "ASVAB reference population" was constructed, it was decided that, "given the growing percentage of females in the enlisted force and changing cultural values, . . . to include both males and females" (Maier and Sims, 1986, p. 1-10). There were practically no differences.[30]

Table 13.3 shows how the populations compare in terms of AFQT categories. Figure 13.5 shows the percentile distribution of scores of the World War II and the 1980 populations. With the detailed results in hand, services were now able to "investigate the effects of the separate components of Service aptitude standards on the enlistment eligibility of the general population" (Eitelberg et al., 1984, p. 117).

---

[30] At the 93rd annual convention of the American Psychological Association, a symposium, Janice Laurence observed that

> unanimously concluded, the fact that the distribution of scores from 1944 and 1980 were so close—considering the effect on test performance of age, education, geographic region, social and economic status, and race or ethnic group—and considering that the two tested populations, separated by a span of almost thirty-six years, are so unalike—is truly remarkable. (Laurence and Ramsberger, 1991, pp. 82–83)

Figure 13.5
Conversion of AFQT Raw Scores from ASVAB 8A to Percentile Scores on the World War II and 1980 Scales

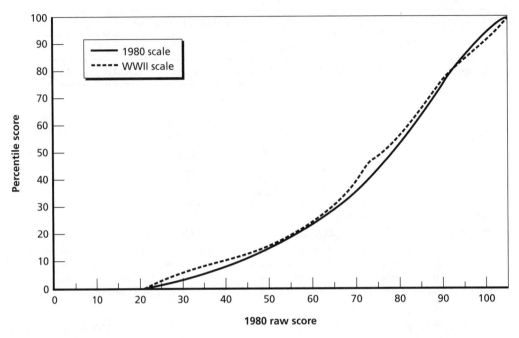

SOURCE: Maier and Sims (1986, p. 1–18).
RAND *MG265-13.5*

Problems with the Revised ASVAB Scoring for 1980 Youth

The 1980 reference population study was itself not without problems, and the new reference population conversion tables were not released until 1985. Studies showed that "the sample of American male youths and the samples of male military applicants and recruits did not differ significantly on . . . eight power subtests. Notable differences in subtest performance were found" on two subtests, Numerical Operations and Code Speed (Waters, 1982, p. 5). Again, it was a team at CNA that noted the discrepancy. Researchers at the Air Force Human Resources Laboratory developed "adjustments from the equation and corrected the speeded subtest discrepancies between the NORC sample and military sample" (Waters, 1982, pp. 6–7). Finally, six years after the 1980 Profile of American Youth tests were administered, DoD announced that, since "scores of Service applicants and recruits who tested on the new [October 1984] forms have been understated by approximately two percentile points, . . . [t]ables adjusting the current scoring . . . will be implemented on July 1, 1986" (Armor, 1986).

Accession Screening and Job Performance

Ever since the CNA report brought the ASVAB to center stage of the all-volunteer force, Pirie had been concerned about the fact that the test was not linked to job performance. He told the service secretaries that

> the Department of Defense should base its standards for enlistment and for assignment to a military specialty upon the probability of successful job performance later in a person's military career. Therefore, I am asking the Services to undertake an effort, in cooperation with OSD, to establish standards for enlistment and assignment to training that are validated against eventual job performance. (Pirie, 1980d)[31]

As Pirie saw it, there would be three stages to the establishment of job performance standards. Phase 1 was to be a pilot project that would demonstrate the feasibility of setting standards; phase 2 was to be a long-term program that would establish and validate standards; and phase 3 was to be "a long-term research effort to improve DoD's measures of potential ability and job performance" (Pirie, 1980d, p. 1). Pirie was calling for a revolution in the way the services had done business for decades, and he knew it. He told the services that they "should plan to initiate or re-orient research work in this general area and to insure that adequate resources are provided to address this problem starting in FY 1981" and that they should have "their personnel research laboratories . . . begin research projects for specific occupations" (Pirie, 1980d, p. 2). This charge would become the focus of much of the personnel research done in the 1980s.[32]

Pirie reported to Congress on the ASVAB and on the issue of job performance just weeks before leaving office.[33] He told Congress about

> the introduction of [the] new ASVAB on October 1, 1980, . . . [the new] independent testing review board, and . . . what has been learned about job performance of Army personnel who would not have been admitted if the previous ASVAB had been correctly calibrated. (Pirie, 1980f, p. i)

---

[31] Pirie's involvement in this issue did not go down well with the Secretary of the Army. Secretary Alexander told Pirie that the

> Secretary of the Army, advised by the Chief of Staff, is in the best position to establish standards for enlistment into the Army. Personnel testing, evaluation and management in each of the Services are too large, complex and unique to be controlled effectively by your office. (Alexander, 1980)

[32] In June 1982, the House Appropriations Committee "requested an annual report outlining plans and program status for the Joint-Service Job Performance Measurement/Enlistment Standards Project be submitted to the House and Senate Armed Services and Appropriations Committees" (Armor, 1986).

[33] The Conference Report on the FY 1981 Authorization Act required a report to the Armed Services Committees "on the implementation of the new testing process, on the correlation between test scores and of the measures of quality and actual job performance, and on the creation of an independent testing review board no later than December 31, 1980" (Pirie, 1980e). Substantially the same report was sent to Brown and Claytor at the beginning of December (Stone, 1980).

Now the services and his office were "cooperating" on a "long-range systematic program of validating the enlistment standards of trainability, aptitude, and educational level against job performance" (Pirie, 1980f, p. 3). While this research would take many years to complete, the focus at this point was on how the ASVAB misnorming had affected "on our ability to man our forces effectively" (Pirie, 1980f, p. 9). Pirie considered the differing performance measures to be "central to the problem of relating screening measures to performance" (Pirie, 1980f, p. 10). Without controlled field testing, which would come later, the only readily available measures were the "gates" of graduation from recruit training, proficiency tests for promotion, and eligibility for reenlistment. He noted that "[c]ontinued successful performance at each of the many gates through which an individual must pass is assumed to be indicative of generally satisfactory performance" (Pirie, 1980f, p. 10).[34] Pirie presented two studies for consideration by the Armed Services Committees: one by CNA and another by an independent contractor, written by Irv Greenberg.

The CNA study by Catherine Hiatt and Bill Sims—the same Bill Sims who had brought the original misnorming problem to center stage—focused on the Marine Corps. They noted the Marine Corps' commitment to constructing and evaluating a prototype job performance test "to set enlistment standards based on job performance rather than on training school performance" (Hiatt and Sims, 1980, p. ii). However, for now, they used "attrition, training school performance, recommendation for reenlistment, promotion and supervisory ratings . . . [for] three occupation areas: infantry, communications maintenance and motor transport."

As shown in Figure 13.6, they found a "strong relationship between ASVAB scores and job performance and an even stronger relationship between educational level and job performance," in which the best measures of job performance were "completion of the first term of service and promotion to corporal" (Hiatt and Sims, 1980, p. ii).

Irv Greenberg produced the other study that Pirie presented to the Armed Services Committees. While he found the same basic pattern extended beyond the Marine Corps, he drew somewhat different conclusions. He was more concerned with the large number of low-scoring recruits whose "job performance" was acceptable and who would be lost to the services if standards were raised. His focus reflected his decade-long experience working with Project 100,000. In what was essentially a replay of the

---

[34] Secretary of the Army Alexander fundamentally disagreed with what Pirie was doing and told him that the test was

> principally a training diagnostic instrument. Use of results from the Skill Qualification Test to describe personnel performance, as has been done recently in a number of papers from your office, should be made only with extreme caution if at all. The results reflect the effectiveness of training as much as or more than the individual's ability and capabilities. (Alexander, 1980)

In a thinly veiled threat, Alexander told Pirie that, if he did not come around "on reflection," "the Chief of Staff and I will be happy to discuss this matter with Secretary Brown" (Alexander, 1980). Brown did get involved in a number of ways. In response to several of his questions, Danzig sent Brown a memorandum to clarify the relationship between aptitude testing and job and training performance (Danzig, 1980). The acrimony between Pirie and Alexander got so bad that Deputy Secretary of Defense Claytor had to get involved and bring the issue to Secretary Brown (Claytor, 1980).

Figure 13.6
Assessment of ASVAB AFQT Categories and "Job Performance"

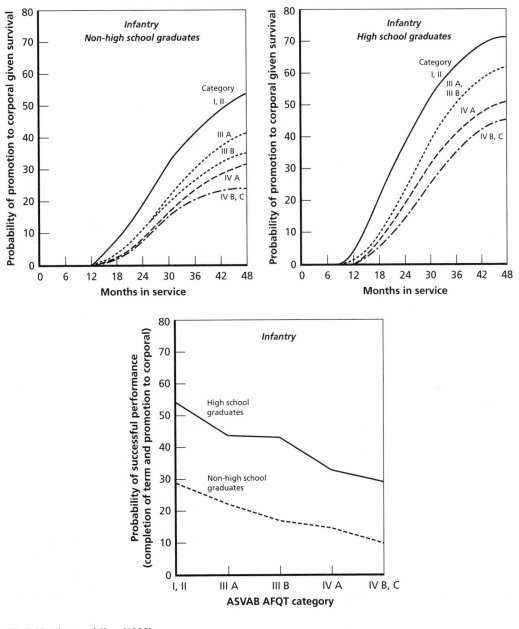

SOURCE: Hiatt and Sims (1980).

RAND *MG265-13.6*

planned experiment of the 1960s, Greenberg, recently retired and now a contractor, was asked to review the "natural experiment" of the 1970s as he had the "planned experiment" of the 1960s. Greenberg summed up the dilemma that DoD faced:

> If the performance data show[s] that most of the people who were inadvertently enlisted performed satisfactorily, it would make sense to continue accepting the best of them to meet recruiting goals. (Greenberg, 1980, p. 2)

From the population of Army recruits, Greenberg identified "those who would have failed a correctly calibrated ASVAB," calling them the "Potential Ineligibles (PIs)" (Greenberg, 1980, p. 58). These included low-scoring high school graduates and the lower-scoring category IIIB, non–high school graduates. Much as had been the case with the New Standards Men of a decade earlier, the PI group "did not perform as well" as other recruits. They had higher attrition and lower scores on the skill qualifying test (SQT). However, and here was the rub, "the majority of the PIs were successful." Greenberg recited the statistics: "58 percent passed their SQT, 52 percent completed their first term, 72 percent of those were eligible for reenlistment." Greenberg found that

> 76 percent of those who completed their first term achieved grade E-4 or E-5 [and] 23 percent of the PIs who enlisted in FY 1977 entered the career force. . . . The performance of the Category IIIA soldiers was better than that of the PIs especially on SQTs, promotion, and graduation from skill training courses of average complexity. (Greenberg, 1980, p. 64)

Greenberg's findings notwithstanding, the debate about quality and eligibility standards continued to be addressed in the job performance studies each of the services carried out, especially the massive Project A studies undertaken by the Army Research Institute starting in the early 1980s.

The Legacy

The research that began during the Carter administration, particularly the work addressing the misnorming problem, would take years to complete. The various test programs provided clear evidence of the value of advertising and the benefits of educational incentives to encourage enlistment. The research on job performance would not finally be completed until the end of the decade and would settle the questions about accession testing and job performance. What seems so logical now—people who score higher on standardized tests do better on the job than those who score lower—was once very controversial. By focusing on quality, the all-volunteer force became a self-fulfilling prophecy. As the quality of the force increased, it became easier to recruit quality people, and those who were recruited were more willing to stay and reenlist. Like the mythological phoenix, the all-volunteer force would rise from the misnorming fiasco to soar once more.

References

Alexander, Clifford L., Jr., "Plan for Validating Enlistment Standards Against Job Performance," memorandum to Assistant Secretary of Defense (M&RA), Washington, D.C., July 15, 1980. G0443.pdf.

Armor, David J., "Fifth Annual Report to Congress—Department of Defense Efforts to Link Enlistment Standards and Job Performance," memorandum to Assistant Secretaries of the Military Department (M&RA), Washington, D.C., July 18, 1986. G0980.pdf.

———, "Implementation of Adjusted Scoring Tables for ASVAB Forms 11/12/13," memorandum to Assistant Secretaries of the Military Department (M&RA), Washington, D.C., May 23, 1986. G0919.pdf.

———, interview with Bernard Rostker, October 3, 2002.

Asch, Beth J., and John T. Warner, *A Policy Analysis of Alternative Military Retirement Systems,* Santa Monica, Calif.: RAND Corporation, MR-465-OSD, 1994. S0570.pdf.

Ausink, John, Jonathan Cave, and Manuel Carrillo, *Background and Theory Behind the Compensation: Accessions and Personnel Management (CAOM) Model,* Santa Monica, Calif.: RAND Corporation, 2003. S0890.pdf.

Black, Matthew, Robert Moffitt, and John T. Warner, "Reply to Comment by Glenn Gotz on 'The Dynamics of Job Separation: The Case of Federal Employees'," *Journal of Applied Econometrics,* Vol. 5, No. 3, July–August 1990, pp. 269–272.

———, "The Dynamics of Job Separation: The Case of Federal Employees," *Journal of Applied Econometrics,* Vol. 5, No. 3, July–August 1990, pp. 245–262.

Brehm, William K., "Standardized Testing of Enlistees," information memorandum to Deputy Secretary of Defense, Washington, D.C., June 9, 1975. G0664.pdf.

Buddin, Richard, *Enlisted Effects of the 2+2+4 Recruiting Program,* Santa Monica, Calif.: RAND Corporation, R-4097-A, 1991. S0694.pdf.

Bureau of Labor Statistics, *National Longitudinal Survey: The ASVAB,* Washington, D.C.: United States Department of Labor, October 21, 2002. S0538.pdf.

Carroll, Vincent P., Ambar G. Rao, Hau L. Lee, Arthur Shapiro, and Barry L. Bayus, "The Navy Enlistment Marketing Experiment," *Marketing Science,* Vol. 4, No. 4, Autumn 1985, pp. 352–374.

Claytor, W. Graham, Jr., "Unsuccessful Attempts to Get Robin and Cliff to Agree on an Appropriate Program," memorandum to Secretary of Defense, Washington, D.C., July 30, 1980. G0368.pdf.

Cooper, Richard V. L., "AVF vs. DRAFT: Where Do We Go From Here?" in William J. Taylor Jr., Eric T. Olson and Richard A. Schrader, eds., *Defense Manpower Planning: Issues for the 1980s,* New York: Pergamon Press, 1981.

Danzig, Richard, "Aptitude Testing," information memorandum to Secretary of Defense, Washington, D.C., July 23, 1980. G0468.pdf.

Duncan, Charles W., "First-Term Attrition," memorandum to Secretaries of the Military Departments, Washington, D.C., February 10, 1978. G0012.pdf.

Eitelberg, Mark Jan, Janice H. Laurence, Brian K. Waters, and Linda S. Perelman, *Screening for Service: Aptitude and Education Criteria for Military Entry*, Washington, D.C.: Office of the Assistant Secretary of Defense (Manpower, Installations, and Logistics), September 1984. S0659.pdf.

Fernandez, Richard L., *Issues in the Use of Postservice Educational Benefits as Enlistment Incentives*, Santa Monica, Calif.: RAND Corporation, N-1510-MRAL, July 1980. S0681.pdf.

———, *Enlistment Effects and Policy Implications of the Educational Assistance Test Program*, Santa Monica, Calif.: RAND Corporation, R-2935-MRAL, 1982. S0677.pdf.

Flyer, Eli S., *Factors Relating to Discharge for Unsuitability Among 1956 Accessions to the Air Force*, Lackland Air Force Base, San Antonio, Tex.: U.S. Air Force Personnel Research Laboratory, WADC TN 59201, December 1959.

———, "Abridged History of Personnel Research in the Department of Defense," from an interview with Bernard Rostker, Monterey, Calif., August 13 and 15, 2002. S0633.pdf.

Goldberg, Lawrence, "Recruiters, Advertising, and Navy Enlistment," *Naval Research Logistics Quarterly*, Vol. 29, No. 2, June 1982, pp. 385–398. S0674.pdf.

Gotz, Glenn A., "Comment on 'The Dynamics of Job Separation: The Case of Federal Employees'," *Journal of Applied Econometrics*, Vol. 5, No. 3, July–August 1990, pp. 263–268.

Gotz, Glenn A., and John J. McCall, *The Retirement Decision: A Numerical Analysis of a Dynamic Retirement Model*, Santa Monica, Calif.: RAND Corporation, WN-9628-AF, March 1977. S0436.pdf.

Greenberg, I. M., *Mental Standards for Enlistment Performance of Army Personnel Related to AFQT/ASVAB Scores: Final Report*, Monterey, Calif.: McFann Gray Associates, Inc., MGA0180WRD02, December 1980. S0540.pdf.

Haggstrom, Gus W., Thomas J. Blaschke, Winston K. Chow, and William Lisowski, *The Multiple Option Recruiting Experiment*, Santa Monica, Calif.: RAND Corporation, R-2671-MRAL, 1981. S0673.pdf.

Headquarters, U.S. Marine Corps, Deputy Chief of Staff for Manpower, "ASVAB Experimental Testing Analysis: Request for Marine Corps Operations Analysis Group (MCOAG) Support of," memorandum to Deputy Chief of Staff for Research Development and Studies, Washington, D.C., September 7, 1976.

Hiatt, Catherine M., and William H. Sims, *Armed Forces Vocational Aptitude Battery (ASVAB) and Job Performance*, Alexandria, Va.: Center for Naval Analyses, CNA 803121, November 20, 1980. S0539.pdf.

Hidalgo, Edward, Navy Manpower, hearing before the House Armed Services Committee, 95th Cong., 2nd Sess., February 24, 1978. S0448.pdf.

Kim, Choongsoo, Gilbert Nestel, Robert L. Phillips, and Micahel E. Borus, *Summary and Fact Sheet, The All-Volunteer Force: An Analysis of Youth Participation, Attrition, and Retention*, Columbus, Ohio: Center for Human Resource Research, The Ohio State University, Undated. S0532.pdf.

Laurence, Janice H., and Peter F. Ramsberger, *Low-Aptitude Men in the Military*, New York: Praeger, 1991.

Lockman, Robert F., *Enlisted Selection Strategies,* Alexandria, Va.: Center for Naval Analyses, CNS 1039, September 1974. S0837.pdf.

———, *Chances for Surviving the First Year of Service: A New Technique for Use in Making Recruiting Policy and Screening Applicants for the Navy,* Alexandria, Va.: Center for Naval Analyses, CNS 1068, November 1975. S0346.pdf.

Lockman, Robert F., and Patrice L. Gordon, *A Revised Screen Model for Recruit Selection and Recruitment Planning,* Arlington, Va.: Center for Naval Analyses, August 1977.

Lockman, Robert F., and John T. Warner, *Predicting Attrition: A Test of Alternative Approaches,* Arlington, Va.: Center for Naval Analyses, March 1977. S0525.pdf.

Maier, Milton H., *Military Aptitude Testing: The Past Fifty Years,* Monterey, Calif.: Defense Manpower Data Center, D Md.C TR 93007, June 1993. S0384.pdf.

Maier, Milton H., and William H. Sims, *The ASAB Score Scales: 1980 and World War II,* Alexandria, Va.: Center for Naval Analyses, CNR 116, July 1986. S0385.pdf.

Martin, Albert J., "Significant Events—Week of 7 May 1979," memorandum to Captain Fleeson, Washington, D.C., May 11, 1979. S0517.pdf.

———, "Significant Events—Week of 19 November 1979," memorandum to Jr. Major General Dean Tice, Washington, D.C., November 19, 1979. S0513.pdf.

———, *Miscellaneous Manpower Files,* Washington, D.C.: Office of the Assistant Secretary of Defense (MRA&L), September 9, 1980a. S0317.pdf.

———, "Significant Events—Week of 4 August 1980," memorandum to Major General Dean Tice Jr., Washington, D.C., August 8, 1980b. S0533.pdf.

———, "Significant Events—Week of 15 September 1980," memorandum to Major General Dean Tice Jr., Washington, D.C., September 18, 1980c. S0534.pdf.

Moskos, Charles C., Jr., "It's A New Ball Game: Changing Expectation of Military Service," in H. Wallace Sinaiko, ed., *First Term Enlisted Attrition,* Washington, D.C.: Smithsonian Institution, 1977. S0321.pdf.

———, "Serving in the Ranks: Citizenship and the All-Volunteer Force," in Martin C. Anderson, ed., *Registration and the Draft: Proceedings of the Hoover-Rochester Conference on the All-Volunteer Force,* Stanford, Ca.: Hoover Institution Press, Stanford University, 1982.

Nelson, Gary R., *The Costs of Defense Manpower: Issues for 1977,* Washington, D.C.: Congressional Budget Office, January 1977. S0458.pdf.

———, "CNA Support for the PCMC Analysis," memorandum to Richard Danzig, Washington, D.C., April 25, 1978. G0022.pdf.

Nixon, Richard M., *The Real War,* New York: Warner Books, 1980.

Nunn, Sam, Status of the All-Volunteer Force, hearing before the Senate Armed Services Subcommittee on Manpower and Personnel, 95th Cong., 2nd Sess., Washington, D.C., U.S. Government Printing Office, June 20, 1978. S0444.pdf.

OASD[M&RA]—*See* Office of the Assistant Secretary of Defense for Manpower and Reserve Affairs.

Office of the Assistant Secretary of Defense for Manpower and Reserve Affairs, *Investigation of Test Compromises—TALKING POINTS,* Washington, D.C.: U.S. Department of Defense, June 4, 1979. G0476.pdf.

Pirie, Robert B., Jr., "Weekly Activity Report (23–27 October 1978)," information memorandum to Secretary of Defense, Washington, D.C., November 1, 1978. G0414.pdf.

———, "Enlistment Mental Testing," memorandum to Secretary of Defense, Washington, D.C., February 13, 1980a. G0367.pdf.

———, "Enlisted Mental Testing," memorandum to Secretary of Defense, Washington, D.C., February 19, 1980b. G0469.pdf.

———, "Impact of Nonpay Factors on Retention," memorandum to Secretary of Defense, Washington, D.C., March 24, 1980c. G0416.pdf.

———, "Plan for Validating Enlistment Standards Against Job Performance," memorandum to Secretaries of the Military Department, Washington, D.C., July 7, 1980d. G0371.pdf.

———, "Report to the Secretary and the Congress on Relation of Entrance Standards to Job Performance," memorandum to Assistant Secretaries of the Military Departments (M&RA), Washington, D.C., November 7, 1980e. G0460.pdf.

———, *Implementation of New Armed Services Vocational Aptitude Battery and Actions to Improve the Enlistment Standards Process: A Report to the House and Senate Committees on Armed Services,* Washington, D.C.: Office of the Assistant Secretary of Defense (MRA&L), December 31f, 1980. S0338.pdf.

Pirie, Robert B., Jr., and Richard Danzig, Testimony on the ASAVB Misnorming, hearing before the Subcommittee on Manpower and Personnel, Senate Armed Services Committee, Washington, D.C., U.S. Government Printing Office, March 10, 1980. S0567.pdf.

Rostker, Bernard D., Statement in Support of Fiscal Year 1979 Recruiting Reprogramming Request, hearing before the Subcommittee on the Department of Defense of the Committee on Appropriations, House of Representatives, 96th Cong., 1st Sess., Washington, D.C., U.S. Government Printing Office, June 13, 1979. G1223.pdf.

Sims, William H., *An Analysis of the Normalization and Verification of the Armed Services Vocational Aptitude battery (ASAVB) Forms 6 and 7,* Vol. I: *Main Text,* Arlington, Va.: Center for Naval Analyses, 1978. S0277.pdf.

———, *CNA's Role in Finding and Fixing the ASVAB Misnorming,* Alexandria, Va.: Center for Naval Analyses, CRM 94151, January 1995. S0347.pdf.

———, interview with Bernard Rostker, August 8, 2004.

Sinaiko, H. Wallace, ed., *First Term Enlisted Attrition,* Washington, D.C.: Smithsonian Institution, 1977. S0321.pdf.

Stone, Robert A., "Progress Report on ASVAB 8, 9, and 10 Implementation and on Validation of Enlistment Standards," information memorandum to Secretary of Defense, Washington, D.C., December 2, 1980. G0423.pdf.

Tice, R. Dean, "Weekly Activities Report—Military Personnel Policy," memorandum to Robin Pirie, Washington, D.C., Undated (Approximately March 20, 1980). S0530.pdf.

Warner, John T., *Analysis of the Retention Impact of the Proposed Retirement System,* Alexandria, Va.: Institute of Naval Studies, Center for Naval Analyses, CNA 780362, April 5, 1978. S0584.pdf.

———, *Models of Retention Behavior,* Alexandria, Va.: Institute of Naval Studies, Center for Naval Analyses, CNA 791139, July 30 1979a. S0434.pdf.

———, *Alternative Military Retirement Systems: Their Effects on Enlisted Retention,* Alexandria, Va.: Center for Naval Analyses, CRC 376, September 1979b. S0433.pdf.

———, *Military Compensation and Retention: An Analysis of Alternative Models and a Simulation of a New Retention Model,* Alexandria, Va.: Center for Naval Analyses, CRC 436, August 1981. S0453.pdf.

Warner, John T., and Matthew S. Goldberg, "The Influence of Non-Pecuniary Factors on Labor Supply: The Case of Navy Enlisted Personnel," *The Review of Economics and Statistics,* Vol. 66, No. 1, February 1984, pp. 26–35.

Warner, John T., and Philip M. Lurie, *A Simulation of a New Model of Compensation and Retention,* Alexandria, Va.: Institute of Naval Studies, Center for Naval Analyses, CNA 791350, September 12, 1979. S0431.pdf.

Waters, Brian K., *The Profile of American Youth: Annotated Bibliography of Department of Defense Related Publications,* Washington, D.C.: Directorate of Accession Policy Office of the Secretary of Defense, Technical memorandum 821, March 1982. S0575.pdf.

White House Press Secretary, *Announcement of the President's Commission on Military Compensation,* Washington, D.C.: The White House, June 27, 1977. S0590.pdf.

White, John P., "First-Term Attrition," action memorandum to Secretary of Defense, Washington, D.C., November 12, 1977. G0011.pdf.

Wigdor, Alexandra K., and Bert F. Green, Jr., eds., *Performance Assessment for the Workplace,* Washington, D.C.: National Academy Press, 1991.

Zwick, Charles J., *President's Commission on Military Compensation: Background Papers,* Washington, D.C.: President's Commission on Military Compensation. S0580.pdf.

CHAPTER FOURTEEN

Sustaining the All-Volunteer Force: The Reagan-Bush Years (1981–1992)

> In the late 1970s the recruiting and retention of qualified personnel for the Armed Forces had deteriorated to the point where many were questioning the effectiveness of the All-Volunteer Force. We are pleased to report that there has been a dramatic improvement during the last two years. . . . The Task Force is confident that the higher active and reserve strengths planned for the next five years can be achieved without a resumption of the draft.
>
> —Caspar W. Weinberger
> Secretary of Defense
> Military Manpower Task Force[1]

Introduction

If the Carter administration had inherited an all-volunteer force that was not as robust as public pronouncement at the time suggested, it left an all-volunteer force that was not as moribund as had been portrayed in the campaign of 1980. Just days after the Reagan administration took office, the first report on the status of the all-volunteer force was surprisingly positive. Acting Assistant Secretary of Defense for Manpower, Reserve Affairs and Logistics Robert Stone announced that the military services had "achieved 101% of the DoD-wide recruiting objective for the first quarter of FY 1981 (October–December) as compared to 96% for the same period a year ago" (Stone, R., 1981a). Even the Army had "achieved 99% of its overall objective."

This first good news boded well for the new administration's aggressive defense buildup program. The Reagan administration planned an infusion of new equipment but also an increase in military end strength. Revitalizing the all-volunteer force was an important part of its developing program. Having run against Jimmy Carter's record

---

[1] October 18, 1982 (Weinberger, 1982b, p. i).

and his presumed lack of support for the military and their families, the new administration wanted to do something to signal to those in uniform that they had a friend in the White House. Their most visible signal was an unscheduled pay raise of 5.3 percent which they wanted to take place that July.[2]

The First Reagan Pay Raise: Across the Board for "Morale and Self-Image"

The Nunn-Warner pay increase of 11.7 percent had just gone into effect in October 1980. This was the pay raise that President Carter had belatedly supported the previous June. Now, not willing to wait to see what effects the pay increase might have had—were the improving accession and retention numbers related to the pay raise?[3]— the Pentagon asked Congress for a 5.3 percent across-the-board pay raise to be effective that July. Larry Korb, a former professor at the Naval War College and the new Assistant Secretary of Defense for Manpower, Reserve Affairs, and Logistics, told the Manpower and Personnel Subcommittee of the Senate Armed Services Committee, that the

> 5.3 percent pay raise will demonstrate in a convincing manner to the men and women of the armed services that this administration cares and is committed to work with Congress in making up for a decade of neglect of their needs. (Armstrong et al., 1981, p. 18)

While at least one member of the Senate, William Armstrong (R-Colorado), was unsure that an across-the-board increase was justified, he conveyed the feelings of many that "the administration is on the right track by suggesting an increase in military compensation . . . [as] a wholesome and welcome change from that of the prior administration" (Armstrong et al., 1981, p. 2).

Senator Armstrong was, however, concerned that the across-the-board pay increase

---

[2] The administration's pay package, part of President Reagan's March 10, 1981, revised FY 1982 budget, included not only the 5.3 percent pay raise for all military personnel effective July 1981, as noted by the Congressional Budget Office, but also

> increases in the maximum allowable enlistment bonus and a broadening of eligibility requirements for the bonus, higher aviation bonuses, and numerous other changes. Finally, the Administration . . . proposed a contingency fund of $370 million for further pay initiatives, with specific proposals to be provided. (Armstrong et al., 1981, p. 42)

[3] The Congressional Budget Office estimated

> that the number of enlisted career personnel will increase in each of the services over the next five years, even without a special pay increase. . . . Without a special pay increase, the outlook for enlisted recruiting is less favorable than that for career retention, particularly in the Army. (Armstrong et al., 1981, p. 41)

would compound the existing problem of compensation. In addition it could be that an across-the-board pay increase would put us in a position of overpaying at both ends of the military spectrum, that is at the bottom and top, while continuing to underpay in the noncommissioned officer grades where the personnel shortages are the most acute. (Armstrong et al., 1981, p. 4)

While Korb did not disagree that there were problems with the compensation for noncommissioned officers, he told the committee that

> [t]argeting the raise is not the answer. The purpose of targeting is to deal with specific needs and problems. More targeting will simply raise the frustration level of the "have-nots" who will perceive they have been left out in the cold. (Armstrong et al., 1981, p. 18)[4]

Korb saw "[t]he raise as a matter of equity and not an attempt to deal with specific problems. A 5.3 percent pay raise will help to restore military compensation to the level we committed ourselves to when we created the AVF" (Armstrong et al., 1981, p. 18). It agreed that a portion of the 9.1 percent pay increase put into the budget by the outgoing Carter administration and still scheduled to take effect the following October might be targeted "after we have had months to assess the particular situation" (Armstrong et al., 1981, p. 25). In all, base pay was increased across the board by 11.7 percent in FY 1981 and by 14.3 percent in FY 1982, for a total increase of 26 percent in two years.

Support for the All-Volunteer Force Within the Administration and the Military Manpower Task Force

In early May, shortly before Korb testified on the new pay initiatives that had been included in President Reagan's revised FY 1982 budget, Korb was "summoned," without notice or preparation, to the White House to meet with senior staff from the Vice

---

[4] The issue of the type of military pay raise was not at all settled within the Reagan administration. The Military Manpower Task Force discussed the issue at its second meeting on September 14, 1981 (Korb, 1981i). The Chairman of the Counsel of Economic Advisors (CEA), Murray Weidenbaum, told Anderson that

> all of us at CEA share strongly the view . . . [i]f Korb's analysis is correct, the most efficient way to attract sufficient recruits and thus to avoid pressures for a draft is to target the pay raise on the enlisted force, especially first termers, especially Army first termers. Giving cash bonuses to selected enlisted personnel, perhaps spread over the four years of service, is probably the best type of targeting. (Weidenbaum, 1981)

At the time, two pay-raise bills were before Congress. The Jepsen bill (S.1181) provided higher pay raises for the career force than for first-termers. The Nichols bill (H.R. 3380) provided an across-the-board pay raise of 14.3 percent but allowed some limited targeting. The administration was on record supporting the Nichols bill. The CEA staff noted that, "if the Nichols bill passes, there will almost certainly be a fight about which group to favor" (Weidenbaum, 1981).

President's office, the Chief of Staff's office, the National Security Council (NSC), and the Office of the Assistant to the President for Policy Development, to discuss the status of the all-volunteer force. The Assistant to the President for Policy Development was Martin Anderson,[5] the same Martin Anderson who had first broached the idea of the all-volunteer military to would-be presidential candidate Richard Nixon in 1967. This was the same person who had so skillfully organized the Gates Commission and oversaw the initial implementation in the early 1970s.

Korb reported the meeting to Deputy Secretary of Defense Frank Carlucci and told him he was "surprised" that "the White House, or at least those present, had very little idea about our program to make the military 'first class citizens'" (Korb, 1981b). Korb recommended that the new Secretary of Defense, Caspar (Cap) Weinberger, "discuss the subject [of the all-volunteer force] at an upcoming cabinet or NSC meeting" (Korb, 1981b).[6] In fact, what Korb did not know was that even before his visit to the White House in May, the White House staff had been discussing what to do about "issues in the area of military manpower," including draft registration, combat capability, compensation and incentives, enlistment options, and defense dependent living conditions (McClaughry, 1981b). Before the end of the month, President Reagan directed Weinberger "to form a Defense Manpower Task Force to review the entire military manpower question and make proposals that will increase the effectiveness of the active and reserve all-volunteer force" (Reagan, 1981a).[7]

Irv Greenberg, the retired senior executive from DoD who was brought back to be the Executive Director of the task force, remembers that the driving force behind the creation of the task force was Martin Anderson. Anderson thought the task force was the best way to counter pressure from the Army to return to conscription. "The Army," Greenberg remembers, "hoped the new administration would increase authorized

---

[5] *Author's Note:* Besides his early association with the all-volunteer force during the Nixon administration, Anderson orchestrated candidate Reagan's opposition to draft registration. Now, as Assistant to the President for Policy Development, he was in a position to help breathe new life into his creation. In 1993, Richard Nixon told a friend that "Martin Anderson deserves the major credit for conceiving the idea, implementing it, despite . . . very stubborn opposition" (Nixon, 1993).

[6] Apparently unaware of the discussions about a task force, Korb provided Frank Hodsoll, the Deputy to the Chief of Staff at the White House, an update on the current military manpower situation and told him he "enjoyed the meeting and look[ed] forward to future discussions in this area" (Korb, 1981a). Additional material was also provided some days later (Waller, 1981). Anderson had more in mind for Korb than "future discussions." He already envisioned Korb as a key member of the working group (McClaughry, 1981b).

[7] Also cited by Secretary Weinberger in the final report of the Military Manpower Task Force (Weinberger, 1982b, p. xiii). Reagan's tasking was part of the 1981 commencement speech he gave at West Point on May 27, 1981. This was one of his first appearances after his recovery from an attempted assassination (Reagan, 1981a). The task force Korb originally proposed to Weinberger would have included outside experts (Korb, 1981c). Martin Anderson had other ideas, and Korb finally recommended to Weinberger a "cabinet council" type organization, as Anderson had suggested (Korb, 1981c).

military strength significantly, but doubted they could recruit enough volunteers to sustain such a large force" (Greenberg, 2004).[8]

The task force was formally established on July 8, 1981 (Reagan, 1982b). It was chaired by the Secretary of Defense and included the secretaries of the military departments, the Chairman of the Joint Chiefs of Staff, the head of the Office of Management and Budget, and the National Security Advisor. Anderson was also a member. Greenberg remembers that Anderson was confident that he could "educate the members on the status of the AVF and all related manpower issues" (Greenberg, 2004).[9] When established, the task force first addressed the unresolved issues of draft registration and then moved on to consider the viability of the all-volunteer force. A working group chaired by Larry Korb supported the task force.[10]

Military Manpower Task Force: Draft Registration

The first issue the Weinberger task force took up was draft registration.[11] Two of the members of the task force, Edwin (Ed) Meese, the Counselor to the President, and

---

[8] Anderson's staff told him that Steve Herbits and others felt "strongly that the campaign to bring back the draft is heading into high gear" (McClaughry, 1981a). Often cited were an op-ed article in the *Wall Street Journal* by former Army Chief of Staff General William C. Westmoreland (1981) and the position of some major newspapers, such as the *Los Angeles Times* (Editorial Staff of the *Los Angeles Times*, 1981). Besides Anderson's staff, Senator Mark Hatfield (R-Oregon) was also concerned about the all volunteer force and draft registration. On April 3, 1981, he wrote Reagan about his concerns that a new Director of Selective Service had not been selected and that registration was continuing:

> In my view, Dr. Rostker should be replaced with an individual who is prepared to carry forth your policy, not that of the last Administration. I have no doubt that the most effective way to lay the draft issue to rest is to dismantle the Carter registration program. (Hatfield, 1981)

Senator Hatfield's request notwithstanding, the work of Selective Service continued, including a radical revision of the Selective Service regulations that was reviewed by the White House staff (Bandow, 1981a).

[9] Time was also on Anderson's side. Between February 1980 and October 1981, support for a return to a draft dropped from 59 percent, as reported by Gallup, to 43 percent, as recorded in a ABC-*Washington Post* poll (McClaughry, 1981d).

[10] The first meeting of the working group was scheduled for July 1, 1981. Korb provided materials ahead of time (Korb, 1981d). McClaughry summarized the meeting for Anderson and told him that the senior-level task force would hear the same presentation at its first meeting, scheduled for July 8 (McClaughry, 1981c). The meeting was changed to August 7, and, in preparation for the meeting, Korb circulated his report of the July 1 working group meeting, as well as a briefing he had given the working group the previous month (Korb, 1981). The second task force meeting was set for September 14, 1981 (Korb, 1981). Anderson's staff told him that they thought that the pay raises would be the most important issues that would be discussed (Bandow, 1981b).

[11] *Author's Note:* Sometime during the spring of 1981—I do not recall the exact date—I was summoned to the Pentagon to talk to Secretary Weinberger about draft registration. It was a private conversation, involving only the Secretary, one of his military aides, and me. I think the aide might have been Brigadier General Colin Powell, who had worked military manpower issues in the Office of the Secretary of Defense (OSD) and the Army and was very familiar with the issue. (Years later, he recalled meeting me when I was Director of Selective Service, but I had no specific recollection of meeting him.) We sat at a small round table off to one side of an immense office. It was the first time I was in the Secretary of Defense's office. The office was at least four times the size of the office of my former Pentagon boss, the Secretary of the Navy. It would be another 11 years before I returned to that office to talk to Secretary Les Aspin about RAND's study of gays in the military. It appeared to me that everything was in about the same place it had been a decade earlier. During the following years, through the tenure of four Secretaries of Defense, I was in that office many times. The physical office never seemed to change. The permanency of it seems to suggest how little impact each secretary had on the institution of the Pentagon.

Martin Anderson, the Assistant to the President for Policy Development, probably represented the most extreme views concerning draft registration. Anderson opposed draft registration and was instrumental in candidate Reagan's stand against the program leading to candidate Reagan's May 5, 1980 letter to Senator Mark Hatfield in which Reagan stated, "draft registration may actually decrease our military preparedness, by making people think we have solved our defense problems—when we have not" (Reagan, 1980). Moreover, in words that most likely were written for Reagan by Anderson—they had a clear ring of Anderson to them—he said that

> perhaps the most fundamental objection to draft registration is moral. Only in the most severe national emergency does the government have a claim to the mandatory service of its young people. In any other time, a draft or draft registration destroys the very values that our society is committed to defending. (Reagan, 1980)

Now in the early months of his presidency, his Military Manpower Task Force would take up the issue.

Besides Secretary Weinberger and Deputy Secretary Carlucci at the Pentagon, the strongest voice for retaining registration came from Meese. By summer, it was clear that Meese had gained the upper hand. In July, the administration named Major General Thomas K. Turnage of the California National Guard to be the new Director of Selective Service. Meese had served under Turnage when both were active in the California National Guard. By early December, and with Turnage in place, a draft report was circulated among task force members that contained options to be presented to the President.[12] This draft included an option to retain registration and three alternatives to have some form of standby program without continuing registration. In commenting on the options, the Chairman of the Joint Chiefs, General David C. Jones, told Weinberger the chiefs "strongly support continuation of Selective Service registration because it is essential to the capability to mobilize manpower swiftly in an emergency" (Jones, 1981). As they saw it, peacetime registration was part of the all-volunteer force. There was no "philosophical debate" here, they said: "The AVF policy provides peacetime manpower; Selective Service registration supports mobilization for war."

General Shy Meyer, the Army Chief of Staff, was so concerned about the issue going against the Pentagon that he sent a handwritten note to Weinberger complaining

---

[12] Turnage and Meese had worked together when both were National Guard officers in California. On November 16, 1981, Turnage circulated the first draft of the task force's report on draft registration (Turnage, 1981). This version did not contain explicit options that the President might consider but provided general background information. Secretary Weinberger signed a revised version with four specific options on November 20 (Weinberger, 1981d). Martin Anderson's assistant, Doug Bandow, described some of the back-room maneuvering in a memorandum to Anderson on November 25 (1981c). Members of the task force voted on four options, with votes due on December 11, 1981. Anderson voted to "discontinue peacetime registration" (Military Manpower Task Force, 1981a).

that the task force's draft report was biased against registration and was not "as objective as I believe the President deserves" (Meyer, 1981).[13] He told the Secretary the non-registration options present "very serious questions" that the report did not answer "concerning their ability to be implemented"; in addition, the report did not mention "the favorable impact on our Armed Services recruiting this year of having registration . . . [or] the impact on our Services of canceling registration" (Meyer, 1981). The task force's report, with the recommendations of the Joint Chiefs of Staff, went to President Reagan on December 15, 1981.

The options presented to the President clearly reflected the experience of the previous year. In 1979, Selective Service had been charged with developing a credible and effective postmobilization registration program. While the White House initially accepted the plan, President Carter decided to order registration because of the message it would send about the resolve of the American people to resist the Soviet invasion of Afghanistan. When that argument rang hollow, senior members of the Carter administration made some attempts to justify peacetime registration as the only workable mobilization scheme.

The task force report presented to President Reagan came to a different conclusion. It virtually endorsed the postmobilization plan Selective Service had been working on before President Carter's 1979 State of the Union Address. Ignoring the conclusions the former director of Selective Service had drawn that, based on the experience of putting things in place in 1980, the plan was overly optimistic, the task force argued that whatever logistics problems there were could be overcome and postmobilization registration could be accomplished in four weeks, just two weeks more than if registration was continued. Was a two-week saving enough justification to retain registration and go back on a campaign promise? The main arguments in favor of maintaining registration were the strong endorsement among those in Congress who supported the administration's defense program, a September 1981 Harris poll showed that "83 percent of US families support[ed] registration, including families with draft age males" (Military Manpower Task Force, 1981b, p. 7).

The debate within the administration was a microcosm of the debate over the philosophical underpinnings of the all-volunteer force. The Joint Chiefs of Staff argued

> the act of registration has tended to remind [young men] . . . of the obligation of citizenship and helps to rekindle pride in service and country. Thus, peacetime registration is an important element in terms of civic responsibility—an element that does not run against the grain of the American public. (Jones, 1981)

---

[13] *Author's Note:* In the etiquette of the Pentagon, a handwritten note signifies special importance. General Meyer's even commented that "I've written this by hand & to you personally because I was concerned that were I to forward it as a CJCS paper it would be circulated too freely" (Meyer, 1981).

By contrast, the task force report to the President noted,

> Those who oppose peacetime registration argue that a draft or draft registration destroys the very values that our society is committed to defending, and is justified only in the most severe national emergency. (Weinberger, 1982b, p. 11)

As in the larger world, the black and white of conscription were civic responsibility and obligation contrasted against individual freedom. In this case, civic responsibility and obligation, backed by the majority of the administration's supporters in Congress, won out over individual freedom. On January 7, 1982, President Reagan announced his decision to continue peacetime registration:[14]

> I have decided to continue [peacetime] registration. Make no mistake: The continuation of peacetime registration does not foreshadow a return to the draft. . . . However, we live in a dangerous world. In the event of a future threat to national safety, registration could save the United States as much as *6 weeks* in mobilization emergency manpower. (Reagan, 1982) [Emphasis added]

Military Manpower Task Force: Report on the Status and Prospects of the All-Volunteer Force

Almost a year after the task force reported to President Reagan on registration, it submitted its report on the all-volunteer force.[15] The report reflected the positive trends in manning the all-volunteer force. In FY 1982, all the services achieved 100 percent of their recruiting objectives; test scores and educational levels were up, meeting congressional standards imposed in 1980; the career force was growing and even the selected reserves had "succeeded in recovering the strength lost earlier in the AVF period" (Weinberger, 1982b); discipline had improved; and AWOL and desertion rates were

---

[14] The issue would be raised again in 1988, when the Director of the Office of Management and Budget and the Chairman of the Council of Economic Advisors wrote to Colin Powell, no longer the military assistant to the Secretary of Defense but now National Security Advisor to President Reagan, to express their belief that "the time has come to end draft registration" (Sprinkel and Miller, 1988). Powell asked his old boss, Secretary of Defense Frank Carlucci, for his "views on the . . . proposal" (Powell, 1988). Carlucci wrote that he supported "continuation of the requirement for young men to register with the Selective Service System. . . . I am hopeful that peacetime draft registration can be continued without interruption" (Carlucci, 1988).

[15] With the issue of draft registration resolved, Anderson's staff thought that major military manpower issues would be "the quality cap imposed by Congress" and the Army's

> recent regulations . . . which will deny reenlistment to some soldiers who score poorly on the enlistment exam (strange!), and who don't make C-4 within three years (as long as the soldier performs well, we shouldn't expect every recruit to be NCO). Reducing reenlistments will put upward pressure on the number of new recruits needed. (Bandow, 1981d)

down (Weinberger, 1982b).[16] Moreover, the report reflected the majority attitudes of the American people. The National Opinion Research Center found that

> a majority (59%) rate the AVF as working well or fairly well, . . . a third (35%) rate the AVF as not working well. . . . In the absence of a national emergency, less than half (42%) of the American population would choose a return to the draft. (Korb, 1983a)

Any misgivings that some in the administration might have had, such as Secretary of State Alexander Haig, Jr.,[17] were put aside when the task force expressed strong support for the all-volunteer force "if the required resources [were] made available" (Weinberger, 1982b, p. A-1). Given that the task force members included not only the Secretary of Defense but also the director of the Office of Management and Budget, it seemed likely that the all-volunteer force would no longer be starved for resources as it had been since the last year of the Ford administration and during the Carter administration. Citing his chairmanship of the Presidential Military Manpower Task Force, Weinberger wrote the editors of the *New York Times:*

> The revitalization of our All-Volunteer Force has been a success. We remain committed to and view the AVF as the prime peacetime option for both now and the foreseeable future. On its tenth birthday, the AVF gets high marks. Today, more than ever, we have every right to be proud of our people in uniform. (Weinberger, 1983)

---

[16] Weinberger was particularly proud and "noted with pleasure the decline in incidents of absenteeism and desertion. . . . DoD-wide the rates are the lowest experienced during the last 14 years," he told the secretaries of the military departments, attributing this to their "improvement efforts in selecting volunteers for military service" (Weinberger, 1982a).

[17] The Secretary of State had long been a critic of the all-volunteer force. At the beginning of the Nixon administration, when he was the military assistant to Henry Kissinger, Haig told Kissinger that

> an all-volunteer force under certain concepts would be totally incompatible with the traditions of the military in our society. . . . The only reason I am not more concerned about this campaign promise is the fact that I know a Republican budget could not sustain the simple economics of such a force, even if the Vietnam conflict were settled tomorrow. (Haig, 1969)

In 1981, no longer a colonel working on the National Security Council but the Secretary of State, Haig inserted himself into the discussion at a conference in California, where Korb told Weinberger that Haig had "broached the possibility that a return to the draft could reduce costs" (Korb, 1981h). Korb also told Weinberger that, "if we returned to the draft, added a GI Bill, but did not drastically reduce first-term pay, such a draft system would be considerably more costly than the AVF" (Korb, 1981h). In a courteously worded letter to Haig, Weinberger presented Korb's arguments and concluded that "a return to the draft would not automatically generate savings. . . . I am confident that with appropriate support from the Congress the AVF will continue to succeed" (Weinberger, 1981c). In a handwritten addendum to his letter Weinberger added, "Al, if you would like us to look at other aspects of this, etc., we'll be glad to do so" (Weinberger, 1981c), which, in Washington's clear but never stated parlance of one equal talking to another, meant "please, next time, consult me first before you talk about something for which you are neither responsible nor have the facts."

Making the All-Volunteer Force Work: Educational Benefits, Bonuses, and Advertising

From the beginning, it was clear to some members in the new administration that, if the all-volunteer force was to become viable, many of the supporting programs that had been starved for support would have to be expanded. In fact, it was the consistent position of the Office of the Secretary of Defense that a well-implemented

> strategy requires a mix of resources that include recruiters, retention counselors, advertising, basic entitlements, as well as enlistment and reenlistment incentives. . . . In general, discretionary incentives (cash bonuses, educational supplements to the Montgomery GI Bill or Army College Fund) provide two benefits. They expand the market by attracting more high quality people to the service than would otherwise apply, and they help channel them to longer enlistment terms than they would otherwise choose and to less popular skills. (Green, G., 1988c)

This was just the first of a number of initiatives undertaken to increase the attractiveness of military service and the effectiveness of the recruiting efforts of the services.

Educational Assistance Benefit

In early December 1979, Major General Max Thurman, Commander of the Army's Recruiting Command, traveled to Stanford, California, to attend the Hoover-Rochester Conference on the All-Volunteer Force (Anderson, 1982). One might have expected that a person in his position would be making the keynote address or, if not that, presenting a paper or making a report. In fact, Thurman was just one of many sitting in the audience. He did not even join into the floor discussions after the formal papers were presented and critiqued. He just listened. The usual presenters made the usual points, and Thurman listened. Little came out of the conference except that Thurman met Charlie Moskos.[18] After meeting Moskos, Thurman became a strong proponent of a two-market strategy for the Army—one being work-oriented, for which traditional promises of skill training, security, and pay would have great appeal, and the other being college-oriented, for youth who might look for a short hiatus between high school and college but whose main objective was a college education.

Charles Moskos, of course, was the loudest voice in favor of educational benefits. He originally proposed them in 1974 (Janowitz and Moskos, 1974). As a frequent witness before Senator Nunn's personnel subcommittee, he eventually got a very reluctant John White to agree to test the program (Nunn, 1978). Moskos's arguments had

---

[18] Moskos recalls that he

> first met Max Thurman there [at the conference] and we became very close. When he was based in the DC area, I always stayed at his digs at Ft. McNair. At his invitation, I flew down with him during the Panama invasion. He was super keen on the Montgomery GI Bill. (Moskos, 2004)

another champion besides Max Thurman: the new Secretary of the Army, John Marsh, Jr. Within days of taking office, Marsh asked Deputy Secretary of Defense Frank Carlucci for his support in continuing and expanding a number of educational incentive programs,[19] even before the test program that had begun in the last days of the Carter administration (December 1980) was evaluated or its results were translated into new legislative programs. At the very minimum, he told Carlucci, "the Army will need the legislative authority to continue with those programs currently available" (Marsh, 1981). Carlucci agreed and instructed Korb to "prepare appropriate legislation" (Marsh, 1981).

When Thurman became the Army's Deputy Chief of Staff for Personnel in early 1981, he asked Curt Gilroy from ARI to "work with Charlie Moskos and others to come up with a strategy for army recruiting success in the 1980s. . . . [They] structured an incentives package to segment the market, and the Army College Fund (ACF) was key to it" (Gilroy, 2004).[20]

Testing Educational Benefits

After the discouraging results of the Multiple Option Recruiting Experiment in 1979 and early 1980, members of the House Armed Services Committee made it clear that they thought the existing benefits were too small to be very helpful. In their Authorization Report for FY 1981, they noted that

> [t]he recruiting force needs new tools to attract enlistees. Continual increases in the recruiting and advertising budget miss the heart of the problem. For most youth today, the military no longer holds out an image of providing an opportunity for personal development. The loss of a substantial non-contributory educational assistance benefit as a concomitant to military service has left the military incapable of reaching a large segment of society. (U.S. House of Representatives, 1980, pp. 116–117)

---

[19] As noted in Marsh's memorandum to Carlucci,

> [t]he Veterans Educational Assistant Program (VEAP) was enacted by Congress after the GI Bill was terminated. This program, into which the soldier contributes up to $100 a month in return for which the Veterans Administration contributes $2 for every $1, ends on 31 December 1981. If the VEAP program is to be extended, the President must make such a recommendation to the Congress before 1 June 1981.

> A key provision of the VEAP program provides authority for SECDEF to supplement the basic benefit for critical skills in which the Services are having difficulty in attracting individuals.

> In conjunction with OSD, the Army is currently testing three variations of the Basic VEAP educational incentives. These are: The "Basic" VEAP, nationwide—maximum benefit $8,100; the "Super" VEAP in 52% of the country with "kickers" of $2,000, $4,000, and $6,000 for enlistments of 2 years, 3 years, and 4 years respectively—maximum benefit $14,100; and the "Ultra VEAP" in 18% of the country with "kickers of $8,000, $8,000, and $12,000 for 2, 3, and 4 year enlistments respectively—maximum benefit of $20,100."

> In addition, Congress directed the testing of three additional educational assistance incentives. (Marsh, 1981, p. 1)

[20] At Thurman's request, Gilroy documented the dual-market strategy and the role of educational benefits in Gilroy et al. (1990).

The Senate did not support the new program suggested by the House but agreed to a

> one year "pilot test" of three new programs: (1) a program of DoD payments of student loans held by Active and Reserve enlistees and reenlistees; (2) a noncontributory version of [Veteran's Educational Assistance Program] VEAP ... and (3) a retention plan under which the Secretary [of Defense] was authorized to make payments from an enlistee's VEAP account to his spouse or children. (Fernandez, 1982, pp. 9–10)

These options, as well as the VEAP and Ultra VEAP—a more-generous program—for the Army, were tested between December 1980 and September 1981. The test showed that the new Ultra VEAP with its "kickers" or supplemental benefits of as much as $12,000 that were given to certain "high quality" recruits for longer enlistments or agreeing to service in certain occupations

> raised Army enlistments by a statistically significant amount; about 9 percent ... and did not appear to come at the expense of the other services. . . . Results for the Noncontributory VEAP program were disappointing. None of the services registered a substantial relative gain. (Fernandez, 1982, pp. 56–57)

The Noncontributory VEAP and tuition-and-stipend programs were terminated with the end of the test in September 1981. The Army extended the "Ultra VEAP" program, renamed the Army College Fund, as the other services reverted to the Basic VEAP. In Congress, however, members were pressing for a new GI Bill.

The Montgomery GI Bill

On October 19, 1984, Congress passed the Veterans' Educational Assistance Act of 1984, as part of the FY 1985 Defense Authorization Act. The new program provided for a "contributory educational program for all active duty, non prior service accessions after June 30, 1985" (ASD[FMP], 1988, p. 1). The program became known as the Montgomery GI Bill (MGIB), after Congressman Sonny Montgomery (D-Mississippi), its primary sponsor.[21] It provided for automatic enrollment, unless a soldier opted out, and a reduction in a participant's pay by $100 a month for the first 12 months of service. The returns for two- and three-year enlistments, with four years in the Selected Reserve, were very generous. When a participant completed an enlistment, the Veterans Administration matched his or her $1,200 with $9,600 for a three-year enlistment and

---

[21] Moskos also recalls that

> Jack Marsh called me into is office sometime in the early 1980s and said he liked my AVF GI Bill proposal. But he could not publicly oppose the OSD party line. He said I should see his good friend Sonny Montgomery and say go ahead. I met with Montgomery and the rest is history. When the Montgomery Bill passed the Congress, Sonny called me up personally at home to relay the news. (Moskos, 2004)

$7,800 for a two-year enlistment. So, after military service, a participant who had enlisted for three years would receive $300 a month for 36 months, and a two-year enlistee would receive $250 a month for 36 months. A noncontributory program was also established for members of the Selected Reserves.

While the services were perfectly willing to stay with the VEAP program, DoD would report several years later that the "MGIB has become a valuable part of the . . . broad program of recruiting incentives" (ASD[FMP], 1988, p. 2). In reporting to Congress in 1988,[22] DoD said that it would be

> facing a more challenging recruiting effort over the next few years. The youth population will continue to decline causing increased competition with private employers and institution of higher education. In light of reduced recruiting budgets and the increasing gap between military and civilian pay, educational benefits and other quality of life programs take on increasing importance. The Congressional Budget Office has estimated that the MGIB basic benefit has a 4 to 5 percent effect on increasing the number of enlistments of high quality personnel. This effect will help maintain the recruiting momentum established over the last 5 years. (ASD[FMP], 1988, p. 2)

Others in Congress, however, did not share the enthusiasm for these programs and even went so far as to "[prohibit] payment of Army College Fund (ACF) benefits for 2-year enlistments into noncombat skills" (Green, G., 1988a). The problem was, as the House Appropriations Report for FY 1988 noted, that

> the Army . . . offer(s) a two-year enlistment and Army College Fund to recruit high quality, obviously college-bound individuals into the seriously shortage skill area of combat arms. There is something incongruous with a program that brings high quality individuals into the Army, while at the same time offering them a great incentive to leave.[23]

The Appropriations Committee believed that the Army did not have "a consistent strategy to recruit and retain the number and quality of people it needs to sustain the force" and so directed the Army "to develop a comprehensive, sound and economically feasible approach to an incentive package to enlist and reenlist high quality individuals" (attachment to Green, G., 1988a).

---

[22] Interestingly, while the report to Congress on the MGIB cited the findings of the Congressional Budget Office that the program had a very positive effect on recruiting, the 1988 Biennial Report to Congress by the Secretary of Defense apparently gave "all credit (for better recruiting results) to increased compensation and increased funds for enlistment and reenlistment bonuses." Congressman Montgomery "was very disappointed," and so told Secretary of Defense Carlucci. As far as he was concerned, there was "no doubt that educational incentives are the most important factor in recruiting the bright young men and women in today's society. [Your] [r]eport writers should understand that" (Montgomery, 1988).

[23] From the House Appropriations Committee Report for FY 1988, provided as an attachment to Green, G. (1988a).

The Army countered by proposing the 2+2+4 Recruiting Options Test—two years on active duty, two years in the reserves, and four years in the Individual Ready Reserve pool—to see if the shorter initial term of service could "increase high-quality enlistments in the active-duty forces" that would also "increase the . . . [flow] of trained manpower from the active forces into the Army reserve" (Buddin, 1991). The final results supported both Moskos's contentions and the Army's expectations that a short-term option tied to the Army College Fund would be "market expanding."[24] RAND's assessment of the Options Test was that the

> 2+2+4 program expanded the market for high-quality male recruits, . . . about 25 to 30 percent of the men taking the program were new recruits. . . . The program did channel recruits into those hard-to-fill noncombat skills that participated in the 2+2+4 program. . . . [T]he program attracted additional high-quality recruits into the Army and caused only a small number to change from a long term of service to a shorter term. These results suggest that many people were willing to make the commitment to reserve service, in the process providing an additional supply of manpower to both the active and reserve components. (Buddin, 1991, pp. 38–39)

Contrary to the fears of the House Appropriations Committee and many managers in OSD, Buddin estimated that there was actually an increase in active-duty obligated man-years of 2 percent (Buddin, 1991, p. 37).

The 1990 DoD Report to Congress recognized that

> the MGIB has become a valuable part of the Department's broad program of recruiting incentives. Despite projections of reduced force structure as a result of emerging developments in Eastern Europe and elsewhere, we anticipate continued maintenance of excellence in the All-Volunteer Force. . . . In light of reduced recruiting budgets, now estimated to be a reduction of 11 percent, and the increasing gap between military and private sector pay, education benefits and other quality-of-life programs take on increasing importance. (Jehn, 1990a, p. 3)

During the first five years, over 71 percent of those eligible enrolled in the program. It was estimated that the MGIB would pay 49.5 percent of the costs for enrollees who "serve 3 or more years enlistment and pursue a program of education on a full-time basis" (Jehn, 1990a).

---

[24] As recently as 2003, Moskos was still advocating a 15-month enlistment option. For "college attendees and college graduates," see Moskos (2003, p. 1).

The Bonus Programs

The second part of the all-volunteer force program, in addition to educational benefits, was economic incentives or bonuses.[25] In the early days of the all-volunteer force, there was a decided lack of enthusiasm for bonus programs; some argued that they were inconsistent with and broke the historic ties between pay grades.[26] Critics of the all-volunteer force, such as Charlie Moskos, saw such monetary incentives as undermining the institutional commitment to serve. They would rather have had a vacancy than use bonuses to help recruit or retain qualified service members. Despite such views, the bonus programs proved extremely popular. For example, in the dark days of 1980, the Navy had to suspend its Selective Reenlistment Bonus program—it was too popular. As Danzig told Secretary Brown, "[m]ore sailors have been signing up for the bonuses than expected, and the Navy now estimates . . . if they do not curtail the program" they will run out of funds (Danzig, 1980).

Given the results of the Educational Assistance Test, the Congressional Budget Office and the administration, even in the face of strong support for a new GI Bill, expressed preferences for the more-selective bonus programs. On September 10, 1981, the lead witness for the CBO told a House Committee that, as

> a general rule, manpower costs can be held down by focusing improvements in pay and benefits on those skills with the greatest recruiting and retention problems. Most of the legislative proposals on educational benefits, including H.R. 1400 [introduced by Congressman Montgomery], do not fully adopt this approach. Instead, they extend eligibility to all military personnel after a specific period of service, regardless of recruiting and retention conditions. (Hale, 1981, p. 35)

Korb followed, noting that, "[l]ike the Congressional Budget Office, we believe that postservice educational assistance programs create a retention disincentive once a member has earned his basic entitlement" (Korb et al., 1981, p. 53). Congress ordered a test of the bonus program, which began on June 29, 1982.

---

[25] All-volunteer force bonus programs are usually associated with attracting and retaining enlisted personnel. Bonuses, however, were also important for the management of aviators and submariners. Since there was no problem attracting qualified people to sign up for pilot training, the aviation bonus program was used to retain pilots and provide an incentive to the services to assign them to jobs that met "operational flying duty requirements" so that pilots might meet flying hour "gates"—cumulative flying hour goals at various stages in their careers—to receive the aviation bonus. In 1992, Jehn estimated that

> over 275 pilots remained in the service who would have left if there was no bonus. When contrasted with a jet pilot's initial training cost of about $1 million, the bonus investment is a bargain. Nonetheless, the Navy and Air Force were unable to retain sufficient numbers of experienced pilots to meet their desired goal, despite the lower requirements resulting from force structure reductions. (Jehn, 1992f)

[26] The lack of enthusiasm apparently did not extend to General George Washington. A report to Congress noted that

> General Washington, recognizing the desirability of retaining personnel in the Army who were already trained, wrote the Congress on February 9, 1776, urging that a reenlistment "bounty" be established. (OASD[MRA&L], 1982, p. 4)

Method of Payment

During the 1980s, the method by which a bonus was to be paid became a point of controversy between the services and Congress. These methods are controlled by Congress and "because of concern over recoupment of unearned portions of bonuses, Congress has, at times, directed that bonuses be paid on an installment basis" (Korb, 1982e, p. 2). The FY 1982 Defense Appropriations Bill Conferees, in an application of "economic theory and discount rates" and responding to research that suggested the same number of reenlistments "could be obtained by offering a smaller bonus paid in a lump sum rather than a larger bonus paid over time," directed "all selective reenlistment bonuses . . . [be] paid on the modified lump sum/installment basis" (OASD[MRA&L], 1982).

Joint Advertising

While Carlucci was willing to support educational assistance and the bonus program, he and Weinberger were wary of how expensive the all-volunteer force might be. In redoing the FY 1982 budget, Korb reminded them that the Congressional Budget Office had "recommended significant increases in the Joint Recruiting Advertising Program with resultant savings from single-Service advertising" (Korb, 1981e). Joint advertising programs were not new. Al Martin had established a joint advertising program when he first went to work for Bill Brehm in 1974. He had argued that joint advertising could be used to make prospective recruits aware of the opportunities DoD was offering and would complement the efforts of the individual services, which focused on how each of their programs were unique.[27] With the services in competition for high school graduates, they were not interested in blurring their message by telling prospects that there was a common core of benefits. They were interested in gaining the most advantage over their competition and resisted anything that was joint, including advertising. Now the services' fears were coming true. Weinberger and Carlucci decided to cut their advertising program below the FY 1981 program level they were then executing—the only exception was the Army, which got a slight increase over FY 1981 levels but lost almost all the additional funds it had been promised for the FY 1982 program. The budget for the joint program more than tripled, from

---

[27] Martin's arguments notwithstanding, the case for joint advertising was not all that strong. There might be some cost saving from joint advertising, the idea being that one joint advertisement could do the work of four service-specific advertisements. But there was little recognition of the value of emphasizing the individuality and uniqueness of each service. In economics, the services can be thought of as an oligopoly (highly concentrated industry) with differentiated products (they all produced national security, yet each has its own role and heritage). Arguably, service-specific advertising reinforced the "brand" of each service and would prove more cost-effective than advertising that was entirely joint. There was also the more-practical question of what message the joint advertising should convey and what themes and slogans would be memorable.

$8.0 million to $24.7 million.[28] While joint service advertising appeared to be "more cost-effective," Korb predicted, "[t]he Military Departments remain opposed to any increase in joint advertising" (Korb, 1981e).

Secretary of the Navy John Lehman quickly expressed his opposition to reducing the Navy's budget in favor of a joint program. He wanted no change in the FY 1982 program and would consider change for FY 1983 "only after a complete review of the joint and Service advertising programs and their relative efficiencies is completed" (Lehman, 1981b). As far as he was concerned, "[e]xpanding joint service recruiting advertising at the expense of individual service-oriented advertising efforts would run counter to our efforts to correct manning deficiencies and increase our capabilities" (Lehman, 1981b). In addition, he told Weinberger that he had heard rumors—"it has come to my attention," was the way he put it—"that the Army would be given an additional competitive edge over the other services" and he urged that such a change "not be approved" (Lehman, 1981a).[29]

Support for service advertising programs was certainly not what Weinberger had in mind. Not only did the joint program go forward, but, that September, he asked Korb if it were possible to create a "centralized recruiting command and a single advertising agency?" In a long memorandum, Korb explained that, "at no time did any review" of the advertising program "favor a single recruiting agency." Such a change, he explained to the secretary "would create an untenable situation for the Services in that it denies the Service Chiefs the command and control authority and flexibility needed to address specific Service recruiting problems" (Korb, 1981j). With regard to Weinberger's notion of a single advertising contract, Korb told him it was unlikely that

---

[28] *Author's Note:* It is somewhat ironic that, shortly after the Secretary of Defense had tripled the joint advertising program, the creator of the program, Al Martin, decided to leave DoD. Martin had fought with the services for years over the issue of joint advertising—no less than with me when I was Principal Deputy Assistant Secretary of the Navy. No one wanted to lose control of resources, and as Korb had told Carlucci and Weinberger, the joint program was consistently opposed. Now, after Martin had been on the job for five years, Weinberger wrote him to express the department's appreciation for his efforts:

> Your leadership has produced innovative and effective military manpower procurement policies and programs for the all-volunteer force. Your contributions in a key policy-making position have had major influence on national public policy and national security. (Weinberger, 1981b)

Martin may have physically left the department, but he never ceased to stay involved. His presence at the 30 anniversary conference for the all-volunteer force in September 2003 attested to his continued commitment almost 22 years after leaving government service.

[29] On July 13, 1981, Lehman met with Carlucci and Korb to discuss his concerns that the Army had been given a competitive edge over the other services. In his memorandum to Carlucci four days later, he recounted what he considered "my understanding of the results of our meeting." As he remembered it, they had agreed to a number of things decidedly to the Army's disadvantage—specifically, that DoD would not allow the "Ultra VEAP" program to be extended. This would have negated the agreement Carlucci had made with the Army months earlier to support extension of the VEAP program. Carlucci asked Korb: "Is this accurate on Ultra VEAP?" Korb told him it was not (e.g., "John [Lehman] is wrong on Ultra VEAP") and agreed to get with the Army Secretary when he returned to Washington to make sure he understood the situation. There would be some problems, however, because as he said, "this memo [containing Lehman's version of events] is already on the Hill." In other words, the memorandum had been leaked to members of Congress (Lehman, 1981c).

any advertising agency "would be willing to have a significant amount of its business tied up in a single account that could require rebidding every year (with the potential for loss)." The secretary asked whether a "joint campaign, divided among 3 or so agencies . . . [would] save us anything" (Korb, 1981j).[30] Korb admitted that, "simply stated we do not know" and pressed for a joint advertising test program which would help him "find out" (Korb, 1981m).

On November 18, 1981, Weinberger approved Korb's "four part plan to determine the best mix of joint vs. Service specific advertising" (Korb, 1982d). The plan included (1) monitoring the effects of increased joint program funding, (2) a review of previous research, (3) the development of an advertising effectiveness test for FY 1983, and (4) increased the funding for FYs 1983 and 1984 to the program levels approved for FY 1982.[31]

Korb approved the concept design for the test on July 8, 1983, which included $68 million for service-specific advertising and $6 million for joint advertising (Korb, 1983b, p. 4). The advertising effectiveness test started on October 1, 1983, the first day of FY 1984.[32] By the time the FY 1985 budget was being developed in December 1983, the DoD Comptroller was complaining that, "[g]iven current recruiting success," there was "uncertainty whether the test underway in FY 1984 will need to continue in FY 1985" (Puritano, 1983). Korb believed that any cuts would put the program in jeopardy. He told the Deputy Secretary that there was

> no doubt in my mind that the test must continue in FY 1985, if I am to be able to establish the best levels of Service and Joint advertising in the future. The test was carefully designed to provide valid information on reasonable alternative mixes and levels of advertising with the objective of finding an alternative which would reduce total DoD advertising dollars while maintaining an adequate level of effectiveness. (Korb, 1983c)

Korb "felt the additional year was needed to compare the effects of advertising in the highly favorable recruiting environment of FY 1984 with those in FY 1985, to

---

[30] Marginal note on Korb's memorandum (1981j).

[31] *Author's Note:* In April 1982, Korb told Weinberger that the Wharton School of Business had done the best advertising effectiveness study. The study was done for the Navy (Korb, 1982d). It was nice to read that, since I had ordered, and the Office of Naval Research had paid for, the study when I was Principal Deputy Assistant Secretary of the Navy.

[32] According to Cox,

> [t]he test measured the effects of different levels of total DoD advertising as well as different mixes of Service-specific and Joint advertising. . . . [T]he research design divided the country into a control cell, and three test cells, each composed of about 8 percent of the country's male, enlistable population. The test focused only on the active, enlisted portion of the total DoD advertising budget.
>
> The test was designed so that any change in measures of recruiting effectiveness could be attributed to the level and mix of advertising associated with each cell. The budget levels simulated in the study ranged from a low of $31 million in one cell to a high of $84 million in the control cell. (Cox, 1986b, p. 1)

analyze the lagged effects of recruiting and to provide a stronger data base for analysis" (Korb, 1984). His request to continue the test into FY 1985 was denied. Before the end of January 1984, he asked permission to end the test the following September, at the end of FY 1984. Although "the final results of the FY 1984 advertising test will not be available until the fall of 1985," he told Weinberger that he would "have sufficient preliminary data to make recommendations on the sizing of the FY 1986 advertising budgets" (Korb, 1984). Weinberger agreed and said he still thought "a joint advertising campaign is better for the most part and saves money. Certain unmet needs can be met by specific ads, but they should be few and far between. Besides, I don't think we need to test advertisement now" (Korb, 1984).[33] Weinberger's decision was vindicated when the results of the joint advertising test finally came through.[34]

Results of the Test

On March 31, 1986, Chapman Cox, Larry Korb's replacement as Assistant Secretary of Defense, reported to Secretary Weinberger the results of the DoD Advertising Mix Test. These confirmed the services' worst fears. From the beginning, the services had been concerned that the test would result in "a reduction in their advertising budgets and an increased reliance on Joint advertising" and that this would "adversely impact their recruiting efforts" (Cox, 1986b, p. 1). With the results in, Cox told Weinberger:

> The principal conclusions from the test are that in the current environment (1) total DoD recruiting goals can be accomplished with a lower level of total DoD advertising; (2) large increases in advertising spending do not necessarily produce substantial increases in recruiting results; and (3) to achieve optimal results, lower levels of total DoD advertising require higher proportions of Joint advertising.

---

[33] Weinberger's comment was written across Korb's memorandum in such illegible handwriting that his senior military assistant, Major General Colin Powell, had to decipher it, have it retyped, and send it to Korb as a "note." See marginal comments and note attached to Korb (1984).

[34] In fall 1985, Weinberger complained that "the Advertising Mix test was taking 'much too long'" (Calhoun, 1985a). The acting Assistant Secretary, Jerry Calhoun, in a renamed organization, Force Management and Personnel, tried to explain the delays:

> [M]any of the delays experienced . . . are directly attributable to our efforts to overcome Service objections and obtain their agreement on how to proceed.

> In addition, unforeseen technical difficulties arose—such a test had never before been undertaken by either the military or the civilian advertising communities. Thus, we need extra time to design the test and to locate a contractor capable of performing such a pioneer effort. (Calhoun, 1985a, p. 1)

Even before the results of the test were in, Calhoun pressed to reduce service-specific advertising and increase joint advertising. He told the Deputy Secretary,

> [W]e share the Secretary of Defense's view that certain economies and efficiencies are inherent in Joint advertising, particularly in the area of national awareness advertising. We believe a moderate reduction in the total Service-specific advertising program and, perhaps, a slight increase in the Joint program for FY 1987 is possible without adversely affecting Service recruiting results. . . . [H]owever, we recommend that any major shift from Service-specific to Joint advertising be deferred until the results of the Advertising Mix test are available early next year. (Calhoun, 1985c, p. 2)

The conclusions suggest that we could lower the total DoD advertising budget by about 18 percent. At that level, Joint advertising should increase from its current 9 percent to 23 percent of the total DoD advertising budget. . . .

The test suggests that a cost-effective role for the Services could be to support their recruiters by focusing on local and regional advertising using local radio and television, specific magazines, and direct mail aimed directly at the primary youth audience. A cost-effective role for the Joint program could be to support all the Services with national awareness advertising in mass magazines and national television aimed at both the primary youth audience and the adults who influence these youth. (Cox, 1986b, p. 2)

Cox recommended that the issue of reducing the services' advertising budget be raised during the next programming and budget cycle, but Weinberger would not wait. There was little that could be done during the remainder of FY 1986, Cox told him, because the services had "already developed their advertising programs . . . and obligated their funds," but he would monitor their programs "to ensure compliance with your guidance" (Cox, 1986d).[35]

In a "draft" memorandum Cox proposed a 25-percent cut from the original FY 1987 levels, with an 11-percent cut coming in FY 1987 itself (Cox, 1986f).[36] The service with the largest program, the Army, was cut 14 percent. The largest percentage cut, 15 percent, was to the Marine Corps. The Navy and Air Force were cut 13 percent and 9.6 percent, respectively. The joint program was increased by 3 percent. The Marine Corps objected, citing "our advertising budget in constant FY 1987 dollars is at a 10 year low" (Mangale, 1986) and got some funds restored. Its final cut was 10 percent. The Navy also objected—"the proposed reductions in FY-87 would cause disproportionate harm to Navy's recruiting efforts" was the way the Chief of Naval Personnel put it (Carlson, 1986).

Cox relented, reducing the cuts he had proposed for the Navy and Air Force. He told Weinberger that he wanted to hold the line as far as the eventual cuts for FY 1990 were concerned but that "we could provide additional flexibility by reducing by one-third the currently planned cuts to the Navy and the Air Force" (Cox, 1986g). Only the Army did not get relief (Taft, 1986b). Now, the Army argued, "the adverse recruiting impact portrayed in the Navy presentation will likely be reflected in the Army," and they too wanted relief (Marsh, 1986a). By August, to use two popular metaphors, Cox was ready to "throw in the towel, and kick the can down the road." Complaining to Taft, Cox noted that, "traditionally, the Services have opposed efforts by OSD to

---

[35] Taft was concerned about the Navy. On June 5, 1986, he told Weinberger that he was "very concerned about the effect of this [the cut in advertising funds] on the Navy, whose figures are showing weakness now. They have not been doing enough in recent years" (Taft, 1986a). Weinberger was willing to "allocate a bit more to the Navy" (Taft, 1986a).

[36] "Draft" memoranda were often circulated to give interested parties a chance to express their concerns before a senior official actually signed a directive (Cox, 1986a).

restrict their advertising budgets," and now they were trying to discredit the Joint Advertising Mix Test. Specifically, Cox was concerned the Army,

> in coordination with the other Services, . . . [had] funded an independent analysis of the test by researchers from the University of Texas that . . . concluded that joint advertising contributes nothing to Service recruiting efforts. (Cox, 1986h)

The Army told the Secretary of Defense that "[a]dvertising is the key to communicating these incentives to our Nation's young people and their influencers—parents, teachers, and counselors" (Marsh, 1986b). The service suggested that, if Cox did not like the results of the Texas reassessment, another "third party . . . be engaged to conduct yet another independent analysis of the test data" (Cox, 1986h). Cox's recommendation to Taft was that "all the Services be permitted to defer for one year the reductions," and he said he would task RAND to "undertake an independent analysis of the DoD Advertising Mix Test data and present its views on the appropriate levels and mix of joint and Service-specific advertising" (Cox, 1986h).[37] RAND's reexamination of the Advertising Mix Test produced strikingly different results. RAND was critical of the test design and research methodology the Wharton team had employed and came to a very different set of conclusions and recommendations, based on both a reassessment of the data (Dertouzos, 1989) and a separate study of Army advertising (Dertouzos et al., 1989). Dertouzos's reassessment found that the results of the Wharton study were not warranted because of "inadequate data, a failure to consider systematic differences between Services, and questionable judgment in the choice of methodologies" (Dertouzos, 1989, p. v). In addition, using Army advertising data from 1981 to 1985, he found that, "[a]dvertising expenditures in a given month have a significant and immediate effect on the number of high-quality enlistments in the Army (Dertouzos et al., 1989, p. v).

The House Appropriations Committee held hearings on joint advertising in early March 1988. The Committee did not invite anyone from the Office of the Secretary of Defense to testify, but directed the Department of Defense to report to them on "the RAND analysis and the rationale used for determining the recruiting advertising budget for fiscal year 1989 the outyears" (as noted in Staff of the Directorate for Accession Policy, 1989, p. 1). Even before the report was prepared, Grant S. Green, Jr., Chapman Cox's replacement as Assistant Secretary of Defense for Force Management and Personnel, felt compelled to write the chairman to "explain the Department's position" (Green, G., 1988d). Earlier in the year he had told Congress, "The Joint Recruitment Advertising Program (JRAP) is projected to grow $7.2 million after inflation to offset Service budget reductions," (Green, G., 1988b) he now told Congress

---

[37] In September, Cox reported that the House Appropriations Committee had proposed an $8.1 million general cut against the Office of the Secretary of Defense, with 60 percent ($4.8) specifically made against the Joint Recruiting Advertising Program (JRAP). He asked the Comptroller that "the JRAP be exempt from the planned general reduction to the OSD account" (Cox, 1986i).

that while the "Joint Recruiting Advertising Program performs those functions centrally that would cost more for each Service to accomplish individually," without strong research findings, he had little to refute the services' opposition to joint advertising. Almost apologetically, he expressed his "hope [that] this information will help your committee in its review of the Defense manpower budget for FY 1989" (Green, G., 1988d).

When the dust finally settled, Korb's initiative and Cox's plan to slash the services' advertising budgets by 25 percent and to increase the JRAP budget by 38 percent did not come to pass (Cox, 1986d). Deputy Secretary Taft reduced the services' FY 1987 budgets about 10 percent—14 percent for the Army—and increased JRAP budget by a little over 3 percent (Taft, 1986b). The service's advertising program having survived the move by the Secretary of Defense to shift their resources to JRAP would face a new threat, peace. When the Defense Department finally reported to congress in March 1989 they reported a bleak future for all recruiting budgets. They admitted "the financial ceilings established by the Department of Defense as a result of the advertising mix test . . . constrained [service] recruitment advertising budgets, [current] pressure to reduce Defense spending . . . [resulted in budget levels] well below the ceiling . . . Given available recruiting and advertising resources . . . achieving recruitment goals in . . . will be difficult" (Staff of the Directorate for Accession Policy, 1989, p. 24). [38]

Good News

The 1980 election not only brought a new political administration, it also brought a new environment as far as the all-volunteer force was concerned. Military pay was up, with the largest increase since the advent of the all-volunteer pay rises a decade before. Also, the rate of unemployment among males between the ages of 16 and 24 was sharply higher because of the recession, making the military that much more attractive.[39] While there was some concern that military pay increases were not keeping pace with overall wage growth, the wage growth for those not going on to college was

---

[38] With the fall of the Soviet Union and with the services trying to reduce their end strength, senior officials wanted to know why advertising should remain at high at Cold War levels. The FY 1992 advertising program, which reflected the military drawdown, saw the services' advertising budgets decline. The Air Force's budget was reduced by 47 percent and the Army's by 40 percent compared to the FY 1987 budget. The JRAP budget, "the corporate advertising voice of the Department," received "no resources for paid television and advertising" (Jehn, Carney et al., 1992, p. 163) and was reduced by 80 percent. Jehn was concerned and pointed out to Congress that the drop in advertising came at a time when the most recent results from the Youth Attitude Tracking Survey (YATS) indicated "that the percentage of youth who said they would 'definitely' or 'probably' enlist over the next years . . . [showed] a 10-percent decline in interest in just 1 year" (Jehn, Duncan et al., 1992, p. 830). The cuts took their toll, and by 1994, Congress was urging DoD "to increase recruiting resources, if required to meet quality goals" (Dorn, 1994, p. 1). However, there would be another round of inquiries during the late 1990s, when Secretary of Defense William Cohn brought in outside consultants to recommend fundamental changes to the program.

[39] The United Nations Statistics Division reports that youth unemployment in the United States in 1980 was 14.6 percent. By 1982, the rate had risen to 19.1 percent.

lagging. The total economic picture was promising. Each month in the early 1980s, the Assistant Secretary of Defense for Manpower, Reserve Affairs, and Logistics sent to the Secretary of Defense an "information memorandum" that carried the unimposing name, "Monthly Report on Recruiting and Retention." This was the assistant secretary's report card. Often bureaucrats wonder if they are doing a good job or if anyone notices how well or how poorly they are performing. In the personnel business, especially in 1981, everyone cared and everyone noticed. Each month, the spotlight fell on the service personnel chiefs, their recruiting command commanders, and especially the Assistant Secretary of Defense. On June 4, 1981, for the first time in his tenure as assistant secretary, Larry Korb sent the report to the Special Assistant to the Secretary of Defense—the secretary's principal civilian executive assistant.[40] As would become his custom, Korb put a personal endorsement on the "routine" memorandum: "Note to CAP [Secretary Weinberger] the vast improvement in the HSG [High School Graduate] and CAT [category] IVs compared to year ago." He was proud, and he had reason to be. Through April 1981, the Army was within 100 recruits of making its accession goal for FY 1981. The other services had exceeded their goals. Most importantly, especially given the quality standards Congress had imposed,[41] 75 percent of all recruits had earned high school diplomas, while only 58 percent had the year before. Even the Army, which had only recruited 43 percent high school graduates at this time the previous fiscal year, had recruited 71 percent high school graduates—almost 20 percent more than the previous year. The number of category IV recruits was cut almost in half. Reenlistments were also up; first-term reenlistments increased from 42 to 46 percent, and career reenlistment increased from 72 to almost 80 percent. His conclusion:

> The Services should meet their recruiting goals in FY 1981 with substantially improved quality over FY 1980. This should permit the Services to meet the Congressional recruiting quality constraints in FY 1981. The career reenlistment picture is particularly encouraging. (Korb, 1981f)

The next month, he added to the report his personal observation that "so far things continue to go well. For two thirds of FY 81—quality of recruits is up and retention percentages is high" (Korb, 1981f). His August report noted that things

---

[40] The Acting Assistant Secretary, Robert Stone, had been sending the reports forward since February. They also showed positive trends (Stone, R., 1981b).

[41] Section 520, of Title 10 of the U.S. Code placed limits on the number of non–high school graduates and category IV people who could be accessed each year: not more than 35 percent non–high school graduate and only those that score above the 35th percentile on the AFQT test (U.S. Code, 1983). In April, Weinberger, in responding to a series of questions from Senator Carl Levin on "the effect of the legislative recruit quality constraints" and their effects on the "ability to meet annual accession requirement," said that he was

> in complete agreement with the Congress that we must recruit and maintain the highest quality military force possible. I nevertheless strongly believe that the management of recruit quality control is most appropriately left to the Department of Defense. (Weinberger, 1981a)

"still look good" (Korb, 1981f). In November, in a summary of his office's "accomplishments," he observed that all the services had "achieved overall recruiting goals with the highest number of high school graduates since the start of the AVF" (Korb, 1981k).

Korb started 1982 with a note to Weinberger: "CAP, Figures still look good—particularly noteworthy are drop in Category IVs and increased reenlistments. One sour note is decline in Army H.S. [high school] graduates. We will continue to monitor" (Korb, 1982a). The Army had actually recruited more high school graduates than in the previous year, but as a percentage of the total, their numbers were down, from 77 to 68 percent. The Navy's high school graduate numbers, both absolute and as a percentage of the total, were also down. By February, the Army's numbers, both absolute and as a percentage of the total, were up, and Korb told Weinberger, "CAP, Things continue to go well. Most encouraging development is decline in CAT IVs and higher reenlistment rates" (Korb, 1982b). His report in March was that things were "still going well" (Korb, 1982b). In May, he told the secretary that "[t]hings seem to get better every month. Retention is at an all time high" (Korb, 1982b).

After almost a decade, had the all-volunteer force finally turned the corner? In June, Korb told Weinberger that the figures continued to look good: "They are close to being historic highs in every category" (Korb, 1982f). In June, nine years after the official end of the draft and three years after the dark days of the misnorming problem, the all-volunteer force numbers were nothing short of amazing. Every service had met or exceeded its accession goals. The Army, which had always been the "litmus test" for the all-volunteer force, had achieved 105 percent of its goal. Almost 66,000 of its 89,000 recruits held high school diplomas, and less than 20 percent of its recruits had scored in the category IV zone. Korb told Weinberger that, "with one quarter to go we are still above FY 81 in every respect" (Korb, 1982f).

In July, Korb reported that both "recruiting and retention are still better than FY 1981, which was a good year" (Korb, 1982h). Possibly reflecting on those that thought the all-volunteer force would only be made up of the poor and uneducated, Korb reminded Weinberger, in the October report, that the services continued to do well: "In fact, better than when we had conscription" (Korb, 1982). In his end-of-year report for FY 1982, he noted that nearly

> 86 percent of our new enlisted accessions had a high school diploma. This is the highest proportion ever—under either conscription or the AVF. Nearly nine percent had attended or graduated from college, the highest level since 1973. The percentage scoring average or above on the enlistment test (Category I thru IIIA) was over 87 percent, which was greater than any year under conscription. (Korb, 1982g)

October 1982 also was the month that Secretary Weinberger, in his capacity as chairman of the Military Manpower Task Force, reported the results of the task force to President Reagan. The numbers had silenced all, or almost all the critics of the all-volunteer force.[42] Weinberger's transmittal letter to the President told the story:

> In the late 1970s the recruiting and retention of qualified personnel for the Armed Forces had deteriorated to the point where many were questioning the effectiveness of the All-Volunteer Force. We are pleased to report that there has been a dramatic improvement during the past two years. In fact, the fiscal year just completed, FY 1982, has been the best year for recruiting and retention that the All-Volunteer Force has ever experienced.
> - All of the Services are achieving 100 percent of their recruiting objectives, and many additional qualified people have signed up for entry into the service when vacancies become available.
> - Test scores and educational levels of new enlistees now compare quite favorably with those of the civilian youth population.
> - Excessive losses from the career force have been stopped, and the career force is growing in size and experience.
> - The Selected Reserve has succeeded in recovering the strength lost earlier in the AVF period. The Task Force has identified solutions that can, over a period of time, provide enough Individual Ready Reservists to meet mobilization needs.
>
> The Task Force is confident that the higher active and reserve strengths planned for the next five years can be achieved without a resumption of the draft. (Weinberger, 1982b, p. i)

Korb's end-of-year report for FY 1983 was no less glowing as the numbers continued to improve. An official news release covering FY 1983 highlighted the fact that

> [t]he Army, which historically has had the greatest recruiting difficulty, fared better in FY 1983 than during conscription and set new records. The high school diploma graduate rate for new Army recruits was 88 percent, a record high, as was the combined AFQT categories I and II rate of 37 percent. The latter is especially significant as those scoring in this category usually have the option of directly attending the best colleges versus enlisting. (ASD[PA], 1983)

An accompanying report, *Fiscal Year 1983 Results* (ASD[MRA&L], 1983), compared the AFQT category distribution for FY 1983 accessions with the 18- to 23-year-old youth population from the 1980 tests reported in *Profile of American Youth* (Korb, 1982c). The top two categories (I and II) accounted for 37 percent of the youth population but 41 percent of new accessions. The bottom two categories (IV and V) accounted for 31 percent of the youth population but only 8 percent of new accessions, and these were all in category IV (ASD[MRA&L], 1983). Korb reminded

---

[42] In December 1982, Korb did express one note of caution. He told Weinberger that they were

off to a good start, 110% of quota, which should provide us a cushion later in [the] year if we need one. [The] Army first term reenlistments are down, but I think they are tightening standards because in 1979 many more CAT IVs were taken in than they realized. (Korb, 1982h)

Weinberger that, while the department was still under congressional quality controls, "we do not anticipate difficulty in meeting these constraints" (Korb, 1983a).

A Turn of Fortune

When Weinberger sent the Military Manpower Task Force report to President Reagan in October 1982, he predicted that, "by Fiscal Year 1985 the Army may encounter some difficulty in recruiting the required number of well-qualified enlistees, but this problem can be overcome through enlistment incentives" (Weinberger, 1982b, p. ii). Early in 1985, Korb reported to Weinberger that the fortunes of the services had started to change and that

> [t]he Services have experienced difficulties in meeting new contract[s]. . . . The Army DEP [delayed entry pool] is about 6,000 below desired levels. . . . The Army has been authorized an additional $28 million in FY 1985 to enable them to respond more effectively to changing market conditions." (Korb, 1985, p. 1)

Korb was also alarmed because the recently received results from the 1984 Youth Attitude Tracking Study (YATS) indicated that the propensity to enlist, a key indicator of the recruiting environment, was "substantially lower than in the previous three years" (Korb, 1985). These results, he noted, "are consistent with the more difficult recruiting environment we are currently experiencing" (Korb, 1985). He remained confident, however, that "we will achieve our FY 1985 enlistment objectives, provided we continue our initiatives to provide comparable compensation and adequate recruiting resources" (Korb, 1985).

By September 1985, things seemed to have stabilized as the services "adjusted to the more difficult recruiting conditions resulting from the improving economy and reduced youth unemployment" (Calhoun, 1985b). Acting Assistant Secretary Jerry Calhoun, who was running the manpower office after Korb's departure, was particularly impressed by the Army. He told Weinberger that the

> improved performance by the Army is particularly encouraging—they are meeting their accession requirements while making substantial improvements in their new contract production and increasing their DEP to the desired levels. (Calhoun, 1985b)

The Navy, however, remained a problem. In a story that would become all too familiar in the years ahead, Calhoun told the secretary that the "Navy's difficulty is attributable largely to inadequate resource levels" (Calhoun, 1985b).[43] By spring 1986, Chapman Cox, the New Assistant Secretary of Defense (Force Management and Personnel) and the former Assistant Secretary of the Navy for Manpower and Reserve

---

[43] *Author's Note:* The same situation repeated itself several times in the 1990s, when I was Assistant Secretary of the Navy for Manpower and Reserve Affairs. The Navy consistently underfunded recruiting resources, particularly the staffing of recruiters.

Affairs, reported that the Navy had the lowest high school diploma graduation rate and the lowest AFQT I–III rate of any of the services. Its high school diploma graduation rate was 10 full percentage points lower than that for the previous year (Cox, 1986e). That June, Cox's new principal deputy, David Armor,[44] summed up a growing problem in military compensation in a memorandum for the Secretary of Defense:

> One of the great successes of the Reagan Administration has been the dramatic turnaround in the military manning posture. . . .
> Though a number of factors contributed to the turnaround, certainly a major one—if not *the* major one—was the significant improvement made to military compensation in FY 1981 and FY 1982, capped by a 14.3% pay raise in the FY 1982 which restored military pay to competitive levels.
> Since FY 1982, however, military pay raises have been less than private sector pay raises each year resulting in a cumulative gap of 8.3%. The gap is the largest since the AVF began. . . .
> While we have been fortunate that recruiting and retention has [sic] held up despite the pay caps, there is obviously a limit to how long we can continue to give military members pay raises below the private sector before damage is done.
> In recognition of this fact, the Administration requested a 4 percent military pay raise in FY 1987 to match civilian wage growth. It appears, however, that Congress will limit the raise to 3 percent, thus widening the pay cap even further.
> It is imperative that we not allow military pay to decline relative to civilian pay to the point that a repeat of the 1970s occurs. (Armor, 1986, emphasis in the original)

The results for FY 1986, however, while showing the Navy to have the poorest record of all the services, still found that each of the services had "met its enlistment goal for the fiscal year" (Cox, 1986j). The Air Force reported that it had "completed the most successful recruiting year in our history" (McCoy, 1986). What was particularly troublesome, however, was that, despite the difficult recruiting environment, Congress had reduced the FY 1987 recruiting and advertising budget by 8 percent ($47 million). Almost one third of that, $15 million, was taken against the Navy, cutting its budget by 14 percent. Cox told the secretary, however, that "the Navy staff is confident they can meet their FY 1987 accession requirements with recruits of acceptable quality" (Cox, 1986j). The Secretary of the Navy, John Lehman, thought that the combination of additional recruiters, increasing their levels of support, and returning to national television would help the Navy "meet or exceed . . . [the FY 1986] performance in the coming year" (Lehman, 1986).

Lehman and the Navy's staff optimism notwithstanding, as FY 1987 moved to completion, each service had "achieved its overall accession goal . . . with recruits of

---

[44] *Author's Note*: David Armor and I were colleagues at RAND during the 1970s. When I returned to RAND in 1985, David was in the process of leaving to take on the responsibilities of Principal Deputy Assistant Secretary. To take the position, David had to resign as a member of the School Board of the Los Angeles Public Schools. He was a leader of the conservative wing of the school board, and his resignation set off a firestorm of criticism, as discussed in Cox (1986c).

outstanding quality" with the exception of the Navy. While the Navy's high school diploma graduate rate was "nine percentage points higher than this time last year, . . . their percentage with average or above aptitude has declined by three points" (Armor, 1987, p. 1). The following year, FY 1988, was also considered an excellent year, especially given the "turbulence in strength management programs associated with last year's force structure reductions" (Green, B., 1987). FY 1989 saw some reductions in the quality of the average recruits—"both the proportion of high school diploma graduates (92 percent) and individuals scoring average or above average on the enlistment tests (94 percent) fell 1 percentage point when compared to FY 1988" (Jehn, 1989). Chris Jehn, the Bush administration's Assistant Secretary of Defense (Force Management and Personnel), thought the results *satisfactory,* "[i]n view of the turbulent manpower environment and likelihood of reduced recruiting objectives" (Jehn, 1989, p. 3).

Was There a Military Pay Gap?

When the Reagan administration came into office, it added an across-the-board pay increase of 5.3 percent to the 9.1 percent already programmed by the outgoing Carter administration for FY 1982. This, together with the 11.7 percent from the previous year (FY 1981), meant that pay had increased by 26 percent in two years. With things looking up, the willingness of the Reagan administration to put even more money into DoD for military pay was limited. Military pay was capped at a 3 percent growth rate. Unfortunately, civilian pay kept rising. The result was that by 1985 there was an estimated pay gap of 8.8 percent. In the summer of 1985, the issue came to a head during the annual review of the services' program objective memorandum (POM). The "issue paper" prepared that summer noted:

> Military pay raises have again fallen behind civilian wage growth because of caps imposed in each year since FY 1982. Including an assumed 3 percent pay raise cap in FY 1986, military pay raises will have fallen 8.3 percent behind private sector wage growth since comparability was restored in FY 1982. This expanding pay gap, acting in conjunction with an improving economy, potentially jeopardized the Services' achievement of their manning objective and raises the specter that we are once again entering a period like that of the late 1970s. (OASD[MRA&L], 1985, p. 5)

When the Defense Resource Board met on August 5, 1985, a lively debate ensued that pitted those who saw this as an issue of keeping a commitment to service members and those concerned with the high cost of personnel. Surprisingly, since the services were making their personnel numbers, there was little discussion of the negative impact that the reported gap had on recruiting or retention. The service secretaries were not in favor of continuing the cap. They wanted a 6-percent increase for FY 1987, somewhat higher than the 5.8-percent increase in military pay that was programmed. Given that civilian wages were expected to grow just 5.2 percent the next year, this would start to reduce the pay gap. Some expressed concern about the high cost of people, which Larry

Korb placed at $600 million for each 1-percent increase in pay. Deputy Secretary Taft decided on the POM's 5.8-percent increase and promised to talk with Weinberger about further increases in the out-years. However, this is not the way things worked out.

When the budget went to Congress the following January, it contained only a 4.0-percent increase for military pay. Even with a revised estimate that civilian wages would grow only 4.2 percent, there would be no progress in reducing the pay gap. Moreover, DoD expected that Congress would continue the 3-percent cap, thereby further increasing the pay gap. An issue paper the following summer, 1986, reflected the limited effect the gap was having:

> Though the current 8.3 percent gap is the largest since the beginning of the All-Volunteer Force, thus far no serious damage has been done to DoD's ability to recruit and retain the numbers and quality of personnel that it requires. While first term reenlistment rates have declined since FY 1982 and the percentage of high school graduates jointing the Navy have [sic] turned down somewhat recently, overall recruiting and retention have remained at or near historical highs. (OASD[MRA&L], 1986, p. 1)

In the resulting debate, the relative benefits of putting more into bonuses rather than across-the-board pay increases was discussed. Taft finally decided to provide some catch-up over the POM years. The issue of the gap continued to make headlines in the *Army Times* and the other service newspapers, causing morale problems but having little effect on the ability of the services to attract or retain the people they needed.

Too Much of a Good Thing

All through the 1980s, reports of high levels of career retention to the Secretary of Defense were one indication of the improving fortunes of the all-volunteer force.[45] According to a RAND report prepared for the Force Management Policy office, by 1988,

> [w]hile only 3–4 percent of enlisted personnel reached retirement eligibility for the draft era cohort (FY67–70), current estimates project about 18 percent of the FY87 cohort reaching retirement eligibility. (Grissmer et al., 1989, pp. 4–5)

The unconstrained growth in the career force, however, came with a commensurate increase in the cost of personnel. On two occasions, it was the subject of Defense

---

[45] For example, Korb reported to Weinberger that first-term reenlistments increased from 42 to 46 percent and that career reenlistment increased from 72 to almost 80 percent: "The career reenlistment picture is particularly encouraging" (Korb, 1981f). In November 1983, at the Tenth Anniversary conference, Hosek, Fernandez, and Grissmer warned of the "dramatic increase in senior career force manning" (1984, p. 19): "This near doubling in first-term retention created a 'bow wave' of personnel moving toward the senior force. We are now [1983] seeing that wave penetrate the ten-plus year of service group" (Hosek, Fernandez, and Grissmer, 1984, p. 21). They observed that "[d]etermining the 'optimal' experience mix . . . means striking the right balance between productivity and effectiveness on the one hand and costs on the other" (Hosek, Fernandez, and Grissmer, 1984, p. 17).

Resources Board reviews.[46] Senior officials clearly understood that reducing the seniority of the force would reduce personnel costs in four areas (Grissmer et al., 1989, p. 13)—current basic military pay, grade-specific personnel support costs, reenlistment bonuses, and future retirement costs as reflected in current accrual charges. This, however, would be offset by an increase in accession requirements and accession related costs, as well as separation pay for those who leave before retirement.[47]

Grant Green, the new Assistant Secretary of Defense (Force Management & Personnel), was concerned that the involvement of the Defense Resource Board would mean that the budget process, rather than policy, would be determining the future personnel structure of the enlisted force. In late October 1988, Taft told the service secretaries to work with Green to develop policies that would "address the relationship between grade structure and strength" (Taft, 1988). Taft wanted each service to provide recommendations and supporting rationale on the

> relationship between strength and grade structure . . . promotion timing and opportunity for each of the top five enlisted grades . . . [a]nd separation policies for those who substantially lag their peers in advancement, and any potential role that separation pay might play in implementing those policies. (Taft, 1988)

The measures Taft was asking for should have been familiar to the services, since they were the same type of parameters that were used to manage their officer corps. Promotion timing and opportunity, strength, and grade structure and severance policies for those who did not progress through the up-or-out system were the stuff that the Officer Personnel Management Act (DOPMA) imposed on the services. In December 1988, Green asked the services to review the draft document outlining a new enlisted personnel management system for the 90s (EPMS-90) (Green, G., 1988e). The system had four policy components:

1. the grade structure
2. the relationship between the size of the force and the distribution of grades— "[w]hen strength is reduced the grade structure should be adjusted on a scale similar to that associated with officers grade structure adjustments" (Green, G., 1988e, p. 2)
3. the experience profile of the force
4. the rules for an enlisted up-or-out system

---

[46] The Principal Deputy Secretary of Defense for Force Management Policy brought a proposal to constrain the enlisted seniority to the 1988 Defense Resources Board Implementation Review in 1988. The proposal is described in Grissmer, Hosek, and Eisenman (1989, p. 26).

[47] The trade-offs associated with reducing high-cost careerists and increasing lower-cost first-terms, with their associated recruiting and training costs is discussed in Grissmer, Hosek, and Eisenman (1989, pp. 8–9).

Anticipating what would be a point of contention between his office and the services in the years ahead, Green also told them that "[f]orce renewal is an integral part of force sustainment. Repeatedly low accession levels necessarily drive future experience shortfalls and impair force sustainment" (Green, G., 1988e, p. 2).

The services' reaction to imposing DOPMA-like rules on how they managed *their* enlisted forces was not favorable. The Army complained that the proposal was

> short on analysis and long on assumptions. . . . We are facing a period of unprecedented uncertainty. . . . These proposals, using historically based assumptions and estimates, will tend to limit our options, and potentially our successes, in coping with these uncertainties. (Clark, 1989, pp. 1–2)

With faint praise, the Assistant Secretary of the Navy called the "attempt to provide DoD policies . . . worthy" (Bergquist, 1989). He then complained that "[a]ny attempt to lump all services into one homogeneous entity is wrong because a single methodology cannot be used to develop unique differences and grade structures for all the services" (Bergquist, 1989). The Air Force was somewhat more favorable, but said that it was not certain that

> [T]hey [the proposals] would serve the Air Force well in the event of significant strength changes. . . . We have not had the opportunity to test these concepts. . . . Given this lack of information and insight, we believe it is unreasonable to rush to closure on this complex issue to meet a basically artificial deadline. (Keesling, 1989)

Green invited the assistant secretaries and the personnel chiefs of the services to a meeting to discuss the EPMS proposals. He organized the meeting around a series of "issues" and suggested a number of "alternatives" for each. The issues and alternatives were presented in a working paper that was circulated before the meeting (Green, G., 1989). At the meeting, the Chief of Naval Personnel, Vice Admiral Jeremy M. (Mike) Boorda, presented a particularly tight summary of the tenure rules, arguing that "implementing a separation pay would in effect be a negative SRB [Selected Reenlistment Bonus] paying people to leave the Navy who have the skill and experience we can least afford to lose, and boost accession requirements in a market where demand already exceeds supply" (Boorda, 1989).[48] Without the agreement of the services, Green

---

[48] Bill Carr, who was the Deputy Director (Enlisted Policy) in the Officer and Enlisted Personnel Management Directorate in Green's office at the time, remembers that Boorda's arguments followed almost word for word a paper he had sent to Bergquist, which was forwarded to Green's office. At the meeting, the services split. Carr recalls Green's decision to proceed:

> While it did not go, it certainly helped shape the 1989 "drawdown guidance." In particular OSD demanded sustainment of accessions sufficient to sustain the force "in the steady state"—those four words were a real fight to put aboard but the words were kept, making the recruiting glide path during the drawdown both auditable and enforceable. (Carr, 2004)

decided he could not proceed with the full EPMS-90 proposal. Later, William Carr, one of the architects of EPMS-90, recalled what happened next:

> Staff principals in the Office of the Secretary of Defense initially concurred in the provision of EPMS-90. However, most of the manpower representatives of the Military Departments urged against EMPS-90, believing that the dynamic nature of requirements militated against establishment of seniority objectives with DoD policy. It was recommended that the budget process should remain the forum for establishing appropriate enlisted seniority patterns—the case for enlisted seniority plans would rest on its merits in each budget review. DoD objectives would not be established in advance; future increases in grade or longevity patterns would require justification drawn from requirements-based, skill-specific analyses. (Carr, 1989, p. 8)

In February 1989, Taft told the services that after January 1990, rather than a prescribed goal the services would have to achieve "[s]eniority increases must be explained along two dimensions . . . [1] explicit cost- and combat-effectiveness considerations and . . . [2] increases in grade posture must define where the growth will occur, and the specific bases for the increases" (Taft, 1989, p. 2). The push for a officer-like enlisted personnel system was over.

Testing the All-Volunteer Force in War and Peace

Toward the end of the Bush administration, the all-volunteer force was tested in two very different and unexpected ways. First, since the days of the Gates Commission, the ultimate question concerning the all-volunteer force was whether it would fight. Sociologists, such as Charlie Moskos, suggested that it might not. Military action in Panama and in the Persian Gulf answered that question. The volunteer force was arguably the finest military force the United States had ever sent into battle.

Second, a situation developed that the Gates Commission never contemplated: peace. New questions arose: (1) With the end of the Cold War, would Congress be willing to sustain the costs of an all-volunteer force? (2) Given the decision by Congress to reduce the size of the military, would personnel managers be able to maintain the career and incentive structures that had made the volunteer force possible? (3) Finally, would the youth of America continue to volunteer for service without the motivating threat of the Soviet Union?

Testing the All-Volunteer Force in War: Operation Desert Storm

A great deal has been written about Operation Desert Storm, and it is not our purpose to recount the war in these pages.[49] After the war, "one of the highest priorities of

---

[49] See the Army's official history of Operation Desert Storm, *Certain Victory* (Scales, 1993).

[Secretary of Defense Dick Cheney was] . . . to develop 'lessons learned' from Desert Storm, and to take action based on those lessons." Orders went out to safeguard documents, and each staff office was asked to "contribute detailed lessons in the established format." Nick Timenes, the principal director in Chris Jehn's office of Military Manpower and Personnel Policy, did not believe that the "established formats" were adequate to sum up the manpower story. He proposed taking a different perspective that would directly address the issue of the all-volunteer force. Jehn agreed and forwarded Timenes's staff paper to the secretary to give him "another way of looking at the issue" (Jehn, 1991f)."[50]

Complaining that most reviewers were either "self-congratulatory or far down in the weeds," Timenes made a number of critical observations that would dominate actions to improve manpower and personnel planning for the next decade. One of these was that "we were unprepared for partial mobilization . . . mobility forces were inadequate . . . mobilization and deployment take time" (Timenes, 1991). The following, however, was his first observation:

> The all-volunteer force worked. It took a generation to get here, but in Desert Storm: The enlisted force exhibited unprecedented skill, commitment, maturity, and professionalism. The entire officer corps (including general-, field-, and company-grade officers) consistently demonstrated skill, excellence, leadership, and professionalism we have not seen in this century—if ever. . . . The role and performance of minorities in the enlisted force is a huge success. This ought to be a source of enormous pride both to black Americans and the military services. . . . while our policies with respect to women and single parents are well-reasoned and generally effective, pressure for change (in both directions) will continue. (Timenes, 1991)

A lingering issue was how the war would affect recruiting in both the long and short terms. In December 1990, before combat actually started, Secretary of the Army Mike Stone responded to speculation in the media that "Desert Shield is having a negative impact on Defense, and more significantly Army, recruiting" (Stone, W., 1990, p. 1). He reported that "Desert Shield appears to have had some short-term impact on recruiting as prospects took a 'wait and see' attitude towards contracting" (Stone, W., 1990, p. 3). He assured the Deputy Secretary of Defense, however, that "the Army's total FY 91 requirement for replacement soldiers will be met." In a show of how sophisticated management of the all-volunteer force had become, he reported that "the Army did enhance bonuses by $2,000 in 27 MOSs [military occupation specialties] critical

---

[50] Jehn and Timenes were, of course, not the only ones who commented on how well the all-volunteer force did during the Gulf War. The former Chairman of the Joint Chiefs noted in his memoir,

> The Gulf War also demonstrated the significance of having good people. The main reason we did so well once we got there was the skill of our people. That was the result of many factors, but primarily it is the great benefit of having a volunteer professional force. The men and women who participated in Desert Shield and Desert Storm were members of the oldest, most experienced [in length of service] fighting force the United States has ever fielded. (Crowe, 1993, p. 324)

to Desert Shield to increase enlistments and to advance the reporting dates to those already contracted" (Stone, W., 1990). [51]

After the war recruiting rebounded, and the expected turndown in reserve personnel did not materialize. In August, Jehn reported the recruiting results for the third quarter of FY 1991 (April, May, and June 1991): All the services met their recruiting objectives. "High school diploma graduates increased from 92 percent . . . to 97 percent for the same time this year, and the percent of individuals who scored average or above on the enlistment test . . . rose from 96 percent to 99 percent" (Jehn, 1991n).

Desert Storm and the Issue of Race

Timenes's comments notwithstanding, the issue of race was a point of contention during the Gulf War. Robert Goldich laid out the arguments in a Congressional Research Service report to Congress on the eve of the land campaign, when the result was still in doubt and some were projecting that as many as 10,000 might die, with 35,000 casualties. Blacks were overrepresented in the all-volunteer force. He noted that those who wanted a return to the draft were arguing that

> [i]n time of war, . . . it is important that the most discriminated-against members of American society do not bear more than their fair share of fighting and casualties, and that those who have benefited the most do not bear less than their fair share. (Goldich, 1991)

Some saw more-sinister reasons. Jesse Jackson, president of the National Rainbow Coalition, complained to Cheney that he had

> some unsubstantiated information that neither the targeted recruitment to the military nor the disproportionate number of African Americans assigned to the Persian Gulf is accidental. . . . [I]f it were found that African Americans and poor whites were being deliberately targeted to serve "voluntarily" in the military . . . that would be scandalous. (Jackson, 1991)

Jehn, responding for Cheney, assured Jackson that the services did "not have racial or ethnic goals for recruiting. Accordingly, they do not target specific groups as a part

---

[51] Stone's assessment was echoed in a white paper prepared by Jehn's Directorate for Accession Policy, which found "that non–prior service recruiting will be successful in the immediate future, providing adequate resources are applied to support the programs" (Staff of the Directorate for Accession Policy, 1991, p. i). In one area that would repeat itself during the second Gulf War, Jehn's group also found that

> [i]n the area of Reserve Component recruiting and mobilization issues, clearly Operations Desert Shield and Desert Storm provided a far greater 'test' of our capability than ever imagined during post-exercise critiques of past mobilization simulations. . . . [They reported that] the Army and Air Force Reserve Components have not recovered from the recruiting slowdown . . . . However, retention is all Reserve Components is better than expected so there should be no endstrength problems for FY 1991. (Staff of the Directorate for Accession Policy, 1991, p. i)

of their recruiting strategies, nor do they condone unethical recruiting practices of any kind, to include racial discrimination" (Jehn, 1991a). His explanation for the relatively large number of blacks in the military, he told Jackson, was that the

> Department of Defense had led the way in equal opportunity . . . [and] this success is reflected by the presence of significant numbers of minority members who chose to join, reenlist, and make the military a career. . . . Military service . . . is an honorable profession offering challenges, rewards, and opportunities for those who volunteer. . . . Our African-American Service members are not victims needing protection. They are capable, willing, patriotic Americans. (Jehn, 1991a)[52]

What Jehn did not know at the time was that the number of blacks killed during the Gulf War would be substantially less than the percentage of blacks in the active Army. In fact, examining the more-general claim "that Afro-Americans have been used by their country as cannon fodder," Jehn might have quoted Moskos and Butler: "No serious case can be made that blacks suffer undue casualties in America's wars and military interventions" (Moskos and Butler, 1996, p. 9). Nevertheless, that would not prevent the emotional charge being leveled again more than a decade later, during the Iraqi war of 2003. It would be as untrue then as it had been for each military operation since the advent of the all-volunteer force.

Testing the All-Volunteer Force in Peace

One might date the end of the Cold War to the fall of the Berlin Wall or the formal end of the Soviet Union, but dating the beginning of the end is much more problematic. Bill Crowe, former Chairman of the Joint Chiefs recalls that in "1986 and 1987 no branch of the government foresaw the dissolution of the Soviet Union. Rather, we were negotiating with what was still very much a cohesive, if troubled, superpower" (Crowe, 1993, p. 264). After the minisummit at Reykjavik, Iceland—October 11–12, 1986—things changed. Things also changed with the election of President George H. W. Bush. Crowe describes the 1989 change in administrations as resembling a Democrat-Republican shift, with "the Bush administration . . . determined to distinguish itself from its predecessor" (Crowe, 1993, p. 312). Nowhere was the change more apparent than in the defense budget. Crowe had hoped "that President Bush would

---

[52] What Jehn did not know at the time was the DoD was experiencing declines in black enlistments and in the "propensity of Black youth toward military service." In a memorandum to the Joint Chiefs of Staff, he explained:

> Black accessions dropped significantly in FY 1991, at 33,574 or 16.5 percent of total active enlistments compared to 45,893 or 20.6 percent of the total for the preceding year. The downward trend now appears to have stopped. Through the first half of this fiscal year, 16.7 percent of new recruits were Black. There are two possible explanations for the decline: (1) higher recruit quality requirements as we downsize the force and (2) lower enlistment propensities among 16- to 21-year-old Black men. Our analyses estimate that one-third of the 4-point decline in FY 91 can be attributed to higher standards and two-thirds can be assigned to lower enlistment propensity among Blacks. (Jehn, 1992e)

accept the 3 percent increase embodied in the Carlucci proposals," referring to the departing Secretary of Defense, Frank Carlucci, "rather than the new OMB zero growth budget for the next 4 years." As far as Crowe was concerned, "[g]iven inflation and several other uncontrollable factors, zero growth actually meant a sizable decrease in funding" (Crowe, 1993, p. 314). When President Bush finally agreed to a "zero, one, one, two"—zero the first year, one percent the second and third years, and two percent the fourth year—"percent growth in the four-year defense program, the downturn had started.

In his memoir, Crowe also reflected that growth is much easier to manage than decline and that, while "the United States has gone through the builddown process many times, . . . most often we have handled it miserably" (Crowe, 1993, p. 328). In 1989 and 1990, we started out without the tools and policies in place to manage the drawdown effectively. In the manpower hearings of spring 1990, Senator John Glenn (D-Ohio) summed up the dilemma DoD and Congress faced: "[W]e are . . . caught between a couple of philosophies, about how fast we should scale down and whether now is the time, or whether we should be waiting until we get comparable cuts in certain areas from the Soviets" (Jehn, Wincup et al., 1990, p. 5). The initial cut in active-duty military personnel during the first year of the Bush administration (FYs 1989–1990) was almost 54,000, to be followed by an additional 38,000 the following year (FY 1991). The politically powerful reserve forces actually *gained* almost 100,000 people during FY 1991. The Army was scheduled to take almost half of the reductions. Jehn recalled that, once it was clear that the long-term prospects were for a reduced defense budget, pressure mounted for "immediate budget adjustments and end strength reductions prior to the identification of specific programs for elimination" (Jehn, Wincup et al., 1990, p. 5). The problem, as he saw it, was that when we had conscription, "it was relatively easy to rapidly reduce our force simply by not drafting or letting people go home, who wanted to go home anyway." With the all-volunteer force, however,

> everyone in the military wants to be there, and many have made career commitments. When we draw down now . . . [w]e must preserve our professional officer and noncommissioned officer corps, and to the greatest extent possible, meet our commitment to career members. (Jehn, Wincup et al., 1990, pp. 5–6)

He told the senators that the department was working on personnel policies for the enlisted force based on "equity, early notice, and other factors that will serve to cushion adverse effects" of the drawdown (Jehn, Wincup et al., 1990). Officers, however, were another issue. Their personnel system, including tenure and promotion policies, was set in law by the Defense Officer Personnel Act of 1980. Jehn wanted Congress to consider "legislation that would modify certain restrictions involving the voluntary and involuntary retirement or discharge of commissioned officers" (Jehn, Wincup et al., 1990, p. 6). The world had truly turned upside down.

A World Turned Upside Down

Since the days of the Gates Commission, military personnel managers and the research community that supported them had tried to construct a program that would encourage young men and women to enlist or get those already in service to remain. Now, with the drawdown, their job was to construct a program that would encourage members to leave; service members who just a few months earlier would have been pressed to stay would now be encouraged to leave or, in some instances, forced to leave. For service personnel managers, the easiest way to manage the drawdown, and the way the Air Force tried initially, was to cut accessions to almost zero.[53]

The Air Force believed its best policy would be to "keep faith" with its career force and honor the implicit contract, which promised continued employment and retirement for continued good and faithful service.[54] How, in good conscience, argued the Chief of Staff of Air Force, could they be hiring and training new airmen and especially pilots, and firing fully qualified airmen and pilots just to meet some arbitrary personnel profile for the ideal distribution of years of service?[55] Moreover, drastically reducing

---

[53] In 1992, the Deputy Assistant Secretary of Defense for Military Manpower and Personnel Policy explained this to the Senate Subcommittee on Defense Appropriations:

> [I]t became very clear during our planning for the drawdown that we should not accomplish the reduction solely by substantially reducing or even discontinuing officer and enlisted accessions in order to allow those already in the Service to continue to retirement.

> We decided against this approach because . . . it would result in severe shortages of our future officer and enlisted leaders. . . . [S]uch a policy would result in acute seniority or experience deficits in the future and severely distort the future force. This situation could not be corrected and would grossly mis-align our personnel profiles for years to come. (Alexander, 1992b, pp. 524–525)

[54] This was the first time that the Air Force had had such a problem. In the 1950s, the Air Force "allowed most airmen to remain in the service as long as they desired. Once past the initial reenlistment point, airmen were not removed from the service except for cause until they reached retirement eligibility." This resulted in the "Korean Hump," and the "large experience deficits once the Korean War hump disappeared [and] required that the Air Force change its method for managing the enlisted force" (Jones, 1973, pp. A-1 and A-8).

[55] *Author's Note:* Sometime in 1991, David Grissmer and I published a paper in the *American Defense Annual: 1991–1992* (Grissmer and Rostker, 1992). It took the Air Force to task for not maintaining a balanced drawdown program. The Secretary of the Air Force, Donald Rice, my old boss at RAND, invited Grissmer and me to brief the Air Force Chief of Staff, General Larry Welch, in the Secretary's office. (I have no recollection of the specific date.) From his body language and the tone of his voice, it was clear to us that the chief resented having been directed to be there. He was totally unmoved by our presentation and reiterated the most important thing for the Air Force was not breaking its commitments to its career force. His policy, and that of his predecessor, was no involuntary separation, if at all possible. The future would take care of itself. He would not access anyone if it meant more involuntary separations.

enlisted recruiting and pilot training would save money in the short run.[56] They viewed the future as dynamic and uncertain, and something would come along and change even the best of plans, so, the Chief argued, let the future take care of itself. At the least, he felt, the Air Force could retain more pilots from their smaller drawdown-period training class and could manage the future through better pilot retention—which, as it turned out, was a hope and a prayer but not reality. In the boom years of the 1990s, the retention rate for pilots fell as many accepted jobs with the airlines.

Jehn believed that such sentiments were laudable, but given the closed military personnel system, they could only lead to long-term problems, putting any service that tried it into cycles of personnel skill overages and personnel skill shortages, recruiting periods of bust and boom, and oscillating personnel costs. The Air Force believed the long-term problems were manageable, that the cycles of boom and bust were not so great that they justified losing experienced personnel, and that any oscillating personnel costs would dampen quickly.[57] The lines were drawn between those who had to make the gut-wrenching decision to cut friends and colleagues with what they believed was a very inadequate and unfair severance and retirement system (no retirement for those separated before 20 years of service) and those somewhat removed from the decisions who believed that concern for the immediate problem could not be allowed to ruin the long-term viability of the personnel structure. Ultimately, however, the decision would left in the hands of Congress.[58]

---

[56] Senator John McCain (R-Arizona) was concerned about short-term recruiting budget cuts. He wrote Secretary Cheney to remind him that

> our experience with the Vietnam draw down clearly shows that declining or stable end strength may be accomplished by wide swings in accession levels. If we don't protect our capital investment in recruiting capability during this transition, the Services could fairly quickly find themselves unable to meet recruit quality requirements. (McCain, 1990)

Writing for Secretary Cheney, Jehn replied to Senator McCain: "We are working with the Services to find smart ways to streamline our recruiting infrastructure" (Jehn, 1990d). McCain's colleagues, however, did not necessarily share his long-term view. In a memorandum to Cheney, Jehn noted that "several members of Congress have expressed concern we have not made sufficient cuts in recruiting objectives and resources in light of the projected reductions in end-strength" (Jehn, 1990b). In fact, as McCain had feared, recruiting would become a problem by the mid-1990s.

[57] Al Robbert, then a colonel in Air Force Personnel, was the lead analyst for the Air Force on the issue of accession controls. His analysis showed that drastically reducing accessions would have a smaller effect in the future than Jehn and his staff expected. His results bolstered the resolve of the Air Force's uniformed leadership to manage the drawdown through accession cuts and to hold the line, as far as possible, on separating career personnel. RAND's analysis, which came well after Jehn had set his policy direction, tended to bolster Jehn's conclusions. There was no question that the optimal personnel profile could not be maintained. The Air Force believed that any of the most likely future personnel profiles would produce an effective force, although some profiles might be more expensive than others (Robbert, 2003).

[58] In spring 1990, Senator Glenn wrote Jehn that the "Subcommittee on Manpower and Personnel is evaluating a number of proposals that would provide compensation and benefits to military personnel who are involuntarily separated" (Glenn, 1990). He asked Jehn to "provide a description of your current loss management authorities . . . and the compensation and benefits provided to individuals affected by these authorities" (Glenn, 1990). The list Jehn provided (1990c) clearly illustrated why some felt that the current system was inadequate and refused to force people out of the military.

The Senate Armed Services Committee gave specific guidance on where the cuts should be made, e.g., "prudently adjusting the intake of new recruits, selectively retiring senior personnel, and selectively releasing first term personnel before completion of their first term of service" (Senate Armed Services Committee, 1990, p. 157). The House Armed Services Committee took a less-prescriptive stance and directed that

> the force drawdown [be] accomplished in a balanced and equitable fashion that will preserve the integrity of the military, maintain adequate force readiness, and cushion the blow for adversely affected career personnel. (House Armed Services Committee, 1990, p. 264)

On January 11, 1990, Deputy Secretary of Defense Donald Atwood issued a memorandum concerning the management of the military manpower reductions. He directed the services to maintain "annual accession flows . . . sufficient in quality and quantity to sustain future forces in a steady state" and to develop "procedures to involuntarily separate career [enlisted] Service members prior to expiration of their contract after other management alternatives have proven inadequate" (Atwood, 1990).

In early summer, DoD asked Congress for support in expanding its transition-assistance programs. Jehn told the House Armed Services Committee that the programs the department than had in place were

> not adequate to support the anticipated military and civilian downsizing. We are, therefore, moving out on those items we have the authorities to implement, and request your support for initiatives requiring legislation. (Jehn, Ono et al., 1990)

That December, following action by Congress to provide new temporary rules for the management of commissioned officers during the drawdown period,[59] Jehn prepared "a set of uniform reduction policy objectives which instilled a balance between readiness and personnel considerations" (Jehn, 1990e). The nine objectives were designed to "ensure that we carefully consider how our decisions today will impact the force tomorrow" (Jehn, 1990e):

> Officer-Enlisted Proportional Reductions. Officer reductions should be proportional to enlisted reduction by the end of FY 1997. . . .
> Skill Alignment. Use the drawdown as an opportunity, wherever possible, to balance officer and enlisted skills. . . .
> Accessions (YOS 0 [Year of Service Zero]). Establish nonprior service enlisted and officer accessions at levels consistent with the force planned for FY 1995. . . . Annual accessions will not be programmed to less than 85 percent of the levels required to sustain the FY 1995 force levels in any given year. . . .

---

[59] Congress gave the Secretary of Defense the authority to reduce the time-in-grade requirements and the required length of commissioned service for voluntary retirements. Deputy Secretary Atwood delegated the authority to the secretaries of the military departments (Atwood, 1991a), with additional guidance from Jehn's office (Silberman, 1991).

Initial Term Members (YOS 1–6). Establish policies and procedures to limit the retention or continuation of members who have completed between 2 and 6 years of service (YOS 2–6) to levels not greater than that required to sustain the FY 1995 force structure levels . . .

Retirement Eligible Members (YOS 20+). Establish policies and procedures to limit the retention or continuation of members who are immediately eligible for retirement or retainer pay to levels not greater than that required to sustain the FY 1995 force. . . .

Protect Careerists Near Retirement. Services should protect all qualified service members with 15 years or more until they are eligible for retirement. In addition, Services should minimize, wherever possible, the involuntary separation or members with 12 years of service or more until they are eligible for retirement.

Promotions (Enlisted). Control senior enlisted grades (TOP5) growth . . . .

Career Content (Enlisted). Services should establish retention programs to limit career growth to no more than 4 percent (above FY 1989 level). . . .

Promotion and Strength Plans (Officer). Services should establish officer strength reduction plans so that DOPMA guidelines for promotion opportunity and timing are achieved by the end of FY 1997. (Jehn, 1990e, pp. 4–5)

The proposed guidance for the management of manpower reductions was controversial, reflecting the very different priorities of OSD and the services, particularly the Air Force, over the issues of accession controls and involuntary separations. The DoD Comptroller, Sean O'Keefe, "fully support[ed] the proposed guidance to the Services and believe[d] that the guidance represent[ed] a balanced approach in achieving strength reductions during the downsizing of the force" (O'Keefe, 1990). The Director of the Joint Staff, Air Force Lieutenant General Michael Carns, on the other hand, told Jehn that

the Joint Staff [continues to] share Service concerns over the potential for inflexible application of the policies. Specifically, the force management advantages of requiring the Air Force to maintain annual accessions at level that could lead to unnecessary involuntary separations of non–retirement eligible career officers and noncommissioned officers. (Carns, 1990)

While each of the services had some concern about one or more of the objectives, the particular issue the Director of the Joint Staff raised was uniquely made by the Air Force and was at the heart of the issue of managing the all-volunteer force during the drawdown. In a separate memorandum, the Air Force told Jehn that it did not

see any need for additional guidance beyond that provided by Congress. In fact, we are seriously concerned that compliance with the proposed policy objective would lead to a clear contradiction of Congress' intent to limit involuntary separation of non–retirement eligible career officers and NCOs to the greatest extent possible. [Our] . . . analysis . . . demonstrated that compliance with your proposed policy objectives could lead to over 20,000 unnecessary involuntary separations. (Cooper, 1990)

Their specific comments concerning "Objective 3" were that

> Congress provided guidance for Services to use a balanced approach in achieving reductions. It gave thresholds above which we couldn't go. Concurrently, they sent a clear signal, particularly for officers, to avoid involuntary separations if at all possible. Applying an 85% floor on accessions forces large scale reductions . . . at a time when we need the experience to sustain us through the large scale reduction period. A 75% floor, if a floor is necessary, will provide the flexibility to avoid involuntary separation actions against the senior career force. (Cooper, 1990)

Jehn told Atwood that, if he accepted the Air Force's position and allowed them to recruit only 75 percent of the steady-state requirement, "this effectively eliminates the intent of the objective . . . [to] establish nonprior service enlisted . . . accessions at levels consistent with the force planned for FY 1995" (Jehn, 1990e).

The following February, the Air Force submitted its personnel plan. To Jehn's dismay, it was a reversal of the plan the Air Force had briefed to him the previous March. He thought the earlier plan had been "farsighted." It

> achieved reductions not just by reducing accessions, but also by establishing initial term objectives to control entry into the career force . . . [it contained] several years of accession levels . . . well below those required to sustain the future force [and reduced] mid-career and retirement eligible inventories. (Jehn, 1991i)

The new plan included "several years of accession levels at well below those required to sustain the force." Jehn told the Air Force Assistant Secretary for Manpower that he was particularly concerned with the program the Air Force laid out and that its

> overriding commitment to its career force results in a plan in which grade and experience content is largely unbounded, regardless of force requirements. Although the plan states a . . . career objective of 57 percent, the plan results in career content fluctuating from 73 percent to 53 percent and promotions occurring without regard to grade and skill requirements. (Jehn, 1991i)

While he knew he would have little success moving the Air Force to his position, he expressed his concern in a handwritten note to his Air Force counterpart, saying that he hoped "our current initiatives will give us the means to resolve this to everyone's satisfaction" (Jehn, 1991h).

The Voluntary Severance Incentive and the Selective Severance Bonus Initiative

The "initiatives" Jehn was talking about were the "voluntary severance incentives" (VSIs) he and his staff had been working on for months. In a letter to Senator McCain, Jehn summed up the problem they had been working to address:

> In particular, the Services have significantly more members in a mid-career status (e.g., sergeants, staff sergeants, captains and majors with more than 6 years of

service but less than 20) than will be required for the smaller force in 1995 and beyond. With current personnel management tools, the Services must choose between retaining too many of these members (at significant cost to promotion opportunity, force shaping, and budget outlays), or separating involuntarily members who have made significant personal commitments to their Service and to the nation.

We have developed personnel plans which reduce strengths without the use of additional involuntary separation actions wherever possible. To date, we have reduced the Department's military strength by over 130,000 from its 1987 peak exclusively through reduced accessions, voluntary separations, and early retirements. Over the next 4 years, we plan to continue this approach as much as possible. In fact, about 85 percent of the remaining 400,000 strength reductions will still be achieved in this manner. However, to maintain a vibrant, effective force with the proper mix of skills, grades, and experience, some involuntary separations will be necessary. (Jehn, 1991m)

The VSI program was basically designed to "encourage people with 6 to 19 years of service to leave voluntarily and help ... minimize involuntary separations" (Alexander, 1992b, p. 526). It was the logical alternative to an accession-heavy reduction program. Jehn estimated that, for the services to meet their FY 1995 end-strength goals, they would have to cut one-quarter of their force structures. This meant the services would have to "separate a total of 26,000 more members each year than would be expected to leave under normal conditions" (Jehn, 1991j). The services had many more members between 6 years of service and 20 years of service than would be required in the future.

Jehn briefed Deputy Secretary Atwood on April 15, 1991. Atwood thought it a pretty good plan and commented that it was better than industry would offer. He asked Jehn to give the services a chance to comment, as OSD would need the support of the services with Congress.[60] The basic plan Jehn circulated to the services on May 14, 1991 incorporated cash payments of various amounts for varying periods, depending on each member's length of service before taking the VSI option (Jehn, 1991c).[61] The Army thought the plan not generous enough, particularly for those with more than 15 years of service, to encourage the required number of people to leave voluntarily. The Air Force and Navy felt the plan too generous.[62] In addition to the VSI

---

[60] See the briefing in Jehn (1991b).

[61] The VSI annual payment was equal to final base monthly pay times 12 months times 2.5 percent times the years of service. The annual payment would be received for twice the number of years of service. Atwood told Cheney "a lieutenant colonel with 15 years of service who volunteered to separate and receive the financial incentive would be entitled to receive [$15,934] each year for 30 years" (Atwood, 1991b). Cheney approved the program as long as it did not add cost to the defense budget. Atwood would later tell him that the "cost of the incentive will be offset by the lower cost of the more junior personnel who will replace the service member who voluntarily separated under the plan" (Jehn, 1991k).

[62] See the Air Force response in Secretary of the Air Force (1991) and the Navy response in Pope (1991).

program, the Army wanted a 15-year early retirement option.[63] Jehn worried that the costs of such a program might be hard to control and that future service members might press to make this a permanent entitlement. All agreed, however, while they "would prefer that the drawdown reflect voluntary actions, . . . the Department should strongly oppose any effort to suspend involuntary separation authorities" (Jehn, 1991j). Jehn told Atwood that the services "would like to be able to use a 'stick'—such as the threat or actuality of involuntary separations—in conjunction with the 'carrot' of the incentive" (Jehn, 1991j).

Jehn briefed Attwood again on May 20, 1991 to get him ready for a number of design issues he would be called on to decide, such as whether the incentives should be used to permit increased involuntary separations of the senior career force. This time, the briefing did not go as well. The large number of involuntary separations Jehn was projecting, some 114,000, and the large payments some would receive concerned Attwood.[64] In a follow-on briefing two days later, they got more into the details of force shaping, and Attwood, after having lunch with the service secretaries, was concerned that they were "all over the map on how to proceed."[65] At the next meeting, on May 31, 1991, Jehn explained how he had accommodated some of the concerns the services had expressed. Attwood polled his senior staff. The general consensus was positive. Attwood summed up his view by saying that he liked it. It was creative, a long-term solution; it let the services shape their forces as they liked; and it was voluntary.[66] On June 17, 1971, Attwood told the staff he was ready to go.[67] He wanted to see the final decision package they would take to Secretary Cheney. Final decisions were made on June 20, 1991,[68] and legislation was sent to Congress on July 25, 1991.[69]

One of the very creative provisions of the DoD proposal was transferability. The transferability provision of the VSI proposal was designed to give the service member an option between an annuity and cashing out the future stream of payments by selling the annuity on the open market. On first proposing this provision, Jehn explained to Atwood that transferability would allow "the member to capitalize his annuity, and use the capital to buy or put a down payment on a house, to start a business, to educate himself or his children, or for any other purpose" (Jehn, 1991j). He was concerned,

---

[63] See the Army response in Wincup (1991).

[64] See the briefing in Jehn (1991d).

[65] The follow-on briefing is in Jehn (1991e).

[66] The meeting was scheduled for June 1, 1991, but actually took place on May 31, 1991 (see Jehn, 1991).

[67] See the briefing in Jehn (1991g).

[68] See Jehn (1991j).

[69] See the transmittal letter, the proposed bill, and Craig College's summary in Cheney (1991).

however, that the details of this option might be too confusing and that some members might not understand how it would operate.[70]

Congress also found the proposal confusing and stripped the transferability provision from VSI and crafted a new alternative. The Special Separation Benefit (SSB) was a lump-sum payment equal to 15 percent of the member's base pay times the number of years of service at the time of separation.[71] An objective analysis of the VSI annuity and the lump-sum payment of the SSB showed that the value of the VSI, if it could be transferred freely and sold on the open market, would be considerably greater than the cash received for the SSB. For example, an officer in grade O-4 with 14 years of service would receive a yearly annuity payment of $14,640 for 28 years. The SSB lump-sum payment was $87,840. Given that the VSI annuity was an obligation of the U.S. government, a bank, for example, should have been willing to buy the VSI annuity for much more than the cash received by a member who opted for the SSB. Estimates by John Warner and Saul Pleeter suggested that those who took the SSB had a preference for cash much like those willing to pay interest rates of about 16 percent, the typical interest rates paid on credit card balances.[72]

The VSI and SSB programs were enacted as Sections 661 and 662 of the National Defense Authorization Act for Fiscal Years 1992 and 1993. The program started on January 1, 1992. Jehn's first biweekly report to Atwood and Cheney was upbeat; for the first six weeks of the program, "almost 2,900 personnel have applied for separation under VSI and 13,000 under the SSB.[73] . . . [T]he results thus far are encouraging and indicate our goals . . . are achievable" (Jehn, 1992a). He reminded them, however, that this was just part of the program and that "Retirements beyond normal numbers are generated by actions of Selected Early Retirement Boards (SERBs) and enforcement of Service up-or-out policies" (Jehn, 1992a). Involuntary separations were still possible. In March he reported, "since not enough [Army] majors applied [for VSI or SSB], the RIF [Reduction-in-Force] Board for Army majors convened as scheduled on

---

[70] Jehn told Atwood that

> the unfamiliarity of the option may reduce its attractiveness to members, and may result in too few volunteers. The transferability may lead some members to cash in their incentive, and use the proceeds in ways which could leave them, some years from now, with no tangible benefits from their military service. The complexity of this option, coupled with a concern for protecting members against misuse of their capital, may make this proposal difficult to enact. (Jehn, 1991j, pp. 5–6)

[71] The PA&E staff prepared an assessment of the changes Congress made to the original DoD proposal in Beland (1991).

[72] Asch and Warner, citing the unpublished estimates of Warner and Pleeter, noted that the "relative size of the discounted present value of VSI and SSB depends on the member's personal discount rate, but for real discount rates below 16 percent, the discounted present value of VSI, exceeds that of the SSB payment" (Asch and Warner, 2001, p. 5). Warner and Pleeter's work was later published in *American Economic Review* (Warner and Pleeter, 2001).

[73] Jehn would report that "about 80% of the applications to date [March 12, 1992] are for the Special Separation Bonus (SSB) which is the primary choice of junior enlisted members. Officers and senior enlisted are opting for the Voluntary Separation Incentive (VSI)" (Jehn, 1992b).

March 10" (Jehn, 1992b).[74] The Air Force followed with its own SERB Board for captains and majors, which affected all "captains and majors who are either retirement eligible as an officer, or will be within 2 years, and are not on a promotion selection list" (Alexander, 1992a). In the June report to Congress, the department reported that, in "most cases," it would be able to "avoid the previously planned mid-career involuntary separations. In addition, these programs [VSI and SSB] are proving effective in reducing over strength inventories in which strength reductions were not previously planned" (ASD[FMP], 1992, p. 7).[75]

Temporary Early Retirement Authority (TERA)

The Congress not only passed the VSI and SSB program but also showed an interest in a possible early retirement program. The conference report that accompanied the authorization act asked DoD to "explore" an early retirement option for members with between 15 and 20 years of service. In preparing the report to Congress, Jehn told Atwood that

> the disadvantages of an early retirement more than offset any advantage. We are seriously concerned it would actually increase retention, resulting in a more senior and costly force, and create a perception that it was a permanent entitlement, which could severely distort the future force. Finally, early retirement would undoubtedly reduce the effectiveness of our VSI and SSB force shaping efforts, especially for members with 10 to 14 YOS. This could ultimately result in more involuntary separations—something we have worked very hard to avoid. (Jehn, 1992c)

That fall, over the objections of the department,[76] Congress passed the temporary early retirement authority (TERA). But, as a result of the November 1992 elections, it would fall to a new administration to carry out the program and the rest of the drawdown.[77]

---

[74] In May, the Army told Jehn that, "although the RIF board has already adjourned, all RIF-eligible officers were offered VSI/SSB and could apply up to May 1, 1992" (Alexander, 1992c). Jehn told his Army counterpart that he applauded the "effort to minimize the number of involuntary separations by leaving your VSI and SSB applications window open for RIF Eligible officers until May 1, 1992" (Jehn, 1992d).

[75] Asch and Warner estimated that

> half of the personnel who left in 1992 with the separation pay would have left without it; therefore our results indicate that half of the eligible personnel earned economic rents. Consequently, this analysis suggests that a separation-pay program such as the VSI/SSB program can be an effective means of inducing separations over and above what would have occurred without such a program. (Asch and Warner, 2001, p. xii)

[76] Jehn told Deputy Secretary Atwood the Senate Armed Services Committee proposal was "unnecessary, counterproductive, unfair and too expensive and unnecessarily generous." Other than that, at the request of Legislative Affairs, he proposed "conference report language to provide the SECDEF latitude to use this new retirement authority selectively" (Jehn, 1992g). He noted it would be particularly unfair to the "7,000 members with 15 or more years currently separating with VSI/SSB [and] 18,000 members with 12 to 14 years" for whom the early retirement option would have been more lucrative (Jehn, 1992g).

[77] Jehn listed this program as one of the major issues remaining (1992h).

The Legacy

Karl Haltiner and Paul Klein, in commenting on how the end of the Cold War had affected the countries of Western and Eastern Europe, identified a number of "waves of reform." They argued that "most European countries by and large follow the same pattern on modernizing their armed forces in the post–Cold War period" (Haltiner and Klein, 2005, p. 9). They did not have to limit their observation to Europe, however, and might well have included the United States, at least in the first wave of reform. According to Haltiner and Klein, the first wave started in 1990 and lasted to about 1995. In Europe, as in the United States, it was characterized by a "rapid, predominantly cost-motivated downsizing. . . . As a rule," they noted "this first generation of reform lacked strategic vision and was devoid of a serious questioning of the mass-army principle" (Haltiner and Klein, 2005, p. 9). Certainly, in this country, the drawdown of the early 1990s "lacked strategic vision." The drawdown was all about saving money and did not leave the military well prepared for the new missions of the new millennium.

The American military skipped the second wave of reform that swept conscription from country after country in Europe, having already moved to an all-volunteer force a generation earlier. Haltiner and Klein's description of the third wave in Europe, however, applies equally well to the United States and to Europe. The third wave was and continues to be about "modularization and flexibilization" (Haltiner and Klein, 2005, p. 13). For Europe, the wake-up call was the air campaign against Serbia and the NATO Kosovo Force [KFOR] mission in Kosovo. Serbia and Kosovo were also catalysts for the U.S. Army's first round of transformation in the late 1990s, a program that has been accelerated more recently as a result of military operations in Iraq and Afghanistan.

References

Alexander, Robert M., "FY93 USAF Captain/Major Selective Early Retirement Board (SERB)," memorandum to Principal Assistant Secretary of Defense (FM&P), Washington, D.C., March 12, 1992a. G0777.pdf.

———, Testimony on Explanation of Department of Defense Plan for Reducing Military Forces, hearing before the Senate Appropriations Committee, 92S18132 No. 4, March 26, 1992b. G0888.pdf.

———, "Army Reduction in Force (RIF) Board—Coordinate Army's FY 92 RIF Board Instructions," memorandum to Assistant Secretary of Defense (FM&P), Washington, D.C., May 1, 1992c. G0930.pdf.

Anderson, Martin C., ed., *Registration and the Draft,* Stanford, Ca.: Hoover Institution, Stanford University, 1982.

Armor, David J., "Decline in 1985 First Term Reenlistment Rates," information memorandum to Secretary of Defense, Washington, D.C., June 18, 1986. G0796.pdf.

———, *Military Manpower Recruiting and Reenlistment Results for the Active Component—Third Quarter Fiscal Year 1987,* Washington, D.C.: Acting Assistant Secretary of Defense (FM&P), August 6, 1987. G0989.pdf.

Armstrong, William L., Kenneth J. Coffey, Robert F. Hale, and Lawrence J. Korb, Testimony on Pay Increases for Military Personnel, hearing before the Senate Armed Services Committee, Subcommittee on Manpower and Personnel, 97th Cong., 1st Sess., Washington, D.C., U.S. Government Printing Office, May 7, 1981. G1165.pdf.

Asch, Beth J., and John T. Warner, *An Examination of the Effects of Voluntary Separation Incentives,* Santa Monica, Calif.: RAND Corporation, MR-859-OSD, 2001. S0646.pdf.

ASD[FMP]—*See* Assistant Secretary of Defense for Force Management Policy.

ASD[MRA&L]—*See* Assistant Secretary of Defense for Manpower, Reserve Affairs, and Logistics.

ASD[PA]—*See* Assistant Secretary of Defense for Public Affairs.

Assistant Secretary of Defense for Force Management Policy, *A Report to the Congress on the Montgomery GI Bill Education Benefits Program,* Washington, D.C.: Office of the Secretary of Defense, January 1988. G0761.pdf.

———, *Report to Congress: Department of Defense Assessment of the Voluntary Separation Incentive (VSI) and the Special Separation Benefit (SSB): January 1–May 20,* Washington, D.C., June 1, 1992. G0786.pdf.

Assistant Secretary of Defense for Manpower, Reserve Affairs, and Logistics, *Fiscal Year 1983 Results,* Washington, D.C., November 23, 1983. G1185.pdf.

Assistant Secretary of Defense for Public Affairs, *Military Manpower Strength Assessment, Recruiting and Reenlistment Results Fiscal Year 1983 (October 1982 Through September 1983),* Washington, D.C.: 58083, November 23, 1983. G1184.pdf.

Atwood, Donald J., "Management of Military Manpower Reductions," U.S. Senate to Secretaries of the Military Departments, Washington, D.C., January 22, 1990. G1193.pdf.

———, "Additional Flexibilities in Officer Personnel Management," memorandum to Secretaries of the Military Departments, Washington, D.C., January 16, 1991a.

———, "Voluntary Separation Incentive Legislation," memorandum to Secretary of Defense, Washington, D.C., June 28, 1991b. G1198.pdf.

Bandow, Doug, "Selective Service [Proposed] Regulations," memorandum to Martin Anderson, Washington, D.C., June 19, 1981a. R0009.pdf.

———, "Military Manpower Working Group," memorandum to Martin Anderson, Washington, D.C., September 4, 1981b. R0013.pdf.

———, "Military Manpower Task Force," memorandum to Martin Anderson, Washington, D.C., November 25, 1981c. R0018.pdf.

———, "Upcoming Issues in Military Manpower Policy," memorandum to Martin Anderson, Washington, D.C., December 31, 1981d. R0020.pdf.

Beland, Russell, "Recent Changes in the Voluntary Separation Incentive," memorandum to David Chu, Washington, D.C., December 3, 1991. G1410.pdf.

Bergquist, Kenneth P., "Enlisted Personnel Management System for the Nineties (EPMS 90)," action memorandum to Assistant Secretary of Defense (Force Management and Personnel), Washington, D.C., January 12, 1989. G1354.pdf.

Boorda, J. Michael, *Views on EPMS-90,* Washington, D.C.: Chief of Naval Personnel, January 12,1989. G1357.pdf.

Buddin, Richard, *Enlisted Effects of the 2+2+4 Recruiting Program,* Santa Monica, Calif.: RAND Corporation, R-4097-A, 1991. S0694.pdf.

Calhoun, Jerry L., "FY 1984 Advertising Mix Test," information memorandum to Secretary of Defense, Washington, D.C., September 23, 1985a. G0996.pdf.

———, "FY 1985 Recruiting Results," information memorandum to Secretary of Defense, Washington, D.C., September 25, 1985b. G1002.pdf.

———, "Department of Defense Recruiting and Advertising Trends—FYs 1981–1987," information memorandum to Secretary of Defense, Washington, D.C., October 7, 1985c. G0827.pdf.

Carlson, Dudley L., "Service Recruiting Advertising Budgets for FY-87," memorandum to Assistant Secretary of Defense (MM&PP), Washington, D.C., May 28, 1986. G1183.pdf.

Carlucci, Frank C., "Discontinuation of Draft Registration," memorandum to Assistant to the President for National Security Affairs, Washington, D.C., April 18, 1988. G0854.pdf.

Carns, Michael P. C., "Service Force Reduction Plans for FY 1991," memorandum to Principal Deputy Assistant Secretary of Defense (FM&P), Washington, D.C., November 1, 1990. G1195.pdf.

Carr, William J., *Managing Enlisted Seniority,* Washington, D.C.: Office of the Assistant Secretary of Defense (Force Management & Personnel), May 10, 1989. G1358.pdf.

———, interview with Bernard Rostker, September 22, 2004.

Cheney, Richard, "Voluntary Separation Incentive Act" memorandum to President of the United States Senate and Speaker of the House of Representatives, Washington, D.C., July 25, 1991. G1411.pdf.

Clark, William D., "Enlisted Personnel Management System for the Nineties (EPMS 90)," information memorandum to Assistant Secretary of Defense (Force Management and Personnel), Washington, D.C., January 13, 1989. G1353.pdf.

Cooper, J. G., "Military Manpower Reductions," memorandum to Assistant Secretary of Defense (FM&P), Washington, D.C., November 19, 1990. G1196.pdf.

Cox, Chapman B., "Service Recruitment Advertising Budgets for FY 1987 (Draft)," memorandum to Assistant Secretaries of Defense, Washington, D.C., March 27, 1986a. G1181.pdf.

———, "Results of the Department of Defense Advertising Mix Test," information memorandum to Secretary of Defense, Washington, D.C., March 31, 1986b. G0823.pdf.

———, "Appointment of Dave Armor," memorandum to Secretary of Defense, Washington, D.C., April 7, 1986c. G1003.pdf.

———, "Implementation of the Department of Defense Advertising Mix Test Findings," information memorandum to Secretary of Defense, Washington, D.C., May 9, 1986d. G0998.pdf.

———, *First Half FY 1986 Recruiting Results,* information memorandum, Washington, D.C.: Assistant Secretary of Defense (FM&P), May 28, 1986e. G0822.pdf.

———, "Service Recruitment Advertising Budgets: FY 1987–FY 1990," action memorandum to Secretary of Defense, Washington, D.C., June 4, 1986f. G0830.pdf.

———, "FY 1987 Navy Advertising Budget Cut," action memorandum to Secretary of Defense, Washington, D.C., July 1, 1986g. G1008.pdf.

———, "Funding for Recruiting Advertising," memorandum to Deputy Secretary of Defense, Washington, D.C., August 19, 1986h. G0928.pdf.

———, "FY 1987 Joint Recruiting Advertising Program (JRAP) Funding Reductions," memorandum to Assistant Secretary of Defense (Comptroller), Washington, D.C., September 5, 1986i. G0932.pdf.

———, "FY 1986 Recruiting Results," information memorandum to Secretary of Defense, Washington, D.C., November 25, 1986j. G1004.pdf.

Crowe, William J., Jr., *The Line of Fire: From Washington to the Gulf, the Politics and Battles of the New Military,* New York: Simon and Schuster, 1993.

Danzig, Richard, "Navy Suspension of Selective Reenlistment Bonuses," information memorandum to Secretary of Defense, Washington, D.C., June 19, 1980. G0392.pdf.

Dertouzos, James N., *The Effects of Military Advertising: Evidence from the Advertising Mix Test,* Santa Monica, Calif.: RAND Corporation, N-2907-FMP, March 1989. S0688.pdf.

Dertouzos, James N., J. Michael Polich, Ani Bamezai, and Thomas Cestnutt, *Recruiting Effects of Army Advertising,* Santa Monica, Calif.: RAND Corporation, R-3577-FMP, January 1989. S0689.pdf.

Dorn, Edwin, "Balanced Recruiting Programs," to Assistant Secretaries of the Military Departments, Washington, D.C. , January 21, 1994. P0004.pdf.

Editorial Staff of the *Los Angeles Times,* "Drafting for Defense," *Los Angeles Times,* May 28, 1981.

Fernandez, Richard L., *Enlistment Effects and Policy Implications of the Educational Assistance Test Program,* Santa Monica, Calif.: RAND Corporation, R-2935-MRAL, 1982. S0677.pdf.

Gilroy, Curtis L., interview with Bernard Rostker, September 15, 2004.

Gilroy, Curtis L., Robert L. Phillips, and John D. Blair, "The All-Volunteer Force: Fifteen Years Later," *Armed Force and Society,* Vol. 16, No. 3, Spring 1990, pp. 329–350.

Glenn, John S., Jr., "Request for Current Loss Management Authorities," memorandum to Assistant Secretary of Defense (FM&P), Washington, D.C., May 21, 1990.

Goldich, Robert L., *The Persian Gulf War and the Draft,* Washington, D.C.: The Library of Congress, Congressional Research Service, January 22, 1991. S0016.pdf.

Green, Bert F., Jr., *Military Manpower Recruiting and Reenlistment Results for the Active Components—End of Fiscal Year 1988,* Washington, D.C.: Assistant Secretary of Defense (FM&P), December 11, 1988. G0759.pdf.

Green, Grant S., Jr., "Army Enlistment and Reenlistment Incentives," memorandum to Assistant Secretary of the Army (M&RA), Washington, D.C., February 25, 1988a. G0793.pdf.

———, Recruiting, Retention, and Compensation, hearing before the Subcommittee on Manpower and Personnel Senate Committee on Armed Services, Washington, D.C., Assistant Secretary of Defense (Force Management and Personnel), March 24, 1988b. P0013.pdf.

———, "Recruiting, Retention and Quality in Today's Army," memorandum to Chairman Senate Appropriations Committee John C. Stennis, Washington, D.C., July 7, 1988c. G0914.pdf.

———, "Department of Defense Position on Joint Advertising," letter to Bill Chappell, Jr., Chairman House Appropriations Committee, Washington, D.C., December 11, 1988d. G0760.pdf.

———, "Enlisted Personnel Management System for the Nineties (EPMS 90)," memorandum to Assistant Secretary of Defense (PA&E), Assistant Secretary of Defense (Comptroller) and Assistant Secretaries of the Military Departments, Washington, D.C., December 28, 1988e. G1352.pdf.

———, *Working Paper,* Washington, D.C.: Office of the Assistant Secretary of Defense (Force Management and Personnel), January 1989. G1356.pdf.

Greenberg, I. M., "Technical Comments," memorandum to Bernard Rostker, Washington, D.C., July 2004.

Grissmer, David W., James R. Hosek, and Richard L. Eisenman, *Trimming the Senior Enlisted Force: Estimating Cost Savings and Structural Institutional Incentives,* Santa Monica, Calif.: RAND Corporation, WD-4616-FMP, October 1989. S0854.pdf.

Grissmer, David W., and Bernard D. Rostker, "Military Manpower in a Changing World," in Joseph Kruzel, ed., *American Defense Annual: 1991–1992,* New York: Lexington Books, 1992, pp. 127–145.

Haig, Alexander M., "Speech by General William C. Westmoreland," memorandum to Henry Kissinger, Washington, D.C., May 2, 1969. G1171.pdf.

Hale, Robert, New Educational Assistance Program for the Military to Assist Recruiting, hearing before the House Armed Services Committee, Subcommittee on Military Personnel and Compensation, 97th Cong., 1st Sess., Washington, D.C.: U.S. Government Printing Office, September 10, 1981.

Haltiner, Karl W., and Paul Klein, "The European Post–Cold War Military Reforms and Their Impact on Civil-Military Relations," in Franz Kernic, Paul Klien and Karl Haltiner, eds., *The European Armed Forces in Transition,* New York: Peter Lang, 2005.

Hatfield, Mark O., "Opposition to Continued Registration, together with draft response," letter to the President, Washington, D.C., April 3, 1981. R0007.pdf.

Hosek, James R., Richard L. Fernandez, and David W. Grissmer, *Active Enlisted Supply: Prospects and Policy Options,* Santa Monica, Calif.: RAND Corporation, P-6967, 1984. S0653.pdf.

House Armed Services Committee, *Defense Authorizations Report for Fiscal Year 1991,* Washington, D.C.: U.S. House of Representatives.

Jackson, Jesse L., "African Americans Assigned to the Persian Gulf," memorandum to Secretary of Defense, Washington, D.C., February 25, 1991. G0779.pdf.

Janowitz, Morris, and Charles C. Moskos, Jr., "Racial Composition in the All-Volunteer Force," *Armed Forces and Society*, Vol. 1, No. 1, November 1974, pp. 109–123.

Jehn, Christopher, *Fiscal Year 1989 Active Component Recruiting and Reenlistment Results,* information memorandum, Washington, D.C.: Assistant Secretary of Defense (FM&P), December 18, 1989. G0819.pdf.

———, *A Biennial Report to Congress on the Montgomery GI Bill Education Benefits Program,* Washington, D.C.: Office of the Secretary of Defense, February 1990a. G0985.pdf.

———, "Military Recruiting Expenditures," information memorandum to Assistant Secretaries of the Military Department (M&RA), Washington, D.C., April 20, 1990b. G0999.pdf.

———, "Department of Defense Involuntary Loss Management Authorities/Policies and Compensation and Benefits," memorandum to Senator John Glenn, Washington, D.C., May 30, 1990c. G0973.pdf.

———, "Recruiting Issues in a Period of Transition," memorandum to John McCain, Washington, D.C., May 18, 1990d. G0825.pdf.

———, "Military Manpower Reductions," policy memorandum to Deputy Secretary of Defense, Washington, D.C., December 5, 1990e. G0772.pdf.

———, "African Americans Assigned to the Persian Gulf," letter to Jesse L. Jackson, Washington, D.C., March 21, 1991a. G0780.pdf.

———, *Voluntary Separations by the Senior Career Force as a Tool in the Drawdown: A Briefing for the Deputy Secretary of Defense,* Washington, D.C.: Assistant Secretary of Defense (Force Management Policy), April 15, 1991b. G1408.pdf.

———, "Voluntary Severance Payment Options," memorandum to Secretary of the Military Departments, Washington, D.C., May 14, 1991c. G0763.pdf.

———, *Voluntary Severance Payment Initiative: A Briefing for the Deputy Secretary of Defense,* Washington, D.C.: Assistant Secretary of Defense (Force Management Policy), May 20, 1991d. G1415.pdf.

———, *Drawdown Characteristics and Issues and a Voluntary Separation Initiative: A Briefing for the Deputy Secretary of Defense,* Washington, D.C.: Assistant Secretary of Defense (Force Management Policy), May 22, 1991e. G1413.pdf.

———, "Desert Storm Lessons Learned—A Second Opinion," memorandum to Secretary of Defense, Washington, D.C., May 28, 1991f. G0768.pdf.

———, *Managing the Drawdown—Force Shaping and Timing Issues: A Briefing for the Deputy Secretary of Defense,* Washington, D.C.: Assistant Secretary of Defense (Force Management Policy), June 1, 1991g. G1412.pdf.

———, "Air Force Enlisted Personnel Plan," memorandum to Deputy Secretary of Defense, Washington, D.C., June 7, 1991h. G0767.pdf.

———, "Enlisted Personnel Plan," memorandum to Assistant Secretary of the Air Force (MRAI&E), Washington, D.C., June 7, 1991i. G1197.pdf.

———, "Voluntary Severance Incentive Initiative," memorandum to Deputy Secretary of Defense, Washington, D.C., June 20, 1991j. G0765.pdf.

———, "Voluntary Separation Incentive (VSI) Legislation," memorandum to Secretary of Defense, Washington, D.C., July 10, 1991k. G0782.pdf.

———, "Reduced Manning Levels," memorandum to Senator John McCain, Washington, D.C., July 19, 1991m. G0978.pdf.

———, *Military Manpower Recruiting Results for the Active Components—Third Quarter Fiscal Year 1991,* Washington, D.C.: Assistant Secretary of Defense (FM&P), August 9, 1991n. G0769.pdf.

———, "Voluntary Separation Incentive (VSI) and Special Separation Benefit (SSB) Status Report," memorandum to Secretary of Defense, Washington, D.C., February 14, 1992a. G0776.pdf.

———, "VSI/SSB Program Status," memorandum to Secretary of Defense, Washington, D.C., March 12, 199b2. G0775.pdf.

———, "Voluntary Severance Incentive Initiative," memorandum to Deputy Secretary of Defense, Washington, D.C., May 4, 1992c. G0774.pdf.

———, "Army Reduction in Force (RIF) Board," memorandum to Assistant Secretary of the Army (M&RA), Washington, D.C., May 5, 1992d.

———, "Decline in Black Enlistments," memorandum to Chairman of the Joint Chiefs of Staff, Washington, D.C., May 7, 1992e. G0931.pdf.

———, "Aviation Bonus Program," memorandum to Chairman Senate Armed Services Committee, Washington, D.C., June 3, 1992f. G0785.pdf.

————, "15-Year Early Retirement," memorandum to Deputy Secretary of Defense, Washington, D.C., September 24, 1992g. G0778.pdf.

————, "Significant Actions During Transition Period," memorandum to Secretary of Defense, Washington, D.C., November 20, 1992h. G0972.pdf.

Jehn, Christopher, Thomas P. Carney, Ronald J. Zlatoper, Billy J. Boles, Matthew T. Cooper, Status of Programs for Reducing and Restructuring Military Forces, hearing before the House Armed Services Committee, 102nd Cong., 2nd Sess., 93-H201-1 No. 4, March 26, 1992. G0898.pdf.

Jehn, Christopher, Stephen M. Duncan, Barbara S. Pope, Gary J. Cooper, and Paul L. Jones, Status of Programs for Reducing and Restructuring Military Forces, hearing before the Senate Armed Services Committee, 93S2011 No 11, June 2, 1992. G0893.pdf.

Jehn, Christopher, Allen K. Ono, Thomas J. Hickey, Jeremy M. Boorda, Involuntary Separations, hearing before the Senate Appropriations Committee, 91-H2011-4 No. 12, June 26, 1990. G0891.pdf.

Jehn, Christopher, Kim G. Wincup, Barbara S. Pope, Jerome G. Cooper, Allen K. Ono, Jeremy M. Boorda, Norman H. Cooper, Thomas J. Hickey, U.S. Congress, Status of Programs for Reducing and Restructuring Military Forces, hearing before the Senate Armed Services Committee, 91-S201-8 No. 1, March 5, 1990. G0903.pdf.

Jones, David C., *TOPCAP: USAF Personnel Plan,* Annexes, Washington, D.C.: U.S. Air Force, May 1, 1973. S0485.pdf.

————, "Selective Service Registration," memorandum to Secretary of Defense, Washington, D.C., December 4, 1981. G0850.pdf.

Keesling, Karen R., "Enlisted Personnel Management System for the Nineties (EPMS 90)," action memorandum to Assistant Secretary of Defense (Force Management and Personnel), Washington, D.C., January 9, 1989. G1355.pdf.

Korb, Lawrence J., "Military Manpower," memorandum to Frank Hodsoll, Washington, D.C., May 4, 1981a. R0002.pdf.

————, "White House Meeting—Status of the AVF," memorandum to Secretary of Defense, Washington, D.C., May 12, 1981b. G0842.pdf.

————, "Defense Manpower Task Force," action memorandum to Secretary of Defense, Washington, D.C., June 3, 1981c. R0008.pdf.

————, "Working Group Meeting, July 1, 1981," memorandum to Interagency Working Group of the Military Manpower Task Force, Washington, D.C. , June 30, 1981d. R0010.pdf.

————, "Secretary of Defense Decisions on Efficiency and Economy Actions—Joint Recruiting Advertising Programs," action memorandum to Secretary of Defense, Washington, D.C., July 1, 1981e. G0815.pdf.

————, "Monthly Report on Recruiting and Retention," information memorandum to Special Assistant to the Secretary of Defense, Washington, D.C., July 6, 1981f. G0816.pdf.

————, "Information for the Task Force Meeting," memorandum to Members of the Military Manpower Task Force, Washington, D.C., August 4, 1981g. R0012.pdf.

————, "Response to Secretary of State on the Question of Cost Reductions Associated with a Return to the Draft," action memorandum to Secretary of Defense, Washington, D.C., September 8, 1981h. G0992.pdf.

————, "Military Manpower Task Force Meeting #2," memorandum to Members of the Military Manpower Task Force, Washington, D.C., September 11, 1981i. R0014.pdf.

————, "Secretary of Defense Decision on Efficiency and Economy Actions: Streamlining of Military Recruiting Support Operations," action memorandum to Secretary of Defense, Washington, D.C., October 6, 1981j. G1022.pdf.

————, "MRA&L Monthly Report of Department of Defense Accomplishments," memorandum to Special Assistant to the Secretary of Defense, Washington, D.C., November 2, 1981k. G0835.pdf.

————, "Response to Your Joint Advertising Comments on Our October 6, 1981 Recruiting Support Memorandum," action memorandum to Secretary of Defense, Washington, D.C., November 13, 1981m. G0802.pdf.

————, "Active Forces Recruiting and Reenlistment FY 1982 Thru November 1981," monthly report to Secretary of Defense, Washington, D.C., January 6, 1982a. G0911.pdf.

————, "Recruiting and Reenlistment," monthly report to Special Assistant to the Secretary of Defense, Washington, D.C., February 10, 1982b. G0852.pdf.

————, *The Profile of American Youth Study: 1980 Nationwide Administration of the Armed Services Vocational Aptitude Battery,* Washington, D.C.: Office of the Assistant Secretary of Defense (MRA&L), March 1982c. S0576.pdf.

————, "Status Report on FY 1982 Recruiting Advertising Program," information memorandum to Secretary of Defense, Washington, D.C., April 9, 1982d. G1020.pdf.

————, "Report on the Review of the Department of Defense Enlisted Bonus Program," memorandum to Director Defense Audit Service, Washington, D.C., August 9, 1982e. G0968.pdf.

————, "Recruiting and Reenlistment," monthly report to Secretary of the Department of Defense, Washington, D.C., August 17, 1982f. G1015.pdf.

————, "Press Conference—FY 1982 Recruiting Results," decision memorandum to Secretary of Defense, Washington, D.C., November 19, 1982g. G1011.pdf.

————, "Monthly Report on Recruiting and Reenlistment," information memorandum to Secretary of Defense, Washington, D.C., December 27, 1982h. G1019.pdf.

————, "Survey of Attitudes Toward the Military," information memorandum to Secretary of Defense, Washington, D.C., June 22, 1983a. G0883.pdf.

————, "FY 84 Advertising Mix Test Concept Design," memorandum to Assistant Secretary of the Military Departments, Washington, D.C., July 8, 1983b. G1224.pdf.

————, "FY 1985 Funding for Advertising Mix Test," action memorandum to Deputy Secretary of Defense, Washington, D.C., December 6, 1983c. G0995.pdf.

————, "Monthly Report on Recruiting and Reenlistments (FY 1983)," information memorandum to Secretary of Defense, Washington, D.C., December 27, 1983d. G0879.pdf.

———, "Recommendation to Discontinue the Advertising Mix Test at the End of FY 1984," decision memorandum to Secretary of Defense, Washington, D.C., January 11, 1984. G0857.pdf.

———, "Recruiting Results," information memorandum to Secretary of Defense, Washington, D.C., February 1, 1985. G0821.pdf.

Lawrence J. Korb, Robert Hale, Maxwell R. Thurman, and G. V. Montgomery, New Educational Assistance Program for the Military to Assist Recruiting, hearing before the House Armed Services Committee, Subcommittee on Military Personnel and Compensation, 97th Cong., 1st Sess., Washington, D.C., U.S. Government Printing Office, September 10, 1981. G1304.pdf.

Lehman, John, "Proposed Competitive Edge for Army Recruiting in FY-82," action memorandum to Secretary of Defense, Washington, D.C., July 10, 1981a. G0863.pdf.

———, "Secretary of Defense Decision on Efficiency and Economy Actions—Joint Recruiting Advertising Program," action memorandum to Secretary of Defense, Washington, D.C., July 10, 1981b. G0867.pdf.

———, "Meeting of 13 July 1981 Regarding Army Recruiting," information memorandum to Deputy Secretary of Defense, Washington, D.C., July 17, 1981c. G0864.pdf.

———, "Recruiting 'Good News'," memorandum to Secretary of Defense, Washington, D.C., October 24, 1986. G0829.pdf.

Mangale, J. J. M., "Service Recruitment Advertising Budgets for FY 1987," memorandum to Deputy Assistant Secretary of Defense (MM&PP), Washington, D.C., May 29, 1986. G1182.pdf.

Marsh, John O., Jr., "Educational Incentives for Army Recruiting," action memorandum to Deputy Secretary of Defense, Washington, D.C., March 16, 1981. G0844.pdf.

———, "Advertising Levels," information memorandum to Secretary of Defense, Washington, D.C., August 8, 1986a. G1006.pdf.

———, "Advertising," information memorandum to Secretary of Defense, Washington, D.C., September 30, 1986b. G1005.pdf.

McCain, John, "Recruiting Issues in a Period of Transition," memorandum to Secretary of Defense, Washington, D.C., April 10, 1990. G0824.pdf.

McClaughry, John, "Military Manpower and the Draft," memorandum to Martin Anderson, Washington, D.C., April 8, 1981a. R0024.pdf.

———, "Proposed Defense Manpower Task Force and Working Group," memorandum to Martin Anderson, Washington, D.C., April 24, 1981b. R0001.pdf.

———, "Military Manpower Task Force Working Group Meeting," memorandum to Martin Anderson, Washington, D.C., July 1, 1981c. R0011.pdf.

———, "Poll Results on the AVF and the Draft," memorandum to Martin Anderson, Washington, D.C., October 33, 1981d. R0022.pdf.

McCoy, Tidal W., "Air Force Recruiting Good News Report," information memorandum to Secretary of Defense, Washington, D.C., September 29, 1986. G1007.pdf.

Meyer, Shy, "Selective Service Registration," memorandum to Secretary of Defense, Washington, D.C., December 11, 1981. G0990.pdf.

Military Manpower Task Force, Poll of Task Force Members on Registration Options (Martin Anderson's Ballot), Washington, D.C.: December 11, 1981. R0019.pdf.

———, *A Report to the President on Selective Service Registration,* Washington, D.C.: U.S. Department of Defense, December 15, 1981. G1167.pdf.

Montgomery, Gillespie V., "Montgomery GI Bill," letter to Secretary of Defense, Washington, D.C., February 20, 1988. G0762.pdf.

Moskos, Charles C., Jr., "15-Month Enlistment Option," memorandum to Acting Secretary of the Army Les Brownless, Evanston, Ill, October 14, 2003. S0824.pdf.

———, interview with Bernard Rostker, September 15, 2004.

Moskos, Charles C., Jr., and John Sibley Butler, *Be All You Can Be: Black Leadership and Racial Integration the Army Way,* New York: Basic Books, 1996.

Nixon, Richard M., "Volunteer Army," letter to John C. Whitaker, Woodcliff Lake, N.J., November 4, 1993. S0481.pdf.

Nunn, Sam, Status of the All-Volunteer Force, hearing before the Senate Armed Services Subcommittee on Manpower and Personnel, 95th Cong., 2nd Sess., Washington, D.C., U.S. Government Printing Office, June 20, 1978. S0444.pdf.

O'Keefe, Sean, "Military Manpower Reduction," policy memorandum to Assistant Secretary of Defense (FM&P), Washington, D.C., November 29, 1990. G1194.pdf.

OASD[MRA&L]—*See* Office of the Assistant Secretary of Defense for Manpower, Reserve Affairs, and Logistics.

Office of the Assistant Secretary of Defense for Manpower, Reserve Affairs, and Logistics, *Report on Selective Reenlistment Bonus Program,* Washington, D.C.: U.S. Department of Defense, May 1, 1982. G1210.pdf.

———, *Program Review FY 1987–1991: Issues Book—Manpower,* Washington, D.C.: U.S. Department of Defense, Summer 1985. G1403.pdf.

———, *Program Review FY 1988–1992: Issues Book—Manpower—Military Compensation Program,* Washington, D.C.: U.S. Department of Defense, Summer 1986. G1404.pdf.

Pope, Barbara Spyridon, "Voluntary Severance Payment," memorandum to Assistant Secretary of Defense (Force Management Policy), Washington, D.C., May 17, 1991. G1406.pdf.

Powell, Colin L., "Views of the Director of the Office of Management and Budget and the Chairman of the Council of Economic Advisers on Discontinuation of Draft Registration," memorandum to Secretary of Defense, Washington, D.C., March 30, 1988. G0913.pdf.

Puritano, Vincent, "FY 1985 Funding for Advertising Mix Test," memorandum to Assistant Secretary of Defense of Defense (MRA&L), Washington, D.C., December 2, 1983. G1179.pdf.

Reagan, Ronald, "Draft Registration," letter to Mark O. Hatfield, Los Angeles, Ca., May 5, 1980. G0352.pdf.

———, *Address at Commencement Exercises at the United States Military Academy,* Washington, D.C.: The White House, May 27, 1981a. G1166.pdf.

————, *Announcement of the Establishment of the Military Manpower Task Force,* Washington, D.C.: The White House, July 8, 1981b. R0026.pdf.

————, *Statement on Continuation of the Registration Program Under the Military Selective Service Act,* Washington, D.C.: The White House, January 7, 1982. R0025.pdf.

Robbert, Al, "Comments on Air Force Personnel Policies During the Drawdown," memorandum to Bernard Rostker, Washington, D.C., November 25, 2003.

Scales, Robert H., Jr., *Certain Victory,* Washington, D.C.: U.S. Army, Office of the Chief of Staff, 1993.

Secretary of the Air Force, "Voluntary Severance Payment Options (draft)," memorandum to Deputy Secretary of Defense, Washington, D.C., May 1991. G1407.pdf.

Senate Armed Services Committee, *Defense Authorizations Report for Fiscal Year 1991,* Washington, D.C.: U.S. Senate.

Silberman, Robert S., "Officer Personnel Management Authorities," memorandum to Assistant Secretaries of the Military Department (M&RA), Washington, D.C., February 5, 1991. G1217.pdf.

Sprinkel, Beryl W., and James C. III Miller, *Discontinuation of Draft Registration,* Washington, D.C.: Executive Office of the President, February 29, 1988.

Staff of the Directorate for Accession Policy, *Military Recruitment Advertising: Joint and Service-Specific Roles and Funding,* Washington, D.C.: Office of the Assistant Secretary of Defense (Force Management and Personnel), March 1989. P0002.pdf.

————, *Military Recruiting Issues for 1991-1993: Accession Plans and Policies,* Washington, D.C.: Office of the Assistant Secretary of Defense (Force Management and Personnel), September 1991. P0001.pdf.

Stone, Robert A., *Military Manpower Strength Assessment, Recruiting and Reenlistment Results for October–December 1980 (Active Force),* Washington, D.C.: Acting Assistant Secretary of Defense (MRA&L), February 11, 1981a. G0845.pdf.

————, "Monthly Report on Recruiting and Retention," information memorandum to Special Assistant to the Secretary of Defense, Washington, D.C., May 1, 1981b. G0810.pdf.

Stone, W. P. W., "Army Recruiting Effectiveness Since the Start of Operation Desert Shield," memorandum to Deputy Secretary of Defense, Washington, D.C., December 6, 1990. G1000.pdf.

Taft, William Howard, IV, "Service Recruitment Advertising Budgets: FY 1987–FY 1990—concerns," memorandum to Secretary of Defense, Washington, D.C., June 5, 1986. G0831.pdf.

————, "Service Recruitment Advertising Budgets," memorandum to Secretaries of the Military Departments, Washington, D.C., July 9, 1986. G1013.pdf.

————, "Managing Enlisted Seniority," memorandum to Secretaries of the military Departments, Washington, D.C., October 11, 1988. G1350.pdf.

————, "Managing Enlisted Seniority," memorandum to Secretaries of the Military Departments, Washington, D.C., February 22, 1989. G1351.pdf.

Timenes, Nick, "Desert Storm Lessons Learned—A Second Opinion," memorandum to Assistant Secretary of Defense, Washington, D.C., May 21, 1991. G1192.pdf.

Turnage, Thomas K., "Military Manpower Task Force," close hold draft of the proposed report to the President on the registration issue, memorandum to Task Force Members, Washington, D.C., November 16, 1981. R0016.pdf.

10 USC 520, Armed Force, January 14, 1983.

U.S. House of Representatives, Committee on Armed Services, Subcommittee on Military Personnel and Compensation, *Department of Defense Authorization Act, 1981,* Report No. 96916, April 30, 1980.

Waller, C. A. H., "Information for the Manpower Meeting," memorandum to Barbara Honeggar, Washington, D.C., May 14, 1981. R0003.pdf.

Warner, John T., and Saul Pleeter, "The Personal Discount Rate: Evidence from Military Downsizing Programs," *American Economic Review,* Vol. 91, No. 1, March 2001, pp. 33–53. S0880.pdf.

Weidenbaum, Murray L., "Targeting of the Military Pay Raise," memorandum to Martin Anderson, Washington, D.C., September 18, 1981. R0015.pdf.

Weinberger, Caspar W., "Recruit Quality Constraints," memorandum to Carl Levin, Washington, D.C., April 21, 1981a. G0839.pdf.

———, "Congratulations for a Job Well Done," letter to Albert J. Martin, Washington, D.C., August 24, 1981b. G0865.pdf.

———, "Response to Secretary Haig Concerning a Possible Return of the Draft," memorandum to Secretary of State, Washington, D.C., September 16, 1981c. G0991.pdf.

———, "Military Manpower Task Force Report," close hold revised draft of the Report to the President on selective service registration, memorandum to Military Manpower Task Force Members, Washington, D.C., November 20, 1981d. R0017.pdf.

———, "Decline in Absenteeism and Desertion," memorandum to Secretaries of the Military Departments, Washington, D.C., January 8, 1982a. G0970.pdf.

———, *Military Manpower Task Force: A Report to the President on the Status and Prospects of the All-Volunteer Force,* Washington, D.C.: U.S. Government Printing Office, November 1982b. S0004.pdf.

———, "Tenth Anniversary of the All-Volunteer Force," letter to the editor of the *Washington Post,* to Editor The Washington Post, Washington, D.C., July 19, 1983. G0909.pdf.

Westmoreland, William C., "U.S. Military Readiness Requires the Draft," *The Wall Street Journal,* May 26, 1981.

Wincup, G. Kim, "Voluntary Severance Payment Option," action memorandum to Assistant Secretary of the Defense (Force Management Policy), Washington, D.C., May 17, 1991. G1405.pdf.

CHAPTER FIFTEEN

The Role of Women in the All-Volunteer Force

> The greatest change that has come about in the United States Forces in the time I've been in the military service has been the extensive use of women.
>
> —General John W. Vessey, Jr.
> Chairman, Joint Chiefs of Staff[1]
> February 2, 1984

Introduction

Arguably the single group most responsible for the success of the all-volunteer force has been women. Much has been written on the increasingly large number of women who have volunteered for service in the armed forces. At the beginning of FY 2005, 15.4 percent of active duty enlisted personnel and 14.8 percent of active-duty officers were women. The success of the all-volunteer force may, however, be even more attributable to the support that spouses, largely women, give to their service members.[2] At the beginning of FY 2005, almost half of all enlisted personnel were married (49.8 percent), and 69 percent of all officers were married (Defense Manpower Data Center, 2004). The numbers are even greater if you consider only the career force. At the end of September 2005, 73 percent of the enlisted career force in grades E-5 and above were married, and 79 percent of officers in grades O-3 and above were married. Of these, 12 percent of career-enlisted marriages were between service members, and 9 percent of officer marriages were dual-service marriage (Defense Manpower Data Center, 2004). In both roles, as members and supporters, the women of the all-volunteer force broke sharply with past traditions.

---

[1] "Gen. Vessey Sees Women as Biggest Military Change" (1984).

[2] For example, Kirby and Naftel report that after Desert Storm "nonmobilized reservists who perceived that their spouses have a very unfavorable attitude have a retention rate of 37 percent; the retention rate among those with spouses who are very positive is about twice that: 73 percent" (Kirby and Naftel, 1998, pp. 29–30).

Women as Members of the All-Volunteer Force

In 1983, Secretary of Defense Caspar Weinberger reflected on the first decade of the all-volunteer force at the Tenth Anniversary All-Volunteer Force Conference: "The most rewarding development we have seen in our armed forces over the past decade has been the tremendous expansion of opportunities for women" (Weinberger, 1986). When Weinberger spoke those words, the role that women play as the partners of male service members was less obvious than it is today. The largely unexpected consequence of moving to a professional military with better pay was the higher rate of reenlistment and a sharp increase in the size of the career force. Today, the all-volunteer force is, on average, older and much more likely to have families than was the mixed force of volunteers and draftees of the 1960s. Today, the all-volunteer force is a force of families. In retrospect, the Gates Commission not only failed to consider the role women would play in the all-volunteer force, it never considered that the military would have to become a more family-friendly institution.[3]

Women and the Early All-Volunteer Force

At the Tenth Anniversary Conference, William Meckling, Staff Director of the Gates Commission, told the meeting that he was sure, when reading the Brookings Institution monograph on the role of women in the military (Binkin and Bach, 1977), that the authors, Martin Binkin and Shirley Bach, were wrong when they said that the Gates Commission had not addressed the role of women. He described how he was "shocked" when he reviewed the report to "find no record anywhere that we seriously considered the question of expanding the number of women in uniform" (Meckling, 1986, p. 112).

What might have appeared shocking in 1983 seemed to have reflected the prevailing values in 1969. The Air Force's "Project Volunteer Implementation Plan,"[4] written at the time the Gates Commission was doing its work, observed that, despite the fact that

> hundreds of thousands of women qualified for service enter the labor force each year, there can be no appreciable increase in the recruitment of enlisted women for the Air Force beyond that currently programmed unless there is a significant change in public attitudes toward the military services in general and unless military service

---

[3] For example, Meredith Leyva, founder of CinCHouse.com and cofounder of Operation Homefront, has argued that, in 2005,

> retention problem[s] . . . stem from the military's shortcomings in transitioning to an all-volunteer force and the continuing treatment of wartime personnel as draftees. The key to keeping troops is recognizing that they are professionals with personal commitments who are concerned with the care their families receive. (Leyva, 2005, p. 84)

[4] As indicated in the "first draft" of the implementation plan, which had survived in the files of the Office of the Secretary of Defense.

becomes more attractive to young qualified women as a source of employment. (Air Force DCSP Staff, 1969, p. 7)

The comparable Army report of the period, the so-called Project PROVIDE report, did envision an increase in the number of women in the Army if the draft were eliminated,[5] subject to "the social and biological limitations of women" (Directorate of Personnel Studies and Research, 1969b, p. 9-8). As the Army saw it,

> In the military service, the woman finds herself the minority among males; she requires separate facilities and is precluded for social reasons, and for her own safety, from performing duties within the confines of an all-male atmosphere. Physically, the military woman is not well suited for the rigors of field duty or capable of performing fatigue details normally performed by men, and cannot be considered self-sufficient enough in this regard to perform under the conditions experienced by maneuver elements in tactical operations. For this reason, the utilization of women in units below Corps level is not considered feasible. (Directorate of Personnel Studies and Research, 1969b, p. 9-8)[6]

Implementation of the Project PROVIDE recommendations started in June 1971 with a funded "plan to increase WAC to a strength of 1,400 officers and 18,700 enlisted women" (Kerwin, 1971), a number smaller than the authors of PROVIDE had envisioned.

The full appreciation of the role that women could play in the successful implementation of the all-volunteer force fell to Stephen Enke in his "private" report to Secretary Laird (December 14, 1971). Enke told Laird that every time a woman was enlisted, it saved the DoD over $10,000 "if the alternative is extra pay to attract an extra . . . [man]. As substitutes at the margin, Servicemen cost many times more than Servicewomen" (Enke, 1971a, p. 3). He acknowledged that women were more costly than draftees, an argument that was

> quite irrelevant when the draft ended. The choice may . . . be between enlisting more women or giving an extra general pay increase to over a million first-termers. . . . Compared with such a substantial increase in aggregate military compensation, enlisting additional Service women is really the most economical way to fill the projected annual shortfall. (Enke, 1971b)

---

[5] The Army report called for the development of a "detailed plan for the phased increase in the strength of the Women's Army Corps (WAC) from 1,100 officers and 12,400 enlisted women to 2,000 officers and 22,400 enlisted women" (Directorate of Personnel Studies and Research, 1969a, p. vi).

[6] The notion that it was unsafe for women to be in the male dominated military because service women could not be protected from being sexually assaulted was a common stereotype held by those opposed to women in nontraditional military jobs. It was repeated at the end of the decade during testimony before the House Armed Services Committee concerning the Carter administration's proposal to register women for a possible military draft. Mrs. Kathleen Teague, representing Phyllis Schlafly and the *Coalition Against Drafting Women* characterized "the Army environment [as one] where there is little or no privacy, where the rape rate is considerably higher than in civilian life, [and] where there is open toleration of immoral sex" (White, 1980, p. 108).

In fact, by 1972, there were not only projected but actual shortages. The Navy, citing its inability to fill recruiting quotas, opened "enlisted ratings to women to enhance their status and provide increased assignment flexibility" (Finneran, 1972). Allowing women to serve at sea was an important step Chief of Naval Operations Elmo Zumwalt took with Z-Gram 116, "Equal Rights and Opportunities for Women in the Navy."[7] The first women ever were assigned to a ship, the USS *Sanctuary*, a hospital ship, that November.[8]

One follow-up to the Enke report was the creation of the Central All-Volunteer Force Task Force in early 1972. One of the issues the task force was charged with studying was "women in the military." The topic seemed most appropriate when Congress passed the Equal Rights Amendment to the Constitution on March 22, 1972. Several weeks later, on April 6, 1972, Assistant Secretary Kelley instructed the services to "take action to eliminate all unnecessary [restrictions] applying to women" (Central All-Volunteer Force Task Force, 1972, p. 8). At the end of the year, the task force "conclud[ed] that the potential supply of military women could sustain a substantial increase in accession of military women" (Central All-Volunteer Force Task Force, 1972, p. 22).[9] The task force set a goal to increase the number of women in each service. The Navy and the Air Force submitted "action plans" that exceeded the task force's expectations. The situation is summarized in Table 15.1.

The goals, however, kept rising steadily. In February 1975, Bill Brehm's Manpower Office reported service goals for FY 1978 of 52,700 for the Army, and 24,800 for the Navy (OASD[M&RA], 1975). The Marine Corps remained unchanged, while the Air Force was the most aggressive. From an initial position of "no appreciable

---

[7] In his autobiography, *On Watch: A Memoir,* Admiral Zumwalt observed that, with the war in Vietnam winding down and the end of the draft in sight, "the Navy would have to compete head on for able young people not only with the other services but with the civilian economy." He was determined to "make the service more attractive and more satisfying" by addressing the "regulations and practices dealing with personal behavior," by reducing the time sailors spend away from their families, and by improving promotion opportunities for the brightest and most talented. He thought, however, that the "most important" thing he could do was to

> throw overboard once and for all the Navy's silent but real and persistent discrimination against minorities—not only blacks, the chief victims, but Puerto Ricans, American Indians, Chicanos, Filipinos, Orientals and, indeed, women as well—in recruiting, in training, in job assignment [and] in promotion. (Zumwalt, 1976, p. 168)

[8] Admiral Zumwalt discusses the opposition to assigning women to the USS *Sanctuary* (Zumwalt, 1976, p. 264). The 30-month pilot program on this hospital ship, which was scheduled to be decommissioned in 1975, demonstrated "that women were capable of serving in ships" (Ebbert and Hall, 1993, p. 215).

[9] The recommendation of the task force to almost double and the plans of the services to almost triple the number of women in uniform was not anticipated by at least some military sociologists. In a January 1973 article in the *American Journal of Sociology,* Nancy Goldman of the University of Chicago commented on "the profound organizational resistance and role strains associated with increasing the concentration of women in the armed forces" (Goldman, 1973, p. 892). She saw

> no reason to believe that the proportion of women in the armed forces will increase or that the range of their employment and responsibility will expand rapidly or dramatically with the advent of the all-volunteer force. However, . . . there is ample reason to expect a gradual increase in numbers and a slow but steady expansion of assignment. (Goldman, 1973, p. 910)

Table 15.1
Service Action Plans Compared to Task Force Goals,
Female Officer and Enlisted End Strength, FYs 1972 and 1977

| Military Services | End FY 1972 Actual | End FY 1977 | | |
		Task Force Goal	Service Action Plan	Over or Under Goal
Army	12,886	26,650	25,130	−1,520
Navy	6,724	11,400	20,921	+9,521
Air Force	12,766	22,800	38,007	+15,207
Marine Corps	2,329	3,100	2,800	−300
DoD	34,703	63,950	86,858	+22,908

SOURCE: Central All-Volunteer Force Task Force (1972, p. 46).

increase," the Air Force Personnel Chief, Lieutenant General John Roberts, told the DoD Committee on Women in the Services (DACOWITS) in 1974, the Air Force's program was "an ambitious one leading to a strength of approximately 50,000 women by the end FY 78. . . . This will be more than triple the number of women we had on board when we launched our program in FY 73" (Roberts, 1974, p. 2). In 1975, the decision was made and endorsed by Congress to open the service academies to women.[10]

The Carter administration's initial review of this issue was the May 1977 report, *Use of Women in the Military* (Hunter, 1977), that Secretary Brown had ordered within a week of taking office. The findings were updated with the publication of *America's Volunteer* in December 1978. As far as the administration was concerned "women are demonstrating that they are capable of playing an even larger part in national defense" (Nelson, 1978, p. 77). The goal for women as a percentage of the active-duty enlisted force for FY 1984 was set at 11.6 percent, with 80,000 enlisted women in the Army.[11] The manifestations of this "larger part in national defense" that women would play were everywhere to be seen. While in 1969 the Army's Project PROVIDE did not consider it feasible for women to be assigned to units below the corps level, the Army was telling unit commanders by September 1977 they were "authorized to employ women to accomplish unit missions throughout the battlefield. . . . Women are not excluded from performance of mission duty forward of the brigade rear boundary."[12] In the Navy, Judge John Sirica's decision on July 27, 1978, that Section 6015, which restricted

---

[10] Jeanne Holm, who was the Director of Women in the Air Force (WAF) at the time, has provided a firsthand account (1992, pp. 305–312). While the issue was settled in law and the first graduating class that included women was the class of 1980, women have not always been welcome at the academies; for example, see Conahan (1994). More recently the issues has highlighted sexual misconduct at the Air Force was examined in Fowler (2003).

[11] By the end of the Carter administration, the goal had risen to 87,500 for FY 1986, which was 12.5 percent of the enlisted force (Korb, 1981; Powell, 1981).

[12] Army Message quoted in Nelson (1978, p. 75).

women from all but hospital ships, like the USS *Sanctuary*, was unconstitutional because it "was premised on the notion that duty at sea is part of an essentially masculine tradition . . . more related to the traditional ways of thinking about women than to military preparedness" (Frontline, 1993) promised to open new opportunities for women at sea. With what at the time seemed the imminent passage of the Equal Rights Amendment to the Constitution, the Navy's most senior leaders, Secretary of the Navy Graham Claytor, Chief of Naval Operations James Holloway, and Chief of Naval Personnel James Watkins pressed Congress to allow women to serve on "ships that normally do not perform combat missions [and] temporarily on any ship for a period of no longer than six months" (Ebbert and Hall, 1993, p. 223). Congress agreed and amended the law accordingly. Still, by 1980, there were warnings that "the honeymoon is over."[13] The failure of the Equal Rights Amendment to gain the requisite number of states for approval, the Carter administration's decision not to allow women to register for the draft, and the strong opposition of the new Chief of Naval Operations, Thomas Hayward, to the complete repeal of the Section 6015 restrictions were warnings of things to come.[14]

The Army Takes a Pause: The WOMANPAUSE of 1981

Many, however, thought that the increased role women were playing, particularly in the Army, would be fleeting. In her landmark book, *Women in the Military: An Unfinished Revolution*, Major General Jeanne Holm, the first female general officer in the Air Force, observed that it seemed "a temporary condition that would pass with the demise of a misguided Carter administration." She summed up the attitude of "many military leaders, including *some senior women*" (emphasis added)[15]:

> It was no secret that, just below the surface of the military ranks at all levels, there persisted a deep well of resistance and even resentment toward women and their growing incursions into previously all-male preserves. Many . . . believed that military policy decisions were being made by well-meaning amateurs, with little or no service experience, who were motivated more by political expediency and misguided desires for social equity than by the requirements of national defense. (Holm, 1992, pp. 387–388)

---

[13] The term was attributed to Air Force Assistant Secretary (Manpower, Reserve Affairs and Installations), Joseph C. Zengerle, and used in a speech to DACOWITS on November 17, 1980 (cited in Stiehm, 1984, p. 182).

[14] *Author's Note:* The leadership in the Navy changed in fall 1978, with Edward Hidalgo replacing Graham Claytor as Secretary of the Navy, Tom Hayward replacing James Holloway as Chief of Naval Operations, and Robert Baldwin replacing James Watkins as Chief of Naval Personnel. During this period, I was the Principal Deputy Assistant Secretary of the Navy for Manpower and Reserve Affairs. I saw much of this play out before I left the Navy Secretariat to become Director of Selective Service in late November 1979. The issue came to a head on December 11, 1979, when Hayward openly broke with Hidalgo (Holm, 1992, p. 343). In my opinion, what was missing most was the leadership and vision of Graham Claytor and, most critically, Jim Watkins. Watkins was the most forward-looking senior officer I encountered in my 12 years of service at the Pentagon. He would also serve as the Chief of Naval Operations (1972–1976) and Secretary of Energy (1989–1993).

[15] For example, Ebbert and Hall (1993, p. 223) describes the opposition of some female naval officers to even the amendment of Section 6015 to allow women to serve on noncombatant ships.

With the defeat of the Carter administration, the Army decided the time was right to roll back the Carter program. The rollback was hinted at when, on February 26, 1981, Acting Assistant Secretary of the Army (Manpower and Reserve Affairs) William Clark told Congress that the "Army Staff is currently taking a new look at the entire issue of women soldiers" (Clark, 1981a). The next day, the extent of the rollback became clear when Clark told the Acting Assistant Secretary of Defense that the Army planned

> to level out the number of enlisted women in the Active Army at 65,000. . . . These modifications [reductions in projected end strength] were prompted by indications from field commanders that combat readiness is being affected by such factors as attrition, pregnancy, sole parenthood, and strength and stamina, which have come to light during the recent rapid increase in the number of women in the Army. (Clark, 1981b)[16]

This brought an immediate negative reaction from some in Congress and raised concerns within the new Weinberger team.[17] The new Senior Military Assistant to the Deputy Secretary of Defense, Brigadier General Colin Powell, recognized that "women make an enormous and indispensable contribution to the Army" but explained to his bosses that there was "a legitimate policy question of how many [women] should be in the force." As he saw it, the "misdemeanor the Army is guilty of is objecting to Congress about the OSD goal of 85,000 before objecting to the Secretary [of Defense] about the OSD goal of 85,000" (Powell, 1981).

Almost immediately, Deputy Secretary of Defense Frank Carlucci acted to take control of the situation. He told all the services that he wanted "a joint [OSD and the services] assessment of . . . female officer and enlisted accession and retention policies, [and] [t]he implications of the current and projected numbers of women in the force on readiness and mission effectiveness" within two months (Carlucci, 1981). As usual with such things, this would take a lot longer than two months. Within days, a subsequent memorandum formally changed the report originally due on May 15, 1981, to a "progress report," with a "final report" due no later than the following December or January. The memorandum pressed the dual purposes of the study squarely. The first issue reflected the services' concern for readiness, asking, for instance, how readiness and mission capability were affected by the existing or proposed levels of women in each service. While improved readiness was certainly a theme of the new administration, the

---

[16] According to General Holm, the Air Force feared that if the Army was allowed to reduce the number of women it was to recruit, the Air Force might have to take up the slack. General Holm has noted that "to forestall this possibility, the Air Staff set out to convince the Reagan transition team that the Air Force had as many women as it could take. But if the Army's case was weak, the Air Force's was weaker" (Holm, 1992, p. 391).

[17] The point was made in Senator Proxmire's news release of March 4, 1981 (Proxmire, 1981).

While the Army did not coordinate this position with the Secretary of Defense, it was widely reported that it had sent a confidential memorandum about its plans to the Reagan transition team (Stiehm, 1984, p. 187). However, as is often the case during a transition period, communications between the transition team and the new Pentagon administration were not always the most cordial. In any event, as the Army learned, communication with a transition team is not the same as communicating with the new Secretary of Defense.

services were reminded that viability of the volunteer force was also an issue of priority. The services were asked whether, if women's accession goals were lowered, what the cost of recruiting additional males to meet the required end strengths would be. Having been caught off guard by the Army's precipitous announcement of its intention to decrease its planned number of women, the administration told the services that this was an "excellent forum . . . to express and document concerns about the impact of women on mission capability and to consider the implications of revising existing accessions programs" (Stone, 1981).

In October 1981, Assistant Secretary of Defense Larry Korb's office published *Background Review: Women in the Military* (OASD[MRA&L], 1981). A staff summary noted the primary conclusions:

> (1) In general, military women are doing an excellent job; (2) military women are an integral part of the entire manpower issue and should not be addressed in isolation from all other aspects of personnel management; and (3) since the understanding and evaluation of Service-unique issues is complex and difficult, more latitude should be given the Services in their management of women as a part of their total force, although continuing oversight should be exercised by OSD functional area managers. (Thie, 1982)

Holm thought the report "added little to what was already known on the subject" (Holm, 1992, p. 393). While she noted that the document gave the Army and the other services "essentially what [they] . . . had hoped for," it put the Army on notice that "should the Army fail to meet its recruiting, end strength, or quality goals . . . it will be necessary for them to demonstrate why female accessions should not be increased." The Army was told that it could "continue recruiting the number of women required to stabilize its end strength at 65,000 women until such time as it completed its review of policies concerning women" (ASD[MRA&L], 1981, p. 96).

If some saw in the report a vindication of the Army's position, particularly endorsing the claim that the Carter administration had acted arbitrarily in setting a series of goals without "full consideration of Service mission requirements and other personnel management concerns" (ASD[MRA&L], 1981, p. 10), the notion that equal opportunity or accession requirements of the all-volunteer force would not be important was misplaced. A headline in the *Washington Post* in July, just as the administration announced the formation of the All-Volunteer Force Task Force under the leadership of Secretary Weinberger, hinted at how far the Army had miscalculated. The headline was: "Army Hints Draft May Be Required." As reported, the Army wanted 100,000 more soldiers "to carry out President Reagan's military strategy and that it [the Army] doubts they can be recruited under 'the volunteer concept' suggesting a return to the draft" (Wilson, 1981, p. 1). Holm reported that even the hint of bringing back conscription "landed like a live grenade on the third floor of the Pentagon," noting that one DoD official had "described the Secretary's reaction as livid" (Holm, 1992, p. 395).

Weinberger's spokesman told the *Washington Post*, "the draft is not anything anybody is considering" (Wilson, 1981). If anything, the new group of civilian leaders in the Pentagon saw the increased, rather than decreased, use of women as important to the Reagan buildup and the sustainment of the all-volunteer force policy. Within weeks of the publication of the background review, Secretary Weinberger set the definitive statement on the policy of the Reagan administration on women in the military:

> Women in the military are a very important part of our total force capability. Qualified women are essential to obtaining the numbers of quality people required to maintain the readiness of our forces. This Administration desires to increase the role of women in the military, and I expect the Service Secretaries actively to support that policy.
>
> While we have made much progress, some institutional barriers still exist. I ask that you personally review your Service Policies to ensure that women are not subject to discrimination in recruiting or career opportunities. This Department must aggressively break down those remaining barriers that prevent us from making the fullest use of the capabilities of women in providing for our national defense. (Weinberger, 1982)

Removing Institutional Barriers for Women

From now on, Weinberger told the services, their focus should not be on rolling back the gains women had made since the advent of the all-volunteer force or even on limiting the gains to levels achieved at the end of the previous administration. Their focus should be on "eliminating barriers." Korb explained, however, that central to the issue of eliminating barriers was the question of combat exclusions. If combat exclusions were legitimate, he told the Secretary of Defense that summer, "the barriers that result are neither artificial nor discriminatory" (Korb, 1982b). To implement Weinberger's policy, his office became "involved in the time-consuming process of reviewing each of the Services' complex methodologies . . . to determine [appropriate] levels of women" for them (Korb, 1982b). On September 2, 1982, Korb reported to Deputy Secretary Carlucci on his review of accession methodology and enlistment standards for enlisted women (Korb, 1982c).

Table 15.2 shows the projected end-strength of enlisted women based on the service methodologies developed during 1982, compared with the numbers the Central All-Volunteer Force Task Force recommended, the services' end FY 1977 projections, and the goals of the Carter administration for FY 1984. While the new projections were substantially greater than what was thought possible during the early years of the all-volunteer force, they were substantially lower than the Carter administration's projections. The numbers, however, were more rigorously derived from a widely reviewed methodology and, coming from a Republican administration, represented a floor on which further expansion might build in the future.

Table 15.2
Service Action Plans Compared to Task Force Goals,
Female Officer and Enlisted End Strength

Military Services	End FY 1972 Actual	End FY 1977 Task Force Goal	End FY 1977 Service Action Plan	FY 1984 Goal[a]	Maximum Projected End Strength[b]
Army	12,886	26,650	25,130	80,000	70,000
Navy	6,724	11,400	20,921	40,000	45,000
Air Force	12,766	22,800	38,007	80,000	63,000
Marine Corps	2,329	3,100	2,800	8,000	9,100
Total DoD	34,703	63,950	86,858	208,000	187,100

SOURCES: Central All-Volunteer Force Task Force (1972, p. 46), Korb (1982c), and Nelson (1978, p. 70).

[a]As set by the Carter administration.

[b]As set by the Reagan administration.

The Women in the Army Policy Review

The Army confirmed its new methodology for determining the number of women it would take by publishing its long-awaited report, *Women in the Army Policy Review,* on November 12, 1982 (Deputy Chief of Staff for Personnel, 1982).[18] The preparation of the report had been very controversial.[19] This was the report that the Army had promised would be prepared when it asked for the "womenpause" at the beginning of the Reagan administration almost two years earlier. It was the report that Korb had deferred to when he published his background study more than a year before. In some ways, it was a shadow of what was expected. The report focused on only two issues: military occupational specialty (MOS) physical demands and direct combat probability (the combat exclusion policy). The burning social issues that many saw to be at the heart of the debate and which were captured in the term "truly radical social experiment" were either passed to the Office of the Secretary of Defense (such as the pregnancy policy[20]) or not dealt with at all (such as single parents and military couples[21]).

---

[18] It was actually released at the DACOWITS meeting at Fort Bragg on November 18, 1982, after what Stiehm described as "a dramatic showdown with substantial press coverage, flights by generals from the Pentagon, and public statements by uniformed women stationed at Fort Bragg" (Stiehm, 1984, p. 195).

[19] There were particular concerns because without waiting for the report the Army had decided to resegregate basic training. The issue of gender mixed training would surface again during the Clinton administration. For a discussion of the events around the resegregation of Army basic training, see Stiehm (1984).

[20] See Tice (1982) and Korb (1982d).

[21] In a review for the Secretary of Defense in 1984, Korb noted that while "OSD does not have a policy on single-parent enlistments" for the Navy and Marine Corps, "single parents are not eligible for enlistment unless they place their children in the legal custody (by court order) of other individuals" (Korb, 1984). The issue, however, was the subject of litigation.

The issue of effectiveness was reserved to an inquiry of physical strength and the legislative restriction on exposure to direct and close combat was all that was left of issues of military effectiveness, readiness, and unit cohesion. Apparently, the systematic research prepared for the OSD and Army studies did not support the dire anecdotal tales of an ineffective and less-ready military that some had counted on. What Justice Marshall had referred to as "the old canard" about women—"the inherently weaker female who left to her own devices will probably [become] pregnant, is most concerned with parenting and can't be relied upon at certain times of the month" (Stiehm, 1984, p. 192)—was absent from the final report.

The number of women that the Army might be able to use, projected to be 70,000—5,000 above the "womanpause" number of 65,000, but 17,000 less than the number the Carter administration had projected—was still controversial. Korb told Weinberger, "Nothing could do more to dispel the wide-spread impression that the Review has been 'rigged' . . . [than to] proceed to raise the number of women in the Army to 70,000" (Korb, 1982a). On the other hand, the chairperson of DACOWITS, Mary Evelyn Blagg Huey, writing for the committee, expressed concern that

> [t]he elimination of women from participation in a broad spectrum of military occupations because of calculations of the potential for involvement in the "forward" battle area deprives our Army of many skilled soldiers. This reduces available manpower, both because "combat risk" women are removed from the specialties and because the jobs they otherwise do must be assumed by male soldiers. . . . [W]e are concerned that the closing of military occupations impacts negatively on career development for women, making their advancement difficult if not impossible and closing the higher ratings and rankings to women. In addition, . . . this "domino effect" poses concerns for morale, enlistments, and the continued success of the all-volunteer Army. (Huey, 1983)

The Army reassessed the coding system, restoring some jobs but eliminating others, and briefed DACOWITS the following fall (1983). In response to an inquiry on the subject from the United States Commission on Civil Rights, Weinberger told its chairman that "the Army has done everything in its power to be objective and it will implement the combat coding with great care and sensitivity" (Weinberger, 1983b).

The last phase of this chapter of women in the military came in summer 1983, when Secretary Weinberger, alarmed by reports in the news media of changes in the policy for the utilization of women, felt it necessary to send a reminder to the services:

> I want to state it again. It is the policy of this Department that women will be provided full and equal opportunity with men to pursue appropriate careers in the military services for which they can qualify. This means that military women can and should be utilized in all roles except those explicitly prohibited by combat exclusion statutes and related policy. This does *not* mean that the combat exclusion policy can be used to justify closing career opportunities to women. The combat exclusion rules should be interpreted to allow as many as possible career opportunities for women to be kept open. (Weinberger, 1983a, emphasis in the original)

He put to rest the challenge that Army leaders had brought in the name of force effectiveness and readiness three years before. Weinberger found

> Women contribute significantly toward the high state of *readiness* we currently enjoy under the all-volunteer force. While [the utilization of women] . . . must be predicated on Service needs and individual capabilities, no artificial barriers to career opportunity for women will be constructed or tolerated. (Weinberger, 1983a, emphasis added)

The next chapters of the saga would now be fought out over the issue of combat exclusions.

Combat Exclusion

While Weinberger's words were strong and clear—"military women can and should be utilized in all roles expect those explicitly prohibited by combat exclusion statutes and related policy" (Weinberger, 1983a)—could these words be carried out in the face of the combat exclusions that, in the views of many, made women second-class citizens?

Even before Weinberger issued his clarifying memorandum to the service secretaries, Korb provided him an indication of things to come. In April 1983, noting his staff's review of a 192-page listing of company-size "units which were closed to women because they were evaluated as units in which all members would be exposed to direct combat in the main battle area," Korb told Weinberger that there appeared "to be some inconsistencies in the way the Army went about applying its methodology. . . . [W]e found units whose composition and mission made their closure based on individual position classification suspect" (Korb, 1983). The issue was raised in fall 1987, after "a particularly negative DACOWITS report following their trip to the Pacific" (Armor, 1988, p. 1). Weinberger established a task force under the leadership of the Principal Deputy Assistant Secretary of Defense David Armor to "review policies and recommend changes . . . in three areas: attitudes toward and treatment of women; consistency in application of combat exclusion statutes and policies; and career development" (Armor, 1988). Within months, the task force had confirmed DACOWITS's misgivings and reported that, "despite vigorous institutional efforts to prevent it, sexual harassment remains a significant problem in all Services" (Armor, 1988). In fact, it would remain a significant problem well into and through the 1990s. Such future events as the Navy's Tailhook affair, the Army training scandals at Aberdeen, and the sexual assault cases at the U.S. Air Force Academy into the early years of the 21st century attest to the persistency of this issue.

The task force also found problems concerning the implementation of the combat exclusion rules. It made specific recommendations concerning a number of occupations, but most importantly, found the need for new and "clear guidance on the grounds for closing noncombatant positions or units, since such closings are not required by law and they have created our major consistency problems" (Armor, 1988). Apparently, the task force reported, Secretary Weinberger's pronouncement that "the combat exclusion rules should be interpreted to allow as many as possible career opportunities for women to be kept open" (Weinberger, 1983a) was not clear enough for some people. "Social and organization inhibitors," they told the Weinberger successor, Frank Carlucci, "as well as laws concerning combat exclusion, have resulted in assignment and classification policies based on gender" (Armor, 1988, p. 2). As result, in what David Armor would remember years later as its "most significant recommendation" (Armor, 2002), the task force proposed a new "at risk rule . . . to permit closure of noncombatant positions or units if their risks of exposure to hostile fire or capture are equal or greater than the risk for land, air or sea combat units with which they are associated in a theater of operations" (Armor, 1988).

This, more than any other change, opened up new jobs for women. In less than two years, Assistant Secretary Jehn reported to Congress that, as a result of the new "at risk" rule, "31,000 new positions were opened to women in both the active and reserve components [and] over 63 percent of all positions in the Services are now open to women" (Jehn, 1990, p. 17).

Tested in War: Operation Just Cause and Operation Desert Storm

The incursion into Panama (Operation Just Cause) in December 1989 raised concerns about what the combat exclusion meant. It was clear from firsthand reports that women were serving in a hostile place and that some were taking and returning fire. Was this not combat? Jehn explained:

> Female service members are not absolutely prohibited by law or policy from taking part in hostilities. In accordance with the combat exclusion statutes and related Army policy, women are not assigned direct combat roles; the support and service support units to which they are assigned, however, may still encounter hostilities to varying degrees in the performance of required missions. All members of such organizations are trained to operate and employ weapons issued under unit tables of organization and equipment. Accordingly, military women are authorized and expected, if necessary, to use assigned weapons in self-defense, to protect the lives of others, or in the line of duty (e.g., military police, sentries). The female soldiers in Panama were not members of combat units; they performed combat support duties. Thus, no combat exclusion law or policies were violated. The women in Panama performed the duties expected of them, and they performed them quite well. (Jehn, 1990, p. 23)[22]

In a little over a year, Jehn was back before Congress, this time discussing the performance of women during Operation Desert Storm "and our views regarding the proposed changes to the combat exclusion statutes" (Jehn, 1991b, p. 805). He told the Senate Armed Services Committee that, by all indications, "women who served in the

---

[22] *Author's Note:* In 1999, when I was Under Secretary of the Army, my military aide-de-camp was Major Sabrina Sanfillipo, a female military policeman. When she was a young captain, she parachuted into Panama during Operation Just Cause. A decade later, the fact that she "saw action" gave her a further measure of respect in her community.

Gulf performed their duties magnificently. They served in hundreds of different [skilled positions] on land, at sea, and in the air. Many served as commanders and as key staff officers" (Jehn, 1991b, p. 806). In a larger sense, he told the senators, the "expanded career opportunities for women in the military . . . [had] reached the point where further expansion of opportunities is very difficult within the current combat exclusion laws" (Jehn, 1991b, p. 806). Noting the moves in both the Senate and the House to relax the combat exclusion rules, particularly with regard to women flying combat aircraft, he expressed concern that such a change, without addressing the issue of women serving on combat vessels, would "inadvertently create inequalities or inconsistencies" (Jehn, 1991b, pp. 806–807).

Importantly, Jehn was passive concerning the possible changes to the combat exclusion statutes Congress was considering, except in his desire to have "maximum flexibility" in managing any change they passed, and assured the senators that he would use their guidance "as the benchmark for our efforts" (Jehn, 1991b, p. 807). Senator McCain, for one, was not satisfied, wanting DoD "to make recommendations to the Congress" (Jehn, 1991b, p. 811). Jehn pushed back: "I do not think the Department of Defense ought to be a sole actor here. . . . If you want to engage us in a dialogue. . . we look forward to discussing this with you" (Jehn, 1991b, p. 811). But a mere dialogue was not what Senator McCain had in mind. Senator Kennedy expressed the committee's "disappoint[ment] that the administration has not got a position and some recommendations on this issue [combat exclusion] so that we could give some consideration to it" (Jehn, 1991b, p. 815). In fact, Jehn was following a strategy that he and Secretary of Defense Dick Cheney had agreed to weeks before. Jehn had told Cheney that

> [u]nless we wish to take the lead in altering current policy (and hence, implicitly endorse repeal of the combat exclusion laws), . . . the Department should continue to insist that any major change in law or policy governing women in combat be made only after full, open, and inclusive national debate—and that debate should take place in Congress. (Jehn, 1991a)

The debate would take place in many forums, including the Presidential Commission on the Assignment of Women in the Armed Services.

Presidential Commission on the Assignment of Women in the Armed Services

In 1991, Congress repealed the combat exclusion as it pertained to women flying combat aircraft and, in a compromise move, established a commission to study the issue further.[23] Representative Beverley Byron, the Chairman of the Military Personnel and Compensation Subcommittee of the House Armed Services Committee, reacting to criticism that the House had passed the measure without adequate public notice or

---

[23] Holm (1992, pp. 473–510) covers the action by Congress.

debate, saw the change as "the logical next step in an incremental process to expand the role of women in the Armed Forces . . . fueled by the evolution in attitudes over the last decade" (Jehn, 1992, pp. 1–2). She told her critics that there was

> no backroom political [plot]. There are no women's rights conspiracies involved in this issue. Just the simple recognition by the American people that it is acceptable of women to endure the same hardships and the same dangers as men, and to volunteer for military duties for which they are capable. (As quoted in Jehn, 1992, p. 2)[24]

In hearings before Congress, Jehn delivered DoD's response:

> The Department is pleased with the new authority and flexibility provided by the recent repeal of most of the statuary limitations on the assignment of women to aircraft engaged in combat missions. As a result of the lifting of these restrictions the services are currently evaluating the many issues associated with potential changes involved with expanding opportunities for women in combat aircraft. . . . Many of the areas being looked at by the services concerning the placement of women into combat aircraft will be addressed by the Presidential Commission. . . . We also think the Commission will be helpful in resolving many of the issues that need to be addressed. . . . We look forward to working with the Presidential Commission, assisting it in its deliberations and, finally, to reviewing its recommendations. (Jehn, 1992, pp. 5–6)

The commission, consisting of nine men and seven women, spent seven months taking testimony from more than 300 witnesses. It solicited comments from more than 3,000 retired officers, considered 11,000 letters and statements, and visited 22 military installations. The commission, however, will most be remembered for the acrimony it generated, both within and outside.[25] From the beginning, the commission was criticized for focusing on "cultural issues" rather than on issues of military effectiveness as Congress had directed (Sagawa and Campbell, 1992) "and stood accused of being weighted in favor of conservative factions opposed to relaxing the combat exclusion rule for women" (Cilliers, 1993). In fact, many of the commissioners were known to have well-formed views on the subject.[26] While some believed that "no one who had

---

[24] Culler (2000, pp. 64–74) provides an accounting of the legislative process that led to the repeal of the combat exclusion for assignment to aircraft flying a combat mission.

[25] For a more complete accounting, see Culler (2000, pp. 75–80).

[26] Two commissioners had long associations with the all-volunteer force, Charlie Moskos and now-retired Army General Max Thurman. Thurman, noted for the recruiting turnaround of the early 1980s, had subsequently been the Army's Deputy Chief of Staff for Personnel when the Direct Combat Probability System was installed in 1983. Retired Army Colonel Darryl Henderson, former commander of the Army Research Institute and author of *Cohesion: The Human Element in Combat*, had written extensively on the subject of unit cohesion and had argued that it was best achieved when members of a unit were from the same socioeconomic class. He had concluded that cohesion could not be developed in mixed gender units. Elaine Donnelly is president of the Center for Military Readiness and a frequent critic of defense personnel policies. All four would again be central figures in the debate on homosexual rights in the military.

actively advocated increasing women's roles was appointed" (Sagawa and Campbell, 1992), the most politically active commissioner, Elaine Donnelly, complained to Secretary of Defense Cheney that the chairman, Robert Herres, a retired Air Force general and former Vice Chairmen of the Joint Staff, was a "strong supporter of women in air and sea combat" (Donnelly et al., 1992) and that the "close Commission votes all provided clear indications that there are strong differences of opinion on the subject of women in combat" (Donnelly et al., 1992).

Despite the charge that the commission was stacked with conservatives, the majority report was seen as too liberal for several of its more conservative members. Five commissioners signed an "Alternative View Section" that summarized what they thought was "a consistent case against the use of women in any kind of combat role" (Donnelly et al., 1992). Their main argument was the "Commission's limited support for the assignment of women to some combatant ships," which they saw as "inconsistent with the other major recommendations" (Hoar, 1993). They asked Secretary Cheney for an appointment to press their case. Even if the majority of the commission could not see it, they believed that "the solid record of testimony and facts which were presented during the Commission's hearings and deliberations provided a significant amount of convincing new evidence that it would be unwise as well as unnecessary to assign women to combat roles" (Donnelly et al., 1992). Since the report was finished after the 1992 Presidential elections, Cheney, as the outgoing Secretary of Defense, would not be drawn into the debate. It would fall to the new Secretary of Defense, Les Aspin, to respond to Donnelly, to review the recommendations of the commission, and to implement whatever changes were to be forthcoming.

While the majority report was too liberal for the five commissioners who signed the Alternative View Section, many found the same majority report too conservative. They objected to the major recommendations, which Jakkie Cilliers (Cilliers, 1993, pp. 2–3, emphasis in the original) described as

- the retention of existing policies which did not allow for the assignment of Service women to Special Operations Forces apart from service in a medical, linguistic or civil affairs capacity;
- that the military services adopt "gender-neutral assignment policies" to ensure that no one is denied access to a post open to both men and women on the basis of gender;
- urging the Pentagon to consider adopting policies that would disallow assignments that would separate single parents from children too young for school or take more than one parent in a dual-military service family away from home;
- acknowledging the physiological differences between men and women, and calling on services to *retain gender-specific physical fitness tests and standards to promote the highest level of general fitness and wellness.* In a military well known for its quantification of every aspect of military duties this is bound to result in a large

number of specific physical, mental and moral standards for every conceivable military job open to both genders.

- a new law banning women from air combat positions (18 months after Congress repealed an identical law) as well as urging legislation to exclude women from ground combat assignments in the infantry, artillery and armor, as well as certain assignments in air defense and combat engineers;
- opening non-flying jobs to women on Navy combat ships while disqualifying women from service in submarines and landing aircraft.

Once the new administration took office, the role of women quickly took backstage to the heated issue of homosexual rights as President Clinton tried to fulfill his campaign promise to allow openly gay men and women to serve in the armed forces. While most activists focused on the issue of gays in the military, Secretary Aspin and Clinton acted to expand opportunities for women. On April 23, 1993, President Clinton ordered the services to open combat aviation to women and to investigate other opportunities for women to serve. Five days later Aspin ordered the services to "permit women to compete for assignments in aircraft including aircraft engaged in combat missions" (Aspin, 1993). He told the Navy to

> open as many additional ships to women as is practicable within current law [and to] develop a legislative proposal . . . to repeal the existing combat exclusion law and permit the assignment of women to ships that are engaged in combat missions. (Aspin, 1993)

He told the Army and Marine Corps "to study opportunities for women to serve in additional assignments, including, but not limited to, field artillery and air defense artillery" (Aspin, 1993) and established a high level "Implementation Committee" to look at "the appropriateness of the 'Risk Rule'" (Aspin, 1993).[27]

As one might expect, Aspin's actions met with conflicting reactions. The former Chief of Naval Operations, Admiral Zumwalt, offered his

> [h]eartiest congratulations and my sincere compliments . . . concerning [the] . . . new policy on the assignment of women on the armed forces. I consider your actions to be the logical fruition of the highly controversial programs that I initiated in the early 1970s—sending women to sea on the USS Sanctuary and

---

[27] The Deputy Assistant Secretary (Military Manpower and Personnel Policy), Air Force Major General Robert (Minter) Alexander established the Implementation Committee. He told the Deputy Secretary of Defense that

> the study panel [was] reviewing the DoD Risk Rule . . . focusing their efforts on developing a definition of direct combat on the ground. . . . [W]e are [also] reviewing occupational physical standards as we deem this to be an important element regarding assignment policies. (Alexander, 1993a)

In August, Assistant Secretary of Defense (Personnel and Readiness) Edwin Dorn reported to Aspin "good progress in implementing your April 28 memorandum" (Dorn, 1993).

through pilot training. Your action took administrative courage and I salute you. (Zumwalt, 1993)

Elaine Donnelly saw in the new policy

little evidence that [your] . . . Administration has given serious consideration to the Commission's majority vote on combat aviation, or to the significant and consistent findings summarized in the Alterative Views Section of the Commission report. (Donnelly, 1993)[28]

With regard to the former commission's findings, Aspin had a response. On May 11, he wrote Congressman Ike Skelton, Chairman of the Military Force and Personnel Subcommittee: "My direction is . . . consistent with the . . . [commission's] recommendations. The one position I took that was contrary to the commission's recommendations was on the issue of assigning women to combat aircraft" (Aspin, 1993).

Using the same logic that Donnelly had tried to use on Secretary Cheney, the closeness of the vote, Aspin argued the opposite case. As he saw it, since "the Commission's recommendation on this issue was based on a very close vote, with eight members supporting the continued exclusion, and the remaining seven supporting the assignment of women to combat aircraft" (Aspin, 1993), he was not totally outside the spirit of the commission when he ignored this recommendation. Donnelly, of course, saw it differently. She later complained that the "Clinton administration ignored the commission's report," and chided a Congress that "failed to schedule full-scale hearings on its findings and recommendations" (Donnelly, 2003).

In early 1994, Aspin was ready to announce the results of the committee he had chartered the previous spring. The committee recommended establishment of a ground combat rule for assigning women in the armed forces. The following would be DoD's policy henceforth:

Women shall be excluded from assignment to units below the brigade level whose primary mission is to engage in direct combat on the ground . . . with individual or crew served weapons, while being exposed to hostile fire and to a high probability of direct physical contact with hostile force's personnel. (Aspin, 1994)

---

[28] A deputy assistant secretary, a person considerably lower in bureaucratic stature than the person Donnelly had addressed, signed the formal response to Donnelly's letter to the Secretary of Defense. General Alexander assured Ms. Donnelly that the secretary was

familiar with the detailed "Alternative Views Section" . . . you co-authored and considered its contents in his deliberations on this issue. In addition, while in Congress, he reviewed many of these same issues before voting to repeal the combat exclusion provisions regarding the assignment of women to aircraft engaged in combat missions. (Alexander, 1993b)

After the "risk rule" was changed, Donnelly again wrote to the Secretary of Defense—this time to Aspin's successor, Secretary of Defense William Perry.[29] She thought the change betrayed "a civilian-oriented mindset that puts the career ambitions of a few women ahead of the needs of the Army and the armed forces as a whole" (Donnelly, 1994). This time, Secretary of the Army Togo West responded for the department, stating that "the Department of Defense rescinded the 'risk rule' . . . because it was no longer realistic given the nature of the modern battlefield" (West, 1994). The issue of the nature of the modern battlefield would, however, be raised again a decade later, during the war in Iraq.

In spring 2005, with the traditional lines between areas of combat and rear support areas blurred by the insurgencies in Iraq and Afghanistan, the House Military Personnel Subcommittee moved to "ban women from serving in certain support units in a bid to keep them out of 'direct ground combat'" (Tyson, 2005a). The Subcommittee Chairman, Duncan Hunter (R-California) declared that the "American people have never wanted to have women in combat and this reaffirms that policy" (Tyson, 2005a). In a move that showed how much things had changed since the days of Project PROVIDE in 1969, the Army, in a public statement, told the committee that the proposed legislation was "unnecessary [and] does not provide further clarification, and may in fact lead to confusion on the part of commanders and Soldiers" (Department of the Army, 2005b). In the face of overwhelming opposition from Secretary Rumsfeld and the leadership of the Army, Chairman Hunter relented somewhat by insisting only that DoD give Congress "60 days of continuous session" notice of any change in policy or practice before it opens or closes positions to women (Tyson, 2005b). Hunter's move, however, was a trap, because the "60 days of continuous session" (unbroken by an adjournment of either chamber) requirement would effectively mean a delay of six months or longer. Moreover, the demand that DoD notify Congress of changes in practice, not merely changes in policy, was a new reporting requirement that would effectively stall even the most mundane change. While DoD hoped to have this provision overturned in conference with the Senate, the final bill maintained the general provision reducing the notice period to 30 days of continuous session (Ground Combat and Other Exclusion Policies, Section 541 of the National Defense Authorization Act of 2006).

---

[29] After the "risk rule" was changed, Congress expressed "concern that that current DoD training standards were not, in fact, gender-neutral and could therefore potentially have a negative effect on morale and readiness" (Staff of the Directorate for Accession Policy, 1995, p. 1). In the spirit of equal opportunity, DoD responded by telling Congress "that readiness will be enhanced, not degraded, by accounting for individual differences in physical abilities, but . . . additional formal standards [by occupation] are not necessary" (Staff of the Directorate for Accession Policy, 1995, p. 10). The issue of gender-neutral standards was raised again during President Clinton's second term as part of a broader inquire on gender-integrated training.

Women as Supporters of the All-Volunteer Force: The Military as a Family-Friendly Institution

Traditionally, military life has not been "family friendly." The American Army first took note of members' families in 1794, when a death allocation of cash was provided "widows and orphans of officers killed in battle" (Department of the Army, 2005a, p. 28). The "benefit" was later extended to the families of noncommissioned officers (NCOs). Married soldiers were expected to provide for their families' needs.

> Wives, known as "camp followers," could receive half-rations when they accompanied their spouse and performed services such as cooking, sewing, cleaning barracks, working in hospitals, and even loading and firing muskets. (Department of the Army, 2005a, p. 29)

In 1802, the Army authorized company laundresses, and many of these ladies married NCOs. By regulation, however, the Army barred officers from marrying until their captaincy; NCOs and enlisted men required permission from their company commanders to marry. Starting in 1847, Congress prohibited the enlistment of married men in the Army.

After the Civil War, the Army followed a policy of discouraging married men from serving. In an effort to reduce the number of families, the Army provided family quarters only for senior officers. Married men could not enlist, and the Army provided little assistance to service members with wives and children. The Army did not provide housing for married enlisted men, did not provide transportation for families when soldiers permanently changed duty stations, and "obstructed" the reenlistment of married soldiers. Whatever support the families of married enlisted personnel got came from the largesse of the wives of officers and NCOs (Department of the Army, 2005a, p. 29). Up until World War II, with the exception of the World War I period, the adage that "if the Army had wanted you to have a wife, it would have issued you one" aptly summed up the Army's attitude toward families.

During World War I, while most married men were not drafted, the government still had to provide support for those who were. As a result, during World War I, the first program of family allotments for officers and enlisted personnel, voluntary insurance against death and disability, was started. It was not until the of the 1940s, however, that Congress provided government housing for soldiers E-4 and above with family members and, after the start of hostilities, authorized a basic allowance for quarters for military families residing in civilian communities. During World War II, when the exclusion of married men from the service was no longer feasible, Congress provided a monthly family allowance for a wife and each child. Married females, however, continued to be barred from enlistment and could be separated from the service because of pregnancy, marriage, and parenthood, a policy that remained in effect until 1975. In February 1942, to deal more effectively with family emergencies, the Secretary of War created the Army Emergency Relief (AER) program. The AER adopted the slogan, "The Army

Takes Care of its Own," a slogan that would have more meaning with the advent of the all-volunteer force two decades later (Department of the Army, 2005a, p. 30).

After World War II, the Cold War–era Army in no way resembled the prewar organization of the same name. The postwar Army was many times the size of the prewar Army and had worldwide responsibilities. The Army's approach to addressing family concerns, however, remained reactive and piecemeal. The development of the Army Community Services (ACS) organization in 1965, at the start of the buildup for Vietnam, was the Army's first attempt to create an umbrella approach for family support. It took the move to the all-volunteer force to really change things.

Recruiting Soldiers and Retaining Families: The Development of Army Family Programs in the All-Volunteer Force

On the eve of the all-volunteer force, the *Fiscal Year 1971 Department of the Army Historical Summary* made no mention of military families per se, except by implication. It expressed concern that "the Army needs a total of 353,440 housing units for eligible families [when] available family housing on and off post totals 220,600 units" (Bell, 1973, p. 55). By 1978, however, the Army understood that its approach to its Quality of Life Program, originally established "to improve services and activities for enlisted personnel in their daily life," needed to be expanded "to bolster community life support activities" (Boldan, 1982, p. 91). Citing the all-volunteer force, the Army noted that, before the end of the draft,

> less than half of the soldiers were married. By the end of 1977, over 60 percent fell into that category, many more were sole parents, and a considerable number were married to other soldiers. The changing composition of the Army has necessitated increased attention to community services to sustain morale and retain highly qualified personnel. (Boldan, 1982, p. 91)

In 1979, the Army, recognizing that even the most junior enlisted members had families, established "a family separation allowance for service members in grades E-1 to E-4" (Brown, 1983, p. 110).

Even as the Army was trying the curtail the increases in the number of women soldiers, the leadership understood that families were here to stay. The Deputy Chief of Staff for Personnel told the Army in March 1980 that their

> commitment to the Army family has been made at the highest level. We know that the Quality of Life impacts on readiness and on attracting and retaining quality soldiers the Army needs. We've got to continue to get better in this vital area, and through our efforts, provide meaning to the [resurrected World War II] slogan: "The Army Takes Care of Its Own." (Brown, 1983, p. 92)

By resurrecting that slogan about taking care of its own, the Army made a major commitment to child-care programs. By FY 1980, the Army had 281 child-care programs (159 day care and 122 preschool) in operation.

In October 1980, the first Army Family Symposium was held in Washington, D.C., sponsored by the Army Officers' Wives Club of the Greater Washington Area and the Association of the United States Army. Almost 200 delegates and observers attended. The symposium resulted in the creation of the Family Action Committee. Following their recommendations, the Chief of Staff of the Army established the Family Liaison Office within the Office of the Deputy Chief of Staff for Personnel to oversee all family issues. On September 8, 1981, the Adjutant General's Office opened the Army Family Life Communications Line at the Pentagon and developed a quarterly family newsletter to be distributed to Army families worldwide (Hardyman, 1988, p. 109).[30]

On August 15, 1983, Army Chief of Staff John A. Wickham signed the *Army Family White Paper—The Army Family,* which has been described as a "landmark document [that] underscored the Army's recognition that families affect the Army's ability to accomplish its mission" (Department of the Army, 2005a, p. 30). It provided for the annual Army Family Action Plan; the Army theme for 1984, "Year of the Family"; and the establishment of installation-based Family Centers.

With the end of the Cold War and with America at peace, the issues the delegates brought to the Army Family Action Plan (AFAP) conference in the early 1990s seemed rather mundane[31]:

> inadequate housing allowances, comprehensive dental care, and enhanced family programs for the Total Army were among top issues identified in 1990. Inequitable military pay, the need for increased marketing of CHAMPUS, and underutilized teen programs were issues identified in 1991. (Janes, 1997, p. 49)

The situation changed, however, when Iraq invaded Kuwait in summer 1991.

The Army's Volunteer Families Go to War: Family Assistance Centers

Simultaneous with the initial deployment of troops to Saudi Arabia and as a harbinger of things to come, the ACS established and operated 24-hour Family Assistance Centers (FACs) at the seven stateside posts from which large numbers of troops deployed.

---

[30] Attitudes were also changing as the *Army Historical Summary* notes,

> The Chief of Staff also directed the general use in Army publications of the terms *family member* or *souse* [sic] in place of *dependent,* and he issued a policy statement supporting the right of family members to be employed without limiting a service member's assignment or position in the government. The policy statement read in part: "The inability of a spouse personally to volunteer services or perform a role to complement the service-member's discharge of military duties normally is a private matter and should not be a factor in the individual's selection for a military position." (Hardyman, 1988, pp. 109–110, emphasis in the original)

[31] It should be noted that

> [i]n November 1989 Congress passed the Military Child Care Act (MCCA). This legislation stipulated minimum appropriated funding and staff levels, higher wages, and better training for child care staffs; user fees based on family income; national accreditation of child development centers; and unannounced inspections of local child development services (CDS) programs and facilities. (Janes, 1997, pp. 50–51)

The FACs brought together, "under one roof," chaplains, lawyers, relief workers, and other social service specialists to provide information and counseling. The ACS trained "unit support groups" and provided relocation information, consumer and financial advice, employment counseling, aid to exceptional family members, and other services. Unit support groups and such traditional support groups as the United Services Organization (USO), American Legion, Young Men's Christian Association, and American Red Cross provided information and helped with child care, housing, and financial problems. From August 1990 through January 1991, AER helped 31,000 soldiers and their families with $17 million in grants and interest-free loans (Janes, 1997).

Soon after the first troops went to the Middle East in August 1990, the Army established a toll-free hotline in an operations center in Alexandria, Virginia, to support the reserve components and families at installations without FACs. The hotline was manned 24/7 through April 1991, and after that on reduced hours until July 1991. The center logged 80,000 calls during these nine months.

For the Army, the lessons of Desert Storm were that "family members of deployed service members had innumerable problems and questions, felt confused and abandoned, and often did not know where to turn to obtain resolution or answers" (Reeves, 1998, p. 122). To address these needs and to "create self-sufficient and self-reliant individuals and families who could cope with the stress of deployment," the Army developed the Family Team Building Program, established family support groups as a major source of support for every deployment and declared that "[q]uality of life is the Army's third highest priority, immediately behind readiness and modernization" (Reeves, 1998, p. 122).

Meeting the Continuing Needs of Military Families

A 2001 Morale and Quality of Life Study found, however, that the "family support system has not kept pace with the changing family structure. Nor has it kept pace with the higher aspirations and expectations of an increasingly better educated workforce and their families" (Leyva, 2005, p. 87). As a matter of policy, in 2002, DoD confirmed its commitment to service members and their families in a new social compact that committed the President and DoD "to improving life in the military, to underwrite family support programs, and to work in partnership with families to accomplish the military mission. America's noble warfighters deserve no less" (Molino, 2002, p. 1). Notwithstanding this policy statement, however, funding family support programs remains a challenge in periods of increased military operations and tight budgets, just as the needs of families are the greatest. As a result, self-help and family advocacy groups have dramatically increased.

To partially fill the void created by tight service budgets, unofficial and grass-roots organizations started to spring up. One group of Navy wives in Washington organized the CinCHouse.com—"A Nonprofit Community of Military Wives and Women"—the title taken from Navy jargon for a spouse who is the "Commander in Chief of the House," and turned it into a national self-help program with chapters throughout the country. After the attacks on September 11, 2001, CinCHouse organized a support network, Operation Homefront.[32] Another example of the growth of unofficial support organizations is the very popular commercial Web site Military.com, which complemented the official DoD and service family Web sites. The National Military Family Association (NMFA) gave voice to the concerns of military family as a powerful and well-respected lobbying organization in Washington. Even before 9/11, with the deployments to the Balkans, the Clinton administration developed Military One-Source as a hotline open 24 hours a day, 7 days a week that provided direct professional help to all military families. Military OneSource can find a spouse access to a everything from a local plumber to a counselor that can help a spouse cope with the stress of a deployment. Military OneSource is sponsored by the Office of the Under Secretary of Defense for Personnel and Readiness. This ensures that every military family, regardless of service component—active duty or reserve—has access to support services, no matter where the military family resides.

The Special Burdens of the Military Spouse

Even as the military elevated family quality of life as a priority issue, the stories of the special problems of military spouses came into sharper focus. Anthologists, sociologists, and economists viewing spouses from the vantage points of their separate disciplines provided a picture of the unique challenges that come with being a military spouse. Several examples only illustrate how persistent and difficult the special burdens are.

In 1978, the Bureau of Naval Personnel hired a young anthologist, Sabra Woolley, to help the Navy better understand the lifestyles of young Navy and Marine families and to evaluate then-current family programs—"the personal service centers, Navy Wives Information Clubs, wives associations, etc." (Woolley, 1978, p. 1). Woolley interviewed the wives of junior enlisted sailors and Marines in Navy housing in the District of Columbia. This was a group of some of the most vulnerable young wives anywhere in the Navy, and her report helped shape future Navy programs. Here is a summary of what she reported:

> [T]he majority expressed repeatedly the perception that they were caught up in a system characterized by inconsistency, ambiguity and arbitrary decisions. Their families were at the mercy of a system that made decisions that impacted violently on their lives, moved them, sent their husbands away from them, enmeshed them in a tangle of rules and regulations which changed constantly. Decisions made by the system were then redecided by the system . . . . Over and above the uncertainty was the feeling of helplessness created by the fact that there is no place or person in the system that dependents can go to for information. Their husbands, some of them, learned how to "beat the system" but that is because they are inside it. Dependents are outside it far enough so that the cannot learn the ways to work through it

---

[32] The founder of CinCHouse, Meredith Leyva, also published a popular self-help guide for "military wives, girlfriends, and women in uniform" (2003).

or around it; at the same time they are far enough outside that it does not impinge daily on their lives. (Woolley, 1978, p. 11)

Two decades later, sociologist Margaret Harrell told the compelling story of five women married to Army junior enlisted men. From a different place and time, the stories these women told reflected the same environment and showed the same challenges the Navy wives faced in 1978, such as "lack of education, financial difficulties, emotional and physical distance from extended family, and invisibility in a large bureaucracy" (Harrell, 2000, p. xi). Although told as individual stories and in a highly personal manner, the situations they depict were representative of those that many wives of young servicemen face. For example, Harrell describes Dana, one of the five, as the "stereotypical junior enlisted spouse" and concludes, in much the same way Woolley had earlier, that "her physical isolation, limited financial means, and lack of knowledge about the insular culture her husband has joined combine to reinforce her own sense of invisibility" (Harrell, 2000, p. 15).

The personal and anecdotal reports of Navy and Army wives were reinforced by the economic analysis of military wives that James Hosek and his colleagues undertook for the Office of the Under Secretary of Defense for Personnel and Readiness. They found that

> compared with civilian wives, military wives are less likely to work in a year; less likely to work full-time; have fewer weeks of work; and have similar, though lower, hours of work per week. . . . Their wages are lower, whether measured by weekly wage or hourly wage. (Hosek et al., 2002, pp. xii–xiii)

Identification of these and other problems lead to a wide range of support programs and a new social compact that recognized "the challenges of military life and the sacrifices service members and their families make in serving of their country" (Pirie, 1979, p. 1). Problems, however, continue, and notwithstanding the stresses of military life, support from military wives remains critical for the continued sustainment of the all-volunteer force. After more than 30 years of the all-volunteer force, change will not only require an increasing budgetary commitment, which has often been lacking, but what may even be harder:

> an attitude adjustment toward spouses and an overarching strategy for genuinely addressing their needs. The military must be comfortable dealing with spouses if it wishes to retain experienced, professional servicemembers and complete its mission. (Leyva, 2005, p. 91)

The Legacy

By the time of the fall of the Berlin Wall and after Desert Storm, it was clear that women were playing critical roles in the success of the all-volunteer force. These roles, both as service members and supporting families, would be tested during the deployments of the 1990s and operations in Iraq and Afghanistan in the new century. It was not just in the United States that women were taking on new roles in the military. On January 11, 2000, the European Court of Justice decided that limiting women to medical units and military bands was "a violation of the principle of equal opportunity [and] . . . in about half of all European armed forces women are admitted to combat units without restrictions" (Haltiner and Klein, 2005, pp. 22–23). While the American military still does not allow women in combat units, their proximity to combat is still the subject of concern and debate even as Operation Iraqi Freedom places new burdens on the all-volunteer force.

References

Air Force DCSP Staff, *Personnel Operating Plan: Project Volunteer Task Group,* first draft, Washington, D.C.: U.S. Air Force Headquarters, Directorate of Personnel Planning, June 30, 1969. G0275.pdf.

Alexander, Robert M., "Implementation Committee Report on the Assignment of Women in the Armed Forces," memorandum to Deputy Secretary of Defense, Washington, D.C., June 4, 1993. G0790.pdf.

————, "Women in Combat," memorandum to Elaine Donnelly, Washington, D.C., July 2, 1993. G0788.pdf.

Armor, David J., "Report of the Task Force on Women in the Military," action memorandum to Secretary of Defense, Washington, D.C., January 21, 1988. G0910.pdf.

————, interview with Bernard Rostker, October 3, 2002.

ASD[MRA&L]—*See* Assistant Secretary of Defense for Manpower, Reserve Affairs, and Logistics.

Assistant Secretary of Defense for Manpower, Reserve Affairs, and Logistics, *Background Review: Women in the Military,* Washington, D.C., October 1, 1981.

Aspin, Les, "Policy on the Assignment of Women in the Armed Forces," memorandum to Secretaries of the Military Department, Chairman of the Joints Chiefs of Staff, Assistant Secretary of Defense (FM&P) and Assistant Secretary of Defense (RA), Washington, D.C., April 28, 1993. G0869.pdf.

————, "Direct Ground Combat Definition and Assignment Rule," memorandum to Secretaries of the Military Department, Chairman of the Joints Chiefs of Staff, Assistant Secretary of Defense (Force Management and Personnel) and Assistant Secretary of Defense (Reserve Affairs), Washington, D.C., January 13, 1994. G1425.pdf.

Bell, William G., "Chapter 5—Personnel," in *Department of the Army Historical Summary: Fiscal Year 1980,* Washington, D.C.: U.S. Army Center of Military History, 1973. G1419.pdf.

Binkin, Martin, and Shirley J. Bach, *Women and the Military,* Washington, D.C.: Brookings Institution, June 1977.

Boldan, Edith M., "Chapter 6—Human Resources Development," in *Department of the Army Historical Summary: Fiscal Year 1979,* Washington, D.C.: U.S. Army Center of Military History, 1982. G1420.pdf.

Brown, Lenwood Y., "Chapter 6—Human Resource Development," in *Department of the Army Historical Summary: Fiscal Year 1980,* Washington, D.C.: U.S. Army Center of Military History, 1983. G1421.pdf.

Carlucci, Frank C., "Women in the Armed Forces," memorandum to Secretaries of the Military Department, Washington, D.C., March 19, 1981. G0808.pdf.

Central All-Volunteer Force Task Force, *Utilization of Military Women: A Report of Increased Utilization of Military Women, FYs 1973–1977,* Washington, D.C.: Office of the Assistant Secretary of Defense (M&RA), AD764510, December 1972. S0026.pdf.

Cilliers, Jakkie, "Feminism and the Military: Developments in the United States of America," *South African Defense Review,* No. 9, 1993. G1205.pdf.

Clark, William D., *Army Manpower Request: Statement Before the Subcommittee on Manpower and Personnel Senate Armed Services Committee,* Washington, D.C.: Office of the Acting Assistant Secretary of the Army (M&RA), February 26, 1981a. G0848.pdf.

———, "Women in the Army," memorandum to Acting Assistant Secretary of Defense (MRA&L), Washington, D.C., February 27, 1981b. G0806.pdf.

Conahan, Frank C., *DOD Service Academies: More Action Needed to Eliminate Sexual Harassment,* Washington, D.C.: General Accounting Office, GAO/NSIAD946, January 1994. G1434.pdf.

Culler, Kristen W., *The Decision to Allow Military Women into Combat Positions: A Study in Policy and Politics,* Monterey, Calif.: Naval Postgraduate School, 2000. G1177.pdf.

Defense Manpower Data Center, *Active Duty Demographic Profile: Assigned Strength, Gender, Race-Ethnic, Marital, Education and Age Profile of Active Duty Force, September 2004,* Washington, D.C.: Office of the Under Secretary of Defense (Personnel and Readiness), December 2004. G1416.pdf.

Department of the Army, *Consideration of Others (CO2) Handbook,* Washington, D.C.: Office of the Deputy Chief of Staff for Personnel, 2005a. G1418.pdf.

———, *Army Statement on Proposed Legislation,* Washington, D.C., May 19, 2005b. G1482.pdf.

Deputy Chief of Staff for Personnel, *Women in the Army Policy Review,* Washington, D.C.: Department of the Army, Office of the Deputy Chief of Staff for Personnel, November 12, 1982. G0927.pdf.

Directorate of Personnel Studies and Research, *Provide: Project Volunteer in Defense of the Nation,* Vol. 1, Washington, D.C.: Office of the Deputy Chief of Staff for Personnel, 1969. G0334.pdf.

———, *Provide: Project Volunteer in Defense of the Nation,* Vol. 2, Washington, D.C.: Office of the Deputy Chief of Staff for Personnel, 1969. G0335.pdf.

Donnelly, Elaine, "Women in Combat," memorandum to Secretary of Defense, Washington, D.C., May 27, 1993. G0787.pdf.

———, "Women in Combat," letter to Secretary of Defense, Livonia, Mich., June 23, 1994. G0701.pdf.

———, "Female Trouble: Women in War Face Worse Risks Than Men," *National Review Online,* March 27, 2003. S0802.pdf.

Donnelly, Elaine, Kate Walsh O'Beirne, and Sarah F. White, "Alterative View in the Report of the Presidential Commission on the Assignment of Women in the Armed Forces," memorandum to Secretary of Defense, Washington, D.C., November 25, 1992. G0877.pdf.

Dorn, Edwin, "Assignment of Women in the Military," memorandum to Secretary of Defense, Washington, D.C., August 27, 1993. G0817.pdf.

Ebbert, Jean, and Marie-Beth Hall, *Cross Currents: Navy Women from WWI to Tailhook,* Washington, D.C.: Brassey's, 1993.

Enke, Stephen, "Recommended Actions," preliminary memorandum to Robert E. Pursley, Washington, D.C., December 14, 1971a. G0669.pdf.

———, *Innovations for Achieving an AVAF,* Washington, D.C.: GE/TEMPO, December 15, 1971b. G0338.pdf.

Finneran, John G., "All Volunteer Force Recruiting Problems," memorandum to Deputy Assistant Secretary of Defense (Manpower Research and Utilization), Washington, D.C., January 31, 1972. G0137.pdf.

Frontline, *Women in the Navy: A Half Century Chronology,* Public Broadcasting System, 1993. S0874.pdf.

"Gen. Vessey Sees Women as Biggest Military Change," *Washington Post,* February 3, 1984, p. A12.

Goldman, Nancy, "The Changing Role of Women in the Armed Services," *American Journal of Sociology,* Vol. 78, No. 4, January 1973, pp. 892–911.

Ground Combat and Other Exclusion Policies, Section 541 of the National Defense Authorization Act of 2006, January 3, 2006. G1483.pdf.

Haltiner, Karl W., and Paul Klein, "The European Post–Cold War Military Reforms and Their Impact on Civil-Military Relations," in Franz Kernic, Paul Klien and Karl Haltiner, eds., *The European Armed Forces in Transition,* New York: Peter Lang, 2005.

Hardyman, Christine O., "Chapter 6—Human Resources Development," in *Department of the Army Historical Summary: Fiscal Year 1981,* Washington, D.C.: U.S. Army Center of Military History, 1988. G1422.pdf.

Harrell, Margaret C., *Invisible Wives: Junior Enlisted Army Wives,* Santa Monica, Calif.: RAND Corporation, MR-1223-OSD, 2000. S0894.pdf.

Hoar, William P., "Case Against Women in Combat," *The New American,* Vol. 9, No. 3, February 8, 1993. S0803.pdf.

Holm, Jeanne, *Women in the Military: An Unfinished Revolution,* rev. ed., Novato, Ca.: Presidio, 1992.

Hosek, James R., Beth J. Asch, C. Christine Fair, Craig W. Martin, and Michael G. Mattock, *Married to the Military: The Employment and Earnings of Military Wives Compared with Those of Civilian Wives,* Santa Monica, Calif.: RAND Corporation, MR-1565-OSD. S0895.pdf.

Huey, Mary Evelyn Blagg, "DACOWITS Concern About 'Women in the Army Report'," memorandum to Secretary of Defense, Washington, D.C., June 6, 1983. G0906.pdf.

Hunter, Richard W., *Use of Women in the Military: Background Study,* Washington, D.C.: Office of the Deputy Secretary of Defense (Programs and Requirements), May 2, 1977. G1440.pdf.

Janes, W. Scott, "Chapter 4—Support Services," in *Department of the Army Historical Summary: Fiscal Years 1990 and 1991,* Washington, D.C.: U.S. Army Center of Military History, 1997. G1423.pdf.

Jehn, Christopher, Women in the Military, hearing before the House Armed Service Committee, Subcommittee on Military Personnel and Compensation, 101st Cong., 2nd Sess., Washington, D.C., March 20, 1990. G0894.pdf.

———, "Recent Developments Concerning Women in Combat," memorandum to Secretary of Defense, Washington, D.C., May 15, 1991. G0874.pdf.

———, Women in the Military, hearing before the Senate Armed Service Committee, 101st Cong., 1st Sess., Washington, D.C., 91-S201-24 No. 7, June 18, 1991. G0902.pdf.

———, Testimony of Christopher Jehn on Implementation of the Repeal of the Combat Exclusion on Female Aviators, hearing before the House Armed Service Committee, 2nd, Washington, D.C., January 29, 1992. G0895.pdf.

Kerwin, Walter T., Jr., "Women's Army Corps (WAC) Authorizations for the Baseline Force," memorandum to U.S. Army Chief of Staff, Washington, D.C., June 10, 1971. G0212.pdf.

Kirby, Sheila Nararaj, and Scott Naftel, *The Effect of Mobilization on Retention of Enlisted Reservists After ODS/S,* Santa Monica: RAND, MR-943-OSD. S0908.pdf.

Korb, Lawrence J., "Women in the Armed Forces," memorandum to Secretary of Defense, Washington, D.C., May 14, 1981. G0832.pdf.

———, "Draft Release on Women in the Army Review," memorandum to Secretary of Defense, Washington, D.C., August 12, 1982a. G0967.pdf.

———, "Women in the Military," information memorandum to Secretary of Defense, Washington, D.C., August 16, 1982b. G0966.pdf.

———, "Accession Methodology and Enlistment Standards for Enlisted Women," information memorandum to Deputy Secretary of Defense, Washington, D.C., September 2, 1982c. G1010.pdf.

———, "Department of Defense Pregnancy Separation Policy," memorandum to Secretary of the Army (M&RA), Washington, D.C., December 23, 1982d. G0926.pdf.

———, "Women in the Army," information memorandum to Secretary of Defense, Washington, D.C., April 25, 1983. G0884.pdf.

———, "Single-Parent Enlistment Policies," information memorandum to Special Assistant to the Secretary of Defense, Washington, D.C., December 28, 1984. G0860.pdf.

Leyva, Meredith, *Married to the Military: A Survival Guide for Military Wives, Girlfriends, and Women in Uniform,* New York: Simon & Schuster, 2003.

———, "Transforming the 'Retention Sector,'" *Joint Force Quarterly,* No. 38, 3rd Quarter 2005, pp. 84-91. S0907.pdf.

Meckling, William H., "Comment on 'Women and Minorities in the All-Volunteer' Force," in Rodger Little and G. Thomas Sicilia William Bowman, ed., *The All-Volunteer Force After A Decade: Retrospect and Prospect,* New York: Pergamon-Brassey's, 1986.

Molino, John M., *A New Social Compact: A Reciprocal Partnership Between the Department of Defense, Service Members and Families,* Washington, D.C.: U.S. Department of Defense, July 2002. G1275.pdf.

Nelson, Gary R., *America's Volunteers: A Report on the All-Volunteer Armed Forces,* Washington, D.C.: Office of the Assistant Secretary of Defense (M&RA), December 31, 1978. S0194.pdf.

OASD[M&RA]—*See* Office of the Assistant Secretary of Defense for Manpower and Reserve Affairs.

OASD[MRA&L]—*See* Office of the Assistant Secretary of Defense for Manpower, Reserve Affairs, and Logistics.

Office of the Assistant Secretary of Defense for Manpower and Reserve Affairs, *Two Years with the Volunteer Force—FACT SHEET,* Washington, D.C.: U.S. Department of Defense, February 1, 1975. G0492.pdf.

Office of the Assistant Secretary of Defense for Manpower, Reserve Affairs, and Logistics, *Background Review: Women in the Military,* Washington, D.C.: U.S. Department of Defense, October 1981. G1173.pdf.

Pirie, Robert B., Jr., "Study of Military Pay Adequacy," memorandum to Secretary of Defense, Washington, D.C., November 13, 1979. G0354.pdf.

Powell, Colin L., "Women in the Army," memorandum to Carl Smith, Washington, D.C., March 6, 1981. G0847.pdf.

Proxmire, William, *Army's Decision to Restrict Enlistments of Women,* Washington, D.C.: U.S. Senate, March 4, 1981. G0834.pdf.

Reeves, Connie L., "Chapter 8—Support Services," in *Department of the Army Historical Summary: Fiscal Year 1996,* Washington, D.C.: U.S. Army Center of Military History, 1998. G1424.pdf.

Roberts, John W., "Women in the Air Force Report: DACOWITS Request for Information," memorandum to Gus C. Lee, Washington, D.C., July 27, 1974. G0044.pdf.

Sagawa, Shirley, and Nancy Duff Campbell, *Women in the Military paper: Women in Combat,* Washington, D.C.: National Women's Law Center, October 30, 1992.

Staff of the Directorate for Accession Policy, *Gender Neutral Standards,* Washington, D.C.: Office of the Assistant Secretary of Defense (Force Management Policy), April 1995. P0012.pdf.

Stiehm, Judith Hicks, "Trends in Utilization of Women 1980–82: End of a Honeymoon?," in Nancy H. Loring, ed., *Women in the United States Armed Forces: Progress and Barriers in the 1980s,* Chicago: Inter-University Seminar on Armed Forces and Society, 1984. G1174.pdf.

Stone, Robert A., "Women in the Armed Forces," memorandum to Assistant Secretaries of the Military Department (M&RA), Washington, D.C., March 25, 1981. G0809.pdf.

Thie, Harry, *Women in the Military,* Washington, D.C.: Office of the Assistant Secretary of Defense (MRA&L), August 20, 1982. G1172.pdf.

Tice, R. Dean, "Review of Pregnancy Separation Policy," memorandum to Assistant Secretary of Defense (MRA&L), Washington, D.C., December 21, 1982. G0925.pdf.

Tyson, Ann Scott, "Panel Votes to Ban Women From Combat: Army Leaders Strongly Oppose House Subcommittee's Action," *Washington Post,* May 12, 2005a, p. A08.

———, "Bid to Limit Women In Combat Withdrawn," *Washington Post,* May 26, 2005b, p. A01.

Weinberger, Caspar W., "Women in the Military," memorandum to Secretaries of the Military Departments, Washington, D.C., January 14, 1982. G1170.pdf.

———, "Women in the Military," memorandum to Thomas K. Turnage, Washington, D.C., July 19, 1983a. G0885.pdf.

———, "Combat Exclusion Policy," letter to Chairman U.S. Commission on Civil Rights, Washington, D.C., October 26, 1983b. G0907.pdf.

———, "The All-Volunteer Force in the 1980s: Department of Defense Perspective," in William Bowman, Roger Little, and G. Thomas Sicilia, eds., *The All-Volunteer Force After a Decade: Retrospect and Prospect,* New York: Pergamon-Brassey's, 1986.

West, Togo D., "Response to Elaine Donnelly: Army Women in Direct Ground Combat," action memorandum to Secretary of Defense, Washington, D.C., July 25, 1994. G0702.pdf.

White, Richard C., Testimony on the Registration of Women, hearing before the Military Personnel Subcommittee of the House Committee on Armed Services, 96th Cong., 2nd Sess., Washington, D.C., U.S. Government Printing Office, March 5, 1980. G1175.pdf.

Wilson, George C., "Army Hints Draft May Be Required," *Washington Post,* July 9, 1981, p. 1. S0640.pdf.

Woolley, Sabra, *Survey of a Navy Housing Area,* unpublished, Bureau of Naval Personnel. G1426.pdf.

Zumwalt, Elmo R., Jr., *On Watch: A Memoir,* Arlington, Va.: Admiral Zumwalt & Associates, Inc., 1976.

———, "Women in Combat," memorandum to Secretary of Defense, Washington, D.C., May 17, 1993. G0789.pdf.

CHAPTER SIXTEEN

The Reagan-Bush Years: Analytic Studies (1981–1992)

As we look back on the first decade of the All-Volunteer Force, I feel that we have learned how to make it work. *We have found the levers to pull.* We have determined the influences of bonuses and education incentives. We have seen the power of effective advertising. . . . In short, we have a better understanding of the supply of available youth, the recruiting environment, and the use of recruiting resources. [Emphasis added]

—General Maxwell R. Thurman
Vice Chief of Staff of the Army[1]

Introduction: Finding the Levers to Pull

The research agenda of the 1980s in support of the all-volunteer force was all about "finding the levers to pull." It was dominated by the ASVAB misnorming and the assessment of many of the recruiting-related incentive programs initiated in the late 1970s, including joint advertising, educational incentives, and monetary bonuses. The two issues reflect the continuing dialogue concerning *supply* of and *demand* for personnel that managers of the all-volunteer force faced from the very beginning.

On the demand side, the requirement for "quality" people was a topic the Gates Commission (1970), the Central All-Volunteer Force Task Force (1972), and Congress, with its frequent pronouncements on recruiting problems, had all addressed.[2] On the

---

[1] November 2, 1983 (Thurman, 1986, p. 274).

[2] Pirie reviewed the subject in a letter to Senator Carl Levin in June 1980. At the time, the Senate Armed Services Committee was considering placing a 20-percent limit on category IV accessions by each service (Pirie, 1980a). Previously, the FY 1974 Appropriations Bill contained the so-called Section 718 restrictions on who could be recruited—no more than 45 percent of new recruits could be non–high school graduates, and only 18 percent in each service could score at the mental category IV level. Fortunately for the services, recruiting started to pick up about this time, and they were able to meet the congressionally imposed limitations. For a more complete discussion, see Griffith (1997, pp. 243–245).

supply side, issues of compensation, bonuses, and the recruiting process, including the effects of advertising, had been central to the debate from the very beginning. Unlike the early years, however, the assessments of the 1980s were long term and empirically based, incorporating both readily available data, as well as data generated uniquely for these specific research efforts.

At the end of the decade, the fall of the Soviet Union and the drawdown of the force structure presented a new set of challenges for researchers, who for years had struggled to keep qualified personnel *in* service and now had to try to develop programs to get *some of them* to leave voluntarily.

Responding to the ASVAB Misnorming: "How Much Quality is Enough?"

In a report entitled *Performance Assessment for the Workplace* (Wigdor and Green, 1991), the National Research Council characterized the debate that focused the research agenda of the 1980s[3]:

> In the economic climate of the 1980s, the old "more is better" way of doing business was no longer credible. As the decade progressed, Congress became increasingly insistent in asking: How much quality is enough? . . . Whether their quality goals are realistic and necessary, as the Services maintain, or too high, as Congress often claims, has been difficult to ascertain. One of the major weaknesses of DoD's position is that quality requirements have been related to the aptitude of recruits rather than to realized on-the-job performance. . . . The AFQT categories do not denote levels of job mastery and, indeed, the link from recruit quality to job performance has been largely unknown. (Wigdor and Green, 1991, p. 55)

In 1981, the Reagan administration inherited both the misnorming problem and a set of management actions designed to provide a new reference population that related test scores to the current profile of American youth and that attempted to improve the selection and classification instruments so that they related more closely to actual performance on the job. Unfortunately, what originally had been tasked for completion "by the end of FY 1983" would take a great deal longer and would be more problematic to implement.

Job Performance and ASVAB Qualification Standards

Four months after the Reagan administration took office, the House Armed Services Committee expressed "dissatisfaction with . . . efforts to develop an evidentiary base

---

[3] The National Research Council, commissioned to provide "scientific oversight" of the Joint-Service Job Performance Measurement/Enlisted Standards (JPM) Project, created the Committee on the Performance of Military Personnel composed of prominent researchers and academics in the field.

concerning the relationship between factors such as ASVAB scores, levels of education, etc., and potential for effective service" (OASD[MRA&L], 1981, p. 3). The new Assistant Secretary of Defense, Larry Korb, was on the hot seat with Congress. The previous administration had raised expectations, but the new administration had done little. In his first report in December 1981, almost a year after taking office, Korb described "a new DoD initiative to relate enlistment standards to job performance, and plans to determine the appropriate aptitude levels for military personnel" (OASD[MRA&L], 1981, p. 3). Korb told Congress that, historically, for "technical as well as economic considerations, most selection and classification procedures have been developed and validated against success in training rather than performance on the job" (OASD[MRA&L], 1981, p. 5). He admitted that job performance research had gotten off to a slow start despite directions to redirect funds (Pirie, 1980b) and was not currently in the research budget. He asked for congressional support for "reprogram[ming] funds originally earmarked for other areas of personnel research" (OASD[MRA&L], 1981, p. 6) for FYs 1982 and 1983. It would be FY 1984, he explained, before the budget process would catch up with changing priorities and "project[s] will be available through regular budget channels" (OASD[MRA&L], 1981, p. 6).

Even if DoD did not have the kind of "evidentiary base" Congress seemed to want, Korb was willing to share with Congress some conclusions based on ongoing research that was guiding Department of Defense policy. He told Congress it was "well-known that non–high school graduates have substantially higher first-term attrition rates than graduates" (OASD[MRA&L], 1981, p. 8). He cited the results of "a recent DoD-sponsored study of enlistment standards in the Army" (OASD[MRA&L], 1981, p. 9), done by David Armor and his colleagues at RAND, to the effect that

> low-aptitude personnel are less likely to meet minimum requirements as measured by on-the-job performance tests . . . [such as the] Skill Qualification Test (SQT) results for Army Infantry as well as special hands-on job performance tests for four other Army jobs. (OASD[MRA&L], 1981, p. 9)

It was his hope that such work would lead to an Enlistment Standards Model to determine the most cost-effective "ability mix" of new recruits.

The Joint Performance Measurement Project

The process of preparing the report to Congress in fall 1981 illustrated how disorganized DoD was when it came to measuring job performance.[4] The responses of the services showed their widely differing levels of commitment to addressing the job-performance

---

[4] There would eventually be a series of yearly reports to Congress, starting in 1982: Staff of the Directorate for Accession Policy (1982), Staff of the Directorate for Accession Policy (1983), Staff of the Directorate for Accession Policy (1985a), Staff of the Directorate for Accession Policy (1985), Staff of the Directorate for Accession Policy (1985b), Staff of the Directorate for Accession Policy (1985c), Staff of the Directorate for Accession Policy (1987), Staff of the Directorate for Accession Policy (1990), and Staff of the Directorate for Accession Policy (1991).

measurement problem that Pirie had laid out in summer 1980. The Army was the most enthusiastic, telling Korb that the Army Research Institute (ARI) had developed a program through FY 1987 to

> screen applicants for potential and to optimize the match between individual's aptitude and MOS [military occupational specialty] classification based upon probability of successful performance during training and later on the job. (Wright, 1981)

As ARI saw it, the Army needed

> a system whereby it can assure the optimal match between the available manpower resources and its manpower requirements. At the individual level, personnel should be trained and assigned to duties for which they are best suited, within certain constraints. (Eaton et al., 1981, p. 2)

The Air Force was less supportive. In its response to Korb, it noted that the Air Force Human Resources Laboratory had "proposed a large scale project to explore several alternate means of assessing quality of job performance" but complained that "previous research to establish the relationship between enlistment standards and job performance was of minimal value, and current research still bears a high risk of failure due to the complexity of this task" (Lucus, 1981). The Navy was concerned because this line of research had "already proven to be time consuming and extremely costly . . . [and the] Navy . . . is currently unable to fund new/long range job performance research work" (Grayson, 1981). The Deputy Assistant Secretary of the Navy (Manpower), in providing the Navy's input to the report, did propose that Korb charter a Joint Service Executive Oversight Committee and a working group; he thought that "some cost efficiencies or reduction in duplicating efforts might be achieved by such an oversight" (Grayson, 1981). In fact, this is what happened. Korb chartered the JPM Project and a working group that was chaired by Tom Sicilia, who filled the position that Al Martin had vacated in summer 1981 (Weinberger, 1981). In addition, he contracted with the National Academy of Sciences to form a committee to "provide technical oversight" (Maier, 1993, p. 82).

In at least one very important and very expensive way, the JPM Project and associated service efforts were unique. For years, researchers had tried, with varying degrees of success, to correlate performance on the job with the characteristics of jobholders using available sources of both performance and demographic data. The JPM studies would develop their own data-collection instruments to describe job incumbents in new and different ways and to measure job performance. Each step, however, was breaking new ground.

Not only was the JPM Project expensive, measured in millions of dollars, and time-consuming, measured in decades, the application of these new data instruments to carefully randomized groups of subjects was often disruptive.[5] It was the general view of research psychologists, however, that to do it right, these costs were unavoidable. Two of the Army's lead psychologists, Joyce Shields and Larry Hanser, argued, for example, that available data are less appropriate for the kinds of studies that are most useful, since such data are "cross-sectional rather than longitudinal" (Shields and Hanser, 1990, p. 242). Milton Maier and Catherine Hiatt explained that, while

> job performance appears to be a simple concept readily observable and quantifiable; . . . in practice, records of performance by individual workers usually are not available, or if they are, the entries are not reliable. Furthermore, the definition of the term job performance is itself not precise. (Maier and Hiatt, 1984, p. 2)[6]

They provided some indications of the difficulties surrounding the measurement of job performance:

> The starting place for determining content of the proficiency tests is, of course, job requirements. After that general statement, divergent points of view abound about how to define job requirements. One point of view is that the content should be based on the specific requirements in a specific duty assignment. . . . A second point of view is that the content should enable generalization from the content of the measures to performance on all requirements in the skill. Another consideration is whether the content should cover peacetime or combat requirements. The positions are not necessarily mutually exclusive and there are arguments to support each point of view. (Maier and Hiatt, 1984, p. 6)

The Army Research Institute's Project A

More than any of the other services, the Army was committed to an ambitious expansion of performance-measurement research even before the congressional mandate and the requirements of the JPM Project were known. In 2001, looking back over the previous two decades, John P. Campbell, principal scientist of what would become known as Project A, wrote the following:

> The Army viewed the Congressional mandate as an opportunity to address a much larger set of personnel research questions. Could other selection and classification

---

[5] During the implementation of Project A, for example, one of the responsibilities of the Army's Assistant Deputy Chief of Staff for Personnel, Major General Norman Schwarzkopf, was to ensure that subject units were available to the HumRRO researchers to take the tests they and their team of "subject-matter experts" had so carefully developed (Shields, 2004). In total, "9,430 entry-level personnel in 19 MOS were finally tested" (Young et al., 1990, p. 303).

[6] The Maier and Hiatt study for the Marine Corps used hands-on and written tests especially developed for this study by Marine Corps experts with the technical assistance of the Navy Personnel Research and Development Center (NPRDC) in San Diego (Maier and Hiatt, 1984, p. 10). Maier also used training grades.

A decade before, Bob Lockman had discussed the importance and difficulties of grounding the selection process on job performance in Lockman (1974).

measures be developed to supplement the predictive power of the ASVAB? Could selection tests be used to identify individuals more likely to complete their tour of service? Given the declining manpower pool, could tests be designed to more efficiently use the available resources via better classification and allocation? These questions . . . grew from the need to address some very real policy issues and to improve the design and functioning of the Army's selection/classification decision procedures. (Campbell, 2001b, pp. 26–27)

Campbell recalled that, in spring 1981, "a team from . . . ARI's Manpower and Personnel Research Laboratory," the organization that Dr. Joyce Shields was heading which was trying to make ARI more responsive to the needs of General Max Thurman's Army Recruiting Command, "began to prepare the design specifications that were to become Project A" (Campbell, 2001b, p. 27). About the time of Wright's October 1981 memorandum to OSD providing the Army's input to the December 1981 report to Congress, the Army awarded the overall contract for Project A to HumRRO, supported by the American Institute for Research and the Personnel Decisions Research Institute:

The overall goal of Project A was to generate the criterion variables, predictor measures, analytic methods and validation data that [were] . . . necessary for developing an enhanced selection and classification system for all entry-level positions in the United States Army. (Campbell, 1990, p. 232)

One of the most interesting aspects of Project A was that it focused not only on predicting training performance but also on post-training performance during the initial term of service, first-term attrition, the reenlistment decision, and even performance during the second term. Such an analysis required longitudinal data. Figure 16.1 shows the resulting research design.

The Results of Project A: The Importance of Getting the Policy Question Right

Project A was the largest, and probably most ambitious, single research effort ever undertaken in the history of personnel research. It was made up of a coordinated number of separate research tasks that included the development of new test batteries and the collection of data on thousands of soldiers over many years. A full examination of its many facets would take, and in fact has taken, a book as large, if not larger, than the present volume. Two comprehensive examinations are available. An entire issue of *Personnel Psychology* was devoted to "Project A: The U.S. Army Selection and Classification Project."[7] In addition, John Campbell and Deirdre Knapp edited a comprehensive accounting of Project A, *Exploring the Limits in Personnel Selection and Classification,* which was published in 2001.

Given the project's size and ambitious agenda, one can reasonably ask whether it had the desired effect on the Army. If by that we mean the fielding of an entire new

---

[7] The issue was Volume 43, Number 2, Summer 1990.

Figure 16.1
Schematic Portrayal of the Research Design Framework for the Army Selection Classification Project (Project A)

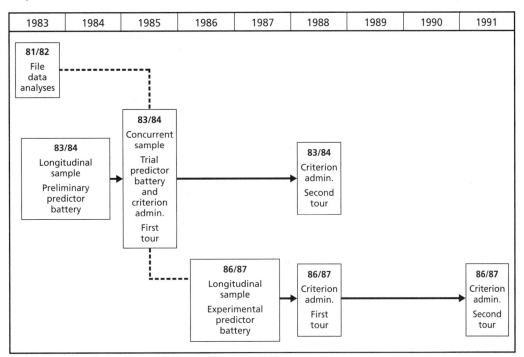

SOURCE: Campbell (1990, p. 235).
NOTE: Numbers in the boxes indicate the years in which soldiers in the sample entered the Army.
RAND MG265-16.1

means of selection and classification, Project A was not successful. If instead we mean validating the ASVAB, Project A was a success. The most striking result of Project A was that it strengthened the case for retaining the ASVAB. While it also provided "a strong foundation for the use of new temperament, spatial, and psychomotor tests," these tests were not implemented (White et al., 2001, p. 525):

> The Project A research showed that the personality constructs measured by ABLE[8] [Assessment of Background and Life Experiences] were predictive of enlisted performance and first-tour attrition . . . and that ABLE tapped qualities needed for successful performance that were captured by currently used screening tools [i.e., the ASVAB]. These findings generated much enthusiasm for further evaluating ABLE's potential for use in the Army's personnel selection and classification decision system. . . . [However,] the prospect of using ABLE for operational decisions raised questions pertaining to selection utility, fakability, and the logistics of test administration. . . . Given the pressures to minimize testing time in preenlistment screening and elsewhere, an early implementation concern was that the full,

---

[8] ABLE includes scales for achievement, adjustment, dependability, and something called "social desirability" to detect faking (see White et al., 2001, p. 537).

199-item ABLE required nearly one hour for some examinees to complete, which exceeded the time available for most, if not all, potential operational uses. (White et al., 2001, p. 527–528)

[T]he Services decided not to implement ABLE-based selection procedures . . . largely due to concerns about its fakability and potential compromise. Some individuals believed that any large-scale operational screening using self-reported measures, like ABLE, would lead to widespread faking and degradation of predictive validity over time. . . . There was also concern that applicants might receive outside guidance (i.e., coaching) on how to score well on ABLE. (White et al., 2001, p. 546–547)

Walker and Rumsey summed up the situation:

ASVAB performs its selection function very effectively; it strongly distinguishes those who can perform the job well from those who cannot, and it is an excellent predictor of the future job performance of applicants for enlistment. (Walker and Rumsey, 2001, p. 560)

The irony did not escape them. They clearly understood that "the success of Project A in demonstrating the validity of ASVAB worked to discourage implementing new selection tests. In the eyes of many, it would be hard for new tests to improve on that level of functioning" (Walker and Rumsey, 2001, p. 560).

Hanser, one of the designers of Project A and one of the authors of its statement of work, as well as the senior Army scientist responsible for overseeing Project A after Kent Eaton took over from Joyce Shields as head of the Manpower and Personnel Research laboratory at ARI, remembers meeting with General Thurman in 1988 after he became the commander of the Army's Training and Doctrine Command. Thurman, Hanser recalls, was less than fully enthusiastic with the results of Project A that were briefed to him. Hanser thought it was because "he wanted to know more than the ASVAB was, in fact, related to individual performance" (Hanser, 2004). The JPM Project and Project A addressed individual performances, and while such issues were and continue to be important, the issues du jour had started to change. The JPM Project was criticized by the National Research Council for focusing on "norm-referenced standards, rather than criterion-referenced standards." Moreover, it did not address several issues that had become important to decisionmakers in the late 1980s: unit readiness under combat conditions and the cost-effective mix of recruits. In retrospect, for Project A at least, ARI's original concept seemed to be more applicable to the era of the draft than it was to the era of an all-volunteer force. Its focus was on "available manpower resources and [the Army's] manpower requirements" (Eaton et al., 1981, p. 2) rather than on managing an all-volunteer force.

"Norm-Referenced" Rather Than "Criterion-Referenced" Standards

The National Research Council was critical of the JPM Project and Project A decisions to develop "norm-referenced" standards" rather than "criterion-referenced" standards:

> An early and largely implicit decision in the JPM Project [and the Army's Project A] was that the proficiency measures would be developed in the style of the usual norm-referenced tests used in prediction. That is, the research paradigm was to rank each job incumbent relative to his peers, rather than determining how well the incumbent could do the job in an absolute sense. . . . [The criterion]-referenced approach would have been more appropriate to the long-term goal of the JPM Project, which was not simply to validate the ASVAB, but to link enlistment standards to job performance. Had this approach been adopted, the tests would have been designed to measure individual performance against a scale of competence or job mastery, and the scores would have indicated how well the incumbent could do the job. . . . This challenges the traditional research paradigm, but offers more compelling evidence to policy makers concerned with the question of how much quality is enough. As it is, inferences cannot be made directly from the JPM data about the competence of individuals relative to a job, but only about competence relative to others who perform the job. (Wigdor and Green, 1991, p. 8)

For many in the field the use of "criterion-referenced" standards was not warranted. Maier and Hiatt made the counter argument:

> In recent years, a movement has grown to use "criterion-referenced" standards to evaluate performance. With criterion-referenced standards, an a priori passing score is established on the measure. Examinees who meet the passing score are said to be satisfactory, or competent, or to have "mastered" the domain. The number of examinees who attain a passing score is irrelevant to the setting of criterion-referenced standards. . . .
>
> In "norm-referenced" scales, the meaning of the scores is determined by the relative performance of examinees on the measure. We compare scores relative to the other scores in the distribution. We use the mean as the zero point, and assign meaning to scores based on their distance away from the mean. . . .
>
> Given the types of performance measures used in this study, we are willing to assume a norm-referenced scale, and then drive standards from that type of scale. We are unwilling to assume an absolute dichotomy between satisfactory and unsatisfactory performance that is based on realistic job requirements. We plan to continue with norm-referenced scales in future research efforts unless new evidence emerges that criterion-referenced standards are meaningful for military skills. (Maier and Hiatt, 1984, pp. 72–73)

The Cost Effective Mix of Recruits

The National Research Council also endorsed "the development of techniques for modeling the policy maker's need to balance performance requirements and personnel costs" (Wigdor and Green, 1991, p. 185). The council considered several approaches, including the "seminal" work done by Armor reported below (Wigdor and Green, 1991, pp. 194–203). The council felt it had

> spoken at some length . . . of the need to provide an absolute, or competency, inter-
> pretation of performance in a particular job to set enlistment standards—so that
> policy makers can address the question of how much performance is enough.
> (Wigdor and Green, 1991, p. 209)[9]

Using the readily available absolute pass-fail data of the Army's Skill Qualification Test (SQT), e.g., a "criterion-referenced" standard, Armor and his colleagues at RAND reached substantially the same conclusion Project A had reached for the Army and Maier and Hiatt had reached for the Marine Corps.[10] They concluded that recruit "aptitude levels strongly affect subsequent job performance, not only for Infantrymen but for a representative variety of other Army personnel as well" (Armor et al., 1982). However, for Armor and his colleagues, this finding was only the beginning of the process of setting enlistment standards that were "cost-effective" and relevant to an all-volunteer force:

> Merely showing a correlation between recruit aptitude and on-the-job performance
> does not itself establish aptitude standards for a given job. . . . The SQT is not the
> only indicator of personnel effectiveness; other performance indicators, especially
> training results and attrition, must be considered. Persons who fail training courses
> or who separate before the end of their enlistment term also detract from effective-
> ness by increasing training loads and by creating job turbulence. Nor should the
> factor of cost be ignored. High-ability enlistees may out-perform low-ability enlist-
> ees, but they also cost more to recruit. The cost trade-offs between higher recruiting

---

[9] It is worthwhile to note earlier work that focused not on issues of recruit quality but on the critical question of the mix of first-term and career personnel. Mark Albrecht estimated the parameters of a constant elasticity of substitution production function using survey data on relative productivity of first-term and career personnel. He found that "an overall Air Force proportion of first term to career personnel of around 50 percent at [then] current strength levels would be consistent with cost minimization criteria" (Albrecht, 1979, p. 70). Also see work by C. Robert Roll and Glenn Gotz for the Defense Resources Management Study in Rice (Rice, 1979).

[10] Armor's work at RAND (Armor et al., 1982) and the work by Irv Greenberg that had been reported the previous year to Congress (Greenberg, 1980) were similar. They both used an existing source of performance data, the SQT. This test dated from 1978, when it replaced the MOS Proficiency Test. The RAND study, however, found the relationship between AFQT and SQT to be more important and also developed the first cost-performance trade-off model. As a cost-saving initiative, the Self-Development Test (SDT) replaced the SQT in 1991. The SDT was later also discontinued.

costs of high-ability personnel and their superior performance must therefore be considered. (Armor et al., 1982, p. 3)[11]

Given the measures of job performance—training success, attrition, and the SQT—and the policy-relevant measures of ASVAB scores and high school status, trade-offs were needed because "no entry characteristics other than high school status were found that correlate strongly with either training completion or post-training attrition in the Army" (Armor et al., 1982, p. 6), while "the strongest predictors of passing the SQT were Combat Arms (CO) and the AFQT scores" (Armor et al., 1982, p. 7), both derived from the ASVAB.

Armor developed the concept of the *qualified man-month,* equal to "each month of post-training duty time contributed by a person who can pass the SQT at the minimum standard" (Armor et al., 1982, p. 14). Given the costs of recruiting, training, and force maintenance, which were dependent on ASVAB scores and high school status, the optimal enlistment ability standards are the ones that

> minimize cost for a given level of . . . performance, both with respect to attrition and on-the-job effectiveness. . . . Therefore, an optimal aptitude standard depends upon the trade-off between the more costly but better-performing higher-ability recruits versus the less costly but poorer-performing low-ability recruits. (Armor et al., 1982, p. 24)

While Armor's results were "preliminary" and based on a limited sample of Army specialties, they illustrated the dilemma the Army and Congress faced. Armor found:

> Generally speaking, the model shows that optimum ability mixes require higher ability standards than those used between 1976 and 1980. Moreover, the standards mandated by Congress for the 1982 fiscal year, when applied to the Infantry, also generated a more cost-effective ability mix than pre-1981 standards. The Congressional mandate ultimately calls for a maximum of 20 percent category IV personnel and 35 percent non–high school graduates. . . . If the Congressional mandate were

---

[11] According to Armor, it needed to

> be emphasized that SQT does not capture all aspects of actual on-the-job performance. . . . Nevertheless, it captures more of the essential aspects of on-the-job performance than any other objective measure available at this time, and it is therefore a serviceable tool for evaluating enlistment standards. (Armor et al., 1982, pp. 5–6)

Also note that Maier and Hiatt did point out the changing military environment of the all-volunteer force:

> During the draft environment, when procuring people was relatively easy, recruiting costs could be largely ignored. In the all-volunteer environment, where the Services must compete with civilian employers and academic institutions, procurement costs are substantial . . . [while] the validity of standards is still the fundamental issue, . . . issues of costs and even social policy need more systematic consideration. (Maier and Hiatt, 1984, p. 54)

However, they limited their conclusions, calling the ASVAB "a valid qualification predictor of job performance, as measured by hands-on proficiency tests, written proficiency tests, and grades in skill training" (Maier and Hiatt, 1984, p. 78).

applied to all Army jobs, this increment . . . [increases] costs on the order of $280 million to $370 million per year. Moreover, as the number of 18-year-olds in the general population declines throughout the 1980s, coupled with plans to increase the size of the Army, the competition for high-ability personnel may become even more intense. Recruiting costs may then have to rise even further to attract enough persons to meet these new ability standards.

Notwithstanding these seemingly high costs, . . . higher ability standards make sense. . . . The additional costs are only a small increment to the total cost of recruiting and maintaining the first-term force [and] . . . the return to these additional expenditures is a substantially more capable force. Higher standards ensure that more of the Army's recruits are able to perform their jobs adequately, reduce the cost of obtaining each month of qualified job performance, and hence may justify the cost they impose. (Armor et al., 1982, pp. 30–31)

Personnel Quality and Unit Performance

By the late 1980s, policymakers in the Army and Congress were turning their interest to unit performance and combat readiness. There had been a number of prominent examples of research, using available data, linking the characteristics of personnel in units with the performance of their units.[12] In the late 1970s, Stanley Horowitz and Allan Sherman at the Center for Naval Analyses (CNA) were "successful in attributing variation among ships in the level of maintenance [required] to differences in the make-up of the portion of the crew responsible for maintenance" (Horowitz and Sherman, 1976, p. 1). They reported that "crew characteristics that influence the productivity of enlisted men include high school graduation, entry test scores, race, marital status, length of service, sea experience, and advanced training" (Horowitz and Sherman, 1980).

More-recent work at CNA and the Institute for Defense Analysis (IDA) examined aviation units. An early analysis demonstrated that training was positively related to better performance, as measured by scores on the Operational Readiness Evaluations achieved by air wings aboard aircraft carriers (Horowitz, 1984). Another study showed that personnel in upper pay grades are much more productive than junior personnel in maintaining aircraft. A shift in manning toward the top three pay grades could result in significantly lower costs yet maintain the same level of effectiveness (Marcus, 1982). Later work demonstrated that experience is important for determining bombing accuracy, the quality of landings aboard aircraft carriers, and kills in air-combat maneuvering exercises (Hammon and Horowitz, 1990). An analysis of ship readiness showed that more experienced crews and crews that had been together longer reduced the amount of time ships could not perform their missions due to equipment failures (Quester, 1989; Quester et al., 1989). All this work strongly suggests the importance of experienced personnel and thus of retention.

---

[12] Colin Hammon and Stanley Horowitz provided a catalogue of performance data in their report (1987).

In the early 1980s, a team from the U.S. Military Academy at West Point's Office of Economic and Manpower Analysis used

> a large data set consisting of tank-crew firing scores . . . [from] a standardized Tank Table 8 (individual crew qualification) course at Grafenwohr Training Area, Federal Republic of Germany (FRG) for 1,131 crews equipped with M-60 series and M-1 tanks. (Scribner et al., 1986, p. 194)

The team collected information on the individual members of the tank crews and matched the crews with their "enlisted master file. . . their biographic and demographic information" (Scribner et al., 1986, p. 195). Its statistical analysis—ordinary least squares— showed tank commanders' and gunners' AFQT scores were "numerically important and statistically significant (Scribner et al., 1986, p. 198).

While such studies showed a significant relationship between AFQT and small- unit performance, General Thurman, now the commander of the Army's Training and Doctrine Command (TRADOC), commissioned the Soldier Performance Research Project in 1988 (Block et al., 1989) "to show how individual AFQT levels promote combat performance and readiness of units" (Block et al., 1989, p. 1). Like the JPM Project and Project A before them, the studies ARI and RAND's Arroyo Center did for this project did not use available performance data. They carefully constructed perfor- mance data taken from combat simulations and recorded the group's performance on simulators as proxies for actual combat. Experience during the Gulf War suggested that proficiency in these simulations was a good measure of how combat soldiers performed in battle.

The ARI and RAND studies done for General Thurman not only validated the close association between quality and both individual and group job performance, they also showed how such research could help the services manage the all-volunteer force. The tank gunnery study by ARI used a

> [h]igh-fidelity tank gunnery simulat[ion], . . . the Instructional-Conduct of Fire Trainer (I-COFT) . . . to measure a full range of target engagement tasks, including acquisition, laying the main gun, and issuing fire commands. (Graham, 1989, p. 4)

The study found that

> Soldiers with higher mental ability were faster and more accurate on the I-COFT gunnery test than soldiers with lower mental ability. Analyses using a soldier per- formance model demonstrated that differences in performance levels would likely have a large impact on unit combat effectiveness. Furthermore, the model showed category IV soldiers performed at approximately 78% of category I & II soldiers. (Graham, 1989, p. 15)

Another ARI project focused on the determinants of unit performance at the National Training Center, a tough, realistic combined-arms environment. The perfor- mance measure used was the percentage of missions successfully accomplished, as assessed by trained observer-controllers.[13] It found that units performed better at the center if they had realistic training facilities, more opportunities to train, and better-trained opposing forces at their home stations. The results on AFQT scores were the most interesting. Low-AFQT personnel degraded the performance of platoons with low experience. AFQT was not found to matter in platoons with more experience.

RAND's study of job performance on the Patriot system used a high-fidelity simulator, the Patriot Conduct of Fire trainer, and four 20-minute specially constructed simulated air battles to measure performance, defined in terms of "success in the missions of point defense and area defense" (Orvis et al., 1992, p. vi). In the case of communications operators, RAND used a high-fidelity tactical communications simulator, the Reactive Electronic Equipment Simulator, as the test platform to assess how "various soldier characteristics, such as aptitude, experience, and demographic and educational background" affected group outcomes, defined as success or failure in establishing a functioning system (Winkler et al., 1992).

While the results of the three studies were consistent with the findings of Project A, they went further, addressing the critical questions of the cost-effective mix of personnel, as reflected in the report on the Patriot system:

> The results provide considerable evidence that Armed Forces Qualification Test (AFQT) score has a direct and consistent effect on the outcomes of air battles, both in terms of knowledge assessed by written tests and in actual performance in simulations. . . .
>
> We also found substantial tradeoffs between AFQT and both operator experience and training days for many of the outcome measures: a one-level change in AFQT category equaled or surpassed the effect of a year of operator experience or of frequent training according to these data. These tradeoffs have significant readiness and cost implications in that higher quality soldiers, as measured by AFQT scores, require less training and operator experience to perform as well as lower quality soldiers. . . .
>
> The findings suggest the importance of unit training along with personnel quality, in affecting mission performance. (Orvis et al., 1992, p. vi)

The report on communications operators showed the extent to which the position of the services concerning their need for quality personnel was supported by the research:

> [A] change in accession standards that causes a shift in average AFQT category from IIIA (close to current levels) to IIIB will substantially reduce the probability of operator success in operating and troubleshooting communications systems. The results are significant—reductions of 16 to 17 percentage points in the probability of successful operation and troubleshooting—and imply that a reduction in

---

[13] Keesling (Hammon and Horowitz, 1987) provides a full discussion of the work.

average AFQT levels would carry a penalty in battlefield performance and readiness, an effect that should be considered in making budget and resource allocation decisions. (Winkler et al., 1992, p. x)

Looking Back: Good Practice and Good Science

Looking back on a decade of the most intense and costly research on classification, selection and job performance in the history of military manpower, several reviewers expressed satisfaction with the science but were less than satisfied with the practical outcomes. Attempts to share data among the services with the establishment of the Defense Training and Analysis Center (DTAC) foundered on distrust of OSD and with the claims that DTAC was an "unacceptable [intrusion] into the military departments' prerogatives" (Lehman, 1986).[14] The new selection and classification instruments ARI developed were rejected as not being practical. Research using readily available measures of job performance linked to data maintained in the automated personnel files provided substantially the same results and insights as the JPM Project and Project A's carefully designed and tailored studies, at a fraction of the cost.

Years later, the designers of Project A recalled their "hope" that they had

> designed a research program that would bear directly on the major policy and design parameters of the selection/classification decision process such that the research results would be directly useful [and] . . . simultaneously, . . . the science of industrial and organizational psychology would also be served. (Shields et al., 2001, p. 29)

---

[14] Tom Sicilia, Director of Procurement Policy, was the architect of DTAC and its first director. In its fourth annual report to the House Committee on Appropriations, on joint-service efforts to link enlistment standards and job performance, the Office of the Assistant Secretary of Defense (Force Management and Personnel) admitted that sharing data among the services was problematic and that they wanted "an explicit policy and agreement with TDAC allowing each service to approve the release of data to any other agency outside that service, and to review any analyses proposed by OSD or TDAC" (ASD[FMP], 1985, p. 10). In January 1986, the Secretary of the Navy called DTAC an "unacceptable intruder into the military departments' prerogatives concerning training management" (Lehman, 1986), after it had tried to catalogue training simulators in what the Navy perceived as an attempt to centralize training system management under OSD. He recommended, "strongly that TDAC be disestablished" (Lehman, 1986). In May 1986, Assistant Secretary Cox told the Deputy Secretary of Defense that the Navy's

> recommendation to disestablish TDAC appear[s] extreme . . . the expressed positions of the Services cannot be ignored without crippling TDAC's effectiveness. Training and performance data and tools cannot be compiled or improved without the cooperation of all four Services. (Cox, 1986a)

He proposed to

> narrow the focus of TDAC to emphasize its role as a tool generator and data repository, and remove the term "analysis" from its name. . . . And assign . . . [the TDAC Director] to a different post after a fixed period (maximum of three years from now). (Cox, 1986a)

Neither a change in name to the Defense Training and Performance Data Center nor a revised charter that reflected its "role as a training and job performance data repository and builder of tools for evaluating training and job performance" was enough to save it (Cox, 1986b).

In 1991, the National Research Council concluded that these hopes were only partially met. Commenting on the six years of the JPM Project, the council found that the

> full implication of the job performance measurement research for military policy makers—and for civilian-sector employers—remain to be worked out in coming years. It has produced a rich body of data and a wealth of methodological insights and advances. Most important of all, the JPM Project . . . defined the challenges for the next generation of research on performance assessment. (Wigdor and Green, 1991, p. 210)

John Campbell, writing in 2001 from a perspective almost two decades after Project A began, found that

> the original objectives set by the sponsor [for Project A] were met. Using well-developed measures and large representative samples, it was possible to estimate the validity of the current system and to estimate the degree of selection validity and classification efficiency that could be achieved from the current state-of-the-art. . . . However, there was not immediate wholesale implementation of the project's findings into the enlisted personnel and classification system. (Campbell, 2001a, pp. 587–588)

His final words were that continually "trying to improve our models of relevant domains, as well as the interrelationship among them, is as critical for [good] practice as it is for [good] science" (Campbell, 2001a, p. 589).

The Legacy of JPM

The 10-year, multimillion dollar JPM Projects demonstrated that cognitive ability, as measured by AFQT, is a strong predictor of job performance across a variety of occupations.[15] The best predictor of successful adjustment to military life is the procession of a high school diploma. The problem, however, as ODS Director of Accession Policy Steve Sellman found, was that even after the supportive findings about AFQT scores and perseverance of high school, the DoD was "virtually defenseless to justify those requirements and the associated budget" (Sellman, 1994). The policy question had shifted. It was no longer good enough to answer the question about how much quality was enough. The question now turned to how much quality we could afford. Sellman, working with the National Academy of Sciences and others

> developed a mathematical model that links job performance to recruit quality and recruiting resources; this model specifies the number of high-quality recruits who will provide the desired level of job performance for the least cost . . . [DoD selected] the level of performance provided by the 1990–91 enlisted cohort, a group that

---

[15] Laurence has said that "Project A found that the benefits of selection and classification using the ASVAB held not only over the course of the first enlistment term but also into the career force as a predictor of non-commission officer effectiveness" (1992, pp. 36–48).

produced satisfactory performance during Operations Desert Shield and Desert Storm. (Sellman, 2004, p. 9)

Using the results of the cost-performance trade-off model that David Smith and Paul Hogan (1994) had developed, Sellman and William Carr put forward new recruiting guidelines known as the "60/90 rule." The Defense Planning Guidance for 1993 (and subsequent years) contains the following passage:

> Service programs will ensure at least 90 percent of non–prior service recruits are high school diploma graduates with 60 percent . . . drawn from Armed Force Qualifications Test Categories I–IIIA. No more than 4 percent of the recruits will come from Category IV. (As quoted in Carr, 2004)

Managing Recruiting

The Reagan administration is most often remembered for the pay increase it pushed through Congress in the months after first taking office. That increase, coupled with the Nunn-Warner pay increases in 1980 and the pay changes that the Carter administration had included in its version of the FY 1982 budget, resulted in a pay increase of 25 percent in two years.[16] What was also important to General Max Thurman, commander of the Army's Recruiting Command (and later when he was the Army's Deputy Chief of Staff for Personnel) were the various bonus programs and programs that increased resources available to recruiters and that supported the recruiting process. In remarks at the U.S. Naval Academy (November 2–4, 1983) commemorating the tenth anniversary of the end of conscription, he highlighted these programs: "We have found the levers to pull" (Thurman, 1986, p. 274). He then gave a number of examples of how he had used research to show what worked—the Youth Attitudinal Tracking Survey (YTS), educational benefits, bonuses, recruiters, and advertising—in sustaining the all-volunteer force.

Youth Attitudinal Tracking Survey

A decade later, again at Annapolis, but this time at a conference celebrating the second decade of the all-volunteer force (September 15–17, 1993), the now-retired General Thurman again highlighted the important contribution research played in making the all-volunteer force a success.[17] Of the 13 "major actions" that "turned the Army's 1979 recruiting failure into the success story of the 1980s," one of them was

> developing a "research program" involving the Army's advertising agency, . . . the RAND Corporation, DoD's Youth Attitudinal Tracking Survey (YATS), the U.S.

---

[16] While the 25 percent increase took place during the Reagan administration, the majority of the change, a 19.6 percent increase, was in place or programmed before President Reagan took office.

[17] The conference proceedings were dedicated to the memory of General Thurman, who died from leukemia on December 1, 1995, just before they were published.

Military Academy at West Point, and the Army Research Institute to advise the Army about what the youth of America were thinking. This led to a normative approach to the Army's advertising strategy. *Understanding the market is critical to business success.* (Thurman, 1996, p. 60, emphasis added)

YATS was a national survey of military eligible non–prior service youths between the ages of 16 and 21. It was started in 1975 as a semiannual survey; in 1980, women were included for the first time; in 1981 and for the rest of the period, it was administered annually.[18] While individual versions of YATS provided valuable information gained from the answers to specific questions and assessment of specific options were tested,[19] the managers of the all-volunteer force most often used the results of the survey to track changes in the answers to the "propensity to enlist" questions. During these years, YATS became the barometer for military enlistment.

The question of the validity and usefulness of the enlistment intentions portion of YATS as a predictor of actual enlistments was answered in a series of studies by Bruce Orvis and his colleagues at RAND during the 1980s. In 1992, Orvis published a "synthesis" of the results of his decade-long research (1992). His analysis was based on matching the records of individuals who took test against information on whether the respondents had enlisted or had taken the ASVAB to qualify for military service. Between spring 1976 and fall 1981, over 43,000 records were matched. Table 16.1 "shows the relationship between strength of enlistment intention" and the percentage actually tested; the "actual behavior of the respondents shows a very strong and statistically significant relationship to strength of enlistment intention" (Orvis et al., 1992, p. 10).

Table 16.1
Enlistment and Written Testing Rates by Intention Level,
Combined YATS Surveys, Spring 1976–Fall 1980

Enlistment Intention Level	Percentage Enlisting by March 1984	Percentage Testing by March 1984
Positive intention and unaided mention	37	55
	(0.05)	(0.05)
Positive intention, no unaided mention	16	29
	(0.23)	(0.29)
Negative intention	6	12
	(0.72)	(0.72)

SOURCE: Orvis (1992, p. 11).

NOTES: Results are weighted to ensure representativeness (N = 33,909). The proportion of the sample classified at each level is shown in parenthesis.

Unaided mention means that the question asked the respondent what he or she planned to do in the next few years.

---

[18] It ended in 1999 as part of Secretary of Defense William Cohen's general move to "revitalize" military recruiting.

[19] Orvis discussed this in Chapter 4 (Orvis et al., 1992, pp. 36–48).

Table 16.2
Sample Distribution and Sources of Enlistees by Intention Level, Combined YATS Surveys, Spring 1976–Fall 1980

Enlistment Intention Level	Percentage of Sample	Percentage of Enlistees
Positive intention and unaided mention	5	18
Positive intention, no unaided mention	23	36
Negative intention	72	46

SOURCE: Orvis (1992, p. 17).

NOTE: Results are weighted to ensure representativeness (N = 39,909; N = 3,258 enlistees).

One of the most interesting and important results of the research was that the negative intentions group, which accounted for an overwhelming majority of respondents—over two-thirds of all respondents had no plans to join the military—made up almost half of the respondents who eventually enlisted. Table 16.2 shows the numbers.

Orvis answered the question of validity and usefulness in six seminal points:

- Intention information is a significant predictor of enlistment behavior.
- Individual service enlistment intentions predict which service will be selected as well as whether an individual will enlist.
- Intention data provide information about a person's probability of enlisting not known from his demographic characteristics.
- Aggregate intention data are a significant predictor of geographical enlistment rates.
- The relationship between intention and enlistment depends on the frequency of enlistment in the population, the period between measurement of intention and enlistment, and demand constraints on enlistment.
- Because it represents a larger percentage of the population, the negative intention group is an important source of enlistees. (Orvis et al., 1992, pp. 49–50)

Why Do People Enlist?

The YATS studies clearly showed that a higher propensity to enlist makes recruiting easier. However, it also shows that not everyone with a high propensity to enlist actually enlists, and almost half of those who do enlist were likely to have expressed disinclination earlier. Our understanding of how to manage the enlistment process begins by understanding why people enlist. James Hosek and Chris Peterson at RAND thought that eligible youth population "consists of groups of individuals who make decisions regarding school, work, and military service" and that "knowing how enlistment determinants differ by market segment should aid the efforts both of recruiters and enlistment policymakers" (Hosek and Peterson, 1985, p. v). They examined how these choices are made by two distinct segments of the youth population, the high school *senior* and the nonstudent high school *graduate* in the labor market. The popular image in most people's minds of military recruiting is a recruiter working with a high school senior as he struggles to decide whether he wants to go to college or wants to go to work for either the military or a civilian employer.

In the 1980s, however, the majority of young men who were eligible to enlist from any given cohort did not come from this pool. These were the young men who decided to work for a civilian employer rather than go on to college or join the military. Hosek and Peterson estimated that the 1979 cohort was made up of 1.55 million seniors and 3.0 million graduates (Hosek and Peterson, 1985, p. 7).[20] Using microdata on enlistment behavior of individuals, rather than aggregate data they found that

> seniors and graduates do differ substantially in the empirical determinants of their enlistment decisions. Graduates appear more sensitive to work-related variables such as employment status, wage rates, labor force experience, job tenure, and, if not currently employed, duration of joblessness. Seniors, by contrast, appear more sensitive to education-related variables representing learning proficiency, ability to finance further education, and parental influences. (Hosek and Peterson, 1985, pp. v–vi)[21]

By segmenting the market, Hosek and Peterson were able to obtain results that should be very helpful to recruiters as they plan their strategies for reaching their goals. For example, Hosek and Peterson found that, while

> *seniors* expecting more education are less likely to enlist, *graduates* expecting more education are more likely to enlist . . . *seniors* from higher income families [generally] have lower enlistment probabilities unless they happen to come from a large family; or that a *graduate's* enlistment probability is unrelated to family income. (Hosek and Peterson, 1985, p. 51, emphasis added)

---

[20] This is somewhat misleading, since a person gets to be a senior once, but graduates remain in the pool of graduates for many years, until they are too old to enlist. The pool of graduates that recruiters face at any given time is the culmination of many of Hosek and Peterson's graduate cohorts. As a result, in any year the age distribution of enlistees looks like a Poisson distribution with a mean of about 19—the seniors—and a long tail extending to the enlistment cutoff age, 26. The tail is made up of enlistees from Hosek and Peterson's graduate cohorts. For example, while seniors from the 1979 cohort could have enlisted in 1979, the last of the 1979 cohort could have enlisted in 1987. Given that graduates get to make the decision about enlisting again and again and given that seniors make it once, the cumulative probability of enlisting for graduates is much higher than for seniors, as Hosek and Peterson report (Hosek and Peterson, 1985, p. 7).

[21] Hosek and Peterson noted their work was

> distinctive in several respects. First, we analyze[d] actual enlistment behavior, not enlisted intentions. Second, unlike most enlistment studies, we analyze[d] the behavior of individuals, not aggregates. And third, we use[d] a large, specially constructed database that permitted us to analyze behavior closely in distinct segments of the recruiting market. (Hosek et al., 1986, p. v)

Specifically, they created a choice-based sample of young male enlistees and nonenlistees combining observations from the 1979 DoD Survey of Personnel Entering Military Service (AFEES) and from the 1979 wave of the National Longitudinal Survey of Labor Force Behavior, Youth Survey (NLS), as discussed in Hosek and Peterson (Hosek and Peterson, 1983).

Table 16.3
Relationship Between Race/Ethnicity and Enlistment Probability

Race	All	Expect More Education		AFQT Group	
		Yes	No	Upper	Lower
Seniors					
White	0.020	0.020	0.033	0.018	0.058
Black	0.032	0.018	0.094	0.021	0.106
Hispanic	0.031	0.013	0.163	0.014	0.125
Graduates					
White	0.024	0.054	0.015	0.016	0.027
Black	0.038	0.086	0.017	0.040	0.026
Hispanic	0.019	0.039	0.021	0.010	0.019

SOURCE: Hosek (1985, p. 47).

Hosek and Peterson's results can provide some insights into the potential drawing power of educational benefits as an incentive to enlist. Writing about their concern for the racial composition of the all-volunteer force, Janowitz and Moskos (1974) proposed an improved educational benefit because they believed it would be attractive to the white middle class, not to blacks. Hosek and Peterson found that,

> [f]or a given level of recruiting effort, a recruiter [wishing] to maximize the expected number of recruits . . . might work the graduate expect-more-education market more heavily since 70 percent of the males in that subsegment have higher enlistment probabilities. (Hosek et al., 1986, p. 23)

Their results (Table 16.3) showed that black graduates who "expect more education" have the highest enlistment probability of any group. Contrary to the speculations of Janowitz and Moskos, an improved educational benefit would be attractive to this group. Moreover, since blacks have lower family incomes, the educational benefit might attract more blacks, on the margin, than whites.

Educational Benefits as an Incentive to Enlist

In 1976, the GI Bill came to an end and was replaced by the Veterans Education Assistant Program (VEAP). Under this program, the government matched 2 for 1 the dollars a soldier contributed to an education fund. Over a career, a soldier could "contribute a maximum of $2,700; after matching, this yields a total of $8,100 to support postservice education" (Polich et al., 1982, p. 5).

The VEAP program, by itself and with a lump sum addition of funds (the VEAP "kicker") that was given to high-quality personnel who enlisted in a critical occupational specialty, was tested in 1979 (Haggstrom et al., 1981). The test confirmed that the basic VEAP was not very attractive and that the "kickers probably produced [only] a small increase in enlistments" (Polich et al., 1982, p. 6). Some in the Army and Congress thought the kicker was not large enough, and in 1980 Congress directed that two noncontributory plans be tested. In all, four options were tested in different parts of the country between December 1980 and September 1981. The base case, the program that was in effect before and throughout the test period, was the basic VEAP program, with the Army allowing additional payments—for 2-year enlistments ($2,000), 3-year enlistments ($3,000), and 4-year enlistments ($6,000) for high-quality, high school graduates in the top 50th percentile or above and who enlisted in a critical occupational specialty. An Army "Ultra VEAP" in select areas paid $8,000 for 2-year enlistments and $12,000 for 3- and 4-year enlistments. Noncontributory programs were used in other regions; one region received

> the same total amount as basic VEAP (plus the kickers of up to $6,000 in the Army), without requiring any payment by the individual. The fourth program is considerably more generous, providing a payment for tuition and a stipend for living expenses. In addition . . . the benefit is indexed to rise with the cost of education; and if the service member later decides to reenlist, he may transfer his benefit to a dependent or to "cash out" of the program to obtain 60 percent of its value. (Polich et al., 1982, p. 8)

Like the 1979 test before it, RAND carried out the test for the Office of the Secretary of Defense. The country was divided into a number of treatment regions and a control region, as shown in Figure 16.2. RAND used an allocation algorithm to assign the test program to the various geographic areas, which "ensured geographic balance, and matched all test cells to 1979 enlistment rates, local unemployment rates, and local civilian wage rates" (Polich et al., 1982, p. 10).

This test, with educational assistance levels higher than those in 1979, "demonstrated that educational benefits did bring about substantial increases in enlistments" (Polich et al., 1982, p. 32). The test provided some very interesting results that were useful both for designing the details of specific options for the future and for addressing the troublesome issue of interservice competition for recruits:

> The Army's Ultra-VEAP Kicker program increased Army enlistments by [at least] 9 percent. . . .
> The Tuition/Stipend Program, which offered equal benefits to all services, also increased Navy and Air Force enlistments by smaller amounts. However, the program *reduced* Army enlistments by 6 percent, compared with the results in the control program, in which the Army was able to offer larger benefits than the other services. We concluded that the removal of the differences between the Army and the other services explained the Army's loss of enlistments under the Tuition/Stipend Plan. . . .
> We found evidence that recruiting for the combat specialties was hurt when the Army added noncombat skills to the test. . . . [M]ilitary applicants were much more responsive to the basic level of benefits than to any of the other specific provisions such as loan repayment or indexing. Finally, the survey results indicate that

Figure 16.2
Educational Assistance Test Design

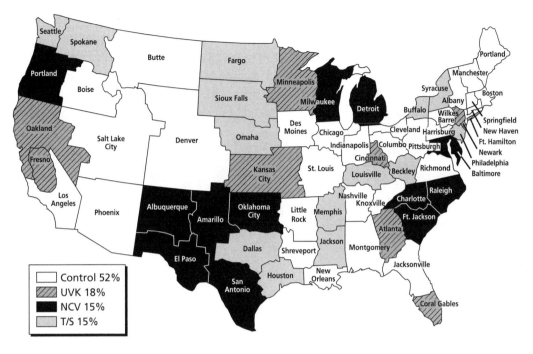

SOURCE: Polich et al. (1982, p. 10).
RAND *MG265-16.2*

cash bonuses, as well as educational benefits, can be an effective incentives for recruiting high-quality personnel. (Polich et al., 1982, pp. 32–33, emphasis in the original)[22]

Even though the results of the Educational Assistance Test Program were promising, the services were not prepared to "invest" their own funds in a new and permanent educational assistance program. On September 10, 1981, Korb told Congress that DoD "continues to believe that it is premature to consider enactment of H.R. 1400" (Korb et al., 1981, p. 54)—the bill authored by Congressman Sonny Montgomery of Mississippi.

Opposition to a new program continued through the following year. On February 1, 1982, Deputy Secretary of Defense Frank Carlucci met with the services and subsequently asked Korb "to put together a proposal for an educational benefits program, based on the particular needs of each of the military departments, to begin in FY 83" (Carlucci, 1982). Korb polled the services: The Army wanted to keep the VEAP program. It would fund a new program only if its budget was increased. The Air Force,

---

[22] The survey polled 3,700 applicants who took the military aptitude test.

citing "good recruiting and retention," also wanted to keep the current VEAP program. As an indication of how far things had turned around, the Air Force thought "funding for a new education benefits program would not compete with more urgent manpower programs" (Juliana, 1982). The Navy, ever wary of giving a competitive advantage to the Army, also wanted to continue the VEAP program, but "will not support ultra VEAP" because it "provides too great an advantage to the Army." In September 1982 Korb told Carlucci "none of the Services support funding a new educational benefit program at this time" (Juliana, 1982). Nevertheless, in the years ahead, Congress would provide an ever-expanding series of educational benefits, and by 1990, the Navy had implemented its own Navy College Fund (NCF).

Enlistment Bonuses

The educational assistance program, while popular with some members of Congress, has several built-in problems. On July 24, 1981, Korb told Congress that the program had advantages over other incentive programs:

> The bonus levels and skills for which bonuses are offered can be adjusted to changes in supply and demand. The bonus can be promoted to satisfy many needs and desires of the target population; and to a segment of the market, the bonus offers an immediate payoff which is valued more highly than a benefit that is delayed such as educational benefits received after satisfactory completion of the enlistment. (Korb, 1981, p. 13)[23]

With the Uniformed Services Pay Act of 1981, Congress expanded the enlistment bonus program and ordered a test of "the effectiveness of various bonus levels for four-year enlistments, . . . three-year enlistments, and the interaction between [t]hem" (Korb, 1982b, p. 500).

To meet the congressional mandate and test for *market expansion effects, skill channeling effects,* and *term of enlistment effects,* DoD and the Army undertook a two-year test from July 1982 to June 1984. As directed by Congress, the Enlistment Bonus Test was modeled after the Educational Assistance Test of the previous year and was also to be carried out by RAND (Polich et al., 1986, p. 8).

Coming soon after the Educational Assistance Test, the Bonus Test was a not-very-thinly veiled competition between the two types of incentives—a competition that reflected the very different views of the Army and OSD and "some groups in Congress" about the possible effects of a cash bonus on the behavior of a prospective recruit. Trying to measure these differences was a critical factor to be considered in designing the test. Mike Polich and his colleagues recorded the differing perspectives in RAND's final report. They described the OSD and congressional view as being that

---

[23] In September 1981, when he testified on DoD's position on Congressman Montgomery's new GI Bill, Korb observed that "post-service educational assistance programs create a retention disincentive once a member has earned his basic entitlement" (Korb et al., 1981, p. 53).

Table 16.4
Test Cells

Test Cell	Percentage of Nation in Test Cell	Bonus Amount ($)[a]		
		Four Years	Three Years	Two Years
A	70	5,000	0	0
B	15	8,000	0	0
C	15	8,000	4,000	0

SOURCE: Polich et al. (1986, p. 13).

[a]This is the bonus for high-quality recruits entering test-eligible skills.

larger bonuses should encourage more high-quality young people to enter the Army. . . . [T]he $4,000 three-year bonus would attract enough new people signing three-year contracts to offset any tendency of the three-year bonus to draw recruits away from four-year commitments. (Polich et al., 1986, pp. 10–11)

And described the Army view as being that

cash incentives . . . appeal much less than educational benefits to prospects in the early stages of the enlistment decision process. . . . [L]arge bonuses may be expected to produce only small increases in total enlistments, but should generate major changes in recruits' choices of skills. (Polich et al., 1986, p. 11)

The test design provided three "test cells," a control group and two "treatment" groups (see Table 16.4). Military Enlistment Processing Stations were the unit of analysis. They were randomly assigned to test cells

based on a statistical model that also imposed matching or balancing constraints on certain variables . . . that could be measured during the year immediately preceding the experiment and that might be expected to exert an important influence on the number of Army enlistments during the experiment. (Polich et al., 1986, p. 14)

Table 16.5 shows the variables that were "balanced." The test cells were assigned to individual Military Enlistment Processing Stations (MEPSs) throughout the United States in such a way as to protect "against extraneous factors that might complicate comparisons among cells" (Polich et al., 1986, p. 17). Figure 16.3 maps the final assignments.

Given the critical role that awareness of bonus options might have on the results of the experiment, the Army provided its recruiting battalions with advertising kits that contained

newspaper "glossy" ads, radio tapes and scripts, and press releases with messages specific to each test cell. [The RAND team] verified that the battalions did, in fact,

Table 16.5
Test Cell Balancing

Balancing Variable	Value, by Cell		
	A	B	C
Male high-quality enlistments, per 100 males age 17–21 in population	1.14	1.14	1.13
Unemployment rate (number of unemployed per 100 in labor force)	7.69	7.66	7.45
Wage ratio (civilian hourly pay divided by military hourly pay)	1.48	1.52	1.48
High-quality military available persons, per 100 population	15.25	15.22	15.23
Nonwhite persons, per 100 population	14.80	16.37	16.22
Number of Army recruiters, per 1,000 population	0.87	0.89	0.89
High-quality recruiting quotas, per 100 population	1.21	1.18	1.18
Percentage of cell population in east	28	13	16
Percentage of cell population in west	19	12	25
Percentage of cell population in south	19	29	22
Population in cell, as a percentage of the total U.S. population	69.1	15.5	15.4

SOURCE: Polich et al. (1986, p. 15).

Figure 16.3
Educational Assistance Test Design, Final Map Assignments

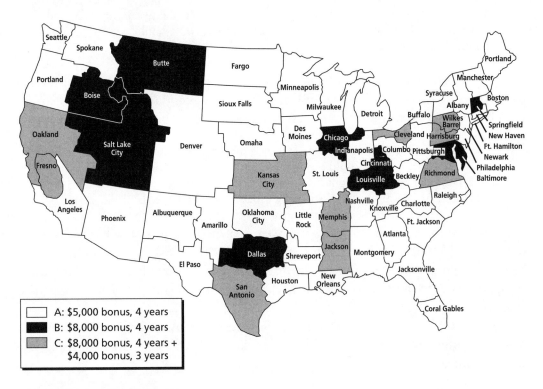

A: $5,000 bonus, 4 years
B: $8,000 bonus, 4 years
C: $8,000 bonus, 4 years +
   $4,000 bonus, 3 years

SOURCE: Polich et al. (1986, p. 18).

place bonus advertising in their local media; an examination of all local advertising purchases during the experiment showed that ads . . . were appropriately balanced across the test cells. (Polich et al., 1986, p. 19)

Most studies of this type simply compare raw data in the treatment and control cells. However, as the RAND team noted, "complexities in both the test and real-world recruiting systems, make such a simple analysis inappropriate." Introducing a level of sophistication not before seen in these type of studies, the RAND team developed an analytic strategy "that employs (1) differences between the test and base periods, (2) adjustments for changes in exogenous factors that affect enlistment supply, and (3) a system of simultaneous equations representing the behavior of recruiters as they react to supply changes" (Polich et al., 1986, pp. 21–22). Specifically,

- To control for differences in the base and test periods, RAND used the change in enlistments between the two periods as the output measure, rather than the absolute level of enlistments in the test period. Incorporating this measure in the analysis suggested "that factors unrelated to bonuses led to a 20 percent increase in recruiting supply, since bonuses remained constant in the control area" (Polich et al., 1986, p. 23).
- To control for unobserved factors that were not accounted for by balancing in the assignments of MEPS to test cells, RAND used a "change-analysis approach [that] has the advantage that it 'nets out' any differences between areas that are stable over time and that might be present even though we tried to balance cells" (Polich et al., 1986, p. 23).[24]
- To control for the "direction and intensity" of recruiters (Polich et al., 1986, p. 28), RAND incorporated the pioneering work of Jim Dertouzos (1985) and developed a simultaneous equation system to represent the joint effect of recruiters' behavior and enlistment supply.

The results of the RAND analysis were striking and provided important insights into the design of an optimal program of recruiting resources, e.g., recruiters, different types of bonuses, and advertising. The study found the following:

- How recruiters responded to supply changes could "significantly alter enlistment outcomes and, consequently, affect estimates of the bonus expansion effects" (Polich et al., 1986, p. 38).
- With the Army's new bonus program, it had to "pay an extra $3,000 to all recruits who enter the eligible skills for four years, not just to the 'newly attracted' recruits,"

---

[24] In effect, the change-analysis approach using log-differences controls for factors that are often explicitly entered as independent or explanatory variables in nonexperimental studies using regression techniques (Polich et al., 1986, p. 24).

which worked out to "$16,000 per new high-quality recruit" (Polich et al., 1986, p. 40).

- Conversely, increasing the recruiting staff meant that "it would cost about $5,400 to obtain an additional high-quality recruit" (Polich et al., 1986, p. 40).
- With advertising, "the marginal cost of obtaining a high-quality recruit is about $6,000 using national advertising and about $5,900 using local advertising" (Polich et al., 1986, p. 40).[25]
- RAND felt that the effects of the bonus and educational benefits tests could not be compared "without making cost assumptions that are difficult to justify" (Polich et al., 1986, p. 41).
- The test program did influence skill choices: "[M]any people who would have joined the Army in noneligible skills without the test program chose to move into the test-eligible skills because of the enhanced bonuses offered" (Polich et al., 1986, p. 44).
- Given that some had "feared that the program would 'cannibalize' four-year contracts by converting them into three-year contracts," that is not what actually happened: "Instead, the program's main effect on term of service choices was to persuade recruits who otherwise would have signed up for two years to sign for three years" (Polich et al., 1986, pp. 44–45).

The total effects were:

1. Market expansion: A 4.1 percent increase in Army high-quality contracts.
2. Skill channeling: A 31.7 [percent] increase in test-eligible skill contracts.
3. Term of service: A 15.3 percent increase in four-year terms. (Polich et al., 1986, p. 46)

RAND further observed that the man-year

percentage increases are larger than the market expansion effects for recruits because the test bonus programs did more than attract new people to the Army; they also persuaded some recruits who would have enlisted anyway to enlist for longer terms. . . . In addition, the Army obtained the benefit of shifting people from noneligible skills into test-eligible skills, which have chronically been difficult to fill. (Polich et al., 1986, p. 48)

RAND's final conclusion is noteworthy:

Of all the alternative policy options available, bonuses are the most flexible. Without altering the fundamental structure or level of military compensation, bonuses can be swiftly changed in response to critical shortfalls in particular personnel categories. The high degree of flexibility, combined with the dramatic impact of bonuses on occupations and term of service choices, make enlistment bonuses a

---

[25] The RAND authors call these "crude calculations" and warn that "such comparisons are extremely complex and to make them properly would require information that is not now available" (Polich et al., 1986, p. 50).

useful option for short-term management of enlistment flows and for targeting incentives toward particular subgroups. (Polich et al., 1986, p. 50)

Recruiters

The Bonus Experiment Study clearly pointed to the importance of recruiters as one, if not the most critical, element in the recruiting process. While there had been a number of earlier studies that explicitly considered the number of recruiters, with some even accounting for the effects quotas on their performance, the treatment of recruiters was rudimentary. The work of Jim Dertouzos in the early 1980s, however, stands out as the most rigorous examination of recruiters and the way they reacted to goals and quotas and other details of the recruiting process.[26] The lack of attention up to this time was all the more difficult to explain because of the wide variance in individual recruiter productivity within recruiting units and across the nation.

For most of the post–Gates Commission period, estimates of the supply of recruits remained focused on the effects of wages and unemployment on enlistments. While many cross-section studies did consider the number of recruiters, they did not consider factors that influenced the way recruiters did their job, that is, recruiter behavior. Recruiter behavior, however, was not lost on Major General Max Thurman when he took over the Army Recruiting Command in 1979. Under Thurman, the command developed models to determine the number of recruiting stations, allocate recruiters to them, and provide explicit recruiting goals, trade-off incentives, and rewards to recruiters. Thurman gave much credit for his success to a simple device he invented called the "mission box" (Thurman, 1996, p. 59). This was a card each recruiter carried to remind him of the number of high-quality recruits he was responsible for enlisting each month. Thurman wanted his recruiters to concentrate on quality, not quantity; no credit was given for low-quality recruits unless the recruiter also met his goal for high school graduates with above-average aptitude. The "mission box" was the key way he communicated to his recruiters what he expected of them.[27]

---

[26] Nelson (Nelson, 1986) reported the results of a large number of time-series and cross-sectional studies of the supply of first-term enlistees at the tenth-anniversary conference in November 1983. Few of the time-series studies, but most of the cross-sectional studies, include the number of recruiters as an important explanatory variable:

> The results from the cross-section studies and joint cross-section and time-series studies show strong positive effects due to increases in the number of recruiters. Although the results vary, the preponderance of studies show recruiter elasticity of 0.50 or larger. . . . Diminishing returns are inevitable, but we have not reached the point where investment in greater numbers of recruiters is uneconomic. In fact, studies typically show that increasing recruiters is the most cost-effective method of increasing enlistment supply. (Nelson, 1986, p. 45)

[27] Thurman put it this way

> If you told a guy, "Here's your mission card," you don't get any credit for anything unless it is in the mission box. The mission box was the tool to radiate the standards down and get people to do what was needed. You tell them to go out and get a 1-3A, they go get one. If you don't tell them to go get a 1-3A, then you get just anything. You get what you don't order. You get something, but you don't get what you had in mind. (Thurman, 1992, pp. 219–220)

Polich, J. Michael, James N. Dertouzos, and S. James Press, *The Enlistment Bonus Experiment,* Santa Monica, CA: RAND, R-3353-FMP, April 1986, pp. 29–30

The ultimate mix of enlistments chosen will depend on the incentives he faces and the relative rewards for securing different categories of enlistments. For illustrative purposes, let us assume that he moves to point A, representing H_A high-quality recruits and L_A low-quality recruits, respectively.

A changing economic or social environment or level of recruiting resource expenditures alters the range of feasible outcomes facing recruiters. For example, because the bonus test causes larger enlistment bonuses to be offered, recruiters will be able to secure increased numbers of enlistments. Suppose, for the time being, that recruiters continue to put forth the same level of effort as they did before the test began. The new level of enlistment supply, reflected in choices available to the recruiter, is indicated by the outermost solid line in Fig. 3. Of course, the observed effect of the larger bonuses on high-quality enlistments will depend not only on the magnitude of the shift in potential supply, but also on the allocation of effort among various recruiting activities. For example, the observed bonus effect on high-quality contracts will be dampened if recruiters decide to simultaneously increase

enlistments in lower-quality categories. Since identical outward shifts in supply can result in a variety of actual outcomes, test and pretest comparisons must control for movements along the tradeoff curve. Thus, we wish to identify point B, representing the potential increase in high-quality enlistments, holding the number of low-quality individuals constant.

In addition to holding low-quality enlistments constant, the movement to point B assumes that recruiters have incentives to maintain the degree of effort at the pretest level. However, there is compelling evidence that recruiters lack strong incentives to exceed quotas (see Dertouzos, 1983, 1985). Although achieving goals ("making mission") is viewed as essential for career advancement, *over*production has a distinct disadvantage: future quotas may be increased in response to present success. If this is true, recruiters might respond to the increase in the supply of enlistments by reducing their effort. The resulting range of choices, at the lower level of recruiting intensity, is represented by the dashed line falling between the initial tradeoff curve and the range of outcomes that would be feasible with constant effort.

Thus, even after controlling for the direction of recruiter effort, the resulting increase in high-quality enlistments, indicated by point C, may significantly underestimate the potential increase to point B. Of course, if recruiters have incentives to secure additional low-quality enlistments, the observed outcome would be at a point such as D, representing even fewer high-quality enlistments. Consequently, the measured bonus effect can be quite small even though the latent supply effect is significant. The degree of divergence between D and B will depend on levels and changes in quotas for different categories of recruits as well as the incentive systems in place during the initial and bonus test periods. However the importance of recruiter behavior remains an empirical question pending our analysis below.

Fig. 3—Potential effects of recruiter choices on bonus results

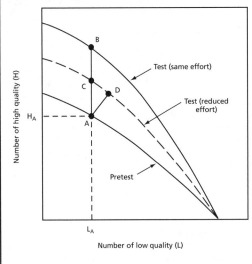

Early Research. The first consideration of the role recruiters play in the recruiting process was Alvin Cook and John White's efforts to estimate a supply curve for the Air Force during the draft period. They noted the role that Air Force recruiters played in "creaming" the volunteer population and stated that by examining "variations in recruiter force quality," they could "predict quality changes in recruits and, by extension, in volunteers, as a function of the draft and economic considerations" (Cook and White, 1970, p. 2).

Christopher Jehn and Hugh Carroll did one of the earliest studies of the "recruiting process," at CNA in 1972, "to determine the proximate causes of the [Navy] Recruiting Command's difficulties in FY 1972" (Jehn and Carroll, 1974, p. 1). At the time, they thought that "the question of recruiter productivity was especially interesting and . . . sought to determine not only how many recruiters were necessary but also where they should be stationed." They pooled monthly time-series and cross-sectional data for eight Navy recruiting regions for the eight months from October 1971 to June 1972, a period when no Navy recruiting area made its recruiting objective. They had data on the number of recruiters and unemployment rates for each area for each month. They controlled for population density and accounted for differences in relative wages across areas and changes over time with dummy variables. Their results showed that "the number of recruiters had little effect on the enlistment rate" (Jehn and Carroll, 1974, p. 10). Rather than draw the conclusion that "recruiters were not important," they interpreted the results as suggesting that the "*number* of recruiters is not nearly so important as might be their selection, training, motivation and management" (Jehn and Carroll, 1974, p. 14, emphasis in original).

Jehn and William Shughart extended the initial study using data from 43 Navy Recruiting Districts for CY 1973 and FY 1975. This time, recruiters "had a positive and strongly significant effect on enlistments" (Jehn and Shughart, 1979, p. 143). They also considered the effects of quotas and found that they "always had a positive and strongly significant coefficient" (Jehn and Shughart, 1979, p. 144). They "interpreted" their results to mean that there was a strong interaction between quotas and recruiters.

The concept of "density of recruiters" (recruiters divided by the eligible population) was added to the studies David Grissmer and his colleagues conducted at the General Research Corporation, the successor organization to the Research Analysis Corporation, the defunct Army federally contracted research center. They did not explicitly treat quotas and found inconsistent results for the influence of recruiters that they attributed to "shortcomings in the recruiter data" (Grissmer, 1974, p. 38).

Lawrence Goldberg, who used data from Navy Recruiting Districts for 1976 through 1981, "found that a service's recruiters increase its enlistments and the supply for DoD as a whole: the elasticities range between 0.30 and 0.88, averaging 0.52" (Goldberg, 1982, p. 37). His study did not explicitly consider recruiting goals set by the recruiting command as a separate explanatory variable because, as he argued, the

> goal is highly correlated with recruiters; indeed, one does not add a recruiter without giving him a goal, an implicit assumption on the other cross section studies. To estimate the recruiter elasticity from these . . . studies, goals per recruiter were held

constant. In so doing, they yielded recruiter elasticities that are similar to those in other studies [which did not control for the goal]. Thus it appears that omitting goals per recruiter does not cause a serious bias of the recruiter elasticity in cross section studies." (Goldberg, 1982, p. 11)

Goldberg's assertion notwithstanding, the issue of recruiter goals and how to treat them would become a significant issue in the estimation of military enlistments during the 1980s, as seen in the work of James Dertouzos (1983) and of Tom Daula and Dave Smith (1985a). As Dertouzos saw it, the failure to account for how the goal affects the behavior of recruiters was "a fundamental flaw in the methodology employed in [Goldberg's and] most manpower studies" (Dertouzos, 1984b, p. 1). He argued that

> the observed production of enlistments is assumed, at least implicitly, to be deter-mined solely by supply factors. But recruiters do not passively process enlistments; rather, allocating their time differently in response to quotas [goals] and to rewards for achieving and exceeding them, they alter both the quantity and quality of enlist-ments. By affecting recruiter behavior, demand factors such as goals and incentives can play a critical role in the determination of enlistments. (Dertouzos, 1985, p. 1)

A New Way of Looking at the Supply of New Recruits. The issues Dertouzos and Daula and Smith raised reflected fundamental advances in econometric theory suggested by Tom Sargent that question the stability and interpretation of data itself.[28] The basic argument was that observed variables did not change just because of a change in the environment but also as "the result of private agents' optimizing choices." This is clear from this extract from Sargent's groundbreaking article "Interpreting Economic Time Series," if we substitute the term *recruiter* for *agent,* the recruiter being the agent of the recruiting command. Sargent shows how important it is to understand what drives a recruiter's behavior and how his objectives and the constraints he faces could be just as important in determining enlistments as changes in level of compensation the military offers recruits.[29] Sargent wrote that the

---

[28] *Author's Note:* Tom Sargent and I served together as economists in the Office of the Assistant Secretary of Defense (Systems Analysis) in the late 1960s.

[29] It should be noted that recruiters are not the only recruiting professionals who interacted with prospective enlist-ees before a contract was signed. Beth Asch and Lynn Karoly found that

> While the key purpose of recruiters is to sell to youth the idea of military service, the role of the coun-selor is to "close" the enlistment sale and sell the specific terms of the enlistment contract such as the occupation and term of service. (Asch and Karoly, 1993, p. 1)

Since their job is to close the sale and to do it

> at the least resource cost to the service by emphasizing lower rather than higher-cost enlistment incen-tives . . . counselors are managed by incentive plans that are intended to ensure that counselor incen-tives coincide with service priorities. (Asch and Karoly, 1993, p. 2)

Their study provided estimates of how Army counselors affect enlistments into high-priority jobs, and

> estimates of the effectiveness of recruiting incentives, such as the Army College Fund (ACF) and enlist-ment bonuses, on occupational enlistments. . . . These estimates, unlike previous research, take into account the role of the counselor in channeling recruits into occupations. (Asch and Karoly, 1993, p. 4)

practice of dynamic econometrics should be changed so that it is consistent with the principle that people's rules of choice are influenced by their constraints. . . . The body of doctrine associated with the "simultaneous equation" model in econometrics properly directs the attention of the researcher beyond reduced-form parameters to the parameters of the "structural equation," which presumably describes those aspects of the behavior of people that prevail across a range of hypothetical environments. Estimates of the parameters of structural equations are needed in order to analyze an interesting class of policy interventions. . . . The basic idea is to interpret a collection of economic . . . [data] as resulting from the choices of private agents interacting in markets assumed to be organized along well-specified lines. . . . The reason for interpreting . . . [data] this way is practical: potentially it offers the analyst the ability to predict how agents' behavior and the random behavior of the market-determined variables will each change when there are policy interventions or other changes in the environment that alter some of the agents' dynamic constraints. (Sargent, 1981, pp. 214–215)

Past . . . studies should usually be regarded as having been directed at providing ways of summarizing the observed behavior of interrelated variables, without attempting to infer the objectives, opportunities, and constraints of the agents whose decisions determine those variables. Most existing studies can be viewed, at best, as having estimated parameters of agents' decision rules for setting chosen variables as functions of the information they process. . . . Dynamic economic theory implies that these decision rules cannot be expected to remain invariant in the face of policy interventions that take the form of changes in some of the constraints facing agents. . . . [H]istorical econometric estimates of such decision rules will provide poor predictions about behavior in a hypothetically new environment. . . . [T]he formulation, identification, and estimation of the models must . . . be approached in substantially new and different ways. Most existing models simply cannot be saved by simulating them a little more shrewdly. . . . Prior information about agents' criterion functions and constraints is what should be used in estimation. (Sargent, 1981, pp. 215–217)

Dynamic economic theory has forced us to reexamine whether objects long thought to be "structural," including the parameters of decision rules, . . . are correctly taken to be invariant with respect to changes in the environment. (Sargent, 1981, p. 233)

As Sargent might put it, Dertouzos's groundbreaking work approached "the formulation, identification, and estimation of the models in substantially new and different ways" (Sargent, 1981, p. 217). Moreover, Sargent's admonition that this new way of looking at things would mean "a substantial undertaking and involves major adjustments in the ways that we formulate, estimate and simulate econometric models" (Sargent, 1981, p. 233), was certainly true of Dertouzos's work.

Dertouzos on Recruiting.[30] Dertouzos's challenge to the traditional way supply elasticities were estimated was based on three insights. First, recruiters make a difference,

---

[30] Dertouzos presented an early version of his work at the May 1983 Joint Service Workshop on Recruiter Productivity, held at the Naval Postgraduate School in late February 1983. His work was well received by the "Services' policy people . . . because it quantifies previously missing information, i.e., individual choices" (Goodstadt et al., 1983, p. 8).

both by being there and by the choice of activities they could undertake. Some activities are more productive than others, and focusing on different types of potential recruits makes a difference in the total number and quality mix of accessions. Second, recruiters will choose a set of activities that will maximize the points they are awarded by their goal system, subject to the constraints of time, the environment, and the resources they are given. While the goal systems are usually specified in terms of minimum absolute numbers of recruits a recruiter must bring under contract in any month, relative points for high-quality and low-quality enlistments sometimes depend on whether or not a recruiter has reached this minimum acceptable level. Third, a single-equation estimate of the supply function would provide biased results because the proper specification of the supply of high quality recruits, for example, would include the number of low-quality recruits. Therefore, a two-stage simultaneous estimation of parameters would be required.

The economic model Dertouzos suggested provided a rich framework for understanding how the behavior of recruiters affects the number of people the services are able to recruit and the likely effects of alternative incentive systems on recruiter behavior. His insights were like letting the proverbial genie out of the bottle. They were so simple and fundamentally correct that, once stated, subsequent research could never be judged by the old standards. Dertouzos' argument was that, in the past,

> research on aggregate military enlistments has focused primarily on the factors affecting the labor supply of the youth population. In contrast, recent efforts[31] strongly suggest that recruiters behaving as agents on behalf of their service, are not merely processing enlistments. . . . [Past studies,] at least implicitly . . . assume that quotas affect recruiters in a straightforward and predictable manner. . . . Little attention has been paid to the status of aggregate performance. The relationships between quotas, market potential, reward programs, and recruiting effort are likely, in reality, to be quite complex. These complexities could have profound implications for the analysis of aggregate enlistments. (Dertouzos, 1984, p. 127)

Dertouzos's theoretical model can be used to analyze recruiter behavior when recruiters act alone and under a team concept. He found that

> the relationships between enlistments and quota levels will depend on several factors, including the feasibility of the mission, the relative rewards and difficulty of securing different categories of recruits, and whether the recruiter belongs to a successful command unit. (Dertouzos, 1984, p. 135)

Dertouzos provided three sets of estimates for 1980 using monthly data from 33 MEPS areas. The first set of estimates, reflecting "the common research approach" (Dertouzos, 1984, p. 12), reports ordinary regression coefficients for an equation that

---

[31] Dertouzos cited four documents (Daula and Smith, 1985a; Daula and Smith, 1985b; Dertouzos, 1984; Dertouzos, 1985).

does not include quota variables. The second set includes the quota variables and "can be interpreted as the reduced-form relationship between the high-quality enlistments and factors which characterized both supply and demand" (Dertouzos, 1985, p. 12). The third set "reports results from the joint maximum likelihood estimation of the supply relationship along with the reduced-form expression" for the low-quality enlistments (Dertouzos, 1984, p. 12).

The estimates Dertouzos obtained using his third specification provided uniformly larger elasticities because "they represent partial elasticities or the expected percentage increase in high quality enlistments holding the number of low-quality enlistments constant" (Dertouzos, 1985, p. 18). The specification also allows for the estimation of the "trade-off parameter" that showed "a 10-percent increase in low-quality enlistments would result in nearly a 4-percent decline in the number of high-quality enlistments." Dertouzos evaluated the elasticities "at the mean values for high- and low-quality graduates, . . . [which] yields a trade-off of slightly greater than four to one" (Dertouzos, 1985, pp. 18–19).

One of the most important issues Dertouzos raised was how the system of goals and quotas affected the total effort recruiters put forward, especially after the goal had been reached. He noted that, "although recruiter success and subsequent promotion depend on production relative to quota allocations, the rewards for overproduction may not, for a variety of reasons, be sufficient to induce maximum effort at all times" (Dertouzos, 1985, p. 19). Given that leisure is always a trade-off with work, the issue was not only the return a recruiter might get for exceeding his goal today but also how such behavior might influence the goals set for him in the future. He found that "[r]ecruiters who exceeded quotas in 1980 confronted relatively higher quotas in 1981. If production in one period redefines standards in the next, extreme success may guarantee failure in the future." He estimated that "overproduction by 20-percent in 1980 could . . . [result in] a 10-percent increase in quotas the next year" (Dertouzos, 1985, p. 20, n. 8).

Dertouzos tested this proposition by dividing his sample between areas that had achieved their goals and those that had not. The results for the two groups were strikingly different from each other and from the results obtained when all areas were analyzed together. He found that there was "a strong implication" that recruiters in areas that achieved their goals had "few incentives to increase production because of an improved climate once quotas have already been achieved" (Dertouzos, 1985, p. 24). This means that estimates of what effects positive changes—such as in the economic environment and/or an increase in recruiting resources, including advertising or enlistment bonuses—would have on enlistments would underestimate the true potential of such changes. So, as more resources are put into recruiting relative to the goals given to recruiters and as the job becomes somewhat easier, recruiters who may now be able to make their goals will respond by cutting back on their efforts. This is the classic problem of a minimum goal or floor becoming a ceiling. Writing in the mid-1980s, Dertouzos could observe that since, at that time, recruiting success is at an unprecedented level. . . . In such an environment, recruiters who are given the extra advantage of an enlistment bonus or increased advertising expenditures may not respond as they would under conditions marked by underproduction relative to quota. Thus, any evaluation of the potential effectiveness of these resource expenditures must consider their likely impact. (Dertouzos, 1985, p. 31)

In fact, at the time DoD was engaged in a very large-scale test of service-specific and joint advertising.

Dertouzos, James N., "Microeconomics Foundation of Recruiter Behavior: Implications for Aggregate Enlistment Models," in Curtis L. Gilroy, ed., *Army Manpower Economics*, Boulder, Colo.: Westview Press, 1984

Recruiter Preferences

Recruiter preferences will depend on the rewards associated with different combinations of enlistments. Under the assumption that a station commander wishes to maximize points, potential enlistment outcomes can be ranked in order of preference. This ordering can be represented by a series of "isopoint" lines that indicate all combinations of high- and low-quality contracts that provide equivalent point totals for a representative station commander with a staff of 10 recruiters.

For this illustration, I assume that each recruiter receives a quota of one high- and one low-quality recruit. In Figure 4-1, Q represents the commander's mission of 10 high-quality and 10 low-quality enlistments. If the station achieves these quotas, the commander receives 40 bonus points for making mission. For recruiter overproduction,

30 points are received for each high-quality enlistment and 20 points for each low-quality enlistment. Thus, each in a series of parallel isopoint lines for both under- and overproduction outcomes will have a slope of 2/3, reflecting the relative value of high-quality versus low-quality enlistments. For example, the line closest to the origin represents all combinations of enlistments that earn the commander 6 points. Recall, commanders receive points based on average production. If the 10 recruiters sign four high-quality contracts only, they earn a total of 60 points (1/2 of 4 times 30). However if the recruiters instead sign six low-quality recruits, the commander will also receive 6 points based on the same total of 60 (1/2 of 6 times 20). The line connecting these extremes represents all combinations of high- and low-quality recruits worth 6 points.

Note that the isopoint line passing through the quota represents 25 points. Securing 17 high- or 25 low-quality recruits yields an average point production of about 25 points. However, attracting 10 recruits of each category, also worth 25 points at the underproduction rates, earns the commander the bonus of 40 points. Thus, the isopoint line if discontinuous at the quota.

In addition, the 45-degree line passing through the quota point, Q, represents all combinations of high- and low-quality recruits that sum to 20 enlistments. Because of the substitution rules, choices representing a higher quality composition along the

Figure 4-1. Isopoint curves in the absence of a team concept.

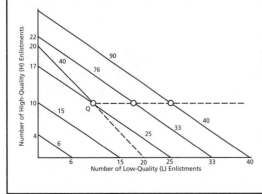

Dertouzos, James N., "Microeconomics Foundation of Recruiter Behavior: Implications for Aggregate Enlistment Models," in Curtis L. Gilroy, ed., *Army Manpower Economics*, Boulder, Colo.: Westview Press, 1984—continued

45-degree volume-mission line are on the isopoint locus representing 40 points. Lower quality composition, of course, results in lower points because of underproduction. In order to earn 40 points while not making the quality mission, it is necessary to sign several additional low-quality enlistments. In this example, the bottom portion of the isopoint line to the extreme right also represents enlistment combinations worth 40 points.

For overproduction, the isopoint lines retain the slope of 2/3, but represent higher per contract point totals. In addition, the discontinuity at the high-quality quota remains, which is illustrated by the dashed horizontal line extending from point Q. The discontinuity exists because enlistments are worth half as much when high-quality quotas are not achieved. For underproduction combinations in the vicinity of this discontinuity, the marginal value of high-quality enlistments is very high. Clearly, recruiters have few incentives to overproduce low-quality enlistments if high-quality missions are not being made. For example, the extreme isopoint line represents 90 points if the high-quality mission is achieved. By choosing a point just above the high-quality mission, 40 bonus points and full overproduction points for the excess are earned. For points just below, half points are earned and no bonus points are received. Thus, recruiters have strong incentives to make their high-quality missions before adding excess low-quality enlistments.

Applying the Model to the Navy and the Freeman Incentive Plan. The Freeman Plan was a Navy unique incentive system that operated in parallel with a traditional monthly quota system used by all of the recruiting commands. The Navy wanted to encourage sustained long-term performance. Under the provisions of the Navy system developed for the Navy Recruiting Command by retired Admiral John Freeman awards were given to recruiters whose average accumulated points for a 12-month period exceeded predetermined award levels. Those who failed to qualify for an award were put on a 12-month moving average until they did qualify. After receiving an award, the 12 month cycle started again. Additional awards were available based on multiyear performance.

Beth Asch built on earlier insights about supply and demand factors and used a two-stage least-squares estimation model to "determine whether the Freeman Plan results in a pattern of behavior in recruiters consistent with the Navy's recruiting goals" (Asch, 1990, p. vi). Clearly, as Asch noted, the recruiters wanted "to maximize their chances of winning a reward, and to that end develop a strategy for earning points" (Asch, 1990, p. v). The particular features of the Freeman Plan allowed Asch to examine how recruiters allocated their efforts over time, both over a one-year production cycle and over their tenures as recruiters—normally three years. As one might expect, Asch found that recruiters gamed the system. For example, Ashe found that,

> [w]ith a 12-month production cycle, recruiters can win only three awards at most. Recruiters aiming to win all three must supply sufficient effort to win every 12 months. Those who have the usual three-year tour and who fail to win immediately after the first year become ineligible to win all three awards. Such recruiters may

reduce effort because they have more than 12 months to win each of the two awards for which they remain eligible. (Asch, 1990, p. 15)

She found several patterns of recruiter behavior:

- Recruiter productivity appeared to increase over the 12-month production cycle, with production becoming the highest after a recruiter qualified for a Freeman Plan award.
- Recruiters may have stockpiled future enlistments at the beginning of the cycle and drawn down the stockpile after qualifying for an award.
- Recruiter productivity dropped immediately after receiving an award.
- Recruiters who were eligible for a Freeman award did not display the usual end-of-tour decline in productivity.
- The point differential between high- and low-quality enlistment was such that "there is some incentive to recruit low-quality enlistments under certain circumstances"(Asch, 1990, p. viii).

The one-year Freeman production cycle encouraged periods of low and high productivity, reduced productivity after awards were received, and reduced effort at the ends of tours. Asch found that "Shortening the production cycle . . . may cause recruiter productivity to be more stable over time" (Asch, 1990, p. ix).

Asch noted that recruiters differed in both their ability and effort. To estimate the effects of quotas and the Freeman plan, she needed to "eliminate the effects of differences in recruiter ability while ensuring that the effects of variations in effort remain" (Asch, 1990, p. 23). By assuming that ability and effort were not correlated and using a fixed-effect model to exclude attributes that changed over time, Asch was able to isolate recruiter effort and the effects of tenure, tour length, experience—time as a recruiter—and the Freeman point structure had on making quotas, e.g., under- or overproduction relative to the quota. She addressed the simultaneous supply-and-demand relationship of low- and high-quality production and Freeman points using a two-stage least-squares regression model. Her findings suggested that "quality mix regresses toward the mean. . . . Recruiters who are in a good position for winning a reward reduce effort while poorer performers increase effort" (Asch, 1990, p. 34). She found that production rose over the first production cycle, then fell off at the beginning of the second production cycle, only to rise again toward its end. This pattern is consistent with recruiters who

> initially stockpile future recruits and deplete their stock at the end of a cycle when they become eligible to win a reward. Alternatively, recruiters may vary their level of effort over the cycle. They may simply procrastinate until they near the reward point in the cycle, thereby supplying less effort initially and more effort at the end of the cycle. (Asch, 1990, p. 38)

Clearly, the Freeman Plan was having an effect, but not always the effect the Navy wanted. Recruiters adjusted their performance to the plan's cycle. Fine-tuning the plan by increasing the point differentials between high and lower quality recruits or reducing the cycle to discourage periods of slack production seemed appropriate.

Advertising: The Joint Advertising Mix Test

In May 1983, Assistant Secretary of Defense Larry Korb awarded a contract to the Wharton Applied Research Center at the University of Pennsylvania to organize and run the Advertising Mix Test that Secretary of Defense Weinberger had ordered in fall 1981. Korb selected Wharton because, in his review of completed studies of advertising effectiveness, he particularly liked the study Wharton had done for the Navy (Korb, 1982a).

The Wharton team included a number of other organizations: RAND helped in the selection and assignment of "areas of dominant influence" (ADIs), ensuring that the test cells were balanced; CACI Inc. coordinated the management tasks; PEP, Inc. analyzed advertising data; Arthur D. Little, Inc. developed several interview protocols; and Rao Associates prepared several reports reviewing "empirical studies of enlistment response to advertising [and] conducted a series of independent analyses of the experimental data" (Carroll, 1987, p. 4). Wharton developed a "four-cell design," with the ADIs as the "unit of analysis" based on television markets. Each ADI consisted of one or more counties,

> the plurality of whose households received electronic media from one common location. Taken together, ADIs uniquely account for each county in the continental United States. . . . [RAND] provided technical assistance in assigning (ADIs) to test cells. (Carroll, 1987, pp. 8–9)

RAND used the experimental design methodology it had developed for the Enlistment Bonus Test (Polich, 1983). RAND's designs were created by randomly assigning ADIs to the test program, "subject to constraints stipulating that the means of certain variables be closely matched across the four test cells." Constraints were imposed on

> (1) enlistment rates for each of the four military services and DoD; (2) minority populations; (3) unemployment rate; (4) propensity (intention) to enlist, as expressed in surveys; (5) geographic region; and (6) population in large, medium, and small sized ADIs. (Polich, 1983, pp. 1–2)
>
> Three measures of effectiveness were chosen:
> - Number of applicants taking the enlistment test
> - Number of contracts signed
> - Applicant-to-contract ratio, i.e., the number of applicants required per contract. Advertising may increase applicants without a corresponding increase in contracts, leading to inefficiency. Conversely, advertising may increase the yield of a given applicant pool, thus enhancing system efficiency. (Carroll, 1987, p. 48)

Separate assessments were made for the DoD as a whole and individually for each service, as well as for high school and non–high school graduates and nongraduates, and graduates in AFTQ categories I–IIIA and I–III.

In sharp contrast to previous studies of military recruiting, the methodology used was an analysis-of-variance framework,[32] which emphasized the treatment cells using total aggregate data for the whole period, rather than individual monthly data for each ADI area, as the unit of observation. As a result, the researchers asked whether the Army's share of total applicants changed from one cell to another rather than how changes in advertising funds affected the number of Army applicants (Carroll, 1987, p. 49). Such an approach did not make the maximum use of the data, which was generated at considerable expense; did not take into account the important role the recruiters and recruiting quotas play in the enlistment process[33]; and did not adequately account for regional differences in economic environment. By aggregating data over time and into treatment regions, the researchers ended up with 72 observations rather than the 2,520 independent observations that were available to them. This dampened the variations in the observed data used in the analysis and masked the underlying interactions between the variables. Given their aggregation scheme, it is no wonder that they found few factors to be statistically significant.

The test started on October 1, 1984, at a time when the economy was improving and unemployment was declining. Across the board, in test and control cells alike, "military enlistment contracts for all categories of recruits . . . [were] dropp[ing]" (Carroll, 1987, p. 13). The Wharton team reported the following:

- The test cell with the lowest total advertising spending . . . produced applicant and enlistment results equal to, or occasionally better than, the control cell.
- Other test cells with considerably larger total spending . . . produced results no better than, and occasionally poorer than, the control cell . . . .
- None of the test cells provided results in terms of enlistment or applicant share by Service that differed to a statistically significant degree from the shares observed in the control cell.

---

[32] *Author's Note:* Wharton originally proposed an analysis-of-variance approach for the Navy Advertising Mix Test in 1978. When, as the Principal Deputy Assistant Secretary of the Navy I reviewed their work plan I objected on the grounds that analysis-of-variance was a statistical technique that did not make the best use of the information being collected and did not provide us with the information that we needed for policy decisions. Wharton changed its methodology to make better use of the data. Its analysis for the Navy (Carroll et al., 1985) was much more robust than that for the Advertising Mix Test. Apparently, Wharton returned to its original selection of an analysis-of-variance type use of test cells, rather than a more-appropriate econometric analysis.

[33] The Wharton team was well aware of this problem, but decided to ignore it. Carroll noted,

> Recent efforts suggest that recruiter behavior variables might be important in manpower supply models. . . . Accounting for such factors simultaneously for all four Services is a demanding task well beyond the scope of this study. Accordingly, any effect that recruiter behavior variables might have had on the findings of this experiment are unknown. (Carroll, 1987, p. ES-5)

Carroll apparently thought that he was just leaving a little more of the variance unexplained. Unfortunately, by ignoring recruiters behavior the parameters he estimated were biased.

- In the first year of significant changes to advertising spending levels, it appears that the combination of advertising to recruiting system performance is either quite small or virtually non-existent. (Carroll, 1987, p. ES-6)

Given these results, Wharton made a very strong and controversial policy recommendation to the Secretary of Defense: "Reduce DoD recruiting budgets while increasing the proportion of those budgets allocated to Joint advertising" (Carroll, 1987, p. 95). In its 1987 report, Wharton noted that,

[i]n July 1986, the Deputy Secretary of Defense reviewed the findings of the DoD Advertising Mix Test. After full consideration of the findings and the recruiting environment, he decided to phase in reductions to total DoD advertising and to effect cost savings by reducing Service and slightly increasing the Joint advertising budgets. Specifically, the Deputy Secretary established a goal to achieve a 25-percent reduction in the total DoD advertising budget by FY 1991. (Carroll, 1987, p. 95)

What Wharton did not say was how controversial its analysis was or how the services fought back.

Chapman Cox, Korb's successor as Assistant Secretary of Defense for Force Management and Personnel, told Deputy Secretary Taft that the Army, "[i]n coordination with the other Services, . . . funded an independent analysis of the [Advertising Mix] Test by researchers from the University of Texas" (Cox, 1986c). In contrast to the Wharton analysis, the University of Texas group found that "joint advertising contributes nothing to Service recruiting efforts" (Cox, 1986c). The Air Force backed the Army's request that a "third party . . . conduct an independent assessment" and tasked RAND to take a second look (Cox, 1986c).

RAND's Reassessment of the Advertising Mix Test

Jim Dertouzos led RAND's reassessment. He summed up the problem:

The 1984 Advertising Mix Test (AMT) [was] an ambitious field experiment . . . Unfortunately, initial analysis based on observed enlistments during the period was inconclusive because of inadequate data, a failure to consider systematic differences between services, and questionable judgment in the choice of methodologies. In particular, the exclusion of 60 percent of the control group, the use of annual instead of monthly information, and the emphasis on broad "test-cell" effects rather than actual fluctuations in advertising expenditures militated against finding statistically significant relationships. As a result, policy conclusions were not warranted. (Dertouzos, 1989, p. v)

RAND noted that, despite the fact that this was a controlled test, many data elements that were needed for a completed assessment were not collected. For example, the data the Wharton team provided RAND did not include market demographics or "data on separate recruiting goals for different quality enlistments (except for the Army). In addition, there was no information on local advertising expenditures"

(Dertouzos, 1989, p. 10). Some of the data received were "not usable. Data oddities included monthly quotas of several thousand for a single ADI market and negative missions for some Marine Corps recruiters" (Dertouzos, 1989, p. 11). RAND used all the 2,520 available observations—210 markets for 12 months:

> [v]ariables that influence[d] individuals to supply enlistments include economic conditions, numbers of recruiters, and advertising expenditures. Demand factors include recruiting quotas that affect both the magnitude and direction of recruiter effort. (Dertouzos, 1989, p. 11)

In an example of how important a correct specification of the basic model is, the conclusions RAND was able to draw from its analysis differed markedly from what Wharton was able to draw from its assessment, even though both used substantially the same data. RAND concluded that,

> [f]irst, service and joint advertising both appear to be powerful tools to help meet the recruiting requirements of the active duty forces . . . [A]dvertising appears to compare favorably with more expensive options such as cash bonuses or pay. Second, our results do not provide unequivocal conclusions about the relative . . . equivalent effects. There is no obvious reason to either cut the budget or reallocate funding. Finally, competition among the Services does not diminish the usefulness of advertising from the DoD perspective . . . The drawing power of an individual service's advertising program often benefits other services as well. . . .
>
> [T]he empirical results appear quite robust with respect to alternative model specifications. In addition, estimates of advertising effectiveness for the Army program are remarkably similar to those obtained from earlier studies, even though the latter used different data, models of the underlying recruiting and advertising process, and statistical methodologies. (Dertouzos, 1989, p. 21)

Previous Study of Army Recruiting and Advertising

The previous study that Dertouzos referred to was one he and Michael Polich had led that looked at three years (1981–1984) of advertising data for the Army (Dertouzos et al., 1989). While the results were consistent with the reassessment of the Advertising Mix Test, the results of this study were sharply at odds with the results of Wharton's assessment of the same data. Given the encouraging results RAND reported, it is no wonder the Army was so concerned about the conclusions the Wharton team had reached. The resulting attempt by the Deputy Secretary of Defense to cut their advertising funds was wrong.

During the period covered by the RAND study (1981–1984), the Army spent between $40 and $45 million annually, an amount equal to two-thirds of all the advertising money DoD spent. To assess the data from that period, RAND developed an econometric model of Army monthly advertising expenditures that controlled for economic conditions, local area characteristics, the magnitude and direction of recruiter effort, and levels of other recruiting resources [the model] permitted identification of the independent effects of different advertising purchases on the short-run supply of high-quality enlistees. (Dertouzos et al., 1989, p. v)

The results of the assessment of the Army advertising data found the following:

[A]dvertising expenditures in a given month have a significant and immediate effect on the number of high-quality enlistments in the Army. Moreover, the advertising has a lagged effect, increasing enlistments for as long as six months, although the effect dampens out over time. The enlistment effect of advertising in a given month falls by 42 percent each month after the advertising appears.

The effects found . . . imply that the Army's national and local advertising programs compare favorably with other recruiting tools in terms of cost per high-quality enlistee. . . . [T]he marginal cost of recruiting a high-quality person through increased advertising [was found] to be between $5,000 and $6,000. The marginal cost of achieving the same goal by increasing the recruiting staff was about $5,700, and the cost of using bonuses was much higher (about $16,000 per recruit). . . . [N]ational magazine and local newspaper advertising are the most cost effective in promoting short-run enlistment responses, costing between $2,000 and $3,400 per additional recruit. National broadcasting purchases, both network television and radio, also have strong effects . . . [but] cost somewhat more than the print media ($7,000 to $10,000 per marginal recruit). (Dertouzos et al., 1989, pp. v–vi)

The Army 2 + 2 + 4 Option Test

In 1988, the House Armed Services Committee used the word *incongruous* to describe the Army's use of the two-year enlistment option coupled with the Army College Fund (ACF). They questioned a program that brought high-quality individuals into the Army for only two years, in noncritical skill areas and with an incentive, the ACF, that was also a great incentive to leave.[34] This problem had bothered personnel managers in the Office of the Secretary of Defense since the early 1970s, when Charles Moskos had argued for it before Congress. Despite the fact that it had been tested and found wanting several times, Moskos's notion still found favor with the Army. Personnel managers in the Army believed "a significant number of young people are willing to enter Army service to obtain educational benefits such as the ACF, provided that they must serve only a short tour" (Buddin, 1991, p. 1).

Even so, the House Appropriations Committee prohibited the Army from making further ACF payments to two-year enlistees in noncombat skills. The Army countered by suggesting a program that would prove advantageous for the total force. The service wanted to test a two-year enlisted program with ACF for high-quality

---

[34] The ACF became a very important recruiting tool largely because of the increase in the economic returns to colleges and the concurrent increase in the number of high school graduates seeking postsecondary education. College attendance rates were rising, and the services faced the challenge of learning how to "penetrate the college market."

Table 16.6
ACF Choices Applicants Face ($)

Term of Service (years)	Program-Eligible Skills	
	Combat	Noncombat
Four	14,400	14,400
Three	12,000	12,000
Two	8,000	0
Two (2+2+4 program)		8,000[a]

SOURCE: Buddin (Buddin, 1991, pp. 6–7).

NOTE: Amounts in addition to the "GI Bill."

[a]To receive ACF benefit in a noncombat skill, the recruit must accept a two-year additional reserve commitment.

recruits in hard-to-fill occupations with short training times. It would require a recruit to serve two years on active duty, after basic and advanced individual training, then two years in the Selected Reserve, followed by four years in the Individual Ready Reserve (IRR)—the so-called "2 + 2 + 4 option." ACF payments were contingent on joining and serving in the Selected Reserve. To be judged "cost-effective," the new option would have to be market-expanding, e.g., "attracting an untapped, college bound youth market that is unwilling to commit to other Army programs" (Buddin, 1991, p. 2), that is, draw prospective recruits to the hard-to-fill occupations, have a minimal effect on those who would have enlisted for four years, and increase the flow of trained soldiers into the Selected Reserve. Congress approved a limited test for 15 months, and RAND was selected to design and run the test (Buddin, 1991). This was just one of many programs available to prospective high-quality recruits. Table 16.6 shows the options available in July 1989 when the test started.

The test incorporated a "*job-offer experiment* that randomly assigned qualified Army applicants to various program conditions" and a "*geographic experiment* . . . [in which] matched sets of areas were assigned to different program cells" (Buddin, 1991, pp. 6–7) to test overall market expansion. The geographic experiment was designed to ensure that recruiters actively sold the program and that the "true" expansion effect was recorded. The job-offer experiment utilized the job counselor sessions to offer the specific 2 + 2 + 4 option to a randomly selected group—70 percent—of qualified applicants. The geographic experiment "was based on a randomized assignment of dispersed sets of areas to the three test cells. The assignment algorithm resembled that employed previously in the Educational Benefits Test and the Enlistment Bonus Test" (Buddin, 1991, p. 12) and the Advertising Mix Test. Unlike the Advertising Mix Test, however, a more-complete set of data was collected at each recruiting battalion each month.

RAND obtained a "rough picture of the enlistment pattern across cells" that showed "high-quality enlistments did increase substantially during the test period" (Buddin, 1991, pp. 21–22). This may have been the result of a sharp reduction in the recruiting mission as a result of the force reductions at the end of the Cold War, but "[p]erhaps the main factors affecting a battalion's recruiting success are local economic conditions" (Buddin, 1991, p. 23). A full examination of possible effects required a multivariate analysis along the lines Dertouzos had suggested in his original paper (Dertouzos, 1984) and in his reanalysis of the Advertising Mix Test data (Dertouzos, 1989). Buddin extended the analysis by specifying the transformation between high-quality and low-quality recruits as a "constant elasticity transformation (CET) production frontier" (Buddin, 1991, p. 25).

He noted that the traditional approach used is a simpler formulation of the production trade-offs—a so-called Cobb-Douglas transformation function—that holds the marginal rate of transformation between the two production options equal to one and provides for constant returns to scale.[35] There are no such constraints with the CET production frontier. Testing both models on his data, Buddin found the CET-produced results were

> quite similar to those that would have been obtained from the more traditional specification. . . . This similarity reflects the fact that the estimated transformation frontier is virtually linear over the range of high- and low-quality enlistments observed in the data. (Buddin, 1991, pp. 41–42)

Buddin's results gave some support to Moskos's thesis and the expectations of Army recruiters. The 2 + 2 + 4 program was very popular. It "expanded the market for high-quality male recruits by about 3 percent" (Buddin, 1991, p. 42). While smaller than the expansion effects of the more-lucrative educational benefits associated with a four-year enlistment, estimated at 9 percent, or bonuses, estimated at 5 percent, "the 3 percent is comparable with that of the . . . [other] programs after controlling for the scale of the programs. The results imply that about 25 to 30 percent of the men taking the program are new recruits" (Buddin, 1991, p. 38). The analysis showed that there was a minimal amount of "buying-down" from the longer terms of service to the two-year term. The option did "channel" recruits into hard-to-fill noncombat jobs, and recruits were willing to buy additional college funds by committing to two years in the Selected Reserve. The effects of expanding the market on the expected obligated active-duty man-years of service appeared to be positive, even though the average length of service per recruit was somewhat lower. The 2 + 2 + 4 option provided "additional supply of manpower to both the active and reserve components" (Buddin, 1991, p. 39).

The Navy Tries a "College Fund" Type Program

In 1990, the Navy set up the NCF, initially limiting the number of eligible recruits to 2,000 per year. The size of the program was increased to 4,700 per year in FY 1994 and

---

[35] The analogous case is the constant elasticity of substitution production function and the Cobb-Douglas production function. The Cobb-Douglas production function is a special case of the more-general constant elasticity of substitution production function in which the elasticity of substitution is equal to one; there are constant returns to scale; and the isoquant is perfectly concave to the origin.

to 10,800 in FY 1995 (Warner et al., 2001, p. 12). OSD commissioned John Warner and a team from Clemson University to undertake an "evaluation study of the new NCF," as well as other trends in recruiting in the 1990s. They found "the impact of the NCF program was positive, but smaller" than that of the ACF program because

> the average term of enlistment of ACF recipients was 3 to 3.5 years compared with 4 to 4.5 years for NCF recipients. The present value of college fund benefits was therefore higher for Army recruits than for Navy recruits. (Warner et al., 2001, pp. iv–v)

Warner and his colleagues provided a very useful summary of some of the econometric issues that had arisen since the first estimates of supply were developed for the 1964 Pentagon Draft Study and the Gates Commission:

> Some researchers developed highly structured models in which there is a very tight relationship between economic theory and the estimated parameters. To the extent that the theory is correct, the structural approach is preferable. If, however, the theory makes invalid assumptions, the resulting estimates may be no more accurate than those obtained using a reduced-form approach. (Warner et al., 2001, p. 82)

The earliest examples of structural models are Fisher's original supply model (Fisher, 1970), Altman and Barro's estimates of officer supply (Altman and Barro, 1970), and my estimates of the supply to the Air National Guard and the Air Force Reserve (Rostker, 1974). The model Warner developed was based on Dertouzos's original work (Dertouzos, 1985) and the model Polich, Dertouzos, and Press used to analyze the enlistment bonus experiment (Polich et al., 1986). Warner, however, addressed the issues that Goldberg had raised with regard to the colinearity of recruiters and goals (Goldberg, 1982). He noted that a number of researchers had extended Dertouzos original formulation but that Dertouzos's model "is easily implemented provided that data on low-quality enlistment quotas are available to serve as an instrument" (Warner et al., 2001, p. 87).[36]

Managing Attrition

Attrition is defined as the separation from the military—a loss—before an individual reaches the end of his or her initial term of obligated service. There is an initial surge of losses during training—approximately one in ten—and then a steady trickle of losses

---

[36] Daula and Smith (Daula and Smith, 1985a) estimated within a switching regression framework. This allowed for the possibilities that some units were supply constrained and others demand constrained. Berner and Daula (Berner and Daula, 1993) extended the model used in the enlistment bonus experiment to account for possible nonlinearity and endogeneity of enlistment quotas. Warner noted, however, that implementing their model is "daunting" (Warner et al., 2001, p. 87).

However, since it is likely the services set quotas in response to the past performance of the recruiting station and the current contract requirement (if, for instance, recruiting is below target) quotas are increased, there could be a correlation between the low-quality quotas and the error term, and autocorrelation in the error could result. Dertouzos continues research at RAND about how best to model recruiter behavior in response to goals and incentives.

during the remainder of the initial term of service until about 30 percent of the entering cohort is gone. There has been a tendency for the attrition rate to be higher since the end of the draft, leading some to claim that the all-volunteer force is an easy-in, easy-out form of service. As reported to Congress during the early days of the all-volunteer force (Nelson, 1978, p. 65), attrition rates for the Army at the three-years-of-service point rose from 26 percent in FY 1971 to 38 percent in FY 1974. Similar changes were recorded for the other services; for example, the Navy's three-year attrition rate rose from 28 percent in FY 1971 to 38 percent in FY 1974. High attrition has persisted despite substantial management attention over the years. Nevertheless, attrition of between 30 and 35 percent, with attrition during training of between 10 and 15 percent, has become the enduring norm and has been little effected by the numerous and repeated tries to reduce it.

Reducing attrition was a management priority of the Carter administration. In February 1978, the Deputy Secretary of Defense "directed the services to program for reduced first-term attrition rates in order to reduce accession requirements," noting that "DoD must reduce the number of people who are being separated prior to the end of their enlistments" (Duncan, 1978). The general approach was to try to find a set of recruiting standards and policies to allow the services to screen out the recruits most likely to leave before the ends of their initial obligated terms of service. The Navy commissioned work at CNA by Robert Lockman that led to the development of screening tables based on the odds that a prospective recruit "would still be in the Navy one year after he went on active duty" (Lockman, 1978, p. 171).

In the early 1980s, Richard Buddin at RAND undertook a study of military attrition

> designed to assess the contribution of demographic background, prior experience, job match and satisfaction, entry point decisions, alternatives to the military, and socioeconomic factors to early attrition of enlisted males. The framework was based on recent firm-specific human capital and job matching models that analyze the dynamics of job separation. Comparisons are drawn between the determinants of early military attrition and civilian job separations of young workers. (Buddin, 1984, p. v)

The inclusion of information from the survey recruits took at the Armed Forces Examination and Entry Stations (AFEES), which covered such ground as prior experience, job satisfaction, and information on alternatives, allowed Buddin to better compare military and civilian separations. Buddin found that attrition was considerably greater than for a comparable civilian population. Specifically, "[e]arly attrition *increases* about 1 percentage point per year for each year at enlistment beyond age 17"; this compares with "a 3 percentage point decline in annual civilian separations for each yearly increment in age" (Buddin, 1984, p. 24). While it may be true that those who join the military later in life have less of a taste for military service, Buddin suggests that higher attrition among older recruits may reflect the continuation of old behavior.

Older recruits tried the civilian labor market and did not make a go of it, and now they find they also cannot succeed in the military.

The dominant finding concerning high school diploma graduates also came through in Buddin's results for the military. He found that

> [t]he most persistent attrition finding is that high school diploma graduates have markedly lower attrition than nongraduates. . . . The early attrition rates of non–high school graduates and recruits with certificates of general educational development (GED) are 8 percentage points higher than for high school graduates. . . . [However,] in contrast to military attrition, civilian job separations of young workers is not affected by educational level. (Buddin, 1984, pp. 24–26)

A history of either frequent job changes before enlistment or prior periods of unemployment are indications of higher levels of attrition. Buddin found that, "[a]lthough high school graduation status is the primary *single* factor affecting attrition, age and previous employment stability together have comparable influences on early attrition" (Buddin, 1984, p. 29, emphasis in original). In a finding that directly addressed Moskos's contention that attrition would be higher in the all-volunteer force than in a draft force because draftees are "not subject to profound disillusionment after service entry" and "accepted military service on its own terms," while a volunteer is "subject to post-entry disillusionment if expectations are not met" (Moskos, 1977, p. 1), Buddin found that "[r]ecruits whose interests are redirected into unexpected or less desirable occupations because of aptitude or service requirements are no more attrition-prone than those who get their first occupational choice" (Buddin, 1984, p. 51). Employment history also makes a difference: "Recruits who changed jobs frequently before enlistment are more prone to early attrition" (Buddin, 1984, p. v).[37]

Matthew Black and Thomas Fraker (Black and Fraker, 1985) also used the National Longitudinal Study (NLS) in their study of attrition. In a paper presented at a conference organized by the Manpower and Personnel Policy Research Group at ARI, they presented results from an analysis using matched records from the NLS of the High School Class of 1972 (NLS-72) and the 1972–1979 Accession, Master, and Loss files.[38] The Defense Manpower Data Center matched 1,274 cases. They used an

---

[37] Specifically, "[o]ther things equal, a 19-year-old recruit with four previous employers has a predicted separation rate of 12.7 percent compared with 9.6 percent for a recruit with a single previous employer (Buddin, 1984, p. v).

[38] *Author's Note:* The 1984 Conference on Army Manpower Economics brought together the most senior researchers in the field. The majority of the papers came from RAND, the Office of Economic and Manpower Analysis at West Point, IDA, and CNA. While there were pockets of excellence in the private sector, the Systems Research and Applications Corporation (SRA) was the only commercial firm that consistently produced a high volume of high-quality studies. Gary Nelson, who had previously worked at IDA and RAND and had been a Deputy Assistant Secretary of Defense in the Carter administration, headed the SRA group. I was a discussant at the conference and set off a firestorm by criticizing the focus of some of the accessions research, resulting in a sharp reply (Goldberg and Greenston, 1985; Rostker, 1985, pp. 95–96). At the time, I was just returning to RAND after spending four years at CNA and SRA and had not been actively engaged in personnel research since leaving Selective Service in 1981. It would be another five years before I returned to manpower research as head of the Defense Manpower Research Center at RAND.

"event-history analysis . . . to estimate the instantaneous rate of transition from one state to another" (Black and Fraker, 1985, p. 265). They found grade-point average to be

> a strong predictor of attrition, but only for the non-blacks, . . . postsecondary educational goals and the planned use of the GI Bill by high school seniors to be a strong predictor . . . [and] work experience while in high school is [also] highly correlated with low attrition in the military. (Black and Fraker, 1985, p. 279)

The work of Lockman, of Buddin, and of Black and Fraker all point to the same policy conclusion, quality matters. Surely, as the services increased the quality of accessions during the 1980s, attrition was bound to come down. Unfortunately, as Buddin noted in a 1988 study for the Assistant Secretary of Defense, while "the active enlisted forces have sharply increased the proportion of high-quality enlistments, . . . the improved recruit quality has not led to the anticipated reduction in recruit attrition" (Buddin, 1988, p. iii). While it remained true that the high-quality recruits had lower attrition than low-quality recruits, "trends in cohort attrition are not well predicted from trends in cohort quality" (Buddin, 1988, p. v). Buddin concluded that the "training commands and training bases may essentially grade on a curve rather than against a fixed performance standard, so they expect comparable losses in each cohort, and these expectations are self-fulfilling" (Buddin, 1988, p. 58). Clearly, the management policies of the services, their institutional environment, and the incentives they offered those who control attrition, such as drill instructors at basic training, may have as much to do with reducing attrition as the quality mix of new recruits.[39]

Force Management and the Post–Cold War Drawdown

The paradigm for managing the all-volunteer force shifted over the 1980s. The success of the all-volunteer force was originally seen as rising or falling on the number of non–prior service recruits who could be induced to join and limited by the shrinking size of the youth population. Little attention was given to how higher retention might affect the personnel force structure. At the tenth-anniversary conference in 1983, James Hosek, Richard Fernandez, and David Grissmer sounded a warning that went largely unheeded. They told the conference that it was

---

[39] *Author's Note:* Buddin's research was consistent with Admiral Mike Boorda's experience as Chief of Naval Personnel. Mike complained to me that the drill instructors at the Navy's basic training programs believed their job was to weed out those who should not be in the Navy, and they had informally told him they thought that was about 15 percent of every cohort. Buddin's numbers reflected the same pattern. He found that,

> after controlling for differences in recruit characteristics, the basic training (BT) attrition rate of high-quality Navy men rose about 1.5 percentage points between FY 1982 and FY 1985 on a base BT attrition rate of 6 percent. . . . The cohort and training base effects suggest that differences in Navy policies and practices over time and across bases may have an effect on Navy attrition rates. (Buddin, 1988, p. 57)

time to recognize that the traditional method of assessing its [the all-volunteer force's] success has been too limiting. The picture of the AVF's future painted by a single line tracing high-quality supply leaves equally important parts of the canvas blank. Our work draws attention to major trends within the entire enlisted force. Absent any major policy change, the current decade will see a shift toward a more-senior force, requiring fewer and fewer new enlistees. . . . The movement toward a more senior force, however, raises some fundamental questions, among them: How is such a force to be managed? Is it sustainable? Is a more-senior force desirable? If it is not desirable, what can be done to forestall it? . . . Delaying actions to trim the force until the late 1980s will deny policymakers much of the leverage they could exercise today. (Hosek et al., 1986, pp. 201–203)

By 1990, three things were clear: First, nothing had been done during the previous decade to reduce the growing size of the career military force. Second, the size of the military would be cut by about 22 percent over a four-year period, with the Army taking a 30-percent reduction. Third, there was considerable disagreement on how and where to make the cuts and much unhappiness about the possibility that such cuts would be a hardship on the people involuntarily separated to meet reduced force levels.

The Mershon Center at Ohio State University publishes the *American Defense Annual* to offer a critical examination of administration thinking about U.S. defense needs. In a chapter in the *1991–1992 Defense Annual,* David Grissmer and Bernard Rostker provided a summary assessment of the situation the personnel managers at the Pentagon faced in the early 1990s:

Different approaches about how to reduce force levels can be seen in the "guidance" the Department of Defense received from the two Armed Services Committees of the Congress. The Senate Armed Service Committee gave specific guidance on where the cuts should be made, e.g. "prudently adjusting the intake of new recruits, selectively retiring senior personnel, and selectively releasing first term personnel before completion of their first term of service." The House Armed Services Committee took a less prescriptive stance and emphasized "the force drawdown (be) accomplished in a balanced and equitable fashion that will preserve the integrity of the military, maintain adequate force readiness, and cushion the blow for adversely affected career personnel. (Grissmer and Rostker, 1992, p. 131)

At the time, the critical issue was whether the drawdown would be largely managed by reducing accessions or by initiating a balanced program of accession cuts and the separation of personnel who had already committed to making the military a career. The drawdown plan for the Marine Corps that produced a balanced force is shown in Figure 16.4.

The Air Force, however, planned to manage its drawdown by sharply curtailing accessions, resulting in a projected force profile that was badly out of balance, as shown in Figure 16.5.

Figure 16.4
Marine Corps Enlisted Personnel Profile, 1990–2000

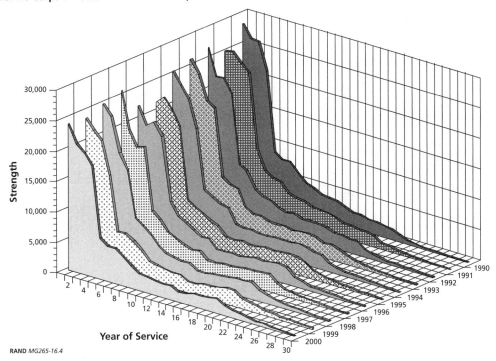

Figure 16.5
Air Force Enlisted Personnel Profile, 1990–2001

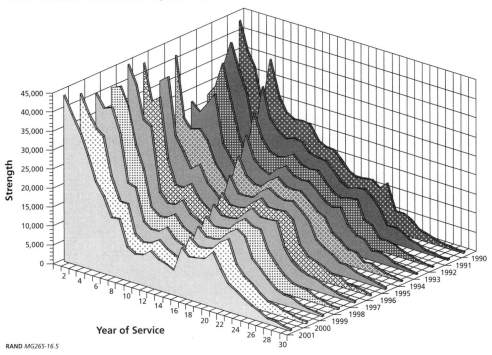

Figure 16.6
Percentage of Force with Ten or More Years of Service: Accessions-Only Policy

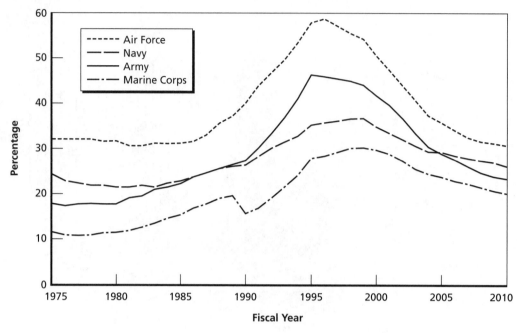

The Air Force wanted to "keep faith" with its service members, cut accessions, and minimize separations from the career force. Such a policy was projected to be a sharp increase in the seniority of the force, as shown in Figure 16.6.

OSD wanted to keep the age-experience profile of the force in balance over time. This would require the services to maintain new accessions at a level that would sustain the force over time and to reduce the uncontrolled growth in the number of career personnel on active duty project during the drawdown. Such a program of "force shaping" would of course mean that the services would have to cut people already in the force. Russell Beland and Carl Dahlman, working for Assistant Secretary of Defense Chris Jehn, tried to develop a workable and affordable voluntary separation incentive (VSI) program to provide the flexibility needed to shape the force during the drawdown.

Beland's initial proposal was a VSI that would consist of an immediate separation payment and an annual annuity for a period equal to twice the service member's years of service. Benefits were not extended, and there was no cost-of-living adjustment, but a unique feature of the plan was that it was transferable, thus creating a negotiable instrument, much like a bond, which was then returning between 8 and 9 percent. Congress approved the VSI without the transferability provision and added its own alternative, the Special Separation Benefit (SSB), a lump-sum payment equal to 15 percent of the member's base pay times the number of years of service at the time of separation.

VSI and SSB as a Natural Experiment

In the days leading up to the drawdown, a critical factor that was widely debated by the analysts building the VSI program was the personal discount rate service members would use when they considered their options to stay or leave, options that had very different income streams. Not only would the discount rate affect the estimates of the number of service members who would voluntarily leave the service, it would also affect the cost the government would have to bear to get the needed numbers to leave and the very design of the program itself. For example, if the government's discount rate, usually thought to be the cost the government pays to borrow money, was less than the individual's discount rate, it would be foolish to offer a program with a long payout.

When Congress authorized two buyout programs—the VSI annuity and the SSB lump-sum payment—with very different benefit streams, it serendipitously set up a natural experiment as 11,000 offices and 55,000 enlisted selected one program or the other. Working with the results of the two programs, John Warner and Saul Pleeter— Pleeter was the chief economist of the OSD's compensation office—noted that, despite break-even discount rates (the rate which equated the present value of the annuity with the present value of the lump-sum payment) that were between 17.5 and 19.8 percent, most of the separatees selected the lump sum. This implied "that the vast majority of personnel had discount rates at least 18 percent." In fact they found "discount rates rang[ing] from 0 to over 30 percent" that varied "with education, age, race, sex, number of dependants, ability test score, and the size of payment" (Warner and Pleeter, 2001, p. 33).

Before the fact, those who designed the VSI program believed that half of the enlisted and almost none of the officers would take the lump-sum payment, preferring the annuity. They believed that, for most people, the personal discount rate was below 18 percent. In fact, 90 percent of the enlisted personnel and half the officers took the lump-sum payment, implying a personal discount rate of over 18 percent for the vast majority of those who decided to leave (Warner and Pleeter, 2001, p. 33). Warner and Pleeter estimated that the SSB option saved the government $1.7 billion dollars.[40] Since the government's interest rate was lower than the personal discount rate for a majority of those being offered the program, an up-front program (in particular, the SSB Congress had developed) would cost the government $1.7 billion less and would have the same effect as the more costly, longer-term VSI annuity.

---

[40] They noted,

> Using the 7-percent discount rate on government bonds prevailing at the time of the program, we calculate[d] that if only the annuity alternative had been available, the present value of the annuity payments would have been $4.2 billion. The present value of the actual annuity payments plus lump-sum payments was $2.5 billion. The lump-sum alternative thus saved the federal government $1.7 billion. (Warner and Pleeter, 2001, p. 49)

The Legacy

When Ronald Reagan became President, the military was struggling to recruit quality personnel, and few thought the all-volunteer force could succeed. Twelve years later, as George H. W. Bush left the White House, the new volunteers had proven themselves in battle. The experiment of the all-volunteer force was a success. Moreover, the partnership between policymakers and researchers provided the tools needed to manage the force. Experiments and careful analysis of the results of the experiments showed how the services could attract and retain the right men and women. The most immediate problem in 1993, as the new Clinton administration took over, was managing the drawdown. The challenge for the future was restructuring the force to the emerging post–Cold War world. Would young men and women still want to serve without the threat of the Soviet Union? What would military service be like without the routines established by a half century of the Cold War? The new administration would soon find that the demands on the force not only exceeded what was expected after the end of the Cold War but would even exceed the demands of the Cold War. There would be no lack of challenges for personnel managers ahead.

References

Albrecht, Mark J., *Labor Substitution in the Military Environment: Implications for Enlisted Force Management,* Santa Monica, Calif.: RAND Corporation, R-2330-MRAL, November 1979. S0896.pdf.

Altman, Stuart H., and Robert J. Barro, "A Model of Officer Supply Under Draft and No Draft Conditions," in *Staff Papers for the Presidents Commission on an All-Volunteer Force,* Washington, D.C.: U.S. Government Printing Office, 1970, pp. II-10-11 to II-10-31. S0469.pdf.

Armor, David J., Richard L. Fernandez, Kathy Bers, Donna Schwarzbach, S. Craig Moore, and Leola Cutler, *Recruit Aptitudes and Army Job Performance: Setting Enlistment Standards for Infantrymen,* R2874MRA&L, 1982. S0658.pdf.

Asch, Beth J., *Navy Recruiter Productivity and the Freeman Plan,* Santa Monica, Calif.: RAND Corporation, R-3713-FMP, June 1990. S0697.pdf.

Asch, Beth J., and Lynn A. Karoly, *The Role of the Job Counselor in the Military Enlistment Process,* Santa Monica, Calif.: RAND Corporation, MR-315-P&R, 1993. S0693.pdf.

ASD[FMP]—*See* Assistant Secretary of Defense for Force Management Policy.

Assistant Secretary of Defense for Force Management Policy, *Fourth Annual Report to the House Committee on Appropriations: Joint-Service Efforts to Link Enlistment Standards to Job Performance,* Washington, D.C.: Office of the Assistant Secretary of Defense (FM&Pl), December 1985. G1222.pdf.

Berner, J. Kevin, and Thomas V. Daula, "Recruiting Goals, Regime Shifts and the Supply of Labor to the Army," *Defense Economics,* Vol. 4, No. 4, 1993, pp. 315–328.

Black, Matthew, and Thomas Fraker, "First-Term Attrition of High School Graduates in the Military," in Curtis L. Gilroy, ed., *Army Manpower Economics,* Boulder, Colo.: Westview Press, 1985.

Block, David, J. Michael Polich, and David K. Horne, *Soldier Performance Research Project,* Fort Monroe, Va.: United States Army Training and Doctrine Command, August 31, 1989. G1219.pdf.

Buddin, Richard, *Analysis of Early Military Attrition Behavior,* Santa Monica, Calif.: RAND Corporation, R-3069-MIL, July 1984. S0701.pdf.

———, *Trends in Attrition of High-Quality Military Recruits,* Santa Monica, Calif.: RAND Corporation, R-3539-FMP, August 1988. S0709.pdf.

———, *Enlisted Effects of the 2+2+4 Recruiting Program,* Santa Monica, Calif.: RAND Corporation, R-4097-A, 1991. S0694.pdf.

Campbell, John P., "An Overview of the Army Selection and Classification Project (Project A)," *Personnel Psychology,* Vol. 42, No. 2, Summer 1990, pp. 231–239.

———, "Implications for Future Personnel Research and Personnel Management," in John P. Campbell and Deirdre J. Knapp, eds., *Exploring the Limits in Personnel Selection and Classification,* Mahwah, New Jersey: Lawrence Erlbaum Associates, Publishers, 2001a.

————, "Matching People and Jobs: An Introduction to Twelve Years of R&D," in John P. Campbell and Deirdre J. Knapp, eds., *Exploring the Limits in Personnel Selection and Classification*, Mahwah, N.J.: Lawrence Erlbaum Associates, Publishers, 2001b.

Carlucci, Frank C., "Department of Defense Educational Benefits Program," Christopher Jehn to Assistant Secretaries of the Military Department (M&RA), Washington, D.C., February 5, 1982. G0935.pdf.

Carr, William J., *Recruit Quality (The '60/90' Rule)*, Washington, D.C.: Office of the Under Secretary of Defense (Personnel and Readiness), September 22, 2004. G1359.pdf.

Carroll, Vincent P., *Department of Defense Advertising Mix Test: Comparison of Joint-Service with Service-Specific Strategies and Levels of Funding*, Washington, D.C.: Office of the Assistant Secretary of Defense (FM&P), July 1987. G1225.pdf.

Carroll, Vincent P., Ambar G. Rao, Hau L. Lee, Arthur Shapiro, and Barry L. Bayus, "The Navy Enlistment Marketing Experiment," *Marketing Science*, Vol. 4, No. 4, Autumn 1985, pp. 352–374.

Central All-Volunteer Force Task Force, *Qualitative Accession Requirements: A Report on the Qualitative Accession Needs of the Military Services*, Washington, D.C.: Office of the Assistant Secretary of Defense (M&RA), AD764511, November 1972. G1226.pdf.

Cook, Alvin A., Jr., and John P. White, *Estimating the Quality of Air Force Volunteers*, Santa Monica, Calif.: RAND Corporation, RM-630-PR, September 1970. S0301.pdf.

Cox, Chapman B., "Defense Training Data and Analysis Center (TDAC) Review and Recommended Actions," action memorandum to Deputy Secretary of Defense, Washington, D.C., May 28, 1986a. G0770.pdf.

————, "Defense Training and Performance Data Center (TPDC)," memorandum to Assistant Secretaries of Defense and the Military Departments, Joint Staff Director and Program Analysis and Evaluation Director, Washington, D.C., July 8, 1986b. G0982.pdf.

————, "Funding for Recruiting Advertising," memorandum to Deputy Secretary of Defense, Washington, D.C., August 19, 1986c. G0928.pdf.

Daula, Thomas V., and David Alton Smith, "Estimating Supply Models for the US Army," in R. Ehrenberg, ed., *Research in Labor Economics*, Greenwich, Conn.: JAI Press, 1985a, pp. 261–309.

————, "Recruiting Goals, Enlistment Supply, and Enlistments in the U.S. Army," in Curtis L. Gilroy, ed., *Army Manpower Economics*, Boulder, Colo.: Westview Press, 1985b.

Dertouzos, James N., "Recruiter Incentives and the Marginal Cost of Accessions," in Barry E. Goodstadt, G. Thomas Sicilia and H. Wallace Sinaiko, eds., *Proceedings of the Joint Service Workshop on Recruiter Productivity*, Washington, D.C.: Office of the Assistant Secretary of Defense (MRA&L), 1983, pp. 60–63. S0710.pdf.

————, "Microeconomics Foundation of Recruiter Behavior: Implications for Aggregate Enlistment Models," in Curtis L. Gilroy, ed., *Army Manpower Economics*, Boulder, Colo.: Westview Press, 1984a.

————, *Enlistment Supply, Recruiter Objectives, and the All-Volunteer Force*, Santa Monica, Calif.: RAND Corporation, P-7022, 1984b. S0683.pdf.

————, *Recruiter Incentives and Enlistment Supply,* Santa Monica, Calif.: RAND Corporation, R-3065-MIL, 1985. S0679.pdf.

————, *The Effects of Military Advertising: Evidence from the Advertising Mix Test,* Santa Monica, Calif.: RAND Corporation, N-2907-FMP, 1989. S0688.pdf.

Dertouzos, James N., J. Michael Polich, Ani Bamezai, and Thomas Cestnutt, *Recruiting Effects of Army Advertising,* Santa Monica, Calif.: RAND Corporation, R-3577-FMP, January 1989. S0689.pdf.

Duncan, Charles W., "First-Term Attrition," memorandum to Secretaries of the Military Departments, Washington, D.C., February 10, 1978. G0012.pdf.

Eaton, N.K., H. Wing, L.M. Hanser, N.S. Dumas, and J.L. Shields, *ARI's Program for Improving the Selection, Classification and Utilization of Army Enlisted Personnel,* Alexandria, Va.: United States Army Research Institute, Working Paper 826, November 1981. G1220.pdf.

Fisher, Anthony C., "The Cost of Ending the Draft: Reply," *The American Economic Review,* Vol. 60, No. 5, December 1970, pp. 979–983. S0234.pdf.

Gates, Thomas S. Jr., *The Report of the President's Commission on an All-Volunteer Armed Force,* Washington, D.C., February 1970. S0243.pdf.

Goldberg, Lawrence, *Enlisted Supply: Past, Present, and Future: Executive Summary & Main Text,* Arlington, Va.: Center for Naval Analyses, CNS 1168Vol. 1, September 1982. S0682.pdf.

Goldberg, Lawrence, and Peter Greenston, "Economic Analysis of Enlistment: Rely to Rostker's Comment," in Curtis L. Gilroy, ed., *Army Manpower Economics,* Boulder, Colo.: Westview Press, 1985.

Goodstadt, Barry E., G. Thomas Sicilia, and H. Wallace Sinaiko, "Overview," in Barry E. Goodstadt, G. Thomas Sicilia and H. Wallace Sinaiko, eds., *Proceedings of the Joint Service Workshop on Recruiter Productivity,* Washington, D.C.: Office of the Assistant Secretary of Defense (MRA&L), 1983. S0700.pdf.

Graham, Scott E., *Assessing the Impact of Mental Category on Simulated Tank Gunnery Performance,* Alexandria, Va.: United States Army Research Institute for the Behavioral and Social Sciences, 1515, March 1989. S0675.pdf.

Grayson, E.C., "Navy Input into 'Department of Defense Efforts to Develop Quality Standards for Enlistment: A Report to the House and Senate Committees on Armed Services'," in Office of the Assistant Secretary of Defense (MRA&L), ed., *Department of Defense Efforts to Develop Quality Standards for Enlistment: A Report to the House and Senate Committees on Armed Services,* Washington, D.C.: Office of the Assistant Secretary of Defense (MRA&L), 1981. G1211.pdf.

Greenberg, I. M., *Mental Standards for Enlistment Performance of Army Personnel Related to AFQT/ASVAB Scores: Final Report,* Monterey, Calif.: McFann Gray Associates, Inc, MGA0180WRD02, December 1980. S0540.pdf.

Griffith, Robert K., Jr., *The U.S. Army's Transition to the All-Volunteer Force 1968–1974,* Washington, D.C.: U.S. Army Center of Military History, 1997. S0186.pdf.

Grissmer, David W., *An Econometric Analysis of Volunteer Enlistment of Service and Cost Effectiveness Comparison of Service Incentive Programs,* McLean, Va.: General Research Corporation, October 1974. S0355.pdf.

Grissmer, David W., and Bernard D. Rostker, "Military Manpower in a Changing World," in Joseph Kruzel, ed., *American Defense Annual: 1991–1992,* New York: Lexington Books, 1992, pp. 127–145.

Haggstrom, Gus W., Thomas J. Blaschke, Winston K. Chow, and William Lisowski, *The Multiple Option Recruiting Experiment,* Santa Monica, Calif.: RAND Corporation, R-2671-MRAL, 1981. S0673.pdf.

Hammon, Colin P., and Stanley A. Horowitz, *Relating Personnel and Training Resources to Unit Performance,* Washington, D.C.: Institute for Defense Analyses, September 1987. S0671.pdf.

———, *Flying Hours and Aircrew Performance,* Alexandria, Va.: Institute for Defense Analyses, P2379, March 1990. S0849.pdf.

Hanser, Larry, interview with Bernard Rostker, March 12, 2004.

Horowitz, Stanley A., *Airwing Training Readiness,* Arlington, Va.: Center for Naval Analyses, CNA84-0817, May 25, 1984. S0847.pdf.

Horowitz, Stanley A., and Alan Sherman, *Maintenance Personnel Effectiveness in the Navy,* Arlington, Va.: Center for Naval Analyses, PP143, January 1976. S0343.pdf.

———, "A Direct Measure of the Relationship Between Human Capital and Productivity," *Journal of Human Resources,* Vol. 15, No. 1, Winter 1980.

Hosek, James R., Richard L. Fernandez, and David W. Grissmer, "Active Enlisted Supply: Prospects and Policy Options," in William Bowan, Roger Little, and G. Thomas Sicilia, eds., *The All-Volunteer Force After a Decade: Retrospect and Prospect,* New York: Pergamon-Brassey's, 1986.

Hosek, James R., and Christine E. Peterson, *The AFEESNLS Database: A Choice-Based Sample for Studying Enlistment and Post-Enlistment Outcomes,* Santa Monica, Calif.: RAND Corporation, N-1930-MRAL, January 1983. S0692.pdf.

———, *Enlistment Decisions of Young Men,* Santa Monica, Calif.: RAND Corporation, R-3238-MIL, July 1985. S0690.pdf.

Hosek, James R., Christine E. Peterson, and Rick A. Eden, *Educational Expectations and Enlistment Decisions,* Santa Monica, Calif.: RAND Corporation, R-3350-FMP, March 1986. S0691.pdf.

Janowitz, Morris, and Charles C. Moskos, Jr., "Racial Composition in the All-Volunteer Force," *Armed Forces and Society,* Vol. 1, No. 1, November 1974, pp. 109–123.

Jehn, Christopher, and Hugh E. Carroll, *Navy Recruiting in an All-Volunteer Environment,* Arlington, Va.: Center for Naval Analyses, CRC 235, April 25, 1974. S0342.pdf.

Jehn, Christopher, and William F. Shughart, III, "Modeling Recruiting District Performance," in Richard V. L. Cooper, ed., *missing,* Santa Monica, Calif.: RAND Corporation, 1979.

Juliana, James N., "Department of Defense Education Benefits Program," action memorandum to Deputy Secretary of Defense, Washington, D.C., March 2, 1982. G1180.pdf.

Korb, Lawrence J., Recruiting and Retention Activities, hearing before the Senate Appropriations Committee, Subcommittee on Defense Appropriations, 97th Cong., 1st Sess., Washington, D.C., U.S. Government Printing Office, July 24, 1981. G1294.pdf.

———, "Status Report on FY 1982 Recruiting Advertising Program," information memorandum to Secretary of Defense, Washington, D.C., April 9, 1982a. G1020.pdf.

———, Recruiting and Retention Activities, hearing before the Senate Appropriations Committee, Subcommittee on Defense Appropriations, 97th Cong., 2nd Sess., Washington, D.C., U.S. Government Printing Office, May 19, 1982b. G1293.pdf.

Lawrence J. Korb, Robert Hale, Maxwell R. Thurman, G.V. Montgomery, New Educational Assistance Program for the Military to Assist Recruiting, hearing before the House Armed Services Committee, Subcommittee on Military Personnel and Compensation, 97th Cong., 1st Sess., Washington, D.C., U.S. Government Printing Office, September 10, 1981. G1304.pdf.

Lehman, John, "Training Data and Analysis Center (TDAC)," action memorandum to Secretary of Defense, Washington, D.C., January 6, 1986. G1221.pdf.

Lockman, Robert F., *Enlisted Selection Strategies,* Alexandria, Va.: Center for Naval Analyses, CNS 1039, September 1974. S0837.pdf.

———, "A Model for Estimating Premature Losses," in Richard V. L. Cooper, ed., *Defense Manpower Policy: Presentations from the 1976 RAND Conference on Defense Manpower,* Santa Monica, Calif.: RAND Corporation, R-2490-ARPA, 1978. S0702.pdf.

Lucus, James L., "Air Force Input into 'Department of Defense Efforts to Develop Quality Standards for Enlistment: A Report to the House and Senate Committees on Armed Services'," in Office of the Assistant Secretary of Defense (MRA&L), ed., *Department of Defense Efforts to Develop Quality Standards for Enlistment: A Report to the House and Senate Committees on Armed Services,* Washington, D.C.: Office of the Assistant Secretary of Defense (MRA&L), 1981. G1211.pdf.

Maier, Milton H., *Military Aptitude Testing: The Past Fifty Years,* Monterey, Calif.: Defense Manpower Data Center, D Md.C TR 93007, June 1993. S0384.pdf.

Maier, Milton H., and Catherine M. Hiatt, *An Evaluation of Using Job Performance Tests to Validate ASVAB Qualification Standards,* Alexandria, Va.: Center for Naval Analyses, CNR 89 / May 1984, May 1984. S0396.pdf.

Marcus, Alan J., *Personnel Substitution and Navy Aviation Readiness*, Alexandria, Va.: Center for Naval Analyses, PP 363, October 1982. S0848.pdf.

Moskos, Charles C., Jr., "It's A New Ball Game: Changing Expectation of Military Service," in H. Wallace Sinaiko, ed., *First Term Enlisted Attrition,* Washington, D.C.: Smithsonian Institution, 1977. S0321.pdf.

Nelson, Gary R., *America's Volunteers: A Report on the All-Volunteer Armed Forces,* Washington, D.C.: Office of the Assistant Secretary of Defense (M&RA), December 31, 1978. S0194.pdf.

———, "The Supply and Quality of First-Term Enlistees Under the All-Volunteer Force," in William Bowman, Roger Little and G. Thomas Sicilia, eds., *The All-Volunteer Force After a Decade: Retrospect and Project,* New York: Pergamon-Brassey's, 1986.

OASD[MRA&L]—*See* Office of the Assistant Secretary of Defense for Manpower, Reserve Affairs, and Logistics.

Office of the Assistant Secretary of Defense for Manpower, Reserve Affairs, and Logistics, *Department of Defense Efforts to Develop Quality Standards for Enlistment: A Report to the House and Senate Committees on Armed Services,* Washington, D.C.: U.S. Department of Defense, December 1, 1981. G1211.pdf.

Orvis, Bruce R., Michael T. Childress, and J. Michael Polich, *Effect of Personnel Quality on the Performance of Patriot Air Defense System Operators,* R3901A, 1992. S0666.pdf.

Orvis, Bruce R., Martin T. Gahart, Alvin K. Ludwig, and Karl F. Schutz, *Validity and Usefulness of Enlistment Intention Information,* Santa Monica, Calif.: RAND Corporation, R-3775-FMP, 1992. S0698.pdf.

Pirie, Robert B., Jr., "Limits on Category IV Accessions," memorandum to Carl Levin, Washington, D.C., June 28, 1980a. G0448.pdf.

———, "Plan for Validating Enlistment Standards Against Job Performance," memorandum to Secretaries of the Military Department, Washington, D.C., July 7, 1980b. G0371.pdf.

Polich, J. Michael, *Design Options for the Department of Defense Advertising Mix Test,* Letter, Santa Monica, Calif.: RAND Corporation, April 22, 1983. S0687.pdf.

Polich, J. Michael, James N. Dertouzos, and S. James Press, *The Enlistment Bonus Experiment,* Santa Monica, Calif.: RAND Corporation, R-3353-FMP, April 1986. S0678.pdf.

Polich, J. Michael, Richard L. Fernandez, and Bruce R. Orvis, *Enlistment Effects of Military Educational Benefits,* Santa Monica, Calif.: RAND Corporation, N-1783-MRAL, 1982. S0676.pdf.

Quester, Aline O., *Enlisted Crew Quality and Ship Material Readiness,* Alexandria, Va.: Center for Naval Analyses, CRM 88254, April 1989. S0864.pdf.

Quester, Aline O., Russell Beland, and William Mulligan, *Ship Material Readiness,* Alexandria, Va.: Center for Naval Analyses, PP467, March 1989. S0850.pdf.

Rice, Donald B., ed., *Defense Resource Management Study: A Report Requested by the President and Submitted to the Secretary of Defense—February 1979,* Washington, D.C.: U.S. Government Printing Office, 1979. S0488.pdf.

Rostker, Bernard D., *Total Force Planning, Personnel Costs and the Supply of New Reservists,* Santa Monica, Calif.: RAND Corporation, R-1430-PR, October 1974. S0796.pdf.

———, "Economic Analysis of Enlistment: Comment," in Curt L. Gilroy, ed., *Army Manpower Economics,* Boulder, Colo.: Westview Press, 1985.

Sargent, Thomas J., "Interpreting Economic Time Series," *The Journal of Political Economy,* Vol. 89, No. 2, April 1981, pp. 213–248.

Scribner, Barry L, D. Alton Smith, Robert H. Baldwin, and Robert L. Phillips, "Are Smart Tankers Better? AFQT and Military Productivity," *Armed Forces & Society,* Vol. 12, No. 2, Winter 1986, pp. 193–206.

Sellman, Wayne S., "The Nexus Between Science and Policy," in Bert F. Jr. Green and Anne S. Mavor, eds., *Modeling Cost and Performance for Military Enlistment: Report of a Workshop,* Washington, D.C.: National Academy Press, 1994.

———, *Predicting Readiness for Military Service: How Enlistment Standards Are Estimated,* paper, Washington, D.C.: U.S. Department of Education, September 30, 2004. G1360.pdf.

Shields, Joyce L., interview with Bernard Rostker, March 5, 2004.

Shields, Joyce L., and Lawrence M. Hanser, "Designing, Planning and Selling Project A," *Personnel Psychology,* Vol. 43, No. 2, Summer 1990, pp. 241–247.

Shields, Joyce L., Lawrence M. Hanser, and John P. Campbell, "A Paradigm Shift," in John P. Campbell and Deirdre J. Knapp, eds., *Exploring the Limits in Personnel Selection and Classification,* Mahwah, N.J.: Lawrence Erlbaum Associates, Publishers, 2001.

Smith, David A., and Paul F. Hogan, "The Accession Quality Cost/Performance Trade-off Model," in B.F. Green and A.S. Mavor, eds., *Modeling Cost and Performance for Military Enlistments,* Washington, D.C.: National Academy Press, 1994. S0835.pdf.

Staff of the Directorate for Accession Policy, *First Annual Report to the Congress on Joint-Service Efforts to Link Enlistment Standards to On-The-Job Performance,* Washington, D.C.: Office of the Assistant Secretary of Defense (Manpower, Reserve Affairs and Logistics), December 1982. P0019.pdf.

———, *Second Annual Report to the Congress on Joint-Service Efforts to Link Enlistment Standards to On-The-Job Performance,* Washington, D.C.: Office of the Assistant Secretary of Defense (Manpower, Reserve Affairs and Logistics), December 1983. P0015.pdf.

———, *Defense Manpower Quality: Volume I,* Washington, D.C.: Office of the Assistant Secretary of Defense (Manpower, Installations, and Logistics), May 1985a. P0007.pdf.

———, *Defense Manpower Quality: Volume II, Army Submission,* Washington, D.C.: Office of the Assistant Secretary of Defense (Manpower, Installations, and Logistics), May 1985b. P0008.pdf.

———, *Defense Manpower Quality: Volume III Navy, Marine Corps and Air Force Submissions,* Washington, D.C.: Office of the Assistant Secretary of Defense (Manpower, Installations, and Logistics), May 1985c. P0006.pdf.

———, *Joint-Service Efforts to Link Enlistment Standards to On-The-Job Performance,* Washington, D.C.: Office of the Assistant Secretary of Defense (Force Management and Personnel), December 1987. P0014.pdf.

———, *Joint-Service Efforts to Link Enlistment Standards to Job Performance,* Washington, D.C.: Office of the Assistant Secretary of Defense (Force Management and Personnel), January 1990. P0017.pdf.

———, *Joint-Service Efforts to Link Enlistment Standards to Job Performance,* Washington, D.C.: Office of the Assistant Secretary of Defense (Force Management and Personnel), January 1991. P0018.pdf.

Thurman, Maxwell R., "Sustaining the All-Volunteer Force 1983–1992: The Second Decade," in William Bowman, Roger Little and G. Thomas Sicilia, eds., *The All-Volunteer Force After a Decade: Retrospect and Prospect,* New York: Pergamon-Brassey's, 1986.

————, *Oral History,* unpublished RAND research, 1992.

————, "On Being All You Can Be: A Recruiting Perspective," in J. Eric Fredland, Curtis L. Gilroy, Roger D. Little and W.S. Sellman, eds., *Professionals on the Front Line: Two Decades of the All-Volunteer Force,* Washington, D.C.: Brassey's, 1996.

Walker, Clinton B., and Michael G Rumsey, "Application of Findings: ASVAB , New Aptitude Tests, and Personnel Classification," in John P. Campbell and Deirdre J. Knapp, eds., *Exploring the Limits in Personnel Selection and Classification,* Mahwah, N.J.: Lawrence Erlbaum Associates, Publishers, 2001.

Warner, John T., and Saul Pleeter, "The Personal Discount Rate: Evidence from Military Downsizing Programs," *American Economic Review,* Vol. 91, No. 1, March 2001, pp. 33–53. S0880.pdf.

Warner, John T., Curtis J. Simon, Deborah M. Payne, and J. Michael Jones, *Enlistment Supply in the 1990's: A Study of the Navy College Fund and Other Enlistment Incentive Programs,* Washington, D.C.: Defense Manpower Data Center, D Md.C 2000015, April 2001. S0699.pdf.

Weinberger, Caspar W., "Congratulations for a Job Well Done," letter to Albert J. Martin, Washington, D.C., August 24, 1981. G0865.pdf.

White, Leonard A., Mark C. Young, and Michael G. Rumsey, "ABLE Implementation Issues and Related Research," in John P. Campbell and Deirdre J. Knapp, eds., *Exploring the Limits in Personnel Selection and Classification,* Mahwah, N.J.: Lawrence Erlbaum Associates, Publishers, 2001.

Wigdor, Alexandra K., and Bert F. Green, Jr., *Performance Assessment for the Workplace,* Washington, D.C.: National Academy Press, 1991.

Winkler, John D., Judith C. Fernandez, and J. Michael Polich, *Effect of Aptitude on the Performance of Army Communications Operators,* RAND Corporation, Arroyo Center, R-4143A, 1992. S0667.pdf.

Wright, Elden H., "Army Input into 'Department of Defense Efforts to Develop Quality Standards for Enlistment: A Report to the House and Senate Committees on Armed Services'," in Office of the Assistant Secretary of Defense (MRA&L), ed., *Department of Defense Efforts to Develop Quality Standards for Enlistment: A Report to the House and Senate Committees on Armed Services,* Washington, D.C.: Office of the Assistant Secretary of Defense (MRA&L), 1981. G1211.pdf.

Young, Winnie Y., Janis H. Houston, James H. Harris, R. Gene Hoffman, and Lauress L. Wise, "Large-Scale Predictor Validation in Project A: Data Collection Procedures and Data Base Preparation," *Personnel Psychology,* Vol. 43, No. 2, Summer 1990.

CHAPTER SEVENTEEN

Pax Americana and the New World Order: The Clinton and Bush Years (1992–2004)

The United States possesses unprecedented—and unequaled—strength and influence in the World. . . . The U.S. national security strategy will be based on a distinctly American internationalism that reflects the union of our values and our national interests.

—George W. Bush
President of the United States[1]

The All-Volunteer Force has proven itself. We have the highest caliber men and women in our Armed Forces. . . . The days of conscript military personnel are over.

—Melvin Laird
Secretary of Defense[2]

We're not going to reimplement a draft. There is no need for it at all. The disadvantages of using compulsion to bring into the armed forces the men and women needed are notable.

—Donald H. Rumsfeld
Secretary of Defense[3]

Introduction

The war in Iraq is the latest and, in some ways, the severest test of the all-volunteer force. It is a test that actually started with the end of the Cold War, during the administration of the first President Bush. The first Gulf War seemed to definitively answer the question of the efficacy of the all-volunteer force. Together, the decision to end

---

[1] The National Security Strategy of the United States of America, September 17, 2002 (Bush, G. W., 2002)

[2] Letter to Secretary of Defense, William Perry, October 6, 1995 (Laird, 1995)

[3] DoD News Briefing January 7, 2003 (Rumsfeld, 2003a)

conscription and the policies of the 1980s produced a military capable of defeating a large enemy army and air force using Soviet equipment and employing Soviet tactics. While the fight took place on the sands of the Middle East rather than the plains of Germany as had been assumed for most of the post-World War II period of the Cold War, the overriding consensus was that the all-volunteer force was a success. In retrospect, however, the Gulf War may not have been the ultimate test of the all-volunteer force, and the conclusion that the all-volunteer force has been a success may yet prove to be premature. The conflict in Iraq and Afghanistan is proving to be much more trying, and the ultimate success of the all-volunteer force may depend not only on the traditional measures of recruiting, retaining, and motivating our active and reserve service members but on force-planning decisions made in the years immediately following the end of the Cold War.

Rethinking American Military Posture After the Cold War

The end of the Cold War precipitated a rethinking of America's role in the world and reconsideration of the military force structure. Initially, Secretary of Defense Dick Cheney and Chairman of the Joint Chiefs Colin Powell developed what they called the *Base Force;* the Clinton administration made some modifications with its Bottom-Up Review (BUR) and first Quadrennial Defense Review (QDR); and Secretary of Defense Donald Rumsfeld has, more recently, pushed his notion of *Transformation.* At their core, all these views of the American military had a vision of future warfare largely modeled after Operation Desert Storm and generalized by the term *major theater war* (MTW)—a vision that at the time a small minority called a "mistake."[4] Disagreement on this fundamental vision of the future lies at the heart of any assessment of the future of the all-volunteer force as a force largely restructured to fight a conventional major regional conflict (MRC) found itself increasingly engaging in nonconventional conflicts.

The Base Force

In January 1990 President Bush proposed that the nation "transition to a restructured military" that would incorporate "a new strategy that is more flexible, more geared to

---

[4] The 2000 National Defense University study called this a "divergent view" and noted that its holders

> point out the relative rarity of American military involvement in major theater warfare against cross-border aggression. From this perspective, *Desert Storm* is an exception rather than a rule. Given the apparent increase in the number and frequency of nonstate threats and the potential for asymmetric operations, it has been suggested that the primacy of the DoD focus on preparing for classic MTWs [Major Theater Wars] is a mistake. The threats of the future, according to this view, will be significantly different and will require a different emphasis in preparation. . . . A major proponent of the forecast of future warfare in chaotic environments has been a former Commandant of the Marine Corps, General Charles C. Krulak. (Tangredi, 2000, pp. 100–101)

In addition, see General Anthony Zinni's comments on Desert Storm and Somalia in Zinni (2000).

contingencies outside of Europe while continuing to meet our inescapable responsibilities to NATO and while maintaining the global balance."[5]

Chairman Powell, seeing a consensus develop around a substantially smaller military, developed his concept of a minimum, or *base,* force.[6] As so often happens, the Base Force quickly became a ceiling. President Bush endorsed the crisis response and reconstitution strategy of the Base Force. He told those gathered under the tent at the Aspin Institute in Colorado on August 2, 1990, that

> [o]ur task today is to shape our defense capabilities to these changing strategic circumstances. In a world less driven by an immediate threat to Europe and the danger of global war, in a world where the size of our forces will increasingly be shaped by the needs of regional contingencies and peacetime presence, we know that our forces can be smaller. . . . What we need are not merely reductions but restructuring. (Bush, G. H. W., 1990)

The following September, Secretary of Defense Dick Cheney told a defense think tank that, "under the world as it is developing in the 1990s, [we can] assume that we would have significant time, sufficient [warning] time, before a global conflict to reconstitute forces" (Cheney, 1990).

A review of the 1990s suggests that the Base Force missed the mark in several ways that have implications for the all-volunteer force. In an assessment of the Base Force, Eric Larson and his colleagues at RAND found "little evidence that substantial involvement in peacekeeping and other peace operations was anticipated during the development of the Base Force" (Larson et al., 2001, p. iv).[7] They further noted that

> one of the Base Force's key premises—that the post–Cold War world would not be occasioned by large-scale, long-duration contingency operations—was [immediately] cast in doubt by the post–Gulf War stationing of Air Force . . . aircraft in Southwest Asia. (Larson et al., 2001, p. 38)

The Clinton Administration's Bottom-Up Review and the Quadrennial Defense Review of 1997

The legacy from the Bush administration to the new administration that took office in January 1993 was the entire intellectual construct of the Base Force, e.g., the dominance of MTW planning and the notion that engagements like the then-ongoing

---

[5] As quoted by Senator Sam Nunn in his March 22 floor speech, "Defense Budget Blanks" (1990).

[6] Jaffe (1993) discusses the development of the Base Force more fully.

[7] Leslie Lewis et al. had earlier observed that the "Army's strategy was to protect force structure by sustaining O&M [operations and maintenance] accounts, bringing down Research and Development (R&D) and making modernization programs the offsets for its force structure budget requirements" (1992, p. 41). Part of the reluctance may well go back to the Army's reaction to Vietnam. Certainly, the Abrams Doctrine, on the Active-Reserve Force Mix, and the Powell Doctrine, emphasizing the overwhelming use of force and the need for an exit strategy, are direct reflections of the Vietnam experience.

deployment to Somalia were simply "lesser included cases" requiring little if any deviation from the conventional norm. The legacy, together with a Presidential campaign promise to reduce the cost of the military, dominated the Clinton administration's efforts to design a new military for the 1990s. When the BUR was finally unveiled on September 1, 1993, the new force incorporated the MTWs of the Base Force (but now referring to them as MRCs). Even with American troops struggling in Somalia and recognition of the importance of such missions as peacekeeping and peace enforcement, humanitarian operations, and disaster relief, the design of the force changed little, as no new funds or forces were provided. Through the rest of the decade, operations other than war and small-scale contingencies remained the "lesser-included-cases" of a force designed primarily to fight and win a conventional MTW/MRC war.

As events progressed, it became clear that the BUR force and budget were not adequate. Readiness problems emerged as peacekeeping and other small-scale operations increased, and these negatively affected warfighting and readiness because, as the Congressional Research Service found (Ryan, 1998, p. 10–13), the cumulative level of peacetime operations approximated a force structure equivalent to a full MRC or more.[8] The Clinton administration had a chance to revise the BUR with the QDR of 1997, but again rhetoric won out over resources. Larson observed that the QDR did not "change . . . [any of] the BUR's basic approach" but "relied on management review to minimize SSC [small-scale contingency]-related deployment and personnel tempos, readiness, and other risks to warfighting capabilities" (Larson et al., 2001, p. 90).

The Administration of George W. Bush: Transformation and the Global War on Terrorism

The path that George W. Bush's administration would follow was laid out at the Citadel on September 23, 1999, when then Governor Bush promised to transform the American military. Lamenting what he saw as the deplorable state of the all-volunteer force—"undermined [morale caused] by back-to-back deployments, poor pay, shortages of spare parts and equipment, and rapidly declining readiness" (1999)—Bush promised that if elected the new administration would provide

> better pay, better treatment and better training. . . .
>   But our military requires more than good treatment. It needs the rallying point of a defining mission. And that mission is to deter wars—and win wars when deterrence fails. Sending our military on vague, aimless and endless deployments is the swift solvent of morale.
>   As president I will order an immediate review of our overseas deployments . . . . we will not be permanent peacekeepers, dividing warring parties. This is not our strength or our calling. . . .

---

[8] Eric Larson et al. (2001, p. 80) make similar observations and provide a complete review of the Base Force, Bottom-up and Quadrennial Defense reviews.

And this review of our deployments will also reduce the tension on an over-stretched military. (Bush, G. W., 1999)[9]

Bush promised "a revolution in the technology of war" in which size would be replaced by "mobility and swiftness." As he saw it, "[t]his revolution perfectly matches the strengths of our country—the skill of our people and the superiority of our technology. The best way to keep the peace," he told his audience, "is to redefine war on our terms" (Bush, G. W., 1999). However, the events of September 11, 2001, and the Global War on Terrorism that followed have changed these initial ideas, as events in Iraq and Afghanistan brought into question the program for transformation and the viability of the all-volunteer force.[10] But none of this was anticipated as the Berlin Wall came down and the Soviet Union came apart.

Managing the All-Volunteer Force After the Cold War, "Steaming as Before"

When the Clinton administration took over in January 1993, the tenor of the confirmation hearing for the new Secretary of Defense, Les Aspin, made it clear that reducing the size of the military and developing the new administration's version of the Base Force would be the major focus of the new defense team. There were, of course, hold-over issues, such as the report of the President's Commission on the Assignment of Women in the Armed Forces, what to do about women in combat, and recruiting. These issues, however, would take a back seat when "gays in the military" inadvertently became the defense issue that marked the Clinton administration.

---

[9] A Congressional Research Service has reported that, "during the first 16 months of his administration, Bush sought and achieved a reduction of over 50% of U.S. forces in the Balkans" (Serafino, 2003, p. 2).

[10] The Congressional Research Service reviewed the post–Cold War commitment to operations other than traditional combat and, in light of the events of September 11, 2001, the Global War on Terrorism and concluded that the

> post–Cold War defense drawdown and the expanding demands of manpower-intensive peacekeeping and humanitarian operations . . . are placing at risk the decisive military edge that this nation enjoys at the end of the Cold War. . . . Many suggested fewer overseas commitments, but neither Democratic nor Republican administrations could stem demands on U.S. forces. Congress mandated DoD to compensate soldiers who were deployed too long or too often, but September 11, 2001, caused that law to be waived. Technological advances made transforming U.S. forces even more combat effective against conventional forces, but could not yet substitute for all the manpower needs in the unconventional and asymmetric environments of "stability" operations. In contrast, some charged that the Army, in particular, was resisting such "constabulary" operations and therefore managed its personnel inefficiently. (Bruner, 2004, p. 2)

Sexual Orientation and Military Personnel Policy

In his memoir, President Clinton reflects on

> the major shortcoming of the transition. . . . I hardly spent any time on the White House staff, and I gave almost no thought to how to keep the public's focus on my most important priorities, rather than on competing stories that, at least, would divert public attention from the big issues and, at worst, could make it appear that I was neglecting those priorities. (Clinton, 1993, p. 467)

For those who wanted a change, allowing gays to serve in the armed forces was an equity-of-service issue for the all-volunteer force. For those favoring the continuation of the policy of banning gays from the military, this had nothing to do with the all-volunteer force but affected the moral integrity of the armed forces. Like the issue of draft registration in the late 1970s, the gay issue was a "sideshow" that took center stage. While it had little tangible influence on either the short-term fortunes of the all-volunteer force or on the longer-term issues of restructuring for the post–Cold War environment, it set the tone for the relationship between the new commander in chief and those who served. Subsequent personnel decisions at the Pentagon were made in light of the perception that many in the military held negative views of President Clinton.

Lifting the ban on gays in the military had been one of Governor Clinton's campaign pledges. In retrospect, Clinton thought it unwise to raise such a divisive issue so early in his Presidency—he would later say, "[w]e were denied the honeymoon traditionally given new Presidents, partly because of the way the gays-in-the-military issue surfaced early" (1993, p. 516). However, when the issue came up at his first press conference, just three days after he took office, he could not resist taking the bait and committing his new administration to regulations allowing homosexuals to serve.

An "urgent request" from the Joint Chiefs of Staff for a meeting on the subject the following day challenged Clinton's authority in ways that could not be easily ignored. The chiefs objected to any change and "made it clear" to him that if he went ahead and "ordered them to take action they'd do the best job they could, although if called to testify before Congress they would have to state their views frankly" (Clinton, 1993, p. 484). The lines were drawn. Four days later (January 29, 1993), he signed a memorandum directing Secretary of Defense Les Aspin to "submit . . . prior to July 15, 1993 a draft Executive Order ending discrimination on the basis of sexual orientation in determining who may serve in the Armed Forces" (Clinton, 1993). Reflecting what would become one of the major concerns for those opposing the change in policy, he asked Secretary Aspin to ensure that the new policy would be "carried out in a manner that is practical and realistic, and consistent with the high standards of combat effectiveness and unit cohesion our Armed Forces must maintain."[11]

It soon became clear that, while the President had the legal authority to issue an executive order, his actions could not be sustained. As President Clinton later noted, the

> House passed a resolution opposing my position by more than three to one. The Senate opposition was not as great but was still substantial. . . . If I persisted, the Congress would overturn my position. . . . With congressional defeat inevitable, Les Aspin worked with Colin Powell and the Joint Chiefs on a compromise. (Clinton, 1993, p. 485)
> The compromise was "don't ask; don't tell."[12]

On July 19, 1993, President Clinton stepped before what can only be described as a cold and hostile audience at the National Defense University to formally announce the new policy. While he later saw this as "moving a long way, to 'live and let live,'" he

---

[11] *Author's Note:* In February 1993, Aspin asked the president of the RAND Corporation to "research" the issue of gays in the military. RAND documented the scope of its activities:

> Staff members visited military organizations in seven foreign countries and police and fire departments in six American cities, seeking insights and lessons from analogous experiences of other organizations and institutions. The team considered the historical record, focusing on the integration of African-Americans and on the development of the current policy that prohibits homosexuals from serving in the military. It reviewed public opinion data and the data concerning the views of current active-duty military personnel. It also reviewed the scientific literature on group cohesion, sexuality, and related health issues. It examined a number of legal and enforcement issues, as well as the literature that deals with implementing change in large organizations. (Rostker et al., 1993, p. 2)

In April, the RAND team briefed Aspin and Deputy Secretary William Perry on their findings:

> Only one policy option was . . . consistent with the findings of this research and the criteria of the Presidential memorandum, and . . . logically and internally consistent. That policy would consider sexual orientation, by itself, as not germane to determining who may serve in the military. The policy would establish clear standards of conduct for all military personnel, to be equally and strictly enforced, in order to maintain the military discipline necessary for effective operations. (Rostker et al., 1993, p. 2)

Within weeks of the briefing to Aspin, the pressure from the Pentagon to have RAND write up its findings suddenly changed. While RAND was never told not to publish its findings, it became clear that, once the administration adopted the "don't ask, don't tell" policy, DoD would have been just as happy if the RAND material was never made public. After the President's speech at the National Defense University, some members of Congress insisted on seeing RAND's work, and the report was released to the public in August.

[12] Moskos has pointed out that, in 1993, he

> first suggested the "Don't Ask, Don't Tell, Don't Pursue" policy to then Senate Armed Forces Committee Chairman Senator Sam Nunn. Then Secretary of Defense Les Aspin approved the policy and it was recommended to the President. In the following months, I worked with the White House, the Armed Forces and Senator Nunn's committee to draft the policy, which eventually was codified into law. (Moskos, 1998)

While Clinton eventually accepted the policy, he was concerned because he saw a problem with Moskos's and Nunn's arguments: "that they could have been used with equal force against Truman's order on integration or against current efforts to open more positions to women in the military" (Clinton, 1993, p. 484). Moskos had, in fact, recently used the same arguments against expanding the role of women in the military as a member of President Bush's Commission on Women in the Armed Forces.

admitted, "I got the worst of both worlds—I lost the fight, and the gay community was highly critical of me for the compromise" (Clinton, 1993, p. 486). He could also have added that the compromise did not go down well with many in the military.[13] They saw it as hypocritical, and this intensified their dislike and, in some quarters, open disrespect for the new commander in chief.[14]

Recruiting

Recruiting is the heart of sustaining the all-volunteer force. However, with the change in the world order, a perceived reduction in the threat to the Nation and the drawing down of the force the focus of attention shifted to getting people out of the military, rather then getting them into the military. The recruiting commands became a target for cuts and no longer were up and coming officers finding themselves assigned to

---

[13] *Author's Note:* My involvement in preparing the RAND report on gays in the military came up when I was nominated to be Assistant Secretary of the Navy for Manpower and Reserve Affairs, a position requiring Senate confirmation. Before being nominated, I was asked to meet with the Marine Corps Commandant, General Carl Mundy. General Mundy was one of the most outspoken critics of the proposal to lift the ban as President Clinton explained in his memoir (Clinton, 1993, p. 483). I explained to General Mundy, as I would to the members of the Senate Armed Services Committee, that I understood the law and was prepared to carry it out if nominated and confirmed.

The facts that RAND's recommendations were fully based on our documented research and that we did not try to sell our results seemed to mitigate any fear that I would be on some kind of a crusade to change things regardless of the imposition of don't ask, don't tell. In November 1994, I left RAND and took the oath of office to rejoin the Navy Secretariat I had left 15 years before. In many ways a lot had changed, but in some ways, things were very familiar. My office was just one door down the hall on the E-ring from my old office. My old Executive Assistant, Mike Boorda, was now the Chief of National Operations, filling the position I had always thought he was destined to fill. I would be working with my old friends, Richard Danzig and Robin Pirie. Unfortunately, I also found the quality of decisionmaking much less analytic and rigorous than it had been when I had served earlier. This was true not only in the Navy Secretariat but also in OSD. The golden days of "Systems Analysis" had long passed.

[14] *Author's Note:* In 2004, Clinton wrote, "In practice it [don't ask; don't tell] often did not work out. . . . Many anti-gay officers simply ignored the new policy and worked even harder to root out homosexuals" (Clinton, 1993, p. 485). That was not my experience serving as Assistant Secretary of the Navy from 1994 to 1998, when I was most directly involved in reviewing the policy and approving all officer discharges.

It was true that, before 1993, such organizations as the Naval Criminal Investigation Service actively targeted homosexuals. However, after the change in policy, as far as I could tell from the cases I reviewed, organized "witch hunts" stopped. Almost all the discharges granted to homosexuals that I saw involved service members who voluntarily identified themselves, particularly when the new policy put in place by Deputy Secretary John Deutch in 1994 cancelled the outstanding financial obligation of discharged homosexuals. As a result, some thought that claiming to be a homosexual was a quick and financially lucrative way of getting out of the military. In fact, I handled a number of cases where claims of homosexuality were rejected, forcing those making the claim to complete their service obligations.

In 1998 Charles Moskos, the person who originally suggested the "don't ask, don't tell" policy, reviewed the status of the gay issue in the military and concluded that, while it remained contentious, "the general movement is toward increased toleration and acceptance" (Moskos, 1998, p. 15):

> For both sexes, homosexual discharges were much more likely to be due to "telling" than by authorities "asking." For fiscal year 1997 in the Army, 171 homosexuals were discharged for "admissions" compared to four for "acts." Although the lifting of the full ban seemed unlikely, the United States has clearly moved toward greater acceptance of homosexuality than would have been imagined a decade or so earlier. (Moskos, 1998, pp. 16–17)

recruiting. As the drawdown drew to a close and recruiting goals were increased it became apparent that recruiting would be more difficult than during the Cold War. The demographics of the primary age group had changed and there was an apparent reduction in the propensity to enlist. Recruiting became a concern once again taking a great deal of the time of senior defense leaders, including the Secretary of Defense, himself.

The Senior Panel on Recruiting. Initially, things looked good for the new administration, in fact, so good that Aspin agreed to go along with the initiative by the Office of Management and Budget to reduce the substantial pay raise that had been budgeted by the outgoing Bush administration. Even with the less than expected pay raise, in November 1993, Aspin announced,

> [t]he Department of Defense achieved its FY93 recruiting goal. . . . Overall, recruit quality was excellent: 95 percent of FY 1993 new recruits were high school diploma graduates . . . [with] [t]he proportion of individuals who scored in the upper half of the enlistment test . . . [at] 71 percent. The percentage of "high quality" recruits (those who have both a high school diploma and also score in the upper half of the enlistment test) was 67 percent. Finally, less than 1 percent of new recruits scored in the lowest acceptable category (AFQT Category IV). (Aspin, 1993)

Reflecting on the change in the military since the initial transition to an all-volunteer force 20 years before, Aspin noted that females made up 15 percent of total accessions and "black accessions" were 17 percent, generally in line with their proportion of the population. "We want well educated, highly professional, highly motivated teams, and we're getting them," he told the press (Aspin, 1993). By the following April (1994), however, Deputy Secretary of Defense John Deutch was concerned enough about the drop in a number of "leading indicators" for recruiting that he established a Senior Panel to oversee and, if necessary, change the way recruiting was being managed.

The new Under Secretary of Defense for Personnel and Readiness, Edwin Dorn explained "the rationale and anticipated direction for the [Senior] Panel" (Sellman, 1994),[15]

> annual youth attitude surveys show that young people's interest in the military (their enlistment propensity) has dropped. . . . We have indications of apprehensiveness in the force—the result of the drawdown, changes in mission, high operating tempo in some units, and concerns about pay and benefits. There is a perception by many of our young people that the military is no longer a source of long-term career opportunity. . . .

---

[15] *Author's Note:* The following "talking points" were prepared by the Director of Procurement Policy, Steve Sellman, at the direction of Ed Dorn and sent "through" Dorn to the Deputy Secretary of Defense, John Deutch, to be approved by him and forwarded to the Public Affairs office for its use in explaining to the press why DoD had established a Senior Panel. This "chain" is typical and illustrates the whimsical definition of government as a place where you "write things you do not sign, and sign things you do not write."

The panel . . . will consider potential reasons for declining enlistment propensity (i.e., lack of advertising, effects of downsizing on attitudes toward military as a viable career option and stable employer).

Continued economic growth, coupled with falling propensity and slightly more ambitious accession goals will challenge our recruiting efforts next year. . . . The panel will consider the need to increase the number of recruiters and to reprogram additional funds for advertising, educational incentives, and enlistment bonuses. (Sellman, 1994)

In June, Dorn reported a mixed picture. He told Deputy Secretary Deutch that, in April, "the Services missed their monthly new contract goals, varying from 86 percent (Navy) to 98 (Air Force)" (Dorn, 1994a).[16] Even though it looked as though the services overall would have a "successful recruiting year" they were eating into their Delayed Entry Program (DEP). A similar picture was reported for the third quarter of FY 1994 (Dorn, 1994b).[17]

The contradictory picture of meeting goals in the face of drops in the reported "propensity to enlist" and complaints about poor morale and stress among recruiters continued into 1995. Assistant Secretary of Defense (Force Management) Fred Pang reported a "continuing decline in the enlistment propensity of 16-21 year old men" (Pang, 1995a) from the 1994 Youth Attitude Tracking Study (YATS), and the "propensity to join the Army . . . declined most sharply, from 17 percent in 1991 to 11 percent in 1994" (Pang, 1995a). At the March 13, 1995, meeting of the Senior Panel on

---

[16] Secretary Dorn asked the Defense Manpower Research Center at RAND to look at the decline in propensity estimates and recruiting results. RAND briefed Deputy Secretary Deutch and the Senior Panel in May 1994. RAND explained that it did not believe there had been a fundamental shift in the underlying propensities, which was the popular explanation. They reported that the

> more likely explanation for the reported recruiting difficulties is that important changes in resource management or recruiting practices could have occurred as recruiting resources were substantially reduced during the drawdown. . . . Our research supports increases in advertising and the removal of the ceiling on the number of recruiters. (Asch and Orvis, 1994, p. 28)

A subsequent, more-detailed study found that,

> if anything, the supply of potential high-quality enlistees had generally increased since the beginning of the drawdown . . . relative to the accession requirement. Thus, the recent difficulties reported by recruiters in FY94 and FY95 came at a time when potential supply appears to have been adequate; this suggests problems in converting supply into enlistments. Notwithstanding the results for FY94–95, there has been some downturn in youth interest in military service. When that downturn is coupled with the large postdrawdown increase in accession requirements . . . we find that the potential supply of high-quality enlistees could fall short of its pre-drawdown levels. (Orvis et al., 1996)

[17] *Author's Note:* Edwin Dorn originally held the position of Assistant Secretary (Personnel and Readiness). The position was changed to under secretary, making him the fourth and junior under secretary, rounding out the structure of four under secretaries reporting to the secretary and the deputy secretary. With the assistant secretaries for Health Affairs and for Reserve Affairs reporting to the new under secretary, DoD had come full circle. This was the arrangement that existed 20 years earlier, but this time all positions were elevated by one grade. The assistant secretary of the 1970s had become the under secretary and the deputy assistant secretaries had become assistant secretaries.

Recruiting, Dorn stressed that, departmentwide, "we are meeting our FY 1995 quality/quantity objective, but face increasing accession mission in FY 1996–1997." He was, however, concerned about "the low quality of Navy women" and wondered whether the Navy needed "to set aptitude goals for women." He further noted the continuing decline in the propensity of youth to join the military, "especially among Blacks, although still higher than Whites." Observing that recruiters were showing "higher stress and dissatisfaction than in 1989 and 1991," he wondered whether there was a need for more recruiters or to increase resources or management emphasis. He concluded with the observation that "[r]ecruiting continues to need attention by senior OSD and Service officials" (OUSD[P&R], 1995b).

One set of data presented at the Senior Panel meeting was particularly revealing. As reported, the services had reduced the number of production recruiters since FY 1990. While the overall plan for FY 1995 was to start to increase the number of recruiters, only the Marine Corps planned to have more recruiters in the field than they had had in September 1993. In fact, the Air Force, despite the fact that it had been recruiting only 91 percent of it monthly goal, was still planning on reducing recruiters in FY 1995 and again in FY 1996 (OUSD[P&R], 1995a, Tab I).

Deputy Secretary Deutch was particularly concerned about results of the 1994 Recruiter Survey. After the March meeting, he wrote the service secretaries to ask that they "[c]onduct a thorough review of recruiting policies and practices to improve recruiter quality of life, and to reduce the pressures that may lead to potential improprieties" (Deutch, 1995). He reminded them of his personal commitment and DoD's policy: "Successful recruiting is a centerpiece of personnel readiness; as such it requires the close attention of senior OSD and Service officials" (Deutch, 1995).

The Senior Panel on Recruiting was not the only venue at which recruiting problems were discussed. They also became a topic of discussion during meetings of the Senior Readiness Oversight Council. While it might seem somewhat redundant to cover the same ground at meetings of two "senior" forums, different people attended the different meetings. The service secretaries, the civilian leaders of the military departments, sat on both the panel and the council, but the service chiefs were members only of the council. In spring 1995, linking recruiting to readiness, the service chiefs "mentioned" their growing concerns for recruiting. However, as Dorn noted, "under current plans the Services would spend less per recruit in 1996 and 1997" than they did in 1995 (Dorn, 1995b). Dorn reminded the service chiefs that "investment per recruit is a strong determinant of the quality mix" and that there was "an imbalance between recruiting goals and resources" (Dorn, 1995a).

When the Senior Readiness Panel next met on September 5, 1995—the first meeting chaired by the new Deputy Secretary, John White—Dorn reported, "increases in Army and Navy accessions levels were not matched by increased resources, depressing their investment-per-accession" even further (OUSD[P&R], 1995c).[18] White wrote the Secretary of the Army to express his concern about the "apparent underfunding of Army recruiting" (White, 1996):

> Between Fiscal Years 1995 and 1997, your active-force enlisted recruiting mission rises by nearly 40 percent; but that rise is not matched by a complementary increase in recruiting resources. As a result, your investment per recruit drops by about 20 percent. Given the strong historical correlation between the investment per recruit and the resulting quality mix, it is important that you closely review that resource-mission balance to confirm the Army's ability to accomplish its stated recruiting goal. (White, 1996)

White wanted the Army to "identify any specific actions you intend to take" and "the specific controls . . . [you] have put in place to trigger periodic resource reviews should your recruiting thresholds be violated" (White, 1996).

Recruiter Quality of Life. One addition to the discussion of recruiting during the 1990s was the issue of "recruiter quality of life." In October 1994, Assistant Secretary Pang responded to the imminent release of a General Accounting Office report entitled *Military Recruiting: More Innovative Approaches Needed* (Gebicke, 1994) by establishing the Joint Recruiting Support Study Group, which was to "evaluate the viability and cost effectiveness of a variety of joint recruiting support concepts" (Pang, 1996a). The following March, Deputy Secretary Deutch reminded the service secretaries that the 1994 Recruiter Survey had indicated "that recruiter morale is down while stress and dissatisfaction are up" (Deutch, 1995). He wanted them to "[c]onduct a thorough review of recruiting policies and practices to improve recruiter quality-of-life, and to reduce the pressures that may lead to potential improprieties" (Deutch, 1995).

Work on recruiter quality of life went forward both in the Joint Recruiting Group and as part of the DoD Quality of Life Executive Committee that Secretary of Defense William Perry set up as one of his major initiatives. Four specific areas were identified for action: special-duty assignment pay, health care, housing, and child care.[19] Several lesser issues, such as out-of-pocket expenses, were also considered. A number of actions were undertaken to improve the living and working conditions for recruiters:

---

[18] Anita Lancaster, the Assistant Director of the Defense Manpower Data Center (DMDC), remembers this meeting as the first time senior officials were made aware of the "college propensity problem." She told the panel that "youths know we are hiring" but that "most young men thought college was their next step in life." While "youths knew the military had programs to fund college expenses," they felt the sacrifices of going into the military "were too great" (OUSD[P&R], 1995c).

White had been the Assistant Secretary of Defense (Manpower, Reserve Affairs and Logistics) and then the Deputy Director of the Office of Management and Budget during the lean days of the late 1970s. He well understood the fragility of the all-volunteer force and was committed that DoD would not make the same mistakes again.

[19] The executive committee decided that, since the more generic problem was "independently assigned personnel" (Pang, 1996a, p. 2), the results should be made applicable to this larger group, which included not only recruiters but instructors at college ROTC programs and Marine Corps inspectors and instructors (I&Is) serving with reserve units.

- In FY 1996, Congress approved an increase in recruiters' Special Duty Assignment Pay from $275 to $375 per month, effective April 1, 1996.
- In addition, an expanded health benefit was tested by offering TRICARE Prime for service members and dependants in areas beyond the normal 30-minute driving time [from quarters to the recruiting station].
- A modification to normal housing policy let recruiters and other independently assigned personnel get higher priority for on-base housing.
- Recruiters would later benefit from the new Secretary of Defense William (Bill) Cohen's initiative to phase in an improved Variable Housing Allowance (VHA) that phased in full coverage based on local market surveys (Sellman, 1997, p. 39).

A Fresh Look at Recruiting and Advertising: Eskew-Murphy, YATS, and the National Academy of Sciences. Each year, DoD publishes the *Annual Report to the President and the Congress;* each year, the report has a chapter on personnel; and each year during the 1990s, the chapter told substantially the same story.[20] The reference in the 1999 report to "new initiatives," however, was a faint indication of Secretary Cohen's initiatives, which were shaking the recruiting world to its very foundations.[21]

In July 1998, Cohen visited several of the advertising agencies that represented the military departments. He did not like what he saw. He returned to the Pentagon and started to ask questions (Lancaster, 2000): "Do we have the right business practices and messages structured to connect to today's kids? Shouldn't DoD review current advertising programs before committing increased resources to them?" In March 1999, Cohen ordered a review of advertising and the public relations that supported recruiting and of the contractual processes for advertising.

---

[20] The first annual report, signed by former Senator and new Secretary of Defense William S. Cohen, President Clinton's choice to run DoD during his second term, the chapter on personnel said:

> Over the past several years, enlistment propensity has declined . . . as the Services experienced serious cuts in recruiting resources. In 1994, 1995, and 1996, recruitment advertising was increased, and the 1995 and 1996 YATS results indicate that the decline [in] propensity may have stabilized. Continued investment in recruiting and advertising resources is required, however, to assure that the pool of young men and women interested in the military will be available to meet Service personnel requirements in the future. (Cohen, 1997a)

[21] The report contained the following passage on challenges in a changing recruiting environment:

> Given that the increases in advertising were successful in raising youth awareness about military opportunities, continued investment in recruiting and advertising resources is required to assure that the pool of young men and women interested in the military will be available to meet Service personnel requirements. . . .
>
> The Department has several initiatives underway to address the challenges of recruiting. . . . [T]he Department is sponsoring research to determine the optimal allocation of advertising dollars between television, radio, and newspapers at the local vs. national level, the development of a plan to test privatization of recruiting, and an analysis of college-bound youth with emphasis on how best to recruit in this lucrative market. The Department will continue to closely monitor the recruiting climate and is committed to maintaining the appropriate levels of recruitment and advertising resources necessary to ensure an adequate flow of young men and women into the armed forces. (Cohen, 1999)

Rudy DeLeon, who replaced Edwin Dorn as the Under Secretary of Defense for Personnel and Readiness during President Clinton's second term, hired two advertising consulting organizations—Bozell/Eskew and Pintauk-Murphy-Gautier-Hudome, collectively referred to as Eskew-Murphy—to review the market research, creative approaches, media tactics, contract management, and program oversight for services' advertising agencies. In spring 1999, the Eskew-Murphy team interviewed 20 senior DoD officials, met with the advertising agencies, and held "focus group meetings" with "recruiters, potential recruits and recent recruits" (Bozell/Eskew Advertising and Pintauk-Murphy-Gautier-Hudome, 1999). Their findings were briefed to Secretary Cohen on August 4, 1999, and subsequently were widely briefed throughout DoD, including to each of the services.

The Eskew-Murphy team was particularly critical of what it saw as a lack of appropriate research and what it perceived to be the minimal value of the venerable annual YATS. They felt that the "largest recruiter of youth does not adequately understand its target," and observed that "each service branch is left to do their own research" (Bozell/Eskew Advertising and Pintauk-Murphy-Gautier-Hudome, 1999). Specifically, they found that YATS, "DoD's principal means of gathering market research information, did not satisfy the needs of recruiting advertising" and concluded that the survey "did not provide all the information advertising agencies need in sufficient detail" (ASD[FMP], 2000, p. 5). In March 2000, DoD reported to Congress that the survey would "not be conducted in 2000. Rather, it will be replaced with quarterly polls of both youth and influencers" (ASD[FMP], 2000).[22]

The issue of YATS and its follow-up was also the subject of a review by a group at the National Research Council (NRC) of the National Academy of Sciences. In 1999, Steve Sellman convinced Vice Admiral Patricia Tracy, Deputy Assistant Secretary for Military Personnel Policy, to engage the NRC to "recommend various recruiting and advertising strategies and incentive programs based on sound scientific data with the goal of increasing propensity and facilitating enlistment" (Sackett and Mavor, 2004a, p. vii). In a letter report on YATS dated June 16, 2000, the Committee on the Youth Population and Military Recruitment made a number of recommendations to improve the survey (Sackett and Mavor, 2004a, pp. 288–298). In a subsequent report, after the YATS had been cancelled, the committee reviewed the youth and influencer surveys. It concluded that, while the "youth surveys provided information necessary for testing some of the relations in the theoretical model . . . [t]here is little evidence that variables of this type are in any way related to the propensity to enlist or to actual enlistment behavior" (Sackett and Mavor, 2004b, pp. 42–43).[23]

---

[22] The 1999 YATS was the last in a series that began in 1975 (Wilson et al., 2000).

[23] This report provides a very useful comparison of alternative views of enlistment behavior, taken from behavioral theory, economic theory and adolescent development theory, and their implications for intervention design. It discusses the role and use of surveys, as well as the econometric approach to enlistment supply and the potential effects of enlistment incentives (see Sackett and Mavor, 2004b).

In the final analysis, surprisingly little came of the Eskew-Murphy study. With the administration change in 2001, plans for a Department of Defense Marketing Director of Advertising were not implemented. The Army made the most changes, competing its advertising contract and eventually hiring a new agency. It dropped its long-standing advertising slogan, *Be All You Can Be*—which Max Thurman had developed in 1979—and adopted a new slogan, *An Army of One*.

Quality of Life

William Perry succeeded Les Aspin as Secretary of Defense in 1994.[24] He had served in the Carter administration as Director of Defense Research and Engineering and Under Secretary of Defense for Acquisition and Technology and had been Deputy Secretary of Defense during Aspin's short time in office. He was a soft spoken and popular secretary who will long be remembered for his efforts to improve the quality of life of soldiers.

When Perry spoke of quality of life, he not only meant the traditional programs of "commissaries, exchanges, . . . schools, child care, family counseling and transition services . . . [but] pay, health care and housing" (Dorn, 1994d). In fall 1994, Dorn prepared a $375 million annual quality-of-life funding increment of the "biggest bang for the buck" items: such things as housing and barracks maintenance and revitalization, as well as a move to close the gap in the housing allowance, with additional monies for child care, family advocacy, and a number of other traditional quality-of-life programs (Dorn, 1994c); (USD[FMP] et al., 1994); (USD[FMP] and Carr, 1994).

Perry also established a Defense Science Board task force to "study military housing, personnel tempo and community and family services," and to recommend "ways and means to improve Service quality of life" (Marsh, 1995, p. xi). Referred to as the Marsh Report, after the chairman of the task force, former Secretary of the Army John O. Marsh, Jr., the task force included a number of distinguished former DoD officials, both civilian and military.[25]

The task force tied its work to the fortunes of the all-volunteer force with these words:

> Opinion polls continue to show time and time again that the American public considers its military volunteers to be among the country's most skilled, dedicated and courageous professionals. To ensure this perception remains accurate, military volunteers must be provided a quality of life that encourages the skilled and disciplined

---

[24] Aspin had resigned shortly after the debacle in Somalia. It was widely believed that his decision in trying to limit the scope of that conflict and the resulting problems with the performance of American troops were at least partly responsible for his resignation; he unexpectedly died of a stroke shortly after leaving DoD.

[25] The formal report is dated October 1995. The task force's findings and recommendations were briefed throughout the Pentagon well before the report was published. Just days before the report's formal release, Assistant Secretary Pang sent Secretary Perry an informational memorandum on the quality-of-life initiatives his office had already started to undertake (Pang, 1995b). In February 1996, Pang provided another update on actions to implement the Marsh Report (Becraft, 1996), as well as a fact sheet (ODASD[PSF&E], 1996).

to stay and attracts promising young people to join. Voluntary service is inexorably linked to quality of life. (Marsh, 1995, p. 4)

Housing. Probably the most distinguishing feature of the Marsh report was its emphasis on housing as a quality-of-life issue. In the final report, housing featured prominently as the first issue the task force addressed. In one way, this was ironic because, as Under Secretary Dorn had observed when Secretary Perry identified quality of life as one of the major initiatives of his administration (Dorn, 1994d), responsibility for housing had been transferred from the personnel office to the Under Secretary of Defense for Acquisition in the early 1980s. For the last decade, housing had been treated as a military construction line item rather than as a matter of quality of life. Now, following Perry's views—"there are few human needs in life more basic or important than a decent place to live" (Marsh, 1995, p. 3)—the task force took a new look at housing.

To no one's surprise, the task force found that military housing "fails to meet the Defense Department's intended goal," and "correcting deficiencies will be expensive" (Marsh, 1995, p. 3). What was new, however, was the finding that

the delivery system is so intrinsically flawed that it should be replaced with an entirely new system. The system should be *run* by a *Military Housing Authority* . . . [and that] the proposed *Authority* would be empowered to raise operating and investment money from private sources. (Marsh, 1995, p. 5, emphasis in original)

Ultimately, the idea of a housing authority threatened too many entrenched interests in the defense bureaucracy and in Congress. The service chiefs of staff, fearing the loss of control over a portion of their bases, opposed the creation of a housing authority, even though they would be members of the authority's board of directors.[26] There were also those in Congress who opposed a housing authority because it would mean that decisions about how much, where, and when housing would be constructed would no longer be a part of the yearly appropriations process, causing some subcommittee staff members to lose their claim on resources. In the final analysis, and despite the strong support of a well-respected and popular Secretary of Defense, the housing authority proposal died without any action.[27]

---

[26] The Deputy Assistant Secretary of Defense for Installations told the Quality of Life Executive Committee on February 29, 1996 that the

Military Housing Authority idea expressed in the Task Force report is not acceptable to the Services, so at SECDEF direction, they are looking at reengineering housing with individual Service housing authorities that would be controlled by each of the Services. (Pang, 1996b)

[27] Eventually, the services would put forth a program for privatizing military housing with long-term, 50-year leases to private developers to make the up-front investment need to revitalize military housing. This was essentially base-by-base creation of housing authorities, without the umbrella of a single authority that could have allowed borrowing under more favorable terms.

Personnel Tempo: Forward Basing to Deploying Forward. Anticipating what would become one of the most important quality-of-life issues in the years ahead, Perry directed the task force to focus on personnel tempo (perstempo).[28] During the Iraq War starting in 2003, the focus would be on the Army, but at the time of the 1995 task force report, the focus was on the Air Force. According to the task force, the number of Air Force "deployed away from home units was four times higher" in September 1994 than it had been five years before (Marsh, 1995, p. 8).

For the task force, five basic facts stood out as being indicative of the general understanding of perstempo at the time (Marsh, 1995, p. 65):

> First, no clear, universally accepted definition of personnel tempo exists. Second, the profile of the active force and its operating environment have changed dramatically over the past decade. Third, the means of measuring personnel tempo varies widely among the Services. Fourth, while some personnel tempo is beyond the control of the Department of Defense, other elements can be influenced. Fifth, the consequences of excessive personnel tempo impair readiness and every other aspect of quality of life. (Marsh, 1995, p. 65)

As the task force saw it,

> [f]requent unprogrammed deployments, numerous training activities generated by Combatant Commanders in Chief, and traditional inspection activities directed by the Military Departments all lead to increased personnel and operational tempo and challenges in managing the Active Force in uncertain operational environments. (Marsh, 1995, p. 68)

In emphasizing recommendations and corrective actions—such as quick reimbursement for contingency operations to eliminate the migration of funds from support to operating accounts, the judicious management of noncontingency training activities, the use of distance learning and simulations to cut deployment time and costs, and numerous reporting requirements—the task force failed to address one of the most fundamental causes of high perstempo: a force structure of inadequate size that did not contain enough of the skills in high demand.

During the 1990s, the phrase "low density, high demand" was heard many times in the Pentagon to describe situations in which military police units, psychological operations units, or electronic jamming aircraft and their crews, to name just a few, were constantly on deployment because, while the demand for their services was great, the active forces had fewer such units than were needed. Such jobs, it was argued, should be left to the reserve forces, but even there too few units were available.

---

[28] While perstempo refers to personnel, *operational tempo* (optempo) refers to units. Generally, the two go hand in hand, but on occasion they can differ, such as when a personnel community has enough individuals so that it can change assignment policies to better manage perstempo.

The services were loath, however, to increase the number of these units because they were judged not to contribute to the war-fighting mission and were seen as "peacekeeping" elements, which by definition were to be provided as a byproduct of conventional force units.

One significant exception to the business-as-usual approach to perstempo was the Air Force's reorganization into a number of Aerospace Expeditionary Forces (AEFs). One reason the Air Force developed the new organizational system was to address the optempo-perstempo dilemma. Lieutenant General Lawrence P. Farrell, Jr., Air Force Deputy Chief of Staff for Plans and Programs, saw the problem this way:

> The problem is that since about 1990, we found ourselves continuing to rotate forces to enforce the protocols from the desert war and for other purposes. We got involved in Northern Watch and Bosnia and, without really realizing it, we found ourselves in a series of ongoing, expeditionary operations. . . .
>
> [W]e have been approaching such deployments on what amounts to an ad hoc schedule basis . . . .
>
> Recent USAF quality-of-life surveys confirmed that the impact of deployments has been almost as severe on some of the support specialists at domestic bases as on the overseas participants. Moreover, the polls show a close connection between increased optempo and falling retention rates. (As quoted in Callander, 1998)

The Air Force's answer to these problems was to structure "the forces into standing units [that] in peacetime . . . would train together, plan together. . . . Then, when their turn came to go on deployment, they would know a year ahead so they could plan on it" (Callander, 1998).[29] In 2003, Air Force Chief of Staff John P. Jumper, an early proponent of the concept when he was Central Air Force commander in the late 1990s, told the Air Force Association of the benefits of the AEF in managing the all-volunteer force: "The AEF is allowing us to highlight our stressed career fields. We are able to pinpoint them and able to size the level of our stress. . . . We are working hard to rightsize our force" (Jumper, 2003).

Community and Family Services. The Marsh task force recognized that with the all-volunteer force the military would "no longer . . . be largely a force of short-term enlistees . . . [and] therefore [would] have to address the quality of life of their members" (Marsh, 1995, p. 95). They started with a call for the services to "determine the true need. Validate departmental goals and requirements to ensure they represented the level and type of services wanted in the field." Unfortunately, what constituted the "true needs" of the services was often quite controversial.

Probably the most controversial of all "community and family service" programs was child care. The task force noted that

---

[29] For a history of the AEF concept, see Titus and Howey (1999).

[a]ctive-duty service members have approximately 1 million children younger than 12 years of age most of them needing some form of care. . . . Since the All-Volunteer Force began, the number of dependent preschool children in the Services has steadily grown, reaching more than 575,000 in December 1994. (Marsh, 1995, p. 98)

The services had a large number of single-parent families—approximately 10 percent—as well as dual-military couples—9 percent. While child-care services did not meet the entire needs of service families—child-care programs provided about 52 percent of the estimated requirement—they were still a substantial investment of resources. In 1994, child care was provided at 346 locations, serving over 155,000 children (Marsh, 1995, p. 98). Many commanders, however, resented spending money on child care, resented the direction from Congress in the Military Child Care Act of 1989, and resented having to deal with the family issues they thought compromised their flexibility and the readiness of their troops. For many commanders, child care was a surrogate for their opposition to the increased role women were playing in the military workplace. In their view, when the DoD provided child care services, it was just making it easier for single mothers to be in the military, *where they did not belong.* The issue of women in the military remained, often under the surface, one of the most volatile issues of the all-volunteer force. It would again come to the surface with the "highly-publicized difficulties involving inappropriate senior/subordinate relations" (Ashcroft, 1997).

The Role of Women Is Raised Again in the Aftermath of Reported Sexual Misconduct at Army Training Centers

During the first six months of the new administration, all attention was on the issue of gays in the military, and Clinton and Aspin took advantage of the intense focus to deal with the inherited report of President Bush's Presidential Commission on the Assignment of Women in the Armed Forces. By the end of August 1993, the new Assistant Secretary for Personnel and Readiness, Edwin Dorn, could report "good progress" to Aspin, in opening "nearly all combat aircraft position to women," drafting "legislation to repeal the existing naval combat exclusion law," and "developing a definition of 'direct combat on the ground' and an interim assignment rule" (Dorn, 1993). The issues of women in the military were *off the front page*—at least temporarily.

However, on November 7, 1996, the *New York Times* reported that "[m]ore than two dozen female privates have come forward to complain that they were raped or harassed at the [Army Training] Center in Aberdeen, Md." (Wald, 1996). While the Army would later be praised for being "much more [aggressive] in Aberdeen" (Board, 1996) than the Navy was in handling the Tailhook investigations, neither a quick nor an energetic investigation could erase the damning headlines that appeared day after day in the nation's leading newspapers. On November 13, 1996, the headline in the *Times* was: "One Sergeant Pleads Guilty as Army Widens Sex Inquiry" (Weiner,

1996).[30] Ten days later, the Secretary of the Army ordered a wider investigation and created an outside panel to "review all policies dealing with sexual harassment" (Schmitt, 1996a). When the panel reported in September 1997, it concluded that the Army "lacks the institutional commitment" to treat men and women equally.[31]

The events at Aberdeen and the other training centers renewed the contentious debate over the role of women in the military, particularly the Army. John Eisenhower, a former Army colonel and son of the former wartime leader, onetime Chief of Staff of the Army, and former President of the United States, saw "outrage and pledges to punish those who committed the abuses" as not enough. In an op-ed piece published by the *Times,* he wrote that

> [s]omehow all military men must be made to recognize women as equals and to appreciate the contributions that women can make to overall military efficiency. . . . The military must find a way to finally reconcile itself to accepting women in the ranks. (Eisenhower, 1996)

But not everyone agreed with Eisenhower. The situation at Aberdeen and the other training centers rekindled the "debate" that had been relatively quiet since the Presidential commission at the end of the Bush administration, and action in both the House and Senate foretold a heavy involvement by Congress (Schmitt, 1996a).

DoD Reacts. In early summer 1997, Senator John Ashcroft wrote his former colleague and now Secretary of Defense Bill Cohen about the "renewed congressional interest in the role of women in the Armed Forces and its effect on military readiness" (Ashcroft, 1997). Citing the "allegations of sexual misconduct at Fort Leonard Wood and elsewhere" and the "compelling" testimony of Elaine Donnelly about "co-ed field tents in Bosnia" and the resulting "required emergency evacuations for pregnancy every three days" from that theater, the senator told Cohen that, "while equal opportunity for men and women in the Armed Forces is a worthy goal, it must not come at the cost of our military readiness" (Ashcroft, 1997). Challenging the policies of the Clinton administration, he bluntly said: "I cannot help but believe that in a rapidly expanding, wartime military, the notion of placing women and men together in combat is a recipe for disaster" (Ashcroft, 1997).

Secretary Cohen was also concerned, and several weeks later, he told Senator Ashcroft of the three initiatives he had ordered to address "sexual misconduct and inappropriate relationships in our Armed Forces" (Cohen, 1997b). The purpose of his initiatives, he explained to his former colleague, was to "maintain the effectiveness and readiness of U.S. military forces and to ensure that . . . policies governing good order

---

[30] At the 35th Annual Tailhook Symposium of the Tailhook Association (September 5 to 7, 1991) at the Las Vegas Hilton Hotel, 83 women and 7 men were assaulted. The investigation was taken over by the DoD Inspector General, and the Secretary of the Navy was fired, not only because of the event itself but, more important, because of the perception that the Navy was not conducting a proper investigation but was protecting those responsible.

[31] As quoted in Priest (1997a).

and discipline are clear and fair" (Cohen, 1997b). Two of the three initiatives were internal to the Pentagon. He asked Under Secretary of Defense Rudy DeLeon to head a group to review "personnel policies and practices concerning good order and discipline," and he asked "the General Counsel . . . to review the clarity of existing guidance on adultery under the Uniform Code of Military Justice" (Cohen, 1997b). In what would turn out to be the most controversial of his initiatives, he asked former Senator Nancy Kassebaum-Baker to head a panel to "study the training programs and policies of the armed services, examine related morale and discipline issues, and . . . recommend . . . any necessary changes or improvements to assure the readiness and effectiveness of our forces" (Cohen, 1997b).

The Kassebaum-Baker Panel. The Kassebaum-Baker panel saw the issue squarely in terms of the all-volunteer force:

> The demographics of the all-volunteer force have . . . been undergoing a major transition. Since 1972, when women comprised about 2 percent of the military, the number of women has increased in the total force to about 13.5 percent and recent policy changes have opened up more than 260,000 new positions for women. . . . It is the committee's intention, during this time of transition, to contribute to the effort to craft a sound policy for training our young men and women today for tomorrow's mission. (Kassebaum-Baker, 1997)

When the Kassebaum-Baker committee submitted its report on December 16, 1997 (Baker, 1997), its members thought they were "strongly support[ing] a gender-integrated military force" (Kassebaum-Baker, 1997). Even though they said they "firmly believe that gender-integrated training must continue to be an important element of the training program," their call for gender-separate basic training set off a firestorm. The headlines in the *Washington Post* that day told the story: "Civilian Committee on Military Favors Separate Female Training; Need to Bolster Cohesion Discipline Cited" (Priest, 1997b). In fact, they had endorsed one of the demands of conservatives in Congress. The *New York Times* reported, "conservative[s] . . . in Congress say the Army abuses . . . warrant an end to sex-integrated barracks and combat warships and a return to the days when male and female recruits were always trained at separate boot camps" (Schmitt, 1996b).[32]

Secretary Cohen gave the services 90 days to review the Kassebaum-Baker report. The services objected to the panel's recommendations on gender-separate basic training. Not only would the cost of building new facilities be prohibitive, they argued, the goal should be "to train [as we] fight" (Priest, 1998). Immediately after basic training, women and men would be living and working together, and the time to learn how that needed to be done, they argued, was from the very beginning, at basic training.

---

[32] The powerful chairman of the House Appropriations Committee told a New Orleans newspaper soon after the events at Aberdeen became public that the "facts indicate that the complete integration of men and women in all aspects of military life has proven to be a disaster" (as quoted in Schmitt, 1996b).

On March 16, 1998, Cohen provided the services guidance, telling them to increase the numbers of female recruiters and trainers, improve the selection processes for trainers, and to make their authority clearer. He asked the services to "[r]eexamine recruiting advertising to put more emphasis on patriotism and challenge," and to "[p]lace greater emphasis on core military values in training" (Cohen, 1998a). They were to "[d]evelop more consistent training standards between the genders," and to "[i]nstitute training to produce professional relationships between the genders without use of such expedient gender-based policies as 'no talk, no touch'" (Cohen, 1998a). While he directed the services to "ensure that male and female basic trainees live in separate areas, if not separate buildings . . . [and] have after-hours supervision by training professionals," he did not order the gender separate basic training recommended by the Kassebaum-Baker panel. "The goal is a basic training system which provides gender privacy and dignity in safe, secure living conditions," he explained in his press briefing (Cohen, 1998a).

Congress Reacts. Even before the Kassebaum-Baker Panel made its report to the Secretary of Defense, Congress established its own group to look at gender-integrated training, on November 18, 1997. The Defense Authorizations Act of 1998 established the Commission on Military Training and Gender-Related Issues (Blair, 1999, p. xvii). Prominent among the ten private citizens (five appointed by the Senate and five by the House) were Fred Pang, the former Assistant Secretary of Defense for Force Management Policy, and Barbara Pope, who had experience dealing with the aftermath of Tailhook when she was Assistant Secretary of the Navy in 1991. Two military sociologists were on the commission, Charles Moskos and Mady Segal. Two other commissioners were retired military officers, both Marines; this was thought to be significant since the Marine Corps was the only service that had not done any gender-integrated basic training. The chairperson of the commission was Anita K. Blair, a member of the Virginia Military Institute's Board of Visitors, where she chaired the Assimilation Review Task Force, which monitored the process of integrating women into the previously all male institution, and President of the Independent Women's Forum, a conservative women's organization.[33]

When the commission first met on April 13, 1998, it knew Secretary Cohen had already decided what he wanted to do. Nevertheless, it went forward with an ambitious agenda of 10 research projects, including surveys of approximately 9,000 recruits and 2,300 recruit trainers. When the commission finally reported its results on July 30, 1999, it made a number of unanimous recommendations on cross-gender relationships—adultery and fraternization—and on the nature of initial entry training. In the area of "gender-integrated and gender-separate basic training," the commissioners could not

---

[33] On July 8, 1997, the Independent Women's Forum published a position paper, *Improve Effectiveness of Military Basic Training by Separating Men and Women Recruits* (Independent Women's Forum, 1997).

come to a unanimous position. A bare majority—six out of the ten members—endorsed the following statement:

> The Commission concludes that the Services are providing the soldiers, sailors, airmen, and Marines required by the operating forces to carry out their assigned missions; therefore, each Service should be allowed to continue to conduct basic training in accordance with its current policies. This includes the manner in which basic trainees are housed and organized into units. This conclusion does not imply the absence of challenges and issues associated with the dynamics found in a gender integrated basic training environment. Therefore, improvements to Initial Entry Training that have been made by the Services or are currently being considered must be sustained and continually reviewed. (Blair, 1999, p. xlii)

When the final vote was taken, the two retired Marine generals split. Major General Ron Christmas (ret.), a former Marine Corps Deputy Chief of Staff for Personnel, voted with the majority. The military sociologists were also split. Mady Segal voted with the majority; Charles Moskos abstained from the vote. Moskos's position was he was "not in full accord with the overall tone of the recommendation as it implies there are no serious problems in Initial Entry Training beyond those identified by the Services" (Blair, 1999, p. 189). He noted that

> persistent complaints among the trainers are that their concerns are not being attended to . . . [Therefore,] I abstain from the recommendation that each Service be allowed to conduct initial entry training as it presently does. (Blair, 1999, p. 190)

Moskos did not, however, sign up for the minority position. He did conclude that "not only is there evidence of serious problems in gender-integrated training, but there is also substantial evidence that gender-separate training produces superior results" (Blair, 1999, p. xliii).

Reforming the Military

By summer 1998, Secretary Cohen knew something was wrong. The deployment of troops to Bosnia, continued air patrols over Iraq, and naval patrols in the Persian Gulf were generating a din of complaints. On August 17, 1998, Cohen flew to Moody Air Force Base to learn firsthand from the troops what was bothering them. He chose Moody, the first of a series of bases he planned to visit, because the 347th Fighter Wing stationed there was the most frequently deployed Air Force unit. Cohen took away from the visit the airmen's concerns for spare parts and equipment shortages, and, he told a reporter, "[s]ome of the people we talked to are leaving because of their deployment schedules . . . . For others, it's a question of compensation, or they may find housing unavailable on base and too expensive off base" (as quoted in Gillert, 1998a). Two weeks later, at Fort Drum, Cohen "heard an earful of soldiers concerns about pay, health care, retention, personnel tempo, Bosnia, housing, and, especially, military retirement" (Garamone, 1998a). The 1986 retirement changes that had reduced the payout for a 20 years of service from 50 to 40 percent of base pay, while not effective for anyone about to retire, had produced a two-level compensation system and were a particular irritant to the troops. After hearing complaints from Army Community Service volunteers, Cohen said he was "embarrassed" that so many families were on food stamps. The increasing gap between military and civilian pay was also cited.

Within days of his visit to Fort Drum, Secretary Cohen, the Joint Chiefs of Staff, and the heads of the unified commands met with President Clinton to discuss what Joint Chiefs chairman General Henry Shelton called the "nose-dive" in readiness (as quoted in Gillert, 1998b). While they discussed the need to balance readiness and procurement, Cohen's spokesman, Ken Bacon, said the challenge was not to overlook "retention issues like military pay and retirement benefits" (Gillert, 1998b).

Cohen's trips resulted in a number of initiatives to address the problems he saw first hand. First, concern that a sizable number of service members were on food stamps brought into question the adequacy of military compensation and sent proposals and counterproposals bounding between the Pentagon and Congress. Second, complaints about the level of military pay in general led DoD to reconsider the recommendations of the 7th Quadrennial Review of Military Compensation (QRMC) and make adjustments to selected portions of the basic military pay table in 2000. This was followed by further and more fundamental changes recommended by the 9th QRMC, discussed later in this chapter. Third, there was also concern about the deleterious effects of increases in optempos service members faced. Congress attempted to initiate perstempo pay, both to compensate service members for extra work and to penalize the services for causing the extra working in the first place—an idea that was abandoned after the events of September 11, 2001. Finally, within days of the Fort Drum trip, Under Secretary Jacques (Jack) Gansler asked the Defense Science Board to undertake a comprehensive evaluation of DoD's human resources strategy (Gansler, 1998).

The Defense Science Board. The Defense Science Board Task Force on Human Resources Strategy was established "to review trends and opportunities to improve DoD capacity to attract and retain civilian and military personnel with the motivation and intellectual capabilities to serve and lead" (Foster and Welch, 2000, p. A-1). Under Secretary of Defense for Personnel and Readiness Rudy DeLeon joined in on sponsoring the task force, which was cochaired by Johnny Foster, a legendary figure in DoD history who had served as the Director of Defense Research and Engineering—then the number three position in the civilian leadership of the Pentagon—in the 1960s under Secretary of Defense Robert McNamara and General Larry Welch, USAF (ret.), the former Air Force Chief of Staff and, at the time, head of the Institute for Defense Analysis. The task force saw that

> [t]he human resource challenges facing DoD have changed rapidly over the last decade as a result of . . . a robust economy, civilian sector competition . . . to fill high-technology positions, declining American public interest in public service, major changes in the Department's mission and operational tempo, and a significant downsizing of the Department's workforce. (Foster and Welch, 2000, p. iii)

The task force was alarmed at what it saw as

> evidence that the quality and capability of the force is beginning to erode from the record highs of the mid-1990s. . . . As the Department transforms its force structure to meet the needs of the 21st century, transforming the character and management of the human element of the force is critical. (Foster and Welch, 2000, p. v)

It called for "action[s] to promote more understanding of the value of public service" (Foster and Welch, 2000, p. viii). It wanted a comprehensive "strategic human resources plan" and new "force-shaping tools . . . appropriate for the 21st century" (Foster and Welch, 2000, p. x). Noting that the all-volunteer force is, "in reality, a recruited force" (Foster and Welch, 2000, p. 52), the task force provided a cogent review of the then-current state of recruiting and retention (Foster and Welch, 2000, pp. 52–64). It endorsed continued improvement in quality of life, noting that "a good quality of life is an essential component of military morale" (Foster and Welch, 2000, p. 64). Reflecting the kind of policy the Air Force had initiated with the AEF organization, the task force urged DoD "to develop effective ways to manage operational and personnel tempo that recognize the anticipated operating patterns of the force and the family-oriented interest of service members" (Foster and Welch, 2000, p. 68).

In the area of compensation, the task force recommended "moving beyond a 'one-size-fits-all' approach to compensation and providing the Services with more flexibility to deal with recruiting and retention problems" (Foster and Welch, 2000, p. 70). This took on one of the most sacrosanct features of the existing military compensation system. The task force acknowledged the "long-standing tenet" of equal reward for all personnel who hold the same rank and level of responsibility regardless of skill, but argued that "changes are necessary in the military pay system to accommodate continuing technological changes that increase the diversity of skill requirements which will inevitably lead to the need for more differentiation in pay by skill" (Foster and Welch, 2000, p. 71).

Compensation. The task of addressing compensation and retirement fell to Under Secretary of Defense DeLeon and his team.[34] Addressing the change in retirement was reasonably straightforward. Joint Chiefs Chairman Shelton had personally focused on the retirement question, and all agreed that the reduction of retirement to 40 percent of basic pay for those who retire at 20 years of service, known as REDUX, would be rolled back. It was clear that reducing the perceived pay gap would require an across-the-board pay increase. This would not, however, address what appeared to be a growing problem among midlevel and senior officers and enlisted personnel. DeLeon's staff set to work looking at different budget levels and different combinations of pay cells for the basic pay table—each cell represented a specific combination of grade and years of service—to see what might reasonably be done (Pleeter, 2004). Fortunately, they had the work of the 7th QRMC to guide them.[35] The 7th QRMC had looked at restructuring the basic pay table to change the emphasis from longevity to promotion, stressing the principle of pay for performance. By November 1998, Secretary Cohen was confident enough on the direction of the changes that he would be taking forward that he told a group of sailors at the Norfolk Naval Base that the package would "include a 4.4 percent pay raise, targeted pay hikes for mid-level and senior officers and enlisted

---

[34] *Author's Note:* The team included Acting Assistant Secretary of Defense for Force Management Policy, Frank Rush; Deputy Assistant Secretary of Defense for Military Manpower and Personnel Policy, Vice Admiral Patricia Tracy; Director of Compensation, Navy Captain Elliott Bloxom; his deputy, Charles Witschonke; and the Compensation Directorate's Chief Economist, Saul Pleeter. In fact, I was originally supposed to be part of that team, but I was diverted and at the time was serving as Under Secretary of the Army. Here is the story:

In September 1996, Under Secretary John White asked my boss, Navy Secretary John Dalton—I was the Assistant Secretary of the Navy for Manpower and Reserve Affairs—if he could borrow me to help review his options in dealing with the Gulf War Illness problem. By November, the temporary additional assignment had turned into a second job as the Special Assistant to the Deputy Secretary of Defense for Gulf War Illnesses and head of the Gulf War Office, which would eventually number over 200 people and have a budget of about 35 million a year. When Bill Cohen became Secretary of Defense in spring 1997, he asked if I would like to become the Assistant Secretary of Defense for Force Management Policy under Rudy DeLeon, in addition to running the Gulf War program. Since I was completely engaged in setting up the Gulf War office, I declined his offer. The following November (1997), Cohen's Special Assistant, Bob Tyrer, tracked me down on a trip to Kuwait and again asked if I would move from the Navy to DoD. This time, with the majority of the travel for the Gulf War program complete, I accepted. By the end of January 1998, the FBI had completed its background investigation and the papers were in the White House. The nomination was not formalized until May, and the Senate Armed Services Committee scheduled a confirmation hearing for early July. If I had gone through the hearing and been confirmed, I might have accompanied Secretary Cohen on his trip to Moody Air Force Base in August. As it was, in August, I was still the Assistant Secretary of the Navy.

In early June, with a confirmation hearing only weeks away, Bob Tyrer called to say that an unexpected vacancy had developed in the Army, and would I *mind* if they nominated me to be Under Secretary of the Army. He was sure that, since my papers were already before the Senate, a quick change in the cover sheet was all that was necessary and that I would be confirmed in July to this new post. I agreed, but it was not all that simple. Eventually, Secretary Cohen had to threaten to go to see the President over the matter before the White House staff would move on my nominations. The paperwork would have to go back to the FBI for an update of its investigation, and the Senate process would have to start all over again. It was not until November 1998 that I was finally confirmed as the 25th Under Secretary of the Army. And that is why I was not on DeLeon's team in fall 1998. I did, however, succeed DeLeon in the spring of 2000, when he moved up to be Deputy Secretary of Defense and I became the Under Secretary for Personnel and Readiness.

[35] Charles Witschonke, Deputy Director of Compensation, had worked on the 7th QRMC.

personnel, and changing REDUX. . . . Even in a balanced budget environment, the president has made this a priority" (Garamone, 1998b).

On December 21, 1998, Secretary Cohen and Joint Chiefs Chairman Shelton announced the pay package would be part of the President's fiscal 2000 budget (Cohen, 1998b). Effective January 1, 2000, pay would go up 4.4 percent, with increases through 2005 tentatively set at 3.9 percent per year. The principle of pay for performance was stressed, with an emphasis on "merit, performance and promotion versus just simply being in the service for long periods of time" (Garamone, 1998c). The targeted pay increases, ranging from 0.5 to 5.5 percent, were to take effect on July 1, 2000.

Despite the support the proposals received among service members (Kozaryn, 1998), the issue was still not settled. On February 24, 1999, within days of the FY 2000 budget reaching Congress, the Senate passed the *Soldiers', Sailors', Airmen's and Marines' Bill of Rights Act of 1999*, which "would have provided a substantially larger pay and benefits package than the Administration ha[d] proposed" (Daggett, 1999, p. 14). While the House did not go along with this special legislation, preferring to address the issues in the normal legislative process, the final plan Congress enacted included higher future pay raises—the Employment Cost Index plus 0.5 percent through FY 2006—and the larger pay and benefits package included a voluntary thrift savings plan benefit, albeit without an "employers" contribution.

On July 20, 1999, President Clinton signed the charter for the 9th QRMC. Noting the "triad of reforms" included in his FY 2000 budget, then being considered by Congress, the President said the new review

> should encompass a strategic review of the military compensation and benefits system [and] . . . assess the effectiveness of the current military compensation and benefits in recruiting and retaining a high-quality force in light of changing demographics, a dynamic economy, and the new military strategy. (Clinton, 1999)

As far as many senior enlisted leaders were concerned, this was an opportunity to further reform the compensation system. At the Senior Enlisted Advisors Forum, called by Secretary Cohen the following June, a spokesperson for the group asked "Pentagon officials to take a look at the pay table for promotion from E-4 to E-5 and to look at pay for the top three enlisted ranks . . . [who] have far more education today than they did in the past" (Kozaryn, 1998). In fact, that was exactly what the 9th QRMC was doing (as discussed in Chapter Eighteen).

Food Stamps. One of the most disturbing specters of the all-volunteer force was how many were on food stamps. In 1999, Senator John McCain (R-Arizona) told his colleagues that "over 12,000 military families on food stamps, and the potential of more than double that number eligible for the program. . . . I find it an outrage that enlisted families line up for free food and furniture" (McCain, 1999). He railed against the administration's "lack of foresight and the Congress' lack of compassion. . . . Our service members . . . deserve our continuing respect, our unwavering support, and a living wage." Few would disagree. The question, however, was less foresight and compassion than it was the facts of the case—facts that had been debated for more than two decades.

In the early 1980s, the General Accounting Office (GAO) reported a charge by former Secretary of Defense Melvin Laird that "at least 100,000, and possibly as many as 275,000 military families were eligible for food stamps" (as quoted in Gould, 1983, p. 3). The GAO put the problem succinctly: "The implication [of Laird's charge] was that the Government was paying its members poverty wages, which would adversely affect the services' ability to attract and retain personnel" (Gould, 1983). By 1983, with three rounds of pay increases enacted by Congress, the GAO concluded the following:

> Only a small percentage of military families [about 1.3 percent] are eligible for and receiving food stamps. Most families are eligible because part of their pay—Government-furnished housing—is not counted as income. GAO believes that all components of military pay, including Government-furnished housing, should be counted in determining food stamp eligibility. This could result in substantial savings in the food stamp program and more equitable treatment of all military personnel—those living on bases, as well as off bases. (Gould, 1983)

In 1992, DoD, responding to concerns in Congress and reports that as much as $1.6 million of food stamps were being redeemed at military commissaries each month, performed a "computer match" of Department of Agriculture and DoD records from January 1991 for six states and Guam (Pleeter, 1992). This computer match suggested that an estimated 19,740 members received food stamps. In 1991 that was 0.9 percent of the force (Gilroy, 2002, p. 141). The numbers decreased throughout the 1990s, as determined by subsequent computer matches. In 1995, it was estimated that 11,900 members were on food stamps—0.8 percent of the force. The 1998 match produced an estimate that only 6,300 members were on food stamps—0.5 percent of the force (Directorate of Compensation, 2003).[36]

During 1999, the Senate twice passed, and the defense authorizations conference rejected, Senator McCain's proposal to provide "an additional $180 a month subsistence allowance to any service member eligible for food stamps" (McCain, 2000). Senator McCain, however, was not put off. On March 29, 2000, Senator McCain reintroduced the same proposal, as S. 2332. Some in the Senate and at the Pentagon thought Senator McCain's proposal created an equity problem. Senator Carl Levin (D-Michigan) noted that, since government quarters came with free utilities and were "not counted as income under the Department of Agriculture rules for eligibility" (as discussed in Rostker, 2000), there would be a problem of unequal benefits between members of similar grade and family circumstances living on base and off base. In addition,

---

[36] The 9th QRMC reported that, between 1998 and 2001,

> military pay increased by a cumulative total of 15 percent . . .When adjustments using these relative gains in military income were made to the FY 1998 food stamp population, the number of members estimated to be eligible for food stamps fell to about 4,200 in FY 2001. (Gilroy, 2002, p. 142)

the eligibility for food stamps was directly tied to the number of dependants living with a service member, and some felt that family size should be a private matter.

In fact, DoD had not endorsed Senator McCain's proposal because it exacerbated the equity issue Senator Levin had raised. At the Pentagon, Secretary Cohen believed that the proper thing to do was to lift all poor families. On April 19, 2000, he proposed to "work with the Agriculture Department leadership to amend current rules so as to exclude the cash housing allowance paid to our people living off-base from the computation for eligibility" (Cohen, 2000).

In July, unable to get the Department of Agriculture to change the way it counted eligibility, Cohen decided to solve the problem himself. Rather than food stamps, Cohn proposed to give additional compensation to all low-income service members based on their rank and family size, regardless of housing situation (Rhem, 2000a). Under Cohen's proposal, the value of on-base housing would not be counted but neither would the housing allowance provided to those who live off base. In addition, the new DoD proposal would not give out food stamps but would issue a debit card that could be used at military commissaries. Cash would be provided only for those living in remote locations that did not have ready access to a commissary.

Congress, however, was in no mood to compromise on the food-stamp issue or even to consider Secretary Cohen's proposal. The FY 2001 Defense Authorization Act created the Family Subsistence Supplemental Allowance (FSSA) for low-income members of the armed forces and provided "a cash allowance in the amount of the food stamp allotment or $500, whichever is less" (Rhem, 2000b). In an attempt to address the equity issue, the new legislation provided that the value of base housing would be included in computing eligibility for the new allowance. The law, however, did not guarantee that military families would no longer be on food stamps. The day after President Clinton signed the authorization act, Assistant Secretary of Defense for Public Affairs Ken Bacon reminded reporters that qualified families "would still be able to get food stamps, but the cash payment would make it less likely that some families would qualify for food stamps than today" (Bacon, 2000). In the end Bacon, concluded that the plan Congress passed was "more complex then the plan we [DoD] proposed" (Bacon, 2000), and the very poorest families would most likely remain on food stamps, and overall, fewer poor families would receive FSSA payments than would have under the DoD proposal.

The new law required a yearly report of the number of service members, including the Coast Guard, who had received the subsistence supplemental allowance any time during the previous year. On February 1, 2002, DoD estimated that 2,100 members were still on food stamps—0.15 percent of the force—with an additional 610 members receiving FSSA (Directorate of Compensation, 2002). In FY 2002, DoD estimated that 2,084 members were receiving food stamps—still 0.15 percent of the force—with an additional 755 members receiving FSSA (Directorate of Compensation, 2003). For FY 2003, DoD did not report an estimated number of members receiving food stamps but did report that 647 members received FSSA payments.

Concern for High Optempo and Perstempo: Congress Acts. In April 1996, the General Accounting Office documented for the House Committee on National Security that all services had experienced increased deployments since the late 1980s, but "DoD systems are inadequate to assess the full impact of high PERSTEMPO on readiness" (Gebicke, 1996, p. 11). In 1997, the House Committee on National Security complained that the drawdown and

> the expanding demands of manpower intensive peacekeeping and humanitarian operations known collectively as "operations other than war" . . . are having a significant [negative] impact on the readiness of U.S. military forces. (Spence, 1997, p. 1)

The committee was concerned that this readiness problem "over the long-term [was] more serious than the modernization shortfall" (Spence, 1997, p. 3). What concerned the committee most was an unsustainably high operational pace (optempo) and personnel being deployed or otherwise away from home for too many days per year (perstempo). The Congressional Research Service report the following winter provided a more analytic picture (Ryan, 1998). While research done for DoD raised questions about the connection between perstempo and retention,[37] Congress tried to control perstempo by limiting deployments and training days away from home base without compensating service members for days away above a stated norm. Specifically, the Senate Armed Services Committee found

> that excessive time away from home station and families is the reason most cited by service members and their families for dissatisfaction with military service. The United States military is deployed to more places doing more missions now than at any time in our history. In testimony, military and civilian leaders within the Department of Defense recognized the deleterious effects of repeated deployments. Unfortunately, in spite of urging by the Congress, as in section 565 of the National Defense Authorization Act for Fiscal Year 1996, these leaders have not taken aggressive steps to reduce the burdensome personnel tempo. (Senate Armed Services Committee, 1999, p. 326)[38]

---

[37] For instance, while many people assumed that deployment would reduce retention, Mark Totten and James Hosek found that personnel who had been deployed were typically more likely to reenlist, not less likely. This finding might have also helped in other ways. Under Secretary of Defense David Chu recently (2005) told a class on policy analysis at the Pardee RAND Graduate School that Totten and Hosek's work on deployment provided a framework that changed the way people thought about deployment and how it entered the decision to enter or stay in the military (see Fricker, 2002; Fricker et al., 2003; Hosek and Totten, 1998; Hosek and Totten, 2002; Koopman and Hattiangadi, 2001; Sticha et al., 1999).

[38] The Senate bill would have required that

> the first general or flag officer in the chain of command approve the deployment of a member who would be deployed more than 180 days of the past 365 days. The recommended provision would also require that deployments of members who would be deployed more than 200 days of the past 365 days be approved by a four-star general or flag officer. The recommended provision would require that service members deployed in excess of 220 days of the past 365 days be paid $100 per day for each day over 220 days. The recommended provision would authorize the Secretary of Defense to suspend applicability of this section when the Secretary determines that such a waiver is in the national security interests of the United States. (Senate Armed Services Committee, 1999, p. 325)

The House-Senate conference committee agreed:

> [T]he first general or flag officer in the chain of command . . . [must] approve any deployment in excess of 182 days. Approval of a general or flag officer in the grade of general or admiral would be required for any deployment that would be in excess of 220 days. Service members deployed in excess of 250 days would be paid $100 per day for each day over 250 days. . . .The Secretary of Defense [should develop] a common method to measure operations tempo and personnel tempo.[39] . . .The service chief . . . [could] suspend applicability of the provision when the service chief determines that it is in the national security interests of the United States. The senior officer approval requirements would be effective October 1, 2000. The . . . payment of the $100 per diem [would be] effective October 1, 2001. (Conference Committee, 1999, pp. 746–747)

The conferees wanted to send a message to the Pentagon about the management of perstempo for each and every service member. They wanted the Pentagon to "track the perstempo of individual service members and consider the effects of perstempo when assigning service members to deployments and other temporary duties away from the service member's home station" (Conference Committee, 1999, p. 747). In early September 2001, the House Armed Services Committee acknowledged that the Navy and Marine Corps were concerned that the new program would have "unintended fiscal and readiness consequences" (House Armed Services Committee, 2001, p. 325). The committee objected to the decision "to pay high-deployment per diem out of military personnel accounts." In a move that might pit the committee against the uniformed leaders of the Navy and Marine Corps, the committee indicated that it "strongly believes that deploying service members in excess of 400 days out of any 730-day period is fundamentally an operational decision driven by operational requirements. As such, the committee considers high-deployment per diem an operational cost that should be paid from operations and maintenance accounts" (House Armed Services Committee, 2001, p. 325). The potential conflict never really came to a head because, on October 8, 2001, the Deputy Secretary of Defense suspended the program as a result of the terrorist attacks of September 11, 2001 (Burlas, 2001a).[40]

A New Team on Watch

In the days immediately after the administration change in 2001, the new Secretary of Defense, Donald Rumsfeld, focused on recruiting his staff. The confirmation process

---

[39] The conferees said they would "entertain a recommendation by the Secretary of Defense to adjust these points to accommodate deployment cycles or other operational considerations" (Conference Committee, 1999, p. 747).

[40] The Army continued to track perstempo data (Burlas, 2001b).

had become interminable since his previous service in the Pentagon,[41] and Rumsfeld could not wait for this process to run its course before he set the agenda for the new administration. Following up on issues the new President had raised in the campaign, National Security Presidential Directive #2 charged Rumsfeld with improving the quality of life of service members. Even before his team was in place, Rumsfeld asked retired Admiral Dave Jeremiah to put a group together to focus on improving morale and quality of life. The group was not only to be responsive to National Security Presidential Directive #2, which tasked the Secretary of Defense to study quality of life; Rumsfeld broadened its charter to include morale.

By late March, Jeremiah had a broad outline. As he saw it, the problem was to maintain an all-volunteer force when "[m]ore young people are going to college, reducing the pool of qualified high school graduates that could be going into [the] military" (Jeremiah, 2001a, p. 1). He singled out "[f]requent military deployments, pay that lacks comparability to the private sector particularly for individuals with some college" and observed that shortages of spare parts and equipment breakdowns also "threaten morale" (Jeremiah, 2001a, p. 1). He thought a leadership message that conveyed "the nobility and value of military service" would "enhance morale and esprit de corps, [improve] recruiting and retention and enhance support of the American people for the administration's defense objectives" (Jeremiah, 2001a, p. 2).[42]

Picking up on the issues highlighted by the Defense Science Board in its 2000 report on human resources strategy (Foster and Welch, 2000), Jeremiah also called on the Pentagon to "transform its military forces to meet the diverse challenges of the future strategic environment." He called on DoD to reform the way it managed its "facilities and infrastructure" (Jeremiah, 2001a, p. 5). Finally, citing the President's promise to service members that they would have "a decent quality of life," he suggested that the "Administration must implement a comprehensive program of improvements in family support, to include housing, health care and other family support activities" (Jeremiah, 2001a, p. 6), together with improved pay.

By the early part of May, Jeremiah's group had added specific programs that it thought should be part of the broad initiatives (Jeremiah, 2001b). It prioritized the programs, made a guess at the costs associated with its recommendations, and assigned responsibilities to lead agencies within the Office of the Secretary of Defense. By mid-June, Jeremiah was ready to brief the Pentagon press corps on his activities (Jeremiah, 2001c). He started his June 13, 2001, presentation by reviewing the problems our

---

[41] *Author's Note:* In the 1970s, Bill Brehm recalled it took only one week to get his nomination out of the White House and only a month or so for the Senate to take action on his nomination. In 2000, six months passed from the time I was asked to become the Under Secretary of Defense for Personnel and Readiness, functionally the same job Brehm had held, to my confirmation by the Senate. In 2001, David Chu was sworn in on June 1, 2001, a little over four months after the new administration came into office.

[42] It is somewhat ironic that the very effort Admiral Jeremiah headed, together with other special panels and the way these panels operated, apparently made many senior military leaders in the Pentagon feel like "second-rate citizens." *Washington Post* reporter Dana Priest wrote about this (Priest, 2004, pp. 23–25).

military personnel faced, then outlined in broad terms the recommendations his panel had developed. When asked about the long-term implications of the pay gap, he agreed that military pay would have to rise in the future, but told reporters that he and his team "deferred that to the Quadrennial Review of Military Compensation, because they're working on the same track, but with more precision than we have" (Jeremiah, 2001d). He was also asked about high optempos and the fact that, despite the recent Presidential campaign, it did not look like the troops would be pulled out very soon.[43] He offered an answer that went far beyond the work of his panel, but went to the heart of the issue:

> The solution rests in the transformation and general purpose force question, because . . . it's fundamentally a question of the force structure you have and the missions you believe you have to undertake, and if you believe you have to undertake the number of missions we have there, then we have to change force structure. (Jeremiah, 2001d)

Jeremiah also noted that, on a trip to Fort Stewart, President Bush had already committed the new administration to $1.4 billion in increased military pay and allowances, housing improvements totaling $400 million, and expanded health benefits costing $3.9 billion (Bush, G. W., 2001).[44] The President's promise and the work of the Jeremiah panel, however, were never coordinated—the President's promise came months before the Jeremiah panel developed its recommendations—and it would be the task of the new Under Secretary, David Chu, sworn into office just days before Jeremiah's briefing, to press for a new personnel program and budget.

Under Secretary of Defense David S. C. Chu

Returning to the Pentagon after an absence of 8 years, David S. C. Chu was sworn in as the fourth Under Secretary for Personnel and Readiness on June 1, 2001 (ASD[PA], 2001). Previously, Chu had served 12 years in the Reagan and Bush administrations as the Director and then Assistant Secretary of Defense for Program Evaluation. Characterizing his former position as "mostly an inside job, . . . the Secretary's internal advisor" (Chu, 2001b), Chu told reporters in the Pentagon pressroom in early August, he found his new "responsibilities . . . very energizing, challenging" (Chu, 2001b). His background both in government and at RAND made him ideally suited to help Secretary of Defense Rumsfeld "rethink many of the precepts on which the Department has operated for the last 50 years." Chu noted, with the Cold War having ended ten years earlier, DoD was "still in many of its endeavors practicing along the lines established

---

[43] Peacekeeping duties in the Balkans were the subject of a news article by the Armed Forces Information Service, which reported that troops would continue to be needed in the Balkans (Gilmore, 2001).

[44] In fact, while this was "new spending" above the then-current budget, according to the *Washington Post*, the "$5.7 billion . . . would fall within the $310 billion budget that President Clinton had outlined for [DoD] for the fiscal year that begins in October [2001]" (Myers, 2001).

during that long historical conflict," then rhetorically asked, "shouldn't we be reconsidering these practices?" (Chu, 2001b).

What was particularly on Rumsfeld's mind as he put together his new team was, as one reporter commented, "re-looking in the personnel areas . . . [of the] 'up-or-out' [policy]" (Chu, 2001b). Chu explained that Rumsfeld's concerns were

> not so much a challenge to "up or out" as it is a challenge . . . [to understand] the appropriate length of a career in the military, especially in a technocratic age where the skill set in senior personnel we're calling on is not as physically dependent. (Chu, 2001b)

"The Europeans do it differently," he told reporters, and while he was "not saying the European model is right," he did believe that "some of the alternatives that are out there in other militaries have proven effective." "What the Secretary is really doing," he told reporters, "is challenging us to think about have we got the right model for the 21st century and for some of the kinds of skills we want. He's particularly thinking of senior leaders, executive skills" (Chu, 2001b). This would eventually lead to new legislation extending the tenure of flag and general officers.

When Chu went before his Senate oversight committee for the first time on July 18, 2001, he not only defended the revised FY 2002 budget, which contained the changes recommended by the new administration, he also provided them with a cogent report on the state of military personnel: "Despite improvement in FY 2001 recruiting achievement, the recruiting and retention war for talent continues" (Chu, 2001a). One measure of the "war" was the cost the services had to bear to meet their FY 2000 active-duty recruiting goals. "We budgeted over $2.3 billion this year for enlisted recruiting including advertising, incentives, and recruiter salaries," he told the committee:

> Our expenditure-per-recruit will be at an all time high of $11,471, 53 percent higher than 10 years ago, accounting for inflation. Recruiter manning is higher than before the drawdown with more than 15,000 active component production recruiters. Advertising budgets have increased 55 percent since FY 1997. (Chu, 2001a)

He identified several programs to "expand the market," including several that allow some youths who had earned GEDs to enlist.[45] Most noteworthy was the National Guard Challenge program that took disadvantaged youths and provided a residential program leading to a GED. "In general," he noted, "12-month attrition rates for [program] holders appear to be similar to those of high school diploma graduates" (Chu,

---

[45] Even consideration of the General Equivalency Diploma high school graduate reversed a long-standing DoD policy, which treated the GED graduate as a high school dropout for purposes of meeting recruiting standards (Staff of the Directorate for Accession Policy, 1996).

2001a).[46] He also highlighted the Army's "College First Program," which had been started by Army Secretary Louis Caldera before he left office the previous January.

Foreshadowing the results of the 9th QRMC (Gilroy, 2002), which would not be officially published until the following March,[47] and breaking with the long tradition of across-the-board pay raises, Chu defended the decision to start to restructure pay:

> While targeted bonuses may be the most economic manner to achieve improved retention in specific skill areas, we believe the pay table imbalances, due to educational change alone, is of sufficient magnitude that immediate permanent corrections are required. . . . Additional money has been budgeted to provide a minimum pay raise of 6 percent for all enlisted personnel, 5 percent for officers, and larger increases targeted for mid-grade and senior NCO's and mid-grade commissioned officers. . . . Senior enlisted pay was increased, not only to avoid pay compression, but to recognize increased responsibility and, consistent with the advice of senior enlisted NCO leadership, larger raises were provided to E-5 and E-7 in recognition of the achievement of NCO and senior NCO status. (Chu, 2001a)

He also indicated the new administration's intent to carry forward a particular commitment of Secretary Cohen, the improvement of military housing allowances and the elimination of "out-of-pocket costs" by 2005. At the time, the allowance covered only an estimated 75 percent of housing costs. By 2005, it would cover all the estimated costs.

An unintended consequence of high retention of the all-volunteer force was that the vast majority of career military members had families. The Army saying that "we enlist an individual and reenlist a family" had become a nearly universal reality. One of the cornerstones of the new program would be quality of life. Chu summed it up for the committee:

> Providing a high quality of life for our military members and their families is essential to our effort to attract and retain a quality force. Considering changes in the composition of military families (such as the increasing number of dual income families), and realizing that continued service is a family decision (because how

---

[46] While this was true at the time, attrition rates were growing, bringing into doubt the long-term benefit of the program (Gilroy, 2004).

[47] *Author's Note:* The 9th QRMC started in summer 1999 and is extensively discussed in the next chapter. When I became Under Secretary of Defense for Personnel and Readiness in June 2000, I reviewed the review's progress and was very impressed with its work. I attribute the outstanding quality of this work to the leadership of Curt Gilroy, the QRMC's executive director. He assembled the best economists from the federally funded research and development centers and independent contractors. After the 2000 election and before I left office, I was eager to see their work published, fearing that the new administration might try to change some of the more-important recommendations. Vice Admiral Pat Tracy, Deputy Assistant Secretary for Military Personnel Policy and Curt's boss, convinced me not to jump the gun. She was afraid that, if the results came out from the old administration, the new administration might reject them out of hand. We compromised, and I sent out an interim report to document the progress we had made (Rostker, 2001). Not only was Pat right, of course, but also the new Under Secretary was David Chu. In one way, David came full cycle. In 1973, when David was at RAND he provided analytic support for the 4th QRMC. Now, he was responsible for the 9th QRMC, and some of his early testimony to Congress incorporated the outstanding work of the 9th QRMC.

families feel affects their satisfaction with military life), force management and retention strategies must focus on the entire military family. (Chu, 2001a)

As a result, as Chu's Principal Deputy, Charles Abell, would later testify,

DoD has entered into a new social compact—a written commitment to improve life in the military, and underwrite family support programs. We acknowledge the reciprocal nature of the relationship between the accomplishments of the DoD mission and quality of life. Families also serve. (Abell, 2004)

The issue of families would become particularly important over the coming years with new and extended deployments to Afghanistan and Iraq.

September 11, 2001

Ask an American who was alive on December 7, 1941, and 60 years later he or she can tell you exactly where they were and what they were doing when they heard that the United States was attacked by Japan and America was in World War II. The same is true for the day President Roosevelt died and the day President Kennedy was assassinated. The events of September 11, 2001, have similarly been burned into the consciousness of this generation of Americans.

David Chu remembers where he was that Tuesday morning.[48] He was en route to the Army-Navy Club in downtown Washington to talk to the Reserve Forces Policy Board when he heard that a plane had hit one of the towers of the World Trade Center in New York. He remembers thinking that it must have been a private plane. Surely commercial jetliner pilots were too experienced to be so off course over New York. When the news came that the second tower had also been hit, he knew that his assumption was badly wrong. He immediately started back to the Pentagon. As he approached the building, so did American Airlines Flight 77. By the time he arrived, the building was already being cordoned off, and he and his executive assistant, Navy Captain Steve Wellock, headed for the nearest DoD facility that he thought would have secure communications. Minutes later, they arrived at the old Navy Annex, on a hill overlooking the Pentagon in plain view of the crash scene. This "temporary" World War II building had escaped the wrecker's ball many times and still supplied offices for members of the Headquarters, U.S. Marine Corps staff.[49]

As Under Secretary for Personnel and Readiness, Chu was a staff officer to the Secretary of Defense, but he instinctively knew that he had to pull together the humanitarian response to help the families of what he could see would be many victims. He was able to contact Meg Falk, from his Military Community and Family Support staff,

---

[48] The following is based on an interview with David S. C. Chu, September 12, 2004.

[49] After more than a half century of avoiding a move into the Pentagon, Navy Secretary John Dolton had persuaded Marine Corps Commandant, Chuck Krulak, to move to the Commandant's office to the Pentagon in 1997. Most of his staff, however, remained at the annex.

who oversaw "policy" in this area. He asked her to secure hotel space immediately so that the relatives would have a place to go and to make arrangements to set up what would become known as the Pentagon Family Support Center. He told her to have things operational by early the next morning.

Chu's instincts were right on target. At 6:00 a.m. the next morning, he received a call from the public affairs office, which had already been inundated with calls for help and support. "What are you going to do?" he was asked. He responded that he had already taken steps, including making hotel arrangements for people who would be coming from out of town and setting up a toll-free phone number so families could obtain information about their loved ones. At 9:00 a.m. on September 12, 2001, less than 24 hours after the attack on the Pentagon and while rescue and recovery operations at the building continued, the staff office, now transformed into the first-ever Joint Military Service Family Assistance Center, was operational. The evolving center continued to operate until November 1, 2001. That is not to say that there were no policy decisions to be made. With no more guidance than the public pronouncements of the President, Chu and his reserve affairs office made critical decisions concerning the mobilization of National Guard and Reserve personnel. As the President said, this was war. Call-ups would not be for 30 or 60 days but, to control expectations and provide flexibility, for one year initially.

What has all of this to do with the all-volunteer force? Chu would later explain that it was in the spirit of the all-volunteer force that he decided to act:

> Collectively, . . . [we] reinvented the DoD tradition of "taking care of our own" by supporting the families of our fallen comrades, as well as the families of the passengers and crew of American Airlines Flight 77. (Chu, 2004b)

Those in the Pentagon were all volunteers, whether professional solders, civilians, or contractors. They were all part of the DoD family, and Chu was the senior DoD personnel official on the scene. It did not matter whether a victim worked for the Office of the Secretary of Defense or one of the services, was a passenger on the airliner or a member of its crew; the families would look to the Secretary of Defense for support since this was his headquarters. Chu meant to provide them that support. The details of those heroic days are captured in an after-action report (Chu, 2003).

The Iraq War

Early on the morning of March 20, 2003, American and coalition troops attacked Iraq. Halfway around the world, it was still March 19 when, at 10:16 p.m., President Bush addressed the American people and "all the men and women of the United States Armed Forces now in the Middle East." He told them, "the peace of a troubled world and the hopes of an oppressed people now depend on you," and ended by saying "[t]hat trust is well placed" (Bush, G. W., 2003a). The men and women he spoke to that night were from every branch of the military, including both active and reserve personnel. Besides being in uniform, they had at least one other thing in common: They were all volunteers. And it was the fact that they were volunteers that would be the subject of debate and concern for months to come.

Initially, the war was the catalyst for a renewed debate over the legitimacy of the all-volunteer force concept itself. Some immediately called for a return to conscription as a means of sharing the burden equitably. When the conventional phase of the war ended with the rapid collapse of the Baghdad regime, those calls subsided. As time went on, however, and as the military was called on to undertake the largest "nation-building" program since the reconstruction of Germany and Japan after World War II and the bloodiest ever, many worried about the long-term viability of the volunteer Army. While strains have appeared, the all-volunteer force has to date proven its resilience. This ongoing story is the most recent test of the all-volunteer force—a test that continues.

Bring Back the Draft

The headline on the op-ed page of the *New York Times* on the last day of 2002 proclaimed, "Bring Back the Draft." The author, Representative Charles Rangel (D-New York), observed, as had military sociologist Charlie Moskos on countless occasions, that "only one member [of Congress] . . . has a child in the enlisted ranks of the military—just a few more have children who are officers" (Rangel, 2002). Rangel had voted against the congressional resolution giving the president authority to go to war in Iraq—a war still three months away, but one he was sure would come. In a replay of the Gates Commission debate on whether the all-volunteer force would lead to adventurism, Rangel openly wondered whether

> those calling for war knew that their children were likely to be required to serve—and to be placed in harm's way—there would be more caution and a greater willingness to work with the international community in dealing with Iraq. A renewed draft will help bring a greater appreciation of the consequences to go to war. (Rangel, 2002)

He seemed less concerned than Jesse Jackson had been more than a decade before, during the first Gulf War, that the poor and minorities had been tricked into risking their lives for a bowl of pottage in the form of bonuses and educational benefits, although he did mention their overrepresentation in the Army Force. He was concerned, however, that "going to war against Iraq will severely strain military resources already burdened by a growing number of obligations, . . . stretching them to the limit" (Rangel, 2002).

Within days, the rhetorical battle was joined with op-ed pieces by former Secretary of Defense Cap Weinberger in the *Wall Street Journal* (2002) and former Army Secretary Louis Caldera in the *Los Angeles Times* (2003). Caldera saw some possible benefit from universal service and teaching "America's young people that the benefits of military service far outweigh its burdens" (Caldera, 2003), but chided Rangel for "tapping into these fears" of conscription for his own purpose. Rangel, however, found an ally in Senator Ernest Hollings (D-South Carolina), who introduced a companion bill and was quoted as saying that one way "to avoid a lot more wars to come is institute the draft. You will find that this country will sober up, and its leadership too" (as quoted in Hulse, 2003).

At the Pentagon, Secretary of Defense Rumsfeld wanted no part of a draft. When asked about the legislation that Representative Rangel had introduced, Rumsfeld explained:

> We're not going to reimplement a draft. There is no need for it at all. The disadvantages of using compulsion to bring into the armed forces the men and women needed are notable. . . .
>
> If you think back to when we had the draft, people were brought in; they were paid some fraction of what they could make in the civilian manpower market because they were without choices. Big categories were exempted—people that were in college, people that were teaching, people that were married. It varied from time to time, but there were all kinds of exemptions. And what was left was sucked into the intake, trained for a period of months, and then went out, adding no value, no advantage, really, to the United States armed services over any sustained period of time, because the churning that took place, it took enormous amount of effort in terms of training, and then they were gone.
>
> Now, are we able today to maintain a force that is at the appropriate size with the appropriate skills by paying people roughly what they'd be making in the civilian manpower market? Yes. Are we doing it today? Yes. Are we meeting the recruiting goals? Yes. Have we been able to attract and retain people in the Guard and the Reserves who can augment that force when necessary, such as today? Yes, we have. (Rumsfeld, 2003b)

Within days, amid a volley of criticism, Rumsfeld apologized to veterans for his remarks. In a response to an open letter from the American Legion that was posted on its Web site—"retraction and an apology to the families of those 'draftees' who served America with honor and gave their very lives for this country"—Rumsfeld told the veterans groups, "The last thing I would want to do would be to disparage the service of those draftees" (as quoted in Loeb, 2003). However, his position was clear.

Rangel's contention that the poor and minorities were overrepresented in the military and the old canard that they were cannon fodder also came into scrutiny. *USA Today,* citing Rangel's claims, reported on the tendency for black soldiers to be underrepresented in front-line combat units. They reported that a

> close examination of Pentagon statistics suggests that at least some of the conventional wisdom about who is most at risk during wartime is misleading. For example, although blacks account for 26% of Army troops, they make up a much smaller percentage of those in front-line combat units, the most likely to be killed or injured in a conventional war. (Moniz and Squitieri, 2003a)

In fact, blacks were underrepresented in the infantry and in such specialized jobs as Armored Cavalry Scouts and Green Berets (Moniz and Squitieri, 2003b). The *New*

York Times' analysis of the first 1,000 troops who died in the war in Iraq showed that 13 percent were black, 12 percent Hispanic, 70 percent white, and 5 percent "other" (Werschkul et al., 2004). Keeping with the demographics of the all-volunteer force, 47 percent were married, and 48 percent were older than 24. Enlisted personnel made up 88 percent of the dead; 82 percent came from the full-time military; and relative to their populations, the rural states of Oregon, Idaho, Wyoming, North and South Dakota, Nebraska, Oklahoma, Mississippi, and Maine had by far the greatest numbers of deaths. Among the first 1,000 deaths, 25 were women.

With the fall of Baghdad on April 10, 2003, the talk of the draft also seemed to come to an end. The "embedded" reporters who traveled with Army and Marine Corps units saw firsthand the professionalism of the all-volunteer force. On May 1, 2003, on board the USS *Abraham Lincoln* off the coast of San Diego, President Bush announced, "Mission Accomplished: Major Combat Operations Have Ended" (Bush, G. W., 2003b).

The War Enters a New Phase: 2004—Testing the Viability of the All-Volunteer Force

With the end of conventional combat operations, the Army and Marine Corps entered a period that some have called nation-building. It has also been a period of great danger and instability, and a period that again brought into question the viability of the all-volunteer force.

Rather than reducing troop levels in Iraq as planned, Secretary Rumsfeld announced on May 4, 2004, that the "overall U.S. troop strength in Iraq will be stabilized at approximately 138,000 as requested by the combatant commander." The announcement also confirmed that "[v]arious units from the National Guard and Reserve are in the deployment. . . . All Army National Guard and Reserve units being deployed will be given sufficient time to train in preparation for their service in Operation Iraqi Freedom" (OASD[PA], 2004a). The units would be deployed up to 12 months in Iraq, but the total time they would be away from home would "depend upon training requirements and the requirements of the Central Command commander" (OASD[PA], 2004a).

Concern for the increased casualities and optempo was evident in both the popular press and in reports to Congress.[50] Even before the end of the conventional phase of the war was declared, the *New York Times* editorialized that the "pacification and rebuilding of Iraq will eventually require tens of thousands of part-time, civilian soldiers in the National Guard and various military reserves" and complained that "overused reservists are experiencing personal and professional problems that could eventually drive many of them out of the service" (*New York Times* Editorial Staff, 2003). The

---

[50] A February 16, 2003, the *Washington Post* headline read: "Unrivaled Military Feels Strains of Unending War" (Ricks and Loeb, 2004). On January 18, 2004, the headline in the *Post* was: "Rotation to Cut U.S. Presence, Reservists to Assume Greater Share of Duties in Iraq" (Spayd and Ricks, 2004). Several days later, a headline in the *Post* read: "Reserve Chief Fears Retention Crisis" (Loeb, 2004).

Times was wrong on two accounts. The May 4, 2004, deployment order brought "the total National Guard and Reserve on active duty to 168,197 including both units and individual augmentees" (OASD[PA], 2004b), far exceeding the tens of thousands they had speculated about the previous year. They were also wrong in that retention in the National Guard and Reserve remained surprisingly high.

Members of Congress were also concerned. Responding to a request by the ranking member of the Senate Appropriations Committee, the head of the Congressional Budget Office (CBO) told senior members of Congress on September 3, 2003, that the

> active Army would be unable to sustain an occupation force of the present size [180,000, about 150,000 deployed in Iraq itself and the rest supporting the occupation from neighboring countries] beyond about March 2004 if it chose not to keep individual units deployed to Iraq for longer than one year without relief. . . . After [that] . . . the United States could sustain—indefinitely, if need be—an occupation force of 38,000 to 64,000 . . . .
>
> A larger occupation force could be sustained in . . . Iraq if DoD employed additional forces, including Marine Corps units, Army special-forces groups, and combat units from the Army National Guard. (Holtz-Eakin, 2003, pp. 1–3)

CBO also considered the option of creating new units, noting that it "would take several years to accomplish and thus would not assist in the occupation of Iraq as soon as other options" (Holtz-Eakin, 2003, p. 19). The office analyzed the impact of deploying a larger part of the force by increasing "time away from home for active deployable units to levels higher than the all-volunteer force has ever experienced" (Holtz-Eakin, 2003, p. 25). To sustain such deployments, though,

> DoD could seek the authority to use temporary financial incentives to increase the number of personnel that could be sent to Iraq. Such incentives could encourage current selected-reserve and active-duty personnel to voluntarily accept higher deployment tempo and induce new categories of reserve personnel or prior service members to volunteer for deployment. (Holtz-Eakin, 2003, p. 26)

They admitted, however, that "DoD does not have experience using bonuses to encourage military personnel to deploy voluntarily to a hostile area . . . [and] [t]hus the effects of offering such financial incentives are unknown" (Holtz-Eakin, 2003, p. 26).

The analysis CBO presented to Congress assumed the Army would maintain its preferred policy of rotating units rather than individuals, which has been common during such long-term military operations as World War II, the Korean War, and the war in Vietnam. In addition, stationing of troops overseas in Europe and Korea was generally accomplished by rotating individuals, rather than units.[51] CBO concluded, however, that rotating individuals would have "disadvantages." A one-year tour of duty

---

[51] The Army had tried several times to move to unit rotations with such programs as Gyroscope, Overseas Unit Rotation Plan, Long Thrust, ROTAPLAN, Brigade 75–76, and COHORT, but these efforts could not be sustained, and the Army returned to individual rotation to man these overseas locations.

in Iraq would mean that units in Iraq would "experience 100 percent annual turnover in personnel," and this would be "detrimental to units' cohesion and ability to perform in combat" (Holtz-Eakin, 2003, pp. 32–33).

The Military Takes Extraordinary Steps

Even before the invasion of Iraq, in support of post–September 11 operations, the Secretary of Defense started to take steps to make sure that it had the necessary skills. The stop-loss policy allowed the services to keep individuals on active duty beyond their scheduled separation dates. The affected individuals "generally cannot retire or leave the service as long as reserves are called to active duty or until relieved," by a waiver to the policy from their service. The policy generally targets those with "critical military skills" (OASD[PA], 2001).[52]

In June 2004, in addition to the stop-loss policy in effect, DoD announced it would take the highly unusual step of ordering members of the Individual Ready Reserve (IRR) to active duty.

PERSTEMPO. On October 8, 2001, the Deputy Secretary of Defense invoked §991(d) of Title 10, U.S. Code (USC), to suspend the perstempo management program in the wake of the terrorist attacks on September 11, 2001. This suspension terminated the accumulation of deployment days for purposes of determining eligibility for high deployment per diem payments and the statutory requirement for general and flag officers to personally manage the deployment of certain members. Chu's office reexamined existing policies in light of the current operations. The review suggested (1) that high deployment tempos can not be eliminated altogether, (2) that high deployment may take the form of extraordinarily long periods or even frequent deployments for short periods, and (3) that either must be recognized through compensation. The staff suggested a revision to the perstempo law to "streamline current management thresholds and required actions . . . [and] improve [the] structure, levels and flexibility of compensation to members" (Chu, 2002, p. 5).

The National Defense Authorization Act of 2004 incorporated the changes Chu had suggested. It allowed flexibility in the employment of military forces and, at the same time, provided fair and reasonable compensation for the relatively few who would unavoidably have to be deployed beyond service norms. The new law

> authorize[s] payment of a monthly high-deployment allowance of up to $1,000, instead of the $100 high-tempo per diem allowance . . . for service members each month during which the member is deployed for 191 or more consecutive days

---

[52] Stop-loss originally required the president's action, but was delegated to the secretary of defense in 1990, during Operation Desert Shield. It was used during Operation Allied Force over Kosovo. On September 24, 2001, Secretary Rumsfeld "delegated his 'stop-loss' authority to the heads of the military departments" (OASD[PA], 2001). The policy does not, however, affect most involuntary or administrative discharges.

or for 401 days out of the preceding 730 days. (Conference Committee, 2003, p. 694)[53]

Stop-Loss. The term *stop-loss* refers to a military service keeping a service member on active duty beyond the date he or she was scheduled to leave, usually because the force is engaged in a critical operation and cannot afford to lose the services of a trained and skilled individual. In the face of an all-volunteer force, this is a decidedly nonvoluntary action. It violates the spirit of the all-volunteer force and sets aside the terms of the contract that the service member, sometimes an active-duty service member and sometimes a member of the National Guard or reserves serving on active duty, has with the government. It is decidedly short term and immediate and often results in unhappy service members, whose plans for jobs or school must be put on hold when they are told they cannot leave. Immediately after the events of September 11, 2001, the military moved to stabilize the force and initiated stop-loss on November 30, 2001, in support of Operations Noble Eagle and Enduring Freedom.

While all the services used stop-loss, the Army got the most attention and was the focus of press scrutiny because it had the largest number of personnel involved. In the Army, soldiers subject to the stop-loss rules were kept on active duty or in the Selective Reserves for 12 months longer than they had originally planned. Reviewed periodically, even before Operation Iraqi Freedom, stop-loss affected over 51,000 soldiers. On February 14, 2003, stop-loss was authorized for active component units supporting Operation Iraqi Freedom. On May 27, 2003, the Army ended stop-loss for active component units but continued it for 16,000 active Army; 4,900 Army Reserve; and 675 National Guard soldiers until October 2003 (U.S. Army, 2003b). A further partial lifting of stop-loss took place in early July 2003 (U.S. Army, 2003a). By November, however, the Acting Secretary of the Army announced that

> [t]he current operational situation warrants that the Army implements [sic] the Active Army Unit Stop Loss Program based on the commitment to pursue the Global War On Terrorism for the immediate future, to provide our combatant commanders the force to decisively defeat those that threaten our security, and to ensure our unit formations are ready, cohesive and at their best to effect forthcoming rotational plans. Retaining the Reserve Component (RC) Unit Stop Loss and re-instituting the Act Army Unit Stop Loss and Stop Movement provides equity for all Components and ensures unit stability from alert through redeployment/demobilization. (U.S. Army, 2003c)

---

[53] While the new monthly High Deployment Allowance (HDA) authorizes the services to compensate members for excessive deployments based on both their duration and frequency, work is under way on a new proposal, *Triple Backstop*. The new system would consist of three components: First, members who are sent to less-desirable locations are compensated using High Deployment Pay—Location. The rates are established by country. Second, High Deployment Pay—Tempo will compensate those who are deployed excessively long and/or too frequently, with the amount and definition of "too long and/or too frequently" left to each service to determine. The existing Selective Reenlistment Bonus would also be made part of this program. The goal of all these efforts is to "adequately" compensate members who are subject to long and/or frequent deployments and to have positively influence the decision to reenlist (Carr, 2004).

In June 2004, the Army decided that, to "ensure our formations remain a cohesive element throughout their deployment it is necessary to stop personnel losses from the deploying units until after they return to their permanent duty station" (U.S. Army, 2004). The policy effectively froze soldiers in place for a period of 90 days before a deployment, during the one-year deployment, and for up to 90 days after the unit retuned home. The policy drew some sharp criticism. The *New York Times* reported one defense analyst's comments:

> The Army is just running out of creative ideas for coping with the level of commitment that Iraq requires. . . . It's clear there was a fundamental miscalculation about how protracted and how intense the ground commitment in Iraq would be. (Schmitt, 2004)

An op-ed in the *New York Times* by a veteran of Operation Iraqi Freedom raised questions about the compatibility of stop-loss and the all-volunteer force:

> [T]he stop-loss policy is wrong, it runs contrary to the concept of the volunteer military set up in the aftermath of the Vietnam War. Many if not most of the soldiers in this latest Iraq-bound wave are already veterans of several tours in Iraq and Afghanistan. They have honorably completed their active duty obligations. But like draftees, they have been conscripted to meet the additional needs in Iraq. (Exum, 2004)

The Individual Ready Reserve. If stop-loss was unpopular, calling members of the IRR was even more so, even though it had been done during Operations Desert Shield and Desert Storm in larger numbers than for Operation Iraqi Freedom. On June 30, 2004, the Army announced that, beginning July 6, it would start calling 5,600 solders of the IRR. Soldiers in the IRR have finished the initial period of active duty but have time remaining before the expiration of the eight-year military service obligation they incurred when they first enlisted. Members of the IRR do not drill and usually have no ongoing association with the military. Calling them to return to active duty is highly unusual. One day after the call-up of the IRR started, Under Secretary Chu and the Army Vice Chief of Staff, General Richard Cody were before the House Armed Services Committee explaining the new policy.

Chairman Duncan Hunter opened the hearing by noting that

> the continued heavy reliance on the reserve components, which . . . make up 43 percent of the force going into Iraq and the reasons behind the Army's need to involuntarily mobilize 5,600 people in the Individual Ready Reserve, the IRR. (Chu and Cody, 2004)

He accepted "that the Army and Marine Corps are under stress because of deployments," but wanted to know more "about the measures being taken to preserve what we would call the 'elasticity' of the force." He expressed concern "that insufficient force structure and manpower are leaving the services to make decision[s] . . . to make it through today . . . that mortgage the future" (Chu and Cody, 2004). The ranking member of the committee, Representative Ike Skelton (D-Missouri) expressed his concern that "we're wearing our people out" (Chu and Cody, 2004). He acknowledged what he called the "drastic measures" DoD was taking "to man the next rotation [of] forces to Iraq and Afghanistan," but thought that they posed "a serious alarm" (Chu and Cody, 2004).

When it was his turn to make his opening remarks, Chu thanked the committee for their support over the years.[54] Agreeing with the committee that calling on the IRR was not done often, Chu pointed out, "Individual ready reserve service . . . is part of the obligation of military service that each entrant in the military assumes. The fact that it is rare that we call up an individual ready reservist does not . . . mean that it is inappropriate." He told the committee that "it is important to our military readiness. . . . It allows us to fill holes quickly with a trained person in the appropriate skill. And it avoids tearing up other units that we may need at a later stage of the mobilization process" (Chu and Cody, 2004). Skelton, however, was clearly disturbed that the IRR call-up was going on when "the Pentagon continues to oppose an increase in end strength" (Chu and Cody, 2004). He asked Chu, "Once you used these measures of last resort, what happens when you need to reuse them in subsequent rotations, . . . I think every member of this committee is concerned. . . . How do we keep going?" (Chu and Cody, 2004).

Chu explained that the disagreement was not about end strength, but how it was going to be financed, with a temporary increase financed by a supplemental appropriation. He took exception with Skelton's characterization of the personnel actions DoD had undertaken as "measures of last resort." "These are measures that keep the burden equitably shared among the various components of our military. These are . . . the way we would sustain this over a long-term future if that is, indeed, the requirement" (Chu and Cody, 2004), he told the congressman. In an uncharacteristically sharp tone Skelton told Chu, "I just don't—I just don't think you understand the seriousness of the situation. . . . Talk with some of the folks that tell us, 'We are stretched, Congressman'" (Chu and Cody, 2004).

Rebalancing and Restructuring the Force

Invoking stop-loss and calling up the IRR were admittedly short-term means of addressing the immediate shortage of skilled personnel by adding to the available supply. Some, however, questioned their legitimacy because they required people to serve involuntarily in the era of an all-volunteer force. They were not, however, the only programs DoD undertook to ease the stress on the force, as programs to rebalance and restructure the services were put in place.

---

[54] In his formal statement for the record, Chu reviewed the guidelines the Secretary of Defense and Chairman of the Joint Chiefs of Staff use to assess the requests for troops by the combatant commanders (Chu, 2004a).

Rebalancing the Force. The need to rebalance the force was recognized in a December 2002 review of the reserve components' contributions to national defense (Office of the Assistant Secretary of Defense for Reserve Affairs, 2002), even before the beginning of Operation Iraqi Freedom. The report highlighted a number of "indicators" that suggested something was wrong:

> [R]outine use of involuntary recall of the reserves; increased operational tempo in selected areas; anecdotal evidence that the ongoing partial mobilization may have a negative impact on reserve recruiting and retention in the future; the apparent mismatch between the new defense strategy and current force structure; and the length of time it takes to adapt force-mix allocations in today's rapidly changing security environment. (Office of the Assistant Secretary of Defense for Reserve Affairs, 2002, p. 22)
>
> Contingencies such as peacekeeping and humanitarian operations place a high demand on some capabilities—[civil affairs, military police and security forces, public affairs units, air traffic control services, deployable air control squadrons, and the reserve intelligence community]—that are low in density to overall available forces. (Office of the Assistant Secretary of Defense for Reserve Affairs, 2002, p. 26)

The authors attributed this to the assumptions that these capabilities would be needed "only in the later phases of a conflict under the two-major-theater-war strategy." The Global War on Terror required the force to be rebalanced.

In early 2004, John Winkler, the Deputy Assistant Secretary of Defense for Reserve Affairs, reported on efforts to rebalance forces by moving people from low-demand positions to fill vacancies in high-demand positions. The theme of the program, he noted, was "to improve the responsiveness of the force and to help ease stress on units and individuals with skills in high demand" (Winkler, 2004, p. v). Over the previous three-year period, he reported, the services had changed 50,000 military spaces—10,000 in FY 2003 and 20,000 in each of the two subsequent years. The reported rebalancing was based on the December 2002 review (Office of the Assistant Secretary of Defense for Reserve Affairs, 2002) and the secretary of defense's directions of early July 2003 (Rumsfeld, 2003c).

Secretary Rumsfeld was very sensitive to the stress that frequent deployments place on both the active and reserve forces and how critical it is for the future of the all-volunteer force. On the occasion of the 30th anniversary of the all-volunteer force, he addressed this subject:

> Personnel tempo has to be set at a level that is rational, that does not wear people out, and that does not drive people away, because we need to continue to attract the best people available. . . . We must provide our reserve forces with more predictability and take care to use this important component of the force judiciously— in a way that is fair to our reservists, to their families, and to their employers. (Rumsfeld, 2004)

He directed the services to

> [r]estructure active and reserve forces to reduce the need for involuntary mobiliza-tion, . . . [e]stablish a more rigorous process for reviewing joint requirements . . . to provide timely notice of mobilization [and to] make the mobilization and demobi-lization process more efficient. (Rumsfeld, 2003c)

Among other things, in a proactive move, Rumsfeld also established the planning goal of using a guardsman or reservist "not more than one year every 6 years" (Rumsfeld, 2003c).[55] Rumsfeld was trying to get ahead of the problem, but the enormity of the task of maintaining such a large force in Iraq with reasonable and predictable deploy-ment schedules would not be easy to accomplish.

While the rebalancing is being carried out by all the services, it is the Army that has drawn the most attention, given the situation in Iraq. To increase Army readiness without having to call up reserve forces with little or no warning, a report on force rebalancing observed that the

> Army is converting 5,600 spaces of lower priority active structure to higher priority active structure. These conversions will add capabilities in chemical, military police, engineer (bridging and fire fighting units), medical, quartermaster (fuel, water, and mortuary affairs units), and transportation specialists. (Winkler, 2004, pp. 10–11)

Recognizing that the "global security environment" was putting stress on certain career fields, in FY 2001 the Army reprogrammed 30,000 spaces,

> providing additional capabilities in the areas of civil affairs, psychological opera-tions, special operations forces, intelligence, and military police. . . . Beginning in fiscal year 2006, the Army will undertake a major rebalancing effort involving over 80,000 spaces to further relieve stress on the force and continue to improve its Reserve component capabilities and readiness. (Winkler, 2004, pp. 13–14)

Restructuring the Army. The rebalancing of spaces is complemented by an even more radical plan. Employing the new force-generation concept, the Army plans to

---

[55] Rumsfeld also challenged a basic tenet of reserve force design, commonly known as the Abrams Doctrine: "If we go to war again, we're taking the reserves with us." After the war in Vietnam, Army Chief of Staff Creighton Abrams wanted to make sure that, in the future, the political leadership could not commit the Army to combat without paying the political price of calling up the reserves (See Pullen, 2003). His design for the active-reserve force mix put important support elements in the reserves—elements that were absolutely required to move the active Army were made part of the Army Reserve. Rumsfeld's July 9, 2003, instructions were that the new "structure [of] active and reserve forces [should] . . . eliminate the need for involuntary mobilization during the first 15 days of a rapid response operation (or for any alerts to mobilize prior to the operation)" (Rumsfeld, 2003c). Subsequently, the Army decided to restructure itself so the active Army could "execute the first 30 days of any deployment" (Brownlee and Schoomaker, 2004, p. 17), rather than just the first 15 days. The Reserve Officers Association, as well as other military service organizations, questioned this part of Rumsfeld's plan—the "concept that recalling citizen soldiers before a conflict begins is, in fact, good for our country. "In our view," the association said in a public position paper, "we need to consider this concept as an integral part of force planning" (McIntosh, 2003).

restructure itself to become an "expeditionary" force so that it can provide a continuous supply of forces more effectively than it has in the past. The Secretary of the Army and the Chief of Staff of the Army recently wrote about their plans for changing the Army. When implemented, these plans will finally address how the world has changed since the fall of the Soviet Union and will radically transform the Army from the Cold War force, which has lingered for 15 years, to one designed to address the realities of the current environment. In the summer 2004 issue of the Army's senior professional journal, *Parameters,* the Acting Secretary of the Army and the Chief of Staff wrote:

> In the Cold War, the United States was committed to reinforce Europe with ten divisions within ten days, but no one perceived that responsiveness as expeditionary. The reason for this is significant: in the Cold War we knew where we would fight and we met this requirement through prepositioning of units or unit sets in a very developed theater. The uncertainty as to where we must deploy, the probability of a very austere operational environment, and the requirement to fight on arrival throughout the battlespace pose an entirely different challenge—and the fundamental distinction of expeditionary operations. (Brownlee and Schoomaker, 2004, p. 9)

In simple terms, the results of these changes will radically alter the Army of the future. In effect, the Army is adopting the deployment cycle strategy that the Navy and Marine Corps have used for years and the AEF concept that the Air Force has adopted more recently. Instead of having all active combat units of the Army constantly at a high state of readiness and all available to deploy, two-thirds of the active combat units of the Army would be available to the President at any time. Moreover, only one-sixth of reserve component troop units would be available to be deployed at any given time. Short of the "deployment for the duration of operations" manning that was used during World War II, accommodating the continuous operations of any limited-tenure force, whether all-volunteer or a mix of volunteers and draftees, requires a rotational base that is very expensive to maintain.

Michael O'Hanlon, a senior fellow at the Brookings Institution, however, has noted what may be the critical weakness in the expeditionary model the Army is moving toward. In *Parameters,* he poses a central question: "How does one determine the appropriate . . . size of the Army?" This brings the discussion back to the very heart of the Army's plan. He answered his own question:

> There is no definitive method because it is impossible to determine exactly how large a rotation base will be needed to continue the Iraq mission over a period of years while avoiding an unacceptable strain on the all-volunteer force that could drive large numbers of people out of the military. (O'Hanlon, 2004b, p. 10)

So, if the deployment rotations, as envisioned in the specific design of the expeditionary force, supply an inadequate number of troops to carry out the sustained mission, the Army will find itself back in the same place Representative Skelton was complaining about earlier. If this happens, volunteers and would-be volunteers may no longer trust DoD to limit the frequency and duration of deployments to bearable levels. The British understand this and even have a term for it; the period between deployments is called the "harmony" period—the time necessary to restore balance and harmony in one's military life and family life. The harmony period in the Army and the Marine Corps is quite short at present but ultimately has as much to say about the future of the all-volunteer force as pay, enlistment, and reenlistment bonuses do.

The Legacy: Waiting for the Other Shoe to Drop

Despite the House vote of 402 to 2 to reject a return to the draft—a move that even Representative Rangel voted against—the issue will not die (Babington and Oldenburg, 2004). What seems to fuel speculation about the draft is the talk about the over-extended military. For example, meeting with reporters on September 16, 2004, the Chief of the Army Reserve warned that, at the current pace of operations, "the Army faced a serious risk of running out of crucial specialists in the Reserves who can be involuntarily called up for active duty" (Schmitt, 2004). O'Hanlon argues bluntly: "Today's policies for deploying forces abroad risks breaking the all-volunteer force" (O'Hanlon, 2004b, p. 10). He even proposes that, to

> minimize the chances of a draft, it makes sense to increase the size of today's armed forces now, *before* a personnel crisis occurs. We're already deploying today's soldiers and Marines at a pace that is unrivaled in the history of the all-volunteer force, at considerable risk to the staying power of that force. (O'Hanlon, 2004a)

Ultimately, however, the ability to grow the all-volunteer force will depend on the willingness of young men and women to join. Increased incentives have always proven to stretch enlistments, but there is a limit.

So far the all-volunteer force has proven to be very resilient, but the all-volunteer force does not lend itself to guarantees. Those charged with managing the force are vigilant and with the knowledge gained from over 30 years certainly will do their utmost to ensure its continued success. However, only time will tell.

References

Abell, Charles S., *The Needs of Military Families: How Are States and the Pentagon Responding, Especially for Guard and Reservists?* Washington, D.C.: U.S. Department of Defense, July 21, 2004. G1274.pdf.

Asch, Beth J., and Bruce R. Orvis, *Recent Recruiting Trends and Their Implications: Preliminary Analysis and Recommendations,* Santa Monica, Calif.: RAND Corporation, MR-549-A, 1994. S0744.pdf.

ASD[FMP]—*See* Assistant Secretary of Defense for Force Management Policy.

ASD[PA]—*See* Assistant Secretary of Defense for Public Affairs.

Ashcroft, John, "Sexual Misconduct," memorandum to Secretary of Defense, Washington, D.C., June 17, 1997. G0861.pdf.

Aspin, Les, *Military Manpower Recruiting Results for the Active Components Fiscal Year 1992,* Washington, D.C.: U.S. Department of Defense, November 17, 1993. G0818.pdf.

Assistant Secretary of Defense for Force Management Policy, *Report to Congress: A New Focus for Military Advertising and Market Research,* Washington, D.C.: Office of the Assistant Secretary of Defense (Force Management Policy), March 2000. G1328.pdf.

Assistant Secretary of Defense for Public Affairs, *Under Secretary for Personnel and Readiness Sworn In,* Washington, D.C.: Department of Defense, 22501, June 8, 2001. G1269.pdf.

Babington, Charles, and Don Oldenburg, "House GOP Brings Up Draft in Order to Knock It Down," *Washington Post,* October 6, 2004, p. 1.

Bacon, Kenneth H., "DoD News Briefing," Washington, D.C., October 31, 2000. G1372.pdf.

Baker, Nancy Kassebaum, "On the Report of the Federal Advisory Committee on Gender-Integrated Training and Related Issues," transmittal letter to William S. Cohen, Washington, D.C., December 16, 1997. G1250.pdf.

Becraft, Carolyn, "Response to the Report of the Task Force on Quality of Life," information memorandum to Assistant Secretary of Defense (Force Management Policy), Washington, D.C., February 26, 1996. G0700.pdf.

Blair, Anita K., *Final Report of the Congressional Commission on Military Training and Gender-Related Issues,* Washington, D.C.: Congressional Commission on Military Training and Gender-Related Issues, July 30, 1999. G1248.pdf.

Bozell/Eskew Advertising, and Pintauk-Murphy-Gautier-Hudome, *Topline Findings: Recruitment Advertising Review,* Washington, D.C.: RAND Corporation, August 4, 1999. G1330.pdf.

Brownlee, Les, and Peter J. Schoomaker, "Serving a Nation at War: A Campaign Quality Army with Joint and Expeditionary Capabilities," *Parameters,* Vol. XXXIV, No. 2, Summer 2004, pp. 5–23. S0808.pdf.

Burlas, Joe, "Terrorist Attacks Prompt Danger Pay, Suspend PERSTEMPO Clock," *ARNEWS: Army News Service,* October 11, 2001a. G1342.pdf.

———, "Army Will Continue to Track PERSTEMPO," *ARNEWS: Army New Service,* November 6, 2001b. G1343.pdf.

Bush, George W., *Speech on Defense Strategy at the Citadel,* Citadel, S.C.: The Citadel, September 23, 1999. S0742.pdf.

———, *Remarks by the President to the Troops of Fort Stewart,* Washington, D.C.: The White House, February 12, 2001. G1264.pdf.

———, *The National Security Strategy of the United States of America,* Washington, D.C.: The White House, September 17, 2002. G1231.pdf.

———, *President Bush Addresses the Nation: Operation Iraqi Freedom,* Washington, D.C.: The White House, March 19, 2003a. G1278.pdf.

———, *President Bush Announces Major Combat Operations in Iraq Have Ended,* Washington, D.C.: The White House, May 1, 2003b. G1280.pdf.

Bush, George H. W., "Remarks," Aspen Institute Symposium in Aspen, Colorado, August 2, 1990. G1237.pdf.

Caldera, Louis, "Talk of a Draft Is Nothing but Hot Air," *Los Angeles Times,* January 13, 2003. S0599.pdf.

Callander, Bruce D., "The New Expeditionary Force," *Air Force Magazine: Journal of the Air Force Association,* Vol. 81, No. 9, September 1998. S0766.pdf.

Carr, William J., *Briefing: Triple Backstop,* Washington, D.C.: Office of the Under Secretary of Defense (Personnel and Readiness): Military Personnel Policy, 2004. G1321.pdf.

Cheney, Richard R., "Remarks to the International Institute for Strategic Studies," Washington, D.C., September 6, 1990.

Chu, David S. C., *Army Military Personnel Posture: Prepared Testimony Before the Senate Committee on Armed Services Personnel Subcommittee,* Washington, D.C.: U.S. Department of Defense, July 18, 2001a. G1283.pdf.

———, *Transcript of Department of Defense News Briefing—Dr. David S. C. Chu, USD (Personnel and Readiness),* Washington, D.C.: U.S. Department of Defense, August 8, 2001b. G1271.pdf.

———, *Report to Congress: Management of Deployments of Individual Members—Personnel Temp (PERSTEMPO),* Washington, D.C.: Office of the Under Secretary of Defense (Personnel and Readiness), October 22, 2002. G1349.pdf.

———, *Response to the Terrorist Attack on the Pentagon: Pentagon Family Assistance Center (PFAC),* after-action report, Washington, D.C.: Office of the Under Secretary of Defense (Personnel and Readiness), March 2003. G1277.pdf.

———, Prepared Statement of the Honorable David S. C. Chu Under Secretary of Defense (Personnel and Readiness), hearing before the House Armed Services Committee, Washington, D.C., U.S. Department of Defense, July 7, 2004a. G1305.pdf.

———, interview with Bernard Rostker, September 12, 2004b.

Chu, David S. C., and Richard Cody, Troop Rotations In Iraq and Afghanistan and Mobilization of the Army's Individual Ready Reserve, hearing before the House Armed Services Committee, Washington, D.C., The Federal News Service, Inc., July 7, 2004.

Clinton, William J., "Ending Discrimination on the Basis of Sexual Orientation in the Armed Forces," memorandum to The Secretary of Defense, Washington, D.C., January 29, 1993.

———, "Ninth Quadrennial Review of Military Compensation," memorandum to The Secretary of Defense, Washington, D.C., July 20, 1999. G1376.pdf.

Cohen, William S., "Chapter 10: Personnel," in *1997 Annual Defense Report*, Washington, D.C.: U.S. Department of Defense, 1997a. G1335.pdf.

———, "Sexual Misconduct," letter to John Ashcroft, Washington, D.C., August 5, 1997b. G0862.pdf.

———, "Secretary Cohen Issues Guidance to Services on Kassebaum Baker Panel Recommendations," news release, March 16, 1998a. G1249.pdf.

———, *The Statement of the Secretary of Defense and the Chairman of the Joint Chiefs of Staff Concerning Military Pay and Retirement*, Washington, D.C.: U.S. Department of Defense, 64698, December 21, 1998b. G1384.pdf.

———, "Chapter 9: Personnel and Quality of Life," in *1999 Annual Defense Report*, Washington, D.C.: U.S. Department of Defense, 1999. G1337.pdf.

———, *Secretary Cohen Statement on Food Stamp Benefits*, Washington, D.C.: U.S. Department of Defense, News Release 19700, April 19, 2000. G1370.pdf.

Conference Committee, *National Defense Authorization Act for Fiscal Year 2000 Conference Report: Section 586—Members Under Burdensome Personnel Tempo*, Washington, D.C.: United States House of Representatives, Report 106301, August 6, 1999. G1341.pdf.

———, *National Defense Authorization Act for Fiscal Year 2004 Conference Report: Section 541—High-Tempo Personnel Management and Allowance*, Washington, D.C.: U.S. House of Representatives, Report 108-354, November 7, 2003. G1346.pdf.

Daggett, Stephen, *Appropriations for FY 2000: Defense*, Washington, D.C.: The Library of Congress, Congressional Research Service, RL30205, October 27, 1999. G1381.pdf.

Deutch, John M., "Senior Panel on Recruiting," memorandum to Secretaries of the Military Department, Washington, D.C., March 23, 1995. G0908.pdf.

Directorate of Compensation, *Report to Congress: Family Subsistence Supplemental Allowance*, Washington, D.C.: Office of the Assistant Secretary of Defense for Force Management Policy (Military Personnel Policy), August 27, 2002. G1373.pdf.

———, *Report to Congress: Family Subsistence Supplemental Allowance*, Washington, D.C.: Office of the Assistant Secretary of Defense for Force Management Policy (Military Personnel Policy), August 2003. G1374.pdf.

Dorn, Edwin, "Assignment of Women in the Military," memorandum to Secretary of Defense, Washington, D.C., August 27, 1993. G0817.pdf.

———, *Recruiting Statistics—April 1994*, information memorandum, Washington, D.C.: Under Secretary of Defense (Force Management Policy), June 19, 1994a. G0798.pdf.

———, *Military Personnel Recruiting Results for the Active Components—Third Quarter of Fiscal Year 1994*, Washington, D.C.: Office of the Under Secretary of Defense (Force Management Policy), August 1994b. G0792.pdf.

———, "Quality of Life (QoL)," action memorandum to Secretary of Defense, Washington, D.C., October 12, 1994c. G0745.pdf.

———, "Quality of Life—A Matter of Definition," memorandum to Director of Defense Program Analysis and Evaluation, Washington, D.C., November 1, 1994d. G0738.pdf.

———, "Recruiting," memorandum to Service Chiefs of Staff, Washington, D.C., May 26, 1995a. G1326.pdf.

———, "Problem-Solving in Senior Readiness Oversight Council—Information," memorandum to Secretary of Defense, Washington, D.C., June 5, 1995b. G1325.pdf.

Editorial Board, "The Army Investigates Rape," *New York Times,* November 10, 1996.

Eisenhower, John, "The Military's Moment of Truth," *New York Times,* November 16, 1996.

Exum, Andrew, "For Some Soldiers The War Ever Ends," *New York Times,* June 2, 2004.

Foster, John, Jr., and Larry D. Welch, *The Defense Science Board Task Force on Human Resources Strategy,* Washington, D.C.: Defense Science Board, Office of the Under Secretary of Defense for Acquisition, Technology, and Logistics, February 2000. G1263.pdf.

Fricker, Ronald D., Jr., *The Effect of Perstempo on Officer Retention in the U.S. Military,* Santa Monica, Calif.: RAND Corporation, MR-1556-OSD, 2002. S0814.pdf.

Fricker, Ronald D., Jr., James R. Hosek, and Mark Totten, *How Does Deployment Affect Retention of Military Personnel?* Santa Monica, Calif.: RAND Corporation, RB-7557-OSD, 2003. S0815.pdf.

Gansler, Jack, "Terms of Reference-Defense Science Board Task Force on Human Resources Strategy," memorandum to Chairman of the Defense Science Board, Washington, D.C., September 15, 1998. G1380.pdf.

Garamone, Jim, "Cohen Meets, Listens to Drum Soldiers," *American Forces Press Service,* September 8, 1998a. G1378.pdf.

———, "DoD Compensation Package Coming, Cohen Tells Sailors," *American Forces Press Service,* November 16, 1998b. G1382.pdf.

———, "DoD Proposes Largest Military Pay Hike in Generation," *American Forces Press Service,* December 21, 1998c. G1383.pdf.

Gebicke, Mark E., *Military Recruiting: More Innovative Approaches Needed,* Washington, D.C.: U.S. General Accounting Office, GAO/NSIAD9522, December 1994. G1429.pdf.

———, *Military Readiness: A Clear Policy Is Needed to Guide Management of Frequently Deployed Units,* Washington, D.C.: U.S. General Accounting Office, GAO/NSIAD96105, April 1996. G1344.pdf.

Gillert, Douglas J., "Readiness Concerns Underscore Cohen Visit to Georgia," *American Force Press Service,* August 21, 1998a. G1377.pdf.

———, "Clinton Briefed on Potential Readiness 'Nose Dive'," *American Force Press Service,* September 17, 1998b. G1379.pdf.

Gilmore, Gerry J., "Rumsfeld: Balkans Still Need Peacekeeping Troops," *Armed Forces Information Service,* June 6, 2001. G1270.pdf.

Gilroy, Curtis L., *Report of the Ninth Quadrennial Review of Military Compensation,* Washington, D.C.: U.S. Department of Defense, March 2002. G1276.pdf.

———, *Report to Congress: Enlistment Eligibility Priorities for Home School and National Guard Youth ChalleNGe GED Credentials-Evaluation of a Pilot Program,* Washington, D.C.: Office of the Under Secretary of Defense (Personnel and Readiness), 2004. G1394.pdf.

Gould, Clifford I., *Small Percentage of Military Families Eligible for Food Stamps,* Washington, D.C.: General Accounting Office, GAO/FPCD8325, April 19, 1983. G1366.pdf.

Holtz-Eakin, Douglas, *An Analysis of the U.S. Military's Ability to Sustain an Occupation of Iraq,* Washington, D.C.: Congressional Budget Office, September 3, 2003. G1282.pdf.

Hosek, James R., and Mark Totten, *Does Perstempo Hurt Retention? The Effect of Long or Hostile Perstempo on Reenlistment,* Santa Monica, Calif.: RAND Corporation, MR-990-OSD, 1998. S0813.pdf.

———, *Serving Away from Home: How Deployments Influence Reenlistment,* Santa Monica, Calif.: RAND Corporation, MR-1594-OSD, 2002. S0816.pdf.

House Armed Services Committee, *National Defense Authorization Act for Fiscal Year 2002 Report: Section 590—Per Diem Allowance for Lengthy or Numerous Deployments,* Washington, D.C.: U.S. House of Representatives, Report 107-194, September 4, 2001. G1345.pdf.

Hulse, Carl, "A New Tactic Against War: Renew Talk About Draft," *New York Times,* February 9, 2003.

Independent Women's Forum, *Improve Effectiveness of Military Basic Training by Separating Men and Women Recruits,* Independent Women's Forum, July 8, 1997. S0875.pdf.

Jaffe, Lorna S., *The Development of the Base Force 1989–1992,* Washington, D.C.: Joint History Office, Office of the Chairman of the Joint Chiefs of Staff, July 1993. G1236.pdf.

Jeremiah, David, *Defense Morale and Quality of Life Study: Improving Morale & Quality of Life,* Washington, D.C.: U.S. Department of Defense, March 1, 2001a. G1244.pdf.

———, *Improving Morale & Quality of Life,* Washington, D.C.: U.S. Department of Defense, May 7, 2001b. G1246.pdf.

———, "Department of Defense Morale and Quality of Life Study," press briefing slides, Washington, D.C., June 13, 2001c. G1245.pdf.

———, "Special Department of Defense News Briefing on Morale and Quality of Life," press briefing transcript, Washington, D.C., June 13, 2001d. G1268.pdf.

Jumper, John P., *The Future Air Force: Remarks by the Chief of Staff of the Air Force at the Air Force Association Air Warfare Symposium,* Washington, D.C., February 13, 2003. G1265.pdf.

Kassebaum-Baker, Nancy, *Report of the Federal Advisory Committee on Gender-Integrated Training and Related Issues to the Secretary of Defense,* Washington, D.C.: U.S. Department of Defense, December 16, 1997. G1247.pdf.

Koopman, Martha E., and Anita U. Hattiangadi, *Do the Services Need a Deployment Pay?* Alexandria, Va.: Center for Naval Analyses, CRM D0004458.A2/Final, December 2001. S0868.pdf.

Kozaryn, Linda D., "'We Hear You,' Cohen Tells Troops," *Armed Force Press Service,* December 28, 1998. G1385.pdf.

———, "Top NCOs Call for Pay, QOL Reforms," *Armed Force Press Service,* June 26, 2000. G1386.pdf.

Laird, Melvin R., "25th Anniversary of the All-Volunteer Service," memorandum to Secretary of Defense, Washington, D.C., October 6, 1995. G0708.pdf.

Lancaster, Anita R., *Recruitment Advertising Review: Study Overview and Topline Findings: Briefing for the National Academy of Sciences,* Washington, D.C.: Defense Manpower Data Center, January 28, 2000. G1331.pdf.

Larson, Eric V., David T. Orletsky, and Kristin Leuschner, *Defense Planning in a Decade of Change: Lessons from the Base Force, Bottom-Up Review, and Quadrennial Defense Review,* Santa Monica, Calif.: RAND Corporation, MR-1387-AF, 2001. S0741.pdf.

Lewis, Leslie, C. Robert. Roll, Jr., and John D. Mayer, *Assessing the Structure and Mix of Future Active and Reserve Forces: Assessment of Policies and Practices for Implementing the Total Force Policy,* Santa Monica, Calif.: RAND Corporation, MR-133-OSD, 1992. S0888.pdf.

Loeb, Vernon, "Rumsfeld Apologizes for Remarks on Draftees," *Washington Post,* January 22, 2003, pp. A1, A4.

———, "Army Reserve Chief Fears Retention Crisis; Helmly Faults Open-Ended Deployments, Shortages of Equipment in Iraq War," *Washington Post,* January 21, 2004, p. A4.

Marsh, John O., Jr., *Report of the Defense Science Board Task Force on Quality of Life,* Washington, D.C.: Office of the Under Secretary of Defense for Acquisition and Technology, October 1995. G1230.pdf.

McCain, John, *McCain: Defense Bill Ignores 12,000 Military on Food Stamps, Renews Goldwater Range,* Washington, D.C.: Office of Senator John McCain, September 23, 1999. G1365.pdf.

———, *McCain to Offer Amendment Ending 'Food Stamp Army',* Washington, D.C.: U.S. Senate, April 5, 2000. G1368.pdf.

McIntosh, Robert A., *Position Paper on Rebalancing Forces,* Washington, D.C.: Reserve Officers Association of the United States, July 2003. S0807.pdf.

Moniz, David, and Tom Squitieri, "Experts Seek Roots of Military's Racial Makeup," *USA Today,* January 21, 2003a, p. 6A.

———, "Front-Line Troops Disproportionately White, Not Black," *USA Today,* January 21, 2003b, p. 1A.

Moskos, Charles C., Jr., *The American Soldier after the Cold War: Towards a Post-Modern Military?* Washington, D.C.: United States Army Research Institute for the Behavioral and Social Sciences, October 1998. S0199.pdf.

Myers, Steven Lee, "Bush Seeks $5.7 Billion Increase For Military Salaries and Benefits," *Washington Post,* February 12, 2001.

New York Times Editorial Staff, *Overextended Military Reserves,* New York: The New York Times, April 6, 2003.

Nunn, Sam, Defense Budget Blanks, hearing before the Senate, 101st Cong., 2nd Sess., Washington, D.C., 32, March 22, 1990. G1316.pdf.

O'Hanlon, Michael, "Opinion: Nobody Wants a Draft, but What If We Need One?" *Los Angeles Times,* October 13, 2004a.

———, "The Need to Increase the Size of the Deployable Army," *Parameters: The U.S. Army War College Quarterly,* Vol. XXXIV, No. 3, Autumn 2004b. S0833.pdf.

OASD[PA]—*See* Office of the Assistant Secretary of Defense for Public Affairs.

ODASD[PSF&E]—*See* Office of the Deputy Assistant Secretary of Defense for Personnel Support, Families, and Education.

Office of the Assistant Secretary of Defense for Public Affairs, "Department of Defense Authorizes Stop Loss," press release, Washington, D.C., September 24, 2001. G1286.pdf.

———, "Secretary of Defense Approves Iraq Troop Deployment," press release Washington, D.C., May 4, 2004a. G1284.pdf.

———, "National Guard and Reserve Mobilized as of May 5, 2004," press release, Washington, D.C., May 5, 2004b. G1285.pdf.

Office of the Assistant Secretary of Defense for Reserve Affairs, *Review of Reserve Component Contributions to National Defense,* Washington, D.C., December 20, 2002. G1310.pdf.

Office of the Deputy Assistant Secretary of Defense for Personnel Support, Families, and Education, Quality of Life Office, *Quality of Life—Issues/Accomplishments/Initiatives: Department of Defense Fact Sheet,* Washington, D.C.: U.S. Department of Defense, April 19, 1996. G0712.pdf.

Office of the Under Secretary of Defense for Personnel and Readiness, *Backup Book: Senior Panel on Recruiting—March 13, 1995,* Washington, D.C.: U.S. Department of Defense, March 13, 1995a. G1324.pdf.

———, *Talking Points: Senior Panel on Recruiting—March 13, 1995,* Washington, D.C.: U.S. Department of Defense, March 13, 1995b. G1323.pdf.

———, *Talking Points and Backup Book: Senior Panel on Recruiting—September 5, 1995,* Washington, D.C.: U.S. Department of Defense, September 5, 1995c. G1327.pdf.

Orvis, Bruce R., Narayan Sasty, and Laurie L. McDonald, *Military Recruiting Outlook: Recent Trends in Enlistment Propensity and Conversion of Potential Enlisted Supply,* Santa Monica, Calif.: RAND Corporation, MR-677-A/OSD, 1996. S0745.pdf.

OUSD[P&R]—*See* Office of the Under Secretary of Defense for Personnel and Readiness.

Pang, Fred, "1994 Youth Attitude Tracking Study (YATS)," information memorandum to Deputy Secretary of Defense, Washington, D.C., February 27, 1995. G0880.pdf.

———, "Status Report on Quality of Life Initiatives," memorandum to Secretary of Defense, Washington, D.C., September 25, 1995b. G0732.pdf.

———, *Recruiter Quality of Life Initiatives: Joint Recruiting Support Study Group,* Washington, D.C.: Office of the Assistant Secretary of Defense (Force Management Policy), March 30, 1996a. G0725.pdf.

————, "Quality of Life Executive Committee Minutes of the February 28, 1996 Meeting," memorandum to Members of the Defense Quality of Life Executive Committee, Washington, D.C., June 7, 1996b. G0711.pdf.

Pleeter, Saul, *The Food Stamp Program and the Military,* Washington, D.C.: Directorate of Compensation Military Manpower and Personnel Policy, February 21, 1992. G1367.pdf.

————, interview with Bernard Rostker, November 10, 2004.

Priest, Dana, "Army Finds Wide Abuse of Women; Panel Report Faults Leaders' Commitment," *Washington Post,* September 12, 1997a, p. A1.

————, "Civilian Committee on Military Favors Separate Female Training; Need to Bolster Cohesion, Discipline Cited," *Washington Post,* December 16, 1997b, p. A1.

————, "Defense Chief Opposes Separating Sexes in Basic Training," *Washington Post,* June 9, 1998, p. A9.

————, *The Mission: Waging War and Keeping Peace With America's Military,* New York: W.W. Norton & Company, 2004.

Pullen, Randy, *Keep the Reserves in the Fight,* OPED, Carlisle, Pa.: Strategic Studies Institute, U.S. Army War College, September 2003. S0806.pdf.

Rangel, Charles B., "Bring Back the Draft," *New York Times,* December 31, 2002. S0591.pdf.

Rhem, Kathleen T., "Defense Officials Announce Plan to Replace Food Stamps," *American Forces Press Service,* July 28, 2000a. G1369.pdf.

————, "Troops on Food Stamps May Get Special Allowance," *American Forces Press Service,* October 31, 2000b. G1371.pdf.

Ricks, Thomas E., and Vernon Loeb, "Unrivaled Military Feels Strains of Unending War: For U.S. Forces, a Technological Revolution and a Constant Call to Do More," *Washington Post,* February 16, 2003, p. A1.

Rostker, Bernard D., Testimony on Nominations, hearing before the Senate Armed Services Committee, Washington, D.C.: FDCHeMedia, Inc., April 11, 2000.

————, "Enlisted Pay—Interim Report of the 9th Quadrennial Review of Military Compensation (QRMC) Coordination," memorandum to Commandant U.S. Coast Guard, Assistant Secretaries of the Military Department (M&RA), Washington, D.C., January 18, 2001. G1266.pdf.

Rostker, Bernard D., Scott Allen Harris, et al., *Sexual Orientation and U.S. Military Personnel Policy, Options and Assessment,* Santa Monica, Calif.: RAND Corporation, MR-323-OSD, 1993. S0743.pdf.

Rumsfeld, Donald H., *Department of Defense News Briefing—Secretary Rumsfeld and Gen. Myers,* Washington, D.C.: U.S. Department of Defense, January 7, 2003a. G1232.pdf.

————, *Department of Defense News Briefing—Secretary Rumsfeld and General Myers,* Washington, D.C.: U.S. Department of Defense, January 7, 2003b. G1279.pdf.

————, "Rebalancing Forces," memorandum to Secretaries of the Military Departments, Chairman of the Joint Chiefs of Staff and Under Secretaries of Defense, Washington, D.C., July 9, 2003c. G1309.pdf.

————, "Forward," in Barbara A. Bicksler, Curtis L. Gilroy and John T. Warner, eds., *The All-Volunteer Force: Thirty Years of Service,* Washington, D.C.: Brassey's, Inc., 2004.

Ryan, Michael C., *Military Readiness, Operations Tempo (OPTEMPO) and Personnel Tempo (PERSTEMPO): Are U.S. Forces Doing Too Much?* Washington, D.C.: The Library of Congress, Congressional Research Service, 98-41 F, January 14, 1998. G1311.pdf.

Sackett, Paul R., and Anne S. Mavor, eds., *Attitudes, Aptitudes, and Aspirations of American Youths: Implications for Military Recruiting,* Washington, D.C.: The National Academies Press, 2004a. S0827.pdf.

————, eds., *Evaluating Military Advertising and Recruiting: Theory and Methodology,* Washington, D.C.: The National Academies Press, 2004b. S0828.pdf.

Schmitt, Eric, "Army Broadens Its Inquiry of Sex Abuse Accusations," *New York Times,* November 23, 1996a.

————, "Role of Women in the Military Is Again Bringing Debate," *New York Times,* December 29, 1996b.

————, "Army Extending Service for G.I.s Due in War Zone," *New York Times,* June 3, 2004.

Sellman, W. S., "Senior Panel on Recruiting (Talking Points)," action memorandum to Deputy Secretary of Defense, Washington, D.C., April 21, 1994. G0742.pdf.

————, *Senior Panel on Recruiting READ AHEAD,* Washington, D.C.: Office of the Under Secretary of Defense (Personnel and Readiness), March 7, 1997. G1347.pdf.

Senate Armed Services Committee, *National Defense Authorization Act for Fiscal Year 2000 Report: Section 672—Members Under Burdensome PERSTEMPO,* Washington, D.C.: United States Senate, Report 10650, May 17, 1999. G1340.pdf.

Serafino, Nina M., *Peacekeeping: Issues of U.S. Military Involvement,* Washington, D.C.: The Library of Congress, Congressional Research Service, IB940491, August 6, 2003.

Spayd, Liz, and Thomas E. Ricks, "Rotation to Cut U.S. Presence; Reservists to Assume Greater Share of Duties in Iraq," *Washington Post,* January 18, 2004, p. A1.

Spence, Floyd D., *Military Readiness 1997: Rhetoric and Reality,* Washington, D.C.: House Committee on National Security, April 9, 1997. G1315.pdf.

Staff of the Directorate for Accession Policy, *Education Enlistment Standards: Recruiting Equity for GED Certificates,* Washington, D.C.: Office of the Assistant Secretary of Defense (Force Management Policy), April 1996. P0011.pdf.

Sticha, Paul J., Robert Sadacca, Ani S. DiFazio, C. Mazie Knerr, Paul F. Hogan, and Marisa Diana, *Personnel Tempo: Definition, Measurement, and Effects on Retention, Readiness, and Quality of Life,* Washington, D.C.: United States Army Research Institute for the Behavioral and Social Sciences, ARI Contractor Report 9904, September 1999. S0858.pdf.

Tangredi, Sam J., *All Possible Wars? Towards a Consensus View of the Future Security Environment, 2001–2025,* Washington, D.C.: Institute for National Strategic Studies, National Defense University, McNair Paper 63. G1235.pdf.

Titus, James R. W., and Allan W. Howey, *The Air Expeditionary Force in Perspective,* Montgomery, Ala.: Airpower Research Institute, January 15, 1999. G1258.pdf.

Under Secretary of Defense for Force Management Policy and W. J. Carr, "Quality of Life," information memorandum to Deputy Secretary of Defense, Washington, D.C., September 22, 1994. G0705.pdf.

Under Secretary of Defense for Force Management Policy, Al Conte, and Bill Carr, "Quality of Life," action memorandum to Secretary of Defense and Deputy Secretary of Defense, Washington, D.C., October 12, 1994. G0699.pdf.

U.S. Army, Public Affairs, "Army Announces Changes in 12-Month, Skill-Based Stop Loss," press release, May 29, 2003a. G1288.pdf.

———, "Army Announces Changes in Stop Loss," press release, Washington, D.C., May 29, 2003b. G1287.pdf.

———, "Army Announces Implementation of the Active Army Unit Stop Loss/Stop Movement Program," press release, November 17, 2003c. G1289.pdf.

———, "Army Announces Changes to the Active Army Unit Stop Loss/Stop Movement Program," press release, Washington, D.C., June 2, 2004. G1290.pdf.

USD[FMP]—See Under Secretary of Defense for Force Management Policy

Wald, Matthew L., "2 Are Charged with Rapes at an Army Training Center," *New York Times,* November 8, 1996.

Weinberger, Caspar W., "Dodgy Drafters," *Wall Street Journal,* January 10, 2003.

Weiner, Tim, "One Sergeant Pleads Guilty as Army Widens Sex Inquiry," *New York Times,* November 13, 1996.

Werschkul, Ben, Matthew Ericson, and Tom Torok, "Interactive Graph: A Look at 1000 Who Died," *New York Times,* September 17, 2004.

White, John P., "FY 1997–98 Recruiting," memorandum to Secretary of Army, Washington, D.C., November 21, 1996. G0791.pdf.

Wilson, Michael J., James B Greenlees, Tracey Hagerty, Cynthia v. Helba, D. Wayne Hintze, and Jerome D. Lehnus, *Youth Attitude Tracking Study: 1999 Propensity and Advertising Report,* Arlington, Va.: Defense Manpower Data Center, Report No. 2000-019, June 14, 2000. G1332.pdf.

Winkler, John D., *Rebalancing Forces: Easing the Stress on the Guard and Reserves,* Washington, D.C.: Office of the Deputy Assistant Secretary of Defense for Reserve Affairs (RT&M), January 15, 2004. G1260.pdf.

Zinni, Anthony C., "A Commander Reflects," *Proceedings: The U.S. Naval Institute,* Vol. 126, No. 7, July 2000, pp. 34–37. S0739.pdf.

CHAPTER EIGHTEEN

Reaping What You Sow: Analytic Studies of the Clinton and Bush Years (1992–2004)

The successes of military personnel management over the last generation offer four potential explanations for success:

- First, in each area a clear, measurable set of objectives was set.
- Second, military personnel outcomes were seen to be the product of a system . . .
- Third, quantitative analysis was employed widely and aggressively to try to understand the relationship between causes and effects. . . .
- Fourth, policymakers came to understand early that incentives— bonuses, compensation, promotion opportunity, and the like— rather than "rules and regulations" would be the main instruments to achieve the outcomes they desired. . . .

—David S. C. Chu and John P. White[1]

Introduction

Since 1964, personnel managers have used research to help develop, implement, and sustain the all-volunteer force. The research has been a balance of empirical studies and basic research on the very nature of decisionmaking as young men and women decide to join or not to join the military and as serving members decide to stay or leave. The research has been policy-relevant and has drawn on a *spectrum* of behavioral models and empirical techniques, often extending theory and method in innovative ways. The design of field experiments of enlistment incentives was essential. The mixture of different disciplines—psychology, social psychology, sociology, and economics—produced a comprehensive and credible assessment of alternative policies.

The research of the 1960s and early 1970s, both theoretical modeling and empirical studies, reassured decisionmakers that an all-volunteer force might be possible at

---

[1] Ensuring Quality People in Defense in Chu and White (2001).

acceptable budget outlays. That of the late 1970s helped the services develop programs to end their reliance on the draft. In the 1980s, carefully designed experiments helped hone such tools as education benefits and recruiting advertising. Since the end of the Cold War, personnel research has helped managers make the adjustments that were needed to transition the larger post–Cold War military to a smaller, more-agile and more-engaged force. There is probably no better example of this than the changes in compensation policy in the late 1990s and the work of the 9th Quadrennial Review of Military Compensation (QRMC), which came in time to help meet the challenge of sustained operations in a hostile Iraq.[2]

Reforming Military Compensation in the Post–Cold War Era: The 9th QRMC

By law, since 1967, the President must submit to Congress a review of military compensation every four years. The history of these quadrennial reviews, however, has been very spotty. Some have focused narrowly on parts of the compensation system; the 6th QMRC, for instance, focused on reserve affairs and resulted in significant changes to the system of reserve compensation and passage of the Reserve Officers Personnel Act. Some have ambitiously recommended significant reform to one or more parts of the military personnel system; the 4th QRMC, for instance, reflected the recommendations of the 1978 President's Commission on Military Compensation. Congress never acted on those recommendations. The ill-fated 8th QRMC set out to explore "modern principles" of personnel management but succeeded in drawing nearly universal negative reviews.

Some QRMCs took on controversial issues, such as the 7th QRMC's attempt to reform the basic pay table by giving larger pay increases for promotions than for additional years of service. While it might seem that shifting the pay table from one favoring longevity to one favoring promotions would not be significant, in fact it was. The Air Force—which had higher retention, promoted more slowly, and relied on longevity step increases to keep compensation high for its personnel—was opposed to the change. The Navy—which had lower retention, promoted more quickly, and wanted a new pay table to reward its sailors for the jobs they were doing and to encourage flagging retention—wanted the pay tables changed. When the 7th QRMC made its report in 1992, without agreement from all the services, reform was dead or at least seemed dead. But more was to come.

---

[2] In 2005, Secretary Rumsfeld decided before moving forward with the 10th QRMC, which by law should have started work 2003, that he would establish a blue ribbon panel to assist and advise him and Dr. Chu

> on matters pertaining to military compensation. More specifically, the Committee shall identify approaches to balance military pay and benefits in sustaining recruitment and retention of high-quality people, as well as a cost-effective and ready military force. (Secretary of Defense, 2005)

To facilitate the work of the Committee, the Office of the Under Secretary of Defense for Personnel and Readiness also published an extensive reference on military compensation (Pirie, 1980).

The Assessment of the TRIAD Pay Reforms of FY 2000

As so often happens with research and analysis, the initial effects are not always the final ones. In 1998, facing a rising number of complaints about the inadequacies of compensation from noncommissioned and midlevel officers, Secretary of Defense William Cohen wanted to focus his response on where he thought the problem was most critical. The work of the 7th QRMC got a new look, and Cohen settled on a series of changes that very much reflected the thinking of the earlier study group. The FY 2000 budget included targeted pay raises and greater rewards for performance. It increased bonus ceilings and special pays, especially for aviators, and adjusted the REDUX retirement program. In late 1998, Secretary Cohen told the press that this would "enable us to do a better job of rewarding performance, compensating people for their skills, education and experience and encouraging them to continue their military service. We are also reforming the pay table to make raises for promotion bigger than those for longevity" (Cohen, 1998). For example, under the old pay table, officers get "only 37 percent of raises over a career coming from promotions and the rest through longevity," Cohen noted, saying that the "preponderance" of the new target raises would be "based on merit, performance, promotion versus just simply being in the service for long periods of time" (Garamone, 1998).[3]

A provision of the FY 2000 authorization act required DoD to provide Congress a yearly assessment of TRIAD reforms. OSD asked RAND to prepare the initial report. RAND based the report on the "empirical estimates of behavioral response from previous studies" and focused on "high-quality recruits, reenlistment of junior and early midcareer enlisted members, and the continuation of junior and early midcareer officers" (Asch, Arkes et al., 2001, p. xiii). The report, *Military Recruiting and Retention After the Fiscal Year 2000 Military Pay Legislation,* is a good example of how decades of research and a sophisticated understanding of the factors that affect recruiting and retention pay off in developing programs to address problems before they become critical. The following excerpt from that report describes the recruiting difficulties of the late 1990s and the actions taken to address them (Asch, Arkes et al., 2001, p. xiv); the citations are additions to point out some of the research that informed the analysis:

> From the mid-1990s onward, a set of supply-side factors made recruiting increasingly difficult. First, entry-level military pay declined relative to civilian pay (see Hosek et al., 1994). Second, the unemployment rate declined to record lows, indicating that job opportunities were excellent (see Hosek and Sharp, 2001). Third, the college attendance rate had risen substantially in the 1980s and continued to rise in the 1990s, though much more slowly. The high college attendance rate

---

[3] Joint Chiefs Chairman Henry H. Shelton also noted that

the revision in pay tables would reward the "fast burners." If you take one of our great staff sergeants [E-6] that has eight years of service, you'll find that one of his subordinates, who may be a sergeant, an E-5 pay grade, who has 14 years of service, makes as much or more than he does. (Garamone, 1998)

This would change under the new pay table.

reduced the size of the traditional high-quality recruiting market (see Kilburn and Asch, 2003). Fourth, family incomes rose, making it easier to support a son or daughter's job search or college education.

There were a number of demand-side responses to the supply-side trends. By the late 1990s, the services were increasing their advertising (see Dertouzos and Garber, 2003), enlistment bonuses (see Hansen, 2000), and college fund awards (see Asch, Fair, and Kilburn, 2000) . . . and adding recruiters (see Dertouzos, 1985).

Using a model John Warner and colleagues developed for the Defense Manpower Data Center (Warner et al., 2001), the RAND team "found that TRIAD increased high-quality contracts in FY00 and FY01 above what they would have been under an ordinary military pay increase" (Asch, Arkes et al., 2001, p. 32). The researchers were less sanguine, however, about retention "due to uncertainty about the responsiveness of reenlistment to pay and the effective size of the pay increase" (Asch, Arkes et al., 2001, p. 34). In fact, the Senior Enlisted Advisors made that point clear at a meeting in late June 2000.

On June 22, 2000, at the First Annual Senior Enlisted Advisors Forum, a spokesperson for the group addressed Secretary Cohen:

> When I first came in the Army 29 years ago, it was very common to see an NCO with anywhere from a seventh to ninth-grade education. Today most NCOs have some college or have a college education. (quoted in Kozaryn, 1998)

Secretary Cohen told the forum that the 9th QRMC would be looking at just that situation.

The Ninth Quadrennial Review of Military Compensation

The 9th QRMC was one of the more productive QRMCs. The changes it recommended were implemented and, by at least one account, are an important reason military retention has remained high in the face of extended deployments and combat casualties in the war in Iraq.[4]

The 9th QRMC has been a success for a number of reasons. First, there was continuing demand for reform, and the success of the FY 2000 program had set the stage. Second, unlike several previous QRMCs, this review did not get bogged down with arguments about the limitations of the current pay and allowance system and the benefits of a salary system. The study team accepted the current system and, working within its bounds, tried to make improvements. The theme of its work, *balance* and *flexibility*, was just what the times demanded. The team understood that the

> first priority is to "get basic pay right." It is the foundation of the compensation system and the basis for maintaining *balance*. Once basic pay is set, special and

---

[4] This view was expressed by Bill Carr (2004), the Acting Deputy Under Secretary of Defense for Military Personnel Policy.

incentive pays and bonuses provide needed *flexibility* in creating pay differentials to attract and retain personnel in particular career fields. (Gilroy, 2002, p. xxxiii, emphasis in original)

Third, the QRMC's assessment of the current system and recommendations for change were built on a foundation of 30 years of research and drew on the experience of researchers who had spent most of their professional careers in the manpower and personnel research business. The study's executive director, Curtis Gilroy, had previously headed the economic analysis group at the Army Research Institute; had worked in the areas of recruiting, retention, compensation, and force management; and understood the importance of policy-relevant research. He drew from the federally funded research and development centers that have supported the all-volunteer force for almost thirty years. The RAND Corporation, the Institute for Defense Analyses (IDA), and the Center for Naval Analyses (CNA) were fully engaged, as were a small number of private-sector researchers who have developed expertise over many years. The QRMC report provided a roadmap of the all-volunteer force as it researched its 30th anniversary and a blueprint for the future. Table 18.1 summarizes the topics the 9th QRMC's report covered and the studies that informed its assessments and recommendations.

Table 18.1
Research the 9th QRMC Cited

QRMC Section	Research	Supporting Organization
The Need for Quality Personnel—The Link Between Quality & Performance	Curtis L. Gilroy and W. S. Sellman, "Recruiting and Sustaining a Quality Army: A Review of the Evidence," in Robert L. Phillips and Maxwell R. Thurman, eds. *Future Soldiers and the Quality Imperative: The Army 2010 Conference* (1995).	OSD
	Bruce R. Orvis, Michael T. Childress, and J. Michael Polich, *Effect of Personnel Quality on the Performance of Patriot Air Defense System Operators* (1992).	RAND
	John D. Winkler, Judith C. Fernandez, and J. Michael Polich, *Effect of Aptitude on the Performance of Army Communications Operators* (1992).	RAND
	Barry L. Scribner, D. Alton Smith, Robert H. Baldwin, and Robert L. Phillips, *Are Smart Tankers Better? AFQT and Military Productivity* (1986).	West Point
	Stanley Horowitz and Alan Sherman, *A Direct Measure of the Relationship Between Human Capital and Productivity* (1980).	CNA
	Aline O. Quester, *Enlisted Crew Quality and Ship Material Readiness* (1989).	CNA

Table 18.1—continued

QRMC Section	Research	Supporting Organization
The Military Personnel System and Compensation	Beth J. Asch and John T. Warner, *A Theory of Military Compensation and Personnel Policy* (1994b).	RAND
	Beth J. Asch and John T. Warner, *A Policy Analysis of Alternative Military Retirement Systems* (1994a).	RAND
	Beth J. Asch, Richard Johnson, and John T. Warner, *Reforming the Military Retirement System* (1998).	RAND
	James R. Hosek and Jennifer Sharp, *Keeping Military Pay Competitive: The Outlook for Civilian Wages and Its Consequences* (2001).	RAND
The Military Personnel System and Compensation	James R. Hosek, Christine E. Peterson, and Joanna Z. Heilbrunn, *Military Pay Gaps and Caps* (1994).	RAND
	Richard L. Fernandez, *What Does The Military "Pay Gap" Mean?* (1999).	Congressional Budget Office
	Thomas A. Husted and Michael L. Hansen, *Standard of Living of Enlisted Personnel* (2001a).	CNA
	Aline O. Quester and Gary Lee, *Senior Enlisted Personnel: Do We Need Another Grade?* (2001).	CNA
	Beth J. Asch, James R. Hosek, and Craig W. Martin, *A Look at Cash Compensation for Active Duty Military Personnel* (2002).	RAND
	Richard L. Fernandez, *The Warrant Office Rank: Adding Flexibility to Military Personnel Management* (2002).	Congressional Budget Office
Creating Differentials in Military Pay	Heidi L. Golding and Susan C. McArver, *Navy Sea Pay: History and Recent Initiatives* (2001).	CNA
	Martha E. Koopman and Anita U. Hattiangadi, *Do the Services Need a Deployment Pay?* (2001).	CNA
	John T. Warner and Beth J. Asch, *The Economics of Military Manpower*, in Keith Hartley and Todd Sandler, eds., *Handbook of Defense Economics* (1995).	RAND
	John T. Warner, Curtis J. Simon, Deborah M. Payne, and J. Michael Jones, *Enlistment Supply in the 1990s: A Study of the Navy College Fund and Other Enlistment Incentive Programs* (2001).	DMDC
	Matthew S. Goldberg, *A Survey of Enlisted Retention: Models and Findings* (2001).	CNA
	Carol S. Moore, Heidi L.W. Golding, and Henry S. Griffis, *Manpower and Personnel IWAR 2000: Aging the Force* (2001).	CNA

Table 18.1—continued

QRMC Section	Research	Supporting Organization
Special Pays		
Deployment Pay	James R. Hosek and Mark Totten, *Does Perstempo Hurt Retention?—The Effect of Long or Hostile Perstempo on Reenlistment* (1998).	RAND
	Ronald D. Fricker, Jr., *The Effect of Perstempo on Officer Retention in the U.S. Military* (2002).	RAND
Thrift Savings Plan	Thomas A. Husted and Michael L. Hansen, *Thrift Savings Plans: Effect on Savings and Tax Revenues* (2000b).	CNA
Financing Well-Being	James R. Hosek, Beth Asch, C. Christine Fair, Craig Martin, and Michael Mattock, *Married to the Military: The Employment and Earnings of Military Wives Compared to Civilian Wives* (2002).	RAND

A Theory of Compensation

Implicit in the deliberation of each of the QRMCs is a proverbial question: "What is the purpose of compensation?" While it seems that the answer should be very straightforward, disagreements over it scuttled the 4th QRMC, with one faction arguing that the purpose was to attract and retain the required personnel and another looking for the elusive "X factor" to reward people for taking on the burdens of military service. By the time of the 9th QRMC, it was generally understood that the "military compensation system . . . [enables] us to recruit and retain enough dedicated men and women to achieve the highest quality uniformed forces in the Nation's history" (Clinton, 1999). The QRMC, however, went beyond "recruit and retain" and recognized that the function of the compensation system was to attract, retain, motivate, and separate personnel (Gilroy, 2002, p xxii). This had already become clear in 1994 with the publication of *A Theory of Military Compensation and Personnel Policy* by Beth Asch and John Warner. The purpose of their work was to

> develop a unified model that will permit an analysis of all the various issues relating to the military compensation system. To do so, we marry recent advances in the modeling of military compensation and retention with the emerging economic literature on compensation and incentives in large, hierarchical organizations. The latter literature examines how large organizations use compensation and other personnel policies to motivate work effort and induce the proper *ability-sorting* (i.e., the motivation of high-quality personnel to stay and seek higher ranks) with the organization. (Asch and Warner, 1994b, p. xiv, emphasis in the original)

They noted that this allowed them to

> address the traditional macroeconomic issue of the force-structure and -size implications of alternative military pay and personnel policies . . . [and] the microeconomic

issues of effort supply and ability-sorting that heretofore have been ignored. (Asch and Warner, 1994b, p. xiv)

Asch and Warner provided, for the first time, a consistent rationale—or, as they called it, a "unified framework"—not only for the level of military compensation that would allow the services to attract and retain the required personnel but also for the internal structure of the basic pay table, the formal rules codified in the Defense Officer Personnel Management Act, and the less-formal rules that govern the management of enlisted personnel.

Asch and Warner modeled the flow of personnel through the closed hierarchical military system and the ability of the hierarchy to produce the *work effort* that provides the output of the organization. In their model, the individual service member is still the critical decisionmaker, basing decisions about whether to stay or go and how much effort to put out on the available incentives and rewards. To model the individual's decision process, they used the dynamic program framework pioneered by Gotz and McCall (1984), adding to it the work-effort decision service members make.[5] Given that the military does not allow lateral entry, Asch and Warner found that

> individuals in the [military] organization are valuable for what they produce in their current grades and for what they are capable of producing in higher grades in the future. The [military] organization must access, train, and retain a large enough pool of workers in the lower ranks to maintain the flow of workers necessary to staff the upper ranks. (Asch and Warner, 1994b, p. 116)

They demonstrated the essential importance of the kind of system rules incorporated into Defense Officer Personnel Management Act and the rationale for the "up-or-out" system, observing, for example, that the military organization "must generate some turnover at the higher levels, even among qualified personnel, to maintain effort and retention incentives at the lower levels " (Asch and Warner, 1994b, p. 116). They found that, first,

> in a hierarchical system, pay spreads need to rise with rank to provide personnel with continuing incentives to work hard and seek promotion, and to induce the

---

[5] While Asch and Warner owe a debt to Gotz and McCall for including individual heterogeneity in the form of a distribution of taste for military service, they also owe a debt to Sherwin Rosen for his work on tournament models of compensation (Rosen, 1986), (Rosen, 1992). In their report, Asch and Warner described the military promotion system as a tournament. The tournament model shows how the incentive structure can induce the most-able workers to seek high-ranking positions, thereby creating the greatest value for the firm. Similarly, their model suggests that the military compensation structure should be capable of attracting high-quality individuals and eventually sorting the most capable into the highest ranking positions. Asch and Warner track this sorting via simulation, looking at the retained distribution of ability by grade.

Their work also built on Edward Lazear's development of personnel economics (Lazear, 1995) and his research into why firms have a mandatory retirement age (Lazear, 1979). Rosen and Lazear worked together at Chicago before Lazear went to Stanford (Lazear and Rosen, 1981). Beth Asch was a student of each while at Chicago. This is an example of how outstanding policy work builds on developments in pure theory.

most able personnel to stay. Second, intragrade pay should to some extent be contingent upon performance and not be provided lockstep with seniority. Third, up-or-out rules are necessary to induce the separation of unpromotable personnel when pay is set administratively and one-on-one bargaining is costly. Fourth, although there is no unique theoretical role for retired pay, it may be offered for a number of reasons: to provide old-age insurance, encourage effort and retention of nonvested personnel, encourage the voluntary separation of senior personnel, and reduce *ex post* regret arising from earning losses individuals may suffer when transitioning to other employment rather than full retirement. (Asch and Warner, 1994b, p. xv, italics in the original)

Their assessment of the military basic pay table helped the 9th QRMC understand where changes needed to be made:

The current active-duty pay table is very "flat"; that is, the pay system is not skewed to any great extent: Compared with private-sector pay, entry pay is fairly high, but the rank differentials are not large and they do not increase much with rank, certainly not enough to offset declining probabilities of promotion. Intergrade pay rises with length of service (YOS, years of service), and there are a number of instances in which lower-ranking personnel with more longevity are paid more than higher-ranking personnel with less. Furthermore, the intragrade increases are automatic and not based on performance. All in all, the active-duty pay system appears more aimed at attracting and retaining personnel than at providing them with effective incentives to work hard and seek advancement. (Asch and Warner, 1994b, pp. xv–xvi)

The Environment of 2000

As the 9th QRMC set to work in fall 1999, it faced a number of "realities." DoD had submitted the TRIAD pay reform package to Congress. While that package had not yet been acted on, major changes had already been made to the basic pay tables. There was still a sense among the senior enlisted advisors that additional changes were needed. Among the OSD staff there was also a sense that the TRAID reforms had been somewhat *ad hoc* and that a more systematic look was needed. Indeed, the charter of the 9th QRMC was to "determine whether the structure and level of military compensation remains adequate to meet the manning requirements of the military" (Asch, Hosek, and Warner, 2001, p. v). RAND was asked to look at the question and prepare a briefing that would help focus the work of the QRMC and provide a rationale for its work so soon after the TRIAD was submitted, a rationale that could not be used to sidetrack the TRIAD as it moved through the legislative process.

The RAND briefing highlighted trends that would affect recruiting and retention. First, was the "dramatic rise in college attendance." The problem they laid out was that, in 1980, "only about 48 percent of high school seniors enrolled in a college," compared to "almost 70 percent" today. "Unless the services can penetrate the market for college-bound youths," RAND reported, the recruiting pool would be "limited to about 3 of every 10 youth. In 1980, the services could recruit from 5 of every 10 youths without resorting to recruitment of college-bound youth" (Asch, Hosek, and Warner, 2001, p. 5).

Second, the briefing noted that "[t]he traditional image of the enlisted force is one of high school graduates, but this depiction has become less and less accurate. . . . In the 1999 survey, 21 percent of E-8s and 27 percent of E-9s reported having either a college degree or an advanced degree" (Asch, Hosek, and Warner, 2001, p. 8).

Third, "[e]ducational attainment is strongly related to Armed Forces Qualifications Test (AFQT) scores" and "[h]igh-scoring personnel pay off in terms of higher performance" (Asch, Hosek, and Warner, 2001, pp. 10–11).

Fourth, a life-cycle comparison of military and civilian earning shows that, in FY 2000, enlisted regular military compensation compared "favorably" with the earnings of high-school graduates but "less favorably" with the earnings of those with some college education. Relative to civilians with some college, enlisted pay growth was "slower in mid-career even with the FY 01–FY 05 reforms" (Asch, Hosek, and Warner, 2001, pp. 19–22).

Fifth, despite the rising value of an enlisted career, "attracting those with some college may prove difficult" to recruit (Asch, Hosek, and Warner, 2001, p. 27).

Sixth, recruiting was problematic—recruiting requirements were increasing, the services were struggling to make accession goals, and recruit quality was down, with the percentage of high-quality recruits dropping from a high in 1992 of 74.4 percent to a 1999 level of 59.1 percent (Asch, Hosek, and Warner, 2001, pp. 30–34).

Seventh, first-term retention for the Army and Air Force was falling, and with the small cohorts of the early 1990s for the Air Force and Navy, a future large increase in recruiting would be needed to maintain end strength (Asch, Hosek, and Warner, 2001, p. 38).

Eighth, to react to these "realities," RAND recommended a graduated pay raise. Such a pay raise would bolster "incentives to continue in service after obtaining some college," would "generally cost less because only a subset of personnel would receive more money," and would

> address inequities associated with the . . . [TRIAD] target pay raise, critics of which argued that enlisted non-commissioned officers in their mid-career received lower raises than junior commissioned officers, even though the duties of NCOs have entailed more responsibilities in recent years. (Asch, Hosek, and Warner, 2001, p. 45)

Following the theory of compensation discussed earlier, the RAND team suggested that pay raises be graduated throughout the ranks, eliminating any "notch" or discontinuity by extending the pay raise to the most-senior enlisted ranks:

If the promotion system successfully identifies the most-productive and best-performing personnel, a graduated system increases the incentives for members to work hard and effectively, and it motivates the performers who are the most likely to get promoted to remain in the organization. (Asch, Hosek, and Warner, 2001, p. 48)

Achieving Balance in the Basic Pay Table

The QRMC essentially incorporated the insights from the RAND briefing as the core of its findings. Its final report highlighted the following: *"To compete in this environment, the Department must reexamine all of its recruiting and retention tools, the foundation of which is regular military compensation"* (Gilroy, 2002, p. 29, emphasis in the original).

The QRMC team put its story forward in a series of graphs (see Figure 18.1). Regular military compensation today is roughly equivalent to the earning of a person in the 70th percentile of high school graduates.

This certainly would have been good news in the 1970s, but in the 21st century, with an increasing number of midcareer enlisted personnel having at least some advanced education, the enlisted pay profile compares "far less favorably with comparable wage opportunities in the private sector" (Gilroy, 2002, p. 44).

Figure 18.2 illustrates these points well, comparing the high school profile computed by Rick Cooper in 1977 (Cooper, 1977, p. 369) with the high school profile computed by the 9th QRMC (Gilroy, 2002, p. 42). The 2000 high school and "some college education" (Gilroy, 2002, p. 44) data are also shown. In the case of 2000 high school graduates with some college education, the profile parallels the 50th percentile, rather than the 70th percentile.

The 9th QRMC reached the following conclusions:

[C]omparing enlisted [regular military compensation] with the earnings of high school graduates in the civilian population is no longer appropriate for much of the enlisted force. (Gilroy, 2002, p. 41)

A modest pay adjustment for junior enlisted personnel, coupled with strong enlistment incentives through bonuses and educational benefits, should help to improve recruiting success. (Gilroy, 2002, p. 43)

This analysis highlights a clear need for pay table adjustment in the mid-level enlisted grades. (Gilroy, 2002, p. 45)

Figure 18.1
Personnel Environment in 2000 from Report of the 9th QRMC

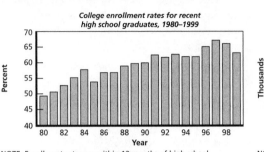

College enrollment rates for recent high school graduates, 1980–1999

NOTE: Enrollment rates are within 12 months of high school graduation.

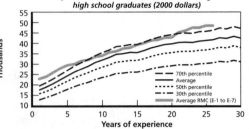

Comparison of enlisted RMC to civilian earnings for high school graduates (2000 dollars)

NOTE: Data reflect July 2000 enlisted pay (RMC) for E-1 to E-7 compared with predicted year 2000 earnings of male high school graduates.

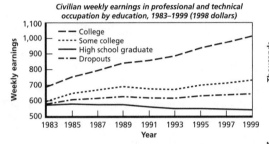

Civilian weekly earnings in professional and technical occupation by education, 1983–1999 (1998 dollars)

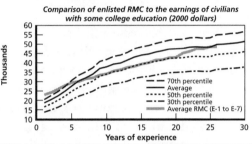

Comparison of enlisted RMC to the earnings of civilians with some college education (2000 dollars)

NOTE: Data reflect July 2000 enlisted pay (RMC) for E-1 to E-7 compared with predicted year 2000 earnings of males with some college.

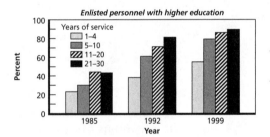

Enlisted personnel with higher education

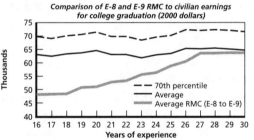

Comparison of E-8 and E-9 RMC to civilian earnings for college graduation (2000 dollars)

NOTE: Data reflect July 2000 E-8 and E-9 enlisted pay (RMC) compared with predicted year 2000 earnings of male college graduates.

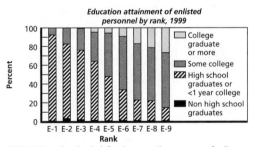

Education attainment of enlisted personnel by rank, 1999

NOTE: Higher education is defined as more than one year of college.

SOURCE: Gilroy (2002).

RAND *MG265-18.1*

Figure 18.2
Comparison of Regular Military Compensation 1977 and 2000
for High School and "Some College Education"

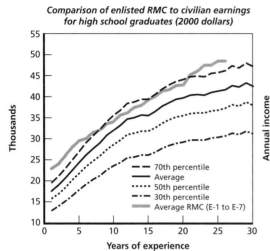

Comparison of enlisted RMC to civilian earnings for high school graduates (2000 dollars)

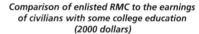

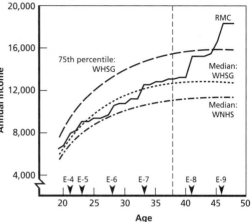

Enlisted RMC versus civilian wage and salary earnings for white high-school graduates and white non–high-school graduates: calendar year 1974

NOTE: Data reflect July 2000 enlisted pay (RMC) for E-1 to E-7 compared with predicted year 2000 earnings of male high school graduates.

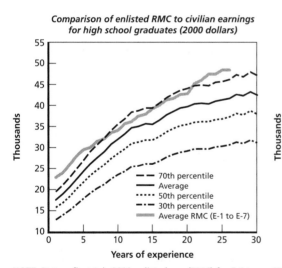

Comparison of enlisted RMC to civilian earnings for high school graduates (2000 dollars)

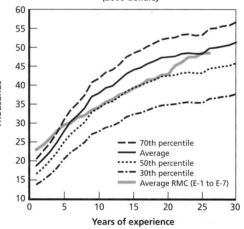

Comparison of enlisted RMC to the earnings of civilians with some college education (2000 dollars)

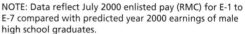

NOTE: Data reflect July 2000 enlisted pay (RMC) for E-1 to E-7 compared with predicted year 2000 earnings of male high school graduates.

NOTE: Data reflect July 2000 enlisted pay (RMC) for E-1 to E-7 compared with predicted year 2000 earnings of male high school graduates.

SOURCES: Gilroy (2002) and Cooper (1977).

RAND *MG265-18.2*

Achieving Flexibility in the Compensation System: The Post–Cold War Problem of Increased Time Away from Home

Given the centrality of the common basic pay table, many have complained that the compensation system is too rigid and does not give management the tools it needs to use financial incentives to induce desired behaviors, so they have favored a salary system. In fact, while the base pay discussed in the previous section accounts for 77.8 percent of cash enlisted members receive, it accounts for only 20.2 percent of the variance among enlisted members.[6] The 9th QRMC concluded, however, that

> the wide variety of special and incentive (S&I) pays and bonuses that service members receive during their careers . . . provide *flexibility* in the military compensation system. . . . [S]pecial pays have generally allowed the Services to remain competitive and respond to changing military missions and changing conditions in the civilian labor market. (Gilroy, 2002, p. 77, emphasis in original)

Special pays and bonuses account for 7 percent of the level of cash received but for 23 percent of the variance (see Tables 5.9 and 5.10 in Kilburn et al., 2001, p. 39). Table 18.2 shows the enlisted total pay, by category and service, for 1999, including base pay, special and incentive pays, and bonuses.

From the time of the 2nd QRMC, which examined special and incentive pays, research has played a critical role in helping the compensation system remain competitive. Since the end of the Cold War, what to do about the unexpected increase in the tempo of operations has been a central issue. As so often happens, it was service members in the field with their complaints to Congress that first alerted personnel managers that there was a problem. The chairman of the House Subcommittees on Military Readiness and Military Personnel pointed out

> that the time military personnel are spending away from home on deployments—commonly called personnel tempo (PERSTEMPO)—has increased and is stressing portions of the military community and adversely affecting readiness. (Gebicke, 1996, p. 1)

In response, the General Accounting Office showed how sharply deployments had increased over the period 1990–1995, especially for the Army and the Air Force (see Figure 18.3). In fact, as early as 1995, the General Accounting Office had been warning of a mismatch between force structure and mission requirements, pointing out what became known as the "high-demand and low-density" problem:

---

[6] In fact, Kilburn et al. found that the

> components that make up the bulk of enlisted compensation account for a smaller portion of the variance in enlisted compensation than they contribute to the levels. While the largest contributor to the levels of Cash Compensation is Basic Pay, the largest contributor to variance in Cash Compensation is the Enlistment/Reenlistment Bonus. (Kilburn et al., 2001, p. 42)

Table 18.2
Enlisted Total Pay by Category and Service, 1999

Type of Pay	Army Percent Rec'g	Army Avg. Amount ($)	Air Force Percent Rec'g	Air Force Avg. Amount ($)	Marine Corps Percent Rec'g	Marine Corps Avg. Amount ($)	Navy Percent Rec'g	Navy Avg. Amount ($)
RMC								
Basic Pay	100.0	19,542	100.0	20,371	100.0	17,611	100.0	19,757
Basic Allowance for Housing	100.0	6,497	100.0	6,559	100.0	6,245	100.0	6,453
Basic Allowance for Subsistence	100.0	2,738	100.0	2,738	100.0	2,738	100.0	2,738
Tax Advantage	100.0	1,732	100.0	1,731	100.0	1,647	100.0	1,707
S&I Pays								
Certain Places Pay/ Hardship Duty Pay-Location	28.1	73	25.2	65	10.3	35	5.3	90
Special Duty Assignment Pay	6.1	2,699	3.0	2,285	5.8	2,583	9.4	2,108
Overseas Extension Pay	0.4	696	0.1	434	1.5	1,212	0.4	675
Career Sea Pay	0.1	1,314	<1.0	112	9.0	205	40.5	1,624
Career Sea Pay Premium	<1.0	742	0.0		<1.0	734	5.1	684
Hostile Fire/Imminent Danger Pay	15.7	633	19.8	570	12.1	468	26.1	511
Diving Duty Pay	0.1	1,744	0.3	1,687	0.3	1,800	1.7	2,007
Submarine Duty Pay	0.0		0.0		0.0		7.5	2,094
Foreign Language Proficiency Pay (1)	1.5	675	1.5	806	0.7	620	0.5	715
Foreign Language Proficiency Pay (2)	0.2	332	0.1	360	0.0		<1.0	373
Flying Pay (Crew)	1.0	1,688	3.1	1,979	1.3	1,847	1.9	2,120
Flying Pay (Noncrew)	0.0		0.0		0.8	1,003	0.0	
Parachute Duty Pay	10.1	1,471	0.2	1,078	0.7	1,095	0.3	1,417
High Alt. Low Opening	0.3	2,297	0.3	2,399	0.2	2,207	0.5	2,498
Flight Deck Duty Pay	<1.0	1,200	<1.0	85	2.4	471	9.0	591
Demolition Duty Pay	0.4	1,567	0.4	1,641	0.3	1,475	0.5	1,406
Experimental Stress Duty Pay	<1.0	870	0.2	1,261	<1.0	1,387	0.2	747
Toxic Fuels Duty Pay	<1.0	261	0.3	1,507	0.0		<1.0	303
Toxic Pesticides Duty	<1.0	532	<1.0	1,166	0.0		<1.0	998
Chemical Munitions Duty Pay	0.1	927	<1.0	813	0.0		<1.0	546

Table 18.2—continued

Type of Pay	Army		Air Force		Marine Corps		Navy	
	Percent Rec'g	Avg. Amount ($)	Percent Rec'g	Avg. Amount ($)	Percent Rec'g	Avg. Amount ($)	Percent Rec'g	Avg. Amount ($)
Bonuses								
Enlistment Bonus	3.0	5,193	1.7	3,749	0.5	2,137	2.2	4,139
Selective Reenlistment Bonus	11.2	1,949	10.1	3,167	<1.0	5,329	15.4	4,452
Miscellaneous Allowances and COLAs								
Family Sep. Allow. I	1.4	181	0.7	308	0.0		0.8	180
Family Sep. Allow. II	19.9	417	17.1	333	19.2	385	23.0	399
CONUS COLA	0.6	730	0.6	355	1.4	612	0.7	697
Oversea COLA	24.6	1,849	24.1	2,904	21.4	2,240	19.4	2,748
Clothing/Uniform Allowance	87.2	329	90.8	281	97.9	229	99.7	336

SOURCE: Gilroy (2002, p. 82).

Figure 18.3
General Accounting Office Estimates of Service Deployments 1990–1995

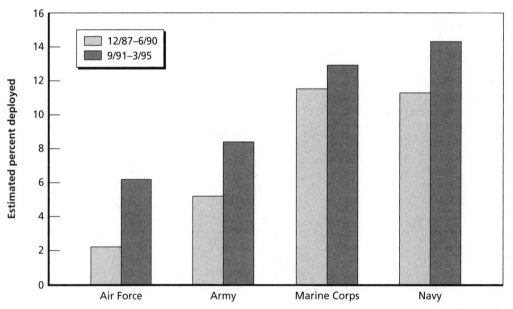

SOURCE: Gebicke (1996, p. 4).
NOTE: Data from July 1990 through August 1991 was excluded to eliminate effects of the Gulf War. Marine Corps data for September 1991 through March 1992 was excluded due to inaccurate reporting of family separation allowances.

RAND *MG265-18.3*

[p]eace operations heavily stress some U.S. military capabilities. . . . Repeated use of these forces, of which there are relatively few in the active force, has resulted in some units and personnel deploying more than once to an operation or to consecutive operations, increas[ing] the tempo of operations. (Davis, 1995, p. 3)

In March 1997, Army Chief of Staff Dennis Reimer told Congress that manpower in the Army had decreased 3 percent since the end of the Cold War and that deployed operations had gone up some 300 percent. He estimated that

officers and senior non-commissioned officers from deployable units now spend 180–190 days away from home annually, while junior soldiers spend 140–155 days away. (As recounted in Ryan, 1998, p. 3)

Personnel managers were keen to know whether increased personnel use had decreased or increased retention. Several studies at RAND, CNA, and the Army Research Institute tried to answer this question.

In a review of growing literature on perstempo prepared for the Army Research Institute, researchers at HumRRO and the Lewin Group found the following:

1. The effects of PERSTEMPO on retention, readiness, and quality of life are relatively small.
2. The effects of PERSTEMPO are often not linear.
3. Different ways of measuring PERSTEMPO and outcome variables produce different assessments of the magnitude of relationships between them. (Sticha et al., 1999, p. 66)

They reported their

results appear to be generally consistent with Hosek and Totten . . . . Measuring PERSTEMPO as the number of months deployed over a 24 month period, . . . deployments generally have a positive effect on first term Army retention, . . . but . . . the effect diminished with increasing deployment. (Sticha et al., 1999, p. 64)

Jim Hosek and Mark Totten at RAND developed a rigorous model of deployments by adding perstempo to the dynamic retention model originally developed by Glenn Gotz and John McCall (Gotz and McCall, 1984) and later modified by Beth Asch and John Warner (Asch and Warner, 1994b). Critical to their approach is the expectation of service members that they will work hard and spend a great deal of time away from home. The notion that a service member making career choices might have a *preferred* level of deployment and an *expected* level of deployment and that these will eventually be compared with the *actual* level of deployments is critical to their analysis, or as they put it,

the individual [service member] takes stock and makes a decision to stay or leave. The decision depends on expected and actual deployment. Expected deployment had guided the choice of service and occupation, and actual deployment is used to update the expectations. (Hosek and Totten, 1998, p. 34)

Noting that they did not have time-series data but only a look through a 24-month window, they found results that were consistent with a seemingly contradictory statement by the Army's Deputy Chief of Staff for Personnel in March 1997: "To date, PERSTEMPO has not impacted on retention. In fact, soldier[s] . . . in our most-deployed units are reenlisting in rates higher than those that do not deploy" (as quoted in Hosek and Totten, 1998, p. 56). Hosek and Totten observed the following:

> Our model and findings help reconcile these contrary positions. First, we find that having some perstempo—in our case, a separation of 30 days or longer or duty in a hostile area—is in fact associated with a higher reenlistment probability, as compared with not having *any* such perstempo. This aligns with survey findings that indicate many persons are interested in military service for adventure, travel, patriotism, and an opportunity to serve actively. It is also possible perstempo has a positive effect on promotion, as compared with no perstempo; this remains a topic for future study. Second, we find that the extent and nature of long or hostile duty matter. More months away from home, especially on hostile duty, reduce the positive impact of having long or hostile duty. Thus both the length and danger of duty have a negative effect on reenlistment. Putting the two main points together, we see that having some long or hostile duty has a positive effect on reenlistment, but as the duty lengthens or involves danger it may cause stress and disrupt personal life, thereby lowering morale and potentially reducing reenlistment. (Hosek and Totten, 1998, pp. 56–57, emphasis in the original)

These results seem to be very robust. Using a logistic regression model and calculating the odds ratio for junior officers (the ratios of the odds of separating for a given deployment pattern) and the hazard ratios for midgrade officers (the comparison of the probability of separation for an officer with a certain level and type of deployment with a similar individual without any deployment), Fricker found similar results for officers (Fricker et al., 2003). He found "a clear and positive association between increasing amounts of nonhostile deployment and junior and midgrade officer retention" (Fricker et al., 2003, p. 45).

A CNA team led by Timothy Cooke found similar results using time-series data. Cooke and his colleagues examined the personnel records of sailors on deployed naval ships from 1976 to 1988. With the deployment history, they were able to determine the influence of deployments—length and frequency—on sailors' reenlistment decisions:

> [V]ery long deployments, and more time under way when not deployed are associated with lower first-term retention. The effects are largest for married sailors (about one-third of those making reenlistment decisions), and sailors in relatively sea-intensive occupations. (Cooke et al., 1992, p. ix)

Most importantly, they concluded "that the retention reductions associated with substantial increases in deployment length or time under way when not deployed could be offset by increasing relative military compensation" (Cooke et al., 1992, p. ix).

Given that a number of special and incentive pays already existed, the effect of which is to give service members who are deployed extra compensation, the 9th QRMC asked whether it was really necessary to initiate yet another special pay for deployment. CNA took on the question the 9th QRMC was asking. The first problem they pointed out was finding an acceptable definition of *deployment*.[7] Each of the services had its own definition, which they attributed to "differences in the services' missions, equipment, and operating procedures" (Koopman and Hattiangadi, 2001, p. 5), and Congress imposed a new definition imposed in 2000. CNA noted that

> Navy deployments required that a unit be away from its home port for at least 56 days. Marine Corps deployments were defined as 10 or more days away from the home station. The Army counted 7 days or more away from home base as a deployment. Finally, the Air Force counted 1 day or more of away time as a deployment because of its ability to accomplish flight missions in a single day by flying out and back. (Koopman and Hattiangadi, 2001, pp. 5–6)

CNA quoted the definition Congress had included in the 2000 National Defense Authorization Act (10 USC 991):

> any day on which pursuant to orders the member is *performing service in a training exercise or operation* at a location or under circumstances that make it impossible or infeasible for the member to spend off-duty time in the housing in which the member resides when on garrison duty at the member's PDS [permanent duty station] or homeport. (Koopman and Hattiangadi, 2001, p. 6, emphasis in original)

Congress also had its own version of deployment pay—any person deployed more than 250 days in the previous year would receive $100 per day for each additional deployment day (36 USC 435)[8]—which was to go into effect in 2002, but was suspended on October 8, 2001, after the terrorist attack on September 11, 2001. Since this would have been yet another special pay a member would qualify for if deployed, it added to a confusing array of pays the services would have to cope with. Table 18.3 summarizes the existing "away pays."

This new congressionally mandated Burdensome Tempo Pay, also called High Deployment Per Diem, however, was unique. Unlike the other pays, which generally went into effect or were terminated at the start or end of an event and could be handled by submitting a list of members assigned to a unit, Congress required that each member's deployment status be tracked individually. Given the state of clerical support in

---

[7] The problem of Service-specific definitions is also discussed in Sticha et al. (1999, pp. 4–10).

[8] In 2001, Congress changed the threshold for the new pay from 250 days out of 365 days to 400 days out of 730 days.

Table 18.3
Department of Defense "Away Pays"

Pay	Paid for	Amount	Varies with	Other restrictions	FY01 budget ($M)[a]
Career Sea Pay[b]	Assignment to ship	$50-$520/ month, avg. $200 for E-6	Paygrade and cumulative sea duty	Paygrade E-4 and above	216 combined
Career Sea Pay Premium[c]	Extensions at sea beyond 36 months	$100/month	Fixed	Paid to E-4s and a few E-5 and above	
Submarine Duty Pay	Operational sub duty for lower PGs, sub qualification for higher PGs	$75-$355/ month, avg. $230 for E-6	Paygrade and years of sub service		46
Family Separation Allowance	Enforced family separations	$100/month prorated daily	Fixed	Must have spouse and/or dependents, be away >30 days	84
Hostile Fire/ Imminent Danger Pay	Subjected to hostile fire or hostile mine	$150/month	Fixed	IDP plus HDP-L shouldn't exceed $250/month	28
Hardship Duty Pay—Mission	Designated hardship mission, e.g., POW remains recovery	$150/month	Fixed		26 combined
Hardship Duty Pay—Location	Poor living conditions	$50-$150/ month	Severity of hardships	OCONUS locations[d]	
Overseas Tour Extension Incentive Pay	Extending OCONUS tour at least 1 year	$80/month or extra leave[e]	Fixed	Paid to specific MOSs	5
Combat Zone Tax Exclusion	Serving in designated combat zone	Taxes on basic and some special pays	Income level	Officer income exclusions have upper limits	N/A
Burdensome Tempo Pay	Days deployed in excess of 400/730	$100/day	Fixed		0 for 2001

a. The amounts are in millions of dollars and are enlisted military personnel appropriations only.

b. These amounts and restrictions were in effect before 1 October 2001. See the CSP section for a description of changes since that time.

c. These amounts and restrictions were in effect before 1 October 2001. See the CSPP section for a description of changes since that time.

d. Permanent duty assignments collect pay from first day. TAD/TDY must be there at least 30 days; then they get pay retroactively.

e. Some locations and MOSs qualify for $2,000 lump sum payments.

SOURCE: Koopman and Hattiangadi (2001, p. 12).

some units, particularly the Army, this was virtually impossible. CNA concluded "any new deployment pay should be integrated into existing pays so that troops in similar circumstances get the same benefits and any differences can be explained and defended" (Koopman and Hattiangadi, 2001, p. 37). DoD tried to do this by suggesting to Congress it change its mandated program. The National Defense Authorization Act of 2004 incorporated the changes DoD recommended. The new law "authorize[s] payment of a monthly high-deployment allowance of up to $1000, instead of the $100 high-tempo per diem allowance . . . for service members for each month during which the member is deployed for 191 or more consecutive days or for 401 days out of the preceding 730 days" (Conference Committee, 2003, p. 694).

Research, Leading the Way into the Future

Former Assistant Secretary of Defense Chris Jehn addressed the 30th Anniversary Conference for the All-Volunteer Force:

> Effective recruiting and retention is extraordinarily important, indeed essential, for sustaining the all-volunteer force. If the Department of Defense is unsuccessful in attracting and retaining quality people, other successes are unimportant. . . . Success . . . requires that the department understand how external factors such as economic conditions and demographic changes . . . affect recruiting and retention. (Jehn, 2003, pp. 55–56)

At the same conference, Martha Farnsworth Riche and Aline Quester from CNA provided a cogent summary of the population trends and characteristics that will shape the recruiting market the military services will face in the future:

- While the "average American thinks the U.S. youth population is declining in size, . . . it is not" (Riche and Quester, 2003, p. 109).
- The size of the 15–19 age group "will continue to decline relatively, but not absolutely, into the future" (Riche and Quester, 2003, p. 10).
- Substantial waves of immigration in late 20th century "increased the racial and ethnic diversity of the U.S. population" (Riche and Quester, 2003, p. 118).
- The 15- to 19-year-old group, the target for advertising and recruiting, "will contain more Hispanics than previously estimated" (Riche and Quester, 2003, p. 119).
- The educational requirements for accessions "call for careful thinking about the interaction of trends in education attainment and in recruiting and retention strategies" (Riche and Quester, 2003, p. 121).
- The preference for recruits with high school diplomas "has been well tested and justified. . . . At the same time increasing numbers of Americans are pursuing higher education" (Riche and Quester, 2003, p. 121).

- Offering "educational benefits and useful job-related learning," means that the military is becoming "one stop on a young adult's increasingly long transition from school to adult career" (Riche and Quester, 2003, p. 121).
- New educational credentials raise questions about how these should be categorized for accession purposes: "Recruiters can assume GED holders and youth with other nontraditional credentials will make up an increasing share of high school completions, making it more difficult for recruiters to find youths who meet existing enlistment standards" (Riche and Quester, 2003, pp. 124–125).

Significant research since the end of the Cold War has been undertaken to help the services adjust to these trends. Several topics stand out: adjusting to the increased propensity of high school graduates to go on to either college or junior college, rather than going into the military first; the increased cohort of Hispanic youths as a potential source of new recruits; and attempts to make better selections from those not usually permitted to join, e.g., non–high school graduates and those who have obtained a General Educational Development (GED) certificate.

Recruiting from the College Bound. The 9th QRMC called the rise in college attendance "dramatic" and the "most significant trend in the youth labor market . . . over the past 20 years" (Gilroy, 2002, p. 35), a trend that cut the primary pool of new, eligible youths almost in half.[9] Figure 18.4 illustrates the trend. Researchers at both RAND and CNA have examined the college trend.

A group at RAND studied this trend and also noted that

> the military college-benefit program that boosts education the most requires participants to separate from the service [the Montgomery GI Bill] has not kept pace with college costs . . . [and] [e]xisting college-first programs in the military, such as the loan repayment program, are small in scale and serve few enlistees. (Asch, Kilburn, and Klerman, 1999, p. 33)[10]

Besides expanding existing programs, they suggested "entirely new programs," such as "expand the recruitment of college dropouts" and "increase the presence of recruiters on two-year campuses" (Asch, Kilburn, and Klerman, 1999, pp. 34, 37–38). In a subsequent analysis, Asch and Kilburn found "recruiters are more likely to find young men with desirable eligibility characteristics among four-year entrants than other groups" (Asch and Kilburn, 2003, p. 178)—two-year college or certificate students. They estimated, however, that two-year students are more likely to have the "decision characteristics" more associated with joining the military. Taken together,

---

[9] While significant, the QRMC overstated the problem. Each year, half of Army enlistees are 20 years of age or older. In effect, the high school graduate who chooses not to join the military after graduation gets the chance to reaffirm that decision over and over again each year until his or her 26th birthday, the nominal cutoff for enlistments. While the number going to college immediately after high school has sharply increased, many who make that decision and others who go to work after high school eventually do join the military.

[10] Also see Fair (2003).

Figure 18.4
College Enrollment Rates for Recent High School Graduates, 1980–1999

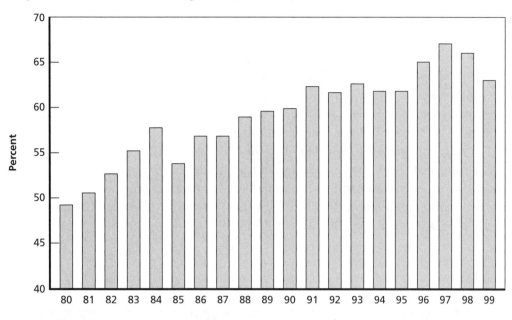

SOURCE: Gilroy (2002, p. 35).
NOTE: Enrollment rates are within 12 months of high school graduation.
RAND *MG265-18.4*

their "findings on enlistment potential suggest that recruiting efforts should be targeted toward two-year students and two-year dropouts" (Asch and Kilburn, 2003, p. 186).

Beth Asch and Rebecca Kilburn argued that "[o]ne way to develop new recruiting policies designed to attract youth in the college market is to consider approaches that make enlisting and attending college a joint choice rather than an 'either/or' choice" (Asch and Kilburn, 2003, p. 192). In fact, the Army has developed a new program aimed at the two-year vocational college market, and the Army and the Navy have substantially increased their in-service voluntary education programs.

The 1999 Army Secretary, Louis Caldera, the first Hispanic Secretary of the Army, established the Army's College First program to try to attract highly qualified high school graduates who are interested in attending two-year colleges or vocational schools with financial assistance and advanced pay grade on graduation, if they committed to join the Army when they were finished. He asked RAND to evaluate the program. The initial results reported to the Under Secretary of Defense show this program "expanded Army recruiting among high school graduates with less than one year of college by 43 percent. However, the Army has not seen similar expansion among high school graduates who have not attended college, or those who have one or more years of college" (Rutherford, 2002). The Army expanded the program in FY 2002, increasing the stipend from $150 per month to $250 per month and increasing the length of the program from 24 to 30 months (Rutherford, 2002).

In-Service Voluntary Education Program. Secretary Caldera also started an enhanced in-service education program that he called *eArmyU*. Figure 18.5 shows the home page of the eArmyU Web site, which is an example of the use of the Internet in today's military. The program offered 100-percent funding for tuition, books, fees, email, and individual access to the Internet and a laptop computer. Unlike traditional in-service programs (in which a service member–student takes responsibility for the design and progress of his or her program, working through the available on-base voluntary education office), this program provided an online service with common application and registration forms, a library, tutoring, and an academic counseling service. To stay enrolled in the program, Army enrollees had to complete 12 semester hours during the first two years of enrollment. In 2003, with the Army in the lead, DoD changed its in-service program to provide 100-percent tuition assistance, rather than 75 percent.

Figure 18.5
eArmyU Home Page

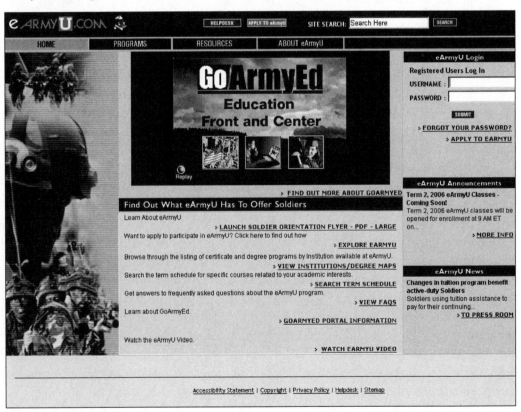

SOURCE: http://www.earmyu.com/

RAND *MG265-18.5*

In FY 1997, the year CNA studied the Navy's in-service Voluntary Education Program (VOLED),[11] it found that the program had "a significant positive impact on retention" (Garcia et al., 1998, p. 3). Among first-term sailors who do not take the opportunity to take some college courses, the reenlistment rate was 31 percent. The number grew to 37 percent for those with 15 college credits. Sailors with 60 college credits—enough for an associate degree or half the number needed to receive a baccalaureate diploma—had a reenlistment rate of 55 percent. "This . . . should lay to rest," CNA noted, "the argument that college education hastens the departure of Sailors seeking employment in the private sector" (Garcia et al., 1998, p. 3). In addition to higher retention, CNA found that sailors taking college courses were promoted faster and at a higher rate than those not enrolled, even though no accommodations were made to provide those enrolled with additional off-duty time to facilitate their enrollment. "College education . . . helps Sailors score higher on the advancement rating tests," CNA reported (Garcia et al., 1998, p. 28). Also, demotions—discipline problems—are "significantly less likely for Sailors who participate in the [VOLED] Program than for those who did not" (Garcia et al., 1998, p. 31).

Expanding the Pool of Potential New Recruits. Throughout the 30-year history of the all-volunteer force, personnel managers have tried to expand the pool of potential recruits as a means of ensuring the success of the program. Originally, the focus of recruiting was on white males. In a series of monographs, Martin Binkin of the Brookings Institution raised the issues of women (Binkin and Bach, 1977) and blacks (Binkin et al., 1982). In a 1986 revision (Binkin and Eitelberg, 1986), Binkin again asked who would fight the next war, and the focus remained on women, blacks and members of the reserve components. A group Binkin did not identify but that is becoming increasingly important to the future of the all-volunteer force is Hispanics. The Census Bureau reports that, between 2000 and 2050, the white population will grow by 7.4 percent, the black population will grow by 71.3 percent and the Hispanic population will grow by 187.9 percent (U.S. Census Bureau, 2004a). In 2000, Hispanics were 12.6 percent of the population. By 2050, Hispanics will make up 24.4 percent (U.S. Census Bureau, 2004b).

In FY 2002, the most recent year reported, 12.0 percent of Army and 14.1 percent of male Marine Corps accessions were Hispanic (Chu, 2004, p. 2-7).[12] Hispanics, however, are underrepresented, "with 11 percent among [total] NPS [non–prior service] accessions compared with nearly 16 percent for comparable civilians" (Chu, 2004, pp. iii–iv). A National Research Council study found that the underrepresentation of

---

[11] *Author's Note:* I can attest to the effect this study had on the Navy. When I was the Assistant Secretary of the Navy for Manpower and Reserve Affairs, the people preparing the annual Navy budget wanted to cut this program. When they saw the results CNA reported, they instead expanded the program.

[12] The *New York Times* report on the first 1,000 casualties of Operation Iraqi Freedom, 25 percent were women, 13 percent were black, 18 percent were National Guard or Reservists, and 12 percent were Hispanic (Werschkul et al., 2004).

Hispanics could not be explained by differences in family characteristics—a parent in the military or the educational attainment of the mother in the household or region of the country—that are often used to explain the variance in the probability to enlist in the armed services (Sackett and Mavor, 2004, p. 65).

The service that has had the most success recruiting Hispanics has been the Marine Corps. A team from CNA documented the Hispanic experience in the Marine Corps in depth. They demonstrate that

> Hispanics have done very well in the Marine Corps. Their boot camp attrition rates are substantially below average rates and they have lower attrition in the first term of service. . . . Our field work analysis suggests some possible reasons for lower attrition, such as reluctance to disappoint family and friends and unwillingness to treat the enlistment opportunity lightly. (Hattiangadi et al., 2004, p. 73)

In the report, the authors discuss how Hispanics relate to the whole concept of the "Marine Corps family." While they do have some specific recommendations for ways DoD can enhance "the continued success of Hispanics in the military, e.g., translate the Services' recruiting brochures and materials" (Hattiangadi et al., 2004, p. 75), one is left with the impression that the relationship between Hispanics and Marine Corps may be hard to duplicate in the other services. Other approaches, however, have been tried. Army Secretary Caldera, a Hispanic himself, targeted Hispanics with the College First program and also with a revised GED program called GED Plus.

Recently, the services have also tried to increase the pool of potential recruits by improving their screening tools to improve their ability to increase enlistments from groups they do not normally recruit. Specifically, pilot programs have focused on high-quality GED holders, those enrolled in the National Guard ChalleNGe program, and those who have been home schooled.

In the FY 1999 Defense Authorization Act, Congress mandated a five-year test of graduates of home schooling and the ChalleNGe Program. CNA was asked to evaluate these programs. Initially, the researchers found "relatively low 12-month attrition rates for ChalleNGe . . . and for all homeschooled recruits with above-average scores on the Armed Forces Qualifications Test." They also found, however, "that attrition rates rise sharply for these groups by the 24- and 36-month points" (Wenger and Hodar, 2004, pp. 1–2). A 2004 DoD report to Congress concluded: "Based on the results of this Pilot Test, as well as our historical experience, there is no empirical support for treating either home school or ChalleNGe GED recruits on a par with high school diploma graduates for determining enlistment eligibility" (Gilroy, 2004, p. 14).

The Impact of Operation Iraqi Freedom

In 1969, one member of the President's Commission on the All-Volunteer Armed Force wrote to Chairman Thomas Gates: "While there is a reasonable possibility that a peacetime armed force could be entirely voluntary, I am certain that an armed force involved in a major conflict could *not* be voluntary" (Greenewalt, 1969, emphasis in original). While it is too early to tell how the all-volunteer force will fare, given the current situation in Iraq, the last half century of experience suggests that one thing is certain: Those charged with managing the all-volunteer force will turn to the research community to help them decide what programs to establish and to evaluate what programs are working.

References

Asch, Beth J., Jeremy Arkes, James R. Hosek, C. Christine Fair, Jennifer Sharp, and Mark Totte, *Military Recruiting and Retention After the Fiscal Year 2000 Military Pay Legislation,* Santa Monica, Calif.: RAND Corporation, 2002. S0876.pdf.

Asch, Beth J., C. Christine Fair, and M. Rebecca Kilburn, *An Assessment of Recent Proposals to Improve the Montgomery GI Bill,* Santa Monica, Calif.: RAND Corporation, DB-301-OSD/FRP, 2000. S0747.pdf.

Asch, Beth J., James R. Hosek, and Craig W. Martin, *A Look at Cash Compensation for Active Duty Military Personnel,* Santa Monica, Calif.: RAND Corporation, MR-1492-OSD, 2002. S0866.pdf.

Asch, Beth J., James R. Hosek, and John T. Warner, *An Analysis of Pay for Enlisted Personnel,* Santa Monica, Calif.: RAND Corporation, DB-344-OSD, 2001. S0860.pdf.

Asch, Beth J., Richard Johnson, and John T. Warner, *Reforming the Military Retirement System,* Santa Monica, Calif.. RAND Corporation, MR-748-OSD, 1998. S0859.pdf.

Asch, Beth J., and M. Rebecca Kilburn, "The Enlistment Potential of College Students," in M. Rebecca Kilburn and Beth Asch, eds., *Recruiting Youth in the College Market: Current Practices and Future Policy Options,* Santa Monica, Calif.: RAND Corporation, 2003. S0877.pdf.

Asch, Beth J., M. Rebecca Kilburn, and Jacob A. Klerman, *Attracting College-Bound Youth into the Military,* Santa Monica, Calif.: RAND Corporation, MR-984-OSD, 1999. S0885.pdf.

Asch, Beth J., and John T. Warner, *A Policy Analysis of Alternative Military Retirement Systems,* Santa Monica, Calif.: RAND Corporation, MR-465-OSD, 1994a. S0570.pdf.

———, *A Theory of Military Compensation and Personnel Policy,* Santa Monica, Calif.: RAND Corporation, MR-439-OSD, 1994b. S0571.pdf.

Binkin, Martin, and Shirley J. Bach, *Women and the Military,* Washington, D.C.: Brookings Institution, June 1977.

Binkin, Martin, and Mark Jan Eitelberg, "Women and Minorities in the All-Volunteer Force," in William Bowman, Rodger Little and G. Thomas Sicilia, eds., *The All-Volunteer Force After A Decade: Retrospect and Prospect,* New York: Pergamon-Brassey's, 1986.

Binkin, Martin, Mark Jan Eitelberg, Alvin J. Schenider, and Marvin M. Smith, *Blacks and the Military,* Washington, D.C.: The Brookings Institution, 1982.

Carr, William J., interview with Bernard Rostker, September 22, 2004.

Chu, David S. C., *Population Representation in the Military Services—Fiscal Year 2001,* Washington, D.C.: Office of the Under Secretary of Defense (Personnel and Readiness), March 1, 2004. G1392.pdf.

Chu, David S. C., and John P. White, "Ensuring Quality People in Defense," in Ashton B. Carter and John P. White, eds., *Keeping the Edge: Managing Defense for the Future,* Cambridge, Mass.: MIT Press, 2001.

Clinton, William J., "Ninth Quadrennial Review of Military Compensation," memorandum to The Secretary of Defense, Washington, D.C., July 20, 1999. G1376.pdf.

Cohen, William S., *The Statement of the Secretary of Defense and the Chairman of the Joint Chiefs of Staff Concerning Military Pay and Retirement,* Washington, D.C.: U.S. Department of Defense, 64698, December 21, 1998. G1384.pdf.

Conference Committee, *National Defense Authorization Act for Fiscal Year 2004 Conference Report: Section 541—High-Tempo Personnel Management and Allowance,* Washington, D.C.: U.S. House of Representatives, Report 108-354, November 7, 2003. G1346.pdf.

Cooke, Timothy W., Alan J. Marcus, and Aline O. Quester, *Personnel Tempo of Operations and Navy Enlisted Retention,* Alexandria, Va.: Center for Naval Analyses, CRM 91150, February 1992. S0821.pdf.

Cooper, Richard V. L., *Military Manpower and the All-Volunteer Force,* Santa Monica, Calif.: RAND Corporation, R-1450-ARPA, September 1977. S0177.pdf.

Davis, Richard, *Peace Operations: Heavy Use of Key Capabilities May Affect Response of Regional Conflicts,* Washington, D.C.: General Accounting Office, GAO/NSIAD9551, March 8, 1995. G1391.pdf.

Dertouzos, James N., *Recruiter Incentive and Enlistment Supply,* Santa Monica, Calif.: RAND Corporation, R-3065-MIL, May 1985. S0684.pdf.

Dertouzos, James N., and Steve Garber, *Is Military Advertising Effective? An Estimation Methodology and Application to Recruiting in the 1980s and 90s,* Santa Monica, Calif.: RAND Corporation, MR-1591-OSD, 2003. S0878.pdf.

Fair, C. Christine, "Paying for College: A Survey of Military and Civilian Financial Aid Programs and Postsecondary Education Costs," in M. Rebecca Kilburn and Beth Asch, eds., *Recruiting Youth in the College Market: Current Practices and Future Policy Options,* Santa Monica, Calif.: RAND Corporation, 2003. S0877.pdf.

Fernandez, Richard L., *What Does the Military "Pay Gap" Mean?* Washington, D.C.: Congressional Budget Office, June 1999. G1388.pdf.

———, *The Warrant Office Rank: Adding Flexibility to Military Personnel Management,* Washington, D.C.: Congressional Budget Office, February 2002. G1387.pdf.

Fricker, Ronald D., Jr., *The Effect of Perstempo on Officer Retention in the U.S. Military,* Santa Monica, Calif.: RAND Corporation, MR-1556-OSD, 2002. S0814.pdf.

Fricker, Ronald D., Jr., James R. Hosek, and Mark Totten, *How Does Deployment Affect Retention of Military Personnel?* Santa Monica, Calif.: RAND Corporation, RB-7557-OSD, 2003. S0815.pdf.

Garamone, Jim, "DoD Proposes Largest Military Pay Hike in Generation," *American Forces Press Service,* December 21, 1998. G1383.pdf.

Garcia, Federico E., Ernest H. Joy, and David L. Reese, *Effectiveness of the Voluntary Education Program,* Alexandria, Va.: Center for Naval Analyses, CRM 9840, April 1998. S0886.pdf.

Gebicke, Mark E., *Military Readiness: A Clear Policy Is Needed to Guide Management of Frequently Deployed Units,* Washington, D.C.: U.S. General Accounting Office, GAO/NSIAD96105, April 1996. G1344.pdf.

Gilroy, Curtis L., *Report of the Ninth Quadrennial Review of Military Compensation,* Washington, D.C.: U.S. Department of Defense, March 2002. G1276.pdf.

―――, *Report to Congress: Enlistment Eligibility Priorities for Home School and National Guard Youth ChalleNGe GED Credentials-Evaluation of a Pilot Program,* Washington, D.C.: Office of the Under Secretary of Defense (Personnel and Readiness), 2004. G1394.pdf.

Gilroy, Curtis L., and W. S. Sellman, "Recruiting and Sustaining a Quality Army: A Review of the Evidence," in Robert L. Phillips and Maxwell R. Thurman, eds. *Future Soldiers and the Quality Imperative: The Army 2010 Conference,* T. Knox, Ky.: U.S. Army Recruiting Command, 1995, pp. 53–70.

Goldberg, Matthew S., *A Survey of Enlisted Retention: Models and Findings,* Alexandria, Va.: Center for Naval Analyses, CRM D0004085.A2/Final, November 2001. S0869.pdf.

Golding, Heidi L., and Susan C McArver, *Navy Sea Pay: History and Recent Initiatives,* Alexandria, Va.: Center for Naval Analyses, CRM D0003611.A2/Final, December 2001. S0867.pdf.

Gotz, Glenn A., and John J. McCall, *A Dynamic Retention Model for Air Force Officers: Theory and Estimates,* Santa Monica, Calif.: RAND Corporation, R-3028-AF, December 1984. S0879.pdf.

Greenewalt, Crawford H., "I Have Concerns," memorandum to Thomas Gates, Wilmington, Delaware, December 31, 1969. A0001.pdf.

Hansen, Michael L., *Compensation and Enlisted Manning Shortfalls,* Alexandria, Va.: Center for Naval Analyses, CRM D0001998.A2/Final, September 2000. S0871.pdf.

Hattiangadi, Anita U., Hary Lee, and Aline O. Quester, *Recruiting Hispanics: The Marine Corps Experience Final Report,* Alexandria, Va.: Center for Naval Analyses, CRM D0009071. A2/Final, January 2004.

Horowitz, Stanley A., and Alan Sherman, "A Direct Measure of the Relationship Between Human Capital and Productivity," *Journal of Human Resources,* Vol. 15, No. 1, Winter 1980.

Hosek, James R., Beth Asch, C. Christine Fair, Craig Martin, and Michael Mattock, *Married to the Military: The Employment and Earnings of Military Wives Compared to Civilian Wives,* Santa Monica, Calif.: RAND Corporation, MR-1565-OSD, 2002. S0873.pdf.

Hosek, James R., Christine E. Peterson, and Joanna Z. Heilbrunn, *Military Pay Gaps and Caps,* Santa Monica, Calif.: RAND Corporation, MR-368-P&R, 1994. S0865.pdf.

Hosek, James R., and Jennifer Sharp, *Keeping Military Pay Competitive: The Outlook for Civilian Wages and Its Consequences,* Santa Monica, Calif.: RAND Corporation, IP-205, 2001. S0861.pdf.

Hosek, James R., and Mark Totten, *Does Perstempo Hurt Retention? The Effect of Long or Hostile Perstempo on Reenlistment,* Santa Monica, Calif.: RAND Corporation, MR-990-OSD, 1998. S0813.pdf.

Husted, Thomas A., and Michael L. Hansen, *Standard of Living of Enlisted Personnel,* Alexandria, Va.: Center for Naval Analyses, CRM D0002907.A2/Final, March 2001a. S0862.pdf.

―――, *Thrift Savings Plans: Effect on Savings and Tax Revenues,* Alexandria, Va.: Center for Naval Analyses, CRM D0002891.A2/Final, December 2001b. S0872.pdf.

Jehn, Christopher, "Introduction," in Barbara A. Bicksler, Curtis L. Gilroy, and John T. Warner, eds., *The All-Volunteer Force: Thirty Years of Service,* Washington, D.C.: Brassey's, Inc., 2003.

Kilburn, M. Rebecca, and Beth Asch, eds., *Recruiting Youth in the College Market: Current Practices and Future Policy Options,* Santa Monica, Calif.: RAND Corporation, 2003. S0877.pdf.

Kilburn, M. Rebecca, Rachel Louie, and Dana P. Goldman, *Patterns of Enlisted Compensation,* Santa Monica, Calif.: RAND Corporation, 2001. S0882.pdf.

Koopman, Martha E., and Anita U. Hattiangadi, *Do the Services Need a Deployment Pay?* Alexandria, Va.: Center for Naval Analyses, CRM D0004458.A2/Final, December 2001. S0868.pdf.

Kozaryn, Linda D., "Top NCOs Call for Pay, QOL Reforms," *Armed Force Press Service,* June 26, 2000. G1386.pdf.

Lazear, Edward P., "Why Is There Mandatory Retirement?" *Journal of Political Economy,* Vol. 87, No. 6, 1979, pp. 1,261–1,284.

———, *Personnel Economics,* Cambridge: The MIT Press, 1995.

Lazear, Edward P., and Sherwin Rosen, "Rank Order Tournaments as Optimum Labor Contracts," *The Journal of Political Economy,* Vol. 89, No. 5, October 1981, pp. 841–864.

Moore, Carol S., Heidi L. W. Golding, and Henry S. Griffis, *Manpower and Personnel IWAR 2000: Aging the Force,* Alexandria, Va.: Center for Naval Analyses, CRM D0003079.A2/Final, January 2001. S0870.pdf.

Orvis, Bruce R., Michael T. Childress, and J. Michael Polich, *Effect of Personnel Quality on the Performance of Patriot Air Defense System Operators,* Santa Monica, Calif.: RAND Corporation, R-3901-A, 1992. S0666.pdf.

Pirie, Robert B., Jr., "More Data on ASVAB Norming Problem," memorandum to Deputy Secretary of Defense, Washington, D.C., February 23, 1980. G0366.pdf.

Quester, Aline O., *Enlisted Crew Quality and Ship Material Readiness,* Alexandria, Va.: Center for Naval Analyses, CRM 88254, April 1989. S0864.pdf.

Quester, Aline O., and Gary Lee, *Senior Enlisted Personnel: Do We Need Another Grade?* Alexandria, Va.: Center for Naval Analyses, CRM D0005072.A2/Final, December 2001. S0863.pdf.

Riche, Martha Farnsworth, and Aline O. Quester, "The Effects of Socioeconomic Change on the All-Volunteer Force: Past, Present, and Future," in Barbara A. Bicksler, Curtis L. Gilroy and John T. Warner, eds., *The All-Volunteer Force: Thirty Years of Service,* Washington, D.C.: Brassey's, Inc., 2003.

Rosen, Sherwin, "Prizes and Incentives in Elimination Tournaments," *American Economic Review,* Vol. 76, No. 4, 1986, pp. 701–715.

———, "The Military as an Internal Labor Market: Some Allocation, Productivity, and Incentive Problems," *Social Science Quarterly,* Vol. 73, No. 2, 1992, pp. 227–237.

Rutherford, Gwen, *Recruiting from the College-Oriented Market,* Washington, D.C.: U.S. Department of Defense, January 25, 2002. G1393.pdf.

Ryan, Michael C., *Military Readiness, Operations Tempo (OPTEMPO) and Personnel Tempo (PERSTEMPO): Are U.S. Forces Doing Too Much?* Washington, D.C.: The Library of Congress, Congressional Research Service, 98-41 F, January 14, 1998. G1311.pdf.

Sackett, Paul R., and Anne S. Mavor, eds., *Attitudes, Aptitudes, and Aspirations of American Youths: Implications for Military Recruiting,* Washington, D.C.: The National Academies Press, 2004. S0827.pdf.

Scribner, Barry L., D. Alton Smith, Robert H. Baldwin, and Robert L. Phillips, "Are Smart Tankers Better? AFQT and Military Productivity," *Armed Forces & Society,* Vol. 12, No. 2, Winter 1986, pp. 193–206.

Secretary of Defense, *Charter of the Defense Advisory Committee on Military Compensation,* Washington, D.C.: U.S. Department of Defense, March 14, 2005. G1433.pdf.

Sticha, Paul J., Robert Sadacca, Ani S. DiFazio, C. Mazie Knerr, Paul F. Hogan, and Marisa Diana, *Personnel Tempo: Definition, Measurement, and Effects on Retention, Readiness, and Quality of Life,* Washington, D.C.: United States Army Research Institute for the Behavioral and Social Sciences, ARI Contractor Report 9904, September 1999. S0858.pdf.

U.S. Census Bureau, *U.S. Interim Projections by Age, Race, and Hispanic Origin: Population Change,* March 18, 2004a. G1395.pdf.

———, *U.S. Interim Projections by Age, Race, and Hispanic Origin: Projected Population,* March 18, 2004b. G1396.pdf.

Warner, John T., and Beth J. Asch, "The Economics of Military Manpower," in Keith Hartley and Todd Sandler, eds., *Handbook of Defense Economics,* New York: Elsevier, 1995, pp. 348–394. S0241.pdf.

Warner, John T., Curtis J. Simon, Deborah M. Payne, and J. Michael Jones, *Enlistment Supply in the 1990's: A Study of the Navy College Fund and Other Enlistment Incentive Programs,* Washington, D.C.: Defense Manpower Data Center, D Md.C 2000015, April 2001. S0699.pdf.

Wenger, Jennie W., and April K. Hodar, *Final Analysis of Evaluation of Homeschool and ChalleNGe Program Results,* Alexandria: Center for Naval Analyses, CRM D0009351.A2/Final, January 2004. S0883.pdf.

Werschkul, Ben, Matthew Ericson, and Tom Torok, "Interactive Graph: A Look at 1000 Who Died," *New York Times,* September 17, 2004.

Winkler, John D., Judith C. Fernandez, and J. Michael Polich, *Effect of Aptitude on the Performance of Army Communications Operators,* RAND Corporation, Arroyo Center, R-4143A, 1992. S0667.pdf.

CHAPTER NINETEEN

Why Has the All-Volunteer Force Been a Success?

> We're not going to reimplement a draft. There is no need for it at all.
> The disadvantages of using compulsion to bring into the Armed
> Forces the men and women needed are notable.
>
> —Donald H. Rumsfeld
> Secretary of Defense[1]

Introduction[2]

When the United States moved to an all-volunteer force in 1973, it marked the culmination of years of public debate about how the United States should procure its military manpower—continue conscription or institute a volunteer force. The dominant theme of the debate was summed up in the title of a 1966 landmark study by the Presidential Advisory Commission on Selective Service: *In Pursuit of Equity: Who Serves When Not All Serve?* Indeed, the major theme of the President's Commission on an All-Volunteer Armed Force in 1970, which provided the final push toward an all-volunteer force, was that the draft was inherently unfair.

The Time for Change Was Right

Through most of its history, America has had a volunteer force. The draft has been used only to obtain military personnel during major wars requiring very large armies, e.g., our Civil War (1861–1865) and World Wars I and II. Accordingly, the draft was ended after World War II for a period of 18 months but was reinstated at the beginning

---

[1] DoD News Briefing, January 7, 2003 (Rumsfeld, 2003).

[2] An earlier version of this chapter, coauthored with Curtis Gilroy, was given at the Building Military Capability: The Transformation of Personnel Policies Conference in Brussels in June 2004. The conference was sponsored by the Under Secretary of Defense for Personnel and Readiness (United States) and the U.S. mission to NATO.

of the Cold War. It lasted for another 25 years, through the Korean conflict and most of the Vietnam War. So the U.S. has had conscription for only 35 of its 228 years, and nearly all of it was in the 20th century. The American people generally accepted the draft when service was universal or nearly so. The credibility of the draft began to change in the mid-1960s. There were several reasons.

The first reason was the changing demographics in America. The size of the eligible population of young men reaching draft age each year was so large and the needs of the military so small in comparison that, in practice, the draft was no longer universal. It also meant that obtaining enough volunteers was possible at budget levels that were seen as acceptable. Another reason was the rising voices of conservatives and libertarians, who questioned the moral and economic rationale for conscription. To them, the state had no right to take the services of young men involuntarily, that is, without their consent. At the same time, many liberals believed that the draft imposed unfair burdens on the less-advantaged members of society, who were unable to obtain educational or occupational deferments. Finally, the growing unpopularity of the Vietnam War meant the country was ripe for a change to a volunteer force.

The economic arguments the Gates Commission used also played a critical role in bringing about an all-volunteer force.[3] They presented a totally new paradigm for evaluating military organizations. These arguments were coherent, integrated, and intellectually sound. They addressed all the issues of demand and supply, attrition and retention, and the mix of career and noncareer members in the context of management efficiency and personal equity. As a result, the proponents of an all-volunteer force were able to muster persuasive arguments at a time when the need for change was strongly felt and the demographics made change feasible. Both factors were critical for the recommendation of the Gates Commission: "We unanimously believe that the nation's interest will be better served by an all-volunteer force, supported by an effective standby draft, than by a mixed force of volunteers and conscripts" (Gates, 1970).

What Lessons Did We Learn?

It would be less than honest to report that the transition to a volunteer military was smooth and swift. It was not. Mistakes were made—in some cases, the same mistakes more than once. In fact, ten years after the inception of the all-volunteer force, there were still those who called for a return to the draft on both moral and efficiency grounds. Some still believed that every young man had a moral obligation to serve in the military, while others were concerned that we were attracting a low-quality force overrepresented by the poor and minorities. The situation at the time was so dire that

---

[3] At the 30th Anniversary Conference on the All-Volunteer Force, former Deputy Secretary of Defense John White argued: "In contrast to the social, psychological models of testing and evaluation that grew out of WWII, this free market model could deal effectively with the macro operational issues of manning the force" (White, 2003, p. 2).

former President Richard Nixon, the person most responsible for our move to an all-volunteer force, wrote in 1980:

> I considered the end of the draft in 1973 to be one of the major achievements of my administration. Now seven years later, I have reluctantly concluded that we should reintroduce the draft. . . . [T]he volunteer army has failed to provide enough personnel of the caliber we need. (Nixon, 1980)

It would take another ten years of concerted effort and the conclusive success of the Gulf War before Nixon would again call the all-volunteer force a success. In 1993, Nixon noted the "dramatic improvement in the quality of the men and women who joined the armed forces" and felt that he could, consequently, "endorse the all-volunteer Army approach without qualification" (Nixon, 1993).

Today, with 150,000 troops engaged in Iraq and Afghanistan, the all-volunteer force is being tested again. Military commanders continually attest to the outstanding job the volunteer force is doing in this nontraditional military conflict. Remarkably, retention has remained high, but enlistments have fallen off. The last 30 years have demonstrated that an all-voluntary military can be sustained in peace and during the initial periods of military conflict. Whether or not an all-volunteer force can be sustained over longer periods of sustained conflicts and recurring deployments has yet to be determined.

Reflecting on the last 30 years of the all-volunteer force suggests four broad reasons that it has been as successful as it has been. Short of the current situation of sustained conflicts and recurring deployments, the all-volunteer force has faltered when any one of the following factors was missing:

- Top management attention—leadership—is essential.
- Understanding the problem requires research.
- Managing the problem requires a new breed of skilled practitioners.
- A commitment to maintaining the solution requires adequate budgets.

Top Management Attention—Leadership

The all-volunteer force would not have come about when it did without the leadership of President Richard Nixon. In 1968, as a candidate for President, Nixon publicly declared his support for an all-volunteer force in a radio address on October 17, 1968:

> Today all across our country we face a crisis of confidence. Nowhere is it more acute than among our young people. They recognize the draft as an infringement on their liberty, which it is. To them, it represents a government insensitive to their rights, a government callous to their status as free men. They ask for justice, and they deserve it. (Nixon, 1971, p. 8)

Within weeks of taking office, he began the planning for a volunteer military and, on March 27, 1969, announced the formation of a commission charged to "develop a comprehensive plan for eliminating conscription and moving towards an all-volunteer armed force" (Nixon, 1969).

Writing to a friend in 1993, Nixon gave "the major credit for conceiving the idea and implementing" the all-volunteer force to "Martin Anderson . . . despite . . . very stubborn opposition" (Nixon, 1993). The credit Nixon gave to Anderson was well deserved. It was Anderson who first broached the idea to Nixon's advisors and prepared the critical issue paper for Nixon in 1967 (Anderson, 1967). Anderson was with Nixon at the University of Wisconsin when he endorsed a professional military corps (Semple, 1967) and on the campaign trail when Nixon made his most public statement favoring an all-volunteer force (Nixon, 1971). Anderson was instrumental in setting up the Gates Commission and, equally important, making sure that its recommendations were put before the American people with government and commercial printings of the commission's report. Anderson shepherded the Gates Commission's recommendation through the White House decisionmaking process leading to the fateful meeting of the National Security Council on March 25, 1970 (Anderson, 1970). A decade later, Anderson— then Assistant to the President [Reagan] for Policy Development—was a member of the Military Manpower Task Force, which recommended the continuation of Selective Service registration and support for continuing the all-volunteer force. In both 1970 and 1981, Anderson was the most articulate advocate for a volunteer army against concerted opposition from many in Congress and much of the uniformed leadership at the Pentagon. Critical to the successful process, Anderson was the White House insider who was there at the most decisive times and who made sure that the pro–all-volunteer force positions of Secretary Laird and Secretary Weinberger were not belittled, as can happen so often on controversial issues, by negative voices in the President's inner offices.

To complement Anderson inside the White House, Nixon had a very strong Secretary of Defense at the Pentagon in Melvin Laird. A former congressman, Laird knew how to work with Congress and, at critical points, personally interceded with his former colleagues who, if left on their own, would not have supported the volunteer military. It was Laird who made it clear to the military leaders at the Pentagon that, if they wanted to remain the heads of their respective services, the price was continued support for the all-volunteer force. It was Laird who held the decidedly negative National Security Advisor, Henry Kissinger, at bay and pressed the issue through to completion. While Anderson could work behind the scene, it was Laird who was on center stage engaging powerful protagonists in Congress and the administration until the play was over and the final curtain came down. On January 27, 1973, it was Laird who made the announcement: "Use of the draft has ended."

The Gates Commission, which recommended to Nixon that the nation move to an all-volunteer force, was greatly influenced by one of its members, Professor Milton Friedman of the University of Chicago. Friedman was the most articulate spokesman for the view that the draft was "inconsistent with a free society" (Friedman, 1967). It is generally agreed that Friedman—later a Nobel laureate—was the intellectual father of the all-volunteer force.

During the initial period, two Assistant Secretaries of Defense managed the transition from the draft to the all-volunteer force at the Pentagon. Even before the Gates Commission reported its recommendations, Assistant Secretary Roger Kelley established the Project Volunteer Committee at the Pentagon to develop "a comprehensive action program for moving toward a volunteer force" (Laird, 1969). Kelley's philosophy was to have the services (Army, Navy, Marine Corps, and Air Force) be the prime agents for implementing the all-volunteer force. He asked them to develop their "own proposed program and recommendations," which he would approve. Ultimately, and often overcoming the opposition of his colleagues who wanted more central management and the reluctance of the services, Kelley was proven right.

During this critical first period, the uniformed leaders of the military services were supportive. By 1973, however, with the pressure from Vietnam reduced, segments within the Army were questioning the all-volunteer force and the quality of those enlisting. Kelley was so concerned that before he retired from the Pentagon, he wrote his boss, Deputy Secretary of Defense William Clements, that there was "one thing only that can keep the All-Volunteer Force from being a success, and that is a lack of complete and positive commitment on the part of those responsible for its operation" (Kelley, 1973).

Fortunately, William K. Brehm succeeded Kelley as Assistant Secretary of Defense. Brehm had been part of the team that brought quantitative analysis to the Pentagon during the tenure of Secretary of Defense Robert McNamara. He was the first Assistant Secretary of the Army for Manpower and was instrumental in the Army's early support for the all-volunteer force. Probably the most important thing Brehm provided was a high level of leadership when it was most needed. In the February 28, 1974, "Special Report" in the *Commanders Digest,* he told them in blunt language that whatever shortfall might exist in the all-volunteer force, it was "not . . . enough to cause us to think about returning to the draft" (Brehm, 1974, p. 3).

Important support at critical times often came from the most unexpected places. The most outspoken critics of the all-volunteer force in Congress were Senators Sam Nunn and John Warner. Nunn believed that everyone had an obligation to serve and that the all-volunteer force was "to a large extent a political child of the draft card burning, campus riots, and violent protest demonstrations of the late 1960s and early 1970s" (Nunn, 1973). He believed that the concept of the all-volunteer force was "a clear result of the Vietnam war . . . because [i]t caused the President and Congress to yield to the tremendous pressure to end the draft at almost any price" (Nunn, 1973). In 1978, Nunn argued that the

> real question we must face is the future capability to meet our national security problems. . . . Do we choose to continue increases in manpower costs? . . . Instead of adding potentially larger costs for the current structure of the AVF, shouldn't we recognize that . . . alternative structures should be examined? The only alternative

is not to return to the draft as previously constituted. Management initiatives by DoD can help, at least in the short term. (Nunn et al., 1978)

By late 1979—six years into our volunteer military—there was a growing realization in the Pentagon and in Congress that the level of military compensation had fallen so far behind civilian pay that it was inadequate to attract and retain personnel to staff the services with the numbers and quality of the people they needed. All four services failed to achieve their recruiting goals; the Army was in the worst position as it fell short of its recruiting mission by 17 percent, and the quality of the recruits was at an all-time low. The White House under President Jimmy Carter was more concerned with double-digit inflation and holding down the overall size of the federal budget than in military recruiting and compensation. The action Senators Nunn and Warner took to improve military pay over the initial objections of the White House is generally credited with saving the all-volunteer force at that time.

When President Ronald Reagan took office in 1981, he directed his new Secretary of Defense, Caspar Weinberger, "to form a defense manpower task force to review the entire military manpower question and make proposals that will increase the effectiveness of the active and reserve All-Volunteer Force" (Weinberger, 1982b). In 1982, the task force concluded the following:

> In the late 1970s the recruiting and retention of qualified personnel for the Armed Forces had deteriorated to the point where many were questioning the effectiveness of the All-Volunteer Force. We are pleased to report that there has been a dramatic improvement during the last two years. . . . The Task Force is confident that the higher active and reserve strengths planned for the next five years can be achieved without the resumption of the draft. (Weinberger, 1982b)

Weinberger played a particularly important part in the success of the volunteer military and displayed very strong leadership concerning the increased role of women. For many in uniform the increased role that women were playing, particularly in the Army, was "a temporary condition that would pass" (Holm, 1992). Weinberger, reflecting on the first decade of the all-volunteer force, addressed the Tenth Anniversary All-Volunteer Force Conference: "The most rewarding development we have seen in our armed forces over the past decade has been the tremendous expansion of opportunities for women" (Weinberger, 1986). Rather then reduce the role of women in the armed forces, he made it clear in a major policy statement: "This Department must aggressively break down those remaining barriers that prevent us from making the fullest use of the capabilities of women in providing for our national defense" (Weinberger, 1982a). This was important because women have made the transition to a volunteer force in the United States easier than it might otherwise have been, since their relatively high level of interest and participation in the military was a phenomenon the Gates Commission had overlooked (Quester and Gilroy, 2002). Held to a maximum of 2 percent in the draft era, women made up 9 percent of the enlisted force in

1983 when Weinberger spoke. Today, women make up 15 percent of the active enlisted force, more than in any other country. They account for about 18 percent of new recruits.

Army General Maxwell Reid Thurman is considered by many as the single most important person in the history of the all-volunteer force because he taught the Pentagon how to recruit and, by dint of personality and intellect, made the all-volunteer concept work throughout the 1980s. While Thurman would be the first to credit the increasing pay levels and educational benefits in "selling" the Army, the period is most noted for his leadership. There were no "school solutions" before Max Thurman; he was the school. He wrote the book and delivered the lessons for all to see. He recognized, more than any other uniformed leader, that the military had to compete aggressively in the civilian labor market for American youth, and it had to do so with the right tools based on market research and statistical analysis.

Understanding the Problem: The Need for Research

In 2000, former Deputy Secretary of Defense John White and the current Under Secretary of Defense for Personnel and Readiness David S. C. Chu wrote that the success of the all-volunteer force can, at least partially be related to the "quantitative analysis [that] was employed widely and aggressively to try to understand the relationship between cause and effects. . . . [Policymakers] were willing to use experiments to test, evaluate and adjust policies" (Chu and White, 2001).

Research had been a critical part of the all-volunteer force from its very beginning. Starting with World War I, military psychologists pioneered the fields of selection and classification. The research staff of the Gates Commission was largely drawn from economists who had worked on the Pentagon's 1964 study of the draft, which President Lyndon Johnson had ordered. Many of these economists filled key positions at the Pentagon. Important to the success of the all-volunteer force, research into the measurement of job performance and the optimum mix of quality and cost has focused recruiters and sustained the quality force we have today. Almost every change to the all-volunteer force has been made only after research had demonstrated its likely effect, and most programs have been formally evaluated through research.

A number of organizations have provided research to the Office of the Secretary of Defense and each of the services. The Center for Naval Analyses, the Institute for Defense Analyses, and the Air Force's Project RAND all worked to support the Gates Commission. At the beginning of the All-Volunteer Force, the Defense Advanced Projects Research Agency funded the development of a manpower studies program at the RAND Corporation. When he took over the position of Assistant Secretary for Manpower and Reserve Affairs, William Brehm took over the sponsorship of the RAND program and established the Defense Manpower Studies Center at RAND

> to engage in high-priority studies and analysis to support DoD-wide manpower policy decisions . . . with diverse academic backgrounds (e.g., economics, operations

research, psychology, math, etc.) and experience in manpower and personnel studies and analysis. (Greenberg and Flyer, 1976, pp. 1–2)

Research, however, has little effect unless defense personnel managers use it to help them ask the right questions and make the decisions at appropriate and critical points. It is a partnership that has worked particularly well at the Pentagon for almost 40 years.

Personnel research and decisions must be grounded on the personnel data the services routinely collect. Brehm understood, however, how important is to maintain and archive these data and was supportive of a data center to develop and maintain computerized personnel files for analysis and reporting. The Defense Manpower Data Center was soon established to provide historical time-series and longitudinal data on the force in great detail to serve as the warehouse for much of the survey data that has been collected on the force and the civilian population.

Managing the Problem: Developing New Programs

The transition from a conscripted force to a volunteer military presented special challenges for which new programs had to be developed. The military had to learn whom to recruit, and then it had to learn how to recruit.

Whom to Recruit. Although there are approximately 25 million youth 18 to 24 years of age in the United States, the military is interested in only a small subset of this population. General Thurman believed that the all-volunteer force would only be judged a success if it could attract "high quality" men *and* women—those who have completed high school and who score above average on our Armed Forces Qualification Test (AFQT). He rejected arguments that the only way to get the required number of recruits was to lower standards. He called this "bottom fishing" and was confident that if his recruiters were given the proper tools and good programs that were attractive to young men and women completing high school, these individuals would join the Army. He believed that, if he did not set standards, his recruiters would, and the standards they would set would not be congruent with those of the Army. So, he forced his recruiters to concentrate on quality, not quantity. A recruiter got no credit for more recruits unless he had already brought into the Army the designated number of high school graduates with above average aptitude.

Today's volunteer military has a higher proportion of high school graduates and above-average scores on the AFQT and, in that sense, is of higher quality than our draft force was over 30 years ago. It is also, in the same sense, of higher quality than the civilian population of today from which the force has been drawn. In FY 2003, 95 percent of new recruits were high school diploma graduates, and 72 percent scored above average on the enlistment aptitude test. Overall, less than 80 percent of American youth have a high school diploma and, by definition, 50 percent of the youth population scored in the upper half of the AFQT.

How to Recruit. In their review, Chu and White argued that an important factor leading to the success of the all-volunteer force was that

> policymakers came to understand that incentives—bonuses, compensation, promotion opportunity, and the like—rather than "rules and regulations" would be the main instruments to achieve the outcomes they desired. (Chu and White, 2001)

The services had to develop appropriate marketing strategies and advertising programs to get high-quality youths to join. The services found they needed to explain to potential recruits the benefits and opportunities of military service. But the media only conveyed the message; the military learned it had to offer money for education and bonuses to enlist in certain occupations or for enlistment tours of different lengths. To be attractive, the military found it need to develop career opportunities that had civilian relevance and were a good preparation for adulthood. A mix of economic benefits and educational programs helps channel youths into hard-to-fill occupations, hazardous duty assignments, and undesirable locations. Educational benefits proved particularly important. Members can use these while in service or use them when they leave; they can use them to further their education or their military careers or to train for a civilian job. Recruiters learned they needed to offer useful training and in-service professional military education, as well as rewarding assignments to get the most highly qualified people to join. Advertising also portrays the intangibles of the military, such as service to country, honor, courage, commitment, and the chance to learn discipline and to mature. Over time, advertising became a big and expensive business. In 2003, DoD spent nearly $400 million on enlisted recruitment advertising.

The services also had to develop a professional, highly trained and motivated recruiting staff. It may be called an all-volunteer force, but General Thurman taught that it was really an all-recruited force. There are currently about 14,500 recruiters across the U.S. representing all four services, and each one is responsible, on average, for about 12 new recruits each year—or one each month. These recruiters are assigned recruiting goals in terms of quantity and quality of recruits and are held accountable for achieving these goals. Accountability is established through a management system characterized by face-to-face meetings between recruiter and supervisor.

After enlisting new members, the services found reenlisting the most outstanding members who completed their initial period of service was the key to truly high quality force. Besides good pay, these careerists demanded quality-of-life benefits, such as good housing, child care, health benefits, family advocacy programs, and military stores. The mantra became "the military recruits individuals, it retains families." Programs needed to be developed that made the services "family friendly." Under the all-volunteer force, the force is more senior and experienced than under the draft. Currently, careerists make up over 50 percent of the active enlisted force. This contrasts sharply with about 40 percent during the draft years.

Commitment to Maintaining the Solution: Adequate Budgets

The final lesson is to ensure that adequate resources are available to support the all-volunteer force. The defense budget must be large enough to support pay raises to keep pace with both inflation and civilian-sector pay increases; for recruiting resources to support advertising, recruiters, bonuses, and educational benefits; and to fund the military retirement program and quality-of-life initiatives. On various occasions since 1973, military pay was allowed to fall too far behind civilian earnings, and recruiting and other programs were reduced too much. Each time, recruiting and retention suffered, and the viability of the all-volunteer force was threatened. This was because policymakers did not understand the fragile relationship between recruiting and economic factors—specifically, the aspects of the labor market in which the military competes for manpower and in which pecuniary and nonpecuniary incentives allocate labor supply. The story of what happened after the early success of the all-volunteer force is instructive.

The early years of our volunteer force were successful primarily because they were adequately resourced. Following the recommendations by the Gates Commission, Congress enacted the largest pay raise ever (over 60 percent) in 1972 to provide new recruits pay comparability with their civilian peers. Recruiting resources were increased to place more recruiters across the country, enhance recruiting facilities, and expand and improve advertising. Educational benefits for service members were still generous and popular. A growing youth population and rising unemployment in the early years together resulted in a richer manpower pool from which the services—particularly the Army—could draw. In 1973 the prospects for an all-volunteer force looked so bright that on January 27 of that year, Secretary of Defense Laird announced that the use of the draft had ended (Laird, 1973).

After several years of success, however, Congress became concerned with the increasing budget costs of personnel. It created the Defense Manpower Commission with a charter to "focus on the substantial increase in the costs of military manpower" (Tarr, 1976). When the commission reported to the President and Congress in 1976, it did not prove to be the cost cutting zealot that some had hoped. Nevertheless, the Ford administration took cost-cutting actions that imperiled the all-volunteer force. Clearly, the most problematic cost-cutting came in the sensitive area of recruiting. On reflection years later, General Thurman observed that "recruiting resources as a whole were thought to be at least adequate, if not excessive, and thus became targets for cost-cutting" (Thurman, 1986). These cuts in resources occurred at a time when the civilian economy was robust and youth unemployment was low. Rather than cutting recruiting budgets in this tight labor market, resources should have been increased to counter its challenges. The recruiting difficulties that resulted should not have been a surprise (Gilroy et al., 1990), but by 1979, all four services failed to achieve their recruiting goals. The Army and Marine Corps suffered most, and the Army was in the worst position, falling short of its recruiting mission by 17 percent. The quality of the recruits also fell to an all-time low. For the Marine Corps, only 27 percent of new recruits were high quality; for the Army, that figure was a dismal 19 percent. During the late 1970s and early 1980s, the quality of new recruits was below the minimum levels DoD had established.

The Gates Commission had predicted that the Army would have the greatest difficulty in obtaining volunteers:

> Voluntary enlisted deficits are the highest in the Army. This . . . is to be expected, given that entry level pay is lowest for enlisted personnel and that the non-monetary conditions of service are less attractive in the Army than in the other three services. (Gates, 1970, p. 56)

The White House under President Jimmy Carter was more concerned about fighting inflation and holding down the overall size of the federal budget than about military recruiting and compensation. To remedy the situation, Congress legislated two large pay raises for the military in 1980 and 1981—11.7 and 14.3 percent, respectively—to help restore military-civilian pay comparability. The solution was to raise basic pay for all service members to a level that would enable the Army to meet its manpower objectives. The Gates Commission had argued that the "evidence is overwhelming that, if compensation is set at levels which satisfy Army requirements, the other services will be able to attract enough qualified volunteers to meet their respective requirements" (Gates, 1970, p. 57).

Interestingly, we made the same mistake in the late 1990s, when we cut recruiting budgets too much at a time when the economy was strong and unemployment low. The U.S. military had just undergone a drawdown of its active-duty force by about 25 percent. Concomitantly, recruiting resources were cut as the recruiting mission was reduced. Unfortunately, budgets were cut too much, and, with unemployment reaching a 30-year low, the services found it difficult to achieve their recruiting goals. It took a large infusion of resources to correct this oversight in 1978 and 1979 before recruiting turned around in 1980, and it took even larger increases in 1998 and 1999 before it rebounded in 2000.

The problem, as John White noted at the 30th Anniversary Conference is that the all-volunteer force is fragile, and

> it takes some time for the system to detect any important shifts in program effectiveness. Monitoring mechanisms are "weak and imperfect, leading to an unfortunate lag between changes in conditions and changes in policy." . . . Second, once the remedies are fashioned there is a further, inevitable, lag in the time it takes to make either internal, programmatic adjustments or legislative changes such as authorizing pay increases. (White, 2003, p. 5)

White was particularly sensitive to the problem because, as senior decisionmaker in the Carter administration, he was unable to convince the President to increase military pay in 1978 when it was plain to all that it needed to be increased. President Carter, while a supporter of the all-volunteer force, had a strategy for fighting inflation that included limiting all federal pay raises, including those for the military. The experience in the late 1970s and early 1980s proved, as White noted, that a volunteer military "requires an ongoing institutional commitment to assure its continued success" (White, 2003, p. 3).

Looking Ahead

In 2004, with the all-volunteer force under hostile fire and strained by long deployments and with a vote pending in House of Representative to bring back the draft, Secretary of Defense Donald Rumsfeld wrote the Chairman of the House Armed Services Committee, offering his assessment of the all-volunteer force and the need for the country to return to conscription:

> A draft simply is not needed. We have 295 million people in the United States of America and there are some 2.6 million active and reserve forces serving. We are capable of attracting and retaining the people we need, through the proper use of pay and other incentives. . . .
>
> In danger zones across the globe, the all-volunteer, professional force is performing superbly—as typified by operations in Afghanistan and Iraq. I have met with many of these men and women as they carry out their missions. They are committed, enthusiastic, and proud to be contributing to the defense of the nation. Most importantly, they want to be doing what they are doing. Every single one of them stepped forward, raised their hand, and said, "I'm ready. I want to serve." They are serving most professionally and proudly. (Rumsfeld, 2004)

The vote was 400 to 2 to reject a return to conscription (Babington and Oldenburg, 2004). For them, at least, the all-volunteer force was judged a success in peace and war. Now, two years later, with casualties rising[4] and enlistments decreasing,[5] but reenlistments at a five-year high, and with a majority of the public, as reported by a *Washington Post*–ABC News poll, believing the war in Iraq was "not worth fighting,"[6] one might ask again: Is the all-volunteer armed force sustainable? The answer, as it has always been: Only time will tell.

---

[4] At the end of calendar year 2005, DoD reported 2,173 U.S. dead in Iraq, with an additional 7,529 wounded in action and not returned to duty. The numbers for Afghanistan were 253 dead and 400 wounded who did not return to duty (Department of Defense, 2005).

[5] In a January 18, 2006, report, Army Secretary Francis J. Harvey was quoted as follows:

> Re-enlistments for the Army in fiscal 2005 [the year ending September 30, 2005] were the highest they've been in five years, nearly enough to make up for a shortfall of about 7,000 new recruits last year, said ... the Army has already recruited 25 percent more new troops this year [2006] than at the same point in fiscal 2005. (Brown, 2006)

[6] On November 11, 2005, a *Washington Post*–ABC News poll reported the highest level of disapproval for the war when its "not worth fighting" index spiked at 60 percent (*Washington Post* Staff, 2006).

References

Anderson, Martin C., "An Analysis of the Factors Involved in Moving to An All-Volunteer Armed Force," unpublished paper, New York, July 4, 1967. S0032.pdf.

———, "All-Volunteer Force and Draft Reform," decision memorandum to John Ehrlichman, Washington, D.C., March 31, 1970. G1142.pdf.

Babington, Charles, and Don Oldenburg, "House GOP Brings Up Draft in Order to Knock It Down," *Washington Post,* October 6, 2004, p. 1.

Brehm, William K., "A Special Status Report: All Volunteer Force," *Commanders Digest,* Vol. 15, No. 9, February 28, 1974. G0040.pdf.

Brown, Drew, "Army Re-Enlistment Figures Up, but Recruiting Lags," *Knight Ridder Newspapers,* January 18, 2006.

Chu, David S. C., and John P. White, "Ensuring Quality People in Defense," in Ashton B. Carter and John P. White, eds., *Keeping the Edge: Managing Defense for the Future,* Cambridge, Mass.: MIT Press, 2001.

Department of Defense, *Operation Iraqi Freedom (OIF) and Operation Enduring Freedom (OEF) as of December 28, 2005,* Washington, D.C.: Department of Defense, December 30, 2005. G1484.pdf.

Friedman, Milton, Statement, hearing before the 90th Cong., 1st Sess., Washington, D.C., U.S. Government Printing Office, Vol. 113, March 9, 1967.

Gates, Thomas S., Jr., *The Report of the President's Commission on an All-Volunteer Armed Force,* Washington, D.C., February 1970. S0243.pdf.

Gilroy, Curtis L., Robert L. Phillips, and John D. Blair, "The All-Volunteer Force: Fifteen Years Later," *Armed Force and Society*, Vol. 16, No. 3, Spring 1990, pp. 329–350.

Greenberg, I. M., and Eli S. Flyer, *Proposal for an In-House Defense Manpower Studies Center—FY 1977,* Washington, D.C.: Office of the Assistant Secretary of Defense (M&RA), January 1, 1976. G0717.pdf.

Holm, Jeanne, *Women in the Military: An Unfinished Revolution,* rev. ed., Novato, Ca.: Presidio, 1992.

Kelley, Roger T., "The All-Volunteer Force: As I Leave My Job Today, . . ." memorandum to Deputy Secretary of Defense, Washington, D.C., May 31, 1973. G0609.pdf.

Laird, Melvin R., "Project Volunteer (Committee)," memorandum to Secretaries of the Military Departments, Chairman of the Joint Chiefs of Staff and Assistants Secretaries of Defense, Washington, D.C., April 10, 1969. G0269.pdf.

———, "Use of the Draft Has Ended," news release Washington, D.C., January 27, 1973. G0103.pdf.

Nixon, Richard M., *Statement by the President Announcing a Commission on an All-Volunteer Armed Forces,* Washington, D.C.: Office of the White House Press Secretary, March 27, 1969. G0266.pdf.

———, "The All-Volunteer Armed Force: A Radio Address, October 17, 1968," in Harry A. Marmion, ed., *The Case Against a Volunteer Army,* Chicago: Quadrangle Books, 1971, pp. 75–82. G0251.pdf.

———, *The Real War,* New York: Warner Books, 1980.

———, "Volunteer Army," letter to John C. Whitaker, Woodcliff Lake, N.J., November 4, 1993. S0481.pdf.

Nunn, Sam, "Remarks before the Georgia General Assembly," news release, Washington, D.C., March 5, 1973. S0118.pdf.

Nunn, Sam, et al., Costs of the All-Volunteer Force, hearing before the Senate Armed Services Subcommittee on Manpower and Personnel, 95th Cong., 2nd Sess., Washington, D.C., U.S. Government Printing Office, February 6, 1978. S0443.pdf.

Quester, Aline O., and Curtis L. Gilroy, "Women and Minorities in America's Volunteer Military," *Contemporary Economic Policy,* Vol. 20, No. 2, April 2002, pp. 111–121.

Rumsfeld, Donald H., *Department of Defense News Briefing—Secretary Rumsfeld and Gen. Myers,* Washington, D.C.: U.S. Department of Defense, January 7, 2003. G1232.pdf.

———, "Opposition to Re-institute of the Draft," memorandum to Chairman House Armed Services Committee, Washington, D.C., October 5, 2004. G1364.pdf.

Semple, Robert B., Jr., "Nixon Backs Eventual End of Draft," *New York Times,* November 18, 1967, p. 21.

Tarr, Curtis W., *Defense Manpower: The Keystone of National Security—Report to the President and Congress,* Washington, D.C.: Defense Manpower Commission, April 1976. S0113.pdf.

Thurman, Maxwell R., "Sustaining the All-Volunteer Force 1983–1992: The Second Decade," in William Bowman, Roger Little and G. Thomas Sicilia, eds., *The All-Volunteer Force After a Decade: Retrospect and Prospect,* New York: Pergamon-Brassey's, 1986.

Washington Post Staff, "Washington Post–ABC News Poll," *WashingtonPost.com,* January 11, 2005.

Weinberger, Caspar W., "Women in the Military," memorandum to Secretaries of the Military Departments, Washington, D.C., January 14, 1982a. G1170.pdf.

———, *Military Manpower Task Force: A Report to the President on the Status and Prospects of the All-Volunteer Force,* Washington, D.C.: U.S. Government Printing Office, November 1982b. S0004.pdf.

———, "The All-Volunteer Force in the 1980s: Department of Defense Perspective," in William Bowman, Roger Little and G. Thomas Sicilia, eds., *The All-Volunteer Force After a Decade: Retrospect and Prospect,* New York: Pergamon-Brassey's, 1986, p. 3.

White, John P., "Comments," 30th Anniversary Conference, Washington, D.C., September 2003. S0717.pdf.

Index

Page numbers followed by *n* refer to footnotes